JN320461

財務情報英和辞典

Dictionary of Financial Statements in English

菊地義明 ▶著

三省堂

© 2008 菊地義明

DICTIONARY OF FINANCIAL STATEMENTS IN ENGLISH

財務情報英和辞典

Printed in Japan

装幀・組版設計————————宗利淳一

組版————————原島康晴（エディマン）

はじめに

　この『財務情報英和辞典』は，製造，販売・流通，銀行，保険，証券，情報技術(IT)など各専門分野の企業の年次報告書(annual report)と四半期報告書(quarterly report)に用いられている基本用語と重要語句をまとめたものです。
　そのため，これには株主や債権者，政府など企業外部の利害関係者に対する財務報告に用いられる財務会計用語のほかに，経済，金融，経営，マーケティングやビジネス用語が多数収録されています。また，本書は基本的に見出し語とその語義，見出し語の関連語句と文例とで構成されていますが，英字新聞・雑誌やビジネス・レポートなどを読み解く上で必要とされる財務情報関連の語句も幅広く収録されています。
　このほか，見出し語には同意・同義語を含めて語義の後に適宜，簡単な説明が加えてあり，最新性と実用性を考慮してカレントなトピックを豊富に盛り込んだ文例も，この辞典の特長です。文例にはその的確な訳文が付してあるため，専門用語辞典のほかに「翻訳事典」として利用することもできます。

　この『財務情報英和辞典』は，わたしの40年にわたる広範な翻訳の実務経験と十数年に及ぶこの分野での制作活動の成果で，日本初の年次・四半期報告用語辞典として，またビジネスピープルにとって真の実用ビジネス用語辞典として活用していただければうれしく思います。

　なお，文例の作成にあたっては，企業のビジネス・レポートや各種英字新聞などの記事も参考にさせていただきました。ここに，心からお礼申しあげます。

2008年8月
菊地義明

目次

はじめに ──────────────────────────────── iii

凡例 ──────────────────────────────── iv–v

A—Z ──────────────────────────────── 001–410

資料 ──────────────────────────────── 412–416

和英索引 ──────────────────────────────── 417–531

凡例

1. 見出し語
単一の語のほかに，2語以上からなる語句（分離複合語）も重要なものは見出し語として立てた。同じつづりで語源が異なるもの，複数の品詞を持つものはそれぞれ見出し語としたが，番号などで区別することはしていない。

1.1 配列
見出し語の配列は原則としてアルファベット順としたが，分離複合語およびハイフンで結合された複合語は，構成要素の最初の語を基準としてひとまとまりで示した。
数字は，アルファベットとは別種の文字として扱い，アルファベットよりも前に昇順で置いた。

1.2 品詞
単一の語には品詞を略記した。
- **名** 名詞
- **形** 形容詞
- **動** 動詞
- **副** 副詞
- **前** 前置詞
- **接** 接続詞

2. 語義
語義の区分はカンマで示した。

2.1 括弧類
括弧類を次の原則に基づいて使用した。
- （　） 注記，参照，略語の成り立ちなどを示す。
- 〈　〉 他動詞の目的語や語の内包的意味を補助的に示す。
- 〚　〛 使用域や文法・語法上の制限を示す。
- ［　］ 交換可能であることを示す。
- 《　》 《略　》の形で略語を示す。

2.2 その他記号類
- ⇒ 当該の見出し語を含む例文が参照先に存在することを表す。
- ＝ ほぼ同義で用いられる語句を示す。

3. 副見出し
分離複合語および文の形をとっていない用例を副見出しとして示した。
配列と語義の書式は見出し語と同様の規則に基づく。

4. 用例
用例は原則として完全文の形で示した。見出し部分を斜字体で示した。

4.1 用例の訳
語義と同様の括弧類を用いた。ただし，次の例外がある。
- ［　］ 交換可能を示すほか，解説的な言い換えを示すのにも用いた。

A a

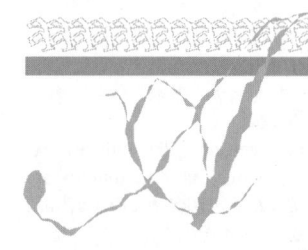

AAA company トリプルAの会社, トリプルAの格付けの会社, 超一流企業
▶We are a *AAA* company. 当社は、トリプルAの超一流企業です。

abandonment 名 除却, 放棄, 遺棄, 引渡し, 中断, 中止, 保険委付
  abandonment cost 固定資産の除却費
  abandonment method 除却法, 廃棄法（＝retirement method, retirement system）
  asset abandonment 資産除却
▶These provisions include $110 million for closing facilities, lease terminations and asset *abandonments* associated with centralizing customer support services. この引当金には、顧客支援サービス部門の集中化に関連した施設閉鎖費、リース解約費と資産除却費用の1億1,000万ドルも含まれています。

ABC 活動基準原価計算, ABC管理（**activity based costing**の略）
  ABC analysis ABC分析

ABCP 資産担保CP, 資産担保コマーシャル・ペーパー, アセットバックCP（**asset-backed commercial paper**の略）

ability 名 能力, 力
  ability to buy back shares 自社株を買い戻す能力, 自社株買戻し能力, 買戻し能力
  ability to control costs コスト管理能力
  ability to finance 資金調達力
  ability to generate cash 収益力, キャッシュフロー生成能力, キャッシュフローを生み出す能力
  ability to meet cash capital requirements 資金需要を賄う能力
  ability to pay down debt 債務返済能力（＝ability to meet debt payments due）
  ability to refinance 借換え能力
  debt-paying ability 債務返済能力（＝debt servicing capacity）
▶This company has demonstrated its *ability* to deal with change and challenge throughout all of its history. 当社は、創立以来こんにちに至るまで、変革と課題に対応する当社の能力を示してきました。

ABM 活動基準管理（**activity based management**の略）

abnormal 形 異常な
  abnormal cost 異常原価
  abnormal item 異常項目（＝extraordinary item：企業の非経常的活動から生じた損益項目。固定資産の売却による損益など）
  abnormal loss 異常損失
  abnormal settlement of accounts 異常決算
  abnormal shrinkage 異常減損, 異常減耗
  abnormal waste 異常減損

above 前 …を上回る, …より上の, …以上の
  above-average 平均を上回る
  above-normal earnings 超過収益力, 超過利益
  above-normal profit 超過利益, 超過利潤
  above par 額面超過, 額面以上, 額面以上の状態, 割増
  above the line 経常損益計算, 経常収支, 経常支出, 範囲内, アバブ・ザ・ライン（事業の経常的な収益と費用を指し、lineは損益計算書の経常利益または当期純利益を指す）
  above the line profit 経常利益
  above the market strategy 市価以上戦略, 高価格市場戦略

above trend growth トレンドを上回る成長率

ABS 資産担保証券, 商業用不動産証券, アセットバック証券 (**asset-backed securities**の略)

absorb 動 吸収する, 吸収合併する, 配賦(はいふ)する, 填補(てんぽ)する, 〈税金などを〉負担する, 解消する
 absorb fixed overhead as a cost of product 固定間接費を製品原価の一部として配賦する
 absorb losses 損失を吸収する
 absorb the withholding tax 源泉課税を負担する
 absorbed cost 全部原価, 配賦済み原価, 配賦原価
 absorbed overhead 製造間接費配賦額 (＝absorbed burden, applied overhead)
▸We will *absorb* the company as a wholly owned subsidiary. 当社は,同社を完全子会社として吸収する[同社を完全子会社化する]方針です。

absorption 名 吸収, 吸収合併, 配賦, 賦課, 填補
 absorption cost 全部原価 (＝full cost：製品の製造過程で生じる原価をすべて製品原価に算入する計算方法)
 absorption income 全部原価計算に基づく損益
 actual absorption costing 実際全部原価計算
 mergers and absorptions 吸収・合併
 overhead absorption 間接費の配賦
 tax absorption fee 課税負担手数料
▸All mergers are regarded as *absorption* in the United States, even if some are effectively on an equal basis. 実際には対等の立場での合併であっても,米国では合併はすべて吸収合併と見なされる。

a/c 勘定 (**account**の略)

accelerate 動 加速する, 加速させる, 促進する, 推進する, 拍車をかける (⇒**bad loan**)
 accelerated amortization 加速償却, 加速減価償却, 加速なし崩し償却
 accelerated cost recovery system 加速原価回収制度[回収法], 加速償却制度, 加速償却法, エイカーズ《略 **ACRS**》
 accelerated depreciation 加速償却, 加速減価償却, 加速償却法 (⇒**facility**)
 accelerated disposal of bad loans 不良債権処理の加速
 accelerated method 加速償却法 (＝accelerated depreciation method)
▸A series of accounting scandals and delays in the recovery of corporate performance are *accelerating* falls in stock prices on the U.S. markets, along with the weakening of the dollar. 一連の[相次ぐ]企業会計の不祥事と企業業績回復の遅れで,米国の株安とドル安が加速している。

accept 動 承諾する, 受諾する, 受け入れる, 同意する, 〈手形や注文などを〉引き受ける, 認める, 容認する (⇒**buyout offer**)
 accept a bill 手形を引き受ける
 accept a risk 危険を引き受ける, リスクをとる
 accept an offer 申込みを受諾する
 generally accepted 一般に認められた, 一般に公正妥当と認められた
▸Applications have been *accepted* with few exceptions as long as necessary documents are submitted. 必要な書類が提出されていれば,申請はほぼ例外なく受理されてきた。
▸The consolidated financial statements have been prepared in accordance with accounting principles generally *accepted* in Canada. 連結財務書類[連結財務諸表]は,カナダで一般に公正妥当と認められた会計基準に従って[会計基準に準拠して]作成されています。

acceptable 形 一般に認められている, 公正妥当と認められている, 認められている, 許容できる, 容認できる, 許容範囲の, 採択可能な
 acceptable actuarial cost method 一般に認められている保険数理上の原価計算法
 acceptable actuarial cost method for financial purposes 財務会計上認められている保険数理上の原価計算法
 acceptable acturial method 一般に認められている[認められている]保険数理法

acceptance 名 引受け, 容認, 受諾
 acceptance commission 手形引受手数料
 acceptance commitment 引受債務
 acceptance payable 手形債務, 支払手形
 acceptance receivable 手形債権, 受取手形
 acceptance receivable discounted 割引手形

access 動 接続する, 利用する, 〈データを〉閲覧する, 入手する, 参加する, 参入する, 加入する, 立ち入る, 接近する
 access cash 資金を調達する
 access external sources of cash 外部から資金調達する (＝access external sources of funding, access external funding sources)
 access foreign technology 海外技術を導入する
 access information on ... …の情報を入手する
 access the capital markets 資本市場で資金を調達する, 資本市場で調達する
 access the market 起債する, 市場で資金を調達する
▸Yahoo Japan Corp. provides free detailed disaster

information via its Web site that can be *accessed* by cell phone.　ネット検索大手のヤフージャパンが，携帯電話でアクセスできるサイトで詳しい災害情報を，無料で提供している。

access 名　参入，参入機会，市場アクセス，加入，参加，利用，閲覧，〈コンピュータシステムやネットワークへの〉接続，アクセス　（⇒**audit committee**）
　access charge　接続料金，通信事業者間接続料金，アクセス料金，ネットワーク利用料金
　access to assets　資産の取扱い　（⇒**authorization**）
　access to funding　資金調達，資金源の確保
　access to markets on an unsecured basis　無担保ベースでの資金調達
　access to records and books of account　会計記録と会計帳簿の閲覧
　access to the market　市場への参入，市場への参入機会，市場進出，市場アクセス，市場へのアクセス　（＝market access）
▸The shareholders' auditors have full *access* to the audit committee, with and without management being present.　経営者の同席の有無にかかわらず，監査委員会とは会計監査人が密接に連絡を取っています［監査委員会には会計監査人が毎回参加することができます］。
▸We have easy *access* to financing when we need it.　資金調達については，当社は必要な時にたやすく資金調達ができます。

accommodation 名　融通，融資，便宜
　accommodation bill　融通手形　（＝accommodation paper）
　accommodation paper　融通手形　（＝accommodation bill）
　accommodation purpose　融通目的

accompanying 形　添付した，付属する
　accompanying consolidated balance sheet　添付の連結貸借対照表
　accompanying notes　添付の注記，添付した注記事項
　accompanying notes to financial statements　添付の財務書類［財務諸表］注記　（⇒**integral part**）
▸We have audited the *accompanying* consolidated balance sheets of ABC Corporation and subsidiaries as of December 31, 2007 and 2006.　私どもは，ここに添付されているABCコーポレーションおよび子会社の2007年12月31日現在と2006年12月31日現在の連結貸借対照表について監査しました。
▸The *accompanying* notes should be read in conjunction with these financial statements.　添付の注記は，これらの財務書類［本計算書］と関連づけてお読みください。

accomplishment 名　業績，成果，達成，成就，遂行，完了，完遂，熟練技術，技能
▸This *accomplishment* is especially gratifying given the current climate.　この業績［成果］は，とくに現在の経営環境を考えますと，まことに喜ばしい限りです。

accord 名　合意，同意，合意書，合意文書，協定，意見の一致，和解，代物弁済
▸Under the *accord*, the banking, trust and brokerage units of the financial group will be the surviving companies, respectively.　合意書によると，同金融グループの銀行，信託，証券会社がそれぞれ存続会社となる。

account 名　口座，預金，勘定，勘定書，計算，計算書，収支，決算，決算書，会計，取引関係，取引先，投資家，説明，報告，理由，考慮，重要性《略 a/c》
　account books　会計帳簿，売掛債権帳，売掛帳，決算書　（＝accounting books, books of account, financial books; ⇒**books of account**）
　account due　未収金
　account executive　〈広告会社の〉営業責任者，〈証券会社の〉セールスマン《略 AE》
　account of business　営業報告書
　bank account　銀行口座，銀行勘定，預金
　branch account　支店勘定
　call ... to account　…に釈明を求める，…に責任を問う
　fund account　資金勘定
　head office account　本店勘定
　off-the-book account　簿外口座
　open account　当座預金，当座勘定，交互計算
　open an account　口座を開設する
　ordinary account　普通口座
　settlement account　決済口座，決算
　specified account　特定口座
　trade account　貿易収支
　two sets of account books　二重帳簿
　Web account　ウェブ口座
▸Customers can choose a settlement-specific or a savings deposit when they open an *account*.　口座を開設する際，顧客は普通預金か決済用預金かを選択することができる。
▸The brokerage firm manages client assets of ¥520 billion in about 150,000 *accounts*.　この証券会社は，口座数約15万で顧客預かり資産は5,200億円に達する。

account balance　差引残高，勘定残高，口座残高

▶The 2007 condensed consolidated balance sheet reflects full consolidation of ABCD's *account balances*. 2007年度の要約連結貸借対照表は、ABCD社の勘定残高の完全連結を反映しています。

account for ... 計上する, 処理する, 会計処理する, …を占める, 説明する

▶In the past, the finance subsidiaries of the Corporation were *accounted for* by the equity method. これまで、当社の金融事業を営む子会社は、持分法で会計処理していました。

▶Intellectual assets *account for* about 70 percent of the total market value of all corporate assets in the United States. 知的資産は、米国では全企業資産の総時価評価額の約70%を占めている。

account payable 買掛金, 未払い金, 支払い勘定, 支払い債務, 買入れ債務, 購入債務, 仕入債務
  account-payable-trade 買掛金, 営業支払い勘定 (＝trade accounts payable)
  accounts payable-other 未払い金
  accounts payable to affiliated companies 関係会社買掛金, 関係会社未払い金, 関係会社支払い勘定

▶*Accounts payable* are lower because of reduced access and other interconnection costs. 買掛金は、アクセス料とその他の中間接続原価の減少に伴って減少します。

account receivable 売掛金, 未収金, 未収入金, 受取勘定, 売掛債権, 売上債権, 受取債権 (＝account due, sales credit)
  account receivable-misc 未収入金
  accounts receivable balances 売掛金残高
  accounts receivable collection 売上債権[売掛金]の回収
  accounts receivable discounted 割引売上債権
  accounts receivable sold 売掛金の売却
  accounts receivable-trade 売掛金, 営業上の未収金, 営業受取勘定

▶The growth in *accounts receivable* comes from our higher sales levels. 売掛金の増加は、当社の販売額の増加によるものです。

account settlement 決算 (＝settlement of accounts; ⇒confidence)
  account settlement term 決算期
  account settlement term ending in March 3月決算期, 3月期
  annual account settlement ending in March 3月期決算, 3月終了の年次決算
  March account settlement 3月期決算
  midyear account settlement 中間決算 (＝midterm account settlement)
  the latest account settlement 今決算

▶The end-of-year *account settlements* of Japanese companies are generally announced in May or June. 一般に日本企業は、5, 6月に3月期決算の発表を行う。

▶All business sectors registered year-on-year increases in earnings and profit for the *account settlement* term ending in March. 3月期は、前年同期比で全業種が増収増益だった。

accountability 名 義務, 責任, 実施義務, 説明責任, 報告責任, 会計責任, 企業責任, アカウンタビリティ
  accountability of assets 資産に対する企業責任
  accountability to customers 顧客への説明責任
  business accountability 独立採算
  corporate accountability 企業の説明責任
  management accountability 経営の説明責任, 経営の説明責任能力
  operational accountability 経営責任
  stewardship accountability 受託責任

▶Corporation's internal controls are designed to adequately safeguard, verify and maintain *accountability* of assets. 当社の内部統制は、資産に対する企業責任を十分に保証・確認・維持するよう図られています。

accountable 形 (…する)責任がある
  accountable for ... …に対して責任がある, …の責任がある
  be held accountable for ... …の責任を問われる, …について責任がある
  hold accountable for ... …に責任を持たせる

▶Executives will be held *accountable* if the low-rated government bonds they have purchased fail to produce profits. 経営者が購入した格付けの低い国債が利益を生み出さなかったら[経営者が格付けの低い国債への投資で失敗したら]、経営者が(株主から)その責任を問われることになる。

▶The bank's investigation committee is compiling a report that holds several former executives *accountable* for the enormous losses. 同行の調査委員会は、旧経営陣数名に多額の損失の責任を問う内容の報告書をまとめている。

accountancy 名 会計の専門領域

accountant 名 会計士, 会計[経理]担当者, 会計専門家, 監査人 (⇒independent accountant)
  accountant general 経理部長
  accountant's certificate 監査報告書
  accountant's fee 監査報酬
  accountant's office 会計事務所
  certified accountant 公認会計士

certified management accountant 公認管理会計士

certified public accountant 公認会計士

chartered accountant 勅許会計士

chief accountant 会計主任, 経理課長, 主任会計審査官

continuing accountant 継続会計士

public accountant 公認会計士, 公共会計士, 職業会計士［会計人］

reporting accountant 報告会計士

tax accountant 税理士

▸Four certified public *accountants* at ChuoAoyama PricewaterhouseCoopers were involved in the window dressing. 中央青山監査法人の4人の公認会計士が, 粉飾決算に関与していた。

accounting 名 会計, 会計処理, 決算処理, 会計処理方法, 会計学, 経理, 計算, 算定 (⇒**change in accounting, corporate accounting principles, mark-to-market**)

accounting audit 会計監査

accounting consolidation 連結会計

accounting control 会計上の統制

accounting date 決算日

accounting department 経理部, 経理部門, 会計部門 (=accounting division, accounting section)

accounting elements 財務諸表の基本要素

accounting entity 会計実体, 会計主体

accounting equation 会計等式

accounting firm 会計事務所, 会計士事務所, 監査法人

accounting income 会計上の利益 (⇒**provide**)

accounting interpretations APB意見書解釈

accounting manual 会計手続書, 会計規程(集), 会計便覧

accounting policy 会計方針, 経理方針(財務書類の作成にあたって採用した会計処理や表示方法)

accounting profit 会計上の利益(一般に公正妥当と認められた会計原則に従って測定・計算された利益)

accounting qualities 会計情報の特質

accounting record 会計記録, 会計帳簿

accounting reports 会計報告書, 財務諸表, 有価証券報告書, 財務情報

Accounting Research Bulletin 会計調査公報《略 ARB》

accounting scandal 〈不正経理や粉飾決算などの〉企業会計疑惑, 会計疑惑, 会計処理疑惑会計不祥事, 会計スキャンダル, 不正会計事件

Accounting Series Release 会計連続通牒

accounting term ending in September 2008 2008年9月期, 2008年9月中間決算, 2008年9月に終了する会計期間

accounting theory 会計理論

accounting year 会計年度 (=accounting period, business year, fiscal year, operating period)

corporate accounting 企業会計

current cost accounting 現在原価会計, 時価主義会計

current cost/constant dollar accounting 現在原価・統一ドル会計, 現在原価・恒常ドル会計

current cost/constant purchasing power accounting 現在原価・統一購買力会計

current value accounting 現在価値会計, 時価主義会計

▸The *accounting* books and other data have been leaked. 会計帳簿や他のデータが流出してしまった。

accounting change 会計処理の変更, 会計基準の変更, 会計上の変更, 会計処理方法の変更, 会計見積りの変更 (⇒**change, cumulative effect**)

an accounting change that should be reported by restating the financial statements of all prior periods presented 表示するすべての過年度財務書類［財務諸表］を再表示して報告しなければならない会計上の変更

an accounting change that should be reported prospectively 見込みで報告しなければならない会計上の変更

▸Income taxes for 2007 have not been restated for this *accounting change*. 2007年度の法人所得税額は, この会計処理の変更による修正・再表示を行っていません。

▸We made three *accounting changes* this past year. 当社は, 当年度に三つの会計処理の変更を行いました。

accounting for ... …の会計, …の会計処理, …の決算処理

accounting for changing prices 物価変動会計

accounting for contingencies 偶発事象の会計, 偶発事象の会計処理

accounting for corporate social responsibility 社会責任会計

accounting for equities 持ち分会計

accounting for foreign currency translation 外貨換算会計

accounting for impaired assets［**the impairment of assets**］ 減損会計 (=asset impairment accounting)

accounting for retirement benefit 退職給付会計
▶In 2008 we are to adopt SFAS No.115, "*Accounting for* Certain Investments in Debt and Equity Securities."　2008年度から当社は, SFAS（財務会計基準書）第115号「負債証券および持ち分証券への特定の投資に関する会計処理」を採用することになっています。

accounting for income taxes 法人税等に関する会計処理, 法人所得税会計
▶In 2006, the Company adopted SFAS No. 109, "*Accounting for income Taxes*."　2006年度に当社は, 財務会計基準諸（SFAS）第109号「法人税等に関する会計処理基準」を採用しました。

accounting for postemployment benefits 退職後給付会計, 退職後給付についての会計処理, 退職後給付に関する会計処理
▶Our new *accounting for postemployment benefits* is very similar to our new accounting for retiree benefits.　退職後給付に関する当社の新会計処理方法は, 退職者給付に関する当社の新会計処理方法に極めて近いものです。

accounting for retiree benefits 退職者給付会計, 退職者給付についての会計処理
▶We changed our *accounting for retiree benefits*, postemployment benefits and income taxes.　当社は, 退職者給付, 退職後給付と法人税についての会計処理方法を変更しました。

accounting manipulation 会計操作（＝accounting fraud）
▶Such an *accounting manipulation* can be done simply by doctoring the books.　このような会計操作は, 帳簿に手を加えるだけで簡単にできる。

accounting method 会計処理方法, 会計方法
▶We sometimes decide to change our *accounting methods* because of trends in our business or industry.　当社は, 当社の事業や業界の動向に応じて会計処理方法の変更を決定することもあります。

accounting period 会計期間, 会計年度, 事業年度（＝financial period, financial year, fiscal period, fiscal year：財務書類［財務諸表］の基本会計期間は1年となっている）
　the accounting period ending March 31 3月31日終了会計年度, 3月期決算
　the latest accounting period 当事業年度, 当期
▶Major corporations' percentage of the drop in after-tax gains significantly exceeded that of the fall in recurring profits during the latest *accounting period*.　当期は, 大手企業の税引き後利益の減少率が経常利益の減少率を大きく上回った。

accounting practice 会計実務, 会計慣行, 会計処理
　specialized accounting practice 特殊な会計実務
　statement of recommended accounting practices 会計実務勧告書

accounting principle 会計原則, 会計基準, 会計処理基準, 会計処理の方法（⇒**generally accepted accounting principles**）
　accounting principle change 会計原則の変更
　accounting principles and practices 会計原則, 会計方針と手続き
　Accounting Principles for Business Enterprises 企業会計原則
▶The financial statements have been prepared in accordance with Canadian generally accepted *accounting principles*.　この財務書類は, カナダの会計基準に準拠して［カナダの一般に認められた会計基準に従って］作成されています。

accounting rule 会計規則, 会計基準
▶Under the new *accounting rules* introduced in April 2001, banks are required to deduct 60 percent of appraisal losses on shareholdings from retained earnings.　2001年4月から導入された会計規則（時価会計）で, 銀行は保有株の評価損［含み損］の6割を剰余金から差し引かなければならない。

accounting standards 会計基準, 会計原則（＝accounting criteria; ⇒**current value accounting**）
　Accounting Standards for Business Enterprises 企業会計原則
　Accounting Standards for Consolidated Financial Statements 連結財務諸表原則
　accounting standards for foreign currency translation 外貨換算基準, 換算基準
　U.S. accounting standards 米国会計基準
▶For the business year ending in March 2008, we will post more than ¥3 trillion in consolidated operating profits based on U.S. *accounting standards*.　2008年3月期連結決算で, 米国会計基準に基づく当社の連結営業利益は3兆円を上回る見通しだ。

accounting system 会計制度, 会計組織, 会計システム, 計算制度, 計算体系
▶In financial institutions, an *accounting system* to evaluate assets based on market values was introduced in April 2004.　金融機関の場合は, 時価会計制度（時価に基づいて資産を評価する制度）が, 2004年4月から導入された。

▸Internal auditors continually review the *accounting* and control *systems*.　内部監査人は、継続して当社の会計処理システムと管理システムを検討しています。

accounts　財務書類, 財務諸表, 計算書類, 勘定, 会計記録, 決算　（＝financial statements; ⇒**group accounts**）

   abridged accounts　略式財務諸表

   accounts settlement ending in March　3月期決算

   annual accounts　年次財務諸表

   book of accounts　会計帳簿, 財務帳簿　（＝accounts book）

   closing of accounts　決算

   corporate accounts　会社財務諸表

   current cost accounts　現在原価財務諸表, カレント・コスト財務諸表

   final accounts　決算財務諸表

   historical cost accounts　取得原価主義財務諸表

   income and expenditure accounts　収支計算書

   individual accounts　個別財務諸表

   interim accounts　中間財務諸表, 中間財務書類, 半期財務書類　（＝interim financial statements, interim statements）

   midyear accounts　中間決算

   modified accounts　修正財務諸表

   periodic financial accounts　期間財務諸表

   profit and loss accounts　損益計算書

   statement of accounts　決算報告書

   the half-year closing of fiscal 2008 accounts　2008年度中間決算

   the last period of settlement of accounts　最終決算期

▸The consolidated financial statements include the *accounts* of the corporation and all subsidiary companies.　連結財務書類には、当社と全子会社の財務書類(経営成績と財政状態に関する情報)が含まれています。

▸This midranked general contractor is said to have window-dressed *accounts* for four years.　この中堅ゼネコンは、4年間、決算を粉飾したといわれている。

accrual　〈利子や権利などの〉発生, 未払い金, 未払い費用, 未払い額見越し, 見越し額, 見越し項目, 引当金, 見積り額, 増加額, 増加部分

   accrual basis　発生主義, 発生基準　（＝accrual concept, accrual method, accrual principle）

   accrual expense　発生費用, 見越し費用

   accrual rate　経過金利

▸Current liabilities increased due primarily to increased *accruals* resulting from the restructuring and other actions taken in the fourth quarter.　流動負債の増加は、主に第4四半期に実施した事業再編成などの施策に伴って発生した引当金の増加によるものです。

accrue　生じる, 発生する, 付加する, 付与する, 増加する, 計上する, 見越し計上する　（⇒**current service cost**）

   running royalty accruing under this agreement　本契約により生じるランニング・ロイヤルティ

▸The Corporation has fully *accrued* on its books all income taxes for any period which is not yet due.　当社は、まだ支払い期日が到来していない期間のすべての法人税等を、当社の会計帳簿に全額計上しています。

accrued　発生した, 未払いの, 未収の

   accrued and other liabilities　未払い費用およびその他の負債

   accrued basis　発生主義, 発生基準

   accrued bonuses　賞与引当金, 未払い賞与

   accrued compensated absences　未払い有給休暇

   accrued compensation　未払い報酬

   accrued depreciation　減価償却累計額, 発生減価　（＝accumulated depreciation, allowance [reserve] for depreciation）

   accrued dividend　未払い配当金

   accrued expenses　発生経費, 未払い費用　（＝accrued charges, accrued payables, accrued liabilities）

   accrued expenses and liabilities　未払い費用および負債

   accrued income taxes　未払い法人税, 未払い税金

   accrued payables　未払い費用　（＝accrued charges, accrued expenses, accrued liabilities）

   accrued payroll　未払い給与

   accrued pension cost　未払い年金費用　（＝accrued retirement benefits for employees, allowance for retirement benefits for employees）

   accrued plan benefits　年金給付債務額

   accrued postretirement benefit cost　未払い退職後給付費用

   accrued postretirement benefit obligation　未払い退職後給付債務

   accrued property taxes　未払い固定資産税

   accrued receivables　未収収益, 見越し債権　（＝accrued income, accrued revenues）

   accrued revenues　未収収益　（＝accrued income, accrued receivables）

accrued taxes on incme 未払い法人税等, 未払い法人所得税

accrued charges 未払い費用（＝accrued expenses, accrued payables, accrued liabilities：すでに役務の提供を受けているが, 決算日時点でまだ支払いがなされていない費用で, 当期の費用として計上されるもの）

accrued income 未収収益（＝accrued receivables, accrued revenues）

accrued income to subsidiaries 子会社未収収益

accrued interest 発生済み利息, 発生利息, 未払い［未収］利息, 経過利息（＝interest accrued）

accrued interest expenses on bonds payable 社債の未払い利息

accrued interest on loan 貸付け未収利息

accrued interest payable 未払い利息

accrued interest receivable 未収利息

▶This amount includes the appropriate *accrued interest*. この金額には, 適切な未収利息が含まれています。

accrued liabilities 未払い負債, 未払い債務, 未払い費用, 見越し負債

▶Interest expense is the interest on short-term and long-term debt and *accrued liabilities*. 支払い利息は, 短期および長期負債と未払い債務に対する利息です。

accumulate 動 蓄積する, 累積する

accumulated 形 蓄積した, 累積した

accumulated and accrued plan benefits 累積年金給付債務額（⇒**weighted average discount rate**）

accumulated deficit 累積赤字（＝accumulative deficit）

accumulated dividend 累積配当, 累積利益配当, 累積未払い配当

accumulated earnings 利益剰余金, 留保利益, 累積利益, 積立利益（＝accumulated income, accumulated profit）

accumulated charged expenditure 累計支出額

accumulated income 利益剰余金, 留保利益, 累積利益（＝accumulated earnings, earned surplus, retained earnings）

accumulated other comprehensive income その他の包括利益累計額

accumulated plan benefits 年金未支給額, 年金給付累積額, 累積給付, 累積給付債務額（⇒**pension liability, prepay**）

accumulated postretirement benefit obligation 累積退職後給付債務

accumulated profit 利益剰余金, 留保利益（＝accumulated income）

accumulated depreciation 減価償却累計額, 減価償却引当金（＝accrued depreciation, allowance [reserve] for depreciation; ⇒**net of ...**）

accumulated depreciation and amortization 減価償却累計額, 減価償却引当金

▶When we sell or retire plant that was depreciated using the group method, we deduct the original cost from the plant account and from *accumulated depreciation*. グループ償却法を用いて償却した工場を売却もしくは除却する場合, 当社は当該工場の取得原価を当該資産勘定と減価償却累計額から控除します。

accumulated liability 累積債務

▶When we adopted the new standard, we had an *accumulated liability* related to past service from retirees and active employees. 当社が新基準を採用した時点で, 当社には退職者と現従業員の過去勤務に関する累積債務がありました。

accumulation 名 蓄積, 増加, 累積, 蓄財, 積み増し, 利殖, アキュムレーション

accumulation plan 積立プラン

capital accumulation ［accumulation of capital］ 資本蓄積

cost accumulations 原価累積額

debt accumulation 累積債務

inventory accumulation ［accumulation of inventories］ 在庫の増加, 在庫の積み増し

accuse 動 告発する, 告訴する, 起訴する, 訴える, 非難する, 責める, 指摘する

▶A major credit guarantor company has been *accused* of concealing taxable income by the Tokyo Regional Taxation Bureau. 大手の信用保証会社が, 東京国税局から課税所得隠しを指摘された。

ACE 調整後当期利益（adjusted current earningsの略）

achieve 動 達成する, 完了する, 獲得する, 確保する, もたらす（＝rack up）

achieve improved results 業績が改善する

achieve one's planned growth 成長目標を達成する

achieve profitability 黒字転換を果たす, 黒字化する

▶This improvement in revenues was *achieved* despite a lower rate of growth in the number of network access services. この収益改善は, ネットワーク・アクセス・サービス利用件数の伸び率が低下したにもかかわらず達成しました。

achievement 名 成績, 業績, 達成, 成果

achievement value 業績価値

actual achievement 実績
corporate achievements 企業の業績
employee achievements 従業員の功績
financial achievement 業績
performance achievement 業績達成
▸The compay, aiming to expand its financial *achievement*, will open a new factory in Texas in May 2008.　業績拡大を目指す同社は、2008年5月に米テキサスの新工場を稼働させる。

acid test
厳しい検査、最終的な厳しい考査、厳しい試験、酸性試験、吟味、厳しい試練、試金石、正念場　（＝severe test）
▸All major banking groups now face the *acid test* of whether they can regain profitability this fiscal year.　大手銀行・金融グループは、すべて今期の収益力回復に向けて正念場を迎えている。

acid test ratio
当座比率、酸性試験比率　（＝quick ratio：企業の短期的な支払い能力を示す財務指標の一つで、流動負債に対する当座資産（現金・預金、受取勘定、市場性有価証券などの合計額）の割合）

acquire 動
取得する、購入する、引き受ける、買収する　（＝buy, purchase；⇒controlling stake, veto）
acquired company 被買収会社、被買収企業　（＝acquiree company, acquired firm）
acquired entity 被獲得主体
▸Under the new Corporate Law, a subsidiary of a foreign company is allowed to use shares of the parent to *acquire* a Japanese company.　新会社法では、外国企業の子会社が親会社の株を用いて日本企業を買収することができる。
▸We *acquired* shares in the company.　当社は、同社の株式を取得しました。

acquirer 名
買収会社、買収企業、買収者、取得者、購入者、買取り手
▸A foreign *acquirer* of a Japanese company is allowed to pay shareholders of the Japanese entity "merger consideration" in the form of cash and the parent company's shares.　日本企業を買収する外国企業は現在、「合併の対価」を、現金や親会社の株式の形で日本企業の株主に支払うことができる。

acquiring entity 獲得主体

acquisition 名
取得、購入、買取り、買付け、買収、企業取得、企業買収、事業買収
acquisition and development アクイジッション・アンド・ディベロプメント《略 A&D》（買収により新技術や商圏を取り込み、成長戦略の武器にすること）
acquisition by gift 贈与による取得
acquisition cost 取得原価、買収コスト、新契約費　（＝cost）
acquisition of businesses 事業の買収
acquisition of fixed assets 固定資産購入、固定資産の取得
acquisition offer 買収の申込み、買収提案
acquisition price 取得価格、買付け価格、取得原価、買収価格
acquisition strategy 買収戦略
corporate acquisition 企業買収、企業取得　（＝acquisition of business, business acquisition, corporate buyout）
discount on acquisition 買入のれん
friendly acquisition 友好的買収
hostile acquisition 敵対的買収
major acquisition 大型買収
neutral acquisition 中立的買収
share-swap acquisition 株式交換による買収
stock [share] acquisition 株式取得、株式購入
▸We made some important adjustments and *acquisitions* in the area of telecommunications in 2007.　2007年度は、通信事業の分野で、重要な調整と買収をいくつか実施しました。

ACRS
加速原価回収制度［回収法］、加速償却制度、加速償却法（**accelerated cost recovery system** の略）

action 名
行動、活動、実行、動き、〈行政上の〉処分、措置、対応、決議、決定、訴え、訴訟、判決、行為、作為、アクション
action point 行動提案
adminstrarive action 行政処分
affirmative action 積極的優遇措置、積極的是正措置、差別修正措置、差別撤廃措置、少数民族の優遇措置、アファーマティブ・アクション
antidumping actions 反ダンピング措置
business action 業務行為
disciplinary actions 懲戒処分
line of action 行動方針
price action 値動き
▸We have taken many *actions* in the last five years to streamline our business and reduce the number of employees.　事業の合理化と従業員数削減のため、当社はここ5年間に多くの施策を講じてきました。

action program
行動計画、実行計画、アクション・プログラム　（＝action plan）
▸We have a written *action program* which includes everything posing a threat to the environment: plant, use of products and even their journey to the rubbish tip.　当社の文書化したア

クション・プログラムには，生産設備や製品の使用から製品の廃品処理場に行き着くまでの過程にいたるまで，環境を脅かすあらゆる要因が盛り込まれています．

activity 名 活動，動き，働き，活動範囲，活動度，操業，事業，業務，取引，活気，活況，景気，好景気
 activity level 操業度
 activity method 生産高比例法（＝production method）
 business activities 事業活動，企業活動，営業活動，経営活動，景気，商況，業況
 core activities 中核事業，主力事業，主力業務（＝core business, main activities）
 credit activities 与信業務
 financial activity 資金調達活動
 financing activities 財務活動
 international activities 国際事業
 investing activities 投資活動
 local citizenship activities 社会貢献活動
 operating activities 営業活動
 pick-up in activity 景気回復
 principal areas of activity 中核事業
 profit or loss from[on]ordinary activities 経常損益
 quality control activity QC活動
 regional activity 地域活動
 report of activity 営業報告書，活動報告書
 statement of activity 営業報告書，活動報告書
 trading activities 業務展開
▸Much of the financing *activities* shown on our statement of cash flows relates to these refinancing *activities*.　当社のキャッシュ・フロー計算書に示した資金調達活動の大半は，負債の借換え関連です．
▸This amount of cash was provided by business *activities*.　この現金額は，営業活動で得られたものだ．

activity based costing 活動基準原価計算，活動基準原価管理，ABC管理《略 **ABC**》（一つの作業にかかった時間を計測して，かかった時間に応じて人件費などの間接コストを配賦し，製品の正確な原価を割り出す手法．隠れた不採算製品の洗い出しなどに効果がある，とされている）

activity based management 活動基準管理《略 **ABM**》（活動基準原価計算(ABC)を利用して業務改革につなげる取組み）

actual 形 実際の，実地の，現実的，現実の，実質的，事実上の，現行の
 actual cost 実際原価，取得原価
 actual cost method 実際原価法，実価法，個別法
 actual demand 実需
 actual expense 実際経費，実費
 actual growth rate 現実成長率
 actual inventory 実地棚卸し
 actual losses 実際の損失額，実損
 actual margin 実効証拠金率
 actual overhead rate 実際配賦（はいふ）率，製造間接費実際配賦率
 actual rate of interest 実際利率
 actual record 実績
 actual transaction 実際取引
 actual value method 実価法，個別法
▸The taxes banks pay in writing off their nonperforming loans are refunded to banks after the amount of the *actual* losses is determined.　銀行が不良債権処理の際に納める税金は，実際の損失額が確定した後，銀行に戻ってくる．

actuarial 形 年金数理計算上の，年金数理上の，保険数理上の
 actuarial asset value 保険数理による資産価値
 actuarial assumption 年金数理計算上の仮定，保険数理上の計算基礎，年金数理計算上の基礎率（⇒salary projection）
 actuarial gains and[or]losses 保険数理上の損益，年金数理上の誤差，数理計算上の差異（年金基金の運用時に生じる見積り額と実際額との差額）
 actuarial liability 保険数理上の債務
 actuarial measurement of pension cost and obligation 年金費用および年金債務額の統計的手法による測定
 actuarial method 年金数理法，保険数理法
 actuarial valuation 保険数理評価，保険数理価値
▸Pension cost in 2007 was lower than in 2006 principally due to *actuarial* assumption changes in the U.S. and several non-U.S. plans.　2007年度の年金費用は，主に米国内制度と一部の米国外制度の年金数理上の仮定の変更により，前年度より減少しました．

actuarial cost method 保険数理原価法，保険数理による原価計算法，年金数理計算方式
▸Under the noncontributory defined benefit plans, pension costs are funded through contributions based on various *actuarial cost methods* as permitted by pension regulatory bodies.　非拠出型確定給付年金制度[非拠出型給付金規定方式による年金制度]のもとでは，年金の所轄官庁により認められた各種の保険数理原価法[年金数理計算方式]に基づいて算定される拠出金[年金掛金]により，年金費用を賄う[積み立てる]ことになっています．

actuarial present value 年金数理上の現在価値, 保険数理上の現在価値
  actuarial present value of accumulated benefit obligation 累積給付債務の保険数理上の現在価値
  actuarial present value of accumulated plan benefits 保険数理計算による年金未支給額の現在価値［現価］, 年金制度上の将来給付額の年金数理現価, 累積年金給付額の保険数理上の現在価値, 年間給付累積額の保険数理現在価値
  actuarial present value of benefit obligation 給付債務の保険数理上の現在価値, 保険数理に基づく給付債務の現在価値
  actuarial present value of plan benefits 年金給付の年金数理現価
  actuarial present value of projected benefit obligation 予測給付債務の保険数理上の現在価値
  actuarial present value of vested accumulated plan benefits 受給権の発生していない累積年金給付額の保険数理上の現在価値
▶The *actuarial present value* of the accrued plan benefits and the net assets available to discharge these benefits at December 31 are as follows: 12月31日現在の年金給付債務額の年金数理原価と年金給付債務に充当可能な年金純資産は, 以下のとおりです。

actuarially computed value 保険数理上の計算価値

actuary 名 保険数理士, 保険計理士, 保険数理専門家, 年金数理人, アクチュアリー
▶An *actuary* applies the theory of probability to the business of insurance and is responsible for the calculation of premiums, policy reserves and other values. 保険数理士は, 保険業に確率論を適用して, 保険料, 保険契約準備金やその他の価値を計算するのが仕事だ。

ad 広告（**advertisement, advertising**の略）

ADD: Deposit in transit 加算：未記入の預け入れ

add back 加算戻しをする, 振り戻す
▶For the computation of the earnings per share, assuming full dilution, dividends on convertible preferred shares have been *added back* to income. 完全希薄化を仮定した場合の1株当たり純利益［利益］の計算では, 転換可能優先株式への配当は利益に振り戻してあります。

add-back 加算戻し, 振戻し

add（deduct）noncash items 非金銭［非現金］項目増加(減少)

ADD—Net income 加算―当期利益
added value 付加価値, 付加価値額（＝value added）
  added value per employee 従業員1人当たりの付加価値額（⇒**manpower**）
  added value statement 付加価値計算書
  added value tax 付加価値税
▶Our affiliate program offers your Web site the opportunity to generate profit while providing *added value* to your customers. 当社のアフィリエイト・プログラムは, あなたの顧客に付加価値を提供しながら利益を生み出す機会を, あなたのウェブサイトに提供します。

addition 名 追加, 追加投資, 付加, 加算, 増築, 増設, 増加, 拡大
  addition to reserves 積立金繰入れ
  additions and betterments [improvements] reserves 増改築積立金, 増設改良積立金
  additions to long-term debt 長期債務の増加
  capital additions 追加資本, 追加投資, 追加設備投資（⇒**reliability**）
  plant additions 工場の増設
▶We had lower depreciation expense because we reduced plant *additions*. 工場の増設を手控えたため, 減価償却費は低下しました。

additional 形 追加的な, 付加的な, 特別の
  additional allowance 割増手当
  additional charge 追加料金, 追加費用, 割増料金
  additional equity capital 増資（＝additional equity）
  additional expense 追加費用
  additional fund 追加資金
  additional paid-in capital 株式払込み剰余金, 払込み資本剰余金, 資本剰余金, 払込み剰余金, 付加的払込み資本, 追加払込み資本（＝capital surplus）
  additional paid-in capital from treasury stock 株式払込み剰余金・自己株式より
  additional share 追加株式, 増資株, 増資, 株式数の増加
  additional tax 追徴税, 加算税, 増税
  additonal working capital 追加的運転資金
additional capital 増資資本
▶As in the past, the Corporation and its subsidiaries raised *additional capital* during this year's first half. 従来どおり, 当社と子会社は当上半期も追加資本を調達しました。

additional investment 追加投資
▶The principal requirement for funds is for capital expenditures and to acquire new and *addi-*

tional investments. 資金需要は, 主に資本的支出と新規および追加投資を行うにあたって発生します。

adjust 動 修正する, 調整する, 調節する, 補正する
 adjusted bank balance 修正後銀行残高
 adjusted current earnings 調整後当期利益《略 ACE》
 adjusted gross income 調整後総所得
 adjusted net profit 修正後純利益
 value of assets adjusted to market 時価に修正した資産価額
 ▶We recognized a $80 million benefit from *adjusting* our deferred tax assets for the new tax rate. 新税率を適用して当社の繰延べ税金資産を調整した結果, 8,000万ドルの利益を認識しました。

adjustment 名 調整, 修正, 照合, 整理, 査定, 精算 (⇒foreign currency translation)
 accounting adjustment of prior periods 過年度修正, 前期損益修正
 adjustment for fractional differences 四捨五入による調整
 adjustment for taxable income 税務調整, 申告調整
 adjustment of financial statements of prior periods 過年度の財務諸表修正
 adjustments to reconcile net earnings to cash provided from operating activities 純利益と営業活動から生じた資金との調整
 backlog adjustment 遡及修正
 capital adjustment 資本修正
 closing adjustment 決算整理, 決算整理事項 (=close adjustment)
 currency translation adjustment 外貨換算調整勘定
 downward adjustment 下方修正, 減額修正, 下方調整
 exchange rate adjustment 為替レートの調整
 experience adjustment 実績による修正
 inventory adjustment 在庫調整
 loss adjustment expense 損害査定費
 prior period adjustment 過年度修正, 過年度損益修正, 前期損益修正
 production adjustment 生産調整
 seasonal adjustment 季節調整
 upward adjustment 上方修正, 増額修正
 ▶We make all the *adjustments* needed to catch up with these new accounting methods. これらの新会計処理方法に対応するにあたって, 必要な修正はすべて行っています。

administration 名 経営, 経営管理, 管理, 運営, 事務, 事務管理, 業務, 執行, 政権, 政府, 行政
 administration cost [expense] 一般管理費 (=administration overhead)
 administration of shares 株式事務 (⇒consign)
 administration process 社内手続き, 事務手続き
 board of administration 理事会
 business administration 企業経営, 商工経営, 経営管理 (=business management)
 capital and administration 資本と経営
 department administration 部門管理
 financial administration 財務管理, 財政
 human resources and administration department 人事・総務部
 personnel administration 人事管理
 ▶We continued to consolidate support activities for manufacturing, development and *administration*. 当社は, 引き続き製造, 開発と事務部門に対する支援活動を統合しました。

administrative 形 経営管理上の, 経営上の, 運営上の, 管理上の, 管理的, 行政の
 administrative and general expense 一般管理費
 administrative and maintenance expenses 維持管理費, 維持管理費用
 administrative and selling expenses 一般管理費および販売費
 administrative cost 一般管理費, 管理費, 運営経費, 運営管理費
 administrative expenses 一般管理費, 管理費, 経費 (=administration costs, administration overhead, administrative and general expense)
 ▶Operating profit, or sales minus the cost of goods sold and *administrative* expenses, rose 1.4 percent to ¥161 billion from ¥159 billion a year ago. 売上高から販売した製品の製造原価 [売上原価] と一般管理費を差し引いた収益を示す営業利益は, 前期の1,590億円に対して1.4％増の1,610億円でした。

administrator 名 管理者, 管財人

adopt 動 採用する, 採択する, 可決する, 〈計画などを〉実施する, 選出する, 指名する
 ▶We *adopt* SFAS No.106, "Employers' Accounting for Postretirement Benefits Other Than Pensions." 当社では, 財務会計基準書 (SFAS) 第106号「年金以外の退職後給付に関する事業主の会計処理」を採用しています。

advance 動 進歩する, 発展する, 前進する, 進出する, 増加する, 上昇する, 向上する, 値上がりする, 進める, 促進する, 〈提出する予定を〉繰り上げる, 前渡しする, 前払いする, 提供する

advance funds 資金を提供する
advance strongly 力強く伸びる, 力強く値上がりする, 大幅に伸びる, 大幅の伸びを示す, 力強い伸びを示す
▶The firm's consolidated sales *advanced* 13.4 percent to ¥21.04 trillion. 同社の連結売上高は, 前期比13.4%増の21兆400億円となった。

advance 名 進歩, 発展, 進展, 革新, 前進, 進出, 増加, 上昇, 向上, 騰貴, 値上がり, 前払い, 前渡し, 前貸し, 融資, 借入れ, 前払い金, 前渡し金, 前貸し金, 前受金, 前金, 仮払い金, 借入金
advance accounting 前倒し計上
advance corporation tax 前払い法人税, 予納法人税 《略 ACT》
advance from customers 顧客からの前受金
advance in profits 増益
advance in productivity 生産性の伸び, 生産性の向上
advance of funds 資金の提供
advance payments 前払い金
advance premium 前払い保険料
advance redemption 繰上げ償還
advance refunding 〈社債の〉満期日前償還, 借換え債務の事前負担（期中償還と同義）
advance sales 予約販売
advances from customers 顧客からの前受金, 顧客前受金, 得意先前受金
advances or loans to directors/employees 役員・従業員に対する貸付け金
advances payable 借入金, 前受金
advances receivable 貸付け金, 前渡し金
advances to affiliates 関係会社貸付け金, 関係会社立替金, 関係会社前渡し金
advances to employees 従業員貸付け金, 従業員立替金
bank advance 銀行貸出
economic advance 経済進出
generate a strong advance 業績を大幅に伸ばす
make a liquidity advance 資金を提供する, 流動性を供与する
strong advance 力強い伸び, 大幅の伸び
technical advances 技術革新, 技術の進歩 (＝advances in technology)
▶Another strong *advance* will be seen. 今後は, もう一段の力強い伸び［もう一段の上げ相場］が期待されます。
▶Deferred tax assets are essentially taxes paid in *advance* that are expected to be refunded when the bank incurs losses, for instance by writing off bad loans resulting from the bankruptcy of corporate borrowers. 繰延べ税金資産は本質的に前払いした税金で, 例えば融資先企業の倒産などで不良債権を処理して, 銀行が損失を被った時点で戻ってくる。

advanced 形 進歩した, 高等の
advanced technology 先進技術, 最新技術, 高度な技術, 技術の進歩, 技術革新
products of advanced technology 先端技術製品, ハイテク製品

advantage 名 有利, 利点, 強み, メリット, 利益, 優勢, 優位, 優位性, 競争力, 優遇措置 (⇒**competitive advantage**)
comparative advantage 比較優位
cost advantage コスト面での競争力
gross advantage 総利益
net advantage 正味利益
tax advantages 税制上の優遇措置, 節税効果
▶An urgent task facing each financial group is to improve its financial conditions and profitability on the strength of *advantages* gained from merger. 合併・統合の相乗効果を生かして, 財務内容と収益力を向上させることが, 各金融グループの現在の急務だ。
▶We hope to retain our *advantages* by slowing down the technology drain. 当社としては, 技術流出を遅らせて当社の優位性を保ちたい。

advertisement 名 広告, 広告宣伝 (＝ad, advertising)
▶The company's earnings for Web site *advertisements* in the July–September period last year were almost three times that of the April–June period. 同社の昨年7-9月期のホームページ広告［ネット広告］収益は, 同年4-6月期の約3倍だった。

advertising 名 広告, 広告宣伝, 広告宣伝費 (＝ad, advetisement)
advertising and promotion costs 広告宣伝費
advertising campaign 広告キャンペーン, 広告・宣伝活動 (＝advertising drive)
advertising expense 広告宣伝費
advertising jingle 宣伝文句, 宣伝のかけ声
advertisng revenue 広告収入
B2B advertising ビー・ツー・ビー広告（広告主も広告の受け手も企業である広告活動）
business advertising 企業広告, ビジネス広告
classified advertising 案内広告, 求人・求職広告
corporate advertising 企業広告, 会社の広告
full page advertising 全面広告
mass media advertising マスメディア広告
new product advertising 新製品広告
retail advertising 小売広告

sales promotion advertising SP広告
virtual advertising バーチャル広告
▸A major reason for the slide in USEN's stock price was the company's inaccurate business estimates for the Gyao operation, which depends entirely on *advertising* revenue. USENの株価下落の主因は，完全に広告収入に依存している同社のギャオ事業の業績[収益]見通しの甘さだ．

advisory 形 諮問の，顧問の，投資顧問の，助言の，勧告の
　advisory board 諮問委員会，諮問機関，アドバイザリー・ボード
　advisory council 理事会，参事会，諮問委員会
　advisory income 投資顧問収益
　advisory service 顧問業務
　financial advisory service 財務顧問サービス
　investment advisory service 投資顧問業務，投資顧問サービス
▸The *advisory board* composed of external experts convenes regularly and reports to the executive committee. 社外の有識者を委員とする諮問委員会は，委員会を定期的に開催して，経営委員会に報告書を提出しています［社外の有識者を委員とするアドバイザリー・ボードは，経営委員会の諮問機関として，委員会を定期的に開催しています］．
▸An *advisory* report by Sumitomo Mitsui Banking Corp. said "both tie-up plans are almost the same." 三井住友銀行の意見書は，「両社の提携案は優劣つけがたい」としていた．

AE 〈広告会社の〉営業責任者，〈証券会社の〉セールスマン（**account executive**の略）

affair 名 仕事，業務，事務，事業，事態，情勢，状況，事柄，問題，事件，出来事，事項，関心事，関係（⇒**ethical standard**）
　affairs entrusted 委任事項
　affairs of state 国事，政務
　as affairs stand 現状では
　business affairs 仕事，業務，企業事象
　community affairs 社会事業
　get one's affairs straight 財務を整理する
　international affairs 国際問題，国際関係，対外関係，国際情勢
　on business affairs 商用で，所用で（＝**on business**）
　public affairs 公務，公報
　social affair 会合，パーティ
　state of affairs 事態，形勢，財政状態
　statement of affairs 状況報告書
　wind up one's affairs 店じまいをする
　world affairs 国際問題，国際社会

affect 動 影響を及ぼす，影響を与える
　negatively affect マイナス影響を与える，悪影響を及ぼす
　unfavorably affect 不利な影響を与える，マイナス影響を与える，悪影響を及ぼす
▸This accounting change does not *affect* cash flows. この会計処理の変更は，キャッシュ・フローには影響しません．

affiliate 動 提携する，合併する，傘下入りする，加入する，加盟する，友好関係を結ぶ，提携させる，合併させる，系列[傘下]に置く，加入させる
　affiliated card 提携カード，共用カード
　affiliated company 関連会社，関係会社，系列会社，系列企業，傘下企業（＝**affiliate firm, associated company**）
　affiliated nonblank 系列ノンバンク
　affiliated transaction グループ内取引
　bank-affiliated securities subsidiary 銀行系証券子会社
　foreign-affiliated company 外資系企業
　government-affiliated financial institution 政府系金融機関
▸Both companies are *affiliated* with Mizuho Financial Group. 両社は，みずほフィナンシャルグループの系列会社だ．

affiliate 名 関係会社，関連会社，系列会社，子会社，関係者，提携者，加入者，参加者，アフィリエイト（＝**affiliate firm, affiliated company, associate**; ⇒**consolidated affiliate**）
　関係会社とは➡20％以上，50％以下の議決権株式を所有され，持ち分法を適用される会社のことを関係会社という．これに対して，50％超の議決権株式を所有されている会社が子会社で，米国の会計実務では親会社が連結財務諸表（連結財務書類）を作成する際に原則として連結の範囲に含められる．
　consolidated affiliate 連結対象関連会社
　investment in affiliate 関係会社への投資，関係会社株式（＝**investment in affiliated company**）
　unconsolidated affiliate 連結対象外関連会社
▸Due to the brand's popularity, the number of shops of the company's *affiliate* in Japan has grown to about 70 as of the end of 2007. ブランドの人気で，同社の日本子会社の店舗数は，2007年末現在で約70店にまで拡大した．

affirmative action 積極的優遇措置，積極的是正措置，差別修正措置，差別撤廃措置，少数民族優遇措置，アファーマティブ・アクション
　affirmative action compliance program 積極的優遇措置遵守プログラム

after 前 …差引き後, …控除後, …を控除した[差し引いた]うえで, 事後の
  after cost 事後費用, 事後経費, アフターコスト
  after dividends on preferred shares 優先株式配当額を控除したうえで (⇒**dividend on preferred shares**)
  after giving effect to taxes and minority interest 関連税額と少数株主持ち分利益控除後
  after-hours trading 時間外取引 (=off-hours trading; ⇒**buy up**)
▶*After* taxes, this charge was $1,200 million. 税引き後で, この費用は12億ドルでした。
▶The provisions, *after* giving effect to taxes and minority interest, reduced 2007 earnings by $200 million. これらの引当金繰入れで, 関連税額と少数株主持ち分利益控除後の2007年度の純利益は, 2億ドル減少しました。

after market [aftermarket] 名 販売後市場, 〈有価証券の〉流通市場, 二次市場, 補修部品市場, 関連ハードウエア/ソフトウエア/周辺装置の市場, アフターマーケット (=aftermath market)

after-tax 形 税引き後の, 税引き後で
  after-tax earnings 税引き後利益 (=earnings after tax)
  after-tax effect 税引き後の影響
  after-tax gain 税引き後利益, 税引き後の手取り額 (⇒**accounting period**)
  after-tax income 税引き後所得, 税引き後利益

after-tax balance 税引き後利益
▶The two banks' total *after-tax balance* will move into the red from the previous projection of a ¥125 billion profit. 2行合算ベースの税引き後利益は, これまでの1,250億円の黒字予想から赤字に転落する見通しだ。

after-tax loss 税引き後損失, 税引き後赤字
▶The JAL Group is expected to declare *after-tax losses* of ¥47 billion in the current fiscal year. 日本航空(JAL)グループは, 今期は470億円の税引き後損失を計上する見通しだ。

after-tax margin 税引き後利益率
▶Worldwide net earnings for the nine monts were $3 billion in 2007, with *after-tax margins* of 7.5 percent. 2007年度1-9月期の世界全体での純利益は30億ドルで, 税引き後利益率は7.5％でした。

after-tax profit 税引き後利益, 税引き後黒字 (決算書上では一般に「当期純利益」と表記され, 企業の収益から諸費用や税金を差し引いて残った最終的な利益のこと)

▶The state-funded Japan Post Holdings' *after-tax profits* are expected to be ¥508 billion in fiscal 2008. 政府出資の持ち株会社, 日本郵政グループの2008年度の税引き後利益は, 5,080億円が見込まれている。

age 名 年数, 年齢, 経過期間, 経過年数, 耐用年数
  effective age 実効築後経過年数
  entry age cost method 加入年齢方式
  pensionable age 支給開始年齢
  remaining economic age 経済的残存耐用年数
  weighted average loan age 加重平均ローン経過期間

aggregate 名 総計, 総額, 合計, 総数
  aggregate amount 総額, 合計金額, 総計, 累計
  aggregate basis 一括基準
  aggregate method 総和法
▶Miscellaneous other activities, in the *aggregate*, represent less than 10% of revenues, operating income and identifiable assets. その他の各種事業は, 合計しても, 収益, 営業利益と識別可能資産の10％未満となっています。

aggregate cost method 原価総額方式, 総額原価法, 総合保険料方式 (=aggregate method)
  closed aggregate cost method 閉鎖型総合保険料方式
  open aggregate cost method 開放型総合保険料方式
▶Pension contributions are principally determined using the *aggregate cost method*. 年金拠出額は, 基本的に総額原価法を用いて決定される。

aggregate market value 時価総額 (=aggregate market price, market valuation, total market value)
▶An *aggregate market value* represents a corporate value in terms of stock price. 時価総額は, 株価による企業価値を示す。

aging 高齢化, 加齢, 老化, 老朽, 老朽化, 熟成, 年齢調べ, 年数調べ, 経過期間, エイジング
  accounts-receivable aging 売掛金の年齢調べ, 未収金の経過期間 (=aging of accounts receivable)
  aging of receivables 債権の経過期間
  rapid aging of the population 急速な高齢化
▶The *aging* of small business owners may prove to be a turn of events in the Japanese economy. 中小企業経営者の高齢化は, 日本経済の一つの転機になる可能性がある。

AGM 年次株主総会, 定例株主総会, 定時株主総会, 年次社員総会 (=shareholder AGM: **annual general meeting**の略)

agreement 名 契約, 契約書, 合意, 合意書, 合意事項, 同意, 同意書, 協定, 協約, 取決め （⇒commitment, swap agreement）
  basic agreement 基本的合意, 基本合意, 大筋合意, 基本合意書, 基本契約, 基本契約書
  credit agreement 借入契約 （＝financing agreement）
  currency swap agreement 通貨スワップ契約
  debt agreement 借入契約 （＝financing agreement）
  interest rate swap agreement 金利スワップ契約
  loan agreement 借入契約, 融資契約, 貸付け契約
  reach an agreement 合意に達する, 合意する
  revolving loan agreement 回転融資契約
  sign an agreement 契約を締結する, 契約書[合意書]に署名する, 基本合意する
  software license agreement ソフトウエア使用許諾契約
  underwriting agreement 引受契約
  ▶GM reached a tentative contract *agreement* with the United Auto Workers. GMは, 全米自動車労組（UAW）と暫定協定で合意した。

AICPA 米国公認会計士協会（**American Institute of Certified Public Accountants**の略）

alien 形 外国の, 外国人の, 異質の
alien corporation 外国会社, 外国企業
alliance 名 提携, 提携関係, 連携, 連合, 統合, 同盟, 同盟関係, 同盟国 （＝tie-up; ⇒**business alliance, capital alliance, strategic alliance**）
  alliance pact 提携契約
  capital and business alliance 資本・業務提携, 資本提携を含む業務提携
  comprehensive alliance 包括的提携, 包括提携 （＝broad alliance）
  equity alliance 資本提携関係
  three-way alliance 3社提携
  ▶General Motors Corp.'s board has decided to explore an *alliance* with Renault SA and Nissan Motro Co. ゼネラル・モーターズ（GM）の取締役会は, 仏ルノー・日産自動車連合との提携について調査することを決めた。
  ▶The Nissan-Renault *alliance* and GM has called off *alliance* talks. 日産・仏ルノー連合とGMは, 提携協議を取り止めた。

allocate 動 割り当てる, 配分する, 配賦（はいふ）する, 割り振る （＝allot; ⇒**plan participant, unrealized exchange gains and loses**）
  amounts allocated to income tax liabilities 未払い税金に配分された額
  fully allocated cost 全部配賦原価
  tax effects allocated to stockholders' equity 資本勘定に配分される税効果額
  ▶Hokuetsu Paper Mills Ltd. decided to *allocate* 50 million new shares to trading house Mitsubishi for ¥607 per share and form a business tie-up with the trading house. 北越製紙は, 三菱商事に1株607円で新株5,000株を割り当て, 三菱商事と業務提携することを決めた。

allocation 名 割当て, 配分, 期間配分, 配賦（はいふ）, 原価配賦, 割振り, 配当 （＝allotment）
  allocation of burden 製造間接費の配賦, 間接費の配分
  allocation of capital 資本の投入
  allocation of cost 原価配分, 費用配分, 原価の配賦 （＝cost allocation）
  allocation of income taxes 所得税[法人税]の期間配分
  allocation of new shares to a third party 第三者割当て, 第三者割当て増資 （＝third party allocation, third-party share allotment）
  allocation of revenue 収益の配分
  allocation of shares 株式割当て （＝share allocation）
  asset allocation 資産配分, 資金の割当て
  foreign exchange allocation 外貨割当て, 外貨資金割当て
  fund allocation 資金配分
  liquidity allocation 資金供給
  private allocation 縁故者割当て
  resource allocation 資源配分
  systematic and rational allocation 体系的で合理的な配分
  ▶We intend to rebuild its financial structure by a large-scale *allocation* of the new shares to the third parties. 当社は, 大規模な第三者割当増資で資本構成を再構築する考えだ。

allotment 名 〈株式の〉割当て, 株式配当, 配分, 割当金 （＝allocation; ⇒**recapitalize, third-party allotment**）
  allotment of new shares 新株割当て （＝new share allotment）
  final allotments 最終割当額
  over-allotment option 超過引受オプション
  ▶With a fair and balanced *allotment* of shares, the Corporation laid the foundation for a stable and long-term shareholder securities. 公正でバランスのとれた株式割当てにより, 当社は安定した長期的株主構成の基盤を据えることとなりました。

allowance 名 引当金, 見込み額, 値引き, 控除,

手当, 承認, 許可, 排出権, 排出割当て （⇒length of service, retirement allowances）

allowance for credit losses 貸倒れ引当金 （＝allowance for bad debts, allowance for doubtful debts, allowance for uncollectible debts）

allowance for depreciation 減価償却累計額減, 減価償却引当金 （＝accrued depreciation, accumulated depreciation, depreciation allowance, reserve for depreciation）

allowance for expected returns and allowances 売上戻りおよび値引き見込み額

allowance for inventory price decline 評価損失の記帳

allowance for investment losses 投資損失引当金

allowance for outstanding discounts 売上割引見込み額

allowance for retirement benefits for directors and corporate auditors 役員退職慰労引当金

allowance for uncollectible receivable 回収不能見込み額

allowance method 引当金法, 引当金方式, 引当金設定法

▶We use the *allowance* method based on credit sales to estimate bad debts. 当社は, 不良債権の見積りに掛売りをもとにした引当金設定法を採用しています。

ALM 資産負債総合管理, 資産負債管理, バランスシート管理（asset liability managementの略）

alteration 名 変更, 改変, 修正, 改造, 変造, 改修, 改築, 模様替え

alternative 名 代案, 代替策, 選択肢, 代わるべき手段

　alternative method 代替方式
　alternative source of funds 代替流動性源
　financial alternative 資金調達手段
　investment alternative 投資手段

▶We looked for *alternatives* that would improve prospects for longer-term profits and growth. 私ども経営陣は, 長期的な利益と成長見通しの好転につながる代替策を模索しました。

amalgamation 名 合併（一般に新設合併をconsolidation, 吸収合併をmergerというが, amalgamationは両方の意味で使われる）

American Institute of Certified Public Accountants 米国公認会計士協会 《略 AICPA》

American Stock Exchange アメリカ証券取引所, アメックス《略 AMEX》

AMEX アメリカン証券取引所（American Stock Exchangeの略）

amortization 名 償却, なし崩し償却, 減価償却, 定額償却, 償却額, 償還, 年賦（ねんぷ）償還, 割賦償還, 減算, アモチゼーション （⇒depreciation, depreciation expense）

　amortization of bond discounts 社債発行差金償却
　amortization of deferred asset 繰延べ資産の償却
　amortization of [on] goodwill 営業権の償却
　amortization of past service cost 原始過去勤務原価の償却
　amortization of principal 元本の返済
　amortization of software ソフトウエア償却費
　amortization of transition asset 移行時資産の償却, 移行時差額の償却
　amortization of unrecognized prior service costs 未認識過去勤務債務の償却
　amortization period 元利払い期間

▶*Amortization* of the excess of cost over the net assets acquired is to be recorded over sixty months. 取得した純資産に対する取得価額超過額の償却は, 60か月にわたって行う予定です。

amortize 動 償却する,〈負債などを〉割賦償還する, 定期的に返済する,〈不動産を〉譲渡する （⇒goodwill）

▶For financial reporting purposes, we *amortize* investment tax credits as a reduction to the provision for income taxes over the useful lives of property that produced the credits. 財務報告上, 投資税額控除については, 当社は対象資産の耐用期間にわたって法人税繰入れ額の減少項目として償却しています。

amount 名 金額, 数値, 総額, 合計, 総計, 総数, 総量, 額, 量, 高 （⇒carrying amount）

　accumulated amount 累積額, 累計額
　amount capitalized 資産計上金額, 資産化金額
　amount due 満期支払い高, 満期決済額, 期日受渡し高
　amount earned for equity 普通株主持ち分利益, 株主持ち分利益
　amount of annuity 年金終価, 複利年金終価
　amount payable 支払い金 （⇒amount receivable）
　amount receivable 受取金
　amounts in millions 単位：100万［百万］ドル
　amounts in millions, except per share data 単位：100万ドル。ただし, 1株当たりの金額は除く。単位：1株当たりの金額を除き100万ドル

carrying amount 帳簿価額
dollar amount of direct investment ドル・ベースでの直接投資
face amount 額面
future amount 複利終価
nominal amount 額面金額, 名目元本
principal amount 元本
recorded amount 計上金額
tax amount 税額
▶For the business we transact in currencies other than U.S. dollars, we translate income statement *amounts* at average exchange rates for the year. 米ドル以外の通貨で取引している事業については, 当社はその事業年度の平均為替レートで損益計算書の金額を換算しています.

amount receivable or payable 受取金と支払い金
▶*Amounts receivable or payable* and gains or losses realized under swap agreements are recognized as yield adjustments over the life of the related debt. スワップ契約に基づいて実現した受取金や支払い金と利益, 損失は, 当該債務が存続する間, 利回り調整して認識されます.

amount to ... …に達する, …になる
▶Our contributions to the savings plans *amounted to* $400 milliom in 2006. 当社の貯蓄制度への拠出金額は, 2006年度は4億ドルでした.

angel 名 ベンチャー企業への個人投資家, エンジェル（ベンチャー企業育成のため, ベンチャー企業に個人投資家が投資をしやすくする税制を「エンジェル税制」という）

announce 動 発表する, 公表する, 告示する
▶We *announced* a discount plan for new services in October 2007. 当社は, 2007年10月に新サービスの割引制度を発表しました.

announcement 名 発表, 公表, 告示
announcement of business results 業績発表, 決算発表, 決算短信 (=results announcement)
dividend announcement 配当発表
earnings announcement 利益発表, 業績発表
results announcement 業績発表

annual 形 年間の, 年次の, 通期の, 年1回の, 毎年の, アニュアル
annual accounting 年次決算
annual closing 年次決算, 年度決算, 年度締切り (=annual closing of accounts)
annual consolidated financial statements 年次連結財務書類, 年次連結財務諸表
annual earnings 年次利益, 年間所得
annual financial report 年次財務報告
annual financial statements 年次財務諸表, 年次財務書類, 年次報告書, 年次有価証券報告書 (=annual accounts)
annual growth rate 年成長率, 年間伸び率［成長率］
annual loss 年間赤字, 通期での赤字
annual pension cost expense 年間年金費用
annual profit and loss 年次損益
annual summary 年次営業概要書

annual accounts 年次財務諸表, 年次財務書類, 年次計算書類 (=annual financial statements, final accounts)
annual accounts settlement 年次決算
▶A large majority of First Section-listed companies close their books at the end of March for their *annual accounts* settlement. 東証1部上場企業の大半が, 年次決算のため3月末に帳簿を締める.

annual meeting 定時総会, 年次総会, 定時株主総会, 年次株主総会 (⇒annual report)
annual general meeting of shareholders 年次株主総会, 定例株主総会, 定時株主総会, 年次社員総会《略 **AGM**》(=annual general meeting, annual shareholders meeting, annual shareholders' meeting)
annual general shareholders meeting 年次株主総会, 定時株主総会 (=annual general meeting of shareholders)
annual meeting of policyholders' representatives 総代会 (⇒policyholders' representative meeting)
annual meeting of shareholders [stockholders] 年次株主総会 (=annual shareholders meeting)
▶The *annual meeting* of the shareholders of this corporation will be held on May 15, 2008. 当社の年次株主総会は, 2008年5月15日に開催します.

annual report 年次報告書, 年次決算報告書, 年次営業報告書, 有価証券報告書, 年報, アニュアル・レポート (⇒quarterly report)
年次報告書とは ➡ 日本の営業報告書に相当するものに, 英米では一般に年次報告書（annual report: アニュアルレポート）と四半期報告書（quarterly report）がある.

年次報告書（アニュアルレポート）は, イギリスではannual report and accountsともいわれるが, とくにアメリカの場合はSEC（米国証券取引委員会）向け年次報告書と株主向け年次報告書がある. SEC向け年次報告書は, SECに登録している企業が株式, 社債などの証券を発行した後, 決算期ごとに毎年提出する報告書で, その様式は米国企業がForm 10-

K（様式10-K），外国企業がForm 20-F（様式20-F）となっている。SECへのその提出期限は，様式10-K（米国企業）が60日以内，様式20-F（外国企業）が6か月以内となっている。

米国企業の提出期限を従来の90日以内から60日以内に変更することにSECが決定したのは2002年8月27日で，これは米エネルギー大手エンロンや長距離通信大手ワールドコムなど，エンロンの経営破綻をきっかけに相次いで発覚した米国企業の経営者による不正な会計操作を時間的に難しくするのが目的である。

また，会計不祥事の再発防止に向けて，年次決算報告書の提出期限の短縮化とともに，企業幹部による自社株取引の報告期限も従来の40日以内から2日以内に大幅に短縮された。

これら報告期限の短縮のほか，一連の会計不祥事の再発を防ぐため，米国企業だけでなく米株式市場に上場する外国企業に対しても，決算報告の正確さを保証する宣誓書の提出が義務付けられた（米国企業の場合，2002年7月に成立した企業改革法（サーベンス・オクスレー法：Sarbanes-Oxley Act）に基づくSECの措置として，2002年8月29日から年次報告書だけでなく四半期報告書についても決算宣誓書の提出を義務づけている）。

SECの会計基準で作成されるこれらのSEC向け年次報告書に対して，「一般に公正妥当と認められた会計原則（会計基準）」（generally accepted accounting principles：GAAP）に従って作成されるのが，株主向け年次報告書である。株主向け年次報告書は，各企業が毎年1回，定期的に作成して，年次株主総会（the annual meeting of shareholders）の委任状説明書（proxy statement：株主総会の議案内容などを説明した文書）を送る前に，株主その他利害関係者（stakeholder）に送付することになっている。

これには通常，財務ハイライト（financial highlight），会長または社長の株主宛メッセージ（letter to the shareholders），事業活動状況（operating activities），営業成績（operating performance）と財政状態（financial state or condition）に関する情報（財務書類：financial statements），財務書類注記（notes to financial statements）が記載されるほか，会計士または会計士事務所の監査報告書（auditor's report），取締役会（board of directors）と役員（officers）などが記載される。

なお，株主総会には年次株主総会と臨時株主総会（special meeting of shareholders）の二つがあり，年に1回開催される年次株主総会の開催地と日時はアニュアル・レポートにも掲載されるが，the annual meeting of shareholders（年次株主総会）は日本語では会社によって定例株主総会とも定時株主総会とも訳されている。

annual report and accounts 年次報告書
annual report on Form 10-K 様式10-Kに基づく年次報告書 （⇒**annual report**）
annual report to stockholders [**shareholders**] 株主向け年次報告書, 年次報告書
▸Form 10-K is our *annual report* to the Securities and Exchange Commission. 様式10-Kは，当社が米証券取引委員会に提出する年次報告書です。
▸The board of directors carries out its responsibility for the financial statements in this *annual report* principally through its audit committee, consisting solely of outside directors. 取締役会は，主に社外取締役だけで構成される監査委員会を通じて，この年次報告書の財務書類に対する責任を遂行しています。

annual salary system 年俸制
▸We are considering the introduction of an *annual salary system*, which does not pay bonuses. 当社は現在，ボーナスのない年俸制の導入を検討しています。

annual securities report 年次有価証券報告書
▸The presence of investment funds on the share register is generally unknown until their names are listed in *annual securities reports*. 株主名簿上の投資ファンドの存在は，一般にそのファンド名が年次有価証券報告書に記載されるまで分からない。

annual shareowners [**shareholders, stockholders**] **meeting** 年次株主総会
▸In Japan, *annual general shareholders meetings* are generally held in June. 日本では，一般に年次株主総会は6月に開かれる［6月に集中する］。
▸The 69th *Annual Shareowners Meeting* will be held 10:30 a.m., April 20, 2008 at the World Congress Center. 第69回年次株主総会は，2008年4月20日，ワールド・コングレス・センターで午前10時30分から開催されます。

annualized terms 年率換算, 年換算, 年率 （＝annualized basis）
▸The real growth in *annualized terms* was 5.6 percent, showing clear signs of an economic recovery. 年率換算での実質成長率は5.6％で，明らかに景気回復基調を示した。

annuitant 名 年金受給者, 年金受給権者
annuity 名 年金, 年金保険制度, 年金受領権, 年賦金, 出資金, 掛金
　amount of annuity 年金終価
　annuity cost 年金費用
　annuity due 期首払い年金 （＝annuity in ad-

vance)
annuity in arrears 期末払い年金
annuity scheme 年金制度（⇒**defined-contribution annuity scheme**）
fixed annuity 定額年金
occupational annuity 企業年金
present value of annuity 年金現価
retirement annuity 退職年金
variable annuity 変額年金

▶In the corporate type of defined-contribution pension plans, companies pay *annuities* for employees. 企業型の確定拠出年金制度では、企業が従業員のために掛金を支払う。

anticipate 動 〈負債を〉期限前に返済する、〈資金の入金を〉見越して使う、予想［予期］する
　anticipated loss 見込み損失、予想損失（＝anticipatory loss）
　anticipated profit 見込み利益、予想利益、期待利益（＝anticipatory profit）
anticipatory 形 予想の
antidilution 名 反希薄化、逆希薄化
APB ［米］会計原則審議会（Accounting Principles Boardの略）
APB Opinions APB意見書（米国公認会計士協会（AICPA）の会計原則審議会（APB）の意見書）（Opinions of the Accounting Principles Boardの略）
append 動 付加する、書き添える
appended footnote 添付の脚注
applicable to ... …に帰属する、…に適用可能な、…に適格な、…に配賦（はいふ）可能な、…に配分される、…に係わる
　amounts applicable to ... …に配分された額
　applicable to the year 当該年度
　income taxes applicable to extraordinary items 特別損益に係る税金
　net income applicable to common shares 普通株式に帰属する当期純利益
　net loss applicable to common shares for the company 同社の普通株式に帰属する当期純損失

▶Net income *applicable to* common shares for 2007 was $882 million, down 16 percent, compared with $1,054 million in 2006. 普通株式に帰属する当期純利益［2007年度の純利益］は、前期の10億5,400万ドルに対して16％減の8億8,200万ドルでした。

application 名 申込み、申請、出願、申請者、申込者、願書、信用状開設依頼書、運用、適用、応用、使途、配賦、予定配賦、割賦適用業務、アプリケーション・ソフト、応用ソフト、応用システム、適用業務、アプリケーション（⇒**accept, full cost**）
　application for registration 登録申請
　application of funds 資金運用、資金の使途、資金の適用
　commercial application 商用化、実用化、商用アプリケーション
　listing application 上場申請
　preliminary application for listing 上場の仮申請

▶We have completed the transformation into an *application*-oriented high-tech group. 当社は、アプリケーション志向のハイテク集団への変革を成し遂げました。

apply 動 適用する、応用する、利用する、当てはめる、配賦（はいふ）する
　applied cost 配賦原価、原価配賦額、賦課済み原価、適用原価
　applied overhead 製造間接費配賦額（＝applied factory burden, applied factory overhead, applied manufacturing burden）

▶New accounting rules *apply* to all U.S. companies. 新会計規則は、すべての米国企業に適用されている。

appoint 動 指名する、任命する、選任する、指定する、定める

▶In the proposal, the investment fund requests nine people be *appointed* board members. この提案で、同投資ファンドは、9人を取締役に選任するよう求めている。

▶The FSA *appointed* three administrators to take charge of the failed bank's administration, operations and asset management. 金融庁は、破綻した銀行の経営、業務と資産の管理に当たる金融整理管財人3名を指名した。

appointment 名 任命、指名、指定、官職、地位、役職、取決め、約束、予約、アポイントメント
　appointment and removal of ... …の任免
　appointment of a trustee 管財人の指名
　appointment of representative 代表者の選任
appointment of auditors 監査役指名

▶A majority of the votes cast is required to ratify the *appointment of auditors*. 監査役指名の承認を得るには、投票総数の過半数の賛成投票が必要です。

appointment of outside directors 社外取締役選任

▶Recently, shareholders' proposals have come from investment funds seeking higher dividends and the *appointment of outside directors*. 最近の株主提案は、増配や社外取締役選任などを求め

る投資ファンドから出されている。

appraisal 名 評価, 査定, 鑑定, 見積り
- **appraisal of asset** 資産の鑑定
- **appraisal profit** 含み益, 評価益（＝appraisal gain, latent profit; ⇒**basic profit**）
- **appraisal profits and losses** 含み損益, 評価損益（＝latent profits and losses, unrealized profits and losses）
- **appraisal surplus** 評価剰余金, 評価替剰余金, 再評価積立金
- **appraisal value** 評価額, 評価価値, 鑑定評価額, 査定価値（＝appraised value, assessed value）
- **performance appraisal** 業績評価

appraisal gain 含み益, 評価益（＝appraisal profit, latent gain）
▸The nine insurers booked about ¥5 trillion in combined *appraisal gains* on their shareholdings. 生保9社の保有株式の含み益は, 総額で約5兆円となった。

appraisal loss 含み損, 評価損, 保有株の評価損を損失に計上する減損処理額（＝latent loss, valuation loss; ⇒**accounting rule**, **mark to market**）
▸The nine nonlife insurers suffered total *appraisal losses* on securities of ¥360 billion. 損保9社が, 9社合計で3,600億円の有価証券評価損を計上した。

appreciate 動 上昇する, 騰貴する, 高く評価する
▸Tokyo stocks *appreciated* across the board. 東京株[東京株式市場の株価]は, 全面高となった。

appreciation 名 〈価格・相場の〉上昇, 騰貴, 急騰, 増価(資産価値の増加), 平価切上げ, 正当な評価, 評価増, 評価切上げ, 評価益, 増加額（⇒**negative effect**）
- **appreciation surplus** 評価剰余金, 評価替剰余金, 再評価積立金（＝appraisal surplus）
- **benefits of the yen's appreciation** 円高差益
- **capital appreciation** キャピタル・ゲイン
- **equity appreciation** 株価上昇
- **sharp yen appreciation** 急激な円高
- **yen's appreciation against the dollar** 円高・ドル安, ドルに対する円相場の上昇

▸A rapid *appreciation* of the yen is not desirable to the U.S. economy. 急激な円高は, 米国経済には好ましくない。

appropriation 名 充当, 充用, 配分, 処分, 収用, 利益処分, 剰余金処分, 充当金, 支出金, 積立金, 承認済み予算額, 割当予算額, 配分額, 歳出予算, 政府支出金
- **appropriation of earned surplus** 利益剰余金の処分
- **appropriation of surplus** 剰余金の処分, 利益処分
- **appropriation statement** 利益処分計算書
- **appropriations for redemption of bonds** 社債償還積立金
- **budgetary appropriation** 予算の計上
- **capital appropriations account** 資本処分勘定
- **profit appropriation** 利益の処分
- **surplus appropriation statement** 利益処分計算書

approval 名 承認, 承諾, 是認, 賛成, 賛同, 同意, 支持, 認可, 許可
- **approval rate [rating]** 支持率（＝popularity rating, support rate）
- **blanket approval** 一括承認
- **conditional approval** 条件付き認可
- **conversion approval** 転用認可
- **credit approval** 与信承認
- **investment approvals** 投資承認額, 投資認可額
- **official approvals** 許認可

▸Companies should obtain shareholder *approval* when introducing methods to counter hostile takeover attempts. 敵対的買収への対抗策を導入する場合, 企業は株主の承認を得なければならない。
▸The Tokyo Stock Exchange has canceled its *approval* for the company's plan to go public on the Mother's market. 東京証券取引所は, 同社の東証マザーズへの上場計画承認を取り消した。

approve 動 承認する, 承諾する, 賛成する, 賛同する, 同意する, 支持する, 認可する, 許可する
▸The executive compensation committee of the board of directors *approves* the compensation of all executive officers. 取締役会の役員報酬委員会は, 業務執行役員全員の報酬について承認しております。

approved 形 認可された, 承認された, 定評のある
- **approved invoice** 承認済みの請求書
- **approved pension scheme** 適格年金制度

approximate 動 概算する, 見積もる, 概算値を得る, 近似計算をする, …に相当する, …にほぼ等しい
▸The securities are stated at cost, which *approximates* fair value. 有価証券は, 時価にほぼ等しい原価で評価されています。

April-December period 4-12月期（＝the nine months to Dec. 31）
▸Our group net profit in the *April-December period* soared 50 percent from a year earlier mainly due to a robust performance in our mobile phone business. 当社の4-12月期の連結税引き後利益[純利益]は, 主に当社の携帯電話事業の業績が

好調だったため,前年同期比で50%急増した。

April–June quarter 4–6月期 (3月期決算企業の第1四半期,12月期決算企業の第2四半期)
▶In the *April–June quarter*, major high-tech companies suffered losses or profit declines. 4–6月期は,主要ハイテク企業が赤字や減益に苦しんでいる。

April–June revenue 4–6月期の売上高,4–6月期の収益
▶Nissan Motor's *April–June revenue* rose 3.1 percent to ¥2.21 trillion, but global unit sales fell 6 percent to 826,000 units. 日産自動車の4–6月期の売上高は,前年同期比3.1%増の2兆2,100億円だったが,世界販売台数は6%減の82万6,000台だった。

April–September fiscal first half 〈3月期決算企業の〉上半期,4–9月期の上半期,4–9月期の上半期決算,9月中間決算 (⇒**combined group net profit**)

April–September period 4–9月期,9月中間決算 (=the six months to September 30)
▶The firm posted a net profit of ¥1.5 billion for the *April–September period*. 同社は,9月中間決算で15億円の税引き後利益を計上した。

ARB 〈米国公認会計士協会(AICPA)の〉会計研究公報,会計調査公報 (**Accounting Research Bulletin**の略)

arithmetical average cost method 算術平均原価法,単純平均法

arm 名 子会社,部門,部局,支店 (=unit)
　brokerage arm 証券子会社,証券会社,証券部門
　consulting arm コンサルティング部門,コンサルティング会社
　long-arm jurisdiction 域外適用管轄権
　research arm 研究所,研究部門
　treasury arm 財務部門
▶General Motors Acceptance Corp. (GMAC), GM's finance *arm*, is giving the boost to the struggling automaker's bottom line. GMの金融子会社GMACが,経営再建に取り組む米自動車メーカーGMの業績の後押しをしている。

arm's length [**arm's-length**] 公正な,独立した,独立当事者間の,独立企業間の,独立第三者間の,第三者間取引にかかわる,商業ベースの (⇒**intersegment**)
　arm's length bargaining 公正な取引,独立当事者間の取引
　arm's length basis 純然たる商業ベース,商業ベース
　arm's length price 独立当事者間の価格,独立企業間価格,第三者間との取引価格
　arm's length pricing basis 第三者に対する取引価格基準 (⇒**intersegment**)
　arm's length relationship 商業ベースの取引関係
　arm's length transaction 第三者間の公正な取引,独立当事者間の取引,独立第三者間取引,対等取引,商業ベースの取引
▶In the case of sale by the licensee to an affiliated company thereof, such royalties shall be calculated based upon the price which would be charged if the transaction were an *arm's length transaction*. ライセンシーの関係会社に対するライセンシーの販売の場合,このロイヤルティは,その取引が第三者間の公正な取引[純然たる商業ベースの取引]であった場合に請求する価格に基づいて計算するものとする。

arrangement 名 手配,準備,打合せ,取決め,協定,合意,契約,取りまとめ,調整,解決
　arrangement plan 設備配置計画
　business arrangement 業務協定,業務契約,業務提携
　correspondent arrangement コルレス契約
　formal arrangement 正式取決め
　market sharing arrangement 市場協定
　reciprocal arrangement 相互協定
　standby arrangement スタンドバイ協定,スタンドバイ取決め,借入予約協定
　supply arrangement 供給契約
▶The two firms have built a relationship during a three-year business *arrangement*. 両社は,3年前からの業務提携で信頼関係を築いた。

arrears 名 延滞,遅滞,遅延,滞納,延滞金,未納金,未払い金
　arrears on loan repayments 延滞債権
　in arrears 延滞している,未払いの,未納の,遅れが出ている
　interest for arrears 延滞利息
▶The bank has about ¥2.6 trillion in loans to firms that are in *arrears* on principal and interest payments. 同行には,元利の返済に遅れが出ている企業向け融資額[債権]が約2兆6,000億円ある。

articles of association 米企業の基本定款 (=**articles of incorporation**), 英企業の通常定款 (英企業の基本定款は**memorandum of association**), 団体規約

articles of incorporation 企業の基本定款,設立定款,定款 (=**articles of association**: 会社の方針を定めたもの。日本は単一定款制度をとっているのに対して,欧米では基本定款 (**articles of association, articles of incorporation**) と付属定

款(bylaws)の二つの定款制度をとっている)
initial articles of incorporation 設立時の定款, 設立定款
revised articles of incorporation 変更定款
▶We will amend our *articles of incorporation* at our shareholders meeting in June to shift to the new management system. 当社は6月の株主総会で基本定款を改定して, 新経営システムに移行する。

as a percentage of ... ...に対する比率[割合], ...に占める比率
as percentages of total revenues 総収益[総売上高]に対する比率[百分率]
current assets as a percentage of current liabilities 流動負債に対する流動資産の比率, 流動比率
net income as a percentage of average assets 平均資産に対する純利益の比率, 総資本純利益率
net income (loss) as a percentage of revenues 収益[売上高]に対する純利益(損失)の比率
operating income (loss) as a percentage of revenues 収益[売上高]に対する営業利益(損失)の比率, 対売上高営業利益[損失]率, 営業利益[損失]率
total debt as a percentage of total capitalization 資本総額に対する債務総額の比率
▶Total debt *as a percentage of* total capitalization was 20 percent at yearend 2007. 資本総額に対する債務総額の比率は, 2007年末現在で20%でした。

as incurred 発生時に, 発生時点で, 発生基準で (⇒**selling expenses**)
▶Costs to support or service licensed programs are charged against income *as incurred* or when related revenue is recognized, whichever occurs first. ライセンス・プログラムの使用に伴う技術支援またはサービスに要する原価は, 発生時か関連収益の認識時のうちどちらか早い時点で原価に賦課されています。

as of ... ...現在で, ...の時点で, ...現在の, ...の日付で, ...の日付に
▶The bank reported a capital adequacy ratio of 4.54 percent *as of* the end of fiscal 2007. 同行の2007年度末現在[時点]の自己資本比率は, 4.54%だった。

assembly 名 組立て, 集合, 会議
assembly operations 組立技術
assembly plant 組立工場 (⇒**stream**)

assertive 形 主張する, 意見をはっきり言う
assertive shareholder モノ言う株主
▶The pension fund association is an *assertive* shareholder that makes tough demands on corporate managements. 企業年金連合会は, 企業の経営姿勢に厳しい注文をつけるモノ言う株主でもある。

assess 動 評価する, 査定する, 審査する, 算定する, 判断する
▶Managers must continuously *assess* their resource needs and consider further steps to reduce costs. 経営陣は, つねに資源の必要性を評価して, コスト削減のための一段と進んだ方法を考える必要がある。

assessed value 査定価額, 査定評価額, 査定価, 課税価額
assessed value of fixed assets 固定資産税評価額

assessment 名 評価, 事前評価, 鑑定, 査定, 審査, 算定, 課税, 賦課, 更正, 判断, 評価額, 鑑定額, 査定額, 賦課金, 追徴金, アセスメント
assessment of taxes 税の賦課
assessment plan 賦課方式
asset assessment 資産査定, 資産評価 (＝asset appraisal, asset evaluation)
basis of assessment 課税標準
collateral assessment 担保評価
credit assessment 信用評価, 信用分析
damage assessment 損害査定
official assessment method 賦課課税方式
rating assessment 格付け評価
self-assessment 申告納税
▶Outstanding nonperforming loans held by banks are increasing due to poor business results of borrowers and the strict asset *assessment* methods. 金融機関が抱える不良債権残高は, 貸出先[融資先]の業績不振や資産の査定方法の厳格化で増加している。

asset 名 資産, 財産, アセット (⇒**assessment**)
asset contra accounts 試算対照勘定
asset deficiency 債務超過
asset disposition 資産処分
asset investment 資産運用
asset value 資産価値, 資産価格, 純資産 (⇒**consolidated after-tax deficit**)
assets acquired 取得資産
assets and liabilities 資産と負債
bad assets 不良資産
capital asset 資本資産, 資本的資産, 固定資産 (＝fixed asset, fixed capital, long-lived asset, permanent asset)
commercial assets 商業資産
customer assets 預かり資産, 顧客からの預かり

資産
foreign asset 在外資産
freezing terrorist-related assets テロ関連資産の凍結
hidden assets 含み資産
intangible asset 無形資産, 無形固定資産
out-of-book assets 簿外資産
quick assets 当座資産
real assets 不動産
securitized assets 証券化資産, 証券化した資産
tangible asset 有形資産, 有形固定資産
▶The Corporation will put all its efforts into increasing its profitability and promptly selling its unnecessary *assets*. 当社は, 利益水準の向上や不要資産の即時売却などに全力を挙げる方針です。

asset-backed commercial paper 資産担保コマーシャル・ペーパー, 資産担保CP, アセットバックCP《略 **ABCP**》
▶*Asset-backed commercial paper* refers to commercial paper whose creditworthiness is guaranteed by sales credit that the corporate issuer has with its debtors. 資産担保CPとは, 企業発行体がその債務者に対して保有する売掛金によって信用度が保証されるコマーシャル・ペーパーを指す。

asset-backed securities 資産担保証券, 商業用不動産証券, アセットバック証券《略 **ABS**》(銀行の貸出債権や企業の売掛債権などを担保に発行される証券)

asset base 資産基盤
▶ABC Inc. management took vigorous steps during 2007 to reinforce the performance of ABC's *asset base*. ABCの経営陣は, 資産運用実績を強化するため, 2007年度に思い切った措置をとりました。

asset impairment accounting 減損会計
(=accounting for the impairment of assets: 企業が保有する土地やビル, 工場, 店舗などの固定資産から生じる収益が, 投資額に見合うかどうかを判断する会計基準)
▶This extraordinary loss of ¥581.06 billion stems partly from the write-offs of appraisal losses in fixed assets under an *asset impairment accounting* rule. この5,810億6,000万円の特別損失の一因は, 減損会計基準に基づく固定資産の減損処理によるものだ。

asset liability management 資産負債総合管理, 資産負債管理, バランス・シート管理《略 **ALM**》

asset management 資産管理, 資産運用, 投資顧問
asset management services 資産運用サービス

▶All these events are part of a larger strategy of our *asset management*. これらの措置は, 当社の資産運営戦略の一環としてとられたものです。
▶The new firm will offer *asset management services* to individual investors whose net worth is ¥100 million or more. 新会社は, 純資産が1億円以上の個人投資家に資産運用サービスを提供する。

asset provision 資産評価損引当金, 資産評価損引当金繰入れ額
▶ABC Inc.'s share of the loss and the *asset provision* amounted to $60 million. この損失と資産評価損引当金のうちABCの負担分は, 6,000万ドルになりました。

assign 動 委託する
▶The pension fund association *assigns* other institutional investors to manage the rest of its funds for domestic equity investment. 年金基金連合会は, 国内株式投資資金の残りを, 他の機関投資家[外部の運用機関]に委託している。

assignment 名 割当て, 譲渡, 差し入れ
assignment of receivables 債権譲渡
assignment of contract 契約の譲渡
cost assignment 原価配分

associate 名 関連会社, 関係会社, 系列会社, 同系会社, 半数所有会社, 持ち分法適用会社 (=affiliated company, [associate] associated company)

associate company 関連会社, 系列会社
(=associated company)

associated company 関連会社, 系列会社
(=associated company)

assume 動 〈任務・義務・債務を〉引き受ける, 〈債務などを〉肩代わりする, 負担する, 就任する, 就く, 責任を負う, 責任をとる, 引き継ぐ, 継承する, 占有する, 〈…と〉仮定する, 推定する, 想定する, 予想する, 予定する, 見込む, 考慮する
assume A to be B AをBとみなす, AをBと仮定する
assume liquidity risk 流動性リスクを負担する
assume office 就任する
assume responsibility for ... …の責任を負う, …の責任を取る
assume the risk リスクを負う, リスクを引き受ける
earnings per common share—assuming full dilution 普通株式1株当たり利益—完全希薄化[希釈化, 希釈効果]を考慮した場合, 完全希薄化後普通株式1株当たり利益
▶We *assumed* that the growth in the per capita cost of covered health care benefits (the health

care cost trend rate) would gradually decline after 2008.　当社は、計上済み医療給付費用の1人当たりの伸び率(医療費用の傾向値)は、2008年度以降はゆるやかに減少するものと予想しています。

assumed 形　引き受けた、引き継いだ、予想の
  assumed bond　保証社債
  assumed liability　引継ぎ負債、債務引受未払い金
  assumed loans　債務の肩代わり
  assumed rate of interest　予定利率
  assumed rate of return　予想収益率、予想運用利益率
  assumed rates of return on pension funds　予想年金基金運用収益率
  assumed trend rate　予想傾向値
  assumed yield　予想利回り
▶Increasing the *assumed* trend rate by 1% in each year would raise our accumulated postretirement benefit obligation at December 31, 2006 by $700 million.　予想傾向値が毎年1%ずつ上昇すると、当社の累積退職後給付債務は、2006年12月31日現在で7億ドル増加します。

assumption 名　〈義務や債務の〉引受け、〈債務などの〉肩代わり、負担、就任、引継ぎ、継承、占有、仮定、前提、公準、想定、予想、考慮
  assumption of accounting　会計上の仮定
  assumption of going concern　継続企業の前提
  basic assumption　基礎的仮定
  debt assumption　債務引受け、債務引受契約、債務履行引受け、債務の肩代わり、債務引受契約に基づく債務譲渡、デット・アサンプション
  economic assumptions　経済見通し
  going concern assumption　継続企業の公準
  risk assumption business　リスク負担型ビジネス
▶To use the new accounting method, we made *assumptions* about trends in health care costs, interest rates and average life expectancy.　新会計処理方法を採用するにあたって、当社は医療給付コスト、金利と平均寿命の傾向について仮定を設けました。
▶We made the following *assumptions* in valuing our postretirement benefit obligation at December 31, 2007.　2007年12月31日現在の退職後給付債務の評価にあたって、当社は以下の仮定を行いました。

at cost　原価で、取得原価で　(=at historical cost; ⇒state)
  at cost (approximates market)　取得原価(ほぼ時価に一致)
  at cost which approximates market　時価に近い取得原価評価
  buildings—at cost　建物—原価評価
  investment in bonds—at cost　投資社債—原価評価
▶We state property, plant and equipment *at cost* and determine depreciation using the group or unit method.　当社では、有形固定資産は取得原価で計上し、減価償却費はグループ償却法または個別償却法を用いて算定しています。

attorney 名　弁護士
  attorney's fee　弁護士報酬
  letter of attorney　委任状、弁護士の書簡
  power of attorney　委任状

attributable to ...　…に起因する、…に帰属する、…による
  be partially attributable to ...　…の一因である
  be primarily attributable to ...　…の主因である
▶These increases in consolidated revenues were *attributable* primarily *to* volume growth rather than price increases.　この連結売上高の伸びは、価格引き上げによるものではなく、主に販売数量の拡大によるものです。

attribution 名　帰属、属性
  attribution of revenue to periods　収益の期間帰属
  cost attribution　原価配分

auction 名　競売、競り売り、公売、入札、公募入札、オークション　(⇒online auction)
  30 year auction　30年物入札
  auction price　入札価格
  auction site　オークション・サイト、競売サイト(売り手が出品した品物を、買い手が落札するウェブサイトのこと)
  competitive auction　競争入札
  e-auction　eオークション
  Internet [Net] auction　ネット・オークション
  open auction　公開競売
  reverse auction　逆オークション、リバース・オークション
▶Dealers are allowed to bid for Treasury bonds by a quarterly *auction*.　ディーラーは、四半期ごとの入札[四半期入札]で米財務省証券への入札が認められている。

auction business　オークション事業、オークション・ビジネス
▶NTT DoCoMo will take a 40 percent stake for about ¥4.2 billion in a new company to be set up by splitting off Rakuten's *auction business*.　楽天のネットオークション・ビジネスを分社化して設立される新会社に、NTTドコモは4割(約42億円)出資する。

auction item オークション出品物
▶Companies that operate auction sites and collect charges from users should monitor *auction items* more thoroughly. オークション・サイトを運営して(落札時に)手数料を徴収する会社が、オークション[競売]に出品される品物を十分監視すべきだ。

audit 動 監査する、会計検査する (⇒**accompanying, book** 名)
▶The auditing firm *audited* the accounts of failed companies Yamaichi Securities Co. and Yaohan Japan Corp. この監査法人は、経営破綻した山一証券やヤオハンジャパンの財務書類の監査を担当した。

audit 名 監査、会計検査 (=auditing; ⇒**auditing standards**)
- **accounting audit** 会計監査
- **audit certificate** 監査証明、監査証明書、監査報告書
- **audit year** 監査年度
- **audit of financial statements** 財務諸表監査、財務書類監査
- **audit opinion** 監査意見
- **audit procedure** 監査手続き (=auditing procedure)
- **audit report** 監査報告書 (=auditor's report)
- **audit test** 監査上の試査、監査テスト
- **audit trail** 監査証跡
- **book audit** 帳簿監査
- **checking audit** 照査
- **external audit** 外部監査
- **final audit** 期末監査
- **financial audit** 会計監査、財務諸表監査
- **independent audit** 独立監査、独立的監査
- **interim audit** 期中監査、中間監査
- **internal audit** 内部監査
- **managerial audit** 経営監査 (=managerial auditing)
- **operation [operational] audit** 業務監査
- **regular audit** 正規監査
- **running audit** 連続監査
- **site audit** 現場監査
- **statutory audit** 法定監査

▶We plan and perform the *audit* to obtain reasonable assurance about whether the financial statements are free of material misstatements. 私どもは、監査を計画・実施して、財務書類に重大な虚偽記載がないかどうかについての合理的な確証を得ます。

audit committee 監査委員会
▶The independent auditors and the internal auditors have full and free access to the *audit committee*. 独立監査人と内部監査人は、監査委員会に毎回、自由に参加することができます。

audit firm 監査法人 (=audit corporation, auditing firm)
▶The FSA gave an official warning to this *audit firm* under the Certified Public Accountants Law over negligence in its checking of the bank's accounts. 金融庁は、同行の財務書類の監査内容が不十分であったとして、公認会計士法に基づきこの監査法人に対して正式に戒告処分を出した。

audited 形 監査済みの
- **audited amount** 監査済み金額
- **audited balance sheet** 監査済み貸借対照表

auditing 名 会計監査、会計検査、監査 (⇒**conflict of interest**)
- **auditing company [firm]** 監査法人、会計事務所 (=audit corporation, audit firm, auditing house, auditor; ⇒**book** 名)
- **auditing operations** 監査業務 (=auditing services, cease and desist order)
- **auditing principles** 監査原則
- **auditing procedure** 監査手続き (=audit procedure)
- **auditing services [business, operations, work]** 監査業務
- **complete auditing** 全部監査
- **computer auditing** コンピュータ監査
- **EDP auditing** EDP監査
- **functional auditing** 機能別監査
- **internal auditing** 内部監査
- **managerial auditing** 経営監査 (=managerial audit)
- **purchase [purchasing] auditing** 購買監査

▶The outside corporate auditors contribute to improving the quality of *auditing* activities by corporate auditors by expressing their opinions at the meeting of the board of corporate auditors. 社外監査役は、監査役会で意見を表明して、監査役による監査活動の質の向上に貢献しています。

auditing standards 監査基準 (=audit standards)
▶We conducted our audits in accordance with generally accepted *auditing standards*. 私どもは、一般に認められた監査基準に準拠して[従って]監査を実施しました。

auditor 名 監査人、監査役、監査法人、会計検査官、監査機関 (⇒**access** 名, **accounting system, audit committee, independent auditor**)

auditor's certificate 監査証明書, 監査報告書 (=auditor's report)
auditors' opinion 監査意見 (=audit opinion)
auditor's [auditors'] report 監査報告, 監査報告書 (=audit report, auditor's certificate)
certified internal auditor 公認内部監査人《略 CIA》
change of auditors 監査人の交代
EDP auditor EDP監査人 (=system auditor)
external auditor 外部監査人
outside auditor 社外監査人, 社外監査役 (=nonexecutive internal auditor)
predecessor auditor 前任監査人
primary auditor 持ち株会社の監査人, 親会社の監査人
shareholders' auditors 会計監査人
statutory auditor 法定監査人
system auditor システム監査人
successor auditor 後任監査人
temporary auditor 一時監査人
▶An independent *auditor* found problems with the way Time Warner accounted for a number of transactions. タイム・ワーナーの一部取引の会計処理方法に問題があることに, 独立監査人が気づいた。
▶*Auditors* conduct unannounced site inspection after ISO certification each year. ISO（国際標準化機構）の認定後も, 監査機関が毎年, 予告なしの現場検査を実施します。

authorisation (⇒authorization)

authority 名 権限, 権力, 権威, 権威者, 専門家, 公共機関
▶To assist it in carrying out its duties, the Board has delegated certain *authority* to several committees. 取締役会は, その職務遂行を補佐する機関として, 複数の委員会に特定の権限を委譲しています。

authorization 名 承認, 承諾, 認可, 公認, 権限, 授権, 検定, 委任, 委任状
▶Access to assets occurs only in accordance with management's *authorization*. 資産の取扱いは, 必ず経営陣の承認に基づいて行われています。

authorize 動 承認する, 権限を与える
authorized capital 授権資本, 授権株式, 授権株式数, 公称資本, 株式発行可能枠 (=authorized capital stock, authorized share capital)（株式会社がその基本定款に基づいて株式発行により調達できる資本の限度額）
authorized minimum 必要最低資本額
authorized shares [stock] 授権株式, 授権株式数

▶We have 100 million *authorized* shares of preferred stock at $1 par value. 当社には, 額面1ドルの優先株式1億株の授権株式があります。

available 形 利用可能な, 使用可能な, 処分可能な, 充当可能な, 入手可能な, 調達可能な
available asset 利用可能資産
available earned surplus 利用可能利益剰余金, 処分可能利益剰余金
available for investment 投資に運用可能
available profit 処分可能利益
available time 使用可能時間, 可用時間, 納品期間, 納期
be commercially available 実用化される
net assets available for plan benefits 年金給付債務に充当可能な純資産
net income available for common stock 普通株主に帰属する当期利益
profit available for dividend 配当可能利益
▶The Annual Report on Form 10-K is *available* from the date of its filing with the Securities and Exchange Commission in the United States. 様式10-Kに基づく当社の年次報告書は, 米国の証券取引委員会（SEC）への提出日以降に入手できます。

available-for-sale securities 売却可能証券

average 動 相殺する, 合算する
▶Under the new securities taxation system, gains and losses on stocks and investment trusts will be *averaged* before being taxed. 新証券税制では, 株式の損益［株式譲渡損益］と投信の損益（投資信託の償還・解約に伴う損益）を合算［相殺］して課税する。

average 名 平均, 海損
arithmetic average [mean] 算術平均
arithmetic weighted average 加重平均
compound yield based on weighted average 加重平均利回り
moving average 移動平均
weighted average price 加重平均価格
weighted average share 加重平均株式数

average 形 平均の
average markup 平均値入れ率
average number of listed stocks [shares] 平均上場株式数, 上場株式総数の平均（(期初の上場株式数＋期末の上場株式数)÷2で算出する）
average rate of profit 平均利益率
average rate of return 平均資本利益率
average remaining service period of employees 従業員の平均残存勤続[勤務]期間
average return on invetment 平均投資収益率,

平均投資収益

return on average equity 平均株主資本利益率

stock price average 平均株価
▸The *average* market price of the company's common stock was $20 per share during 2007.　同社の普通株式の平均株価は，2007年度は1株当たり20ドルであった．

average common shares outstanding 発行済み普通株式の平均数，発行済み普通株式の平均株式数
▸The number of *average common shares* outstanding in the third quarter 2007 declined because shares were purchased for cancellation.　2007年第3四半期の発行済み普通株式平均株式数が減少したのは，株式を買い戻して消却したためです．

average daily balance 平均残高，1日平均残高
▸The *average daily balance* of bank lending fell 4.7 percent in October from a year earlier.　10月の銀行貸出の平均残高は，前年同月比で4.7％減少した．

average number of shares outstanding 期中平均発行済み株式数，平均発行済み株式数［株式総数］（＝average shares outstanding）
▸For the nine months ended September 30, 2007, the *average number of shares outstanding* was 582.8 million.　2007年1-9月期の平均発行済み株式総数は，5億8,280万株でした．

average return on capital 平均資本利益率
▸The *average return on capital* of Britain's business rose 26 basis points to 4.95 percent in this year's first quarter.　今年第1四半期の英国企業の平均資本利益率は，（前年同期比）0.26％増の4.95％だった．

average shares outstanding 期中平均発行済み株式総数
▸*Average shares outstanding* were 581.1 million in 2007.　期中平均発行済み株式総数は，2007年度は5億8,110万株でした．

award 動　与える，授与する，査定する，裁定する
▸Supplier will pay all damages and costs *awarded* therein against Distributor or its customers.　供給者は，これについて裁定された損害賠償額と費用を全額，販売店またはその顧客に支払う．

B b

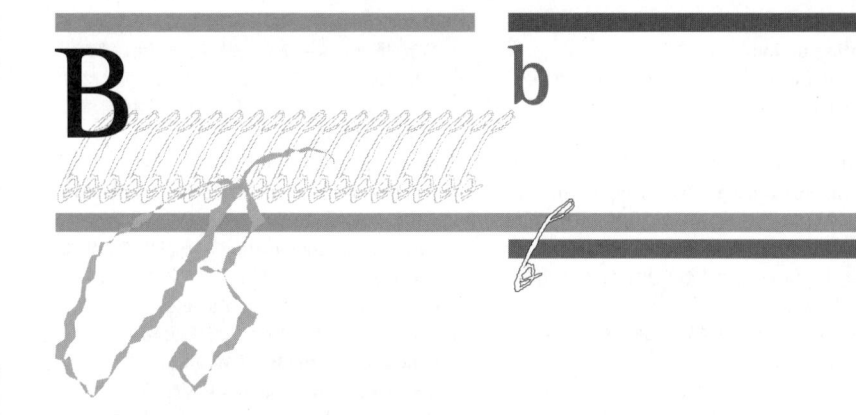

back burner 後回し, 先送り, 二の次, 棚上げ状態, 保留 (⇒front burner)
▸The current reconstruction plan was put on the *back burner*. 現在の再建計画は, 先送りされた。
back cover 〈書籍の〉表4
back cover inside 〈書籍の〉表3
back-to-back 形 連続の, 続けざまの, 相次ぐ, 背中合わせの, 見返り信用状の
▸Japan's industrial output climbed for a second straight month in June, the first *back-to-back* rise in two years. 日本の6月の鉱工業生産高は, 2か月連続で増加し, 2年ぶりに2か月連続の増加となった。
backdrop 名 背景, 事情
▸Against this *backdrop*, we reported a 4% increase in total revenues in 2007. これを受けて[こうした事情から], 2007年度の当社の総営業収益は4%の伸びを示しました。
background and history of the company 会社の沿革と組織
backlog 名 未処理部分, 残務, 在庫, 残高, 受注残高 (＝backlog figure), 注文残高, 手持ち注文, 予備貯蔵, 蓄積, 山積, バックログ (＝back-logging)
　backlog adjustment 遡及修正 (＝catch-up adjustment)
　backlog depreciation 遡及償却額, 取戻し償却額, バックログ償却 (＝catch-up depreciation)
　factory backlog 製造業の受注残高
　order backlog 受注残高
▸The continuing global acceptance of our products and our record *backlog* indicate an improved second half of the year. 当社の製品が引き続きグローバル市場で受け入れられ, 受注残高も過去最高であることから, 下半期[下期]の業績は改善する見込みです。

bad debt 不良債権（銀行などが融資して回収困難となった貸出金）, 不良貸付け, 貸倒れ, 焦げ付き, 貸倒れ損失 (＝bad loan, doubtful debt, nonperforming loan, uncollectible loan, unrecoverable loan)
　bad-debt clean-up charge 不良債権処理額
　bad debt loss 貸倒れ損失
　bad debt provision[reserve] 貸倒れ引当金, 貸倒れ準備金
　bad debt recovery 償却債権の取立て
　bad debts written off 貸倒れ償却
▸The major financial and banking groups achieved the *bad-debt* reduction goals six months earlier than initially planned. 大手金融・銀行グループは, 当初の計画より半年早く不良債権削減の目標を達成した。
bad debt expense 貸倒れ費用, 貸倒れ損失, 貸倒れ償却
▸During 2007 the Corporation estimated that its *bad debt expense* should be 1% of all credit sales. 2007年度は, 当社の見積もりで, 掛売り総額の1％について貸倒れ損失を計上することになりました。
bad loan 不良債権, 不良貸付け, 不良貸出, 不良融資, 貸倒れ (＝bad debt, nonperforming loan, uncollectible loan, unrecoverable loan)
　bad loan charges 不良債権処理額
　bad loan costs 不良債権処理費用, 貸倒れ損失, 貸倒れ償却
　bad loan securitization 不良債権の証券化

bad loan write-offs 不良債権処理 （⇒**accounting period**）
▶The accelerated disposal of *bad loans* will augment deflationary pressures on the economy. 不良債権処理の加速は、デフレ圧力を強める。

bad loan disposal 不良債権処理 （=disposal of bad [nonperforming] loans, write-off of bad loans）
▶Many expect losses from *bad loan disposals* to increase drastically. 大方の予想では、不良債権処理に伴う損失額は今後大幅に増えそうである。

bailout 图 救済, 緊急援助, 金融支援, 債務棚上げ, 救済措置
▶We withdrew from a *bailout* of the company. 当社は、同社への金融支援を打ち切りました。

balance 图 収支, 差額, 残高, 勘定残高, 残金, 残り, 貸借勘定, 帳尻, 不足額, 繰越金残存価額, 均衡, 釣合い, バランス （⇒**account balance, after-tax balance, cash balance, outstanding balance of contracts**）
  account balance 差引残高, 口座残高
  balance at beginning of year 期首残高 （=balance at the beginning of the period）
  balance at end of year 期末残高 （=balance at the end of the period, balance at the term-end）
  bank balance 銀行側残高
  beginning balance [the 〜]期首残高
  cash balance 現金預金残高
  certificate of bank balance 預金残高証明書
  clearing balance 交換尻
  clearing house balance 手形交換尻
  closing balance [the 〜]期末残高
  credit balances 貸方残高, 預金残高
  declining balance 定率法
  financial balance 金融収支
▶The consortium intends to raise funds to cover one-third of its development costs and expects the government will pay the *balance*. この共同事業体は、開発費の3分の1は独自に資金調達する方針で、残りは政府の支援を見込んでいる。
▶The worsening *balance* of supply and demand is mainly due to the surplus of production equpment. 需給バランス悪化の主因は、過剰設備である。

balance sheet 貸借対照表, 財務基盤, 財務体質, 財務内容, 財務状況, 財務状態, 財務, 資産, バランス・シート《略 BS, B/S》 （=position statement, statement of financial condition, statement of financial position; ⇒**consolidated balance sheet**）
貸借対照表とは ➡ 企業の一定時点（貸借対照表日）の総資産と負債, 資本など企業の財政状態を示す財務表（計算書）で, 損益計算書とともに財務書類［財務諸表］の中心をなす。

balance sheet adjustment バランス・シート調整 （収益力向上のため、企業が過剰な設備や雇用の調整を進めること）
balance sheet composition 貸借対照表の構成
balance sheet date 貸借対照表日, 決算日 （=closing date; ⇒**monetary assets**）
balance sheet equation 貸借対照表等式
balance sheet growth 資産の増加
balance sheet management 財務管理, バランス・シート管理
balance sheet ratio 財務指標, 貸借対照表比率
branch balance sheet 支店貸借対照表
classified balance sheet 分類貸借対照表, 区分式貸借対照表
combined balance sheet 合併貸借対照表, 本支店合併貸借対照表
combined balance sheet of home office and branch 本支店合併貸借対照表 （=combined balance sheet）
common-size balance sheet 百分率貸借対照表, 比率表示貸借対照表, 共通型貸借対照表
comparative balance sheet 比較貸借対照表
consolidated balance sheet 連結貸借対照表
constant dollar balance sheet 恒常ドル貸借対照表
credit balance sheet 信用貸借対照表
damaged balance sheet 資産の質の悪化
estimated balance sheet 見積り貸借対照表
improve one's balance sheet 財務体質を改善する, 資金ポジションを改善させる
post-balance sheet date 決算日後
post-balance sheet event 後発事象
preparation of balance sheet 貸借対照表の作成
restatement of balance sheet 貸借対照表の再表示
strengthen one's balance sheet 財務体質を強化する
strong balance sheet 健全な財務内容, 健全な財務状態
trim the balance sheet 資産を減らす
▶We first figure out what our *balance sheet* would look like if we had always used the new accounting methods. 新会計処理方法を常時採用した場合、私どもはまず貸借対照表がどのような

影響を受けるかを考えます。

balance sheet information 貸借対照表情報

[貸借対照表情報]の表示例

Dollars in millions	単位：百万ドル
Working capital	運転資本
Cash and temporary cash investments	現金および短期投資
Total assets	資産合計
Total debt	債務合計
Total shareowners' equity	株主持ち分合計
Days sales outstanding for core business	中核事業の平均売掛債権滞留日数
Inventory turnover	棚卸し資産回転率

balanced scorecard バランスト・スコアカード（財務会計的な項目のほかに、顧客満足度や業務プロセスなどの非財務的な項目を数値化して評価する業績評価法）

bank 名 銀行, バンク
　agent bank 幹事銀行
　bank balance 銀行預金残高, 銀行残高 （＝balance at the bank）
　bank card 銀行発行のクレジット・カード, バンク・カード （＝bankcard）
　bank charge 銀行手数料, 銀行諸費用
　Bank for International Settlements 国際決済銀行《略 BIS》（⇒minimum capital adequacy ratio）
　bank interest 銀行利子
　bank loan [loans] payable 銀行借入金
　bank prime rate 銀行プライムレート（一流企業に対する最優遇貸出金利）
　bank rate 公定歩合, 銀行利率, 金利 （＝official discount rate：中央銀行が定める貸出金の基準金利）
　bank reconciliation 銀行勘定調整
　bank refinancing 銀行融資の借換え
　bank service fee 銀行手数料
　bank transfer 銀行振替え, 口座振替え, 銀行間振替え, 銀行送金, 銀行決済, 銀行振込み （＝credit transfer）
　commercial bank 商業銀行, 民間銀行, 都市銀行, 都銀
　core bank 主力銀行
　custodian bank 保管銀行, カストディ銀行
　financially healthy bank 健全行
　funding bank 貸出銀行, 貸出行
　leading banks 大手銀行
　main bank 主力取引銀行
　merchant bank マーチャント・バンク, 引受銀行
　mortgage bank 住宅金融会社
　national bank [米]国法銀行, 国立銀行, 全国銀行
　nonbank ノンバンク （＝nonbank financial in-stitution：銀行以外の金融機関）
　one bank policy 一行取引主義
　prime bank 一流銀行, 有力銀行
　retail bank リテール・バンク
　state bank [米]州法銀行, 国営銀行
　top banks 上位行, 上位銀行
　trust bank 信託銀行
　wholesale bank 法人向けの銀行
▸Several major *banks* have recently received upgraded ratings.　大手銀行数行の格付けが最近、上方修正されている。

bank agent system 銀行代理店制度 （＝banking agent system）

▸A *bank agent system* obliges business corporations acting as bank agents to offer time-consuming and costly staff training programs.　銀行代理店制度では、代理店になる事業会社は、人材育成にかなりの手間とコストをかけなければならない。

bank credit 銀行借入れ, 銀行貸出, 銀行融資, 銀行当座貸し, 銀行信用, 銀行信用状 （＝bank lending, bank loan, banker's credit）

bank lending 銀行貸出, 銀行融資 （＝bank accomodation, bank advance, bank credit, bank loan）

▸The average daily balance of domestic *bank lending* expanded 1.8 percent to ¥390.95 trillion in January 2007 from a year earlier.　国内銀行（民間銀行）の2007年1月の貸出平均残高は、前年同月比1.8％増の390兆9,500億円となった。

bank line of credit 銀行与信枠, 銀行信用枠, 銀行与信限度額, 銀行借入れ枠, 利用限度額 （＝bank line）

▸At December 31, 2007, we had available unused *bank lines of credit* with a number of U.S. and non-U.S. banks permitting borrowings up to an aggregate of $4,000 million.　2007年12月31日現在、当社が米国内および米国外の多数の銀行から与えられた銀行借入限度枠の未使用分は、総額で40億ドルでした。

bank loan 銀行貸付け, 銀行融資, 銀行貸付け金, 銀行借入れ, 銀行借入金, 銀行間借款, 銀行ローン, バンク・ローン （＝bank lending）

▸Germany's financial sector used to rely on *bank loan*-centered indirect financing.　ドイツの金融業界は、以前は銀行融資中心の間接金融に頼っていた。

bankcard 名 銀行発行のクレジット・カード（＝bank card）

bankrupt 形 破産した，倒産した，経営破綻した，破綻した，支払い不能の
- **be declared bankrupt** 破産宣告を受ける
- **be nearly bankrupt** 倒産寸前
- **go bankrupt** 破産する，倒産する，破綻する（＝go under）
▸The company was officially declared *bankrupt* by the Tokyo District Court. 同社は，東京地裁から正式に破産宣告を受けた。

bankrupt 名 破産者，破綻者，破産宣告を受けた者，債務支払い不能者

bankruptcy 名 倒産，破産，経営破綻，破産手続き（＝business failure, insolvency）
- **bankruptcy procedure** 破産手続き
- **Bankruptcy Reform Act of 1978** 1978年米連邦改正破産法，1978年改正破産法
- **corporate bankruptcy** 企業倒産（＝corporate failure）
▸U.S. subprime mortgage lender New Century Financial filed for *bankruptcy* protection. 米住宅ローン会社のニューセンチュリー・フィナンシャルが，会社更生手続きの適用を申請した。

bargain 名 取引，取引契約，商談，交渉
- **bargain price** 割引価格
- **bargain purchase option** 廉価買取選択権，割安購入選択権
- **bargain renewal option** 割安更新選択権

bargaining power 交渉力
▸In the background of the global steel industry's consolidation is the intention of steelmakers to enhance their *bargaining power* against both upstream and downstream industries by increasing their size. 世界的な鉄鋼業界の再編成の背景には，巨大化で川上・川下産業［上・下流部門］との交渉力を強めたい，という鉄鋼メーカーの思惑が働いている。

base 動 拠点を置く，…を拠点とする，根拠を置く，…を根拠に据える，…をベースにする
- **be based in [at] ...** …に拠点［本部・本店・本社］を置く，…を拠点とする，…を活動の基盤とする
- **be based on [upon] ...** …に基づく，…に基づいて算出［算定］される，…を根拠に置く，…に基づいて構築する
▸Earnings per share for the third quarter were *based* on 305 million average common shares outstanding. 第3四半期の1株当たり純利益は，発行済み普通株式の平均株式数3億500万株に基づいて計算されています。

base 名 基準，基本，基礎，基盤，拠点，基地，ベース（⇒**asset base, capital base, customer base, enhancement**）
- **at the parent base** 単独ベースで
- **base of taxation** 課税標準
- **base stock inventory valuation** 基準棚卸し法，正常在り高［有り高］法，基礎在り高法（＝base stock inventory, base stock method）
- **base year** 基準年，基準年度，基準年次
- **business base** 営業基盤，経営基盤
- **earnings base** 収益基盤
- **equity base** 株主資本基盤
- **export base** 輸出拠点
- **funding base** 資金調達源
- **liabilities base** 債務の範囲
- **manufacturing base** 生産拠点（＝production base）
- **tax base** 課税基準
▸Sony's technology center in Shanghai is its *base* for the development of software in China. ソニーの上海のテクノロジー・センターは，中国国内でのソフトウエア開発拠点である。

base period 基準期間，基準時，基準年次

base rate 基本料金，基準金利，基準利率，最低貸出利率，基本給，基礎賃率
- **base rate increase** 基準金利の引上げ

basic fund 〔保険〕基金（一般企業の資本金に相当する）
▸*Basic fund* is equivalent to the capital of a joint-stock company. 基金は，株式会社の資本金に当たる。

basic material 原材料，素材
▸Factors that could damage corporate performance are creeping up on industrial firms, including higher prices of oil and *basic materials* and increasingly intense end-product price competition. 石油や原材料の値上がり，最終製品の価格競争の激化など，企業の業績を悪化させる要因が製造業に忍び寄っている。

basic net earnings per common share 基本的普通株式1株当たり純利益

basic profit 基礎利益（＝fundamental profit）
▸The *basic profit* excludes appraisal profits and losses from liquidation of securities holdings and write-offs of problem loans. 基礎利益には，保有有価証券の売却や不良債権の処理による評価損益は含まれない。

basis 名 方針，基準，根本原理，主義，方式，基礎，根拠，論拠，土台，主成分，ベース（⇒**consolidated basis**）

accrued basis 発生主義, 発生基準
basis of consolidation 連結方針, 連結の基準
basis of recognition 認識基準
constant dollar basis 実質ベース
cost basis 原価基準
customs basis 通関ベース
delivery basis 出荷基準
denominated basis ドル表示で
equity basis 持ち分法
first-in, first-out basis 先入れ先出し法
full cost basis 全部原価法
fully diluted basis 完全希薄化法
historical cost basis 取得原価基準
lower of cost or market basis 低価法, 低価主義, 低価基準
market price [value] basis 時価主義
on a dollar denominated basis ドル表示で
on a full year basis 通年で, 通期で
on a group basis 連結ベースで
on a moment-to-moment basis 瞬間瞬間ベースで
on a monthly basis 単月で
on a nominal basis 名目で
on a preliminary basis 暫定段階で
on a same-store basis 既存店ベースで
on a seasonally adjusted basis 季節調整済みで
on an all-store basis 全店舗ベースで
on an annualized basis 年率換算で, 年換算で
on an optional basis 選択制で
on the basis of IMF formula IMF方式で
parent-basis earnings outlook 単独ベースの収益見通し
production basis 生産基準
profitable basis 収益基盤
receipts and payments basis 現金基準, 現金主義（＝cash basis）
settlement date basis 決済日ベース
straight-line basis 定額法
tax basis 課税標準
▶Toyota became Japan's first manufacturer to post sales of more than ¥10 trillion on a half-year *basis*. 売上高が半期ベースで10兆円を突破したのは, 日本企業でトヨタが初めてだ。

basis point ベーシス・ポイント, b.p.（為替・金利変動の基準単位で, 1ベーシス・ポイント＝0.01％, 100ベーシス・ポイント＝1％。⇒**average return on capital, percentage point**）
▶Spending on research and development dipped by 10 *basis points*. 研究開発費は, 10ベーシス・ポイント（0.1％）減少しました。

basket 名 一括, 集合, かご, バスケット方式集合
basket purchase 一括買取
B/D [b/d] 〔簿記〕前期繰越し, 一括購入（brought downの略）
bear hug ベア・ハッグ（条件のよい株式公開買付けなどの買収提案）
beef up 強化する, 増強する, 補強する, 拡充する, 向上させる, 食肉処理する（＝strengthen）
▶We will *beef up* overseas production capacity. 当社は, 海外での生産能力を強化［拡充］する方針です。
beef-up 名 強化, 増強, 補強, 食肉処理
▶The *beef-up* of the early warning system is expected to enable insurers to make decision on the decrease of guranteed yields before the companies fail. 早期警戒制度の強化で, 生保は破綻前に予定利率引下げを決断できるようになる。
before 前 …前, …考慮前, …差引き前, …控除前（⇒**income before income taxes**）
before cumulative effect of accounting change 会計処理変更に伴う累積的影響額考慮前, 会計処理変更の累積効果控除前
before equity in undistributed income of subsidiaries 子会社の未処分利益に対する持ち分差引き前
before extraordinary items 異常項目前
before interest and taxes 利子・税金控除前
before the impact of the restructuring provision 事業再編引当金の影響額控除前, 事業再編に伴う引当金繰入れの影響額控除前
income before income taxes 税引き前利益
income before minority interests 少数株主持ち分控除前利益
income before provision for income tax 税引き前利益, 税引き前当期利益
income before provisions 引当金繰入れ前利益
income before provisions and loss on disposal of assets 引当金繰入れ額および資産処分損失控除前
income before taxes 税引き前利益
income before taxes on income 税引き前利益
▶The U.S. and foreign components of income *before* income taxes and the provision for income taxes are presented in this table. 以下に示すのは, 米国と外国の税引き前利益と法人税繰入れ額の内訳です。
beginning 名 最初, 初め, 初期, 期首
beginning and ending balances 期首残高と期末残高
beginning equity 期首株主資本

beginning inventory 期首棚卸し高, 期首棚卸
資産, 期首在庫, 期首在庫品
beginning of (the) period 期首
beginning of (the) year 期首, 年度初め, 年初
《略 **BOY**》（=beginning of fiscal year）
below-par company 赤字会社
below the line 異常損益項目, 利益処分, 範囲
外（lineは「損益計算書の経常利益」をさす）
benchmark 動 基準にする, 尺度とする
▸These performance objectives are *benchmarked* and evaluated against companies within industries similar to the Cororpation, and with similar internal objectives. これらの業績目標は, 当社と類似の業界にあって当社と類似の社内目標を掲げている会社を基準として評価されています。
benchmark 名 基準, 尺度, 基準値, 測定基準, 基準指数, 基準銘柄, 指標, 指標銘柄, 節目, ベンチマーク
　benchmark federal funds rate 短期金利の指標であるフェデラル・ファンド金利
　benchmark interest rate 基準金利, 指標金利, 政策金利
　benchmark reserves 基準準備金
▸The Fed raised the *benchmark* short-term federal funds rate a quarter percentage point to 4.75 percent per annum. 米連邦準備制度理事会（FRB）は, 短期金利の指標となるフェデラル・ファンド（FF）金利を［短期金利の指標となるFF金利の誘導目標］0.25%引き上げて年4.75%とした。
beneficiary 名 〈年金や保険金, 為替などの〉受取人, 〈信用状の〉受益者, 受給者
　beneficiary right to the trust 信託受益権
　contingent beneficiary 偶発受益者
　letter of credit beneficiary 信用状の受益者
　pension beneficiary 年金受給者
　pension fund beneficiary 年金基金の受益者
benefit 動 利益を与える, …の利益になる, …のプラスになる, …に貢献する, 利益を得る, 恩恵を受ける, 利益が発生する（⇒**goodwill**）
　benefit existing shareholders 株主の利益になる
　benefit from ... …から利益を得る, …の恩恵を受ける, …のメリットを受ける, …が追い風になる
▸Automobile and electric appliance industries have *benefited* from these windfalls. 自動車と電機業界は, これらの追い風の恩恵を受けた。
▸Goodwill is amortized on a straight-line basis over the periods estimated to be *benefited*, currently not exceeding five years. 営業権は, その効果が及ぶと見込まれる期間にわたり, 現在は5年を超えない期間で定額法で償却されています。

benefit 名 利益, 利得, 便益, 利点, 効果, 給付, 給付金, 給付額, 年金, 手当, 受益, 受益金, 税減額効果, ベネフィット（⇒**career-average pay, defined benefit, employee, health care benefits, pension benefits**）
　accumulated benefit 累積給付
　benefit cost 給付コスト（⇒**benefit-related liabilities**）
　benefit-cost [benefit/cost] analysis 費用便益分析, 便益・費用分析, 効果・費用分析, 収益原価分析（=cost benefit analysis）
　benefit formula 給付額計算方式
　benefit security 給付保障
　benefits earned during the period 当期に発生した給付
　benefits from declining interest rates 金利低下の効果, 金利低下の恩恵
　benefits of cost cutting [reduction] 経費削減効果, コスト削減効果
　fringe benefit 付加給付
　non-vested benefit 受益権非確定給付
　retirement benefit 退職給付
　right to benefits 受給権
▸We estimated the future payments for *benefits* to all present retirees and for accumulated benefits of active employees. 現在の全退職者に対する給付と現職従業員の累積給付の将来支払い額については, 予測を行いました。
benefit obligation 給付債務
▸We use a weighted-average discount rate, the rate of increase in future compensation levels and assumptions to calculate the projected *benefit obligation*. 当社では, 加重平均割引率, 将来の昇給率と仮定を用いて, 予測給付債務を計算しています。
benefit plan 給付制度（⇒**defined benefit**）
　benefit plans expense 年金制度費用
　fixed benefit plan 定額給付制度
　fringe benefit plan 付加給付制度
　postretirement benefit plan 退職後給付制度
　retirement benefit plan 退職給付制度, 退職給与制度
benefit-related liabilities 給付関連債務
▸Payroll and *benefit-related liabilities* are higher mainly due to increases in the associated expenses and benefit costs. 給与と給付関連債務は, 主に関連費用と給付コストの増大で膨らんでいます。
benefits of shareholders 株主の利益, 株主利益

▶Japanese companies tend to attach greater importance to favorable relations with customers than to boosting *benefits of shareholders*.　日本企業は, 株主の利益を高めることより, 顧客との好ましい関係を重視する傾向がある.

best efforts　最善の努力, 委託募集
best-efforts 形　最善の努力をする条件の
　　best-efforts issue　売出発行
　　best-efforts selling　委託販売
best estimates and judgments　最良 [最善] の見積りと判断
▶The financial statements include some amounts that are based on *best estimates and judgments*.　財務書類には, 最善の見積りと判断に基づく数値が一部含まれています.

betterment expense　改良費
B/F [b/f]　〔簿記〕次期繰越し, 次頁繰越し (=carried forward : **brought forward**の略)
BI　企業経営情報, 企業情報 (business intelligenceの略)
bid 名　入札, 申込み, 〔入札の〕付け値, 落札価格, 競り, 提案, 買収提案, 買収案件, 買収, 株式公開買付け, 買い注文, 買い呼び値, 買い気配, 買い唱え (証券などの売買で買い手が希望する値段), ビッド (=bidding, tendering; ⇒**bidding, buy out, hostile takeover, takeover bid**)
　　accepted bid　落札価格
　　agreed bid　合意による株式公開買付け
　　bid for a company　企業買収, 企業買収案
　　bid price　買い手の指し値, 買い値, 買い呼び値, 買い気配, 入札価格, せり値, 付け値 (=buying price ; ⇒**buy order**)
　　bid target　買収の標的
　　competitive bid　競争入札 (=competitive bidding)
　　hostile bid　敵対的TOB
　　make a successful bid　落札する, 受注する
　　submit bids　入札に応じる (=send in a bid)
　　win the bid　受注する, 落札する
▶Aoki Holdings Inc. made a *bid* to take over Futata on Aug. 7, 2006.　AOKIホールディングス (アオキ) は, フタタに対して2006年8月7日にTOB [株式公開買付け] を提案した.
▶The company's winning *bid* is subject to the approval of AT&T Wireless shareholders.　同社が獲得した買収案件は, AT&Tワイヤレス株主の承認を得なければならない.
bid winner　落札業者, 落札予定会社, 受注業者, 受注会社
▶The four companies negotiated and agreed in advance the *bid winner* and the bidding price.　4社は, 事前に談合を行って落札予定会社や入札価格を決めていた.

bidder 名　入札者, 入札業者, 入札参加企業, 入札行, 競り手, 〈参加などの〉申込み国
　　bidder for a contract　請負仕事の入札
　　designated bidder　指名入札業者
　　highest bidder　最高入札者, 最高入札企業
　　lowest bidder　最低入札者, 最低入札企業
　　potential bidder　入札参加予定者
　　preferential bidder　一番札
　　preferred bidder　優先入札者
　　select bidders　入札業者を選定する, 入札参加業者を選定する
　　star bidder　最有力の入札参加企業
　　successful bidder　落札業者
bidding 名　入札, 競り, 申込み, 買収提案, 命令 (=bid, tender, tendering)
　　bidding among designated companies　指名競争入札 (=designated bidding)
　　bidding expense　入札費, 入札経費
　　bidding price　入札価格 (⇒bid)
　　bidding procedures　入札手続き
　　bidding system　入札方式, 入札制度
　　bidding war　競り, 競争, 買収戦争, 買収提案戦争
　　collusive bidding　馴れ合い入札
　　competitive bidding　競争入札
　　designated bidding　指名競争入札
　　e-bidding　電子入札 (=Net bidding)
　　interfering in the bidding process for ...　…の入札妨害をする
　　Net bidding　ネット入札, 電子入札 (=e-bidding)
　　noncompetitive bidding　非競争入札
　　open bidding　公開入札, 一般競争入札
　　open bidding anew　入札をやり直す
　　participate in the bidding　入札に参加する
　　postpone the bidding　入札を延期する
　　public bidding　公開入札
　　unsolicited bidding　直接入札
　　winner of the bidding　落札業者, 受注者, 受注業者
▶Before *biddings*, the construction firms decided which firm would win the bid.　入札前に, これらの建設会社は受注業者を決めていた.
▶Each bid was submitted during competitive *bidding*, with the bidding price being between 95 percent and 99 percent of the estimated winning price.　入札はいずれも競争入札で行われ, 入札価格は予定落札価格の95-99%だった [落

札率（予定落札価格に占める落札価格の割合）は95-99％だった］.
▸The *bidding* for the public works project was held in July 2007 among designated construction firms. この公共工事の入札は、2007年7月に指名建設会社間で行われた［この公共工事の競争入札は、2007年7月に行われた］.

bill 名 手形, 為替手形, 証券, 法案, 訴状, 紙幣
  bill of exchange 為替手形
  bill of material 部品表, 材料表
  bills payable 支払手形
  bills receivable 受取手形
billing 名 請求書の送付, 勘定書の作成, 広告取扱高 （⇒**one-stop shopping**）
BIS 国際決済銀行（**Bank for International Settlements**の略; ⇒**capital adequacy ratio**）
  BIS requirements BIS基準, BISの自己資本比率基準 （＝BIS equity standards, BIS standard）
black 名 黒字 （＝black figure; ⇒**red**）
  in the black 黒字で
  keep one's balance in the black 黒字を確保する
  operate in the black 黒字経営する
  return to the black 黒字に戻る, 黒字に転換する, 黒字に転じる
  swing back into the black 黒字に転換する
▸The company's after-tax profit returned to the *black* for the first time in six years. 同社の税引き後利益は、6期ぶりに黒字に転換した.

blue-chip 形 優良な
  blue-chip subsidiary 優良子会社
  blue-chip stock 優良株
BN 銀行券（**bank note**の略）
board 名 取締役会 （＝the board of directors）, 重役会, 理事会, 審議会, 委員会, 会議, 省・庁・局・部, 掲示板, ボード （⇒**authority**）
  Big Board ニューヨーク証券取引所, ビッグボード
  bill board 広告掲示板, ビルボード
  board meeting 取締役会, 取締役会会議, 役員会, 評議員会
  board minutes 取締役会議事録
  board of executive officers 常務会
  board of managing directors 常務会
  board of statutory auditors 監査役会
  board of trade 商業会議所
  board of trustees 理事会
  chairman of the board 取締役会会長, 取締役会長 （＝chairman of board of directors）
  Chicago Board of Trade シカゴ商品取引所
  committee of the board 理事会
  executive board 重役会, 常務会, 理事会, 執行委員会
  extraordinary board meeting 臨時取締役会
  fall across the board 全面安になる, 全面的に下落する
  full board 取締役会の全体会議 （⇒**submission**）
  go on the board 上場する
  independent oversight board 独立監視委員会
  join the board 取締役会に加わる, 取締役に就任する, 取締役に選任される
  management board 取締役会, 重役会
  managing board 運営委員会, 運営理事会
  rise across the board 全面高になる, 全面的に上昇する
  second board companies 二部上場企業
  Securities and Investments Board 〚英〛証券投資委員会
  sit on the board 取締役を務める, 役員［委員］を務める
  special precinct board 特別委員会
  staggered board スタガー取締役会
  supervisory board 監査役会
  U.S.-style board structure 米国型の取締役会制度
▸Four new directors joined the *board* at last year's annual meeting. 昨年度の定時株主総会で、新取締役4名が取締役会に加わりました［新たに4名が取締役に選任されました］.

board member 取締役, 役員, 重役, 理事, 執行委員 （＝board director）
  board members' bonus 役員賞与
  board members' pay [**compensation**] 役員報酬
  board members' salaries 役員報酬
▸At the general meeting of shareholders, *board members* are required to hold earnest dialogues with shareholders and clarify their strategies to win their approval. 株主総会では、経営陣は株主と真剣に対話し、経営陣の経営方針を明らかにして株主の承認［賛同］を得なければならない.
▸The two companies will send *board members* to each other. 両社は、役員を相互派遣する.

board of corporate auditors 監査役会
▸The *board of corporate auditors* has five members, with the three outside corporate auditors comprising a majority. 監査役会は監査役5名で構成され、このうち3名の社外取締役が過半数を占めています.

board of directors 〈会社の〉取締役会, 役員会, 重役会, 財団などの理事会 《略 **BOD**》
|　取締役会とは ➡ アメリカの会社の場合、取締役会は

会社経営の最高意思決定機関で、株主総会で選任された取締役数名で構成される。会社役員（corporate officer）の選任、株式の発行、配当宣言などについての決定権がある。また、社内取締役（inside director）と社外取締役（outside director）を含めて取締役（director）は株主が選任し、役員は取締役が選任することになっている。

the extraordinary meeting of the board of directors 臨時取締役会

the permanent committees of the board of directors 取締役会の常設委員会、常設の取締役会付属委員会

the regular meeting of the board of directors 取締役会の定例会議、定例取締役会

▶The *Board of Directors* is responsible for the overall affairs of the Corporation. 取締役会は、当社の全体的な問題に関して責任を負っています。

▶The *board of directors*' audit committee consists solely of outside directors. 取締役会の監査委員会は、社外取締役だけで構成されています。

board proposal 取締役会の提案

▶We will oppose every *board proposal* for an increase in the authorized capital scale. われわれとしては、取締役会の株式発行可能枠（授権株式数）の拡大提案には、全部反対します。

boardroom 名 証券取引所の立会場、立会所、役員室、会議室

bond 名 債券、社債、公社債（「債券」には、国や地方公共団体が発行する公債と、事業会社が発行する社債があり、これを一括して「公社債」という）、債務証書、借用証書、保証証書、支払い保証契約、保証、保証金、保釈（⇒convertible bond）

accrued bond interest to date of sale 外部発行時までの社債経過利息

active bond 利付き債券

blank bond 無記名債券

bond authorized 授権社債

bond expenses 社債発行費

bond holder 社債権者、社債保有者、債券保有者（=bondholder, debenture holder）

bond interest paid 支払い社債利息

bond interest received 受入社債利息

bond issue expenses 社債発行費、債券発行費（=bond issue costs, bond issuing expenses, issue costs on bonds）

bond issued at a discount 割引発行社債（社債の発行価額が額面金額［額面価格］より低い社債）

bond issued at a premium 割増発行社債、プレミアム発行された社債（社債の発行価額が額面金額より高い社債）

bond outstanding 債券発行残高、発行済み社債、未償還債券、流通社債

bond payable 未償還社債、社債、社債勘定（=bonds payable, corporate bond）

bond redemption 社債償還、発行済み社債の買戻し、債券の償還（=redemption of bonds）

bond refunding 社債借換え（発行済み社債と新規社債を交換すること）

bond with detachable stock warrant 分離型の新株引受権付き社債

bond with nondetachable stock warrant 非分離型の新株引受権付き社債

collateral bond 担保付き社債

collateral for bonds 社債の担保

consolidated bond 整理社債

debenture bond 無担保社債、無担保債（=debenture）

discount bond 割引発行債、割引債

discount on bonds payable 社債発行差金（=premium on bonds payable）

high yield bond 高利回り債

interest bearing bond 利付き債

issue of bonds 社債発行、社債の発行（=issuance of bonds）

mortgage bond 担保付き社債

premium on bonds payable 社債発行差金

private placement bond 私募債

public bond 公債

U.S. longer-term bond 米国の長期国債

yuan-based bond 人民元建て債

zero coupon bond ゼロ・クーポン債

▶We raised ¥100 billion from the *bond* issue to finance our restructuring. 当社は、社債発行で1,000億円を調達して、リストラの資金に充てました。

bond issuance [issue] 社債発行、債券発行

▶Livedoor planned to raise about ¥80 billion, about half the value of all outstanding shares of Nippon Broadcasting System's shares, through *bond issuance*. ライブドアは、社債を発行して、ニッポン放送株の時価総額の約半分にあたる約800億円の資金を調達する計画だった。

bond premium 社債発行差金（「社債発行差金」=発行価額－額面金額。社債の発行価額［売買価格］が額面金額［額面価格］を上回ったときの差額）、社債発行割増金、社債割増金、社債プレミアム、打ち歩（ぶ）料

bond with stock purchase warrant 株式買取り権付き社債、新株予約権付き社債、ワラント債

▶The investment fund converted *bonds with*

bonus 名 手当, 賞与, 特別配当, 助成金, ボーナス (⇒annual salary system, corporate earnings)
　bonus dividend 特別配当 （＝capital dividend）
　bonus issue 特別発行, 無償新株発行, 無償増資（特別配当株の発行）
　bonus payment reserve 賞与引当金
　bonus payments 賞与支給額
　bonus plan 賞与制度, 課業賞与制度
　bonus share [stock] 特別配当株, 無償株式, ボーナス株, 景品株
　bonus system 報奨制度
　bonus to directors 役員賞与
　bonus to employees 従業員賞与
　bonuses payable 未払い賞与, 未払いボーナス
　capital bonus 株式配当 （＝stock dividend）
　directors' bonuses 役員賞与
　employee's bonus 従業員ボーナス
　export bonus 輸出助成金
　incentive bonus 奨励手当, 奨励特別手当
　officer's bonus 役員賞与
　premium bonus 割増手当, 割増賞与
　reserve for bonuses [bonus payment] 賞与引当金
　stock bonus plan 株式賞与制度
　winter bonus 冬季賞与, 冬のボーナス
　year end bonus 年末賞与
▶Since bonuses directly reflect corporate performance, most companies have announced reductions in bonus payments. 賞与は企業の業績を直接反映するので、大半の企業が賞与支給額の削減をすでに打ち出している。

book 動 計上する, 会計処理する, 帳簿に載せる, 記入する, 記帳する, 記録する,〈資産や債権を〉積み増す, 予約する （＝post, record; ⇒recall 名）
　book a special profit 特別利益を計上する
　book assets 資産を積み増す, 債権を積み増す
▶KDDI booked a group net profit of ¥136.03 billion in the fiscal first half. KDDIは、今年度上期に1,360億3,000万円の連結税引き後利益を計上した。
▶New accounting rules changed the way we book expenses for retiree benefits, separation payments and income taxes. 新会計規則により、当社の退職者給付、中途退職金と法人税の各費用の会計処理方法が変わりました。

book 名 帳面, …帳,〈従業員などの〉名簿, 帳簿, 会計上 （⇒accounting, accounting manipulation, cash book, close the [one's] books, cook 動）
　assets out of book 簿外資産
　book balance 預金者側残高
　book loss 帳簿上の損失, 含み損, 評価損
　book profit 帳簿上の利益, 帳簿利益, 紙上利益, 含み益, 評価益
　book surplus 帳簿上の剰余金, 帳簿剰余金
　books of account 会計帳簿 （＝account books, financial books）
　closing of books 決算, 帳簿の締切り （＝book-closing, closing of accounts, closing the books）
　financial books 会計帳簿, 帳簿
　liability off the book 簿外負債
　make up the books 帳簿を締め切る
　stock transfer book 株主名簿
▶The nation's big four audiding firms audit the books of about 80 percent of listed companies. 国内の4大監査法人が、上場企業の約8割の会計監査をしている。

book-closing 名 決算
　book-closing period 決算期
▶We will disclose our earnings forecasts on a consolidated basis, starting with our March 2009 book-closing. 当社は、2009年3月期決算から、連結ベースの業績予想を開示する方針だ。

book income 帳簿上の利益, 会計上の利益
▶The provisions for income taxes increased mainly because of higher "book income," that is, the income before income taxes and cumulative effects of accounting changes. 法人税繰入額は、主に「会計上の利益」、すなわち法人税および会計処理の変更による累積的影響額考慮前利益が増加したため、増大しました。

book inventory 帳簿棚卸
　book inventory method 帳簿棚卸法
　book inventory system 帳簿棚卸法

book value 簿価, 帳簿価額 [価格], 帳簿上の価格, 純資産額, 取得価格, 純資産 （＝book price, carrying amount, effective book value）
　adjusted book value method 修正純資産方式（バランス・シートの資産と負債を時価に換算して純資産を計算する方法）
　asset book value 資産簿価
　be below book value 取得価格を下回る
　book value approach 帳簿価額方式
　book value at beginning of year 期首簿価
　book value per common share [stock] 普通株式1株当たり純資産, 普通株式1株当たり持ち分額, 普通株式1株当たり帳簿価額, 普通株1株当たり簿価
　book value per share 1株当たり純資産, 1株当

たり純資産額, 1株当たり簿価《略 BPS》(企業の純資産を発行済み株式数で割った指数。BPSの数値が高いほど, 企業の安定性も高いといわれる)
book value stock plan 帳簿価格株式プラン
book value stock purchase plan 帳簿価格株式購入制度
excess of cost over book value 簿価に対する原価超過額
fixed percentage of book value method 定率法
net book value 正味簿価
price book-value ratio 株価純資産倍率
▸We sold eqipment costing $50,000, with a *book value* of $25,000, for $20,000 cash on October 15, 2007. 当社は, 2007年10月15日に, 原価5万ドル(簿価2万5,000ドル)の設備を2万ドルの現金で売却しました。

book value method 簿価法, 帳簿価額法
▸Under the *book value method*, the carrying value of the convertible bonds at the date of the conversion would be used to account for the conversion. 簿価法では, 転換時の転換社債の簿価が, 転換の会計処理に使われる。

boost 動 推進する, 引き上げる, 増加させる, 拡大する, 押し上げる, 積み増す, 高める, 向上させる, 増強する, 強化する, 拡充する, 〈需要などを〉喚起する, 活気づかせる, 刺激する
▸The company will be split into a food supermarket chain and a real estate company to *boost* profitability. 同社は, 収益力を高めるため, 食品スーパーと不動産会社の2社に分割される。
▸The depreciation of the yen has *boosted* profits for exporting companies. 円安が輸出企業の利益を押し上げた。

boost 名 押し上げ, 後押し, 増強, 活気づけ, 発展, 向上, 増大, 急増, 上昇, 急上昇
▸The strong performance was supported by a *boost* in sales, mainly in the U.S. market. この好業績の要因は, 主に米国内市場での販売急増です。

boot 名 交換差金

borrow 動 借り入れる, 融資を受ける, 資金を調達する, 借金する (⇒**carry trade**)
borrowed capital 他人資本, 借入資本
borrowed money 借金, 借り
borrowed security 借入有価証券
borrowed stock 借り株
▸The company will *borrow* ¥56 billion to fund the introduction of new models. 同社は, 新型車導入の資金を調達するため, 560億円の融資を受ける。

▸The syndicated loan is part of our plan to *borrow* about ¥80 billion. 協調融資は, 当社の約800億円の資金調達計画の一環です。

borrower 名 借り手, 資金の借り手, 貸付け先, 貸出先, 融資先, 融資先企業, 債務者, 発行体, ボロワー (⇒**leverage** 名)
AAA rated borrower トリプルA格の発行体
borrower limit 与信限度
corporate borrowers 融資先, 融資先企業
major borrower 大口融資先, 主要発行体 (= large borrower)
premium borrower 優良発行体
▸Japan's economic recovery helped improve the business conditions of corporate *borrowers*. 日本の景気回復で, 融資先企業の業況が改善した。
▸The banks have categorized *borrowers* based on their financial health. 銀行は, 経営の健全度に基づいて融資先[債務者]を区分している。

borrowing 名 借入れ, 資金調達, 借入金, 借金, 負債, 債務 (⇒**bank line of credit**, **paper**)
banking borrowing 銀行借入れ (= bank borrowing)
borrowing capacity 資金調達能力, 借入れによる資金調達能力, 借入能力 (= borrowing power)
borrowing facilities 信用枠
borrowing needs 借入需要, 資金調達需要, 調達額
borrowing power 借入能力, 資金調達能力 (= borrowing capacity)
interest rate on borrowings 借入金の金利, 借入金の利率
long-term borrowings 長期借入金
net short-term borrowings 短期借入金純額
securitized borrowings 借入れの証券化
unsecured borrowing 無担保借入れ
▸Interest rates on *borrowings* would vary from country to country depending on local market conditions. 借入金の金利は, 各国の市場の状況に左右され, 国によって異なります。

borrowing cost 資金調達コスト, 借入コスト, 借入費用
▸The sale of car and truck loans may lower *borrowing costs* for General Motors Acceptance Corp. 自動車ローン債権の売却は, GMAC(GMの金融子会社)の資金調達コストを低減するねらいもある。

bottom line (損益計算書の最終行の意味から) 純損益, 純利益, 利益, 当期利益, 純損失益性, 取引の収支, 業績, 最終損益, 総決算, 最終結果[成果], 結論, 最終決定, 最重要事項, 要点, カギ, 問題

の核心, ぎりぎりの線, 本音 （⇒**arm**）
  bottom line results 純利益
  bottom lines 業績, 収益
  company's bottom line 企業［会社］の損益
  contribute to the bottom line 利益［当期利益］に貢献する, 利益に寄与する
  corporate [corporations'] bottom lines 企業収益
  enhance the bottom line 利益を押し上げる, 利益を増やす
  flow through to the bottom line 利益に直結する
  ▶Our *bottom line* shows a loss of $2.80 a share. 当社の最終損益は, 1株当たり2.80ドルの損失を示しています。
  ▶This is a *bottom-line* confirmation of the improvements of efficiency and competitiveness. これは, 効率性の改善と競争力の向上を決算で確認したことになります。

bourse 名 証券取引所, 取引所, 株式市況, 株式相場 （＝securities exchange）
  ▶A company listed on the Fukuoka *bourse* is subject to delisting after two straight years of negative net worth. 福岡証券取引所に上場している企業は, 2年連続債務超過になると, 上場廃止の対象になる。

BOY 期首, 年度初め, 年初 （beginning of (the) yearの略）

BPS 1株当たり純資産, 1株当たり純資産額 （book value per shareの略）

brand 名 商標, 銘柄, 特定の銘柄品, ブランド, ブランド品, ブランド商品, ブランド店
  barnacle brand バーナクル・ブランド（製品ライフサイクルの後半段階で市場に参入する競合ブランド）
  brand loyalty 商標忠実性, ブランドに対するこだわり, 銘柄忠実度, 商標信頼度, ブランド・ロイヤルティ
  brand name 商標名, 商品名, ブランド名, ブランド力, ブランド・ネーム
  brand name products ブランド品, ブランド商品 （＝branded goods, designer goods）
  brand switching 商標変更, ブランド・スイッチング
  character brand キャラクター・ブランド（大手メーカーの個性や特徴を強く打ち出した製品）
  consumer brand preference 消費者ブランド選好
  corporate brand 企業ブランド
  fashion brand ファッション・ブランド
  fighting brand 競争的ブランド, 競争的商標
  generic brand 非銘柄商品, 無印商品, ノーブランド商品, ジェネリック・ブランド, ジェネリック・ラベル
  individual brand 個別ブランド, 個別商標
  luxury foreign brands 海外高級ブランド
  manufacturer's brand 製造業者商標
  own brand 自社製品ブランド
  private brand プライベート・ブランド
  unified brand 統一ブランド
  ▶It's normal to maintain the independence of several cosmetics *brands* among major cosmetic firms in Europe and the United States. 欧米の化粧品大手では, 化粧品の複数ブランドの独立性を維持するのが普通だ。
  ▶U.S.-based Wal-Mart Stores Inc. suggested a merger with Daiei and Seiyu to create a unified *brand* in the future. 米ウォルマート・ストアーズは, ダイエーと西友を経営統合して, 将来は統一ブランドに一本化する案を示した。

break even 損得なしになる, 収支がとんとんになる, 五分五分になる, 辛うじて採算が取れる, 採算ラインになる
  ▶If the price of naphtha, which currently is about ¥35,000 per kiloliter, rises ¥1,000, the company's profit and costs will fail to *break even*. 現在1キロリットル当たり約35,000円のナフサ（粗製ガソリン）が, 1,000円値上がりすると, 同社の利益とコストは採算が取れなくなる。

break-even (point) 損益分岐点, 採算ライン, 採算点, 収支とんとん （＝breakdown point）
  break-even price 損益分岐点価格
  break-even time 損益分岐期間
  break-even yield 損益分岐点利回り
  profit and loss break-even point 損益分岐点
  return to break-even 収支とんとんに戻る, 採算ラインに戻る, 赤字を解消する

breakdown 名 分類, 内訳, 構成, 明細書, 故障
  breakdown of revenue 売上構成, 売上の内訳

briefing 名 説明会, 投資家向け説明会, 投資家説明会, 経過報告, 概要報告, 概況・状況説明, 背景説明, 要約書, セミナー
  ▶Our *briefing* for foreign investors was held in London. 当社の海外投資家向け説明会は, ロンドンで開きました。

brisk 形 活発な, 好調な
  brisk business performance 好業績, 好決算 （＝brisk performance, buoyant performance）
  ▶Buoyed with *brisk* business performance, one in every two companies will increase or resume

dividends. 好決算を受けて, 2社に1社は増配や復配[配当の再開]に踏み切る見通しだ。

brokerage 名 証券業, 証券会社, 仲介, 仲介業, 仲買, 仲買業, 証券仲買会社, 仲介手数料, ブローカー
 brokerage commission 株式委託売買手数料, 委託売買手数料, 委託手数料, 仲介手数料, ブローカー手数料 (＝brokerage fee)
 brokerage firm 証券会社 (＝brokerage house, securities company)
▸Many banks and *brokerage* houses have formed business alliances in launching stock brokerage business at the banks. 銀行での証券仲介業務を開始するにあたって, 銀行や証券会社の多くは業務提携している。

brought down [簿記]前期繰越し《略 B/D [b/d]》(＝carried down)

brought forward [簿記]次期繰越し, 次頁繰越し《略 B/F [b/f]》(＝carried forward)

BS [B/S] balance sheetを参照

B2B 企業対企業, 企業間取引 (business to businessの略)

BTO 受注生産, 受注生産方式 (build to orderの略)

bubble 名 バブル, 泡沫 (⇒business diversification, business strategy)
 asset bubble 資産のバブル
 bubble economy burst バブル経済の崩壊, バブル崩壊 (＝bubble burst, bursting of the bubble economy, collapse of the bubble economy)
 dot-com bubble ドットコム・バブル
 economic bubble 経済のバブル, バブル
 IT bubble IT投資バブル, ITバブル
 Net bubble ネット株バブル, ネット・バブル
▸We had about 10,000 people at our *bubble* economy era peak. 当社には, バブル期のピーク時に約1万人の従業員がいました。

bubble economy period バブル期 (＝bubble economic era, bubble period, bubble years)
▸The company followed an aggressive business strategy during the *bubble economy period* of the late 1980s. 同社は, 1980年代終わりのバブル期に積極的な事業戦略を展開した。

budget 名 予算, 財政, 家計, 経費
 budget consolidation 財政建て直し
 budget goal 予算目標
 budget guideline 予算編成方針 (＝budgeting policy)
 budget outlays 財政支出
 budget planning 予算計画
 incremental budget 増分主義予算
 long-range budget 長期予算

budgetary 形 予算上の
 budgetary appropriation 予算の計上
 budgetary procedure 予算手続き

budgeting 名 予算編成, 予算管理
 budgeting policy 予算編成方針 (＝budget guideline)

build to order 受注生産, 受注生産方式, 注文生産方式《略BTO》(顧客の注文を受けてから顧客の好みの仕様に応じて生産する方式)

building 名 建物, 建築, 建造
 building expense 建築費
 building maintenance expense 建物維持費
 buildings and accessories 建物および付属施設, 建物・付属施設
 buildings and building fixtures 建物および付属設備, 建物・付属設備 (＝buildings and fixed equipments)
 buildings and improvements 建物および付属設備, 建物および改良費, 建物・改良費

buoy 動 活気づかせる, 浮揚させる, 支える
 be buoyed by ... …で活気づく, …に支えられる
 buoy the economy 景気を浮揚させる
▸Sharp Corp. posted a 14 percent gain in quarterly profit, *buoyed* by robust demand for its liquid crystal display TVs. シャープの四半期利益は, 同社製液晶テレビの需要の大幅の伸びに支えられて, 14%増加した。

burden 名 負担, 費用負担, 重荷, 間接費, 製造間接費, 経費
 absorbed burden 製造間接費配賦額, 配賦済み製造間接費 (＝absorbed overhead, applied burden, applied overhead)
 burden charge 負担金
 burden of debt service 金利負担
 burden of disposing of bad loans 不良債権処理の負担, 不良債権処理損失
 burden rate 間接費配賦率, 製造間接費配賦率, 配賦率
 debt burden 債務負担, 債務超過
 factory burden 製造間接費
 interest payment burden 金利負担, 利払い負担 (＝the burden of interest payment)
 overhead burden 経費
 tax burden 租税負担
 wage burden 人件費
▸Major banking groups reported after-tax losses

for the second consecutive business year due to the *burden* of disposing of bad loans and slumping stock markets. 不良債権処理の負担[不良債権処理損失]や株式市況の低迷で、大手銀行は2期連続の税引き後赤字となった。

burnout 名 燃え尽き、燃え尽き症候群、虚脱感、心身の衰弱
▶More multinational firms' workers are experiencing *burnout* as they work longer hours. 多国籍企業の社員の場合、労働時間の増加に伴って燃え尽き症候群の経験者が増えている。

business 名 事業、商売、商業、取引、営業、業務、業容、職務、職業、実務、実業、実業界、会社、企業、経営、業績、ビジネス（⇒**core business**, **transfer of business**）
 banking business 銀行業、銀行業務
 big business 大企業、巨大企業
 branch business 支店業務
 business combination 企業結合
 business enterprise 企業、営利企業、経営事業体
 business entity 企業体、事業体、企業、企業実体、企業主体
 business line 業務分野、事業分野、事業部門、事業の種類、業種、営業品目、営業項目、営業科目、事業ライン（⇒**line of business**）
 business management 企業経営
 business planning head office 経営企画本部
 business statistics 経営統計、経営分析
 business to business 企業対企業、企業間取引（=b to b, B2B, business to business EC）
 business to consumer 企業対消費者、企業対消費者間の取引（=b to c, B2C, business to consumer EC）
 business to government 政府調達（=b to g, B2G）
 credit business 信用業務、信用事業、与信業務
 deterioration in the business situation 経営悪化
 dot business [dot-com] business ドットコム・ビジネス、IT関連ビジネス
 e-business eビジネス、Eビジネス
 exchange business 為替業務
 expanding business 事業拡大
 extension of business 業務拡張
 failed business 経営破綻した企業
 fashion business ファッション事業
 financial business 金融業務、金融ビジネス
 food business 食品事業
 forward business 先物取引
 global business strategy グローバル経営戦略、企業の世界戦略、世界的企業戦略
 government-business cooperation 官民協調
 investment advisory business 投資顧問業
 IT business ITビジネス、IT企業
 leading business 先導企業
 life and reinsurance business 生保・再保険事業
 mortgage business 住宅ローン事業、不動産担保金融
 Net business ネット・ビジネス
 niche business 得意分野
 noncore business 非中核事業
 online business オンライン業務、オンライン・ビジネス
 scope of business 業務範囲
 securities business 証券業務
 solution business 問題解決型営業、ソリューション・ビジネス
 start-up business 新興企業、ベンチャー分野
 suspension of business 取引停止、営業停止
 tax on business 企業課税
 transfer of business 営業譲渡
 troubled business 経営の行き詰まり、経営不振企業
 volume of business 取引高
 water treatment business 水処理事業
▶Revenues increased across our *business*. 当社の事業全般にわたって、収益は増加しました。

business alliance 業務提携（=business tie-up）、経済団体（⇒**brokerage**）
▶The two firms will continue their *business alliance*. 両社は、業務提携を今後とも継続する。

business climate 事業環境、企業環境、経営環境、企業風土、経営風土、企業の体質、景況、商況、景気（=business environment）
▶This accomplishment is especially gratifying given the current *business climate*. この成果は、現在の経営環境を考えますと、まことに喜ばしい限りです。

business confidence 景況感、業況感、業況判断、企業マインド、企業心理（=business mind, business sentiment）
▶*Business confidence* among major manufacturers improved marginally in the three months to December. 10-12月期の大企業・製造業の景況感が、小幅ながら改善した。

business cost 経費、事業コスト
▶The payment is not a *business cost* but constitutes a social expense which should be taxed. 支払った金は、経費ではなく、課税対象の交際費にあたる。

business development ビジネス開発，ビジネスの展開，業務展開
▸We will continue our effort to promote our global *business development*.　当社は，今後も引き続きグローバルな業務展開に取り組む方針です．

business diversification 事業多角化，経営多角化　(⇒**diversification**)
▸Rising debts are mainly due to our *business diversification*.　借入金の増大は，主に事業多角化によるものです．

business group 企業グループ，企業集団　(=corporate group)
▸Hankyu will work with Hanshin to create a new *business group* that can contribute to shareholders and local communities.　阪急は，株主や地域社会に貢献できる新しい企業集団になれるよう，阪神と力を合わせて行く方針だ．

business method 経営手法
▸Many corporate managers often praise *business methods* used in the United States.　とかく，米国流の経営手法をもてはやす経営者が多い．

business model ビジネス手法，事業モデル，事業計画，ビジネス・モデル
▸The loan was the first of its kind to be extended with a *business model* patent as collateral.　今回の融資は，ビジネス・モデル特許を担保にした融資としては初めてだ．

business operation 業務運営，企業運営，企業経営，経営，営業活動，営業運転，業務，事業，業容
▸Rakuten Inc. and Livedoor Co. have expanded their *business operations* through corporate mergers and acquisitions.　楽天とライブドアは，企業の合併・買収(M&A)で業容を拡大してきた．

business performance 営業成績，業績，決算，経営　(=business results)
▸*Business performance* has improved since the latter half of last year.　昨年後半から，業績は向上しています．

business plan 事業計画，経営計画，経営構想　(=business planning)
　long-term business plan 長期事業計画，長期経営計画，長期経営構想
　midterm business plan 中期事業計画
▸Our midterm *business plan* includes 4,300 job cuts and pay cuts of up to 60% for executives.　当社の中期経営計画には，社員の4,300人削減と役員報酬の最大60%カットが含まれている．

business quarter 四半期
▸The company will hold a press conference every *business quarter* to explain its business results.　同社は今後，四半期ごとに記者会見を開いて業績内容について説明する．

business restructuring 事業再編成，事業再編，企業のリストラ
　business restructuring activities 事業再編成作業
　business restructuring costs [charge] 事業再編成費用　(=restructuring costs)
▸We are undertaking a major *business restructuring* which will improve our competitive position.　当社は現在，競争力強化をめざして大規模な事業再編に着手しています．

business results 営業成績，企業業績，業績，決算　(=business performance, operating results; ⇒**assessment, business quarter, results**)
　improved business results 業績向上
　poor business results 業績の落ち込み，業績不振，業績低迷
　unprecedentedly good business results 空前の好決算
▸Many listed companies announce their midterm consolidated *business results* for the six months up to September in October.　上場企業の多くは，10月に9月中間連結決算[4-9月期の中間連結決算]を発表する．

business strategy 経営戦略，事業戦略，企業戦略，ビジネス戦略
▸The company's figures are the fruit of its global *business strategy*.　同社の業績は，同社のグローバル経営戦略の成果である．

business suspension 業務停止
▸During the period of *business suspension*, the company is not allowed to extend new loans, solicit new customers or call in loans.　業務停止期間中，同社は新規の融資や新規顧客の勧誘，貸出の回収などの業務はできない．

business term 事業期間，決算期

business term ending in December 12月終了事業年度，12月期，12月期決算，12月決算期
▸During the *business term ending in December*, the company is expected to register a sixth consecutive quarterly increase in revenue and profits on a consolidated basis.　今年12月期決算では，同社は連結ベースで6四半期連続の増収増益を達成する見通しだ．

business term ending in March 3月期，3月決算期
▸Toyota's consolidated sales, which surpassed ¥10 trillion in the *business term ending in March*

1997, doubled to ¥21 trillion in the following nine years.　トヨタの連結売上高は,1997年3月期に10兆円を突破した後,9年間で21兆円に倍増した。

business term ending in September
9月期, 9月決算期, 9月中間決算
▶During the *business term ending in September*, Nippon Steel Corp. achieved a fivefold increase in its recurring profits from a year earlier.　9月中間決算で,新日本製鉄の経常利益は前年同期比で5倍増となった。

business terms [terms and conditions]
取引条件

business tie-up　業務提携, 事業の提携, 事業連携　(=business alliance)
▶Through the multilateral *business tie-up*, the three leading newspapers of Japan will bolster their ability to disseminate information as news media.　この多角的な事業提携により,日本の大手新聞3社は,報道機関としての情報発信力を強化する。

business tie-up plan　業務提携計画
▶The firm withdrew the capital increase and *business tie-up plans* during the tender offer.　同社は,TOB(株式公開買付け)期間中に増資と業務提携計画を撤回した。

business year　営業年度, 事業年度, 会計年度, 年度, 会計期間　(=accounting year, financial year, fiscal year; ⇒accounting standards, burden)

business projection for the business year ending in May　5月期決算の業績見通し, 5月終了事業年度の業績見通し

during the business year　期中

the business year ending in February 2008　2008年2月期, 2008年2月期決算, 2008年2月終了事業年度

the business year ending in March 2009　2009年3月期, 2009年3月期決算, 2009年3月終了事業年度, 2008年度

the business year that ended in December 2008　2008年12月決算, 2008年12月終了事業年度, 2008年度

the current business year ending March 2008　2008年3月期, 2008年3月に終了する今年度, 2008年3月終了の今期

the next business year　来期, 来年度

the settlement of accounts for the business year ending in March　3月期決算, 3月終了事業年度の決算

the settlement of accounts for the business year ending March 31　3月期決算, 3月31日終了事業年度の決算

the whole [entire] business year　通期

this business year　今期, 今年度

▶The brokerage firm inflated its consolidated earnings for its *business year* through March 2008.　同証券会社は,2008年3月期の連結利益を水増ししていた。

business year ending in August　8月終了の事業年度, 8月期決算
▶The company revised downward its *business projection* for the *business year ending in August* this year.　同社は,本年8月期決算の業績見通しを下方修正した。

business year to March 31　3月31日までの事業年度, 3月期, 3月期決算
▶The major banking groups announced the consolidated accounts for the *business year to March 31.*　大手銀行グループが,3月期の連結決算を発表した。

buy　動　買う, 購入する, 取得する, 買い取る, 買収する,〈株などを〉引き受ける　(=acquire, purchase; ⇒buyout firm)
▶Mitsui Fudosan will *buy* 9.85 million shares in Imperial Hotel from current top shareholder Kokusai Kogyo Co.　三井不動産は,現在の筆頭株主の国際興業から帝国ホテルの株式985万株を取得する。

buy back　買い戻す, 買い取る　(=repurchase)
▶The company plans to *buy back* its own shares in a bid to completely control its subsidiaries.　同社は,子会社の100%経営支配権を得るため,自社株買いをする方針だ。
▶To date, we have *bought back* about 26 million shares–close to 4.5 percent of the outstanding shares of the company.　これまで当社は,約2,600万株(当社の発行済み株式総数の約4.5%)を買い戻しました。

buy order　買い注文
▶No deals were struck and the issue ended at a bid price of ¥3.15 million due to a massive wave of *buy orders.*　売買が成立せず,大量の買い注文が殺到したため,同銘柄は315万円の買い気配で終了した。

buy out　〈権利などを〉買い取る, 買い占める, 買い上げる, 買収する, 乗っ取る
▶Oji Paper Co.'s bid to *buy out* Hokuetsu Paper Mills Ltd. did not succeed.　王子製紙が実施している北越製紙株の株式公開買付け(TOB)は,成立[成功]しなかった。
▶On Jan. 30, 2004, Kao announced it wanted to *buy out* Kanebo's cosmetics division.　2004年1

月30日に、花王は、カネボウの化粧品事業部門を完全買収する方針を発表した。

buy up 買い占める、買い取る
▸Former head of the Murakami Fund instructed Livedoor to *buy up* Nippon Broadcasting System Inc.'s shares during after-hours trading.　村上ファンドの元代表が、ライブドアに対して、時間外取引でニッポン放送株を買い占めるようニ指南していた。

buyback 名　買戻し、買取り、自社株買戻し、自社株買い、自社株取得
▸Stock *buybacks* are commonly aimed at raising profits per share and enhance dividend payouts to shareholders.　株式買戻しのねらいは、一般に1株当たり利益の引上げと株主への配当支払いの増額にある。

buyout 買収、〈会社・経営権の〉買取り、買占め、乗っ取り、〈株式の〉買付け、金を払って引き取らせること、金を払って退職させること、早期退職奨励金　（＝buy-out；⇒**leveraged buyout, management buyout**)
buyout fund 買収ファンド
buyout of minorities 少数株主持ち分の買取り
buyout plan 買収計画
corporate buyout 企業買収　（＝corporate acquisition）
corporate buyout strategy 企業買収戦略
employee buyout 従業員の会社買取り、従業員の経営権買取り　（＝worker buyout）
leveraged buyout レバレッジド・バイアウト
management buyout 経営者による自社買収
strategic buyout 戦略的買収（経営戦略に基づいて行われる企業買収）
worker buyout 従業員の経営権買取り
▸Ford Motor Co. will cut about $5 billion in operating costs mainly by offering early retirement and *buyout* packages to all hourly workers and to white-collar employees.　米フォード・モーターは、主に工場従業員［時間給労働者］とホワイトカラー従業員を対象に早期退職優遇制度を導入して、営業経費約50億ドルを削減する方針だ。

buyout firm 企業買収(M&A)専門会社
▸Sony Corp. and two U.S. *buyout firms* are in talks to buy U.S. film studio Metro-Goldwyn-Mayer Inc. for about $5 billion.　ソニーと米国の企業買収専門会社2社が共同で、米国の映画会社MGM（メトロ・ゴールドウィン・メイヤー）を約50億ドルで買収する交渉を進めている。

buyout offer 買収提案
▸Tribune Co. has accepted a *buyout offer* from a real estate investor.　米トリビューン（米新聞業界2位）は、不動産投資家による買収提案を受け入れた。

buyout strategy 買収戦略
▸The firm's corporate *buyout strategy* took full advantage of the effect of stock splits.　同社の企業買収戦略は、株式分割の効果を最大限、利用した。

bylaw 名　付属定款

C

calculate 動 計算する, 算定する, 算出する, 計上する, 評価する （=compute; ⇒**stock dealing**）
　calculate credit risk 信用リスクを評価する
　calculate the estimated ending inventory 期末棚卸し資産の見積り高を計算する
▸The change in the method of *calculating* deferred tax assets has driven each of the banking groups into a corner. 　繰延べ税金資産の算定方式の変更が, 銀行グループ各行を窮地に追い込んでいる。

calculation 名 計算, 算定, 算出, 計上, 評価, 計算方法
　book calculation of inventory 帳簿棚卸し高
　calculation of goodwill 営業権の計算
　calculation of sources of funds and uses of funds 資金の源泉と資金運用の計算
　cumulative calculation 累積的計算
　depreciation calculation 減価償却の計算
　sectional calculation 部門計算
▸Pension cost *calculations* were based on a value of assets adjusted to market over periods ranging from 3 to 5 years. 　年金原価［年金費用］は, 過去3-5年間の時価に修正した資産価額に基づいて計算されています。

calendar year 暦年, 年度, 12月期決算 (1月1日から12月31日までの1年で, a full calendar yearは1暦年, 満1暦年を指す。⇒**business year, quarter**)

call 動 償還する,〈貸付け金の返済［返還］を〉求める
　call in loans 貸付け金を回収する, 貸出を回収する
　call the existing bonds 既発債を償還する
　call the loan 貸付け金の返済を請求する, ローンの償還を請求する

　call the preferred issue at a premium プレミアムを払って優先株を償還する
▸During March 2007, the Corporation *called*, at a rate of 101%, its 11.5% Eurodollar notes due 2010 with a carrying value totaling $93 million. 　2007年3月に当社は, 帳簿価格総額が9,300万ドルで2010年満期11.5%のユーロ・ドル債を101%で償還しました。

call 名 償還, 貸付け金の返済［返還］請求
　call premium 任意償還プレミアム, 償還プレミアム, 繰上げ償還時に支払われる割増金, コール・オプションを買うときに支払うオプション料, コール・プレミアム
　call price 償還価格, 繰上げ償還価格, 任意償還価格, 期前償還価格, 買入れ価格, 買戻し価格, コール価格
　call provision 償還条項, 任意償還条項
▸The benefits of refinancing were partly offset by cost of that refinancing such as *call premiums*. 　借換えの効果は, 償還プレミアムのような資金再調達関連費用によって, 一部相殺されています。

callable 形 償還できる, 償還可能な, 繰上げ償還可能な
　callable bond 任意償還条項付き債券, コーラブル債
　callable preferred stock 償還優先株式
▸These notes are *callable* by the Company at the carrying value at any time. 　これらの債券は, 当社がいつでも帳簿価格で繰上げ償還することができます。

CalPERS カリフォルニア州公務員退職年金基金, カルパース（California Public Employees' Retirement Systemの略）

CALS 生産・調達・運用支援統合情報システム，継続的調達と製品のライフサイクルの支援（Continuous Acquisition and Lifestyle Supportの略）

CALS 瞬時電子取引，キャルス（Commerce at Light Speedの略）

CAMEL 資本（capital），資産内容（asset quality），経営（management），収益（earnings），流動性（liquidity）の略

cancel 動 〈株式を〉消却する，取り消す，解除する，解約する，中止する
▸The creditor banks are considering having the company reduce its capital by *canceling* a portion of its preferred shares held by them. 同社の取引銀行は現在，各行が保有する同社の優先株（議決権がない代わりに配当が高い株式）の消却による同社の資本金引下げ［減資］を検討している。

cancelable [cancellable] 形 解約可能な
  cancelable lease 解約可能リース，解約可能賃貸借，解約可能賃貸借契約
  non-cancelable lease 中途解約不能リース
  unconditionally cancelable 無条件解消可能な
▸We lease equipment to others through operating leases, the majority of which are *cancelabel*. 当社はオペレーティングリース方式で設備を他社にリースしており，その大部分は解約可能です。

cancelation [cancellation] 名 〈株式の〉消却，〈契約の〉解除，解約，免除，破棄，抹消，中止（⇒repurchase）
  cancelation before maturity 中途解約
  cancelation money 解約金
  cancelation of indebtedness 負債の免除
  cancelation of license 実施権の解除
  cancelation of stocks 株式消却（＝cancellation of shares, stock cancellation）
  debt cancelation 負債の帳消し，負債の棒引き（＝write-off）
  mark down cancelation 値下げ取消高
  mark up cancelation 値上げ取消高
  policy cancellation 保険の解約
▸The Company repurchased for *cancelation* its own common shares for an aggregate amount of $300 million. 当社は，消却の目的で，総額3億ドルの自社普通株式を買い戻しました。

cap 名 上限，最高限度，最高，上限金利，キャップ
  interest rate cap 金利キャップ
  life-of-loan cap 貸出期間中の上限金利
  market cap 時価総額
  set a cap on ... …に上限を設ける
  small cap index 小型株指数
▸The new law of California imposes a first-in-the-nation emissions *cap* on utilities, refineries and manufacturing plants. 米カリフォルニア州の新法は，発電所［公共事業体］や製油所，製造工場などの温室効果ガス排出量に米国内で初めて上限を設けている。

capacity 名 能力，資本，資金，設備，生産能力，操業度，発電容量，収容力，収容能力，地位，資格，立場，キャパシティ（⇒production capacity）
  average capacity 平均操業度
  business capacity 営業力
  capacity ratio 設備稼動率，稼動率，創業率，操業度比率（＝capacity usage ratio）
  capacity utilization 設備利用，設備稼働，設備稼動率，操業，操業度
  capacity yield 最大産出高
  debt capacity 借入余力
  debt servicing capacity 債務返済能力
  dividend paying capacity 配当支払い能力
  excess capacity 過剰設備，超過設備，過剰能力
  dividend capacity 配当支払い能力
  expand capacity 設備を拡張する
  full capacity 完全操業度，全能力，完全能力，完全利用
  idle capacity 遊休生産能力
  increase production capacity 生産能力を拡大する
  installed capacity 稼動発電能力
  operate at full capacity フル稼働する，フル稼働状態にある
  output capacity 生産能力
  produce at full capacity フル生産体制を取る
  supply capacity 供給能力
▸Technological advances permit us to use existing *capacity* more efficiently. 技術の進歩で，既存の設備を一段と効率的に使用することが可能になっています。

capex [CAPEX] 名 設備投資（capital expenditureの略）
  capex growth 設備投資の増加
  heavy capex 大型設備投資，多額［巨額］の設備投資
▸The company raised its *capex* budget for semiconductors in the current business year to meet rapidly growing demand for flash memory chips. フラッシュメモリ・チップの需要急増に対応するため，同社は今年度の半導体の設備投資予算を増額した。

capital 名 資本，自己資本，資本金，資金，元金，出資金，〈保険会社の〉基金（株式会社の資本金に相当），正味財産，純資産，キャピタル

bank capital 銀行の自己資本
bank capital requirements 銀行の自己資本比率規制（＝bank capital standards）
capital adequacy 資本充実度, 資本要件, 自己資本比率
capital and liabilities ratio 資本負債比率
capital authorized 公称資本金
capital constraints 自己資本比率規制（＝capital adequacy rule, capital requirements）
capital employed 使用資本
capital formation 資本形成, 資本構成
capital introduced 拠出資本, 出資金, 資本金
capital issue 株式発行, 新株発行, 資本発行, 増資, 株券, 株式
capital maintenance adjustments 資本維持修正額
capital management capabilities 資産運用力
capital shortfall 資本不足, 資金不足（＝capital shortage）
debt capital 借入資本, 固定負債（＝borrowed capital, loan capital）
declared capital 公示資本, 表示資本, 法定資本
development capital 開発資金
increase of capital 増資（＝capital increase）
initial capital 当初資金
invested capital 投下資本
issued share capital 発行済み株式資本
reduction of capital 減資（＝reduction in capital）
share capital 株式資本
short-term working capital 短期運転資金
▶The company aims to achieve its rehabilitation by asking its largest shareholder and group companies to increase its *capital* by ¥200 billion. 同社は, 筆頭株主とグループ企業に2,000億円規模の増資引受けを仰いで, 再建を目指している。

capital adequacy ratio 自己資本比率（＝capital-asset ratio, capital-to-asset ratio, net worth ratio）
　自己資本比率とは ➡ 銀行の融資残高などの総資産に対する資本金などの比率をいう。国際銀行業務の銀行の自己資本比率はBIS（国際決済銀行）基準で8％以上, 国内銀行業務の銀行の自己資本比率は4％以上とされている。
▶The *capital adequacy ratio* is used to determine the financial health of financial institutions. 自己資本比率は, 金融機関の経営の健全性［財務の健全性］を判断するのに用いられる。

capital alliance 資本提携（＝capital tie-up）
　資本提携とは ➡ 企業が提携関係を強化するため, 株式を互いに取得したり, 交換したりすること。業務関係だけの提携に比べて, 一段と強い関係を構築できる。新株を発行して割り当てる第三者割当て増資や, 新株予約権の引受けなどの手法も使われる。

capital and business partnership 資本・業務提携（＝capital and business alliance, capital and business links, capital and business tie-ups, capital and business ties）
▶Yamato Holdings Co. and Nippon Yusen K.K. will launch a *capital and business partnership*. ヤマトホールディングスと日本郵船が, 資本・業務提携する方針だ。

capital base 資本基盤, 自己資本, 資本金
▶Especially companies with fragile *capital bases* are using schemes such as private placements of convertible bonds, known as multiple private offerings (MPOs). 特に資本基盤が弱い企業は, MPOと呼ばれる転換社債の第三者割当て発行のような資金調達方式を活用している。

capital boost plan 増資計画
▶The share purchase price of Oji Paper Co.'s hostile tender offer will be raised to ¥860 per share if Hokuetsu Paper Mills ltd. drops its *capital boost plan*. 王子製紙の敵対的TOB［株式公開買付け］の株の買付け価格［TOB価格］は, 北越製紙がその増資計画を撤回した場合には, 1株860円に引き上げられる。

capital expenditure 設備投資, 固定資産投資, 資本支出, 資本的支出, 資本投資, 設備投資額, 固定資産投資額, 資本支出額, 資本投資額（＝capex, capital investment, capital spending）
consolidated capital expenditures 連結資本的支出, 連結資本的支出額
consolidated net capital expenditures 連結資本的支出純額
gross capital expenditures 資本的支出総額
▶ABC Inc., experiencing major growth in demand for communication services, made record *capital expenditures* in 2007. ABCの2007年度の資本的支出は, 通信サービス需要の著しい伸びに伴って, 過去最高を記録しました。
▶We reduced *capital expenditures* for the network in 2007. 2007年度は, 通信ネットワーク向けの資本的支出額を削減しました。

capital gain 資本利得, 資産売却益, 資産譲渡益, 株式売買益, 譲渡所得, 値上がり益, キャピタル・ゲイン
capital gain tax 資本利得税, キャピタル・ゲイン税《略 CGT》
capital gain taxation 資本利得課税, キャピタ

ル・ゲイン税
capital gain yield 資本利得率
capital gains and losses 資本利得および損失, 資産譲渡損益, 株式譲渡損益, 譲渡損益, 株式売買損益
▸The tax rate on *capital gains* from stock sales and on dividend income was lowered to 10 percent from 20 percent.　株式譲渡益［株式売却益］と受取配当金の税率は、20％から10％に引き下げられた。
capital increase 増資, 資本増強, 〈保険会社の〉基金の積み増し［増額］, 基金増資 （＝capital expansion, capital increment, capital injection）
　増資とは➡会社が資本金を増やすことを増資という。これには、払込み金を取って新株を発行する有償増資と、株主から払込み金を取らない増資がある。
▸We spent the additional fund collected through the *capital increase* on debt repayment.　当社は、増資で集めた追加資金を債務返済に充てました。
capital increment 増資 （＝capital increase）
▸Through 83 rounds of *capital increment* since the listing of its stocks in 2000, Livedoor swelled its capital base from ¥60 million to ¥86.2 billion.　2000年の株式上場以来、83回に及ぶ増資で、ライブドアは資本金を6,000万円から862億円まで膨らませた。
capital-intensive 形 資本集約型, 資本集約的
▸The list of major Japanese corporations operating in China is dominated by *capital-intensive* businesses, including consumer electronics, information technology and car manufacturers.　中国に進出している主要日本企業は、家電、情報技術(IT)や自動車メーカーなど資本集約型の企業が中心だ。
capital investment 設備投資, 資本投資, 公共投資, 資本投下, 出資, 出資金 （＝capital expenditure, capital spending, investment in plant and other facilities）
▸Corporate *capital investment* and individual consumption are healthier than expected.　企業の設備投資や個人消費は、予想以上に好調だ。
capital lease 資産型リース, 資本化リース, 資本リース, キャピタル・リース
　debt excluding capital leases キャピタル・リースを除く債務
　sales-type capital lease 販売型キャピタル・リース
▸Lower long-term debt, including *capital leases*, was the net result of our refinancing and redemption activities.　キャピタル・リースを含めて長期負債の減少は、最終的に当社が負債の借換えと償還を実施した結果です。
capital loss 資本損失, 資産売却損, 資産譲渡損, 譲渡損失, 固定資産処分損, キャピタル・ロス （⇒**deduction**）
capital market 資本市場（一般的には株式・債券の発行市場(primary market：新規発行の株式や債券が、発行者から投資家に売り渡される市場)と流通市場(secondary market：すでに発行された株式や債券が投資家間で売買される市場)を含めた証券市場とほぼ同義）, 長期金融市場, キャピタル・マーケット　（⇒**money market**, **securities market**）
▸The Japanese *capital market* is not transparent enough.　日本の資本市場は、透明とは言いがたい。
capital raising 資金調達
▸Japan's equity and equity-linked *capital raising* volume for the six months to June slipped 46.7 percent from a year earlier.　日本の1-6月期の株式と株式リンク債の発行による資金調達の取引高は、前年同期に比べて46.7％減少した。
capital ratio [rate] 自己資本比率　（＝capital adequacy ratio, capital-asset ratio, net worth ratio; ⇒**capital adequacy ratio**）
▸Mizuho Financial Group's *capital ratio* as of Sept. 30, 2006 stood at 11.01 percent, above the international standard of 8 percent.　みずほフィナンシャルグループ(FG)の2006年9月末現在の自己資本比率は11.01％で、国際基準［国際銀行業務のBIS基準］の8％を上回っている。
capital reduction 減資 （＝capital decrease, reduction of capital：資本金を減らして捻出した資金を企業再建に使う措置）
▸The *capital reduction* will allow the company to raise the ¥15 billion needed to implement its restructuring plan.　減資を行うことで、同社は会社再建案の実施に必要な150億円を調達［捻出］することができる。
capital requirements 資金需要, 資金の必要額, 自己資本規制, 自己資本比率規制
　cash capital requirements 資金需要
　initial capital requirements 当初自己資本比率規定
　working capital requirements 必要運転資金
▸These *capital requirements* will continue growing in 2008.　これらの資金需要は、2008年度も増大するものと思われます。
capital reserve 資本準備金, 資本剰余金 （＝additional paid-in capital, legal capital reserve）
▸The bank transferred about ¥500 billion in *capi-*

capital spending 設備投資, 資本的支出 （= capex, capital investment）
▶The company plans to make about ¥300 billion worth of *capital spending* in fiscal 2008. 同社は, 2008年度に約3,000億円の設備投資を予定している。

capital stock 株式資本, 株式資本金, 資本金, 資本ストック, 法定資本, 総株式数, 資本株式, 株式, 普通株, 外部の人々が所有する株式
　capital stock authorized 授権資本, 授権資本金
　capital stock cut 減資 （= capital decrease, capital reduction）
　capital stock issued 発行済み資本金
　capital stock issued under employee plans 従業員プランによる株式の発行
　capital stock of subsidiary and affiliated companies 従属会社および関係会社出資金
　capital stock outstanding 発行済み株式数, 流通株式, 社外資本金
　capital stock, par value $1.25 per share 資本金, 額面1株当たり1.25ドル
　capital stock premium 株式発行差金, 株式割増金
　capital stock subscribed 引受済み資本金, 引受済み資本金勘定
　capital stock unissued 未発行資本金, 資本未発行分
　distribution of capital stock 株式資本の分配
　full-paid capital stock 全額払込済み株式
　increase in capital stock 資本ストックの増加
　increase of capital stock 増資
　large capital stock 大型株
　premium on share stock 株式発行差金
　reduction of capital stock 減資 （= reduction of capital）
　total capital stock 資本金合計, 総資本ストック
▶The *capital stock* of the Corporation is its only class of voting security. 当社の資本株式［当社株式］は, 当社の唯一の議決権付き証券です。

capital structure 資本構成［構造］（総資本に占める自己資本と他人資本（負債）の割合で, バランスシート上の資本（純資産（net worth）＋優先株式）と長期債務（long-term debt）の合計額を指す）, 財務基盤
▶The Corporation's *capital structure* as of December 31, 2007 was as follows. 当社の2007年12月31日現在の資本構成は, 次のとおりです。
▶The upgrade reflects Moody's expectation that the company will continue to exhibit an excellent operating performance and outstanding *capital structure*. この格上げは, 同社が引き続き好業績と際立った財務基盤を示すとのムーディーズの期待感を反映している。

capital surplus 資本剰余金, 資本準備金, 資本積立金, 差益
　capital surplus reserve 資本積立金
　capital surplus statement 資本剰余金計算書
▶Profits generated through selling shares of an owned company are included in the amount of capital or *capital surplus* shown on a company's balance sheet. 自社株の売却益は, 会社の貸借対照表上の資本金や資本剰余金に計上される。

capital tie-up 資本提携 （= capital alliance, capital link, capital ties）
▶The *capital tie-up* of Nissin Food Products and Myojo Foods aims at thwarting a U.S. investment fund's hostile takeover bid for Myojo. 日清食品と明星食品の資本提携は, 明星に対する米系投資ファンドの敵対的TOB（株式公開買付け）阻止が狙いだ。

capital-to-asset ratio 株主資本比率, 自己資本比率 （= capital adequacy ratio, capital-asset ratio, net worth ratio）
▶The *capital-to-asset ratios* at Japanese major banks are above an 8 percent global standard. 日本の大手銀行の自己資本比率は, グローバル・スタンダードの8％を上回っている。

capitalization 名 資本構成, 資本総額, 資本化, 株式資本化, 資本調達, 収益の資本還元, 資本組入れ, 発行済み株式の時価総額, 長期資本, 資本計上, 資本化, 〈会社・事業などへの〉投資, 資本基盤 （= capitalisation）
　asset capitalization 資産計上
　authorized capitalization 授権株式総数
　capitalization issue 資本金組入れ発行, 資本組入れ株式発行, 無償発行
　capitalization of earnings 収益の資本還元, 収益力の資本還元
　capitalization of interest 利息の資産化, 利息の資産計上 （= interest capitalization）
　capitalization period 資産化期間, 資産計上の期間
　capitalization requirements 必要資本金額, 資本金制度 （= capital requirements）
　core capitalization コア資本
　direct capitalization 直接収益還元法
　improved capitalization 資本基盤の改善

large capitalization stock　大型株
low [weak] capitalization　資本基盤が弱いこと，脆弱な資本基盤
overall [total] market capitalization　市場の時価総額，株式時価総額
strengthen capitalization　資本の充実化，資本を充実させる
▸Depreciation expenses increased due to higher average depreciable plant and the effect of the change in the *capitalization* and amortization policy for switching machine software.　減価償却費の増加は，減価償却の対象となる有形固定資産の平均残高が高水準に達したほか，交換機ソフトウェアの資本化と償却方針の変更の影響によるものです。

capitalize 動　資本化する，資産化する，資産に計上する，現価計上する，資本として使用する，〈資本に〉組み入れる，〈資本を〉投入する，出資する，投資する（⇒**indirect cost**）
　amounts capitalized　資産化金額
　capitalized costs　資産に計上した費用，資産化費用，費用の資産化（＝capitalized expenses）
　capitalized leases　資産に計上したリース，資産化リース，資本化リース，リースの資産化
　capitalized surplus　組入れ資本金，資本化された剰余金
▸The new company will be *capitalized* at ¥100 billion.　新会社の資本金は，1,000億円になる見通しだ。
▸We *capitalize* the remaining software production costs as other assets.　当社は，残りのソフトウェア制作費用については，その他の資産として資産化しています。
▸Certain indirect costs, including financing costs, are *capitalized*.　特定の間接費は，利息［資金調達コスト］を含めて資産計上されています。

capitalize on　利用する，活用する，生かす，つけ込む，〈需要などを〉見越す
　capitalize on a market opportunity　市場の機会をとらえる，市場の機会を生かす
　capitalize on one's market share　市場シェアを生かす，シェアを生かす
▸Japan's major automakers are *capitalizing on* improved quality at production plants overseas as part of their global strategies.　日本の大手自動車メーカーは，自動車各社の世界戦略の一環として，海外生産拠点での品質向上を活用している。

care service　介護サービス，ケア・サービス
▸Our family care development fund improves the quality and supply of child- and elder-*care services* by funding community-based organizations.　当社の家族介護会基金は，地域密着型組織［地域社会ベースの組織］に資金を提供することにより，幼児・高齢者介護サービスの質と量の向上を図っています。

career-average pay　職歴平均給与方式
▸Benefits for management employees are principally based on *career-average pay*.　管理職に対する給付は，主に職歴平均給与方式に基づいています。

career compensation　職務給（⇒**retirement benefits**）

carry 動　計上する，算定する，［帳簿に］記載しておく，記帳する，転記する，〈保険などを〉付ける，設定する，〈債務を〉負う
　be carried at cost　取得原価で計上される
　be carried at FIFO cost　先入れ先出し法で算定される
　be carried to ...　…に転記される
　carry back　繰り戻す，欠損［欠損金］を前期［前年度以降］に繰り戻す
　carry down　前期へ繰り越す
　carry forward　繰り越す，欠損［欠損金］を次期［翌年度以降］に繰り越す（＝carry over）
　carry over　繰り越す（＝carry forward），持ち越す，引き継ぐ，延期する
▸Currently, companies are allowed to *carry forward* their losses for up to five years and offset part of any profit incurred in following fiscal years with the losses.　企業は現在，欠損金を最高5年繰り越し，翌年度以降に生じた利益の一部をこの欠損金と相殺することができる。
▸Plant, rental machines and other property are *carried* at cost.　工場設備，賃貸機械，その他の固定資産は，取得原価で計上されています。

carry trade　キャリー取引，キャリー・トレード
▸In yen-*carry trades*, hedge funds borrow yen at low interest rates to invest into financial assets of other major currencies at higher interest rates.　円キャリー取引では，ヘッジ・ファンドが低金利で円を借りて，円以外の高金利の外貨建て金融資産に投資している。

carryback 名　繰戻し
　carryback and carryforward of operating losses　欠損金［営業損失］の繰戻しと繰越し
　operating loss carryback　繰戻し欠損金，欠損金［営業損失］の繰戻し（＝carryback of operating loss）
　tax [tax loss] carryback　欠損金の繰戻し
▸Net loss has been determined after giving recognition to recoverable federal income taxes

resulting from *carryback* of operating losses to prior years. 純損失は、欠損金の過年度への繰戻しにより発生する米連邦所得税の未収還付税額を算定して計上されています。

carryforward 名 繰越し，繰延べ（⇒loss carryforward）
　carryforward of operating loss 欠損金［営業損失］の繰越し（＝operating loss carryforward）
　operating loss carryforward 繰越し欠損金，欠損金繰越し
　tax (loss) carryback and carryforward 欠損金の繰戻しと繰越し

carrying amount 帳簿価額，簿価（＝book value, carrying value）
▶The Company's finance subsidiary purchases customer obligations under long-term contracts from the Company at net *carrying amount*. 当社の金融子会社は、当社との長期契約によって、顧客の債務を当社から帳簿価格で購入しています。

carrying value 帳簿価額，簿価，繰越し価額，未償却残高（＝book value, carrying amount; ⇒ book value method）
▶We reduced the *carrying value* of this investment by $70 million because of a sustained decline in its market value. 当社は、この投資の市場価格が長期にわたって下落しているため、その帳簿価額を7,000万ドル引き下げました。

cash 動 現金に換える，換金する
▶Quasi money refers to savings at banks that cannot be immediately *cashed*. 準通貨とは、即時に換金できない［現金に換えられない］銀行預金のことをいう。

cash 名 現金，預金，現金預金，現預金，通貨，資金，キャッシュ（会計上，銀行預金のほかに小切手，手形，郵便為替なども含むが，流動資産（current assets）に含まれるcashは手元現金と銀行の要求払い預金を指す）
　cash and short-term investments 現金預金［現金・預金］および短期投資
　cash at bank and in hand 要求払い預金と手元現金
　cash basis 現金基準，現金主義（＝receipts and payments basis）
　cash capital requirements 資金需要
　cash from operations 営業収益
　cash in [on] hand 手元現金
　cash income 現金収入
　cash on hand and in banks 手元現金および銀行預金，現金および預金
　Cash paid during the year for ... 当期現金支払い額：…
　cash provided from (used for) financing activities 財務活動に伴う資金の調達（使途），財務活動から生じた（財務活動に使用した）資金
　cash provided from (used for) investing activities 投資活動に伴う資金の調達（使途），投資活動から生じた（投資活動に使用した）資金
　cash provided from (used for) operating activities 営業活動［事業活動］に伴う資金の調達（使途），営業活動［事業活動］から生じた（営業活動に使用した）資金
▶We used the *cash* from operations to pay dividends and to invest in R&D. 配当の支払いと研究開発投資には、営業活動により生じたキャッシュを充てました。

cash and cash equivalents 現預金および現金同等物［現金等価物］，金および現金等価物，現金および現金同等物（「現預金および現金同等物」とは、短期間に現金化できる投資資産で，財務省証券やマネー・マーケット・ファンド，他社発行のコマーシャル・ペーパーなど3か月以内に現金化できる短期の有価証券も含まれる）
　cash and cash equivalents at beginning of year 現金預金および現金同等物［現金等価物］期首残高，期首の現金預金および現金同等物
　cash and cash equivalents at end of year 現金および現金同等物期末残高，期末の現金預金および現金同等物
　net change in cash and cash equivalents 現金および現金同等物の純増減高
　net increase [decrease] in cash and cash equivalents 現金および現金同等物の純増［減］

cash balance 現金預金残高，現預金残高，現金残高，キャッシュ・バランス（⇒results）
▶We raised our *cash balance* in 2007 so that we could act quickly on new opportunities outside the U.S. 当社は2007年度の現預金残高を増やしましたが、これは米国外での新たな事業機会に即応できるようにするためです。

cash dividend 現金配当，配当金
　cash dividends declared 現金配当宣言額，現金配当金
　cash dividends paid 現金配当支払い額，現金配当金，配当金の支払い
　cash dividends per share 1株当たり現金配当，1株当たり配当金
▶The Corporation declared a *cash dividend* of $0.07 per common share in the first two quarters of 2006. 2006年第1四半期と第2四半期に、当社はそれぞれ普通株1株当たり0.07ドルの現金

配当を宣言しました。

cash equivalents 現金同等物, 現金等価物, 現金預金同等物, 現金等価額
▸The Corporation considers all highly liquid investments purchased with an original maturity of three months or less to be *cash equivalents*. 当社は, 取得日から満期日までの期間が3か月以内の流動性の高い投資を現預金等価物としています。

cash flow 現金の収入と支出, 現金収支, 資金収支, 資金の流出入, 資金の運用・調達, 資金繰り, 現金資金, 純収入, キャッシュ・フロー (現金収入と現金支出の総称で, 企業の一定期間の現金などの流れを指す)
  annual cash flow 年間資金収入
  cash flow problems 資金難, 資金繰りの問題
  cash flows from financing activities 金融[財務]から生じた資金フロー, 財務活動によるキャッシュ・フロー, 財務活動に伴う資金収支[現金収支]
  cash flows from investing activities 投資活動から生じた資金フロー, 投資活動によるキャッシュ・フロー
  cash flows from operating activities 営業活動から生じた資金フロー, 営業活動によるキャッシュ・フロー
  current cash flow 手元流動性
  discounted cash flow キャッシュ・フロー割引
  discretionary cash flow 裁量可能キャッシュ・フロー
  excess cash flow 余剰キャッシュ・フロー, 超過キャッシュ・フロー
  exchange a series of cash flows 各種のキャッシュ・フローを交換する
  expected cash flow 期待キャッシュ・フロー
  fixed cash flow 固定金利のキャッシュ・フロー
  floating cash flow 変動金利のキャッシュ・フロー
  generate cash flow 現金収入を得る
  future cash flow 将来の資金繰り
  historical cash flow 過去のキャッシュ・フロー
  internal cash flows 内部キャッシュ・フロー
  negative cash flow 負のキャッシュ・フロー
  net cash flow 純キャッシュ・フロー
  retained cash flow 手元キャッシュ・フロー《略 RCF》
  statement of cash flows 資金収支表, 資金収支計算書, 資金フロー表, キャッシュ・フロー表
  tightened cash flow 資金繰りの悪化
▸These accounting changes do not affect *cash flows*; they only change the expenses we report. これらの会計処理方法の変更は, キャッシュ・フローには影響しません。当社が計上する費用の額が, 変動するだけです。

cash flow statement 資金収支表, 現金収支計算書, 収支計算書, 現金資金計算書, キャッシュ・フロー計算書 (＝statement of cash flows)
  キャッシュ・フロー計算書とは ➡ 財務諸表 (financial statements)の一つで, 売上や仕入れ, 借金などを通じた純粋なお金の増減を計算したもの。企業の現金支払い能力が分かるため, 企業の成長力を示す重要な指標となっている。

cash merger 現金合併, キャッシュ・マージャー (企業の買収・合併の手段として, 存続会社が, 合併で吸収される会社の少数株主に対して存続会社の株式ではなく現金を交付する方法。⇒**stock exchange merger**)

cash on delivery 代金引換え渡し, 現金払い《略 COD》
  cash on delivery sale 代金[現金]引換販売 (＝COD sale, collect on delivery sale, sale for cash on delivery)

cash outlay 現金支出額
  cash outlay cost 現金支出原価
  initial cash outlay 当初支出額

cash provided by operations 営業活動[事業活動]で得られる現金, 営業活動[事業活動]によって得られる現金収入, 営業活動[事業活動]による資金の調達
▸In 2007, we will meet our cash requirements through *cash provided by operations*, refinancing of $158 million of long-term debt maturing in 2007 and external financing. 2007年度は, 事業活動[営業活動]によって得られる現金収入と, 2007年に満期[期日]が到来する長期債務1億5,800万ドルの借換えのほか, 外部資金の調達で必要資金をまかなう予定です。

cash requirements 必要資金, 現金必要[所要]量, 現金必要見込み額, 資金必要額
▸We will meet our *cash requirements* in 2007 by refinancing debt maturing in 2007. 当社は, 2007年に満期が到来する債務の借換えで, 2007年度の必要資金をまかなう方針です。

catch-up 形 追い上げの
  catch-up depreciation 遡及償却

category 名 部類, 種類, 部門, 分野, 範疇, 分類, 区分, 項目, カテゴリー
  emerging growth categories 急成長分野
  product category 製品分野, 製品カテゴリー
  rating category 格付けの分類
  special category company 特別区分会社
▸A growing number of women and elderly people

have been starting business in such *categories of industry* as the service, wholesale and retail sectors.　サービス業や卸売り・小売り業などの業種で, 女性や高齢者層の開業が増加している.

CB　転換社債（**convertible bond**の略）
CC　現在原価, 時価（**current cost**の略）
CCA　現在原価会計, 時価主義会計（**current cost accounting**の略）
CD　預金証書, 譲渡可能定期預金証書（**certificate of deposit**の略）
C/D　[c/d]　前期繰越し（**carried down**の略）
cell phone service provider　携帯電話会社
▶All *cell phone service providers* spend hefy sums on sales promotions to bring in new subscribers.　携帯電話会社はいずれも, 新規加入者の獲得のため, 多額の販売促進費を投入している.
central and administrative expenses　管理費
central corporate expense　本社費用, 本部費, 一般管理費
CEO　最高業務執行役員, 最高経営責任者, 最高業務執行理事（＝**chief executive**：**chief executive officer**の略）
certainty 名　確実性
　certainty equivalent　確実性等価, 確実性等価額
　certainty equivalent return　確実性等価収益率
certificate of deposit　預金証書, 譲渡可能定期預金証書《略 **CD**》
certificate of the auditor　監査報告書
certified check　支払い保証小切手, 銀行保証小切手, 預金小切手
certified public accountant　公認会計士《略 **CPA**》
▶*Certified public accountants* and auditing firms are responsible for preventing corporate managers from window-dressing business results.　公認会計士や監査法人には, 企業経営者の粉飾決算を止めさせる責任がある.
CESR　欧州証券規制委員会（**Committee of European Securities Regulators**の略）
C/F　[c/f]　次期繰越し, 次頁繰越し（**carried forward**の略）
CFC　在外子会社, 在外従属会社（**controlled foreign corporation**の略）
CFO　最高財務担当役員, 最高財務担当者, 最高財務責任者, 財務担当責任者（**chief financial officer**の略）
chairman 名　会長, 委員長, 議長, 社長, 司会者（＝**chairperson**）
　Chairman and CEO　会長兼最高経営責任者

chairman emeritus　名誉会長
chairman of board of directors　取締役会長
chairman's report　会長報告書
chairman's review　会長報告書
chairman's statement　会長報告書, 社長報告書, 社長声明
Fed Chairman　米連邦準備制度理事会（FRB）議長
▶Sony Corp. named Vice Chairman Howard Stringer as the company's new *chairman* and group chief executive officer.　ソニーは, ハワード・ストリンガー副会長を, 同社の新会長兼グループ最高経営責任者（CEO）に任命した.
chalk up　収益を上げる, …を記録する, 計上する, 獲得する, 達成する
▶The Company *chalked up* a group net profit of ¥224 million in the first half of the business year.　当社の今年度上半期の連結純利益は, 2億2,400万円でした.
challenge 名　挑戦, 課題, 難題, 難問, 脅威, やりがいのある仕事, 任務, 要求, 〈競技などへの〉参加勧誘［参加呼びかけ］, 〈陪審員に対する〉拒否, 忌避, 異議, 異議申立て, チャレンジ　（⇒**raise**）
challenging 形　挑戦の, 試練の, 難しい, 厳しい, やりがいがある
▶This is likely to be a *challenging* year for our corporation.　今期［今年度］は, 当社にとって挑戦の年となりそうです.
change 名　変動, 変化, 変更, 改正, 改革, 増減, 釣銭, 小銭　（⇒**accounting change**）
　adjustment for the change　変更による修正
　capital change　資本の変動, 資本の増減
　change fund　両替資金
　change in accounts receivable　受取債権の増減
　change in cash and cash equivalents　現金および現金同等物の増減
　change in investment securities　投資有価証券の増減
　change in other operating assets and liabilities　その他の営業資産および営業負債の増減
　change in short-term debt　短期債務増減
　change in value　評価換え
　changes during the year　期末の増減
　changes in accounts payable, accrued and other liabilities　買掛金, 未払い費用およびその他の負債増減
　changes in capital　資本の増減, 資金勘定の変動, 資本の変動（＝**capital change**）
　currency changes　為替相場の変動
　dividend change　配当変更
　financial change　金融改革

interest rate change　金利変動, 金利の変更
  rating change　格付け変更
  structural change　構造的な変化, 構造的変化
change in accounting　会計処理の変更
  change in accounting estimate　会計上の見積りの変更
  change in accounting policy　会計方針の変更
  change in accounting principle and practice　会計原則・会計手続きの変更
▸The *change in accounting* reduced operating income by $300 million in 2006.　この会計処理の変更で, 2006年度の営業利益は3億ドル減少しました.
change of control　資本拘束, 経営権の変更
▸Nippon Steel is currently negotiating with its domestic capital partners to conclude *change-of-control* agreements.　新日鉄は現在, 国内の資本提携先とチェンジ・オブ・コントロール［資本拘束］条項の契約を結ぶ交渉を進めている.
change of control clause　資本拘束条項, チェンジ・オブ・コントロール条項（ライセンス契約や代理店契約を結ぶ際, 買収などで一方の会社の支配権が変わった場合には, 相手方の会社が契約を破棄できるとする条項）
Chapter 10 of the National Bankruptcy Act　［米］連邦破産法第10章
Chapter 11　［米］連邦改正破産法第11章, 米連邦破産法11章, チャプター・イレブン, 会社更生手続き（＝Chapter 11 bankruptcy, Chapter 11 of the U.S. Bankruptcy Code, Chapter 11 of the U.S. Bankruptcy Reform Act：日本の民事更生法に相当）
  Chapter 11 bankruptcy　米連邦破産法第11章に基づく倒産
charge　動　請求する, 課する, 要求する, 支払わせる, 負担させる, 借方に記入する, 借記する, 計上する, クレジット・カードで買う, 告発する（⇒**selling expense**）
  be charged to cost of sales　売上原価に計上される
  be charged to expenses as incurred　発生時に費用に計上される, 発生基準で費用に計上される
  be charged to income　費用として計上される, 費用計上される（＝be charged to earnings）
  charge against　費用として差し引く, 損失とみて差し引く
  loans and leases charged off　償却された貸出金とリース, 貸出とリースの償却額
▸Research and development costs are *charged* to earnings in the periods in which they are incurred.　研究開発費は, それが発生した期間に費用として計上されています.
▸The bank stopped *charging* its cash-card holders remittance fees when they send money from its ATMs to accounts at its head and regional branches.　同行は, キャッシュカード会員を対象に, 現金自動預け払い機（ATM）から同行の本支店の口座に金を振り込む場合の振込み手数料を無料化した.
charge　名　費用, 料金, 税金, 課税金, 手数料, 代価, 代金, 請求金額, 借方記入, 借記, 負債, 借金, 責任, 義務, 任務, 担保, 担保権, 管理, 監督, 保管, 運営, 処理, 告発, 提訴,〈陪審に対する裁判官の〉説示, チャージ（⇒**comparison**）
  accrued charges　未払い費用
  advising charge　通知手数料
  capital charge　資本費, 資本費用, 資本コスト
  charge against revenues　損金
  charge customer　掛売りの顧客
  charge sales　掛売り, 掛売上（＝credit sales）
  charge to income　損失の計上
  charges for special pension options　特別退職勧奨制度の費用
  deferred charges　繰延べ費用, 繰延べ資産
  discount charge　割引料
  eligible charges　給付額
  estimated charge　見積り費用
  finance charge　財務費用
  first legal charge　第一順位の抵当権
  fixed charge　金融費用, 固定費用, 固定担保
  floating charge　浮動担保
  interest charges　支払い利息
  lifting charge　取扱い手数料
  maintenance charge　維持費
  management charge　管理費
  one-off charge　特別損失, 一時的費用
  one-time charge　一時的費用
  repair charge　修繕費
  surrender charge　解約手数料
  taxes and public charges　公租公課
  transferring charge　振替手数料
▸Our bottom line includes company-wide *charges* that we took for accounting changes.　当社の業績［最終損益］には, 会計処理方法の変更のために計上した全社的な費用も含まれています.
charge off　損費として処理する, 費用または損失として処理する, 償却する
▸The obsolete portion of the inventory was *charged off* during the year.　陳腐化した棚卸し資産は, 当期に損失として処理しました.
charge-off　[**chargeoff**]　名　貸倒れ償却, 資産の費用処理

gross charge-offs 総貸倒れ償却
investor charge-off 貸倒れ償却
net charge-off as a percentage of loans 貸出金に対する純貸倒れ償却の比率
net charge-offs 純償却額
net losses (charge offs) 純損失(償却額)

chargeable 形 課税の対象となる，課税扱いとなる，賦課的，税を課される，請求することができる，負担すべき
　chargeable expense 付帯費用
　chargeable gain 課税対象となる資産売却益[資産処分益]
　chargeable labor cost 賦課的労務費
　chargeable transfer 課税対象となる資産譲渡

chart 名 表，図表，罫線，チャート
　bar chart 棒グラフ
　circular chart 円グラフ
　contol chart 管理図
　chart of accounts 勘定科目表

charter 名 定款，認証定款，貸借契約，特許状
　charter hire 用船料
　charter of ethics 企業行動憲章
　corporate charter 会社定款

check register 小切手記入帳
checkbook 名 小切手帳
checking transaction 小切手取引（=check trading）
▶If a financial institution goes under, companies that have checking accounts at that financial institution will become unable to conclude *checking transactions* or settle bills and will go bankrupt. 金融機関が破綻すれば，そこに当座預金を持つ企業は，小切手取引の決済や手形の決済ができなくなり，倒産してしまうことになる。

chief executive officer 最高経営責任者，最高業務執行役員，最高業務執行理事《略 CEO》（経営戦略や経営ビジョンを決める企業のトップ．米国では，CEOが会長を兼ねることが多い）

claim 名 請求，請求権，請求事項，特許請求の範囲，信用，未収の債権，債権の届出，保険金，権利，権利の主張
　amount of claim 請求額
　asset claim 資産請求権
　categorization of loan claims 債権区分
　claim adjustment expense 保険金支払い費
　claim cost recognition 保険金費用の認識
　claim for a refund 還付請求
　claim for reimbursement 未収払戻し金，償還請求
　claims for damages 損害賠償請求，求償請求
　claims of creditors 債権者の請求権
　claims of owners 企業主の請求権
　claims paid 保険金
　housing loan claim 住宅ローンの債権
　initial unemployment claims 新規失業保険申請件数
　junior claim 劣後請求権
　money claim 金銭債権
　policy claims 保険金請求，保険金
　refund claim 還付申請書
　senior claim 上位請求権
　warranty claim 保証債務，品質保証に基づく支払い請求

▶The Japan Housing Finance Agency plans to securitize housing loan *claims* bought from financial institutions. 住宅金融支援機構(独立行政法人で，旧住宅金融公庫が2007年4月1日に改称)は，金融機関から買い取った住宅ローンの債権を証券化する方針だ。

class action 集団代表訴訟，集団訴訟，クラス・アクション（=class action suit, class action lawsuit; ⇒**compensation**）

cleanup costs 浄化費用，環境の整備費（⇒**communication**）
▶There are other "potentially responsible parties (PRPs)" who can be expected to contribute to the *cleanup costs*. 浄化費用を分担するものと思われる「潜在責任当事者」は，当社以外にも存在します。

clerical and administrative expenses 事務と管理のための諸費用

client 名 顧客，お得意，得意先，得意客，取引先，依頼人，依頼者，監査依頼会社，被監査会社（=examinee corporation），クライアント（=customer）
▶Banks are allowed to sell insurance policies to *clients*. 銀行は，顧客に保険を販売することができる。
▶Consulting services under contract to *clients* are included in other operations. 得意先との契約に基づくコンサルティング・サービスは，その他の事業に含めてあります。

client information 顧客情報
▶Leakage of *client information* by businesses has gone unabated. 企業による顧客情報の漏洩は，依然として相次いでいる[一向に減らない]。

climate 名 気候，風土，条件，環境，状況，情勢，傾向，風潮，思潮，雰囲気，空気，地方，地帯（⇒**business climate**）
　changing climate 環境の変化

Climate Change Levy 気候変動税
climate for acquisition 買収条件
economic climate 経済環境, 経済情勢, 景況, 景気
financial climate 金融環境
investment climate 投資環境
management climate 経営環境
organizational climate 組織風土, 組織環境, 経営風土
the climate of opinion 世論
▶The declining income and sales result from the changing *climate* in the mobile phone and digital camera businesses. この減収減益は, 携帯電話事業とデジタル・カメラ事業の環境の変化によるものです。
▶Those corporations that will succeed and flourish will be those that create a *climate* encouraging exploration of new business possibilities and encouraging active listening to new ideas. これから成功して繁栄する企業は, 新規事業の可能性を積極的に追求し, 新しいアイデアの導入を積極的に進める企業風土を創出できる企業でしょう。

close 動 〈取引を〉終える, 引ける, 取り決める, 決める, 締め切る, 閉鎖する, 整理する, 清算する, 解散する (⇒abandonment)
  close a factory 工場を閉鎖する
  close off 勘定などを締め切る
  close out 処分する, 締め切る
  close to [into] ... …に振り替える
  close the day at ... …で取引を終える
  close the day lower 下落して引ける
  close unprofitable stores 不採算店舗を閉鎖する
▶As jittery investors sold blue-chip holdings, Chinese share prices *closed* 2.91 percent lower. 不安にかられた投資家が優良な持ち株を売却したため, 中国の株式相場は2.91%安で取引を終えた。
▶Mother Rock, a U.S. hedge fund, *closed* in August due to losses incurred by the plunge in the natural gas prices. 米国のヘッジ・ファンド「マザーロック」は, 天然ガス相場の下落に伴う損失で, 今年の8月に解散した。
▶The company plans to *close* or consolidate 46 stores by the end of this fiscal year. 同社は, 今年度末までに46店舗の統廃合を計画している。

close 名 終値, 引け値, 引け, 終了
  close of business 営業終了, 営業時間の終了
  market on close 引け注文
▶The corporation's regular quarterly dividend will be payable June 30, 2007 to shareholders of record at the *close* of business on June 9, 2007. 当社の通常四半期配当は, 2007年6月9日営業終了時の登録株主に対して2007年6月30日に支払われます。

close 形 近い, 密接な, 閉じた, 徹底的な
  close company 閉鎖会社 (基本的に, 株主やパートナーなどの構成員が5名以下の会社)
  close cooperation and coordination 密接な協力体制
  close corporation 株式非公開会社, 非公開会社, 閉鎖会社 (=closed corporation)

close the [one's] books 〈決算などのために〉帳簿を締める, 株式名義の書換えを停止する, 申込みを締め切る (=close one's accounts; ⇒**annual accounts settlement**)
▶These companies *close their books* between April and June. これらの企業は, 4-6月期決算だ[これらは, 4-6月期決算企業だ]。

closed 形 閉ざされた, 非公開の
  closed company 非公開会社, 非上場会社 (=private company, privately held company)
  closed corporation 閉鎖会社, 非公開会社 (=closing corporation)
  closed-end company 閉鎖式投資信託会社, クローズドエンド型投資信託会社

closely held 少数者[少数株主]に支配されている
  closely held company 少数株主支配会社, 閉鎖的会社

closing 名 決済, 期末, 決算, 締切り, 取引完了, 終値, 〈正式契約書の〉調印式, 正式契約書の作成・署名, クロージング, 〈不動産売買の〉最終手続き, 株式の譲渡手続きと代金の払込み手続きの同時履行, 〈工場などの〉閉鎖, 休会, 結語 (⇒**sale and purchase**)
  after-closing [post-closing] trial balance 繰越し試算表
  closing balance 期末残高
  closing date 払込み日, 払込み期日, 締切り日, 売上締切り日, 決算日, 証券の引渡し日, クロージング日 (=closing day)
  closing of accounts 決算, 勘定の締切り (=closing account, closing books, closing of books)
  closing procedure 決算手続き (=closing process)
  closing rate 終値, 引け値, 決算日レート, クロージング・レート 《略 CR》
  closing statements 決算書類
  closing stock 棚卸し資産期末在り高[有り高] (=ending inventory)
  interim closing 中間決算

June mid-term book-closing　6月中間決算
plant closing　工場閉鎖（＝plant closure）
▶GM's plant *closings* and job cuts in the United States will generate annual savings of roughly $2.5 billion.　GMの米国での工場閉鎖と人員削減で，年間約25億ドルのコストが削減される。

closing account　決算勘定，決算
　closing account for the half year ending March 2009　2009年3月中間決算
　closing accounts for the year　年次決算

closing balance sheet　クロージング貸借対照表，クロージング時現在の貸借対照表
▶The *closing balance sheet* fairly presents the financial position of the Corporation at the closing date in conformity with United States GAAP.　クロージング時現在の貸借対照表は，米国の一般に認められた会計原則［米国の会計基準］に従って，クロージング日の「会社」の財政状態を適正に表示している。

closing price　終値，引け値（＝closing market price）
▶Based on the firm's *closing price*, its market capitalization stands at ¥219 billion, making the second-largest issue on the Mothers market.　終値ベースで，同社の時価総額は2,199億円で，新興企業向け市場の東証マザーズ上場銘柄としては第2位となった。

closure 名　〈工場や店舗，事業などの〉閉鎖，封鎖，閉幕，閉会（⇒**money-losing store**）
▶This restructuring program includes streamlining marketing and selling organizations, *closure* and consolidation of several manufacturing facilities and a general streamlining of operations throughout the Corporation.　この事業再編計画には，マーケティング組織と販売組織の効率化，一部製造工場の閉鎖・統合や全社レベルでの業務全般の効率化が含まれています。

COD　代金引換渡し（**cash on delivery, collect on delivery**の略）
　COD sale　代金［現金］引換販売

code 名　規則，規約，基準，規範，法，略号，情報，コード
　code of conduct　行動規範，倫理綱領，倫理規定（＝code of ethics）
　code of ethics　倫理規定，倫理綱領（＝business conduct code, code of conduct）
　code of professional ethics　職業倫理規程
　Internal Revenue Code　内国歳入法
　Uniform Commercial Code　統一商事法典，統一商法典

▶The *code* of conduct for battery manufacturers will stipulate the methods of production, including process management, to protect consumers.　電池メーカーに対する行動規範では，消費者保護のため，工程管理など電池の製造方法を定めることになった。

collapse 動　経営破綻する，破綻する，倒産する（＝fail），暴落する，急減する，崩壊する
▶Ashikaga Bank *collapsed* and was temporarily placed under state control.　足利銀行は，経営破綻して一時国有化された。

collapse 名　経営破綻，破綻，倒産，崩壊，暴落，急落，下落，急減，悪化
　collapse of financial institutions　金融破綻，金融機関の経営破綻
　collapse of the dollar　ドルの下落
　collapse of the economic bubble　バブル崩壊
　collapse of the stock market　株式市場の急落，株式相場の下落（＝stock market collapse）
　corporate collapse　企業倒産，企業の経営破綻（＝corporate failure）
　credit collapse　信用崩壊（＝the collapse of credit）
　earnings collapse　業績悪化，大幅減益，収益の落ち込み
▶Distrust of corporate accounting was ignited by the *collapse* of major energy trader Enron.　企業会計への不信感は，米エネルギー大手エンロンの経営破綻に端を発した。

collateral 名　担保，担保物件，担保品，担保財産（＝mortgage, security）
　collateral assessment　担保評価
　collateral bond　担保付き社債
　collateral value　担保価値（⇒**collection of debts**）
　fixed collateral　根（ね）抵当，根抵当権
　foreclosed collateral　担保権の実行，担保権の行使
　offer ... as collateral　…を担保として提供する
　pledge ... as collateral　…を担保として差し出す
　post collateral　担保を差し入れる，担保を設定する，担保を積む
▶We usually do not require *collateral* or other security from other parties to these financial instruments.　これらの金融商品については，当社は通常，相手方に当該商品に対する担保その他の保証を要求してはいません。

collect 動　〈債権や代金，資源などを〉回収する，〈年金や保険料，税金などを〉徴収する，〈預金などを〉獲得する

▶ *Collecting* receivables helps us to pay our suppliers.　売掛債権を回収すると, 当社の納入業者への支払いが楽になります。

collect on delivery　代金引換渡し《略 COD》

collection 名　〈債権や代金などの〉回収, 代金取立て, 集金, 〈年金や保険料, 税金などの〉徴収, 〈預金などの〉獲得

　bill for collection　代金取立手形
　cash collection　現金回収, 回収額
　collection and distribution services　集配業務
　collection basis　回収基準
　collection expense [**cost**]　回収費, 集金費, 代金回収費
　collection of debts　債権回収 (＝debt collection)
　collection of premiums　保険料の徴収
　collection of principal　元本回収
　collection of receivables　売掛金の回収
　collections from customers and others　顧客その他からの回収
　debt collection　債権回収, 貸金取立て, 借金取り (＝collecting the debt, collection of debts)
　loan collection　債権回収
　tax collection　徴税, 税の徴収 (＝collection of taxes)
　transfer of collections　回収金の送金

▶ The *collection* of debts has been delayed due to falling collateral value.　担保価値の下落などで, 債権の回収は遅れている。

▶ Yamato Transport Co. and Sagawa Express Co. temporarily suspended their *collection* and distribution services in Kyushu.　ヤマト運輸と佐川急便は, 九州での集配業務を一時見合わせた。

combination 名　合併, 連結, 企業結合, 企業連合, 相互利益協定, 結合, 組合せ, 関連性

　business combination　企業結合, 企業合同, 合併, 統合, 企業買収 (＝combination of business)
　combination of cap and swap　キャップとスワップの組合せ
　combination of factors　要因の関連性
　combinations of companies　企業結合, 企業グループ
　deferred taxes in a purchase combination　パーチェス法による合併での繰延べ税金
　industrial combination　企業結合

▶ Goodwill is the difference between the purchase price and the fair value of net assets acquired in business *combinations* treated as purchases.　営業権は, パーチェス法により会計処理した企業買収で取得した純資産の購入価格と公正価格との差異です。

combined 形　合算した, 結合した, 統合した, 連結した, …の合算, …の合計 [合計額]

　combined income and retained earnings statement　損益および留保利益結合計算書 (＝combined statement of income and retained earnings)
　combined income statement　合併損益計算書
　combined losses　赤字合計額
　combined net profit　税引き後利益の合計額, 純利益の合計額
　combined profits or losses　損益の合算, 損益の通算 (＝combined profits and losses)
　combined revenue　連結収益, 総合収益
　combined sales　売上高の合計, 全社合計の売上高, 全社合わせての売上高, 総売却額

▶ The consolidated tax system calculates taxes based on *combined* profits or losses.　連結税制は, 企業グループの損益を合算 [結合] して税額を算定するシステムだ。

combined amount　合算した数値, 合算数値

▶ After a merger, financial statements and all other financial information show the two companies' *combined amounts*.　合併後の財務書類とその他の財務情報は, すべて両社の合算数値を示しています。

combined group net profit　連結税引き後利益の合計額, 連結純利益の合計額

▶ *Combined group net profit* at Japan's six top banking grouops totaled a record ¥1.74 trillion for the April–September fiscal first half.　9月中間決算 [4–9月期の上半期決算] で, 日本の大手銀行・金融6グループ合計の連結税引き後利益が, 過去最高益の1兆7,400億円となった。

combined net loss　純損失の合計, 税引き後損失の合計額, 全社合わせての赤字

▶ The major banking groups posted a combined loss of ¥5.2 trillion incurred by writing off bad loans, while chalking up a *combined net loss* of ¥4.6 trillion.　大手銀行グループの不良債権処理に伴う損失額は総計5兆2,000億円で, 最終赤字は計4兆6,000億円に上った。

combined pretax profit　経常利益合計

▶ Companies listed on the TSE's First Section posted a year-on-year increase of 33.2 percent in *combined pretax profit* in the first half of the current fiscal year.　東証一部上場企業の今年度上期 (4–9月期) の経常利益合計は, 前年同期比33.2％増となった。

comfort letter　財務内容に関する意見書, 調査

報告書, コンフォート・レター （=letter of comfort)
comfort letter for underwriter 証券引受人への書簡, 証券引受業者［幹事証券会社］に対する調査報告書 (=letter for underwriter)
coming year 来年度, 来期, 新年度
▸We won't make predictions for the *coming year*. 来期の予測をするのは, 差し控えます。
commercial draft 商業為替手形
commercial note 商業手形
commercial paper 商業証券, 商業手形, コマーシャル・ペーパー《略 **CP**》(為替手形(bill of exchange, draft), 約束手形(note, promissory note), 小切手(check)や預金証書(certificate of deposit)などを指し, 米国では資金調達のために優良企業が発行する通常2日-270日以内の短期約束手形のことをいう。⇒**asset-backed commercial paper**)
　commercial paper issuance CPの発行
　commercial paper outstanding CP発行残高
　tax-exempt commercial paper 免税［非課税］CP
▸Higher debt maturing within one year chiefly reflects *commercial paper* we issued to support financial services. 1年以内返済予定の負債の増加は, 主に金融サービス部門の支援のため, 当社がコマーシャル・ペーパーを発行したことを反映しています。
commission 名 手数料, 株式引受手数料, 報酬, 口銭, 委任, 委任状, 委託, 代理業務, 授与, 授権, 任命, 任命書, 委員会, 責務, 任務, 権限, 職権, 過失, 作為, コミッション (⇒**liberalization**)
　acceptance commission 手形引受手数料
　accrued commission 未払い手数料
　agent [agency] commission 代理店手数料
　amount of commission charged 請求手数料額
　commission and expenses on capital shares 株式発行費用
　commission and fee 報酬
　commission expense 手数料費用
　commission income and expense 受入手数料および支払い手数料
　commission payable 未払い手数料
　commission receivable 未収手数料 (=accrued commission receivable)
　commission revenue 手数料収入
　discount commission 割引手数料
　fee and commision received 受入手数料
　opening commission 発行手数料
　placement commission 販売手数料
　prepaid commission 前払い手数料
　selling [sales] commission 販売手数料
　underwriting commission 引受手数料
▸Brokerage *commissions* on commodity futures trading are completely liberalized. 商品先物取引の委託手数料は, 完全自由化されている。
▸Securities firms are free to set the price for all *commissions*. 売買委託手数料は, すべて証券各社が自由に設定できる。
commit 動 約束する, 公約する, 確約する, 取り組む, 専念する, 全力を挙げる, 引き受ける, 委託する, 委任する
　committed bank facilities 契約に基づく銀行借入枠
　committed bank lines of credit 銀行の信用供与枠
▸We *commit* to these values to guide our decisions and behavior. 私たちは, 私たちの意思決定と行動の基準としてこれらの価値観を大切にしています。
commitment 名 委任, 委託, 公約, 誓約, 約束, 約定, 立場の明確な表明, 必達目標, 〈協調融資団への〉参加意思表示, 〈融資参加の〉意向表明, 〈銀行の〉融資承認, 融資先, 売買約定, 売買契約, 取引契約, 契約債務, 契約義務, 未履行債務, 姿勢, 取組, コミットメント
　acceptance commitment 引受債務
　capital commitments 出資, 資本参加
　commitment fee 約定料, 契約手数料, 保証手数料, コミットメント・フィー
　commitments and contingent liabilities 契約債務および偶発債務
　commitments to extend credit 信用供与契約
　customor financing commiments 顧客融資契約
　financial commitment 資金協力, 金銭の支払い
　firm commitment 確定契約, 成約済み取引
　lease commitme nt 賃貸借契約
　loan commitments 貸出約定, 融資契約, 融資確約
　new loans commitments 新規融資契約, 新規融資承認額
　underwriting commitment 引受額
　unused portions of commitments 貸出枠未実行残高
▸These lease *commitments* are pricinpally for the rental of office premises. これらのリース契約は, 主に事務所施設の賃貸を対象としています。
▸We are continuing our *commitment* to the Corporation's research and development programs. 当社は, 当社の研究開発計画にも引き続き取り組んでいます。

commitment line 融資枠の設定, コミットメント・ライン
コミットメント・ラインとは ➡ 銀行から一定の範囲で自由に借入れができる融資枠の設定のこと。コミットメント・ラインを設定すると, 金融機関は安定した手数料収入が得られるほか, 優良企業との取引拡大を期待できる。また, 企業にとっては, 手数料を払う代わりに金利ゼロで融資を受けられるメリットがある。緊急の資金需要に備えられるほか, 資金効率の改善効果もある。最近は, 経営不振の企業が, 信用不安を解消するため主力取引銀行とコミットメント・ライン契約を結ぶことが多い。

committee 名 委員会, 協議会, 部会 (⇒**audit committee, management executive committee**)
advisory committee 諮問委員会
audit committee 監査委員会
business conduct committee 業務委員会
committee on employee benefits 従業員待遇委員会
committee on internal auditing 内部監査委員会
corporate value assessment special committee 企業価値評価特別委員会
executive committee 経営委員会
internal audit and compliance committee 内部監査・法令遵守委員会
investigation committee 調査委員会 (⇒**accountable**)
management executive committee 経営執行委員会
managing committee 経営委員会
Nomination and Compensation Committee 指名報酬委員会
operating committee 常務会
social responsibility committee 社会的責任委員会
steering committee 運営委員会
third party committee 第三者委員会
voluntary committee 任意の委員会

▶Audit *Committee* of the board of directors is composed of directors who are not employees. 取締役会の監査委員会は, 社外取締役で構成されています。

commodity 名 商品, 市況品, 日用品, 物品, 生産物, 財貨, 財
marketable commodity 市場性のある商品
nonmarketed commodity 非市場性商品
taxed commodity 課税品, 課税商品
commodity exchange 商品取引所

Commodity Exchange Law 商品取引所法
commodity futures 商品先物, 商品先物市場
commodity futures trading 商品先物取引 (金や石油などの商品について, 一定の値段で将来売買することを約束して行う取引で, 価格は取引契約を結ぶ時点で決める)

▶Foreign players also are expected to enter the *commodity futures* market in line with the improvement in investment conditions. 投資の環境改善で, 外資 [海外企業] の商品先物市場への参入も見込まれる。

commodity market 商品市場, 商品相場

▶Primary factors behind the buoyant performances were price increases in *commodity markets* such as steel, and increased exports. 好業績 [好決算] の主因は, 鉄鋼など商品相場の上昇と輸出の増大である。

common 形 共通の, 共有の, 共同の, 普通の, 通常の
common dividend 普通株式配当金, 普通株配当金
common equity 普通株
common interests 共通の利益
common voting stock 普通議決権株式
common control 共通の支配

▶In 2007, no single customer or group under *common control* represented 10% or more of the Company's sales. 2007年度は, 共通の支配下にある単一顧客またはグループで, 当社売上高の10%以上を占めるものはありません。

common cost 共通費, 共通原価 (費用のうち, 2つ以上の製品・部署などに共通で, いずれか1つの製品・部署などに帰属させることが不適当なもの)

common share 普通株, 普通株式, 普通株資本金, 資本金 (=common equity, common stock, ordinary share, ordinary stock:普通株は, 優先株 (preferred share, preferred stock) や後配株 (deferred share, deferred stock) のように特別の権利内容を持たない一般の株式)
common shares purchased for cancellation 消却のための普通株式の購入
dividends on common shares 普通株式に対する配当金

▶Consolidated net income applicable to *common shares* for the third quarter of 2007 was $295 million. 2007年第3四半期の普通株式に帰属する連結純利益は, 2億9,500万ドルでした。

▶The increase in the number of *common shares* was due mainly to conversion of the $2.70 preferred shares in March. 普通株式数が増加したのは, 主に3月に行われた額面2.70ドルの優先株式の

転換によるものです。

common shares outstanding 発行済み普通株式, 発行済み社外流通株式, 普通株式発行総数
▸First quarter earnings per share were based on 320 million average *common shares outstanding*. 第1四半期の1株当たり純利益は, 発行済み普通株式の平均株式数に基づいて計算されています。

common stock 普通株[普通株式], 普通株資本金, 資本金 (=common share, ordinary share, ordinary stock)
    affiliated common stock 関連会社普通株式
    authorized common stock 授権普通株式数
    common stock at par 額面普通株資本
    common stock in treasury 自己普通株式, 自己株式
    common stock issued and outstanding 普通株式発行済み株式数
    common stock outstanding 発行済み社外流通普通株式 (=common shares outstanding)
    common stock with par value 額面株式 (⇒ par value)
    common stock without par value 無額面株式
    dilutive common stock equivalents 希薄化準普通株式
    junior common stock 劣後普通株式
    net income available for common stock 普通株主に帰属する当期利益
    outstanding common stock 発行済み普通株式
    puttable common stock プット・オプション付き普通株式
▸On November 1, 2007, the Company's Board of Directors approved a 43% increase in the quarterly dividend on *common stock*. 2007年11月1日, 当社取締役会は, 普通株式の四半期配当金の43%増額を承認しました。

common stock equivalents 普通株式相当証券, 普通株式等価物, 準普通株式 (⇒convertible bond)
    common stock equivalents from stock option ストック・オプションからの準普通株式
    common stock equivalents from warrants ワラントからの準普通株式
▸*Common stock equivalents* are stock options that we assume to be exercised for the purposes of computing earnings per common share. 普通株式等価物とは, 1株[普通株式1株] 当たり純利益を計算するにあたって行使されると仮定したストック・オプションです。

common stockholder 普通株主
    common stockholders's equity 普通株主資本, 普通株主資本の部
    common stockholders' equity per share 1株当たり普通株主持ち分

communication 名 通信, 伝達, 意思疎通, 相互理解, やり取り, 協議, 連絡, 手紙, コミュニケーション
▸Our efforts for environmental improvement include environmental cleanup costs and *communication* programs. 当社の環境改善策には, 環境の浄化整備費や住民とのコミュニケーション・プログラムも含まれています。
▸The Company, experiencing major growth in demand for *communication* services, made record capital expenditures in 2007. 当社の2007年度の資本的支出は, 通信サービス需要の著しい伸びに伴って, 過去最高を記録しました。

community 地域社会, 共同社会, 社会, 共同体, 団体, 業界, …界, コミュニティ
    business community 経済界, 財界, 産業界, 実業界 (=business circles, business world)
    community relations 地域社会との関係, 対地域社会関係, 地域社会PR
    economic community 経済界, 財界, 経済圏
    financial community 金融業界
    global [international] community 国際社会
    industrial community 経済界, 産業界, 実業界
    international community 国際社会
    investment community 投資業界
    local community 地域社会
    Net community ネット社会
    virtual community 仮想現実社会
    Web-based community ウェブ上のコミュニティ
    world community 世界共同体, 国際社会
▸We are responsible to our people and to the *community* where they live and work. 当社は, 従業員に対して責任を負うと同時に, 従業員が生活し働いている地域社会に対しても責任を負っています。

community-based 形 地域社会ベースの, 地域密着型の
    community-based sales 地域密着型の営業
    community-based services 地域密着型のサービス, 地域密着型の営業活動
▸The Company will enhance *community-based* sales. 当社は今後, 地元密着型の営業を強化します。

community of interest 関心の一致, 利害の一致, 利害の調整, 利益共同体
▸The alliance is a *community of interest* based on new growth opportunities in the global telecommunications equipment markets. この提携

は，世界の通信機器市場で新たな成長の機会をめざす両社の関心が一致したことによるものです．

company 名 会社，企業，社団 （⇒**holding company, listed company, publicly held company, targeted company, unlisted**）
  acquiring company 買収会社
  blue-chip company 優良企業 （＝**successful company**）
  business company 事業会社
  Companies Act 会社法
  company credit quality 企業の信用の質，企業の信用力
  company limited by guarantee 英国の保証有限会社 （＝**guarantee company**）
  company profile 会社概要 （＝**company description**）
  company profit 企業利益，法人利潤，企業収益
  company results meeting 決算発表時の記者会見
  company spokesperson 企業の広報担当者
  comparable company 類似会社，類似企業
  fifty-percent-owned company 半数所有会社，50％所有会社
  friendly company 友好的な企業
  majority owned company 過半数所有会社
  mutual company 相互会社
  nonpublic company 非公開企業 （＝**private company**）
  offeree company 買付け対象会社
  operating company 事業会社
  outstanding company 超優良会社
  parent company 親会社
  peer companies 同業他社
  private company 非公開会社，民間企業
  public company 株式公開企業
  quoted [listed] company 上場企業，上場会社
  regulated company 規制対象企業
  stand alone company 独立企業
  subsidiary company 子会社
  unquoted [unlisted] company 非上場企業，非上場会社
  utility company 公益事業会社
▶We are a *company* ever-strengthening its customer partnerships, product line and efficiency. 当社は，つねにお客さまとの連携および製品ラインの強化と効率性改善に取り組んでいる会社です．

company system カンパニー制，社内企業制 （企業の事業部制に市場原理を導入して，独立の会社に近づけた形態の擬似会社制．そのメリットとして，意思決定と実施の迅速化，組織の活性化，本業の責任の明確化などが挙げられる）
▶*Company system* of independent divisions is a management system that Sony pioneered as a major company in Japan. 独立事業部門のカンパニー制は，ソニーが日本の大手企業として初めて導入した経営システムである．

company's value 企業価値
▶The market capitalization of a company determines the *company's value*. 企業価値の決定要因は［企業価値を決めるのは］，企業の時価総額だ．

comparability 名 〈会計データなどの〉比較可能性

comparative advantage 比較優位，比較優位性 （＝**relative advantage**）
▶*Comparative advantage* in this new global market depends not only on superior R&D, but also on speed in making management decisions. この新しいグローバル市場で比較優位性を確立できるかどうかは，高度な研究開発だけでなく，経営の意思決定を迅速に行えるかどうかにかかっている．

comparative figures 前期の比較対応数値，前期の対応額

comparative financial results 財務書類の期間比較

compared to a year earlier 前年比で，前期比で，前年同期比で

compared with ... …と比べて，…に対して，…比で （＝**compared to ...**）
▶Revenues were $4,860 million, *compared with* $4,728 million the previous year. 売上高［収益］は，前期［前年度］の47億2,800万ドルに対して48億6,000万ドルでした．

comparison 名 比較，対照，例示，照合，突合せ （⇒**depreciation expense**）
  comparison schedule 比較表
  financial comparison 財務比較
  in the year-on-year comparison 前年同期比で，前年同月比で
  one-for-one comparisons 個別照合チェック
  one-to-one comparisons 個別データの突合せ比較
▶By *comparison* to 2006, expenditures during 2007 included a significantly lower level of expenses for charges resulting from the Company's ongoing evaluation of its operations and asset valuation. 2006年度と比べて，当年度の費用は，会社の業務活動と資産評価の継続的評価から生じた諸経費に対する費用負担の水準がかなり低くなっています．

compensation 名 報酬，対価，給与，手当，報

償, 補償, 賠償, 代償, 相殺, 報償金, 補償金, 賠償金, 慰謝料 （⇒approve）
claim compensation from ... …に賠償金を請求する
compensation and benefits 給与および給付金
compensation for damages 損害賠償, 損害賠償金
compensation for losses 損害賠償, 損害賠償金 （＝compensation for damages）
compensation for technical services 技術サービスの対価
compensation system 給与体系
compensation expense 報償費用
employee compensation 雇用者所得, 勤労者所得, 従業員給与 （＝compensation of employees）
executive compensation 役員報酬
incentive compensation 奨励報償, インセンティブ報酬
net compensation amount 差額決済金額
seek [claim] compensation from ... …に補償を求める, …に賠償請求する
total compensation 給与総額
unemployment compensation 失業給付
welfare compensation plan 福利厚生費制度
worker's compensation insurance 労災保険

▶The *compensation* to the individual was taken care of largely out of our pension fund. 個人に支払われた退職金は, 主に当社の年金基金から拠出しました。

▶Victim firms have entered into talks to file a class action suit for *compensation*. 被害企業が, 損害賠償に向けて集団訴訟のための協議を開始した。

compensatory 形 代償の, 補償の, 償いの
compensatory plan 報酬制度

compete 動 競争する, 競う, 争う, 張り合う, 渡り合う, 競合する
▶The best way to *compete* is to get closer to each customer. 競うための最良の方法は, お客さまにそれぞれもっと近づくことです。

competition 動 競争, 競合, 競業, 競争相手, ライバル
cost reduction competition コスト削減競争
cutthroat competition 熾烈な競争, 激烈な競争, 激しい競争, のど元をかき切る競争
demands competition 需要間競争, 需要競争
excessive [excess] competition 過当競争
export competition 輸出競争
fair competition 公正競争
global [international] competition 国際競争

growing competition 競争の高まり, 競争激化
intensifying competition 激しさを増す競争, 競争の激化
inter-industry competition 産業間競争
market competition 市場での競争, 市場競争
non-price competition 非価格競争
open competition 公開競争
price competition 価格競争
quality competition 品質競争
sales competition 販売競争
unfair competition 不正競争

▶All our business units face stiff *competition*. 当社の事業部門は, すべて苛烈な競争に直面しています。

competitive 形 競争的, 競争上の, 競争力のある, 他社に負けない, 安い, 低コストの （＝cost-competitive）
competitive dynamics 競争環境 （＝competitive environment）
competitive moves 競争力
competitive position 競争力, 競争上の地位, 競争上のポジション
competitive pressure 競争圧力
competitive price 競争価格, 競争値段, 低価格, 安い価格 [値段]
competitive strength 競争力
cost-competitive 価格競争力がある, 価格競争力が高い, コスト競争力がある
highly competitive 競争力が高い
hold a competitive advantage 競争上の優位性を維持する, 競争上の優位性を保つ
improve competitive position 競争力を高める
international competitive position 国際競争力
remain [stay] competitive 競争力を維持する, 競争力を保つ

▶Our customers rely on vast amounts of business information to thrive in *competitive* environments. 当社の顧客は, 競争環境にあって勝ち残るため, 膨大な量のビジネス情報に依存しています。

competitive advantage 競争上の優位, 競争上の優位性, 競争力, 比較優位, 比較優位性, 競争有利性

▶We believe our new, patented technology gives us a *competitive advantage* that will help us attract and keep customers. 当社の特許取得済みの新技術は, 当社に競争力を与え, 当社の今後の顧客獲得と顧客離れを防ぐのに役立つと考えています。

competitive edge 競争力, 競争上の優位, 競争上の優位性, 競争力での優位
add additional competitive edge さらに競争

力を高める
lose competitive edge 競争力を失う

competitive environment 競争環境
▸The *competitive environment* inside and outside the nation has been changing drastically. 国内外の競争環境は, 激変している。

competitive product 競争力のある製品
▸In our drive for more *competitive products* and services, we are making essential investments in research, development and engineering. 一段と競争力のある製品とサービスの提供をめざして, 当社は研究, 開発とエンジニアリングに重要な投資を行っています。

competitiveness 名 競争力, 競争
  corporate competitiveness 企業競争力
  cost competitiveness コスト競争力, 費用競争力
  export competitiveness 輸出競争力 (=trade competitiveness)
  external competitiveness 対外競争力
  industrial competitiveness 産業競争力
  international competitiveness 国際競争力 (=global competitiveness)
  market competitiveness 市場競争力
  non-price competitiveness 非価格競争力
  price comepetitiveness 価格競争力 (=competitiveness in prices)
  product competitiveness 製品競争力
▸Famly-friendly programs help us attract and retain top-notch people, which is essential to our *competitiveness*. 家庭にやさしいプログラムは, 一流の社員を引き付け, これらの社員を長期的に確保する上でも有益で, これは当社の競争力維持に欠かせないものです。

competitor 名 競争相手, 競合他社, 同業者, ライバル企業, ライバル (⇒**disadvantage**)
▸We won many contracts from our *competitors*. 当社は, 競争相手から多くの契約を勝ち取りました。

complete 動 完全にする, 完成させる, 仕上げる, もれなく記入する

complete 形 完全な, 完成した
  complete checking 完全照合
  complete inventory 一斉棚卸し
  complete specialization 完全特化

completed contract method 工事完成基準 (請負工事などの長期契約の収益認識基準で工事完了の年度に認識するもの), 完成基準, 完了基準 (=completed contract basis, completed job method, completed job method of accounting for long-term contracts)
▸The *completed contract method* requires that provision should be made for an expected loss. 工事完成基準では, 見込まれる損失について引当金の計上が必要である。

completion 名 完成, 完工, 達成, 成立 (⇒**percentage of completion method**)
  completion basis 工事完成基準
  completion of production method 生産基準, 完成基準
  estimated costs at completion 完成時の見積り原価
  estimated percentage of completion 見積り完成比率
  percentage-of-completion earnings 工事進行基準売上

complex capital structure 複合的資本構成(社外流通するdilutive securities (希薄性証券) が企業にある状態。Basic EPSとDiluted EPSの開示を義務付けられる)

compliance 名 承諾, 受諾, 遵守, 遵守性, 準拠性, 適合, 服従, コンプライアンス
  affirmative action compliance program 積極的優遇措置遵守プログラム
  compliance of financial statements 財務諸表［財務書類］の準拠性, 財務諸表の会計原則準拠性
  compliance officer 法令・規則遵守担当役員, 業務監査役, コンプライアンス・オフィサー
  compliance program 法遵守プログラム, 規制遵守プログラム (⇒**planning**)
  compliance with rules 規則の遵守
  legal compliance 法令遵守
  tax compliance 税務の法令遵守
▸Costs related to ongoing *compliance* with present laws will not have a material effect on our future expenditures, earnings or competitive position. 現在進めている現行法遵守の関連費用が, 当社の将来的支出, 利益や競争力に重大な影響をもたらすことはないでしょう。

component 名 構成部品, 部品, 構成要素, 成分, 内訳, 部分, 項目, コンポーネント (⇒**before**)
  component of stockholders' equity 資本の部
  component percentage 構成比率 (=component proportion ratio)
  components of income tax expense 所得税費用の内訳
  debt component 債券部分
  earnings-related component 報酬比例部分
  interest component 金利部分
  separate component 独立した構成要素
▸We show the adjustments from balance sheet transaction as a separate *component* of share-

owners' equity. 貸借対照表の取引から生じる換算差益額は、株主持ち分の独立した構成要素として示してあります。

composition 名 構成, 一部返済金, 示談金, 債務一部免除契約, 和解, 和議, 示談
　asset composition 資産の構成
　balance sheet composition 貸借対照表の構成
　capital composition ratio 資本構成比率
　compulsory composition 強制和議
　value composition of capital 資本の価値構成

compound interest 複利(預金などに適用される金利で、元本と利息に金利が付く)

comprehensive 形 総合的な, 包括的な, 広範な, 幅広い
　comprehensive annual financial report 包括的年次財務報告
　comprehensive financial services 総合金融サービス
　comprehensive income 包括利益, 包括的利益
　comprehensive income tax allocation 完全税効果会計, 所得税の完全期間配分, 総合的繰延べ課税 (＝comprehensive tax allocation)
　comprehensive loss 包括損失, 包括的損失
　comprehensive tie-up [alliance] 包括提携, 包括的提携 (＝broad alliance)

▸The natin's mega banking groups have been realigning their securuites units to offer *comprehensive* financial services. 国内の大手金融グループは、総合金融サービスを提供するため、グループ各社の証券会社を再統合している。

comprise 動 …を含む, …から成る, …を構成する, …で構成される, …を占める, 内訳は…

▸Other revenues *comprise* principally research and development for other companies and interest income of the finance subsidiaries. その他の売上高には、主に他社から委託された研究開発の収益と金融子会社の受取利息などが含まれています。

comptroller 名 経理部長, コントローラー (⇒controller)

compute 動 計算する, 算定する, 算出する (＝calculate)
　actuarial computed value 保険数理上の計算価値, 保険数理上で計算した価値
　actuarially-computed pension liabilities 年金数理上の年金債務算出額

▸We use the weighted average number of shares of common stock and common stock equivalents outstanding during each period to *compute* earnings per common share. 当社は、各会計期間の発行済み普通株式および普通株式等価物の加重平均株式数を用いて、1株当たり純利益を計算しています。

concentrate 動 集中する, 集中させる, 全力を傾ける, 力を注ぐ, …に照準を合わせる (⇒concept)

▸Kanebo now is *concentrating* on its three core businesses of daily commodities, pharmaceuticals and food. カネボウは現在、日用品、薬品、食品の主力3事業に集中している。

concept 名 基本的な考え方, アイデア, 基本思想, 主義, 構想, 概念, 理念, 観念, 基準, 公準, コンセプト
　accounting concept 会計概念
　attributable concept 帰属主義
　auditing concepts 監査上の諸概念
　business concept 企業理念
　cash concept 現金主義
　concept of matching costs with revenues 費用・収益対応の概念
　cost concept 現価概念
　founding concept 会社設立構想
　fundamental accounting concepts 会計の基礎概念
　going concern concept 継続企業の公準, 継続企業の概念
　management concept 経営理念
　money measurement concept 貨幣[貨幣的]測定の公準
　one-year concept 1年基準
　periodicity concept 会計期間の公準
　product development concept 商品開発のコンセプト, 製品開発コンセプト
　time period concept 会計期間の概念

▸We work with a clear business *concept* geared toward innovation and concentrating on special fields. 当社は、革新と特定分野への集中に照準を合わせた明確な企業理念を掲げて事業を行っています。

concern 動 …に関係する, 利害関係がある, 重要である

concern 名 関心, 関心事, 関係, 利害関係, 心配, 懸念, 懸念材料, 不安, 不安材料, 配慮, 問題, 会社, 企業, 企業体, 事業, 業務, 責務, 任務, 重要性 (⇒going concern)
　commercial concerns 経済的利益
　concern for employees 従業員への配慮
　concern interested 関係会社
　credit concerns 信用リスクに対する懸念
　inflationary concerns インフレに対する懸念
　political concerns 政局不安
　quitting concern 非継続企業, 終了企業 (⇒

going concern)
▸There are serious *concerns* that the strong yen and the weak U.S. dollar could hurt the current economic upturn led by exports. 大きな懸念材料は、円高・ドル安の進行で現在の輸出主導の景気回復が打撃を受けることだ。

condensed 形 要約された、凝縮した
　condensed consolidated balance sheet (unaudited) 連結貸借対照表要約(未監査)
　condensed income statement 要約損益計算書、損益計算書要約 (＝condensed statement of income)
　condensed statement of consolidated income 要約連結損益計算書

condition 名 条件、状態、状況、情勢、動向、環境 (⇒borrower, borrowing, financial condition)
　business condition index 景気動向指数
　business conditions 景気、商況、業況、業況判断、業態、事業環境、経営の実態、営業状況
　credit conditions 信用状態
　economic conditions 経済状態、経済情勢、景気
　financial terms and conditions 財務条件
　market conditions 市場環境、市況
　monetary conditions 金融情勢、金融環境
　operating conditions 事業環境
　qualifying conditions 年金受給資格
　technical conditions 技術的条件、テクニカル要因
▸Many major customers demand ISO certification as a *condition* of doing business. 主要顧客の多くは、取引の条件としてISO (国際標準化機構) の認定を求めます。
▸The company's financial statements did not correctly reflect its financial *condition*. 同社の財務諸表は、財務状況を適正に表していなかった。

conditional payment 条件付き支払項目

conduct 名 行為、行動、遂行、実施、活動、管理、運営、処理、運営方法、規範、指針、紀律
　business conduct 業務活動、業務遂行、業務、営業上の指針
　code of conduct 行動規範
　professional conduct 職業行為、職業倫理
　rules of conduct 紀律規則

confidence 名 信頼、信用、信任、秘密、内密、秘密保持 (⇒business confidence)
▸The firm reviewed its account settlement in an attempt to regain consumer *confidence*. 同社は、消費者の信頼回復に向けて決算の洗い直しをした。

conflict of interest 利害の対立、利害の衝突、利益相反、利益相反行為
▸The auditing firm's independent oversight board ordered the firm to split its auditing and consulting services to eliminate any *conflicts of interest*. 同監査法人の独立監視委員会は、業務上の利害の対立を排除するため、監査業務と経営コンサルタント業務の分離を同社に命じた。

conflict of risk 利害関係

conform to [with] … …に従う、…に準拠する、…に適合する、…に一致する、…に合致する、…に従わせる、…に適合させる、…に合わせる (⇒reclassify)
▸Certain prior year amounts on the consolidated statements of earnings and financial position have been reclassified to *conform to* the 2007 presentation. 連結損益計算書と連結貸借対照表上の一部の過年度金額は、2007年度の表示方法に従って組み替えられています。

conformity 名 適合、一致、順応、適合性、準拠性
　conformity with GAAP 一般に認められた会計原則 [会計基準] への準拠性 (⇒closing balance sheet)
　in conformity with … …に従って、…に準拠して、…に適合して
　lack of conformity 不適合性、契約不適合性
▸These consolidated financial statements present fairly the financial position of the corporation as at December 31, 2007 in *conformity* with Canadian GAAP. これらの連結財務書類は、カナダの会計基準に準拠して [従って]、2007年12月31日現在の同社の財政状態を適正に表示しています。

conglomerate 名 コングロマリット、巨大複合企業、複合企業、複合企業体、複合体、多角化企業、企業グループ (＝conglomerate company)
　conglomerate company 多角化企業、コングロマリット
　conglomerate financial statements 複合企業財務諸表
　conglomerate merger 複合的合併、コングロマリット合併 (無関係な業種あるいは無関係な商品の生産者同士の合併)
▸The FSA's guideline for supervising financial *conglomerate* is aimed at urging operators of financial *conglomerates* to reinforce their corporate governance to prevent irregularities. 金融庁の金融コングロマリット (複合体) 監督指針の狙いは、不正防止に向けて、金融コングロマリットの経営者に経営監視の強化を促すことにある。

consecutive 形 連続した、通しの、論理の一貫した

a consecutive dividend 安定配当
consecutive numbers 通し番号
for X consecutive years X年連続して, X年連続で, X年連続
mark the sixth consecutive quarterly growth 6四半期連続の増加[プラス成長]となる
register a third consecutive quarterly contraction in the growth rate 成長率が3四半期連続で縮小する

▸The settlements of accounts to March 31 for the companies listed on the First Section of the Tokyo Stock Exchange will show record highs for the third *consecutive* year. 東証1部上場企業の3月期決算は, 3年連続で過去最高を更新する見通しだ。

consensus 名 多数意見, 意見の一致, 合意
conservatism 名 保守主義, 保守主義の原則, 慎重性の原則(資産と収益は実現するまで計上せず, 負債と損失は予測に基づいて早めに認識する会計原則)
consider 動 考える, 考慮する, 見なす, 尊重する
consideration 名 対価, 代金, 手付け金, 〈契約の〉約因, 考慮
　as consideration for the services rendered pursuant to this agreement 本契約に従って提供されたサービスの対価として
　good consideration 有効な約因
　in consideration for the license of the trademark 商標の使用許諾の対価として, 商標使用許諾の対価として
　in consideration of the payment of ... …の支払いを約因として
　merger consideration 合併の対価 (⇒**acquirer, pay**)
　sufficient consideration 十分な約因, 有効な約因

▸We acquired 100 percent of the common shares outstanding of the company for a total *consideration* of $850 million. 当社は, 対価総額8億5,000万ドルで, 同社の発行済み普通株式を100%取得しました。

consign 動 委託する, 任せる, 委ねる, 引き渡す, 割り当てる

▸Since July 1971, all newly listed companies must *consign* the administration of their shares to third parties, such as trust banks. 1971年7月以降, 新規上場企業はすべて株式事務を信託銀行などの第三者に委託しなければならない。

consignment 名 委託販売, 委託売買, 委託販売品

consistency 名 継続性
consistency principle 継続性原則
consistent with ... …と一致する, …と整合する, …と矛盾しない, …と一貫性がある

▸Financial information used elsewhere in the annual report is *consistent with* that in the financial statements. この年次報告書の他の項(財務書類以外の項)で示した財務情報は, 財務書類上の財務情報と一致しています。

consistently 副 一貫して, 首尾一貫して

▸These financial statements have been prepared in accordance with the U.S. GAAP *consistently* applied throughout the periods indicated. これらの財務書類は, 当該期間中に一貫して適用した米国の一般に公正妥当と認められた会計原則[会計基準]に従って[準拠して]作成されています。

consolidate 動 連結する, 連結計上する, 連結対象にする, 整理統合する, 統廃合する, 統合する, 合併する, 一元化する, 一体化する, 整理する, 集約する, 強化する (⇒**consolidation**)

▸Steps to reduce costs include *consolidating* facilities, disposing of assets, reducing workforce or withdrawing from markets. コスト削減策としては, 施設の統合, 資産の処分, 人員削減や市場からの撤退などが考えられています。

▸When we raise our ownership in 2008, we will fully *consolidate* this venture in our financial statements. 2008年度に当社の持ち株比率が増加した時点で, 当社はこの事業を当社の財務諸表に全部連結[100%連結]する方針です。

consolidated 形 連結対象の, 連結した, 整理統合した, 統合した, 一本化した, 一元化した
　companies consolidated 連結対象子会社
　consolidated accounting period figures 連結決算 (=group accounting period figures)
　consolidated business profits 連結経常利益 (=consolidated pretax business profits)
　consolidated company 連結対象会社, 連結会社
　consolidated current account profit 連結計上利益
　consolidated entity 連結事業体, 連結主体
　consolidated equity 連結持ち分, 親会社持ち分 (=majority interest)
　consolidated excess 連結のれん, 連結超過額 (=consolidated goodwill, consolidation goodwill)
　consolidated funds statement 連結資金計算書
　consolidated income statement 連結損益計算書
　consolidated profit 連結利益

consolidated ratio 合併比率
consolidated recurring profit 連結経常利益, 企業グループの経常利益
consolidated return 連結納税申告, 連結納税申告書（＝consolidated tax return）
consolidated stockholders' equity 連結株主持ち分, 連結持ち分
consolidated tax provision 連結納税引当金
consolidated tax return 連結納税申告, 連結納税申告書（＝consolidated return）
consolidated tax system 連結税制, 連結納税制（＝consolidated tax payment system, consolidated tax return system, consolidated taxation system, corporate group tax system）
consolidated accounts 連結決算（＝consolidated accounting period figures）, 連結財務書類, 連結財務諸表（＝consolidated financial statements, group accounts）, 財務書類の連結（⇒account）
▶In its *consolidated accounts*, the Toyota group posted ¥21 trillion in sales with a net profit of ¥1.37 trillion, marking a record high for the fourth consecutive year. トヨタの連結決算で, トヨタ・グループの売上高が21兆円, 税引き後利益が1兆3,700億円となり, 4年連続で過去最高を記録した。

consolidated affiliate 連結対象の関連会社, 連結対象関連会社, 連結対象の持ち分法適用会社
▶We made the company our *consolidated affiliate*. 当社は, 同社を連結対象の関連会社としました。

consolidated after-tax deficit 連結税引き後赤字（＝consolidated after-tax loss）
▶The company's *consolidated after-tax deficit* reflects its sluggish sales and reduced asset values. 同社の連結税引き後赤字は, 販売不振や資産価値の低下を反映している。

consolidated after-tax loss 連結税引き後損失, 連結税引き後赤字
▶The company suffered ¥61 billion in *consolidated after-tax losses* at the end of fiscal 2007. 同社は, 2007年3月期［2007年度］に, 610億円の連結税引き後赤字に陥った。

consolidated after-tax profit 連結税引き後利益, 連結税引き後黒字
▶Sony has revised its projection for its fiscal 2005 *consolidated after-tax profit* from the ¥10 billion to a ¥10 billion loss. ソニーは, 2006年3月決算の連結税引き後利益の見通しを, 100億円の黒字から100億円の赤字に修正した。

consolidated balance sheet 連結貸借対照表（⇒**accompanying**）
▶We have audited the accompanying *consolidated balance sheets* of ABC Corporation and consolidated subsidiaries as of December 31, 2007 and 2006. 私どもは, 本報告書に記載されているABCコーポレーションと連結子会社の2007年および2006年12月31日現在の連結貸借対照表について監査を実施しました。

consolidated basis 連結ベース（＝group basis）
on a consolidated basis 連結ベースで, 一括して
▶We posted a record net profit of ¥1.18 trillion on a *consolidated basis* for the year ending March 31. 当社の3月期連結決算は, 税引き後利益［純利益］が過去最高の1兆1,800億円になりました［当社の3月期決算は, 連結ベースで税引き後利益が過去最高の1兆1,800億円になりました］。

consolidated earnings 連結利益, 連結純利益, 連結当期利益
▶Last fiscal year, earnings at the parent company accounted for 56 percent of Toyota's *consolidated earnings*. 前期［前年度］は, トヨタ本体の利益［トヨタの単独ベースの利益］が, 連結利益の56％を占めた。

consolidated earnings report 連結決算報告, 連結決算報告書, 連結業績報告書, 連結決算
consolidated earnings report for the April-September period 〈3月期決算企業の〉9月連結中間決算, 4-9月期の連結決算
▶According to the *consolidated earnings reports* of listed companies, 277 companies saw an average 2.4 percent increase in their sales for the year ended Mach 31. 上場企業の連結決算［決算報告］によれば, 277社が3月期決算で売上高が平均2.4％の増収となった。
▶In its *consolidated earnings report* for the April-September period, Yahoo Japan posted a net profit of ¥26.8 billion. ヤフーの9月連結中間決算で, ヤフーの税引き後利益は268億円となった。

consolidated financial statements 連結財務書類, 連結財務諸表, 合併財務諸表（＝consolidated accounts, group accounts）
連結財務書類について ➡ アニュアル・レポートや四半期報告書などで公表される米国企業の財務書類［財務諸表］は, ほぼ連結財務書類である。これは, 親会社（他の会社の発行済み株式の50％超を直接・間接に所有している会社）の財務書類と子会社の財務書類を合算して, 親会社を中心とした企業グループとしての経営成績と財政状態を表したものであ

る。なお、英国では、連結財務書類[連結財務諸表]のことをgroup accountsと呼んでいる。
▸The *consolidated financial statements* include the accounts of all majority owned subsidiaries, either direct or indirect. 連結財務書類には、直接所有と間接所有を問わず、過半数所有の全子会社の財務書類が含まれています。

consolidated first-half net profit 上半期[上期]の連結税引き後利益、上半期の連結純利益
▸*Consolidated first-half net profit* at the bank dropped 28 percent. 同行の上半期の連結税引き後利益は、28%減少した。

consolidated income 連結利益
▸The proportional contribution to *consolidated income* of individual ABC Inc. companies was somewhat skewed this year, largely due to the various provisions. 連結利益に対するABC各社の比例貢献度は、主に各種引当金の繰入れで、当期[当年度]はいくぶん片寄った結果となりました。

consolidated interest-bearing debt 連結有利子負債
▸We will reduce our *consolidated interest-bearing debts* to less than ¥1 trillion by the business term ending in March 2009. 当社は、2009年3月期までに連結有利子負債を1兆円以下に削減する方針です。

consolidated net capital expenditures 連結資本の支出純額
▸*Consolidated net capital expenditures* for the first six months of 2007 were $1,500 million. 2007年度上期[上半期]の連結資本的支出純額は、15億ドルでした。

consolidated net income 連結純利益、連結当期純利益(連結損益計算書上の利益)
consolidated net income applicable to common shares 普通株式に帰属する連結純利益
▸*Consolidated net income* applicable to common shares for the third quarter of 2007 was $294 million, compared with $337 million in the same period last year. 2007年第3四半期の普通株式に帰属する連結純利益は、前年同期の3億3,700万ドルに対して、2億9,400万ドルでした。
▸These provisions, after deducting the related tax and minority interest, reduced *consolidated net income* by $150 million. これらの引当金繰入れ額により、関連税額と少数株主持ち分利益控除後の連結純利益は、1億5千万ドル減少しました。

consolidated net loss 連結純損失、連結税引き後赤字、連結税引き後損失
▸The firm chalked up a *consolidated net loss* of ¥91.58 billion for the April-June quarter. 同社は、4-6月期は915億8,000万円の連結税引き後赤字となった。

consolidated net profit 連結純利益、連結税引き後利益、連結ベースの税引き後利益 (=consolidated net income, group net profit)
▸Sony's *consolidated net profit* rose 60.2 percent from a year earlier to ¥33.97 billion on sales of ¥3.60 trillion. ソニーの連結税引き後利益は、3兆6,000億円の売上高に対して、前年同期比60.2%増の339億7,000万円となった。

consolidated operating profit 連結営業利益、連結業務利益、金融機関の業務純益
▸In the year through March 31, the Corporation's *consolidated operating profit* plummeted 38 percent. 3月期決算で、当社の連結営業利益は38%減少しました。

consolidated operating profit margin 連結営業利益率
▸Sony expects to post more than 8 trillion in con-

年次報告書で開示される連結財務書類の例	
A社の場合	
Consolidated Balance Sheets	連結貸借対照表
Consolidated Statements of Income	連結損益計算書
Statements of Changes in Consolidated Financial Position	連結財政状態変動表
B社の場合	
Consolidated Statement of Cash Flows	連結資金フロー表
Consolidated Statement of Earnings	連結損益計算書
Consolidated Statement of Financial Position	連結貸借対照表
Consolidated Statement of Stockholders' Equity	連結株主持ち分計算書
C社の場合	
Consolidated Balance sheet	連結貸借対照表
Consolidated Statement of Changes in Financial Position	連結財政状態変動表
Consolidated Statement of Operations	連結損益計算書
Consolidated Statement of Retained Earnings	連結利益剰余金計算書

solidated sales and to mark a *consolidated operating profit margin* of 5 percent by the end of fiscal 2007.　ソニーは、2007年度末までに、連結売上高8兆円超と連結営業利益率5％の達成を目指している。

consolidated payout ratio　連結配当性向
▶Toyota is planning to bolster its *consolidated payout ratio* to around 30 percent on a net profit basis under its midterm business strategy.　トヨタは、中期経営戦略に従って、税引き後利益ベースで連結配当性向を約30％まで高める方針だ。

consolidated pretax profit　連結経常利益、連結税引き前利益
▶Sony's *consolidated pretax profit* in the first half of fiscal 2006 plunged by 74.2 percent from a year earlier.　ソニーの2006年度上期［2006年9月中間決算］の連結税引き前利益は、前年同期比で74.2％減少した。

consolidated revenues　連結売上高、連結収益（親会社と子会社とで構成されている連結企業グループ全体としての売上高［収益］）
▶*Consolidated revenues* in 2007 were $5.41 billion, up 10 percent from $4.91 billion in 2006.　2007年［2007年度］の連結売上高は54.1億ドルで、前年［前年度］の49.1億ドルから10％増加しました。

consolidated sales　連結売上高、連結ベースの売上高　（⇒consolidated operating profit margin）
▶Toyota's *consolidated sales*, which surpassed ¥10 trillion in the business term ending in March 1997, doubled to ¥21 trillion in the following nine years.　トヨタの連結売上高は、1997年3月期に10兆円を突破した後、9年間で21兆円に倍増した。

consolidated statement　連結計算書
consolidated statement of cash flows　連結資金フロー計算書、連結キャッシュ・フロー表［計算書］
consolidated statement of changes in financial position　連結財政状態変動表
consolidated statement of earnings　連結損益計算書
consolidated statement of financial position　連結貸借対照表
consolidated statement of income　連結損益計算書
consolidated statement of operations　連結損益計算書　（＝consolidated statement of earnings）
consolidated statement of retained earnings　連結利益剰余金計算書、連結剰余金計算書
consolidated statement of source and application of fund　連結資金計算書　（＝consolidated funds statement）
consolidated statement of stockholders' [shareholders'] equity　連結株主持ち分計算書、連結資本勘定計算書、連結資本勘定表

consolidated subsidiary　連結子会社、連結対象子会社
▶Hanshin became Hankyu's *consolidated subsidiary* on June 27.　阪神は、6月27日付けで阪急の連結子会社になった。

consolidated taxation　連結納税　（＝consolidated tax payment）
▶In this *consolidated taxation*, losses from one company in a group are subtracted from the profits of another group company in calculating taxable income, reducing the group's overall tax burdens.　この連結納税では、グループ内の会社の損失［赤字］を同じグループ内の別会社の利益［黒字］から差し引いて［控除して］課税所得を算出するため、グループ企業全体の税負担が軽くなる。

consolidation　名　連結、連結決算、新設合併、統合、企業統合、整理、再編、強化、地固め　（⇒full consolidation）

「連結（consolidation）」について　➡会計用語の［連結］は、簡単にいえば、親会社を中心とする企業グループを一つの企業とみなして、親会社（parent company）と子会社（subsidiary）の損益を合算することをいう。

しかし、子会社が全部連結の対象になる［連結の範囲に含まれる］わけではない。米国企業の場合は、親会社が保有する子会社の株式保有の割合によって連結の範囲が決まり、連結の対象になった子会社を連結対象子会社・連結子会社（consolidated subsidiary）、連結の対象から外された子会社を非連結子会社（unconsolidated subsidiary）という。

連結の範囲の基準としては、基本的に「他社の発行済み議決権株式（outstanding voting stock）の50％超（過半数）を直接間接に所有している場合、その会社を連結の範囲に含める」ことになっている。ここで議決権とは、株主が会社の総会で取締役の選任などの決議に参加する権利のことで、株主の議決権はその持ち株1株について1個与えられる。ただし、会社が持っている自社株や優先株に議決権はない。また、議決権株式の過半数を所有していても、その企業支配の関係が一時的なものや、更生会社や破産会社など過半数所有が実質的な企業支配に当たらない場合には、連結の範囲に含めないことになっている。

accounting consolidation　連結会計
accounting for consolidation　連結決算

budget consolidation 財政建て直し
capital consolidation 資本連結
consolidation and closure 統廃合, 統合と閉鎖
consolidation basis 連結の基準, 連結の方針 (＝basis of consolidation)
consolidation by purchase 買収方式による連結, パーチェス方式(purchase method)による買収
consolidation date 連結決算日
consolidation excess 連結のれん, 連結超過額 (＝consolidated excess, consolidated goodwill, consolidation goodwill)
consolidation goodwill 連結のれん (＝consolidated excess, consolidated goodwill)
consolidation group 連結企業グループ, 連結対象の会社グループ, 連結集団 (＝consolidated group)
consolidation of all majority-owned subsidiaries すべての過半数所有子会社の連結
consolidation of corporations 会社の新設合併
consolidation of shares 株式併合 (＝consolidation of stocks)
consolidation of stocks 株式併合 (＝consolidation of shares)
consolidation surplus 連結剰余金
debt consolidation fund 国債整理基金
economic consolidation 経済調整
facility consolidation 工場統廃合
full consolidation 全部連結, 総額連結
in consolidation 連結上, 連結決算上
industry consolidation 業界統合, 業界再編
line-by-line consolidation 全科目連結, 各行連結
market consolidation 市場再編, 市場統合
one-line consolidation 1行連結, 純額連結 (＝equity method：非連結子会社と関連会社の株式に対して持ち分法(equity method)を適用すること)
partial consolidation 部分連結
principles of consolidation 連結の方針
proportional [proportionate] consolidation 比例連結
staff consolidation 人員整理
scope of consolidation 連結の範囲 (＝consolidation criteria)
stock consolidation 株式併合 (＝share consolidation)
▶The company will be urged to pursue a large-scale *consolidation* of its stores and cut its workforce.　同社は今後, 大規模な店舗の統廃合や人員削減を迫られるのは必至だ。
▶The summarized financial information includes transactions with the company that are eliminated in *consolidation*.　要約財務情報には, 連結では消去されている同社との取引が含まれています。
consolidation criteria 連結の範囲, 連結範囲の基準 (＝scope of consolidation：米国企業の場合は, 親会社が保有する子会社の株式保有の割合によって連結の範囲が決まり, 連結の対象になった子会社を連結対象子会社・連結子会社(consolidated subsidiary), 連結の対象から外された子会社を非連結子会社(unconsolidated sub-sidiary)という)
consolidation policy 連結方針, 連結の方針 (＝principles of consolidation)

連結方針の表示例

関連会社所有比率		会計処理方法	
More than 50%	50%超	Fully consolidated	全部連結
20% to 50%	20%～50%	Equity method	持ち分法
Less than 20%	20% 以下	Cost method	原価法

consortium 名 国際借款団, 〈銀行の〉協調融資団, 債権国会議, 共同事業体, 共同連合体, 企業連合, 組合, コンソーシアム (⇒accept, balance, investment consortium)
　a consortium of companies 合弁企業
　a consortium of lenders 融資団, 融資グループ (⇒revolving credit facility)
▶The Japanese *consortium* will be responsible for production of nearly 50 percent or more than 10 million cubic meters of natural gas per day in the Pars South gas field.　日本の企業連合体は, イランの南パルス・ガス田については, 約50％, 日量1,000万立方メートル以上の生産に当たることになっている。
constant dollar 統一ドル, 恒常ドル, 一定ドル (＝constant purchasing power)
　constant dollar accounting 統一ドル会計, 恒常ドル会計, 一般購買力会計, 安定価値会計 (＝constant purchasing power accounting)
　constant dollar basis 実質ベース, 恒常ドル基準, 恒常ドル・ベース
　constant dollar reporting 統一ドルによる報告, 実質ベースの報告
constituent company 構成会社 (連結グループに含まれる会社)
construction 名 建設, 工事, 建造物, 構築物, 〈契約や条項の〉解釈 (⇒construe)

advance on construction 建設工事前渡し金
construction in progress 建設仮勘定, 未成工事支出金 （＝construction in process）
construction loan 建設借入金, 建設融資, 建設ローン
construction of completion 完成工事高
construction of cost 原価構成
construction revenue 工事収益 （＝construction in progress）
construction-type contract 請負工事契約
construction work account receivable 建設工事未収金
estimated cost of construction work 見積り工事原価
income on construction 工事利益
interest on construction 建設中の支払い利息
reserve for construction work guarantee 工事補償引当金
▸The Company has executed two contracts with the firm for the *construction* and operation of the global communications system. 当社は, 国際通信システムの建設と運用のために同社と2件の契約を結びました。

construe 動 解釈する
consumer 名 消費者, コンシューマー
▸Companies should recycle their profits to *consumers*. 企業は, 利益を消費者に還元すべきだ。

Consumer Credit Protection Act of 1968
〖米〗1968年消費者信用保護法（信用条件の開示, 強要的信用取引や信用情報などに関する規定がある）

consumer electronics 家電製品
▸NEC's first-quarter net loss narrowed as it sold more semiconductors used in *consumer electronics*. NECの第1四半期の税引き後赤字は, 家電製品に用いられる半導体の販売増で縮小した。

consumer product 消費者製品, 消費財
▸The company plans to make drugs and other *consumer product* operations the company's core business. 同社は, 医薬品などの消費者製品事業を同社の主力事業にする方針だ。

contain 動 抑える, 抑制する, 阻止する, 歯止めをかける, 削減する, 含む, …に等しい
▸The Company's increased profitability continued to be primarily affected during 2007 by significant volume increases combined with its efforts to *contain* costs. 当社の2007年度の収益向上は, 前年度に続いて主に経費削減努力と大幅な販売数量の増加によるものです。

contender 名 競争相手, 対抗馬, 候補, ライバル

content 名 情報の内容, 情報の中身, 情報, 著作物,〈ラジオやテレビの〉番組, 番組の内容, コンテンツ
▸As the *content* of our products shifts from hardware to software, we require less manufacturing, assembly and test facilities. 当社の製品内容がハードウェアからソフトウェアに移行するに伴い, 当社では製造・組立施設や試験施設の必要性が減少しています。

contents 名 内容目次, 目次 （＝table of contents）

株主向け年次報告書の目次内容表示例

Financial highlights	財務報告ハイライト
Letter to shareholders	株主の皆さまへ（会長・社長の挨拶）
A year of global achievement	グローバル化推進の1年
Financial review	財務概況
Consolidated financial statements	連結財務書類
Consolidated Income Statement	連結損益計算書
Consolidated Balance Sheet	連結貸借対照表
Consolidated Statement of Retained Earnings	連結利益剰余金計算書
Consolidated Statement of Changes in Financial Position	連結財政状態変動表
Notes to consolidated financial statement	連結財務書類注記
Management's responsibility for financial statements	財務書類に対する経営者の責任
Auditors' report	監査報告書
11-year review	11年間の財務概況
Directors	取締役
Officers	役員
Principal subsidiaries	主要子会社

contingency 名 偶発事象, 偶発事項, 不測の事態, 緊急事態, 臨時費用
accounting for contingencies 偶発事象の会計
contingency fund 偶発資金, 偶発危険準備金 （＝contingent fund）
contingency reserve 偶発損失引当金［準備金］, 偶発損失積立金
disclosure of loss contingencies 偶発損失の開示
gain contingency 偶発利益事象, 偶発利益
loss contingencies 偶発損失事象
off-balance-sheet contingencies オフバランスの偶発債務
reserve for contingencies 偶発損失引当金, 偶

contingent

発損失積立金（＝reserve for possible future losses）

transaction-related contingencies 取引関連偶発債務

▶We provided $30 million for legal *contingencies* in 2007. 2007年度は、法的偶発債務費として3,000万ドルを計上しました。

contingent 形 偶発の、不確定の、不確かな、臨時の、…を条件とする、…に付随する

　contingent annuity 不確定年金、臨時払い年金
　contingent charge [cost] 偶発費用（＝contingent expense）
　contingent fee 成功報酬
　contingent gain 偶発利益、偶発利得（＝contingent profit, gain contingency）
　contingent issues 臨時発行証券、条件付き証券
　contingent liability 偶発債務（現時点で債務は発生していないが、係争事件で賠償義務が生じるとか保証付きで商品を販売する場合など、将来発生する可能性がある未確定の債務）
　contingent loss 偶発損失
　contingent profit 偶発利益（＝contingent gain）
　contingent rent 偶発賃借料、条件付賃借料
　contingent reserve 偶発損失引当金、偶発損失積立金（＝contingency reserve, reserve for contingencies, special contingency reserve）

▶The Company is likely to suffer *contingent* liabilities as it will face a damages suit. 当社は今後、損害賠償訴訟を起こされるので、偶発債務が生じる可能性がある。

continue to ... 引き続き…する、継続して…する、今後とも…する、…を維持する

▶If we are to *continue to* deliver improved financial results, we must continue to enhance our competitiveness. 今後とも業績[財務成績]向上を図るには、当社の競争力を引き続き高める必要があります。

continuity 名 連続性、継続性
　business continuity 経営継続性
　continuity of existence 永続性
　continuity of sales 安定した売れ行き
　continuity principle 継続性原則

contract 名 契約、契約書、規約、協定、協定書、請負、契約商品、契約品、約定品
　contract amount 契約高
　contract charge 契約手数料
　contract construction 請負工事
　contract deposit paid 契約前渡し金
　contract deposit received 契約前受金

contract winner 元受業者、契約獲得企業、受注者、施工業者（＝the winner of a contract）

contract work account receivable 請負工事未収金

▶Companies have been entering into *contracts* with the temporary staffing agency that can offer the lowest dispatch fees. 企業は、いちばん安い派遣料を提示できる人材派遣会社と契約[派遣料契約]を結んでいる。

contractual obligation 契約義務、契約上の義務

▶Provisions for business restructuring include the estimated costs of specific plans to close offices, consolidate facilities, relocate employees and fulfill *contractual obligations*. 事業再編成引当金には、事業所の閉鎖や施設統合、従業員の再配置、契約義務の履行など特定の計画に対する見積り費用が含まれています。

contribute 動 出資する、払い込む、納付する、拠出する、寄与する、貢献する、協力する、支援する、…に一役買う、…の要因になる（⇒**guideline**）
　contributed capital 払込み資本、拠出資本（株主が払い込んだ資本）（＝paid-in capital）
　contributed surplus 払込み剰余金、資本準備金

▶It is our goal to increase the proportion of earnings *contributed* by the non-regulated business sector. 規制対象外の事業部門の利益貢献度拡大が、当社の目標です。

contributing factor 貢献要因、…をもたらした要因

▶Another *contributing factor* of the increase in operating expenses was an increase in salaries and wages for employees. 営業費用の増加をもたらした他の要因としては、従業員の給与・賃金の引上げを挙げることもできます。

contribution 名 出資、拠出、寄与、貢献、寄付、協力、支援、貢献額、寄付金、拠出金、負担金、掛け金、分担金、共同海損分担金、負担部分、求償権、保険料、納付金（⇒**defined contribution pension scheme, match**）
　additional contribution 追加拠出
　associate contribution 関連会社の利益寄与
　capital contribution 資本拠出、出資
　contribution profit or loss 貢献損益
　contribution to capital 出資金、資本への拠出額
　contribution to affiliated companies 関係会社出資金
　contributions and equity 出資と持ち分
　contributions to retirement funds 退職基金への拠出金

defined contribution plan 確定拠出制度
divisional contribution 事業部貢献利益 （= divisional contribution margin）
employee contributions 従業員の拠出金
equity contribution 出資
national contribution ratio 国民負担率(個人と企業の所得に占める税金と社会保険料の割合)
profit contribution 利益貢献度, 利益寄与
social insurance contribution 社会保険料

▶Our *contributions* to the savings plans amounted to $330 million in 2007. 当社の貯蓄制度に対する会社側の拠出額は, 2007年度は3億3,000万ドルでした。

▶The company's *contributions* to our net income in the third quarter were $250 million ($230 million in 2006). 当社の第3四半期の純利益に対する同社の貢献額は, 2億5,000万ドル(前年同期は2億3,000万ドル)でした。

contributor 名 貢献要因, 貢献[寄与]したもの （=contributing factor）

▶The main *contributors* to revenue growth were increased product and system sales outside the U.S. 収益の伸びに主に貢献したのは, 米国外での製品とシステムの売上の増加です。

contributory plan 拠出型制度, 拠出型年金制度, 拠出制年金制度

control 動 支配する, 経営権を握る, 経営支配権を得る, 掌握する, 管理する, 抑制する, 抑える, 操作する （⇒**buy back**）
　completely control one's subsidiaries 100％経営支配権を得る, 完全に経営権を握る
　control quality 品質管理をする
　control working capital 運転資金を抑える
　controlled company 被支配会社, 傘下企業, 従属会社, 子会社 （=subsidiary）
　controlled foreign corporation 在外子会社, 在外従属会社《略 CFC》

▶Stock swaps allow the acquirer to purchase the company it wants to *control* without preparing a large sum of cash. 株式交換だと, 買収企業は多額の現金を用意しなくても, 相手先企業[経営権を握りたいと思う企業]を買収することができる。

control 名 支配, 統制, 管理, 経営支配権, 経営権, 規制, 抑制, 制御, コントロール （⇒**cost control**, **internal control**, **quality control**）
　administrative control 管理統制, 管理上の統制, 業務統制, 行政監査, 運営管理コントロール
　capital control 資本規制, 資本取引規制
　change of control 資本拘束
　control environment 統制環境

control of ownership 経営権
corporate control 企業経営
credit control 与信管理, 信用管理, 信用規制, 信用制限, 信用統制 （=credit management）
inventory control 在庫管理
majority control 過半数所有支配, 過半数子会社
management control 経営支配
minority control 少数支配, 少数派支配
monetary control 金融調節 （=monetary adjustment）
process control 工程管理
separation of ownership and control 所有と経営の分離
take control of ... …の経営権を握る[掌握する], …の経営権を支配する, …の主導権を握る
take full control of ... …の経営権を完全に掌握する, …を完全子会社化する
under state control 国の管理下にある, 国有化されている

▶The purpose of issuing a sizable amount of new shares is to maintain the *control* of a specific stockholder over the company. 新株の大量発行は, 同社に対する特定株主の支配権[経営支配権]確保が目的だ。

▶We will focus on even more rigorous credit *control* to avoid risks. 当社は, 一段と厳しい与信管理を徹底して, リスク回避を図る方針です。

controller 名 経理部長, 財務部長, 管理部長, 会計監査役, 会計検査役, コントローラー （=comptroller：米大手企業の「コントローラー(controller)」は, 会社の資金調達や運用などの財務部門を統括する役員の「トレジャラー(treasurer)」と違って, 会社の経理や会計監査など経理部門の統括者。中小企業の場合は, トレジャラーがコントローラーを兼務することもある。⇒**treasurer**）
　chief controller [**comptroller**] 財務部長, 経理部長
　controller of audit 監査責任者

controlling company 支配会社, 親会社
controlling interest 支配(的)持ち分, 支配株主持ち分, 経営支配権, 経営支配株 （=controlling stake：「経営支配権」とは, 一般には他社を支配できる議決権株式(voting stock)の過半数(50%超)を所有することをいう）

▶GM may sell a *controlling interest* in its profitable finance arm, General Motors Acceptance Corp. (GMAC). GMは, 同社の収益性の高い金融子会社GMACの経営支配株を売却する可能性もある。

controlling shareholder 支配株主
controlling stake 支配持ち分, 支配株主持ち

分, 経営支配権 （＝controlling interest）
▸The tender offer to acquire a *controlling stake* of more than 50 percent in the company will last through December 10. 同社の50％超の経営支配権[支配持ち分]取得をめざした株式公開買付け(TOB)の期限は, 12月10日までの予定だ。

conversion 图 転換, 換算, 両替, 交換, 借換え, 〈公債などの〉切替え, 加工 （⇒**book value method**)
　about 6 million tons (in liquefied natural gas conversion) of natural gas 約600万トン（液化天然ガス換算）の天然ガス
　bond conversion 社債転換, 社債の転換, 転換社債の株式への転換
　conversion clause 転換条項
　conversion issue 借換え発行
　conversion of convertible debentures 転換社債の転換, 転換社債の株式への転換
　conversion of stock 株式転換
　conversion of warrants ワラントの権利行使
　conversion period 転換期間
　conversion price 転換価格（転換証券を普通株式に転換する場合の株式1株当たり価格）
　conversion privilege 転換条項, 転換特約
　conversion rate [ratio] 外貨換算率, 交換比率, 転換比率（転換証券を普通株式に転換する場合に何株と交換できるかを示す比率）, 転換割合 （＝**convertible rate [ratio]**)
　conversion value 転換価値（転換によって入手できる普通株式の時価）
　date of conversion 転換日, 転換時
　debt-equity conversion 債務の株式化
　effective conversion price 実効転換価格
　interest rate conversion agreement 利率[利子率]変更契約
▸On May 10, 2007, individuals holding $50,000 face value of of the Corporation's bonds exercised their *conversion* privilege. 2007年5月10日に, 当社の社債権者が, 額面5万ドル分の転換権を行使しました[額面5万ドル分の株式への転換を行いました]。

convert 動 転換する, 変える, 加工する, 改造する, 流用する, 〈公債などを〉切り替える, 振り替える, 換算する, 両替する, 元金に繰り入れる （⇒**inflate**)
▸The shares were *converted* into approximately 18 million shares of our common stock upon consummation of the merger. この株式は, 合併完了時に約1,800万株の当社普通株式に転換されました。

convertible 形 転換可能な, 転換できる, 転換性のある, 変換[交換]可能な
　convertible class A preferred stock 転換権付きクラスA優先株式
　convertible preferred stock 転換優先株式, 転換権付き優先株式
　convertible stock [share] 転換株式
▸All the first preferred shares are *convertible* into common shares. 第一優先株式は, すべて普通株式への転換が可能です。

convertible bond 転換社債《略CB》 （＝convertible debenture, convertible debt, convertible loan stock; ⇒**book value method**)
　convertible bond payable 転換社債
　convertible bonds with put option プット・オプション付き転換社債
▸These *convertible bonds* are not considered common stock equivalents. これらの転換社債は, 準普通株式とは考えられていません。

convertible note 転換社債, 兌換券
▸Ford increased the amount of *convertible notes* it is offering to $4.5 billion from $3 billion announced previously. フォードは, 転換社債の発行規模を当初計画[当初発表]の30億ドルから45億ドルに引き上げた。

convertible subordinated debenture 転換劣後社債, 劣後転換社債, 後順位転換社債
▸The Company completed a $100 million 8% *convertible subordinated debenture* issue during 2007. 当社は, 2007年に利率8％の転換劣後社債1億ドルの発行を完了しました。

COO 最高業務運営役員, 最高業務運営責任者, 最高執行責任者（chief operating officerの略）

cook 動 〈帳簿などを〉ごまかす, 〈勘定を〉手加減する
　cook books 帳簿に手を加える, 帳簿をごまかす, 帳簿を改竄する, 粉飾する （＝cook the books）
▸The company *cooked* books to cover loss. 同社は, 帳簿を改竄して損失[赤字]を補塡した。

cooperation 图 協力, 協同, 協調, 協業, 共同作業, 提携, 提供, 援助
　business cooperation 事業提携, 業務提携
　capital cooperation 資本提携 （＝cooperation by holding capital）
　patent cooperation 特許協力
　simple cooperation 単純協業
　technical cooperation 技術提携, 技術提供
▸Mitsui Fudosan and Imperial Hotel are considering *cooperation* in redeveloping Tokyo's Hibiya area. 三井不動産と帝国ホテルは, 東京・日比谷地区の再開発での提携を検討している。

core 名形 核, 中心, 核心, 芯, 中核, 中枢, 主力, 主軸, 基本モデル, 基本設計, 〈原子炉の〉炉心, コア, 核となる, 軸となる, 中心的な, 中核的な, 核心的な, 基本的な, 本業の
 core activities 中核事業
 core bank 主力銀行, 主力行, 主力取引銀行
 core capital 中核的自己資本, 自己資本の基本的項目, 基本的資本項目, コア資本
 core capitalization コア資本
 core company 中核企業
 core deposit intangibles コア預金無形資産
 core element 中核の要素
 core ideology 基本理念
 core inflation コア・インフレ率, 基礎インフレ率, コア指数 (＝core rate of inflation)
 core issue 核心的な問題
 core operation 中核事業, 主力事業, 基幹事業 (＝core business; ⇒fundamental profit)
 core portion of one's capital base 中核的自己資本, 自己資本
 core producer prices 生産者物価のコア部分の指数, 生産者物価指数コア部分
 core product line 主要製品, 主力製品
 core profit コア利益, 主力事業の利益, 生命保険会社の基礎利益
 core profitability 主力事業の収益性, コア収益性, コア収益
 core values 基本的価値観
▸JAL's *core* aviation business posted an operating loss of ¥3.4 billion in the six months through September 2006. 日本航空の本業の航空事業は, 2006年9月の中間決算で, 34億円の営業損失［営業赤字］を計上した。
▸Mizuho Financial Group Inc. will float preferred securities to domestic institutional investors to enhance the *core* portion of its capital base. みずほフィナンシャルグループ（FG）は, 自己資本［中核的自己資本］を増強するため, 国内の機関投資家向けに優先出資証券を発行する。
core business 中核事業, 中核業務, 中核企業, 主力事業, 基幹事業, 根幹業務, 本業, コア・ビジネス (＝core activities, core operation)
▸Our *core business* is to meet the communications and computing needs of our customers by using networks to move and manage information. 当社の中核事業は, 情報の伝送と処理にネットワークを利用して, 顧客のコミュニケーションとコンピューティングの必要性に応えることです。
core capital rate [ratio] 中核的自己資本比率 (＝Tier 1 capital rate, tier-one capital ratio)

▸The bank's *core capital rate* falls behind those of many major European and U.S. banks. 同行の中核的自己資本比率は, 欧米の多くの大手銀行を下回っている。
core competence 中核的業務, 中核能力, 企業固有の技術（スキルや技術）, 企業固有の競争力の核, 自社ならではの強み, コア・コンピテンス (noncore competence＝非中核業務, ノンコア業務)
core earnings 中核事業収益, 主力事業の収益, コア収益
▸Group operating profit shows a company's *core earnings* strength. 連結営業利益は, 企業の主力事業の収益力［本業のもうけ］を示す。
core operating profit 〈生命保険会社の本業のもうけに当たる〉基礎利益 (＝core profit; ⇒**dividend income**)
▸The increase in seven insurers' *core operating profits* is due to appraisal gains in their stockholdings. 生保7社の基礎利益の増加は, 保有株式の含み益によるものだ。
core strategy 基本戦略, 主力戦略, 中核戦略
▸Customer focus is our *core strategy* for weathering the forces of competition. 顧客志向は, 競争圧力に対応するための当社の基本戦略です。
corporate 形 企業の, 会社の, 共通の, 共同の, コーポレート
 corporate bond 社債 (＝corporate debenture)
 corporate breakup 企業分割
 corporate costs 企業経費, 一般管理費
 corporate credit quality 企業の信用力, 企業の信用の質
 corporate defensive measure 企業防衛策 (⇒**defensive measure**)
 corporate enterprise 法人企業
 corporate enterprise tax 法人事業税, 法人税 (＝corporate tax)
 corporate financial health 企業の財務健全性
 corporate loans 法人向け融資, 企業向け融資, 企業向け貸出
 corporate rebuilding plan 企業再建計画, 経営再建計画, 再建計画
 corporate reconstruction 企業再建, 企業再生
 corporate reconstruction fund 企業再生ファンド (＝corporate turnaround fund)
 corporate safeguards 企業防衛策
 corporate social report 企業社会報告
 corporate spending 企業の支出, 設備投資
 corporate turnaround fund 企業再生ファンド
corporate accounting 企業会計, 企業の会計処理, 企業の会計処理方法, 企業の経理, 会社会

計 (⇒collapse)

corporate accounting principles 企業会計原則
▸*Corporate accounting principles* prohibit companies from including profits gained through selling their own shares in their gains in a profit and loss statement. 自社株の売却益を損益計算書で自社の利益に計上することは、企業会計原則[企業会計基準]で禁じられている。

corporate assets 全社一般資産, 本社資産, 会社資産, 企業資産, 本部資産
▸*Corporate assets* are principally cash and temporary cash investments. 本社資産は、主に現金と短期投資です。

corporate charter 会社定款 (=corporation charter)
▸The power of a veto is used to make important management decisions such as mergers or revision of *corporation charters* at shareholders meetings. 拒否権は、株主総会で合併や会社定款などの重要な経営の意思決定を行う際に行使される。

corporate citizen [**citizenship**] 企業市民, 市民としての企業, コーポレート・シティズン
▸We are committed to being a good *corporate citizen* and a responsible neighbor in the communities in which we live and work. 当社は、生活や労働の場としている地域社会の善良な企業市民であると同時に責任感の強い隣人でありたいと考えています。

corporate culture 企業文化, 企業の体質, 企業風土, 社風, コーポレート・カルチャー
▸*Corporate culture* can be a hurdle in a merger. 統合では、企業風土が障害になる場合もある。
▸It does not reflect the reality of Japanese *corporate culture* to define all mergers as takeovers. 合併をすべて吸収合併と見なすやり方は、日本の企業風土の実態を反映していない。

corporate debt securities 債券
▸The assets of the various plans include corporate equities, government securities, *corporate debt securities* and income-producing real estate. 各種制度の年金資産は、株式、政府証券、債券や収益を稼得する不動産などで構成されています。

corporate earnings 企業収益, 企業業績
　corporate earnings growth 企業収益の改善
　corporate earnings performance 企業収益
▸A rise in *corporate earnings* will stimulate private spending, as it will boost individual income through wage raises and bigger bonuses. 企業業績の上昇は、賃上げやボーナス増で個人所得を増大させ、個人消費を刺激することになる。

corporate employee pension insurance 〖日〗厚生年金保険
▸The Pension Fund Association restarted operations as a special privately owned corporation based on a law on *corporate employee pension insurance* in 2005. 企業年金連合会(旧特殊法人「厚生年金基金連合会」)は、厚生年金保険法に基づく特別民間法人として2005年に再スタートした。

corporate employee pension plan 〖日〗厚生年金制度, 厚生年金
▸The Employees Pension Fund supports the public *corporate employee pension plan*. 厚生年金基金は、公的な厚生年金制度を支えている。

corporate employee pension system 〖日〗厚生年金制度, 厚生年金
▸The Social Insurance Agency paid out less in *corporate employee* and basic *pension system* benefits to elderly subscribers. 社会保険庁が、高齢加入者に厚生年金や基礎年金(国民年金)の給付金を少なく支給していた。

corporate finance 企業金融, 企業財務, 企業の資金調達, 法人金融, コーポレート・ファイナンス
　corporate finance sector 企業金融部門

corporate goal 企業目標, 会社目標
▸When we look to our quarterly results, we are always reminded of our longer term *corporate goals*. 各四半期の業績を検討するにあたって、私たちがつねに想起するのは、当社の長期的な企業目標です。

corporate governance 会社の管理・運営, 会社管理法, 企業統治, 企業支配, 経営監視, コーポレート・ガバナンス(株主や取締役、監査役などによる経営チェック・システム)
　corporate governance reform bill 企業統治改革法案
　corporate governance system コーポレート・ガバナンス体制
▸We have developed a *corporate governance* framework based on a system comprising corporate auditors, directors and outside direcors and a system of voluntary committees. 当社は、監査役、取締役と外部取締役を置く制度と任意の委員会制度に基づくコーポレート・ガバナンス体制を構築しています。
▸We regard the establishment and operation of properly functioning *corporate governance* systems as an important management issue. 当社は、適切に機能するコーポレート・ガバナンス体制の確立と運営を経営の重要課題の一つと位置付けて

います。

corporate income 法人所得, 企業所得
  corporate income tax 法人所得税, 法人税, 企業所得税
  corporate income taxes payable 未払い法人税等
  ▸China's *corporate income* tax is similar to Japan's corporate tax. 中国の企業所得税は, 日本の法人税に相当する.

corporate management 企業経営, 会社経営
  ▸Under the Commercial Code, to gain approval for an important resolution that directly affects *corporate management*, shareholders holding at least 50 percent of shares with voting rights must cast ballots, and two-thirds must back the motion. 商法で, 企業の経営に直接影響を及ぼす重要決議の承認を得るには, 議決権株式の少なくとも50%を保有する株主が投票し, 提案に対してその3分の2の支持を得る必要がある.

corporate officer 〈企業の〉業務執行役員, 執行役員, 株式会社の役員, 会社役員
  ▸The firm will introduce a *corporate officer* under a new system. 同社は, 新たに執行役員制度を導入する.

corporate pension plan 企業年金制度（⇒**employee pension**）
  ▸Companies are responsible for the pension fund investment under conventional *corporate pension plans*. 従来からの企業年金制度では, 企業が年金積立金の運用に責任を負っている.

corporate performance 企業収益, 企業業績, 会社業績, 決算 （⇒**accelerate**）
  ▸*Corporate performance* has improved at varying rates in different industries and companies. 企業の業績回復には, 業種間, 企業間で差がある.

corporate reform 企業改革
  ▸There also is a growing trend for shareholders to press for *corporate reform*. 株主が企業改革への圧力を高める傾向も, 強まっている.

corporate rehabilitation 企業再建, 経営再建
  corporate rehabilitation fund 企業再建ファンド, 企業再建基金
  Corporate Rehabilitation Law [日]会社更生法
  corporate rehabilitation plan 経営再建計画, 企業再建計画

corporate report 会社報告書, コーポレート・レポート（英国の会社の営業報告書と財務諸表の総称）

corporate social responsibility 企業の社会的責任《略 CSR》(企業の社会的責任には, 地域社会に対する責任のほかに, 環境や法令遵守, 社員の権利尊重などが含まれる)
  ▸The Corporation is responsible for its people and to the communities where they live and work as a *corporare social responsibility*. 当社は, 企業の社会的責任として, 従業員のみならず従業員が生活して働いている地域社会に対しても責任を負っている.

corporate strength 企業体質, 企業力, 企業の強み
  ▸Businesses need to reinforce their *corporate strength*. 企業は, 企業体質を強化する必要がある.

corporate tax 法人税, 法人事業税(企業の利潤に対して課される国税)
  corporate tax on gross operating profit 外形標準課税(業務粗利益への法人事業税[法人税]の課税)
  corporate tax rate 法人税率

corporate value 企業価値
  corporate value assessment 企業価値の評価
  raise corporate value 企業価値を高める
  ▸Market capitalization is the only fair indicator of *corporate value* for stock companies. 時価総額は, 株式会社の企業価値を示す唯一の公正な指標である.

corporation 名 会社, 企業, 法人, 株式会社, 団体, コーポレーション
  audit corporation 監査法人
  business corporation 事業会社, 法人企業, 営利法人, 株式会社（＝stock company）, 商社（＝trading corporation）, 会社
  corporation income 法人所得, 法人利益, 会社の利益
  corporation income tax 法人税
  Corporation Tax Act 法人税法
  mutual corporation 相互会社
  open corporation 公開会社, 株式公開会社
  ordinary corporation 普通法人
  profit corporation 営利企業, 営利会社, 営利法人, 会社 （＝profit organization）
  public corporation 株式公開企業, 公共企業体
  special purpose corporation 特別目的会社 （＝special purpose company）
  stock corporation 株式会社 （＝joint stock company, stock company）
  twenty percent corporation 20%所有法人
  ▸The power of veto is used to make important management decisions such as mergers or revi-

sion of *corporation* charters at shareholders meetings.　拒否権は、株主総会で合併や会社定款などの重要な経営の意思決定を行う際に行使される。

correct 動　訂正する, 是正する, 補正する, 調整する
▸The company will *correct* financial statements on its portfolio since March 2003.　同社は、2003年3月以降の有価証券報告書の財務諸表を訂正する。

cost 動　〈費用などが〉かかる, 必要とする, 要する, 原価計算をする, 原価を見積もる
▸The recall and replacement would *cost* as much as ¥50 billion.　今回のリコール［自主回収と無償交換］の負担額は、500億円規模に達する。

cost 名　原価, 費用, 経費, 原価法, コスト　(⇒ **borrowing costs, credit cost, production cost**)
　abandonment cost　固定資産の除却費
　at factor cost　要素費用表示
　business costs　事業コスト
　capital cost　資本費用, 資本コスト　(＝cost of capital, cost of equity：資金調達にかかった費用で、借入金の金利や株主への配当などが含まれる)
　cost accounting　原価計算
　cost allocation　原価配分, 原価配賦（はいふ）, 費用配分　(＝cost assignment, cost distribution)
　cost basis　原価基準, 原価主義, 取得原価基準
　cost-benefit analysis　費用便益分析, 費用対効果分析　(＝benefit-cost analysis, cost and benefit analysis)
　cost center　原価中心点, 原価部門, コスト・センター
　cost depletion　取得原価に基づく減耗償却, 減耗償却費, 産高比例減耗償却法
　cost depreciation　減価償却
　cost distribution　原価配分, 費用配分, 原価［費用］の配賦, 費用［原価］の流れ　(＝cost allocation)
　cost of capital　資本費用, 資本コスト, 資本用役費, 資本利子　(＝capital cost)
　cost of debt　借入コスト, 借入資本の調達費用
　cost of equity　持ち分コスト, 自己資本コスト(持ち分資本の調達費用)
　cost of goods manufactured　製造原価, 完成品原価　(＝cost of manufacture, cost of production, output cost)
　cost or market principle　低価主義
　cost or market, which is lower　低価主義, 低価法　(＝cost or market principle, lower of cost or market (basis［method］))
　cost or market, whichever is lowere basis［method］　低価基準, 低価法, 低価主義, 原価時価比較低価法　(＝cost-or-market-whichever-is lower)
　cost percentage　原価率
　cost saving　原価節約, 原価節減, 経費節減, コスト削減, コストの節約
　cost-volume-profit analysis　原価・営業量［売上高］・利益関係分析, 原価・操業度・利益分析, CVP分析(原価・販売量・利益の関係に対する分析)
　cut operating costs　営業費用を削減する
　lower cost of funds　資金調達コストの軽減
　managing cost　経営コスト
　manufactured cost　自製部品費
　net cost of funding　実質上の資金調達コスト
　order-getting cost　注文獲得費
　reduce overhead costs　経費を削減する
　service department cost　補助部門費
　set-up cost　段取り費用
　shipping transportation cost　発送運賃
　unit labor cost　単位労働コスト
▸A lower *cost of funds* due to lower interest rates also contributed to the improved margin percentage.　金利の低下で資金コストが下がったことも、利益率の改善に貢献しました。
▸*Costs* related to the conceptual formulation and design of licensed programas are expensed as research and development.　ライセンス・プログラムの概念形成と設計に要した原価は、研究開発費として費用処理されています。

cost calculation　原価計算
▸Pension *cost calculations* were based on a value of assets adjusted to market over periods ranging from 3 to 5 years.　年金原価の計算は、過去3–5年間の時価に修正した資産価額に基づいています。

cost control　原価統制, 原価管理, コスト管理, コスト削減, コスト・コントロール
▸*Cost controls*, coupled with our revenue growth, caused our gross margin percentage to improve the past two years.　コスト管理と増収により、当社の売上総利益率は過去2年間上昇しました。

cost cut　経費削減, 費用削減, コスト削減　(＝cost cutting)
▸Continued *cost cuts* and sales promotion efforts offset a ¥70 billion loss generated by the yen's appreciation against the dollar.　引き続き行ったコスト削減と営業努力で、円高ドル安で生じた700億円の為替差損は相殺されました。

cost effective　費用効果が高い, 費用効率がよい, コスト効率がよい　(＝cost efficient)
▸To us, our approach of partnering with national

cost cut / **create**

carriers and upgrading existing networks is the most *cost-effective way*. 当社にとって，世界各国の通信事業者と提携して既存のネットワークの向上を図るという当社のアプローチの仕方は，最も費用効果の高い手段です。

cost method 原価法, 原価基準, 原価主義（= cost basis, cost convention, valuation at cost）
▸Other investments are accounted for by the *cost method*. その他の投資は，原価法で会計処理［処理］されています。

cost of goods sold 売上原価（= cost of sales：卸売り・小売り業の場合は販売した商品に対応する原価，製造業の場合は販売した製品の製造原価）
▸The company's operating loss, or sales minus the *cost of goods sold* and administrative expenses, totaled ¥31.9 billion in the first quarter. 第1四半期（決算）は，売上高から売上原価と一般管理費を差し引いた同社の営業赤字が，総額で319億円だった。

cost reduction コスト削減, 経費削減, 費用削減, 原価削減［低減］, 原価引下げ, 原価控除（= cost cutting）
　cost reduction efforts コスト削減努力, コスト削減策
　cost reduction method 原価控除法
▸The increase in gross profit was mainly due to the success of *cost reduction* and improved productivity programs. 売上総利益の増加の主な要因は，コスト削減計画と生産性向上計画の成功です。

counterpart 图 同じ立場・地位にある人, 同等物, 同業者, 片方, 副本, 正副2通のうちの1通
▸The Japanese financail institutions are more vulnerable to corporate takeovers than their U.S. and European *counterparts*. 日本の金融機関は，欧米の金融機関に比べて企業買収の標的になりやすい。

coupon 图 商品券, 景品引換券, クーポン
　coupons and trading stamps 景品引換券とスタンプ

cover 動 〈保険を〉かける［付ける］,〈費用や金額などを〉賄う,〈損失の〉穴埋めをする,〈損失などを〉補填する, …を抵当とする, …を担保に入れる,〈問題などを〉取り扱う, …を対象とする, 含む, 表示する, 報道する, 取材する
▸We expect operating cash flows to continue *covering* capital expenditures and dividends in 2008. 当社は，営業活動によるキャッシュ・フローで2008年度も資本的支出と配当をカバーできるものと思います。

▸We sponsor noncontributory defined benefit plans *covering* the majority of our employees. 当社は，従業員の大多数を対象とする非拠出型確定給付年金制度を設けています。

coverage 图 〈保険の〉担保, 担保範囲, 付保範囲, 適用範囲, 範囲, 負担能力, カバレッジ
　benefit coverage 給付内容
　debt coverage 返済余力
　earning coverage 収益カバレッジ
　extended coverage 拡張担保
　fixed charge coverage 金融費用カバレッジ, 固定費カバレッジ
　insurance coverage 保険担保, 保険の担保範囲, 保険填補範囲, 保険の付保, 付保危険
　loan loss coverage 債券損失カバレッジ
▸Major nonlife insurers have introduced terrorism *coverage* exemption clauses for new contracts and contract renewals. 大手損保は，新規契約と契約の更改分について「テロ免責条項」を導入した。

CP 商業証券, 商業手形, コマーシャル・ペーパー（**commercial paper**の略）

CPA 公認会計士（**certified public accountant**の略）

CR 終値, 引け値, 決算日レート, クロージング・レート（**closing rate**の略）

create 動 創造する, 創出する, 創作する, 作り出す, 開発する, 生み出す, 引き起こす, 発生させる,〈会社などを〉設立する, 新設する, 設ける,〈担保権などを〉設定する, 構築する, 伸ばす, 高める
　create a market 市場を開拓する
　create a portfolio of securities 証券ポートフォリオを構築する
　create a security interest 担保権を設定する
　create an idea アイデアを生み出す
　create deals 案件を組成する
　create jobs 雇用を創出する, 職場［仕事］を作る
　create sales 売上を伸ばす
　create value for shareholders 株主の価値を創出する, 株主の価値を高める, 株主の利益を高める, 株主に対する資産価値を創出する
　create value in diverse markets 広範な市場で収益を生み出す
▸We want to *create* Japan's first media group that will pass as a global player. われわれとしては，グローバル企業として通用する日本初のメディア・グループを設立したい。
▸The restructuring will allow us to continue to *create* value for our shareholders. この事業再編によって，当社は，当社の株主価値を今後とも高めることができます。

creativity 名　創造性, 創作性, 独創性, 創造力, 独創力, 制作, クリエイティビティ　(⇒**culture**)
▸Through enhancing the skills of our people and our portfolio of technologies, we draw on the *creativity* and wealth of experience of our people in all cultures.　社員の技能と当社の各種製品技術を高めることによって, 当社は多様な文化背景をもつ社員の創造性と豊かな経験を引き出しています.

credit 動　貸方に記入する, 計上する, 差し引く, 控除する
　　credit A against B　AをBから差し引く, AをBに充当する, AとBを相殺する
　　credit to ...　...に計上する, ...に貸記する, , ...に入金する, ...に充当する
▸Any unpaid balance will be *credited* to outstanding receivables between the two companies.　一切の未払い残高は, 両社間の未収売掛金扱いとします.
▸Under the offset provisions, depositors at a failed bank can have their deposits *credited* against outstanding loans, including mortgages.　相殺規定によると, 破綻した銀行の預金者は, 預金を住宅ローンなどの借入金残高を相殺してもらえる.

credit 名　信用, 与信, 債権, 貸方, 貸金, 融資, 預金, 利益, 信用状, 支払い猶予期間, 税額控除, 金融, クレジット　(⇒**revolving credit facility**)
　　bank credit　銀行借入れ
　　banker's credit　銀行信用状 (=bank credit, banker's letter of credit)
　　credit agency　信用格付け機関, 信用調査機関, 格付け会社 (=credit rating agency, rating agency)
　　credit approval　信用供与承認, 与信承認 (⇒**delinquent balances**, **exposure**)
　　credit criteria　与信基準
　　credit crunch　貸し渋り, 信用危機, 信用不安, 信用逼迫, 金融逼迫, 金融危機, クレジット・クランチ (=credit crisis)
　　credit demand　信用需要
　　credit department　債権管理部門, 債権管理部, 信用調査部
　　credit for expected return on plan assets　予想される年金制度資産運用益
　　credit grantor　与信者
　　credit limit　信用限度, 与信限度, 信用貸出限度, 貸出限度額, 信用供与限度額 (⇒**credit line**)
　　credit period　与信期間, 支払い期限
　　credit profile　信用力, 信用情報
　　debit and credit　借方・貸方

direct credit　直接控除
documentary credit　荷為替信用状
extend credit　信用を供与する
outstanding credits　融資残高
raise credit　資金を調達する
relaxation of credit　金融緩和
tightening in the credit policy　金融引締め
▸A large amount of *credit* cannot be removed from the balance sheets of banks even though loan-loss reserves have been set aside.　貸倒れ引当金を積んでも, 多くの債権は銀行のバランス・シートから切り離せない状況にある [銀行で最終処理できない債権が多い].
▸The firm's debt has been issued using its own *credit*.　同社の負債 [債務] は, 同社の信用で調達しています.

credit card　クレジット・カード
　　credit card transaction　クレジット・カードの取引
▸The growth in costs of financial services and leasing over the last two years came from the higher volume of financing and *credit card* transactions.　過去2年間の金融サービスとリース部門のコスト増の要因は, 資金調達とクレジット・カード取引量の増加です.
▸We also offer a general-purpose *credit card* and financial and leasing services.　当社は, 汎用のクレジット・カードや金融サービス, リース・サービスも提供しています.

credit cost　与信費用, 債権処理費用, 不良債権処理額 (=loan loss charge)
▸Increases in interest payments on deposits outweighed *credit cost* falls.　預金の利払い増加のほうが, 与信費用の低下より大きかった.

credit enhancement　信用補填, 信用補完, 信用補強
　　credit enhancement provider　信用補強提供者
　　provide credit enhancement　信用補完を提供する, 信用リスクをカバーする

credit facilities　信用枠, 信用供与枠, 与信枠, 融資枠
▸At December 31, 2007, the Company's total domestic and foreign *credit facilities* aggregated $2.5 billion.　2007年12月31日現在, 当社の国内および国外与信枠の総額は, 25億ドルとなっています.

credit line　貸出限度 (額), 貸付け限度 (額), 与信限度 (額), 信用限度, 信用保証枠, 信用供与限度, 信用供与枠, 融資枠, 融資限度額, 利用限度額, クレジット・ライン (=credit limit, line of credit)

▸At December 31, 2007, the corporation and certain subsidiaries companies had unused *credit lines*, generally available at the prime bank rate of interest, of approximately $400 million.　2007年12月31日現在、当社と一部の子会社が一般にプライム・レートで利用できる銀行与信枠未使用残高は、約4億ドルとなっています。

credit loss　信用損失、貸倒れ、貸倒れ額、貸倒れ予想額
▸This accounting standard requires us to compute present values for impaired loans when determining our allowances for *credit losses*.　この会計基準は、貸倒れ引当金を決定するにあたって、不良債権の現在価値を計算するよう要求しています。

credit rating　信用格付け、企業の信用等級、格付け評価、格付け（=rating）
　　格付けとは➡民間の格付け機関［格付け会社］が、債券を発行する企業や国、公社などの財務を分析して債務返済能力を判定して、トリプルA（AAA）やB,Cなどとランク付けする仕組み。投資家はこのランク付けに基づいて投資判断をすることができるのに対して、企業にとっては高い格付けが得られれば低利で債券を発行できるといった利点がある。
　　bank letter-of-credit ratings　銀行信用状の格付け
　　long-term credit ratings　長期格付け
　　credit rating agency　格付け機関、信用格付け機関、格付け会社、信用調査機関（=credit agency, rating agency）
　　credit rating service　信用格付けサービス
▸Declines in *credit ratings* will prevent businesses from acquiring capital from the market or financial institutions.　信用格付けが低下すると、企業は市場や金融機関から資金を引き出せなくなる。

credit standing　信用状態、信用度、信用力（=credit strength, creditworthiness）
　　high credit standing　高い信用力、高い信用度（=good credit standing）
▸The company is a customer of good *credit standing*.　同社は、信用度の高い得意先です。

creditor　名　債権者、債権国、債権保有者、資金供与者、取引銀行、貸方、貸主、仕入先、クレディター（⇒**panel**）

crisis　名　危機、経営危機、重大局面、暴落、恐慌、不安、不足、リスク（⇒**financial crisis**）
　　bank crisis　銀行恐慌（取付け騒ぎで銀行閉鎖を迫られる事態のこと）
　　cash flow crisis　資金繰りが苦しくなること、資金繰りがつかないこと

credit crisis　金融恐慌、信用恐慌、信用危機（=credit crunch）
crisis-stricken　経営危機に陥っている
currency crisis　通貨危機
debt crisis　債務危機、累積債務危機
liquidity crisis　流動性危機、資金繰りの悪化（=crisis of liquidity）
monetary crisis　通貨危機、金融危機、貨幣恐慌
stock crisis　株価暴落
stock market crisis　株式市場の暴落、株式市場の混乱
▸A U.S. financial crisis would undoubtedly trigger a global *crisis*.　米国の金融危機は、間違いなく地球規模の（同時）危機を誘発するものと思われる。

criterion　名　基準、標準、尺度
▸At the firm, curbing repayment amounts is regarded as a *criterion* for in-house personnel evaluation.　同社では、返済額を抑えることが社内の人事評価基準と見なされている。

critical mass　最低限の経済規模、採算の取れる規模、望ましい成果を十分得るための確固たる基盤、限界質量、臨界質量、限界量、臨界量、臨界、クリティカル・マス
▸This strategic alliance is a major step toward building *critical mass* that will benefit both companies in the highly competitive and rapidly growing global telecommunications markets.　この戦略的提携は、クリティカル・マス［望ましい成果を十分得るための確固たる基盤］を構築するための大きなステップで、競争が激しく急成長を見せるグローバル通信市場での両社の事業展開に有利に働くものと思われます。

cross license　クロス・ライセンス、特許権交換による特許

cross licensing agreement　クロス・ライセンス契約、特許相互利用契約、交互実施許諾契約（=cross licensing contract）
▸*Cross licensing agreements* are expected to help forestall patent disputes that could delay the development of new products.　クロス・ライセンス契約には、新製品の開発を遅らせる可能性がある特許紛争を未然に防ぐ効果がある。

cross-sectoral tie-up　業態を超えての統合、業態超え統合

crossheld shares　持ち合い株、持ち合い株式（=cross-held shares, crossheld stocks）

crosshold　[**cross-hold**]　動　〈株式を〉持ち合う
▸The Corporation *crossholds* shares with other two steel companies.　当社は、他の鉄鋼2社と株式を持ち合っています。

crossholding [**cross-holding**] 名 株式持ち合い（＝cross-holding shares, cross shareholding, crossholding of shares）
▶ *Crossholding* is a practice in which financial institutions and their client companies own a large amount of stock in each other. 株式持ち合いは、金融機関とその取引先企業が相互に大量の株式を保有する慣行である。

crown jewel クラウン・ジュエル（「王冠の宝石」の意。買収される会社の特に魅力のある重要資産）

crown jewel defense クラウン・ジュエル防衛、有望資産売却戦略、重要資産売却作戦

CS 顧客の満足、顧客満足度（**customer satisfaction** の略）

CSR 企業の社会的責任（**corporate social responsibility** の略）

CTO 最高技術責任者（**chief technology officer** の略）

CTO 受注仕様生産（**configure to order** の略。受注生産方式の一種で、メーカーの販売代理店が注文を受け、自らメーカー・ブランドの製品を組み立てて販売する方式）

CTT 資本移転税、資産譲渡税、贈与税（**capital transfer tax** の略）

culture 名 文化、風土、体質、耕作、培養、養殖、カルチャー（⇒**corporate culture**）
　enterprise culture 企業文化、企業社会、起業文化、起業社会、起業精神
　management culture 経営体質、経営文化
　risk-tolerance culture リスク許容度
▶ Our *culture* embraces creativity, seeks different perspectives and risks pursuing new opportunities. 創造性を積極的に受け入れ、さまざまな物の見方を求めて、新たな事業機会の追求に果敢に挑戦するのが、当社の企業文化です。

cumulative 形 累積した、累積的な、累加した、累計的な、漸増的な、追加方式の
　cumulative accounting adjustment 累積的会計修正
　cumulative income statement 累計的損益計算書（＝cumulative statement of profit and loss）
　cumulative preferred stock [**share**] 累積優先株式、累加優先株式
　cumulative stock 累積株
　cumulative translation adjustment 累積換算調整額

cumulative dividend 累積配当、累加配当、積置き配当
▶ The first preferred shareholders are entitled to *cumulative* annual dividends per share in the amount set out in the titles of each series. 第一優先株式の株主には、シリーズごとに規定された［各シリーズの証券に記載された］レートで1株当たり年間累積配当を受ける権利が与えられています。

cumulative effect 累積効果、累積的影響、累積的影響額
　cumulative effect of a change in accounting principle 会計原則の変更による累積影響額、会計原則変更の累積効果
　cumulative effect of an accounting change 会計方針［会計処理］変更の累積的影響
　cumulative effect of change in accounting for income taxes 法人所得税の会計処理変更に伴う累積的影響額
　cumulative effect on prior years of changing to a different depreciation method 減価償却方法変更の過年度への累積影響額
　cumulative effects of accounting changes 会計処理の変更による累積的影響
　cumulative effects on prior years of changes in accounting 会計処理の変更による累積的影響額
▶ The *cumulative effects* come from earlier years. 累積的影響額は、過年度のものです。
▶ Our income statement shows the net impact of all these adjustments as "*cumulative effects* on prior years of changes in accounting." 当社の損益計算書では、これらすべての修正による最終的な影響額が、「会計処理の変更による累積的影響額」として表示されています。

curb 動 抑制する
curb 名 抑制、拘束
currency 名 通貨、為替、為替相場、流通、流行
　currency changes 分離、為替相場の変動、為替変動（＝currency exchange fluctuation, currency fluctuation, currency movements, currency swings, exchange fluctuation）
　currency movements 為替相場の動き、為替相場の変動、為替変動（＝currency changes, exchange fluctuation）
　foreign currency loan 外貨建て借入金
　hard currency 交換可能通貨、ハード・カレンシー（＝hard money：米ドルや金と交換できる通貨）
　home currency 自国通貨
　key currency 基軸通貨、国際通貨、キー・カレンシー（＝international money）
　local currency 現地通貨（建て）
　major currencies 主要通貨
　soft currency 交換不能通貨、軟貨、ソフト通貨、

ソフト・カレンシー（米ドルやその他の主要通貨と直接交換できない通貨）

strong dollar against other currencies ドル全面高

▶For the businesss we transact in *currencies other than U.S. dollars*, we translate assets and liabilities at year-end exchange rates. 米ドル以外の通貨で行う取引については、当社は資産と負債について事業年度末の為替レートに基づいて換算しています。

currency exchange rate 為替相場, 為替レート, 通貨交換レート (＝exchange rate)

▶We enter into foreign currency exchange contracts, including forward, options and swap contracts, to manage our exposure to changes in *currency exchange rates*. 当社は、為替相場の変動によるリスクを管理するため、先物予約、オプションやスワップなどの契約を含めて、外国為替予約を締結しています。

currency translation 通貨換算, 外貨換算

　currency translation adjustment 為替換算調整, 外貨換算調整, 為替換算調整勘定, 外貨換算調整勘定

current 形 現在の, 当座の, 当期の, 短期の, 臨時の, 経常的, 流動的 (⇒delivery)

　current balance 当座残高
　current bank loan 短期借入金
　current cash price 現金正価
　current deposit 当座預金 (＝checking account, current account, current account deposit)
　current fair value 現在公正価格
　current loan receivable 短期貸付け金
　current net income 当期純利益 (＝current earnings, current income)
　current operating basis [concept] 当期業績主義
　current operating income 当期営業利益, 当期操業利益
　current operating performance theory [basis, concept] 当期業績主義
　current operating profit 当期営業利益, 当期操業利益
　current payment 当月支払い
　current proceeds 当期収入, 当期収益, 当期売上高, 現在現金受領額
　current rate 決算日レート, カレント・レート (＝closing rate)
　current replacement cost 再調達時価
　current revenue 当期収益, 当期収入, 当期歳入
　current sales 当月売上

current term net loss 当期純損失
current term settlement 当期決算
deferred tax asset/current 繰延べ税金資産・短期
deferred tax liabilities/current 繰延べ税金負債・短期

▶*Current* international markets have lower margins because of higher start-up and operating costs. 現在の国際市場は、営業開始コスト[初期費用]と営業コストの増大で利益率が低下しています。

current 名 流動, 流動性, 1年以内返済予定額, 当期分 (⇒previously reported figures)
　current ratio 流動比率
current account profit 経常利益 (⇒current profit)

▶The Corporation's consolidated *current account profits* stood at ¥80 billion for the current year. 当社の連結経常利益は、今期は800億円でした。

current account surplus 経常黒字, 経常収支の黒字, 経常収支の黒字額

▶We recorded a *current account surplus* of about ¥2 billion in the fiscal period ending December 2007. 当社は、2007年12月期決算で、約20億円の経常黒字を計上しました。

current assets 流動資産 (＝floating assets, near-cash assets, liquid assets：比較的流動性が高く、1年以内に現金化される可能性がある資産)

流動資産に含まれるもの

accounts receivable-net	売掛債権[売掛金]—純額
cash and cash equivalents	現金預金および現金同等物
inventories	棚卸し資産
notes and accounts receivable-trade	受取手形および売掛金
other current assets	その他の流動資産
other securities	その他の有価証券
prepaid expenses and other current assets	前払い費用およびその他の流動資産
short-term investments	短期投資
trade notes and accounts receivable	受取手形および売掛金

▶*Current assets* and current liabilities are translated at the exchange rates in effect at the balance sheet date. 流動資産と流動負債は、貸借対照表日[決算日]現在の実効為替レートで換算してあります。

current business year 今年度, 今期, 当年度, 当事業年度 (＝current fiscal year, current year)

▶For the *current business year*, the Company anticipates rises in consolidated sales and operating profit, but a fall in group net profit. 今期は、

当社の連結売上高と営業利益は増加するが、連結税引き後利益[連結純利益]は減少する見込みです。

current cost 現在原価, 時価, 現在取替原価, 再調達原価, 当期原価, 当期費用, カレント・コスト《略 CC》
 current cost accounting 現在原価会計, 時価主義会計《略 CCA》
 current cost basis 現在原価基準, 時価主義
 current cost depreciation 時価償却, 現在原価に基づく減価償却, カレント・コスト減価償却費（⇒replacement cost）
 current cost profit 現在原価利益
▶*Current cost* depreciation is used by the manufacturing companies for cost calculations. 時価償却[現在原価に基づく減価償却]は、製造会社がコスト計算のために使用しています。

current fiscal year 今年度, 今期, 当会計年度, 当事業年度, 当年度 （＝current business year, current year; ⇒**combined pretax profit**）
▶Net profit per share fell as a result of a 2-for-1 stock split carried out at the beginning of the *current fiscal year*. 1株当たり純利益は、今年度の初めに実施した1対2の比率による株式分割のため、減少しました。

current fund 〘~s〙流動資金, 当座資金, 運営資金, 〘~〙一般財政

current income 当期利益 （＝current earnings, current net income）, 経常収益, 経常収入, インカム・ゲイン
▶The costs of these benefits are paid out of *current income*, as benefits are received. これらの給付費用は、実際の給付時にその期間の経費として処理されています[実際の給付時に当期利益から支払われています]。

current liabilities 流動負債, 短期負債(1年以内に返済しなければならない債務)

流動負債に含まれるもの

accounts receivable	買掛金, 買掛債務
accrued expenses	支払い費用, 未払い費用
commercial paper	コマーシャルペーパー, CP
compensation and benefits	給与および給付金
current installments of long term debt	1年以内返済の長期債務
dividends payable	未払い配当金
income taxes	未払い税金
income taxes payable	未払い税金
loans payable	借入金
notes payable	支払い手形
other accrued expenses and liabilities	その他の未払い費用および負債
other current liabilities	その他の流動負債
payroll	未払い給与
short-term bank loans	短期銀行借入金
short-term debt	短期債務
short-term loans	短期借入金
trade notes and accounts payable	支払い手形および買掛金

▶Other *current liabilities* declined because some restructuring reserves were reclassified to post-employment liabilities. その他の流動負債は、事業再編成引当金の一部が雇用後債務に振り替えられたため、減少しました。

current maturity 残存期間, 当期支払い額
 current maturities 1年以内返済長期債務
 current maturities of long-term debt 1年以内返済長期借入金

current net earnings 当期純利益 （＝current net income）
▶There is no change in the *current* or previously reported *net earnings*. 当期純利益と過年度に計上した純利益に、変動はありません。

current portion 1年以内返済(分), 1年以内償還(分), 1年以内回収(分)
 current portion of bonds 1年以内償還社債
 current portion of lease receivables 1年以内回収予定のリース受取債権
 current portion of long term debt 1年以内返済長期借入金

current profit 経常利益 （＝current account profit, pretax profit, recurring profit）
▶Listed companies saw double-digit growth in their sales and *current profits* from a year earlier. 上場企業の売上高と経常利益は、前年比[前年同期比]で2桁増加した。

current results 当期業績
▶Many investors set aside the cumulative effects of changes in accounting when looking at *current results*. 当期業績を見る場合、多くの投資家は、会計処理の変更による累積的影響を除外して考えます。

current service cost 現在勤務費用, 当期の勤務費用
▶*Current service costs* of retirement plans are accrued currently. 退職金制度の当期勤務費用は、当期に処理されています。

current value accounting 現在価値会計, 時価主義会計《略 CVA》（＝mark-to-market accounting, market value accounting）
 current value accounting standard 時価主義会計基準

▶The Financial Services Agency's Business Accounting Council adopted a U.S.-style *current value accounting* standard for corporate mergers to increase transparency of accounting rules. 金融庁の企業会計審議会は、会計規則の透明性を高めるため、会社合併については米国式の時価主義会計基準を採用した。

current year 今年度, 今期, 当年度, 当期 （= current fiscal year）
▶Both *current* and prior *year* results conform with Statement of Financial Accounting Standards Number 94, "Consolidation of All Majority-Owned Subsidiaries.". 当年度と過年度の業績は、いずれも財務会計基準書第94号の「すべての過半数株式所有子会社の連結」に適合しています。

customer 顧客, 得意先, 得意客, 取引先, 需要家, 加入者, ユーザー
▶Our strategy of listening to our *customers* and improving the competitiveness of our products and services is working. お客さまのご意見を取り入れ、製品とサービスの競争力強化に取り組んでいる当社の経営戦略が、功を奏しています。

customer base 顧客基盤, 顧客層
▶The biggest advantage for the bank in entering the venture will be to increase its *customer base* without having to open expensive new branch offices. 同行にとってこの新規事業への参入の最大の利点は、コストのかかる新店舗を開設するまでもなく、顧客基盤を拡大できることだ。

customer needs 顧客のニーズ, 顧客の要求
▶We are required to become a global company in order to meet *customer needs* in a world where companies do business around the globe. 世界全域で事業を展開している企業社会にあって、お客さまのニーズを満たすには、当社自体がグローバルな企業にならなければなりません。

customer requirements 顧客の要求
▶Not only must researchers develop new technologies, they must apply them to products which respond to specific *customer requirements*. 研究者は、新技術の開発だけでなく、開発した技術を製品に応用して顧客の特定の要求に応えなければならない。

customer satisfaction 顧客の満足, 顧客満足度《略 CS》（⇒growth strategy）
▶*Customer satisfaction* is giving customers what they want. 顧客の満足を得るということは、顧客が欲しいものを提供することである。

customer service 顧客サービス, 顧客への奉仕, 顧客へのサービス, 接客, カスタマー・サービス

▶Seven & I and Millenium Retailing plan to increase their revenues by taking advantage of the combined effect of their product development and *customer services*. セブン＆アイとミレニアムリテイリングは、両社の商品開発や接客［顧客サービス］などの面での統合効果を発揮して、収益力強化を図る計画だ。

customer support services 顧客支援サービス
▶To provide consistent, coordinated solutions and *customer support services*, regional and branch offices have been created. 一貫性と整合性のあるソリューションと顧客支援サービスを提供するため、地域営業本部と営業所を設置しました。

cut 動 削減する, 縮小する, 減らす, 引き下げる, 下げる
　cut inventories 在庫を削減する, 在庫を取り崩す
　cut labor costs 人件費を引き下げる
　cut operating costs 営業コストを削減する, 営業経費を削減する
　cut payrolls 人員を削減する
　cut production 生産を削減する
　cut spending 支出を減らす, 支出を削減する
▶The company succeeded in *cutting* costs by jointly purchasing some of the products with its group firm. 同社は、グループ企業と一部商品の仕入れを共通化して、コスト削減に成功した。

cutting edge 最前線, 最先端, 最新式, 最新型, 最新鋭, 先頭, 主導的地位, 鋭利な刃物 （= leading edge, sophisticated, state-of-the-art, top of the line）
▶We are continuously developing and striving to provide *cutting-edge* software that our end-users can use without worry. 当社は、エンド・ユーザーが安心して利用できる最先端のソフトウエア製品の開発と提供に継続的に取り組んでいます。

CVA 現在価値会計, 時価主義会計（**current value accounting**の略）

CVP 原価・営業量［売上高］・利益関係（**cost-volume-profit**の略）

cyberbusiness 名 サイバービジネス（=e-business：インターネットを使って消費者に直接販売するビジネス）

cycle 名 周期, 循環, 動向, 景気, サイクル
　business cycle 景気循環, 景気変動, 景気 （= trade cycle）
　consumption cycle 消費サイクル
　cycle billing 循環請求
　cycle inventory 循環棚卸
　down cycle 景気悪化

economic cycle 経済循環, 景気循環, 景気動向
life cycle 製品ライフサイクル, 生活循環
ordering cycle 発注間隔
output cycle 生産動向
production cycle 生産サイクル
virtuous cycle 好循環

▸We continue to make essential investments in our drive for more competitive products and services, delivered on ever shorter *cycles*. 当社は、一段と競争力のある製品とサービスを従来より短いサイクルで納入する取組みに対する極めて重要な投資を継続しています。

cyclical [**cyclic**] 形 景気循環の, 周期的な, 循環の

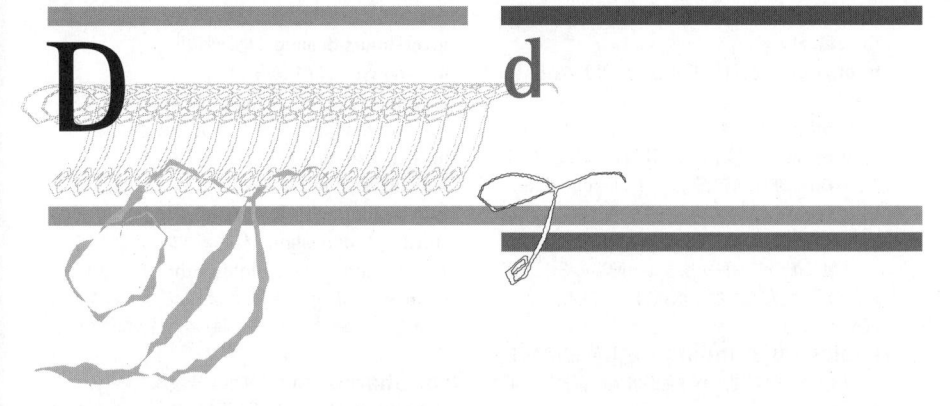

daily average for a month　月中平均
▶In the term-end settlement of accounts at the end of September, most companies use the *daily average for a month* of the share prices in gauging the value of latent gains or losses in their stockholdings.　9月末の期末決算で［9月中間決算で］大半の企業は, 保有株式の含み損益を算出する際に株価の月中平均を使っている。

daily turnover　1日当たりの取引高
▶Average *daily turnover* on the Tokyo Stock Exchange grew 86 percent year-on-year to ¥663 billion during the April-June quarter.　東京証券取引所の4-6月期の1日当たり平均取引高［売買代金］は, 前年同期に比べて86％増の6,630億円に達した。

damage 名　損害, 損害賠償, 被害, 損害賠償金, 損害賠償額, 損害額, 被害額
　　compensation for damages　損害賠償
　　damage claims receivable　損害賠償未収金
　　damage payments　損害賠償金
　　damage [damages] suit　損害賠償訴訟　(⇒contingent)
　　passive damages　逸失利益
▶The trust bank claimed ¥10 billion in *damages*.　同信託銀行は, 100億円の損害賠償を求めた。

damage assessment　損害査定
▶This nonlife insurance company provides the company with know-how on *damage assessment* and product development.　この損害保険会社は, 同社に損害査定や商品開発に関するノウハウを提供している。

damage compensation　損害賠償
▶Toshiba may demand *damage compensation* from Sony, and others may follow suit.　東芝はソニーに対する損害賠償請求を検討しており, 他社もこれに追随する可能性がある。

damage costs　損害費用
▶The liability insurance fell short in covering *damage costs*.　この損害賠償責任保険で, 損害費用を賄いきれませんでした。

data 名　情報, 文書, 資料, 指標, 統計, データ　(⇒accounting)
　　customer data　顧客情報　(＝customer information)
　　data leak　情報漏洩, 情報漏れ, 情報流出
　　data on transactions　取引データ
　　data processing method　情報処理方式, データ処理方式
　　economic data　景気指標, 経済指標, 経済データ
　　employment data　雇用統計
　　financial data　財務情報
　　geographic area data　地域別データ
　　key economic data　主要景気指標
　　market data　市場統計, 市場データ, 市場資料, 相場の動き
　　personal data　個人情報　(＝personal information)
　　public data on issuer　発行体に関する公表データ
　　stock price data　株価資料
　　trade data　貿易統計
▶*Data* on other geographic areas pertain to operations that are located outside of the U.S.　「その他の地域」に関する数値は, 米国外に拠点を置く事業の数値です。

date 名　日時, 日付
　　date of declaration　配当宣言日

date of expiration 満了日(契約期間が円満に終了した場合)

date of issue 発行日, 提出日, 小切手の振出日, 作成日

date of maturity 満期日, 支払い期日, 支払い日

date of payment 支払い日, 決済日, 支払い期日, 払込み期日, 期日, 配当支払い日(＝due date)

date of record 配当基準日(各事業年度に配当を受け取る権利のある株主を決める日のこと。株価は, 一般に配当基準日を過ぎると配当の分だけ価値が下がって安くなる), 名義書換え停止日(＝record date)

days sales outstanding 売上債権回転日数, 売上債権回収期間, 平均売掛債権滞留日数《略 DSO》
▸*Days sales outstanding* in our core business are defined as average accounts receivable divided by average daily revenues in our core business. 当社の主力事業の平均売上債権回転日数[平均売掛債権滞留日数]は, 売掛金の平均額を主力事業の1日当たり平均収益で割ることによって得られます。

DCF 割引キャッシュ・フロー法, 割引現在価値法(**discount**[**discounted**] **cash flow**の略)

de fact 事実上の, 実質的な, ディファクト
▸The investment fund has a *de fact* majority of shareholder voting rights. この投資ファンドが, 実質的に株主議決権の過半数を握っている。

deal 動 分配する, 取引する
　deal a blow to ... …に打撃を与える
▸Appraisal losses on securities holdings *dealt* a blow to the firm's earnings. 保有証券の含み損[評価損]が, 同社の収益に打撃を与えた。

deal 名 取引, 売買, 政策, 計画, 協定, 協約, 労使協約, 取決め, 契約, 協議, 協議書, 案件, 物
　bullet deal 満期一括償還債
　cash deal 現金取引
　compensation deal 補償取引
　exchange deal 為替取引
　financial deal 金融取引
　fund deal 資金取引
　stock deal 株取引, 株式の売買
　structured deal 仕組み取引, 仕組み債
　swap deal スワップ取引
　trust deal 信託契約
▸In May 2007, the ban on foreign firms taking over Japanese companies with stock swap *deals* was lifted. 2007年5月から, 株式交換取引での外資[外資系企業, 外国企業]による日本企業買収が解禁となった。

dealing 名 売買取引, 取引, 売買, 自己売買, ディーリング
　after-hours dealing 時間外取引
　dealing cost 取引費用
　foreign exchange dealing 外国為替取引
　forward dealing 先物取引, 先物為替取引
　insider dealing インサイダー取引
　outside dealing 場外取引
　spot dealing 直物取引, 直物為替取引
　stock option dealing 株式オプション取引
▸We are honest and highly ethical in all our business *dealings*. 私たちは, あらゆる事業取引で誠実かつ高い企業倫理に基づいて行動しています。

Dear Shareowner 株主の皆様へ, 株主各位

debenture 名 社債; [米]無担保債券, [英]不動産担保付き債券(⇒**bank debenture**, **subordinated debenture**)
　bank debenture 金融債, 銀行債, 銀行債券(金融機関が資金調達のために発行する債券)
　capital debenture 劣後債
　convertible debenture 転換社債
　corporate debenture 社債(＝corporate bond)
　debenture bond 無担保社債, 無担保債(＝debenture)
　debenture interest 社債利息, 社債利子
　debenture stock 社債, 担保付き社債(＝debenture bond)
　debentures issued 社債券発行高
　profit debenture 収益社債
　unsecured corporate debenture 無担保社債
▸During the first half of the 2007, we completed a public offering in Canada of $150 million of *debentures*, due 2017. 2007年上半期に, 当社はカナダ国内で満期2017年の社債1億5,000万ドルの公募発行を完了しました。

debit 名 借方(勘定の左側), 負債, 引落し, デビット
　debit balance 借方残高, 貸付け残高, 差引融資残高
　debit equity ratio 負債持ち分比率, 他人資本比率
　debit memorandum 借方記入通知書
　debit note 借方票, 請求書, デビット・ノート
　direct debit 自動引落し, 直接引落し, 口座引落し
　Net-debit service ネット決済サービス, インターネット即時決済サービス
　online debit service インターネット即時決済サービス, オンライン即時決済サービス
▸The life insurer introduced a system that allows customers to pay their first insurance premiums by direct *debit* from their bank accounts. 同保

険会社は, 顧客の銀行口座からの自動引落しで(契約時の)初回保険料を顧客が支払うことができるシステムを導入した。

debt 名 債務, 負債, 借入れ, 借金, 債権, 借入金, 借入債務, 債務証券, 債券, 金銭債務, 金銭債務訴訟, 金融債務, デット (⇒**bad debt, cash requirements, corporate debt securities, interest bearing debt, long term debt, refinance**)

bank debt 銀行借入れ

corporate debt 法人債務, 企業債務

debt and equity securities 負債証券[債務証券]と持ち分証券

debt-asset ratio 負債・資産比率(総負債の総資産に対する比率)

debt due within one year 1年以内に返済予定の債務

debt equity ratio 負債・資本比率, 負債対資本比率, 負債比率, 外部負債比率, 負債倍率, デットエクイティレシオ《略 DER》 (=debt-to-equity ratio)

debt equity swap 債務の株式化, 債権の株式化, デットエクイティスワップ《略 DES》 (=debt-equity swap, debt-for-equity swap)

debt factoring 債権買取り

debt finance デット・ファイナンス, 負債金融, 負債による資金調達

debt-for-bond swap 債務の債券化, デット・ボンド・スワップ (=debt-bond swap)

debt issued with stock purchase warrant 新株引受権付き社債

debt load 債務負担 (=debt burden)

debt maturing within one year 1年以内に償還期限が到来する負債

debt-swap arrangements 債務の株式化

debt-to-equity analysis 負債比率の分析

debt-to-equity ratio 負債比率, 負債資本比率 (=debt equity ratio, debt ratio; ⇒**debt ratio**)

excess of debt 債務超過

financial debt 金融債務

issue debt 債券を発行する, 負債で資金を調達する

large debts 大口債権

massive debts 巨額の債務, 過剰債務

meet one's debt obligations 債務を履行する, 債務を返済する

operating debt 買掛金

pay down debt 債務を返済する (=repay debt)

reduce debt 債務を削減する (=trim down debt)

refinance existing debt 既存債務を借り換える

replace maturing debt 満期を迎える[満期が来た]債務を借り換える

restructuring of debt 債務の再編

retirement of debt 債務の返済

service debt 債務を履行する, 債務を返済する

unconsolidated debt 単独ベースでの借入金, 非連結子会社の負債

▶From time to time, we guarantee the *debt* of certain unconsolidated joint ventures. 当社は, (当社の財務諸表に)連結されていない特定の合弁会社の負債に対して保証を行う場合があります。

debt financing 他人資本調達, 負債による資金調達, 借入金融, 負債金融 (=debt finance:社債の発行や約束手形の振出し, 短期・長期の借入金などで資金を調達する方法。これに対して, 株式発行による資金調達方法をequity financing [finance]という)

debt-for-equity swap 〈貸し手にとっての〉債権株式化, 〈借り手にとっての〉債務株式化, デット・エクイティ・スワップ (=debt equity swap; ⇒**package, waiver**)

債務の株式化とは ➡ 金融機関に融資(借入金)を出資に振り替えてもらい, 株券を渡して増資すること。つまり, 負債を株に変えて増資すること。こうすると, 融資を受けた企業はその借入金を返す必要もなく, また利子を払う必要もない。企業にとっては負債が減る分, 資本金などの自己資本が増え, 金融機関にとっては債権の株式化によって企業が再建を果たせば配当を受けられるし, 株価が値上がりすれば株を売却して利益が得られるメリットがある。債務の株式化は, 貸し手(金融機関)にとっては債権の株式化を意味する。

▶The bank is considering providing financial aid to the heavily indebted automaker, such as waiving debts and conducting a *debt-for-equity* swap. 同行は, 債権放棄や債務(銀行にとっては債権)の株式化などで, 巨額の債務を抱えたこの自動車メーカーへの金融支援を行うことを検討している。

debt forgiveness 債権放棄, 債務の免除, 債務救済 (=debt relief, debt waiver, forgiveness of debt, loan forgiveness, loan write-off)

▶The company increased the amount of *debt forgiveness* by its creditors to ¥98.9 billion from ¥90.9 billion. 同社は, 取引金融機関による債務免除額を909億円から989億円に引き上げた。

debt instrument 債務証券, 債務証書, 債券 (=debt, debt security)

▶One way for a company to accomplish long-term financing is through the issuance of long-term *debt instruments* in the form of bonds. 会社の長期資金調達方法のひとつは，社債の形で長期債務証券を発行して行われる。

debt outstanding 負債残高，借入残高，未払い負債額，未償還債務，未償還負債

▶The growth of our financial services was the primary reason for the increase in total *debt outstanding* and for most of our financing needs. 当社の金融サービスの成長が，主に当社の未償還債務総額の増加と資金需要の増加をもたらしました。

debt rating 債券格付け，社債の格付け，債務証書，債務契約書 (＝bond rating)

▶Fitch Ratings cut General Motors Corp.'s *debt ratings* to "junk." 欧州系格付け会社のフィッチ・レーティングスは，米ゼネラル・モーターズ（GM）の社債格付けを「投資不適格」に引き下げた。

▶Moody's downgraded GM's long-term *debt rating*. 格付け会社のムーディーズは，GMの長期格付けを引き下げた。

debt ratio 負債比率，債務比率 (＝debt-to-equity ratio)

▶Our goal is a 30 percent *debt ratio* for our core business. 当社の中核事業の負債比率を30％にするのが，当社の目標です。

debt repayment 債務返済，借入金の返済 (＝repayment of debt)

▶The dissolution of the nonprofit foundation was considered as one way of resolving the issue of *debt repayment*. 同公益法人の解散は，債務返済問題を解決するための手段の一つとして考えられた。

debt-saddled 形 借金を背負っている，負債［債務，赤字］を抱えた，経営再建中の

▶We are attempting to improve the management of our *debt-saddled* subsidiary. 当社は現在，赤字を抱える子会社の経営改善に取り組んでいます。

debt security 債務証券，債券，債務証書 (＝debt, debt instrument)

債務証券について ➡ 債務証券は，一般に債券などの有価証券を指す。一定の額面金額（par value）と満期日（maturity date）があり，利払いがある利付き証券（interest-bearing securities）と利払いはないが割引方式で発行される割引証券（discount securities）がある。

利払いがある利付き証券のうち，期間が長いものは利付き債（coupon bond）と呼ばれている。また，利払いがなく割引方式で発行される割引証券の場合は，券面に確定利息（fixed interest rate）がなく，額面（par value）より低い割引価格で発行され，満期日には額面価格で返済される。この割引証券は，米国財務省短期証券（Treasury bill）やコマーシャル・ペーパー（CP）がその代表格で，発行から償還（redemption）までの期間の利払いは一切なく，発行価格と額面価格との差額（償還差益）が利息相当分となる。米国では，コマーシャル・ペーパーなどのような短期の債券をpaper, bill, 中期債券（満期までの期間が1年超～10年程度の中期債）をnote, 長期債券（満期までの期間が10年以上の長期債）をbondなどと，期間によって表現を使い分けしている。

▶We sold ¥31 billion of *debt securities* with a maturity of 50 years. 当社は，満期50年の債券［債務証券］310億円を発行しました［満期50年の債券を発行して，310億円を調達しました］。

debt service 元利払い，債務返済，未払い金，債務元利返済額

burden of debt service 金利負担
debt service fund 借入返済基金

debt servicing 債務返済，利息払い (＝debt paying, debt service)

debt servicing capacity 債務返済能力 (＝debt-paying ability)
debt servicing costs [expenses] 債務返済費用，国債費 (＝debt-servicing expenditures)

▶The rise in *debt-servicing* costs is due to the massive issuance of government bonds to prop up the economy. 国債費が増えたのは，景気を支えるため国債を大量に発行したためだ。

debt waiver 債権放棄，債務免除 (＝waiver of debt; ⇒waiver)

▶The remaining ¥20 billion of debt will be repaid through *debt waivers* by the firm's six main banks and three regional banks. 残りの負債200億円は，同社の主力取引銀行6行と地銀3行による債権放棄で返済する。

debtor 名 債務者，融資先，借方，借主，債務国《略 Dr.》

debtor balance 借方残高
debtor company 融資先企業，融資先，債務者

▶*Debtor* companies are currently categorized by the banks into five groups, ranging from normal to bankrupt. 債務者［融資先］は現在，金融機関が正常先から破綻先まで5段階に分類している。

debtor in possession 管理処分権保持債務者，継承破産人《略 DIP》(⇒DIP plan)

debtor in possession finance 事業再生融資，DIPファイナンス，デッター・イン・ポゼション融資 (＝DIP financing, DIP plan：不動産担保がなくても事業の継続可能性などを考慮して新規融資する仕組み)

decentralize 動 分散する, 分散化する, 一極集中を排除する, 多極分散する, 分権する
▸In case of transnational companies, decision making is *decentralized* and coordinated across borders, linking functins for global leverage and competitive advantage. トランスナショナル（超国籍）企業の場合, 意思決定は分散・分権化され, 国境を越えて調整されると同時に, 諸機能を連結して地球規模のレバレッジ効果と競争上の優位性を追求しています。

decision 名 決定, 意思決定, 決断, 判断, 決議, 判定, 判決, 裁決
　　business decision　経営判断, 企業の意思決定, 事業決定
　　decision of a general meeting of stockholders　株主総会決議
　　investment decision　投資判断
　　majority decision　多数決（=decision by a majority）
　　make or buy decision　自製か購入かの決定
　　operating decision　業務上の意思決定（=operation decision）
　　pricing decision　価格決定, 価格設定
　　rating decision　格付け判断, 格付けの意思決定
　　strategic decision　戦略的意思決定
▸*Decisions* regarding small contributions are made by local management. 少額の寄付についての決定は, 各国の経営陣が行っています。
▸We are working with employees and the unions to increase their involvement and input in planning and *decisions*. 私ども経営陣は, 従業員と組合と一緒に, 企画立案と意思決定に参加して意見を述べる機会を増やす努力をしています。

decision making 意思決定, 政策決定, 経営判断
▸Outside directors are appointed to enhance transparency in *decision making* as well as strengthen oversight of directors who have operational responsibilities. 社外取締役任用の目的は, 意思決定の透明性向上と業務執行を担う取締役の監督強化です。

decision-making 形 意思決定の, 政策決定の, 経営判断の

declaration 名 宣言, 申告, 宣告, 公表, 決議
　　declaration date　配当宣言日（=date of declaration）
　　declaration of bankruptcy　破産宣言
　　declaration of default　デフォルト宣言
　　declaration of dividend　配当宣言, 配当決議（=dividend announcement, dividend declaration)

declare 動〈配当支払いなどを〉宣言する, 申告する, 計上する, 公表する, 発表する（⇒bankrupt）
　　be declared bankrupt　破産宣告を受ける
　　declare a cash dividend　現金配当を宣言する
　　declared dividend　宣言配当金, 公表配当金, 配当宣言
　　declared income　申告所得, 所得申告
　　declared profit　計上利益
　　dividend declared　宣言配当金[配当額], 配当金, 配当決議
　　dividends declared per common share　普通株式1株当たり配当
▸Dividends may be *declared* by the board of directors out of the surplus or net profits of the company. 配当金は, 会社の剰余金または純利益から取締役会が宣言することができる。
▸GM *declared* a net deficit of more than ¥1 trillion in the fiscal year ending December 2005. GMは, 2005年度に[2005年12月期決算で]1兆円超の税引き後赤字を計上した。
▸The company made simple accounting errors and failed to *declare* income totaling more than ¥2 billion. 同社は, 単純な経理ミスをして, 総額20数億円の所得を申告しなかった。

decline 形 減少, 低下, 下落, 悪化, 低迷, 縮小（⇒April-June quarter）
　　asset price decline　資産価格の下落
　　bond yield decline　債券利回りの下落
　　decline in capital expenditure　設備投資の減少
　　decline in deficits　赤字削減
　　decline in inventories　在庫の減少
　　decline in losses　赤字縮小
　　earnings decline　利益の減少, 収益の減少, 減益, 収益減（=profit decline）
　　interest rate decline　金利の低下
　　profit decline　減益
　　share price decline　株価の下落
▸Boeing Co. posted a 31 percent *decline* in third quarter profits. ボーイングの第3四半期（7-9月期）の利益は, 前年同期比で31%減少した。

decline 動 減少する, 低下する, 下落する, 悪化する, 低迷する, 縮小する
▸Our interest income *declined* because we had less cash on hand and interest rates were lower. 利息収入は, 手元現預金が少なく, 金利が低下したために減少しました。

declining balance 定率法
　　declining balance depreciation　定率法, 逓減残高法

declining balance method 定率法, 逓減残高法, 残高逓減法 （＝reducing balance method）
▶Depreciation is recorded principally using the *declining balance* method, based on the estimated useful lives of the assets. 減価償却は, 原則として資産の見積り耐用年数に基づき定率法で行っています。

declining birthrate and graying society
少子高齢化 （＝aging society and declining birthrate, declining birthrate and graying of the population）

decontrol 名 規制撤廃, 制限解除, 統制解除, 統制撤廃, 自由化

decrease 動 引き下げる, 軽減する, 減らす, 減少する, 減る, 縮小する, 低下する, 下落する
  decreased margin 利益率の低下
  decreased profitability 収益性の低下
  decreased sales 売上高の減少, 売上の減少
  decreasing birth rate 少子化
▶Earnigs *decreased* for the third quarter. 第3四半期の利益は減少しました。

decrease 名 減少, 縮小, 低下, 下落
  arbitrary increase or decrease method 任意増減算出法
  capital decrease 減資 （＝capital reduction, reduction of capital）
  decrease in accounts receivable (net) 売掛金の減少（純額）, 受取債権の減少（減額）
  decrease in accrued expenses 未払い費用の減少
  decrease in dividends 減配
  decrease in other current assets その他の流動資産の減少
  decrease in other current liabilities その他の流動負債の減少
  (**decrease**) **increase in cash and short-term investments and borrowings** 現金・預金, 短期投資および短期借入金の増加（減少）
  decrease of capital 減資 （＝capital decrease, capital reduction, reduction of capital）
  net decrease in cash and cash equivalents 現金および現金等価物の純減少
  rating decrease 格下げ
▶The *decrease* in revenues in 2007 was mainly due to the reduction of revenues associated with the sale of some European businesses. 2007年度に売上高が減少したのは, 主に欧州事業の一部売却に伴って売上高が減少したためです。

dedication 名 献身, 専念, 専心, 除幕式, 献呈, 献辞
▶The many thousands of employees in our family of companies once again demonstrated their *dedication* and professionalism in support of various corporate goals and activities. 当社のさまざまな企業目標と活動を支えたのは, 当期も当社のファミリー企業に勤務している十数万人の従業員の献身と職業意識です。

deduct 動 差し引く, 控除する, 引き落とす
▶Company employees' pension premiums are automatically *deducted* from their monthly salaries. サラリーマンの厚生年金保険料は, 月給から天引きされる［自動的に差し引かれる］。

deductible 形 控除可能な, 損金算入できる, 経費として認められる, 費用として控除される
  deductible amount 減算額
  deductible expenses 控除可能費用, 損金, 課税控除費目
  deductible for tax purposes 税務上損金となる
  deductible from taxable income 課税所得から控除できる
  dividends deductible as necessary expenses 配当損金算入
  tax deductible 損金算入できる, 経費として認められる, 損金算入項目
▶These expenses are *deductible* for tax purposes in year 5 when the liability is expected to be paid. これらの費用は, 負債を支払う予定の第5事業年度に税務上, 損金となります。

deduction 名 差引, 控除, 控除項目, 差引額, 控除額, 減少額, 減額, 損金, 損金算入, 送り状価格の引下げ, 演繹
  automatic deduction 自動引落し （＝direct debit）
  deduction at source 源泉徴収, 源泉徴収課税
  deduction of foreign tax 外国税額控除 （＝foreign tax credit）
  direct payroll deduction 給与天引き方式
  dividends paid deduction 支払い配当金の控除
  insurance deduction 保険料控除
  profits before tax deduction 税引き前利益
  tax deduction 税額控除, 税控除, 減税, 税引き （＝tax credit）
▶In the United States, a special *deduction* system has been implemented that allows investors to carry over capital losses from stock transactions in their current tax return to future years. 米国では, 税務申告上, 投資家が株式売買による譲渡損失を翌年以降に繰り越すことができる特別控除制度が実施されている。
▶Many of regular premium payments are made

with automatic *deductions* from customers' bank accounts. 定期的な保険料支払いの多くは, 顧客の銀行口座からの自動引落しで行われている。

default 名 債務不履行, 貸倒れ, 支払い停止, 滞納, デフォルト

default premium 債務不履行プレミアム（約定利回りと期待利回りとの差）
default risk 債務不履行リスク, 不履行リスク, デフォルト・リスク
go into default 債務不履行になる

▸Many home mortgages went into *default*. 多くの住宅ローンが債務不履行になった。

▸Subprime lenders are struggling because of rising delinquencies and *defaults*. サブプライム・ローンの融資行は, 返済遅延や債務不履行［焦げ付き］の増加で苦戦している。

defect 名 瑕疵(かし), 欠陥, 欠損, 不良,〈法などの〉不備, 未整備, 欠点, 弱点, 短所, 過失

defect rate 不良率
defects in the law 法の不備
defects in the rules governing mergers and acquisitions M&A（企業の合併・買収）に関するルールの不備
latent defect 隠れた欠陥
production defect 製造上の欠陥
structural defect 構造上の欠陥
zero defects movement 無欠陥運動

▸Our program provides a method for each employee in the company to examine his or her job, apply a criterion of zero *defects* and measure the resuls. 当社の従業員を対象としたこの制度は, 従業員がそれぞれ自分の仕事を検討し, 欠陥ゼロの基準を適用して, 仕事の成果を評価する仕組みになっています。

defer 動 繰り延べる, 遅らせる, 据え置く, 先送りする (⇒feasibility)

defer the payment of share dividend 株式配当の支払いを繰り延べる, 配当を遅らせる
defer the taxes 税金を繰り延べる

deferral 名 繰延べ, 延期

deferral method 繰延べ法

▸Before 2006 our deferred tax accounts reflected the rates in effect when we made the *deferrals*. 2006年度より前は, 当社の繰延べ税金勘定は繰延べを行った年度の税率を適用していました。

deferred 形 繰延べの, 据置きの, 据え置き型の, 未払いの, 延期された

deferred annuity 据え置き年金 (=deferred perpetuity)
deferred asset 繰延べ資産
deferred cost 繰延べ原価, 繰延べ費用 (=deferred charge, deferred debit)
deferred credit 繰延べ収益, 前受収益, 繰延べ税金, 繰延べ貸方項目
deferred deduction 繰延べ控除
deferred dividend 繰延べ配当金, 未払い配当金
deferred expense 繰延べ費用, 前払い費用
deferred gross profit 繰延べ売上総利益
deferred income 繰延べ収益, 前受収益
deferred income tax credit 繰延べ投資税額控除, 投資税額控除の繰延べ
deferred interest 前受利息
deferred investment tax credits 繰延べ投資税額控除, 投資税額控除の繰延べ
deferred liability 長期負債, 繰延べ負債
deferred payment 後払い, 分割払い, 延払い, 支払い繰延べ
deferred premium 未収保険料
deferred revenue 繰延べ収益, 前受収益 (=deferred income, unearned revenue)
deferred share 劣後株, 後配株 (=deferred stock：配当や残余財産の分配など利益配分への参加順位が普通の株式より後位にある株式)

deferred gains and losses 繰延べ利益と損失

▸*Deferred gains and losses* are recognized when the future sales or purchases are recognized or immediately if the commitment is canceled. 繰延べ利益と損失は, 将来の販売もしくは購入を認識した時点で, または契約を解除した場合には即時に認識します。

deferred income taxes 繰延べ法人所得税, 繰延べ税額, 繰延べ税金

▸*Deferred income taxes* arise from difference in basis for tax and financial-reporting purposes. 繰延べ法人所得税は, 税務上と財務会計上の認識基準の差異から生じます。

deferred method 繰延べ方式, 繰延べ法, 損益法

▸Two ways to account for timing differences under the *deferred method* are gross change method and net change method. 繰延べ法に基づく期間差異の会計処理の方法としては, 変動総額方式と変動純額方式の二つがある。

deferred tax 繰延べ税金 (=deferred income tax)

deferred tax accounting 税効果会計 (⇒net worth)
deferred tax expense 繰延べ税金費用
deferred tax liabilities 繰延べ税金債務, 繰延べ

税金負債

▸Using our former accounting method, we held *deferred tax* assets and liabilities at their original values even when tax rates changed. 当社の従来の会計処理方法では、税率が変更された場合でも、繰延べ税金資産および負債は、当初の価額で計上していました。

deferred tax asset 繰延べ税金資産《略 DTAs》
(=potential tax credits; ⇒**adjust**, **advance**)

▸*Deferred tax assets* are taxes we expect to get funded in future periods. 繰延べ税金資産は、将来に払戻しされる税金のことです。

▸The banks' equity capital is inflated by so-called "*deferred tax assets.*" 銀行の自己資本は、いわゆる「繰延べ税金資産」でかさ上げされている。

deficit 名 欠損、損失、欠損金、損失金、営業損失、赤字、不足、不足額、債務超過 (⇒**operating deficit**)
　accumulated deficit 累積赤字
　capital deficit 債務超過、資本不足 (=net capital deficiency)
　consolidated deficit 連結赤字
　deficit at the beginning of a period 前期繰延べ欠損金
　deficit-ridden 赤字に悩む
　deficit settlement of accounts 赤字決算
　financial deficit 経営赤字
　fiscal deficit 財政赤字
　government deficit 財政赤字
　net deficit 税引き後赤字
　operate at a deficit 赤字経営をする
　projected deficit 赤字見通し
　trade deficit 貿易赤字
　unappropriated deficit 未処理欠損金

▸The company expects to post a capital *deficit* of ¥8 billion for the year ending this March. 当社は、今年3月期決算で、80億円の債務超過に陥る見通しだ。

▸Though the seven banking groups increased their capital, the effects of the capital increase were offset by the *deficit* settlement of accounts. 銀行・金融グループ7行は、資本増強を実施したが、赤字決算でその増強効果は吹き飛んでしまった。

define 動 明らかにする、明確にする、定義する、示す、規定する

▸Corporate value is *defined* as "the total of profits one company will earn in future." 企業価値は、「ある会社が将来稼ぐ利益の合計」と定義される。

defined benefit 確定給付、給付建て
　defined benefit pension plan 確定給付年金制度、確定給付企業年金、給付建て年金制度 (=defined benefit plan)
　defined benefit plan 確定給付年金制度、確定給付制度、給付建て年金制度、給付建て制度 (=defined benefit pension plan, defined benefit scheme：退職後の年金給付額またはその決定方法があらかじめ明示してある年金制度。⇒**funded status**)
　noncontributory defined benefit (pension) plan 非拠出型確定給付制度

▸We sponsor non-contributory *defined benefit* plans covering the majority of our employees. 当社は、従業員の大多数を対象とする非拠出型確定給付年金制度を設けています。

defined-contribution annuity scheme 確定拠出年金制度

▸Under the *defined-contribution annuity scheme*, workers who will receive pension payouts in the future decide how the pension fund is invested. 確定拠出年金制度では、将来年金の支払いを受ける従業員が年金積立金の運用方法を決める。

defined-contribution corporate pension plan 確定拠出型企業年金制度

▸This *defined-contribution corporate pension plan* is considered to be a Japanese version of the 401(k) sceme used in the United States. この確定拠出型企業年金制度は、米国で採用している401k制度の日本版と考えられる。

defined contribution pension 確定拠出型年金［日本版401k］、確定拠出年金、拠出建て年金制度 (=defined contribution annuity)(退職後の年金給付額が、基金に対する掛金の額と基金の投資収益に基づいて算定される退職給付額。運用の成否で、将来の年金額が増減する)

defined contribution pension plan 確定拠出型［確定拠出］年金制度、確定拠出型年金、確定拠出制度、定額拠出年金制度、拠出建て年金制度 (=defined-contribution annuity scheme, defined contribution pension scheme, defined contribution plan：掛金の運用方法を株式や投資信託、預貯金などの金融商品から加入者自身が決める企業年金の一種。⇒**pension asset**)

▸The pension assets of the *defined-contribution pension plans* are basically required to be managed until subscribers turn 60. 確定拠出年金の年金資産は、原則として加入者が60歳になるまで運用を続ける必要がある。

defined contribution pension scheme 確定拠出型年金制度、確定拠出年金制度

▸The number of companies that have introduced

the *defined-contribution pension scheme* now exceeds 7,000.　確定拠出年金[日本版401k]制度を導入している企業は現在, 7,000社を超えている。

defined contribution plan　確定拠出制度, 拠出建て年金制度, 保険料建て方式, 定額拠出制度, 掛金建て制度, 拠出金制度

deflation 名　デフレーション

deflationary 形　デフレーションの
　deflationary environment　デフレ環境
　deflationary process　デフレ

defray 動　支払う, 支出する, 負担する
▸The estimated costs of ¥600 million will be *defrayed* by medical device manufacturers and financial institutions.　6億円の見積り費用は, 医療機器メーカーと金融機関が負担することになっている。

delay 動　延期する, 遅らせる
　delayed disbursement　支払いの遅延
　delayed interest　遅延利息, 遅延金利
　delayed settlement　特約日決済

delay 名　遅延, 遅滞

delegate 動　委任する, 権限を委譲する, 代表として派遣する　(⇒**authority**)

delinquency 名　支払い遅延, 返済遅延, 延滞, 不履行の債務
　credit card delinquency　クレジット・カードの支払い遅延[返済遅延]
　rate of delinquency　支払い遅延率, 返済遅延率 (＝delinquency rate)
▸The percentage of credit card *delinquencies* fell sharply in the first quarter of this year.　今年第1四半期のクレジット・カードの返済遅延率は, 急減した。

delinquent 形　滞納の, 延滞の, 義務不履行の
　delinquent account　滞留債権
　delinquent account receivable　回収遅滞受取勘定, 不良債権勘定
　delinquent amounts　延滞額
　delinquent balances　不良債権残高, 回収遅延残高
　delinquent loan　延滞融資, 延滞債券
　delinquent recievable　支払い遅延債券
▸Our credit approval and monitoring have kept our percentage of *delinquent* balances and write-offs below industry norms.　与信承認条件や検査を厳しくしているため, 当社の不良債権残高と償却額は業界水準以下を保っています。

delist 動　上場を廃止する, 上場を停止する
Mitsubishi UFJ Securities was *delisted* from the First Section of the Tokyo Stock Exchange.　三菱UFJ証券は, 東証一部から上場廃止になった。

delisting 名　上場廃止, 上場停止
▸After *delisting*, shareholders cannot sell their shares on the market, but they can do so through securities houses if there are buyers.　上場廃止後は, 株主は手持ちの株を市場で売却することはできないが, 買い手がいれば証券会社を通じて売却することはできる。

deliver 動　届ける, 配達する, 引き渡す, 渡す, 交付する, 送達する, 納入する, 提供する, 達成する, 実行する, 〈判定や評決などを〉行う, 判定を下す, 〈原油などを〉産出する
▸Both markets *delivered* positive organic growth.　両市場は, プラスの有機的成長率を達成しました。

delivery 名　配達, 送達, 配送, 出荷, 納品, 納入, 完納, 引渡し, 受渡し, 交付, 意見の発表, 陳述　(⇒ **orders on hand**)
　buy for future delivery　先渡しで買う
　delivery expense　配達費, 配送費
　delivery of shares　株式の受渡し, 株式交付
　delivery system　配送システム, 配達システム
　export delivery　輸出出荷
　physical delivery　現物受渡し, 現渡し, 現引き
▸After the restructuring, the group aims to strengthen its profit-making capability by establishing joint frameworks in product *delivery* and development.　再編後, 同グループは商品の配送と商品の開発を共同化して, グループ全体の収益力を強化する計画だ。
▸At *delivery*, the balance sheet will be adjusted for the stock split.　株式の交付時に, 貸借対照表は株式分割による調整を行います。
▸Most of the current orders on hand are scheduled for *delivery* in 2008.　現在の受注残高の大半は, 2008年度に納入することになっています。

delivery interval　納入期間
▸The current orders on hand have shorter *delivery intervals* compared with prior years.　現在の手持ちの受注分[受注残高]は, 過年度[過去数年]に比べて納入期間が短くなっています。

demand 動　要求する, 請求する, 求める, 要する, 必要とする
▸The former head of the Murakami Fund was often dubbed a shareholder who *demands* a lot.　村上ファンドの元代表は,「モノ言う株主」とよく呼ばれた。

demand 名　需要, 要求, デマンド
　capital demand　資金需要, 資本需要 (＝demand for capital)
　credit demand　信用需要, 資金需要

demand deposit 要求払い預金, 当座預金
demand for funds 資金需要 (=demand for capital)
demand for loans 借入需要, 資金需要
institutional demand 機関投資家の需要
investor demand 投資家の需要
loan demand 借入需要 (=demand for loans)
payable on demand 一覧払い
▶Customer *demand* for the products and services of our core business continues to grow despite weak economic conditions worldwide. 世界的な景気低迷にもかかわらず、当社の主力事業の製品とサービスに対する顧客の需要は、引き続き伸びています。

demerger 名 会社分割, 会社からの独立
denominated 形 …建て, …表示の
foreign currency-denominated bonds 外貨建て債券
in dollar-denominated terms ドル建てで, ドル表示で
yen-denominated profits 円建て利益
yuan-denominated bond 人民元建て債券
▶The greater part of the consolidated revenues and assets of the Company is *denominated* in U.S. dollars. 当社の連結売上高と連結資産の大半は、米ドル建てとなっています。

denomination 名 金種, 種類, 名称
denominator 名 分母
department 名 部門, 部, 課, 局, 省, 売り場
accounting department 経理部
department administration 部門管理
department cost 部門費 (=department charge, department expense)
financial department 財務部
legal department 法務部
manufacturing department 製造部門 (=production department)
operating department 事業部門
producing department cost 製造部門費
purchasing department 購買部門
sales department 営業部門
shipping department 配送部
treasury department 財務部門

departmental 形 部門の
departmental cost 部門費
departmental profit 事業部利益, 事業別利益 (=divisional profit)

dependent 名 扶養親族
▶GM pays for health care for 750,000 U.S. hourly employees, retirees and their *dependents*. 米ゼネラル・モーターズ(GM)は, 米国の時間給制従業員, 退職者とその扶養親族75万人の医療費を負担している。

dependent 形 従属する, 依存する
be dependent on ... …に左右される, …に依存する
dependent company 従属会社, 子会社
dependent project 相互依存型[相互依存的]プロジェクト

deplete 動 激減させる, 消耗させる
depleted asset 減耗資産, 涸渇資産
depleted inventories 在庫の減少

depletion 名 低下, 減耗, 減耗償却
depletion allowance 減耗控除, 減耗償却累計額
depletion asset 減耗資産, 涸渇資産 (=depleted asset)
depletion base 減耗償却基準額
depletion expense 減耗償却費
depletion in economic value 経済価値の低下

deposit 動 預ける, 供託する, 手付金として支払う
deposit 名 預金, 預かり, 手付金, 保証金
bank deposit 銀行預金
business deposit 営業預金
current deposit 当座預金
deposit in transit 未達預金, 銀行側未処理の預金
interest on deposit 預金利息

depositor 名 預金者, 供託者
depreciable 名 減価償却の対象となる, 減価償却できる, 償却可能な, 償却性の
depreciable asset 減価償却資産, 償却性資産, 償却資産, 減価償却の対象となる資産 (⇒group method)
depreciable life 減価償却期間, 償却期間, 償却年数, 耐用年数 (=estimated useful life, service life, useful life)
▶The increase in operating expenses was primarily due to depreciation expenses caused by higher average *depreciable* plant. 営業費用増加の主な要因は減価償却費で, 減価償却の対象となる有形固定資産の平均残高の拡大により, 減価償却費は増加しました。

depreciate 動 低下する, 下落する, 価値が下がる, 〈通貨を〉切り下げる, 減価償却する, 償却する, 減価する, 減損して見積もる
▶Assets were *depreciated* using the unit method. 資産は、個別償却法で償却しました。
▶The bridge *depreciates* to zero value after 40 years in terms of tax laws. この橋の耐用年数は, 税法上は40年にすぎない。

depreciation 名 減価償却, 減価償却費, 償却,

償却費, 減価, 価値低下, 平価切下げ

depreciationと**amortization**について➡有形固定資産や陳腐化などによる給付能力の減少を一定の公式で計算して, 費用に計上することをdepreciation (減価償却) という。これに対して, 無形固定資産の取得原価を一定の耐用年数にわたって各会計期間の費用として規則的に配分することをamortization (償却) という。米国では, 一般に有形固定資産(property, plant and equipment)の減価償却にdepreciationを使い, 無形固定資産(intangible assets)の償却にはamortizationを使っている。

accounting depreciation 会計上の償却, 会計上の減価償却
accrued depreciation 減価償却累計額
allowance for depreciation 減価償却引当金, 減価償却積立金 (＝depreciation provision)
declining depreciation method 逓減減価償却法
deferred depreciation 繰延べ償却
depreciation and amortization 減価償却および償却, 減価償却費および償却費, 減価償却費
depreciation, depletion and amortization 減価償却費
depreciation of buildings 建物減価償却費
depreciation of office equipment 事務用備品減価償却費
depreciation of the yen 円安 (＝depreciating yen, yen depreciation)
depreciation on plant and equipment 減価償却費
depreciation on property 資産減価償却
depreciation provision 減価償却引当金 (＝accrued depreciation, allowance for depreciation, depreciation reserve)
depreciation reserve 減価償却引当金 (＝reserve for depreciation)
equal installment depreciation 定額法
item depreciation 個別償却
period of depreciation 耐用年数
replacement cost depreciation 時価償却
reserve for depreciation 減価償却引当金 (＝depreciation reserve)
tax depreciation 税務上の減価償却
▸Cost of revenues, *depreciation*, and amortization are translated at the actual rates in effect when the related assets were manufactured or acquired. 売上原価と減価償却費および償却費は, 当該資産の製造日または取得日の実効為替レートで換算してあります。

depreciation cost 減価償却費 (＝depreciation charge, depreciation expense：減価償却総額のうち減価償却手続きで費用化された部分)
▸Companies will be allowed to fully write off *depreciation costs* as tax-exempt expenses. 企業は今後, 減価償却費を非課税費用[損金]として全額処理できるようになる[減価償却費を100％損金算入できるようになる]。

depreciation expense 減価償却費 (＝depreciation cost)
▸*Depreciation expense* increased 30% in 2007 in comparison to 2006 due to increased fixed asset expenditures. 2007年度の減価償却費は, 固定資産支出額の増加により, 前年度に比べて30％増加しました。

DER 負債・資本比率 (debt equity ratioの略)
deregulate 動 規制を緩和する, 規制を撤廃する, 自由化する, 市場開放する
▸Bank sales of insurance products were *deregulated* in April 2001. 保険商品の銀行窓口での販売は, 2001年4月に自由化された。

deregulation 名 規制緩和, 規制撤廃, 自由化, 市場開放
▸With the *deregulation* of the power industry, U.S. electric power companies are fiercely competing in the retail market. 電力自由化では, 米国の電力会社が小売市場で厳しい競争を繰り広げている。

derivative 名 派生商品, 金融派生商品, デリバティブ (＝derivative financial instrument, derivative product)

デリバティブとは➡相場の変動を予測して行う先物取引など, 特殊な取引を組み合わせた金融派生商品。もともとは株価や金利, 為替などの変動リスクを回避するために開発された。少ない原資で多額の取引ができるため, 投機的に用いると巨額の利益が得られる一方, 判断を誤ると多額の損失を被る危険がある。(2003年8月7日付読売新聞)

commodity derivatives 市況商品の派生商品
credit derivatives 信用派生商品
equity derivatives 株式派生商品
exchange-traded derivatives 上場派生商品
financial derivatives 金融派生商品
interest rate derivatives 金利派生商品
mortgage derivatives モーゲージ派生商品
weather derivatives 天候デリバティブ
▸*Derivatives* such as futures and options are securities that derive their value from another financial assets, such as a share. 先物取引やオプション取引などのデリバティブ(金融派生商品)は, 株など他の金融資産から価値を引き出す有価証券だ。

derivative 形 派生した
  derivative action 派生訴訟, 株主代表訴訟 （＝derivative lawsuit, derivative suit）
  derivative financial instrument 派生商品, 金融派生商品, デリバティブ
  derivative instrument 金融派生商品 （＝derivative financial instrument）
  derivative product 派生商品, 金融派生商品, デリバティブ （＝derivative, derivative instrument, derivative financial instrument）
  derivative transaction 派生商品取引, デリバティブ取引
DES 債務の株式化, 債権の株式化, デット・エクイティ・スワップ（**debt equity swap**の略）
descriptive statement 取引明細付き勘定照合表
deteriorate 動 悪化する, 低下する, 停滞する, 退化する, 老朽化する
  deteriorated earnings 業績の悪化
  deteriorated profitability 収益性の悪化
  deteriorating credit quality 信用の質の悪化, 信用度の悪化, 信用力の低下
  ▶Nomura incurred heavy losses due to the *deteriorating* subprime-loan market. 米サブプライム・ローン[低所得者向け住宅融資]市場の悪化で, 野村[野村ホールディングス]が巨額の損失を被った。
deterioration 名 悪化, 低下, 減少, 停滞, 品質低下, 退化, 劣化, 老朽化
  deterioration in asset quality 資産の質の悪化
  deterioration in balance sheets 財務体質の悪化
  deterioration in financial health 財務体質の悪化
  deterioration in the business situation 経営悪化, 景況の悪化
  deterioration of corporate performance 企業業績の悪化
  earnings deterioration 収益の悪化, 業績の悪化
  profit deterioration 減益, 利益の減少
  ▶An increasing number of loans turn out to be nonperforming due to a *deterioration* in the business situation of the borrowers. 融資先の経営悪化で, 不良債権化する貸出が増えている。
determinable 形 決定できる, 確定できる, 終結すべき, 消滅すべき
  determinable interest 解除条件付き利益
  determinable liability 確定債務
determination 名 決定, 決断, 決断力, 決心, 決意, 確定, 限定, 判断, 解決, 測定, 算定, 計算, 判決, 裁決, 終決, 財産権の消滅[終了]

determination of the actuarial present values 保険数理上の現在価値の測定
determination of net income 純利益の算定
determination of the reportable segment 報告すべきセグメントの決定
vesting percentage applicable at the date of determination 測定日に適用可能な給付額の割合
determine 動 決定する, 決断する, 決める, 決意する, 確定する, 定める, …に制限を設ける, 左右する, 強い影響を与える, 判断する, 〈問題などを〉解決する, 測定する, 算定する
▶The board of directors *determines* dividend payments based on such considerations as earnings from operations, capital requirements, and the corporation's financial condition. 配当の支払い額は, 営業利益, 資金需要や当社の財務状況などを検討した上で, 取締役会が決定しています。
develop 動 開発する, 整備する, 改善する, 改良する, 発展させる, 育成する, 〈土地などを〉造成する, 展開する, 現像する
▶General Motors Corp. and Ford Motor Co. were late in *developing* low fuel consumption cars as the price of crude oil rose. ゼネラル・モーターズ(GM)やフォード・モーターは, 原油高のなかで, 低燃費車の開発が遅れた。
developer 名 開発業者, 開発会社, 不動産開発業者, 宅地造成業者, 宅地開発業者, デベロッパー
▶Real estate *developer* Mitsui Fudosan will acquire a 33.16 percent stake in Imperial Hotel for ¥86 billion. 不動産開発会社の三井不動産は, 帝国ホテルの株式の33.16％を860億円で取得する。
development 名 開発, 整備, 教育, 発展, 進歩, 進展, 展開, 推移, 動き, 情勢, 製品 （⇒**research and development**）
▶Our laboratories engage in basic research as well as product and service *development*. 当社の研究所では, 基礎研究のほかに, 製品やサービスの開発に当たっています。
DI 景気変動指数, 拡散指数, 業況判断 （**diffusion index**の略）
difference 名 差, 差異, 違い, 格差, 差額, 不足分 （⇒**temporary differences, timing differences**）
  difference between taxable income and financial statement earnings 課税所得と財務諸表上の利益との差異
  foreign exchange differences 為替差損益
  real bond yield differences 債券実質利回り格差
  timing differences and deferred tax 〈費用収

益の〉期間差異と繰延べ税金
▶The *difference* was funded by increasing notes payable by $200 million, principally through the sale of commercial paper. 資金の不足分は、主にコマーシャル・ペーパーを発行して、手形借入金を2億ドル増やして補填しました。

differentiation 名 差別化, 差別, 区別, 識別, 分化
  product differentiation 製品差別化, 製品の差別化
  strategic differentiation 戦略的差別化
▶Quality no longer secures strategic *differentiation*, but is an operational necessity. 製品とサービスの質はもはや戦略的差別化を保証するものではなく、業務運営の必須条件となっています。

diffusion index 景気変動指数, 拡散指数, 業況判断《略 DI》

digit 名 桁
  double digit 2桁, 10%超

dilute 動 薄める, 弱める,〈価値などを〉損なう, 希薄化する, 希釈化する, 減少する, 減額する
  dilute the value of the existing shares 既存の株の価値を損なう
  diluted earnings per share of common stock 希薄後普通株式1株当たり純利益
  diluted EPS 希薄済み1株利益
  diluted net earnings per common share 希薄後普通株式1株当たり純利益
  fully diluted 完全希薄化, 完全希薄化後
  on a diluted basis 希薄化ベースで, 希釈化ベースで
  primary and fully diluted earnings per share 単純希薄化と完全希薄化による1株当たり利益
▶Hokuetsu will issue equity warrants to all existing shareholders to *dilute* Oji's voting rights and make it difficult for Oji to take control of the company. 北越製紙は、既有の全株主に新株予約権を発行して王子製紙の議決権を減らし、王子が北越の経営権を握るのを阻止する方針だ。

dilution 名 〈株式などの〉希薄化, 希釈化, 減額, 減少, 落ち込み, 1株当たりの価値が低くなる[薄まる]こと (⇒**per-share value**)
  希薄化[希釈化]とは➡時価発行増資や転換社債の転換, ワラント債の権利行使などによる発行済み株式総数の増加で, 1株当たり利益(earnings per share)の減少や資産価値の目減りを招くことをいう。
  anti-dilution 希薄化防止, 反希薄化
  dilution from new share issues 新株発行による希薄化, 増資による希薄化
  dilution from the conversion of convertible bonds 転換社債の転換による希薄化
  dilution losses 減額による損失 (=losses from dilution)
  dilution of earnings per share 1株当たり利益の希薄化
  dilution of the per-share value of existing stock 既存株式の1株当たり価値の希薄化
  earnings dilution 利益の希薄化, 利益の落ち込み, 減益 (=dilution of earnings)
  losses from dilution 減額による損失
▶The *dilution* in earnings per share from new issuances was not material. 新株発行による1株当たり利益[純利益]の希薄化は, 重要視するほどではありません。

dilutive effect 希薄化効果 (⇒**primary**)
dilutive securities 希薄化証券
diminishing balance method 逓減残高法, 逓減減価法, 逓減償却法, 定率法 (=declining balance method, reducing balance method)

DIP financing 事業再生融資, DIPファイナンス (=debtor-in-possession finance)
DIP plan 事業再生融資制度, DIPファイナンス (⇒**debtor-in-possession**)
▶Under the *DIP plan* widely used in the United States, a failed company can get new loans for continuing its business even if it cannot afford to put up property as security. アメリカで広く利用されている事業再生融資制度(DIPファイナンス)では、経営破綻した企業が, 有体財産[不動産]を担保にすることができなくても事業継続のために新規融資を受けることができる。

director 名 取締役, 理事, 役員, 局長 (⇒**board of directors, independent director, officer**)
  取締役とは➡取締役会のメンバーで, 業務執行についての意思決定をするのが取締役であるが, 日本と違って英米法では必ずしも会社の役員ではない。社内取締役(inside director)と社外取締役(outside director)を含めて, 取締役(director)は株主が選任し, 会社役員(corporate officer)は取締役が選任することになっている。
  acting director 仮取締役, 取締役代行, 代行取締役 (⇒**caretaker**)
  advisory director 相談役, 顧問取締
  alternative director 代理取締役, 取締役代行, 予備取締役 (=alternate director)
  board director 取締役, 委員会などの理事 (=board member)
  board of directors 取締役会
  changes in directors 役員の異動
  company director 会社役員, 役員

deputy managing director 〈英国企業の〉副社長, 業務取締役代行
director of finance 財務担当取締役
directors and auditors' bonus 役員賞与, 役員賞与金
directors' emoluments 取締役報酬
directors' remuneration 役員報酬
directors' report 取締役の報告, 取締役報告書
disclosure of individual directors' remuneration 役員報酬の個別開示
executive director 業務執行取締役
full time director 常勤取締役
inside director 社内取締役, 内部取締役, 内部重役
loan to director 取締役貸付け金
loans repayable to stockholders, directors or employees 株主・役員・従業員借入金
managing director 〈英国企業の〉社長, 業務執行取締役, 専務取締役, 常務取締役《略 MD》
meeting of board of directors 取締役会会議, 取締役会
new director 新任取締役, 後任取締役
outside director 社外取締役, 外部取締役
president and representative director 代表取締役社長
provisional director 一時取締役
representative director 代表取締役
senior managing director 専務取締役, 専務

▸The minimum number of *directors* for a stock company has been reduced from three to one under the new Corporate Law. （2006年5月1日に施行された）新会社法では, 株式会社の最低取締役数が3人から1人に減った。

disability benefit 疾病給付

▸We must book expenses for *disability benefits* when the disabilities occur. 疾病給付については, 疾病が実際に生じた時点で費用として計上しなければなりません。

disadvantage 名 不利, 不都合, 不便な点, 不利な立場, 遅れ, 劣位, 弱点, 不備, 欠陥, 損害, 損失, マイナス

▸GM's current $1,500 per worker health care expense puts the company at a significant *disadvantage* versus foreign-based competitors. GMにとって, 現在同社が負担している従業員[労働者] 1人当たり1,500ドルの医療費が, 海外のライバルとの競争上, 大きなマイナスになっている。

disappointing 形 期待外れの, 期待を裏切る, 予想を裏切る

disappointing growth of income 収益の伸び悩み, 期待外れの収益の伸び
disappointing news 悪材料
disappointing results[performance] 期待外れの業績, 期待を裏切る業績, 予想を裏切る業績

▸This difficult global business environment impacted our business and caused *disappointing* second quarter results. この困難な世界のビジネス環境による当社業務への影響で, 第2四半期の業績は不満足な結果となりました。

disclose 動 開示する, 公開する, 公表する, 発表する, 明示する （⇒book-closing）

▸The Tokyo Stock Exchange obliges listed companies to *disclose* information that concerns investors. 東京証券取引所は, 投資家に関連する情報の開示を上場企業に義務付けている。

disclosure 名 企業内容の開示, 企業経営内容の公開, 企業情報の開示, 情報開示, 情報の公開, 事実の開示, 発明の開示, 開示, 公開, 公開性, 公表, 表示, 内容の特定, 告知, ディスクロージャー （⇒evidence）

disclosure of accounting policies 会計方針の開示
disclosure of financial statements 財務諸表[財務書類]の開示, 企業財務の公開
disclosure of individual directors' remuneration 役員報酬の個別開示
disclosure system 企業内容開示制度, 開示制度, ディスクロージャー制度
fair disclosure 公正表示
financial disclosure 財務内容の開示
full disclosure 完全開示
global standard information disclosure 世界標準の情報開示
risk disclosure リスク開示

▸A proposal by our shareholders seeking *disclosure* of individual directors' remuneration gained 35 percent support. 役員報酬の個別開示を求めて出された株主提案に対して, 35%の支持が得られた。

discontinued operation[business] 非継続事業, 中止事業, 廃止事業, 事業廃止部門

income from discontinued operations 廃止事業利益, 中止事業利益, 非継続事業利益, 廃止事業経常利益
loss on discontinued operations 非継続事業[中止事業]損失

discount 動 割引する, 値引きして売る

discount 名 割引, 割引率, 割引額, 割引料, ディスカウント （⇒employee discount）

bank discount 銀行の手形割引, 銀行割引料
 （＝banker's discount：手形金額×日数×利率）

be issued at a discount of ... …割り引いて発行される
be sold on a discount basis 割引発行される（＝be issued on a discount basis）
bond discounts 社債発行差金, 社債発行割引差金, 社債割引料（社債の発行価額［売買価額］と額面金額［額面価額］との差額）
discount on capital stock 株式払込み剰余金
discount on debenture 社債の発行差額, 社債発行差金
discount period 割引期間
discounts on bonds payable 社債発行差金, 社債割引発行差金, 社債発行割引料（＝bond discount）
original issue discount 発行差金

discount [discounted] cash flow method
割引キャッシュ・フロー法, 割引現在価値法, ディスカウント・キャッシュ・フロー方式, DCF方式（＝discount cash flow system, discounted cash flow formula：貸倒れ引当金の必要額の算定方法として, 融資先企業の将来の予想収益などを考慮して債権の現在価値を割り出す方式）
▶Under the *discount cash flow method* based on the U.S. model, loan values are calculated based on projections of how profitable a borrower is likely to be in the future. 米国流の割引現在価値方式では, 融資先企業の予想収益に基づいて債権の現在価値を算定する。

discount plan 割引制度
▶We expect the effects on revenues of this *discount plan* and 2007 price increases to offset each other. この割引制度と2007年度の値上げの収益への影響は, 相殺されると考えています。

discount rate 公定歩合（＝official discount rate）, 割引率
▶The weighted average *discount rate* was used in determining the accumulated and accrued plan benefits. 累積年金給付債務額の算定には, 加重平均割引率が用いられています。

discretion 名 行動の自由, 自由裁量, 任意
discretionary 形 任意の, 自由裁量の
 discretionary account 一任勘定, 売買一任勘定
 discretionary cost 裁量原価
 discretionary fund 売買一任勘定資金
 discretionary service 選択的サービス
discussion 名 討議, 検討, 議論, 講演
discussion and analysis of our results and operations 業績および営業活動の検討と分析
dishonor 名 不名誉, 恥辱, 支払い拒絶, 不渡り

dishonored bill 不渡り手形
dishonored check 不渡り小切手
disparity 名 格差, 開き, 差, 相違, 差異, 不一致, 不均衡, 不釣り合い, 不平等（⇒timing differences）
▶A *disparity* in income between nonregular workers and regular workers is due to the establishment of merit-based pay systems at many firms. 正社員と非正社員との所得格差の原因は, 多くの企業で成果主義型の賃金制度を採用したことにある。

dispatch 動 派遣する,〈文書などを〉発送する
▶Mitsui Fudosan will *dispatch* its executives to Imperial Hotel Ltd. 三井不動産は, 帝国ホテルに役員を派遣することになる。

display 名 陳列, 展示, 表示, 表示端末装置, 画面表示, ディスプレー
▶A *display* of some of our products will open at the Annual Meeting of StockHolders. 定時株主総会では, 当社製品の展示会が開催されます。

disposable 形 処分できる, 使い捨ての
 disposable income 可処分所得
 disposable personal income 可処分個人所得
 disposable profit 可処分利益, 処分可能利益（利益処分の対象となる利益）
disposal 名 処分, 処理, 売却, 除却（⇒bad loan disposal）
 asset disposal 資産の処分, 資産売却
 disposal of bad [nonperforming] loans 不良債権の処理
 disposal of non-core assets 非中核的事業資産の売却
 disposal of property, plant and equipment 有形固定資産の売却
 disposal of shares 株式の売却
 disposal value 処分価額
 gain on disposal of equipment 設備処分益
disposal of facilities 設備の処分, 設備の廃棄
▶Companies are trying to improve their business foundations or structure through mergers, acquisitions, the establishment of joint ventures, the *disposal of facilities* and the sale of business rights and assets. 企業は, 企業の合併や買収, 合弁会社の設立, 設備廃棄あるいは営業権や資産の売却などによって, 事業の基盤や構造の整備に努めている。

disposal of fixed assets 固定資産の除却
▶There were no *disposals of fixed assets*. 固定資産の除却はなかった。

disposal of nonperforming loans 不良債権の処理

▸With the promotion of the *disposal of nonperforming loans*, corporate failures and joblessness will increase in the short time.　不良債権処理を促進すれば、短期的には企業倒産と失業が増える。

disposition 名　処分、売却、譲渡、使途、自由裁量権
　asset disposition　資産処分、資産譲渡
　capital disposition　資本支出
　source and disposition of funds　資金の源泉と使途、資金運用表
▸The ultimate *disposition* of these matters will not have a material adverse effect on the consolidated financial position of the Company.　これらの案件の最終処分で、当社の連結財政状態に重大な悪影響が出るようなことはありません。

dissolution 名　解散、契約の解除、解消、取消し、解体、廃棄

dissolve 動　解散する、〈契約を〉解除する、解消する、取り消す、解体する、廃棄する　（⇒**management right**）
▸Misuzu Audit Corp. was *dissolved* after several accounting scandals.　会計不祥事［監査不祥事］を受けて、みすず監査法人が解散した。

distressed company　経営不振企業、業績悪化企業

distribute 動　分配する、分売する、販売する、供給する、配給する、配送する、配布する、流通させる、配信する
　distributed cost　配賦原価、原価の配賦
　distributed earnings　分配利益、利益の分配
▸Integrating management will benefit both companies by increasing Internet and TV advertising revenues as well as *distributing* TBS programs through broadband.　経営統合は、インターネットとテレビの広告収入拡大やTBS番組のブロードバンド配信などで、両社にメリットがある。

distribution 名　流通、配分、配賦、〈有価証券の〉分売、分配、配当、配給、配布、交付、分布、配信、分類、区分、ディストリビューション　（⇒**secondary distribution**）
　accounting distribution　会計上の配分
　cost distribution　原価配分
　distribution channel　流通経路
　distribution cost　流通費、流通経費、流通原価、流通コスト、販売費、配給費、配送費物流費、物流コスト　（=**distribution expense**）
　distribution expense　販売費、配給費、物流費、流通費、配送費　（=**distribution cost**）
　distribution of cost　原価配分

　distribution of net profit　純利益処分
　distribution of profits　利益分配
　distribution overhead　取引所分売
　free share distribution　株式の無償交付
　funding distribution　資金調達源の分布
　news distribution　ニュース配信
　required distribution　配当必要額
　revenue distribution　収益分布
▸Nippon Express has expertise in the *distribution* of goods such as how to handle customs clearance and stock control.　日本通運は、通関業務や在庫管理業務など物流のノウハウを持っている。
▸This product will be sold through retail computer *distribution* chains.　この製品は、コンピュータの小売販売チェーン店を通じて販売されます。

distribution and marketing support company　物流・販売支援会社
▸The Toyota group has a research and development company in Thailand, as well as a *distribution and marketing support company* in Singapore.　トヨタグループの場合、タイには研究開発会社、シンガポールには物流・販売支援会社がある。

distribution center　物流センター、流通センター、配送センター　（=**distribution facility**）
▸Nike Inc. plans to close two *distribution* centers in Oregon and Tennessee to save $200 million over 20 years.　ナイキが、20年間で2億ドル削減するため、米オレゴン州とテネシー州の流通センター2か所の閉鎖を計画している。

distribution network　物流網、流通網、流通ネットワーク、販売網
▸Bic Camera and Edion will form a capital tie-up and cooperate in jointly procuring products and using *distribution networks*.　ビックカメラとエディオンは、資本提携して、共同仕入れや物流網の共同利用などの面で協力する方針だ。

distributor 名　販売店、販売代理店、代理店、輸入代理店、総輸入元、流通業者、流通、問屋、卸売り業者、配達人、ディストリビュータ
▸France's Competition Commission has ordered Sony, Matsushita and Philips to pay fines for allegedly concluding price-fixing agreements on retail goods with their local *distributors*.　フランスの競争評価会は、国内販売店と小売電気製品の価格維持協定を結んだとして、ソニー、松下電器産業とフィリップスに罰金の支払いを命じた。

diversification 名　多様化、多角化、経営多角化、分散化、分散投資　（⇒**business diversification**）

asset diversification　資産の分散, 資産分散化
diversification of business lines　事業分野の多角化, 業務の多様化
diversification of shares　株式の多様化
diversification strategy　(事業)多角化戦略
horizontal diversification　水平的多角化
international diversification　国際分散投資
portfolio diversification　分散投資
product diversification　製品の多角化, 製品多様化
vertical diversification　垂直的多角化
▶Business *diversification* at major supermarkets during the bubble years negatively impacted their corporate management.　バブル期に大手スーパーが進めた事業の多角化が, 大手スーパーの企業経営に悪影響を及ぼした。

diversified 形　多様化した, 多角化した, 多角経営の, 分散した, 分散型の

diversified assets　分散化した資産, 分散化された資産, 資産の分散化
diversified company [enterprise]　多角化企業, 複合企業
diversified investment　分散投資, 分散型投資, 投資の分散化
diversified management　多角経営, 経営の多角化
diversified portfolio　分散投資されたポートフォリオ, リスク分散型ポートフォリオ
▶These losses represent a tiny portion of most pension funds' well-*diversified assets*.　これらの損害額は, 大半の年金基金の十分に分散化された資産のごく一部にすぎない。

diversify 動　多様化する, 多角化する, 〈資産などを〉分散する, 分散投資する, 拡大する

diversify customer base　顧客基盤を多様化する, 顧客基盤の多様化, 顧客基盤を拡大する
diversify funding activities　資金調達の多様化を進める
diversify into new areas　新規分野への多角化を推進する
diversify investment risks　投資リスクを分散する
diversify the sources of financing　資金調達源の多角化を進める
▶We will continue working to stabilize and *diversify* our funding activities.　当社は, 今後とも資金調達の安定化と多様性を進めてまいります。

diversity 名　多様性, 多角化, 分散

▶We will bring about the changes we need to be successful in the global marketplace by making *diversity* an integral part of the fabric of our business.　当社は, 多様性を当社のビジネス基盤の不可欠な一部として, グローバル市場で成功を収めるのに必要な変革をもたらす方針です。

divest 動　〈資産などを〉整理する, 売却する, 手放す, 取り除く, 放棄する

divest oneself of ...　…を放棄する, …の権利などを剝奪する, …の事業を整理[売却]する
divest unprofitable operation　不採算部門を整理する
▶We *divested* some of our nonstrategic businesses during the second quarter.　当社は, 第2四半期に当社の非戦略的事業部門を売却[整理]しました。

divestiture 名　企業分割, 資産の分割, 〈事業や不採算店舗などの〉整理[売却], 再編成, 権利などの剝奪

corporate divestiture　企業分割, 分社化, 企業再編成　(＝corporate separation)
divestiture of subsidiaries　子会社再編成, 子会社の再編
mergers, acquisitions and divestitures　企業の合併, 買収と分割
▶These gains were partially offset by a decline in other revenues attributable to the *divestiture* of the non-strategic businesses of the firm.　この増加分は, 同社の非戦略的事業部門の売却[整理]に伴うその他の売上高の減少により, 一部相殺されています。

dividend 名　配当, 利益配当, 配当金, 分配金(米国では一般に会社が四半期ごとに配当を支払う。生命保険の配当金は, 主に保険料の運用収益が契約時の想定を上回った場合に, その差額が契約者に支払われる。⇒cash dividend, quarterly dividend, stock dividend)

accrued dividend　未払い配当金, 経過配当
bond dividend　社債配当
capital dividend　資本配当, タコ配当　(＝bonus dividend)
common stock dividend　普通株式配当金
dividend distribution　配当支払い
dividend earned　受取配当金
dividend fund　配当資金
dividend in arrears　繰越し配当金, 延滞配当金, 未払い優先配当金, 累積未払い配当金
dividend of earnings　利益配当
dividend paid　支払い配当金
dividend payout　配当性向, 配当支払い, 配当金の支払い, 配当支払い率　(＝dividend payout ratio, payout ratio; ⇒share buyback)
dividend policy　配当政策, 配当方針　(⇒policy)
dividend [dividends] receivable　未収配当金

dividend revenue 受取配当金 （＝dividend income）
dividend to policyholders 〔保険〕契約者配当 （＝policyholder dividend）
dividends from associated company 関連会社からの配当金
dividends on stocks 株式配当
dividends payable 未払配当金, 未払い配当金 （＝dividend payable unclaimed）
dividends per common share 普通株式1株当たり配当金
dividends to shareholders 株主配当金
final dividend 期末配当, 清算配当
high dividend 高配当
imputed dividend 見なし配当
increased dividend 増配
interim dividend 中間配当 （＝midterm dividend, regular interim dividend）
no dividend 無配
ordinary dividend 普通配当
pay dividends 配当金を支払う
projected dividend 予想配当
reduce dividend payment 減配する
regular dividend 普通配当, 通常配当, 定時配当
special year-end dividend 特別年度末配当
unclaimed dividend 未請求配当金
unusual dividend 特別配当
year-end dividend 期末配当
▶JAL will resume *dividend* payments by fiscal 2010. 日本航空は, 2010年度までに復配する方針だ。

dividend income 受取配当金, 配当金収入, 配当所得
▶A life insurer's core operating profit consists mainly of income related to insurance and investment operations, including interest and *dividend income*. 生命保険会社の基礎利益の内訳は, 主に受取利息や配当金収入など保険・投資事業の関連収益だ。

dividend on preferred shares 優先株式に対する配当金
▶Earnings per common share were calculated after *dividends on preferred shares*. 普通株式1株当たり純利益は, 優先株式配当額を控除したうえで計算されています。

dividend payment 配当支払い, 配当金の支払い, 配当支払い額, 支払い配当金
dividend payment on equity 株式配当
raising of dividend payments 増配
▶The firm paid dividends although it had no profit available for *dividend payment*. 同社は, 配当の支払いに充てる利益が出ていないのに配当金を支払っていた。

dividend per share 1株当たり配当, 1株当たり配当金, 1株当たり配当額《略 DPS》
▶We increased the projected *dividend per share* to ¥10 for fiscal 2007 from the ¥8 paid the previous year. 当社は, 2007年度の1株当たり予想配当を前期[前年度]の8円から10円に引き上げました。

dividend ratio [rate] 配当率（配当率＝年間配当額÷資本金）
▶Each company is allowed to have its board of directors determine the *dividend ratio* once such a rule is written into its articles of incorporation. 企業の配当率は, その規則を定款で定めれば, 取締役会で決めることができる。
▶The *dividend* rate on the series 3 preferred shares is calculated each quarter. シリーズ3優先株式の配当率は, 四半期ごとに計算されます。

dividend reinvestment 配当金再投資, 株主配当再投資, 配当金株式再投資, 配当再投資
dividend reinvestment plan 株主配当再投資制度
dividend reinvestment and stock purchase plan 株主配当再投資・株式購入制度 （＝shareholder dividend reinvestment and stock purchase plan）
▶The *Dividend Reinvestment* and Stock Purchase Plan provides owners of common stock a convenient way to purchase additional shares. 株主配当再投資・株式購入制度は, 普通株式の株主が株式の追加購入をされるのに便利な方法です。

dividend yield 配当利回り（1株の株価に対する年間配当金の割合。配当利回り（％）＝（1株当たり配当金÷株価）×100）
▶The *dividend yield* on Nissan's shares is expected to climb to 2.1 percent this business year, based on the current stock price of ¥1,140. 今年度の日産の株式配当利回りは, 現在の株価1,140円ベースで, 2.1％に増加する見込みだ。

division 名 事業部, 事業部門, 部門, 部・課, 分野, 分割, 分配, 不一致, 分裂
branch division 支部, 支局
business devision 事業部門, 事業分野
cosmetics division 化粧品事業部門
division capital 事業部資本
division of businesses 企業分割
division of labor 分業
division of profit or loss 損益の配分
division of profits 利益分配
functional division 機能的分割, 職能別部門

horizontal division of labor　水平的分業
independent division　独立事業部門
international division　国際事業部, 国際事業部門
operational administration division　業務本部
regional division of labor　地域的分業
unprofitable division　不採算部門
vertical division of labor　垂直的分業

▶The company expects to recover by the end of fiscal 2007 on the back of proceeds from the sale of its cosmetic *division*.　化粧事業部門の売却益で, 同社は2007年度末までに利益を回復するとしている。

▶The firm downsized its semiconductor and home appliances *divisions* drastically.　同社は, 半導体と家電の事業部を大幅に縮小した。

divisional 形　部門の, 事業部の, 分割上の, 区分上の
  divisional performance　事業部業績
  divisional profit　事業部利益, 事業別利益 (＝departmental profit)
  divisional return on investment　事業部資本利益率
  divisional organization　事業部制 (製品・地域・顧客別に編成された利益責任制を持つ経営単位である事業部を単位とする組織構造)
  divisional sales　部門売上
  divisional system　事業部制 (＝divisional organization)

do business　営業活動を行う, 営業する, 事業を行う, 事業を展開する, ビジネス活動をする, 取引する (＝operate)

▶We *do business* in some 150 countries.　当社は, 約150か国で事業を展開しています。

document 名　書類, 文書, 証拠書類, 帳票, ドキュメント (⇒**accept, minority, unless**)

▶The financial statements and a score of related *documents* show that the company has a negative net worth.　財務書類と約20の関連資料は, 同社が債務超過であることを示している。

doldrums 名　沈滞, 低迷, 不振, 不況, 不景気, 中だるみ
  be out of the doldrums　底を脱する
  in the doldrums　不景気で, 不振の, 厳しい状況の, 意気消沈して

▶Most regional economies still linger in the *doldrums*.　地方経済も, 大半はまだ停滞から抜け出せないでいる。

dollar 名　ドル, ドル相場
  constant dollar basis　恒常ドル・ベース
  dollar-denomnated terms [basis]　ドル建て, ドル表示 (＝dollar terms)
  dollar terms　金額ベース
  dollar unit method　金額後出し先入れ法 (＝dollar value LIFO)
  dollar value method　ドル価値法 (＝dollar value LIFO)
  Dollars in millions　単位：百万ドル
  Dollars in millions per share amounts　単位：1株当たりの金額を除いて百万ドル
  higher dollar　ドル高
  nominal dollar basis　名目貨幣基準, 名目ドル基準
  strong dollar against other currencies　ドル全面高
  the dollar's depreciation　ドル安 (＝lower dollar, the weak dollar)

▶The weaker *dollar* affected the net earnings.　ドル安が, 純利益に影響を及ぼしました。

dollar value LIFO　金額後入れ先出し法, ドル価値後入れ先出し法, ドル価値法 (＝dollar value method)
  dollar-value LIFO inventory　金額後入れ先出し法による棚卸し資産, ドル価値後入れ先出し法による棚卸し資産
  dollar-value LIFO method　ドル価値後入れ先出し法 (＝dollar value LIFO)

domestic 形　国内の, 自国の, 国内産の, 自家製の
  domestic corporation　内国法人, 内国会社, 州内法人, 州内会社
  domestic market　国内市場
  domestic production　国内生産

domestic demand　国内需要, 内需
  growth in domestic demand　内需の伸び
  high domestic demand　内需拡大
  sluggish domestic demand　内需の低迷

▶Expansion of *domestic demand* as a driving force to push up prices is not strong.　物価を押し上げる原動力としての内需拡大は, 強くない。

donation 名　贈与, 寄付, 寄贈, 献金, 提供, 受贈, 寄付金, 寄贈品, 受贈金 (⇒**resume**)
  cash donations　寄付金
  charitable donations　慈善寄付
  corporate donations　企業献金, 政治献金
  donation tax　贈与税
  donations expense　寄付金
  large donations　多額の寄付金
  political donations　政治献金
  under-the-table donations　ヤミ献金

▶The Political Funds Control Law bars businesses and organizations from making *donations* to an individual politician.　政治資金規正法では, 政

治家個人への企業・団体による献金が禁止されている。

double 動 2倍になる、倍増する、倍加する
▶Honda Motor Co. plans to *double* its production capacity in India by next year. ホンダは、来年までにインドでの生産能力を倍増する計画だ。
▶The sales of digital cameras *doubled* those of the previous year, assisted by rapid expansion of markets in the nation and abroad. デジタルカメラの販売台数は、国内外の急速な市場拡大に支えられて、前年の2倍に増えた。

doubtful 形 不確かな、疑わしい
　allowance for doubtful receivables 貸倒引当金
　doubtful debt 不良債権、貸倒れ見積額
doubtful account 貸倒れ、不良債権、不良貸掛金勘定（＝doubtful debt）
　doubtful accounts expense 貸倒れ損失
　doubtful accounts expense as a percentage of sales 売上に対する貸倒れ損失の比率、売上に対する貸倒れ損失発生率
　doubtful accounts expense as a percentage to credit sales 掛売上［信売上高］に対する貸倒れ損失、掛売上に対する貸倒れ損失発生率

dovetail 動 適合する、調和する
dovetailing 名 統合化、適合［調和］すること
▶Professional users are calling for the *dovetailing* of different services to form comprehensive information and telecommunications solutions. 専門事務に携わっているユーザーは、情報通信の包括的なソリューション［問題解決策］として、各種サービスの統合化を求めている。

Dow Jones average [**Average**] ダウジョーンズ平均、ダウジョーンズ平均株価、株式ダウ価平均、ダウ平均
Dow Jones industrial average [**Industrial Average**] ダウ工業株平均、ダウ工業株30種平均、ダウ（工業株30種）平均、ダウ平均《略 DJIA》（＝Dow Jones industrials）

down payment 頭金、手付け金、前渡し金、自己投下資本

downgrade 動 格下げする、格付けを引き下げる、下方修正する
downgrade 名 格下げ（⇒upgrade）
　rating downgrade 格下げ、下方修正、引下げ（＝downgrading）
　review for possible downgrade 格下げの方向で検討する
　under review for possible downgrade 格下げの方向で検討中、格下げの方向で格付けを見直し中
▶The *downgrade* could further hamper GM's access to funding. 今回の格下げで、GMの資金調達はさらに厳しくなる可能性がある。
▶The stock market decline can trigger *downgrades* by credit rating agencies. 株安をきっかけとして、格付け機関による評価が引き下げられる可能性がある。

downsize 動 〈規模を〉縮小する、削減する、人員削減する、〈経営を〉合理化する、リストラする、小型化する、軽量化する
▶We will either *downsize* or sell our unprofitable sections by the end of fiscal 2008. 当社は、2008年度末までに、当社の不採算部門を縮小や売却する方針です。

downsizing 名 規模の縮小、削減、人員削減、小型化、軽量化、合理化、経営合理化、リストラ、脱大型コンピュータ現象、ダウンサイジング
▶Struggling Victor Co. of Japan will implement a major workforce-*downsizing* program. 経営再建中の日本ビクターは、大幅な人員削減プログラムを実施する。

downstream 名 川下部門、下流部門、石油精製・販売部門、親会社から子会社への販売、〔通信〕ダウンストリーム、下り（回線の信号の流れが電話局から利用者の方向）（⇒upstream）
　downstream merger 逆吸収合併、ダウンストリーム合併（子会社による親会社の吸収合併）

DPS 1株当たり配当、1株当たり配当金、1株当たり配当額（**dividend per share**の略）

Dr. 借方（**debtor**の略）

drawer 名 振出人、手形振出人

dress up 粉飾する（＝window-dress）
▶In WorldCom's accounting fraud, it *dressed up* fees payable to other telecoms not as expenses, but as capital investments. 米通信大手ワールドコムの会計操作では、他の通信会社に支払う回線使用料を経費に計上せず、資本投資［設備投資］に計上していた。

drive 動 …の原動力になる、…の牽引力となる、…を動かす、…をもたらす、…を喚起する
　drive customer demand 消費者需要を喚起する
　drive growth 成長をもたらす、成長の原動力となる
　drive the markets 相場を動かす
▶The U.S. and other overseas economies have *driven* Japan's recovery. 米国などの海外経済が、日本の景気回復を牽引してきた。

drive 名 政策、主導、動因、キャンペーン、取組み、組織的運動、募金運動、駆動装置、装置、気力、決意、意欲、指向、原動力、推進力、駆動力、ドライブ

(⇒competitive)
austerity drive 緊縮政策
drive to promote a new product 新製品の販促キャンペーン
efficiency drive 効率向上, 効率性の向上
export drive 輸出ドライブ, 輸出攻勢
nationwide drive 全国運動, 全国キャンペーン
technological drive 技術指向
▶To further improve our competitiveness, we have continued our *drive* to cut costs and expenses. 当社の競争力をさらに高めるため, 当社は継続してコストと費用の削減に全力を挙げて取り組んでいます。

driven 形 …志向の, …主導の, …主導型, …優先の, …中心の, …に徹する (=-led, led by)
be driven by ... …を原動力とする, …が追い風になる, …が大きな意味を持つ
business relationship driven 取引関係優先の
export-driven 輸出主導の, 輸出主導型
futures-driven 先物取引中心の
market-driven 市場原理に基づく
order-driven 注文主導型の
profit-driven 利益志向の, 利益志向の強い, 利益追求型の (=profit-oriented)
retail-driven 個人投資家主導の
scale-driven 数量効果が大きい
swap-driven スワップ主導型の
▶Market-*driven* quality means understanding quality as our customers see it. 市場志向の品質とは, お客さまの立場に立って品質を追求することを意味します。

driver 名 原動力, 推進力, 牽引役, 主因 (=driving force; ⇒profit driver)
▶The growth *driver* for our industry is quite simply increasing global competition. 当業界にとって, 成長の原動力[推進力]はまさにグローバル競争の激化です。

driving force 原動力, 推進力, 牽引役, 牽引車, 主因 (=driver; ⇒production cost)
▶With their advanced technical skills, baby boomers have long been a *driving force* behind firms' research and development efforts. 高い技能を持つ団塊の世代は, 企業の研究開発の原動力[牽引役]となってきた。

drop 動 減少する, 低下する, 下落する, 落ち込む (=decrease)
drop below ... …を割り込む
drop sharply 急減する, 急速に減少する, 急落する
drop 名 減少, 低下, 下落, 落ち込み, 低迷, 悪化
drop in asset quality 資産内容の悪化
drop in earnings 減益 (=drop in profits)
drop in income 減益
▶Sony Corp. saw a large *drop* in profits. ソニーは, 大幅減益となった。

DSO 売上債権回転日数, 売上債権回収期間, 平均売掛債権滞留日数 (**days sales outstanding**の略)
DTAs 繰延べ税金資産 (**deferred tax assets**の略)
dual corporate tax system 外形標準課税 (=local corporate tax formula based on the size of business)
dual-list 動 重複上場する (⇒delist, list)
▶Six NYSE-listed blue-chip companies agreed to *dual-list* on Nasdaq and NYSE. ニューヨーク証券取引所に上場している優良企業6社が, ナスダック(米店頭株式市場)とNYSEへの重複上場に合意した。

dual responsibility 二重責任(財務諸表・財務書類の作成については経営者, 監査報告書の作成については監査人がそれぞれ責任を負うこと)

due 形 正当な, 正式の, 適切な, 適正な, 適法の, 合法の, 十分な, 相当の, 合理的な, 履行義務のある, 支払い義務のある, 支払い期日のきた, 満期の過ぎた, 当然支払われるべき, 予定されている
account due 未収金
amount due 満期支払い
amounts due 債務金額
collateral payment due date 担保の支払い日
due and deferred premiums 未収保険金
due to affiliated and associated companies 関係会社借入金
premium due 未払い保険料
▶On June 2, 2007, we sold U.S. $200 million of 9.25% Notes *Due* June 2012. 2007年6月2日, 当社は2007年満期の利率9.25%ノート2億米ドルを発行しました。

due date 支払い期日, 返済期日, 満期日, 満期, 社債の償還日, 履行期日, 期日, 納期 (=date of payment)
▶Any unpaid amount shall bear interest from *due date* until paid. 未払い金額については, 支払い期日から支払われる日まで利息が付くものとする。

due diligence 相当の注意, 正当な注意, 正当な努力, 監査手続き, 事前精査, デュー・ディリジェンス (=due diligence investigation: 契約締結前, 契約交渉中または契約締結後クロージング前に監査法人や法律事務所によって行われる財務面と法的な監査手続き)

due diligence investigation 事業買収前のデュー・ディリジェンス調査, 事前精査, 資産査定
due to ... …により, …が原因で, …のために, …で (⇒assessment)

durable goods 耐久財

durable product 耐久財, 耐久消費財 (=durable goods)

▶The bank reported a 43.4 percent decline in group net profits mainly *due to* lower stockbroking commission revenues. 同行の連結純利益[税引き後利益]は, 主に株式売買手数料の収入が減ったため, 43.4％減少した。

▶Spending on educational and entertainment *durable products*, such as flat-screen televisions, digital cameras and DVD recorders, has posted double-digit increases year-on-year since December. 薄型テレビやデジタル・カメラ, DVDレコーダーなどの教養娯楽用耐久財への消費支出は, 昨年12月以降, 前年同月比で2桁の伸びを示している。

durable years 耐用年数

durables 名 耐久財

during the period 期中, 当期に, 同期に

▶Earnings per common share are based on the weighted average number of shares outstanding *during the period*. 普通株式1株当たり純利益は, 期中の発行済み株式数の加重平均に基づいて計算されています。

▶The Corporation invested some $450 million in its subsidiary and associated companies *during the period*. 当社は, 同期[当期]に子会社と関連会社に4億5,000万ドル余りを投資しました。

during the year 当期, 今年度, 今期, 年間の (⇒**charge off**)

▶An increased quarterly dividend was declared twice *during the year*. 今年度は, 四半期増配を2回宣言しました。

duty 名 義務, 責任, 任務, 職務, 職責, 勤務,〈一般にdutiesで〉関税, 税

▶Itoham Foods Inc. admitted its involvement in a meat importer's evasion of about ¥940 million in customs *duties* on pork imported from Europe. 大手食肉加工メーカーの伊藤ハムが, 食肉輸入業者がヨーロッパから輸入した豚肉にかかる関税約9億4,000万円を脱税した事件に関与していたことを認めた。

▶Patents obtained as a result of *duties* performed by a corporate employee belong to the employee. 企業の従業員が企業の職務の一環として得た特許権は, その従業員に帰属する。

E e

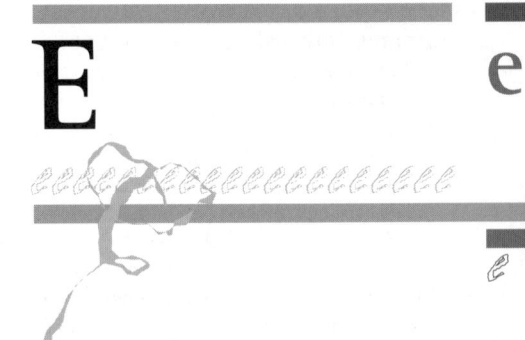

e-book 名 電子書籍 （＝electronic book）
▶Matsushita, Kadokawa and TBS set up a joint firm to sell *e-books*. 松下電器と角川, TBSが, 電子書籍を販売する合弁会社を設立した。
earlier years 過年度 （⇒cumulative effect）
early retirement 早期退職, 早期定年, 希望退職, 期限前返済
　early retirement and buyout packages 早期退職優遇制度 （⇒buyout）
　early retirement of long-term debt 長期債務の期限前返済
　early retirement packages 希望退職プラン［制度］, 早期退職プラン
▶Ford may offer *early retirement* packages to its production workers. フォードは, 生産労働者を対象に希望退職［早期退職］プランを導入する可能性がある。
early retirement program [scheme] 早期退職制度
▶This third straight year of red ink is due to slumps in mobile phone sales and swelling costs for *early retirement programs*. この3年連続赤字の要因は, 携帯電話の販売低迷と早期退職［希望退職］制度の費用増大だ。
earmark 動 予算を組む, 〈…の目的に資金などを〉当てる, 計上する, 指定する, …を区別する
▶We *earmarked* $10 million to promote the study of the emerging environmental field of industrial ecology. 産業エコロジーの新環境分野の研究を促進するため, 当社は1,000万ドルの予算を計上しました。
earn 動 稼ぐ, 稼得(かとく)する, 利益を上げる, 〈報酬などを〉得る, 獲得する, 生む, もたらす （⇒define）
　amount earned for equity 普通株主持ち分利益
　earn a profit 利益を上げる
　earn interest 利息が付く
　earned capital 稼得資本
　earned surplus 利益剰余金 （＝earned surplus reserve, retained earnings）
　income in the period earned 稼得した期間の利益
　interest earned on collateral 担保で付いた利子, 担保から発生した利子
　net premiums earned 正味経過保険料
　pay-as-you-earn 源泉課税
　save-as-you-earn 天引き積立て
▶Seven-Eleven Japan has *earned* more than 90 percent of the operating profit of its parent Seven & I. セブン-イレブン・ジャパンは, 親会社セブン＆アイの営業利益の9割以上を稼いでいる。
▶The firm *earned* $733.4 million, or $2.36 per share, for the three months ended in September. 同社の第三四半期［7-9月期］の利益は, 7億3,340万ドル（1株当たり2.36ドル）でした。
earning 名 利益, 収益 （＝income; ⇒earnings）
　earning capacity 収益力 （＝earning power）
　earning process 利潤獲得過程
　earning rate 収益率
　expected earnings 期待収益
　life-long earning 生涯賃金
　operating earning rate 営業利益率
　revenue-earning activity 収益稼得活動
earning assets 収益性資産, 収益資産
▶Both companies contributed to the growth in these revenues by expanding their portfolios of

earning assets. 両社は，保有収益資産の拡大によってこれらの増収に貢献しました．

earning power 収益力，収益性 （＝earning capacity, earnings power, profitability）
▶An increase in operating profits is said to illustrate the good business results of a company's core business and *earning power.* 営業利益の伸びは，企業の本業の好調さと収益力の高さを示すとされている．

earnings 名 収益，利益，純利益，利潤，所得，収入，投資利益，業績，決算 （＝gains, profits, returns; ⇒**consolidated earnings, corporate earnings, improvement, retained earnings, revenues and earnings**）
　adjusted earnings 調整後利益
　after-tax earnings 税引き後利益
　current earnings 当期純利益 （＝current income, current net income）
　earnings after taxes 税引き後利益《略 EAT》
　earnings before income taxes 税引き前利益《略 EBIT》
　earnings before interest and after tax 税引き後利子控除前利益，税引き後支払い利息控除前利益《略 EBIAT》
　earnings decline 収益の減少，減益
　earnings from continuing operations 継続的営業活動による利益
　earnings from operations 営業利益
　earnings gain 収益の伸び，収益の増加，増益 （＝earnings growth）
　equity in earnings of affiliates 関係会社利益持ち分
　equity in earnings of unconsolidated subsidiaries 非連結子会社の持ち分利益
　increases in earnings and profit 増収増益
　interim earnings 中間利益，中間期の利益
　net interest earnings 投資収益
　parent basis earnings 単独ベースの収益
　robust earnings 業績好調
　sales and earnings gains 増収益
　stagnant earnings 収益の悪化，業績の低迷
　statement of earnings 損益計算書
　statement of retained earnings 利益剰余金計算書
　strong earnings 高収益，高水準の収益
▶The effects of accounting changes on future *earnings* may be quite small once we bring the balance sheet up to date. 将来の利益に対する会計処理変更の影響は，貸借対照表をいったん現状に即したものに修正してしまうと，ごく僅かになる可能性があります．

earnings forecast 業績予想，業績見通し，収益予想，利益予想 （＝earnings estimate, earnings projection, profit forecast）
　full-year earnings forecast 通期の業績予想，通期の業績見通し，通期の収益予想 （＝full-year earnings projection, full-year forecast）
　group earnings forecast 連結業績予想，連結業績見通し，連結収益予想，連結利益予想
▶For the year to March 31, 2007, the company left unchanged its group *earnings forecast* made last November. 2007年3月決算の見通しは，同社が昨年11月に発表した連結業績予想を据え置いた．

earnings growth 収益の伸び［増加］，収益伸び率，利益の伸び，収益率の伸び，増益 （＝earnings gain）
▶Our corporate goal is to achieve at least 10 percent *earnings growth* each year. 毎年少なくとも10％の増益を達成することが，当社の企業目標です．

earnings per common share 普通株式1株当たり利益［純利益］，1株当たり利益 （＝earnings per share）
　　earnings per common shareについて ➡ earnings per share (EPS) と同義で，会社の収益性を分析するうえで重要な指標とされ，当期純利益(net earnings, net income) を外部発行済み普通株式数(common shares outstanding, common stock outstanding) で割って算出する．米国の公開会社は，損益計算書(income statement) に1株当たり利益を表示することになっている．1株当たり利益(EPS)＝当期純利益÷普通株式数
　　earnings (loss) per common share 普通株式1株当たり純利益(損失)
　　earnings per common share―assuming full dilution 普通株式1株当たり利益―完全希薄化［希釈化，希釈効果］を考慮した場合，完全希薄化後普通株式1株当たり利益
▶*Earnings per common share* for the second quarter were $0.72, compared with $0.92 in the same period last year. 第2四半期の普通株式1株当たり純利益は，前年同期の0.92ドルに対して，0.72ドルでした．

earnings per share 1株当たり利益，1株当たり純利益［当期純利益］，普通株式1株当たり純利益《略 EPS》 （＝earnings per common share：1株当たり利益(EPS)＝当期純利益÷普通株式数）
　basic earnings per share 基本的1株当たり利益
　earnings per incremental share EPS増収感度
　first quarter earnings per share 第1四半期の普通株式1株当たり利益［純利益］

fully diluted earnings per share 完全希薄化(後)1株当たり利益, 完全希薄化による1株当たり純利益[利益]

increased earnings per share 濃縮化1株当たり利益

primary earnings per share 基礎的1株当たり利益, 基本的な1株当たり純利益, 単純希薄化による1株当たり利益

reported earnings per share 1株当たり計上利益

▸*Earnings per share* for the first nine months of 2007 were based on 308.4 million average common shares outstanding. 2007年1–9月期の1株当たり純利益は, 発行済み普通株式の平均株式数3億840万株に基づいて計算されています。

earnings projection 業績予想, 業績見通し, 収益予想, 収益見通し (=earnings estimate, earnings forecast)

▸In the revised group *earnings projection* for fiscal 2007 through next March, the firm projects a pretax profit of ¥160 billion. 2008年3月期[2007年度]の連結業績見通しの修正で, 同社は1,600億円の税引き前利益を予想している。

earnings report 業績報告, 業績報告書, 決算, 決算報告, 収益報告, 損益計算書, 財務計算書
　consolidated earnings report 連結決算報告
　earnings report for the first half of fiscal 2007 2007年度上半期決算, 3月期決算企業の9月中間決算
　interim earnings report 中間決算, 中間決算報告[報告書] (=midterm earnings report)
　quarterly earnings report 四半期報告

▸GM released its *earnings report* for the first half of fiscal 2007. GMが2007年9月中間決算を発表した。

EAT 税引き後利益 (**earnings after taxes**の略)

EBIAT 税引き後利子控除前利益, 税引き後支払い利息控除前利益 (**earnings before interest and after tax**の略)

EBIT 利子税金控除前利益, 支払い利息および税金控除前利益, 利払い税引き前利益 (**earnings before interest and taxes**の略)

EBITA 支払い利息・税金・営業権償却費控除前利益 (**earnings before interest, taxes and amortization of goodwill**の略)
　EBITA figure EBITAの数値
　EBITA margin 利息・税金・減価償却控除前利益の利益率, EBITAマージン

▸Through the innovations and contributions of our people, the Corporation's organic growth increased by 11% in 2007 while *EBITA* grew by 26.5 percent. 当社の従業員の技術革新と貢献によって, 2007年の当社の有機的成長率は11%上昇し, EBITAも26.5%増加しました。

▸The *EBITA* figure has been restated following the retrospective application of new International Financial Reporting Standards (IFRS). EBITAの数値は, 国際財務報告基準(IFRS)の新規定を遡及的に適用して再表示されています。

▸The Group's *EBITA* improved 8.9 percent in 2007, leading to an *EBITA* margin improvement of 20 basis points to 12.9 percent of sales. 当グループの2007年度のEBITA(支払利息・税金・営業権償却費控除前利益)が8.9%上昇したのに伴い, EBITAマージンは20ベーシス・ポイント(0.2%)改善して対売上高比が12.9%に拡大しました。

EBITD 支払い利息・税金・減価償却控除前利益, 利払い利息・税金・減価償却前利益 (**earnings before interest, taxes and depreciation**の略)

EBITDA 支払い利息・税金・減価償却・償却控除前利益 (**earnings before interest, taxes, depreciation and amortization**の略)

ECB 欧州中央銀行, 欧州中銀 (**European Central Bank**の略)

economic activities 経済活動

▸Operations whose principal *economic activities* are undertaken in currencies other than the U.S. dollar are classified as either integrated or self-sustaining. 主な経済活動が米ドル以外の通貨で行われている事業は, 一体化した事業か自立した事業に分類されています。

economic conditions 経済状態, 経済状況, 経済情勢, 景気

▸Global *economic conditions* improved last year, but growth was still sluggish. 世界の景気は昨年好転したが, 経済の成長率はまだ低い。

economic environment 経済環境, 景気

▸Earnings for the second quarter reflected a difficult *economic environment*. 第2四半期の純利益は, 厳しい経済環境[経済環境の悪化]を反映しています。

economic globalization 経済のグローバル化

▸An age of *economic globalization* is characterized by intense competition in the pursuit of maximum profit. 経済のグローバル化時代の特徴は, 利益の極大化を求めて繰り広げられる熾烈な競争である。

economic life 経済的耐用年数

economic recovery 景気回復

▸It is natural for interest rates to rise along with an *economic recovery*. 景気回復につれて金利が

上昇するのは, 自然な姿だ.

economic value added 経済的付加価値, 経済付加価値《略 EVA》
▸We look at customer and employee satisfaction, our stock price and *economic value added* (EVA) in measuring our success. 当社の成功の度合いを測る物差しとして, 当社は顧客と従業員の満足度, 当社の株価と経済的付加価値(EVA)を見ます.

education 名 教育, 教養, 学識
    adult education　成人教育
    consumer education　消費者教育
    life-long education　生涯教育
    professional education　専門教育
▸The Corporation's wide-ranging support of *education* includes direct funding and countless hours by its volunteers in schools. 当社の広範な教育助成には, 直接助成金や各種学校での社員の活発なボランティア活動なども含まれています.

EEOA　〔米〕雇用機会均等法, 平等雇用機会法 (Equal Employment Opportunity Actの略)

effect 動 行う, 実施する, 成し遂げる, 手配する, 〈保険を〉付ける
    effect a two-for-one stock split　1対2の株式分割を行う
    effect an insurance　保険を付ける
    effect payment　支払いを行う, 納付する
▸The two-for-one stock splits were *effected* in the forms of 100 percent stock dividends. これらの1対2の株式分割は, 100%株式配当形式で実施しました.

effect 名 影響, 影響額, 発効, 効力, 効果, 施行, 趣旨, 意味 (⇒ripple effect)
    cumulative effect　累積効果
    currency effects　為替の影響
    dilutive effect　希薄化効果
    effect of accounting change　会計処理変更の影響
    effect of exchange rate changes on cash　現金預金に対する為替レート[為替変動相場]変動の影響[影響額], 為替変動による現金への影響
    effect of exchange rate changes on cash and cash equivalents　現金および現金等価物に対する為替レート変動の影響[影響額]
    income taxes excluding effect of accounting change　法人所得税(会計処理変更の影響を除く)
    inventories excluding effect of accounting change　棚卸し資産(会計処理変更の影響を除く)
    leverage effect　他人資本効果
    net of income tax effect　税効果後
    repercussion effect　波及効果
    seasonal effects　季節調整
    size effect　規模効果
    tax effects of timing differences　期間差異の税効果
▸A merger between life insurance companies will have little *effect*, because there is no synergy effect. 生命保険会社同士が合併しても, 相互補完関係が生まれないため, 効果は薄い.
▸Apart from these cumulative *effects* on prior years of the accounting change, our change in accounting had no material effect on net income in 2007. この会計処理の変更による過年度への累積的影響を別にすれば, 当社の会計処理の変更によって, 2007年度の純利益に重大な影響はありませんでした.
▸It would take some time for negative *effects* of the yen's appreciation to become visible. 円高のマイナス影響[悪影響]が出るまでには, 時間がかかるだろう.

effective 形 有効な, 効果的な, 効率的な, 実施されている, 実施中の, 効力をもつ, 事実上の, 実際の, 実動の
    annual effective tax rate　年間実効税率
    cost-effective　コスト効率がよい, 費用効率がよい, 費用効果が高い
    effective demand　有効需要
    effective income tax rate　実効所得税率, 実効税率, 実効法人税率 (=effective tax rate)
    effective exchange rate　実効為替相場, 実効為替レート
    effective management　効率経営
    real effective exchange rate　実質実効為替レート
▸On June 30, 2007, the Corporation concluded the sale of some of its European assets *effective* February 2007 to the firm. 2007年6月30日に当社は, 当社の欧州事業資産の一部を2007年2月付けで同社に売却する手続きを完了しました.

effective book value　実質簿価
▸Bad loans should be bought at market value rather than at *effective book value*. 不良債権は, 実質簿価でなく時価で買い取るべきだ.

effective interest　実効利息, 実質金利
    effective interest method　実効利率法
    effective interest rate　実効利率, 実効金利, 実質利率 (=effective interest, effective rate of interest)

effective tax rate　実効税率, 法定実効税率,

税負担率（税金費用の税引き前当期利益に対する割合）
▸The 2007 provision for income taxes was $128 million (*effective* tax rate of 29 percent). 2007年度の納税引当金［法人税等引当金］は，1億2,800万ドル（実効税率29%）でした。

effectiveness 形 有効性，効率，効果，効力，薬効，成果
　cost effectiveness 費用効果，コスト効果，原価効率，費用有効度
　leveraged effectiveness レバレッジ効果
　managerial effectiveness 経営効率，経営手腕
　operating effectiveness 事業の効率性，運用上の有効性（＝operating efficiency）
▸Our global operations team is responsible for the *effectiveness* of our operations worldwide. 当社のグローバル運営チームは，ワールドワイドな効率の運営に対して責任を負っています。

efficiency 名 効率，効率化，効率性，能率，生産性，有効性（⇒**bottom line**, **operational efficiency**, **return** 名）
　audit efficiency 監査の効率性
　capital efficiency 資本効率
　commercial efficiency 営業効率，営業上の能率
　cost efficiency 原価能率，費用能率，コスト効率
　distribution efficiency 流通効率
　efficiency gain 生産性の伸び，生産性の上昇，生産性の改善
　labor efficiency 作業効率
　market efficiency 市場の効率性
　operating efficiency 営業効率，事業効率
　operational efficiency 経営効率
　plant efficiency 工場の効率性
　production efficiency 生産効率
▸The automaker aims to boost the *efficiency* of development and personnel costs by focusing on the production of midsize and small cars. この自動車メーカーは，中小型車の生産に的を絞りこむことで，開発資金と開発要員費の効率化を目指している。

efficient 形 効率的な，効率のよい，能率的な，有能な，有効な
　cost-efficient 費用効率がよい，費用効率［コスト効率］が高い，コスト効率がよい，低コストの（＝cost-effective）
　cost-efficient source of financing 低コストの資金調達源
　efficient market 効率的市場
　efficient management 効率的経営，経営の効率化

　fuel-efficient 燃費効率のよい，低燃費の
　labor-efficient 労働効率の高い
　more efficient running 運営の効率化
▸Higher gasoline prices have led to brisk sales of fuel-*efficient* cars in North America. ガソリン高騰で，北米での低燃費車の販売は好調だった。
▸We have continued our drive to streamline operations and make ourselves as *efficient* as possible. 当社は，継続して業務運営を簡素化して，できるかぎり効率的な企業になるよう全力を挙げて取り組んでいます。

effort 名 努力，試み，尽力，取組み，動き，活動，作業，仕事，運動，キャンペーン，募集，対策，政策，策，努力の成果，労作，力作，立派な演説
　best efforts 最善の努力，委託募集
　collective effort 総力
　cooperative efforts 協力関係
　cost reduction efforts コスト削減努力
　expense reduction efforts 経費削減努力
　gap-closing efforts 赤字削減努力
　joint effort 提携関係
　reorganization efforts 再編の動き
　restructuring efforts 経営再建策
　sales effort 販売努力
　self-help efforts 自助努力
　streamlining efforts リストラ努力，リストラ策，合理化措置，合理化への取組み
▸The merger plan will not go ahead unless the bank makes unstinting *efforts* to cut its non-performing loans. 同行が不良債権の削減に向けて惜しみない努力をしないかぎり，統合計画が前に進むことはないだろう。
▸Our *efforts* to introduce products that meet the needs of our customers led to increased profits in all regions. 顧客のニーズにマッチした製品を導入するという当社の努力が，全地域での増益につながりました。

elect 動 選出する，選任する，選ぶ，選択する，決める
▸Directors are *elected* by a plurality of votes cast. 取締役は，賛成多数［投票総数の過半数］で選任されます。

election 名 選出，選任，選挙，投票，選択，選択権
　election of directors 取締役の選任
　electon of officers 役員の選任
▸Each of the 12 nominees named in the proxy statement who stood for *election* as a director received a plurality of the votes cast. 委任状に取締役選任候補者として記載されていた12名は，それぞれ投票総数の過半数［大多数］の支持を得ました。

electric appliance maker 電機メーカー
▸*Electric appliance makers* enjoy robust sales of flat-screen television sets and other digital home appliances.　電機メーカーは、薄型テレビなどデジタル家電の販売が好調だ。

electronic money 電子マネー
　electronic money business 電子マネー事業
▸Aeon Co. and Lawson Inc. are also discussing a possible alliance in the *electronic money* business.　イオンとローソンは、電子マネー事業での提携の可能性も検討している。

element 名　要素, 要因, 構成要素, 成分, 項目, エレメント
　accounting elements 財務諸表の基本要素
　cost elements 原価要素
　earnings momentum element 利益のモメンタム要因
　elements of accounting 会計の基本要素
　elements of financial statements 財務諸表の構成要素, 財務諸表の要素
　nonoperating elements 営業外項目
▸Our quality and total cycle-time reduction initiatives remain the key *elements* in achieving superior financial results.　当社の品質に対する方針と全サイクル・タイム(工程期間)短縮の方針は、今でも当社の優れた業績を達成するための中核的要素になっています。

eligible 形　有資格の, 適格の, 受給資格がある
　eligible charges 給付額, 給付対象費用
　eligible employee 有資格従業員, 受給資格のある従業員, 年金加入資格のある従業員　(⇒**RONA**)
　eligible receivables 適格債権
　eligible subscriber 受給資格のある加入者
　fully eligible active plan participant 受給資格取得済み在職制度加入者
▸About 1.24 million *eligible* subscribers to corporate pension plans aged 60 and over had not filed payout requests as of the end of fiscal 2006.　2006年度の時点で、受給資格のある60歳以上の企業年金加入者の約124万人が、年金支払いの請求手続きを取っていない。

eliminate 動　相殺消去する, 消去する, 除去する, 撤廃する, 排除する, 削減する　(⇒**consolidation**, **intercompany**)
　be eliminated in consolidation 連結上, 相殺消去される, 連結で消去される　(⇒**consolidation**)
　eliminate tax incentives 税制上の優遇措置を撤廃する
▸The item Allocations to untaxed reserves has been *eliminated* in the consolidated income statement. 非課税特別準備金繰入れ額の項目は、連結損益計算書から削除されています。

elimination 名　相殺消去, 相殺, 消去, 除去, 撤廃, 排除, 削除
　elimination and adjustments 消去と修正, 相殺消去と修正
　elimination of intercompany profit 会社間利益の消去, 会社相互間の利益の消去
　elimination of intersegment revenues 事業分野間収益の消去
　elimination of transfers between geographic areas 地域間収益移動の消去
　final elimination 最終消去仕訳
　intercompany elimination 会社間取引消去項目
　work sheet elimination 消去仕訳

embark 動　着手する, 〈事業に〉引き入れる
▸We are *embarking* on new ventures to fulfill their different missions.　当社は異なった使命を果たすため新規事業に着手しています。

emerging 形　新興の, 新生の, 最新の
　emerging company 新興企業, 成長企業, 新興のベンチャー企業
　emerging economies 新興経済国, 新興経済地域, 振興経済群
　emerging market 新興市場, 急成長市場, 新成長市場, エマージング・マーケット
　emerging Internet company 新興ネット企業
　emerging technology 新技術, 最新技術
▸The firm received a lot of attention from investors as an *emerging* company.　同社は、新興のベンチャー企業として投資家から大いに注目された。
▸This is the first attempt by television broadcasters to take the initiative to fuse communications and broadcasting to counter the threat from *emerging* Internet companies.　これは、新興ネット企業に対抗してテレビ放送局が主導権を握り、通信と放送の融合を図る初の試みだ。
▸Strategic alliances with and investments in other high-tech firms bolster our position in *emerging* technologies and developing markets. 他のハイテク企業との戦略的提携とハイテク企業への投資により、新技術と急成長市場における当社の地位は向上しています。

employee 名　従業員, 社員, 職員, 雇い人, 使用人　(⇒**career-average pay**)
　active employees 在籍従業員, 現従業員　(⇒**accumulated liability**)
　company employee 会社員
　employee income taxes payable 個人所得税預かり金

employee satisfaction 従業員満足, 従業員の満足, 企業内組織の満足《略 ES》
employee savings plan 従業員貯蓄制度, 従業員貯蓄計画 (⇒**employees' savings plan**)
employee separations 従業員の退職
employee welfare fund 従業員福利厚生基金 (＝employee benefit fund)
inactive employee 休職従業員
managerial employee 管理職
occupational employee 非管理職従業員
part time employee パート社員, パートタイマー, パートタイム労働者
rank-and-file employee 一般社員
regular [full time] employee 正社員
retired employee 退職従業員
▸Benefits for occupational *employees* are not directly pay-related. 非管理職従業員への給付は, 給与と直接的な関係はありません。
▸The efforts of our *employees* are the basis for the success we will achieve in the years to come. 当社従業員の努力こそ, 今後の当社発展を支える礎です。

employee benefit 従業員給付
employee benefit fund 従業員給付基金, 従業員福利厚生基金
employee benefit plan 従業員給付制度, 従業員福利厚生制度, 従業員給付基金
▸It is the company's practice to fund amounts for pensions sufficient to meet the minimum requirements set forth in applicable *employee benefit* and tax laws. 適用される従業員の給付に関する法令と税法に規定されている最小限の要求を十分に満たす額を, 年金基金に積み立てるのが当社の慣行です。

employee director 社内取締役
▸*Employee directors* receive no additional compensation for service on the Board of Directors or its committees. 社内取締役には, 取締役会の取締役またはその付属委員会の委員としての役務に対して, 追加報酬は支払われません。

employee pension 従業員年金
employee pension fund 従業員年金基金, [日] 厚生年金基金
employee pension insurance system 厚生年金
employee pension plan 従業員年金制度
employee plan issuances 従業員持ち株制度への発行
▸The *Employees Pension* Fund is one of many corporate pension plans. 厚生年金基金は, 多くの企業年金制度の一つだ。

Employee Retirement Income Security Act [米]従業員退職所得保障法(1974年に制定), 1974年退職者年金保障法, 企業年金法, エリサ法《略 ERISA》

employee stock compensation 従業員株式報酬制度
▸If not for expenses to cover *employee stock compensation*, the firm would have earned $2.62 per share in the third quarter. 従業員株式報酬制度の費用がなければ, 同社の第3四半期の1株当たり利益は2.62ドルでした。

employee stock option plan 従業員株式購入選択権制度, 従業員株式買取り権制度, 従業員ストックオプション制度《略 ESOP》
▸Under the Company's *employee stock option plans*, shares of common stock have been made available for grant to key employees. 当社の従業員株式購入選択権制度では, 幹部社員に普通株式を購入する権利を付与しています。

employee stock ownership plan [米]従業員持ち株制度, 従業員株式保有制度《略 ESOP》 (＝employee stock ownership trust)
▸The company's *employee stock ownership plan* will be used to finance part of the buyout deal. この買収取引の一部の資金調達には, 同社の従業員持ち株制度が利用される。

employee stock purchase plan 従業員株式購入制度, 従業員持ち株制度《略 ESPP》 (＝employees' stock purchase plan)
▸The *employees stock purchase plan* enables employees who are not participants in a stock option plan to purchase the Corporation's capital stock through payroll deductions of up to 10 % of eligible compensation. 従業員株式購入制度によると, 株式購入選択権制度に加入していない従業員は, 俸給の10％を超えない範囲で給与を積み立てて, 当社株式を購入することができます。

employer 名 雇用主, 雇用者, 雇い主, 使用者, 事業主, 企業
Employers' Accounting for Pensions 雇用主[事業主]の年金会計
employers' accounting for postemployment benefits 退職後[雇用後]給付に関する雇用主の会計
Employers' Accounting for Postretirement Benefits Other Than Pensions 年金以外の雇用給付に関する雇用主の会計処理
employers' contributions to social security schemes 社会保険雇い主負担
▸Under the defined-contribution annuity scheme,

employers do not have to provide additional contributions to cover lower-than-predicted investment yields in the pension funds. 確定拠出年金制度では、年金積立金の運用利回りが予想を下回っても、企業はその穴埋めの追加拠出をする必要がない。

employment 名 雇用, 使用, 利用, 就労, 勤め, 職
- **continuous employment system** 継続雇用性
- **decline in employment** 雇用の低迷, 雇用の悪化
- **employment conditions** 雇用情勢, 雇用環境
- **employment cost** 人件費
- **employment data** 雇用統計（＝employment figures, labor market data）
- **employment insurance program** 雇用保険制度（＝employment insurance system）
- **employment opportunity** 雇用機会
- **employment promotion** 雇用促進
- **employment system** 雇用制度
- **fictitious employment of part-time workers** アルバイトのカラ雇用
- **full employment** 完全雇用
- **increased employment** 雇用の伸び, 雇用の拡大, 雇用の増加
- **lifetime employment** 終身雇用
- **manufacturing employment** 製造業の雇用
- **over-employment** 過剰就業, 人員過剰
- **temporary employment** 一時雇用
▶*Employment* has soared on the strength of strong performance by industries such as the information technology, communications, medical, welfare and services sectors. IT［情報技術］、通信業、医療・福祉・サービス業など各種産業の好調な業績に伴って、雇用も急増している。

empower 動 権限を与える, …できるようにする（⇒**super voting share**）

end 動 終了する
- **ending balance** 期末残高（＝balance at end of the year）
- **ending cash balance** 期末現金残高
- **in the year just ended** 前期
- **year ended December 31, 2007** 2007年12月31日終了事業年度

end 名 期末, 年度末, 終了, 目的
- **balance at end of (the) year** 期末残高
- **end user** 最終使用者, 最終利用者, 一般利用者, 最終投資家, 端末利用者, 最終ユーザー, エンド・ユーザー
- **front end** 短期物, 前段階
- **short end** 短期債

ending inventory 期末棚卸し, 期末棚卸し高, 棚卸し資産期末有り高［期末保有高］, 期末在庫（＝closing stock）
- **estimated ending inventory** 期末棚卸し資産の見積り高

endorsee 名 譲受人, 被裏書人

endorsement 名 裏書, 保証
- **endorsement without recourse** 無担保裏書
- **endorsement in blank** 白地裏書, 無記名裏書

endorser 名 裏書人, 推奨者

engine 名 原動力, エンジン
▶Innovation is the *engine* that will keep us vital and growing. 革新性は、活力と成長の原動力だ。

engineer 動 設計［建設］する, 巧みに処理［管理, 運営, 計画］する, 仕組む, 誘導する
- **engineered security** 仕組み証券
- **genetically engineered food** 遺伝子組換え食品
▶Struggling Victor Co. of Japan will eliminate 1,150 jobs to *engineer* its rehabilitation. 経営不振の日本ビクターは、再建計画を進めるため、1,150人を削減する。

engineering 名 工学, 工学技術, 技術, 設計, 工事, 開発, 手法, エンジニアリング
- **engineering and construction company** エンジニアリング・建設会社, 設計・建設会社
- **engineering estimates** 工学的見積り, 工学的見積り額
- **engineering change** 設計変更
- **engineering, procurement and construction** 設計・調達と建設《略 EPC》
- **engineering program** 開発体制
- **engineering staff** 技術陣, 技術スタッフ
- **engineering team** 技術陣, 研究開発チーム
- **financial engineering** 財テク, 金融手法, 金融エンジニアリング
- **genetic engineering** 遺伝子工学
- **management engineering** 経営工学, 管理工学
- **production engineering** 生産工学
- **sales engineering** 販売工学, セールス・エンジニアリング《略 SE》
- **value engineering** 価値工学
▶Using *engineering* estimates of total cleanup costs, we estimate our potential liability for all currently and previously owned peoperties. 総浄化費用の工学的見積り額を基準に、当社は、現在と過去の所有地すべてについて当社の潜在的債務額を見積もっています。

engineering expense 技術費
▶These charges are included in research, development and *engineering expenses* and in cost of software. これらの費用は、研究、開発および技術

費とソフトウエアの原価に含まれています。

enhance 動 増す, 増やす, 高める, 強化する, 向上させる, 容易にする, 改善する
　enhance cash fow significantly キャッシュ・フローを大幅に改善する
　enhance competitiveness 競争力を高める, 競争力を強化する
　enhance financial health 財務の健全性を高める, 財務内容[財務体質]を改善する
　enhance quality 品質を向上させる
　enhanced earnings 業績向上
　enhanced returns 利益率の改善, 収益向上
▸The restructuring will *enhance* the Corporation's ability to compete more effectively in global markets. この事業再編により, 当社のグローバル市場での競争力は一段と高まるものと思われます。

enhancement 名 増加, 増大, 増進, 向上, 改善, 上昇, 騰貴, 強化, 整備, 補強, 拡張, 改良
　credit enhancement 信用補填
　margin enhancement 利益率の上昇
　quality enhancement 品質向上
▸The *enhancement* of the major banks' revenue bases is essential for the final disposal of bad loans. 不良債権の最終処理には, 大手銀行の収益基盤の強化が欠かせない。

entail 動 必要とする, …を伴う, …をもたらす, …を課す, …を負わせる
▸Both companies expect the integration to *entail* about 5,000 job cuts. 両社は, この統合により約5,000人の人員削減を見込んでいる。

enter 動 記入する, 記載する, 〈市場などに〉参入する, 〈団体などに〉加入する, 加盟する, 入会する, 参加する, 参加登録する, 入る, 提起する, 提出する, 申請する, 申し出る, 申し込む, 〈正式に〉記録にのせる, 〈判決などを〉正式に登録する, 契約を結ぶ, 〈コンピュータにデータなどを〉入力する, 立ち上げる, …にログインする, 〈土地に〉立ち入る, 占取する
　enter in an account book 記帳する
　enter the bond market 債券を発行する
　enter wrongly 誤記入する
▸Of the ¥28 billion to be raised by selling new shares, ¥10 billion will be invested in eMobile Ltd. which is preparing to *enter* the the mobile phone business in Japan. 新株発行で調達する280億円のうち100億円は, 日本での携帯電話事業への新規参入を目指しているイー・モバイル(イー・アクセスの子会社)に出資する。

enterprise 名 事業, 大事業, 事業体, 企業, 会社, 起業家マインド, 進取の気性, 企画, 企て

　accounting for business enterprises 企業会計 (＝enterprise accounting)
　business enterprise 企業
　closely held enterprise 非公開会社
　commercial enterprise 営利企業, 商企業
　corporate enterprise 法人企業
　enterprise fund 事業基金
　enterprise tax 事業税
　enterprise value 企業価値
　issuing enterprise 発行体
　manufacturing enterprise 製造業
　multinational enterprise 多国籍企業
　municipal enterprise 公営事業; 地方公営企業
　national enterprise 国有企業, 国営企業 (＝state-run enterprise)
　private enterprise 私企業
　public enterprise 株式公開会社; 公共企業体
　small and medium enterprises 中小企業
　state-owned enterprise 国有企業 (＝national enterprise)
　state-run enterprise 国営企業
▸There has been no end to the declining number of small and midsize *enterprises*. 中小企業の減少に, 歯止めがかからない。

entertainment expense 交際費
entire 形 全体の
　entire business year 通期, 事業年度全体 (＝entire fiscal year)
　entire fiscal year 通期, 事業年度全体 (＝entire business year, the whole business year)
▸For the *entire* business year to Feb. 28, the firm expects a net profit of ¥1.8 billion and a pretax profit of ¥3.9 billion on sales of ¥136.2 billion. 2月28日までの通期で[2月期決算で], 同社は, 1,362億円の売上高に対して18億円の税引き後利益と39億円の経常利益を予想している。
▸For the *entire* fiscal year to next March 31, the firm targets a net profit of ¥12 billion. 来年3月31日までの通期で, 同社は120億円の連結税引き後利益確保を目標にしている。

entity 名 事業体, 企業体, 組織体, 統一体, 法的存在者, 法主体, 事業単位, 単位
　accounting entity 会計実体
　affiliated entities 関係会社, 関連会社, 系列会社
　business entity 企業主体
　closely held entity 非公開会社
　corporate entity 企業, 企業体, 法人格
　entity equity 企業持ち分, 主体持ち分
　nonfinancial entity 非金融会社, 非金融事業会社
▸The new *entity* created by the merger can be ex-

pected to streamline management. 合併で生まれる新組織は, 経営の効率化を期待できる.

entrepreneur 名 企業家, 起業家, 経営者, 事業家, 興行主
▸This IT *entrepreneur* aimed to push up the aggregate market value of his company shares to the highest level in the world. このIT企業家は, 自社株の時価総額世界一を目指した.

entrepreneurial 形 企業家の, 起業家の, 経営者の, 起業家精神が旺盛な, 企業の
　entrepreneurial skills　経営技術, 起業のノウハウ
　entrepreneurial spirit　企業家精神, 起業家精神 (=entrepreneurialism, entrepreneurship)
　highly entrepreneurial　起業家精神が旺盛な
▸The new company benefits from the management skills, *entrepreneurial* spirit, market penetration and technology contributed by the smaller component companies. 新会社は, 併合した中堅企業のもつ経営技術[経営のノウハウ], 企業家精神, 市場浸透力, 技術力を存分に活かしています[技術力のメリットを受けています].

entrepreneurship 名 起業, 企業家精神, 起業家精神
▸It is important to encourage *entrepreneurship* through various means including assisting corporate ventures. ベンチャー支援などの手だてで起業を促進するのが重要だ.

entry 名 記入, 記帳, 記録, 登録, 登記, 記載, 記載事項, 参加, 参入, 入会, 入場, 入国, 参加者, 出品物, 〈土地への〉立入り, 通関手続き, 通関申告, 入力
　data entry　データ入力
　double entry　複式記入
　entry barriers　参入障壁
　entry cost method　加入年齢方式 (=entry age cost method)
　entry costs　参入コスト (=costs of entry)
　entry machine　初心者用パソコン, 安価なモデル
　entry market　参入市場
　entry strategy　市場参入戦略
　free entry　自由参入
　import entry　輸入手続き
　make an entry　記入する, 記帳する
　order entry　受注
　original entry　原始記入
▸Wal-Mart's *entry* into Japan will accelerate the reorganization of the industry. ウォルマートの日本市場参入で, 業界再編が加速するものと思われる.

environment 名 環境, 情勢, 動向, 局面, 展開
　business environment　経営環境, 企業環境, 事業環境, 景気 (=business climate)
　competitive environment　競争環境
　credit environment　信用情勢
　deflationary environment　デフレ環境
　developing environments　発展途上国, 開発途上国
　economic environment　経済環境
　external environment　外部環境, 外部要因, 事業環境
　falling interest rate environment　金利低下局面, 金利低下環境
　global environment　地球環境
　interest rate environment　金利情勢, 金利動向
　investment environment　投資環境
　issuing environment　起債環境
　market environment　市場環境
　operating environment　営業環境, 事業環境
　organizational environment　組織環境
　political environment　政局
　regulatory environment　規制環境
　rising rate environment　金利上昇局面
▸Non-U.S. subsidiaries which operate in a local currency *environment* account for approximately 90% of the Company's non-U.S. revenue. 現地通貨を用いる経済環境で営業活動を営む米国外子会社は, 当社の米国外収益の約90%を占めています[約90%を稼得しています].

environmental protection 環境保護
▸Calls for *environmental protection*, safer products and corporate cooperation with the local community will continue to grow. 環境保護や製品の安全性, 地域社会との共生への要請は, 今後も強まるものと思われます.

EPC 設計・調達と建設 (**engineering, procurement and construction**の略)

EPS 1株当たり利益, 1株当たり純利益 (**earnings per share**の略)
　basic EPS　基本的な1株利益
　diluted EPS　希薄済み1株当たり純利益
　fully diluted EPS　完全希薄化1株当たり利益, 完全希薄化後1株当たり利益
　primary EPS　基本的EPS

Equal Employment Opportunity Act [米]雇用機会均等法, 平等雇用機会法《略 EEOA》

equipment 名 設備, 施設, 機器, 装置, 用品, 製品, 資産, エクイップメント (⇒**property, plant and equipment**)
　acquisition of equipment　設備購入
　disposal of equipment　設備処分
　equipment and facilities　施設および装置, 施

設・装置
equipment investment 設備投資
equipment purchase obligation 設備購入債務
equipment replacement 設備更新
equipment sales 機器販売
gain on sale of equipment 動産売却益
lease equipment リース資産
loss on sale of equipment 設備売却損
obsolete equipment 老朽設備
premises and equipment net 動産・不動産純額
surplus equipment 遊休設備（＝idle equipment）

▶Other capital expenditures are for *equipment* and facilities used in leasing operations, manufacturing, and research and development. その他の資本的支出は，リース業務，製造部門と研究開発に使用する施設および装置向けでした。

equity 名 株式，持ち分，持ち分権，自己持ち分，自己資本，純資産，純資産価値，正味価額，証券，エクイティ（⇒**partnership interest**）
　at equity 実態による，持ち分価格［価額］で
　corporate equity 企業持ち分
　cross equity holdings 株式の持ち合い
　debt and equity securities 負債証券［債務証券］と持ち分証券
　equity earnings 関係会社利益持ち分，投資損益
　equity holding 株式保有，株式所有，保有株式，持ち株，出資比率，合弁（＝shareholding, stock holding, stockholding）
　equity holding losses 株式含み損，保有株式の含み損
　equity in earnings of unconsolidated subsidiaries and affiliated companies 非連結子会社および関連会社持ち分利益
　equity in net assets of subsidiaries 子会社純資産持ち分
　equity in net income of an associated company 関連会社持ち分利益
　equity ratio 自己資本比率，株主資本比率，株主持ち分比率
　new equity raising 新株発行
　on the equity basis 持ち分法で
　owners' equity 所有者持ち分
　partners' equity パートナーの持ち分
　proprietor's equity 事業主の持ち分
　raise equity 増資する
　stock equity 株式持ち分
　straight equity 普通株，普通株式

▶The accounting changes reduced our *equity* in 2007. 会計処理の変更に伴い，当社の自己資本は，2007年度は減少しました。

▶The *equity* in net assets of non-U.S. subsidiaries amounted to \$4.2 billion at December 31, 2007. 米国外子会社の純資産持ち分は，2007年12月31日現在で42億ドルでした。

equity capital 自己資本，株主資本，持ち分資本，株主の出資資本，株主持ち分，払込み資本，株式資本

　企業の資本について ➡ 企業の資本は，銀行からの借入金などの他人資本と，株主からの拠出資本や利益の蓄積である利益剰余金などの自己資本とに区分される。自己資金には，要するに資本金，資本剰余金（企業の純資産額のうち資本金の額を超える部分）と利益剰余金などが含まれる。

　equity capital to total assets 自己資本比率，株主資本比率
　equity capital to total debt ratio 負債比率

▶In the latest account settlements, some banking groups gave up including sizable deferred tax assets in their *equity capital*. 今決算では，一部の銀行グループが，巨額の繰延べ税金資産の自己資本への計上を見送った。

equity financing エクイティ・ファイナンス，新株発行による資金調達，自己資本金融，株式金融増資，自己資本の調達（＝equity finance：社債発行や借入金によって資本を調達する方法はdebt financingという）

▶We raised \$50 billion through *equity financing* deals in 2007. 当社は，エクイティ・ファイナンス［新株発行による資金調達］の取引で，2007年度は500億ドルの資金を調達しました。

equity in net earnings 持ち分利益，純利益に占める持ち分

▶The increases in earnings were due mainly to the inclusion of *equity in net earnings* of ABC Corp. for the full year 2006 plus foreign exchange gains. この増益は，主にABC社の持ち分利益を2006年度通期で連結計上したことと，為替差益によるものです。

equity in net earnings of an associated company 関連会社持ち分利益，関連会社の純利益に占める持ち分

▶Earnings from *equity in net earnings of an associated company*, investment and other income (net), interest charges and currency exchange gains/(losses) were \$45 million in 2007. 関連会社持ち分利益，投資その他の利益（純額），支払い利息と為替差益（差損）による利益は，2007年度は4,500万ドルでした。

equity interest 持ち分権，株式持ち分（⇒opportunity)

▶We acquired a 20% *equity interest* in the company for cash. 当社は、現金で同社の20%の株式持ち分を取得しました。

equity investment 株式投資, 直接投資, 出資 (=stock investment; ⇒**income from equity investments**)

▶*Equity investments* were a net source of cash in 2007. 2007年度は、基本的に株式投資が現金流入をもたらしました。

equity method 持ち分法, 実価法 (=equity method of accounting; ⇒**account for ...**)
　equity method income 持ち分法利益
　equity method investment 直接投資
　equity method profits 持ち分法収益

▶The finance subsidiaries of the Corporation, which in the past were accounted for by the *equity method*, are now fully consolidated. 前期[前年度]まで持ち分法で会計処理していた当社の金融事業を営む子会社[金融子会社]は、当期[当年度]からすべて連結の範囲に含めてあります。

equity purchase 株式取得, 株式投資

▶Mazda Motor Corp. made its New Zealand marketing subsidiary a wholly owned subsidiary through an *equity purchase*. マツダは、ニュージーランドの販売子会社を株式取得により完全子会社化した。

equity securities 持ち分証券, 持ち分有価証券

▶We must change the way we report and account for investments in *equity securities* in 2008. 2008年度に、当社は持ち分証券への投資に関する報告と会計処理方法を変更しなければなりません。

equity stake 持ち分, 株式持ち分, 保有株式, 出資比率

▶Capital gains from the sale of firm's *equity stake* will amount to about ¥50 billion. 同社の保有株式売却益は、約500億円になる見通しだ。

equity swap 株式交換, 株式スワップ, 株価スワップ
　equity swap contract 株式交換契約
　equity swap deal 株式交換取引 (=share swap deal, stock swap deal)

▶Citigroup Inc. and Nikko Cordial Corp. have altered their *equity swap* contract following the plunge in the stock price of Citigroup in New York. 米金融大手のシティグループと傘下の日興コーディアルグループは、ニューヨーク市場でシティグループの株価が下落したのを受けて、両社の株式交換契約の内容を変更した。

equity tie-up 資本提携

▶Three major steelmakers reached a final agreement to form an *equity tie-up*. 鉄鋼大手の3社が、資本提携を結ぶことで最終合意した。

equivalent 名 同等物, 等価物, 相当額, 相当分, 換算, 換算額, 同意語 (⇒**cash equivalents**)
　annual equivalent 年換算
　cash and equivalents 現金および現金等価物, 現金預金およびその等価物
　cash equivalent value [amount] 現金等価額
　certainty equivalent 確実性等価
　common equivalent shares 普通株式相当証券
　common stock equivalents 普通株式相当証券
　interest equivalents 利息相当分
　profit equivalent 利益同等物

▶Net earnings in 2007 were $1.56 billion, or $2.65 per fully diluted common and common *equivalent* shares. 2006年度の純利益は、15億6,000万ドル(完全希薄化後の普通株式および普通株式相当証券1株当たり2.65ドル)でした。

equivalent 形 ⟨…に⟩相当する, ⟨…に⟩当たる, ⟨…と⟩同等[同価値, 同量]である⟨**to**⟩

▶The company is scheduled to issue new shares *equivalent to* about 35 percent of of its outstanding equities for ¥1,138 per share in an effort to generate ¥30 billion. 同社は、発行済み株式数の約35%に当たる新株を1株当たり1,138円で発行して、300億円を調達する予定だ。

▶The foreign funds purchased the convertible bonds at prices *equivalent to* ¥25 per share. 海外ファンドは、1株25円で転換社債を引き受けた。

ERISA エリサ法 (⇒**Employee Retirement Income Security Act**)
　ERISA plan エリサ年金制度, ERISA年金制度

erode 動 減少させる, 低下させる

▶The meltdown in U.S. subprime mortgages has *eroded* earnings at financial firms. 米国のサブプライム・ローン(低所得者向け住宅ローン)市場の崩壊で、金融機関の収益は減少している。

error 名 誤謬, 誤記, 誤差, 誤り, ミス, 過誤, エラー
　accounting error 経理ミス, 会計上の誤謬 (=accounting mistake)
　calculation error 計算上の誤謬 (=error of calculation)
　clerical error 事務上の誤り, 事務的な誤り, 記帳上の誤謬
　compensating error 相殺誤差
　correction of error 誤謬の訂正, エラーの訂正
　detection of error 誤謬の発見
　error of mistake in writing 誤記上の誤謬, 誤

記による誤謬
error on posting 転記上の誤謬, 転記上の誤り
errors and omissions 誤差脱漏, 誤記・脱漏, 過誤脱漏
standard error 標準誤差
▸The firm failed to report a total of about ¥5 billion including simple accounting *errors*. 同社は, 単純な経理ミスを含めて総額で約50億円を申告しなかった。

escrow 名 第三者預託,〈不動産取引の〉代理人
escrow statement 不動産取引の報告書

ESOP 従業員持ち株制度 (=employee stock ownership trust：**employee stock ownership plan**の略)
ESOP debt guarantee reduction ESOP基金債務保証額の減少
▸We issued 14 million new shares of common stock in connection with the establishment of an *ESOP* feature for the non-management savings plan. 当社は, 非管理職貯蓄制度の一環として従業員持ち株制度(ESOP)を設けたことに関連して, 普通株式新株1,400万株を発行しました。

ESOP 従業員株式購入選択権制度 (**employee stock option plan**の略)

ESPP 従業員株式購入制度, 従業員持ち株制度 (**employee stock purchase plan**の略)

establish 動 設立する, 設置する, 創設する, 創立する, 樹立する, 形成する, 確立する, 制定する, 定める, 規定する,〈引当金や担保権を〉設定する, 設ける, 認定する, 関係を築く,〈制度などを〉導入する, 立証する
▸A pre-tax provision of $200 million ($0.57 per common share, after tax) was *established* to cover the estimated costs of this restructuring program. この事業再編計画の推定費用を補填するため, 税引き前で2億ドル(税引き後で, 普通株式1株当たり0.57ドル)の引当金を設定しました。
▸Each of these major subsidiaries has also *established* an audit committee that reports to their respective directors. これらの主要子会社各社も, それぞれの取締役会傘下の監査委員会を設置しています。
▸In recent years, there has been a rise in the number of women and aged people who want to *establish* enterprises. 最近は, 女性と高齢者の開業希望者が増えている。

estimate 動 見積もる, 推定する, 推計する, 予想する, 予測する, 概算する, 試算する, 評価する
We used our experience over the past five years to *estimate* future separations. 将来の休職を予測するにあたって, 当社は過去5年間の当社の経験値を使用しました。

estimate 名 見積り, 推定, 推計, 予想, 予測, 概算, 試算, 推定値, 推定量, 評価, 判断, 見積り書, 概算書,[～s]見積り金額
accounting estimate 会計見積り, 会計上の見積り
accounting estimate change 会計上の見積りの変更
best estimates and judgments 最良の見積りと判断
collateral value estimates 担保評価額
earlier reported estimate 速報値
estimate of possible loss 予想される損失額
excess over estimate 見積り超過額
full-year parent recurring profit estimate 通期の単独経常利益予想
market consensus estimate 市場のコンセンサス予想
market estimates 市場予想
original [initial] estimate 当初予想, 当初見積り, 当初の見積り額
preliminary estimate 暫定推定值
profit estimate 利益予想, 損益予想, 業績予想 (=profit forecast)
sales estimates 販売予測, 売上予測, 予想売上高 (=estimates of sales)
street estimates 市場予測
▸Capital expenditures for 2007 are now expected to reach approximately $2,750 million from the original *estimate* of $2,200 million. 2007年度の資本的支出は現在, 当初の見積り額22億ドルに対して約27億5,000万ドルに達する見込みです。
▸Toyota revised upward its earnings *estimates* for fiscal 2006 to next March. トヨタは, 2007年3月期の業績予想を上方修正した。

estimated 形 見積りの, 推定の, 概算の
estimated ending inventory 期末棚卸し資産の見積り高
estimated future credit losses 回収不能見込み額, 貸倒れ見積り高
estimated liability 見積り債務, 見積り負債, 引当金
estimated liability under product warranty 製品保証引当金
estimated loss from bad debt 予想貸倒れ損失
estimated loss or expenses 予想[見積り]損失または経費
estimated revenue 見積り収益, 見積り歳入
estimated useful life 見積り耐用年数 (=ex-

pected useful life; ⇒**declining balance**)
estimated value 見積り額, 評価額
estimated cost 見積り費用, 見積り原価, 予定原価, 費用見積り (=cost estimate), 原価見積り, 推定費用 (=estimate cost)
▶The *estimated costs* of specific plans to close offices, consolidate facilities and relocate employees in the provisions for business restructuring. 事業再編成引当金には, 事業所閉鎖や施設統合, 従業員再配置など特定の計画の費用見積りが含まれています。

estimated future postemployment benefits 予測される将来の雇用後給付, 将来の見積り雇用後給付
▶This new standard requires us to accrue *estimated future postemployment benefits*, including separation payments. この新基準は, 休職手当ての支払いを含めて, 予測される将来の雇用後給付を計上するよう要求しています。

estimated future retiree benefits 将来の見積り退職後給付, 予測される将来の退職後給付
▶This accounting standard requires us to accrue *estimated future retiree benefits* during the years employees are working and accumulating these benefits. この会計基準は, 従業員の受給権が発生する在職期間にわたって将来の見積り退職後給付を費用計上するよう要求しています。

estimated life 見積り有効期間, 見積り耐用年数
▶The *estimated lives* of machinery and equipment are 2-12 years. 機械・設備の見積り耐用年数は, 2-12年となっています。

ethical 形 倫理の, 道徳の (⇒**dealing**)
ethical business conduct 倫理的業務活動 (⇒**internal accounting control**)
ethical standard 倫理基準 (=ethics standard)
▶It is essential to conduct business affairs in accordance with the highest *ethical standards* as set forth in our Code of Conduct. 業務は, 当社の「行動規範」に定める最高の倫理基準に従って行うことが絶対必要です。

ethics 名 倫理, 道徳, 倫理体系, 行動の規範 (⇒**code of ethics, stock loss**)
  advertising ethics 広告倫理
  charter of ethics 企業行動憲章
  code of ethics 倫理規程
  corporate ethics 企業倫理 (=business ethics)
  ethics committee 倫理委員会
  ethics standards 倫理基準, 倫理規程 (=etical standards)
  managing ethics 経営倫理
  professional ethics 職業倫理
▶A Harvard University *ethics* committee has given a conditional green light to a research team to grow human embryonic stem cells. ハーバード大学倫理委員会は, 条件付きで研究チームに対してヒトES細胞[ヒト胚性幹細胞]の作製をすでに承認している。

European Central Bank 欧州中央銀行, 欧州中銀《略 ECB》

EVA 経済的付加価値, 経済付加価値 (economic value addedの略。企業価値評価指標で, 1年間に増えた株主の価値のこと。営業利益から税金, 配当金や金利などの資本コストを差し引いた残余利益。米国のスターン・スチュワート社が提唱したもので, 同社の登録商標)
▶*EVA* involves the measurement of economic returns on invested capital to ensure that we are earning more than the cost of capital. 経済的付加価値(EVA)で, 投下資本に対する経済的見返りを測定して, 当社が資本コストを上回る利益を上げていることを確かめることができます。

evaluation 名 評価, 分析, 診断, 判定
  asset evaluation 資産評価
  cost benefit evaluation 費用便益評価
  credit risk evaluation 信用リスク評価, 信用分析
  evaluation of asset values 資産価値の評価
  evaluation of collateral 担保評価
  evaluation of internal control system 内部統制組織の評価
  evaluation of performance 業績評価 (=performance evaluation)
  market evaluation 市場の評価
  stock evaluation losses 株式の評価損
  wage on job evaluation 職能給
▶The firm is suspected of understating its affiliates' stock *evaluation* losses in its financial paper. 同社は, 有価証券報告書で子会社の株式の評価損を過小計上していた疑いがある。

event 名 動き, 動向, 事象, 事態, 発生事項, 出来事, 事件, 成り行き, 結果, 事由, 事柄, 事項, 行事, 催事, イベント
  adjusting events after the balance sheet date 修正後発事象
  economic event 経済の動き, 経済動向, 経済事象
  events occurring after the balance sheet date 後発事象, 貸借対照表日後の発生事項 (=post balance sheet events, subsequent events)
  events subsequent to balance sheet date 後発事象, 貸借対照表日後の発生事項

extraordinary event　異常事象
fortuitous event　偶発的な事象
future events　将来発生する事態
infrequent event　突発事象
internal events　内部取引事象
liquidation event　清算事由
post-balance sheet event　後発事象
reportable event　要報告事項
subsequent event　後発事象
▶A favorable cycle of *events* has begun to emerge, with strong performances leading to an increase in jobs and higher wage, resulting in boosts in consumption.　好業績が雇用改善や賃金の上昇につながり、その結果消費も上向くなど、景気動向に好循環が見えてきた。

evidence 名　証拠、証拠資料、証拠物件　(=evidential matter)
▶An audit includes examining, on a test basis, *evidence* supporting the amounts and disclosures in the financial statements and assessing the accounting principles used.　監査には、財務書類上の金額や開示事項を裏付ける証拠の試査による検証と、適用された会計基準の評価も含まれています。

examination 名　監査、検査、検証、調査
bank examination　銀行監査
examination by reference　照査
examination of financial statements　財務書類監査、財務諸表の監査
interim examination date　中間監査日
scope of examination　監査の範囲
▶Our *examinations* included such tests of the accounting records and such other auditing procedures as we considered necessary in the circumstances.　私どもの監査には、状況に応じて私どもが必要と見なした会計記録［会計報告書・財務諸表］の試査やその他の監査手続きも含まれています。

examine 動　監査する、検査する、検証する、調査する
▶We have *examined* the consolidated balance sheets of ABCD Corp. and subsidiaries as at December 31, 2007 and 2006.　私どもは、ABCD Corp.とその子会社の2006年および2007年12月31日現在の連結貸借対照表について監査しました。

except 前接　…の場合を除いて、…を除いて、…でないかぎり
except per share amounts　1株当たりの金額を除く、1株当たりの金額を除いて
except per share figures　1株当たりの数値［金額］を除く、1株当たりの数値［金額］を除いて

except where otherwise noted [stated]　別段の記載がないかぎり
in millions, except as noted　単位：100万ドル。ただし、特に記載する場合を除く。
in millions, except per share amounts　単位：100万ドル。ただし、1株当たりの金額を除く。
in millions of dollars except per share figures　単位：100万ドル。ただし、1株当たりの金額を除く。
▶Although the firm reports its results in U.S. dollars, they are presented here in Canadian dollars, *except* where otherwise noted.　同社は営業成績を米ドルで表示していますが、別段の記載がないかぎり、この報告書では同社の営業成績はカナダ・ドルで表示されています。

excess 名　超過、超過額、過剰、余剰、過度
capital in excess of par value　株式払込み剰余金、払込み剰余金、資本剰余金、株式発行差金
capital in excess of stated value　株式払込み剰余金、払込み剰余金、額面超過金
excess of assets over projected benefit obligation　資産の予測給付債務超過額
excess over estimate　見積り超過額

excess 形　超過の、余剰の
excess capacity　過剰設備
excess earning power　超過収益力；余剰資金
excess liabilities　債務超過、債務超過額　(= excess of debts, excess of liabilities over assets, excessive liabilities, liabilities in excess of assets)
excess quotas for greenhouse gas emissions　温室効果ガスの削減分、温室効果ガスの排出権
▶*Excess* volatility in exchange rates is undesirable for global economic growth.　為替相場の過度の変動は、世界の経済成長にとって望ましくない。
▶The *excess* quotas for carbon dioxide and other greenhouse gas emissions will be distributed to companies in accordance with the amount of funds each firm provided.　二酸化炭素などの温室効果ガスの排出権［二酸化炭素など温室効果ガス排出量の削減分］は、各企業の基金への出資額に応じて分配される。

excess liquidity　過剰流動性、余剰資金
▶Japanese firms are awash with *excess liquidity* after a decade of post-bubble economic restructuring efforts.　日本企業は、10年に及ぶバブル崩壊後のリストラ策［リストラ努力］で、余剰資金が豊富だ。

excess of cost　原価超過額、取得原価超過額
excess of cost over book value　簿価に対する原価超過額

excess of cost over the net assets acquired 取得した純資産に対する取得価額超過額
▸The *excess of cost* of shares over acquired equity (goodwill) of subsidiary and associated companies is being amortized to earnings on a straight-line basis over its estimated life. 子会社と関連会社の所有持ち分を超える投資額(借方投資差額)は、見積り有効期間にわたって定額法で償却されています。

exchange 動 交換する, 取り替える, 両替する, やり取りする, 〈契約などを〉取り交わす, 〈契約書に〉サインする
▸We had a $200 million gain when we *exchanged* our remaining 70% interest in the company for about 3% ownership of a leading sftware development company. 当社は、同社の70%残存持ち分を大手のソフトウエア開発会社に対する約3%の持ち分と交換して、2億ドルの利益を上げました。
▸We plan to *exchange* one share of the firm for our 1.4 shares, making it a whole subsidiary of us. 当社は、同社株1株に自社株1.4株を割り当てる株式交換を実施して、同社を当社の完全子会社化する方針です。

exchange 名 交換, 両替, 為替, 為替相場, 〈証券や商品の〉取引所, 取引, 交易 (⇒stock exchange)
　exchange contract 為替予約
　exchange distribution 取引所分売
　exchange loss 為替差損
　exchange of shares 株式交換
▸Income and expense items are translated at average rates of *exchange* prevailing during the year. 収益と費用項目は、期中の実勢平均為替レートで換算されています。
▸These interest rate swap agreements generally involve the *exchange* of fixed or floating interest payments without the exchange of the underlying principal amounts. これらの金利スワップ契約では、原則として元本の交換は行わず、固定金利または変動金利による支払い利息を交換する。
▸We computed these combined amounts assuming the merger was already completed using a one-for-one *exchange* of shares. これらの合算数値は、1対1の株式交換方式を用いて合併がすでに完了しているものとして計算しました。

exchange gain 為替差益 (＝currency exchange gain, exchange profit)
　exchange gain from yen appreciation 円高差益

exchange gain (loss) 為替差益(損失)
exchange gain or [and] loss 為替差損益, 為替換算差損益 (＝exchange gains/losses, exchange gains and losses)

exchange market 為替市場
▸It is necessary to keep a watch on large fluctuations on the *exchange market* and changes in stock prices. 為替市場の乱高下や株価の動きを警戒する必要がある。

exchange rate 為替相場, 外国為替相場, 為替レート, 交換レート, 交換比率, 換算レート (＝currency exchange rate, rate of exchange)
　at average exchange rates prevailing during the year 期中の実勢平均為替レートで
　at exchange rates in effect at the balance sheet date 貸借対照表日現在の実効為替レートで, 貸借対照表日現在の為替レートで
　current exchange rate 実勢為替相場, 実勢為替レート, 現在外貨交換レート
　yen-dollar exchange rate 円ドル相場, 円ドル・レート, 円の対ドル・レート, 円とドルの為替レート
▸We forecast an *exchange rate* of ¥120 to the dollar for the current fiscal year. 当社は、今年度の為替レートを1ドル＝120円と想定しています。

execute 動 執行する, 実行する, 実施する, 遂行する, 履行する, 達成する, 完成する, 〈契約書などを〉作成する, 署名する, 調印する
　execute a stock [share] split 株式分割を実施する
　execute a trade 取引を執行する
　execute an obligation created by the contract 契約で生じた義務を履行する
▸We will continue to *execute* our strategy. 私どもは、今後とも当社の経営戦略を推進していく所存です。

execution 名 執行(証券会社などが取引を実行すること), 実行, 実施, 履行, 施行, 達成, 成立, 業務, 署名, 作成, 調印, 締結
　daily execution 日常業務
　execution date of this agreement 本契約締結日
　execution of loan ローンの実行
　execution of stock warrants ワラント[株式ワラント, 新株引受権]の権利行使
　order execution 注文執行, 注文処理 (＝execution of order)
　skill in trade execution 取引執行力
　term of execution 履行期限
▸The responsibilities of the Executive Committee

include the delegation of certain authority for *execution* of bids, proposals and contracts. 経営委員会の権限としては、入札、提議や契約などの履行に関する権限の委譲も含まれています。

executive 名 経営者, 管理職, 重役, 会社役員, 役職員, 執行役員, 執行部, 執行機関, エグゼクティブ
  account executive 〈広告会社の〉営業責任者, 〈証券会社の〉セールスマン
  business executive 企業経営者
  Chief Executive 米大統領
  chief executive 企業などのトップ
  chief executive officer 最高経営責任者
  company executives 会社経営者, 経営者（＝corporate executives）
  current executives 現経営陣, 現役員, 現執行部
  departmental executives 部門別業務執行役員
  executive changes 役員の交代
  executive counselor 取締役相談役
  executive director 業務執行取締役, 執行取締役, [日]専務・常務取締役
  executive office 業務執行室
  executive organization 管理組織
  financial executive 財務管理者, 財務担当経営者, 財務部門の幹部
  former executives 旧経営陣
  managing executive 業務執行役員, 経営業務執行役員, 事務局長
  middle management executive 中間管理者, 中間管理職にある人, 中堅幹部
  rebel executive 造反役員
  senior executive 上級役員, 上級管理者, 経営者
  top executive 最高経営者
▶Ford Motor Co. named Annes Stevens as its No.2 *executive* for the Americas. フォード・モーターは、アン・スティーブンス氏を米州部門のナンバー2（創業102年で初の女性上級副社長）に指名した。

executive committee 経営委員会, 執行委員会, 業務執行委員会（⇒management executive committee）
▶Acting as the Nominating Committee of the Board, the *Executive Committee* recommends qualified candidates for election as officers and directors of the Company. 取締役会付属の指名委員会として機能する経営委員会は、当社の役員、取締役として適格な選任候補者を推薦します。

executive compensation 業務執行役員報酬, 役員報酬
▶*Executive compensation* is directly related to performance. 役員報酬は、業績と直接連動しています。

executive compensation committee 役員報酬委員会, 経営幹部報酬委員会
▶Members of the *executive compensation committee* are directors who are not officers or employees of the Compny or its subsidiaries. 役員報酬委員会の委員は、当社もしくは子会社の役員または従業員でない取締役で構成されています。

executive remuneration packages 執行役員の報酬
▶The company will cut *executive remuneration packages* by 25-50 percent from fiscal 2007. 同社では、2007年度から執行役員の報酬を25~50%カットする。

exercisable 形 権利の行使可能な, 行使できる
▶At December 31, 2007, all of these unexercised SARs were *exercisable*. 2007年12月31日の時点で、この未行使の株式評価受益権(SAR)はすべて行使可能でした。
▶The options are *exercisable* during a period not to exceed ten years. このオプションの行使可能期間は、10年を超えない期間となっています。

exercise 動 〈オプション取引などで権利を〉行使する, 実行する, 〈指導力などを〉発揮する, 〈影響・圧力などを〉及ぼす
▶During 2007 167,747 stock appreciation rights (SARs) were *exercised*. 2007年度は、167,747株分の株式評価受益権(SAR)が行使されました。

exercise 名 権利の行使, 行使, 実行, 努力, 策
  cost-cutting exercise コスト削減策
  refinancing exercise 借換え債の発行
  substitutional exercise of voting right 議決権の代理行使
▶The Corporation will provide the shares available upon *exercise* of options either by issuance or by purchase on the open market. 当社は、選択権の行使に必要な株式を、新規発行または公開市場で購入して提供します。

exercise price 行使価格, 権利行使価格
▶The *exercise price* of each option granted is 100% of market value on the date of the grant. 付与された各購入選択権の権利行使価格は、権利付与日の市場価格の100%となっています。

Exon-Florio provision of the 1988 trade law
1988年通商法のエクソン・フロリオ条項（米国の安全保障を損なう企業買収の禁止）
▶In the United States, the *Exon-Florio provision of the 1988 trade law* can prevent takeover bids that are deemed a threat to national security. 米国では、1988年通商法のエクソン・フロリオ条項で、国家の安全保障上、脅威と考えられる企業買収

を阻止することができる。

expansion 名 拡大, 拡張, 設備拡張, 景気拡大, 成長, 上昇, 多角化
 business expansion 事業拡大, 事業拡張
 capital expansion 増資, 資本増強 (=capital increase, increase of capital)
 credit expansion 信用拡大, 信用拡張, 信用膨張, 貸出の伸び
 economic expansion 景気回復, 景気拡大, 景気上昇, 経済成長
 expansion of domestic demand 内需拡大
 expansion period 景気拡大局面
 factory expansion 工場拡張
 market expansion 市場拡大
 organizational expansion 組織拡大, 企業組織の拡大
 output expansion 生産の増加, 生産の伸び, 生産拡大
 quantitative expansion 量的拡大
 sustained economic expansion 持続的な経済成長, 経済の持続的な成長
 Trade Expansion Act 〚米〛通商拡大法
▸Toyota's growth is supported by the *expansion* of sales overseas. トヨタの成長を支えるのは, 海外での販売拡大だ。

expect 動 期待する, 見込む, 予想する, 見積もる, 推定する
▸We *expect* continuing growth in this segment's revenues, earnings and assets in 2008. 当社は, 2008年度も引き続き当事業部門の収益, 利益と資産の増加を見込んでいます。

expectation 名 期待, 予想, 見通し, 見積り, 推定, 期待値
 expectation of life 見積り耐用年数, 期待耐用年数 (=expected life)
 expectations for the year as a whole 通期予想, 通期見通し, 年間予想

expected 形 期待の, 予想の, 見通しの, 見積りの
 expected earnings 期待収益
 expected income 期待利益, 期待収益, 期待所得
 expected life 見積り耐用年数, 予想耐用年数 (=expectation of life, expected useful life)
 expected loss 予想損失, 損失の予想, 見込まれる損失, 赤字見通し
 expected realizable profit 期待実現可能利益
 expected return on plan assets 年金資産 [年金制度資産] の予想運用利益率, 期待運用収益率, 制度資産の期待収益, 年金資産の予想収益

expected long-term rate of return 予想長期収益率

expected long-term rate of return on plan assets 年金資産 [制度資産] の長期期待収益率, 期待長期資産収益率, 制度資産の予想長期収益率
▸The *expected long-term rate of return* on plan assets is used in the calculation of net periodic pension cost. 年金資産の予想長期収益率は, 期間年金費用純額の計算に使われる。

expected net profit 予想純利益, 予想される [見込まれる] 純利益
▸Decline in the *expected net profit* is attributable mainly to the possible unfavorable effects of the yen's rise against the dollar. 予想される純利益減少の主な要因は, 円高・ドル安の不利な影響である。

expected useful life 見積り耐用年数 (=estimated useful life, expected life)
▸Depreciation is generally computed using the straight-line method, based on the *expected useful lives* of the assets. 減価償却は, 原則として資産の見積り耐用年数に基づいて, 定額法で計算されています。

expenditure 名 支出, 経費, 費消, 消費量, 支払い義務額 (⇒capital expenditure, R&D expenditures)
 consolidated income and expenditure account 連結損益計算書
 current expenditure 当期支出, 当期支払い, 当期費用, 経常的支出
 expenditures for plant and equipment 有形固定資産購入
 expenditures for real estate, plants and equipment 不動産, 工場および設備の取得額
 expenditures for special tools 特殊工具の取得額
 miscellaneous expenditure 雑費
 progress expenditure 製作費
 real expenditure 実質的経費

expense 動 費用処理する, 費用に計上する, 費用として計上する (⇒cost 名)
 amounts expensed as pension costs 年金原価として費用処理した額
 be expensed as written off 貸倒れ損失として費用処理する
▸Previously, we *expensed* life insurance benefits as plans were funded. これまで当社は, 生命保険給付については, 制度に拠出が行われた時点で費用として計上していました。

expense 名 費用, 経費, 支出 (⇒book 動, operating expense)
 business expenses 営業経費, 営業費, 事業費用

central corporate expense 本社費用
compensation expense 報償費用
corporate expense 本部費, 本部経費
current expenses 経常費
debt expense 貸倒れ損失, 社債発行費
deferred expense 繰延べ費用
direct expense 直接経費
distribution expense 物流費
estimated expense 見積り費用
expense arising from outside manufacture 外注加工費
expense on bonds 社債発行費
expense paid 支払い経費, 支払い済み費用
expenses for filing with the SEC SECへの届け出費用
expenses paid in advance 未経過費用
experimental and research expense 試験研究費
factory expense 製造間接費
loss adjustment expense 損害査定費
necessary expenses 必要経費
nonrecurrent expense 経常外費用
normal expense 正常費用
occupancy expense 賃借料
operations expenses 業務経費
secret service expense 機密費
standing expense 経常費

▶In the former accounting method, we booked *expenses* for separations when we identified them. 従来の会計処理方法では, 休職に関する費用は休職を確認した時点で費用として計上していました.

experience 名 経験, 体験, 習得, 実績, 状況, 経緯, 動向
  experience gains and losses 経験的利得および損失
  loss experience 貸倒れ損失実績, 損失率
  purchase experience 購入経験, 購入実績
  write off experience 償却実績

expertise 名 専門知識, 専門技術, ノウハウ, 専門家の報告書
  advanced expertise 先端的ノウハウ, 高度な専門知識・技術
  financial expertise 金融ノウハウ
  manufacturing expertise 生産技術, 生産のノウハウ
  product expertise 製品のノウハウ, 製品知識, 番組などの制作のノウハウ
  technical expertise 技術ノウハウ, 技術的専門意見, 専門技術
  technological expertise 技術的専門知識, 技術ノウハウ

▶By utilizing Imperial Hotel's brand and hotel management *expertise*, Mitsui Fudosan and the Imperial Hotel will cooperate in the hotel and resort facilities business. 帝国ホテルのブランドとホテル運営のノウハウを生かして, 三井不動産と帝国ホテルは今後, ホテル・リゾート施設事業で連携する.

exploratory 形 探索の
  exploratory research 探索的調査 (予備的段階のマーケティング・リサーチ)
  exploratory talks 事前協議

export 名 輸出, 輸出品, 輸出製品, 供給
▶The strong performance of major companies has been achieved because of increases in *exports* to the United States and China. 大企業が好業績を上げているのは, 米国と中国向けの輸出が伸びたからだ.

exposure 名 リスク危険度, 投資, 融資, リスク資産総額, 融資総額, 与信残高, 債権額, エクスポージャー
  currency exposure 為替リスク, 通貨リスク
  exposure limit 与信枠
  exposure threshold リスク限度額
  exposure to interest rates 金利変動リスク
  exposure to losses 損失負担, 損失リスク
  hedge the exposure リスクをヘッジする
  interest exposure 金利リスク, 金利変動リスク, 金利エクスポージャー
  problem exposures 不良債権
  reduce exposure to the risk of loss 損失リスクを減らす, 損失リスクを軽減する

▶We control our *exposure* to credit risk through credit approvals, credit limits and monitoring procedures. 当社は, 信用供与承認, 信用限度と監視手続きを通して信用リスクを管理しています.

express money order 至急為替
extend 動 延ばす, 延長する, 拡大する, 拡張する, 提供する, 差し伸べる, 与える, 供与する
  extend a marketing period 販売期間を延長する
  extend credit 信用を供与する

▶Ford *extended* through Sept. 6 its incentive program reducing customer prices to employee-discount levels. フォードは, 小売価格 [顧客販売価格] を社員向け値引きの水準にまで引き下げる販売促進策を, 9月6日まで延長した.

extended 形 延長した, 拡大した, 拡張した
  extended coverage 〔保険〕拡張担保
  extended fund facility 拡大信用供与

extension 名 拡大, 拡張, 延長, 機能拡張, 拡張工事, 期間延長, 付属電話機, 内線, 範囲, 程度
　double extension　二重計算
　extension of coverage　担保範囲の拡張
　extension of credit　信用供与, 信用の拡大
　extension of employment　雇用延長
　extension risk　期間延長リスク
　reserve for business extension　事業拡張積立金

external financing [funding]　外部調達資金, 外部資金の調達, 外部金融
▸We expect to meet our cash requirements in 2007 from operations and *external financing*. 当社は, 業務活動によってもたらされる資金と外部資金調達で, 2007年度の必要資金を確保する方針です。

extraordinary 形 特別の, 臨時の, 異常な
　extraordinary board of directors meeting　臨時取締役会
　extraordinary charges and credits　特別損益
　extraordinary credit　特別控除, 異常利益
　extraordinary expenses　臨時費用, 臨時費, 特別損失
　extraordinary gain　特別利益, 異常利得
　extraordinary gain or [and] loss　特別損益, 臨時損益, 臨時利得および損失

extraordinary income　特別利益, 臨時利益
　extraordinary income and charge　異常損益
　extraordinary income (expense)　特別損益
▸Sale of buildings to a subsidiary of the firm in which we hold a 25 percent interest, resulted in *extraordinary income* of $5 million. 当社が25％の株式を所有する同社の子会社に建物を売却したのに伴って, 500万ドルの特別利益が生じました。

extraordinary items　特別(損益)項目, 異常(損益)項目, 臨時(損益)項目, 非経常(的)項目

extraordinary items and prior year adjustments　異常損益項目および過年度修正

extraordinary items, less applicable income taxes　臨時損益項目—税引き後

extraordinary items, less applicable tax　税金控除後異常項目

income before extraordinary items　臨時損益項目調整前利益, 異常項目控除前利益, 経常利益
▸Income before *extraordinary items* posted approximately 330.5 billion yen during the fiscal year ended March 31, 2007. 2007年3月期決算で, 経常利益は約3,305億円となった。

extraordinary loss　特別損失, 異常損失, 経常外損失 (=special loss)
▸The company will likely book a total *extraordinary loss* of $170 million for the potential U.S. plant closure. 同社は, 予想される米国工場の閉鎖で, 総額1億7,000万ドルの特別損失を計上する見込みだ。

extraordinary profit　特別利益(保有株式の売却やメーカーの工場売却による利益)
▸The leading banks' loan loss charges were returned as *extraordinary profit*. 大手銀行の貸倒れ引当金は, 特別利益として戻ってきた。

extraordinary shareholders meeting　臨時株主総会 (=extraordinary general meeting, extraordinary meeting of shareholders, special meeting of shareholders, special meeting of stockholders：原則として年1回開く定時株主総会とは別に, 定款変更など株主総会決議が必要な重要事項の決定を行うときに開く)
▸The company will hold an *extraordinary shareholders meeting* in June to choose new directors. 同社は, 6月に臨時株主総会を開いて, 後任取締役[新任取締役]を決める。

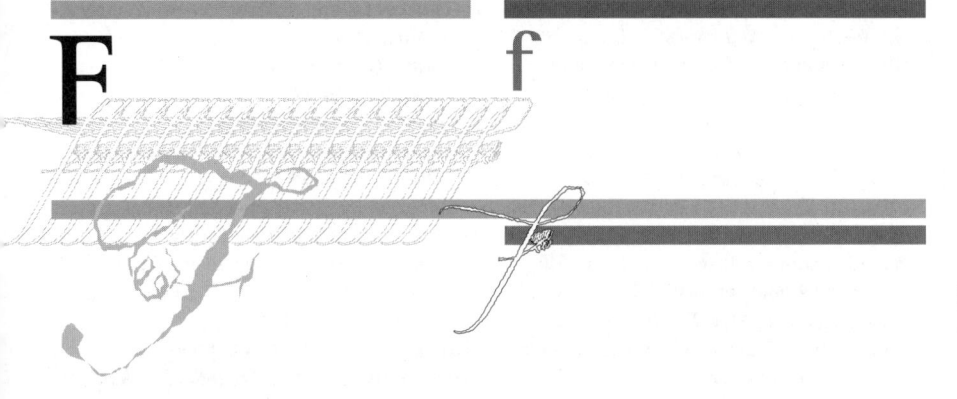

401(k) 米内国歳入庁コード401(k)（米国の企業年金：給与所得者の退職基金積立制度の一つで, 積立金は天引き貯蓄され, 税法上の所得控除が受けられる）

401(k)-style pension scheme 〔日〕確定拠出型年金制度, 日本版401k（米国の企業年金「401(k)プラン」を参考にして作られた年金制度で, 加入者の運用次第で老後の受給額が変動する仕組みになっている）
▶The firm introduced a *401(k)-style pension scheme* for about 10,000 office workers. 同社は, 約1万人の内勤職員を対象に確定拠出型年金制度（日本版401k）を導入した。

face 名 額面, 券面 （⇒**fall**）
  face amount 額面金額, 額面価額, 額面, 券面額（＝face value）
  face value 額面価格［価額］, 額面, 券面額（＝face amount）
▶As of December 31, 2007, the outstanding zero coupon notes due 2022 had a *face value* at maturity of $140 million. 2007年12月31日現在, 2022年満期・発行済みゼロ・クーポン債の満期時の額面総額は, 1億4,000万ドルです。

facility 名 融資枠, 融資, 信用供与, 信用枠, 便宜, 什器, 設備, 施設, 工場, 制度, ファシリティ（⇒**abandonment, credit facilities**）
  borrowing facilities 信用枠
  credit facilities 信用枠
  excess facilities 過剰設備 （＝excess capacity, surplus facilities, unwanted facilities）
  facilities and equipment 設備
  facility management 設備の管理・運用, コンピュータの他社管理, ファシリティ・マネジメント
  factory facilities 工場設備
  idle facility 遊休施設
  loan facility 貸付け, 融資枠
  manufacturing facilities 生産設備
  new facilities 新規融資
  production facility 生産設備
▶The *facility* will be upsized. 融資枠は, 拡大される見込みだ。
▶The segment's fixed costs and production *facility* capacity increased when compared to 2006. 2006年度に比べて, 固定費や生産設備の能力は増大しました。
▶We use accelerated depreciation methods for factory *facilities* and digital equipment used in the telecommunication network. 工場設備と電気通信ネットワークに使用されているデジタル機器については, 当社は加速償却法で償却しています。

factor 名 要素, 要因, 因子, 材料, 原動力, 金融業者, 金融機関, ファクタリング業者, 債権買取り業者, …率, 係数, 指数, ファクター （⇒**basic material, showing**）
  competitive factor 競争要因
  contributing factor 貢献要因
  cost factor コスト要因, 原価要素
  dilution factor 希薄化率
  factor cost 生産要素費用, 要素費用
  multiple factors 複合的な要因
  one-off factor 一時的な要因
  positive factor プラス要因, 好材料, 買い材料
  productive factor 生産要素 （＝production factor）
▶One major *factor* behind lackluster consumption and price increases is the slow increase in wages.

消費の低迷や物価上昇率の伸び悩みの背景にある大きな要因の一つは，賃金上昇の鈍さだ．
▸Other competitive *factors* in the market for the products are service, delivery, technological capability, and product qualty and performance. 市場での製品の競争要因としては，サービスや納入，技術活用能力，品質，性能なども挙げられます．

factoring 名 取立て代理業，債権買取り業，売掛債権売却，ファクタリング
　factoring with recourse 遡求権付きの売却
　factoring without recourse 遡求権なしの売却

factory 名 工場，生産設備，製造業，メーカー
　factory cost 製造原価，製造コスト，工場原価 （＝manufacturing cost）
　factory expense 製造間接費，製造経費，工場経費 （＝factory burden, manufacturing expense）
　factory furniture 工場備品，工場の什器備品 （＝factory fitting, factory furnitures and fixtures）
　factory general expense 工場一般管理費，工場一般経費
　factory supplies 工場消耗品
▸Kirin Brewery Co. plans to take full control of a Chinese unit and build a new *factory* in 2007. キリンビールは，中国の子会社を完全子会社化し，2007年に新工場を建設する計画だ．

factory burden 製造間接費，工場間接費（＝factory expense, factory overhead, manufacturing overhead）
　applied factory burden 製造間接費配賦額
　fixed factory burden 固定製造間接費

factory overhead 工場間接費
　factory overhead cost 製造間接費 （＝factory overhead, factory overhead expense, manufacturing overhead）
　fixed factory overhead 固定製造間接費

fail 動 経営破綻する，破綻する，倒産する，破産する （＝collapse），失敗する，…を怠る
　failed bank 経営破綻銀行，破綻銀行
　failed borrower 融資先企業の経営破綻，経営破綻した融資先
　failed nonlife insurer 破綻損保
▸We *failed* to acquire a majority stake in the company in our tender offer. 当社は，TOB（株式公開買付け）で同社株の過半数株式を取得できませんでした．

failure 名 経営破綻，破綻，倒産，破産，〈債務などの〉不履行，失敗，〈機械などの〉機能停止，故障，障害 （＝collapse）
　bank failure 銀行破綻 （＝bank's collapse）

　business failure 企業倒産 （＝bankruptcy, insolvency）
　corporate failure 企業倒産，経営破綻 （＝corporate bankruptcy）
　financial failures 金融破綻
　system failure システムの故障，システムのトラブル，システム障害
▸One insurance company's *failure* has a great impact on banks that are closely linked to the insurer by means of cross-shareholding. 生保の破綻は，株式の密接な持ち合い関係にある銀行に重大な影響を及ぼします．

fair 形 公正な，適正な，まずまずの
fair value 公正価額，公正価格，公正価値，公正な評価額，適正価値，時価
　current fair value 現在公正価格［価額］，現在公正価値
　equipment fair value 設備適正価額
　fair value gains (losses) on land revaluation 土地再評価差額金 （＝variance of land revaluation）
　fair value of assets acquired 取得資産の公正価格
　fair value of liabilities assumed 引継負債の公正価格
　plan assets at fair value 公正価額による年金資産
▸The *fair value* of our pension plan assets is greater than our projected pension obligations. 当社の年金制度資産の公正価額は，予想年金債務額を上回っています．

fall 動 下落する，低下する，減少する，崩壊する，失墜する，手形の期限が来る
　fall below ... …を割り込む，…を割る
　fall short of ... …を下回る
　falling backlog 受注残高の減少
　falling demand 需要の低下，需要の減少
　falling interest rates 金利の低下
　falling market 下げ相場
　falling prices 物価の下落
　falling stock market 株価の下落
▸Mizuho's first-half profit *fell* 17 percent as credit costs increased and on losses related to investments in U.S. home loans to riskier borrowers. みずほの上半期利益は，与信コストの増加とリスクの高い融資先への米国の住宅ローン投資に関連する損失で17％減少した．
▸The prices of these companies' stock have declined to *fall* below the face value. これらの企業の株価は，額面を下回っている．

fall 名 下落, 低下, 減少, 崩壊 （⇒**accelerate**）
　fall in funding costs 資金調達コストの低下
false 形 虚偽の, 不正確な
　false consolidated financial statements 虚偽の連結財務書類
　▸These four accountants worked with the firm's former executives to produce *false* consolidated financial statements. これら4人の会計士は, 同社の旧経営陣と共謀して虚偽の連結財務書類を作成した。
falsify 動 偽造する, 偽装する, 改竄する, 捏造する, 変造する, 詐称する, 虚偽記載する
　falsified financial documents 虚偽の財務書類
　falsified financial report 有価証券報告書の虚偽記載, 財務報告書の虚偽記載
　falsified stock dealing 株式の偽装売買, 偽装株式取引
　falsified transaction 不正取引, 仮装売買, 偽装売買, 偽装取引 （＝fake transaction, falsified trading）
　▸Four certified public accountants conspired with the firm's former executives to *falsify* accounting reports. 公認会計士4人が, 同社の旧経営陣と共謀して会計報告書［有価証券報告書］に虚偽の記載をした。
FASB ［米］財務会計基準審議会 （**Financial Accounting Standards Board**の略）
　FASB disclosure standards FASBによる開示基準
　FASB pronouncements FASB基準書
　▸The Company adopted the provisions of the *FASB*'s Statement of Financial Accounting Standards (SFAS) No. 106 in 2005. 2005年度から当社は, 財務会計基準審議会(FASB)の財務会計基準書第106号を採用しました。
favorable 形 有利な, 好都合な, 好ましい, 良好な, 好調な, 明るい, 追い風になる （⇒**benefit**名, **maturity**）
　favorable balance of payments 国際収支の黒字
　favorable balance of trade 輸出超過
　favorable economic and political environments 良好な政治・経済環境
　favorable factor 好材料
　favorable inflation outlook 明るいインフレ見通し
　on favorable terms 有利な条件で
　▸China is reviewing its policy of giving *favorable* treatment to foreign companies. 中国は, 外資優遇策を見直している。
feasibility 名 実行可能性, 実現可能性, 企業化可能性, 採算性, フィージビリティ
　economic feasibility 経済的実行可能性
　feasibility study 実行［実現］可能性調査, 実行［実現］可能性研究, 企業化［事業化］可能性調査, 企業化［事業化］調査, 予備調査, 準備調査, 採算性調査, フィージビリティ・スタディ
　financial feasibility 財務上の実現可能性, 経済的実行可能性
　technological feasibility 技術的実現可能性
　▸For contracts involving certain technologies, profits and revenues are deferred until technological *feasibility* is established. 一定の技術を伴う契約(請負契約)については, 技術の実現可能性が確立されるまで, 収益と利益は繰り延べられます。
Fed 米連邦準備制度理事会, FRB （＝Federal Reserve : Federal Reserve Boardの略称。米連邦準備銀行(Federal Reserve Bank)や米連邦準備制度(Federal Reserve System), 米連邦公開市場委員会(Federal Open Market Committee)を意味するときもある）
Federal Employers' Liability Act ［米］連邦雇用者責任法
Federal [federal] funds rate 短期金利, FFレート, FF金利, フェデラル・ファンド金利, フェデラル・ファンド適用金利, フェデラル・ファンド・レート （＝Fed funds rate, key interest rate, key rate : 短期金融市場の状況を最も敏感に反映する指標金利の一つで, 日本のコール・レートに相当。米国の市中銀行同士がフェデラル・ファンドを翌日決済で貸し借りするときに適用する金利）
federal income tax 連邦所得税, 連邦法人税 （⇒**taxable income**）
　federal income tax liability 未払い連邦所得税
　federal income tax return 連邦法人税申告書
　▸The Internal Revenue Service (IRS) has examined the *federal income tax* returns for the Corporation through 2005. 米内国歳入庁(IRS)は, 2005年度までの当社の連邦法人税申告書の調査をしました。
Federal Open Market Committee 米連邦公開市場委員会《略 **FOMC**》 （＝Federal Reserve Open Market Committee : 米国の金融政策の最高意思決定機関で, 短期金融政策と公開市場操作に関する方針を決定する。連邦準備制度理事会の理事7人と地区連邦準備銀行の総裁5人で構成）
Federal Reserve Board 米連邦準備制度理事会, 米連邦準備理事会《略 **FRB**》 （＝Fed, Federal Reserve : 米国の連邦準備制度(FRS)の統括機関で, 正式名称はBoard of Governors of the Federal Reserve System。理事は7人で上院の承認

を経て大統領が任命し、任期は14年)
federal statutory tax rate 連邦法定税率、連邦法人税率 (=federal statutory rate)
Federal Trade Commission [米]連邦取引委員会《略 FTC》(=U.S. federal antitrust regulators:米国の独占禁止法施行機関)
fee 图 料金、入会金、入場料、納付金、会費、手数料、使用料、報酬、謝礼、実施料、対価、所有権、相続財産権、フィー
  after fee 手数料込みで (=at full fees)
  application fee 出願手数料
  audit fee 監査料、監査報酬
  contingent fee 成功報酬
  entrance fee 入会金
  fees and permits 免許料
  fixed fee 固定報酬
  legal fee 弁護士手数料
  medical fees 医療費 (=medical costs)
  redemption fee 解約手数料
  underwriting fee 引受手数料
▶Nomura's net profit jumped 142 percent for the April–June quarter, boosted by gains in commissions, asset management *fees* and interest and dividend revenue. 4-6月期(決算)の野村の税引き後利益は、株式委託手数料や資産運用手数料、受取利息・配当金の増加で、142%急増した。
fictious 形 架空の、虚構の、仮設の
  fictious capital 架空資本、擬制資本
  fictious profit 架空利益 (=paper profit)
field 图 領域、分野、市場、実地、現場、現地、出先、〈天然資源の〉埋蔵地帯、産出地帯、フィールド
  business fields 事業分野
  enter a new field 新分野に参入する
  field engineer サービス技術者
  field office 営業所
  field premises 現地事務所
  field research 実地調査、現地調査、現場調査
  field sales force 外務員、外交販売員 (=field salesman, field salesperson)
  field study 実地調査、現地調査、実地研究、フィールド・スタディ
  field test 実地検査、実地試験
  field work standard 監査実地基準
  gain the field 市場を獲得する
  gas field ガス田
  oil field 油田
  other business fields 異業種
  playing field 事業環境
  regulatory field 規制分野
▶Moves toward a full-scale realignment have been accelerating in the commodity futures trading industry, involving companies from other business *fields*. 商品先物取引業界では、異業種の企業を巻き込んでの総力を挙げての再編の動きが加速している。
field audit 実地監査、現地監査、現場監査、実物監査
▶The Internal Revenue Service has completed its *field audit* of the federal income tax returns of 2005 and 2006. 米内国歳入庁(IRS)が、2005年度と2006年度の連邦法人税申告についての現地監査を終了しました。
fierce 形 熾烈な
  fierce competition 熾烈な競争
FIFO 先入れ先出し法 (=FIFO cost method, FIFO method:**first-in, first-out**の略。⇒**LIFO**)
▶Inventories are valued at the lower of cost (calculated generally on a *FIFO* basis) or net realizable value. 棚卸し資産は、取得原価(原則として先入れ先出し法で計算)と正味実現可能価額のうち、低いほうの価額で評価されています。
figure 图 数値、数量、数字、データ、統計、指数、指標、総額、決算、実績、業績、値段、価格、売上高、計算、図、図案、図形、イラスト、人物、スタイル、プロポーション
  advanced figures 速報値
  corresponding figures 比較対応数値
  figures this quarter 当四半期の業績
  financial figures 財務実績
  net figure 当期利益
  reported figures 公表データ、公表財務データ
  retail sales figures 小売売上高、小売販売の実績
  second quarter figures 第2四半期の実績、第2四半期決算
  trade figures 貿易統計
  year-end figures 年度末の決算、決算
▶*Figures* are on consolidated basis. 数値は、連結ベースです。
▶Previously reported *figures* have been restated. 前期までの報告書に掲げた数値は、修正・再表示[修正して再表示]されています。
▶The *figures* this quarter include the consolidation of the company, a leading United Kingdom telecommunications firm. 当四半期の業績には、同社(英国の大手通信会社)の連結分も含まれています。
file 動 提出する、申請する、申し立てる
  file a damages suit against ... …を相手取り損害賠償を求める、…を相手取り訴訟を起こす
  file a declaration of bankruptcy and a request for asset protection with ... …に破産

宣告と財産保全の処分を申請する, …に破産宣告と財産保全の処分を申し立てる

file a shelf registration statement with the U.S. Securities and Exchange Commisssion 米証券取引委員会(SEC)に一括登録［発行登録］届け出書を提出する (⇒**shelf registration statement**)

file final reports on income for this year 今年度の確定申告書を提出する

file for court protection from creditors 資産保全を申請する, 破綻申請する, 会社更生手続きを申請する (=**file for protection from creditors, seek court protection from creditors**)

▶English conversaton school chain operator Nova Corp. *filed* for court protection from creditors under the Corporate Rehabilitation Law. 英会話学校を運営するNOVAが, 会社更生法の適用［会社更生法に基づく資産保全］を申請した。

▶The firm *filed* for court protection from creditors under the Civil Rehabilitation Law with debts of about ¥60 billion. 同社は, 約600億円の負債をかかえて, 民事再生法に基づく資産保全を［民事再生法の適用を］申請した。

final 形 最終の, 期末の, 確定した, 確定的な, 決定的な, 究極の

  final accounts 決算財務諸表［財務書類］, 決算, 年次財務諸表［財務書類］ (=**annual accounts**)
  final audit 期末監査
  final declaration 確定申告 (=**final return**)
  final dividend 期末配当, 決算配当, 最終配当, 〈清算過程での最後の〉清算配当
  final figure 確定値
  final quarter 第4四半期
  final return 確定申告, 確定申告書
  final sales 最終売上高, 最終需要
  ratio of inventories to final sales 最終売上高在庫率
  real final sales 実質最終需要

final value 終価, 最終価値, 元利合計
  final value of annuity 年金終価

finance 動 融資する, 貸し付ける, 出資する, 資金を出す, 資金を供給する, 資金を調達する, 〈赤字などを〉埋め合わせる, 補塡する, …の資金にあてる
  ability to finance 資金調達力
  amount financed 融資金額, 貸出額, 元金
  be financed by debt 借入れで調達する, 負債による資金調達を行う
  be financed by equity 株式で調達する
  be fully financed by … …が100%出資する
  finance capital needs 資金需要を賄う
  finance government deficits 財政赤字の穴埋めをする, 財政赤字を補塡する
  finance mergers or acquisitions 合併や買収の資金調達をする
  finance stock buybacks 自社株買戻しの資金を調達する
  finance jointly 共同出資する (=**jointly finance**)

▶We raised ¥100 billion from the bond issue to *finance* our restructuring in 2007. 2007年度に当社は, 社債発行で1,000億円を調達してリストラ資金にあてました。

▶The non-U.S. finance subsidiaries *finance* installment receivables in some cases. 米国外の金融子会社は, 割賦債権に対する金融を行う場合もあります。

finance 名 金融, 財務, 財務内容, 財政, 財力, 財源, 資金, 資金調達, 融資, ファイナンス
  asset finance 資産金融, アセット・ファイナンス
  bridging finance つなぎ融資 (=**bridge financing**)
  business finance 企業財務, 経営財務
  capital finance 資本調達
  co-finance 共同融資
  corporate finance 企業金融
  debt finance デット・ファイナンス, 負債による資金調達
  equity finance エクイティ・ファイナンス, 株式発行による資金調達
  external finance 外部資金
  finance committee 財務委員会
  finance income 金融収益
  internal finance 内部資金
  inventory finance 在庫金融
  lease finance リース金融
  loan finance 融資
  project finance プロジェクト金融
  sales finance 販売金融
  self-finance 自己金融
  surplus finance 黒字財政

▶The two banks will tie up in online *finance*. 両行は, オンライン金融で提携する。

finance charge 財務費用, 金融費用, 融資手数料, 金利, ファイナンス・チャージ

▶Any payment not made when due will incur a *finance charge*. 支払い期日までに支払いが履行されない場合には, 金融費用が発生する。

finance receivables 貸出残高, 貸出債権, 金融債権, 金融売掛債権, 債権
  finance receivables-acquisitions 金融債権―

取得

finance receivables-liquidation 金融債権―回収
▸We invested in additional *finance receivables* from our credit card and leasing businesses. 当社は、クレジットカード事業とリース事業から金融売掛債権に追加的投資を行いました。

finance subsidiary 金融子会社, 金融事業を営む子会社
▸In the past, the *finance subsidiaries* were accounted for by the equity method. これまで、金融子会社は持ち分法で会計処理されていました。

financial 形 金融の, 財務の, 財務上の, 金銭的, 金銭面での

Financial Accounting Standards Board 財務会計基準審議会《略 FASB》

financial accounts [英]財務諸表, 財務書類, 財務勘定, 財務報告書

financial activity 資金調達活動, 財務活動

financail adviser [advisor] 財務顧問

financail affairs 財政状態

financial aid package 金融支援策, 財政援助策 (＝financial assistance package, financial rescue package; ⇒package)

financial asset 金融資産, 貨幣性資産

financial assets and liabilities 貨幣性資産と貨幣性負債

financial base 財務基盤, 経営基盤 (＝financial footing, financial foundation; ⇒management buyout)

financial burden 財務負担, 財政負担, 金融負担

financial comments 財務書類注記, 財務諸表注記 (＝notes to financial statements)

financial community 金融業界, 金融界, 金融証券業界

financial comparison 財務比較

financial cost 金融費用, 財務費用, 財務コスト, 資金コスト

financial costs of goods manufactured 製品原価

financial crisis 金融危機, 金融パニック, 金融恐慌, 経営危機, 経営難, 経営破綻 (＝financial difficulties)

financial flexibility 財務弾力性, 財務上の柔軟性, 不測の事態が生じたときの資金調達能力

financial goods 金融商品 (＝financial instruments, financial products)

financial misconduct 不正会計処理, 粉飾決算

financial product 金融商品 (＝financial goods, financial instrument)

financial ratio 財務比率, 財務指標

financial revenue and expense 財務損益

financial situation 財務状態, 財政状態, 財務状況, 財務体質 (＝financial condition, financial position, financial standing)

financial solvency 財務流動性

financial soundness 財務上の健全性, 財政の健全性, 経営の健全性 (＝financial health)

financial status 財政状態, 財務状況, 財務内容, 体力 (＝financial position, financial standing)

financial straits 財政難, 財務困難, 財政危機, 財政逼迫, 財政的苦境, 困難な資金繰り, 金に困ること, 財務力の低下, 金融機関の体力の低下 (＝financial difficulties)

financial year 会計年度, 事業年度, 営業年度, 会計期間 (＝business year, fiscal year)
▸The growth of our *financial* services and leasing business was the primary reason for the increase in total debt outstanding and for most of our financing needs. 当社の金融サービスおよびリース事業の成長が、当社の負債総額の増加と資金需要の大半の主な要因です。

financial assistance 金融支援, 資金援助 (＝financial aid, financial backing, financial support)
▸The company and the six main banks are expected to reach a basic agreement in early November about the scope of the *financial assistance* and asset sales. 同社と主力取引銀行6行は、11月初めに金融支援の枠組みと資産売却について基本合意に達する見込みだ。

financial business 金融業務, 金融事業
▸The company sold all of its *financial businesses* to an investment firm for about ¥20 billion. 同社は、同社の全金融事業を約200億円で投資会社に売却した。

financial condition 財政状態, 財政状況, 財務状態, 財務状況, 財務内容, 財務基盤, 金融情勢 (＝financial position, financial state)
▸Our *financial condition* gives us easy access to financing when we need it. 当社の財務状態からすると、当社は資金需要時にたやすく資金を調達することができます。

financial data 財務データ, 財務情報, 財務資料
▸We included some of these combined amounts at the bottom of the ten-year summary of selected *financial data*. 過去10年間の要約主要財務データの最後に、合算した数値の一部が掲げられています。

financial difficulties 財務悪化, 財政的困難, 財政難, 財政逼迫, 経営危機, 経営難, 経営不振

(=financial disarray, financial distress, financial straits)
▸The Company will reduce its capital by 99.7 percent to ¥100 million to make shareholders accountable for its *financial difficulties*. 当社は, 経営不振の株主責任を明確にするため, 99.7%の減資を実施して資本金を1億円とする。

financial figures 業績, 決算, 財務実績
▸The firm's earnings from May are reflected in our *financial figures* for the April-September period. 同社の5月以降の収益は, 当社の4-9月期の業績[決算]に組み入れてあります。

financial futures 金融先物, 金融先物取引
financial futures instrument 金融先物商品
financial futures market 金融先物市場
financial futures transaction 金融先物取引
▸Under the *Financial Futures* Law, dealers are not allowed to market low-margin foreign exchange products either by directly or by phone. 金融先物取引法では, 少ない証拠金での外国為替商品の直接販売または電話での販売は禁止されている。

financial gearing 財務レバレッジ, ギアリング, 借入比率, 負債比率, 資金調達力比率 (=financial leverage, gearing, trading on the equity: 企業の資本構成に占める負債の額)

financial group 金融グループ, 融資団
▸Today, *financial groups* have come to operate diverse businesses under their umbrella, such as banks, securities firms and insurance companies. 今は, 金融グループが, 銀行や証券会社, 保険会社を傘下に収めて多様な事業を展開するようになってきた。

financial health 財務[財務上]の健全性, 財務内容, 財務状況, 財務体質, 経営の健全度[健全性] (=financial soundness; ⇒borrower, solvency margin)
▸The planned capital increase is designed to strengthen the financial group's *financial health*. 増資計画の目的は, 同フィナンシャル・グループの経営[財務]の健全性強化にある。

financial highlights 財務ハイライト, 財務報告ハイライト, 財務情報要約, 経理ハイライト (一般に年次報告書(annual report)や四半期報告書の最初のページに掲載され, 財務上の主要項目を

財務報告ハイライトの表示例(年度と数値は除く):

Financial highlights for the year ended December 31, 2007 (dollars in millions except per share amounts)	財務報告ハイライト 2007年度(2007年1月1日—12月31日) (単位:1株当たりの金額を除き百万ドル)
Highlights of the year	当期ハイライト
Revenue	総収益
Earnings before income taxes	税引き前利益
Income taxes	法人所得税
Net earnings before cumulative effect of accounting change	会計処理変更に伴う累積的影響額考慮前の当期純利益
Per share	1株当たり利益
Cumulative effect of change in accounting for income taxes	法人所得税の会計処理変更に伴う累積的影響額
Per share	1株当たり影響額
Net earnings	当期純利益
Per share	1株当たり利益
Cash dividends paid	現金配当金
Per share	1株当たり現金配当金
Investment in plant, rental machines and other property	工場設備, 賃貸機械およびその他の固定資産に対する投資
Average number of shares outstanding (in millions)	期中平均発行済み株式数(単位:百万株)
Return on stockholders' equity	株主持ち分利益率
At end of Year:	当期末の状況:
Total assets	資産総額
Net investment in plant, rental machines and other property	工場設備, 賃貸機械およびその他の固定資産に対する純投資
Working capital	運転資本
Long term debt	長期負債
Stockholders' equity	株主持ち分
Number of employees	従業員数
Number of stockholders	株主数

一目で分かるように要約したもの）
この「財務報告ハイライト」の表中, the year ended December 31, 2007は,「2007年12月31日に終了した年度」という意味で, 会社の事業年度(business year, fiscal year)を示している。また, per share amountsの"amounts"は「金額」という意味。「金額」の意味でのamountは, 例えばamount of bill（手形金額）やinsured amount（保険金額）, recorded amount（計上金額）などに使われる。

financial information 金融情報, 財務情報
condensed financial information 要約財務情報 (=summarized financial information)
consolidated financial information 連結財務情報
financial information by segment セグメント別財務情報
general purpose financial information 一般目的財務情報
historical financial information 歴史的財務情報, 取得原価主義財務情報
interim financial information 中間財務情報 (=interim report)
nonfinancial financial information 非財務情報
pro forma [proforma] financial information 見積り財務情報
prospective financial information 将来財務情報
quantified nonfinancial information 定量的非財務情報
quarterly financial information 四半期財務情報
source of financial information 財務情報源
supplemental [supplementary] financial information 補足財務情報

▸The financial statements and other *financial information* included in this annual report were prepared in conformity with generally accepted accounting principles. この年次報告書に記載されている財務書類とその他の財務情報は, 一般に公正妥当と認められた会計原則に従って作成されています。

financial institution 金融機関
▸Swelling losses for U.S. *financial institutions* have pushed down stock prices on the New York market. 米金融機関の損失拡大で, ニューヨーク市場の株価が下落している。

financial instrument 金融商品, 金融資産, 金融手段, 金融証券 (=financial goods, financial product)
▸These *financial instruments* are subject to market risks resulting from exchange rate movements. これらの金融手段[金融商品]は, 為替の変動による市場リスクにさらされています。

financial market 金融市場（資金の供給者である貸し手と資金の需要者である借り手との間で資金取引が行われる場）, 財務管理, 財テク
▸There is a possibility that liquidity demand will increase further depending on *financial market* developments. 金融市場の今後の展開次第では, 資金需要が拡大する可能性もある。

financial performance 財務実績, 財務業績, 財務面での実績, 業績, 財務状態, 財務状況, 財政状況
▸Our *financial performance* met growth targets despite the less favorable business and economic environment. 当社の財務面での業績は, 事業および経済環境が低調だったにもかかわらず, 成長目標を達成しました。

financial position 財政状態, 財務状態, 財務状況, 財務体質, 資金繰り (=financial condition, financial situation, financial standing; ⇒**closing balance sheet**)
▸The financial statements referred to above present fairly the *financial position* of the company in conformity with generally accepted accounting principles. 上記の財務書類は, 同社の財政状態を, 一般に認められた会計原則に準拠して適正に表示しています。

financial pressure 財政難, 金融面の圧力, 経営の圧迫
▸Daiei's business diversification led to rising debts that placed *financial pressure* on the company. ダイエーの事業多角化は, 借入金の増大につながり, それが会社の経営を圧迫する結果となった。

financial records 財務記録
▸*Financial records* are adequate and can be relied upon. 財務記録は, 適切で信頼性がある。

financial reporting 財務報告, 財務会計, 財務報告会計
financial reporting for segments セグメント別財務報告
financial reporting to shareholders 株主に対する財務報告
for financial reporting purposes 財務報告上, 財務会計上
fraudulent financial reporting 不正な財務報告
general purpose external financial reporting 一般目的外部財務報告
interim financial reporting 期中の財務報告

▸The goal of *financial reporting* is to give investors the information they need to understand how we are doing over time and in comparison with other companies.　財務報告の目標は,当社が現在にいたるまで,また他社との比較でどのような経営をしているかを投資家に理解してもらうために必要な情報を,投資家に提供することにあります。

financial results　財務成績,財務実績,業績,金融収支,決算　(⇒goods)
▸Livedoor Co. dressed up the *financial results* of Livedoor Marketing Co. by posting bogus sales in 2004.　ライブドアは,2004年に架空の売上を計上して,ライブドアマーケティングの決算 [業績,財務実績] を粉飾した。

financial review　財務概況,財務状況,財務会計上の説明,財務報告
▸This commentary on *Financial Review* should be read in conjunction the Consolidated Finan-cial Statements and Notes to Cnsolidated Fi-nancial Statements.　この「財務概況」説明の項は,連結財務書類と連結財務書類注記といっしょにお読みください。

financial services　金融サービス
financial services business　金融サービス事業
▸Our *financial services* businesses are growing because we are investing in new assets.　当社の金融サービス業務は,新資産への投資で拡大しています。
▸We are investing in finance receivables, particularly credit card receivables, to increase revenues and earnings from our *financial services* businesses.　当社は,金融サービス事業による収益と利益を増やすため,金融債権,とくにクレジットカード債権に投資を行っています。

financial statement　財務報告書,財務報告,有価証券報告書《略 F/S》financial statements (財務書類・財務諸表)の形容詞として使われることもある)
falsification of financial statements　有価証券報告書の虚偽記載
financial statement amounts　財務書類の数値,財務書類の金額
financial statement date　決算日
financial statement translation　財務書類換算差額
for financial statement reporting　財務書類上,財務諸表上
semiannual financial statement　半期報告書
▸Certain *financial statement* amounts are translated at historic exchange rates.　一部の財務書類の数値は,取引日の為替レートで換算されています。

financial statements　財務諸表,財務書類,企業財務情報,決算書,経営分析,有価証券報告書 (⇒**accompanying, consolidated financial statements**)

　財務書類について ➡ 通常,財務書類にはbalance sheet (貸借対照表), income statement (損益計算書)とcash flow statement (キャッシュ・フロー計算書)のほか, statement of stockholders' equity (株主持ち分計算書)やstatement of changes in financial position (財政状態変動表)などが含まれる。

　米国企業の年次報告書や四半期報告書その他で公表される財務書類は,だいたい連結財務書類で,一般に貸借対照表(balance sheet), 損益および剰余金計算書(statement of income and retained earnings), 財政状態変動表(statement of changes in financial position) 会計処理方針の説明(disclosure of accounting policies)と財務書類注記(notes to financial statements)で構成されている。ただし,会計処理方針の説明は財務書類注記 [財務諸表注記] に盛り込まれることもある。

　このほか,期中に増資(capital increase)や株式の償還(redemption), 自社株取引(treasury stock transaction)などの資本勘定(capital accounts) に変動が生じた場合には,資本勘定計算書(capital statement)が利用される。

　なお,「貸借対照表」は財政状態 (資産内容)を,「損益および剰余金計算書」は経営成績 (営業実績)を,また「財政状態変動表」は資金投下と資金調達 (資金繰り)を示す。

abstract of financial statements　要約財務諸表,財務諸表要約 (=summarized financial statements, summary of financial statements)
account form financial statements　勘定式財務諸表
basic financial statements　基本財務書類,基本財務諸表 (=basic statements, primary financial statements)
certified financial statements　監査済み財務諸表
combined financial statements　結合財務諸表,本支店の合併財務諸表,子会社だけの総合財務諸表,政府会計の財務報告書
common-size financial statements　百分率財務諸表,比率表示財務諸表,共通型財務諸表 (=one hundred percent statements)
comparative financial statements　比較財務書類,比較財務諸表
condensed financial statements　要約財務書類,要約財務諸表
consolidated financial statements in March 2008　2008年3月期の連結決算

corporate financial statements 会社財務諸表
current cost financial statements 現在原価財務諸表, カレント・コスト財務諸表 (＝financial cost accounts)
financial statements and footnotes 財務書類[財務諸表]と注記
financial statements and supplementary data 財務書類と補足データ[補足情報], 経理の状況
forecasted financial statements 見積り財務諸表
foreign currency financial statements 外貨表示財務諸表 (＝foreign statements)
forward financial statements 見積り財務諸表, 未来財務諸表 (＝forecasted financial statements, proforma financial statements, projected financial statements)
general purpose financial statements 一般目的財務諸表
historical cost financial statements 歴史的原価財務諸表, 取得原価主義財務書類
interim financial statements 中間財務諸表, 中間財務書類 (＝interim report, interim statements)
international financial statements 国際財務諸表
summarized financial statements 要約財務書類, 財務書類要約
unconsolidated financial statements 単独財務書類
▶Companies listed on Japan's stock markets are required to release *financial statements* every quarter starting in fiscal 2007. 日本の株式市場に上場している企業は, 2007年度から財務諸表の四半期開示を義務付けられている。

financial strength 資金力, 財力, 財務力, 財務体質, 財務内容, 財務面での健全性, 財政の強み, 支払い能力, 〈金融機関の〉体力
▶The company's *financial strength* has deteriorated since a series of scandals including the mislabeling of beef by its subsidiary. 同社の財務体質は, 子会社による牛肉の偽装表示など一連の事件以来, 悪化している。

financial structure 財務構成, 資本構成, 金融組織
　財務構成と資本構成について ➡ 「財務構成」は資本調達の状態, すなわち資本をどの源泉から調達したかを示すもので, 資本構成(capital structure) に短期債務(short-term debt) や買掛金(account payable) などを加えたもの。これに対して「資本構成」は, 資本総額に占める他人資本(負債) と自己資

本の構成割合をいう。

financial support 金融支援, 資金負担 (＝financial aid, financial assistance, financial rescue)
▶*Financial support* is the prerequisite for the two firms' funding of the issuance of new shares. 金融支援は, 両社の増資引受けの前提条件となっている。

financing 名 資金調達, 資本調達, 金融, 融資, 借入れ, ローン, 財務, 資金
　bridge financing つなぎ融資
　debt financing 負債による資金調達
　direct financing via stock markets 株式市場を通じて資金を調達する直接金融
　equity financing 新株発行による資金調達
　external bond financing 外債発行による資金調達
　financing activities 財務活動, 金融活動, 資金調達活動, 資金調達と返済に関する活動
　financing activities and capitalization 資金調達活動と資本化
　financing agreement 借入契約, 融資契約, 金融協定
　financing demand 借入需要, 資金需要 (＝financing requirements)
　financing operations 融資活動, 金融活動, 金融事業, 財務活動, 財務
　foreign trade financing 外国貿易金融(輸出入必要資金の融通)
　gross financing needs 総調達額
　interim financing つなぎ融資
　joint financing 協調融資
　left-hand financing 資産担保資金調達
　product financing arrangement 製品金融の取決め
　receivables financing 債権融資
　straight financing 直接融資
　tax-exempt financing 免税債での資金調達
　up-coming financing 当面の資金調達
▶Our long-term *financing* was accomplished through the issuance of long-term debt instruments. 当社の長期資金調達は, 長期債務証券を発行して行われた。
▶We sometimes guarantee the *financing* for product purchases by customers outside the U.S. 当社は, 米国外の顧客が製品を購入する際の資金調達に対して保証を行う場合があります。

financing commiment 資金調達契約
▶The Company's financial instruments include foreign currency contracts and other *financing commitments*. 当社の金融手段としては, 外貨取

引契約やその他の資金調達契約もあります。

financing cost 資金調達コスト, 金融費用, 金融コスト
▸Certain indirect costs, including *financing costs*, are capitalized. 特定の間接費は, 資金調達コスト[利息]を含めて資産計上されています。

financing requirements 資金需要, 借入需要, 資金調達必要額
▸*Financing requirements* for 2007 include the purchase for cancellation of a portion of another series of preferred shares for a total amount of $40 million. 2007年度の資金調達必要額には, 他の優先株式シリーズの一部4,000万ドルを消却するための購入資金も含まれています。

finished 形 完成した

finished goods 製品, 完成品, 完成財, 加工品 (=finished product; ⇒**manufacturing overhead**)

finished product 製品, 最終製品, 完成品, 完成財, 加工品 (=end product, finished goods)
▸Costs incurred subsequent to establishment of technological feasibility to produce the *finished product* of software are genarlly capitalized. ソフトウエアの完成品を制作するための技術的可能性が明らかになった後に発生した原価は, 原則として資産に計上されています。

firewall [**fire wall**] 名 防禦壁, 情報隔壁(同グループの銀行と証券会社が顧客情報を共有するのを禁止すること), 情報漏洩防止システム, ネット上のセキュリティ・システム, 不正侵入防止機能[防止装置], ファイアウォール

firm 名 会社, 企業, 法人, 商社, 商会, ファーム
　audit firm 監査法人
　business firm 営利企業
　consulting firm コンサルタント事務所
　controlled firm 傘下企業 (=subordinated firm)
　CPA firm 監査法人
　diversified firm 多角的企業, 多角化企業
　dominant firm 支配的企業, 優越企業
　foreign-affiliated firm 外資系企業, 外資
　law firm 法律事務所
　multi-industry firm 多業種企業 (=multi-market firm)
　target firm 目標会社
▸Thus far restructuring in the domestic pharmaceutical industry has been limited to takeovers by foreign *firms*. これまでのところ国内製薬業界の再編は, 外資による買収に限られている。

first half 上半期, 上期, 前半 (=first six months: 下半期はlatter half, second halfという)

first half of fiscal 2008 2008年上半期, 2008年度上期

first half of the business year 今年度上半期, 今年度上期 (=first half of the year)

first half of the fiscal year to Sept. 30 〈3月期決算企業の〉上半期(4-9月期), 9月中間決算

first half of the year 上半期, 上期, 今年度上半期[上期], 今年度前半, 今年前半 (=the first half, the former half of the year)
▸After declining in the *first half* of the year, net earnings increased during the third quarter. 純利益は, 当年度上半期に落ち込んだ後, 第3四半期に増益基調に転じました。
▸Yahoo Japan Corp. set new highs in both group net profit and operating revenues in the *first half* of fiscal 2006. ヤフーの2008年上半期決算は, 連結税引き後利益も売上高も過去最高となった。

first-half 形 上半期の, 上期の, 前半の
　first-half net profit 上半期の税引き後利益[純利益], 上期の税引き後利益[純利益]
　first-half profit 上半期利益, 上期の利益
　first-half results 上半期決算, 上半期の業績, 中間決算 (=interim closing, interim results, semi-annual results)
　first-half year 上半期, 上期

first-half account settlement 上半期決算, 中間決算 (=first-half results)
▸The company was in the black for its *first-half account settlement* in June. 同社は, 6月中間決算は黒字でした。

first-half loss 上半期損失, 上期の損失[赤字]
▸The Company's *first-half loss* narrowed 85 percent mainly due to the weaker yen. 当社の上半期損失は, 主に円安で85%縮小しました。

first-in, first-out basis [**method**] 先入れ先出し法《略 FIFO》(⇒**lower of cost and net realizable value**)
▸Inventories are valued at the lower of average cost (which approximates computation on a *first-in, first-out basis*) or market, less progress payments on long-term contracts. 棚卸し資産は, 平均法による原価(先入れ先出し法に基づく原価とほぼ同額)または市場価格のいずれか低いほうの価額で評価し, 長期請負契約に関する前受金を控除して表示されています。

first nine months 1-9月期
▸Selling, general and administrative (SG&A) expenses for the *first nine months* were 19 percent of total revenues compared with 19.4 percent in 2005. 1-9月期の販売費および一般管理

費(SG&A)は、2005年同期の19.4％に対して19％でした。

first quarter 第1四半期
  first quarter loss 第1四半期の損失、第1四半期の赤字
  net income for the first quarter of 2008 2008年第1四半期の純利益
  operating expenses in the first quarter of 2008 2008年第1四半期の営業費用
  ▸In the *first quarter* of 2007, both revenue and profits increased. 2007年第1四半期は、増収増益となりました。

first quarter consolidated net income 第1四半期の連結純利益
  ▸The Company's *first-quarter consolidated net income* was $310 million. 当社の第1四半期の連結純利益は、3億1,000万ドルでした。

first quarter earnings per share 第1四半期の1株当たり利益、第1四半期の普通株式1株当たり利益[純利益]
  ▸*First quarter earnings per share* were based on 320 million average common shares outstanding. 第1四半期の普通株式1株当たり純利益は、発行済み普通株式の平均株式数に基づいて計算されています。

first quarter ended March 31 3月31日終了の第1四半期、1-3月期
  ▸Hewlett-Packard earned $1.55 billion, or 55 cents per share, for the *first quarter ended March 31*. ヒューレット・パッカードは、第1四半期(1-3月期)に15億5,000万ドル(1株当たり55セント)の利益を上げた。

first quarter net income applicable to common shares 第1四半期の普通株式に帰属する純利益
  ▸The Corporation's *first-quarter net income applicable to common shares* was $250 million. 当社の第1四半期の普通株式に帰属する純利益は、2億5,000万ドルでした。

first quarter profit 第1四半期の利益、第1四半期の黒字
  ▸The Company's *first quarter profit* was slightly higher than for the same period last year. 当社の第1四半期利益は、前年同期よりいくぶん増加しました。

first quarter results 第1四半期の業績
  ▸*First quarter results* were consistent with expectations. 第1四半期の業績は、当初の予想に沿うものでした。

first six months 上半期、上期(3月決算企業の場合は4-9月期を、12月決算企業の場合は1-6月期を指す)
  ▸During the *first six months* of 2007, the Corporation issued $550 million of debentures in Canada. 2007年上半期に、当社はカナダで5億5,000万ドルの無担保社債を発行しました。
  ▸For the *first six months*, consolidated net income was $495 million. 上半期の連結純利益は、4億9,500万ドルでした。

fiscal 形 財政の、国家財政の、会計上の

fiscal first half 今年度上半期、上半期、上期
  ▸Life insurers customarily do not release financial results for the *fiscal first-half*. 生命保険会社は、慣例として上半期の決算を公表していない。

fiscal first half to Sept. 30 9月中間決算、4-9月期

fiscal year 会計年度、事業年度、営業年度、年度、会計期間《略 **FY**》(=business year, financial year, fiscal period)
  during the fiscal year ended March 31, 2009 2009年3月期決算
  entire fiscal year 通期、事業年度全体
  the first half of the fiscal year 年度前半、今年度前半、上半期、上期 (=the first half)
  the fiscal year ended March 31 3月31日終了事業年度、3月期決算
  the full fiscal year 通期 (=full business year)
  the full fiscal year ending March 31 3月31日終了の通期、3月期決算 (⇒**forecast**)
  the last fiscal year 前年度、前期
  the latter half of this fiscal year 今年度後半、今年度下半期
  this fiscal year 今年度、今期
  ▸We include the accounts of operations located outside the U.S. on the basis of their *fiscal years*, ended either November 30 or December 31. 米国以外の関係会社の財務書類は、11月30日または12月31日に終了する各社の会計年度に基づいて連結されています[連結財務書類に組み入れてあります]。

fiscal year through March 3月期決算
  ▸We now expect group net profit of ¥80 billion for the *fiscal year through March* 2009. 当社は現在、2009年3月期決算で800億円の連結税引き後利益を見込んでいます。

fixed 形 固定した、固定式の、固定型、確定した、変動しない、一定の、安定した
  fixed capital 固定資本 (=capital asset, long-lived asset, permanent asset)
  fixed commission 固定手数料

fixed date 確定日, 約定期日, 指定期日
fixed debt 固定借入金
fixed employee stock option plan 固定型従業員ストックオプション制度
fixed exchange rate 固定為替相場, 固定為替レート, 固定相場
fixed expenditure 固定費, 固定的費用 (＝fixed cost, fixed expense)
fixed interest 固定金利, 確定利子 (＝fixed interest rate)
fixed cost 固定費, 固定的費用, 固定原価 (＝fixed expense)
fixed income 債券, 確定利付き証券 (＝fixed income security), 確定報酬, 固定収入
fixed liability 固定負債, 長期負債
fixed loan 固定貸付け金, 長期貸付け金, 長期借入金
fixed percentage method 定率法 (＝declining balance method, fixed percentage on reducing balance method, fixed rate method)
fixed rate debt 固定利付き債

fixed asset
固定資産 (＝capital asset, fixed capital, long-lived asset：会社の営業活動のために長期的に使用される資産)

固定資産に含まれるもの：

branch networks	支店網
buildings	建物
furnitures and fixtures	什器備品, 家具備品, 営業用備品 (＝fixtures and furnitures)
land	土地
machinery	機械
plant and equipment	工場設備, 設備

fixed asset investment 固定資産投資, 長期投資
fixed assets to net worth 固定比率 (＝固定資産÷純資産)
▶All *fixed assets* are depreciated on the straight line basis. 有形固定資産は, すべて定額法で償却されています。

fixed asset expenditures
固定資産支出額
▶The semiconductor products segment continues to comprise the largest portion of *fixed asset expenditures*. 半導体事業部門が, 引き続き固定資産支出額のうち最大の比率を占めています。

fixed income security
確定利付き証券, 固定金利の証券, 債務証券, 債券 (＝fixed income investment：利率や配当率が証券の発行時から償還時まで一定で変わらない証券)

fixed overhead 固定製造間接費, 固定間接費 (＝fixed factory burden, fixed factory overhead)
fixed overhead allocation 固定製造間接費の配賦
fixed overhead cost 固定間接費 (＝fixed production overhead cost)
▶*Fixed overhead* is absorbed as a cost of product. 固定間接費は, 製品原価の一部として配賦されて[含まれて]います。

fixture 名 備品, 造作, 付帯物

flat 形 単一の, 一律の, 均一の, 変化がない, 横ばい[横ばい状態]の, 伸び悩みの, 平坦化
　be almost [virtually] flat ほぼ横ばい, ほぼ横ばい状態
　flat profits 利益横ばい
　flat rate 定額料金, 均一料金, フラット・レート
　flat yield 直接利回り
▶Business communications systems revenues were essentially *flat* in the second quarter. ビジネス通信システムの売上高は, 第2四半期はほぼ横ばいでした。

flexible 形 変動する, 弾力的な, 融通のきく
　flexible exchange rate 変動為替相場, 屈伸為替相場, 変動相場 (＝floating exchange rate, floating rate)
　flexible rate 変動金利

flight 名 資本逃避
　flight to quality 質への逃避 (市場環境が悪化した際に投資資金がより安全な市場へシフトすること)

float 動 〈株や債券などを〉発行する, 新規に発行する, 株式公開する, 〈会社を〉新規上場する, 会社を設立する, 〈通貨を〉変動相場制に移行する, 変動相場制にする, 変動相場制である, 〈小切手を〉不渡りにする, 提案する, 提示する
　float a loan 起債する
　float an issue of stock 株式を発行する
　float on the stock exchange 証券取引所に上場する
　let the currency float 通貨を変動相場制にする, 通貨を変動相場制に移行する
▶The bank will discontinue issuing bank debentures to companies next March and *float* straight bonds instead. 同行は, 企業向けの金融債発行を来年3月で停止し, それ以降は普通社債を発行する。

float 名 〈証券の〉発行, 〈通貨の〉変動, 変動相場制, 流通量, 未決済小切手取立て中の手形・小切手類, 浮動株数, 小口現金, 設立, フロート
　added float 追加発行
　free float 浮動株, 浮動株式
　public float 公開株

floating 形 流動的, 流動する, 変動する, 流通す

る, 浮動的な
floating asset 流動資産 (＝circulating asset, current asset, near-cash asset)
floating capital 流動資本 (＝circulating capital, net current assets, working capital)
floating charge 浮動担保, 包括担保(社債を発行する場合に設定する担保で, 日々変動する会社の資産を包括して担保にするもの)
floating cost 変動費
floating debt 流動負債 (＝current liability, floating liability)
floating exchange rate 変動為替相場, 変動相場 (＝flexible exchange rate)
floating deposits 流動性預金
floating interest rate 変動金利 (＝floating rate)
floating liability 流動負債 (＝current liability, floating debt)
floating rate 変動金利, 変動利率(＝floating interest rate), 変動相場(＝floating exchange rate), 変動レート
floating rate bond 変動利付き債
floating shares 浮動株 (＝floating stock, floating supply of stocks：安定株の反対で, 市場で転々と流通している株)
▶The Company's finance subsidiary has outstanding *floating* to fixed interest rate commercial paper swaps totaling $50 million at December 31, 2007. 当社の金融子会社には, 2007年12月31日現在, 変動金利を固定金利に変更する総額5,000万ドルの未決済コマーシャル・ペーパー金利スワップ契約があります。
flow 名 流れ, 流出, 移動, 移転, 循環, フロー (⇒cash flow)
capital flows 資本移動, 資本の流れ, 資本流出, 資本流入
capital flows in 資本の流入
capital flows out 資本の流出
cash flow-through 資金の流れ
cross-border capital flows 国際的な資本移動, 国際的な資金フロー
deal flow 取引量, 取引の案件数
financial flow 金融の流れ, 財務フロー, 資金フロー, 資本移動
flow of funds 資金移動, 資金循環, 資金フロー, マネー・フロー
flow of goods and money モノとカネの流れ
money flow 資金循環, マネー・フロー
net long-term capital flow 長期資本収支
new coverage flows 新規保険契約の収益

open capital flows 資本移動の自由化
secondary flows 流通市場の取引
speculative financial flows 投機的な資金移動
▶The international *flow* of goods, services and funds became freer and more globalized. 物, サービスと資金の国際的な流れは, 一段と自由になり, また一段とグローバル化した。
flow-through method フロースルー方式, 流入法
fluctuate 動 変動する, 上がり下がりする, 乱高下する
▶The gain from stock options *fluctuates* depending on the option holder's investment judgment over the timing of purchase and changes of the stock price. ストック・オプション[自社株購入権]の利益は, 購入時期と株価変動に対するオプション保有者[オプションの買い手]の投資判断によって上下する。
fluctuation 名 変動, 変化, 上がり下がり, 乱高下, 騰落, 動き
currency fluctuations 為替変動, 為替レートの変動
economic fluctuation 経済変動, 景気変動
exchange fluctuation 為替変動, 為替相場の変動, 為替の騰落, 為替の乱高下 (＝exchange rate fluctuation)
fluctuations in foreign exchange rate 為替相場の変動, 外国為替相場の変動 (＝foreign exchange fluctuations, foreign exchange rate fluctuations)
foreign exchange fluctuations 為替相場の変動 (＝exchange fluctuation)
market fluctuations 市場変動, 市況の変動
price fluctuation 物価の変動, 価格騰落, 株価の乱高下
seasonal fluctuation 季節変動
▶*Fluctuations* in stock prices could adversely affect major life insurers' finances. 株価の変動は, 大手生保各社の財務内容にマイナス影響を与えかねない。
▶Foreign exchange *fluctuations* are affected not only by economic fundamentals, but also by psychological factors. 為替相場の変動は, 経済のファンダメンタルズだけでなく, 心理的な要因による影響をも受ける。
▶Yen-denominated trade frees domestic companies from the risk of *fluctuations* in foreign exchange rate. 円建て貿易は, 国内企業にとって為替変動のリスクがない。
focus 動 焦点を合わせる, …に集中する, …に焦

点を絞る
▶We are *focusing* our investments to take advantage of the opportunities in our industry. 当社は現在、当業界での事業機会の向上に焦点を絞った投資を展開しています。

focus 名 焦点, 中心, 軸, 集中, 集中化, 傾斜, 注目の的, 震源地, フォーカス
  cost focus strategy コスト集中戦略
  customer focus 顧客中心, 顧客中心主義, 顧客重視, 顧客重視の姿勢, 顧客志向, 顧客の満足度重視, 顧客の満足に力を入れる
  differentiation focus strategy 差別化集中戦略
  effective management focus 経営効率の重視, 焦点を絞った効率経営
  focus on service quality サービスの質の重視
  focus on the bottom line 利益重視, 利益を重視する姿勢[利益重視の姿勢]
  global focus グローバル志向
▶We are building a strong management team with a global *focus*. 当社は、グローバル志向の強力な経営陣を築き上げています。

focus on ... …に焦点を当てる, …に焦点を合わせる, …に焦点を置く, …に的を絞る, …を重視する, …を強調する, …を中核に据える, …を中核事業にする, …に力を注ぐ, …に注目する, …に執着する, …に結集する
▶As our strategy, we *focus on* those product lines vital to our future by streamlining our operations and redeploying assets. 当社の戦略として、当社は業務の効率化と資産の有効利用により、当社の将来を支える製品ラインに焦点を当てています。

FOMC [米]連邦公開市場委員会 (**Federal Open Market Committee**の略)
▶The *FOMC* minutes hinted at the end to Fed rate hikes. 米連邦公開市場委員会(FOMC)の議事要旨は、FRB（連邦準備制度理事会）の利上げ打ち止めを示唆した。

foothold 名 足場, 足がかり, 基盤
▶We have gaind a *foothold* in many markets that are growing faster than those in the U.S. 当社は、米国市場を上回る速度で成長を続ける多くの海外市場で、事業基盤を確保しました。

footing 名 合計, 合算, 突合せ, 合計検算, 締切り, 入会金, 立場, 足場, 足がかり, 地歩, 地盤, 基盤, 関係, 間柄 (⇒**financial footing**)
  financial footing 財務基盤, 経営基盤 (＝financial base)
  forge a solid footing 足元を固める
  on an equal footing 対等の立場で
  verification of footing and posting 計算突合せ

▶To establish a solid financial *footing*, we have been strengthening our shareholders' equity. 磐石な財務基盤[経営基盤]を確立するため、当社は株主資本[自己資本]を強化しています。

footnote 名 注記, 脚注
  footnote to financial statements 財務書類[財務諸表]注記, 財務書類の脚注

for the period 期中, 期中の, 年間の, 事業年度の
▶Revenues and expenses are translated at average rates *for the period*. 収益と費用は、期中平均為替レートで換算されています。

for the year 当年度, 当期
▶We reported a net loss *for the year*. 当年度は、純損失を計上しました[税引き後赤字となりました]。

force 名 力, 勢力, 影響力, 要因, 材料, 有効性, 法的効力, 拘束力, 兵力, 軍隊, 軍
  be put into force 実施される, 施行される, 効力を発生する
  bring ... into force …を実施する
  come into force 実施される, 施行される, 効力を発生する, 発効する
  field sales force 外交販売員
  guiding force 推進力, 指針
  join forces with ... …と協力する, …と力を合わせる
  market forces 市場原理, 市場要因, 市場の力, 市場諸力
  marketing force 営業担当員
  marketing forces マーケティング要因, マーケティング諸力
  negative force 懸念材料, マイナス要因
  productive force 生産力
  sales force 販売員, 販売要員
  sales force recruitment 販売員募集
  underlying forces 構造的要因
▶No company or institution is immune to the *forces* of a paradigm change. どんな企業も機関も、社会的パラダイムの変化の影響力から免れることはできません。
▶We have put more men and women in our customers' plants and laboratories and offices, increasing our worldwide marketing force. 当社は、世界各地の営業担当員を増やして、お客さまの工場や研究所や事務所にさらに多くの当社従業員を派遣しました。

forecast 名 予測, 見通し, 予知, 予見, 予想, 予報 (＝**forecasting**; ⇒**full-year earnings, profit forecast**)
  business forecast 景気予測, 景気見通し, 業績見

通し, 業績予測, 経営予測
cash forecast 資金予測 (=forecast of cash)
company forecasts 会社予想
demand forecast 需要予測
earlier forecast 当初予想
economic forecast 経済予測, 経済見通し, 景気予測
financial forecast 財務予想, 財務予測, 財務見通し, 業績予想, 業績見通し
forecast excess returns 予想超過収益率
forecast of sales 売上高予測, 売上高の見通し, 予想売上高, 販売予測
growth forecast 成長見通し, 伸び率見通し (=growth prospect)
operating profit forecast 営業利益予想
sales forecast 売上高の見通し, 販売予測 (=forecast of sales)

▸For the full fiscal year ending March 2009, the company left its group net profit *forecast* unchanged at ¥3 billion. 2009年3月期決算 [2009年3月終了の通期] については, 同社は30億円の連結税引き後利益見通しを据え置いた。

▸Sharp Corp. kept its full-year *forecasts* unchanged. シャープは, 通期業績見通しを据え置いた。

forecast 動 予測する, 予想する, 予報する
forecasted balance sheet 予測貸借対照表, 見積り貸借対照表
forecasted financial statements 見積り財務諸表, 見積り財務書類, 予測財務諸表 (=projected financial statements, pro forma [proforma] financial statements)
forecasted income statement 見積り損益計算書, 予測損益計算書 (=estimated income statement)
forecasted profit and loss statement 見積り損益計算書, 予測損益計算書

forecasting 名 予測, 予想, 見通し
business forecasting 業績予測 [予想], 事業予測, 企業予測, 景気予測
profit forecasting 利益予測, 利益予想, 収益見通し
technological forecasting 技術予測

foreclosure 名 差し押さえ, 抵当流れ
forefront 名 第一線, 先頭, 最前部, 最前線, 最先端, 中心, 重要部分

▸The fulfillment of a commitment to eliminate an ozone-depleting substance from manufacturing facilities put the Corporation in the *forefront* of corporate environmental responsibility. 製造施設からオゾン層を破壊する物質を取り除く公約を果たして, 当社は環境保護に対する企業責任の面でも業界をリードしています。

foreign 形 外国の, 海外の, 対外
foreign asset 海外資産, 外国資産, 対外資産, 在外資産, 外貨建て資産
foreign bill 外国為替, 外国為替手形 (=foreign bill of exchange)
foreign bond 外債, 外国債券
foreign borrowings 外貨建て債務, 対外借入れ
foreign business income 海外事業所得, 外国での事業所得
foreign capital 外資, 外国資本
Foreign Corrupt Practices Act [米] 海外不正支払い防止法, 海外不正行為防止法
foreign debt 対外債務, 外貨債務, 外貨建て負債
foreign debt servicing 対外債務の返済, 外貨債務の返済
foreign direct investment 外国からの直接投資, 対内直接投資, 対外直接投資《略 FDI》

foreign currency 外国通貨, 外貨
foreign currency bond 外貨建て債, 外貨建て債券 (=foreign currency-denominated bond)
foreign currency earnings 外貨建て収益
foreign currency loan 外貨建て借入金, 外貨ローン
foreign currency obligations 外貨建て債務
foreign currency receivables and payables 外貨建て債権債務, 外貨建て金銭債権債務

▸*Foreign currency*-denominated assets and liabilities are translated at year-end rates in the consolidated financial statements. 外貨建ての資産と負債は, 連結財務書類上, 期末レートで換算されています。

foreign currency exchange contract 外国為替契約, 外国為替予約 (=foreign exchange contract)

▸These financial instruments include commitments to extend credit, letters of credit, guarantees of debt, interest rate swaps and cap agreements, and *foreign currency exchange contracts*. これらの金融商品には, 信用供与契約, 信用状, 債務保証, 金利スワップおよび金利キャップ契約と外国為替予約が含まれています。

▸To manage our exposure to changes in currency exchange rates, we enter into *foreign currency exchange contracts*. 為替相場の変動によるリスクを管理するため, 当社は外国為替予約を締結しています。

foreign currency transaction 外貨建て

foreign currency translation

取引
▸The effects of *foreign currency transactions* and of remeasuring the financial position and results of operations into the functional currency are included in the satement of earnings. 外貨建て取引と財政状態や経営成績の機能通貨による再測定の影響額は、損益計算書に記載されています。

foreign currency translation 外貨換算, 外貨換算差額 (=currency translation, translation of foreign currencies)
　accounting for foreign currency translation 外貨換算に関する会計処理
　accumulated foreign currency translation adjustments 外貨換算修正
　dfference of foreign currency translation 為替換算調整勘定
　effects of foreign currency translation adjustments 外貨換算修正損益
　foreign currency translation adjustments 為替換算調整勘定, 外貨換算調整勘定, 外貨換算調整額 (=translation adjustments)
　foreign currency translation gain and loss 為替差損益
　foreign currency translation gains 外貨換算差益
　foreign currency translation losses 外貨換算差損
▸*Foreign currency translation* adjustments are accumulated in a separate component of stockholders' equity. 外貨換算調整額は、株主持ち分の独立した一項目として累計されています。

foreign exchange 外国為替, 為替, 外国為替取引, 為替差損益, 外貨 (=forex, FX)
　Foreign Exchange and Foreign Trade Law 外国為替及び外国貿易法, 外為法
　foreign exchange contract 外国為替予約 (=foreign currency exchange contract)
　foreign exchange gain(loss) 為替差益(損)
　foreign exchange gains and [or] losses 為替差損益 (=forex gains or losses)
　foreign exchange loss 為替差損 (=forex loss)
　foreign exchange(FX) margin trading 外国為替証拠金取引 (⇒**profit**)
　foreign exchange rate 外国為替レート, 外国為替相場
▸*Foreign exchange* gains and losses on payments during the year are credited to, or charged against, income before taxes in the year they arise. 期中の決済から生じた為替差損益は、発生年度に損益として法人税等前利益に計上されています。

foreign exchange trading 外国為替取引
(=foreign exchange dealing, foreign exchange transaction)
▸*Foreign exchange trading* with low margin requirements is banned. 少ない証拠金での外国為替取引［外国為替証拠金取引］は、禁止されている。

foreign firm 外国企業, 外資系企業, 外資
▸Any acquisition of a Japanese steelmaker by a *foreign firm* could impact Japanese automobile manufacturers. 外国企業による日本の鉄鋼メーカーの買収は、日本の自動車メーカーに影響を及ぼす可能性がある。

foreign subsidiary 外国子会社, 海外子会社, 在外子会社
▸In preparing the consolidated financial statements, all items in the income statements of *foreign subsidiaries* are translated into Swedish kronor at the average exchange rates during the year. 連結財務書類の作成上、外国子会社の損益計算書の項目は、すべて年間［期中］平均換算レートでスウェーデン・クローナに換算されています。

foreign tax credit 外国税額控除
▸Should these undistributed earnings be distributed, *foreign tax credits* would reduce the additional U.S. income tax which would be payable. これらの未処分利益を仮に分配した場合、米国で追加的に生じる法人税等の金額は、外国税額控除により引き下げられます。

forerunner 名 先駆, 先駆者, 前身, 予兆, 前兆
▸Amazon Japan's entry into the online shopping mall business may shake up the customer bases of its *forerunners*, including Rakuten Inc. and Yahoo Japan Corp. アマゾンジャパンの仮想商店街事業への参入は、同事業で先行する楽天やヤフーの顧客基盤を揺るがしかねない。

foresee 動 予想する, 予見する, 見込む
▸Citigroup Inc. *foresees* a sharp fall of about 60 percent in third quarter profit due to failed mortgage investments. 米大手銀行のシティグループは、サブプライム・ローン［米国の低所得者向け住宅融資］関連の担保不動産投資の失敗で、第3四半期(7-9月期)は約60％の大幅減益を見込んでいる。

foresight 名 先見性, 先見の明, 洞察力, 見通し, 計画性, 周到な準備
▸Companies with *foresight* and insight are eager to invest in solutions that will increase their competitiveness. 先見性と洞察力を兼ね備えた企業は、自らの競争力を高める分野に積極的に先行投資します。

forex 名 外国為替, 外貨《略 FX》(foreign ex-

changeの略)
forex gains or losses 為替差損益
forex impact 為替による影響, 為替の影響
forex loss 為替差損
forgiveness 名 放棄, 免除 (⇒debt forgiveness, loan forgiveness)
　forgiveness of liabilities 債務免除
form 動 設立する, 組織する, 組成する, 結成する, 作り出す, 築く, 構築する, 形成する, 設定する
　form a joint venture 合弁会社を設立する
　form a portfolio ポートフォリオを構築する
　form an underwriting group 引受団を組成する
▸Seven & I Holdings Co. was *formed* on Sept. 1, 2005 as the holding company of Ito-Yokado, Seven-Eleven Japan and Denny's Japan Co.　セブン&アイ・ホールディングスは, イトーヨーカ堂, セブン-イレブン・ジャパンとデニーズ・ジャパンの持ち株会社として, 2005年9月1日に設立された.
form 名 様式, 書式, 形式, 表現形式, 式, 形態, 様態, 形状, 外観, 外形, 構図, 構成, 種類, フォーム (⇒**participant, proxy form**)
　bearer form 無記名式
　form of business organization 企業形態, 企業組織の形態
　form of financial statements presentation 財務諸表の表示様式
　graphic form 図表形式
　order form 注文書式
　organization form 組織形態
　statement form 報告式 (＝narrative form, report form)
▸The 2006 and 2007 two-for-one stock splits were effected in the *forms* of 100% stock dividends.　2006年度と2007年度の1対2の株式分割は, 100%株式配当形式で実施されました.
Form 8-K 様式8-K, フォーム8-K (重要事象発生の際に義務付けられている臨時報告書)
Form 10-K 様式10-K, フォーム10-K (⇒**annual report**)
　様式10-Kとは ➡ 米国の有価証券報告書の一種. 米国の公開会社(証券取引所上場企業や店頭公開企業など)が, SEC (米国証券取引委員会)に提出する財務報告の様式で, 株主向け年次報告書と同じく会計監査済み(audited)のものでなければならない.
　Form 10-K Annual Report to the Securities and Exchange Commission 様式10-KのSEC (米証券取引委員会)向け年次報告書
　the annual report on Form 10-K 様式10-Kに基づく年次報告書
▸The Annual Report on *Form 10-K* is available from the date of its filing with the Securities and Exchange Commission in the United States.　様式10-Kに基づく当社の年次報告書は, 米国の証券取引委員会(SEC)への提出日以降に入手できます.
▸*Form 10-K*, our annual report to the SEC, is available without charge by calling or writing.　当社が米証券取引委員会(SEC)に提出している年次報告書のForm 10-Kは, 電話か書面により, 無料で入手することができます.
Form 10-Q 様式10-Q, フォーム10-Q (第1四半期から第3四半期までの特定の財務情報に関する四半期報告書)
▸The *Form 10-Q* Quarterly Report filed with the Securities and Exchange Commission will be available in May.　米国証券取引委員会(SEC)に提出した様式10-Qによる四半期報告書は, 5月に配布可能となります.
Form 20-F 様式20-F, フォーム20-F
▸The Corporation submits an annual report (*Form 20-F*) to the Securities and Exchange Commission (SEC) in the U.S.　当社は, 米証券取引委員会(SEC)に様式20-Fに基づく年次報告書を提出しています.
Form F-1 様式F-1, フォームF-1 (米国外の発行会社が用いる登録届け出書の基本的な様式)
Form F-4 様式F-4, フォームF-4 (外国企業にかかわる企業結合との関連で証券を登録する際の様式)
Form S-1 様式S-1, フォームS-1 (特に様式が規定されていない発行会社の証券を登録する際の一般的な様式)
Form S-8 様式S-8, フォームS-8 (従業員持ち株制度に基づいて発行する証券を登録するための様式)
fortuitous 形 思いがけない, 偶然の
forward 名 先物, 予約取引, 先渡し取引, 先渡し契約, 繰延べ, フォワード
　forward contract 先渡し契約, 先物契約, 予約契約
　forward exchange 先物為替, 先渡し為替, 為替先物
　forward rate 先渡し金利, 先渡しレート, 先物為替相場, 先物相場, 予約相場 (＝forward exchange rate)
　forward trading 先渡し取引, 先物取引 (＝forward bargain)
　forward transaction 先物取引, 先物為替取引, 先物為替予約取引, 為替予約 (＝forward contract, forward dealing)
▸The exporting companies are attempting to

avoid further foreign exchange losses arising from the yen's appreciation by buying *forward* contracts.　輸出企業は, 買い為替予約 [買い予約] で円高による為替差損を避けようとしている。
▶We enter into foreign exchange contract, including *forward*, option and swap contracts.　当社は, 先物, オプション, スワップなどの外国為替予約を締結しています。

foundation 名　基盤, 基礎, 土台, 根拠, 建設, 設立, 創立, 創業, 基金, 維持基金, 奨学基金, 基本金, 財団, 事業団, 基礎化粧品, ファンデーション (⇒allotment, disposal of facilities)
　business foundation　事業基盤, 経営基盤, 経営の根幹, 経営体力
　financial foundation　財務基盤, 経営基盤 (= financial base, financial footing)
▶The survey found about 68 percent of M&As were aimed at strengthening the *foundations* of existing businesses.　調査の結果, M&A [企業の合併・買収] の目的は約68%が既存事業の基盤強化であった。

foundation fund　〈保険会社の〉基金 (株式会社の資本金に相当), 基本積立金
▶Life insurer's *foundation fund* is equivalent to capital for a stock company.　生命保険会社の基金は, 株式会社の資本金に相当する。

fourth quarter　第4四半期
▶Ford Motor Co. lost $45.8 billion in the *fourth quarter* amid slumping sales and huge restructuring costs.　フォード・モーターの第4四半期決算は, 販売不振と多額のリストラ費用で, 458億ドルの赤字となった。

fourth quarter earnings　第4四半期の利益, 第4四半期の純利益
▶*Fourth quarter earnings* were 50 percent greater than the comparable period in 2006.　第4四半期の利益は, 2006年同期と比べて50%増加しました。

fourth quarter results　第4四半期の業績
▶The company's *fourth-quarter results* were hurt by $91 million in income tax expenses.　同社の第4四半期の業績は, 9,100万ドルの法人所得税費用で打撃を受けた。

framework 名　枠組み, 骨組み, 関係, 体系, 制度, 環境
　agreed framework on new trade rules　新貿易ルールの枠組み合意 (= framework agreement on new trade rules)
　economic framework　経済関係
　institutional framework　制度的枠組み
　legal framework　法的枠組み
　new budgetary framework　新予算制度
　regulatory framework　規制の枠組み, 規制上の枠組み, 規制体系, 規制環境

fraudulent 形　不正な, 虚偽の
　fraudulent financial reporting　不正な財務報告, 虚偽の財務報告

FRB　[米] 連邦準備制度理事会 (Federal Reserve Boardの略。連邦準備銀行 (Federal Reserve Bank) を指す場合もある)

free 形　自由な, 制限 [制約] を受けない, 独立の, 任意の, 自主的な, 無料の, 無償の, 免除された
　free balance　正味残高
　free distribution　新株の無償交付, 無償増資 (= free share distribution)
　free distribution of common shares　無償増資, 普通株式の無償交付
　free issue　無償交付 (= bonus issue)
　free market price　市中相場
　free reserve　任意積立金
　free share　無償株
　free share distribution　株式の無償交付
　free surplus　自由剰余金, 処分可能剰余金, 未処分剰余金
　interest free　無利息の
　risk free asset　無リスク資産, 安全資産
　tax-free　非課税の

freehold　不動産所有権, 自由保有権, 自由土地保有

fresh capital　新規資本, 追加資本, 増資
▶Japanese companies actively tapped the stock market to raise *fresh capital*.　日本の企業が, 新規資本を調達するため株式市場で積極的に起債した。

friendly 形　友好的な, 好都合な, 使いやすい
　friendly acquisition　友好的買収 (= friendly takeover)

–friendly　…に役に立つ, …に有利な, …にやさしい, …が使いやすい, …になじみやすい
　customer-friendly market　顧客に有利な市場
　eater-friendly　消費者にとって食べやすい
　eco-friendly　環境にやさしい, 自然環境にあった (= environmentally friendly)
　environment-friendly technology　環境にやさしい技術
　investor-friendly　投資家になじみやすい
　people-friendly justice system　身近な司法制度
　planet-friendly　地球にやさしい
　user-friendly　ユーザーに使いやすい, ユーザーに分かりやすい, 使いやすい, 使い勝手がよい, 操作が簡単な

▶Honda Motor Co. wants to develop bioethanol vehicles as a pillar of the environment-*friendly* technologies that the company promotes, such as hybrid cars.　ホンダは，ハイブリッド車など同社が推進する環境にやさしい技術の柱として，バイオエタノール車の開発を目指している．

friendly offer　友好的買収
▶White knight is a company that saves another firm threatened by a hostile takeover by making a *friendly offer*.　ホワイト・ナイトは，友好的な買収により，敵対的買収の脅威にさらされている他企業を救済する企業のことだ．

friendly tender offer　友好的株式公開買付け，友好的TOB（＝friendly takeover bid）
▶Kirin Brewery Co. will launch a *friendly tender offer* for Mercian shares in a capital and business alliance.　キリンビールは，資本・業務提携としてメルシャン株式の友好的TOB［株式公開買付け］を実施する．

fringe benefit　付加給付，付帯給付，給与外給付，賃金外給付，追加給付，福利厚生費，経済的利益，フリンジ・ベネフィット
　fringe benefit plan　付加給付制度

from a year ago　前年比［前期比］で，前年比，前年［前年度］に比べて，前年から
▶Operating income fell 48 percent in the first half-yeat to ¥8.1 billion *from a year ago*.　上半期の営業利益は，前年比48%減の81億円となった．

from a year earlier　前期比，前年比，前期と比べて，前年から，前年同期比（＝from the previous year; ⇒**group net profit**）
▶Manufacturers' pretax profits rose 11.4 percent in the April-June quarter *from a year earlier*, up for the 16th straight quarter.　4-6月期の製造業の経常利益は，前年同期比11.4%増で，16四半期［4年］連続増加した．

from the year before　前年比［前期比］，前年同期比，前年［前年度］と比べて，前年［前年同期］から
▶Group net profit in the first half of the 2007 business year jumped 37 percent *from the year before*.　2007年度上半期（3月期決算企業の4-9月期）の連結純利益は，前年同期比で37％急増した．

front 名　〈活動の〉最前線，前線，先頭，最前列，冒頭部分，表面，第一面，方面，面，分野，協力，提携，運動，フロント
　be on the front burner　重要視されている，最優先されている
　form [show, present] a united front against ...　…に対して共同戦線を張る

front company　幽霊会社，名目会社，ペーパー・カンパニー，ダミー会社
front cover inside　表2
front money　前金，前払い金
front side　書類の表，表面（裏面＝back side）
labor front　労働運動，組合運動
on both the fiscal and monetary fronts　財政・金融両面で
on the economic front　経済活動の面で
▶As the way to make a real progress on the environmental *front*, we set aggressive goals and used quality control techniques to achieve them.　環境の面［環境問題］で実質的に前進する手段として，当社は積極的な目標を掲げ，その目標を達成するための品質管理手法を採用しました．

front burner　最優先事項，最優先課題，優先的考慮事項，優先事項，最大の関心事，重大な関心事（＝front burner issue; ⇒**back burner**）
　put on the front burner　最重視する，最優先する，優先する

front line　最前線，第一線
▶The two companies' employees are competing on the *front line* of promotion and sales.　両社の社員は，販促や販売の最前線で競いあっている．

front-load 動　前倒しする
▶We plan to *front-load* our current restructuring plan by three years.　当社は，現行のリストラ［人員削減］計画を3年前倒しする方針です．

front-loading 名　前倒し，前倒し執行
front runner [front-runner]　トップ企業，第一人者，最有力候補者，優勝候補，トップランナー
▶Toyota is the *front-runner* among companies that turn out goods using the distinctive Japanese method of production.　トヨタは，日本独特の生産方法で製品を生産している企業のトップ企業だ．

F/S　財務報告書，財務報告，有価証券報告書（financial statementの略）
FSA　［英］金融サービス機構，［日］金融庁（Financial Services Authority, Financial Services Agencyの略）
FTC　［米］連邦取引委員会（Federal Trade Commissionの略）
full 形　完全な，全部の，十分な，全面的，正式の，正規の，詳しい，充実した，総額の
　full actuarial liability　年金数理上の負債総額
　full amount　全額，総額
　full dilution　完全希薄化，完全希釈化，完全希釈効果
　full eligibility　完全受給権取得，完全受給資格取得，完全適格者

full elimination 全額消去
full fair value method 全面時価評価法
full pension 完全年金, 満額年金
full provision basis 完全税効果会計, 所得税の完全期間配分 (＝comprehensive tax allocation)
full turnkey 一括受注・発注方式, フル・ターンキー

full business year 通期 (＝full fiscal year)
for the full business year ending next March 来年3月に終了する事業年度全体で, 来年3月に終了する今年度通期で, 来年3月までの通期で
for the full business year through next March 来年3月までの通期で
▶For the *full business year* ending next March, Takeda expects its group net profit to climb 17.6 percent from fiscal 2006. 来年3月までの通期で, 連結純利益は2006年度比［前期比］で17.6％増加すると武田薬品は予想している。

full capacity 完全操業度, フル稼働
▶Pipeline systems out of Canada have been operating at *full capacity*. カナダ国外のパイプライン・システムは, フル稼働を続けています。

full consolidation 全部連結, 完全連結, 総額連結 (⇒account balance)
▶The 2007 results include the *full consolidation* of SLM's results from March 1, 2007 until March 31, 2007. 2007年度の業績には, 2007年3月1日から2007年3月31日までのSLM社の業績の完全連結分も含まれています。

full cost 全部原価, 総原価, 総括原価, フル・コスト (＝fully allocated cost, fully distributed cost)
full cost accounting 全部原価計算, 総原価計算, 全部原価法 (＝full costing)
full cost basis 全部原価法
full cost method 全部原価法, 総原価法, フル・コスト法 (＝full cost approach, full-cost basis)
full-cost plus method 全部原価プラス価格決定法
▶One of the most significant factors causing these differences between Canadian and U.S. GAAP is the application of *full cost* accounting rules for oil and gas. カナダ会計基準と米国会計基準の間でこれらの差異が生じている最大要因の一つは, ガスおよび石油事業に対して適用される総原価計算の基準です。

full disclosure 完全開示, 完全表示, 十分な開示, 完全公開性
full disclosure principle 完全開示原則

full employment 完全雇用
▶While preserving *full employment*, we have reduced our total work force. 完全雇用を保持しつつ, 当社は全体の従業員数を削減してきました。

full fiscal year to March 31 3月31日までの通期, 3月期決算 (＝full fiscal year ending March 31)
▶For the *full fiscal year to March 31*, the firm expects to post a group net loss of ¥47 billion. 3月期決算で, 同社は470億円の連結税引き後赤字を見込んでいる。

full powers and authority 全権能と権限
▶The Investment Committee is vested with the *full powers and authority* of the board in cases when investment decisions are required urgently. 投資委員会は, 緊急を要する投資の決定［投資判断］について, 取締役会の全権能と権限を付与されています。

full service 完全サービス
▶The new campus includes a *full-service* cafeteria, ATMs and a health center offering comprehensive occupational health and wellness programs to all employees and their families. この新事業施設には, 完全サービスのカフェテリアやATM（現金自動預け払い機）のほか, 従業員とその家族に総合健康管理プログラムを提供する保健センターが設置されています。

full year 通期, 通年, 1年分
▶The equity in net earnings of the company was consolidated for the *full year* of 2007. 同社の持ち分利益は, 2007年度通期で連結計上されています。

full-year 形 通期の, 通年の, 1年分の
full-year net income 通期純利益, 通期税引き後利益
full-year profit and revenue 通期の利益と売上高
full-year profit forecast 通期の利益予想, 通期の利益見通し, 通期の損益予想 (＝full-year profit estimate)
full-year results 通期決算, 通期業績
full-year revenues 通期の売上高
full-year sales 通期の売上高
▶We posted a 15 percent rise in *full-year* net profit. 当社の通期純利益は, 15％増加しました。

full-year consolidated net profit 通期の純利益, 通期の税引き後利益
▶The company expects a *full-year consolidated net profit* of ¥1.55 trillion on sales of ¥23.2 trillion. 同社は, 通期で23兆2,000億円の売上高に対して1兆5,500億円の連結税引き後利益を見込んでいる［予想している］。

full-year dividend 通期配当, 年間配当
▶The firm is considering increasing its *full-year dividend* for the business year to March 31, 2007 to demonstrate its policy of putting greater emphasis on the interests of shareholders. 同社は, 株主利益重視[株主重視]の姿勢を示すため, 2007年3月期決算で通期の増配[年間配当金の増額]を検討している.

full-year earnings 通期の収益, 通期の業績
　full-year earnings forecast 通期の業績予想
　full-year earnings target 通期の収益目標, 通期の業績目標
▶Daiwa Securities Group does not give a *full-year earnings* forecast. 大和証券グループは, 通期の業績見通しは行っていない.

full-year forecast 通期業績見通し, 通期予想, 通期の業績予想 （=full-year earnings forecast, full-year earnings projection, full-year outlook）
▶Honda raised its *full-year forecast* as sales surged in Asia. ホンダは, アジアでの販売急増で通期の業績予想を上方修正した.
▶Mizuho Financial Group Inc. cut its *full-year forecast* to ¥650 billion from ¥750 billion. みずほフィナンシャルグループ(FG)は, 通期業績予想を当初の7,500億円から6,500億円に(1,000億円)下方修正した.

full-year group operating profit 通期の連結営業利益
▶The company's *full-year group operating profit* is now estimated at ¥2.2 trillion. 同社の通期連結営業利益は, 現段階で2兆2,000億円になる見通しだ.

full-year net income forecast 通期の純利益予想, 通期の税引き後利益予想
▶The firm kept its *full-year net income forecast* unchanged. 同社は, 通期の純利益[税引き後利益]予想を据え置いた.

full year to March 31 3月31日までの通期, 3月期, 3月期決算
▶For the *full year to March 31*, 2009, the company's group net and pretax profits are expected to amount to ¥100 billion and ¥170 billion respectively. 2009年3月期の同社の連結税引き後利益と税引き前利益は, それぞれ1,000億円と1,700億円に達する見込みだ.

fully 副 完全に, 全部, 十分に, 正確に, 詳細に, 詳しく, 少なくとも
　fully allocated cost 全部配賦原価 （=full cost, fully distributed cost）

fully eligible active plan participant 受給資格取得済みの在職制度加入者
fully-paid capital stock 全額払い込み済み株式 （=fully paid share）
fully vested 十分受給権が発生している, 受給権が確定している
fully vested employees to pension plan 年金受給権確定従業員
fully consolidated 全部連結されている, すべて連結の範囲に含めてある
▶The company's results are *fully sonsolidated* in our financial statements. 同社の業績は, 当社の財務書類に100%連結されています.

fully diluted 完全希薄化後の, 完全希薄化
　fully diluted average common and common equivalent shares outstanding 完全希薄化後の期中平均発行済み普通株式および普通株式相当証券数
　fully diluted basis 完全希薄化法
　fully diluted common and common equivalent shares 完全希薄化後の普通株式および普通株式相当証券
　fully diluted earnings per common share 完全希薄化による普通株式1株当たり利益, 完全希薄化後普通株式1株当たり利益, 潜在株式調整後1株当たり利益
　fully diluted net earnings per common and common equivalent share 普通株式および普通株式相当証券1株当たりの完全希薄化後純利益
on a fully diluted basis 完全希薄化ベースで
primary and fully diluted earnings per share 単純希薄化と完全希薄化による1株当たり利益
▶Primary earnings per common and common equivalent share were the same as *fully diluted* for all years shown. 普通株式および普通株式相当証券の1株当たりの希薄化前利益は, 表示した全事業年度について完全希薄化後利益と同じでした.

fully diluted earnings per share 完全希薄化1株当たり利益, 1株当たり完全希薄化後純利益, 潜在株式調整後利益 （=fully diluted EPS）
▶*Fully diluted earnings per share* were $2.65, up 49% from $1.78 in 2006. 1株当たり完全希薄化後純利益は, 2006年度の1.78ドルを49%上回って, 2.65ドルとなりました.

fully funded 全額出資の, 全額拠出される, 十分積み立てられている
　fully funded affiliate 全額出資子会社
　fully funded pension 全額年金積立金
fully owned subsidiary 完全所有子会社, 全額所有子会社, 100%子会社 （=fully funded

affiliate, fully owned unit, totally held subsidiary, wholly owned company)

function 名 機能, 職能, 職務, 任務, 業務, 役目, 役割, 働き, 部門, 公式の行事, 関数 (⇒shareholder vote)
 audit function 監査機能
 cost function 費用関数, 原価関数
 investment function 投資業務, 投資関数
 finance function 財務職能
 internal audit function 内部監査機能
 R&D functions 研究開発部門
 wages [pay] according to function 職務給
▸Having sales and marketing, product, and research personnel working in close proximity should permit synergy and closer coordination between the *functions*. 営業・マーケティング, 製品部門と研究部門の従業員が近接して仕事に取り組むことにより, 部門間の相乗効果と一段と緊密な協調関係が生まれるはずです。
▸We want to beef up the original *functions* of futures trading, such as hedging the risk of price fluctuations, and setting proper prices in the market. 相場変動リスクの回避や市場での公正な価格形成など, 先物取引の本来の機能を強化したい。

function 動 機能する, 作動する, 動く, 働く, 職務[機能, 役目]を果たす
▸The managerial system of NHK is considered as having ceased to *function* properly. NHKの経営体制は機能不全に陥ったと見られている。

functional currency 機能通貨, 法貨
▸The Company's European operations use the local currency, instead of the U.S. dollar, as the *functional currency*. 当社の欧州子会社は, 機能通貨として米ドルに代えて現地通貨を使用しています。

fund 動 〈資金を〉調達する, 積み立てる, 〈資金を〉賄う, 〈資金を〉提供する, 拠出する, 出資する, 〈赤字などを〉補塡する (⇒borrow 動)
 amounts funded 積立額
 be fully funded 十分積み立ててある
 be funded equally by ... …が折半出資する
 fund large public expenditures 巨額の財政赤字を賄う
 fund pension costs as accrued 年金費用を発生時に積み立てる
 fund through issuance of debt 債券の発行で資金を調達する

fund 名 資金, 基金, 積立金, ファンド
 advance of funds 資金の提供
 amortization fund 減債基金
 application of funds 資金運用
 assumed rates of return on pension funds 予想年金基金運用収益率
 automated fund transfer account 自動振替口座
 bond fund 債券投資信託, 債券ファンド
 buyout fund 買収ファンド
 capital fund 設備資金, 資金, 基本金, 資本基金
 classified fund 機密費
 collecting and providing of funds for terrorists テロ資金の収集・提供
 consolidated funds statement 連結資金計算書
 cost of borrowed funds 資金調達コスト
 cost of funds 資金調達コスト, 資金調達原価, 資金コスト
 current fund 流動資金, 一般財政
 debt service fund 借入返済基金
 demand for funds 資金需要
 discretionary fund 売買一任勘定資金
 employee's pension fund 従業員年金基金
 endowment fund 寄贈基金
 equity fund 株式ファンド, 投資ファンド (同業他社の平均的収益力を上回る収益力)
 excess fund 余剰資金
 external fund 外部資金, 外部調達資金 (=external funding)
 fund flow 資金フロー, 資金収支, 資金循環, ファンド・フロー
 fund for retirement of bond 社債償還基金 (=bond retirement fund)
 fund from operations 営業活動による資金
 fund in hand 手持ち資金
 fund-of-funds ファンド・オブ・ファンズ (投資信託に投資する投資信託 (「投信の投信」) で, 投資家から集めた資金の運用を, 別の複数の投資信託に再委託する仕組み。⇒investment trust)
 funds borrowed 借入金, 借用金
 funds from external sources 外部資金
 funds from operations 営業活動による資金, 営業活動から得た資金 (=funds provided by operations)
 funds provided by operations 営業活動により得た資金, 営業活動によって供給された資金, 営業活動による資金 (=funds provided from operations)
 funds provided from net earnings 純利益により得た資金, 純利益で得た資金
 funds provided from operations 営業活動から得られた資金, 営業活動による資金, 営業活動から生じた資金 (=funds provided by operations)

income fund　収益配当型投資信託, インカム・ファンド
index mutual fund　インデックス・ミューチュアル・ファンド（＝index fund：株価指数と連動するように設計された株式ポートフォリオを運用対象とする投資信託）
internal fund　内部資金
invest in the fund　ファンドに出資する
invested fund　投下資本
liquid fund　流動資金
loanable fund　貸付け資金, 貸出の原資
operating fund　運転資金
pension fund　年金基金
petty fund　小口資金
plant expansion fund　工場拡張基金
redemption fund　償還基金
revolving fund　回転資金
shareholders funds　株主資本
shift of funds　資金の移動
slush fund　不正資金
source and application of funds　資金の源泉と使途（＝source and disposition of funds）
sources and uses of funds　資金収支表
urgent fund　緊急資金
use of funds　資金の運用
▸*Funds* provided from net earnings, depreciation, and amortization were offset primarily by investment outflow and increased working capital requirements.　純利益と減価償却［減価償却および償却］で得た資金は, 主に投資支出額と必要運転資本の増加額で相殺されました。

fundamental profit　基礎利益（＝basic profit)
▸The *fundamental profit* represents earnings from core insurance operations like policy sales.　基礎利益とは, 保険の販売など, 本業の保険業務による収益［利益］を意味する。

fundamentals 名　基本, 原理, 根本原理, 基礎, 基礎的条件, 基本的指標（国の成長率, インフレ率, 財政収支, 金融情勢, 為替レート, 経常・貿易収支の6つ), ファンダメンタルズ
company fundamentals　企業のファンダメンタルズ
economic fundamentals　経済のファンダメンタルズ, 経済の基礎的条件, 景気のファンダメンタルズ（＝fundamentals of the economy）
financial fundamentals　財務面のファンダメンタルズ, 財務体質
▸We do not see anything in the *fundamentals* of our business that would cause us to change our strategy of investing for profitable growth.　当社の事業基盤に, 高い利益を生む成長をめざした当社の投資方針の変更を迫るような要素は, 見当たりません。

funded 形　資金化した, 積み立てた, 資金を供与[提供]された
funded debt　固定債務, 長期負債, 外部負債, 社債発行借入金,〖英〗有期国債, 確定公債
funded pension plan　積立年金制度, 年金基金制度, 年金基金制
funded status　基金の状態, 積立状況, 拠出状況
jointly funded organization　共同出資の組織
liability for pension expense not funded　未積立年金費用債務
net funded debt　純借入債務
▸This joint news Web site will be operated by a jointly *funded* organization.　この共同ニュース・サイトは, 共同出資の組織が運営する。

funding 名　資金調達, 調達, 調達手段, 積立て, 資金化, 資金源, 長期債化, 長期国債の借換え, 基金設立, 融資, 拠出, 資金供与, 資金提供, 出資, 事業費, 財政援助
advance funding method　事前積立方式
cost of floating rate funding　変動金利による資金調達コスト
direct funding　直接融資
employee pension funding　従業員年金基金への拠出
external funding　外部資金調達（＝external financing）
funding capacity　資金調達能力
funding cost　資金調達コスト（＝cost of funding）
funding for redemption of corporate bonds　社債の償還資金
investment funding　投資金融
long-term funding　長期資金の調達
terminal funding　年金現価積立方式
terminal funding method　年金現価充足方式
▸During 2007, the Company experienced a significant increase in its cash requirements because of *funding* of the Profit Sharing and Pension Trust plans.　利益分配および年金信託制度への資金拠出により, 2007度は必要資金が増加しました。

funding contributions　年金積立額
▸The cumulative difference between amounts expensed as pension costs and the *funding contributions* is reflected on the consolidated balance sheet.　年金原価として費用処理した額［年金費用］と年金積立額の間の累積差額は, 連結貸借対照表上

に表示されています。

fund raising 資金調達, 資本調達, 募金（= fund procurement）
- **new fund raising** 新規資金調達, 新規調達額

fund-raising 形 資金調達の, 資本調達の
- **fund-raising cost** 資金調達コスト, 資金調達費用（=fund-raising expense）
- **fund-raising plan** 資金調達計画
- ▶The Corporation's ¥560 billion syndicated-loan from 31 banks and leasing companies is part of its *fund-raising* plan.　同社が銀行やリース会社から受ける560億円の協調融資は、資金調達計画の一環だ。
- ▶The firm is expected to fall short of its planned *fund-raising* target by about ¥50 billion due to lower stock price.　同社では、株価の下落で、当初計画の資金調達目標を約500億円下回る見通しだ。
- ▶Banks' *fund-raising* costs have increased, reflecting the rise in market rates after the Bank of Japan abandoned its zero-interest policy.　日銀のゼロ金利政策解除に伴って市場金利が上昇したのを反映して、銀行の資金調達コストが増大した。

further 形 一層の, 一段の, 追加の
- **further cost cutting** 一層のコスト削減
- **further earnings decline** 業績の一段の悪化
- **further payment** 追加支払い
- **further rate cut** もう一段の利下げ

furtherance 名 促進, 推進, 助成, 助長
- ▶Management of the corporation, in *furtherance* of the integrity and objectivity of data in the financial statements, has developed and maintains a system of internal accounting controls.　当社の経営者は、財務書類に含まれる［財務書類上の］データの完全性と客観性を高めるため、会計に関する内部統制組織［内部会計統制組織］を整備［開発］し、これを維持しています。

future 名 形 将来, 未来, 先行き, 今後, 将来性, 将来の, 未来の, 先行きの, 今後の
- **future borrowing** 将来の借入れ
- **future cash flow** 将来キャッシュ・フロー, 将来の資金繰り
- **future collectible amounts** 将来の回収可能額
- **future demand outlook** 今後の需要見通し
- **future losses** 将来の損失
- **future net cash flow** 将来の正味キャッシュ・フロー, 将来の純キャッシュ・フロー
- **future performance** 将来の業績
- ▶The accounts receivable are valued at their *future* collectible amounts.　売掛金は、将来の回収可能額で評価されています。

future value 未来価値, 将来価値, 終価《略 FV》
- **future value table** 終価率法

futures 名 先物, 先物取引, 先物契約, 先物為替（⇒commodity futures）
- **bond futures** 債券先物, 債券先物取引
- **commodity futures** 商品先物
- **currency futures** 通貨先物, 通貨先物取引
- **financial futures** 金融先物
- **futures contract** 先物契約
- **futures trading** 先物取引
- **index futures** 指数先物
- **interest rate futures** 金利先物, 金利先物取引
- **New York Futures Exchange** ニューヨーク先物取引所
- **option on futures** 先物オプション
- **stock futures** 株式先物
- **stock index futures** 株価指数先物
- **synthetic futures** 合成先物
- ▶These financial goods listed on the TSE include convertible bonds, government and corporate bonds, as well as stock index *futures* and options.　東証の上場金融商品には、転換社債や国債、社債のほか株価指数先物、株価指数オプションなどがある。

FV 終価（future valueの略）

FX 外国為替（=foreign exchange, forex）
- **FX margin trading** 外国為替証拠金取引
- **FX market** 外国為替市場
- **FX transaction** 外国為替取引
- **real effective FX rate** 実質実効為替レート
- ▶In *FX* margin trading, investors can expect high returns from a relatively small amount of capital.　外国為替証拠金取引では、投資家は、比較的わずかな資金でハイリターンを期待できる。

FY 会計年度, 事業年度, 営業年度, 年度（fiscal yearの略）

G g

GAAP 一般に認められた会計原則[会計基準]，一般に公正妥当と認められた会計原則，一般会計原則[会計基準]，会計基準 (**generally accepted accounting principles**の略；⇒**generally accepted accounting principles**)
 big [large business] GAAP 大企業向け一般会計基準[会計原則]
 Canadian GAAP カナダ会計基準
 EU GAAP 欧州会計基準
 German GAAP ドイツ会計基準
 in conformity with German GAAP ドイツの会計基準[会計原則]に従って，ドイツの一般会計基準に準拠して
 little GAAP 閉鎖会社および小規模公開会社向け一般会計基準[会計原則]
 small business GAAP 中小企業向け会計基準[一般会計基準]
 U.S. [US] GAAP 米国会計基準，米国の一般会計基準[会計原則] (＝United States GAAP)
▸The consolidated financial statements have been prepared in accordance with German *GAAP*. この連結財務書類[財務諸表]は，ドイツの一般に公正妥当と認められた会計基準[ドイツの会計基準]に従って作成されています。

GAAS 一般に認められた監査基準，一般に公正妥当と認められた監査基準 (**generally accepted auditing standards**の略；⇒**misstatement**)

gain 動 得る，獲得する，入手する，達成する，〈技術などを〉身につける，〈経験などを〉積む，増加する，増大する，増進する，増す，向上する，上がる，上昇する
 gain control [dominance] 支配権を得る，経営権を得る[握る]，主導権を得る

gain experience 経験を積む
gain market share シェア[市場シェア]を伸ばす，シェアを拡大する
gain market share from ... …からシェアを奪う
▸For the April–September period, operating profit *gained* 12 percent from the year before. 4–9月期(3月決算企業の上半期)の営業利益は，前年同期比で12％増加しました。

gain 名 利益，利潤，利得，増加，増大，増進，伸び，拡大，上昇，向上，差益，ゲイン (⇒**buoy, capital gain, latent gain, unrealized gain**)
 contingent gain 偶発利益
 currency gain 為替差益
 earnings gain 収益の伸び
 gain contingency 偶発利益事象
 gain from appreciation of securities 有価証券評価益
 gain from forgiveness of debt 債務免除益
 gain from operations 営業利益
 gain from reduction of capital stock 減資差益 (＝gain from capital reduction)
 gain on bond conversion 社債転換差益
 gain on disposal of equipment 設備処分益
 gain on redemption of stock 株式償還益
 gain on retirement of treasury stock 自己株式消却益
 holding gain 保有利益
 market share gains マーケット・シェアの拡大，市場シェアの拡大
 net realized and unrealized capital gains 純実現・未実現キャピタル・ゲイン
 post net gains 黒字を計上する
 purchasing power gain or loss 購買力損益

gain and loss

productivity gain 生産性の向上
sales and earnings gains 増収増益
secure gains 利益を確保する
stockholding gains 保有株式の含み益
unrealized gains on [in] securities 有価証券含み益
unrecognized net gain 未実現純利益

▶Foreign investors who were exchanging dollars for yen to buy Japanese shares began selling their stocks because of the possible rate hike to secure their *gains*.　ドルを円に換えて日本株を買っていた外国人投資家が，(米国の)利上げ観測で，利益を確保するために日本株を売りはじめた。

▶We had a $50 million *gain* on this sale.　当社は，この売却で5,000万ドルの利益を上げました。

gain and loss [gain or loss] 損益 (⇒other income)

actuarial gains and [or] losses 保険数理上の損益
gain or loss from revaluation of inventories 棚卸し評価損益
gain or loss on exchange 為替差損益，交換差損益
gain or loss on retirement of fixed assets 固定資産処分損益
gains or losses on discontinued operations 中止事業[非継続事業]により生じた損益
hedging gains and losses ヘッジ損益
realized gaind and [or] loss 実現損益，売却損益
recognition of gain and loss 損益認識

▶When we dispose of assets that were depreciated using the unit method, we include the *gains or losses* in operating results.　個別償却法で償却した資産を処分する場合，その利益または損失は営業損益に含めます。

gain in revenues 売上高[収益]の伸び，増収

▶A *gain in revenues* was recorded in 2007 despite the intense competitive environment in North America.　2007年度は，北米市場で競争が激化した[北米市場での熾烈な競争環境]にもかかわらず，売上高の伸びを記録しました。

GDP 国内総生産 (gross domestic productの略)

gearing 名 負債，負債比率，純負債比率，ギアリング (=financial leverage, leverage, trading on the equity)

acceptable gearing 許容範囲の負債比率
financial gearing 財務レバレッジ
gearing adjustments ギアリング調整[修正]，負債調整額，ギアリング調整額
gearing effect レバレッジ効果
gearing proportion 負債調整率，ギアリング調整率
gearing ratio 株主資本負債比率，優先資本比率，ギアリング比率，ギアリング・レシオ (=the ratio of net debt to equity)
group gearing 連結純負債比率
high gearing 大きな負債
increase [boost, improve] gearing 負債比率[借入比率]を引き上げる
net gearing 純負債比率 (=net gearing level)
reduce gearing 負債比率を引き下げる

▶We reduced the ratio of net debt to equity (*gearing* ratio) to 15 percent in 2007.　2007年度は，株主資本純負債比率[ギアリングレシオ]を15％に引き下げました。

general 形 一般の，一般的な，全般的な，総合的，多岐にわたる，概略的な，概略の，通常の，総…

general administrative expense 一般管理費，総務費，本社費 (=general administration cost, general and administrative expense)
general auditing standards 監査一般基準 (=general standards of auditing)
general business credit 事業税額控除
general closing 通常決算
general contractor 総建築請負業者，元請業者，一般請負人，ゼネコン
general control procedures 全般統制手続き
general corporate cost 本社費，会社全体の一般的経費，一般管理費 (=general corporation cost)
general operating expense 一般営業費，一般営業活動費，一般管理販売費 (=selling and administrative expense)
general shareholders [shareholders'] meeting 株主総会 (=general meeting, general meeting of shareholders, shareholders' general meeting, stockholders' meeting)
general syndication 一般シ団の組成
general working capital 一般運転資金

general accounting 一般会計

general accounting principles 一般会計原則[会計基準]，会計一般原則
general accounting purpose 財務会計上

general corporate expenses 一般本社経費，全社共通費，全社一般経費，会社全体の一般的経費，一般間接経費

▶Operating profit excludes *general corporate expenses*, net interest and income taxes.　営業利益に，全社一般経費と支払い利息純額，法人税等は含まれていません。

general corporate purposes 一般事業目的
▶The proceeds from all newly issued shares were used for *general corporate purposes*.　新規発行株式の売却代金は，すべて一般事業目的に使用しました。

general expense 一般費，一般経費，間接費，総経費　(=general cost, general operating expense, selling and administrative expense)
　factory general expense 工場一般経費
　insurance general expense 保険一般経費
　investment general expenses 投資一般経費

general meeting 総会，株主総会　(=general shareholders meeting)
　annual general meeting 年次総会，年次株主総会
　extraordinary general meeting 臨時株主総会　(=extraordinary meeting of shareholders)
　first general meeting 創立総会
　general meeting of stockholders [shareholders] 株主総会　(=general shareholders meeting)
　regular general meeting 定例総会，定例株主総会　(=ordinary general meeting)
▶A majority of businesses that closed their accounts for the year to March 31 plan to hold their respective *general meetings* of shareholders next week.　3月期決算企業の大半は来週，それぞれ株主総会の開催を予定している。

generally 副　一般に，全般的に，原則として，基本的に
　accounting principles generally accepted in the United States of America 米国で一般に認められた[一般に公正妥当と認められた]会計基準
　be stated generally at cost 原則として原価[取得原価]で計上する，基本的に原価[取得原価]で計上する
　generally accepted international accounting practices, standards and procedures 一般に認められた国際会計慣習，基準と手続き
▶Options are not *generally* exercisable during the first twelve months after the date of grant.　オプションは，原則としてオプションが付与された日から12か月間は行使することができません。

generally accepted accounting principles 一般に認められた会計原則，一般に認められた会計基準，一般に公正妥当と認められた会計原則[会計基準]，一般会計基準《略 GAAP》 (=generally accepted accounting practices, generally accepted accounting standards)

米国の一般会計基準について → 米国で一般に認められた会計原則は，基本的にARBs (Accounting Research Bulletins：米国公認会計士協会(AICPA)の会計研究公報・会計調査公報)とAPB Opinions (Opinions of the Accounting Principles Board の略称で，APB意見書。これは米国公認会計士協会(AICPA)の会計原則審議会(APB)の意見書を指す)，FASB Statements (財務会計基準審議会(FASB)基準書のほかに，APB Statement No.4やSEC (米証券取引委員会)のRegulation S-X (規則S-X：様式10-Kの財務書類に関する用語，様式，作成方法などを定めたもの)などを指す。
▶The consolidated financial statements were prepared in accordance with Canadian *generally accepted accounting principles*.　この財務書類は，一般に認められたカナダの会計基準[カナダの一般会計基準]に従って作成しました。

generally accepted auditing standards 一般に認められた監査基準，一般に公正妥当と認められた監査基準《略 GAAS》
▶Our examinations were made in accordance with *generally accepted auditing standards*.　私どもの監査は，一般に公正妥当と認められる監査基準に準拠して行われています。

generate 動　生み出す，生む，創造する，生成する，引き起こす，誘発する，獲得する，…を占める，計上する，発生する
　ability to generate cash 収益力
　generate cash 収益を上げる，キャッシュ・フローを生み出す
　generate cash flow 現金収入を得る，キャッシュ・フローを生み出す[生成する]
　generate foreign exchange 外貨を得る，外貨を獲得する
　generate operating margin 営業収益を計上する
　generate profits 利益を生み出す，利益を生む
▶Cash requirements in 2007 will be met by internally *generated* funds.　2007年度の資金必要額は，内部調達資金でまかなう予定です。
▶Funds *generated* from operations increased to $115 million from $90 million in the first quarter.　事業活動に伴って発生した資金は，第1四半期の9,000万ドルから1億1,500万ドルに増加しました。

geographic area 地域別区分，地域セグメント，地域　(⇒terms and conditions)
▶Busines restructuring and other charges were taken primarily in the information movement and management segment and the U.S. *geographic area*.　事業再編成その他の費用は，原則的に情報伝送および処理セグメントと米国地域セグメントに含

geographic revenue 地域別売上高
▸*Geographic revenues* from customers are based on the location of the selling organization rather than the location of the customer.　地域別顧客売上高は、顧客の所在地ではなく、販売組織の所在地に基づく売上高です。

geographical [geographic] segment information 地域別セグメント情報

global 形 全世界の, 世界の, 全世界的, 国際的な, 世界的規模の, 地球規模の, 地球全体の, グローバルの, 広範囲の, 全体的な, 全面的な, 包括的な, 総合的な, グローバル

　global competition 国際競争, グローバルな競争 (=international competition)

　global productivity 総生産性

　global sales 世界全体での売上

　global standard 世界標準, グローバル・スタンダード

▸One of the aims for the three banks to merge into the Mizuho Financial Group was to survive the *global* competition by exploiting the banks' combined strength.　3行がみずほフィナンシャルグループに合併する目的［狙い］の一つに、3行の統合力を駆使して国際競争に勝ち抜くことがあった。

global company 世界企業, グローバル企業
▸To grow, we have to be a *global company*.　当社が成長するためには、グローバル企業になる必要があります。

global competitiveness 国際競争力
▸The goal of the restructuring is to reinforce our *global competitiveness*.　この事業再構築は、当社の国際競争力の強化を目的としている。

global economy 世界経済, 世界の景気
▸Based on our expectations for the *global economy*, we expect greater sales growth in 2008.　世界景気に対する当社の期待によれば、2008年度は一段と大きな売上の伸びを見込んでいます。

global market グローバル市場, 世界市場, 国際市場, グローバル・マーケット (=global marketplace, international market)
▸The restructuring will enhance the Corporation's ability to compete more effectively in *global markets*.　事業再編により、今後はグローバル市場での当社の競争力が一段と強化されることになりました。

global strategy 世界戦略, 国際戦略, グローバル戦略
▸The export base of Thai is part of Nissan's *global strategy* to include ASEAN countries in its component supply network.　タイの輸出拠点は、ASEAN（東南アジア諸国連合）諸国を日産の部品供給ネットワークに組み込む日産の世界戦略の一環だ。

globalization 名 グローバル化, 世界化, 国際化, 地球的規模化, 全世界一体化, グローバリゼーション
▸Our strategy for the second half of 2008 is to continue the *globalization* of our business while gaining market share in North America.　北米の市場シェアを拡大する一方、事業の国際化を引き続き推進するのが、2008年度下期の当社の経営戦略です。

goal 名 目標, 目的, ゴール
　budget goal 予算目標
　business goal 企業目標
　company goal 企業目標, 会社目標 (=corporate goal)
　earnings goal 収益目標, 業績目標 (=earnings target)
　financial goal 財務目標
　financial sales goal 売上目標
　profit goal 利益目標
▸Our *goal* is to dramatically increase that portion of our revenues coming from international activities.　当社の目標は、当社の収益のうち国際事業により生じる部分の大幅増にあります。
▸The company again failed to meet earnings *goals* in fiscal 2007.　同社は、2007年度も収益目標を達成できなかった。

going concern 継続企業, 営業している企業, 企業の存続可能性, ゴーイング・コンサーン (=ongoing concern)
　going concern assumption 継続企業の公準 (=going concern concept)
　going concern rules 企業の継続能力規定, ゴーイング・コンサーン規定
　going concern value 継続企業としての価値, のれん
▸The *going concern* rules require corporations to state in their financial statements whether they are in danger of net capital deficiency, defaults of obligations and continued operating losses.　ゴーイング・コンサーン［企業の継続能力］規定は、債務超過や債務不履行、継続的な営業損失などが発生する恐れがあるかどうかを財務書類［財務諸表］に明記するよう企業に義務付けている。

going private 株式の非公開化, 株式を非公開にすること, 非公開会社化（一般に、上場会社が外部発行済み株式を買い戻して自社を非公開会社にすること）

going public 株式の新規公開, 株式公開, 機密情報の公開 (＝flotation, IPO, listing：証券取引所や店頭市場に株式を新規公開して, 上場会社になること)

golden share 黄金株, 特権株(株主総会での合併などの提案に拒否権を発動できる「拒否権付き株式(種類株式)」のこと)
▶ *Golden shares* give even holders of a single share the veto right to block hostile takeover bids. 黄金株では, 1株の株主にも敵対的買収案を阻止するための拒否権が与えられる。

good 形 好調な, 堅調な, 優良の, 優秀な, 良好な, 好材料の, 強気な, 十分な, かなりの, 高い, 大幅な, 一流の, 親切な
　be good to customers 顧客に親切にする
　good debt 優良貸付け, 優良債権, 優良貸金, 回収確実な貸金
　good growth 大幅な伸び, 高い伸び率, 高成長
　good liquidity 流動性が良好なこと, 流動性が高いこと
　good news 好材料, 良い知らせ
　good paper 一流商業手形
　good people 優秀な人材, 優秀な社員
　good people company グッド・ピープル・カンパニー (＝healthy company：従業員の幸福を最重視する会社)
　good results 好業績, 好決算, 業績好調
　good years 業績好調時
▶ While these short-term financial results are disappointing, demand for our products and services continues to be *good* worldwide. 短期の財務成績[業績]は満足が得られるものではありませんが, 当社の製品とサービスに対する需要は, 引き続き世界各地で好調です。

good performance 業績好調, 好業績 (＝good business performance, good results, strong performance)
▶ Though the global economy continues to be uncertain, we are cautiously optimistic that 2008 will continue to be another year of *good performance*. 世界経済は依然として不確実な状況が続いていますが, 慎重に見て, 当社は2008年度も引き続き好業績を達成できるものと, 楽観的な見通しを持っています。

goods 名 物品, 商品, 製品, 財貨, 財産, 財, 貨物, 動産, 有体動産
　bonded goods 保税貨物 (＝goods in bond)
　capital goods output 資本財生産
　collateral goods 担保品
　completed goods 完成品
　consigned goods 委託品
　damaged goods 傷物
　defective goods 仕損じ品
　durable goods 耐久財
　electrical goods 電化製品
　electronic goods 電子製品
　final goods price 製品価格
　general consumer goods 一般消費財
　goods and services 財貨とサービス, 財貨・サービス, モノとサービス, 財貨と役務, 財貨と用役 (＝services and goods)
　goods in process 仕掛(しかけ・しかかり)品 (＝goods in progress, product in progress, stock in process, work in process)
　goods in stock 在庫品, 商品在高, 手持ち商品 (＝goods on hand)
　industrial goods 産業財
　intermediate goods 中間財
　luxury goods 贅沢品
　manufactured goods 工業製品
　partially finished goods 半製品
　primary goods 一次産品
　producer goods 生産財; 工業製品
　reserve for returned goods 返品調製引当金
　seasonal goods 季節的商品
　semifinished goods 半製品
　shopping goods 買い回り品(ファッション関連や耐久消費財などの商品)
　speciality goods 専門品 (＝specialty goods)
　taxable goods 課税対象商品
▶ The cost of finished *goods* and work in process comprise material, labor, and manufacturing overhead. 製品と仕掛品の原価は, 材料費と労務費と製造間接費からなっています。

goodwill 名 営業権, のれん, 得意先, 信用, 信頼, 善意, 好意, 親善, 快諾
　営業権[のれん]とは ➡ 企業の超過収益力(同業種の企業の平均を上回る利益を上げることができる能力)をもたらす無形固定資産で, 具体的には企業の有能な人間資産(経営者, 従業員), 優れた技術やノウハウ, 優良なブランド・イメージ, 店舗の立地条件, 有利な仕入れ先や得意先との関係などをいう。営業権は企業の財産であるが, これを貸借対照表に資産として計上できるのは, 有償で譲り受けた場合か, 合併で有償取得した場合に限られる。
　amortization of goodwill 営業権の償却 (＝goodwill amortization)
　consolidated goodwill 連結のれん (＝consolidated excess, consolidation goodwill, goodwill on [from] consolidation)

goodwill and other intangible assets　営業権およびその他の無形固定資産
Goodwill, net of accumulated amortization　営業権(償却累計額控除後)
　internally generated goodwill　自己創設のれん，自己創設営業権(過去の教育訓練費や研究費，開発費，交際費などの支出によって創設されるもので，これらの支出は支出時に費用として処理され，資産としては認識されない)
　negative goodwill　消極のれん
　positive goodwill　積極的のれん
　purchased goodwill　取得営業権，買入のれん，営業件の取得
▶*Goodwill* is amortized over its estimated life.　営業権は、見積り有効期間にわたって償却されています。
▶We amortize *goodwill* on a straight-line basis over the periods benefited, principally in the range of 10 to 15 years.　当社は、営業権を、基本的に10年から15年の利益発生期間にわたって定額法で償却しています。

govern 動　支配する，管理運営する，…が適用される，律する，決定する，規定する，…の基準となる，優先する　(⇒**internal accounting control**)
▶Capital subscription in a Chinese bank is *governed* by foreign currency restrictions.　中国の銀行への出資には、外資規制がある。

governance 名　統治，支配，管理，管理法，経営法，統治能力，ガバナンス　(⇒**corporate governance**)
　information governance　情報ガバナンス，情報統治
　information technology governance　ITガバナンス(IT全般の統治能力のこと)
▶U.S. corporate *governance* regulations are too harsh.　米国の企業統治法[企業改革法]は厳しすぎる。

grant 動　与える，付与する，許諾する，許可する，承諾する，認める，譲渡する，移転する
▶The exercise price of any stock option is equal to or greater than the stock price when the option is *granted*.　ストック・オプションの行使価格は、オプションが付与された時の株価と同等、またはそれを上回る価格になっています。

grant 名　権利の付与，財産の移転，譲渡，譲与，実施許諾，〈政府の〉補助金，助成金，交付金，無償資金，無償給付，研究助成金，奨学金
　block grant　包括補助金
　Federal grants to States　連邦から州への交付金
　grant of an option　オプションの付与

　land grant　土地使用権
　loan grants　借款
　operation grant　運営費補助
　percentage grant　定率補助金
▶Simultaneously with the *grant* of an option, the employee may also be granted the right to a special compensation payment.　オプションの付与と同時に、従業員に対しては、特別報酬の支払いを受ける権利を付与することもあります。

greenhouse gas emissions　温室効果ガス排出量、温室効果ガスの排出量、地球温暖化ガスの排出量　(=emissions of greenhouse gases, greenhouse gas discharge)
▶California's Attorney General Bill Lockyer has sued the six largest U.S. and Japanese automakers for damages related to *greenhouse gas emissions*.　米カリフォルニア州のビル・ロッキャー司法長官は、自動車が排出する温室効果ガスについて日米の大手自動車メーカー6社に損害賠償を求める訴訟を起こした。

gross 名　合計，総額，総…
gross 形　総計の，全体の，控除前の，控除をしない
　estimated gross profit　見積り総利益
　gross amount　総額
　gross average method　総平均法，加重平均法
　gross book value　総帳簿価額，帳簿価額総額，簿価総額，減価償却累計額控除前簿価　(=gross carrying amount)
　gross cost of merchandise sold　総売上原価，売上原価総額
　gross debt　総債務
　gross dividend per share　1株当たり総配当
　gross domestic product　国内総生産《略 GDP》(GNPから海外からの純所得を差し引いたもの)
　gross earnings　総収益，総収入，総所得
　gross eligible charges　給付対象費用発生額
　gross expenditure　総支出
　gross gain　総収益
　gross investment in a lease　総リース投資額，リース投資未回収総額
　gross-less-allowance valuation　引当金控除後価額
　gross loss on sales　売上総損失
　gross manufacturing cost　総製造費用
　gross merchandise margin　売上総利益，商品売上総利益，商品粗利益　(=gross profit, gross profit margin, gross profit on sales)
　gross method　総額法
　gross operating income　営業粗利益
　gross operating revenue　営業粗収入

gross results 経常収益
gross revenue 総収益, 総収入, 益金
gross sales 総売上高, 総売上
in the gross 総計で, 全体として, 概して, 卸売りで (＝in total)
realized gross profit 実現総利益
▸*Gross* deferred tax assets were $1,300 million at December 31, 2007.　繰延べ税金資産総額は, 2007年12月31日現在で13億ドルとなっています。

gross capital expenditures 資本的支出総額
▸*Gross capital expenditures* were $519 million for the first quarter of 2007.　2007年第1四半期の資本的支出総額は, 5億1,900万ドルでした。

gross income 売上総利益, 総収益, 総収入, 総所得, 総益金
▸For 2007 as a whole, net earnings rose by about 10 percent while *gross income* increased approximately 6 percent.　2007年度全体としては［2007年通期で］, 純利益は約10％伸び, 総収益はおよそ6％増加しました。

gross margin 売上総利益, 売上利益, 粗利益, 売上利益率, 粗利益率　(⇒margin, pressure)
　current gross margin 取替え原価による売上総利益
　deferred gross margin 繰延べ総利益
　gross margin method 総利益法, 売価還元法 (＝gross profit method)
　gross margin percentage 売上総利益率, 粗利益率　(＝gross margin ratio, gross profit ratio, operating ratio; ⇒cost control)
　gross margin ratio 売上総利益率, 粗利益率　(＝gross margin percentage, gross profit percentage, gross profit ratio, operating ratio)
▸The *gross margin* of 40.5 percent in 2007 was marginally down from 40.7 percent in 2006.　2007年度の40.5％の売上利益率は, 前年度の40.7％を少々下回りました。
▸The *gross margin* percentage improved since 2005 because of a smaller workforce.　売上総利益率は, 人員削減により2005年度以来, 改善しました。

gross operating profit 業務［営業］粗利益
▸Banks have paid hardly any corporate enterprise tax though they made even larger *gross operating profits* than they did during the bubble economic era.　銀行は, バブル期より大きな業務粗利益を上げたものの, 法人税をほとんど負担して［支払って］いない。

gross premium ［保険］総保険料, 表定保険料, 営業保険料（純保険料(net premium)＋付加保険料(loading)で算出される）
▸*Gross premium* refers to the amount that policyowners actually pay for their insurance.　総保険料とは, 契約者が実際に支払う保険契約料の額のことをいう。

gross profit 売上総利益, 粗利益, 粗利, 差益　(＝gross margin, gross profit margin, gross profit on sales：売上総利益＝純売上高－売上原価)
　gross profit method 総利益法, 総益法, 売価還元法 (＝gross margin method)
　gross profit on sales 売上総利益, 粗利益, 売買差益 (＝gross profit, gross profit margin)
　gross profit ratio［rate］ 売上総利益率, 粗利益率, 総益率　(＝gross margin ratio, gross profit percentage, operating ratio)
　ratio of gross profit to net sales 売上高総利益率
▸This product was the prime contributor to the increase in *gross profit* in 2007.　本製品が, 2007年度の売上総利益の増加にとくに大きく貢献しました。

gross profit margin 売上総利益率, 売上利益率, 売上総利益, 粗利益率, 粗利益　(＝gross margin)
▸*Gross profit margins* for the third quarter of 2007 were 39.8 percent of revenues, compared with 41.5 percent of revenues in the same period last year.　2007年第3四半期の売上総利益率は, 前年同期の41.5％に対して39.8％でした。

groundbreaking 名　起工, 起工式, くわ入れ式
groundbreaking 形　起工(式)の, 革新的な, 草分けの, 新生面開拓の
▸Toyota Motor Corp. held a *groundbreaking* ceremony for its car assembly plant in St. Petersburg.　トヨタ自動車は, ロシアのサンクトペテルブルクで自動車組立工場の起工式を行った。

group 名　企業集団, 集団, 団体, 連結, 企業グループ, グループ
　business group 企業グループ
　consolidated group 連結企業グループ, 連結対象の会社グループ, 連結企業集団, 連結集団 (＝consolidation group)
　corporate group 企業グループ, 企業集団 (＝business group)
　corporate group tax system 連結納税制度 (＝consolidated taxation system, group taxation system)
　financial group 金融グループ
　group accounts 連結財務書類, 連結財務諸表,

グループ財務書類, 企業集団財務諸表 （=consolidated accounts, consolidated financial statements, group financial statements)
group depreciation 組別償却, グループ償却
group earnings forecast 連結業績予想
group financial statements 連結財務書類[財務諸表], 企業集団財務諸表 （=group accounts)
group firm グループ会社, グループ企業, 系列企業 （=group company; ⇒**cut**)
group relief グループ税額控除
group results グループの業績, グループ企業の連結業績, 連結決算 （=consolidated results)
industry group 業界団体, 経済団体, 業界
interest group 利益団体, 利益集団, 圧力団体
investment group 投資グループ
manager group 幹事団, 幹事グループ, 幹事銀行団
on a group basis 連結ベースで, 連結ベースの （=on a consolidated basis)
underwriting group 引受団
▶The *group* will be able to raise its consolidated recurring profits to more than ¥20 billion from the current ¥4 billion or so through the reorganization. 再編により, 同グループは今後, グループ全体で現在の40億円程度の経常利益を200億円以上にすることができる。
▶The *Group*'s share of reported income in associated companies is included in the consolidated income statement. 関連会社の公表利益に対する当グループの持ち分は, 連結損益計算書に表示されています。

group after-tax profit 連結税引き後利益
▶*Group after-tax profit* in the first six months plunged 62 percent to ¥195 billion from a year earlier. 上半期の連結税引き後利益は, 前年同期比62%減の1,950億円でした。
group company グループ会社, グループ企業, 系列企業 （=group firm)
▶Softbank currently provides a social networking service through its *group company* Yahoo Japan Corp. ソフトバンクは現在, グループ企業のヤフーを通じてソーシャル・ネットワーキング・サービス（SNS）を提供している。
group insurance 団体保険
  group insurance payable 団体保険料預かり金
  group insurance program 団体保険
group interim report 連結中間決算報告, 連結中間決算報告書
▶The company's *group interim report* was compiled using U.S. accounting rules. 同社の連結中間決算報告書は, 米国の会計基準を用いて作成された。
group method 組別償却法, グループ償却法 （=group depreciation：同種の資産を一つの集合体として減価償却する方法)
▶The *group method* is used for most other depreciable assets. グループ償却法は, その他の大部分の償却資産に用いられています。
group net income 連結純利益, 連結税引き後利益 （=consolidated net income)
▶*Group net income* in the second quarter fell to ¥81 billion. 第2四半期の連結純利益は, 810億円に減少しました。
group net loss 連結純損失, 当期連結純損失, 連結税引き後赤字 （=consolidated net loss：企業グループ全体の税引き後損失)
▶The firm posted a *group net loss* of ¥1.5 billion for the April-September fiscal first half due to the high cost of warding off a hostile takeover bid. 9月中間決算で同社は, 敵対的TOB（株式公開買付け）を回避するために多額の費用が発生したため, 15億円の連結税引き後赤字となった。
group net profit 連結純利益, 当期連結純利益, 連結税引き後利益 （=consolidated net profit：企業グループ全体の税引き後利益)
▶The firm's *group net profit* plunged 72.3 percent to ¥21.2 billion in the six months through Sept. 30, 2007 from a year earlier. 2007年9月中間決算で, 同社の連結税引き後利益は, 前年同期比72.3%減の212億円となった。
group net sales 連結税引き後売上高, 連結純売上高
▶The Company's *group net sales* are estimated at ¥22.3 trillion for the current business year. 当社の連結税引き後売上高は, 今期は22兆3,000億円に達する見込みです。
group operating loss 連結営業損失, 連結営業赤字 （=consolidated operating loss)
▶We suffered a *group operating loss* of ¥3 billion in the first half of fiscal 2007. 当社の2007年上半期の連結営業収益は, 30億円の赤字でした。
group operating profit 連結営業利益, 連結営業黒字 （=consolidated operating profit)
▶The firm's *group operating profit* forecast for the current year was downgraded to ¥35 billion. 同社の今年度の連結営業利益見通しは, 350億円に下方修正された。
group operating revenue 連結営業収益, 連結営業収入, 連結売上高
▶NTT Corp. incurred *group operating revenue*

and profit falls in fiscal 2004 for the first time since its 1985 privatiztion. NTTは，2004年度の連結決算で，1985年の民営化以来初めて（前期比で）減収減益となった．

group pretax loss 連結税引き前損失，連結経常損失 (=consolidated pretax loss)
▸The firm revised downward its *group pretax loss* estimate for the first half of fiscal 2007. 同社は，2007年度上半期の連結税引き前損失予想を下方修正した．

group pretax profit 連結税引き前利益，連結経常利益 (=consolidated pretax profit)
▸For the April-September period, *group pretax profit* gained 11.6 percent to ¥333 million. 4-9月期の連結税引き前利益は，前年同期比で11.6%増の3億3,300万円でした．

group sales 連結売上高 (=consolidated revenues, consolidated sales)
▸The Company's *group sales* fell 22.3 percent to ¥672.11 billion in the March-August period due to closure of its money-losing stores. 当社の8月中間決算で［当社の3-8月期決算で］，連結売上高は，不採算店舗［赤字店舗］の閉鎖で22.3%減の6,721億1,000万円でした．

grow 動 増加する，増大する，拡大する，高まる，伸びる，成長する，発展する，向上する，栽培する，伸ばす
  fast-growing sector 急成長部門
  grow earnings 利益を増やす，利益を伸ばす
  grow steadily 順調に伸びる
  growing competition 競争激化
  rapidly growing market 急成長市場，急拡大市場
▸Mobile phone subscribers are the fastest *growing* segment of the telephone market. 携帯電話の加入者は，電話市場で最も急成長を遂げている部門である．
▸The combined sales of 813 nonfinancial companies in the April-September period *grew* 6.3 percent over the previous year. 金融を除く企業813社の上期（4-9月期）の売上高の合計は，前年同期比で6.3%増加した．

growth 名 成長，成長率，経済成長，伸び，伸び率，増加，増大
  asset growth 資産の伸び率
  balance sheet growth 資産の増加
  capex growth 設備投資の増加
  consolidated EPS growth 連結ベースのEPS伸び率
  dividend growth 配当の伸び，配当伸び率，増配率
  earnings growth 収益の伸び
  growth in profits 利益の増加，増益
  growth rate 成長率，伸び率
  internal growth 内部成長
  net profit growth 純益の伸び，純益伸び率
  organic growth 有機的成長
  profit growth 利益の伸び
▸Our *growth* comes from competing successfully worldwide, offering new technology and high-quality products and services. 当社の成長は，新技術と高品質の製品・サービスを提供して，グローバル競争に勝ち抜くことから生まれます．

growth in revenues and earnings 収益と利益［純利益］の伸び，増収増益
▸Investments in our network, financial operations and alliances will pave the way for further *growth in revenues and earnings*. 通信ネットワークや金融業務，他社との提携への投資によって，さらなる増収増益が可能になります．

growth opportunity 成長の機会
▸Companies move toward more global markets in search of new *growth opportunities*. 企業は，新たな成長の機会を求めて，一段とグローバル市場への進出を図っています．

guarantee 動 保証する，請け合う，確約する
  guaranteed amount 保証額
  guaranteed bond 保証付き社債
  guaranteed dividend 保証配当，確定配当
  guaranteed payback 確定利回り
  guaranteed yield 予定利率 (=promised yield: 生命保険会社が保険契約者に約束した運用利回り)
▸We sometimes *guarantee* the debt of certain unconsolidated joint ventures. 当社は，当社の財務書類に連結されていない一部の合弁会社の負債に対して保証を行うときもあります．

guarantee 名 保証，保証人，引受人，保証額，保証契約，保証書，保証状，担保，抵当，担保物
  advancing guarantee 融資保証
  bank guarantee cost 銀行保証料
  basic guarantee 根（ね）保証 (=initial guarantee)
  corporate guarantee 企業保証
  debt guarantee 債務保証
  export credit guarantee 輸出信用保証
  financial guarantee 金融保証，信用保証
  guarantee fee [charge] 保証手数料，保証料
  guarntee liabilities 保証債務，支払い保証 (=liabilities for guarantee)
  guarantee money 保証金，差入れ保証金
  guarantee of debt 債務保証 (=debt guaran-

tee)
guarantees of indebtedness of others 第三者の債務に対する支払い保証
loan guarantee 債務保証, 融資保証, 融資の信用保証, 貸出保証
maturity guarantee 満期保証
minimum guarantee 最低保証金
performance guarantee insurance 履行保証保険, 契約履行保証保険
tender guarantee 入札保証
▶The Corporation did not honor the debt *guarantee* on a total of ¥50 billion. 当社は, 総額500億円の債務保証を引き受けませんでした。

guideline 名 基準, 指導基準, 運用基準, 指導, 指針, 指標, 上限, ガイドライン
asset guideline peiod 法定耐用年数
budget guideline 予算編成方針 （＝budgeting policy)
capital guideline 自己資本比率の基準
credit risk guideline 信用リスク基準
management guideline 経営方針
Tier 1 capital guideline 基本的項目基準
▶Savings plans for the majority of our employees allow employees to contribute a portion of their pretax and/or after-tax income in accordance with specified *guidelines*. 大多数の当社従業員のための貯蓄制度では, 従業員は従業員の税引き前所得または税引き後所得 (あるいはその両方) の一部を, 特定の基準に従って拠出することができます。

H h

H1 上半期, 上期
    H1 losses 上半期損失, 上半期の赤字
H2 下半期, 下期
    H2 profits 下半期利益, 下半期の黒字
    H2CY2007 2007年下半期
half 名 中間, 半期, 半分 （⇒first half, second half of the year）
    half-finished goods 半製品
    half-fiscal year account 中間決算
    the first half of the fiscal year 年度前半
    the first half of the January to December business year 1-6月中間期決算, 今年度中間決算, 今年度上半期
    the first half of the year 上半期
    the first half of this business year 今年度上半期［上期］, 中間決算
    the second half of the fiscal year 下半期 （＝the latter half）
    the second half of the year 下半期
▶Resona's 1st-*half* net profit plunged 74% from a year earlier to ¥120 billion. りそなの上半期の連結税引き後利益は, 前年同期比74％減の1,200億円となった。
▶The firm returned to the black in the first-*half* of this business year. 同社は, 今年度上半期に［上期に, 中間決算で］黒字に転換した。
half year 半期, 中間
    half-year earnings report 半期業績報告, 中間決算報告, 中間決算 （＝interim earnins report）
    half-year earnings report for the fiscal period up to September 9月中間決算, 上半期（4-9月期）業績, 上半期決算
    half-year ended Sept. 30 9月中間決算
    half-year financial statements 中間財務書類, 中間企業財務情報
    half-year report 半期報告書, 中間事業報告書, 中間営業報告書
    half year to Sept. 30 4-9月期, 3月期決算企業の上半期［上期］, 9月中間決算
    half-year trading figures 中間決算
▶Loan write-off costs at the bank amounted to ¥450 billion for the *half-year* ended Sept. 30. 同行の9月中間決算の不良債権処理費用は, 4,500億円だった。
half-year revenue 半期売上高, 中間決算での売上高
▶The Corporation's *half-year revenue* increased by 15% to $3,420 million, compared with the same period last year. 当社の半期売上高は, 前年同期比15％増の34億2,000万ドルでした。
half-yearly 形 半期の, 中間の
    half-yearly performance 半期業績, 中間業績, 半期決算, 中間決算
    half-yearly performance until the end of February 2月中間決算
    half-yearly report 半期報告, 半期報告書, 中間報告
▶*Half-yearly* performance was affected by the weakening of the U.S. dollar against the Canadian dollar. 半期業績は, カナダ・ドルに対する米ドル安の影響を受けました。
halve 動 半減させる, 50％削減する, 半分に引き下げる, 半分に減らす, 二等分する, 半額にする
▶With this financial support, along with property sales, the company plans to *halve* its approximately ¥540 billion consolidated interest

hand 名 手元, 手持ち, 管理, 支配, 技量, 職工, 職人, 人手, 担当記者
  cash in hand 手元現金 （＝cash on hand）
  change hands 持ち主[所有者]が変わる, 持ち主を変える, 商品が売れる
  fund in hand 手持ち資金, 手元資金, 資金有り高 （＝fund on hand）
  goods on hand 在庫品
  quantity on hand 手持ち数量
  stock in hand 在庫品
  stock on hand 手持ち在庫
handling 名 取扱い, 運用, 出荷
  handling charge 取扱い手数料 （＝handling expense, handling fee）
head 動 …を率いる, …を統括する, 会社を経営する
  ▶The company's business management and planning headquarters is *headed* by its representative director. 同社の経営企画管理本部は, 代表取締役が統括している。
head 名 責任者, 最高責任者, 指導者, 経営者, 社長, 党首, 〈地位・能力の上での〉人
  department head 部門責任者, 部門担当責任者
  group head グループ代表
  official head 社長
  per head 1人当たり
  section head 部門責任者
  ▶The time vice president of the bank was the *head* of the department in charge of assessing the financial status of large borrowers. 同行の元副頭取は, 大口融資先の財務内容審査部門の最高責任者だった。
heading 名 〈財務諸表の〉タイトル, 表題, 見出し
headquarters 名 本社, 本店, 本部, 統括本部 （＝front office, head office, main office）
  administrative headquarters 管理本部
  area headquarters 地域本部
  regional headquarters 地域統括本部
  ▶In 2007, $800 million was included in selling, general and administrative expenses for manufacturing and *headquarters* consolidations. 2007年度は, 販売費および一般管理費として, 製造部門と本社機構の統合化のための費用8億ドルが含まれています。
health care [**healthcare**] 健康医療, 健康管理, 医療, 医療保険, ヘルスケア
  health care expense 健康医療費, 医療費 （＝health care cost：福利厚生の一環として, 米国の企業は従業員や退職者の医療保険への加入を支援している）
  health care industry 医療産業 （＝health care service）
health care benefits 健康保険給付, 健康管理給付, 医療給付
  ▶Previously, we expensed *health care benefits* as claims were incurred. これまで当社は, 医療給付については請求が生じた時点で費用として計上していました。
health care cost 医療費, 医療費用 （＝health care expense）
  ▶GM has conducted intense discussions with the unions about how to reduce *health care costs*. GMは, 医療費負担の軽減について, 自動車労組 (UAW) と精力的に交渉を進めている。
health insurance 健康保険
  health insurance expense 健康保険料
  health insurance system 健康保険制度, 医療保険制度 （＝health insurance plan）
healthy 形 健全な, 好調な, 順調な, 堅調な, 有益な, 相当な, かなりの
  healthy balance sheet 健全な財務体質
  healthy earnings 好業績
  healthy increase 好調な伸び, 順調な伸び, 堅調な伸び （＝healthy gain, healthy growth）
  healthy sales 好調な販売
  ▶Nicon Corp. posted a 20 percent rise in its first half net profit, helped by *healthy* sales of digital cameras and production equipment for crystal displays. ニコンの上半期の税引き後利益は, デジタル・カメラと液晶ディスプレー製造装置の好調な販売に支えられて, 20％増加した。
heavy 形 重い, 重質の, 大量の, 大規模な, 大型の, 多額の, 巨額の, 重大な, 活発な
  heavy additional tax 重加算税
  heavy investment 大型設備投資, 多額[巨額]の設備投資 （＝heavy capex）
  heavy machinery manufacturer 重機械メーカー, 重機メーカー
  heavy share 値がさ株
  heavy trading 大商い, 活発な取引
hedge 動 損失予防策をとる, 売り[買い]つなぎして損失を防ぐ, 分散投資して損失リスクを少なくする, 掛けつなぎする, 掛けつなぐ, リスクを回避する, ヘッジする （⇒risk）
  hedge against future cash flows 将来のキャッシュ・フローをヘッジする
  hedge exchange risk 為替リスクを少なくする,

為替リスクをヘッジ[回避]する
hedge interest rate risk　金利リスクをヘッジする
hedge one's bond portfolio　債券ポートフォリオをヘッジする
▶Gains and losses on these forward contracts will offset losses and gains on the assets, liabilities and transactions being *hedged*.　これらの先物為替予約から生じる利益と損失は、ヘッジの対象となっている資産、債務と取引から生じる損失および利益と相殺される。
▶Japanese companies can *hedge* exchange risks and improve their business image abroad through external bond financing.　日本企業は、外債発行による資金調達で、為替リスクを回避するとともに海外での企業イメージアップを図ることができる。

hedge 名　備え、損失予防手段、防護策、掛けつなぎ売買、保険つなぎ、為替リスクの防止[軽減]、ヘッジ（＝hedging）
　as a hedge against drops in stock prices　株価下落リスクに備えて
　as a hedge against losses　損失に対するつなぎとして
　hedge-buying　買いつなぎ（＝buying hedge）
　hedge gains and losses　ヘッジ損益
　hedge-selling　売りつなぎ（＝selling hedge）
　hedge transaction　ヘッジ取引
　short hedge　売りヘッジ
▶Gains and losses on *hedges* of existing assets or liabilities are marked to market on a monthly basis.　既存の資産または債務のヘッジに関する損益は毎月、評価替えされます。

hedge fund　ヘッジ資金、短期投資資金、ヘッジ・ファンド（「ヘッジ・ファンド」は、投資家から集めた資金を株式や債券、通貨、原油など幅広い市場で運用し、最先端の経済学理論や数学理論、金融手法を駆使して損失の回避[ヘッジ]に努めながら収益を追求する一種の投資信託：⇒**carry trade**）
▶Many major finance firms as well as pension funds of nonfinancial entities have invested in the *hedge fund*.　このヘッジ・ファンドには、多くの金融大手のほか、非金融事業会社の年金基金も投資している。

held-to maturity securities　満期保有証券、満期保有目的債券
HIFO　最高価格払出し法、最高価格先出し法、最高原価先出し法、高入先出し法（＝highest-in first-out method : highest-in first-outの略）
high 形　高い、高度な、高水準の、高級な、強い、大きな、最重要な、活発な
　high credit standing　高い信用力

high domestic demand　内需
high-grade stock　優良株
high margin business　利益率が高い事業
high profile project　大型プロジェクト
high return　高い運用益、高い利回り、高い収益率、高リターン、ハイリターン（⇒**FX**）
high-tech product　ハイテク製品[商品]
higher cost　費用の増加、コスト増、コストの上昇
higher earnings　増益、高収益
higher prices　値上げ、物価上昇、価格上昇
higher profitability　高収益
higher profits　増益、高収益
higher turnover　売上高の増加、取引の活発化（⇒**turnover**）
higher volume　販売数量の増加
higher yen　円高
highest-in first-out method　最高価格払出し法、最高価格先出し法、最高原価先出し法、高入先出し法《略 HIFO》
▶The segment was generally able to offset *higher* costs by improving yields, increasing factory utilization rates and higher worker productivity.　歩留まりの改善、工場稼動率の上昇や労働者の生産性向上により、当部門は全般にコストの増加分を相殺することができました。

high 名　高値、最高、最高値、最高記録、新記録
　an all time high　過去最高、史上最高値、上場来の高値、過去最多、過去最悪
　from a low of A to a high of B　最低Aから最高Bまで
　hit a record high　過去最高を記録する、過去最高に達する
　rally through the old highs　最高値を更新する
　reach a new historical high　過去最高を更新する
　set [hit] a new high　新記録を樹立する、過去最高を更新する、過去最高となる
▶We set new *highs* in both consolidated net profit and sales in 2007.　2007年度は、連結純利益[連結税引き後利益]も売上高も、過去最高を更新しました。

high performance　好業績、高収益、高性能
▶The increase in sales of digital cameras was crucial to the company's *high performance*.　同社の高収益の原動力は、デジタル・カメラの販売の伸びだ。

hire 動　〈人を〉雇う、〈物を〉賃借する
hire 名　賃金、給料、使用料、賃借料、社員、新入社員
　charter hire　用船料

hire charge 賃借料
hire plan 賦払い, 分割払い, 割賦
hire purchase 分割払い[月賦]購入方式, 買取り選択権付きリース, 買取り権付きリース, ハイア・パーチェス
  hire purchase contract 買取り選択権付きリース契約
  hire purchase lending 割賦ローン
  hire purchase transaction 買取り選択権付きリース取引
historical 形 歴史的, 過去の, 取得時の, 取引発生日の
  historical data 過去のデータ, 過去の実績, 実数値
  historical earnings 過去の業績, 収益[売上高]の実績
  historical information 実績データ
  historical net asset value 前期基準の1株当たり純資産
  historical performance 過去の運用成績, 過去の運用実績
  historical price 歴史的原価(過去の実際の取引価格)
  historical rate 取得時レート, 取引日レート, 発生時レート, 取得時の為替レート, 為替の取引発生日相場
  historical summary 財務の推移(過年度の主要財務数値を比較形式で示したもの), 過去の推移, 過去の状況
▶The various types of accounting changes may significantly affect the trends shown in comparative financial statements and *historical* summaries. 各種の会計上の変更は, 比較財務書類に示されている傾向や過去の財務の推移に重要な影響を及ぼす可能性があります。
historical cost 取得原価, 歴史的原価, 取得時の為替レート (=acquisition cost, actual cost, historical buying price:資産の取得に要した金額。実際の取引価額(historical buying price)を指す場合もある)
  historical cost balance sheet 取得原価主義貸借対照表
  historical cost basis 取得原価基準, 取得原価主義, 取得原価法 (=acqusition cost theory)
  historical cost principle 歴史的原価原則
  historical cost system 歴史的原価計算, 実際原価計算 (=historical costing)
▶The consolidated financial statements have been prepared on the *historical cost* basis in accordance with accounting principles generally accepted in Canada. 連結財務書類は, カナダで一般に公正妥当と認められた会計原則[会計基準]に従い, 取得原価基準に基づいて作成されています。

hit product ヒット商品
▶Sony is on its way to a turnaround in its core electronics business because of *hit products* such as liquid-crystal display TVs and digital cameras. 液晶テレビやデジタル・カメラなどのヒット商品があるため, ソニーの主力のエレクトロニクス事業は, 業績が改善している。
holding 名 所有, 保有, 保持, 占有, 所有持ち分, 保有株, 持ち株比率, 子会社, 所有財産, 保有財産
  cross holding 株式持ち合い (=mutual holding of stocks)
  direct holding 直接所有, 直接保有
  equity holding income 持ち分法利益
  holding gains and losses 保有損益, 保有利得および損失 (=holding gains and/or losses)
  holding period return 所有期間利回り
  inventory holding gain 棚卸し資産保有利得
  land-holding tax 土地保有税
  realized holding gain or loss 実現保有損益
  reciprocal share holding 株式持ち合い
  speculative holding 投機的保有
  stock holding 保有株式, 出資比率
▶The U.S. investment fund will offer 25 percent of its *holding*. この米国の投資ファンドは, 保有する株式の25%を売り出す。
holding company 持ち株会社 (=holding corporation:他の会社の株式を, 投資目的でなく事業活動支配のために保有する会社)
  bank holding company 銀行持ち株会社
  financial holding company 金融持ち株会社
  industrial holding company 製造業持ち株会社
  insurance holding company 保険持ち株会社
  investment holding company 投資持ち株会社
  management holding company 経営持ち株会社
  private industrial holding company 民間持ち株会社
  public utility holding company 公益事業持ち株会社
  pure holding company 純粋持ち株会社
  state-owned holding company 国営持ち株会社
▶Maruha and Nichiro seafood firms will integrate their operations under a *holding company* on Oct. 1, 2007. 2007年10月1日に, 水産会社のマルハとニチロが持ち株会社の下に経営統合する。
▶The *holding company* is expected to take an equity stake of around 10 percent in a consumer credit firm. この持ち株会社は, 消費者金融会社の株式持ち分約10%を取得する見込みだ。

holdings 名 持ち株, 保有株, 保有高, 持ち株比率, 持ち株会社, 資産
　blue-chip holdings 優良持ち株
　cash holdings 現金保有高
　draft holdings 手形保有高
　inventory holdings 在庫保有量
　national holdings 国家資産
▸*Holdings* in associated companies are reported in accordance with the equity method. 関連会社株式は, (連結財務書類上)持ち分法に従って報告されています。

home equity 住宅エクイティ (住宅の評価額と住宅ローン残高の差額)
　hime equity line of credit ホーム・エクイティ・ローン
　home equity loan 住宅エクイティ・ローン, ホーム・エクイティ・ローン(住宅の資産価格からローン残高を差し引いた残余分を担保に融資を行う不動産担保融資)
　home equity loan-backed securities ホーム・エクイティ・ローン証券

home office 本社, 本店, 本部
　home office cost 本部費, 本社費, 一般管理費 (＝home office expense)
　home office control 本店勘定

horizontal 形 水平的, 同業異種間の, 横割りの, 横の
　horizontal combination 水平的企業結合, 同業種間の企業結合
　horizontal consolidation 水平的合併, 水平的新設合併, 同業種間の合併[新設合併]
　horizontal diversification 水平的多角化
　horizontal merger 水平的合併
　horizontal specialization 水平的分業, 水平的国際分業 (＝horizontal international specialization)

hostile 形 敵対的, 敵対する
　hostile acquirer 敵対的買収者 (＝hostile bidder, hostile takeover bidder)

hostile bid 敵対的TOB [株式公開買付け], 敵対的買収, 敵対的買収提案 (＝hostile bid offer, hostile takeover bid)
hostile mergers and acquisitions 敵対的M&A (企業の合併・買収), 敵対的M&A
hostile tender offer 敵対的TOB (株式の公開買付け), 敵対的な株式公開買付け
▸We launched the *hostile* bid for the firm's shares. 当社は, 同社株の敵対的公開買付け(TOB)を実施しました。

hostile takeover 敵対的買収, 敵対的M&A (＝hostile acquisition, unsolicited takeover)
　hostile takeover bid 敵対的株式公開買付け, 敵対的TOB, 株式公開買付けによる敵対的買収, 敵対的買収 (＝hostile bid)
　hostile takeover bidder 敵対的買収者 (＝hostile acquirer, hostile bidder)
▸In order to forestall *hostile takeover* bids, companies should raise their corporate value. 敵対的TOB (株式公開買付けによる企業買収)を未然に防ぐには, 企業が企業価値を高めなければならない。

housing loan 住宅ローン, 住宅融資, 住宅金融 (＝home mortgage)
　housing loan claim 住宅ローンの債権
　housing loan insurance 住宅融資保険
　housing loan rate 住宅ローン金利
▸The additional provisions boosted the bank's credit costs related to the U.S. *housing loan* market woes in the April-September period to ¥19.8 billion. 引当金の積み増しで, 米国の住宅ローン市場低迷関連の同行の与信コストは, 4-9月期で198億円に増加した。

housing start 住宅着工, 〚～s〛住宅着工件数, 住宅着工戸数, 新設住宅着工戸数 (⇒increase 名)
▸Revenue growth in 2007 was primarily due to higher demand as a result of record *housing starts*. 2007年の売上高の伸びは, 住宅着工件数が過去最高に達したことに伴って, 需要が高まったことが主な要因です。

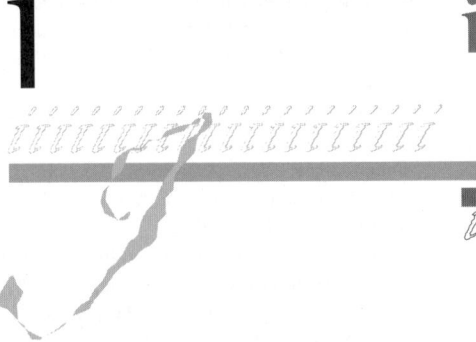

IAS 国際会計基準（**International Accounting Standards**の略。⇒**International Accounting Standards**）
▶Japanese companies listed on the London Stock Exchange will submit financial reports based on the *IAS* or the U.S. GAAP.　ロンドン証券取引所に上場している日本企業は今後, 国際会計基準か米国会計基準に基づく［準拠した］財務報告書を提出することになる。

idea 名　着想, 思いつき, 構想, 発案, 案, 考え, 考え方, 意見, 知識, 認識, 計画, 意図, ねらい, 思想, 概念, 観念, アイデア
　fresh idea　斬新なアイデア
　new idea　新しいアイデア, 新構想, 新しい思想
　outdated idea　時代遅れの思想
　product idea　製品［商品］のアイデア
▶It is to our benefit to be able to use *ideas* that others create.　他社が生み出したアイデアを利用できるのは, 当社にとっても利益になります。

identifiable asset　識別可能資産, 固有資産, セグメント固有資産, セグメント帰属資産, 総資産（⇒**aggregate**, **industry segment**）
　identifiable assets and liabilities　識別できるすべての資産負債
　identifiable assets of an industry segment　産業セグメントの固有資産（＝industry segment's identifiable assets）
▶*Identifiable assets* (excluding intersegment receivables) are the Company's assets that are identified with classes of similar products or operations in each geographic area.　固有資産（部門間受取債権を除く）は, 当社資産を各地域ごとに同種の製品または事業で分類した資産です。

idle 形　遊休の, 不働の
　idle capacity　遊休生産能力, 不働生産能力［生産設備］, 遊休設備, 遊休施設
　idle cash　遊休資金, 余剰資金
　idle equipment　遊休設備
　idle facility　遊休施設, 休止施設
　idle money　遊休資金
　idle plant　遊休設備, 遊休施設, 遊休工場設備
　idle property　遊休資産, 休止資産
　idle real estate　遊休不動産
▶Nonperforming loans will be transferred to the revival account, as well as crossheld shares and *idle* real estate.　不良債権は, 持ち合い株式や遊休不動産などと一緒に「再生勘定」に移されます。

IE　経営工学, 産業工学, 工学技術, インダストリアル・エンジニアリング（**industrial engineering**の略）

IFRS　国際財務報告基準（**International Financial Reporting Standards**の略）

illiquid 形　流動性のない, 流動性に乏しい, 換金しにくい, 容易に現金に転換できない
　illiquid asset　流動性に乏しい資産, 流動性の低い資産, 流動性のない資産
　illiquid issue　流動性の低い銘柄

image 名　画像, 映像, 心像, イメージ
　brand image　ブランド・イメージ, ブランドに対する全体的知覚
　corporate image　企業イメージ, コーポレート・イメージ
　global image　全地球的イメージ, グローバル・イメージ
　image processing　画像処理
　image strategy　イメージ戦略

media image　媒体イメージ
moving image　動画
product image　製品イメージ, 商品イメージ, プロダクト・イメージ
still image　静止画像
▶The company's poor corporate *image* is detrimental to the long-term growth prospects of its corporate group.　同社の悪い企業イメージは, 同社の企業グループの長期成長見通しにはマイナス要因だ.

imbalance 名　不均衡, 差, アンバランス
inventory imbalance　過剰在庫
structural imbalance　構造的不均衡
supply and demand imbalances　需要と供給の不均衡（＝imbalances between supply and demand）
trade imbalance　貿易の不均衡, 貿易不均衡
workload imbalance　作業負担量［仕事量］の不均衡, 労働力の不均衡
▶We prefer to move people to work and work to people as a means of addressing workload *imbalances*.　当社は, 労働力不均衡を是正する手段として, まず人員の配置転換や人員に応じた業務の再配分を行う方針です.

immediate 形　即座の, 即時の, 即刻の, 当面の, 目下の, 目先の, 目前の, 短期的な, 現在の, 隣接した
immediate annuity　即時年金, 即時型年金
immediate earnings outlook　当面の業績見通し, 当面の収益見通し
immediate improvement　目先の業績改善
immediate recognition as an expense　費用としての即時認識
immediate settlement　即時決済

impact 動　影響を及ぼす, 影響［衝撃］を与える, …への効果がある
▶The realignment and streamlining of the Corporation begins to *impact* earnings.　当社の再編と効率化の利益への効果が見られるようになった.

impact 名　影響, 効果, 衝撃, 刺激, インパクト
before the impact of restructuring costs　再編成費用の影響額控除前
financial impact　財務上の影響, 財務的影響
forex impact　為替の影響
impact from currency fluctuation　為替変動による影響, 為替変動の影響
impact of currency swings　為替相場の影響
impact of the declining cycle　景気後退の影響
impact on competitive position　競争力への影響, 競争力に与える影響
negative impact　悪影響

reflationary impact　景気刺激効果
▶Earnings per common share before the *impact* of these restructuring costs would have been $1.30.　これら再編成費用の影響額控除前の普通株式1株当たり利益は, 1.30ドルとなります.

impair 動　損なう, 弱める, 減じる, 劣化する, 制約する
impaired risk　信用リスク
impaired capital　資本の欠損, 資本金の欠損

impaired asset　不良債権
▶Charges included in other accounts were primarily for expenses related to writing down *impaired assets* and merger-related expenses.　その他の勘定科目に計上した費用は, 主に不良資産の評価減と合併関連の費用です.

impaired loan　不良債権, 劣化した貸出金, 貸出金の劣化
▶We compute present values for *impaired loans* when we determine our allowances for credit losses.　当社の貸倒れ引当金を決定するにあたって, 当社は不良債権の現在価値を計算します.

impairment 名　減損, 資本金の欠損, 損耗, 減価, 価値の下落, 劣化, 評価減
accounting for impairment of loans　貸出金劣化の会計処理, 貸出金の劣化の会計
assessment of impairment　価値の下落の評価
impairment losses　減耗損失
impairment of loans　貸出金の劣化, 貸付け金の破損, 不良債権, 貸付け金の評価損
impairment of value　資産価値の損耗
indication of an asset's impairment　減損の兆候
permanent impairment in value　回復不能減価
▶We currently adopt SFAS No.114, "Accounting by Creditors for *Impairment* of a Loan."　当社は現在, SFAS（財務会計基準書）第114号「不良債権に関する債権者の会計処理」を採用しています.

implement 動　実施する, 実行する, 遂行する, 施行する, 適用する
▶In 2007, we *implemented* Statement of Financial Accounting Standards (SFAS) 96.　2007年度から, 当社は財務会計基準書（SFAS）第96号を適用しています.

implement 名　道具, 手段
implicit interest　計算上の利息（＝imputed interest）
import 名　輸入, 輸入品, 輸入製品, 導入
▶The company considered switching purchases of chicken from Thailand to China following the ban on *imports* of Thai chiken.　同社は, タ

イ産鶏肉の輸入停止で，鶏肉の調達先をタイから中国に切り替えることを検討した。

impose 動 課税する，〈税金などを〉課す，〈義務などを〉負わせる，〈危険などを〉与える，〈条件などを〉設ける，売りつける，押しつける
▶No penalty taxes were *imposed* as the company was in the red. 同社は赤字だったので，追徴課税はされなかった。

imprest 名 前払い金，前渡し金
　imprest cash 定額前渡し小口現金
　imprest fund 定額前渡し資金，小口払い資金，手元資金

improve 動 改良する，改善する，改革する，促進する，推進する，強化する，高める，向上させる，拡大する，発展させる，好転させる
　improve competitive position 競争力を高める（＝improve competitiveness）
　improve market share 市場シェアを拡大する，シェアを拡大する
　improve the financial position 財務体質を改善する
　improved productivity 生産性の向上
　improved profit margins 利益率の上昇，利益率の増加
　improved quality 品質向上
　improved results 業績向上，業績改善
▶The company will reduce its interest-bearing debts to *improve* its financial health. 財務体質を改善するため，同社は有利子負債を削減する。
▶We dedicate ourselves to *improved* customer service and strict cost controls. 当社は，顧客サービスの改善とコスト管理の徹底化を図っています。

improvement 名 改良，改善，改革，促進，推進，向上，進歩，増加，伸び，上昇，拡大，〈景気などの〉回復，好転，改良工事，改修工事，整備，付属設備，改良費
　buildings and improvements 建物および付属設備，建物および改良費
　cost improvements コスト削減
　improvement cost 改良費（＝betterment expense, improvement expense）
　improvement in operating margins 営業利益率の向上
　improvement in profitability 収益性の改善，収益力の改善
　interest margin improvement 利ざや改善
　land and improvements 土地および付属設備
　leasehold improvement 賃借物改良費，内装費
　margin improvement 利益率改善
　operating improvements 業績向上
　practice improvement 業務改善
　productivity improvement 生産性向上
　technological improvement 技術力の向上，技術の改善
　yield improvement 利回り改善，利回りの向上
▶Our business in Latin America was good mainly due to economic conditions and our product line *improvements*. ラテンアメリカでの当社のビジネス［業績］は好調で，その主因としては経済環境と当社の製品ラインの改善が挙げられます。
▶We are aiming for a steady annual *improvement* in earnings of five percent or more. 当社は毎年，5％以上の利益増加率の安定確保を目指しています。

imputed interest 計算利子［利息］，適用利息，付加利子，帰属利子，自己資本利子（＝implicit interest）
　imputed interest on equity capital 株主持ち分費用，自己資本利子
　imputed interest on stockholder's equity 自己資本に対する計算利息
▶The net present value of such payments on capital leases was $150 million after deducting estimated executory costs and *imputed* interest. キャピタル・リース支払い額の純現在価値は，見積り管理費用と帰属利子の控除後で1億5,000万ドルでした。

in billions 単位：10億ドル
in millions 単位：100万ドル
　in millions, except as noted 単位：100万ドル。ただし，特に記載する場合を除く。
　in millions, except per share amounts 単位：100万ドル。ただし，1株当たりの金額を除く。
　in millions of dollars except per share figures 単位：100万ドル。ただし，1株当たりの金額を除く。
　in millions of yen and thousands of U.S. dollars 単位：100万円（1,000米ドル）
in our opinion 私どもの意見では（監査報告書の慣用句），当監査法人の意見では
in percentages 単位：パーセント
in thousands 単位：1,000ドル
inauguration ceremony 就任式，発会式，発足式，落成式，開業式，開通式，開会式，除幕式（＝inaugural ceremony）
▶The presidents of the group companies attended the *inauguration ceremony* at the holding company's head office. グループ企業各社の首脳が，この持ち株会社の本社で開かれた発足式に出席した。

incentive 名 刺激，誘因，動機，励み，奨励，販売奨励金，促進策，振興，報奨，報奨金，出来高払

い, 利点, インセンティブ (⇒shareholders incentives)
average incentive per vehicle 1台当たりの平均販売奨励金
export incentives 輸出振興策
financial incentives 特別手当
foreign tax incentives 外国租税優遇措置
incentive fee 成功報酬, 報奨金, インセンティブ・フィー
incentive payment system 奨励給 (＝incentive system)
incentive program 報奨制度, 勤労奨励制度, 促進計画, 販売促進策
incentive stock option 奨励株式オプション《略 ISO》
incentive stock option plan 奨励株式オプション制度, 自社株購入選択奨励制度
incentive to default デフォルトの誘因
incentive trip 報奨旅行, 報奨ツアー
incentive wage 能率給, 奨励給, 報奨金
interest incentive effect 利子刺激効果
refinancing incentive 借換えの利点
sales incentive 販売奨励金, 販売促進策
shareholders incentives 株主優待
tax incentives 税制上の優遇措置
▸We have offered financial *incentives* to individuals retiring or resigning from the company. 当社は, 早期退職を検討している社員に対して, 特別退職手当を支給しています。

incentive award 奨励報酬, 報奨金
▸During 2007, $13 million was provided for *incentive awards*. 2007年度は, 1,300万ドルの報奨金を計上しました。

incentive compensation plan 奨励報償制度(会社が一定以上の利益を上げたとき, 経営者を対象に規定の報酬以外にボーナスを支払う制度)
▸Under the Corporation's *incentive compensation plan*, its president is to receive a bonus equal to 10% of the Corporation's income before deducting income tax. 当社の奨励報償制度では, 社長は, 法人所得税控除前の当社利益の10%相当のボーナスがもらえる。

incentive plan 報奨制度, 報奨金制度 (＝incentive program, incentive scheme; ⇒RONA)
company executive incentive plan 会社幹部報奨金制度
executive incentive plan 幹部報奨金制度
long-range incentive plan 長期報奨金制度
RONA incentive plan 純資産利益率(RONA)報奨金制度
savings incentive plan 貯蓄奨励制度
▸A new long-range *incentive plan* was established to reward participating elected officers for the Company's achieving outstanding long-range performance. 特に際立った長期業績を会社が達成した場合, それに参加した選任役員に報奨を与えるために, 当社は新しい長期報奨金制度を設けました。

inception 名 開始, 開業, 初め, 発端
inception of operations 営業開始, 事業開始, 開業
inception of the pension plan 年金制度の開始, 年金制度開始年度[採用年度]
▸We have carried no allowance for doubtful accounts from the *inception* of operations in 1990. 1990年の開業時から, 当社は貸倒れ引当金の設定は行っていません。

include 動 含む, 算入する, 組み入れる, 計上する, 処理する, 記載する, 表示する, 掲載する, 収録する (⇒prospectus)
▸In the latest account settlements, banking groups gave up *including* sizable deferred tax assets in their equity capital. 今決算で, 銀行グループは, 巨額の繰延べ税金資産の自己資本への計上を見送った。
▸The Company provides for income taxes based on accounting income for tax purposes *included* in the financial statements. 当社は税務上, 財務書類に表示する会計上の利益に基づいて法人所得税を算定しています。

income 名 利益, 収益, 所得, 損益 (＝earnings; ⇒corporate income, dividend income, net income, operating income)
business income 企業利益, 企業収益, 事業所得
capital income 資本所得, 資本的収入
consolidated income 連結利益
corporate income 法人所得
disposable income 可処分所得
earned income 給与所得, 勤労所得
financial income 財務収益, 金融収益
fixed income security 確定利付き証券
income accrued from domestic sources 国内源泉所得
income and profit 収益と利益
income attributable to ordinary activity 経常損益
income available to common share 普通株配当可能利益
income bond 利益社債, 収益社債, 利益債券
income charges 営業外費用
income deductions 利益控除項目, 収益控除項目, 営業外費用・損失

income earned 稼得利益, 実現利益
income earned abroad 海外収益
income forecast 収益見通し, 収益予想（＝earnings forecast, profit forecast）
income gain 金利・配当収入, インカム・ゲイン, 所得の伸び, 増収
income in advance 前受収益
income loss 減収
interest income 受取利息
investment income 投資利益, 投資収益, 投資所得, 投資収入
national income 国民所得
net income 純利益
nonoperating income 営業外収益
occasional income 一時所得
one-time income 一時所得
ordinary income 経常利益
personal income 個人所得
premium income 保険料収入
real income 実質所得, 実質収益
salary income 給与所得
stock option income ストック・オプション利益
taxable income 課税所得
wage income 賃金所得

▸*Income* includes operating income, restructuring costs, income from equity method investments, dividends received, gain (loss) on sale of securities and interest income.　利益には, 営業利益, 事業再編成費用, 持ち分法による投資利益, 受取配当, 有価証券売却損益と受取利息などが含まれています。

▸The firm failed to declare about ¥3 billion in *income*.　同社は, 所得約30億円を申告しなかった。

▸We saw a decline in *income* related to investments and joint ventures in 2007.　2007年度は, 投資とジョイント・ベンチャー関連の利益が減少しました。

income after … …後の利益, …差引後の利益, …控除後の利益, …考慮後の利益
　income after bonuses but before income taxes 賞与［ボーナス］控除後の税込み利益
　income after taxes 税引き後利益（＝after-tax income）

income before … …前の利益, …差引前の利益, …控除前の利益, …考慮前の利益
　income before accounting changes 会計処理［会計方針］変更前の利益
　income before deducting income tax 所得税控除前の利益
　income before depreciation, interest, and lease payments 減価償却費, 利息, リース料控除前利益
　income before income taxes and others 税金等調整前当期利益
　income before underlisted items 下記項目控除前利益
　income or loss before extraordinary items 異常項目前損益

income before cumulative effects of accounting changes 会計方針［会計処理］の変更による累積的影響額控除前利益, 会計処理の変更による累積的影響額考慮前利益, 会計処理変更の累積的影響前の利益

▸Despite the increase in *income before cumulative effects of accounting* changes, operating cash flows declined in 2007.　会計処理の変更による累積的影響額控除前利益が増加したにもかかわらず, 2007年度の営業活動によるキャッシュ・フローは減少しました。

income before income taxes 税引き前利益, 税引前当期利益, 法人税控除前利益, 法人税考慮前利益
　income before income taxes and bonuses 賞与［ボーナス］控除前の税込み利益
　income before income taxes and extraordinary items 税金および臨時損益項目調整前利益
　income before income taxes and minority interest 法人所得税および少数株主持ち分利益控除前利益

▸The tax effects of restructuring charges were magnified by the lower *income before income taxes*.　法人税考慮前利益が低水準だったため, 事業再編成費用の税効果が拡大しました。

income from … …による利益, …利益
　income from consolidated operations 連結利益, 連結会社利益
　income from continuing operations 継続事業利益, 継続事業による利益, 継続的事業活動による利益
　income from discontinued operations 廃止事業利益
　income from equity investments 株式投資収益
　income from operations 営業利益
　income from sales of securities 有価証券売却益
　income from direct investments 直接投資収益

▸*Income from* direct investments reflected profits made from overseas subsidiaries.　直接投資収益は, 海外子会社から上げた利益を反映しています。

連結損益計算書（Consolidated Income Statement）の表示例（年度, 数値は除く）：

Total revenues	収益合計
Telecommunications operations	通信事業
Operating revenues	営業収益
Operating expenses	営業費用
Net revenues–telecommunications operations	営業利益―通信事業
Telecommunications equipment manufacturing	通信機器製造事業
Revenues	売上高
Cost of revenues and expenses	売上原価および費用
Net revenues–telecommunications equipment manufacturing	営業利益―通信機器製造事業
Financial services	金融サービス
Revenues–Investment and loan income	営業収益―投資および貸付収入
–Fees and commissions	―報酬および手数料
Less: Interest expenses	差引：利子費用
Operating expenses	営業費用
Net revenues–financial services	営業利益―金融サービス
Other operations	その他の事業
Operating revenues	営業収益
Operating expenses	営業費用
Net revenues–other operations	営業利益―その他の事業
Total net revenues	営業利益合計
Other income (expense)	その他の収益（費用）
Equity in net income of associated companies	関連会社持ち分利益
Allowance for funds used during construction	通信設備建設付加コスト
Interest charges	未払い利息
Unrealized foreign currency gains	未実現為替差益
Miscellaneous–net	その他―純額
Income before underlisted items	下記項目控除前利益
Income taxes	法人所得税
Minority interest	少数株主持ち分利益
Net income	純利益
Dividends on preferred shares	優先株式に対する配当金
Net income applicable to common shares	普通株式に帰属する純利益
Earnings per common share	普通株式1株当たり純利益
Dividends declared per common share	普通株式1株当たり配当金
Average common shares outstanding (thousands)	発行済み普通株式平均株式数（千株）

▶*Income from* equity investments declined in 2007 after increasing in 2006. 2007年度の株式投資収益は, 2006年度に増加した後, 減少しました。

income statement 損益計算書《略 I/S》（= earnings statement, income account, profit and loss statement, statement of earnings, statement of income, statement of operations）（1年の会計期間の収益と費用をすべて記載して経常利益を示し, これに特別損益項目を加減して当期純利益を表示するもの）

common-size income statement 百分率損益計算書, 比率表示損益計算書, 共通型損益計算書

comparative income statement 比較損益計算書

condensed income statement 要約損益計算書

consolidated income statement 連結損益計算書

cumulative income statement 累計的損益計算書

forecasted income statement 見積り損益計算書

interim income statement 中間損益計算書

▶We divide the revenues and costs of our core business into three categories on our *income statement*. 当社の損益計算書では, 中核事業の収益と費用を3部門に分類しています。

income statement amounts 損益計算書の金額

▶For operations outside of the U.S. that prepare financial statements in currencies other than the U.S. dollar, we translate *income statement amounts* at average exchange rates for the year. 米ドル以外の通貨建てで財務書類を作成している米国外事業については，損益計算書の金額は事業年度の平均為替レートに基づいて換算されています。

income tax 所得税，法人税，法人所得税
　federal income tax at statutory rate 法定税率による連邦法人税
　income tax allocation 法人税期間配分，税金の期間配分，税効果会計，税金配分会計
　income tax bracket 所得区分
　income tax currently payable 当期未払い法人税等
　income tax currently refundable 当期未収法人税等
　income tax deferrals 繰延べ法人税，繰延べ税金（＝income tax deferred）
　income tax effect 所得税効果，税効果
　income tax liability 未払い所得税
　income tax payable 未払い所得税
　provision for income taxes 法人税等引当金
　▶*Income taxes* are generally not provided on cumulative undistributed earnings of certain non-U.S. subsidiaries. 法人税等は，一般に米国外子会社数社の累積未分配利益については計上されません。

income tax expense 法人税額，法人所得税費用，所得税費用，税金費用（⇒**fourth quarter results**）
　income tax expense and liability 税金費用および未払い税金
　income tax expense at statutory rate 法定税率による法人税額
　▶*Income tax expense* is based on reported earnings before income taxes. 法人所得税費用は，決算報告上の税引き前利益に基づいて算定されています。

income tax payments 法人税等の支払い額
　▶*Income tax payments* were $950 million in 2007. 2007年度の法人税等の支払い額は，9億5,000万ドルでした。

income tax rate 法人税率，所得税率
　▶The consolidated effective *income tax rate* was 40 percent in 2007. 連結実効法人税率は，2007年度は40％でした。

income taxes 法人税等，法人所得税，税金費用，法人税，住民税および事業税（＝taxes on income）
　income taxes—current 当期税額，法人税等—当期分
　income taxes—deferred 法人税等調整額
　income taxes expense 法人税等費用
　income taxes paid 税金支払い額
　income taxes payable 未払い法人税等，未払い税金
　income taxes refundable 未収法人税等，未収税金，還付税額，還付所得税
　▶*Income taxes* are generally not provided on cumulative undistributed earnings of certain non-U.S. subsidiaries. 法人税等は，原則として一部の非米国籍［米国外］子会社の累積未分配利益については計上されていません。

incorporate 動 合併する，編入する，合併させる，会社組織にする，法人化する，〈会社を〉設立する，含む，取り入れる，組み入れる，組み込む，具体化する

incorporated [**incorporate**] 形 合併した，合同した，株式会社の，法人［会社］組織の，有限責任の《略 Inc.》
　incorporated association 社団法人
　incorporated foundation 財団法人
　locally incorporated subsidiary 現地法人（＝incorporated local subsidiary）

incorporation 名 合併，合同，編入，法人団体，会社，法人設立，会社設立
　articles of incorporation 企業の基本定款，設立定款
　incorporation fee 法人設立費

increase 動 増やす，上昇させる，引き上げる，押し上げる，拡大する，高める，伸ばす，強化する，増大する，増加する，増える，伸びる，激化する
　increase one's capital 増資する，資本金を増やす
　increase one's equity ownership 持ち株比率を引き上げる
　increase shareholders' value 株主価値を高める，株主の利益を高める
　▶In the first half of the year, Honda *increased* U.S. market share to 8.9 percent from 8.1 percent. 今年度の上半期に，ホンダは米国でのシェア［市場占有率］を8.1％から8.9％に伸ばした。
　▶To *increase* our presence outside the U.S., we are hiring employees, building plants and forming joint ventures. 米国外での当社の事業基盤を強化するため，当社は従業員の雇用，工場建設や合弁会社の設立に取り組んでいます。

increase 名 増加，増大，伸び，上昇，引上げ，拡大，高まり
　base rate increase 基準金利の引上げ
　dividend increase 増配，配当引上げ（＝increase dividend）
　general capital increase 一般増資

increase of capital stock 増資 （＝increase in capital stock, increase of capital）
increase of sales 売上増加
post a healthy increase 好調な伸びを示す
price increase 価格上昇
rating increase 格上げ
tax increase 増税
wage increase 賃上げ, 賃金引上げ, 賃金の上昇
▶The *increase* in 2007 reflected the strong level of new housing starts.　2007年度のこの伸びは, 新規住宅着工件数の大幅増を反映しています。

increase in ...　…の増加, …の伸び
　increase (decrease) in accounts payable　買掛金の増加(減少)
　increase (decrease) in current liabilities　流動負債の増加(減少)
　increase (decrease) in notes payable　手形借入金の増加(減少)
　increase in a revolving credit facility　回転融資枠の引上げ
　increase in accounts payable　買掛金の増加, 仕入債務増加額, 支払い債務の増加
　increase in accounts receivable　売上債権増加額, 売掛金の増加
　increase in revenues and profits　増収増益, 収益と利益の増加
　increases in income and profit　増収増益
▶Concerning their corporate performance, the Japan's business leaders foresee an *increase in* revenues and profits.　企業の業績について, 日本の企業経営者は増収, 増益を見込んでいる。
▶Ford's *increase in* a revolving credit facility is due to overwhelming support by lenders.　米フォードの回転融資枠引上げは, 金融機関の強力な支援によるものだ。

increased 形　増加した, 増大した, 上昇した, 増えた, …の増加, …の上昇, …の拡大
　increased competition　競争の激化
　increased dividends received　受取配当金の増加
　increased investment　投資の拡大
　increased productivity　生産性の向上, 生産性の伸び
　increased quaterly dividend　四半期増配, 四半期配当の引上げ

increased demand　需要の増加, 需要増, 需要の伸び （＝demand growth）
▶An *increased demand* for steel sheet helped major steelmakers, including Nippon Steel Corp., post record high recurring profits.　鋼板の需要増で, 新日本製鐵など鉄鋼大手の経常利益が, 過去最高を記録した。

increased sales　販売の増加, 販売の伸び, 売上［売上高］の伸び
▶There have been *increased sales* in markets overseas.　海外市場では, 販売が伸びている。

incremental 形　漸増する, 増分の, 積み増しの
　incremental borrowing rate　限界借入利率, 限界借入金利子率
　incremental budget　積み増し予算, 増分主義予算
　incremental common stock　普通株式増加数
　incremental profit　増分利益, 差額利益 （＝incremental benefit）
　incremental revenue　増分収益
▶During 2007, the *incremental* borrowing rate of the Company was 13 percent.　2007年度の当社の限界借入利率は, 13%でした。

incur 動　引き起こす, 発生させる, 招く, 〈損失や損害を〉被る［受ける］, 負う, 負担する, 引き受ける, 負債に陥る
　cost incurred　発生原価
　incur a loss　損失を被る
　incur the borrowing costs　借入［資金調達］コストを負担する
　incur unseen liabilities　不測の債務を負う, 不測の債務が発生する
　incurred cost　発生原価, 賦課原価 （＝cost incurred, incurred expense）
　incurred expense　発生費用 （＝incurred cost）
　losses incurred by writing off nonperforming loans　不良債権処理で生じた損失額
▶The company *incurred* ¥2.5 billion of after-tax losses in its semiannual settlement of accounts.　同社は, 中間決算で税引き後損失が25億円に達した。
▶We *incurred* the following interest costs in connection with these activities.　これらの活動との関連で, 次の利子費用が発生しました。

indebtedness 名　負債, 債務, 負債額, 借入金, 貸付け金
　guarantee of indebtedness　債務保証
　indebtedness of affiliates　関係会社貸付け金
　indebtedness to affiliates　関係会社借入金
　net indebtedness　純負債額, 純借入比率
　over-indebtedness　債務過多
▶Thanks to the inflow of funds from the successful share issue, net *indebtedness* has been markedly reduced.　成功を収めた(新規)株式発行による資金の流入により, 正味負債は大幅に縮小しました。

indemnity 名　補償, 損失補償, 損害填補, 損失補償契約, 補償金, 賠償, 賠償金

income indemnity　所得補償
indemnity against a loss　損失に対する補償, 損失補償
indemnity against liability　免責の補償
right of indemnity　求償権
severance indemnity　退職給与
▶Other liabilities consist principally of *indemnity* and retirement plan reserves for non-U.S. employees.　「その他の負債」の主な内訳は, 米国外の従業員に対する補償と退職給付引当金です。

independence　名　独立, 独立性, 自立, 自主性
auditor's independence　監査人の独立性
independence and integrity　独立性と信頼性
▶We would honor the *independence* of the firm's management.　当社としては, 同社の経営の自主性は尊重したいと思っております。

independent　形　独立した, 自立した, 独立系, 個別の, 自主的な

independent accountant　独立会計士, 独立監査人, 独立した会計監査人(一般に公認会計士をいう)
opinion of independent accountant　独立会計士の監査意見
report of independent accountant　独立会計士の監査報告
▶*Independent accountants* are retained to examine our financial statements.　独立した会計監査人が, 当社の財務書類[財務諸表]を監査しています。

independent auditor　独立監査人, 独立した会計監査人, 外部監査人
independent auditors' report　監査報告書, 独立監査人の報告書, 独立監査人の監査報告書（=report of independent auditors）
▶The audit committee meets periodically with management, the internal auditors and the *independent auditors* to review the manner in which they are performing their responsibilities.　監査委員会は, 経営陣, 内部監査人, 外部監査人[独立監査人]と定期的に会合して, これら経営陣や監査人がどのようにその職責を果たしているかについて検討します。

independent director　社外取締役, 独立取締役
▶Comcast Corp., the nation's largest cable operator, called on Disney's *independent directors* to open talks on its all-stock takeover offer.　米ケーブルテレビ最大手のコムキャストは, ディズニーの社外取締役にコムキャストが提出した全株買取り案[全株買取りによる企業買収提案]の協議開始を求めた。

indirect　形　間接の, 間接的, 二次的な
indirect cost　間接費, 工場間接費（=burden, indirect expense, indirect factory cost, overhead cost）
indirect expense　間接経費, 間接費, 工場間接費（=indirect cost, overhead, supplementary cost）
indirect factory cost　製造間接費, 工場間接費（=indirect cost, indirect expense, overhead）
indirect financing　間接金融（=indirect finance）
indirect labor cost　間接労務費
indirect liablity　間接負債, 偶発債務（=contingent liability）
indirect material cost　間接材料費
indirect selling cost　販売間接費
▶The company did not reveal *indirect* expenses, including fixed-asset taxes and depreciation.　同社は, 固定資産税や減価償却費などの間接費は明らかにしなかった。

individual　形　個人の, 個人的, 個別の, 個々の
individual cost　個別原価
individual depreciation　個別減価償却, 個別償却
individual meeting　個別訪問（=face-to-face meeting：IR活動の一つで, 機関投資家や証券会社に出向いて直接会社の業務内容などを説明）
individual retirement account　個人年金退職金勘定, 個人退職所得勘定, 個人退職金口座制度《略 IRA》
individual retirement savings plan　個人退職貯蓄制度
individual tax on income　個人所得税

industrial engineering　経営工学, 産業工学, 工学技術, インダストリアル・エンジニアリング《略 IE》

industry　名　産業, 工業, 産業界, 工業界, 業界, …業, メーカー
▶Automobile and electric appliance *industries* show good business performance.　自動車と電機業界は, 業績好調だ。
▶Our operations in the financial services and leasing *industry* involve direct financing and finance leasing programs for our products and the products of other companies.　金融サービスとリース業界での当社の事業には, 当社製品と他社製品に関する直接融資とファイナンス・リース事業も含まれています。

industry segment　事業別セグメント, 産業別セグメント, 産業セグメント, 事業区分, 事業分野, 事業部門（=industrial segment）
identifiable assets of an industry segment

産業セグメントの固有資産
industry segment information セグメント情報 (＝industry segment reporting)
operating profit or loss of an industry segment 産業セグメントの営業損益
single industry segment 単一の事業分野, 単一の事業区分
▶This *industry segment* represents more than 90% of consolidated revenue, operating profit and identifiable assets. この事業部門は, 連結総売上高[総収益]と営業利益, 識別可能資産[固有資産]の90%以上を占めています。

infinite 形 不定の, 無限の
infinite service life 不定の使用年数

inflate 動 膨らませる, かさ上げする, 〈価格などを〉つり上げる, 上昇させる, 押し上げる, 誇張する
▶The weak yen has also *inflated* the firm's profits, which were converted into Japanese currency from dollars. 円安も, ドルから円に換算した同社の利益を押し上げた。
▶The banks' equity capital is *inflated* by so-called "deferred tax assets." 銀行の自己資本は, いわゆる「繰延べ税金資産」でかさ上げされている。

inflation 名 インフレ, インフレ率, 物価上昇, 物価上昇率, 一般物価変動, 物価高騰, 通貨膨張, インフレーション
▶The U.S. Labor Department's Consumer Price Index is the most widely used gauge of *inflation*. 米労働省が発表する消費者物価指数は, 最も広く使用されているインフレ[物価上昇率]の基準だ。

information 名 情報, 消息, 知識, ニュース, インフォメーション (⇒**financial information**)
benefit information 給付情報
capsule information 要約情報
corporate information 会社情報
false information 虚偽の情報
individual information 個人情報
information about customers 顧客情報
information disclosure 情報開示, 情報公開
information meeting 企業説明会, 会社説明会, インフォメーション・ミーティング(証券アナリストやファンド・マネージャーなどに対して経営方針や経営理念, 業務内容などを定期的に紹介する企業説明会; ⇒**investor relations**)
information technology bubble IT[情報技術]バブル, ネット株バブル (＝IT bubble, Net bubble)
inside information 内部情報, インサイダー情報, 未公開の重要情報, インサイド情報 (＝insider information)

insider trading information インサイダー取引情報
internal information 内部情報
investment information 投資情報
privileged information 内部情報
public information 公開情報, 情報公開, 広報
rating information 格付け情報
sales information 販売情報
summarized financial information 要約財務情報
supplementary financial information 補足財務情報
▶Individual *information* on credit cards was compromised from August to May. クレジット・カードの個人情報の流出は, 昨年8月から今年の5月にかけて発生した[クレジット・カードの個人情報は, 昨年8月から今年5月にかけて漏れた]。

infringe on [**upon**] ... …を侵害する, …に違反する
▶Sharp has accused manufacturers in Taiwan of *infringing on* its intellectual property rights. シャープは, 同社の知的財産権侵害で台湾メーカーを訴えた。

ingredient 名 要素, 要因, 構成要素, 必要な条件, 成分, 成分表示, 材料, 原材料, 原料
expired ingredient 消費期限切れの原材料
ingredient costs 原料コスト
key ingredient 主要要件, 重要な要素[要因]
mix of ingredient 〚the ～〛成分の構成, 構成要素[材料]の組合せ
▶As we move forward, our commitment to the communities in which we work is an essential *ingredient*. 企業活動を推進するにあたって, 私たちが業務展開している地域社会に対する企業責任の遂行は, 必要不可欠の条件となっています。
▶Fujiya Co. used expired *ingredients* in its products. 不二家は, 商品に消費期限切れの原材料を使用していた。

inhouse [**in-house**] 形 社内の, 企業内の, 組織内の, 内部の
inhouse company 社内カンパニー, 分社
inhouse processing 内製, 内部処理
inhouse publication [**newsletter**] 社内報
inhouse rule 社内規則
▶Compliance officers check whether the activities of company executives and employees are legal and comply with *in-house rules*. コンプライアンス・オフィサーは, 経営者と従業員の活動が合法的に行われているかどうか, また社内の規則に従って行われているかどうかをチェックする。

inhouse investigation 社内調査, 内部調査
▶Six major nonlife insurers found the nonpayment of third-sector insurance money through *inhouse investigations*. 損害保険大手6社の第三分野保険の保険金不払いは, 社内調査で判明した.

initial 形 最初の, 初めの, 初期の, 期首の, 当初の, 設立時の
  initial balance 期首残高 (=beginning balance)
  initial investment 初期投資, 初期投資額, 原始投資, 原初投資
  initial measurements 原始計測値(取引を初めて記帳する際の金額)
  initial price 初値(はつね), 初回価格 (=initial share price, initial stock price)

initial capital 当初資本, 期首資本, 当初資金, 〈保険会社の〉基金(株式会社の資本金に相当)
  initial capital requirements 当初自己資本比率規定
▶The new Net bank whose *initial capital* is ¥20 billion started operations in the first half of fiscal 2007. 新ネット銀行は, 当初資本が200億円で, 2007年度上半期から業務を開始した.

initial development 初期開発
▶The company is excellent in its total production system, from the *initial development* and design through to procurement and production. 同社は, 初期開発と設計から調達と生産までのトータルな生産方式が特に優れている.

initial estimate 当初予想, 当初見積り, 当初見積り額 (=original estimate)
▶The firm is lilely to book an operating loss of ¥60 billion in a turnabout from an *initial estimate* of ¥14 billion in profit. 同社は, 当初の140億円の利益予想から一転して, 600億円の営業赤字[営業損失]になる見通しだ.

initial payment 頭金, 一時金, 契約金 (=initial sum)
▶Under the new installment system of the company, purchasers are not required to pay *initial payments*. 同社の新割賦制度では, 購入者は頭金を支払う必要がない.

initial projection 当初予想, 当初の見通し
▶The company's operating profit from cell phone and digital camera operations is expected to be ¥20 billion lower than its *initial projection*. 同社の携帯電話事業とデジタル・カメラ事業の営業利益は, 同社の当初予想を200億円下回ると予想されている.

initial public offering 株式公開, 新規株式公開, 新規株式公募, 新規公募, 上場直前の公募, 第1回株式公募, 株式の公開公募, 上場《略 IPO》 (=debut, initial public offer; ⇒ **public offering**)
  IPO [公開公募・新規公募]とは ➡ 証券取引所に株式を新規公開するなどして, 企業が一般投資家に株式を初めて売り出すこと. 一般には, 引受業務を担当する投資銀行が, 発行会社から株式をまとめて買い取って一般の投資家に売り出す. すでに株式を公開している企業が一般投資家に新規発行株式を売り出す場合を, 公募(public offering)あるいは募集(primary offering)という.
  initial public offering price 公募価格, 売出価格, 公募売出価格
▶In September 2007 we sold 6,000,000 share of common stock in an *initial public offering*. 2007年9月に, 当社は第一回株式公募で600万株の普通株式を売り出しました.

initiative 名 独創力, 独自性, 自主性, 率先, 主導権, 主導, 議案提出権, 発議, 発案, 提案, …案, 政策, 構想, 方針, イニシアチブ
▶The Corporation is trying to restructure itself under the *initiative* of its banks. 当社は, 取引銀行主導のもとに再建を目指しています.

injection 名 注入, 投入, 供給
  capital injection 資本の注入, 資本の増強, 増資, 〈保険会社への〉基金拠出, 〈保険会社の〉基金増資 (=capital increase)
  injection of equity 増資
  injection of public funds 公的資金の注入, 公的資金の投入
  liquidity injection 流動性の供給
▶This life insurer sought capital *injection* of 70 billion yen from financial institutions. この生命保険会社は, 金融機関に700億円の基金拠出[基金増資]を要請した.

ink an agreement 契約書[協定書]に署名する, 契約を結ぶ, 協定を結ぶ
▶NTT DoCoMo and Lawson have *inked* a business and capital tie-up *agreement*. NTTドコモとローソンが, 資本・業務提携契約を締結した.

innovation 名 革新, 革新性, 刷新, 斬新, 改革, 変革, 開発, 新制度, 〈新制度などの〉導入, 画期的な新製品, 新機軸, 新工夫, 新手法, 新発明, 技術革新, イノベーション
  business innovation 経営革新
  capital-intensive innovation 資本集約的技術革新
  export-biased innovation 輸出偏向型技術革新
  innovations in the distribution industry 流通業界の革新
  labor-saving innovation 労働集約的技術革新

pace-setting innovation 先駆的な技術革新
process innovation 生産工程の刷新・革新, 生産工程の技術革新, プロセス・イノベーション
product innovation 製品開発, 商品開発, 画期的な新製品, 製品イノベーション
resource-intensive innovation 資源集約的技術革新
technical innovation 技術革新 (＝technological innovation)
▸The telecommunications business faces continued technological *innovation*. 通信業界は, なお技術革新が続いている.
▸We are a company that not only embraces change, but leads it through pace-setting *innovations*. 当社は, 変化に対応するだけでなく, 先駆的な技術革新を通して変革をリードしています.

innovative 形 革新的な, 斬新な, 新機軸の, 画期的な, 新しい, 最新の (＝innovatory)
▸Japanese firms face the task of developing *innovative* value-added goods and services. 日本企業は, 課題として革新的な付加価値商品とサービスの開発が求められている.
▸The company pioneered a variety of *innovative* promotions to add new accounts. 同社は, 各種の斬新な販促活動によって, 新口座を増やしました.

insider 名 インサイダー (証券の投資判断に影響を及ぼす未公開の重要情報を知ることができる立場にいる公開会社の役員や取締役, 主要株主などをいう), 内部者, 関係者
insider dealing インサイダー取引
insider information インサイダー[内部]情報
insider trading インサイダー取引, 内部者取引 (＝insider dealing, insider stock trading：内部情報(insider information)を利用して証券取引を行うこと)
▸The former head of the company engaged in *insider* trading and obtained unfair benefits. 同社の元代表は, インサイダー取引に手を染め, 不当な利益を上げていた.

insolvency 名 支払い不能, 債務超過, 倒産, 破綻 (＝bankruptcy, business failure)
file for insolvency proceedings with ... ...に破綻処理手続きを申請する
obligor insolvency 債務者の支払い不能
practical insolvency 実質的破産

insolvent 形 支払い不能の, 返済不能の, 債務超過の, 倒産した, 破綻した
▸The Corporation took over millions of yen in personal and corporate debts of the *insolvent* company. 当社は, 債務超過の同社の個人債務や法人債務数百万円の肩代わりをした.

insolvent 名 支払い不能者, 破産者
install [instal] 動 〈設備を〉取り付ける, 設置する, インストールする
installment [instalment] 名 分割払い, 割賦払い, 月賦払い, 割賦金 (＝easy payment)
consumer installment credit 消費者信用残高, 消費者信用
installment (account) payable 割賦未払い金
installment (account) receivable 割賦売掛金, 割賦未収金, 割賦債権
installment acquisition 分割購入
installment basis 回収基準
installment method 割賦基準, 回収基準
installment receivables 割賦売掛金, 割賦未収金
installment sales 割賦販売, 割賦販売高, 割賦売上, 掛売上高, 延べ払い
make payments in installments 割賦返済する
monthly installment sales 月賦販売, 月賦
redemption by yearly installment 年賦償還
▸The principal items making up the deferred tax provision for 2007 included $250 million for sales-type leases and *installment* sales. 2007年の繰延べ税額を構成する主な項目には, 販売型リースと割賦販売の2億5,000万ドルも含まれています.

institution 名 機関, 金融機関, 組織, 法人, 業, 会社, 施設 (⇒financial institution)
▸As ways to fend off takeovers, it is highly likely that Japanese financial *institutions* will aim to become conglomerates. 買収への防衛策として, 日本の金融機関が複合企業化を目指す可能性が高い.

institutional investor 機関投資家 (＝institutional lender)
▸Mitsubishi Tokyo Financial Group Inc. will issue ¥165 billion worth of preferred securities to *institutional investors*. 三菱東京フィナンシャル・グループは, 機関投資家向けに1,650億円の優先出資証券を発行する.

insurance 名 保険, 保険契約, 保険金額, 保険金, 保険料, 保険条件
accident insurance 災害保険
annuity insurance 年金保険
business insurance 事業保険
casualty insurance 損害保険, 災害保険
cargo insurance 貨物保険
corporate employees' pension insurance plan 厚生年金保険
corporate insurance 企業保険
cost, insurance and freight 運賃保険料込み値段《略 CIF》

employment insurance 雇用保険
exchange risk insurance 為替変動保険
financial insurance 融資保険
government-run nursing care insurance system 介護保険制度
group insurance 団体保険
health insurance society 健康保険組合
insurance amount 保険金額
insurance benefits 保険給付金
insurance claims 損害保険の請求額, 未収保険金, 保険金
insurance coverage 保険担保; 保険の付保; 付保危険
insurance dividend 保険契約者配当金
insurance expense 未払い保険料
insurance general expense 保険一般経費
insurance money 保険金
insurance revenue 保険料収入 (＝insurance premium revenue)
keyman insurance 経営者保険
medical insurance 医療保険
mutual insurance 相互保険
nonlife insurance 損害保険
pension insurance 年金保険
prepaid insurance 前払い保険料 (＝prepaid insurance premium)
unemployment insurance 失業保険

insurance contract 保険契約
▶The Insurance Business Law prohibits life insurers from lowering their promised yield rates on existing *insurance contracts* prior to their collapse. 保険業法は, 生命保険会社が破綻前に既契約分の保険契約の予定利率を引き下げることを禁止している。

insurance policyholder 保険契約者
▶There is a negative spread between the yield guaranteed to *insurance policyholders* and their investment returns. 今は, 保険契約者に保証した利回り[予定利率]と運用利回りが逆ざや状態(運用利回りが保険契約者に保証した利回りを下回る状態)にある。

insurance premium 保険料 (＝insurable expense, insurance expense)
  insurance premium revenue 〔保険〕保険料収入 (＝premium revenue : 一般企業の売上高にあたる)
▶The *insurance premiums* are determined by the age and other characteristics of policyholders. この保険料は, 保険加入者の年齢などの特性に応じて決められる。

insurance underwriting 保険引受け
▶The five business fields in the tie-up agreement are product development, marketing, *insurance underwriting*, damage assessment and reinsurance. 提携契約の5業務分野は, 商品開発, マーケティング, 保険引受け, 損害査定と再保険である。

insurer 名 保険会社, 保険業者, 保険者, 保証人 (＝insurance company, insurance enterprise, insurance frim)
▶The *insurer* aimed to improve profitability by being reluctant to pay insurance benefits. この保険会社は, 保険金の支払いを渋って収益の向上を目指した。

intangible 形 無形の, 無体の, 実体のない
  intangible development cost 開発費
  intangible right 無体権
  noncurrent intangible assets 長期の無形資産
  transfer or use of intangible property 無形財産[資産]の譲渡または使用

intangible asset 無形資産, 無体資産, 無形固定資産, のれん (＝intangible property, intangibles : 営業権, 知的所有権(特許権・商標権・著作権・ノウハウ), 借地権, 鉱業権など無形の事実上の資産)

intangibles 名 無形資産, 無形財産, 無形固定資産, 無体項目 (＝intangible asset, intangible property : 特許権や著作権などの無体財産のほか, のれんやフランチャイズ権など)
  amortization of intangibles 無形資産の償却
  intangibles tax 無形財産取引税
  intangibles, deferred charges and other assets 無体項目, 繰延べ項目およびその他資産
  nonfinancial intangibles 非金融無形資産
  valuation and amortization of intangibles 無益資産の評価と償却

integral part 不可欠な一部, 不可分の一体, 構成部分, 構成要素
▶The accompanying Notes to Financial Statements are an *integral part* of the consolidated financial statements. 添付の財務書類注記は, この連結財務書類の不可欠な一部です。

integrate 動 統合する, 一本化する, 一元化する, 一体化する, 統一する, 系列化する, 一貫生産する
  be integrated into ... …に溶け込む
  horizontally integrated 水平統合された, 水平統合
  integrate businesses 経営統合する (＝integrate operations)
  integrated foreign operations 一体化した海外事業
  integrated production site 一貫生産拠点

vertically integrated marketing 販売の垂直統合，一貫販売体制
▶Both insurance companies do not plan to *integrate* their information systems for the time being.　両保険会社は当面，情報システムの統合を行う計画はない。
▶Oji turned to Hokuetsu's shareholders for their decision on whether to *integrate* with Oji or remain independent.　王子製紙は，北越製紙の株主に対して，王子と経営統合するか独立路線を堅持するかの判断を仰いだ。

integrate operations 経営統合する（＝integrate businesses, integrate management）
▶Within one year from the stock transfer, both companies are to *integrate operations*.　株式譲渡から1年以内に，両社は経営統合する。

integrated operations 一体化した事業，統合事業，経営統合，事業統合，一貫した体制，一貫生産体制
▶*Integrated operations* are those whose economic activities have a direct effect on the cash flows and operations of the parent company.　一体化した事業とは，その経済活動が親会社のキャッシュ・フローと事業に直接影響を与える事業のことです。

integration 名　統合，経営統合，一本化，一元化，一体化，統一，〈企業の〉系列化，集約化，環境への適応，一体感，人種統合，人種差別撤廃（⇒ **management integration, process**）
▶We have submitted a business *integration* proposal to the firm to acquire all of its ordinary shares through a takeover bid.　株式公開買付け（TOB）で同社の普通株式を全株取得するため，当社は同社に経営統合案を提出しました［経営統合を申し入れました］。

integrity and objectivity of the financial statements 財務書類の完全性と客観性
▶Management is responsible for the preparation, *integrity and objectivity of the financial statements* and all other financial information included in this report.　経営者は，本報告書に記載した連結財務書類その他すべての財務情報の作成とその完全性および客観性に責任を負っています。

integrity and reliability of the financial statements 財務書類の完全性と信頼性
▶Corporation's internal controls are designed to provide reasonable assurance as to the *integrity and reliability of the financial statements*.　当社の内部統制は，財務書類の完全性と信頼性につい

て十分保証するよう図られています。

intellectual asset 知的資産
▶*Intellectual assets* include industrial expertise and brands, in addition to intellectual properties such as patents.　知的資産には，特許などの知的財産のほかに，企業のノウハウやブランドなどが含まれる。

intellectual property 知的財産，知的所有権，知的財産権（＝intellectual property right）
▶We continually assess the relationship between our company and others in our industry with regard to the protection of our *intellectual properties*.　当社の知的財産の保護に関しましては，私どもは当社と業界他社との関係を絶えず見直しております。

intellectual property dispute 知的財産権紛争
▶Toshiba Corp. has settled an *intellectual property dispute* over flash memory chips with U.S. semiconductor maker Micron Technology.　東芝は，フラッシュメモリ・チップ（電気的に一括消去・再書込みが可能なメモリ・チップ）をめぐるマイクロン・テクノロジー社（米国の半導体メーカー）との知的財産権紛争に決着をつけた。

intellectual property right 知的所有権，知的財産権《略 **IPR**》（＝intellectual property）
知的所有権に含まれるもの：

copyright	著作権
database	データベース
computer program	コンピュータ・プログラム
knowhow	ノウハウ
patent	特許権
registered design	意匠権
registered trademark	商標権
software	ソフトウエア
trade secret	企業秘密，トレード・シークレット
utility model	実用新案権

intensify 動　強める，高める，強化する，増強する，激化する，強くなる，高まる，活発になる
　intensified global competition グローバル競争の激化
　intensified price competition 価格競争の激化
▶GM has been *intensifying* efforts to reduce costs and improve quality.　GMは，コスト削減策と品質改善策を強化している。

interarea accounts receivable 地域間の売掛金
▶*Interarea accounts receivable* and the unamortized portion of service charges have been

eliminated in consolidation. 各地域間の売掛金とサービス料の未償却部分は、連結決算上、消去されています。

interarea transfers 地域間振替え
▶*Interarea transfers* consist principally of completed machines, subassemblies and parts, and software. 地域間振替えの内訳は、主に完成機械、半製品・部品とソフトウエアとなっています。

intercompany 形 会社間の、親子会社間の、内部の
intercompany debt 会社間負債, 内部負債
intercompany interest 会社間利息
intercompany investment 会社間投資, 内部投資
intercompany loan 会社間貸付け, 関係会社からの借入金
intercompany loss 会社間損失, 会社相互間損失
intercompany profit and loss 内部損益, 連結未実現損益
intercompany receivables 会社間債権債務
intercompany sales 会社間売上, 内部取引高

intercompany accounts 会社間[連結会社間]勘定, 親子間勘定
▶All significant *intercompany accounts* and transactions are eliminated in consolidation. 連結上, 連結会社間の重要な勘定と取引はすべて相殺消去されています。

intercompany advances 会社間貸付け金, 親子会社間[連結会社間]貸付け金
▶Revenues and expenses, including gains and losses on foreign exchange transactions other than long-term *intercompany advances*, are translated at average rates for the period. 収益と費用は, 親子[連結]会社間の長期貸付け金以外の外貨建て取引から生じる損益を含めて, 期中平均為替レートで換算されています。

intercompany profit 会社間利益, 会社相互間利益, 内部利益
▶*Intercompany profits* are eliminated in connection with preparation of the consolidated financial statements. 連結財務書類作成上, 内部利益は消去されています。

intercompany transaction 会社間取引, 親子会社間取引, 内部取引, 関係会社間取引, 連結会社間取引(同一会社内の本支店間の取引関係)
▶All other significant *intercompany transactions* have been eliminated in the consolidated financial statements. 他の主要な内部取引は, すべて連結財務書類上, 消去されています。

interest 名 利息, 利子, 金利, 株, 持ち分, 利益, 権益, 利権, 利害関係, 関係者, 同業者, 業界, 企業…側

actual interest 実効金利 (＝actual interest rate)
arrear of interest 遅延利子, 遅延利息 (＝delayed interest)
back interest 未払い利息
bond interest 社債利息, 債券利息
business interests 企業利益
competing interests 競業利益, 利害の対立
compounded interest 複利 (＝compound interest, interest upon interest)
debenture interest 社債利息
ex interest 利落ち
financial interest 財務上の利害関係, 経済的利害関係, 投資関係者
interest accrued 未払い利息, 未収利息
interest advance 前払い利息
interest and dividend income 受取利息および配当金 (＝interest and dividends received)
interest and dividends received 受取利息および配当
interest charge 支払い利息
interest earned 未収利息
interest, gain on securities sold, dividends and other 受取利息, 有価証券売却益, 配当他
interest paid 支払い利息
interest payable 未払い利息
interest prepaid 前払い利息
interest receivable 未収利息
interest received 受取利息
loan interest 貸付け利子
majority interest 過半数持ち分
market interest 市場実勢金利
minority interest 少数株主持ち分
negative interest マイナスの金利
nominal interest 表面利率, 名目金利
paid interest 返済利息
remaining interest 残余権 (＝residual interest)
security interest 有価証券利息, 担保権
simple interest 単利
stock interest 株式持ち分
stockholder's interest 株主持ち分
system of interest 金利体系
vested interest 既得権, 既得権益, 確定権利

▶During 2007, the total amount of *interest* by the Company was $100,000. 2007年度の当社の支払い利息総額は, 10万ドルでした。

▶We have a 49% *interest* in a joint venture with the company. 同社との合弁事業[合弁会社]に対して, 当社は49％の持ち分を所有しています。

▶We seek a healthy balance between business *interests* and environmental protection.　当社は，企業利益と環境保護との健全なバランスを求めています．

interest-bearing 形　利付きの，有利子の，利息条件付きの
　interest-bearing notes　利息付き手形
　interest-bearing notes receivable　利息条件付き受取手形
　interest-bearing receivable　利付き債権
　interest-bearing security　利付き証券

interest-bearing bank deposits　利付き銀行預金
▶Other securities consist of marketable securities and *interest-bearing bank deposits* with varied maturity dates.　「その他の有価証券」の内訳は，市場性ある有価証券と満期日が異なる利付き銀行預金です．

interest-bearing debt　有利子負債（＝interest bearing liability：金利を付けて返済しなければならない債務）
▶We had about ¥1 trillion of *interest-bearing debts* as of the end of December 2007.　2007年12月末時点で，当社は約1兆円の有利子負債を抱えています．

interest cost　利息費用，利子費用，支払い利息（＝interest charge, interest expense）
　interest cost on accumulated postretirement benefit obligation　累積退職後給付債務の利子費用
　interest cost on the projected benefit obligation　予定給付債務の利息費用［利子費用］

interest coverage ratio　利払い余力率，利子支払い保証倍率，インタレスト・カバレッジ比率，インタレスト・カバレッジ・レシオ（＝interest cover, interest coverage, times interest covered, times interest earned ratio：企業の金利支払い能力を見る指標）
▶*Interest coverage ratio* is calculated as income divided by interest expense.　利払い余力率は，利益を支払い利息で割って［除して］算出します．

interest expense　支払い利息，利息費用，利子費用（＝interest charge, interest cost；⇒**accured liabilities, refinancing**）
▶The Company's cash payments for *interest expense* were $200 million in 2007.　当社の支払い利息（計上額）のうち現金支払い額は，2007年度は2億ドルでした．

interest income　受取利息，利息収益，利息収入，金利収入

interest income (adjusted to restate tax-exempt income to a taxable equivalent amount)　受取利息(非課税所得を課税額ベースで調整)
　interest income before amortization　償却前受取利息

Interest Limitation Law　［日］利息制限法
▶Most consumer financing firms offer loans at gray-area interest rates somewhere between the two upper limits under the *Interest Limitation Law* and the Investment Deposit and Interest Rate Law.　ほとんどの消費者金融会社は，利息制限法と出資法の2つの上限金利間のグレーゾーン金利で融資している．

interest on ...　…の利子，…の利息
　interest on borrowings　借入金利子，借入金利息（＝interest on loans）
　interest on debt　支払い利息
　interest on lendings　貸出金利息
　interest on loans　借入金の金利，借入金利息，貸付け金利息，貸付け利子，貸出金利（＝interest on borrowings, interest rate on loans）
　interest on security　有価証券利息
▶During 2007, *interest on* borrowings amounted to $1,100 million.　2007年度の借入金利息は，11億ドルに達しました．

interest payment　利払い，金利の支払い，利子支払い，利息の返済，支払い利息
▶This was considered as *interest payments* and did not reduce the principal of their loan.　これは利払いと見なされたため，借入金の元本は減らなかった．

interest rate　金利，利息，利子率，利率（⇒**borrowing, carry trade, key interest rate, long-term interest rate**）
　compound interest rate　複利
　fixed interest rate　固定金利
　floating interest rate　変動金利
　implicit interest rate　包括利率
　interest rate cut　金利の引下げ，利下げ
　interest rate hike　金利上昇，利上げ，金利引上げ（＝interest rate increase）
　interest rate on loans　貸出金利（＝interest on loans, loan interest rate）
　legal ceiling on interest rates　法定金利の上限（＝legal cap on interest rates, legal interest rate cap, legal interest rate ceiling）
　market interest rate　市中金利，市場金利（＝open market rate）
　preferential interest rate for companies　企

業向け融資の優遇金利
ultralow interest rates　超低金利
upper limit of interest rates　金利の上限, 上限金利
zero-interest rate policy　ゼロ金利政策
▶Should the *interest rate* rise, it will become more expensive for companies to borrow money.　金利が上昇すると［金利上昇局面では］, 企業の資金調達コストが重くなる。

interest rate swap　金利スワップ　(＝interest swap：同一通貨間で固定金利と変動金利の債権または債務を交換する取引)
　interest rate swap agreement　金利スワップ契約　(＝interest rate swap contract)
　interest rate swap bond　金利スワップ債　(＝interest swap bond)
▶We enter into *interest rate swap* agreements to manage our exposure to changes in interest rates.　金利変動リスクに対処するため, 当社は金利スワップ契約を結んでいます。

interest revenue　受取利息, 利息収益, 利息収入, 利子収入　(＝interest received)
▶The finance subsidiary's *interest revenue* is included in the Corporation's consolidated net sales.　金融子会社の受取利息は, 当社の連結売上高［純売上高］に含まれています。

interested persons　利害関係者　(＝interested parties, interest group, interest parties：株主や債権者, 取引先, 顧客などをいう)

intergeographic transfer　(⇒intersegment)

interim 形　中間の, 半期の, 期中の, 中間会計期間の, 暫定的な, 一時的な, 仮の
　interim closing　中間決算, 半期決算　(＝interim earnings report, interim financial results, interim results)
　interim earnings report　中間決算, 中間決算報告, 中間利益報告書　(＝interim financial results, interim results, midterm earnings report)
　interim financial report　中間財務報告, 中間財務報告書　(＝interim report, interim financial information)
　interim net profit　中間期の純利益, 半期の純利益, 中間期の税引き後利益
　interim operating profit　中間期の営業利益, 半期の営業利益
　interim settlement of accounts　中間決算

interim dividend payout　中間配当支払い, 中間配当支払い額
▶Both *interim* and year-end *dividend payouts* are each projected at ¥3 per share.　中間配当と期末配当の支払い額は, それぞれ1株当たり3円となる見込みです。

interim financial results report　中間決算報告
▶Many companies have announced an increase in cash dividends in their *interim financial results reports*.　中間決算報告で, 配当金の引上げを発表する企業が多かった。

interim profit　中間期の利益, 半期利益, 半期決算利益
▶*Interim profit* increased 8 percent from the year before.　同社の半期決算利益は, 前年同期比で8％増加した。

interim report　中間報告, 中間決算報告, 半期報告, 半期報告書　(＝midterm report)
▶The domestic life insurance companies released *interim reports* on the results of their in-house probes.　国内の生命保険各社が, 社内調査の結果に関する中間報告を発表した。

internal 形　内部の, 社内の, 国内の
　internal capital generation　内部資本形成, 留保利益
　internal capital growth　内部資本形成率
　internal cash　内部資金, 内部キャッシュ
　internal fund　内部資金, 自己資金
　internal investigation　社内調査, 内部調査　(＝in-house investigation)
　internal profit　内部利益
　internal rate of return　内部利益率, 内部収益率《略 IRR》
　internal transfer profit　内部振替利益, 本支店振替利益

internal accounting control　内部会計統制, 会計に関する内部統制
▶The *internal accounting control* process includes management's communication to employees of policies which govern ethical business conduct.　会計に関する内部統制の手順には, 経営者の従業員に対する倫理的業務活動に関する方針［倫理的業務遂行の管理方針］の通達も含まれています。

internal audit［**auditing**］　内部監査
▶Outside directors chair the *internal audit* and compliance committee, the nomination committee and the compensation committee.　外部取締役は, 内部監査・法令遵守委員会, 指名委員会と報酬委員会の各委員長を務めています。

internal auditor　内部監査人　(⇒monitor)
▶Periodically, the *internal auditors* and the independent auditors meet privately with the audit committee.　定期的に, 内部監査人と外部監査人

は監査委員会と非公式に会合しています。

internal control 内部統制, 社内管理, 内部チェック, 内部チェック体制 (「内部統制」は, 粉飾決算や経営者の不正・ごまかしなど, 企業の不祥事を防ぐため, 社内の管理・点検体制を整え, 絶えずチェックすることをいう。日本の上場企業は, 2008年度から内部統制に関する報告が義務付けられている。⇒**accountability**)
  assurance on internal control 内部統制についての保証
  evaluation of internal control 内部統制の評定, 内部統制の信頼性の評価
  internal control structure 内部統制機構, 内部統制構造
  ▸To maintain its system of *internal controls*, management carefully selects key personnel and establishes the organizational structure to provide an appropriate division of responsibility. 内部統制組織を維持するため, 経営陣は幹部要員を慎重に選定し, その責任分担を的確に行う組織機構を確立しています。

internal control system 内部統制組織, 内部統制機構 (=system of internal controls)
  ▸Our *internal control system* is reviewed, evaluated and revised as necessary in light of the results of constant management oversight, internal and independent audits, changes in our business and other conditions. 当社の内部統制組織は, 経営者の不断の監視, 内部監査や外部監査, 当社の事業やその他の条件の変動などに照らして随時, 必要に応じて見直し, 評価し, 改善を重ねています。

internal growth 内部成長
  ▸To promote the *internal growth* of ABC Inc. and the value of its shares, the proportion of earnings invested in the corporation should be permitted to grow. ABC社の内部成長を促し, 当社株式の価値を高めるためには, 収益のうち当社自体に対する投資比率を引き上げる必要があります。

internal management system 内部管理体制
  ▸The bank had problems with its *internal management system* and other business schemes. 同行は, 内部管理体制など業務体制に問題があった。

internal resources 内部資金, 手元資金
  ▸The company plans to make initial investments of about ¥200 billion from *internal resources*. 同社では, 当初の約2,000億円の投資額は内部資金 [手元資金] を充てる計画だ。

Internal Revenue Code 内国歳入法, 内国歳入法典《略 IRC》(米国の連邦税法)
  ▸The Company's policy is to fund the maximum amount allowable based on funding limitations of the *Internal Revenue Code*. 当社は, 内国歳入法の拠出限度額に基づいて許容できる最高の金額を拠出する方針です。

Internal Revenue Service 〖米〗内国歳入庁《略 IRS》
  ▸The *Internal Revenue Service* has examined and accepted income tax returns of the Company. 米内国歳入庁は, 当社の所得税申告書を調査して, これを承認しました。

internally generated funds 内部調達資金 (⇒**generate**)

international 国際的, 国際間の, 国際上の, インターナショナル
  international busines activities 国際事業活動, 国際ビジネス
  international business strategy 国際事業戦略, 国際企業戦略, グローバル戦略 (=global business strategy)
  international consortium 国際共同事業体, 国際借款団, 国際融資団
  international double taxation 国際二重課税 (=international double tax)
  international lending 国際融資, 対外融資
  international loan 対外融資, 国際貸付け
  International Organization for Standardization 国際標準化機構《略 IOS》(=International Standardization Organization)
  international tax convention [treaty] 国際租税条約
  ▸*International* businesses performed particularly well, with increased sales in Japan, other Pacific Rim countries and Europe. 国際事業部門の業績はとくに好調で, 日本その他の環太平洋諸国と欧州で売上が増加しました。

International Accounting Standards 国際会計基準《略 IAS》(⇒**International Financial Reporting Standards, material respect**)
  国際会計基準について ➡ 米国の企業会計基準と並ぶ世界の2大会計基準。国際会計基準は, 欧州が主導する国際会計基準審議会(IASB)が作成している。欧州各国のほかに, ロシア, オーストラリア, 中南米諸国など約90か国が採用を決めている。欧州連合(EU)は, 2005年から域内の上場企業に国際会計基準の決算開示を義務付け, 2007年からは域内上場の外国企業にもEUの国際基準と同レベルの開示を求めている。日本の会計基準は, 1999年度に連結会計とキャッシュ・フロー計算書, 税効果会計, 2000年度に退職給付会計や金融商品の時価会計, 2005

年度から減損会計が導入された。その結果，日本の会計基準は現在，国際基準と基本的に同等であるとの評価が得られるようになった。なお，国際会計基準審議会(IASB)が設定する国際会計基準のIASは，2005年1月1日から新しい呼び名として「国際財務報告基準(International Financial Reporting Standards)に改められた。

international activities 国際事業
▸All *international activities* provided 25 percent of consolidated revenues in 2007. 2007年度は，国際事業が連結収益の25%を占めました。

international competition 国際競争 (= global competition)
▸As a measure against drops in sales prices due to *international competition*, Canon has made efforts to emphasize the production of value-added products. 国際競争による売価低下への対抗策として，キヤノンは高付加価値製品の生産に重点を置いている。

International Financial Reporting Standards 国際財務報告基準 《略 IFRS》(国際会計基準審議会(IASB)が設定するIAS（国際会計基準）の新しい呼び名で，2005年1月1日に採択された：⇒**International Accounting Standards**)
▸*International Financial Reporting Standards* (IFRS) were adopted as from 1 January 2005. 国際財務報告基準(IFRS)は，2005年1月1日に採択された。
▸The Group's sales figures have been restated following the retrospective application of new *International Financial Reporting Standards*. 当グループの売上高の数値は，新国際財務報告基準(IFRS)を遡及的に適用して，再表示されています。

international market 国際市場 (= global market)
▸We will expand our presence and improve customer service and support in all markets, particularly the *international market*. 当社は，とくに国際市場を中心に，全市場で当社の事業基盤を拡大し，顧客サービスと顧客支援体制を強化・改善する方針です。

international operations 国際事業，海外事業，海外事業活動，国際業務
▸Revenues from *international operations* in 2007 decreased 16 percent from $242 million (five percent of total revenues) in 2006. 2007年度の国際事業部門の売上高は，前年度の2億4,200万ドル（総売上高の5％）から16％減少しました。

Internet bank ネット銀行
▸The new *Internet bank* will be equally owned by the two firms with initial capital of ¥20 billion. 新ネット銀行は，当初資本が200億円で，両社が折半出資する。

Internet-based banking venture ネット専業銀行業務
▸An *Internet-based banking venture* between the firms will handle deposits, foreign echange, small business and personal loans and sales of securities and other investment products. 両社のネット専業銀行業務では，預金や外国為替，中小企業や個人向け融資のほかに，有価証券その他の投資商品の販売も取り扱う。

Internet business ネット事業，インターネット事業
▸In the *Internet business*, the domestic three leading newspapers will open a joint news Web site early next year. インターネット事業で，国内大手新聞3社が来年（2008年）初めに共同ニュース・サイトを開設する。

Internet service provider business インターネット[ネット]接続サービス事業
▸We span off our *Internet service provider business* on July 1, 2007. 当社は，自社で運営しているインターネット接続サービス事業を，2007年7月1日付けで分社化しました。

Internet shopping mall operator インターネット上の仮想商店街運営会社，仮想商店街の運営会社 (= Net shopping mall operator, online shopping mall operator)
▸NTT DoCoMo Inc. formed a capital tie-up with *Internet shopping mall operator* Rakuten Inc. in the Internet auction business. NTTドコモが，インターネット・オークション事業で電子商取引大手の楽天[仮想商店街を運営している楽天]と資本提携した。

interperiod tax allocation 法人税等の期間配分[期間相互配分]，年度間税配分，税効果 (= interperiod allocation, interperiod income tax allocation, interperiod tax allocation)

interpolation 名 補間，内挿

intersegment 形 事業部門の，部門間の，セグメント間の
intersegment receivables セグメント間の受取債権，部門間受取債権 (= intersegment trade receivables)
intersegment sales or transfers セグメント間の販売または振替え
▸*Intersegment* and intergeographic transfers are accounted for on an arm's length pricing basis. 事業部門間および地域間取引は，第三者に対する取

引価格基準で会計処理されています。

intraperiod income tax allocation 法人税の期間内配分

introduce 動 導入する, 発売する, 売り出す, 公開する, 上場する, 紹介する
▸The company will *introduce* an early retirement scheme in July.　同社は, 7月から早期退職制度を導入する。

introduction 名 導入, 発売, 公開, 持ち込み, 紹介
　introduction of a new product　新製品の発売, 新製品の導入
　introduction of stock　株式公開
▸The segment's revenue growth was achieved through higher sales volumes and the *introduction* of new products.　当部門の増収は, 販売数量の増加と新製品の投入で達成しました。

inventoriable cost　棚卸し資産原価

inventory 名 在庫, 在庫品, 棚卸し, 棚卸し品, 棚卸し資産, 棚卸し高, 棚卸し表, 財産目録, 目録, 保有数 (⇒**charge off**)
一般に「棚卸し資産」に含まれるもの:

finished goods [products]	製品
goods [merchandise]	商品
raw materials	原料, 原材料
supplies	貯蔵品
work in process	仕掛品 (＝goods in process, work in progress)

　book inventory　恒久棚卸し法
　carry inventory　在庫を抱える
　continuous inventory　継続棚卸し
　cuts in inventory　在庫削減, 在庫削減幅
　ending inventory　期末棚卸し高
　finished goods inventory　製品在庫
　initial inventory　期首棚卸し資産, 期首棚卸し高, 期首在庫
　inventory adjustment　在庫調整, 棚卸し修正
　inventory at base year cost　基準年度の価格で積算した在庫金額
　inventory control　在庫管理, 在庫統制, 棚卸し資産統制 (＝inventory management)
　inventory cost flow method　棚卸し資産原価算定の方法 (＝inventory cost flow assumption; ⇒**inventory cost, LIFO**)
　inventory method　棚卸し計算法, 棚卸し法
　inventory profit or loss　棚卸し資産利益または損失, 棚卸し資産損益
　inventory reduction　在庫削減, 在庫圧縮, 在庫整理 (＝reduction of inventories)
　inventory reserve　棚卸し資産引当金, 棚卸し資産評価引当金
　inventory shortage　棚卸し減耗, 棚卸し減耗費, 棚卸し差損費
　inventory turnover　棚卸し資産回転率, 在庫回転率
　inventory valuation　棚卸し資産評価, 棚卸し評価 (＝inventory pricing)
　inventory value　在庫[在庫品]評価額, 棚卸し資産評価額
　liquidate inventories　在庫を削減する, 在庫を取り崩す
　opening inventory　期首残高
　periodic physical inventory　定期実地棚卸し
　rebuild inventories　在庫を積み増す
　right inventory　適正在庫
▸*Inventories* are valued at the lower of average cost (which approximates computation on a first-in, first-out basis) or market (i.e., net realizable value or replacement cost).　棚卸し資産は, 平均法による原価(先入れ先出し法に基づく原価とほぼ同額)または市場価格(正味[純]実現可能価格または再調達価格)のいずれか低いほうの価額で評価されています。

inventory cost　在庫費用, 棚卸し資産原価, 棚卸し資産の取得原価 (＝inventoriable cost)
棚卸し資産取得原価の計算方法:

average method	平均法
moving average method	移動平均法
simple average method	単純平均法
weighted average method	加重平均法
base stock method	規準棚卸し法
dollar value LIFO method	金額後入れ先出し法
first-in, first-out method	先入れ先出し法 (＝FIFO method)
last-in, first-out method	後入れ先出し法 (＝LIFO method)
retail method	売価還元法
specific cost method	個別法

▸*Inventory cost* is generally determined on a first-in, first-out basis.　棚卸し資産の原価は, 原則として先入れ先出し法で算定されています。

inventory level　在庫水準
▸Higher *inventory levels* are associated with our sales growth.　在庫水準が高いのは, 当社の販売増による影響です。

inventory management　在庫管理 (＝inventory control)
▸Improved *inventory management* in 2007 led to increased inventory turnover.　2007年度は, 在庫

管理が改善して在庫回転率が高まりました.

inventory turn 棚卸し資産回転率（＝inventory turnover）
▶*Inventory turns* decreased slightly to 5.7 in 2007 from 5.8 in2006. 棚卸し資産の回転率は，2006年度の5.8から2007年度は5.7にわずかながら減少しました．

invest 動 投資する，出資する，投下する，投入する，運用する
　invest in a joint venture 合弁会社に投資する
　invest in real estate 不動産に投資する
　invested amount 投資額
　invested assets 運用資産
▶We *invest* in the future by investing in education. 当社は，教育に投資することにより，将来に投資しています．

invested capital 投下資本，拠出資本，株主資本（＝contributed capital；⇒**stockholders' equity**）

invested fund 投下資本，投資資金

investee 名 被投資会社（他社に20-50％の株式を所有されている会社）
　investee company 被投資会社

investing activities 投資活動
▶This increase in net cash used for *investing activities* is due to a an increase in the purchase of marketable securities. 投資活動に使用した純キャッシュのこの増加は，市場性ある有価証券の購入量増加によるものです．

investment 名 投資，出資，運用，投資額，投資物，投資事業，投資資産，投資勘定，資金投下，証券，インベストメント（＝investing；⇒**capital investment, equity investment**）
　corporate investment 企業投資，企業の設備投資，民間設備投資
　current investment 短期投資
　early investment 早期投資
　fixed asset investment 固定資産投資
　fixed investment 固定資本投資，設備投資
　foreign investment 外国・海外からの投資，外国資本の投資，対内投資，対外投資
　investment company 投資会社，投資信託会社（＝investment firm, management company：一般から広く資金を集めて証券類に投資する投資信託業務を行う会社）
　investment credit 投資税額控除，投資減税（＝investment tax credit）
　investment decision 投資判断，投資の意思決定，投資決定（⇒**full powers and authority**）
　investment gains or losses 投資利得または損失
　investment in associated company 関連会社に対する投資
　investment tax credit 投資税額控除，投資減税（＝investment credit；⇒**amortize**）
　investments and other property 投資およびその他の資産
　investments in securities 投資有価証券（＝investment securities）
　labor saving investment 省力化投資
　less investment in plant and equipment 設備投資の抑制
　new investment 新規投資
　portfolio investment 証券投資，株式・債券投資，ポートフォリオ投資
　security investment 証券投資
▶In 2007 we made a $500 million *investment* in the company. 2007年度に，当社は同社に5億ドルの投資をしました．
▶The initial *investment* in equipment for the new facility will be ¥1.55 trillion. 新工場設備に対する初期投資額は，1兆5,500億円になる見込みだ．

investment bank 投資銀行（投資銀行の主な業務は，証券引受け（underwriting），新規株式公開（IPO）とM&A（企業合併・買収）の仲介）
▶U.S. *investment bank* Goldman Sachs Group Inc. will invest ¥41 billion in the reconstruction of ailing construction firm Fujita Corp. 米投資銀行のゴールドマン・サックス・グループが，経営不振のフジタ（総合建設会社）の再建に410億円投資する．

investment capital 投資資本（投資に充当する資金）
▶The funds gained from the sale of shares will permit the firm to undertake capital expenditures without calling on further *investment capital* from its parent company. 株式売却で調達した資金によって，同社は親会社に追加投資資本［資本投資］を求めることなく，設備投資ができる状況にあります．

investment costs 投資コスト
▶Huge *investment costs*, such as those for developing environment-friendly technology, have made it difficult for an automaker to survive competition on its own. 環境にやさしい技術の開発費など，巨額の投資コストが見込まれるため，自動車メーカー1社が独力で競争に生き残るのは難しくなっている．

investment fund 投資ファンド，投資信託財産，投資資金
▶The *investment fund*'s investors and investments have yet to be determined. この投資ファンドの出資者と資産の運用内容は，まだ不明だ．

investment in affiliated company
[**concern**] 関係会社投資, 関連会社投資勘定
▸The *investments in affiliated companies* (20% to 50% owned) are accounted for by the equity method.　20~50％所有の関連会社投資勘定は, 持ち分法により会計処理されています.

invetment in home building　住宅建設投資
▸*Investment in home building* in the fourth quarter was slashed by 19.1 percent on an annualized basis.　第4四半期の住宅建設投資は, 年率換算で19.1％減少した.

investment in plant and equipment
設備投資
▸Beset by heavy debts combined with problems of their excessive *investment in plants and equipment*, Japanese corporations are facing stiff competition from Chinese and other Asian companies.　巨額の債務や過剰設備投資の問題に苦しむ日本企業は, 中国などアジアの企業から厳しい競争を仕掛けられている.

investment portfolio　投資ポートフォリオ, 投資資産, 投資資本構成, 投資の内容
▸As of December 31, 2007, the *investment portfolio* was predominantly long-term bonds and equity investments.　2007年12月31日現在, 投資ポートフォリオは主に長期債券と株式投資です.

investment profitability　投資収益性, 投資利益率, 投資収益率
▸We will adhere to our proactive management policies that place the utmost emphasis on *investment profitability*.　当社は, 今後も投資収益性を重視した攻めの経営姿勢を貫く方針です.

investment risk　投資リスク
▸It is a matter of urgency to ensure that banks make profit margins that can meet *investment risk* and that they expand commission revenue as well as promote sweeping restructurings.　抜本的なリストラのほか, 投資リスクに見合う利ざやの確保と手数料収入の拡大などが銀行の急務だ.

investment trust　投資信託, 投信 (一般投資家から資金を集め, 集めた金を専門家が株や債券などに投資して, その運用益を投資家に還元する金融商品)
▸Fund-of-funds do not invest capital directly in stocks and bonds, but reinvest it in other *investment trusts* as a way to minimize risks.　ファンド・オブ・ファンズは, （投資家から集めた）資金を株式や債券に直接投資せず, リスクを最小限に抑える手段として他の複数の投資信託に再投資する.

investment trust fund　投資信託基金, 投資信託
▸Against the backdrop of the liberalization of the financial industry, pension funds and *investment trust funds* grew sharply.　金融自由化を背景に, 年金基金や投資信託基金が急成長した.

investor 名　投資家, 投資者, 投資会社, 出資者, 出資企業, 資本主, 投資側, 投資国, 〈権利などの〉授与者, インベスター　(⇒**institutional investor**)
accountng for investors　投資家のための会計
bloc investor　大口投資家
debt investor　債券投資家, 債券保有者
equity investor　株式投資家
fixed income investor　債券投資家, 確定利付き証券への投資家
institutional investor　機関投資家
professional investor　機関投資家 (＝institutional investor, wholesale investor)
retail investor　小口投資家, 個人投資家, 最終投資家 (＝small investor)
▸Our overseas *investors* account for about 24 percent, which would shrink to 18.6 percent after we raise capital.　当社の外国人株主[外国人投資家]は, 約24％を占め, 増資後は18.6％に減少します.
▸The company has received about ¥780 billion in cash and debt waivers from shareholders and *investors* in two bailouts.　同社は, 2度の金融支援で, 株主と出資企業から約7,800億円の資金提供と債券免除を受けている.

investor [investors] relations　投資家向け広報, 投資家向け広報活動, 投資家向け情報公開, 財務広報, 証券広報, 戦略的財務広報, 対投資家関係, IR活動, インベスター・リレーションズ《略 IR》　(⇒**IR, roadshow**)

　Investor Relations (**IR**) とは ➡ 株主や投資家に対して投資判断に必要な情報を提供することがインベスター・リレーションズで, 一般にIR (アイアール) と呼ばれている.
　全米IR協会 (NIRI) の定義では, IRは「企業の財務機能とコミュニケーション機能を結合して行われる戦略的・全社的なマーケティング活動で, 投資家に対して企業の業績と将来性に関して正確な姿を提供するものである (同友館発行『戦略的IR』参照).
　各企業が実践しているIR活動のツールとしては, アニュアル・レポート (年次報告書), や事業報告書, ファクト・ブック, ニューズ・レターなどの出版物のほか, インフォメーション・ミーティング (証券アナリストやファンド・マネージャーなどに対して経営方針や経営理念, 業務内容などを定期的に紹介する企業説明会), 決算説明会に加えて, 個別訪問 (機関

投資家や証券会社に出向いて直接会社の業務内容などを説明）などがある。会社や工場見学などを, IR活動の一つにしているところもある。

　また、最近の傾向として注目されるのは、インターネットのホームページ上での情報開示である。このホームページには、一般に会社概要や事業内容, 商品情報, 採用情報などが掲載されている。そのメリットとしては、情報伝達の即時性、適時性のほかに個人投資家や潜在投資家を含めてすべての投資家に公正に情報を提供できることや、印刷物や郵便物より安価に情報を発信できること、ウェブ・サイト上でアンケート調査もできること、メールを併用すると投資家の質問や意見を得やすいことなどが挙げられている。

▸The form 10-K annual report for 2007, as filed with the U.S. SEC, is available without charge upon request to *Invetor Relations* of the Corporation.　米証券取引委員会（SEC）に提出した様式10-Kに基づく2007年度年次報告書は、当社のIR担当部署へご請求いただければ無料で提供しています。

invoice 名　送り状, インボイス
invoice 動　インボイスを作る, インボイスを送る,〈貨物を〉積送する
IPO　株式公開, 新規株式公開, 新規株式公募, 公開公募, 新規公募, 上場（**initial public offering**の略。会社が一般投資家に株式を初めて売り出すこと）
IR　投資家向け広報, 投資家向け広報活動, 財務広報（**investor relations**の略。「IR」は、有価証券報告書や決算短信のほかに、決算説明会, 工場見学などの広報活動を含めて、株主や投資家に対して投資判断に必要な情報を提供すること。⇒**investor relations, roadshow**）
　IR activities　IR活動
　IR campaign　IRキャンペーン, IR活動, 投資家説明会
　IR meeting　投資家説明会, IR説明会, 会社説明会, IRミーティング　（＝IR session）
　IR representative　IR担当者
IRC　内国歳入法（**Internal Revenue Code**の略）
IRS　『米』内国歳入庁（**Internal Revenue Service**の略）
ISO　国際標準化機構（**International Standards Organization**の略。 International Organization for Standardizationともいう）
　ISO 9000　品質管理と品質保証に関するISOの国際規格
　ISO 14000　環境管理システムと環境監査に関するISOの国際規格
　ISO 14001　環境管理に関するISOの国際規格（ゴミ分別や節電, コピー用紙の使用枚数などを, 企業などが環境への負荷を減らす数値目標を設けて計画的に取り組んでいることを証明して認証を得る）
　ISO 15408　情報セキュリティに関するISOの国際規格
　ISO certification　ISOの認定
▸Fujiya was found to have failed to meet the *ISO 9001* quality management standard at three factories.　不二家は、3工場でISOの品質管理基準「ISO 9001」を満たしていないことが判明した。
▸*ISO 9001* is the highest quality certification of the International Organization for Standardization.　ISO 9001は、国際標準化機構（ISO）の最高の品質基準である。
▸Our five manufacturing facilities are now *ISO*-certified.　当社の5か所の製造施設は現在, ISOの認定を受けています。

issuance 名　発行, 支給, 配給, 刊行, 入札
　CP issuance　CP発行
　debt issuance cost　社債発行費, 債券発行費
　deficit issuance　赤字国債
　issuance of capital [stock]　株式の発行
　issuance of new shares　新株発行, 増資　（＝new share issuance, new share issue）
　issuance price　発行価格
　issuance volume　発行額
　new bond issuance　起債
　quarterly issuance　四半期入札
　size of the issuance　発行規模
▸During 2007, conversions of convertible debentures resulted in the *issuance* of 968 shares of the Corporation's capital stock.　2007度は、転換社債の転換により, 968株の当社株式を発行しました。

issuance of preferred shares　優先株式の発行
▸During the first nine months of 2007, the Corporation raised $500 million by the *issuance of preferred shares*.　2007年1～9月期に, 当社は優先株式を発行して5億ドルを調達しました。

issue 動　〈証券などを〉発行する, 売り出す, 起債する, 〈手形を〉振り出す, 配当を行う, 発表する, 公表する　（⇒**common share, government bond, ordinary share, privately issue**）
　issued and outstanding　外部発行済み, 発行済み, 発行済み株式
　issued capital　発行済み資本, 発行済み株式　（＝issued share capital）
　issued share capital　発行済み株式資本, 発行済み株式資本金　（＝issued capital）
▸The firm *issued* common stocks to raise capital.　同社は、資金調達のため普通株式を発行した。

issue 名 証券, 株, 銘柄, 発行, 発行債, 発行部数, 交付,〈手形の〉振出し, 問題, 問題点, 争点, 論点 (⇒share issue limit)
  capital issue 株式発行; 株式
  capitalization issue 資本金組入れ発行
  free issue 無償交付
  issue at market price 時価発行
  issue at par 額面発行, 平価発行
  issue capital 発行済み株式資本金
  issue price 発行価格
  issue to stockholders 株主割当て
  share and debenture issue expense 株式・社債発行費
  stock issue cost 新株発行費 (＝stock issue expense)
  ▸The new *issues* of medium and long-term corporate bonds are necessary for investment in plant and equipment. 企業の設備投資には, 中長期社債の新規発行が必要だ。
  ▸The company's shares were included in the 225-*issue* Nikkei Stock Average. 同社の株式は, 日経平均株価(225種)に組み入れられた。
issued shares 発行済み株式, 発行済み株式数, 発行株式数 (＝issued stocks：会社の授権株式(会社が発行できる株式の上限数)のうち, すでに発行された株式の総数)
  ▸Market capitalization is calculated by multiplying the number of a company's *issued shares* by their market price. 株式の時価総額は, 企業の発行済み株式数に株式の時価を掛けて算出される。
issuing enterprise 発行体, 発行企業
IT 情報技術 (information technologyの略)
  IT business ITビジネス
  IT investment IT投資
  IT issues IT関連銘柄
  IT-related plant and equipment IT関連設備
  IT strategy IT戦略
  ▸Microsoft Corp. has used a stock option program to attract talented *IT* professionals. マイクロソフトは, 有能なIT[情報技術]専門家を確保するためにストック・オプション制度を使っている。

item 名 項目, 品目, 種目, 細目, 事項, 商品, 用品, 品物, アイテム
  abnormal item 異常項目
  accrued item 経過項目, 見越し項目
  adjustment item 修正項目, 調整項目
  balance sheet item 貸借対照表項目
  balancing item 調整項目
  base item 基本項目
  cash item 現金項目
  corporate items 本社事項
  expense item 費目
  infrequent item 突発事項
  items deducted from sales 売上高控除項目
  items not affecting cash 資金の流出入を伴わない項目
  items not affecting working capital 運転資本の収支を伴わない項目, 運転資本の増減を伴わない項目, 運転資本に影響しない項目
  items not involving cash 資金の流出[流入]を伴わない項目
  line item 勘定科目
  non-cost item 非原価項目
  offset item 相殺項目
  operating item 営業項目
  prior period item 前期修正項目
  unusual item 特別損益項目
  ▸Among *items* shipping briskly were electronic devices, telecommunications equipment, liquid crystal display TVs and automobiles. 輸出が好調だった品目としては, 電子装置, 通信機器, 液晶テレビや自動車などがある。
  ▸The following table displays the non-cash *items* excluded from the consolidated statement of cash flows. 次表は, 連結キャッシュ・フロー計算書から除外した非現金項目を示したものです。
items of business 議案, 議事
  ▸The Proxy Statement describes the *items of business* to be voted on at the Annual Meeting. 議決権代理行使勧誘状には, 定時株主総会で票決される議案についての説明がなされている。

J j

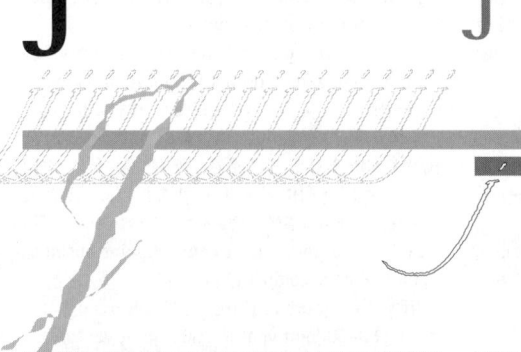

January-to-March quarter 1-3月期,〈12月決算企業の〉第1四半期,〈3月期決算企業の〉第4四半期
▸The percentage of credit card payments that were past due date fell in the *January-to-March quarter*.　クレジット・カードの支払い遅延率［期限を過ぎたクレジット・カードの返済遅延率］は,1-3月期に急減した。

Japan Housing Finance Agency　住宅金融支援機構（独立行政法人で,旧住宅金融公庫が2007年4月1日に改称）

Japanese Welfare Pension Insurance Law　厚生年金保険法

Jasdaq　ジャスダック（**Japan Securities Dealer's Association Quotation**の略。日本の新興企業向け株式店頭市場。2004年12月13日,店頭市場から証券取引所（Jasdaq Securities Exchange）に移行して取引を開始）

JIT　かんばん方式（**just-in-time**の略）

JLL financing　日本型レバレッジド・リース（JLL）方式による資金調達

job　職,職場,職務,業務,雇用,就職口,働き口,仕事,ジョブ
　completed job method of accounting　工事完成基準　（=completed job method）
　job cost method　工事別原価計算,工事別原価計算法
　job development credit　雇用促進税額控除,職業開発税額控除　（=targeted job tax credit）
　job enlargement　職務拡大
　job enrichment　職務充実
　job rate　職務給
　job redesign　職務再設計
　job satisfaction　職務満足
　job tax credit　雇用促進税額控除
　new jobs　新規雇用
　provide jobs　雇用を創出する
　wage on job classification　職階給,職階制賃金,資格給

job cut　人員削減
　speed up job cuts　人員削減を加速する
　white-color job cuts　事務職の削減
▸Ford Motor Co. announced a revised turnaround plan that calls for 10,000 more white-collar *job cuts* and additional plant closures.　フォードは,事務職1万人の追加削減と工場閉鎖の拡大を求める企業再生修正案を発表した。
▸Struggling Sanyo Electric Co. will speed up *job cuts*.　経営再建中の三洋電機が,人員削減を加速する。

job evaluation　職務評価
　wage on job evaluation　職能給　（=wage based on job evaluation）

job training　職業訓練
　job training program　職業訓練プログラム
　off-the-job training　職場外訓練,職場外教育訓練
　on-the-job training　職場内訓練,職場内教育訓練《略 OJT》
▸*Job training* activities required by our society also are important elements of education.　社会が求める職業訓練活動も,教育の大切な要素となっています。
▸We have actively supported *job-training* efforts for disadvantaged and handicapped persons for more than 20 years.　当社は,過去20年以上にわ

たって，経済的に恵まれない人たちや身体障害者のための職業訓練制度を積極的に支援してきました．

join 動 参加する，協力する，提携する
  join forces [hands] 連携する，提携する，力を合わせる，協力する，手を組む，手を結ぶ，勢力を結集する，統一会派を組む
  join the board 取締役会に加わる
  ▶The two companies agreed to *join* forces in developing next generation chip technology. 両社は，次世代半導体チップ技術の共同開発を進めることで合意した．

joint 形 共同の，合同の，連帯の，連合の，合弁の，共有の，共通の，ジョイント
  joint capacity cost 共通固定費
  joint capital 合併資本，共同資本
  joint company [concern] 共同運営会社，合弁会社
  joint delivery 共同配送
  joint effort 提携関係
  joint financing 協調融資 (＝joint finance, cooperative financing)
  joint fixed cost 共通固定費
  joint holding company [firm] 共同持ち株会社
  joint investment 共同投資，合弁
  joint product 連産品，結合生産物 (＝co-product：同一の工程で同一の原料から同時に生産される製品)
  joint production 共同生産
  joint research 共同研究
  joint signature 連署
  joint sponsorship 共同主催，共催
  joint undertaking 共同事業
  ▶Toyota showed GM its advanced production system through *joint* production. トヨタは，共同生産を通じてGMにトヨタの優れた生産システムを証明した．

joint development 共同開発
  ▶Aeon's proposal for business tie-up with Lawson includes the *joint development* of private brand products. イオンのローソンとの業務提携案には，自主開発［プライベート・ブランド］商品の共同開発が含まれている．

joint product development 製品[商品]の共同開発
  ▶Isetan and Tokyu have reached a basic partnership agreement, including *joint product development* and the integration of sales information systems. 伊勢丹と東急百貨店が，商品の共同開発や販売情報システムの統合などを含めて，提携の基本合意に達した．

joint stock 共同資本，共同出資，株式組織
  joint stock association 株式社団，株式会社
  joint stock company 株式会社 (＝joint stock corporation, stock company)
  ▶These annual general meetings are the key decision-making forums for *joint-stock* companies. これらの年次株主総会は，株式会社にとって最も重要な意思決定の場である．

joint venture 合弁会社，合弁事業，合弁，共同企業，共同企業体，共同事業，共同事業体，共同出資会社，共同出資事業，ジョイント・ベンチャー《略 JV》(＝corporate joint venture, joint business, joint venture company)
  fifty-fifty joint venture 折半出資の合弁会社 (＝50-50 joint venture, 50% joint venture)
  joint venture plant 合弁工場
  joint venture statement 共同出資事業計算書
  joint venture tender 合弁株式公開買付け(2社以上の会社が，資本を持ち寄って他社を乗っ取ること)
  ▶Both the Group's sales and EBITA figures have been restated following the creation of a *joint venture*. グループの連結売上高とEBITAの数値は，合弁会社の設立後に再表示されています．
  ▶Softbank and News Corp. will set up a fifty-fifty *joint venture*. ソフトバンクとニューズ・コーポレーション(米メディア・娯楽大手)が，折半出資の会社を新設する．

joint venture company 合弁会社
  ▶The firm will have an initial ownership of forty percent of the voting shares of the *joint venture company*. 同社の当初の出資比率は，合弁会社の議決権付き株式の40%とする方針だ．

jointly 副 共同で
  jointly develop 共同開発する
  jointly own 共同所有する，共同出資する (＝equally own)
  jointly set up a new company 共同出資で新会社を設立する
  ▶Sumitomo Mitsui Banking Corp. has *jointly* developed with American International Group Inc. a foreign bond investment product targeting retired baby boomers. 三井住友銀行が，団塊の世代の定年退職者をターゲットにした外債の金融商品を，米保険最大手のAIGグループと共同開発した．
  ▶GM and Toyota are each set to invest tens of billions of yen in a plant they *jointly* own in California. GMとトヨタはそれぞれ，両社が共同出資する米カリフォルニア州の工場に数百億円を(追加)投資する方針だ．

▸The two companies *jointly* set up a new company. 両社は，共同出資で新会社を設立した。

judgment [judgement] 名 判断，判断力，見識，分別，意見，見解，判決，裁決，審判
  accounting judgment 会計上の判断
  fine judgment 難しい判断
  judgment [judgement] creditor 判決による債権者，判決債権者
  judgment debtor 判決による債務者，判決債務者
  matter of judgment 判断事項
  professional judgment 職業上の判断
  rating judgment 格付け判断
  seasoned judgment 適切な判断
▸Estimates included in the financial statements were based on *judgments* of qualified personnel. 財務書類に記載した見積り額は，有資格者の判断に基づいています。

July–September quarter 7-9月期，〈12月期決算企業の〉第3四半期
▸Nomura expects to book about ¥73 billion in losses related to its residential mortgage-backed securities business in the *July–September quarter*. 野村［野村ホールディングス］は，2007年7-9月期に住宅融資証券事業の関連損失として730億円を計上する見通しだ。

junk 名 投資不適格，ジャンク債
  junk bond [issue] ジャンク債，くず債券，格付けの低い債券，高利回り債
  junk issuer ジャンク債発行体
  junk status 投資不適格のレベル，投機的レベル
▸Standard & Poor's cut its ratings on General Motors Corp. deeper into *junk* status. 米格付け会社のスタンダード・アンド・プアーズは，ゼネラル・モーターズ（GM）の格付け（長期債務格付け）を，投資不適格のレベルに（投資不適格レベルのダブルBからダブルBマイナスに）さらに1段階引き下げた。

junk territory 投資不適格レベル
▸Two influential rating firms lowered Ford Motor Co.'s credit ratings a notch deeper into *junk territory*. 大手［有力な］格付け機関2社が，米フォードの信用格付けを「投資不適格レベル」にさらに1段階引き下げた。

just-in-time 形名 かんばん［カンバン］方式，ジャストインタイム《略 JIT》（＝JIT system, just-in-time system, "Kanban" system：トヨタ自動車の生産管理方式で，部品の在庫ゼロ状態をめざして，必要なときに必要な量だけ部品を納入させる方式）
  just-in-time employee 契約社員，かんばん方式社員
  just-in-time inventory management ジャストインタイムの在庫管理方式，カンバン方式
  just-in-time marketing ジャストインタイム・マーケティング
  just-in-time production system ジャストインタイムの生産方式，かんばん方式
  just-in-time system かんばん方式，ジャストインタイム方式，ジャストインタイム・システム（＝just-in-time method）
▸Car manufacturers are indicating they may emulate Toyota's *just-in-time* system. 自動車メーカー各社は，必要なときに必要な量だけつくるトヨタの「カンバン方式」を見習う姿勢を強めている。

JV 共同事業体，共同企業体，ジョイント・ベンチャー（**joint venture**の略。⇒**joint venture**）

K k

keep 動 維持する, 保持する, 据え置く, 続ける, 保存する, 保管する, 管理する, 経営する, 在庫として持つ, 常備する, 書き記す, 記入する, 〈規則など を〉守る
- **keep hold of market share** シェア［市場シェア］を維持する
- **keep short rates on hold** 短期金利を据え置く, 短期金利を低水準で維持する
- **keep the book** 帳簿に記入する, 帳簿をつける
- **keep the company alive** 会社を存続させる, 生き残りをかける
- **keep the Federal funds rate unchanged** フェデラル・ファンド金利を据え置く
▸Discount rate was *kept* at 1.25 percent. 公定歩合は, 1.25％に据え置かれた。

Keogh 名 自営業者退職年金制度, 個人年金積立奨励制度, キオ・プラン［ケオ・プラン］, キオ (= individual retirement account, qualified pension plan, Keogh plan)
- **Keogh account** キオ口座
- **Keogh plan** キオ・プラン

key interest rate 政策金利, 主要政策金利, 基準金利, 指標金利, 金利の誘導目標, FF金利 (=key rate)
▸The European Central Bank raised its *key interest rate* by a quarter of a percentage point to 3.5 percent. 欧州中央銀行（ECB）は, 主要政策金利を0.25％引き上げて年3.5％とした。

key Nikkei Index 日経平均株価（225種）

key rate 政策金利, 基準金利, 指標金利 (= key interest rate：米国の場合, a key rate (a key interest rate) はフェデラル・ファンド（FF）金利を指し, 複数形のkey ratesは公定歩合（official discount rate）とフェデラル・ファンド（FF）金利の誘導目標の二つを指す。⇒**key interest rate**)
▸The U.S. Federal Reserve Board held a *key rate* steady at 5.25 percent. 米連邦準備制度理事会（FRB）は, フェデラル・ファンド（FF）金利の誘導目標を年5.25％に据え置いた。
▸The U.S. Federal Reserve Board left U.S. *key rates* unchanged. 米連邦準備制度理事会（FRB）は, 米国の基準金利を据え置いた。

knockdown system 現地組立方式, ノックダウン方式

knowhow [**know-how**] 名 ノウハウ, 技術情報, 技術知識, 専門知識, 専門技術, 製造技術, 技術秘密, 技術秘訣, 手法, 秘伝, 奥義, コツ (=expertise)
- **business knowhow** 経営手法, 商売の秘訣［コツ］
- **computer knowhow** コンピュータ技術
- **confidential knowhow** 秘密ノウハウ
- **conveyance of knowhow** ノウハウの供与
- **knowhow fee** ノウハウ料
- **knowhow license agreement** ノウハウ・ライセンス契約
- **knowhow licensing agreement** ノウハウ使用許諾契約
- **knowhow transfer** ノウハウ譲渡, ノウハウの移転
- **management knowhow** 経営のノウハウ, 経営の専門知識
- **technical knowhow** 技術専門知識, 技術ノウハウ
- **transfer of knowhow and technical assistance** ノウハウの移転と技術援助
▸We will organize and lead teams of experts from other companies to provide technical *knowhow* for the global environment problems.

当社は, 他社の技術専門家チームを組織・指揮して, 地球規模の環境問題に関するノウハウを提供することになっています。

Kyoto Protocol 京都議定書 （＝the Kyoto pact, the global climate pact）

▸The *Kyoto Protocol* requires Japan to cut greenhouse gas emissions by 6 percent from the 1990 level by 2012. 京都議定書は, 日本に対して2012年までに1990年比で6％の温室効果ガス排出量削減を義務付けている。

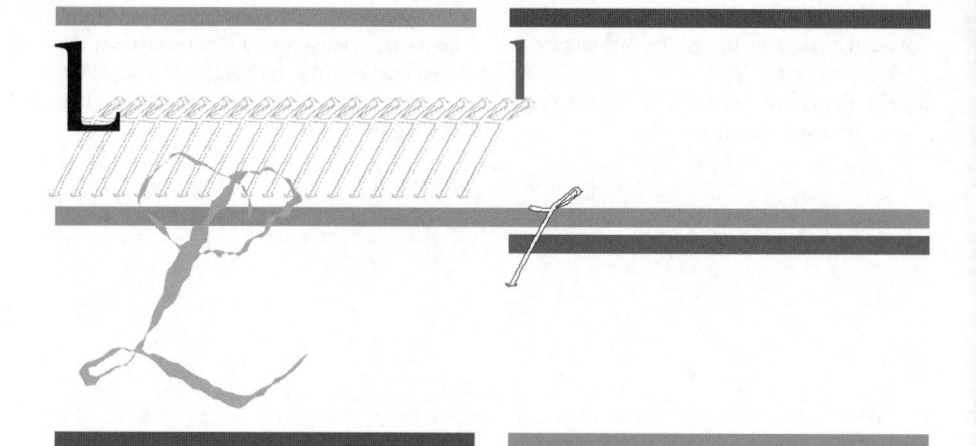

labor agreement 労使協約, 労働協約
▶Our management and union bargainers negotiated innovative *labor agreements* with provisions for employees' career security and well-being as well as higher wages. 当社の経営陣と組合の交渉担当者が, 従業員の雇用確保, 福利厚生と賃上げに関する規定を盛り込んだ革新的な労使協約について協議しました。

labor management 労務管理, 労使
  labor management dispute 労使紛争
  labor management negotiation 労使交渉 (= labor management talks)
▶The burden of medical expenses for current and retired employees, made obligatory through *labor management* accords, hangs heavy on GM. 労使協約で課せられた社員と退職者に対する医療費の負担が, GMに重くのしかかっている。

labor management relations 労使関係
(=labor relations)
▶The company's *labor-management relations* are amicable at present. 同社の労使関係は, 今のところ良好だ。

lag 動 出遅れる, 遅行する, 予定通り進行しない, …に追いつかない, …についていけない, 下回る
  lag behind ... …から取り残される, …より遅れる, …を下回る
  lagging indicator 遅行指標 (=lagging index：現状の景気の動きに半年から1年遅れて動く経済指標)
▶Sales and profits for the handheld PlayStation Portable have also been *lagging*. 携帯型ゲーム機「プレイステーションポータブル (PSP)」の売上高と利益も, 業績予想を下回っている。

land 名 土地, 用地, 国土
  cost of improvements to land 土地改良費
  land, building and equipment 土地, 建物および設備
  land, building and fixtures 土地, 建物および設備
  land improvements 土地改良, 土地付属施設
  leasehold land 賃借地
  loss on land sales 土地売却損
  posted prices of land 地価公示価格
▶We lease *land*, buildings and equipment through contracts. 当社は, 契約により土地, 建物と設備を賃借りしています。

large 形 大規模な, 巨大な, 巨額の, 大型の, 大量の, 大手の, 広範囲な, 主要な, 重要な, 大幅な, 全般的な
  large acquisition 大型買収
  large capitalization [capital] stock 大型株
  large company [firm] 大手企業, 大企業
  large customers 大口顧客
  large deficit 巨額の赤字, 大幅赤字
  large equity holder 大株主 (=large shareholder)
  large gains in productivity 生産性の大幅な伸び, 生産性の大幅上昇, 大幅な生産性向上 (=large productivity gains)
  large merger 大型合併
  large order [lot-order] 大口注文, 大量注文
  large shareholder 大株主, 大口株主 (=large stockholder, major shareholder)
  largest shareholder 筆頭株主, 大株主
  report on large stockholders [shareholders] 大量保有報告書

▶Banks made *larger* gross operating profits than they did during the bubble economic era.　銀行は，バブル期よりも大きな業務粗利益を上げた．

▶We achieved both growth and efficiency, while maintaining a *large* profit.　当社は，成長と効率を両立させる一方，高水準の利益を維持した．

last half　下半期，下期　（⇒first half, latter half）

▶The pressures on gross margins and earnings affected the *last half* of 2007.　売上利益率と利益の低下が，2007年下半期［下期］の業績に影響を及ぼしました．

last-in, first-out　後入れ先出し，後入れ先出し法《略 LIFO》（⇒FIFO）

last-in, first-out basis [method]　後入れ先出し法，後入れ先出し基準，LIFO　（=first in on hand）

last-in, first-out costing method　後入れ先出し原価法

last-in, first-out dollar value method　金額後入れ先出し法

last year　昨年，前年，昨年度，前年度，前期

▶The increased net income for the first nine months of 2007, over the same period *last year*, refects increased contributions from telecommunications operating subsidiaries.　2007年1-9月期の純利益［連結純利益］は，前年同期比で増加していますが，これは通信事業子会社の貢献額拡大を反映しています．

latent 形　潜在的な，表面に出ない，隠れた，含みを持つ《企業保有資産の現在価値［市場価値］が帳簿上の価格を上回っている状態》

latent asset　含み資産《企業保有資産の現在価値［市場価値］が，帳簿上の表示価格より大きい場合の差額》

latent debts　隠れ借金

latent defect　隠れた欠陥，隠れた瑕疵《かし》

latent gains or losses　含み損益，評価損益　（= latent profits or losses）

latent profits and losses　含み損益　（=appraisal profits and losses, latent gains and losses, unrealized profits and losses）

latent stock gains　株式含み益，株の含み益，株式評価益　（=latent profits in stocks）

latent value　含み益　（=latent gain, latent profit）

▶We must charge off *latent* losses on our real estate holdings.　当社は，保有不動産の含み損の処理に迫られています．

latent gain　含み益，評価益　（=appraisal gain, latent profit, unrealized gain）

▶Increases in *latent gains* from these banks' stockholdings are considered far smaller than latent losses in their bond holdings.　これらの銀行が保有する株式の含み益の増加分は，保有債券の含み損よりはるかに小さいと見られる．

latent loss　含み損，評価損　（=appraisal loss, unrealized loss：保有する株式や債券などの有価証券や不動産の取得原価［購入価格］を時価評価額で差し引いて出た損失のこと）

▶The Corporation had a total ¥30 billion in *latent losses* for its stockholdings as of December 31, 2007.　2007年12月31日現在，当社は計300億円の株式含み損を抱えています．

latent profit　含み益，評価益　（=appraisal profit, latent gain, unrealized profit, valuation profit：保有する株式や債券などの有価証券や不動産の取得原価［購入価格］を時価評価額で差し引いて出た利益のこと）

▶*Latent profits* in real estate, stocks or other assets are posted after assessing the assets at market value.　不動産や株などの資産の含み益は，時価で資産を評価した後計上される．

latest 形　最新の，最先端の，今回の，今年度の，最終の

the latest discount rate cut　今回の公定歩合引下げ

the latest purchase cost　最終仕入原価，最終取得原価

▶The *latest* change in tone of the economic upturn is a temporary phenomenon.　今回の景気回復の変調は，一時的な現象である．

latest fiscal first half　今年度上半期，今年度上期，今年度中間決算

▶In the *latest fiscal first half*, the six top banking groups booked as extraordinary profits part of their loan-loss provisions set aside in the past.　今年度中間決算で，大手銀行・金融6グループは，過去に積み立てた貸倒れ引当金の一部を［特別利益］として計上した．

latter half　下半期，下期，後半　（=the latter half of the year, the latter half year, the second half of the year; ⇒first half）

▶In the *latter half* of 2007, we raised our prices and fees.　2007年度下半期に，当社は製品価格と料金を引き上げました．

latter term　下半期，後期　（=the latter half）

launch 動　開始する，着手する，発売する，売り出す，市場に出す，導入する，投入する，上場する，〈コンピュータプログラムを〉立ち上げる［起動する］，〈ロケットなどを〉打ち上げる［発射する］，〈船を〉進

水させる
- The firm plans to *launch* a tender offer from Nov. 16 to Dec. 14. 同社は、11月16日から12月14日までTOB［株式公開買付け］を実施する予定だ。
- Under the new Corporate Law, anyone is allowed to *launch* a publicly traded company even with ¥1. 新会社法では、（資本金）1円でも公開企業を設立することができる。
- Yomiuri, Nikkei and Asahi agreed to *launch* a joint Web site. 読売、日経と朝日が、共同サイト［共同ニュースサイト］を開設することで合意した。

launch 名 発表, 起債発表, 開始, 着手,〈新製品の〉発売, 上市, 導入, 実施, ローンチ（＝launching）
- We have evolved into the country's top retailer since the *launch* of our first outlet in 1990. 当社は、1990年に1号店を開いて以来、国内トップの小売り業に成長しました。

lay off 解雇する, 雇用調整する, レイオフを進める, 削減する, 低減する, 解消する, 回避する
　lay off employees 従業員を解雇する, 従業員のレイオフを進める
　lay off financial risk 金融リスク［財務リスク］を回避する, 金融リスクを低減する, 金融リスクをヘッジする
　lay off risk リスクを軽減する, リスクを回避する
- We have not *layed off* anyone in over 50 years anywhere in the world. 当社は、過去50年以上にわたって、世界のいずれの地域でも1人として解雇したことはありません。

layoff[lay off] 名 解雇, 削減, 低減, 人員削減, 一時解雇, 一時休, 雇用調整, 休養期間, 休暇, レイオフ（＝lay-off, redundancy）
　large-scale layoffs 大規模な雇用調整
　temporary layoff 一時解雇, 一時休
- We resort to *layoffs* only after applying a full range of measures: retraining, early retirement plans, special leaves of absence and opening up other jobs through attrition and other means. 当社が一時解雇に踏み切るのは、再訓練、早期退職制度、特別休暇、（社員の死亡・退職などによる）人員漸減やその他の手段による職場の再配置など、あらゆる手段を尽くしてからのことです。

LBO レバレッジド・バイアウト, 借入資金による企業買収, 企業担保借入買取り（**leveraged buyout[buy-out]** の略）。買収相手先企業の資産や将来のキャッシュ・フローなどを担保にして、金融機関から買収資金を借り入れる方式）
　LBO company 借入比率の高い企業, 負債比率が高い企業, LBO企業（＝highly leveraged company）
　LBO finance LBOファイナンス
　reverse LBO 逆LBO, LBO株の公開, リバースLBO
- New York-based Citigroup has advised on about one-third of the about $61 billion of leveraged buyouts (*LBO*) worldwide this year. シティグループ（ニューヨーク）は、今年の世界のLBO取引高約610億ドルのうち、約3分の1について専門的助言を行った。

L/C 信用状（**letter of credit**の略）

leader 名 経営者, 経営陣, 首脳, 首脳陣, 指導者, 指導部, 党首,〈米議会の〉院内総務, 最大手, おとり商品, 目玉商品, 特売品, 主力株, 一流株, 社説,〈新聞の〉トップ見出し, リーダー
　business leaders 実業界の指導者, 財界の指導者, 財界首脳, 経済界の首脳, 企業経営者, 企業のトップ
　deputy leader ナンバー2
　House Majority leader 下院院内総務
　industrial nations' leaders 先進国首脳, 先進各国の首脳, 主要国首脳（＝leaders of industrial nations）
　industry leader 業界リーダー, 業界最大手
　leader merchandising おとり商品政策, おとり商品戦略
　leader of the business community 財界リーダー
　leader price 指導価格
　leader pricing おとり価格設定
　leaders at the company 同社［当社］の経営陣
　loss leader おとり商品, 特売品, 目玉商品, おとり政策
　market leader 主導株, 先導株, マーケット・リーダー
　political leaders 政府指導者, 政府高官
　price leader 価格先導者, 価格指導者, 目玉商品, プライス・リーダー
　Senate leaders 上院指導部
- We are the world's networking *leader*, providing communications services and products to businesses, consumers and telecommunications services providers. 当社はネットワーキングに関して世界のリーダーであり、通信サービスと通信関連製品を企業、消費者と電気通信サービス事業者に提供しています。

leadership 名 指導, 指揮, 指導力, 統率力, 指導性, 指導者の資質, リーダー性, 体制, 政権,〈同業他社に対する〉優位性, 優位な立場, リーダーシップ
　business leadership ビジネス・リーダーシップ

industry leadership 業界のリーダー
leadership position 主導的地位 （＝leading position)
leadership role 指導者の役割, 指導的役割
new leadership 新体制
price leadership 価格先導制, 価格指導力, 価格指導性（指導的企業が発表した価格を他社が受け入れること）
under the leadership of ... …の指導の下で, …の体制で
union leadership 組合指導者

▶Under the new *leadership*, the top three posts — chairman, president and senior managing director — have been filled by people from departments that have had no links to the president post before. 新体制では, 会長, 社長と専務の経営トップ3人は, これまで社長ポストと縁のなかった部門の出身者で占められている。

▶We continue to maintain our technology *leadership* through a combination of internal investments and selected partnerships with others. 当社は, 社内投資に力を入れる一方, 優れた外部企業との協力関係を通して技術面でのリーダーシップを堅持しています。

leading company 主要企業, 大手企業, 先導企業, 有力企業

▶More than 70 percent of *leading companies* are worried about becoming the target of a hostile takeover. 主要企業の70％以上が, 敵対的買収の対象になる［敵対的買収を仕掛けられる］のを懸念している。

leading edge 主導的地位, 最先端, 最前部, 最前線, 先頭, 最新式, 最新型, 最新鋭, トップ（＝cutting edge, sophisticated, state-of-the-art, top of the line)
leading-edge area 最先端分野
leading-edge technology 先端技術, 最先端技術, 最新技術
leading edges of innovation 技術革新の最先端

lean 形 無駄のない, 乏しい, 貧弱な
lean year 不作の年

▶As the financial results show, the impact of our actions toward creating a *leaner*, more aggressive company has begun to appear. 業績が示すとおり, 当社を一段とスリムで活動的な企業にするために私どもが取った措置の効果が見られるようになりました。

leap 動 跳ね上がる, 急上昇する, 急増する, 急拡大する, 躍進する, 昇進する

▶Intel's profit *leaped* 43 percent in the third quarter. インテルの第3四半期の利益は, 43％急増した。

lease 動 賃貸しする, 賃借りする, 貸し出す, 借り上げる, リースする
leased asset リース資産, 賃貸資産（＝leased property)
leased equipment リース資産（＝lease equipment)
leased equipment under capital leases リース資産, キャピタルリース設備
leased facility 専用設備
leased goods リース物件, 賃貸借物件, 賃貸借件, 貸与物件（＝leased object)
leased machine リース機械

▶We *lease* airplanes, energy-producing facilities and transportation equipment under leveraged leases. 当社は, レバレッジド・リースで航空機, エネルギー生産施設と輸送設備をリースしています。

lease 名 賃貸借, 賃貸借契約(書), 借地・借家契約, 〈鉱物資源の〉開発契約, リース取引, リース契約, リース（⇒leveraged lease, noncancelable, operating lease, sales-type lease)
big-ticket lease 高額物件リース
cancellable lease 解約可能リース契約, 中途解約可能リース
direct financing and sales-type leases 直接金融［直接金融型］ リースと販売型リース
equipment lease 設備機器リース, 設備リース
finance lease 金融リース, 金融性リース, ファイナンス・リース（＝capital lease, financial lease)
financial lease 金融性リース, 融資リース, ファイナンス・リース, ファイナンシャル・リース（＝finance lease)
financial lease financing ファイナンス・リースによる資金調達
inception of the lease リースの開始, リースの開始日
lease agreement 賃貸借契約, リース契約（＝lease contract)
lease commitment 賃貸借契約, リース契約, リース契約債務（＝leasing commitment)
lease expense リース費用
lease financing リース金融
lease liability リース債務（＝lease obligation)
lease revenue 受取リース料
lease term [period] リース期間
lease terms リース条件, 賃貸借条件, リース期間
minimum lease payments receivable 最低リース料債権
net minimum lease payments 正味最低リー

ス料
operating lease 営業型リース
renewal or extension of lease リースの更新または延長
rental expense on operating leases オペレーティング・リースの賃借料
reserve for lease losses リース損失引当金
sales-type lease 販売型リース, 販売金融リース
▸For *leases* which qualify as sales-type *leases*, the sales revenue is recorded at the inception of the *lease*. 販売型リースと定義されるリースについては, リース開始時に売上収益が計上されます。

leased property リース資産, リース物件
estimated economic life of leased property リース資産の経済的見積り耐用年数
estimated residual value of leased property リース資産の見積り残存価値[残存価格]
leased property and commitments リース資産と約定債務
leased property under capital leases 賃借資産, キャピタル・リース資産

lease obligation リース債務, リース契約
▸At December 31, 2007, future minimum *lease obligation*, net of minimum sublease rentals, for the next five years and beyond are as follows. 2007年12月31日現在, 今後5年間とその後の最低転貸し料収入控除後の将来最低リース債務は, 次のとおりです。

lease payments リース支払い額, リース料の支払い, リース料
▸The table below shows our future minimum *lease payments* due under noncancelable leases at December 31, 2007. 次表は, 2007年12月31日現在の解約不能リースの将来における当社の最低リース支払い額を示しています。

lease receivable リース債権
▸*Lease* and loan *receivables* were sold to the company. リース債権やローン債権が, 同社に売却された。

leaseback 名 リースバック, リースによる借戻し, 設備貸与(保有資産を売却して, 売却先から賃借すること)

leasing 名 賃貸借, リース
▸Capital requirements due to the growth of our financial services and *leasing* business will continue to grow in 2008. 当社の金融サービスとリース事業の拡大により, 資金需要は2008年度も引き続き伸びるものと思われます。

leasing income リース料収入, リース収益
▸During the first six years, depreciation costs for the purchased vessels exceeded *leasing income*, leading to a sizable loss. 当初の6年間は, 購入した船舶の減価償却費用がリース料収入を上回ったため, 巨額の赤字となった。

leasing right リース権, 持ち分権
▸The company sold investors *leasing rights* to four vessels, including large container ships. 同社は, 出資者[投資家]に大型コンテナ船など船舶4隻の持ち分権を販売した。

lender 名 貸し手, 貸主, 金融機関, 銀行, 融資行, 融資者, 資金の出し手, 貸金業者
▸The company has been refused additional credit by its *lenders*. 同社は, 融資行から新規融資を拒否された。

lending 名 貸出, 貸付け, 融資, 貸借
bank lending 銀行貸出
commercial lending 商業貸出, 商業貸付け, 民間融資
consumer lending 消費者金融, 消費者ローン
corporate lending 企業向け貸出, 企業向け貸付け, 企業向け融資
direct lending 直接融資
excessive lending 過剰融資
lending interest rate 貸出金利 (=lending rate)
lending period 融資期間, 貸出期間, 貸付け期間
lending standards 与信基準
net lending 資金過不足, 貯蓄差額投資
new lending 新規貸出
restricted lending 貸し渋り
▸The bank's rate of nonperforming loans against overall *lendings* stood at 2.07 percent as of March 31, compared to 3.33 percent a year ago. 同行の貸出全体に占める3月31日現在の不良債権の比率は, 1年前の3.33%に対して2.07%となった。

lending rate 貸出金利 (=lending interest rate)
emergency lending rate 緊急貸出金利
general lending rate 一般貸出金利
minimum lending rate 最低貸出金利
prime lending rate 一流企業向け最優遇貸出金利, 一流企業に対する短期貸付け金利, プライム・レート (=prime rate)
short-term prime lending rate 短期プライム・レート
▸Under the Interest Limitation Law, the upper limit of *lending rates* is set at between 15 to 20 percent per annum. 利息制限法では, 貸出金利の上限は年15-20%に定められている。

lending service 融資業務

▸Rakuten Inc. plans to start the corporate *lending service* with the companies that own the about 44,000 online stores at Rakuten Ichiba. 楽天は，楽天市場にオンライン・ストアを出店している約44,000の出店企業に対し，法人向け融資業務を開始する計画だ．

length of service　勤続年数，在任期間
▸The pension benefits are based on *length of service* and rate of compensation.　年金給付額は，勤続年数と報酬額に基づいて決定されます．

less 副形　差し引いて，差引で，差引，控除して，控除，…控除後，…を除く（＝minus, without）
　　less accumulated depreciation　減価償却累計額控除
　　less allowance for doubtful items　貸倒引当金控除
　　less allowances　引当金控除後
　　less amortization　償却額控除後，償却後
　　less amounts due in one year　1年以内期限到来分控除
　　less cost of common shares in treasury　差引：自己株式
　　Less: accumulated depreciation　控除[差引]：減価償却累計額
　　Less: treasury cost, at cost　控除：自己株式－取得原価
▸Property, plant and equipment are stated at cost *less* accumulated depreciation.　有形固定資産は，減価償却累計額控除後の取得原価で表示されています．

lessee 名　賃借人，借り手，借り主，リース賃借人，レッシー
　　commitments as lessee　リース契約
　　lessee of the property　資産の借り手
　　lessee's improvements　借主造作，借主改良
　　purchase of the machine by the lessee　賃借人による機械の買取り
　　renewal of the lease of the machine by the lessee　賃借人による機械リースの更新
▸When the corporation is the *lessee*, assets recorded under capital leases are amortized on a straight-line method, using rates based on the estimated useful life of the asset or based on the lease term as appropriate.　当社が賃借人である場合，キャピタル・リースとして計上されたリース資産は，その見積り耐用年数またはリース期間にわたって適宜，定額法で償却されています．

lessor 名　賃貸人，貸し手，貸し主，リース賃貸人，レッサー
　　existing assets of the lessor　賃貸人の既存資産

lessor's implicit interest rate　賃貸人の包括利率
nonsubstantive lessor　経済的実体を欠く賃貸人
▸When the corporation is the *lessor*, rental revenue from operating leases is recognized as service is provided to customers.　当社が賃貸人である場合，オペレーティング・リースからの賃貸料収入は，顧客にサービスを提供した時点で認識されます．

letter 名　書簡，書状，文書，証書，証明書，免許状，意見書，報告書，確認書，手紙，レター
　　collections letter　督促状
　　dividend procedure letter　配当手続き書
　　investment letter　投資確認書
　　Letter　ご挨拶（＝Letter to Shareholders）
　　letter for underwriter　証券引受人への書簡
　　Letter from the Chairman　会長からの書簡，株主各位，株主の皆さまへ，ご挨拶
　　letter of allotment　株式割当て通知書
　　letter of attorney　委任状，弁護士の書簡
　　letter of comfort　財務内容に関する意見書，調査報告書，念書，コンフォート・レター（＝comfort letter）
　　letter of procuration　〔株主総会などの〕代理委任状
　　letter of proxy　委任状
　　opinion letter　意見書
　　transmittal letter　送り状

letter of credit　信用状《略 L/C》（⇒commitment）
▸*Letters* of credit are purchased guarantees that ensure our performance or payment to third parties in accordance with specified terms and conditions.　信用状は，特定の条件に従って当社の第三者に対する義務の履行または支払いを確実なものにするために買い取った保証です．

level 名　水準，標準，層，レベル
　　accounting for changes in the general price level　一般物価変動会計
　　accounting for general price-level changes　一般物価指数修正会計
　　at the net level　当期利益で，当期損益レベルで
　　at the operating level　営業利益で
　　be at near record low levels　過去最低に近い水準にある
　　borrowing level　資金調達コストの水準
　　current level of earnings　現在の収益水準
　　debt level　負債[債務]水準
　　historical level of loss　過去の損失水準
　　interest rate level　金利水準
　　inventory level　在庫水準
　　level playing field　共通の土俵，平等の競争条件

middle management level 中間管理層
net level 当期利益ベース
performance level 業績水準
permissible level 許容水準
price level 物価水準
remain at about the same level ほぼ同水準にとどまる
remain at high levels 高水準で推移する
savings level 貯蓄率
share price level 株価水準 (＝stock market level)
volume level 操業度

▸The current stock market *level* is based more on fear than on the economic fundamentals. 現在の株価水準は、経済の基礎的条件というより、不安によるものだ。

leverage 動 借入金で投機をする、…を利用する、生かす、借入金で企業などを買い取る

▸We believe there is an opportunity to *leverage* the strength of the balance sheet to deal with the demands of the business in the future. 財務内容の強みを生かして、将来、事業のニーズに対応する機会はあると思います。

leverage 名 借入れ、借入比率、借入余力、負債、負債比率、借入資本、財務レバレッジ(資本金に対する負債の割合(debt-to-equity ratio：負債自己資本比率、外部負債比率)の高さを示す)、テコ、テコの作用、手段、影響力、力、有利な立場、レバレッジ(投資額に対する借入金の割合)

capital leverage 財務レバレッジ、資本レバレッジ
debt leverage 債務レバレッジ、債務テコ入れ、デット・レバレッジ(金融機関からの借入れで企業買収資金の一部をまかなうとき、自己資金にもたらされる収益を拡大するために用いられる方法)
economic leverage 経済的影響力
financial leverage 財務レバレッジ、借入比率、負債比率、ギアリング、ファイナンシャル・レバレッジ (＝gearing, financial gearing, trading on the equity)
leverage effect 他人資本効果、テコの効果、梃子(ていりつ)効果、レバレッジ効果
leverage ratio 負債比率、レバレッジ比率
risk-adjusted leverage リスク調整後の負債比率

▸Banks could use their *leverage* on borrowers to engage in unfair life insurance sales practices. 銀行が融資先への有利な立場を利用して、不公正な生保販売を行う可能性がある。

leveraged 形 借入金による、借入金を利用した、借入資金による

conservative-leveraged company 負債比率が低い企業
high-leveraged acquisition 多額の借入れによる企業買収
highly leveraged company 負債比率が高い企業
highly leveraged transaction 負債比率が高い取引、ハイレバレッジ取引
leveraged effectiveness レバレッジ効果、他人資本効果 (＝leverage effect)
leveraged finance レバレッジ金融
leveraged recapitalization 借入資金による資本の組換え、レバレッジド・キャピタライゼーション
leveraged buyout [buy-out] 借入資金による企業買収、企業担保借入買取り、レバレッジド・バイアウト《略 **LBO**》 (＝leverage buyout [buy-out]：買収先の会社[ターゲット企業]の資産や収益力を担保にして金融機関から買収資金を借り入れ、ターゲット企業を買収すること)

leveraged lease レバレッジド・リース

▸These *leveraged leases* have original terms ranging from 10 to 30 years and expire in various years from 2008 through 2033. これらのレバレッジド・リースは、当初の期間が10年から30年で、2008年から2033年までの各年度に満期となります。

levy 動 賦課する、徴収する、差し押さえる

▸Corporate income tax is *levied* on the basis of companies' net business profits. 法人事業税[法人所得税]は、企業の業務上の純利益[業務純益]に応じて課税される。

liability 名 責任、義務、負担、負担額、債務、負債、借金、賠償責任 (⇒contingent, current liabilities)

一般的に負債に含まれるもの：

accounts payable	買掛金
loans payable	借入金
notes payable	支払い手形
other liabilities	その他の負債

accrued liabilities 未払い負債
actuarial liability 保険数理上の債務
amount of liabilities 負債金額
auditor's liability 監査人の責任
capital liability 資本負債
external liabilities 対外債務、外部負債
financial liabilities 金融負債
fixed liability 固定負債
hidden liability 簿外債務
income tax liability 未払い所得税、未払い法人税、所得税債務
insurance liabilities 保険契約準備金
interest liability 未払い利息

internal liability 内部負債
joint and several liability 連帯責任
liabilities and capital 負債および資本(他人資本と自己資本)
liabilities and stockholders' equity 負債および株主持ち分, 負債および資本
liabilities assumed 引継負債
liabilities exceeding assets 債務超過 (=excess liabilities, excess of liabilities over assets, liabilities in excess of assets)
liabilities for [on] guarantee 保証債務
liability exposure 債務負担
liability for damages 損害賠償責任
liability for guarantee 保証債務, 債務保証 (=liability on guaranty)
liability for service guarentees 品質保証引当金
liability ratio 負債比率
limited liability company 有限会社, 有限責任会社《略 LLC》 (=limited company)
long term liabilities 長期負債, 長期債務, 固定負債 (=long term debts, long term obligations)
net liabilities 正味負債, 債務超過額
noncurrent liabilities 非流動負債
off-the-book liabilities 簿外債務 (=off-the-book debts)
past service liability 過去勤務債務
product liability 製造物責任《略 PL》
tax liability 租税債務
total liabilities and net worth 総資本
total liabilities and stockholders' equity 負債および資本の部合計

▶Existing limited *liability* companies are allowed to remain intact or change themselves into stock companies under the new Corporate Law. 新会社法では,既存の有限会社はそのまま存続するか,株式会社に(商号を)変更することができる。

▶This charge reflects $12,000 million of *liabilities* less $2,000 million of plan assets. この金額[費用]は,120億ドルの債務額から20億ドルの制度資産を差し引いたものです。

liability method 負債法, 債務法, 負債方式, 債務方式

▶Under United States GAAP, companies are required to adopt the *liability method* for income taxes. 米国の会計基準によれば,企業は,法人所得税の会計処理に債務法[負債法]を採用しなければならない。

liberalization 名 自由化, 規制緩和, 開放, 国際化 (=deregulation)

liberalization of brokerage commissions 委託手数料の自由化
liberalization of brokerage commissions on commodity futures 商品先物取引の委託手数料の自由化
liberalization of interest rates 金利の自由化
liberalization of mail services 郵便事業の自由化, 郵便事業の開放
liberalization of power-supply business 電力自由化
liberalization of the electricity market 電力市場の自由化, 電力自由化, 電力市場の規制緩和 (=power liberalization)
liberalization of the financial industry 金融自由化, 金融の規制緩和 (=financial deregulation, financial liberalization)
liberalization of the Yen 円の国際化
market liberalization 市場の自由化, 市場開放, 市場の規制緩和
price liberalization 価格自由化
total liberalization of brokerage commissions 委託手数料の完全自由化

liberalization of commissions 売買手数料の自由化, 手数料の自由化

▶It was the *liberalization of commissions* that triggered a fierce battle for survival and a stormy realignment in the British securities industry. 英国の証券業界の生き残りをかけた熾烈(しれつ)な戦いと業界再編に火をつけたのは,手数料の自由化である。

liberalization of the labor market 労働市場の開放

▶*Liberalization of the labor market* is, including accepting nurses and caregivers is a tough new issue. 看護師や介護士の受入れなど労働市場の開放は,新たな難題だ。

liberalize 動 自由化する, 規制緩和する, 開放する, 解禁する

▶Brokerage fees on stock and other transactions are fully *liberalized*. 株式その他の取引の売買手数料は,完全に自由化されている。

license 動 免許[認可, 許可, 特許]を与える, 許諾する, 実施許諾する, 使用許諾する, 許可する, ライセンス供与する

▶With regard to our intellectual properties, we will continue to *license* our patents. 当社の知的財産権については,当社は今後とも特許のライセンス供与をする方針です。

license [licence] 名 営業免許権, 許可, 認可, 免許, 特許, 許諾, 実施許諾, 〈商標やソフトウエア

などの〉使用許諾, 実施権, 使用権, 鉱業権,〈不動産の〉立入り権, 許認可, 免許状, ライセンス
business licenses and fees 事業免許料
export license 輸出承認
investment license 投資認可
license contract expense ライセンス契約費用
license expense 免許料
license registration 免許登録
permits and licenses 許認可費用
registration and license tax 登録免許税

▸The banking *license* of the Tokyo branch of Credit Suisse Financial Products was revoked in 1999. クレディ・スイス・ファイナンシャル・プロダクツ銀行の東京支店が, 1999年に銀行免許を取り消された。

license fee 免許料, 免許手数料, 特許権使用料, 実施料, ライセンス料 (＝licensing fee)

▸Revenue is recognized from software when the program is shipped or as monthly *license fees* accrue. 収益は, ソフトウエアについてはプログラムの出荷時に, または毎月の特許権使用料の発生時に計上しています。

licensing 名 実施許諾, 使用許諾, 認可, 免許, 許認可, ライセンス供与, ライセンス契約, 資格認可, ライセンシング

cross licensing クロス・ライセンス, 交互実施許諾, 特許権交換, 特許技術の交換, 相互特許使用権 (＝cross license)

director of patent licensing 特許許諾担当取締役

licensing agreement ライセンス契約, 使用許諾契約

licensing fee 実施料, ライセンス料 (＝license fee)

licensing practice 特許認可手続き, ライセンス契約の手続き

patent licensing 特許実施権, 特許実施認, 特許許諾, 特許のライセンス供与

technology licensing arrangements 技術のライセンス契約

▸We made some adjustments to our *licensing* practices. 当社は, 特許認可手続きを一部変更しました。

life 名 生活, 暮らし, 生命, 寿命, 期間, 活動, 活動期間, 存続, 存続期間, 耐用期間, 耐用年数, 年数, 継続期間, ライフ

actual life 実際耐用年数
asset life 資産の耐用年数
average life 平均期間, 平均残存期間, 平均償還期間

composite life 総合耐用年数 (＝composite useful life)
contractual life 契約期間
economic life 経済的耐用年数
expectation of life 見積り耐用年数
legal life 法定有効期間
life annuity 生涯年金, 終身年金, 生命年金
life period 耐用年数
life span 存続期間
life to call 据置き期間
mean expectation life 平均余命
option life オプション行使期間
physical life 物理的耐用年数
probable life 予想耐用年数
product life 製品寿命, 製品サイクル (＝product cycle)
productive life 生産年数
remaining life 残存期間, 残存年数, 残存耐用年数
remaining life of the issue 社債の残存期間
remaining useful life 残存耐用年数
service life 耐用年数
total economic life 通算経済的耐用年数

▸Amounts receivable or payable and gains or losses realized under swap agreements are recognized as yield adjustments over the *life* of the related debt. スワップ契約に基づいて実現した受取金や支払い金と利益および損失は, 当該債務が存続する間, 利回り調整として認識されます。

life cycle 製品ライフサイクル, 製品寿命, 生活循環, 寿命, ライフサイクル

life cycle costs ライフサイクル・コスト (プロジェクトの全期間にわたって発生する費用)

product life cycle 商品［製品］ライフサイクル, 製品サイクル, 製品寿命

▸We are commited to reducing the environmental impact at every stage of a product's *life cycle*, from design, to manufacture, to use, and to disposal. 当社は, 設計から製造, 使用と廃棄にいたるまで, 製品のライフサイクルの各段階での環境への影響軽減に全力を挙げています。

life insurance 生命保険

life insurance benefits for retirees 退職者に対する生命保険給付
life insurance deduction 生命保険料控除
life insurance in force 生命保険の保有契約高
life insurance premium 生命保険料
life insurance product 生命保険商品, 生保商品

life insurance benefits 生命保険給付

▸*Life insurance benefits* for retirees are expensed as funded, during the post-employment period.

退職者への生命保険給付は, 退職後の期間中に基金が積み立てられた時点で費用として計上されます。

life insurance coverage 保険金額, 保険契約金額, 生命保険給付
▸Our postretirement benefits include health care benefits and *life insurance coverage*. 当社の退職後給付には, 医療給付と生命保険給付が含まれています。

life insurer 生命保険会社 (＝life insurance company, life insurance firm)
▸The top 10 *life insurers* in the nation reported a total of ¥1.46 trillion in valuation losses on their securities holdings. 国内生保の上位(主要)10社の保有有価証券[保有株式]の減損処理額は, 10社合計で1兆4,600億円に達した。

lifetime employment 終身雇用
▸Efforts by the corporate sector to set great value on employees through the *lifetime employment* system has served to accumulate good human resources. 終身雇用制で従業員を大事にする企業の姿勢が, 優れた人的資源の蓄積に役立っている。

LIFO [lifo] 後入れ先出し法 (＝LIFO cost method, LIFO method：last-in, first-outの略。⇒**FIFO**)
　dollor value lifo 金額後入れ先出し法
　LIFO inventory method 後入れ先出し法
　LIFO liquidations 後入れ先出し法の清算
　LIFO method of accounting for inventories 後入れ先出し法による棚卸し資産の会計
　LIFO retail method 後入れ先出し売価還元法 (＝retail LIFO method)
▸We changed our inventory cost flow method to the FIFO cost method from the *LIFO* cost method on January 1, 2007. 2007年1月1日から当社は, 当社の棚卸し資産原価算定の方法を, 後入れ先出し法から先入れ先出し法に変更しました。

like-for-like basis 既存店ベース
▸The sales volume on a *like-for-like basis* fell by three percent. 既存店ベースの売上高は, 3％減少した。

limit 限度, 極度, 限界, 制限, 限度額, リミット
　borrower limit 与信限度
　credit limit 信用限度
　daily price limit 値幅制限 (＝price limit)
　lending limit 貸出限度
　lower limit 値幅制限の下限
　manager's discretionary limit 支店長の専決限度
　order without limit 成り行き注文
　policyholder limits 保険契約者に対する与信限度
　price limit 値幅制限, ストップ値段
　stock-buying limit 株式買入れ枠
　stop limit ストップ・リミット
　stop limit order 指し値注文
　trading limit 取引制限
▸There are legally two different upper *limits* for lending interest rates. 貸出金利の上限が法律上, 二つある。
▸In technology, there are no *limits* in sight for improvements in performance, function and value. テクノロジーの面では, 性能, 機能と価値の向上に限界はなさそうである。

line 商品の種類, 機種, 事業部門, 組立工程, 路線, 方針,〈損益計算書の〉経常利益［当期純利益］, 電話線, 伝送路, 回線, ライン (⇒**bottom line, product line**)
　assembly line 組立ライン, 流れ作業, アセンブリ・ライン
　bank line 銀行与信枠
　below the line 異常損益項目
　line item 勘定科目
　net errors and omissions line 純誤差脱漏項目
　net sales by product line 製品別売上構成
　top line 経常利益
▸Extraordinary losses have also battered the company's bottom *line*. 特別損失も, 同社の業績を直撃した。

line of business 事業の種類, 業種, 事業部門, 事業分野, 事業ライン, 営業品目, 営業項目, 営業科目 (＝business line)
　line of business information 事業の種類別情報, 事業分野別情報, 業種別情報
　line of business reporting 事業の種類別報告, 事業分野別報告, 業種別報告
▸This realignment decentralizes the Corporation into a series of largely autonomous *lines of business*. この再編成により, 当社の組織は, 自主性の高い一連の事業部門に分散されています。

line of credit 信用限度, 信用供与限度, 信用供与枠, 与信限度額, 融資限度, 貸出限度額, 借入限度額, 借入枠, 借入枠中未借入額, クレジット・ライン (＝credit line)
　uncommitted line of credit 未使用信用枠
▸Leverage was increased through a *line of credit*. 与信限度枠を使って, レバレッジを引き上げた。

line of products 製品ライン, 商品ライン, 商品群, 製品系列, 製品種目, 製品品目, 製品構成, プロダクト・ライン (＝product line)
▸Operations involve the design, manufacture and sale of a diversified *line of products*. 当社

の事業には，各種製品品目の設計，製造と販売が含まれています。

linger 動 なかなか消えない，残存する，ぐずぐずする

lingering 形 長引く，ぐずぐずする（⇒recession）

lion's share 最大の比率，最大のシェア，最大の部分，大きい取り分，大部分，一番おいしいところ
▶The *lion's share* of these contributions goes to educational institutions, but we also support health, cultural activities and the like.　この寄付金の大部分は，教育団体に割り当てられますが，当社は保健衛生や文化活動などにも援助を行っています。

liquid 形 流動性がある，流動性の高い
  liquid asset 流動資産，流動性の高い資産，当座資産
  liquid asset ratio 当座資産比率，当座資産構成比率
  liquid capital 流動資本
  liquid fund 流動資金，当座資金
  maintain liquid capital 流動資本を維持する
  net liquid assets 純流動資産
  short-term liquid investments 流動性のある短期投資
▶Temporary cash investments are highly *liquid* and have original maturities generally of three months or less.　短期投資は，非常に流動性が高く，原則として3か月以内に当初の期限が到来するものです。

liquidate 動〈借金や負債を〉弁済する，決済する，清算する，処分する，処理する，〈証券や資産などを〉売却する，現金化する，〈在庫を〉削減する，〈会社などを〉整理する，解散する，破産する
▶The prospects for *liquidating* nonperforming loans are dim.　不良債権処理の見通しは，はっきりしない。

liquidation 名 流動性，流動化（保有資産の支配権を第三者に移転して資金調達すること），決済，清算，処分，処理，整理，解散，破産，売却，現金化，換金（⇒basic profit）
  automatic liquidation 自動決済
  go into liquidation 破産する，清算を開始する，清算する，解散する
  insolvent liquidation 支払い不能による清算
  liquidation of bad debts 不良債権の処理
  liquidation of inventories 在庫削減，在庫整理，在庫取り崩し（＝inventory liquidation）
  liquidation of securities holdings 保有有価証券の売却
  liquidation of the assets 資産の売却（＝asset liquidation）
  profit and loss from liquidation 清算損益（＝liquidation profit and loss）
▶Preferred shares usually do not carry voting rights but have preference over common stocks in the payment of dividends and *liquidation* of assets.　優先株には通常，議決権は与えられないが，配当の支払いや清算時の残余財産の分配を普通株より優先して受けられる権利がある。
▶The Tokyo Stock Exchange (TSE) will move the company's stock to TSE's *liquidation* post from the monitoring post.　東京証券取引所（東証）は，同社株を監理ポストから整理ポストに移す。

liquid investment 流動性の高い投資
▶All highly *liquid investments* with a maturity of three months or less at date of purchase are considered to be cash equivalents.　購入日から3か月以内で満期となる非常に流動性の高い投資は，現金等価物として扱っています。

liquidity 名 流動性，流通性，〈流動資産の〉換金性，〈流動資産の〉換金能力，流動性の高さ，資金繰り，資金（⇒excess liquidity, tax authorities）
  流動性とは ➡ 流動性は，一般に株式や債券などの流通性のことで，marketability（市場性：市場で容易に売買できること）とほぼ同じ意味を持つ。このほかに，自己資産を現金化する能力を意味する場合もある
  ample liquidity 高い流動性，流動性の高さ 豊富な資金，大量の資金，潤沢な資金
  corporate liquidity 企業の手元流動性
  excess liquidity 過剰流動性
  internal sources of liquidity 内部流動性（＝internal liquidity）
  liquidity allocation 資金供給
  liquidity at hand 手元流動性
  liquidity demand 流動性需要，資金需要
  liquidity of investments in corporate securities 投資有価証券の流動性
  liquidity preference 流動性選好
  outside sources of liquidity 外部流動性（＝external liquidity）
  tightened liquidity 資金繰りの悪化

liquidity and capital resources 流動性と資本の源泉
▶Infromation on *liquidity and capital resources* for ABC Inc. and its principal subsidiaries follows.　ABC Inc.とその主要子会社の「流動性と資本の源泉」は，以下のとおりです。

list 動 上場する，上場される，表示する，表記す

る, 記載する, 掲載する, 記録する, 計上する, 名を挙げる, 指定する (⇒**fund procurement, stock buyout [buy-out]**)
listed investment 上場証券に対する投資
listed security 上場有価証券, 上場株式
listed share 上場株式, 上場株 (=listed stock)
▶The company *listed* its shares on the New York Stock Exchange in fiscal 2007 to expedite fund procurement in the U.S. markets. 米市場で機動的に資本調達するため, 同社は2007年度に米ニューヨーク証券取引所に株式を上場した。

list of shareholders 株主名簿 (=list of stockholders, shareholders list)
▶Oji Paper is considering asking the Tokyo District Court to allow it to examine the *list of shareholders* in Hokuetsu Paper. 王子製紙は, 東京地裁に対して北越製紙の株主名簿の閲覧を求めること [閲覧を求める仮処分申請] を検討している。

listed company 上場会社, 上場企業, 公開会社, 公開企業 (=listed corporation, listed firm; ⇒**row**)
▶There are about 1 million stock companies nationwide, and about 4,000 of them are *listed companies*. 国内には株式会社が約100万社あり, そのうち4,000社前後が株式を上場している公開会社だ。

listing 名 上場, 不動産仲介, 不動産仲介契約, 名簿, 表, 表の作成
 backdoor listing 裏口上場 (非上場企業が上場企業を買収して上場を果たすこと)
 eligibility criteria for listing 上場基準
 exchange listing procedures 証券取引所上場手続き
 listing fee 上場手数料
 listing particulars 上場目論見書, 上場明細書, 上場開示項目 (⇒**registration**)
 listing requirement 上場基準, 上場審査基準, 上場要件 (=initial listing requirements, listing rule)
 multiple listing 同時上場
 new listing 新規上場
 official listing 公的相場表
 preliminary application for listing 上場の仮申請
 public listing 上場
 stock exchange listing 上場証券取引所, 証券取引所への上場
 stock listings 株式上場証券取引所
▶Norinchukin Bank can expect large capital gains from the *listing* of Mizuho Securities. 農林中金としては, (みずほ証券に出資することで) みずほ証券の上場により多額の株式譲渡益を期待することができる。

LLC 有限責任会社, 〈日本の〉合同会社
 LLCについて ➡ アメリカのLLCは, ベンチャー企業などが資金調達をしやすくするために考え出された制度で, 構成員間の関係を自由な合意で決めることができる組合 (パートナーシップ) に対し, 企業の法人格と構成員の有限責任を与えたもの。
 LLCでは, 損益が直接, 構成員 (出資者) に配分される。また, LLCには法人所得税が課税されない。 (2003年12月8日付読売新聞「けいざい講座」から一部引用)

LLP 有限責任パートナーシップ, 有限責任事業組合, 有限責任組合 (**limited liability partnership**の略。⇒**partnership**)

loan 動 融資する, 貸し出す, 貸し付ける
▶The bank *loaned* the company a total of ¥5 billion in 25 separate transactions. 同行は, 同社に25回, 総額で50億円を融資した。

loan 名 貸付け, 貸出, 融資, 借入れ, 債権, 貸出債権, 債務, 借款, 債券発行, 貸付け金, 借入金, ローン
 accounting for impairment of loans 貸出債権の劣化
 accounting for loan losses 貸倒れ損失の会計
 arrears on loan repayments 延滞債権
 balance of loans 融資残高
 construction loan 建設借入金
 dead loan 焦げ付き貸金
 debt loan 借入金
 fees on loans 貸出金手数料
 housing loan 住宅金融, 住宅ローン
 interest on loans 貸付け金利息
 loan capital 借入資本 (=long-term loan)
 loan credits 債権 (=loan claims; ⇒**purchasing**)
 loan disposal costs 債権処理費用, 不良債権処理費用 (=credit costs)
 loan from officer 役員借入金 (=loan payable from officer)
 loan funds 貸出資金, 貸付け資金, 融資資金, 借款
 loan guarantee 債務保証
 loan interest rate 貸出金利 (=interest rate on loans, lending rate)
 loan origination fees 貸付け手数料, 貸出金実行手数料
 loan payable from officer 役員借入金 (=loan from officer)
 loan redemption 借入金償還
 loan to affiliated companies 関係会社貸付け

金 (=loan to affiliates)
loan to director 取締役貸付け金
loan to officer 役員貸付け金
loans and discounts 貸出金
loans payable 借入金
loans receivable 貸付け金
loans secured by real estate 不動産担保[抵当]貸付け金
loans secured by stock and bonds 有価証券担保貸付け金
loans to stockholders 株主貸付け金
make a loan 融資する, 貸し出す, 融資を実行する, 貸し付ける
outstanding loan 融資残高
receive loans from ... …から融資を受ける
repay the loan ローンを返済する, 借入金を返済する
securitizing of loans 債権の証券化, 融資の証券化
sound loan 正常債権, 健全債権
troubled loan 不良債権
▶The company plans to use the *loans* mainly to finance its planned capital investment. 同社は, この借入金を使って, 主に予定している設備投資にあてる計画だ.
▶We must change our accounting for the *loans* we make to cutomers by 2008. 当社は, 2008年までに, 顧客に対して行っている融資の会計処理方法を変更しなければなりません.

loan assessment 債権の査定
▶The bank conducted lenient *loan assessments* on borrowers, even those experiencing serious financial trouble. 同行は, 借り手企業に対する債権の査定では, 経営内容が危機的状況にある企業でも, 甘い査定をしていた.

loan assets 貸出資産
▶A U.S.-style formula for calculating loan-loss reserves assesses *loan assets* more strictly. 貸出資産の評価については, 米国流の貸倒れ引当金の算定方式のほうが厳しい.

loan collection 債権回収
▶The financial institutions were asked to temporarily halt *loan collection*. 金融機関は, 債権回収の一時停止を求められた.

loan forgiveness 債権放棄, 債務免除 (=debt forgiveness, debt waiver, loan waiver, loan write-off)
▶The three banks abandoned their initial plan to grant *loan forgiveness* to part of their claims on ¥1.6 trillion in loans to the company. 3行は, 1兆6,000億円の同社向け債権請求の一部について債権を放棄する当初案を断念した.

loan loss 貸倒れ, 貸倒れ損失, 不良債権, 不良貸付け
declare a loan loss 貸倒れ損失を計上する
loan loss provisioning 貸倒れ引当金繰入れ額, 貸倒れ引当金 (=loan loss provisioning charge)
loan loss ratio 貸倒れ実績率
loan losses 貸倒れ損失額

loan loss charge 貸倒れ損失額, 貸倒れ引当金, 不良債権額, 不良債権処理額, 不良債権処理損 (=bad debt clean-up charge, loan loss cost)
▶We expect group *loan-loss charges* of ¥900 billion for fiscal 2008. 当行は, 2008年度は連結で9,000億円の不良債権額を見込んでいます.

loan loss provisions 貸倒れ引当金 (=loan loss reserves)
bolster [hike, increase] loan loss provisions 貸倒れ引当金を積み増す
loan loss provisions of doubtful debts 不良債権に対する貸倒れ引当金
▶Consolidated pretax profit declined 38 percent due to increased *loan-loss provisions* for clients facing declining earnings. 連結税引き前利益は, 収益が低下している取引先[融資先]に対する貸倒れ引当金を積み増したため, 38%減少しました.

loan loss reserves 貸倒れ引当金, 貸倒れ準備金 (=loan loss provisions, reserves for bad loans, reserves for loan losses, reserves for possible loan losses:「貸倒れ引当金」は, 融資などの債権から担保などを差し引いた金額に対して, 貸出先企業が倒産して回収できない確率を考慮して積む. 経営状況が悪い企業向けの債権ほど, 引当率は高くなる)
increase loan loss reserves 貸倒れ引当金を積み増す, 貸倒れ引当金を強化する
reduce the loan loss reserves 貸倒れ引当金を減らす
set aside loan loss reserves 貸倒れ引当金を積む
▶The effective book value is calculated by subtracting amassed *loan loss reserves* from the original amount of money that was lent. 実質簿価は, 債権の元々の額(貸し付けた元々の金額:簿価)から, (銀行が)積み立てた貸倒れ引当金を差し引いて算定する.

loan recipient 融資先, 融資先企業
▶Currently, loan loss reserves are calculated on the basis of the probability of *loan recipients* going bankrupt. 現在, 貸倒れ引当金は融資先企業の(過去の)倒産確率に基づいて算定している.

loan values 債権の現在価値, 借入限度額

▸*Loan values* are calculated based on projections of how profitable a borrower is likely to be in the future.　債権の現在価値は, 融資先企業の予想収益に基づいて算定されています。

loan waiver　債権放棄, 債務免除　(=debt forgiveness, debt waiver, loan forgiveness, loan write-off)

▸The major banks managed to write off ¥5.11 trillion worth of bad loans using financial assistance and legal procedures such as *loan waivers* for large-lot borrowers as well as by selling bad loans to the Resolution and Collection Corporation.　大口融資先への債権放棄などの金融支援や法的整理, 整理回収機構(RCC)への不良債権売却などで, 大手行は最終的に5兆1,100億円の不良債権を処理した。

local currency　現地通貨, 現地通貨建て, 国内通貨(建て), 自国通貨(建て)

▸*Local currencies* are generally considered the functional currencies outside the United States.　米国外では, 一般に現地通貨を機能通貨と見なしています。

local procurement　現地調達

▸The Russian government plans to require Toyota to increase *local procurement* of components.　ロシア政府は部品の現地調達拡大をトヨタに義務付ける方針だ。

locate 動　設ける, 置く, 開設する, 開業する
 be located at …　…に位置する, …にある, …に置いてある
 locate production sites in China　中国に生産拠点を置く

▸We include the accounts of operations *located* outside the U.S. on the basis of their fiscal year.　米国外子会社[関係会社]の財務書類は, 各子会社の事業年度[会計年度]に基づいて連結されています。

▸We *located* a new branch in New York.　当社は, ニューヨークに支店を開設しました。

location 名　立地, 立地条件, 場所, 位置, 配置, 所在地, 拠点, 用地, 敷地,〈データの〉記憶場所, 野外撮影場, ロケーション　(⇒**register**動)
 degree of location　集積度
 fixed location　固定ロケーション(商品を置く場所の固定化)
 free location　フリー・ロケーション(商品を置く場所の自由化)
 geographical location　地理的位置
 industrial location　産業立地, 工業立地, 産業配置　(=location of industry)
 location decision　立地決定
 location factor　立地要因　(=location force)
 manufacturing location　工業立地
 offshore locations　海外拠点
 plant location　工場所在地, 工場立地, 工場用地
 prime location　一等地
 store location　店舗立地, 商業立地
 strategic location　地理的条件, 地理的に有利な条件

▸Revenues from customers (based on the *location* of the selling organization rather than the *location* of the customer) increased in Canada and the United States.　地域別顧客売上高(顧客の所在地ではなく, 販売組織の所在地に基づく売上高)は, カナダと米国で増加しました。

lockup [lock-up] 名　〈約束手形・債務などの〉期限延長, 塩漬け, 塩漬け株, 資本の固定, 損益の確定, 転売禁止, ロックアップ(企業買収交渉で, 買収成立から一切の処理が済むまでのあいだ第三者による買収の脅威をなくすため, 買収する会社と被買収会社が取り交わす取決めのことも「ロックアップ」という)

logistics 名　ロジスティクス(物流管理を含み, 調達・製造・販売のサイクル全体の観点で物流を最適化するシステムおよび最適化に必要な情報のシステムを含む概念)

long-lived asset　長期保有資産, 長期性[長期]資産, 固定資産　(=capital asset, fixed asset, long term asset, plant and equipment, property)

long range　長期, 長距離
 long range budget　長期予算
 long-range business planning　長期経営計画
 long-range cash forecast　長期資金予測
 long range cost　長期的費用, 長期費用, 長期原価　(=long run cost)
 long-range fund [cash] planning　長期資金計画
 long-range management planning　長期経営計画　(=long range planning)
 long-range profit planning　長期利益計画

long run　長期
 long run cost　長期的費用, 長期費用, 長期原価
 long run forces　長期的動向, 長期動向
 long run trend　長期傾向, 長期的動向, 長期トレンド

long term　長期
 long-term accounts payable　長期未払い金
 long term bond　長期債, 長期社債
 long term borrowing　長期借入金
 long-term capital balance　長期資本収支　(=long-term balance of capital account)

long term deposit 長期性預金
long-term note payable 長期支払い手形
long term obligation 長期債務, 長期負債, 長期借入金 (=long term debt)
long term payable 長期支払い債務
long-term contract 長期契約, 長期請負契約, 長期工事契約
　long-term contract balances 長期請負契約支出金
　long-term contract work 長期請負
　long-term contract work in progress 長期請負契約, 長期未完成請負工事 (=long term contract)
▸The Corporation uses the percentage of completion method to recognize revenues and costs associated with most *long-term contracts*. 当社では, 進行基準を用いて大半の長期請負契約に関する収益と費用を認識しています。
long-term debt 長期債務, 長期負債, 長期借入金, 長期借入債務, 固定負債 (=long term borrowings, long term obligation)

長期借入債務に含まれるもの：

convertible bonds	転換社債
long-term contracts	長期請負契約
long-term notes payable	手形借入金
mortgage notes	担保付き長期手形
obligations under capital leases	キャピタル・リース債務
straight bonds	普通社債
debentures	無担保社債
mortgage bonds	担保付き社債
subordinated debentures	劣後社債

　long-term debt obligation 長期債 (=long-term debt securities)
　long-term debt to equity ratio 長期負債対自己資本比率
　long term debts due within one year 1年以内返済長期借入金
　long term debts from affiliated company 関係会社長期借入金
▸About $830 million of *long-term debt* matures during the year. 長期債務のうち約8億3,000万ドルは, 今年度に満期が到来します[満期を迎えます]。
▸The Company's *long-term debt* is rather small. 当社の長期借入金は, どちらかというと少ないほうです。
long-term debt rating 長債格付け, 長期格付け
▸General Motor's *long term debt rating* was slashed one level to Caa1 by Moody's Investors Service. ゼネラル・モーターズ(GM)の長期債格付けを, 米格付け会社のムーディーズ・インベスターズ・サービスが1段階下のCaa1に引き下げた。
long-term debt-to-total capital 長期負債対総資本比率
▸*Long-term debt-to-total capital* is used to gauge a company's financial strength. 長期負債対総資本比率は, 企業の財務力測定に用いられます。
long-term finance receivables 長期金融債権, 長期金融売掛債権
▸*Long-term finance receivables* of $300 million in 2007 are included in other assets. 2007年度の3億ドルの長期金融債権は, その他の資産に含まれています。
long-term financing 長期資金調達
▸*Our long-term financing* was accomplished through the issuance of long-term debt instruments. 当社の長期資金調達は, 長期債務証券を発行して行われた。
long-term incentive program 長期奨励報酬制度, 長期勤労奨励制度
▸In our *Long Term Incentive Program*, we grant stock options, stock appreciation rights (SARs) and other awards. 当社の長期勤労奨励制度には, ストック・オプションや株式評価受益権(SAR)などの奨励制度があります。
long-term interest rate 長期金利
　長期金利とは ➡ 期間1年以上の金利で, 新規発行された10年物国債(長期国債)の流通利回りを指標に使う。国債価格が上がれば長期金利が下がる関係にある。企業向け貸出や住宅ローン金利にも影響する。景気が悪いと経済活動が停滞し, 長期金利も下がる。
▸The rise in *long-term interest rates* may apply the brakes on the recovery. 長期金利の上昇は, 景気回復にブレーキをかけかねない。
long-term loans 長期貸付け金, 長期融資, 長期借入金
　long-term loans payable 長期借入金
　long-term loans receivable 長期貸付け金
　long-term loans to officers and employees 役員と従業員への長期貸付け金
long-term monetary assets 長期貨幣性資産 (⇒monetary assets)
▸*Long-term monetary assets* and liabilities are translated at the exchange rates in effect at the balance sheet date. 長期貨幣性資産および負債は, 貸借対照表日[決算日]現在の実効為替レートで換算されています。
long-term planning 長期経営計画, 長期計画 (=long-range planning)

‣Our *long-term planning* will give us a strong global position in the expanding wireless market. 当社の長期計画によって，当社は拡大する無線通信市場で世界的に強力な事業基盤を確立する方針です．

long-term receivable 長期受取債権，長期債権，長期受取勘定

‣The Corporation's financial instruments include accounts receivable, short-term investments, *long-term receivables*, accounts payable, notes payable and long-term debt. 当社の金融手段［金融資産］としては，売掛金，短期投資，長期受取勘定，買掛金，短期借入金や長期債務などがあります．

lose 動 赤字を出す，損失を被る，失う，〈競争などに〉負ける，下落する

‣GM, the world's largest automaker, *lost* $1.6 billion in the third quarter, or $2.89 per share. 自動車世界最大手のGMの第3四半期（7-9月期）決算は，16億ドル（1株当たり2.89ドル）の赤字となった．

loser 名 負け組，負け組企業，失敗企業，敗者，値下り銘柄

‣What distinguishes the winners from the *losers* is the ability to anticipate and influence these kinds of changes—to be leaders, not victims, of chage. 勝者と敗者を決める大きな要因は，この種の変化を予期し，それに流動的に対応する能力，つまり変化の波に流されずに変化を制する能力です．

loss 名 損失，欠損，欠損金，赤字，赤字額，損害，損失額，減損，減少，ロス
 accounting loss 会計上の損失
 annual profit and loss 年次損益
 book loss 帳簿上の損失
 conditional loss 機会損失
 contingent loss 偶発損失
 credit loss 信用損失
 default loss デフォルト損失
 embedded losses 含み損
 expected losses 予想損失，損失の予想額
 financial loss 財務会計上の損失，財務上［会計上］の損失，金融上の損失，損失
 historical loss experience 過去の損失実績
 holding gain or loss 保有損益
 huge losses 巨額の損失
 interim losses 中間期の損失，半期損失，半期決算損失
 loss carryover [carry-over] 欠損金の繰越し（＝carryover of deficit）
 loss from prior period adjustment 前期損益修正損
 loss from valuation of securities 有価証券評価損（＝loss from securities revaluation, loss from write-down of securities)
 loss of operating earnings 営業利益の減少，営業減益
 loss on bad debt 貸倒れ損失
 loss on bond conversion 社債転換差損
 loss on disposal of property 動産・不動産処分損
 loss on foreign exchange 外国為替差損
 loss on impairment 減損損失
 loss on retirement of fixed assets 固定資産除却損
 loss on sale of real estate 不動産売却損
 loss or gain on retirement of fixed assets 固定資産除却損益
 loss per share 1株当たり純損失，1株当たり損失
 loss projections 損失予想額，予想損失額
 losses from bad loan disposals 不良債権処理損失額，不良債権処理による損失額，不良債権処理に伴う損失額
 losses in stock transactions 株式売買の損失
 normal loss 正常な減損
 periodic loss 期間損失
 potential loss 潜在的損失
 reduced losses 赤字縮小
 special loss 特別損失
 tax loss 税務上の欠損金

‣The bank recorded *losses* in the accounting period ending March 31 due to bad loan write-offs. 同行は，不良債権処理のため，3月期決算［3月31日終了の会計年度］で赤字になった．

‣We incurred a *loss* of $60 million in connection with the sale of U.S. oil and gas interests. 当社は，米国の石油・ガス利権の売却に関連して6,000万ドルの損失を被りました．

loss carryback [carry back] 欠損金の繰戻し

‣No financial recognition is allowed for net deferred tax assets in excess of the amount that could be recovered as income tax refunds through existing *loss carryback* or carryforward provisions. 現行の欠損金の繰戻しまたは繰延べの規定（財務会計基準書（SFAS）第96号の規定）により，還付税金として取り戻すことができる金額を超えて繰延べ税金資産純額を会計上，計上することは認められていません．

loss carryforward [carry forward] 欠損金の繰越し，損失の繰延べ，繰越し欠損金

‣As December 31, 2007, certain non-U.S. subsidiaries had *loss carryforwards* for income tax reporting purposes of $39.7 million, with expiration dates starting in 2008. 2007年12月31日

現在、一部の非米国籍子会社の繰越し欠損金は税務上3,970万ドルで、その繰越し期限は2008年以降到来します。

loss contingencies 偶発損失事象, 偶発［偶発的］損失

loss-making [lossmaking] 形 赤字続きの, 赤字の, 採算が合わない
　loss-making area 不採算部門（＝lossmaking）
　loss-making business results 赤字決算
　loss-making outlet 赤字店舗（＝money-losing outlet）
▶The company window-dressed its *loss-making* business results for the business year to the end of September 2006. 同社は、2006年9月期の赤字決算を粉飾していた。

loss-sharing system ロスシェアリング方式, 損失分担方式
▶The Financial Services Agency applied a *loss-sharing system* when it sold the bank. 同行の営業譲渡の際、金融庁はロスシェアリング方式（国と譲渡先が損失を分担する方式）を適用した。

low 名 安値, 底値, 最低, 底, 最安値, 最低値, 最低記録
　a closing low 終値での最安値
　a new low 新安値
　all time lows 過去最低の水準（＝historic lows）
　an all time low 過去最低, 史上最安値, 上場来の安値, 過去最良
　an intraday low 取引時間中の安値, ざら場の安値
　fall to new lows 史上最安値を更新する（＝set new all-time lows）
▶Tokyo stocks tumbled to a 15-month closing *low* as uncertainties continued to grow about the outlook for the Japanese and U.S. economies. 東京株［東京株式市場の株価］は、日米経済の先行き不透明感の高まりを受け、終値で1年3か月ぶりの最安値となった。

low cost 低コスト, 低費用, 低原価
　low cost labor 低コスト労働力, 低賃金の労働力
　low cost loan 低金利ローン, 低費用融資, 低利融資
▶The company has been building new factories at breakneck speed in *low-cost* countries such as China, Brazil, Hungary and Mexico. 同社は、中国やブラジル、ハンガリー、メキシコなどの低コスト国で、猛スピードで新工場を建設している。

low-interest loans 低利融資
▶The bank will provide the ailing automaker with *low-interest loans* in a bid to help manage its cash flow and conduct its corporate restructuring. 同行は、経営再建中のこの自動車メーカーの資金繰りやリストラを支援するため、低利融資を実施する方向だ。

lower 動 引き下げる, 低減する, 下げる, 下落する, 低下する, 下がる, 減少する
▶The company *lowered* its half-year net profit forecast. 同社は、半期純利益予想を引き下げた。

lower 形 低いほうの, 下部の, 下級の, 下等の, 下層の
　lower aggregate cost or market 総額低価法
　lower realizable value or replacement price rule 実現可能価額取替原価比較低価法
　lower revenues 売上高の減少, 収益の減少, 減収
▶Our earnings per share were affected both by *lower* revenues and reduced gross margins. 当社の1株当たり利益は、売上高の減少と売上利益率の低下の影響を受けました。

lower gross margins 売上利益率の低下, 粗利益率の低下（＝reduced gross margins）
▶Price competition has been a contributing factor to the segment's *lower gross margins*. 当部門の粗利益率の低下をもたらした要因の一つは、価格競争だ。

lower of average cost or market 平均原価または時価のいずれか低いほう（の金額）, 平均原価時価低価法
▶Raw materials, finished goods and work in process are stated at the *lower of average cost or market*. 原材料、製品と仕掛品は、平均原価または時価のいずれか低いほうの金額で計上［評価］されています。

lower of cost and net realizable value （資産の）取得原価と正味実現可能価額のうち低いほうの価額

lower of cost or market 低価法, 低価基準《略 LCM》（＝cost or market, whichever is lower basis [method]）
▶Inventories are stated at the *lower of cost or market*. 棚卸し資産は、低価法で計上しています。
　lower of cost(first-in, first-out)or market 先入れ先出し法に基づく低価法
　lower of cost or market basis [method] 低価法, 低価基準, 低価主義, 原価［資産の取得原価］または時価のいずれか低い金額, 原価時価比較低価法《略 LCM》
　lower of cost or market value 原価時価比較低価法
▶Inventories are valued at the *lower of cost (calculated generally on a first-in, first-out basis) and net realizable value*. 棚卸し資産は、

取得原価(原則として先入れ先出し法で計算)と正味実現可能価額のうち, 低いほうの価額で評価されています。

lucrative 形 利益が得られる, 儲かる, 大変金になる, 利益の大きい, 有利な (＝profitable)
lucrative business 儲かる商売, 有利な事業
lucrative company 有力企業
lucrative investment 有利な投資
lucrative upstream division 利益の大きい原油採掘[原油生産]部門

▸Helping firms go public is a *lucrative* business for securities firms. 企業の上場を手伝う業務は, 証券会社の収益源だ。

lump-sum 形 一括払いの
lump-sum payment 一括支払い
lump-sum repayment 一括返済

M m

M&A 企業の吸収合併, 合併・買収, 企業取得と合併（merger and acquisition [mergers and acquisitions] の略）
 M&A advisory firm M&A [企業の合併・買収] 助言会社
 M&A deal M&A取引, M&A案件 （＝M&A transaction）
▸The recent *M&A* is a strategy with an eye on Asia, which has a great potential for sales growth. 今回のM&Aは, 販売が伸びる可能性が大きいアジアを視野に入れた戦略です。
M&A bid 企業の合併・買収提案, M&Aの提案
▸Those undertaking *M&A bids* are required to make a thorough disclosure of information. 企業のM&A [合併・買収] 提案者は, 情報を十分開示する必要がある。
machinery 名 機械, 機械装置, 機器, 機構, 組織
 electrical machinery 電機
 electronic machinery industry 電機業界
 industrial machinery 産業機械, 産業用機械
 machinery and equipments 機械設備, 機械・設備, 機械装置, 機械および装置
 office machinery オフィス機器, 事務機器
 transport machinery 輸送機器
 transportation machinery 輸送機器, 輸送用機械
▸We depreciate our *machinery* using an accelerated method of depreciation for income tax reporting. 当社では, 税務会計上 [税務上] は加速償却法を使用して機械の減価償却を行っている。
machinery orders 機械受注, 機械受注額
 core private machinery orders 実質民間機械受注, 実質機械受注（船舶・電力を除く民間需要）
 private machinery orders 民間機械受注
 public machinery orders 官公機械受注, 機械受注のうち公共部門の需要
▸*Machinery orders* for the April–June quarter are expected to fall 3.2 percent. 4–6月期の機械受注は, 3.2％減少する見通しだ。
main bank 主要取引銀行, 主力取引銀行, 主力行, メインバンク （＝main financing bank）
▸The firm's *main bank* will swap ¥20 billion in debt into stock. 同社の主力取引銀行は, 200億円分の債権の株式化を行う [200億円分の債権を株式に切り替える]。
main business 主力事業, 中核事業, 本業 （＝core business, main operation, mainstay business）
▸Operating profit from *main businesses* increased 6 percent to ¥950 billion. 本業 [主力事業] による営業利益は, 6％増の9,500億円となった。
mainstay 名 主力, 主力商品, 支え, 支柱, 大黒柱, 頼みの綱, 拠り所
▸Nipponkoa's net premium revenues dropped to 0.9 percent due to declines in its *mainstay* automobile insurance policies. 日本興亜損保の正味収入保険料は, 主力の自動車保険 [自動車保険契約] の減少で, 0.9％減少した。
maintain 動 維持する, 持続する, 保守する, 保全する, 整備する, 据え置く
▸Moody's Investors Service cut Japan's yen-denominated debt rating by one notch to Aa3 from Aa2 and *maintained* a negative outlook. 米国の格付け会社ムーディーズは, 日本の円建て国債の格付けを「Aa2」から「Aa3」に一段階引き下げ, 「ネガティブ（弱含み）」の見通しを据え置いた。
maintenance 名 維持, 保守, メンテナンス

maintenance and inspection 保守・点検
maintenance and repairs 維持修繕費
maintenance charge 維持費, 保守費, メンテナンス費 （＝maintenance cost, maintenance expense）
maintenance reserve 維持費引当金
major shareholder 大株主, 大口株主, 主要株主 （＝large shareholder, major stockholder）
▶According to a listing requirement, *major shareholders* are prohibited from owing more than an 80 percent stake in a company. 上場基準によると, 大株主は80％を超える会社株式の所有は禁じられている。
majority 名 過半数, 大多数, 多数, 大半, 大部分
　majority interest 過半数持ち分, 過半数株式 （＝controlling interest; ⇒**board of corporate auditors**）
　majority owned company 過半数所有子会社 （＝majority owned subsidiary）
　majority owner 過半数株主
　majority ownership 過半数支配
　majority rule 多数決
　majority share 過半数の株式
　majority shareholder［**stockholder**］過半数株主
▶According to the NYSE's new rules, corporate boards must be composed of a *majority* of independent directors. ニューヨーク証券取引所（NYSE）の新上場基準によると, 企業（上場企業）の取締役の過半数は社外取締役にしなければならない。
majority owned subsidiary 過半数所有子会社（50％を超える議決株式を所有する子会社）
▶The consolidated financial statements include the accounts of the Company and those *majority owned subsidiaries* where the Company has control. 連結財務書類［連結財務諸表］には, 当社と当社の支配下にある過半数所有子会社の財務書類が含まれています。
majority stake 過半数株式
▶Aeon Co. has acquired a *majority stake* in Diamond City Co. through a public tender offer. イオンは, 株式公開買付け（TOB）でダイヤモンドシティ（ショッピングセンター開発会社）の過半数株式を取得した。
make up for ... …を補填する, …の穴埋めをする, …を埋め合わせる, 帳消しにする
▶Some banks have been forced to liquidate their legal reserves due to the need to dispose of huge amounts of bad loans and *make up for* latent stock price losses. 巨額の不良債権の処理と株式含み損の補填に迫られ, 一部の銀行は法定準備金の取崩しに追い込まれている。

manage 動 管理する, 経営する, 統括する, 統率する, 監督する, 幹事を務める, 運用する, 運営する, 運用管理する, うまく処理する, 対処する, 取り扱う, 使いこなす, 〈困難などを〉乗り切る, 切り抜ける （⇒**potential**）
　manage liquidity 流動性を抑える
　manage the business 事業を統括する
　manage the portfolio ポートフォリオを運用する
　manage the risk exposure リスクを管理する
　manage the syndication シンジケート団を取り仕切る
▶Investors are buying into the potential of a company, not to *manage* it. 投資家は, 企業の経営権ではなく, 企業の将来性を買っている。
▶We will stay the course, *managing* expenses tightly and pursuing new market opportunities. 私どもは, 当社の経営路線に基づき, 支出管理を強化するとともに, 新たな市場機会を追求していく方針です。

management 名 経営, 管理, 運用, 運営, 取扱い, 業務執行, 経営管理, 経営陣, 経営側, 経営者側, マネジメント （⇒**corporate management**）
　balance sheet management 財務管理, バランス・シート管理
　bond management 債券運用, 債券管理
　business management 企業経営, 企業管理, 経営管理, 業務管理, 経営
　cash flow management キャッシュ・フロー経営 （現金の流れを最大化することを指針として経営の舵取りをする経営手法。流動資産が大きく, 在庫（棚卸し資産）や債権（売掛金や受取手形など）の期間が短ければ, キャッシュ・フローは増大する）
　cash management 現金預金管理, 現金管理, 資金管理, キャッシュ・マネジメント
　corporate management
　credit management 与信管理, 信用管理
　current asset management 流動資産管理
　demand side management 需要管理, デマンド・サイド・マネジメント
　effective management 効率経営, 効率的な経営, 効果的な経営
　expanded management fee 拡大幹事手数料
　financial management 財務管理, 財テク（資金の運用と調達についての検討）
　financial market 金融市場
　financial risk management 金融リスク管理, 金融リスク・マネジメント
　fiscal management 財政運営

fund management 資金運用, 資金管理, 投資運用, 投資管理, 投資顧問
fund management operation 資金運用
investment management 投資管理, 投資運用, 投資顧問
management advisory services 経営助言サービス, 経営者への提案業務《略 MAS》(＝management services)
management control 経営者支配, 経営支配, 経営支配権, 経営管理, 経営統制
management decision 経営者の意思決定, 経営意思決定, 経営判断 (＝managerial decision)
management efficiency 経営効率, 事業効率
management expense 管理費, 運用経費, 運用費用 (＝management charge)
management fees 経営報酬, 役員報酬, 運用報酬, 幹事手数料, 管理手数料
management information 経営情報
management of affairs 事務管理
management of funds 資金繰り, 資金管理, 資金運用 (＝fund management)
management of idle money 余資運用
management report 経営報告, 経営報告書, 経営管理報告書, 経営者の報告, 経営者の報告書
management restructuring plan 経営健全化計画
management system 経営システム, 経営体制, 管理システム, 管理方式, マネジメント・システム
portfolio management 最適資産管理
profit management 利益管理
purchasing management 購買管理
risk management 危険管理, 危機管理, リスク管理, リスク・マネジメント
stock management 株の運用, 株式運用
systems management システム管理《略 SM》
value-oriented management 価値重視の経営
working capital management 運転資本管理

▸Rakuten has proposed integrating the firms' *management* under a joint holding company. 楽天は, 共同持ち株会社の設立による [共同持ち株会社方式での] 両社の経営統合を提案した。

▸The financial statements have been prepared by *management* in conformity with U.S. GAAP (generally accepted accounting principles). 財務書類 [財務諸表] は, 米国会計基準 (米国で一般に公正妥当と認められた会計基準 [会計原則]) に従って, 経営者が作成しました。

management buyout [**buy-out**] 経営者による自社買収, 経営陣による自社株式の公開買付け, 経営者による営業権取得, 経営陣による企業買収, マネジメント・バイアウト《略 MBO》(企業の経営者が, 一般株主や親会社などから自社株を買い取って, 企業や事業部門の経営権を買い取ること)

▸The management has decided to implement *management buyout* to enhance the financial base. 経営陣は, 経営基盤を強化するため, マネジメント・バイアウトの実施を決めた。

management employee 管理職
▸Benefits for *management employees* are principally based on career-average pay. 管理職に対する給付は, 基本的に職歴平均給方式に基づいています。

management executive committee 経営執行委員会
▸The *Management Executive Committee* leads the development and implementation of our mission, values and strategic intent. 経営執行委員会は, 当社の使命, 価値観, 戦略的意図の策定と実施の先頭に立っています。

management integration 経営統合 (＝business integration, management merger, operational integration)
▸Konaka Co. emphasized the advantages of the *management integration* with menswear chain Futata Co. コナカは, 紳士服チェーンのフタタとの経営統合による (経営) メリットを強調した。

management offering 経営陣に対する株式発行 [株式の売出し]
▸We sold approximately 850,000 shares of common stock in a *management offering*. 当社は, 経営陣に対する株式発行で約85万株の普通株式を売り出しました。

management plan 経営計画 (＝management planning)
▸The group's three-year *management plan* slates ¥2 trillion of capital investment for fiscal 2008 on a consolidated basis. 同グループの3か年経営計画では, 2008年度は連結ベースで2兆円の設備投資を予定している。

management renewal 経営刷新, 経営陣の刷新
▸Constant *management renewal* is essential to success. 絶えざる経営刷新 [経営陣の刷新] は, 企業の発展に不可欠である。

management resources 経営資源, 役員人事
▸We must concentrate manpower, money and other *management resources* on profit-making sources. 人材や資金などの経営資源を, 収益源に集中させる [投入する] 必要がある。

management right 経営権

▶Investment funds do not hesitate to dissolve a company and strip its assets after acquiring the *management rights* of the company. 投資ファンドは, 会社の経営権を取得した後, 会社を解散してその資産を売り払うこともいとわない。

management strategy 経営戦略
  long-term management strategy 長期経営戦略
  midterm management strategy 中期経営戦略
▶Foreign companies doing business in China may have to revise their *management strategies* if labor costs continue to climb there. 中国で人件費の上昇が続けば, 中国進出の外国企業は, 経営戦略の見直しを迫られるかもしれない。

management structure 経営組織, 経営機構, 経営形態
▶We announced a new *management structure* in February as a further initiative to align ourselves to compete more effectively in the global marketplace. 当社は2月に, グローバル市場で一段と効果的に競争する体制を整えるためのさらなる施策として, 経営機構 [経営組織] の改革を発表しました。

management style 経営手法, 経営姿勢, 経営スタイル, 経営方式
▶The U.S. business *management style* is characterized by greater transparency and accountability of business management, symbolized by outside directors, corporate executive officers, independent auditors and compliance officers. 米国型企業経営の特色は, 社外重役や業務執行役員, 独立監査人 [外部監査人], コンプライアンス・オフィサー [法令・規則遵守担当役員] などに象徴されるように, 経営の透明性や説明責任にある。

management team 経営陣, マネジメント・チーム (＝management profiles)
  current management team 現経営陣
  new management team 新経営陣
▶Marubeni initially planned to maintain Daiei's current *management team* until next May. 丸紅は当初, 来年5月までダイエーの現経営陣の続行を予定していた。

Management's Discussion and Analysis 経営者の分析・検討 [検討・分析], 経営者の分析・解説, 財務分析と説明, 経営者による事業概況報告 [報告書]《略 MD&A》

management's illegal acts 経営者の違反行為

manager 名 経営者, 管理者, 幹部, 幹部社員, 部長, 理事, 幹事(引受会社), 投資顧問, 支配人, 責任者, 管財人, マネージャー

asset manager 投資顧問業, アセット・マネージャー
bond manager 債券運用者, 債券管理者, 債券運用担当者, 債券管理担当者, ボンド・マネージャー
co-lead manager 共同主幹事 (＝joint lead-manager)
executive manager 執行役員
general manager 総支配人, 全般的管理者, 事業本部長, ゼネラル・マネージャー
investment manager 投資顧問, 投資運用会社, 運用会社, 投資マネージャー
lead manager 主幹事, 引受主幹事, 幹事銀行, 幹事行
personnel manager 人事担当重役
portfolio manager 資産管理者, 資産運用者, ポートフォリオ運用者, ポートフォリオ・マネージャー
▶We have reduced our *managers* by 3,000. 当社は, 管理職を3,000人削減しました。
▶While stock prices shifted upward, the sentiments of corporate *managers* have shown signs of improvement lately. 株価が上昇に転じる一方, 最近は企業経営者の景況感も改善の兆しを見せている。

managerial 形 経営 [管理, 操作, 処理] の, 経営上の, 経営者の
  managerial abilities 経営力, 管理者能力
  managerial control 経営統制, 管理的統制, 経営権
  managerial decision 経営の意思決定, 経営判断 (＝management decision)
  managerial efforts 経営努力
  managerial employee 管理職 (＝management employee)
  managerial functions 経営者の職能
  managerial philosophy 経営理念
  managerial policy 経営方針
  managerial position 管理職 (＝management position)
  managerial problems 経営上の問題
  managerial resources 経営資源
  managerial system 経営体制
▶It is a wise *managerial* decision to give up the profits accrued from the erroneous sell order. 売り注文のミス [誤発注] で得た利益を返上するのは, 賢明な経営判断だ。

manipulate 動 操作する, 操縦する, 巧みに操る (⇒**window dressing**)
▶Stock option programs are seen as leading to financial window-dressing to *manipulate* share prices. ストック・オプション制度は, 株価操作の

ための会計操作につながると見られている。

manipulation 名 操作, 不正操作, 市場操作, 相場操縦
- **accounting manipulation** 会計操作
- **earnings manipulation** 利益の不正操作
- **financial manipulation** 経理操作
- **income manipulation** 利益操作
- **manipulation of accounts** 粉飾 (=equation manipulation)
- **stock price manipulation** 株価操縦, 株価操作 (=stock manipulation; ⇒**stock issue**)

▶Market *manipulation* has been occurring in connection with new share issues. 増資に絡んで, 株価操作が行われている。

▶The accounting *manipulations* went unnoticed by the company's auditors and the board of directors. 会計操作は, 同社の監査役や取締役会が見過ごしていた。

manpower 名 労働力, 労力, 人的資源, 人材, 人手, 労働人員, 人員, 従業員, 従業員数, マンパワー
- **lack of manpower** 人材不足, 人手不足, 労働力不足 (=manpower shortage)
- **manpower management** 労働力管理, 労務管理
- **manpower planning** 人員計画, 要員計画, マンパワー・プランニング

▶Added value per employee indicates the degree of excessive *manpower*. 従業員1人当たりの付加価値額は, 余剰人員の度合いを示す。

manufacture 動 製造する, 生産する, 製作する
- **manufactured goods** 工業製品, 工業品, 加工品, 生産品, 製品 (=manufactured product)
- **manufactured imports** 製品輸入, 工業製品の輸入
- **manufactured material** 自製材料
- **manufactured product** 工業製品 (=manufacturing industry product)

▶Hitachi, Ltd. and Matsushita Electric Industrial Co. are considering jointly *manufacturing* large liquid crystal display panels for flat-screen televisions. 日立製作所と松下電器産業は, 薄型テレビ用の大型液晶パネルの共同生産を検討している。

manufacture 名 製造, 生産, 製作, 製品

manufacturer 名 製造業者, 製造者, 製作者, メーカー, 工場主 (=maker)

▶Like other *manufacturers*, we use, dispose of and clean up substances that are regulated under environmental protection laws. 他の製造業者と同じように, 当社も環境保護法で規制されている物質を使用し, その処分や浄化を行っています。

manufacturing 名 製造, 生産, 加工, 製作, マニュファクチュアリング

- **computer-aided manufacturing** コンピュータ支援[援用]製造
- **computer integrated manufacturing** コンピュータ統合生産(システム) 《略 CIM》
- **economic manufacturing quantity** 経済的生産数量, 最適生産量
- **intelligent manufacturing system** 知的生産システム
- **manufacturing burden** 製造間接費 (=factory burden, factory overhead, manufacturing overhead)
- **manufacturing capacity** 生産能力, 製造能力
- **manufacturing expense** 製造経費, 製造間接費
- **manufacturing facilities** 製造施設, 生産拠点, 生産設備 (=production facilities)
- **manufacturing indirect cost** 製造間接費 (=factory overhead, manufacturing overhead cost)
- **telecommunications equipment manufacturing** 通信機器の製造, 通信機器製造事業
- **virtual manufacturing** 仮想生産, バーチャル・マニュファクチュアリング

▶We have closed some of our *manufacturing* facilities worldwide. 当社は, 当社の世界の製造施設を一部閉鎖しました。

manufacturing cost 製造原価, 製造コスト, 生産コスト (=cost of goods manufactured, output cost, production cost)

▶Our global product organizations helped to improve our margins through product redesign to lower *manufacturing* costs. 当社のグローバル製品事業部門は, 製造コスト低減のための製品再設計により, 当社の利益率改善に寄与しました。

manufacturing cycle time 製造所要時間

▶We have reduced our *manufacturing* cycle time and improved the quality of our products. 当社は, 製造所要時間の削減と当社製品の品質改善[向上]に取り組んでいます。

manufacturing operations 製造事業, 製造部門, 生産子会社[関連会社]

▶*Manufacturing* and distribution *operations* in any one foreign country do not account for more than 10% of consolidated net sales or total assets. 国外で, 製造および販売事業が連結純売上高または総資産の10%を超える国はありません。

manufacturing overhead 製造間接費 (=factory burden, factory overhead, manufacturing burden, manufacturing overhead cost)

- The cost of finished goods and work in process comprise material, labor, and *manufacturing overhead*. 製品と仕掛品の原価は, 材料費と労務費と製造間接費からなっています。

manufacturing process 製造工程, 製造部門
- We are pursuing ambitious efforts to decrease toxic air emissions and *manufacturing process* waste. 当社は, 有毒なガス放出の削減や製造工程での産業廃棄物の削減に意欲的に取り組んでいます。

manufacturing system 生産システム
- Matsushita Electric Industrial Co. has taken the Japanese-style *manufacturing system*. 松下電器産業は, 日本流の生産システムを取り入れている。

March–August period 3-8月期,〈2月期決算企業の〉上半期, 3-8月期決算, 8月中間決算 (⇒**group sales**)
- Pretax profit in the *March–August period* grew 41.3 percent to ¥863 million. 3-8月期［上半期］の税引き前利益［経常利益］は, 41.3％増の8億6,300万円でした。

margin 名 売上総利益, 利益率, 利ざや, 証拠金, 委託証拠金, 委託保証金, 担保金, 手付け金 (⇒ **after-tax margin, gross margin, gross profit margin**)
  additional margin 追加証拠金
  gross margin ratio 売上総利益率
  margin requirement 証拠金, 証拠金所要額, 証拠金規定額, 証拠金率
  margin trading 信用取引, 証拠金取引 (= margin transaction; ⇒**FX margin trading**)
  narrow margin 薄利
  narrow profit margins 利ざやが薄いこと
  net margin 純販売利益, 純売買差益, 純利益
  net profit margin 売上高利益率
  operating income margin 営業利益率
  product margins 製品利益率
  profit margin 利益率, 利ざや
  profit margin on sales 売上高利益率
- We improved our gross and net *margins* on sales with net earnings increasing to 10 percent and earnings per share increasing 12 percent. 当社の純販売利益と販売利益率も改善し, 純利益は10％増加, 1株当たりの利益は12％増加しました。

margin improvement 利益率改善, 利ざやの拡大, 利ざや改善
- In managing the business, we achieved 14 percent growth in earnings per common share through *margin improvement* and prudent expense controls. 業務運営の面では, 利益率の改善と支出抑制の徹底により, 普通株式1株当たり純利

益は14％増加しました。

margin percentage 利益率
- The continuing shift in revenue mix to other services from higher-margin rentals led to a decline in the *margin percentage* in 2007. 高利益率のレンタル事業からその他のサービスへの売上構成の変化が続いたため, 2007年度は利益率が低下しました。

marginal increase 小幅な伸び, 微増
- Business communications systems and terminals revenues showed only a *marginal increase* in 2007 to $1.31 billion (24 percent of total revenues) from $1.30 billion in 2006. ビジネス通信システムと端末装置の2007年度の売上高は, 前年度の13億ドルに対して13.1億ドル(総売上高の24％)で, ほんの微増にとどまりました。

mark 名 水準, 標準, …台, …の大台, 記号, 符号, 標識, 標的, 目標, 成績, 評価, マーク
- Toyota's midterm account settlement will certainly exceed, for the first time, the ¥10 trillion *mark* for the midterm business results. トヨタの中間決算では, 中間期の業績で初めて10兆円台を突破するのは確実となっている。

mark to market 評価替えする, 値洗いする (⇒**hedge**)
  marked-to-market value 時価評価額, 値洗い後の価格

mark-to-market 名形 評価替え, 値洗い (= mark to the market : 手持ち証券などの価値を現在市場価値に評価し直すこと)
  mark-to-market accounting practices 時価による会計処理, 時価会計, 時価主義会計
  mark-to-market accounting standard 時価会計基準
  mark-to-market accounting system 時価会計制度, 時価主義会計制度
  mark-to-market appraisal 時価評価, 時価による評価
  mark-to-market basis 値洗い基準
  mark-to-market method 時価法, 市場連動法
- Since the introduction of the *mark-to-market* accounting system, corporations have been required to report their estimate of losses if the value of their shareholdings has dropped more than 50 percent from their purchasing prices. 時価会計制度の導入以来, 保有株式の価格が取得価格より5割以上下落した場合, 企業は評価損の計上を義務付けられている。

market 動 販売する, 売り出す, 市場に出す
- Honda Motor Co. would be the first to *market*

vehicles that run on bioethanol alone. バイオエタノールだけで走る車を販売するのは、ホンダが初めてだ。

market 名 市場, 市中, 相場, 市況, 売買, 販路, マーケット
 active market 活況市場
 appear on the market 上場する
 bear market 弱気市場, 下げ相場, 売り相場
 bull market 強気市場, 上げ相場, 買い相場
 capture the market シェアを獲得する
 corner the market 市場を買い占める
 credit market 金融市場, 信用市場, 発行市場
 enter the market 市場に参入する, 市場に進出する, 市場を利用する, 市場に加わる
 European-style single market 欧州型単一市場
 exchange market 為替市場
 issue market 発行市場 (＝investment market)
 M&A market M&A市場
 make a market マーケット・メークを行う, 市場を形成する, 値付け業務を行う, マーケット・メーキング (＝market making)
 make inroads in the market 市場に参入する
 market development 市場開発, 市場開拓, 営業開発
 market liquidity 市場流動性, 金融商品市場で株式や債券などを売買するための豊富な資金
 market manipulation 市場操作, 株価操作, 相場操縦
 market method 時価法
 market penetration 市場浸透, 市場浸透力
 market quotes 市場相場価額
 put ... on the market …を売りに出す, …を発売する, …を市販する
 secondary market 流通市場
 security market 証券市場
 sensitive market 不安市況, 不安定市場
 shares on the market 流通している株式
 stock and bond markets 株式・債券市場
 strong market 強気市場, 強気市況
 tap the market 市場に登場する, 市場で調達する
 time the market 市場の好機を選ぶ, 市場のタイミングをとらえる, 市場のタイミングを判断する, 市場のタイミングに合わせる, 市場のタイミングを図る
 trading market 流通市場, トレーディング・マーケット
 weak market 軟弱市況, 軟調市況 (＝soft market)

▸Bandai badly needs to enter new fields due to the shrinking toy market. バンダイは、玩具市場の縮小で, 新分野への参入[展開]が急務となっている。
▸Markets for telecommunication services are extremely competitive. 電気通信サービス市場は, 極めて激しい競争にさらされています。

market capitalization 株式の時価総額 (＝market cap., market capitalization value：株式の外部発行済み株式総数に株式の時価を掛けた額)
▸The fall in the stock price lowers the company's market capitalization. 株価の下落で, 同社の時価総額は目減りしている。
▸The group implemented its creative financial strategy to seek an explosive growth by bloating its market capitalization. 同グループは、時価総額を膨らませて急成長を求める独創的な財務戦略を実行した。

market conditions 市場の状態, 市場環境, 市況
▸Such market conditions, along with a slow-growing economy, make the ongoing need for active cost controls even more urgent. この市場環境と景気低迷で, 継続的に積極的なコスト管理を進める必要性は, 一段と緊急性を増しています。

market demand 市場の需要
▸Because of the strong market demand, the available quantity of some products has been allocated between customers from time to time. 市場需要が大幅に伸びているため, 調達可能な一部の製品は, お客さまの間で割当て配分している状況です。

market-driven 形 市場原理に基づく, 市場志向の, 市場優先の (＝market-oriented)
▸The Corporation made steady progress on its strategy of transforming itself into a more market-driven and efficient company. 当社は, 一段と市場志向の強い効率的な会社に変革する経営戦略を着実に推進した。

market environment 市場環境
▸Even with the demands of a difficult market environment, we have continued to invest in our people. 厳しい市場環境のもとで需要が鈍化しているものの, 当社は引き続き人材開発に投資しています。

market opportunity 市場機会, ビジネス機会, 事業機会
▸We make an acquisition when that seems the most effective way to take advantage of a particular market opportunity to further our growth goals. 当社が企業を買収するのは, 特定の市場機会をとらえて当社の成長目標をさらに推進する上で, それが最も効果的な方法であると思われ

るときです。

market price 市場価格, 市価, 時価, 売価, 相場, 実勢価格 （＝market value; ⇒offered price）
▸Net capital expenditures for the network, at *market price*, were $2.5 billion in 2007. 通信ネットワークの資本的支出純額は, 市場価額で2007年度は25億ドルでした。
▸The offered price was set at levels below *market prices*. 買付け価格[提示価格]は, 時価を下回る水準に設定された。

market principles 市場原理
▸*Market principles* and competition have been emphasized in recent years. 最近は, 市場原理と競争が重視されてきました。

market-related asset value method 市場関連資産価格方式
▸The Corporation uses a three-year, *market-related asset* value method of amortizing asset-related gains and losses. 当社は, 資産関連損益を償却するため, 3年間の市場関連資産価格方式を採用しています。

market share 市場占拠率, 市場占有率, 市場シェア, マーケット・シェア, シェア （＝share）
▸GM has been suffering from declining U.S. *market share*, rising costs for materials like steel and a drop in sales of sport utility vehicles. 米ゼネラル・モーターズは, 米国内シェアの低下や鉄鋼など原材料コストの上昇, スポーツ用多目的車（SUV）の販売減に見舞われている。

market value 市場価値, 市場価格, 市価, 時価, 時価評価額 （＝market price）
　current market value 市場の実勢価格, 現在の市場価格, 現在の市場価値, 現行の市場価格, 時価 （＝current market price）
　estimated market value 見積り市場価値
　market value accounting 現在価値会計, 時価主義会計 （＝current value accounting）
　market value basis 時価主義, 時価基準 （＝market price basis）
　market value method 市場価額法, 市価法, 時価法 （＝market price method）
　market value per share 1株当たり市場価値, 株価
　open market value 公開市場価値
　present market value 時価 （＝current market value）
　secondary-market value 流通市場価格
▸Because of declines in the firm's *market value*, we wrote down this investment by $70 million in 2007. 同社の株価が下落したため, 当社はこの投資について2007年度に7,000万ドルの評価減を計上しました。

marketable 形 市場性ある, 売買可能な
　investment in marketable securities 有価証券投資, 市場性証券への投資
　marketable assets 市場性資産
　marketable commodity 市場性ある商品
　marketable debt security 市場性ある債務証券, 市場性ある債券
　marketable equity securities 市場性ある持ち分証券[有価証券], 市場性ある株式
　marketable investment securities 市場性ある投資有価証券
　marketable issue 市場性証券
　marketable nonequity security 市場性ある債券 （＝marketable debt security）
　marketable product 商品
　marketable securities 市場性ある有価証券, 市場性有価証券, 市場性証券, 有価証券
　marketable securities, at cost, which approximates market 市場性ある有価証券─原価評価で時価とほぼ等しい
　non-marketable securities 市場性のない有価証券, 非市場性証券
▸Corporate assets primarily include cash, *marketable* securities, equity investments and the administrative headquarters of the Company. 全社一般資産の主な内訳は, 現預金, 市場性有価証券, 株式投資と当社の管理本部資産です。

marketing 名 市場取引, 市販, 販売, 売買, 流通, 配給, 分配, 公開, マーケティング（「マーケティング」は, 優れた製品を適正な価格で, 最適な販売チャネルを通じて消費者に提供するための活動）
　marketing cost 販売費, 営業費, マーケティング・コスト （＝marketing expense）
　marketing cost accounting 営業費計算, 営業費会計
　marketing expense 販売費, 営業費, マーケティング・コスト （＝selling expense：広告宣伝費（advertising expense）や販売促進費（sales promotion cost）, 販売手数料（sales commission）, 販売員給料（payroll）, 運賃（freight-out）などが含まれる）
▸Since early 2005, the number of men and women on the front line around the world, principally in *marketing* and programming, has increased by more than 10,000. 2005年初め以降, 世界の第一線で仕事をしている主に営業とプログラミング関連部門の男女従業員の数は, 1万人以上増加しました。

marketing and sales expenses マーケティングおよび販売費, マーケティング・販売費
▶*Marketing and sales expenses* for new services rose in 2007. 2007年度は, 新サービスのマーケティングおよび販売費が増加しました。

markon 名 値入れ, 値入れ率

MAS 経営助言サービス (**management advisory services**の略)

massive 形 巨額の, 多額の, 巨大の, 大量の, 多量の, 多大の, 大規模な, 大がかりな, 大幅な, スケールの大きい, 大きい, 大型の, 旺盛な, 充実した
 massive debt loads 巨額の債務負担, 巨額の債務
 massive demand 旺盛な需要
 massive financial assistance 巨額の金融支援, 巨額の財政援助
 massive investment 大規模投資, 大がかりな投資, 巨額の投資
 massive loss 巨額の損失, 大幅損失, 大幅赤字
 massive outflows of capital and technology 資本と技術の大量流出
▶Loan disposal costs are likely to result in *massive* losses. 債権処理費用で, 大幅な赤字に陥る見通しだ。
▶The *massive* gains in stockholdings' latent value will raise the banks' net worth ratios markedly. 保有株式の含み益の大幅増加で, 銀行の自己資本比率も大きく向上する見込みだ。

match 動 支払う, …と一致する, …と調和する, …に見合う
▶We *match* a percentage of the employee contributions up to certain limits. 当社[会社]は, 従業員拠出金の一定の割合を, 一定限度まで資金援助[負担]しています。

matching 名 突合せ, 照合, 費用・収益の対応, 対応
 concept of matching costs with revenues 費用・収益対応の概念
 matching costs and revenues 費用と収益の対応, 費用収益対応
 matching revenue and related expense 費用収益対応
 revenue-cost matching 収益費用の対応

material 名 材料, 材質, 原料, 資材, 素材, 物質, 構成物質, 服地
 advanced materials 新素材
 hazardous materials 有害物質
 industrial material prices 工業製品価格
 input materials 投入原材料
 material cost 材料費, 材料主費
 material procurement 原材料の調達 (= procurement of materials)
 materials and services 資材と用役
 materials and supplies 原材料および貯蔵品, 材料および貯蔵品, 資材, 原材料
 materials handling 資材運搬, 運搬管理, マテハン
 materials in process 仕掛け材料費, 原材料仕掛け品
 materials inventory 材料棚卸し高
 promotional materials 販促資料 (= sales materials)
▶Rising prices for raw *materials*, such as steel, and crude oil could have an adverse impact. 鉄鋼などの素材や原油の価格高騰が, マイナス材料だ。

material 形 重要な, 大きな影響力のある, 物的[物質的]な, 有形の
▶The impact of this accounting change was not *material*. この会計処理方法の変更による影響は, 重要なものではありません。

material difference 重要な差異
▶With respect to the consolidated statements, there are no *material differences* between German and United States generally accepted accounting principles (GAAP). この連結財務書類に関しては, ドイツと米国の一般に公正妥当と認められた会計基準(GAAP)に, 重要な差異はありません。

material interests in subsidiaries 重要な子会社持ち分
▶We have no present plans to sell *material interests in subsidiaries*. 当社は現在, 重要な子会社持ち分を売却する予定はありません。

material effect 重大な影響, 大きな影響
▶This accounting change will not have a *material effect* on our earnings or financial position. この会計処理方法の変更が, 当社の利益や財政状態に重大な影響を及ぼすことはないでしょう。

material respect 重要な点, 重要事項
▶The financial statements conform in all *material respects* with International Accounting Standards. 財務書類は, すべての重要な点で国際会計基準に適合しています。

matter 名 問題, 主題, 対象, 内容, 事項, 議題, 事態, 事柄, 主要事実, 重要
▶Environmental and other *matters* are subject to many uncertainties, and outcomes are not predictable with assurance. 環境その他の問題は, 多くの不確定要素の影響を受けるため, その帰結を確実に予測するのは不可能です。

▸The Audit Committee reviews accounting, auditing, internal controls and financial reporting *matters*.　監査委員会は、会計、監査、内部統制や財務報告などの問題を検討します。

mature 動　満期になる、期日が到来する、支払い期日になる　(⇒**bank loan**)
　matured bond　満期後社債
　matured bonds unredeemed　期日到来未償還社債
　matured liability　支払い期日到来負債、期日到来債務
　matured note　満期手形
　maturing debt　満期が到来した債券、満期償還額
　refinance maturing debt issues　満期を迎えた債務を借り換える
　repayment [payment] of maturing CP　満期が来た [満期が到来した、満期を迎える] CPの償還
▸Government bonds to be refunded as they *mature* are worth about ¥110 trillion this fiscal year.　今年度は、償還期限が来て借り換える国債が約110兆円もある。

maturity 名　満期、支払い期限、支払い期日、支払い日、弁済期限、償還期限、期限、一括返済
　cancellation before maturity　中途解約
　current maturity　残存期間
　debt maturity　債務支払い日
　final maturity　償還期日、最終満期
　full repayment before maturity　早期完済
　maturity date　満期日、満期、支払い期日、償還日
　maturity value　元利合計、満期日の価額、満期償還価額、満期価値
　original maturity　当初満期
　redemption of maturity　満期償還
　residual maturity　残余期間
▸We took advantage of favorable levels of interest rates to extend debt *maturities* by refinancing a substantial amount of long-term debt.　当社は、有利な金利水準を利用して、長期負債の相当額を借り替えることにより債務の償還期限を延長しました。

maximization of shareholder values　株主価値の最大化
▸In debates about M&A issues, primary importance has so far been given to the concept of *maximization of shareholder values*.　M&A問題の議論では、これまでのところ「株主価値の最大化」という考え方に特に重点が置かれてきた。

maximum 名　最高、最大、最大量、最大数、上限
　maximum commission fees　手数料の上限
　maximum loss　最大損失

maximum pension provision　最高年金計上額
maximum stock　最高在庫、最高在庫量
maximum lending rate　貸出金利の上限
（＝highest lending rate）
▸All four of Japan's major consumer loan firms will lower their *maximum lending rates* to below 20 percent.　国内消費者金融大手の4社すべてが、貸出金利の上限を20％以下（現行の出資法の上限金利は年29.2％）に引き下げる。

maximum limits　発行枠、発行限度、最高限度、最高限度額
▸*Maximum limits* for each type of new shares are: ¥1.5 trillion for convertible preferred shares that can be converted into ordinary shares after a certain period; ¥1.5 trillion for another type of convertible preferred shares; and ¥1.5 trillion for nonconvertible preferred shares.　各種新株の発行枠は、一定期間後に普通株に転換できる転換型優先株が1兆5000億円、その他の転換型優先株が1兆5000億円、それに非転換型優先株が1兆5000億円となっている。

MBI　マネジメント・バイイン（management buy-inの略。買収者がターゲット会社の経営者ではなく、企業投資ファンドなどの部外者で、買収後は一般に取締役会に投資ファンドの代表者を派遣して会社の経営に深く関与する場合をMBIという）

MBO　経営者による自社買収、経営者による営業権取得、マネジメント・バイアウト（**management buyout [buy-out]** の略）
　　MBOとは➡企業の経営者が、一般株主や親会社などから自社株を買い取って、企業や事業部門の経営権を買い取ること。一般に、敵対的買収の防衛や子会社が独立する際に用いられるM&A（合併・買収）の手法。上場企業の場合は、経営陣が買収を実施する会社を別に設立し、自社の資産を担保にして投資会社や金融機関から融資を受け、その資金でTOB（株式公開買付け）を行い、一般株主から株式を広く買い集めることが多い。最近は、非上場にすることを目的に実施する例が目立っている。その背景には、敵対的買収への防衛策のほかに、株式持ち合いが崩れて年金基金のような「物言う株主」が増えてきたことなどの要因があるといわれる。親会社から自社株を買って子会社が独立する際の利点としては、社内体制が変わらないことや、親会社との関係が比較的良好に保たれる点が挙げられる。

MBS　住宅融資証券、モーゲージ担保証券（**mortgage-backed security** の略）

measure 名　対策、措置、対応、政策、施策、方策、策、手段、比率、指標、尺度、基準測定値、測度　（⇒ **negative spread**）

▶This step is being regarded as a *measure* to increase friendly long-term shareholders and discourage a hostile takeover. この措置は，友好的な長期安定株主を増やして敵対的買収を防ぐための手段と考えられている．

measurement 名 測定，計算，算定，計量，測定値，指標，尺度 (⇒**projected benefit obligation**)

MEBO 経営陣と従業員による企業買収 (**management employee buyout**の略)

mecenat 名 文化活動への貢献・寄与，芸術・科学支援活動，文化支援，文化支援事業，メセナ

▶The company carries out four main activities as the basis for its social service: philanthropy, volunteer programs, *mecenat*—patronage of the arts and sciences, and regional environmental protection. 同社では，社会貢献の柱として寄付活動，ボランティア活動，メセナ［芸術・科学支援活動］と地域環境保護の四つの活動を実施している．

meet 動 〈需要や要求などを〉満たす，〈目標などを〉達成する，うまく処理する，対応する，履行する，〈費用などを〉支払う，〈期待などに〉添う

meet a criteria 基準を満たす，基準をクリアする，基準に適合する

meet customer needs 顧客のニーズに対応する，顧客のニーズを満たす

meet expenses 費用を支払う，費用を賄う

meet increasing demand 需要増［需要の増加］に対応する

meet one's obligations 債務を履行する，債務を返済する

meet requirements 必要条件［条件］を満たす，要求に応じる，基準を満たす

▶External funds required to *meet* the additional cash requirements in 2007 will be obtained by offering debt securities in the market. 2007年度内に発生する追加資金必要額を賄うための外部調達資金は，市場で債券を募集発行して調達する予定です．

meeting 名 会議，会，総会，大会，理事会，場，ミーティング (⇒**general meeting**, **shareholders meeting**)

closed meeting 非公開協議

creditors' meeting 債権者会議，債権者集会

due diligence meeting 新証券発行説明会

extraordinary meeting 臨時総会 (=**special meeting**)

inaugural meeting 創立総会

managing directors' meeting 常務会

meeting of representatives of policyholders 〈保険会社の〉総代会 (=meeting of policyholder representatives, policyholders' representative meeting：株式会社の株主総会にあたる)

one-on-one meeting 投資家との個別ミーティング (=one-to-one meeting)

ordinary council meeting 定例理事会 (=regular council meeting)

stockholders [shareholders] meeting 株主総会 (=shareholders' meeting, stockholders' meeting)

▶This issue was settled at the extraordinary *meetings* of both firms' boards of directors. この問題は，両社の臨時取締役会でそれぞれ決議された．

melon 名 利益，所得，余剰利益，特別配当，多額の利益配当

meltdown 名 〈株価などの〉急落，暴落，下落，市場の崩壊，市場の暴落［急落］ (=crash) (⇒**erode**)

memorandum of association 英企業の基本定款 (米企業のarticles of incorporation[association]に相当)

memorandum of understanding 基本合意書，予備的合意書，意思表明状，了解覚書，協定覚書

▶In January 20, 2007, we signed a *memorandum of understanding* for the creation of a new company. 2007年1月20日に当社は，新会社設立の協定覚書に調印しました．

merchandise 動 売買する，販売を促進する

merchandise 名 商品，在庫品

merchant system マーチャント・システム (インターネットで大規模な買い物のサービスを提供するシステム)

merge 動 合併する，吸収合併する，経営統合する，統合する (⇒**operation**)

merge operations 経営統合する，事業を統合する (=integrate operations)

▶Mizuho Financial Group Inc. will *merge* its two securities units in January 2008. みずほフィナンシャルグループは，同社の証券会社2社を2008年1月に統合する．

▶Mizuho Securities Co. and Shinko Securities Co. will *merge* in May rather than January. みずほ証券と新光証券は，1月ではなく5月に合併することになった．

▶TV stations are seeking tie-ups with Internet firms to *merge* their operations with Internet services. テレビ各局は，放送事業とネット事業［通信事業］との融合を目指して，ネット企業との業務提携を求めている．

merger 名 合併, 経営統合, 事業統合, 統合, 吸収合併, 併合, 融合 (⇒triangular merger)
 acquisitions and mergers 企業取得と合併
 business merger 経営統合, 企業の合併 (= merger of businesses)
 corporate merger 企業合併, 会社合併
 debt-financed merger 借入れによる合併
 downstream merger 逆吸収合併
 horizontal merger 水平的合併, 同業他社との合併
 merger agreement 経営統合の合意書, 経営統合の契約[契約書], 合併協議書 (= merger deal)
 merger and acquisition 企業の吸収合併, 合併・買収, 企業取得と合併《略 M&A》(= mergers and acquisitions)
 merger and acquisition deal M&A取引, M&A案件 (= M&A deal)
 merger on an equal basis 対等合併
 merger by purchase 合併
 merger plan 統合計画, 吸収・合併計画, 合併計画
 merger proposal 経営統合案, 経営統合提案, 経営統合の提案書 (= business integration proposal)
 merger rate 統合比率, 合併比率 (= exchange ratio of merger, merger ratio)
 merger talks 合併交渉, 統合交渉, 経営統合交渉 (= merger negotiation)
 mergers and absorptions 吸収・合併
 multi-merger 多角的合併
 stock-for-stock merger 株式交換による合併
 vertical merger 垂直的合併
▸Kiyo Bank and Wakayama Bank agreed to begin *merger* talks. 紀陽銀行と和歌山銀行は, 経営統合交渉を開始することで合意した。
▸The people, assets and capital of the two firms won't change just because of this *merger*. 合併したからといって, 両社の社員, 資産と資本になんら変動はありません。

mergers and acquisitions 企業の合併・買収《略 M&A》(= merger and acquisition; ⇒ corporate merger, M&A)
▸Defects in the rules governing *mergers and acquisitions* are surfacing one after another. M&A[企業の合併・買収]に関するルールの不備が, 次々と表面化している。

merit-based pay plan[**system**] 業績連動型の報酬制度, 成果主義型の賃金制度[報酬制度]
▸More companies are introducing a *merit-based pay plan*. 現在は, 業績連動型の報酬制度を導入する企業が増えている。

message 名 通信文, 伝言, 文面, メッセージ, 電子メールでの通信情報・伝達事項
 Message from the President 株主へのご挨拶, (社長)ご挨拶, 株主の皆様へ
 Message from Top Management 株主へのご挨拶, (会長)ご挨拶, 株主の皆様へ
 Message to (the) Stockholders 株主へのご挨拶, 株主へのメッセージ, 株主の皆様へ, ご挨拶

method 名 方法, 手法, 方式, 手順, 順序, 筋道, 基準, 主義 (⇒accounting method, equity method, percentage of completion method, purchase method)
 account method 帳簿控除方式
 accrued method 発生主義
 declining balance method 定率法
 full cost method 全部原価法
 interest method of amortization 利息法による償却
 liability method 負債法
 method of fixed percentage on cost 定率法
 method of historical cost 原価主義
 method of moving average 移動平均法
 method of price of last purchase 最終仕入原価法
 net of tax method 税引き後法
 normal stock method 基準棚卸し法
 tender panel method 競争入札制度
 terminal funding method 年金現価充足方式
 underwriting method 全額引受方式
▸We use the effective interest *method* of amortization. 当社は, 実効利息法による償却法を採用しています。

mezzanine 形 メザニン型の, 中間的[一時的]に介在する, 中間に位置する
 mezzanine bond メザニン債(優先債と劣後債の中間に位置し, 一般にトリプルB (BBB)以下の格付けとなる)
 mezzanine debt メザニン型負債, 債務メザニン負債, 無担保ローンの借入金
 mezzanine field 中間に位置する分野
 mezzanine finance メザニン融資, メザニン型資金調達, メザニン・ファイナンス (= mezzanine financing, mezzanine funding: 企業買収の際に資金調達方法の一つとして高金利の無担保ローンを利用する方式。また, 会社清算時の受取順位が, 優先債権には劣後するが, 普通株には優先する劣後債(subordinated debenture)などによる資金調達を意味する場合もある)
 mezzanine funds メザニン投資ファンド
 mezzanine money 転換社債
 mezzanine subordination 準劣後請求権

▸Domestic and foreign insurance companies are scrambling to introduce new products in the so-called third sector-a *mezzanine* field between life and nonlife insurance, such as medical, cancer and nursing insurance.　国内外の保険各社は，第三分野（医療やがん，介護保険など生命保険と損害保険の中間に位置する保険分野）と呼ばれる医療保険の商品開発［商品導入］にしのぎを削っている。

midterm 名　中間, 中期

midterm account settlement　中間決算　（＝interim account settlement, midterm settlement of accounts; ⇒**mark**）

midterm business results　中間決算, 半期業績, 中間期の業績　（＝midterm results）

midterm dividend　中間配当　（⇒**sum**）

midterm results　中間決算, 半期の業績　（＝first-half results, interim results, midterm business results, semi-annual results; ⇒**product price**）

midterm settlement that ended Sep. 30　9月中間決算, 9月中間期　（＝September midterm settlement of accounts）

midterm business plan　中期経営計画, 中期事業計画, 中期経営構想, 中期経営プラン

▸The company revealed a new *midterm business plan* for fiscal 2007-2010.　同社は，2007-2010年度の新中期経営構想を発表した。

midterm earnings report　中間決算, 中間決算報告　（＝interim earnings report, midterm financial report）

▸In their *midterm earnings reports*, major banking groups revised initial loss projections resulting from bad loan disposal.　中間決算で，主要銀行グループは不良債権処理に伴う当初の予想損失額を修正した。

midterm financial settlement　中間決算

▸According to its consolidated *midterm financial settlements*, Toyota chalked up more than ¥11 trillion in sales.　トヨタの中間連結決算によると，同社は売上高が11兆円超となった。

midterm management strategy　中期経営戦略

▸Under its *midterm management strategy*, the NTT group aims to further consolidate group companies and lessen duplication of services.　中期経営戦略によると，NTTグループは，グループ企業の一体化を強め，重複業務の解消を目指す。

midterm report　中間決算, 中間決算報告, 半期報告, 中間報告　（＝interim report, midterm business report, midterm earnings report）

▸The fiscal 2007 *midterm reports* for most firms listed on the First Section of the Tokyo Stock Exchange have been released.　東京証券取引所一部上場企業の2007年9月中間決算がほぼ出揃った。

midterm settlement of accounts　中間決算　（＝interim settlement of accounts）

▸In the September *midterm settlement of accounts* for this fiscal year, a number of listed companies registered increrases in profits.　今年度の9月中間決算で，多くの上場企業は増益となった。

midyear accounts　中間決算　（⇒**settle**）

millions of dollars　単位：百万ドル

millions of dollars except per share figures　単位：1株当たりの金額を除いて百万ドル　単位：百万ドル。ただし，1株当たりの金額を除く。

Millions of U.S. dollars except per share figures　単位：百万米ドル。ただし，1株当たりの金額を除く。

minimum 名　最低, 最小, 最小限, 最小値, ミニマム

minimum capital　最低資本金, 最低自己資本

minimum capital adequacy ratio　最低自己資本比率

minimum capital requirements　最低必要資本金額, 会社設立時に必要な最低資本金, 最低資本金の要件　（＝minimum capitalization requirements, minimum regulatory capital requirements; ⇒**stock company**）

minimum guarantee　最低保証金

minimum lease payments　最低リース支払い額, 最低賃借料等支払い額

minimum lending rate　最低貸出金利

minimum margin　最低利幅

minimum order size　最低発注量

minimum pension provision　最低年金計上額

minimum profit　最低利益, 最小利幅

minimum purchase　最低購入量

minimum royalty　最低ロイヤリティ, 最低使用料, ミニマム・ロイヤリティ

minimum stock　最低在庫量, 最低在庫

minimum subscription　最小株式引受限度

minimum tax　ミニマム税, ミニマム・タックス　（通常の法人税, 所得税に追加して課される税）

▸Under the rules of the Bank for International Settlements, the *minimum* capital adequacy ratio required of banks operating internationally is 8 percent.　国際決済銀行（BIS）の規則では，国際銀行業務を行っている銀行に要求される最低自己資本比率は，8％である。

minority 名　少数, 少数派, 少数民族

minority buyout 少数持ち分の買取り
minority equity 少数株主持ち分, 少数株主権
minority shareholder 少数株主 (＝minority stockholder)
minority shareholders' equity 少数株主持ち分
▸A company's stock will be delisted if more than 80 percent of outstanding shares are held by a specified *minority* of owners for more than one year. 流通株式[上場株式数]の80%超を特定の少数株主が1年を超えて保有した場合, その会社の銘柄は上場廃止となる。
▸Our document describes programs in the United States for women, *minorities* and handicapped persons. 当社の小冊子には, 女性, 少数民族と身体障害者に対する当社の米国内プログラムが記載されています。
minority interest 少数株主持ち分, 少数株主持ち分利益, 少数株主損益, 少数利益, 過半数以下の出資, 少数株主権
　income before income taxes, minority interest and cumulative effect of accounting changes 法人所得税, 少数株主損益[少数株主持ち分利益]および会計方針の変更による累積的影響額控除前利益
　minority interest in common stock 少数株主持ち分—資本金
　minority interest in consolidated subsidiaries 連結子会社の少数株主持ち分
　minority interest in net income 少数株主持ち分利益
　minority interests in earnings/loss 少数株主損益
▸*Minority interests* represent other companies' ownership interests in our net assets. 少数株主持ち分は, 当社の純資産に対する他社の所有者持ち分を表します。
minus 前 差し引いて, 引いて, マイナス (＝less)
▸The company had an operating profit, or revenue *minus* the cost of goods sold and administrative expenses, of ¥1.1 billion in the first half. 同社の上半期の営業利益(売上高から売上原価と一般管理費を差し引いた収益)は, 11億円だった。
minutes 名 議事録, 議事要旨, 覚書, 訴訟記録 (＝minutes book)
miscellaneous 形 種々雑多な, 各種の
▸*Miscellaneous* other activities include the distribution of computer equipment through retail outlets. その他の各種事業には, 小売店によるコンピュータ機器の販売も含まれています。

mismatch 名 ミスマッチ (＝mismatching)
▸We must address the improvement of employment situation, particularly in regard to jobs for young people and the *mismatch* between job seekers and job openings. われわれとしては, 特に若年層の雇用や求職者と新規雇用のミスマッチなどの面で, 雇用状況の改善に取り組まなければならない。
misstatement 名 虚偽表示, 虚偽記載, 不実表示, 誤表示 (＝misrepresentation)
　expected misstatement 予想虚偽表示
　financial statement misstatement 財務諸表[財務書類]の虚偽表示, 財務諸表の虚偽記載
　known misstatement 既知の虚偽表示
　material misstatement 重大な虚偽記載, 重要な虚偽表示
　torelable misstatement 許容虚偽表示
▸These GAASs require that we plan and perform the audit to obtain reasonable assurance about whether the financial statements are free of material *misstatement*. これらの一般に認められた監査基準は, 財務書類[財務諸表]に重要な虚偽表示がないかどうかについての合理的な確証を得るため, 私どもが監査を計画して実施することを要求しています。
mix 名 構成, 組合せ, 混合, 比率, 内容, 中身, ミックス
　asset mix 資産構成, 資産配分
　business mix 事業構成, 事業内容 (＝mix of business)
　currency mix of foreign exchange reserves 外貨準備の通貨構成
　merchandise mix 商品構成, 商品ミックス
　portfolio mix ポートフォリオの構成, 有価証券の中身, ポートフォリオ・ミックス
　product mix 商品構成, 製品構成, 製品組合せ, プロダクト・ミックス
　sales mix 売上品目構成
model 名 モデル, 模型, 型, 型式, 車種, 機種, 新案, 模範 (⇒business model, patent)
　buying behavior model 購買行動モデル
　consumer behavior model 消費者行動モデル
　corporate model 企業モデル
　decision model 意思決定モデル
　econometric model 計量経済モデル
　existing models 現行機種
　large models and smaller, lower priced models 大型機種と低価格の小型機種
　leading model 主力車種, 主力車
　linear program(m)ing model LPモデル

market model 市場モデル
Model Business Corporation Act 米国の模範事業会社法
model change 型式変更, モデル・チェンジ
Model T T型フォード
performance model 業績モデル
pricing model 価格決定モデル
role model 手本, 理想像, 理想の姿, 雛型, 模範生, 優等生
simulation model シミュレーション・モデル
stock valuation model 株式評価モデル
successive model 後継機種
utility model 実用新案
valuation model 評価モデル
working model 実用モデル, 実用模型
▶ In cooperation with its parts makers, Toyota has brought one new *model* after another to the market.　部品メーカーとの共同作業で, トヨタは新車種を相次いで市場に投入してきた。

monetary 形 金融の, 通貨の, 貨幣の, 財政上の, 金銭の, マネタリー
monetary donations 企業献金
monetary easing 金融緩和
monetary excess 過剰流動性
monetary gain and/or loss 貨幣利得および／または貨幣損失 (インフレで生じる貨幣項目の損益)
monetary liability 金銭債務
monetary market 通貨市場
monetary policy assessment 金融政策の判断
monetary restraint 金融引締め

monetary assets 貨幣性資産, 金銭債権 (= money asset:「貨幣性資産」は, 貨幣そのものまたは法令や契約によってその金額が固定している資産のことで, 現金, 預金, 売掛金, 受取手形, 貸付け金などがこれに含まれる。これに対して, 将来費用となる棚卸し資産などの資産を「費用性資産」という)
▶ Current assets (excluding inventories and prepaid expenses), current liabilities, and long-term *monetary assets* and liabilities are translated at the exchange rates in effect at the balance sheet date.　流動資産 (棚卸資産と前払い費用を除く), 流動負債と長期貨幣性資産および負債は, 貸借対照表日 [決算日] 現在の実効為替レートで換算してあります。

monetary base マネタリー・ベース, 貨幣的ベース (= high-powered money base, money base: 日本銀行券発行高, 貨幣流通高と日銀当座預金 (民間金融機関の中央銀行預け金) の合計で, 日銀が金融市場に供給している資金の残高を示す)
▶ The *monetary base* shrank 21.1 percent in January from a year ago.　1月のマネタリー・ベース (日銀券発行高, 貨幣流通高, 日銀当座預金の合計) は, 前年同月比で21.1%減少した。

monetary items 貨幣性項目, 貨幣項目 (貨幣性資産と貨幣性負債)
▶ *Monetary items* in the balance sheets are translated at year-end rates.　貸借対照表の貨幣性項目は, 期末レートで換算されています。

money 名 金, 金銭, 通貨, 貨幣, 資金, 金融, マネー
borrowed money
call money コール借入金, 短期資金, 銀行相互間の当座借入金, コール・マネー
call money rate コール・レート
easy money 金融緩和, 低利の金, 低金利
hard money 硬貨
hot money 短期資金, 投機資金, ホット・マネー
hush money 口止め料
key money 権利金, 保証金, 礼金
lose money 赤字を出す, 損失を出す, 損失を被る
make money 利益を生み出す, 利益を上げる, 利益を得る, 資金を稼ぐ
money borrowed for long term 長期借入金
money borrowed for short time 短期借入金
money deposited from customers 得意先預かり金
money deposited from officers 役員預り金
money in hand 手元資金, 手元現金預金
money income 現金収入
money inflow 資金流入
money management 投資運用
money policy 金融政策 (= monetary policy)
money purchase plan 定額拠出年金
money rate of interest 金利, 利子率 (= interest rate, money rate)
money transaction 現金取引, 直取引
money transfer 振替え, 口座振替え, 振込み, 資金の移動, 送金
narrow money 狭義の通貨, 狭義のマネー
raise money 資金を調達する
▶ The challenge in monetary policy for countries now is shifting toward finding a way to move away from ultra-loose *money* policies.　現在, 各国の金融政策の課題は, 超金融緩和政策からいかに転換するかに移りつつある。

money laundering 不正資金の洗浄, 資金洗浄, マネー・ロンダリング (= money washing: 犯罪で得た資金の出所や所有者を隠す行為)
▶ The bank failed to adequately implement anti-*money-laundering* compliance programs.　同

行は, マネー・ロンダリング[資金洗浄] 防止の法遵守プログラムを適正に実施しなかった[同行のマネー・ロンダリングへの監視体制は, 不十分だった]。

money-losing 形 赤字の, 不採算の
　money-losing company 赤字企業, 赤字会社 (=loss-making company, red-ink firm)
　money-losing outlet 赤字店舗 (=loss-making outlet)

money-losing operation 赤字の事業, 不採算事業
▸Hitachi aims to turn its three core *money-losing operations* profitable in fiscal 2007. 日立は, 2007年度[2008年3月期]から赤字の主力3事業の黒字化を目指している。

money-losing store 赤字店舗, 不採算店舗
▸Daiei's group sales fell 22.3 percent to ¥672.11 billion in the March-August period due to closure of its *money-losing stores*. ダイエーの8月中間決算で[ダイエーの3-8月期決算で], 不採算店舗[赤字店舗]の閉鎖により, 連結売上高は22.3%減の6,721億1,000万円となった。

money market 金融市場, マネー・マーケット, 短期金融市場(短期の金融資産であるコール, 手形, 譲渡性預金(DC), 現先などの資金取引が行われる金融市場。長期金融市場はcapital marketという。⇒**capital market, financial market**)
　long-term money market 長期金融市場
　money market instruments 短期金融市場証券, 短期金融商品 (⇒**secondary market**)
　money market management 金融調節
　short-term money market 短期金融市場
▸The *money market* is overheated by massive money inflows from banks on fading concerns over a financial system crisis. 金融システム不安[金融システム危機に対する懸念]の後退により, 短期金融市場は, 銀行からの巨額の資金流入で過熱感が強まっている。

money supply 通貨供給量, 資金供給, マネー・サプライ(中央銀行と市中金融機関が民間に供給する通貨の量で, 通貨にはM2(現金, 要求払い預金, 定期性預金)のほかにCD(譲渡性預金)が含まれる)
▸The *money supply* last year posted its lowest year-on-year growth in 10 years. 昨年の通貨供給量は, 前年比で10年ぶりの低い伸びにとどまった。

monitor 動 監視する, 管理する, 調査する, チェックする, 評価する, 把握する, 分析する, モニターする
▸Our internal auditors *monitor* compliance with the system of internal controls by means of an annual plan of internal audits. 当社の内部監査人は, 内部監査の年度計画により, 内部統制組織が守られているかどうかを監視しています。
▸We will continue to closely *monitor* the market and take appropriate actions as necessary. われわれとしては, 引き続き市場の動向に十分注意して, 必要に応じて適切な対応を取る。

monitoring 名 監視, 監視活動, 監理, モニタリング
　monitoring post 監理ポスト(投資家に上場廃止の可能性を知らせる)
　portfolio monitoring ポートフォリオ管理, ポートフォリオの評価基準
　practice monitoring 業務監視

month 名 月, 1か月 (⇒**nine months ended September 30**)
　be unchanged on the month 前月比で横ばい
　consolidated business results for the six months up to September 4-9月期の連結業績, 4-9月期の連結決算,〈3月期決算企業の〉9月中間連結決算
　for the third consecutive month 3か月連続して
　for the three months ended in June 4-6月期(3月期決算企業の第1四半期, 12月期決算企業の第2四半期)
　in recent months ここ数か月
　in three months 3か月ぶりに, 今後3か月で
　the first nine months of 2008 〈12月期決算企業の〉2008年1-9月期, 2008年の第3四半期
　the 12 months ending March 2009 2009年3月期, 2008年度
▸The Corporation's group operating profit for the six *months* ended June 30 rose to ¥10.86 billion from ¥7.15 billion a year earlier. 当社の1-6月期[上半期, 上期]の連結営業利益は, 前年同期の71億5,000万円に比べて108億6,000万円に増加しました。

month-on-month 前月比で, 前月比 (=**month-on-month figure, on the month**)
▸The CPI continued to drop by close to 1 percent on a *month-on-month* basis. 消費者物価指数の下落幅は, 前月比で1%近い水準で終始した。

morality 名 倫理, 道徳, 道義, 倫理性, 道徳性, 道義性, モラル
▸There is a need to improve the *morality* of corporate executives and more closely monitor companies. 経営者のモラルの向上と, 企業の監視を強化する必要がある。

mortgage 名 抵当, 担保, 担保不動産, 譲渡抵当, 抵当権, 抵当権設定, 抵当証書, 担保付き融資, 住宅

ローン, モーゲージ (⇒**subprime mortgage**)
adjustable mortgage [**mortgage loan**] 変動金利モーゲージ (＝adjustable-rate mortgage, adjustable-rate mortgage loan)
credits for mortgage payments 住宅取得控除
home mortgage 住宅ローン
home mortgage borrowing 住宅ローンの借入れ
lower mortgage rate 住宅ローン金利の低下, モーゲージ金利の低下
mortgage debenture 担保付き社債
mortgage debt 担保付き長期債務, 抵当借り
mortgage deed 担保証券
mortgage loan 抵当貸し, 担保付き貸付け金 (＝mortgage loan receivable, secured loan), 住宅ローン
mortgage note 担保付き長期手形
mortgages payable 担保[抵当]付き借入金
mortgages receivable 担保[抵当]付き貸付け金
residential mortgage market 住宅ローン市場, 住宅用モーゲージ市場
stripped mortgage securities 分離型モーゲージ証券
▶Japan Post is discussing an alliance with Suruga Bank to offer *mortgages* and other loans to individuals. 日本郵政は現在, 住宅ローンなど個人ローン商品の販売に向けて, スルガ銀行と業務提携協議を進めている。

mortgage-backed security 住宅融資証券, モーゲージ担保証券, モーゲージ証券, 不動産証券 《略 MBS》 (＝mortgage-backed certificate)
▶Our quarterly net profit will be lower than the same period a year earlier because of losses tied to *mortgage-backed securities*. 当社の四半期純利益は, 不動産証券関連の損失で前年同期を下回る見込みです。

mortgage-backed securities business
住宅融資証券事業, 不動産証券事業, 不動産証券化事業
▶Nomura will withdraw from the U.S. residential *mortgage-backed securities business*. 野村[野村ホールディングス]が, 米住宅融資の証券化事業[米国の住宅融資証券の関連事業]から撤退することになった。

mortgage bond 担保付き社債, 担保付き債券, 抵当権付き社債, 不動産担保債
　first mortgage bond 第一順位抵当付き社債, 一番抵当付き社債, 第一順位抵当権付き債券
　junior mortgage bond 後順位物上担保付き社債
　second mortgage bond 第二順位抵当付き社債, 二番抵当付き社債

▶The first *mortgage bonds* of the corporation are secured by a first mortgage and a floating charge on the company. 同社の第一順位抵当権付き社債は, 同社の第一順位抵当権と浮動担保権で保証されています。

mortgagor 名 抵当権設定者, 担保提供者
motion 名 提議, 提案, 動議, 発議, 申立て, 動き, 運動, 移動
▶Under the Commercial Code, to gain approval for an important resolution that directly affects corporate management, shareholders holding at least 50 percent of shares with voting rights must cast ballots, and two-thirds must back the *motion*. 商法で, 企業の経営に直接影響を及ぼす重要決議の承認を得るには, 議決権株式の少なくとも50%を保有する株主が投票し, 提案に対してその3分の2の支持を得る必要がある。

movement 名 動き, 行動, 活動, 運動, 移動, 動向, 流れ, 進展, 進行, 変化, 変動
　capital movement 資本移動
　consumer movement 消費者運動
　environmental movement 環境保護運動
　interest rate movement 金利動向, 金利変動 (＝interest rate move)
　market movement 市場の動き, 市場動向, 相場の動き, 相場変動
　movement of funds 資金移動 (＝fund transfer)
　price movement 価格変動, 物価動向
　price movement restriction 値幅制限
　quality movement QC運動
　stock price movement 株価動向, 株価変動
　zero defects movements 無欠陥運動
▶Sharp rises in the price of international commodities and other factors relating to price *movements* have changed significantly. 国際商品の価格高騰など物価動向をめぐる要因が, 大きく変化している。

moving average 〈株価の〉移動平均, 移動平均線 (株価の「移動平均線」は, 当日を起点に, 過去の一定期間をさかのぼって終値の平均値を算出する作業を毎日繰り返し, 値を線で結んだグラフ。株価変動の大まかな傾向をつかむのに有用とされている)
　moving average cost method 移動平均原価法
　moving-average method 移動平均法

moving strike convertible bond 転換社債型新株予約権付き社債 《略 MSCB》
▶Fuji TV issued the *moving strike convertible bonds* (MSCBs) early this year for subscription

by Daiwa Securities SMBC Co. to raise ¥80 billion for its NBS takeover bid. フジテレビは今春, ニッポン放送株の公開買付け(TOB)資金800億円を調達するため, 大和証券SMBCを引受先として転換社債型新株予約権付き社債(MSCB)を発行した.

MPOs MPO (**multiple private offerings**の略. 新株予約権付き社債などを証券会社等への第三者割当てにより発行する資金調達方法)
▸In *MPOs*, a firm issues zero-coupon convertible bonds to brokerages rather than directly to the market. MPOでは, 企業がゼロクーポン社債を市場に直接でなく証券会社などに発行する.

MSCB 転換社債型新株予約権付き社債 (**moving strike convertible bond**の略. 発行した企業の株価下落に伴って, 株式に換える価格を低く修正することができる特別条項が付いた社債)

multinational enterprise 多国籍企業

municipal 形 市の, 地方自治の
  municipal bond 市債, 地方債
  municipal enterprise 公営事業, 地方公営企業

mutual 形 相互の, 共通の, 共同の
  mutual aid pension plan 共済年金, 共済年金制度
  mutual company 相互会社
  mutual fund 投資信託, ミューチュアル・ファンド
  mutual insurance 相互保険
  mutual ownership of shares 株式持ち合い, 株の持ち合い (=mutually held stocks)
  mutual savings bank 相互貯蓄銀行
▸The main purpose of the integration of the corporate employees pension plan and the *mutual* aid pension plan is to eliminate the public-private disparities. 会社員の厚生年金と公務員が加入する共済年金の一元化は, 官民格差の解消がその主な目的だ.

mutual relief operations 共済事業
▸Revenues from commissions of *mutual relief operations* were pooled in off-the-book accounts. 共済事業の手数料収入は, 簿外口座に蓄えられていた.

N n

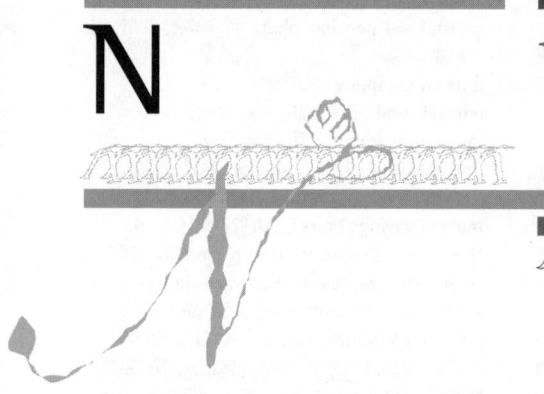

name 動 指名する, 任命する, 選ぶ, 指定する, 命名する, …の名前を挙げる, 公表する, 決める
▸The government has *named* Minoru Murofushi, former chairman of trading house Itochu Corp., as governor of the Development Bank of Japan. 政府は, 日本政策投資銀行の総裁に室伏稔伊藤忠商事前会長を指名した。
▸Under the agreement, France's Danone will *name* two people Yakult Honsha's board of directors and Yakult will name one to Danone's board. 合意事項では, 仏ダノンがヤクルト本社に取締役2名を派遣し, ヤクルトはダノンに取締役1名を派遣する。

name 名 名称, 名前, 名義, 知名度, ネーム (⇒ **register** 動)
 business name 社名
 corporate name 社名
 name borrowing 名義借り
 name gathering 名寄せ
 name lending 名義貸し
 name recognition 知名度
 security name 銘柄名
 single name paper 単名手形 (＝one-name paper)
 trade name 商号
▸After the management integration, the corporate *name* as well as the current management will be retained. 経営統合後も, 社名や現在の経営体制はそのまま残る。

narrow 動 縮小する, 狭まる, 限定する, 狭める, 縮める
▸Japan Airlines' first-quarter loss *narrowed* by 30 percent. 日本航空の第1四半期赤字が, 30％縮小した。

Nasdaq Stock Market ナスダック証券市場, ナスダック (マイクロソフトやインテルなどのハイテク株をはじめ5,000を超える銘柄が上場して取引され, これ以外に数千銘柄が店頭 (OTC) 市場で取引されている)

NAV 純資産価値 (net asset valueの略)
NBV 正味簿価 (net book valueの略)
NCD 譲渡性預金 (negotiable certificate of depositの略)

needs 名 必要, 必要量, 必要額, 要求, 需要, 必需品, 課題, ニーズ
 borrowing needs 借入需要, 調達額
 capital needs 資金需要, 資本必要額, 必要資本
 financing needs 資金調達需要, 資金ニーズ, 調達額
 gross financing needs 総調達額
 market needs 市場の需要, 市場のニーズ
 net borrowing needs 純調達額
 working capital needs 運転資金の必要額, 運転資金のニーズ
▸We build enduring business relationships by understanding and anticipating our customers' *needs*. 当社は, お客さまのニーズを理解, 予測することにより, 長く続く取引関係を築いています。

negative 名 弱気材料, 悪材料, マイナス要因
 structural negatives 構造的マイナス要因

negative 形 マイナスの, 負の, 逆の, 赤字の, 反対の, 弱含みの, 弱気の, 消極的な, 悪影響を与える, 有害な, 否定的な, 悲観的な, 成果が上がらない, ネガティブ (⇒**positive** 形)
 negative amortization 負の返済, 未収利息による元本の増加
 negative assets 消極資産

negative clause 担保提供制限条項（＝negative pledge）

negative currency effects 為替差損

negative factor 悪材料, 懸念材料, 売り材料, マイナス要因

negative growth マイナス成長

negative income tax 負の所得税(所得のない者や一定水準の所得しかない者に国が与える社会保障給付)

negative interest マイナス金利, 逆金利(利息から差し引かれる金)

negative net gearing 純負債比率

negative news 悪材料

negative pledge 担保制限, 担保提供制限条項, ネガティブ・プレッジ条項

negative yield 逆イールド（＝negative spread）

▸Return on shareholders' equity was *negative* in 2007, compared with a return of 13 percent in 2006. 2007年度の株主持ち分利益率は, 前年度の13％に対して, マイナスに転じました。

▸The firm's net operating revenues for the first nine months of 2007 were a *negative* $104 million compared with a positive $41 million in the same period last year. 同社の2007年1－9月期の純営業収益は, 前年同期の4,100万ドルの黒字に対して, 1億400万ドルの赤字でした。

negative effect 悪影響, 悪材料, マイナス影響, マイナス効果, 負の効果, 負の側面（＝negative impact)

▸If the yen starts to appreciate, this will have a *negative effect* on the revenues of exporting companies. 円高に転じれば, 輸出企業の収益は円高のマイナス影響を受けることになる。

negative goodwill 消極のれん, 消極的のれん, 負ののれん, マイナスの営業権

▸*Negative goodwill* is included in Shareholders' equity (Restricted reserves) or in Current liabilities. マイナスの営業権は, 資本の部(拘束予備金)または流動負債に含まれています。

negative impact 負の側面, 負の効果, マイナス効果, マイナス影響, 悪影響, 悪材料（＝negative effect)

▸We cannot ignore the possible *negative impacts* of the regulatory reforms, which may prompt excessive competition and weaken existing industries. 過当競争や既存産業の衰退を招く恐れがある規制改革の負の側面を, 無視することはできない。

negative legacy 負の遺産, ツケ(企業の「負の遺産」としては, 不良債権のほかに, 赤字続きの子会社, 値下がりした株や不動産, 退職金や企業年金の積立て不足といったものが挙げられる)

▸Banks should cut losses—nonperforming loans and other *negative legacies* of the bubble economy. 銀行は, 不良債権その他バブル期の「負の遺産」の損切りをしなければならない。

negative net worth 債務超過, 債務超過額, 税引き後利益の赤字

▸The subsidiary has actually had a *negative net worth* for three consecutive fiscal years. 子会社は, 実際は3期連続債務超過だった。

negative spread 逆ざや（＝negative yield：運用利回りが保険契約者に約束した予定利率を下回ること。⇒**insurance policyholder**)

▸Allowing insurers to lower the promised yields would solve the *negative spread* problem, thus serving as an effective measure to stave off collapse. 生命保険会社の予定利率の引下げを認めれば, 逆ざや問題の解消になり, その結果, 破綻回避の有力な手段になるはずである。

negative wealth effect 逆資産効果(土地や株その他の資産価格の下落)

▸The so-called *negative wealth effect* refers to the drop in the value of land, stocks and other assets. いわゆる「逆資産効果」とは, 土地や株その他の資産価格の下落のことをいう。

negotiable 形 流通可能の, 流通性のある, 手形などを譲渡できる, 譲渡可能な, 買い取ることができる

negotiable asset 譲渡可能資産

negotiable bill of lading 譲渡可能船荷証券

negotiable certificate of deposit 譲渡性預金, 譲渡性預金証書（＝negotiable CD)《略 **NCD**》

negotiable instrument 有価証券, 流通証券, 換金可能証券（＝negotiable securities)

negotiable paper 流通証券（＝negotiable instrument)

Uniform Negotiable Instruments Law 統一流通証券法

negotiation 名 交渉, 協議, 商談, 取引, 流通, 権利の移転, 譲渡, 輸出地の取引銀行による荷為替手形の買取り, ネゴシエーション

conclude negotiations 交渉をまとめる

contract negotiation 契約交渉

enter into final negotiations with ... …と最終調整に入る

first-round negotiations 初協議, 第一回協議

multilateral negotiation 多国間交渉, 多角的交渉

negotiation charge 手形買取り手数料, 買取り

手数料(手形取組み時に銀行が請求する手数料)
negotiation of export bill 輸出手形の買取り
negotiations fall through 交渉が決裂する
negotiations on the capital increase 増資交渉
new round of multilateral trade negotiations 新多角的貿易交渉, 新ラウンド
second-round negotiations 2回目の協議
tie-up negotiation 提携交渉
unified wage negotiation 統一一貫上げ交渉
▶Marubeni Corp. will soon enter into separate *negotiations* with Aeon Co. and Wal-Mart Stores Inc. to choose a partner to assist in the rehabilitation of Daiei. 丸紅は, ダイエー再建に協力する事業提携先として, イオン, 米ウォルマート・ストアーズとそれぞれ近く交渉に入る。

net 動 相殺する, 純益を上げる, もたらす
▶We *netted* these prepaid costs with the liabilities. 当社は, この前払い費用を債務と相殺しました。

net 名 純額, 税引き後金額, 純益, 正味, 正価, 純量
  accounts receivable—net 売掛金—純額
  property, plant and equipment, net 有形固定資産(純額)

net 動 獲得する

Net [net] 名 インターネット[ネット]
  net [**Net**] **auction** ネット・オークション (=Internet auction, online auction)
  Net business ネット・ビジネス (=Internet business)
  Net server ネット事業者

net 形 基本的な, 最終的な, 結局の, 正味の, 掛け値のない, 純粋の, 税引き後の (⇒**equity investment**)
  net accounts receivable 売掛金純額
  net advance 純貸出高
  net amount 純額, 正味金額, 正味資産
  net amount owed 正味負債額
  net balance 純収支残高, 純収支尻(⇒**retained earnings**)
  net basis 配当金[配当]課税後利益法, 純額ベース
  net book value 正味帳簿価額, 正味価, 純簿価《略 NBV》(=net carrying value)
  net borrowing 正味借入金
  net business profit 業務純益, 業務純利益
  net capital deficiency 債務超過, 純資本不足 (=capital deficit; ⇒**going concern**)
  net capital gain 純資本所得, 純キャピタル・ゲイン[資本利得], 純額キャピタル・ゲイン
  net carrying amount 正味繰越し額, 簿価純額, 減価償却費控除後簿価
  net carrying value 正味簿価, 正味帳簿価額
  net current assets 正味流動資産, 純流動資産
  net decrease in cash and cash equivalents 現金および現金等価物の純減少
  net earned surplus forwarded 繰越し利益剰余金
  net effects 正味の影響, 正味の影響額, 純影響額
  net gain (**loss**) **from operations** 純事業利益(損失)
  net gains on the sales of assets 資産売却による正味収益
  net investment 純投資額
  net investment hedges 純投資ヘッジ
▶Substantially increased investments in product and market development, combined with intense global competition, affected our *net* financial performance. 当社の業績は, 最終的に製品開発[商品開発]と市場開拓[市場開発]に対する投資の大幅拡大とグローバル市場における競争[国際競争]の激化の影響を被りました。

net asset 純資産, 正味資産, 正味財産(総資産から総負債を差し引いた資産残高)
  net assets employed 純運用資産
  net assets worth per share 1株当たり純資産 (=net assets worth)
▶Amortization of the excess of cost over the *net* assets acquired is to be recorded over sixty months. 取得した純資産に対する取得価額超過額の償却は, 60か月にわたって行う予定です。

net asset value 純資産価値, 純資産額, 正味資産額, 純資産, 純財産《略 NAV》(=net worth: 貸借対照表上の資産総額から負債総額を差し引いた額で, 自己資本にあたる)

net asset value per share 1株当たり純資産価値, 普通株式1株当たり純資産価値 (=book value per share, net tangible assets per share: 会社が解散した場合, 株主は持ち株数に応じて残った財産が分配されるが, その時の1株当たり資産。解散価値ともいう)

Net bank ネット銀行, ネット専業銀行, ネットバンク (=Internet bank, Internet-based bank, Net-only bank)
▶The new *Net bank* whose initial capital is ¥20 billion started operations in the first half of fiscal 2007. 新ネット銀行は, 当初資本が200億円で, 2007年度上半期から業務を開始した。

net capital expenditures 資本的支出純額, 資本の支出(純額)
▶Operating cash flows covered our *net capital expenditures* and dividend payments for the

two years. 過去2年間は、営業活動によるキャッシュ・フローが、当社の資本的支出（純額）と配当金支払いをまかないました。

net cash 純収支、純キャッシュ、正味現金、現金純額、正味キャッシュ、ネット・キャッシュ
- **net cash from operating activities** 営業活動により得た純キャッシュ、営業活動による資金収入純額
- **net cash inflows** 純現金収入、純資金収入額
- **net cash investment in a lease** リースに係わる正味現金投資額
- **net cash outflows** 純現金支出、純支払い額
- **net cash provided from operating activities** 営業活動［事業活動］から生じた資金—純額
- **net cash received from (used for) acquisitions** 企業買収に伴って受領した（使用した）現金純額

net cash flow 純収入、純支、純資金収入額、純キャッシュ・フロー、正味キャッシュ・フロー（一定期間の現金収入と現金支出との差額、一定期間の企業の営業活動から得られた資金（正味運転資本）、投資の現金収入と現金支出との差額、純利益から株式配当金を差し引いて減価償却費を加算した額、などの意味で用いられる）

net cash provided by ... …により得た資金収入純額［純現金収入、純キャッシュ］、…で得た資金収入純額、…により生じた正味現金、…により調達した資金（純額）
- **net cash provided by financing activities** 財務活動により生じた正味現金、財務活動［金融活動］による純現金収入［現金収入純額］、財務活動により調達した資金（純額）
- **net cash provided by investing activities** 投資活動により得た純キャッシュ［現金預金純額］、投資活動により生じた正味現金、投資活動による純現金収入［現金収入純額］
- **net cash provided by operating activities** 営業活動により生じた正味現金、営業活動により得た純キャッシュ［現金預金純額］、営業活動による資金収入純額［純現金収入］
- **net cash provided by operations** 営業活動により調達した資金（純額）、営業活動により得た資金収入純額 （=net cash provided by operating activities）
  - ▸*Net cash provided by* operations reached a record $3 billion in 2007. 営業活動により調達した資金（純額）は、2007年度は過去最高の30億ドルでした。

net cash provided by (used in) ... …に伴う正味現金収支、…により調達した（…に使用した）

net cash provided by (used in) financing activities 財務活動に伴う正味現金収支、財務活動により得た純キャッシュ、財務活動による資金収入（支出）純額、財務活動により調達した（財務活動に使用した）資金（純額）

net cash provided by (used in) investing activities 投資活動に伴う正味現金収支

net cash provided by (used in) operating activities 営業活動［事業活動］に伴う正味現金収支

net cash used in ... …に使用した現金預金純額［純キャッシュ］
- **net cash used in financig activities** 財務［金融］活動に使用した現金預金純額 （=net cash used for financing activities）
- **net cash used in investing activities** 投資活動に使用した現金預金純額［純キャッシュ］、投資活動に投入した正味現金［純資金額］、投資活動に使用した現金預金純額、投資活動による資金支出［現金支出］純額 （=net cash used for investing activities）

net change in ... …の純増加［減少］、…の増加［減少］額、…の増減、…の正味増減額
- **net change in cash and cash equivalents** 現金および現金同等物の純増加［減少］額、現預金および現預金同等物の純増加［減少］額
- **net change in deferred income taxes** 繰延べ税金の増減
- **net change in short-term debt** 短期債務の純増加［減少］
- **net change in unamortized service charges** 未償却サービス料の正味増減額

net charge 純費用
▸Excluding this *net charge* and a fourth quarter restructuring charge, our per share earnings were $3.45 in 2007. この純費用と第4四半期の事業再編成費用を除くと、当社の2007年度の1株当たり純利益は3.45ドルでした。

net debt 純債務、純負債、金融債務
- **net debt position** 純負債額
- **ratio of net debt to net debt plus equity** 金融債務比率 （=金融債務対金融債務+資本）
  ▸The Company's ratio of *net debt* to net debt plus equity was 15.2 percent at December 31, 2007. 当社の金融債務比率は、2007年12月31日現在で15.2%でした。

Net distribution ネット配信
▸For general viewers, there appears to be no difference between TV broadcasting and *Net distribution*. 一般の視聴者には、テレビ放送とネッ

ト配信に違いはないように見える。

net earnings 純利益, 当期純利益
- **net earnings before cumulative effect of accounting change** 会計処理変更に伴う累積的影響額考慮前の純利益[当期純利益], 会計原則変更の累積効果控除前純利益
- **net earnings (loss) applicable to common shares** 普通株式に帰属する当期純利益(損失), 普通株式に帰属する純利益(損失)
- **net earnings per revenue dollar** 売上高1ドル当たり純利益
- **net earnings per share** 1株当たり純利益, 1株当たり当期純利益
- ▸Worldwide net earnings for the three months ended September 30, 2007 were $0.9 billion compared with 1.2 billion in 2006.　2007年9月30日終了四半期[2007年7-9月期]の国内外の純利益(連結純利益)は, 前年同期の12億ドルに対して9億ドルでした。

net earnings applicable to common shares 普通株式に帰属する当期純利益
- ▸Net earnings applicable to common shares were $330 million ($1.40 per common share) in 2007.　普通株式に帰属する当期純利益は, 2007年度は3億3,000万ドル(普通株式1株当たり1.40ドル)でした。

net financial liabilities 純金融負債
- ▸Net financial liabilities decreased as a result of our debts reduction.　純金融負債は, 当社の負債を削減した結果, 減少しました。

net income 純利益, 当期純利益, 税引き後利益, 純所得, 純収入, 〈日銀の〉剰余金 (=net profit, profit after tax)
- **net income as percent of revenues** 売上高当期純利益率
- **net income available for common stock** 普通株主に帰属する当期純利益
- **net income before taxes** 税引き前当期純利益
- **net income forecast** 純利益[税引き後利益]予想, 純利益見通し
- **net income (losss)** 純利益(損失), 当期純利益(損失)
- **net income per share** 1株当たり純利益
- **net income ratio** 純利益率 (=net income to sales ratio)
- **net income to sales ratio** 売上高純利益率 (=net income ratio)
- **net income to stockholders' equity ratio** 自己資本利益率, 株主持ち分利益率
- **net income to total assets ratio** 総資本利益

率, 総資産純利益率
- ▸Financing arm Ford Credit reported net income of $470 million.　フォードの金融子会社フォード・クレジットは, 4億7,000万ドルの純利益を計上した。
- ▸The decline in net income for the first nine months was affected by lower earnings at the firm.　1-9月期の純利益の減少は, 同社の利益が減少したことが影響しています。

net income applicable to common shares 普通株式に帰属する純利益[当期純利益]
- ▸Net income applicable to common shares for the third quarter of 2007 was $223 million, compared with $283 million for the second quarter of 2007.　2007年第3四半期の普通株式に帰属する純利益は, 第2四半期の2億8,300万ドルに対して2億2,300万ドルでした。

net income for the year 当期純利益 (=net income for the period)
- ▸Net income for the year ended December 31, 2007 was $50 million.　2007年12月31日終了事業年度の当期純利益[2007年度の純利益]は, 5,000万ドルでした。

net increase 純増
- ▸The net increase in gross margin was due principally to improved profit margins in the central office switching business.　売上総利益の純増は, 主に局用交換機事業の利益率改善によるものです。

net interest 純利息, 支払い利息純額 (⇒general corporate expenses)
- **net interest deficit** 純支払い利息
- **net interest income** 純受取利息, 正味受取利息
- **net interest payment** 金融収支
- **net interest revenue** 正味受取利息

net liabilities 正味負債, 債務超過額 (⇒post-retirement)

net loss 純損失, 当期純損失, 税引き後赤字, 最終赤字, 赤字決算 (⇒consolidated net loss, group net loss, quarterly net loss)
- **net loss carried over** 繰越し欠損金
- **net loss from operations** 営業純損失
- ▸The Company likely will dive into the red for the current business year with a group net loss of ¥55 billion.　当社は, 当期は550億円の連結税引き後赤字[連結純損失]で, 赤字に転落する見通しです。

net margin on sales 対売上高純利益率, 売上高純利益率, 売上利益率 (=net profit on sales)
- ▸Net margin on sales was 6% for the full year 2007 compared with 5% a year ago.　対売上高純利益率は, 前期の5%に対して, 2007年度通期で

6%でした。

net of ... …を除いて，…控除後，…差引後，…差引後純額

net of applicable income tax 対応する税金差引後，税引き後

net of depreciation 減価償却差引後

net of pension liabilities 年金債務控除後

net of reserve for doubtful accounts 貸倒れ引当金控除後，貸倒れ引当金控除後の受取債権，貸倒れ引当金差引後の純額 （＝net of loan loss reserves）

net of tax 税引き後，税金差引後，純税額，税控除後，税効果控除後

▶Our plant additions-related expenditures were at about the same level as depreciation, leaving property, plant and equipment, *net of* accumulated depreciation, essentially unchanged. 当社の工場増設関連支出は減価償却額とほぼ同水準で，減価償却累計額控除後の有形固定資産額は実質的に変動しませんでした。

net operating profit 純営業利益，営業純利益，金融機関の業務純益

> 業務純益とは ➡ 銀行など金融機関の「本業によるもうけ」を，業務純益という。これは，貸出金と預金の利息の差から生じる「資金利益」，手数料などの「役務取引等利益」，債券の売買益などの「その他業務利益」の合計から，経費を差し引いて算出する。

▶Bad loan disposal at the end of March next year will be smaller than the *net operating profits* of all the seven major banking groups. 来年3月期の不良債権処理額は，大手銀行・金融7グループ各行の業務純益の範囲内になる見込みだ。

net operating revenues 純営業収益

▶The firm's *net operating revenues* for the second quarter were a negative $106 million compared with a positive $16 million in the same period last year. 同社の第2四半期の純営業収益は，前年同期の1,600万ドルの黒字に対して，1億600万ドルの赤字でした。

net periodic pension cost 期間年金費用純額 （⇒expected long-term rate of return）

net premium revenues 正味収入保険料，正味保険料収入（非金融機関の売上高に当たる）

▶*Net premium revenues* increased at four of the nation's nine major nonlife insurers. 正味収入保険料は，国内大手損保9社のうち4社で増加した。

net proceeds 正味入金額，純売却益，純資金，受取金純額 （⇒proceeds）

▶*Net proceeds* from the public offering were used to reduce notes payable. 公募による純資金［公募発行による受取金純額］は，短期借入金の返済に充てられました。

net profit 純利益，当期純利益，税引き後利益，最終黒字，最終利益，〈日銀の〉当期剰余金 （＝net income）

net profit after tax 税引き後純利益，税引き後の最終利益，法人税控除後純利益

net profit before tax 税引き前純利益，法人税控除前純利益

net profit from operations 営業純利益 （＝income from operations）

▶The confecctionery maker managed to book a *net profit* of ¥1.4 billion through sales of fixed assets. この菓子メーカーは，固定資産の売却で，かろうじて14億円の税引き後利益を計上［確保］した。

net profit per share 1株当たり純利益

▶The Corporation's *net profit per share* in the April-September first half of fiscal 2007 year came to ¥19.95 from ¥34.05 a year before. 当社の2007年度上期(4-9月期)の1株当たり純利益は，前年同期の34円5銭に対して19円95銭だった。

net revenues 純収益，営業利益

▶The decline in *net revenues* is mainly due to higher non-performing loans and reduced spread. 営業利益の減少は，主に不良債権［契約不履行債権］の拡大と利ざや(調達金利と貸出金利との差)の縮小によるものです。

net sales 純売上高

▶In recent years, a large and increasing portion of the Company's *net sales*, operating profits and growth have come from its international operations. ここ数年，当社の純売上高，営業利益と業績の伸びの相当部分が海外活動からもたらされ，その割合は年々高まっています。

net short-term borrowings 短期借入金純額

▶The Corporation's *net short-term borrowings* amounted to $830 million at September 30, 2007. 当社の短期借入金純額は，2007年9月30日現在で8億3,000万ドルに達しました。

net tangible assets 純有形資産

net tangible assets per share 1株当たり純有形資産価値

Net trading ネット取引，ネット販売 （＝Internet trading, online trading）

▶By offering electronic settlement services for *Net* shopping and *trading*, the firm wants to attract funds from Internet users. 同社のねらいは，ネット・ショッピングやネット取引の電子決済業務を行うことにより，インターネット利用者か

ら資金を取り込むことにある。
net working capital 純運転資本, 正味運転資本 (=net current assets：正味運転資本=流動資産-流動負債)
▸*Net working capital* refers to current assets less current liabilities. 正味運転資本は, 流動資産から流動負債を控除した額です。
net worth 自己資本, 資本, 自己資金, 株主持ち分, 純資産, 正味資産, 正味財産 (⇒**negative net worth**)
　net worth agreement 自己資本維持契約
　net worth of collateral 担保余力
　net worth shareholder's equity 所有者持ち分, 株主持ち分, 出資者持ち分
　ratio of total liabilities to net worth 負債対自己資本比率, 負債比率 (=net worth to debts ratio)
　ratio of net worth to fixed assets 固定比率
　ratio of net worth to the total assets 株主資本比率
　return on net worth 株主資本利益率, 自己資本利益率
　sales to net worth 株主資本回転率
　total liabilities and net worth 総資本
　turnover of net worth 株主資本回転率
▸Deferred tax accounting allows banks to calculate their *net worth* by assuming future refunding of excessive tax payments. 税効果会計では, 銀行は, 払いすぎた税金の将来の還付を見込んで自己資本を計算することができる。
net worth ratio 自己資本比率, 株主資本比率 (=capital adequacy ratio, capital-asset ratio, ratio of net worth)
▸The banks are reluctant to lend to small and midsize businesses to protect their capital adequacy and *net worth ratios*. 銀行は, 自己資本比率を守るため[自己資本不足に陥らないための自衛として], 中小企業貸出[中小企業への貸出]に慎重になっている。
network 網状組織, 連絡網, 通信網, 回線網, 回路網, 網, ネットワーク
　branch network 支店網
　communications network 通信網, 通信ネットワーク
　distribution network 流通網, 流通ネットワーク, 販売網
　global network society インターネット社会, ネット社会
　human networks 人脈
　knowledge network 知識ネットワーク

　nationwide network 全国ネットワーク
　network industry ネットワーク産業
　network service provider ネットワーク回線接続プロバイダー
　retail network 小売販売網, リテール販売網
　sales network 販売網
▸Aeon Co. plans to use Maruetsu's *network* of outlets in the metropolitan area to beef up its presence in the grocery store market on the outskirts of Tokyo. イオンは, 首都圏のマルエツの店舗網を活用して, 東京近郊の食品スーパー市場での事業基盤を強化する計画だ。
▸Banks will develop larger sales *networks* for financial products than those of major securities companies. 今後は, 銀行が大手証券会社をしのぐ金融商品の販売網を展開するようになる。
new 形 新規の, 新しい, 新…, ニュー
　new debt 新規借入金
　new debt issues 新発債の発行
　new fiscal year 新年度, 新会計年度
　new funds 新規資金
　new investment 新規投資
　new issuance 新規発行, 新株発行, 新規発行額
　new issue 新規発行, 新規発行株式, 新発債
　new issue of stock 新株発行
　new lending 新規貸出
　new loans 新規融資 (⇒**sluggish performance**)
　new rating 新規格付け
　new share issuance 新株発行 (=issuance of new shares, new share issue)
　new stock [share] issuing expenses 新株発行費
　new technology 新技術, ニュー・テクノロジー
new borrowing 新規借入れ, 新規資金調達
▸Ford Motor Co. will pledge its investment in Mazda Motor Corp. in its *new borrowing*. フォードは, 新規資金調達では保有するマツダ株を担保にする方針だ。
new generation Internet firm 新世代ネット企業
▸Many of these *new generation Internet firms* were established in about 2000, when the so-called IT bubble collapsed. これらの新世代ネット企業の多くは, いわゆるITバブルが崩壊した2000年前後に設立された。
new high 新高値, 最高記録, 空前の高値, 過去最高
▸Excluding these accounting changes, our net income and earnings per share were *new highs*. これらの会計上の変更を除くと, 当社の当期純利益

と1株当たり利益は、過去最高でした。

new product 新製品
▶The company started selling *new products*, including a single-lens reflex digital camera. 同社は、一眼レフ・デジカメなど新製品の販売を開始した。

new share issue 新規株式発行、新株発行、増資 (=new share issuance)
▶The company plans to use the proceeds from *new share issues* to increase its equity ownership in a staff dispatching company. 同社は、新株発行で調達した資金[新株発行による手取金]を、人材派遣会社の株式の追加取得にあてる計画だ。

new share offering 新株発行
▶The firm will raise ¥100 billion in a *new share offering*. 同社は、新株発行で1,000億円を調達する。

new shares 新株、増資
▶Hokuetsu Paper Mills Ltd. issued *new shares* worth about ¥30 billion to Mitsubishi as planned. 北越製紙は、計画どおり、三菱商事を引受先として約300億円の新株を発行した。

New York Stock Exchange ニューヨーク証券取引所《略 **NYSE**》(=**Big Board**)
▶In November 2007, the bank debuted on the *New York Stock Exchange*. 同行は、2007年11月にニューヨーク証券取引所に上場した。
▶The bank will remain listed on the *New York Stock Exchange* after the merger. 「同行は、経営統合後も引き続きニューヨーク証券取引所に上場される。」

newly issued bond 新発債
newly merged firm 合併新会社 (⇒**officer**)
news conference 記者会見
▶The company is to hold a *news conference* to unveil a set of its programs to improve its corporate value. 同社は、記者会見を開いて、企業価値を高めるための一連のプログラムを発表する。

newsletter 名 社報、公報、回報、PR誌、年報、月報、報告書、時事解説、時事通信、ニューズレター
▶The figures for earlier peiods cited in this *newsletter are restated*. この報告書に記載されている当四半期以前の数値は、修正して再表示されています。

niche 名 特定分野、分野、領域、すき間、適所、適した場所[地位]、ニッチ
　niche business 得意分野
　niche market ニッチ市場、市場の特定分野、すき間市場
　niche marketing すき間市場販売戦略、ニッチ・マーケティング（未開発のすき間[ニッチ]市場への適応をめざすマーケティング）
　niche strategy すき間戦略、ニッチ戦略
　specialized niche 得意分野 (=specialised niche)
▶We are ready to take on competitors in every *niche of the marketplace*. 当社は、市場のあらゆる分野でライバル企業と競争する態勢を整えています。

nine months ended September 30 9月30日終了の9か月間、1-9月期、1月から9月までの3四半期
▶Consolidated revenue for the *nine months ended September 30*, 2007 was $42 billion. 2007年9月30日終了の9か月間[2007年1-9月期]の連結収益[連結売上高]は、420億ドルでした。

nine months to Dec. 31 4-12月期、4月から12月末までの3四半期[9か月] (=April-December period：12月期決算企業の場合は第2四半期から第4四半期までの3四半期、3月期決算企業の場合は第1四半期から第3四半期までの3四半期を指す)
▶Kyocera Corp.'s group net profit for the *nine months to Dec. 31* rose 15.6 percent from a year earlier to ¥33.25 billion. 京セラの4-12月期の連結税引き後利益は、前年同期比15.6％増の332億5,000万円でした。

nominee 名 候補者、候補被指名者、被指名者、被任命者、被推薦人、株の名義人、名義上の株式保有
▶Each of the 10 *nominees* named in the proxy statement who stood for election as a director received a plurality of the votes cast. 委任状に取締役選任候補者として記載された10名は、それぞれ投票総数の大多数[過半数]の支持を得ました。

noncancelable [**noncancellable**] 形 解約不能の、中途解約不能の、取消し不能の、解約できない
　noncancelable guarantee 取消し不能保証
　noncancelable lease 解約不能リース、中途解約不能リース (⇒**rental commitments**)
　noncancelable operating lease 解約不能のオペレーティング・リース
▶The Company does lease certain office, factory and warehouse space, and land under principally *noncancelable* operating leases. 当社は、一部の事業所、工場、倉庫や土地などを、主に中途解約不能なオペレーティング・リースにより使用しています。

noncash 形 非現金の、非金銭の、資金以外の、資金を伴わない、現金収支を伴わない

net non-cash items 非現金項目純額
noncash activities 非金銭活動, 資金[現金収支]を伴わない活動
noncash asset 非現金資産, 非貨幣性資産
noncash expense 非現金費用, 非支出費用 (= noncash charge)
noncash financing activities 資金[現金収支]を伴わない財務活動
noncash investing activities 資金[現金収支]を伴わない投資活動
noncash items 非現金項目, 非金銭項目, 現金の収入・支出を伴わない項目
noncash spinoff 現金収入を伴わないスピンオフ
noncash transaction 非現金取引, 現金外取引, 現金決済を伴わない取引
▸The following table displays the *noncash* items excluded from the consolidated statements of cash flows. 次表は, 連結キャッシュ・フロー計算書から除外した非現金項目を示しています。

nonconsolidated 形 非連結, 非連結ベースの
nonconsolidated basis 非連結ベース, 単体ベース
nonconsolidated subsidiaries and affiliates 非連結子会社等
nonconsolidated subsidiary 非連結子会社

noncontributory 形 非拠出, 非拠出型の, 従業員でなく雇用者が負担する
noncontributory defined benefit (pension) plan 非拠出確定給付年金制度
noncontributory pension plan 非拠出型年金制度 (= noncontributory plan)
▸The Company's *noncontributory* pension plan covers most U.S. employees after one year of service. 当社の非拠出型年金制度は, 勤続1年以上のほとんどの米国内従業員を対象としています。

noncontributory defined benefit plan 非拠出型確定給付年金制度, 非拠出型給付金規定方式による年金制度
▸The Corporation and most of its subsidiary companies have *noncontributory defined benefit plans* which provide for service pensions, based on length of service and rates of pay, for substantially all their employees. 当社と子会社の大半は, 実質的に全従業員に対して[全従業員を対象に], 勤続年数と給与額に基づいて年金額を決定する非拠出型確定給付年金制度[非拠出型給付金規定方式による年金制度]を設けています。

noncontributory plan 非拠出年金制度, 非拠出型退職金制度 (= noncontributory pension plan)
▸A *noncontributory plan* is funded by company contributions to an irrevocable trust fund. この非拠出型退職金制度の資金は, 会社の拠出金によって取崩し不能の信託基金に積み立てられています。

noncontributory supplemental retirement benefit plan 非拠出型追加的退職給付制度
▸The Corporation's *noncontributory supplemental retirement benefit plan* for its elected officers contains provisions for funding the participants' expected retirement benefits. 当社の選任役員を対象とする非拠出型追加的退職給付制度には, 制度参加者の予定退職給付額を積み立てる旨の条項が含まれています。

nonconvertible bond 非転換社債
nonconvertible preferred stock 非転換優先株式
noncore assets 非中核的資産, 非中核的事業資産, 周辺資産
noncore business 非中核事業, 非主力事業
▸The company will withdraw from its *noncore* businesses. 同社は, 非中核事業から撤退する方針だ。

noncurrent 非流動的, 長期の, 固定した (= fixed)
deferred tax asset/noncurrent 繰延べ税金資産・長期
deferred tax liabilities/noncurrent 繰延べ税金負債・長期
noncurrent assets 非流動資産, 固定資産 (= fixed assets)
noncurrent liability 非流動負債, 固定負債 (= long-term liability)
noncurrent tangible asset 長期の無形資産
▸Other assets include goodwill, patents, other intangibles, deferred taxes, and other *noncurrent* assets. その他の資産には, 営業権, 特許権, その他の無形固定資産, 繰延べ税金と, その他の非流動資産が含まれています。

nondeductible 形 所得から控除できない, 非控除の
nondeductible expense 非控除費用, 損金として控除できない費用
nondeductible reserves 非所得控除
nondeductible tax 損金不算入の租税課金
nondeductible 名 所得算入
nonfinancial earnings 金融機関の貸出金以外の非金利収入 (⇒pension insurance sales)
nonfinancial statement section 〈アニュアル・レポートの〉非財務書類[財務諸表]情報(株主への挨拶, 財務ハイライト, 事業概況, 経営成績と

財政状態の分析・説明など財務書類[財務諸表]と注記を除いた部分をいう)

nonlife insurer 損害保険会社, 損保会社, 損保 (＝nonlife insurance company)
▶Five major *nonlife insurers* saw their net profits decline in the first half of the fiscal year to Sept. 30 from a year earlier. 9月中間決算で, 損保大手5社の税引き後利益は前年同期を下回った。

nonmanagement Board member 経営権に関与しない取締役
▶The Board of Directors' Audit Cmmittee consists entirely of independent *nonmanagement Board members*. 取締役会付属監査委員会は, 経営権に関与しない独立した取締役だけで構成されています。

nonoperating 形 営業外の, 休眠の
　nonoperating company 休眠会社
　nonoperating expenses 営業外費用
　nonoperating income 営業外収益, 営業外損益 (＝nonoperating revenue)
　nonoperating income or expenses 営業外損益
　nonoperating profit 営業外収益
　nonoperating revenue 営業外収益
　nonoperating section 営業外損益区分

nonpar 形 無額面
　nonpar stock [share] 無額面株式
　nonpar value capital stock 無額面株式
　nonpar value stock 無額面株式 (＝no-par-value stock)

nonparticipating 形 非参加の, 利益不参加の, 無配の
　nonparticipating preferred stock 非参加優先株式
　nonparticipating stock 非参加株

nonpayment 名 不払い
　nonpayment of insurance benefits 保険金の不払い
　nonpayment of insurance money 保険金の不払い (＝nonpayment of insurance benefits, nonpayment of insurance claims)
▶Instances of *nonpayment* involving third-sector insurance products totaled 1,140 for Mitsui Sumitomo Insurance Co. 第三分野(医療保険やがん保険など)の保険商品の保険金不払い件数は, 三井住友海上火災保険で計1,140件もあった。

nonperforming loan 不良債権, 不良貸付け, 貸倒れ (＝bad debt, nonperforming credits, uncollectible loan)
▶Corporate bankruptcies have led to the swelling of *nonperforming loans*, posing a heavy burden on banks. 企業倒産が不良債権の増大を生み, 銀行に重くのしかかっている。

nonqualified plan 非適格年金

nonrecourse 形 遡求権なし, 非遡求 (＝without recourse)
　nonrecourse loan ノンリコース・ローン (責任の範囲が対象案件の収益力や将来キャッシュ・フローによって評価された価値の範囲内に限られる融資)
　nonrecourse obligation 非遡求債務
　on a nonrecourse basis 遡求権なしで
▶The receivables were sold on a *nonrecourse* basis. 債権は, 遡求権なしで売却した。

nonrecurring 形 非経常的な, 非反復的, 経常外
　nonrecurring charge 経常外損失
　nonrecurring cost 臨時費用, 非経常的費用, 非反復的費用 (＝nonrecurring charge)
　nonrecurring gains or losses 経常外損益, 特別損益
　nonrecurring income 経常外収入, 臨時収益
　nonrecurring items 非経常的損益項目
　nonrecurring profit and loss 臨時損益, 非経常的損益, 特別損益

nonresident 名 非居住者
▶Capital gains realized on the Corporation's common shares by individuals who are not resident in Canada for Canadian income tax purposes generally are not taxable in Canada, unless the shares are used or held by a *nonresident* who is carrying on a business in Canada. カナダ所得税法上, カナダ居住者に該当しない個人が実現した当社の普通株式のキャピタル・ゲインは, 非居住者が当社株式をカナダでの事業目的のために[カナダで事業を営んでいる非居住者が当社株式を]使用または保有している場合を除いて, 一般にカナダでは非課税扱いになります。

nonstrategic business 非戦略的事業, 非戦略的事業部門[業務部門]
▶We reported revenues from certain *nonstrategic businesses* of the firm last year. 前期は, 同社の一部の非戦略的業務部門[事業部門]の売上高を計上しました。

nonstrategic division 非戦略的事業部門, 非戦略部門
▶The revenues of these divested *nonstrategic divisions* were included in the second quarter of 2007. 整理・売却したこれらの非戦略的事業部門の売上高は, 2007年第2四半期には計上されていました。

nontaxable 形 非課税の, 無税の

nonvoting class B preferred stock 無

議決権クラスＢ優先株式
nonvoting share 無議決権株，議決権のない株式（＝nonvoting stock）
NOPAT 税引き後営業利益（net operating profit after taxes の略）
norm 名 規範，標準，標準的方式，水準，規準，平均，典型，達成基準，要求水準，規準労働量，基準量，責任生産量，ノルマ
　behavioral norms 行動規範，社会通念
　cultural norms 文化の規範，社会規範
▸Since the bubble economy burst, low interest rates have been the *norm*. バブル崩壊以降，低金利が続いている。

normal course of business 通常の業務過程，通常の事業過程，通常の営業過程，通常の事業活動
▸We use various financial instruments, including derivatives, in the *normal course of business*. 当社は，通常業務で各種の金融商品を利用しており，これには金融派生商品も含まれています。

notch 名 段階，級，程度，順位，0.1ポイント，ノッチ（1ノッチ＝0.1ポイント）
▸Moody's Investors Service Inc. cut its rating on yen-denominated government bonds by two *notches* to A2 from Aa3. ムーディーズ・インベスターズ・サービスは，円建て国債の格付けをAa3からA2に2段階引き下げた。
▸The unemployment rate dipped down a *notch* to 5.5 percent last month, from 5.6 percent in June. 先月（7月）の失業率は，6月の5.6％から5.5％に1ノッチ［0.1ポイント］減少した。

note 名 手形，約束手形，証券（一般に中期の債務証券を指すが，米財務省証券に対して使うときは，償還期限が1年超10年以内の中期証券のことをいう），債券，債権表示証書，紙幣，通知書，伝票，覚書，注釈，注記，注意，ノート
　auditing for note receivable 受取手形監査
　bank note 中央銀行が発行する銀行券《略 BN》
　contract note 契約書
　delivery note 納品書
　fixed and variable rate notes 確定および変動利付きノート
　general notes of financial statements 財務諸表の一般的注記
　heading notes 頭注
　loan on note 手形貸付け
　loans on notes and bills 一般貸付け金
　matured note 満期手形
　notes and accounts receivable-trade, net of allowances 受取手形および売掛金，貸倒れ引

当金控除後
　overdue note 期限経過手形
　sight note 一覧払い約束手形，一覧払い手形
　three-year note auction 米国債3年物の入札，3年物Tノートの入札
　unlisted note 非上場債
　unpaid note 不渡り手形
▸On October 1, 2007, we utilized the shelf registration program to issue US $300 million of 6.0% *Notes* due 2017. 2007年10月1日に当社は，米証券取引所（SEC）の一括登録制度を利用して，満期2017年・利率6.0％のノート3億米ドルを発行しました。

note payable 支払い手形，手形債務，手形借入金，短期借入金，借入金
　note payable to subsidiary 子会社支払い手形
　notes payable-trade 支払い手形（＝acceptance payable）
▸The Corporation has $1 million of *notes payable* due June 10, 2008. 当社は，2008年6月10日期日の100万ドルの支払い手形を振り出している。
▸The difference was funded by increasing *notes payable* principally through the sale of commercial paper. 資金の不足分は，主にコマーシャル・ペーパーを発行して手形借入金を増やして補填しました。

note receivable 受取手形
　note receivable discount 手形割引
　note receivable discounted 割引手形
　note receivable due from employee 従業員手形貸付け金
　notes receivable-trade 受取手形（＝acceptance receivable）

notes to consolidated financial statements 連結財務書類注記，連結財務諸表注記
notes to financial statements 財務書類［財務諸表］に対する注記，財務書類［財務諸表］注記
▸The accompanying *notes to financial statements* are integral part of the finncial statements. 添付の財務書類注記は，財務書類の不可分の一体をなしています。

notice of annual meeting 定時株主総会開催の通知，年次株主総会招集通知（⇒proxy voting card）

number of shares 株式数
　number of shares authorized 授権株式数（＝number of authorized shares）
　number of shares issued 発行済み株式数，発行済み株式総数（＝number of stocks issued）
　number of shares of stock 株式数

number of shares outstanding 発行済み株式数, 社外流通株式数 （＝number of outstanding shares）
number of weighted average shares outstanding 加重平均総発行株式数
numerator 名 〈分数の〉分子
NYSE ニューヨーク証券取引所（New York Stock Exchangeの略）
▶*NYSE* Group struck a deal to buy European bourse operator Euronext for $9.96 billion. （ニューヨーク証券取引所を運営する）NYSEグループは, 欧州（パリやオランダなど）の証券取引所を運営する「ユーロネクスト」を99億6,000万ドルで買収する取引をした。

O

objective 名 目標, 目的, 対象
  business objective 経営目標, 経営目的
  company objective 企業目標, 会社目標
  control objective 内部統制目的
  cost objective 原価対象
  management by objectives 目標別管理, 目標管理, 目標管理制度《略 MBO》
  market objectives 市場目的
  marketing objectives マーケティングの目標, マーケティング目的
  objective of financial reporting 財務報告の目的
  objective of financial statements 財務書類［財務諸表］の目的
  objective tax 目的税
  organization objective 組織目標 (＝objective of organization)
  primary objective 最大の目標
  ▶One of our main *objectives* is to improve the value of our shareholders' investment. 当社の主要な経営目標の一つは, 株主の投資価値を高めることにあります。

objectivity 名 客観性 (⇒integrity and objectivity of the financial standards)
  ▶Management of the Corporation, in furtherance of the integrity and *objectivity* of data in the financial statements, has developed and maintains a system of internal accounting controls. 当社の経営者は, 財務書類に含まれる［財務書類上の］データの完全性と客観性を高めるため, 会計に関する内部統制組織［内部会計統制組織］を整備・維持しています。

obligation 名 債務, 負債, 債務負担, 債務証書, 債権債務関係, 義務, 約束, 金銭
  customer obligations 顧客の債務
  debt obligation 債務, 債務負担, 債務証書, 債務契約書
  estimated future obligations 将来の予測支払い義務額, 予測される将来の支払い義務額
  fund obligation 基金債務, 資金負債
  interest obligation 金利債務
  lease obligation リース債務
  long-term obligation 長期債務, 長期借入金
  obligation outstanding 未決済債務
  obligations incurred 発生債務
  obligations under pension and deferred compensation plans 退職年金債務
  payment obligation 支払い債務, 支払い義務
  pension obligation 年金債務
  short-term obligations 短期債務
  waiver of obligation 債務免除
  ▶The Corporation's finance subsidiary purchases customer *obligations* under long-term cntracts from the Corporation at net carrying value. 当社の金融子会社は, 当社との長期契約によって, 顧客の債務を当社から正味帳簿価格で購入しています。
  ▶We placed this $13 billion liability on the books to reflect those estimated future *obligations* at January 1, 2008, expressed in today's dollars. 2008年1月1日現在の予測される将来支払い義務額を反映させるため, 当社はこの130億ドル（現在のドル価値で）の債務を計上しました。

obsolescence 名 陳腐化, 老朽
obsolete 形 陳腐化した, 廃れた
  obsolete asset 陳腐化資産
  obsolete inventory 陳腐化棚卸し資産, 陳腐化

在庫

obtain 動 取得する, 調達する, 入手する, 獲得する (＝acquire)
  obtain funds 資金を調達する
  obtain in advance 前借りする
  obtain loan finance 借入れで資金調達をする, 借入れによる資金調達
▶We *obtained* a 20 percent stake in the company. 当社は, 同社の株式の20％を取得した。

occupational employee 非管理職従業員
▶Benefits for *occupational employees* are not directly pay-related. 非管理職従業員に対する給付は, 給与と直接的な関係はありません。

occupational pension 雇用年金
  occupational pension scheme 従業員年金制度

October–December period 10-12月期, 〈12月期決算企業の〉第4四半期, 〈3月期決算企業の〉第3四半期
▶The U.S. economy will significantly slow down in the *October–December period* and remain stagnant until spring. 米経済は, 10-12月期にかなり減速し, 来春まで停滞する見通しだ。

October–December quarter 10-12月期, 〈12月期決算企業の〉第4四半期, 〈3月期決算企業の〉第3四半期 (＝October–December period)
▶The company's operating profit rose in the *October–December quarter*. 同社の10-12月期の営業利益は, 増加した［同社の10-12月決算は, 営業利益が増加した］。

OEM 相手先ブランド製造業者, 相手先商標製造業者, 相手先ブランドによる生産方式, 生産委託契約 (**original equipment manufacturer, original equipment manufacturing**の略)

off-balance-sheet 形 貸借対照表に計上［表示］されない, 簿外の, オフ・バランス, オフ・バランスシート
  off-balance-sheet asset 簿外資産
  off-balance-sheet contingencies オフ・バランスの偶発債務
  off-balance-sheet financing 簿外資金調達, オフ・バランスシート資金調達, 簿外金融, オフ・バランス金融, オフ・バランスシート・ファイナンシング (貸借対照表に負債が計上されない形での資金調達)
  off-balance-sheet liability 簿外債務, 簿外負債, オフ・バランス債務
  off-balance-sheet transaction 簿外取引, オフ・バランス取引, オフ・バランスシート取引 (＝off-balance-sheet activity：貸借対照表上に表示されない取引)

▶Other *off-balance-sheet* contingencies aggregated approximately $200 million at December 31, 2007. その他の偶発債務は, 2007年12月31日現在で約2億ドルでした

off-the-book 形 帳簿外の, 簿外の, 記録されていない
  off-the-book account 簿外口座
  off-the-book deal 簿外取引
  off-the-book debts 簿外債務 (＝off-the-book liabilities)
  off-the-book property 含み資産
  off-the-book transaction 簿外取引 (＝off-the-book deal)
▶The company collapsed after its senior management's *off-the-book* deals came to light. 同社は, 経営者の簿外取引が発覚してから倒産した。

offer 動 申し込む, 提供する, 販売する, 〈金利などを〉提示する, 〈買収などの〉提案をする, 〈株式などを〉発行する, 〈株式を〉売り出す (⇒**mortgage**)
  offered price 提示価格, 買付け価格, 売り呼び値
  offered rate 出し手レート, 売り手レート, オファード・レート
▶One of our principal strategies is to *offer* customers the best value. 当社の主要戦略の一つは, 顧客に最大の価値を提供することです。
▶The bank *offered* three types of preferred shares. 同行は, 3種類の優先株を発行した。
▶The company does not *offer* income forecasts for the current business year. 同社は, 今期の収益予想を出していない。
▶The stock, *offered* at ¥235,000 a share in the initial public offering, closed at ¥295,000. 新規株式公開で1株235,000円で売り出された株［株式の新規公開で公開価格が1株当たり235,000円の同株］は, 295,000円で取引を終えた。

offer 名 申込み, 売り申込み, 募集, 売出し, 売り呼び値, 申し出, 提案, 提示, 提示額, 条件, オファー (⇒**public tender offer, tender offer**)
  bid offer price 呼び値
  block offer 一括売出し
  buying offer 買い申込み, 買いオファー
  buyout offer 買収の申込み, 買収提案 (＝acquisition offer)
  counter offer 修正申込み, 逆申込み, カウンター・オファー
  cross offer 交叉申込み
  firm offer 確定申込み, ファーム・オファー
  offer price per share 1株当たり買付け価格, 1株当たり買取り価格 (⇒**proposal**)
  open offer 公募

selling offer 売り申込み, 売りオファー
unseasoned offer 新規公開売出し
▸About 2,500 employees accepted the early retirement *offer*. 従業員約2,500人が, 早期退職提案を受諾しました。
▸Negotiations fell through when Vodafone turned down TEPCO's *offer*. 東電側の提示額をボーダフォンが拒否して, 交渉は決裂した。

offer price 募集価格, 売出価格, 発行価額, 買付け価格, 買取り価格, 提示価格, TOB［株式公開買付け］価格 (⇒**proposal**)
▸The offer will be completed four business days after the *offer price* is fixed. 売却は, 株の売出価格決定の4営業日後に完了する。

offering 图 募集(=primary distribution, primary offering), 売出し(=secondary distribution, secondary offering), 〈株式などの〉発行, 〈株式の〉公開・上場, 入札, 〈教会などへの〉献金, 提供 (⇒**initial public offering**, **public offering**, **stock offering**)
equity offering 株式発行, 株式公開
noncompetitive offering 非競争入札
offering circular 分売案内書
public offering bond 公募債
public stock offering 株式公募, 株式公開, 株式上場, 公募増資 (=public equity offering, public offering, stock offering)
rights offering 株主割当て発行
security offering 有価証券の募集
shelf offering 一括登録
terms of the offering 発行条件
underwrite the offering 売出しを引き受ける
▸The company made a public stock *offering* on the Nasdaq Japan market on the Osaka Securities Exchange in March 2001. 同社は, 2001年3月, 大阪証券取引所のナスダック・ジャパン市場に株式を上場した。

offering price 公募価格, 募集価格, 売出価格 (=offer price:「募集価格」は, 新規発行の有価証券を募集する場合の価格,「売出価格」は, すでに発行された有価証券を売り出す場合の価格)

office 图 事務所, 営業所, 店舗, 省・庁・課, 官職, 公職, 職務, オフィス
foreign office 在外支店
front office 経営陣, 幹部
inter-office account 本支店勘定
marketing office cost 営業事務費
office administration 事務管理
office equipment 事務用設備, 事務用什器備品
office expenses 営業費, 事務所費 (⇒**income and expenditure report**)
office tax 事業所税
▸Info technology has led to the downsizing of *office* administration sections. 情報技術(IT)は, 事務管理部門の縮小を招いている。

officer 图 会社役員, 役員, 業務執行役員, オフィサー

米国企業の役員について ➡ アメリカの会社では, 一般に取締役会の意思決定を受けて実際の業務執行をする会社役員(corporate officer)として最高業務執行役員(chief executive officer), 社長(president), 副社長(vice president), 秘書役(総務担当役員:secretary), 会計役(財務部長, トレジャラー:treasurer), 会計監査役(経理部長, コントローラー:controller, comptroller)やゼネラル・カウンセラー(法務部長:general counsel)などが置かれている。これらの役員(officers)と取締役(directors)は区別され, 取締役会のメンバーで業務執行についての意思決定をするのが取締役で, 日本の場合のように会社の役員は必ずしも取締役でなくてよい。

auditing officer 監査役
chief accounting officer 最高財務担当役員, 財務統括役員《略 CAO》
chief executive officer 最高経営責任者
chief financial officer 最高財務担当役員, 最高財務責任者《略 CFO》
chief information officer 最高情報担当役員, 最高情報責任者, 情報戦略統括役員《略 CIO》
chief information security officer 最高情報セキュリティ担当役員《略 CISO》
chief knowledge officer 最高知識担当役員, ナレッジ担当統括役員, 知識統括役員《略 CKO》
chief operating officer 最高業務運営役員, 最高業務運営責任者, 業務執行役員, 最高執行責任者《略 COO》
chief privacy officer プライバシー保護担当役員, プライバシー統括役員, プライバシー保護最高責任者《略 CPO》
chief technical officer 最高技術担当役員, 最高技術責任者《略 CTO》
chief technology officer 最高技術責任者《略 CTO》
compliance officer 法令・規則遵守担当役員
corporate information officer 情報戦略統括役員《略 CIO》
corporate officer 業務執行役員
elected officer 選任役員 (⇒**pension cost**)
executive officer 業務執行役員, 上席業務執行役員, 執行役員, 業務執行理事

intelligence officer 情報当局者
officer and employee receivables 役員および従業員貸付け金
officers' bonuses 役員賞与, 役員賞与金
officers' remuneration 役員報酬
officers' salaries and bonuses 役員報酬[俸給]および賞与
senior executive officer 常務執行役員, 上席業務執行役員

▶The vice president of Mizuho Corporate Bank will take up the post of president and chief executive *officer* in the newly merged firm.　合併新会社の社長兼最高経営責任者(CEO)には、みずほコーポレート銀行の副頭取が就任する。

offset 動　相殺する, 埋め合わせをする, 帳消しにする, 吸収する, 吸い上げる, 解消する, 打ち消す, 〈リスクなどを〉カバーする　(⇒**discount plan**, **partially**)
　be partially offset by ... …で一部相殺される, …で部分的に相殺される
　more than offset 十分相殺する, かなり相殺する
　offset market risk 市場リスクを吸収する, 市場リスクを相殺する, 市場リスクをカバーする
　offset the loss 損失の穴埋めをする, 損失をカバーする

▶An account payable can be *offset* against an account receivable from the same company.　買掛金は、同じ会社の売掛金と相殺することができる。

offset 名　相殺, 相殺額, 差引勘定, 埋め合わせ
OJT 職場内訓練（on-the-job trainingの略）
one-off 形　一時的, 一回限りの
　one-off charge 特別損失, 一時的費用, 一時的費用計上, 一括処理　(⇒**pension obligation**)
　one-off payment 一時金, 一時支払い, 一回限りの支払い

one-off gains 特別利益, 一回限りの利益
▶Sumitomo Metal Industries Ltd. raised its annual profit forecast by 38 percent on strong demand and *one-off gains*.　需要急増と特別利益で、住友金属工業は年間業績予想を38％上方修正した。

one-off losses 特別損失, 一回限りの損失
▶Earnings fell sharply on *one-off losses* related to changes in accounting standards for fixed assets and a switch in our employee pension system.　固定資産と当社の従業員年金制度変更の会計基準変更に伴う特別損失で、利益が大幅に減少した。

one-stop service ワンストップ・サービス（消費者のニーズを満たすため、主力製品と関連商品をすべて一つのサイトで提供するサービス）
▶We form a global alliance and offer *one-stop service* for multinationals.　当社は、グローバルな提携関係を築いて、多国籍企業にワンストップ・サービスを提供します。

one-stop shopping 一点集中購買, 関連購買, 1か所での同時まとめ買い, 1か所ですべて済ませる買い物, ワンストップ・ショッピング
▶For our customers, our partnership means *one-stop shopping* for service ordering, maintenance and billing.　当社の顧客にとって、当社の提携関係は、サービスの発注、保守と課金がすべてワンストップ・ショッピング（1か所の窓口ですべて済ますことができること）を意味します。

one-time [onetime] charge 一時的費用, 臨時費用
▶The first-half loss of the company widened because of a *onetime charge* from writing down the value of its assets to meet new accounting rules.　同社の上期の赤字は、新会計基準に対応するため同社の資産価値の評価減による一時的費用を計上したため、拡大した。

one-time credit 一括払戻し金
▶Our fnancing requirements for 2007 include the permanent financing requirement of approximately $150 million as a result of the payment of the *one-time credit* to our subscribers.　当社の2007年度の資金調達必要額には、電話加入者への支払いに要する一括払戻し金額約1億5,000万ドルの長期的な資金調達必要額が含まれています。

one-time pretax charge 税引き前臨時費用, 臨時税引き前費用
▶We elected to record a *one-time pretax charge* of $11,000 million to record the unfunded portions of these liabilities.　当社は、この債務の未拠出部分を記録するため、110億ドルを税引き前の臨時費用として計上することにしました。

one-to-one marketing ワン・トゥ・ワン・マーケティング（マス・マーケティングに代わり、インターネットなどを利用して各顧客のニーズに応じた商品を提供して販売促進を図るマーケティング手法。具体的には、顧客の注文やアクセスデータに基づいて顧客1人ひとりのニーズを把握し、それぞれのニーズに合った商品を電子メールで知らせたり、商品の最新情報をホームページに表示したりすること）

online [on-line] 形副　オンライン, オンライン式, 直結, 回線接続中, コンピュータ回線で, コンピュータ回線を使って, コンピュータのネットワークで, インターネットで, ネット上で, ネットで《略 **OL**》

online bank ネット銀行, ネット専業銀行 （＝e-banking, Internet bank, Internet-based bank, Net bank, Net-only bank）
online business オンライン業務, オンライン・ビジネス
online debit service インターネット即時決済サービス, オンライン即時決済サービス
online music distribution services インターネットを通じた音楽配信
online networking オンライン提携
online securities brokerage ネット専業証券会社, オンライン証券会社 （＝e-broker, online broker, online brokerage）
online shopping mall business 仮想商店街事業 （＝Internet shopping mall business）
online stock trading business 株のインターネット取引業務
online trading ネット取引, ネット専業取引, オンライン取引 （＝Internet trading, Net trading）
▶The company plans to bring a new plant *online* in May.　同社では、5月から新工場を稼動させる計画だ。

online advertising オンライン広告, ネット広告 （＝online ad, online advertisement, Web advertisement）
▶The company is also likely to enjoy an expected rise in *online advertising* revenue.　同社の場合は、予想されるオンライン広告の増益も期待できる。

online auction ネット・オークション （＝Net auction：オンライン・オークションには、個人対個人、企業対個人と企業対企業の3種類のオークションがある）
▶Yahoo Japan's quarterly net profit grew 29 percent, helped by its *online auction* and Web advertising business.　ヤフーの四半期税引き後利益は、ネット・オークション［競売］とウェブ広告［ウェブ広告事業］に支えられて29％増加した。

online shopping mall 仮想商店街
▶Thirty percent of the goods the company sold in the first quarter of this fiscal year were sold through the *online shopping mall*.　同社が今年度第1四半期に販売した商品の3割は、仮想商店街を通じて販売された。

open 動 開く, 開設する, 出店する,〈市場などを〉開放する, 初値を付ける
　open an account with ... …に口座を開く, …に口座を開設する
　open up to public ownership 株式を公開する
▶Stock in J-Com *opened* at ￥672,000, but it plunged to its lower limit of ￥572,000.　ジェイコム株は、1株67万2,000円の初値が付いたが、値幅制限［ストップ安］の下限の57万2,000円に下落した。

operate 動 経営する, 運営する, 操作する, 事業を展開する, 営業する, 操業する
　continue to operate 営業を続ける, 運営を続ける, 操業を続ける
　operate at capacity フル稼働を維持する
　operate businesses 各種事業を展開する, 事業を進める
▶Financial institutions *operate* diverse businesses cross-sectionally.　金融機関は、多様な業務を横断的に展開している。
▶The company *operates* an auction sites and collects charges from users.　同社は、オークション・サイトを運営して、（落札時に）利用者から手数料を徴収している。
▶The company's stores, including the 263 it runs directly, will continue *operating*.　同社の店舗は、263の直営店を含めて営業を続ける。

operating 形 経営上の, 営業上の, 業務の
　operating activities 営業活動, 経営活動
　operating capital 運転資金, 運用資本 （＝working capital）
　operating cost 営業費, 営業コスト, 営業上の費用, 営業費用, 営業経費, 業務費, 創業費, 運営費 （＝operating expense）
　operating earning rate 営業利益率, 経営資本利益率 （＝operating income to operating assets ratio）
　operating fund 運転資金, 営業資金 （＝operating capital, working capital, working funds）
　operating leverage 営業レバレッジ, オペレーティング・レバレッジ
　operating liabilities 営業負債
　operating margin percentage 営業利益率
　operating rate 操業度
　operating receipt 営業収入

operating assets 運用資産, 運転資産, 営業資産, 営業用資産
▶After deduction for noninterest-bearing current liabilities, the return on *operating assets* was 5 percent.　運用資産［運転資産］の利益率は、無利息流動負債の控除後で5％でした。

operating cash flow 営業活動によるキャッシュ・フロー, 営業キャッシュ・フロー（企業が外部からの借入れに頼らず、本業で生み出した現金などの出入り）
▶The decline in *operating cash flows* was mainly due to higher inventories and accounts receiv-

able. 営業活動によるキャッシュフローの減少は、主に在庫と売掛金の水準が前期比で高かったためです。

operating company 事業会社 (=business company)
‣We forged this new entity out of three *operating companies*. 当社は、三つの事業会社を統合してこの新会社を設立しました。

operating deficit 営業赤字
‣We posted an *operating deficit* of about ¥25 billion at a settlement term ending March 2008. 当社は、2008年3月期決算で約250億円の営業赤字を計上しました。

operating earnings 営業利益, 業務純益
‣Nissan Motor Co. reported a loss of *operating earnings*. 日産自動車は、営業減益となった。
‣*Operating earnings* represent total revenues less operating expenses. 営業利益は、総収益から営業費用を控除したものです。

operating expense 営業費用, 営業費, 経常経費 (=operating cost; ⇒**operating earnings, organization**)
‣*Operating expenses* grew 8% in 2007 mainly because of marketing and sales efforts. 2007年度の営業費用は、主にマーケティングと販売努力により8%増加しました。
‣This increase in *operating expenses* was primarily due to higher depreciation expenses. この営業費用増加の主な要因は、減価償却費の増加です。

operating income 営業利益, 営業収益, 営業損益 (=income from operations, operating profit, total sales; ⇒**from a year ago**)
  operating income and loss 営業損益
  operating income (loss) 営業利益(損失)
  operating income margin 売上高営業利益率, 営業利益率 (=operating margin)
‣Our *operating income* has decreased since 2005. 当社の営業利益は、2005年度以来減少しています。

operating lease 営業型リース, 営業リース契約, 賃貸性リース, オペレーティング・リース
‣Our rental expense under *operating leases* was $1,500 million in 2007. 当社のオペレーティング・リースの賃借料は、2007年度は15億ドルでした。
‣We lease equipment to others through *operating leases*. 当社は、設備をオペレーティング・リース方式で他社に提供しています。

operating loss 営業損失, 事業損失, 営業赤字, 営業欠損金, 欠損金 (=operational loss)
‣The company's half-yearly performance until the end of February showed an *operating loss* of ¥4 billion. 同社の2月中間決算は、40億円の営業赤字だった。
‣We reported an *operating loss* in our operations outside the U.S. in 2007. 2007年度は、当社の米国外事業で営業損失を計上しました。

operating margin 営業利益率
‣Nissan Motor Co.'s *operating margin* was the highest among domestic automobile manufacturers at midterm settlements that ended Sep. 30. 9月中間期[今年の9月中間決算]で、国内自動車メーカーでは日産の営業利益率が最高だった。

operating plan 業務計画, 事業計画, 営業計画
‣We have reviewd the Corporation's *operating plans* for 2008. 私ども経営陣は、2008年度の当社の事業計画の見直しをしました。

operating profit 営業利益, 営業収益, 〈金融機関の〉業務純益 (=income from operations, operating income：売上高から販売管理費を差し引いた収益で、本業のもうけを示す)
  operating profit and loss 営業損益 (=operating profit or loss)
  operating profit before exceptional items 特別項目前の営業利益, 特別損益計上前の営業利益
‣*Operating profit* from the company's core businesses was ¥5.2 billion. 同社の主力事業の営業利益は、52億円だった。
‣The firm's *operating profits* show the earnings of its core business. 同社の営業利益は、本業のもうけを示す。
‣These banks submitted management restructuring plans with stated targets for net and *operating profits* and other areas. これらの銀行は、当期純利益や業務純益などの目標を掲げて経営健全化計画を提出した。

operating profit forecast 営業利益予想, 営業利益見通し
‣Sanyo revised downward its *operating profit forecast* by a steep 72 percent to ¥18 billion for this business year. 三洋電機は、今年度の営業利益予想を72%急減の180億円に下方修正した。

operating results 営業成績, 経営成績, 営業損益, 業績 (=business results)
‣When we dispose of assets that were depreciated using the unit method, we include the gains or losses in *operating results*. 個別償却法で償却した資産を処分する場合、当社はその利益または損失を営業損益に含めています。

operating revenue 営業収益, 営業収入, 売上高
‣We had an *operating revenue* of ¥224.7 billion

in fiscal 2007. 当社の2007年度の営業収益は、2,247億円でした。

operation 名 営業, 営業活動, 事業, 業務, 作業, 経営, 活動, 操業, 操作, 運用, 公開市場操作, 介入操作, 部門, 子会社, 関係会社, オペ, オペレーション
　business operation 業務運営
　buying and selling operations by hedge funds ヘッジ・ファンドの売り買い操作
　continuing operations 継続事業
　corporate operations 企業経営, 企業の営業活動, 企業の業務
　discontinued operation 廃止事業
　domestic sales operations 国内営業部門
　financial operation 財務活動
　foreign operation 海外事業, 在外事業
　full operation 本格稼働, 完全操業, フル稼働
　go into operation 操業を開始する
　international operations 国際業務
　merge operations 経営統合する
　net operation loss 営業純損失
　normlal operations 通常業務
　operation of a pension plan 年金制度の運用
　operations located outside the U.S. 米国外子会社, 米国外の関係会社
　reduction of operation 操業短縮
　safe operation 安全操業
　take over operations 経営を受け継ぐ
　transfer operation 振替操作
　treasury operation 財務運用
　wholly owned operations 完全所有子会社, 100％子会社
▶The two companies will merge their *operations* under a holding company to be set up next September. 両社は、来年9月に持ち株会社を設立して経営統合する。
▶We expect to meet our cash requirements in 2007 from *operations*, complemented, if necessary, by external financing. 当社は、業務活動によってもたらされる資金で2007年度の必要資金を確保し、必要に応じて外部資金を調達してこれを補う方針です。

operational 形 操作［運転］上の, 運用［運用上］の, 経営［経営上］の, 営業［営業上］の, 戦略［作戦］上の, 機能している, 使用できる
　operational integration 経営統合
　operational loss 営業損失, 営業赤字
　operational profit 営業利益
　operational revenues 営業収益
　operational efficiency 経営効率
▶The serious deterioration of *operational effi-ciency* is caused by excess output capacity and burgeoning workforces. 極端な経営効率の悪化は、生産設備と従業員の過剰によるものだ。

operational funds 営業資金, 運転資金（＝operating funds）
▶We were provided with ¥10 billion in *operational funds*. 当社は、運転資金として100億円の融資を受けました。

operator 名 運営者, 経営者, 事業主, 事業者, 業会社, 運営会社, 会社, 電気通信事業者, 電話交換手, 交換取扱い者, 〈コンピュータを〉操作する人, 運転者, 〈株の〉相場師, 仕手, 演算子, 演算記号, オペレータ
　auction site operator オークション・サイト運営会社, 競売サイト運営業者
　business operator 事業者
　company operator 会社経営者
　major operators 大企業
▶InterContinental Hotels Group PLC is the world's biggest hotel *operator*. インターコンチネンタル・ホテルズ・グループ(IHG)は、世界最大手のホテル運営会社だ。

opinion 名 意見, 監査意見, 意見表明, 判断, 見解, 鑑定, 評価, 〈弁護士の〉意見書, オピニオン
　accountant's opinion 会計士の意見, 監査意見書
　audit opinion 監査意見 (＝auditors' opinion)
　collective opinion 統一意見
　credit opinion 格付け見解 (＝rating opinion)
　express an opinion 意見を表明する
　legal opinion 法律専門家の意見, 法律意見書, 法的見解, 弁護士意見［意見書］
　opinion date 監査報告書の日付
　opinion of independent (public) accountants 独立会計士の意見, 独立会計士の監査意見
　opinion of management 経営陣の見解, 経営者の見解
　Opinions of Accounting Principles Board APB［会計原則審議会］意見書
　overall opinion on the financial statements as a whole 財務諸表［財務書類］全体についての総合意見
　professional opinion 職業専門家の意見
▶Corporations have been limiting shareholders' right to express *opinions* at shareholders' meetings. 企業は、株主総会での株主の発言権を抑えてきた。
▶Our responsibility is to express an *opinion* on these financial statements based on our audits. 私どもの責任は、私どもの監査に基づいてこれらの財務書類［財務諸表］について意見を表明すること

にある。

opportunity 名 機会, 事業機会, 商機, 好機, 場, 環境, 可能性, ビジネスチャンス, チャンス (⇒resize)
 business opportunity ビジネス機会, 事業機会, 商機会, 商機, ビジネスチャンス (＝business chance)
 capitalize on a market opportunity 市場の機会をとらえる
 creation of job opportunities 雇用機会の創出
 employment opportunity 雇用機会, 就労機会
 growth opportunity 成長の機会
 investment opportunity 投資機会, 投資対象, 運用先
 job opportunity 雇用機会, 就労機会, 就業機会, 就業のチャンス, 求人
 market opportunity 市場機会
 merit-based opportunity 実力主義
 opportunity assessment 市場機会の分析・評価, オポチュニティ・アセスメント
 opportunity loss 機会損失 (＝conditional loss, cost of prediction error)
 opportunity of advancement 昇進の機会
 take advantage of opportunities 機会をとらえる, 機会をつかむ, 機会を利用する
 window of opportunity 機会の窓, 機会の手段, 瞬時の好機, 好機
▸We see an abundance of *opportunities* for these new lines of business. これらの新事業部門には, 事業機会が豊富にあります。
▸We sell equity interests in our subsidiaries only when *opportunities* or circumstances warrant. 当社が子会社の株式持ち分を売却するのは, 商機が到来した時または環境が良好な場合に限られています。

opportunity cost 機会原価, 機会費用 (＝imputed cost：ある特定の目的に資源を使う際, 選択可能な複数の方法からその一つを選択した場合に, 採用しなかった他の方法を選択した場合に得られたと思われる収益)
▸We reduced our cash balance and working capital to lower our *opportunity costs* of maintaining that capital. 当社は, 現金残高と運転資本を減らして, 当該資本を維持するための当社の機会費用を削減しました。

option 名 選択, 選択肢, 選択手段, 選択の余地, 選択科目, 選択権, 優先的選択権, 購入選択権, 売買選択権, 〈商品の〉有料付属品, 付加的機能, オプション取引, オプション (⇒exercise 名, stock option)

 exercise of option オプションの行使
 funding option 資金調達の選択肢, 調達手段の選択肢
 option holder オプション保有者, オプションの買い手
 option price オプション価格
 option trading オプション取引 (＝option transaction)
 options cancelled 失効したオプション
 options exercisable 行使可能オプション
 options exercised 行使されたオプション
 options forfeited 失効オプション
 options granted オプション付与 [授与], 許諾オプション
 options outstanding 未行使オプション, オプション残高
 options terminated 期限切れオプション
 put option 売付け選択権, 売る権利, プット・オプション
 stock option transaction ストック・オプション取引
▸Certain land and building leases have renewal *options* for periods ranging from three to five years. 特定の土地と建物のリースには, 3-5年の期間の更新選択権がついている。
▸The right to exercise *options* generally accrues over a period of four years of continuous employment. オプションを行使する権利は, 原則として勤務 [在任] 期間が4年を経過した時点で発生します。

order 動 命じる, 命令を出す, 指示する, 指図する, 注文する, 発注する, 並べる, 陳列する
▸Mitsui Sumitomo Insurance Co. was *ordered* to halt sales of medical insurance products for an indefinite period from July 10. 三井住友海上火災保険が, 7月10日から医療保険商品販売の無期限停止命令を受けた。

order 名 注文, 注文書, 注文品, 受注品, 受注高, 命令, 順序, 秩序, オーダー
 administrative order 行政命令
 budget for order-filling cost 注文履行費予算
 cash with order 現金注文, 注文時支払い条件
 firm order 確定注文, ファーム・オーダー
 manufacture order 製造指図書, 生産指図書
 new orders 新規受注高
 order and advance 前払い注文
 order entry 受注, 注文処理
 order-filling cost 注文履行費, 注文処理費 (包装費や輸送費など)
 order-getting cost 注文獲得費 (＝cost of

getting order：市場調査や製品計画, 広告宣伝, 販売促進などの費用）
order size 発注量 （＝order quantity）
parts production order 部品製造指図書
place a block order 大口注文を出す
place a limit order 指し値注文を出す
place a market order 成り行き注文を出す
shipping order 船積み指図書
specific order costing 個別原価計算 （＝specific-order cost system）
standing order 継続製造指図書
unfilled orders 受注残高, 受注残

▸At the TSE, securities firms input their *orders* for trading on computer terminals. The order is then transmitted via the computer system to the TSE, where the transaction is completed. 東証では, 証券会社がコンピュータ端末で株式売買の注文を入力すると, コンピュータ・システムを通じてその売買注文が東証に送られて, 取引が成立する。

order backlog 受注残高, 受注残 （＝backlog of unfilled orders）

▸*Order backlog* at December 31, 2007 was up six percent to $1.8 billion. 2007年12月31日現在の受注残高は, 6％増の18億ドルに達しました。

orders on hand 受注残高, 手持ちの受注分

▸Nearly half of the *orders on hand* are scheduled for delivery in 2008. 受注残高の半分近くは, 2008年中に納入することになっています。

▸Orders on *hand* at June 30, 2007 were U.S. $1.80 billion from $1.71 billion of orders on *hand* at March 31, 2007. 2007年6月30日現在の受注残高は, 2007年3月31日現在の17億1,000万ドルに対して18億米ドルでした。

ordinary 形 普通の, 通常の, 経常的
　ordinary annuity 普通年金, 期末年金, 年金
　ordinary dividend 普通配当
　ordinary expenditure 経常支出, 経常費用
　ordinary expenses 経常費, 通常費用 （＝ordinary charges）
　ordinary income 経常利益, 経常損益, 通常の所得
　ordinary income and loss 経常損益
　ordinary loss 経常損失
　ordinary profit 経常利益
　ordinary profit and loss 経常損益, 経常損益の部
　ordinary share 普通株 （＝common share, common stock, ordinary stock：優先株や後配株のように特定の権利が与えられていない一般の株式）
　ordinary stock dividend 通常の株式配当

▸During the first nine moths of 2007, we invested $380 million in *ordinary* shares of the company. 2007年1-9月期に, 当社は3億8,000万ドルを投資して, 同社の普通株式を取得しました。

organic growth 有機的成長, 内部成長, 有機的成長率 （＝organic：M&Aによる成長でなく, 自社内で新規事業を成長させること）

▸Above 6% *organic growth* was achieved in the United States, with good performances in all key markets. すべての主要市場で業績が好調だったため, 米国では6％以上の有機的成長率を達成しました。

organization 名 組織, 機関, 機構, 団体, 組織体, 企業, 会社, 組織化, 企画, 企画力, 段取り, 構造, 構成
　business organization 企業, 企業組織, 業務組織, 実業団体, 経済団体, 財界団体
　cost accounting organization 原価計算組織
　divisional organization 事業部制
　functional organization 機能的組織
　investment organization 投資機関
　member organization 会員社
　organization chart 組織図, 会社組織図
　organization cost 創業費, 創立費, 開業費, 設立費 （＝formation expense, organization expense, preliminary expense, promotion expense）
　profit organization 営利企業, 営利事業体, 営利組織, 営利団体 （＝profit corporation）
　voluntary organization 任意組合

▸Many major companies have been streamlining their *organizations*—selling operations, laying off employees, and so forth. 大企業の多くは, 事業の売却, 従業員解雇など, 組織の合理化を進めてきた。

▸Nippon Keidanren (the Japan Business Federation) is the most powerful of the nation's three major business *organizations*. 日本経団連の影響力は, 日本の主要財界3団体のなかでは最も強い。

▸Political *organizations* are required to attach receipts to their funds reports for every operating expense except personnel costs. 政治団体は, 人件費を除くすべての経常経費について, 政治資金収支報告書への領収書添付が求められている。

organizational structure 組織構成

▸The Corporation routinely reviews its business strategies, *organizational structure* and asset valuations, and implements changes deemed appropriate by management. 当社は, 当社の事業戦略, 組織構成, 資産評価をつねに見直し, 経営陣

が適切と判断した変更についてはそれを実施しています。

original 形 原始の, 当初の, 設立当初の, 第一の
  original issue size 当初発行予定額
  original projection 当初予想, 当初見通し （= earlier projection）
  original cost 取得原価, 取得価額, 原始原価, 原初原価, 歴史的原価, 仕入原価, 簿価
  ▸When we sell or retire plant that was depreciated using the group method, we deduct the *original cost* from the plant account and from accumulated depreciation.　グループ償却法を用いて償却した工場を売却もしくは除却する場合, 当社は当該工場の取得原価を当該資産勘定と減価償却累計額から控除します。
  original equipment manufacturer 相手先ブランド［商標］製造業者《略 OEM》
  ▸"OEM's" refer to *original equipment manufacturers*.「OEM業者」とは, 相手先ブランド製造業者のことをいう。
  original equipment manufacturing 相手先ブランドでの生産, 相手先ブランドによる生産方式, 生産委託契約《略 OEM》
  original equipment manufacturing arrangements OEM［相手先ブランドでの生産］契約
  ▸Under the latest corporate rebuilding plan, MMC intends to supply products through *original equipment manufacturing arrangements* to Nissan Motor Co. and Peugeot Citroen group.　今回の再建計画では, 三菱自動車は, OEM［相手先ブランドでの生産］契約により日産自動車やプジョー・シトロエンに製品を供給する方針だ。
  original maturity 当初満期
  ▸The company considers all highly liquid investments purchased with an *original maturity* of three months or less to be cash equivalents.　当社は, 取得日から満期日までの当初期間が3か月以内の流動性が高い投資を, 現預金等価物としています。

other 形 その他の, 他の, その他
  other accounts payable 未払い金
  other accrued expenses その他の未払い費用
  other accrued liabilities その他の未払い費用
  other assets その他の資産, その他資産（流動資産, 投資勘定と有体財産以外の資産で, 日本式貸借対照表での繰越べ資産）
  other capital surplus その他の資本剰余金 （= othe additional paid-in capital）
  other charges その他の費用, 営業外費用 （= other expenses）
  other costs その他の原価, その他のコスト
  other current assets その他の流動資産（前払い保険料や前払い税金, 前払い家賃, 前払い利息などの前払い費用が含まれる）
  other current liabilities その他の流動負債, その他流動負債
  other expenses その他の費用, 営業外費用, 雑収益, 営業外損益
  other expenses and loss その他の費用および損失, 営業外費用および損失
  other interest paid その他の支払い利息
  other interest received その他の受取利息
  other investments—at cost その他の投資—取得原価
  Other, net その他（純額）, その他・純額
  other noncurrent assets その他の非流動資産, その他の固定資産（営業活動のために使用されない投資資産や無形資産が含まれる）
  other noncurrent liabilities その他の長期債務
  other nonoperating income, net その他の営業外収益（純額）
  other operating expenses その他の営業費用
  other payables 未払い金
  other receivables その他の受取債権, その他の受取勘定
  other trade receivables 未収金, 未収入金
  ▸The increase in *other* costs was associated with higher service volume.　その他の原価増は, サービス量の増加との絡みです。
  other income その他の収益, 営業外収益
  other income and expense その他の収益および費用
  other income and loss 営業外損益（受取利息などの金融収益と支払い利息などの金融費用が含まれる）
  other income（deductions） その他の利益（損失）
  other income（expenses） その他の収益（費用）
  other income—net 営業外収益—純額, その他の収益—純額 （⇒results）
  other income or other expenses 営業外損益
  other income, principally interest 営業外収益（主に利息）
  ▸Miscellaneous pretax gains and losses caused the largest shifts in *other income*-net over the three years.　その他の税引き前利益と損失が, ここ3年の「営業外収益—純額」の最大の変動要因でした。
  other liabilities その他の負債, その他負債
  ▸Our recognition of predivestiture retirees' benefits led to higher *other liabilities*.　当社の企業分

割以前の退職者に対する給付を認識した結果、その他の負債は増加しました。

outlay 名 支出, 経費, 出費 (=outgo)
  budget outlays 財政支出
  capital outlay 資本的支出, 資本設備, 資本投資, 設備投資 (=capital expenditure, capital spending)
  cash outlay cost 現金支出原価
  consumer outlays 消費支出
  discretionary outlays 裁量的支出
  entitlement outlays 義務的経費
  initial cash outlay 当初支出額
  outlay for advertisement 広告費
  outlays for capital equipment 設備投資 (=capital outlays)
  outlays for plant and equipment (progress base) 設備投資(進捗ベース)
  public works outlays 公共工事支出
▸The company's group net profit increased significantly against the backdrop of Japanese firms' greater capital *outlays* on factories. 同社の連結税引き後利益は、日本企業の設備投資拡大を背景に、大幅に増加した。

outlet 名 販路, 市場, 小売店, 特約店, 出店, 店舗, 商店, …店, 発表の場, アウトレット
  affiliated sales outlet 系列販売店
  distribution outlet 販路
  giant outlet 大規模小売店
  outlet store 系列販売店
  retail outlet 小売店
  unprofitable outlet 不採算店舗
▸The company is expected to close its unprofitable *outlets* and divisions. 同社は、不採算店舗や事業部門を閉鎖する見通しだ。

outline of business activities 事業概況

outlook 名 見通し, 予測, 予想, 展望, 先行き, …観, 予報
  business outlook 景気見通し, 企業見通し, 業績見通し (=business projection)
  financial outlook 財務見通し
  negative outlook 弱含みの見通し, ネガティブの見通し
  rating outlook 格付け見通し
  strong earnings outlook 力強い増益見通し, 高収益見通し
▸Moody's lowered Merrill Lynch's rating *outlook* to "negative" from "stable." ムーディーズは、メリルリンチの格付け見通しを、「安定的」から「ネガティブ(弱含み)」に引き下げた。
▸Sony left unchanged its fiscal year sales *outlook* at ¥8.23 trillion. ソニーは、今年度の売上高見通しを8兆2,300億円に据え置いた。

outplacement 名 転職斡旋, 再就職斡旋
▸The remaining provisions include $35 million for employee relocation and *outplacement* services. 残りの引当金には、従業員の配置換えや転職斡旋サービスの費用としての3,500万ドルも含まれています。

output 名 生産, 生産量, 生産高, 製作, 産出量, 産出高, 出力, アウトプット (⇒**back-to-back**)
  aggregate output 総生産高, 総生産量, 総産出高
  capital-output ratio 資本・産出量比率, 資本産出高比率
  optimum output 最適操業度 (=optimum capacity)
  output adjustment 生産調整
  output capacity 生産能力, 生産設備 (=manufacturing capacity, production capacity, productive capacity; ⇒**operational efficiency**)
  output cost 製造原価, 製作費
  output method 生産高比例法, アウトプット法
  output volume 生産量
  per-worker output 従業員1人当たり生産高
  real output 実質生産高, 実質産出高, 実質GDP
▸*Output* at domestic factories rose 0.2 percent in April from March. 4月の国内鉱工業生産は、前月比で0.2%増加した。
▸Toyota's global auto *output* is expected to increase 5% from a year earlier to reach 9.95 million units on a group basis in 2008. トヨタのグループ・ベースでの世界全体の自動車生産台数は、2008年には前年比5%増の995万台に達する見込みだ。

outside director 社外取締役, 外部取締役 (=outside board director, outside board member; ⇒**board of directors**)
  社外取締役について➡ 米国企業の場合、取締役会のメンバーで業務執行の意思決定をするのが取締役(director)である。この意思決定を受けて実際の業務執行をするのが役員(officer)であるが、取締役のうち役員を兼務している者を内部取締役(inside director)といって、外部取締役(outside director)と区別している。外部取締役は、経営のチェック機能を高めるために置かれる社外の取締役で、アメリカの会社では取締役の半数を外部取締役にしなければならないことになっている。外部取締役は、一般に大手企業の社長、会長や経営コンサルタント、弁護士、会計士などが株主により選任されることが多い。
▸General Electric Co. has asked two of its *outside directors* to leave as of the end of December.

ゼネラル・エレクトリック(GE)は，12月末日付けで社外取締役2名の退任を求めた。

outsource 動 外部資源を活用する，外部委託する，外注する，社外調達する，業務委託する
▶Sanyo Electric Co. has decided to *outsource* all of its domestic refrigerator production to a top Chinese refrigerator maker. 三洋電機は，冷蔵庫の国内生産をすべて中国の家電大手に委託することを決めた。

outsourcing 名 外部資源の活用，外部委託，外注，社外調達，海外調達，業務委託，アウトソーシング (企業が周辺業務を外部に委託すること)
　outsourcing costs 業務委託料
　outsourcing deal 業務委託契約
▶*Outsourcing* is a strategic method that effectively uses business resources. アウトソーシングは，経営資源を有効に活用するための戦略的手法です。

outstanding 形 未払いの，未決済の，未償還の，未履行の，未解決の，未決定の，未処理の，発行済み，すでに発生している，傑出した，とび抜けた，顕著な，目立った，特に優れた (⇒**debt outstanding**)
　amount outstanding 残高，未払い金，発行残高，市中売却残高
　average number of shares outstanding 期中平均発行済み株式数
　bond outstanding 債券発行残高
　commercial paper outstanding CP発行残高
　contracts outstanding 事業年度末契約高
　loans outstanding 借入金残高，融資残高，貸付け残高
　long term debt outstanding 長期負債残高
　number of shares of stock outstanding 発行済み株式数
　outstanding balance 未払い残高，残高
　outstanding capital stock 株式発行高
　outstanding checks 未決済小切手
　outstanding common shares 発行済み普通株式 (⇒**own**)
　outstanding common stock 発行済み普通株式，外部発行済み普通株式，社外流通の普通株式 (=outstanding common shares)
　outstanding company 超優良企業
　outstanding current accounts 当座預金残高
　outstanding equities 発行済み株式，発行済み株式数
　outstanding loan 融資残高，貸出残高，未決済貸付け金，借入金残高 (=outstanding debt)
　outstanding nonperforming loans 不良債権残高 (=outstanding bad loans)
　outstanding ordinary shares 発行済み普通株式
　outstanding shares 発行済み株式，発行済み株式数，社外株式，社外発行株式，流通株式数 (=outstanding capital stock, outstanding equities)
　outstanding voting stock 発行済み議決権株式
　principal outstanding 残存元本額
　warrant outstanding 発行済みワラント
▶Unexercised stock options to purchase 30,000 shares of common stock at $22 per share were *outstanding* at the beginning and end of 2007. 2007年期首および期末には，1株当たり22ドルで普通株式3万株を購入できる未行使のストック・オプションが存在していた。

outstanding balance of contracts 保有契約高，保有契約，保険の総額 (=outstanding contracts)
▶The 10 life insurers reported a fall in the combined *outstanding balance of* individual life insurance and annuity *contracts* for five straight years. 生命保険10社の個人保険・年金の10社合計での保有契約高[保障の総額]が，5年[5期]連続で減少した。

outstanding debt 借入金残高，借入残高，債務残高，未払い残高，残高，未払い負債額，未償還負債，既存の債務 (=outstanding loan)
▶We unconditionally guaranteed all of the firm's *outstanding debt* at the end of March 2007. 当社は，2007年3月末現在の同社の未払い負債額をすべて保証しました。

outstanding letters of credit 信用状未使用残高
▶*Outstanding letters of credit* aggregated approximately $450 million and $190 million at December 31, 2007 and 2006, respectively. 2007年および2006年12月31日現在の信用状未使用残高は，それぞれ総額約4億5,000万ドルと1億9,000万ドルとなっています。

outstanding performance 際立った業績
▶Canon's *outstanding performance* is based on a rapid increase in the sales of digital cameras and equipment for the production of semiconductors and liquid crystal monitors. キヤノンの際立った業績は，基本的にデジタル・カメラや半導体・液晶パネル製造装置の販売の急成長によるものだ。

over a year ago 前年同期比，前年同月比
over-indebtedness 債務過多
over-the-counter 形 店頭の，店頭市場の，店

頭売買の, 店頭取引の《略 OTC》
- **over-the-counter market** 店頭市場, 店頭株式市場, 場外市場 (=OTC market, over-the-counter stock market)
- **over-the-counter sale** 店頭販売, 店頭売買, 窓口販売 (=OTC sale)
- **over-the-counter stock market** 株式店頭市場
▶FX margin trading can be conducted via *over-the-counter* dealings at securities companies and other financial institutions. 外国為替証拠金取引は, 証券会社など金融機関の店頭取引で行うことができる。

over the previous year 前年と比べて, 前年より, 前年比, 前期比, 前年同期比 (=from the previous year)
▶Our 2007 first quarter net income applicable to common shares showed a slight increase *over the previous year*. 当社の2007年第1四半期の普通株式に帰属する純利益は, 前年同期比で僅かながら増加しました。

overall 形 総合的な, 全体の, 最終の
- **overall balance** 総合収支
- **overall competitiveness** 全体的な競争力
- **overall efficiency** 全体的な効率性
- **overall index** 総合指数
- **overall inflation** 全般的なインフレ
- **overall leverage** 総債務比率
- **slip into the red overall** 最終赤字に陥る

overall 副 計上で, 総額で, 全部で, 全体として, 一般に, 最終的に

overall objective 全社的目標, 全体的な目標
▶Our *overall objective* is to increase value for our shareholders. 当社は, 株主の皆さまの価値利益を高めることを, 全社的目標としています。

overall sales 総売上高, 売上全体
▶Financial services account for about 60 percent of the company's *overall sales*. 金融事業は, 同社の売上全体の6割を占めている。

overdue 形 期限の経過した, 満期の経過した, 支払い遅延の, 支払い期限の過ぎた, 延滞の
- **overdue charge** 延滞金
- **overdue interest** 延滞利子, 延滞金利
- **overdue loan** 延滞債権, 返済期限経過貸付け金
- **overdue penalty** 支払い遅延違約金
▶Ninety-one social insurance offices illegally reduced *overdue* charges by a total of about ¥1.09 billion to improve premium collection. 社会保険庁事務所91か所で, 保険料の徴収実績を上げるため, 延滞金総額約10億9,000万円を不正に減額していた。

overhaul plan リストラ策, 再編策
▶Ford Motor Co. closed its five North American plants as part of its *overhaul plan*. 米フォード・モーターは, リストラ策の一環として同社の北米5工場を閉鎖した。

overhead 名 間接部門, 間接費, 製造間接費, 総経費, 固定費
- **administration overhead** 一般管理費
- **departmental overhead** 部門間接費
- **expenses and overhead** 費用と経費
- **general overhead** 一般間接費, 販売費・一般管理費 (=general expense, selling and administrative expenses)
- **fixed overhead** 固定間接費
- **historical overhead rate** 製造間接費実際配賦率
- **overhead absorption** 間接費の配賦 (=overhead allocation)
- **overhead burden** 経費
- **overhead expense** 製造間接費
- **production overheads** 製造間接費
- **purchasing overhead** 仕入間接費
▶Since early 2005, the *overhead* has decreased by more than 20,000 people. 2005年初め以降, 間接部門の従業員は2万人以上減少しました。

overhead cost 間接製造費, 間接費 (間接労務費, 間接材料費と間接経費から成る)
- **manufacturing overhead cost** 製造間接費
- **overhead cost control** 経費管理
- **reduce overhead costs** 製造間接費を削減する, 経費を削減する, 経費を切り詰める
▶The company plans to slash *overhead costs* both at home and abroad by such measures as reducing advertising expenses, and cutting expenses at its head office and in research and development departments. 同社は, 宣伝費の削減, 本社と研究開発部門の経費削減などで, 国内・海外の製造間接費を削減する方針だ。

overlap 名 重複, 重複部分, 重複関係
▶Material interdependencies and *overlaps* exist among the Company's operating units. 当社の各事業体の間には, 重要な相互依存と重複の関係が存在します。

overseas 形 海外[外国]の, 海外向けの, 海外への, 対外, 海外からの
- **overseas borrowing** 対外借入れ
- **overseas branch** 海外支店
- **overseas debt** 対外債務
- **overseas demand** 外需
- **overseas operations** 海外事業
- **overseas production** 海外生産

overseas shipments　輸出
overseas subsidiary　海外子会社
overseas transaction　海外取引
overseas earnings　海外収益
▸A weaker yen boosted *overseas earnings*.　円安が、海外収益を押し上げた。
overseas investment　対外投資, 海外への直接投資, 海外投資, 海外からの投資
▸The weak dollar may decrease *overseas investment* in the U.S. market.　ドル安で、海外の対米投資が減少する恐れがある。
overseas sales　海外売上高
▸The Corporation's goal is to expand its *overseas sales* to ¥50 billion within three years through mergers and acquisitions.　当社は、M&A（企業の合併・買収）を通じて3年以内に海外の売上高を500億円に拡大する目標を掲げています。
oversight 名　監視, 監督, 手落ち, 手抜かり, 見落とし, 失策　（⇒**conflict of interest**）
　internal independent oversight board　社内独立監視委員会
　oversight agency　所轄官庁
　oversight body　監督機関
▸In order to stem a series of client defections, the internal independent *oversight* board of the accounting firm rushed out an initial set of management reforms for the firm.　一連の顧客離れを食い止めるため、同会計事務所の社内独立監視委員会は、最初の経営改善策を急きょ取りまとめた。
overstatement 名　過大表示, 過大評価, 過大計上, 実際より多く計上すること
▸Freddie Mac revealed its earnings manipulation including billions of dollars of *overstatements* and understatements.　フレディマック（米連邦住宅貸付抵当公社）は、数十億ドルの過大計上と過小計上を含めて利益の不正操作をしていたことを明らかにした。
overvalue 動　過大評価する　（=overstate）
　overvalued dollar　ドル高, ドルの過大評価　（=strong dollar）
　overvalued stock　割高な株式
▸In spite of Mixi's robust performance, traders fear the company has been *overvalued*.　ミクシィの業績好調にもかかわらず、証券業者は同社への過大評価を警戒している。
overview 名　概要, 概観, 概況, 動向
　business overview　事業概況, 事業の概要, 事業概要
　overview of our business operations　営業活動概況, 営業活動のあらまし
　overview of the industry　業界動向
own 動　所有する, 保有する, 持つ　（⇒**wholly**）
　equally owned　折半出資している, 共同所有している　（=jointly owned）
　fully owned subsidiary　完全所有子会社
　jointly owned　共同所有の, 折半出資の　（=equally owned）
　less than 20% owned company　20%未満所有の会社
　majority owned company　過半数所有子会社
　owned capital　自己資本
　privately owned company　株式非公開企業, 非上場会社　（=privately held company）
　publicly owned company　株式公開企業, 上場会社　（=publicly held company, publicly owned corporation）
　real estate owned　所有不動産, 保有不動産
　wholly own　完全所有する
▸Mitsubishi UFJ Merrill Lynch PB Securities Co. is an equally *owned* private banking venture between Mitsubishi UFJ Financial Group and Merrill Lynch Japan Securities.　三菱UFJメリルリンチPB証券は、三菱UFJフィナンシャルグループとメリルリンチ日本証券が折半出資している合弁会社だ。
▸On January 31, 2008, over 15,000 registered shareholders *owned* the remaining 47.2 percent of the outstanding common shares of the firm.　2008年1月31日現在, 15,000名余りの登録株主が、同社の発行済み普通株式の残りの47.2%を所有しています。
-owned　…によって所有されている, …の形で所有されている
　family-owned company　同族経営企業
　fifty-percent-owned company　50%所有会社, 半数所有会社
　government-owned corporation　政府出資企業
　state-owned company　国有企業
owner 名　所有者, 所有権者, 権利者, 株主, 出資者, 企業主, 荷主, 船主,〈プラント輸出契約の〉注文者, 発注者, 施主, オーナー
　at owner's risk　荷主危険持ちで
　beneficial owner　受益者, 実質所有者, 受益株主
　cargo owner　荷主, 貨物所有者
　factory owner　工場主
　joint owner　共有者
　majority owner　過半数株主
　managing owner　経営所有者
　owner control　所有者支配

owner of record 名義上の株主
owner's capital 自己資本, 株主資本, 株式資本
owner's claims 株主の請求権
owner's equity 自己資本, 株主資本, 資本, 所有者持ち分, 株主持ち分, 持ち分権, 所有権 (= net assets, net worth, owners' equity, shareholders' [stockkolders'] equity)
owners' interest 所有者持ち分 (=owners' equity, ownership interest)
stock owner 株式所有者
virtual owner 実質的な所有者, 実質的な保有者, 事実上の保有者
▸Legally speaking, the shareholders are the *owners* of a joint stock company. 法律上は, 株主が株式会社の所有者だ。

ownership 名 所有, 所有権, 所有者, 所有比率, 出資比率, 持ち株比率, 経営権 (⇒ **employee stock ownership plan**)
acquire full ownership 完全子会社化する
acquire ownership stakes in ... …へ資本参加する, …へ一部出資する, …株を一部取得する
capital ownership 出資比率
change of ownership 所有権の移転, 株式の譲渡
control of ownership 経営権
equity ownership 株式所有, 株主所有権, 自己資本, 持ち株比率
equity ownership conditions 持ち株比率状況
foreign ownership 外国人持ち株比率, 外国人保有比率, 外国資本の所有
initial ownership 会社設立時の出資比率, 当初の出資比率 (=initial ownership interest)
joint ownership 共同所有, 共有権
majority ownership 過半数支配
management ownership 経営所有
ownership capital 株主資本
ownership interest in subsidiaries 子会社所有持ち分
ownership interest in the assets 資産の所有権
ownership of affiliates 関連会社[関係会社]株式の所有比率
public ownership 株式公開, 上場企業
▸Minority interests increased mainly because of the sale of 15% *ownership* in the company in June 2007. 少数株主持ち分は, 主に2007年6月に同社所有権の15%を売却したため, 増加しました。
▸Our *ownership* in the company will increase to 80 percent in 2008. 同社に対する当社の持ち株比率は, 2008年度には80%に増加します。

ozone depletion オゾン層破壊
▸We will support industry cooperative efforts to solve industry problems, such as *ozone depletion*. 当社は, オゾン層破壊などの産業活動が引き起こす環境問題を解決するための業界全体の協調努力を支援していく方針です。

P p

pace 名 速度, 速さ, スピード, テンポ, 伸び, 足並み, 足取り, ペース
  be gathering pace スピード[ピッチ]が上がっている, 増えている, 本格化している, 激化している
  keep pace with inflation インフレと足並みを揃える
  pace of economic recovery 景気回復の足取り
  pace of rate reduction 利下げのテンポ
  pace of stockbuilding 在庫積上げのペース, 在庫増加のペース
  ▶We increased our *pace* of growth with revenue increasing nine percent in 2007. 当社の成長のペースは上がっており, 2007年度の売上高は9％増加しました。

package 名 対策, 政策, 策, 案, 計画, プラン, 制度, 包括法案, 装置, 包装, 梱包, パッケージ
  aid package 支援策 （＝rescue package）
  deficit reduction package 赤字削減策
  early retirement and buyout packages 早期退職優遇制度
  fiscal stimulus package 財政面での景気刺激策, 景気対策
  package cost 包装費 （＝packing cost）
  software package ソフトウエア・パッケージ, 汎用ソフトウエア製品
  voluntary separation package 自発的退職案, 希望退職案
  ▶A financial aid *package* that includes a debt-for-equity swap and debt forgiveness was considered by the main banks. 債務の株式化（銀行にとっては債権の株式化）や債権放棄などの金融支援策を, 主力取引銀行が検討した。
  ▶Employees accepting the voluntary separation *package* must respond before February 2008. 自発的[希望]退職案を受諾する従業員は, 2008年2月前に申し出る必要がある。

paid-in capital 払込み資本, 払込み資本金, 発行済み資本金 （＝paid-up capital：株主が会社の株式取得に払い込んだ金額で, これまで発行した株式の総発行価額に相当する。資本金(capital stockまたはcommon stock)と払込み剰余金(paid-in surplusまたはcapital in excess of par value)を合わせたもの)
  additional paid-in capital 株式払込み剰余金
  initial paid-in [paid-up] capital 設立時の払込み資本金, 当初払込み資本金
  paid-in capital in excess of par 額面株式払込み剰余金
  ▶An amount equal to the par value of the additional shares issued has been transferred from additional *paid-in capital* to common stock due to the two-for-one stock splits. 追加発行株式の額面価額相当額が, 1対2の株式分割により, 株式払込み剰余金から普通株式に振り替えられました。

paid-in surplus 払込み剰余金 （＝contribution surplus）

panel 名 討論会, 座談会, 委員会, 小委員会, 審査会, 審議会, 委員団, 審査団, 調査団, 講師団, 専門家集団, 制御盤, 計器盤, パネル
  consumers' panel 消費者パネル, 消費者グループ
  corporate reform panel 経営改革委員会
  disciplinary panel 懲罰委員会
  government advisory panel 政府諮問委員会
  independent panel 独立委員会
  management reform panel 経営改革委員会

tender panel method 競争入札制度
▸The management reform *panel* will seek help from major creditors for the capital increase at the company. 経営改革委員会は、同社の増資に対する支援を、主要取引行に要請する方針だ。

paper 名 手形, 証券, 債券, 文書, 書類, 資料, 論文, 新聞, 紙, ペーパー (⇒commercial paper)
　accommodation paper 融通手形 (＝accommodation bill)
　business paper 業務書類, 商用手形, 商業手形
　corporate paper 社債
　export paper 輸出手形
　financial paper 有価証券報告書, 金融手形
　fine paper 優良手形
　government paper 国債, 政府発行有価証券
　original papers 原本書類
　paper loss 含み損, 評価損
　paper profit 含み益, 架空利益
　paper profit or loss 含み損益, 評価損益
　primary paper 新発債 (＝new paper)
　recycled paper 再生紙
　short paper 短期証券
　valuable paper 有価証券
▸In 2007, the Corporation increased its short-term borrowings by $180 million, principally through the sale of commercial *paper*. 2007年度に当社は、主にコマーシャル・ペーパーを発行して短期借入金を1億8,000万ドル増やしました。

par value 額面, 額面価格, 額面額(株式や社債の券面に記載されている払込みの最低単位), 為替平価
　change in par value 額面変更
　par-value capital stock 額面株式, 額面額資本金 (＝par value capital)
　par value of the stock 株式の1株当たり額面
　par value stock 額面株式, 額面株 (＝share with par value, stock at par, stock with par value)
　stock with par value 額面株
　stock without par value 無額面株
　under-par value investment trust 額面割れ投信
▸The Board of Directors declared a two-for-one stock split in the form of a 100% stock dividend for $1.5 *par value* common stock. 取締役会は、100％株式配当形式で額面1.5ドル普通株式の1株を2株にする株式分割を行うことを公表した。

paradigm 名 理論的枠組み, 枠組み, 構図, 模範, 範例, 典型, 例, 実例, パラダイム (＝example, framework, pattern, typical example)
　conventional paradigm 従来の枠組, 従来のパターン
　paradigm of bid rigging 談合の構図
　paradigm shift 根本的変化, 抜本的変革, 社会の価値観の移行, 社会全体の枠組みの転換・変化, パラダイムの転換・移行, パラダイム・シフト (＝paradigm change)
　regulatory paradigm 規制の枠組
　scientific paradigm 科学的パラダイム
▸The challenge for the management of international companies is that all the aspects of the rapidly changing global economy have driven a *paradigm* shift from an industrial to an information society. 国際企業経営者の課題は、急速に変化する世界経済のあらゆる側面が、工業社会から情報化社会へパラダイムが移行してしまったことである。

parent 名 親会社, 母体, 根源, 単独ベース
　at the parent base [basis] 単独ベースで
　on a parent-only basis 単独ベースで
　parent-basis earnings forecast 単独ベースの収益見通し (＝parent-only earnings forecast)
　parent basis EBITDA multiple 単独ベースのEBITDA倍率
　parent capex 単独ベースの設備投資 (＝parent capital spending)
　parent operating profit 単独ベースの営業利益
　parent recurring profit 単独経常利益
　parent sales 単独ベースの売上高
▸Under the new Corporate Law, a subsidiary of a foreign company is allowed to use shares of the *parent* to acquire a Japanese company. 新会社法では、外国企業の子会社が親会社の株を用いて日本企業を買収することができる。

parent company 親会社
▸All companies that have been listed on the TSE from January 1996 are required to provide management information on their *parent* companies and affiliates. 1996年1月以降に東証に上場した企業は、すべて親会社とグループ企業［関連会社］の経営情報を提供するよう義務付けられている。

parent-only pretax profit 単独ベースの税引き前利益, 単独ベースの経常利益
▸Daiei posted a *parent-only pretax profit* of ¥302 million for the March-August period. ダイエーは、8月中間決算で[3-8月期に]3億200万円の経常利益［税引き前利益］(単独ベース)を計上した。

parenthesis 名 挿入語句, 丸括弧(かっこ), パ

ーレン（複数形はparentheses）
▸Figures within *parentheses* pertain to 2007 operations.　（　）内の数値は、2007年度の事業の数値です。

partially 副　部分的に、一部
　be partially consolidated　部分連結される、一部連結される
　be partially offset　一部相殺される、部分的に相殺される
▸Increases in salaries, wages, and depreciation expenses were *partially* offset by lower pension expenses and by the effect of the strike.　給料・賃金と減価償却費の増加分は、年金費用の減少とストの効果[影響]で一部相殺されています。

participant 名　参加者、参加企業、参加行、参加国、加入者、受講者、出席者、関係者　（⇒plan participant）
　active plan participants　在職制度加入者
　industry participant　業界参加者
　market participant　市場参加者、市場参入企業、市場関係者　（=market player）
　participant in the dividend reinvestment plan　配当金再投資制度加入者
　transaction participant　取引参加者
▸Market *participants* pointed out the issuance of new shares would dilute the value of the company's existing shares.　市場関係者は、増資[新株発行]によって同社の既存株式の価値が損なわれる、と指摘している。
▸The proxy form indicates the number of shares to be voted, including any full shares held for *participants* in the Employee Stock Purchase Plan.　委任状用紙には、従業員株式購入制度加入者のために保有している株式をすべて含めて、行使される議決権数が記載されています。

participate 動　参加する、参入する、進出する、加入する、関与する
▸In order to *participate* in this market in a major way, we are devoting substantial resources to aggressive product development programs.　この市場に本格的に参入するため、当社は現在、大型の製品開発計画に多くの経営資源を投入しています。
▸We *participate* in the general-purpose credit card business through a wholly owned subsidiary.　当社は、完全所有子会社を介して総合[汎用]クレジット・カード事業に関与しています。

participating bond　利益参加社債
participating capital stock　参加株式
participating dividend　参加配当
participating preferred stock　参加優先株式

participation 名　参加、参入、進出、加入、関与、貢献、出資　（=involvement）
　capital participation　資本参加　（=equity participation）
　equity participation　資本参加、出資、株式投資　（=capital participation）
　equity participatin rates　出資比率
　human participation　人的貢献
　management participation　労働者の経営参加
　participation financing　複数の銀行による協調融資、共同融資、参加融資　（=participation loan）
　participation loan　複数の銀行による協調融資、共同融資、参加融資　（=participation financing）
　participation right　参加権、配当権
　profit participation　利益分配
▸This program encourages *participation* and sharing of our results by each employee in the company.　この制度は、当社の業績に各従業員が参加し、その成果をそれぞれが分かち合うことを奨励しています。

partner 名　共同経営者、共同出資者、共同所有者、提携者、提携先、事業提携先、提携企業、組合員、社員、パートナー
　business partner　取引先企業、取引先　（⇒philosophy）
　capital partner　資本提携先　（⇒change of control）
　dormant partner　匿名組合員
　equity partner　資本参加者、出資者
　general partner　無限責任社員
　joint partner　共同出資者、共同パートナー
　rehabilitation partner　再建の提携先
　strategic partner　戦略的パートナー
▸Marubeni, currently holding a 44.6 percent stake in Daiei, will sell up to 20 percentage points of its ownership to the rehabilitation *partner*.　ダイエー株の44.6％を保有する丸紅は、保有株式をダイエー再建の提携先に最大20％売却する。

partnership 名　共同出資、共同所有、共同経営、提携、連携、協力、組合、合名会社、パートナーシップ　（⇒capital and businesss partnership）
　business partnership　業務提携　（=business alliance, business tie-up）
　equal partnership　折半出資、対等提携、対等な協力関係
　form a partnership　提携する、提携を結ぶ

interests in certain partnership 特定パートナーシップの持ち分
limited liability partnership 有限責任事業組合, 有限責任パートナーシップ《略 **LLP**》
partnership shares パートナーシップの株式
public private partnership パブリック・プライベート・パートナーシップ《略 **PPP**》(民間の資金とノウハウを導入して税金の効果的で効率的な活用を図るため、企業や非営利組織が参加して公共サービスを提供する手法の総称)
three-way partnership 3社共同契約
voluntary partnership 任意組合

▸Limited liability *partnership* (LLP) is a new form of business entity that is not a joint stock company or business union. 有限責任事業組合(LLP)は、株式会社でもなく、事業組合でもない新しい事業体だ。

▸We have continued to strengthen our *partnership* with our customers. 当社は、継続してお客さまとの連携を強化してきました。

partnership interest パートナーシップ持ち分, パートナーシップの利権

▸*Partnership interests* are recorded at equity. パートナーシップ持ち分は、持ち分価額で評価しています。

party 名 当事者, 関係者, 契約当事者
employer's liability to third party 使用者責任
interested parties 利害関係者 (＝interest group, interest parties, interested persons: 株主や債権者, 取引先, 顧客などをいう)
party in default 不履行当事者

past service 過去勤務, 原始過去勤務
past service cost 過去勤務年金費用, 過去勤務費用, 原始過去勤務原価 (＝prior service cost)
past service liability 過去勤務債務

▸When we adopted the new standard, we had an accumulated liability for benefits related to the *past service* of active employees. 新基準を採用した時点で、当社は現従業員の過去勤務に関連した給付について、累積債務がありました。

patent 名 特許, 特許権, 特許物件, 特許証, 特権, 権利, 公有地譲渡証書, パテント
BM patent ビジネス・モデル特許, BM特許, ビジネス方法の特許 (＝business method patent, business model patent, patent for a business model)
patent licensing 特許実施権, 特許実施許諾, 特許許諾, 特許のライセンス供与
patent property 特許権 (＝patent right)
pioneer patent 基本特許, 開拓特許, パイオニア特許
product patent 製品特許
share patents on basic techniques 基本技術に関する特許を相互利用する

▸Recent years have seen a sharp rise in the number of companies acquiring business model *patents*. 最近は、ビジネス・モデル特許を取得する企業が急増している。

▸Under the deal, Toyota will license to Volkswagen all its *patents* concerning direct-injection gasoline engines. 両社の取決めによると、トヨタが直噴型ガソリン・エンジンに関するすべての特許をフォルクスワーゲン(VW)にライセンス供与する。

patent 形 明白な, 公開の, 独自の, 新案の, 特許の
patent defect 明白な瑕疵(かし), 明白な欠陥
patent method 独自の方法[手法, やり方]

patent infringement 特許侵害, 特許権侵害, 特許抵触 (＝patent violation)

▸Sony Corp. has agreed to pay $40 million to Ampex Corp. to settle a lawsuit filed by the U.S. visual information technology company over *patent infringement* on its digital camera-related technology. デジタル・カメラ関連技術の特許権侵害をめぐって米国の視覚情報技術会社のアンペックスが起こした訴訟を和解で解決するため、ソニーは、アンペックスに4,000万ドル支払うことに同意した。

pay 動 支払う, 支出する, 負担する, 返済する, 弁済する, 利潤をもたらす, 利益になる, 採算が取れる, もうかる
capital paid in 払込み資本
capital paid-in excess of par value 株式払込み剰余金, 額面超過金 (＝share premium, paid-in surplus)
pay at sight 一覧払い
pay for losses 損失を補填する
pay in advance 前払いする
pay in full 全額支払う, 全額払い込む, 完納する
pay in part 一部返済する, 部分返済する
pay up 完済する, 全額払う, 決済する

▸Foreign firms were allowed to *pay* the merger consideration only in the form of shares of the subsidiary. 外国企業の場合、合併の対価は(日本に設立した)子会社の株式でしか支払うことができなかった。

▸We will *pay* a dividend of ¥50 per share for the first half. 当社は、上半期の配当支払い額を1株当たり50円にする方針です。

pay 名 賃金, 給料, 手当, 報酬

maternity pay fund 出産手当基金
pay according to ability 能力給
pay according to function 職務給
pay cut 減給, 賃金カット, 報酬カット, 減俸
pay-for-age structure 年功序列賃金構造
pay rise 賃上げ, 昇給 (＝pay hike, pay increase, pay raise)
pay system 賃金制度, 賃金体系, 給与制度 (＝wage system; ⇒**merit-based pay plan [system], performance-based pay system**)
▶The company imposed 30 percent *pay* cuts for three months on two senior executive officers. 同社は, 常務執行役員2人について3か月間3割減給の処分にした.

pay as you earn[go] 現金で[即金で]支払う, 賃金から所得税を差し引いて支払う
pay-as-you-earn 形 源泉課税, 即金主義, 現金払い主義, 現金払い方式《略 **PAYE**》 (＝pay-as-you-go)
pay-as-you-go 形 現金払い方式, 現金払い主義, 源泉課税方式, 源泉徴収方式, 独立採算制, 無借金の (＝pay-as-you-earn)
  pay-as-you-go financing plan 賦課方式 (＝pay-as-you-go system)
  pay-as-you-go method 源泉徴収方式, 源泉課税方式 (＝pay-as-you-earn method, pay-as-you-go basis)
pay-as-you-go accounting 現金主義会計
▶In our former *pay-as-you-go accounting*, we booked our contribution to trust funds for life insurance benefits as they occurred. 従来の現金主義会計では, 生命保険給付についての信託基金への拠出額は, その発生時に計上していました.
pay-as-you-go basis 現金主義, 現金基準, 現金払い方式, 現金払い主義, 独立採算制
▶This table shows our actual postretirement benefit costs on a *pay-as-you-go basis* in these years. この表は, これら各年度の実際の退職後給付費用を, 現金基準で表示したものです.
pay-as-you-go formula 賦課方式, 源泉課税方式, 現金払い方式 (＝pay-as-you-go basis)
▶If the younger generation refuses to contribute to the government-run pention program, the pension system, which works on a *pay-as-you-go formula*, will fall apart immediately. 若い世代が政府運営の年金制度への保険料払込みを拒否したら, 賦課方式でうまくいっている年金制度は, たちまち崩壊してしまうだろう.

pay down 即金で支払う, 頭金として支払う
▶New York Times will sell its nine TV stations for $575 million to *pay down* debt. ニューヨーク・タイムズは, 債務返済のため, 傘下のテレビ9局を5億7,500万ドルで売却する.

pay off 借金などを完済する, 借金を返す, 返済する, 償還する, よい結果を生む, うまく行く, 実を結ぶ, 引き合う
  pay off a loan 借入金[ローン]を返済する
  pay off the public funds 公的資金を返済する
▶Maturing commercial paper was *paid off*. 満期を迎えたコマーシャル・ペーパーが償還された.
▶The bank has already *paid off* the injected public funds. 同行は, (国から)注入を受けた公的資金をすでに完済している.

pay out 支払う, 積立金を払い戻す
  pay out a larger percentage of earnings 配当性向を高める
  pay out dividends 配当金を支払う
▶A payout ratio refers to the percentage of a company's profits to be *paid out* to shareholders in the form of dividends. 配当性向とは, 配当の形で株主に支払われる企業の利益の比率[企業の利益のなかから株主への配当に回す比率]のことだ.

payable 形 支払うべき, 支払い満期の, 支払い期限に達した, 支払い期日の到来した, 支払われる
  bill payable at a fixed period after sight 一覧後定期払い手形
  bill payable at sight after a fixed period 確定日後一覧払い手形
  estimated taxes payable 見積り未払い税額
  loan payable from officer 役員借入金
  note payable to subsidiary 子会社支払い手形
  payable period 回収期間 (＝payback period)
  rent payable account 未払い賃借料勘定
▶Interest is *payable* semiannually on December 1 and June 1. 利息は, 12月1日と6月1日の6か月ごとに支払われる.

payable 名 未払い勘定, 仕入れ債務, 買掛金
  payables 債務, 支払い債務, 未払い金, 未払い勘定 (＝debt, liability)
  payables in foreign currency 外貨建て債務

PAYE 源泉課税, 即金主義 (**pay-as-you-earn** の略)

payment 名 支払い, 払込み, 振込み, 決済, 納入, 返済, 弁済, 支払い金額, 債権 (⇒ **interest payment**)
  automatic payment 自動振込み, 自動支払い
  commission payments 手数料収入
  debt payment 債務支払い, 債務返済
  deferred payment 延べ払い, 後払い

installment payment 分割払い, 割賦返済 (= payment in installment)
loan principal payments 借入金返済額
means of payment 支払い方法
on-the-spot payment 即時決済
payment at full 全額払い (= payment in full)
payment by results 業績給, 能率給, 成果配分
payment commission 支払い手数料
payment(s) due 満期支払い金, 満期支払い額, 未払い金
payment in advance 前払い, 前金払い
payment in part 内払い, 部分返済, 一部返済
payment in suspense 仮払い金
payment on demand 要求払い
payment terms 決済条件, 支払い条件, 支払い期限
principal payment 元本返済
security payment 保証金, 敷金
sight payment 一覧払い

▶Common shares may be purchased at the average market price by voluntary cash *payments* of as little as US $40 to a maximum of US $4,000 during a quarter.　当社の普通株式は, 1四半期に最低40米ドルから最高4,000米ドルまでの範囲で任意現金支払いにより, 平均市場価格で購入することができます。

▶The newly introduced installment plan allows purchasers to pay no initial *payments*.　新たに導入された割賦制度では, 購入者は頭金[契約金]の支払いが不要となっている。

pay plan 賃金制度, 報酬制度
▶In return for abolishing retirement allowances for directors, more companies are introducing a merit-based *pay plan*.　役員退職慰労金[役員退職金]を廃止する代わりに, 業績連動型の報酬制度を導入する企業が増えている。

payoff 名 〈給料などの〉支払い, 〈借金などの〉完済, 決済, 〈預金の〉払戻し, 報酬, 利得, 利益, 利益供与, 賄賂, 回収, 成果
▶The *payoff* for this heavy investment in research and development is the acceptance of our products by customers around the world.　この大幅の研究開発投資の成果として, 当社の製品は世界中のお客さまに受け入れられています。

▶There were the *payoff* and falsification of financial statements in a series of scandals involving the company.　同社の一連の企業不祥事としては, 利益供与や有価証券報告書の虚偽記載などがあった。

payout 名 支払い, 支出, 支出金, 〈株式などの〉配当[配当金], 保険金の支払い, 支払い給付金, 〈社会保障の〉給付費, 回収 (⇒**pension payout**)
expected payout ratio 期待配当性向
payout percentage 配当性向, 配当支払い率, 配当比率 (= payout ratio)
payout ratio [**rate**] 配当性向, 実質引受手数料率, ペイアウト比率 (= dividend payout, payout percentage：企業の利益のなかから株主への配当に回す比率。⇒**pay out**)

▶There are moves among listed companies to raise *payout* ratios.　上場企業に, 配当性向を引き上げる動きがある。

payroll 名 従業員名簿, 賃金台帳, 支払給与総額, 賃金, 給与
accrued payroll 未払い給与
cut payrolls 人員を削減する

PBO 予測給付債務, 予定給付債務 (projected benefit obligationの略)

PBR 株価純資産倍率 (price book-value ratioの略。株式投資の主な投資指標の一つ。PBR（倍）は, 株価を1株当たり純資産で割って算出する。純資産は企業の解散価値で, PBRが1倍の企業の場合, その企業を解散したときに株主に分配される額と株価は同じということになる)

PCAOB 米上場企業会計監視委員会, 公開企業会計監視委員会 (Public Company Accounting Oversight Boardの略。民間の独立機関（SECの会計事務局Chief Accountant Officeの直轄）で, 2002年に制定された企業改革法に基づいて2003年に発足。米上場企業を扱う監査法人は, 国内外を問わずPCAOBへの登録を義務付けられている)

▶The *PCAOB* was created by the Sarbanes-Oxley Act of 2002.　米上場企業会計監視委員会（PCAOB）は, 2002年サーベンス・オクスレー法[企業改革法]により設置された。

penalty 名 処罰, 処分, 罰金, 違約金, 延滞金, 反則金, 制裁金, 制裁, 罰則, 刑罰, ペナルティ
penalty charge 遅延損害金
penalty interest 遅延利息
penalty rate 延滞金利
penalty tax 追徴課税, 加算税

▶Kajima Corp. was ordered to pay about ¥800 million in additional tax, including a *penalty*.　大手ゼネコンの鹿島は, 重加算税を含めて約8億円の追徴税の支払い命令を受けた。

▶*Penalties* against insider trading and market manipulation have been strengthened.　インサイダー取引や相場操縦などに対する罰則が, 強化された。

pension 名 年金

annual pension 年金
basic pension 基礎年金
corporate pension 企業年金, 厚生年金
earnings-related pension 所得比例年金
full pension 完全年金
group pension 団体年金
occupational pension 雇用年金
pension beneficiary 年金受給者
pension income 年金利益 (⇒**prepaid pension cost**)
pension payments 年金支給額, 年金給付, 年金給付額 (=pension benefits)
pension plan for company employees 厚生年金 (=company employees' pension plan, corporate employees' pension insurance plan)
pension program 年金制度 (⇒**pay-as-you-go formula**)
pension provision 年金計上額, 年金引当金
pension reserve 年金引当金, 年金積立金
pension subscription period 年金加入期間
pension system benefits 年金の給付金
private pension 企業年金保険, 私的年金
public pension 公的年金
retirement pension 退職年金
supplementary pension 補足年金
transitional pension 経過年金
universal pension 一律給付年金

▸Just as the number of people qualifying for *pensions* is on the rise, the working population, which underpins the *pension* scheme, is on the decline. 年金受給の資格者は増える一方, 年金制度を支える現役世代は減っている。

pension asset 年金資産

▸About ¥21 billion in *pension assets* belonging to more than 80,000 subscribers to defined-contribution pension plans were left unmanaged as of March 2007. 2007年3月末現在で, 8万人を超える確定拠出年金加入者の年金資産約210億円が, 運用されないままになっている。

pension benefits 年金給付, 受取年金, 退職年金給付 (=pension payments; ⇒**pension premium**)

▸In addition to *pension benefits*, the Corporation and its subsidiary companies provide certain health care and life insurance benefits for retired employees. 当社と当社の子会社は, 年金給付のほかに, 退職者を対象に医療給付と生命保険給付を提供しています。

pension contributions 年金拠出額

▸*Pension contributions* are principally determined using the aggregate cost method. 年金拠出額は, 基本的に総額原価法を用いて決定される。

pension cost 年金費用, 年金原価, 年金コスト
(=pension expense; ⇒**actuarial cost method, calculation**)
accounting for pension costs 年金費用の会計
accrued pension cost 未払い年金費用
annual pension cost 年金費用, 年間年金費用
deferred pension cost 繰延べ年金費用
fund pension costs as accrued 年金費用を発生時に積み立てる
net pension cost (credit) 年金費用 (利益) 純額
net periodic pension cost 期間年金費用純額
pension cost accrued 年金コスト発生額
pension credit 年金費用
prepaid pension costs 前払い年金費用 (⇒**pension liability**)
prior pension cost 過去勤務費用, 過去勤務費
provision for pension costs 年金原価計上額, 年金原価繰入れ額, 年金コスト引当金
unfunded accrued pension cost 未払い年金費用

▸The net U.S. *pension cost* for the elected officers' supplemental retirement benefit plan was $27 million in 2007. 選任役員の追加的退職給付制度に対する米国内の純年金費用は, 2007年度は2,700万ドルでした。

▸We compute *pension cost* using the projected unit credit method. 年金費用は, 予測単位積増し方式によって算出します。

pension expense 年金費用 (=pension cost; ⇒**partially**)
annual pension expense 年間年金費用
liability for pension expense not funded 未積立年金費用債務
liability under pension expense 未払い年金債務

pension fund 年金基金, 年金資金, 年金積立金
employee's [employees'] pension fund 従業員年金基金, 厚生年金基金
investment management for pension funds 年金基金の運用
pension fund investment 年金積立金の運用 (⇒**corporate pension plan**)
pension fund reserve 年金基金積立金

▸The *Pension Fund* Association manages about ¥9.9 trillion in pension funds for employees pension fund plans. 厚生年金基金連合会 [企業年金連合会] は, 厚生年金基金 [企業年金] の年金資金約9兆9,000億円を運用している。

pension insurance sales 年金保険の販売

▸Mizuho Financial Group Inc. enjoyed healthy nonfinancial earnings such as commissions on *pension insurance sales*.　みずほフィナンシャルグループは、年金保険の販売手数料など、(貸出金以外の)非金利収入が好調だった。

pension liability　年金債務、年金負債　(⇒ **pension plan assets**)

▸The prepaid pension costs are net of *pension liabilities* for plans where accumulated plan benefits exceed assets.　この前払い年金費用は、累積給付債務額が資産額を超過している場合の年金債務純額を控除したものです。

pension obligation　年金債務　(⇒**fair value**)

▸The firm fell into the red in the first half due to a $1.7 billion one-off charge on *pension obligations*.　同社は、17億ドルの年金債務(共済年金の給付負担額)を一括処理したため、上半期は赤字に転落した。

pension payout　年金の支払い

▸Under the defined-contribution annuity scheme, workers who will receive *pension payouts* in the future decide how the pension fund is invested.　確定拠出年金制度では、将来年金の支払いを受ける従業員が年金積立金の運用方法を決める。

pension plan　年金制度　(＝pension program, pension scheme, pension system; ⇒**corporate pension plan**, **mutual**)

　accounting for pension plans　年金制度の会計
　accounting for the cost of pension plans　年金制度原価に関する会計
　basic pension plan　基礎年金制度、基礎年金
　company-run pension plan　企業年金制度
　defined benefit pension plan　給付建て年金制度
　defined contribution pension plan　確定拠出型年金
　employee pension plan　従業員年金制度
　insured pension plan　保険型年金
　liability under pension plan　未払い年金債務
　qualified pension plan　適格年金制度
　the operation of a pension plan　年金制度の運用

▸It is extremely unusual for a company to take action against the government over company-run *pension plans*.　企業年金制度をめぐって企業が行政を訴えるのは、極めて異例だ。

pension plan assets　年金制度資産、年金資産　(⇒**fair value**)

▸Our *pension plan assets* are earning a return that exceeds the growth in pension liabilities.　当社の年金制度資産は、年金債務の増大を上回る収益を上げています。

pension premium　年金保険料

▸The instability of the pension system has repeatedly experienced increases in *pension premiums* and decreases in pension benefits.　年金制度が不安定なため、年金保険料の負担増と年金給付減が繰り返されてきた。

pension scheme　年金制度、年金供給協定　(＝pension plan; ⇒**pension**)

　approved pension scheme　適格年金制度
　company employees' pension scheme　厚生年金制度、厚生年金　(＝company employees' pension system)
　occupational pension scheme　従業員年金制度

▸Under the company employees' *pension scheme*, subscribing is mandatory for all firms with five or more employees.　厚生年金制度では、従業員5人以上の法人すべてに加入が義務付けられている。

pension subscriber　年金加入者

▸The Pension Fund Association was found not to have paid a total of ¥154.4 billion in pension benefits to 1.24 million *pension subscribers*.　企業年金連合会が、年金加入者124万人に対して計1,544億円の年金[年金給付]を未払いにしていることが分かった。

pension system　年金制度、年金システム　(＝pension scheme; ⇒**pay-as-you-go formula**, **pension premium**)

▸Under the current Japanese *pension system* for company employees, employees and employers each pay half of the insurance premiums worth 17.35 percent of the employee's monthly salary, or 13.58 percent of their annual income.　日本の現在の厚生年金保険制度では、従業員と企業がそれぞれ従業員の月収の17.35％(年収ベースで13.58％)の保険料を半分ずつ負担している。

pensioner 名　年金受給者、年金生活者

people 名　社員、従業員、人々

▸We invest almost $3 million a day in the continuing education, training and development of our *people*.　継続している当社従業員の教育、訓練と開発に、当社は1日当たり約300万ドルを投じています。

PER　株価収益率　(＝P/E, P/E ratio：**price earnings ratio**の略)

株価収益率について ➡「株価収益率(PER)」は、株式投資の主な投資指標の一つで、株価が1株当たり利益(税引き後利益)の何倍に相当するかを示す。株価を1株当たり利益(earnings per share)で割って

算出する。自分の投資した代金を利益で回収すると何年かかるかが分かる。回収期間は短いほうがよいので、PERは小さいほうがよい。
▸Price earnings ratio (*PER*) is obtained by dividing price per share by earnings per share.　株価収益率は、1株当たりの株価を1株当たり利益で割って〔除して〕求められます。

per 前 …につき、…ごとに、…によれば
per annum rate　年利
per capita sales　1人当たりの売上
per contra account　対照勘定

perpetuity 名 終身年金、永続的な支払い

per share 1株当たり (⇒dividend per share, earnings per share, net profit per share)
book value per share　1株当たり純資産、1株当たり簿価
consolidated earnings per share　普通株式1株当たり連結純利益
equity per share　1株当たり資本額
income per share　1株当たり利益
net dividend per share　1株当たり正味配当金
net income or loss per share　1株当たり当期純利益
per-share earning ratio　株価収益率
per share earnings　1株当たり利益（＝earnings per share）
per share effects　1株当たりの影響（⇒unusual item）
per share figures　1株当たりの金額、1株当たりの数値
per-share net profit　1株当たり純利益（⇒year earlier）
per share of common stock　普通株式1株当たり
profit per share　1株当たり利益

▸Hewlett-Packard earned $1.55 billion, or 55 cents *per share*, for the first quarter ended Jan. 31.　ヒューレットパッカードは、第1四半期〔1－3月期〕に15億5,000万ドル（1株当たり55セント）の利益を上げた。

▸Oji Paper Co. will launch a hostile tender offer for Hokuetsu Paper Mills Ltd. shares at ¥800 *per share*.　王子製紙が、北越製紙の株式に対して1株800円で敵対的TOB〔株式公開買付け〕を開始する。

▸The company increased the projected dividend *per share* to ¥6 for fiscal 2007 from the ¥5 paid the previous year.　同社は、2007年度の1株当たり予想配当を前年度の5円から6円に引き上げた〔増配した〕。

per-share group net profit 1株当たり連結純利益
▸*Per-share group net profit* plunged to ¥85.95 from the preceding fiscal year's ¥37,983.95.　1株当たり連結純利益は、前年度の37,983円95銭から85円95銭に激減した。

per-share net loss 1株当たり純損失
▸*Per-share net loss* came to ¥77.92 in a sharp downswing from a profit of ¥10.06 the previous year.　1株当たり純損失は、前期の10.06円の利益から急落して77.92円となった。

per-share value 1株当たり価値
▸The massive issuance of new shares will result in the dilution of the *per-share value* of existing stock, which will then depress share prices on the stock market.　新株が大量に発行されると、既存株式の1株当たり価値の希薄化を招いて、株式市場の株価が下がることになる。

percent 名 百分率、率、割合、パーセント
net income as percent of average stockholders' equity　自己資本当期純利益率
percent depreciated　償却率、償却累計率
percent of capacity use　稼動率

▸The ratio of cash and deposits in total household assets declined 0.7 percentage point to 54.5 *percent* from a year earlier.　家計の金融資産総額に占める現金・預金の割合は、前年比で0.7ポイント（0.7％）減少して54.5％となった。

percentage 名 比率、割合、部分、分け前、歩合〔歩合制〕、百分率、利益、利点、得、パーセント（⇒as a percentage of）
annual percentage rate　実質年率
cost percentage　原価率
fixed percentage method　定率法
gross margin [profit] percentage　売上総利益率、粗利益率
net income (loss) as a percentage of revenues　収益〔売上高〕に対する純利益（損失）の比率、収益対利益率、対収益純利益（損失）率、純利益（損失）率
nonperforming loan percentage　不稼動債権の比率
percentage of capital structure　資本構成比率
percentage profit on turnover　売上高利益率

▸As a *percentage* of revenues SG&A expenses in the second quarter of 2007 decreased to 19.5 percent from 21.0 percent last year.　売上高に占める2007年第2四半期の販売費および一般管理費（SG&A）の比率は、前年同期の21％から19.5％に低下しました。

▸Cost controls, coupled with our revenue growth, caused our gross margin *percentage* to improve the past two years. コスト管理と増収により、当社の売上総利益率は過去2年間上昇しました。

percentage gain 伸び率 (⇒**product line**)
▸Our business communications systems and cable group product lines had strong *percentage gains* in revenue growth. ビジネス通信システムと通信ケーブル・グループの製品系列は、増収の伸び率が大幅に上昇しました。

percentage of completion method 工事進行基準, 進行基準 (=percentage of completion accounting)
▸The Company accounts for this construction work contract under the *percentage of completion method*. 当社は、この請負工事契約については、工事進行基準にしたがって会計処理しています。

percentage point パーセント・ポイント, ポイント, 厘, パーセンテージ・ポイント (one percentage point=1パーセント。⇒**percent**)
 a quarter percentage point 0.25%
 half a percentage point 0.5%
▸The tax rate was reduced by 1.5 *percentage points* in 2007 due to the inclusion of the company's after-tax earnings in the Corporation's earnings before tax. 2007年度の税率は、同社の税引き後利益を当社の税引き前利益に含めたため、1.5%低下しました。

performance 名 実績, 業績, 成果, 〈義務・債務の〉履行, 運用, 運用成績, 動向, 値動き, 収益性, パフォーマンス (⇒**business performance, corporate performance, financial performance, good performance, high performance, robust performance, strong performance**)
 brisk business performance 好業績
 company's performance 企業の業績, 業績 (=company's results)
 consolidated performance 連結決算
 cost performance コスト効率
 cost/performance ratio 費用・性能比
 disappointing performance 期待外れの業績, 予想を裏切る業績
 earnings performance 利益実績, 業績
 economic performance 経済実績, 経済成長率, 景気動向
 high-performance data communications service 高性能データ通信サービス
 historical performance 過去の運用成績
 investment performance 投資実績, 運用成績, 運用実績
 management performance 経営実績, 経営成績, 経営業績, 運用成績

 market performance 市場成果, 相場の動き
 operating performance 営業成績, 経営成績, 営業業績, 業績, 事業効率
 operational performance 業績
 past performance 実績
 performance evaluation 業績評価
 performance measurement 業績測定
 poor performance 業績不振
 portfolio performance 資産運用実績, 資産運用成績, ポートフォリオの運用成績
 price performance 値動き, インフレ動向
 profit performance 利益率
 stock performance 株価の値動き, 株価パフォーマンス, 株価動向 (=share price performance)
▸The downgrade reflects Standard and Poor's concern over the company's ability to avoid a further deterioration in its operating *performance*. この格下げは、同社の一段の業績悪化は避けられないとのスタンダード＆プアーズの懸念を反映している。
▸The firm's financial situation has been aggravated by recent poor *performance* in its main business of developing resorts. リゾート開発の本業がこのところ不振で、同社の財務状況が悪化している。
▸This improved *performance* is due both to steady growth in demand, reflecting a generally prosperous economy, and to efficient management. この業績改善は、好景気を背景にした需要の着実な伸びと経営の効率化によるものです。

performance-based pay system 能力給制度, 成果主義型給与制度, 成果主義型賃金体系 (=merit-based pay system)
▸We plan to make a full-scale shift to a *performance-based pay system* next April. 当社は、来年4月から成果主義型の給与制度に全面的に移行する方針です。

performance plan パフォーマンス制度, パフォーマンス・プラン
▸The long-term *performance plan* provides for incentive awards to be made to officers and other key employees. この長期パフォーマンス・プランは、役員や幹部社員に奨励報酬を与える制度です。

period 名 期間, 時期, 局面, …期, 年度, 年数, 会計期間, 会計年度, 事業年度, ピリオド (⇒**accounting period, March-August period**)
 base period 基準期間
 beginning of the period 期首

current period 当事業年度, 当期 (⇒**reverse**)
fiscal period 会計期間, 会計年度 (＝accounting period)
interim period 中間会計期間, 中間期
July-September period 7-9月期 (⇒**rack up**)
over the same period last year 前年同期比で
period benefited 利益発生期間 (⇒**goodwill**)
period earned 稼得した期間, 稼得した期
period expense 期間費用 (＝period charge, period expense)
period income 期間利益(1会計期間に帰属する利益)
pricing period 価格設定期間
prior period 過年度
production period 生産期間, 製造期間
purchases for the period 当期仕入高
quarterly period 四半期
settlement period 決済期間
the last period of settlement of accounts 最終決算期
throughout the periods indicated 当該期間中に

▶Goodwill is amortized on a straight line method over the *periods* estimated to be benefited, currently not exceeding five years. 営業権は, その効果が及ぶと見込まれる期間にわたって(現在は5年を超えない期間にわたって), 定額法で償却されています。

▶The company's auditing firm approved the firm's accounting for the suspected *periods*. 同社の監査法人は, 問題となっている時期の同社の決算処理を承認していた。

▶The firm posted a pretax profit of ¥30 billion for the April-September *period*. 同社の4-9月期の税引き前利益は, 300億円となった。

period under review 当期

▶In the *period under review*, personnel costs of the Corporation decreased by DM 200 million to DM 9,500 million as compared with the first half of 2006. 当上半期の当社の人件費は, 前年同期比で2億ドイツ・マルク減少して, 95億ドイツ・マルクでした。

periodic 形 定期的な, 周期的な, 期間の
periodic cost 期間費用
periodic income 期間利益, 期間収益
periodic loss 期間損失
periodic pension cost 期間年金費用, 毎期の年金費用 (⇒**expected long-term rate of return**)
periodic profit 期間利益

▶Cost for inventory purposes should be determined by the inventory cost flow method most clearly reflecting *periodic* income. 棚卸し資産の原価は, 期間利益を最も明確に反映する棚卸資産原価算定の方法によって算定すべきである。

permanent 形 永久の, 永久的, 恒久的, 長期的な, 常設の
permanent asset 資本的資産 (＝capital asset, fixed asset, fixed capital, long-lived asset)
permanent committee 常設委員会
permanent differences 永久差異, 永久差異項目
permanent financing 永久資本
permanent financing requirement 長期的な資金調達必要額 (⇒**one-time credit**)
permanent investment 恒久的投資, 永久証券

▶The Corporation has established *permanent* committees of the board of directors to permit continuing review of the areas of auditing, management resources and compensation, pension fund policy, and investment. 当社は, 監査, 役員人事・報酬, 年金基金対策と投資の各分野に関する検討を継続的に行うため, 常設の取締役会付属委員会を設置しています。

perpetual 形 永久の, 終身の, 永続的な
perpetual annuity 終身年金 (＝perpetuity)
perpetual bond 永久債券, 無期限債券(償還期限が定められていない債券)
perpetual preferred stock 永久優先株式 (＝permanent preferred stock)

personnel 名 人員, 要員, 従業員, 職員, 人事
key personnel 基幹人員, 主要人員
management personnel 経営陣
personnel costs 人件費
personnel cuts 人員削減

▶In the closing phases of economic upturns, rises in *personnel* costs and other fixed expenditures caused profits to shrink, leading to a recession. 景気回復期[景気拡大期]の最終局面では, 企業の人件費など固定費の上昇が収益を圧迫して, 景気後退につながった。

petty 形 小口の
petty cash 小口現金
petty fund 小口資金

phase out 段階的に撤廃する, 段階的に廃止する, 段階的に削減する, 段階的に閉鎖する, 段階的に解消する

▶During the fourth quarter of 2007, the Corporation announced a plan to *phase out* certain manufacturing plants. 2007年第4四半期に当社は, 一部の製造施設を段階的に閉鎖する計画を発表しました。

philosophy 名 理念, 方針, 主義, 哲学, 基本的な考え方
　business philosophy 経営理念
　company philosophy 企業理念, 経営哲学, 経営方針
　financing philosophy 資金調達方針, 財務についての考え方
　investment philosophy 投資方針
　management philosophy 経営理念, 経営方針, 経営哲学, 経営思想, 経営者精神 (＝management thought, managerial philosophy)
▸Any listed corporations must convince their customers, business partners and other stakeholders of their business *philosophy* and strategies. 上場企業は, 顧客や取引先などのステークホルダー[利害関係者]に対して, 経営理念と戦略をきちんと説明する必要がある.

physical 形 有形の, 実体のある, 現物の
　physical asset 有形資産, 有形固定資産 (＝tangible asset)
　physical deterioration 劣化
　physical distribution 物流, 物的流通
　physical distribution cost 物流コスト
　physical flow of goods 財貨の流れ
　physical inventory 実地棚卸し
　physical productive capacity 物的生産能力

pick up 景気づく, 景気などが回復する, 復調する, 勢い[はずみ]をつける, 増える, 盛り上がる, 上向く, 改善する
▸Japan's business leaders believe the economy is *picking up* steam. 日本企業のトップ(経営者)は, 景気は上向いていると見ている.

picket 名 〈スト破りを阻止するための〉ピケ隊員, スト破り監視員
▸Workers could return to the *picket* lines if the company rejects the new agreement. 同社が新協約を拒否したら, 労働者はピケライン[監視線]に戻る可能性がある.

pickup [**pick-up**] 名 回復, 改善, 向上, 増加, 伸び, 上昇, 拡大, 活発化
　economic pickup 景気拡大 (＝pickup in economic performance)
　equity pickup 株価の値上がり
　pickup in demand 需要の高まり, 需要の回復
　pickup in inflation インフレ率の上昇
　pickup in production 生産の回復
▸We reported a 5% increase in total revenues in 2007, a *pickup* from the 3% increase in 2006. 当社の2007年度の総営業収益は5％の伸びで, 前年度の3％の伸びを上回りました.

pilot 形 試験的, 実験的, 予備の, 事前の, 先行的, 指標となる, 補助的の, パイロット
　pilot assembly plant 試験組立工場
　pilot experiment 先行的実験, 予備実験
　pilot film 見本用フィルム, 見本フィルム
　pilot plant 実験工場, 試験工場, 試験の生産工場, 試験設備, パイロット・プラント
　pilot production 試験の生産, 試験生産, 試作, パイロット生産
　pilot project [**scheme**] 予備計画, 先行的プロジェクト, パイロット・プロジェクト
　pilot store 実験店, 実験店舗, パイロット店, パイロット・ストア
　pilot survey 予備調査, パイロット・サーベイ
　pilot system パイロット・システム
　pilot test 事前調査, 予備テスト, 先行的試験, パイロット・テスト
▸The chain store opened a *pilot* store in Tokyo in late March. このチェーン・ストアは3月末, 東京都内に実験店を出した.

placement 名 〈株式・債券の〉募集・販売, 売出し, 販売先, 職業紹介, 職業斡旋, 人員配置 (⇒ **private placement**)
　direct placement 直接募集, 直接販売, 私募
　indirect placement 間接募集, 間接販売
　initial placement 募集業務
　public placement 公募発行, 公募, 公募債
　raise cash by a private placement 第三者割当てで資金を調達する
　retail placement 個人投資家への販売
▸Hokuetsu Paper Mills Ltd.'s private *placement* of new shares to allocate a stake of more than 30 percent to trading house Mitsubishi is scheduled for Monday. 三菱商事に30％超を割り当てる北越製紙の第三者割当て増資は, 月曜日に予定されている.

plan 動 計画する, 計画を立てる, 立案する, 設計する
　planned capital increase 増資計画
　planned capital spending 設備投資計画 (＝capital spending plan, planned capex)
　planned expansion 設備拡張計画
▸Nissan *plans* to put about 100,000 units of its Altima Hybrid model on the U.S. market early next year. 日産は来年はじめ, 「アルティマハイブリッド」車約10万台を米国で発売する計画だ.

plan 名 計画, 構想, 提案, 案, 政策, 策, 制度, 方式, 方法, 予定, 段取り, 平面図, プラン (⇒**business plan, noncontributory plan, pension plan, stock purchase plan**)

accumulation plan 積立プラン
acquisition plan 買収計画 (＝acquisition planning)
audit plan 監査計画
bonus plan 賞与制度
capex plan 設備投資計画 (＝capital spending plan)
compensatory plan 報酬制度
contributory plan 拠出型制度
deferred compensation plan 報酬据え置き方式
defined contribution plan 確定拠出制度
employee capital accumulation plan 従業員の資本蓄積プラン
fixed benefit plan 定額給付制度
incentive compensation plan 奨励報償制度
insured pension plan 保険型年金
investment plan 投資計画
management plan 経営計画
production plan 生産計画
profit plan 利益計画 (＝profit planning)
reserve financing plan 積立て方式
stock award plan 株式報奨制度
stock bonus plan 株式賞与制度
▸Fujita Corp. scrapped a *plan* to merge with Sumitomo Mitsui Construction Co. in March 2005.　2005年3月にフジタは、三井住友建設との経営統合計画を白紙撤回した。
▸The *plan* will be officially decided upon at a meeting of representatives of policyholders in July.　この案が、7月の総代会で正式に決定される。

plan assets 年金資産, 制度資産, 年金制度資産, 基金資産 (＝pension plan assets; ⇒**expected long-term rate of return, secured mortgage**)
actual return on plan assets 制度資産の実際運用益
estimated market value of plan assets 基金資産の見積り市場価値
expected return on plan assets 制度資産の期待収益, 年金資産の予想収益
net plan assets 年金プラン純資産
plan assets at fair value 公正価額による年金資産, 年金資産の公正価額, 制度資産時価
plan assets in excess of projected benefit obligation 基金資産の見積り給付債務超過額
▸Our *plan assets* consist primarily of listed stocks, corporate and governmental debt, real estate investments, and cash and cash equivalents.　当社の年金制度資産は、主に上場株式、事業債、国債、不動産投資と現金および現金等価物で構成されています。

plan benefits 年金給付
accrued plan benefits 年金給付債務額
accumulated plan benefits 年金給付累積額, 累積年金給付債務額, 年金未支給額 (⇒**prepay**)
▸The actuarial present value of the accrued *plan benefits* and the net assets available to discharge these benefits at December 31 are as follows:　12月31日現在の年金給付債務額の年金数理原価とこの年金給付債務に充当可能な年金純資産は、以下のとおりです。

plan participant 制度加入者
▸The new shares of common stock are being allocated to *plan participants* over ten years as contributions are made to the plan.　この普通株式新株は、制度への資金拠出と並行して、10年にわたり制度加入者に割り当てられています。

planning 名 企画, 立案, 企画立案, 計画, 計画策定, プランニング
accounting for planning 計画会計
audit planning 監査計画
budget planning 予算計画
business planning 経営計画, 事業計画, ビジネス・プランニング
cash planning 資金計画
corporate planning 経営計画, 企業計画立案
distribution planning 流通計画
financial planning 財務計画, ファイナンシャル・プランニング
intermediate planning 中期経営計画, 中期計画
managerial planning 経営計画 (＝management plan)
manufacturing planning 製造計画
master plan 基本計画, 総合計画, マスター・プラン
office planning 事務計画, 事務改善計画
operational planning 業務計画
organization planning 組織計画 (＝organizational planning)
periodic planning 期間計画 (＝period planning)
planning, program(m)ing, budgeting system 企画計画予算制度, 全計画予算方式, 企画計画予算制度, 費用対効果分析予算方式《略 **PPBS**》
product planning 製品計画
production planning 生産計画
profit planning 利益計画 (＝profit plan)
scenario planning シナリオ・プランニング
short-term planning 短期経営計画, 短期計画 (＝short-range planning)
tax planning 節税計画

tax planning strategy 戦略的税務計画, 税計画戦略, 税務戦略
▸We forecast our expenses and capital expenditures for existing and planned compliance programs as part of our regular corporate *planning* process.　当社の定期的な企業計画立案作業の一環として, 私たち経営陣は, 現在および将来の規制遵守プログラムの費用と資本的支出を予測しています。

plant 名　工場, 生産設備, 工場設備, 施設, 植物, プラント
 assembling plant　組立工場　（＝assembly plant）
 idle plant　遊休設備
 industrial plant　工場設備, 工場
 LCD panel plant　液晶パネル工場, 液晶ディスプレー・パネル工場
 new plant startup　新工場の稼動, 工場の操業開始
 nuclear power plant　原子力発電所　（＝atomic power station, nuclear power station）
 petrochemical plant　石油化学プラント
 plant additions　工場増設　（⇒net of）
 plant asset　工場設備資産, 設備資産
 plant capacity　設備能力
 plant closure　工場閉鎖
 plant expansion　工場拡張
 plant in service　稼動施設
 plant investment　設備投資
 processing plant　加工工場, 加工処理工場
 subcontracting plant　下請工場
 title plant　権原プラント
 utility plant　公益設備
▸The firm's *plants* will be sold or liquidated.　同社の工場は, 売却または清算される。
▸This joint venture *plant* started operating in 1984 with Toyota and GM each providing half the capital.　この合弁工場は, トヨタとGMが折半出資して1984年に生産を開始した。
▸Toyota is estimated to have invested an initial ¥15 billion in the *plant*.　トヨタの同工場への初期投資額は, 推定で150億円と見られる。

plant and equipment　工場設備, 生産設備, 設備, 設備装置, 有形固定資産　（⇒investment in plant and equipment）
 existing plant and equipment　既存設備
 new plant and equipment　新規設備
 plant and equipment investment　設備投資　（＝investment in plant and equipment, plant and equipment funding, plant and equipment spending, spending for plant and equipment）
 producer's plant and equipment　生産設備
 spend on plant and equipment　設備投資する
▸All other *plant and equipment* is depreciated on a straight-line basis.　その他のすべての工場・設備は, 定額法で償却しています。

player 名　参加者, 関係者, 投資家, トレーダー, 専門家, 企業, 要因, プレーヤー, ［playersで］企業グループ, 勢力
 market player　市場関係者, 市場参加者, 市場筋, マーケット・プレーヤー　（＝market participant）
 strong player　有力企業
 top player　最大手
▸Most market *players* and analysts have said the recovery trend would continue for the time being.　市場関係者や経済分析の専門家の間では, 景気回復の動きはまだしばらく続くとの見方が大勢だ。

playing field　事業環境, 競争条件, 競争の場, 土俵

PLC　［英］公開有限公社, 公開有限責任会社　（＝plc, p.l.c.：**public limited company**の略。株式会社（company limited by shares）と保証有限責任会社（company limited by guarantee）のうち, 公開会社（public company）として登録している会社の社名の末尾に表示することになっている）
▸HSBC Holdings *PLC* will shut its subprime mortgage unit and eliminate 750 jobs.　英銀行大手のHSBCホールディングスは, 低所得者向け住宅融資「サブプライム・ローン」事業の子会社を閉鎖して, 従業員750人を解雇する。

pledge 動　入質する, 質入れする, 質を置く, 抵当に入れる, 担保に入れる, 担保に供する, 誓約する, 公約する, 確約する
 amount pledged　譲渡済み金額
 assets pledged　担保資産, 担保提供された資産, 担保として差し入れられた資産
 pledge as collateral for financing　資金調達の担保として提供する［担保として差し出す］
 pledge collateral　担保を差し入れる, 担保を差し出す
 pledged asset　担保資産, 質入資産
 pledged collateral　担保の裏付け, 担保の差し入れ, 差し入れ担保
▸An advance of $100,000 was received from the bank by *pledging* $120,000 of the company's accounts receivable.　同社は, 同社の売掛金12万ドルを担保に供して, 同行から借入金10万ドルを受領した。

pledge 名　担保, 抵当, 質権設定, 入質, 担保・抵当品, 誓約, 公約, 確約, プレッジ

negative pledge 担保制限, 担保提供制限条項, ネガティブ・プレッジ条項 （＝negative clause）
right of pledge 担保権
unconditional pledge（**clause**） 無条件の担保条項

plummet 動 急激に落ち込む

plunge 動 減少する, 下落する, 低下する, 低迷する, 急落する, 安値を付ける, 転落する （＝drop）
plunge into loss 赤字に転落する
plunge to a five month low 5か月来の安値を付ける
▸Citygroup's third-quarter profit *plunged* 57 percent mainly due to fixed-income trading losses and mortgage-backed securuites losses. シティグループの第3四半期の利益は, 債券取引の損失や住宅融資証券［不動産証券］関連の損失で, 57%減少した.

plunge 名 〈市場の〉低迷, 〈株価の〉急落, 下落, 激減, 減少, 急降下, 落ち込み, 突入
plunge in demand 需要の落ち込み
stock market's plunge 株式市場の低迷
the sharp plunge in the dollar's value 急激なドル安
▸If Japanese stock prices continue to fall whenever there is a *plunge* in U.S. stocks, the country might be hit by another financial crisis. 米国株の下落に連動して日本の株価の下落が続けば, 日本は再び金融危機に見舞われかねない.

plurality 名 多数, 過半数
plurality vote 過半数の得票

point of origin 源泉地, 原産地点, 現場渡し
▸The *point of origin* (the location of the selling organization) of revenues and the location of the assets determine the geographic areas. 地域別区分は, 収益の源泉地（販売組織の所在地）と資産の所在地に基づいて行われています.

poison pill 毒薬条項(敵対的買収に対する防衛策の一つ. 既存株主に対して転換優先株式を株式配当の形で発行することを定めた条項を指す), 敵対的買収に対する防衛手段, 買収防衛策, ポイズン・ピル
poison pill defense［**defence**］ ポイズン・ピル防衛, 毒薬条項防衛, 毒入り避妊薬
poison pill plan ポイズン・ピル方式 （＝poison pill scheme）
poison pill scheme ポイズン・ピル防衛策, ポイズン・ピル方式 （＝poison pill plan）
▸If Hokuetsu Paper Mills decides to carry out the *poison pill*, Oji Paper Co. is likely to take legal action against it. 北越製紙が買収防衛策を実施したら, 王子製紙は法的措置を取る可能性が高い.

▸Nireco's *poison pill* scheme carries the danger of inflicting unexpected damage to shareholders. ニレコ(制御機器メーカー)のポイズン・ピル防衛策は, 株主に不測の損害を与える恐れがある.

policy 名 政策, 対策, 方針, 施政方針, 経営方針, 規定, 保険証券, 保険証書, 保険契約, ポリシー （⇒production）
acceptable use policy 〈ネットワークやコンピュータシステムを利用する際の〉方針や約束事《略 AUP》
accounting policy 会計方針
business policy 経営方針, 経営政策, 営業政策, 営業方針
cheap money policy 低金利政策
credit underwriting policy 与信基準
exchange rate policy 為替政策 （＝exchange policy）
financial policy 金融政策, 財政政策, 財務政策, 財務方針, 資金調達方針
financing policy 資金調達方針 （＝financing philosophy：資金の調達と運用についての基本方針）
insurance policy 保険証券, 保険証書, 保険契約, 保険商品, 保険
interest rate policy 金利政策
management policy 経営方針, 経営政策, 経営姿勢
marine insurance policy 海上保険証券
pay-as-you-go policy 無借金経営
policy cancellation 保険の解約
policy dividend 契約者配当
policy obligations 保険契約債務 （⇒unforeseen loss）
policy reserve 保険契約準備金, 責任準備金
pricing policy 価格決定方針, 価格決定政策
stock policy 株価対策
▸During the bubble economy, life insurers sold a large number of *policies* by promising high yields. バブル期に生保各社は, 高い予定利率を約束して多くの保険契約を獲得した.
▸U.S.-based fund Steel Partners is happy at changes in Yushiro Chemical Industry Co.'s dividend *policy* taken to fend off the hostile takeover bid. 米系投資ファンドのスティール・パートナーズは, ユシロ化学工業が敵対的株式公開買付(TOB)の防衛策として行った配当方針の変更に満足している.

policyholder 名 保険契約者, 契約者, 保険加入者 （＝insurance policyholder; ⇒**insurance**

policyholder)
dividend to policyholders 契約者配当 （＝policyholder dividend）
insurance policyholder 保険契約者
meeting of representatives of policyholders 総代会
policyholder benefits 契約者給付金
▶Life insurance companies invest *policyholders' premiums* in stocks. 生命保険会社は，保険契約者の保険料を株式に投資している。

policyholders' representative meeting 〈保険会社の〉総代会 （＝the meeting of representatives of policyholders：株式会社の株主総会にあたる。総代は取引先などから選ばれることが多く，経営へのチェック機能が乏しいとの批判がある）
▶A *policyholders' representative meeting* is akin to a general shareholders meeting for a stock company. 総代会は，株式会社の株主総会にあたる。

political fund revenues 政治資金収入
▶*Political fund revenues* have been decreasing. 政治資金収入は，減少している。

Political Funds Control Law 政治資金規正法
▶The *Political Funds Control Law* was revised in December 2006. 政治資金規正法は，2006年12月に改正された。

pooling of interest [interests] 持ち分プーリング，持ち分プーリング法 （＝pooling of interest method）
▶We accounted for the merger as a *pooling of interests*. This means we combined the financial statements for the two companies. 当社は，この合併を持ち分プーリング法で会計処理しました。これは，2社の財務書類を結合したということです。

pooling of interest [interests] method 持ち分プーリング法，持ち分プーリング方式
▶We used a *pooling of interest method* for the merger with the company. 同社との合併に，当社は持ち分プーリング方式を採用しました。

poor 形 不振の，低迷した，伸び悩みの，不利な，厳しい，乏しい，悪い
　poor economic conditions 景気低迷，景気の悪化
　poor operating revenue 営業収入の低迷
　poor operational performance 業績低迷，業績の悪化
　poor performance 業績不振，業績低迷，業績の伸び悩み （＝weak performance）
　poor-performing company 業績不振の会社

［企業］
　poor profitability 収益性の低迷
poor earnings 減益
▶The major securities house attributed the *poor earnings* to sharp drops in brokerage fees and trading profits amid the extended slump in the domestic stock market. この大手証券会社は，減益の要因として，国内株式市場の長期低迷による株売買手数料と売買益の大幅減を挙げた。

poor sales 販売低迷，販売不振，売上低迷 （＝weak sales）
▶In 2007, we were hit by *poor sales* of digital devices. 2007年度は，デジタル製品［デジタル機器］の販売不振に見舞われました。

popularity rating 支持率 （＝approval rate [rating], support rate）

portfolio 名 所有有価証券，保有株式，有価証券明細表，有価証券報告書，資産内容，資産構成，資産管理，金融資産，投資資産，ポートフォリオ （⇒status）
　bond portfolio 債券ポートフォリオ
　equity portfolio 株式投資
　financial portfolio ローンや証券投資
　investment portfolio 投資ポートフォリオ
　loan portfolio 貸出残高，貸出金ポートフォリオ
　optimal portfolio 最適ポートフォリオ
　portfolio diversification 分散投資
　portfolio gains 資産売却益
　portfolio investment 有価証券投資，証券投資，株式・債券投資，資産運用投資，間接投資，ポートフォリオ投資，投資有価証券
　portfolio management 資産管理，最適資産管理，資産運用，資金運用，ポートフォリオ管理，ポートフォリオ運用，ポートフォリオ・マネジメント
　portfolio of products 製品ポートフォリオ，製品ライン （＝product portfolio）
　portfolio selection 資産選択，資産選好，資産管理，株式銘柄選択
　product portfolio management 製品ポートフォリオ管理 《略 PPM》
　receivables portfolio 債権ポートフォリオ
　troubled loan portfolio 不良債権ポートフォリオ
▶The investment *portfolio* was predominantly long-term bonds and equity investments as of December 31, 2007. 投資ポートフォリオは，2007年12月31日現在，長期債券と株式投資が中心になっています。
▶We are building on the skills of our people and our growing *portfolio* of technologies to create the platforms upon which whole new global

industries will be born.　当社は, 社員の技能と発展を遂げる当社の各種製品技術を構築して, まったく新しいグローバル産業を生み出す基盤を創造しています。

portion 名　部分, 一部, …分, 分け前, 割当て, 分担, 配分額, 計算額
　current portion　1年以内返済分
　portion financed by debt　借入金による調達額, 借入金で調達した分
　portion financed by equity　株式での調達額, 株式で調達した分
　portion of the debt　債務の一部
　portion of the expenses　費用の一部, 費用の分担
　unfunded portions of these liabilities　この債務の未拠出部分
　unused portions of commitments　貸出枠未実行残高
　▸The proceeds were used to repay a *portion* of the debt incurred to finance the acquisition of the company.　(公募で調達した)この資金は, 同社取得のための資金調達の際に発生した債務の一部返済に充てられました。

position 動　〈位置に〉つける, 据える, 〈特定の場所に〉置く, 配置する　(⇒**research and development**)
　be positioned to ...　…する体制を築く, …する態勢を整える
　be well positioned to ...　…する上で有利な立場にある, …する好位置につける, …できる力がある
　position oneself to [for] ...　…への準備を進める, …への対応を進める, …を推進する, …に取り組む
　▸Today, the Corporation is favorably *positioned* to capture an increasing share of the global market for telecommunications equipment and associated services.　こんにち当社は, 通信機器と関連サービスのグローバル市場でシェアを拡大するうえで, 有利な立場にあります。
　▸We will *position* ourselves for new opportunities in Europe.　当社は, 欧州での新たな事業機会に備える方針です。

position 名　有価証券の保有状態, 証券保有高, 持ち高, 経営基盤, 事業基盤, 位置, 地位, 役職, 状態, 地歩, 足場, 勤め口, 職, ポジション　(⇒**financial position**)
　bear position　売り持ち, 投機的売り持ち, 空売り
　bedrock position　基本的立場
　bull position　買い持ち, 投機的買い持ち, 空買い
　cash position　現金持ち高, 現預金, 直物ポジション, キャッシュ・ポジション
　competitive position　競争力
　credit position　信用状態
　debt position　借入状況, 債務状況
　ensure market position　市場での地位を強化する
　equity position　持ち株比率, 出資比率
　exchange position　為替持ち高, 為替ポジション
　hedge position　ヘッジ・ポジション
　leverage position　財務状況
　long position　買い持ち, 買い建て, ロング・ポジション
　management position　管理職, 上級管理職
　negotiating position　交渉力
　operating position　営業状況, 事業基盤
　overbought position　買い持ち
　oversold position　売り持ち
　position paper　特定の問題に関する方針説明書
　position statement　貸借対照表, 財務状態報告書　(=balance sheet)
　short position　売り持ち, 売り建て, ショート・ポジション
　strengthen our position　当社の経営基盤[事業基盤]を強化する
　take long positions in securities　証券の買い持ちをする, 証券のロング・ポジションを取る
　take short positions in securities　証券の空売りをする, 証券のショート・ポジションを取る
　test the market　市場の反応を探る
　▸A derivative contract is also used to hedge an investor's *position*.　デリバティブ契約は, 投資家のポジションをヘッジするために使われることもある。
　▸Following the merger, Nichiro's president will assume the *position* of chairman of the new holding company.　経営統合に伴って, ニチロの社長が新持ち株会社の会長に就任する。
　▸We will strengthen our *position* by reducing costs and improving productivity.　当社は, コスト削減と生産性の向上により, 当社の経営基盤を強化する方針です。

positive 名　強気材料, 好材料, プラス要因　(⇒**negative**)

positive 形　プラスの, 正の, 黒字の, 強含みの, 強気の, 好影響を与える, 明るい, 上昇傾向にある, 積極的な, ポジティブ
　positive earnings　好業績, 好決算
　positive factor　強気の材料, 好材料, 買い材料, プラス要因, 重要なポイント
　positive goodwill　積極的のれん, 積極的営業権
　positive implications　好材料, プラス要因, 格上

げの方向
positive results 好業績, 好決算（＝good results, positive earnings, robust performance）
revise upward the rating outlook from negative to positive 格付け見通しを「ネガティブ（弱含み）」から「ポジティブ（強含み）」に上方修正する
▶Negative factors could affect these *positive* results, such as rapidly falling prices for printers. プリンターの売価の急落などのマイナス要因が, これらの好決算に影響を及ぼす可能性がある。

post 動 …を示す, 提示する,〈赤字や黒字などを〉計上する, 転記する,〈担保や証拠金などを〉差し入れる,〈担保を〉設定する （⇒**row**）
post a healthy growth 好調［順調］な伸びを示す
post collateral 担保を差し入れる［提供する, 設定する, 供与する］
post losses 赤字を計上する
▶In the previous year, we *posted* a group net profit of ¥37.3 billion. 前期に当社は, 373億円の連結税引き後利益［連結純利益］を計上した。
▶The company *posted* ¥44 billion in sales in its business year ending in January 2008. 同社の2008年1月期決算の売上高は, 440億円だった。

post 名 職, 地位, 部署, 持ち場, 任務, ポスト （⇒**president**）
be at one's post 持ち場についている, 任務についている
be relieved of one's post 解任される
liquidation post 整理ポスト
monitoring post 監理ポスト, 監視ポスト（＝supervision post）
presidential post 社長ポスト
trading post 取引ポスト
▶The *post* of president has been vacant. 社長のポストは, 空席になっている。
▶Tokyo, Osaka and Nagoya bourses placed Nikko Cordial stock on their respective supervision *posts* for possible delisting. 東京, 大阪, 名古屋の3証券取引所が, それぞれ日興コーディアルの株式を, 上場廃止の可能性があるため監理ポストに割り当てた。

post- …の後の, 次の, 脱…, 事後の
post-change year 変更後の年度
post-goodwill net profit 営業権［のれん代］償却後の純利益
post-industrial society 脱工業［脱工業化］社会
post-merger 合併後の, 経営統合後の
post-script 追記
post-tax profit 税引き後利益（＝after-tax profit, net profit）

post-balance sheet 貸借対照表日後の, 後発事象の
post-balance sheet day 貸借対照表日後, 決算日後
post-balance sheet event 後発事象, 貸借対照表日後に発生した事象（＝subsequent events）
post-balance sheet review 貸借対照表日後の査閲, 後発事象の監査［査閲］

postemployment [post-employment] benefits 雇用後給付
estimated future postemployment benefits 予測される将来の雇用後給付
▶*Postemployment benefits* include payments for separations and disabilities. 雇用後給付には, 休職と疾病に対する支払いも含まれています。

postponement of credits 債権の棚上げ

postretirement 名 退職後, 雇用後
liabilities for postretirement 退職後債務
postretirement award 退職年金増加額
postretirement benefit plan 退職後給付制度
postretirement liabilities 雇用後債務
▶Our net liabilities for *postretirement* and postemployment liabilities are now combined on our balance sheet. 当社の正味の退職後債務と雇用後債務は現在, 貸借対照表上で合算されています。

postretirement benefit 退職後給付（＝benefit plan for retirees）
Employers' Accounting for Postretirement Benefits 雇用後給付に関する事業主の会計処理
▶The cost of providing *postretirement benefits* is accrued over an employee's service period. 退職後給付費用は, 従業員の勤続年数にわたって引当計上されています。

postretirement benefit cost 退職後給付費用（⇒**pay-as-you-go basis**）
accrued postretirement benefit cost 未払い退職後給付費用
net periodic postretirement benefit cost 退職後給付純期間費用
▶It is the company's practice to fund *postretirement benefit costs*, with an independent trustee, to the extent it is tax deductible. 税務上損金として認められる範囲内で, 退職後給付費用を独立した信託機関に積み立てるのが, 当社の慣行です。

postretirement benefit obligation 退職後給付債務
accrued postretirement benefit obligation

未払い退職後給付債務
accumulated postretirement benefit obligation 累積退職後給付債務
expected postretirement benefit obligation 予想退職後給付債務
▶The Company recognized as expense in 2007 the entire accumulated *postretirement benefit obligation* as of January 1, 2007. 当社は、2007年1月1日現在の退職後給付債務累積額を2007年に費用として全額認識しました。

postretirement health care benefit 退職後の健康保険給付金, 退職後の健康管理給付
▶*Postretirement health care* and life insurance *benefits* are fully accrued, princpally at retirement. 退職後の健康保険と生命保険の給付金は、主に従業員の退職時に全額計上されています。

potential 名 可能性, 将来性, 潜在能力, 潜在力, 潜在成長率, 余力, 余地, 素質, ポテンシャル (⇒strategic investment)
  borrowing potential 借入余力
  cost cutting potential コスト削減の余地
  earnings growth potential 増益力, 増益の余地, 収益増加の可能性
  earnings potential 潜在収益力
  growth potential 成長潜在力, 潜在成長力, 成長余地, 成長能力, 成長ポテンシャル
  investment potential 投資収益力
  market potential 市場の可能性, 市場としての可能性
  production potential 生産能力
  sales potential 販売可能性, 販売可能量, 販売見込み高

potential 形 可能性がある, 潜在的な, 将来起こりそうな
  potential acquisition 買収計画
  potential common stock 潜在株式
  potential demand 潜在需要
  potential growth 潜在成長力
  potential liability 潜在的債務額
  potential market 潜在市場

potential loan losses 予想貸倒れ損失, 予想貸倒れ損失額
▶We took out provisions against *potential loan losses* from non-accrual loans. 不稼動資産から生じる予想貸倒れ損失に備えて、準備金を引き当てました。

potential loss 潜在的損失, 予想損失, 潜在的損失額
▶Our maximum *potential loss* may exceed the amount recognized in our balance sheet. 当社の最大予想損失額は、貸借対照表上で認識された額を上回る可能性があります。

power 名 力, 能力, 権力, 権能, 権限, 法的権限, 支配力, 指名権, 電力, エネルギー (⇒earning power)
  borrowing power 借入能力
  buying power 購買力 (=purchasing power)
  excess earning power 超過収益力
  financial power 金の力
  gain or loss in purchasing power 購買力損益
  historical cost/constant purchasing power accounting 取得原価・統一購買力会計
  power of attorney 委任状, 委任権 (=letter of attorney)
  pricing power 価格支配力, 価格交渉力
  shifting power to price 価格転嫁力
▶Nissan Motor Co.'s board of directors has delegated all the necessary *powers* to Nissan/Renault Chief Executive Officer Carlos Ghosn to conduct any discussions and negotiations with General Motors. 日産自動車の取締役会は、GMとの協議や交渉を行うのに必要な全権限を、カルロス・ゴーン日産/仏ルノー最高経営責任者に委任した。

PPBS 企画計画予算方式 (planning, program(m)ing, budgeting systemの略)
PPP パブリック・プライベート・パートナーシップ (public private partnershipの略)
PR 広報, 広報宣伝活動 (public relationsの略)
practice 名 実行, 実践, 実務, 営業, 開業, 業務, 慣行, 慣習, 習俗, 手法, 仕組み, 法律事務, 訴訟実務, 訴訟手続き (⇒employee benefit, leverage, postretirement benefit cost, raise)
  accounting practices 会計実務, 会計慣行, 会計処理
  banking practice 銀行業務
  best practice 最善の手法, 最良の方法, 卓越した事例, 最善の実施例, 最善の業務慣行, ベスト・プラクティス
  business practice 商慣習, 商慣行, 企業慣行, 取引慣行, 取引方法, 営業手法, 業務
  collection practice 回収業務
  financial practice 金融措置
  financial reporting practice 財務報告実務
  lending practice 融資慣行
  management accounting practice 管理会計実務
  present practice 現行業務, 現行実務 (=current practice)
  Rules of Fair Practice 公正慣習規則, 公正慣行

ルール（全米証券業協会の業界規則）
usual practice 慣例 （⇒**proceedings**）
▶Our *practice* to raise the dividend every year is a signal to investors of our confidence in our future earning power. 毎年増配する当社の慣行は, 投資家にとって, 当社の将来の収益力に当社が確信をもっていることを裏付けるものです。
▶There have been inappropriate accounting *practices* at the subsidiary over the past several years. 過去数年間, 子会社で会計処理の不正が行われてきた。

preceding fiscal year 前年度, 前期 （⇒**per-share group net profit**）

preceding year 前年, 前年度, 前期 （＝previous year）

predominantly 副 優位に, 優勢に, 主に
▶The Company operates *predominantly* in the wireless communication, semiconductor technology and advanced electronic industries. 当社は, 無線通信, 半導体技術と高度電子機器の各分野で優位に事業を展開しています。

preemptive right 新株優先引受権, 新株引受権, 新株先買権, 新株予約権, 先取特権

preferential 形 優先の, 特恵の

preferential nonvoting share 議決権のない優先株式
▶Sanyo will issue *preferential nonvoting shares* worth about ¥50 billion to Sumitomo Mitsui Banking Corp. 三洋電機は, 三井住友銀行を引受先として約500億円の議決権がない優先株式を発行する。

preferential tax treatment 優遇税制措置, 税制優遇
▶Businesses that are recognized as having a highly public nature will be entitled to receive *preferential tax treatment*. 高い公益性を認められた事業は, 優遇税制措置を受けることができる。

preferred 形 優先権を与えられた, 優先権を持つ, 優先的, 優先…
　call the preferred issue at a premium プレミアムを払って優先株を償還する
　preferred dividends 優先配当金
　preferred dividends declared 優先株式の配当宣言額
　preferred securities 優先出資証券

preferred share 優先株式, 優先株 （＝preferred stock：利益の配当や会社解散時の残余財産の分配が普通株式に優先して与えられる株式で, 一般に経営参加権の議決権（voting right）は与えられない。⇒**preferred stock**）
　convertible preferred shares 転換型優先株
　cumulative preferred shares 累積優先株
　first preferred shares 第一優先株
　limited-life preferred shares 期限付き優先株
　nonconvertible preferred shares 非転換型優先株
　nonvoting preferred shares 無議決権優先株
　participating preferred shares 参加型優先株, 受益権付き優先株
　preferred share dividends 優先株式配当金
　preferred shares redeemed 優先株式の償還
　redeemable preferred shares 償還優先株, 償還可能優先株
▶During the first nine months of 2007, the Corporation raised $600 million by the issuance of *preferred shares*. 2007年1～9月期に当社は, 優先株式を発行して6億ドルを調達しました。

preferred stock 優先株式, 優先株 （＝preferred share; ⇒**common stock**）
　accumulated preferred stok 累積的優先株式
　adjustable rate preferred stock 配当率調整型優先株式
　auction rate preferred stock 配当率入札方式優先株式
　authorized preferred stock 授権優先株式数
　callable preferred stock 償還優先株式
　convertible preferred stock 転換優先株式
　cumulative preferred stock 累積優先株式, 累積優先株式
　dividend on preferred stock 優先株式配当, 優先株配当
　dividend preferred stock 配当優先株式
　increasing rate preferred stock 配当率逓増優先株式
　limited-life preferred stock 期限付き優先株式
　nonredeemable preferred stock 非償還優先株式
　nonvoting redeemable preferred stock 無議決権償還優先株式
　participating preferred stock 参加型優先株式
　perpetual preferred stock 永久優先株式
▶No *preferred stock* is currently issued and outstanding. 現在, 優先株式は発行されておらず, 残高もありません。

premium 名 保険料, 保険金, 額面超過額, 割増価格, 割増金, 上乗せ, 手数料, 打ち歩（うちぶ）, 権利金, オプション料, 報奨金, 奨励金, 賞金, 景品, プレミアム （⇒**net premium revenues, pension premium**）
　bond premium 社債発行差金

call the preferred issue at a premium プレミアムを払って優先株を償還する
estimated property premium 推定損害保険料, 概算損害保険料
insurance premium 保険料
premium income 保険料収入, 収入保険料
premium on bonds payable 社債割増発行差金
risk premium 危険負担割増金, 危険度に対する割増金, 危険打ち歩, リスク・プレミアム
single premium 一括払い保険料, 一時払い保険料
up-front premium 前払い保険料, 前払いプレミアム
▶The *premium* revenues are comprised of premiums from both individual and collective insurance contracts. この保険料収入は, 個人保険契約による収入と集団保険契約による収入から成る.

premium revenue 保険料収入(一般事業会社の売上高に相当。⇒**net premium revenues**)
▶*Premium revenues* slipped at seven of the nine major life insurers. 保険料収入は, 主要生命保険9社のうち7社が減少した。

prepaid expenses 前払い費用 (=prepaid costs)
　prepaid expenses and deferred income taxes 前払い費用及び繰延べ税金
　prepaid expenses and other current assets 前払い費用および(その)他の流動資産
一般的に前払い費用に含まれるもの：

prepaid insurance	前払い保険料 (=prepaid insurance premium)	
prepaid interest	前払い利息(=prepaid interest expense)	
prepaid rent	前払い家賃, 前払い賃借料	
prepaid taxes	前払い税金	

prepaid pension cost 前払い年金費用, 前払い年金原価, 前払い年金コスト (=prepaid pension expense; ⇒**pension liability**)
▶Our pension income was added to our *prepaid pension costs*. 当社の年金利益は, 当社の前払い年金費用に加算しました。

prepare 動 作成する, 準備する, 用意する (⇒**accounting principle**, **GAAP**)
▶Small and midsize companies have been stepping up equity financing to fund capital investments and *prepare* for M&A deals. 中小企業は, 設備投資の資金調達とM&A取引に備えて, 株式発行による資金調達を急いでいる。
▶These financial statements have been *prepared* in accordance with the U.S. GAAP consistently applied throughout the periods indicated. これらの財務書類は, 当該期間中に一貫して適用した米国の一般に公正妥当と認められた会計原則[会計基準]に従って[準拠して]作成されています。

prepay 動 前払いする, 前納する, 期限前償還する, 期限前弁済する
　prepaid card 代金前払い式カード, プリペイド・カード
　prepaid cell phone プリペイド式携帯電話, プリペイド携帯 (=prepaid mobile phone)
　prepaid expenses and other receivables 前払い費用およびその他の債権
　prepaid income 前受け収益
　prepaid postretirement healthcare costs 前払い退職後健康保険費用
　prepaid rental 前払い賃借料 (=prepaid rental expense)
　prepaid royalty 前払い特許権使用料, 前払いロイヤルティ
　prepay all or part of the mortgage モーゲージの全部または一部を期限前償還する
　prepay debt 繰上げ償還する
▶The *prepaid* pension costs shown above are net of pension liabilities for plans where accumulated plan benefits exceed assets. 上記の前払い年金費用は, 累積年金給付債務額が資産額を超過している場合の年金債務純額を控除してあります。

prepayment 名 前払い, 前払い費用, 期限前償還, 期限前返済, 借換え
　deferral of prepayments for future services 短期繰延べ法
　income tax prepayments 前払い法人税等, 前払い税金
　long-term prepayments 長期前払い費用 (=long-term prepaid expenses)
　prepayment assumed 期限前返済推定額
　prepayment paid 前払い費用
　prepayment received 前受け収益
　prepayment speed 期限前償還率 (=prepay speed, prepayment rate)
　surge in prepayments 期限前償還の急増 (=prepayment surge)

presence 名 存在, 存在感, 影響力, 地位, 立場, 事業基盤, 経営基盤, 拠点, 進出, 営業網, ポジション, 態度, 姿勢, プレゼンス (⇒**international market**)
　economic presence 経済的影響力, 経済力
　establish a presence in the market 市場での地位を確立する
　global presence 世界の営業網
　market presence 市場での地位, 市場でのプレ

ゼンス, 市場進出
political presence 政治的影響力
▸Leading banks may utilize the banking agent system to increase their *presence* in regional areas. 大手行は, 地方で拠点を増やすため, 銀行代理店制度を活用する可能性がある。
▸Oji Paper Co. ignored the *presence* of the anti-takeover measures and launched a tender offer for Hokuetsu Paper Mills Ltd. 王子製紙は, 買収防衛策の提示を無視して, 北越製紙に対してTOB(株式の公開買付け)に踏み切った。
▸Shiseido Co. is expanding its *presence* in China. 資生堂は, 中国で事業基盤を拡大している。

present 動 表示する, 提示する, 示す, 開示する, 作成する, 提出する, 提供する, 贈呈する, 口頭で説明する, 申し立てる
  fairly present 適正に表示する (=present fairly; ⇒**closing balance sheet**)
  present consolidated financial statements 連結財務書類[連結財務諸表]を作成する
▸In our opinion, these consolidated financial statements fairly *present* the financial position of the corporation as at December 31, 2007. 私どもの意見では, これらの連結財務書類は, 同社の2007年12月31日現在の財政状態を適正に表示しています。

present value 現在価値, 現価《略 PV》 (= present worth)
  actuarial present value 年金数理上の現在価値
  compound present value 複利現価
  discounted present value 割引現価
  net present value 純現在価値, 正味現在価値, 純現価《略 NPV》 (⇒**imputed interest**)
  present value of annuity 年金現価, 複利年金現価
  present value of capital lease payments キャピタル・リース支払い額の現在価値
  present value of net minimum lease payments 最低リース料の現在価値
  present value of the residual value 残存価格の現在価値
  simple present value 単利現価
  total at present value 現在価値総額
  total present value 現在価値合計
▸The net *present value* of capital lease payments was $160 million after deducting estimated executory costs of $1 million and imputed interest of $23 million. キャピタル・リース支払い額の純現在価値は, 見積り管理費用100万ドルと帰属利子2,300万ドルの控除後で, 1億6,000万ドルです。

presentation 名 表示, 表示方法, 表示形式, 提示, 提案, 提出, 手形の提示, 発表, 公開, 説明会, 上演, 贈呈, 進呈, 授与, プレゼンテーション (⇒**previously reported figures**)
  current presentation 当期の表示様式 (⇒**previously reported figures**)
  dual presentation of earnings per share 1株当たり利益の二重表示(普通株式1株当たり利益(earnings per common share)と完全希薄化1株当たり利益(fully diluted earnings per share)の表示)
  fair presentation 適正表示, 公正表示
  financial presentation 財務情報の表示
  financial statement presentation 財務書類[財務諸表]の表示
  graphic presentation 図表による表示, 図表による報告
  manner of presentation 表示方法
  net presentation 純額表示
  partial presentation 部分表示, 部分的表示
  presentation of current assets and liabilities 流動資産と流動負債の表示
▸An audit includes evaluating the overall financial statement *presentation*. 監査には, 財務書類全体の表示についての評価も含まれてます。

president 名 社長, 会長, 会頭, 頭取, 総裁, 議長, 委員長, 学長, 総長, 大統領, 国家主席
  co-president 共同頭取
  company president 会社社長
  president and chief executive officer 社長兼最高経営責任者
  president-designate 次期社長, 新任命社長
  president-elect 次期大統領
  president emeritus 名誉会長
  President's Letter 社長の書簡, 株主各位, 株主の皆様へ, ご挨拶
  President's Message 社長の挨拶, 株主各位, 株主の皆様へ, ご挨拶
▸Following the merger, Maruha's predident will take the post of *president* of the new holding company. 経営統合に伴って, マルハの社長が新持ち株会社の社長に就任する。
▸Takafumi Horie quitted his post as the *president* of Livedoor Co. 堀江貴文氏が, ライブドアの社長を辞任した。

press conference 記者会見 (=news conference)
▸The joint *press conference* was held at the firm's headquarters in Osaka. 共同記者会見は, 大阪市内の同社の本社で行われた。

pressure 圧力, 圧迫, 逼迫, 強要, 強制, 反発, 縮小, 減少, 低下, 悪化, 下落, 伸び悩み, ストレス (⇒**financial pressure, last half, profitability**)
  add to the upward pressure on prices 物価上昇圧力を強める
  asset quality pressures 資産内容の悪化
  be under further pressure 続落する
  business pressure 業務上のストレス, 業務の繁忙 (＝pressure of busines)
  come under heavy pressure 重圧[強い圧力]がかかる
  competitive pressure 競争圧力
  inflationary pressure インフレ圧力 (＝inflation pressure)
  pressure on margins 利益率低下, 利益率への圧力 (＝margin pressure)
  pressure on pricing 価格圧力, 値下げ圧力 (＝pricing pressure; ⇒**mix**)
  pressure on profitability 収益性の悪化
  price pressure 値下げ圧力, 価格低下圧力, インフレ圧力
  pricing pressure 価格圧力, 値下げ圧力 (＝pressure on pricing)
  profit pressure 収益への圧迫
  put [apply, exert, place] pressure on ... …に圧力をかける, …に圧力を加える
  revenue pressure 減収圧力
  sales pressures 販売の伸び悩み
  selling pressure 売り圧力
  upward pressure 上昇圧力, 引上げ圧力, 上昇傾向, 上昇要因
▶Gross margins for all of 2007 were essentially maintained despite severe price *pressures*. 2007年度全体の売上利益率は、値下げ圧力にもかかわらず、実質的に従来と同水準を維持しました。
▶Prices and technology are under continual *pressure*. 価格と技術は、絶えず圧力にさらされています。

pretax [pre-tax] 税引き前の, 税込みの, 経常の
  pretax accounting income 税引き前利益, 税引き前会計利益 (＝income before taxes)
  pretax balance 保険会社の経常収支残高(一般企業の経常利益に相当)
  pretax earnings 税引き前利益 (＝earnings before tax)
  pretax gains and losses 税引き前利益と損失, 税引き前損益 (⇒**other income**)
  pretax income 税引き前所得 (⇒**guideline**)
pretax loss 経常損失, 経常赤字, 課税前損失, 税引き前損失 (⇒**group pretax loss**)
▶UBS SA will post a *pretax loss* of about $690 million in the third quarter mainly because of losses linked to the U.S. subprime mortgage crisis. スイスの最大手銀行UBSは、主に米国のサブプライムローン問題の関連損失で、第3四半期は約6億9,000万ドルの税引き前損失を見込んでいる。

pretax profit 経常利益, 経常収益(民間企業の税引き前利益に相当), 税込み利益, 課税前利益, 税引き前利益 (＝current profit, recurring profit; ⇒**group pretax profit**)
▶This *pretax profit* is mainly due to earnings from our asset management business. この経常利益[税引き前利益]は、主に当社の資産運用業務の収入によるものです。

pretax provision 税引き前引当金
▶The decrease in 2007 net earnings and earnings per share was due mainly to the *pretax provision* of $500 million for restructuring costs. 2007年の純利益と1株当たり純利益が減少したのは、主に事業再編成費用に対する税引き前引当金5億ドルによるものです。

prevailing rate 市場の実勢金利, 市場金利, 実勢相場, 中心相場, 中心レート, 一般賃金, 一般賃率
▶The *prevailing rate* of interest for a note payable of this type is 12%. この種の支払い手形の通常[現行]の利子率は、12%である。

previous year 前年度, 前期, 過年度 (＝preceding year, prior period, prior year)
▶Toyota's operating profit rose 12.3 percent from the *previous year* to ¥1.88 trillion. トヨタの本業のもうけを示す営業利益は、前期比12.3%増の1兆8,800億円となった。

previous years 過年度, 過去の事業年度, 前年度以前, 前年度[前期]までの事業年度 (＝prior periods, prior years; ⇒**reclassify**)

previously reported figures 前期までの報告書に掲げた数値, 前期までに掲げた数値
▶Certain *previously reported figures* have been reclassified to conform with the current presentation. 前期までの報告書に掲げた一部の数値は、当期の表示様式に一致させるために組み替えてあります。

price 価格[値段]をつける, 価格[値段]を決める, 価格形成する
  be fairly priced 適正価格がつけられている, 適正な価格形成が行われている
  be priced in dollars ドル建てである
  be priced into ... …に織り込まれる
▶Interarea transfers are generally *priced* at cost

plus an appropriate service charge. 地域間振替えは、原則として原価に適正サービス料を加えた価格で行われています。

price 名 価格, 値段, 物価 （⇒market price, offer price, stock price）
　adjusted selling price method 修正売価法
　advertising prices 広告費
　agreed price 協定価格
　at constant prices 実質値
　at current prices 当期価格表示
　base period price 基準年の価格
　basis of price 価格条件
　cash price 現金価格
　closing price 終値
　competitive price 競争価格
　consumer prices 消費者物価
　current price 通り相場, 時価, 現行価格
　firm price 確定価格
　issue price 発行価格
　list price 表示価格
　market price of stock 株式相場
　price before tax 税込み前値段, 税金を含めた価格
　price cartel 価格カルテル （＝price agreement）
　price fixing 価格維持, 価格固定, 価格決定, 価格操作, 価格協定, 価格についての取決め, 物価安定
　price fluctuation 物価の変動, 価格騰落, 相場変動, 株価の乱高下, 価格変動
　price maintenance 価格維持
　price margin 売上総利益, 価格差益
　price minus tax 税引き価格, 税引き値段 （＝price less tax）
　price war 価格戦争, 価格競争, 値引き競争, 値引き販売
　public utility price 公益事業料金
　reacquisition price 買戻し価格
　replacement price 取替え価格
　selling price 販売価格, 売却価格, 売価, 売り値
　share price on the first day 初値
　standard price 標準価格, 標準物価, 基準価格
　sticker price メーカー希望小売価格
　stop price 最低落札価格
　strike price 行使価格, 権利行使価格
▶In the transportation industry, the *price* hike in crude oil has led directly to drops in profits. 運輸業界では、原油価格の上昇[原油の値上がり]が収益減に直結している。
▶Many of electrical and precision machinery companies in the country have shifted their production bases overseas to improve their competitiveness in *prices*. 国内電機・精密機械企業の多くは、価格競争力の向上をめざして生産拠点を海外に移している。

price book-value ratio 株価純資産倍率《略 PBR》 （株価を1株当たり純資産(book value per share)で割ったもの。⇒price-to-book value）

price competition 価格競争, 価格引下げ競争, 価格競争力
▶Despite a weak global economy and intense *price competition*, our sales grew 9% in 2007. 世界経済の低迷や激しい価格競争にもかかわらず、2007年度の当社の売上高は9%増加しました。

price competitiveness 価格競争力
▶Seven-Eleven Japan Co. has boosted its *price competitiveness* by mass-purchasing supplies. セブン-イレブン・ジャパンは、商品の大量仕入れで価格競争力を高めてきた。

price cut 値下げ, 価格引下げ （＝price cutting, price reduction）
▶*Price cuts* are afoot in other convenience stores. 値下げは、他のコンビニでも行われている。

price earnings ratio 株価収益率《略 PER》 （＝market multiple, multiple, P/E, P/E ratio）（株式の市場価格(common stock market price)÷1株当たり利益(earnings per common share)＝株価収益率）

price increase 値上げ, 値上がり, 価格上昇, 物価上昇 （＝price hike）
▶We filed for *price increases* of $800 million on an annual basis in late December. 12月末に当社は、年ベースで8億ドルの値上げを申請しました。

price reduction 値下げ, 価格の引下げ （＝price cut）
▶The increase in revenues occurred despite *price reductions* in 2007. 2007年度は、製品価格の引下げにもかかわらず売上高が増加しました。

price-to-book value 株価純資産倍率 （＝price book-value ratio）
▶*Price-to-book value* is obtained by dividing price per share by assets per share. 株価純資産倍率は、1株当たり株価を1株当たりの資産額で割って[除して]求められます。

primarily 副 主に, 元来, 基本的に

primary 形 基本的, 第一順位の, 希薄化前, 単純希薄化による, プライマリー
　primary and fully diluted earnings per share 単純希薄化と完全希薄化による1株当たり利益
　primary earnings per common and common equivalent share 普通株式および普通株式相

当証券1株当たりの希薄化前利益
primary earnings per common share 単純希薄化による普通株式1株当たり利益, 単純希薄化普通株式1株当たり利益, 普通株式1株当たりの希薄化前利益
primary EPS 基本的1株当たり利益, 基本的EPS（＝primary earnings per share, primary earnings per share of common stock）
primary materials 原材料
primary offering 募集（新規発行される有価証券の取得申込みを勧誘すること）
▶Average *primary* common and common equivalent shares outstanding for 2007 includes the dilutive effects of the convertible zero coupon notes. 2007年度の期中平均発行済み普通株式および普通株式相当証券数には, 転換可能なゼロ・クーポン債の希薄化効果も含まれています。

primary earnings per share 基本的1株当たり利益, 基礎的1株当たり利益, 1株当たり希薄化前利益, 単純希薄化による1株当たり利益, 単純希薄化1株当たり利益（＝basic earnings per share, primary EPS）
▶*Primary earnings per share* in 2007 were one cent higher than fully diluted. 2007年度の1株当たり希薄化前利益は, 完全希薄化後利益よりも1セント高かった。

primary market 発行市場, 新規取引市場, 新発債市場, プライマリー市場（新規株式公開や公募など, 企業や国が株や債券を新規発行して資金調達をする市場。⇒capital market）
primary market for securities 証券の発行市場

prime rate 一流企業向け最優遇貸出金利, プライム・レート（＝primary interest rate, prime, prime bank rate, prime lending rate）
▶Short-term *prime rate* is a benchmark for interest rates on loans to small and midsize firms and home buyers. 短期プライム・レートは, 中小企業と住宅取得者向けローンの基準金利である。
▶The long-term *prime rate* is charged on loans of one year or longer to the bank's most creditworthy corporate clients. 長期プライム・レートは, 最も信用力がある銀行の顧客企業に対する1年超の貸付け金に適用される。

principal 🔍 元本, 元金, 基本財産,〈株式の〉額面価額, 主債務者, 本人
　collateral principal payment 担保からの元本支払い［元本返済］
　collection of principal 元本回収
　exchange of principal 元本の交換
　guaranteed principal 元本保証

payment of principal and interest 元利の支払い, 元利払い, 元利の返済, 元利返済
　principal guarantee 元本保証
　principal outstanding 残存元本額
　principal payment 元本返済, 元本の支払い, 元本返済額
　remaining principal balance 元本残存額, 残存元本額（＝principal outstanding）
　repayment of principal 元本の償還, 元本返済
▶Stocks and foreign currency-denominated bonds are financial products which may reduce the *principal*. 株式や外貨建て債券は, 元本割れの恐れがある金融商品だ。
▶We must consider delays or reduced payments of interest as well as *principal* when we value loans that may not be fully repaid. 100%返済されない可能性がある債権を評価するにあたって, 利息や元本の遅延や減額返済を考慮する必要があります。

principal amount 元本, 元金, 額面価額, 額面
▶These convertible debentures are redeemable as of December 2007 at a price of 105% of the *principal amount*. この転換社債は, 2007年12月時点で, 元本の105%の価格で償還できます。

principal and interest 元本と利息, 元利
▶Debt-servicing costs are payments on the *principals and interests* on previously issued government bonds. 国債費は, 過去に発行した国債の元利払いに使われる金だ。

principally 副 主に, 原則として, 基本的に
▶We determine cost *principally* on a first-in, first-out (FIFO) basis. 当社は, 基本的に先入れ先出し法で原価を算定しています。

principle 🔍 原理, 原則, 主義, 方針, 基準, 道義
　accrual principle 発生主義の原則
　alternative accounting principle 代替的会計基準
　arm's length principle 独立企業原則
　business accounting principle 企業会計原則
　cost principle 原価主義
　equal value principle 等価交換の原則
　full cost principle 総括原価主義, フル・コスト原則
　income statement principle 損益計算書原則
　market principles 市場原理
　principle of consistency 継続性の原則
　principle of current operating performance 当期業績主義の原則
　principle of matching costs with revenues 費用収益対応の原則

principles of consolidation 連結方針, 連結の基準 (＝consolidation policy)
profit-first principle 利益至上主義
utility maximization principle 効用最大化の原理
▸We operate on the *principle* that management is accountable to shareholders. 経営者は株主に対して責任がある, というのが当社の経営方針です。

prior period 過年度, 前年度, 前期, 過去の事業年度 (＝previous year, prior year)
　prior period adjustment 過年度修正, 過年度損益修正, 前期修正, 前期損益修正 (＝prior year adjustment)
　prior period adjustment loss 前期損益修正損
　prior period adjustment profit 前期損益修正益, 過年度損益修正項目

prior periods 過年度, 前年度[前期]以前, 前年度[前期]までの事業年度 (＝prior years)

prior service 過去勤務 (＝past service)
　prior service liability 過去勤務債務
　prior service pension cost 過去勤務費用 (＝prior service cost)

prior service cost 過去勤務費用, 過去勤務原価, 過去勤務債務 (＝prior service pension cost)
　amortization of prior service cost 過去勤務原価[費用]の償却
　amortization of unrecognized prior service cost 未認識過去勤務債務の償却
　unrecognized prior service cost 未認識過去勤務費用
▸We amortize *prior service* costs primarily on a straight-line basis. 過去勤務債務は, 主に定額法で償却しています。

prior year 過年度, 前年度, 前期, 前年同期 (⇒prior years)
　certain prior year amounts 特定の[一部の]過年度の金額
　damage to buildings sustained in a prior year 過年度に受けた建物の損害
　financial statements of a prior year 過年度の財務書類[財務諸表]
　prior year adjustment 過年度修正, 過年度損益修正, 前期修正, 前期損益修正 (＝prior period adjustment)
　prior year figures 過年度の数値, 過年度の金額
　prior year income tax returns 過年度の所得税申告書
▸For the first quarter of 2007, our revenue was $14.2 billion, up 11.4 percent from the *prior year's* $12.7 billion. 2007年第1四半期の当社の売上高[収益]は142億ドルで, 前年同期の127億ドルを11.4％上回りました。

prior years 過年度, 前年度[前期]以前, 前年度[前期]までの各事業年度, 過去の事業年度 (＝previous years, prior periods)
　cumulative effect on prior years of changing to a different depreciation method 減価償却方法の変更による過年度への累積的影響(額)
　reduction of income taxes arising from deduction of prior years' accounting loss 過去の事業年度の会計上の損失控除により発生する所得税の減額
▸*Prior years'* statements of cash flows have been reclassified to conform to the new presentation. 前年度までの資金フロー表は, 新しい表示方法に合わせるため, 組み替えて再表示されています。

priority 名 優先, 優先事項, 優先権, 優先順位, 先取権
　cost priority コスト優先, コスト重視
　creditors by priority 優先債権者 (＝priority creditors)
　first priority 最優先
　payment priorities 支払いの優先順位, 元本返済の優先順位
　priority between mortgages 担保権の順位
　priority of claims 請求優先権, 債権先取権
　top priority 最優先課題
▸Existing convenience stores put *priority* on efficiency and forgot about customers. 既存のコンビニは, 効率を重視するあまり顧客のことを忘れていた。
▸Toyota has put *priority* on reducing trade friction with the U.S. トヨタは, 米国との貿易摩擦回避を優先した。

private 形 私的な, 個人的な, 私有の, 私設の, 民営の, 民間の, 非公開の, プライベート
　go private 株式を非公開化する, 非公開会社にする (⇒going private)
　private allocation 縁故者割当て
　private banking プライベート・バンキング
　private consumption 個人消費, 民間消費支出, 民間最終支出 (＝personal consumption)
　private corporation 非公開会社 (＝private enterprise)
　private demand 民需, 民間需要
　private placing 私募発行
　private sector 民間部門, 民間セクター, 民間企業, 民間
▸There has been no sign of increases in the two chief components of *private* sector demand —

private consumption and capital investment. 民間需要の2本柱である個人消費と設備投資に、回復の兆しが見えない。
▸We decided to go *private* in October. 当社は、10月に株式の非公開化を決めました。

private brand プライベート・ブランド、自家製標、商業者商標（＝store brand）
　private brand product 自主開発商品、自社開発商品、プライベート・ブランド商品

private company 非公開会社、株式非公開会社、非上場会社、民間企業、民営会社、私会社、閉鎖会社（＝private corporation, privately held company）
▸Japan Post became a *private company* on Oct. 1, 2007. 日本郵政公社は、2007年10月1日付けで民間企業になった。

private enterprise 私企業、民間企業、一般法人
　private enterprises annuity 企業年金

private offering 株式の直接募集、縁故募集、私募
▸The bonds were for sale by *private offering* and issued by Princeton Global Management Ltd. この債券は、プリンストン・グローバル・マネジメントが発行した私募債である。

private placement 私募発行、私募、私募債、第三者割当て（⇒capital base）
　私募発行とは⇒公募(public offering)と違って、私募(private placement)は株主や取引先、機関投資家など特定少数の投資家を対象に新株を発行、募集するもの。米国では、一定以上の資産・収入のある投資家(accredited investor)に私募発行する場合には、証券取引委員会(SEC)に登録する必要がない。
　bonds offered through private placement 私募債
　debt private placement 私募債発行
　private placement bond market 私募債市場
▸During the first quarter 2007, the Company issued, in *private placements* in Canada, $325 million of preferred shares. 2007年第1四半期に、当社は優先株式をカナダで私募発行して3億2,500万ドルを調達しました。

privately held 株式を公開していない、株式非公開の、非上場の
　privately held company 非公開会社、株式非公開会社、株式未公開会社、非上場会社
　privately held domestic business 民間企業

privately place 私募発行する、第三者割当て発行する、第三者割当て増資する（＝privately issue）

▸In July 2007, the Company *privately placed* two million special warrants to purchase new common shares of the corporation. 2007年7月に当社は、同社の新規発行普通株式引受権付き特別ワラント債200万単位を、私募発行しました。

privatization 名 民営化
▸Japan Post turned into the state-funded Japan Post Holdings Co. as part of the *privatization* of postal services. 日本郵政公社は、郵政民営化の一環として政府出資の持ち株会社、日本郵政グループ[日本郵政株式会社]に生まれ変わった。

pro forma [proforma] 仮定の、見積りの、仮の
　pro forma standard tax 外形標準課税（＝corporate tax on gross operating tax：「外形標準課税」は、法人事業税(都道府県税)について、現行の企業所得(黒字分)ではなく、資本金や人件費、売上高などの事業規模を基準に課税する方法）
▸Under the *pro forma* standard tax, corporate tax is levied on the basis of the number of employees, combined wages, and the size of capital. 外形標準課税では、法人事業税は従業員数や給与総額、資本金の規模などを基準にして課税される。

problem 名 問題、課題、難問
▸Canon's president and other executives hold a meeting every morning to exchange views about management *problems* and the economic situation. キヤノンの社長以下役員は毎朝、会議を開き、経営課題や経済状況について意見交換をしている。

problem borrower 問題融資先（＝problematic borrower）
▸These *problem borrowers* were either consolidated or reorganized. これらの問題融資先は、整理、再編された。

problem loans 問題債権、不良債権、不良債権額、貸倒れ（＝bad loans, loans to questionable borrowers, problem debts）
▸Shinsei Bank set aside an extra ¥8 billion in provisions for *problem loans* to U.S. mortgage business operators. 新生銀行は、米国内の住宅ローン事業を営む融資先に対する貸倒れ引当金として、新たに80億円を積み増した。

procedure 名 手続き、手順、処理手順、慣行、方式（⇒test）
　accounting procedure 会計手続き、会計慣行、会計処理方法
　auditing procedure 監査手続き
　budgetary procedure 予算手続き

clearing procedure 決済手続き
closing procedure 決算手続き
complaint procedures 苦情処理手続き
control procedure 内部統制手続き
credit procedures 与信手続き
external auditing procedure 外部監査手続き
internal procedures 内部規定
judicial procedures 裁判手続き
management procedures 管理手続き
procedures manual 手続きマニュアル, 業務マニュアル
settlement procedure 決済手続き, 決済方式
▸We have to admit there has been an inappropriate accounting *procedure*. 不適切な会計処理［会計処理方法］であったことは, 認めざるを得ない。

proceedings 名 議事進行, 議事録, 決議録, 会議録, 会報, 訴訟手続き, 法的手続き, 手続き, 措置, 訴訟, 弁論
　administrative proceedings 行政手続き, 行政訴訟
　legal proceedings 法律手続き, 法的手続き, 裁判手続き, 法的手段
　receivership proceedings 破産手続き
　take [bring, institute, start] proceedings against ... …に対して訴訟を起こす
　the proceedings of an annual shareholders meeting 年次株主総会の議事進行
▸In accordance with our usual practice, a summary of the *proceedings* of the annual meeting will be mailed to all shareholders. 当社の慣例に従って, 株主総会の議事要項は株主全員に後日, 郵送いたします。
▸In the normal course of business, we are subject to *proceedings*, lawsuits and other claims, including *proceedings* under government laws and regulations related to envirnmental and other matters. 通常の業務過程で当社は, 環境その他の問題に関する政府の法律や規則に基づく措置を含めて, 法的手続きや訴訟その他の請求の対象になります。

proceeds 名 代金, 手取金, 売上, 売上高, 売却収入, 売却益, 所得, 収益, 純利益, 収入, 調達資金, 資金 (⇒**net proceeds, portion**)
　by-product proceeds 副産物からの手取金
　export proceeds 輸出代金
　historical proceeds 実際用役領額
　IPO proceeds 公募による手取金
　proceeds of the sale 売却代金
　use of proceeds 資金の使途
▸We had net *proceeds* of $600 million from selling our shares in the company. 当社は, 同社株を売却して純額で6億ドルの売却益を得ました。
　proceeds from ... …による収入, …による手取金［受取金］, …による利益
　proceeds from asset sales 資産の売却収入
　proceeds from new debt 新規借入金による収入
　proceeds from new share issue 新株発行［起債］による手取金, 新株発行手取額, 新株発行による資金調達 (⇒**new share issue**)
　proceeds from (payments to) employee stock plans—net 従業員ストック・プランによる収入（支払い）―純額
　proceeds from sales of trading and investment securities 商品有価証券・投資有価証券売却額
▸The company will use the *proceeds from* selling its nine TV stations for debt repayment. 同社は, テレビ9局を売却して得た資金を, 債務返済に充てる予定だ。
　proceeds from exercising stock options ストック・オプションの行使による利益, ストック・オプション実行受取金 (＝proceeds from the exercise of stock options)
▸*Proceeds from exercising stock options* are compensation for labor and service rendered and constitute salary income. ストック・オプション［自社株購入権］を行使して得た利益は, 職務遂行の対価なので, 給与所得に当たる。
　proceeds from the public offering 株式公開による手取金, 公募による手取金
▸The net *proceeds* of $973 million *from the public offering* were used to reduce notes payable. 公募による純手取金9億7,300億ドルは, 短期借入金の返済に充当しました。
　proceeds from the sale 売却益, 売却代金
▸*Proceeds from the sale* were in cash. 売却代金は, 現金で入手しました。

process 名 過程, 工程, 流れ, 段階, 部門, 製法, 手続き, 訴訟手続き, プロセス
　beginning work in process 期首仕掛（しかけ・しかかり）品 (＝initial goods in process)
　business process reengineering 業務革新
　closing process 決算手続き
　construction in process 建設仮勘定 (＝construction in process account)
　cost-cutting process コスト削減計画
　decision making process 意思決定の過程, 政策決定の過程
　deflationary process デフレ
　issuing process 起債手続き

labor-intensive manufacturing process　労働集約型の製造部門
loan making process　融資手続き
management process　管理過程, マネジメントプロセス
manufacturing process　製造工程
planning process　計画策定プロセス
process control　工程管理
process industry　加工産業, 装置産業
process production order　継続製造指図書
process sheet　工程表
production process　生産工程
quality processes　品質管理手続き
rating process　格付けの過程
return generating process　収益生成過程
▸The increase in R&D spending reflected new and ongoing programs for new products and *process* developments.　研究開発費の増加は, 新製品とプロセスの開発をめざして, 従来から継続している計画に加えて新規計画を実施したことを反映しています。

processing 名　処理, 加工, 事務処理, 手続き
advanced processing　二次加工
batch processing　バッチ処理, 一括処理
computer processing　コンピュータ処理
data processing　データ処理, 情報処理, データ処理業務
food processing　食品加工
information processing　情報処理
information processing equipment　情報処理機器
inhouse processing　内製
online processing　オンライン処理
outside processing　外注加工
overnight processing　翌日処理
primary processing　一次加工
processing cost　加工費 (= manufacturing cost, processing expense, production cost)
processing industry　加工産業, 食品加工業
▸The plastic parts-*processing* industry and film manufacturers will not be able to shift the raised costs onto product prices.　プラスチック部品の加工業界やフィルムのメーカーは, コスト高［コスト上昇分］を製品価格に転嫁できないようだ。

procure 動　調達する, 購入する, 仕入れる, 取得する, 入手する, 獲得する, 引き起こす
▸We need to *procure* funds by the end of May.　当社は, 5月末までに資金調達［資金繰り］を迫られている。

procurement 名　調達, 購入, 仕入れ, 機器調達,

取得, 入手, 獲得, プロキュアメント
competitive procurement　一般競争による調達
e-procurement　電子調達, eプロキュアメント
enterprise procurement automation software　企業調達オートメーション・ソフト
fund procurement　資金調達, 資本調達 (= fund raising)
government procurement　政府調達
Internet procurement　インターネット調達, ネット調達
local procurement of components　部品の現地調達 (⇒**local procurement**)
mutual procurement　相互調達
noncompetitive procurement　非競争調達
procurement cost　調達費, 調達コスト, 仕入コスト (⇒**profitability**)
procurement department　調達部門
procurement of funds　資金調達 (= fund procurement, fund raising)
procurement of materials　原材料の調達 (= material procurement, procurement of raw materials, raw material procurement)
special procurements　特需
▸The two companies can save a combined ¥15 billion in distribution costs a year through mutual *procurement* of oil products.　両社は, 石油製品の相互調達で, 物流コストを両社合わせて年間150億円節約できる。

produce 動　生産する, 製造する, 製作する, 作成する, 提出する
goods produced　製品
income-producing real estate　稼動不動産
income-producing stock　所得を生む株式
national income produced　生産国民所得
revenue-producing enterprise　営利事業体
▸Import growth outpaced export growth, thus *producing* the trade imbalance.　輸入の伸びが輸出の伸びを上回ったため, 貿易の不均衡が生じた。
▸This increase in recurring profits is largely due to an expansion in domestic demand for steel sheets used to *produce* automobiles and favorable steel exports to the Chinese market.　この経常利益の増加は, 主に自動車生産用鋼板の内需拡大と中国向け鉄鋼輸出の好調によるものだ。

producer 名　生産者, 製造業者, 生産国, 供給者, 企業, メーカー
income producer　収益源, 収入源 (= income source)
industrial commodity producer　素材メーカー
producer goods　生産財, 工業製品

▸We fully expect that the company will be a significant income *producer* in coming years. 同社は今後, 当社の大きな収益源になるものと, 私どもは大いに期待しております。

product 名 製品, 生産品, 産物, 商品, 結果, 成果, プロダクト
  accumulation product 年金商品
  consumer product 消費者製品
  core product line 主力製品
  finished product 製品, 最終製品
  foreign currency product 為替商品 (＝foreign exchange product)
  high-margin product 利益率が高い製品
  high-tech product ハイテク製品
  high value-added product 付加価値の高い製品
  insurance product 保険商品 (＝insurance instrument)
  investment product 金融商品, 投資商品, 投資対象商品
  IT-related products IT関連製品
  joint products costing 連産品原価計算
  low-end product 低価格製品
  manufactured product 工業製品
  medical insurance product 医療保険商品
  popular product 人気商品
  product category 製品分野, 製品カテゴリー
  product cost 製品原価, 生産物原価, プロダクト・コスト
  product financing 製品金融, 製品による資金調達
  structured financial product 仕組み商品
  variable product 変額商品

▸Our strategy of listening to our customers and improving the competitiveness of our *products* and services is working. お客さまのご意見を取り入れ, 製品とサービスの競争力強化に取り組んでいる当社の経営戦略が, 功を奏しています。

▸The good results of the past quarter are the *product* of our people. 当四半期に高水準の業績を記録できましたことは, ひとえに各社員の努力の賜物です。

product development 製品開発, 商品開発 (⇒participate)
▸Restructuring allows us to refocus our resources on *product development*. 事業再編を通して, 当社は経営資源を製品開発に新たに集中することができます。

product financing arrangement 製品金融の取決め, 製品による資金調達方法(製品を買戻し条件付きで販売することで資金を調達する方法)

product line 製品ライン, 商品ライン, 商品群, 製品系列, 製品種目, 製品品目, 製品構成, プロダクト・ライン (⇒focus on ...)
▸*Product line* revenue growth was led by strong percentage gains in business communications systems and terminals. 製品系列の売上高の伸びは, 主にビジネス通信システムと端末機器の大幅な伸び率によるものです。
▸*Product lines* have been refreshed from top to bottom. 製品ラインが, 全面的に一新された。

product performance 製品性能
▸Competitive factors include price, *product performance*, product quality, and service and systems quality and availability. 競争要因としては, 価格, 製品の性能, 製品の品質のほかに, サービスおよびシステムの品質や利用度などもあります。

product price 製品価格
▸What is noteworthy in the midterm results is the 6 percent increase in sales resulting from an increase in *product prices* and sales volumes. 中間決算で特筆できるのは, 製品の価格の上昇と販売数量の拡大で, 売上高が6％伸びたことです。

product related expenses 製品関連費用
▸Expenditures for advertising and sales promotion and for other *product related expenses* are charged to costs and expenses as incurred. 宣伝・販売促進費とその他の製品関連費用は, その発生時に費用に計上されます。

product sales 製品販売
▸For other *product sales*, revenue is recognized at the time of shipment. その他の製品販売については, 収益は出荷時に認識されます。

production 名 生産, 製造, 製作, 制作, プロダクション
  assembly production 組立生産
  industrial production 工業生産, 鉱工業生産, 工業出荷, 鉱工業生産高
  job order production system 個別生産システム
  just-in-time production system かんばん方式
  license production ライセンス生産
  line production 直線生産, 流れ作業生産, 流れ作業
  local production 現地生産, 国内生産
  offshore production 海外生産 (＝overseas production)
  production center 生産拠点, 製造拠点, 生産センター, 生産中心点, 生産の中核拠点
  production control 生産管理, 工程管理
  production facilities 生産設備, 生産拠点 (＝manufacturing facilities)

production labor 製造労務費, 生産労務費, 直接労務費

production level 操業度

production management 生産管理

production method 生産高比例法 （＝activity method, production output method, service yield basis, unit of production method）, 製造方法, 生産方法, 生産方式

production of content コンテンツ［情報の中身］の制作

production output method 生産高比例法 （＝productive output method）

production overhead cost 製造間接費 （＝production overheads）

production process 生産工程, 製造工程, 製造段階, 生産過程, 製造過程, 生産体制, 製造部門 （＝manufacturing process, process of production）

round-about production 迂回生産

surplus production 余剰生産

▶Canon has stuck by its policy of keeping *production* within Japan. キヤノンは, 国内生産を維持する方針にこだわり続けている。

▶Ford Motor Co. will temporarily halt *production* at its assembly plants to reduce bloated inventories. 米フォードは, 増大した在庫を削減［圧縮］するため, 組立工場での生産を一時中止する。

production base 生産拠点, 製造拠点 （＝production center）

▶Canon already has moved its *production base* overseas for products that require a lot of labor but must have a low selling price, such as digital cameras. キヤノンは, デジカメなど手間の割に販売価格が安い製品の生産拠点はすでに海外に移している。

production capacity 生産能力, 生産余力, 生産設備 （＝output capacity）

▶Rapid growth in demand for digital electric appliances led leading electronic and precision equipment manufacturers to enhance investment in their *production capacities*. デジタル家電の需要急増で, 電機, 精密機器などの大手メーカーが, 生産設備への投資を増やした。

production cost 製造費, 製造原価, 製品原価, 生産コスト, 製造コスト （＝cost of production, production expense）

▶Steady efforts toward technological improvement and cuts in *production costs* were the driving forces behind our record net profit for the year ended Dec. 31, 2007. 技術力の向上や生産コスト削減に向けた地道な取組みが, 当社が2007年12月期決算で記録した過去最高の税引き後利益の原動力である。

production cycle 生産サイクル

▶*Production cycles* have been shortened to enable the company to deliver solutions faster. お客様に対するソリューション［問題解決策］の早期提供をめざして, 当社は生産サイクルを短縮している。

production line 生産ライン, 製造ライン, 生産系列, 流れ作業, 生産線 （＝assembly line; ⇒ sales effort, workweek）

▶Toyota and GM will introduce new *production lines* by investing tens of billions of yen in their joint venture plant. トヨタとGMは, 両社の合弁工場に数百億円を追加投資して, 新生産ラインを導入する。

production support company 生産支援会社

▶With the addition of the *production support company* in Thailand, Toyota has strengthened the integration of its development, production and distribution process. タイに生産支援会社を新たに設立して, トヨタは開発, 生産と販売の各部門を一体化する体制を強化した。

production system 生産方式, 生産システム

▶Canon's successful cost-cutting efforts through *production system* reforms of its traditional core products significantly contributed to the company's high performance. キヤノンの伝統的な主力商品の生産方式の改革によるコスト削減策の成功が, 同社の高収益の大きな要因だ。

productivity 🔊 生産性, 生産力, 生産効率, 多様性, プロダクティビティ （⇒position）

capital productivity 資本生産性 （＝productivity of capital）

corporate productivity 企業の生産性

comparative productivity 比較生産性

green productivity 環境にやさしい生産性, グリーン・プロダクティビティ

gross productivity 粗生産力, 粗生産性

improved productivity 生産性向上, 生産性の向上 （＝increased productivity）

labor productivity 労働生産性

marginal productivity 限界生産力, 限界生産性

net productivity 純生産性, 純生産力

productivity improvement 生産性向上, 生産性上昇 （＝improved productivity, increased productivity）

productivity of added value 付加価値生産性

(＝productivity of value added)
productivity of labor 労働生産性 （＝labor productivity)
sales productivity 販売効率
total-factor productivity 全要素生産性
value productivity 価値生産性
▶We will strengthen our position by reducing costs and improving *productivity*. 当社は、コスト削減と生産性の向上により、当社の経営基盤を強化することになりました。

profile 名 構成，構造，輪郭，概要，案内，見通し，予測，特性，地位，方針，プロフィール，プロファイル
credit profile 信用力
earnings profile 収益見通し
financial profile 財務力見通し
investment profile 投資方針
market profile 市場プロフィール，市場特性，市場情報
product profile 製品構成
risk profile リスク特性，リスク構造
▶The credit *profiles* of major Japanese bank groups have improved through falling balance-sheet risk, a plan to repay public funds and other factors. 財務リスクの軽減や公的資金の返済計画などの要因により、日本の大手金融グループ各行の信用力は改善している。

profit 動 〈利益を〉得る，〈教訓を〉得る，利益になる，役に立つ
▶In foreign exchange margin trading, investors repeatedly trade U.S. dollars, euros and other currencies, aiming to *profit* from fluctuations in exchange rates. 外国為替証拠金取引では、為替の変動による利益を狙って、投資家が米ドルやユーロなどの外貨を繰り返し売買する。

profit 名 利益，利得，利潤，黒字 （⇒consolidated net profit, current account profit, current profit, group net profit, net profit, operating profit)
absolute profit 純利益
accounting profit 会計上の利益
advance in profits 増益
all-inclusive profit 包括主義利益
average profit growth 年平均増益率
book profit 帳簿上の利益
business profit 企業収益，企業利益，業務利益 （＝business income)
capital profit 資本利潤
corporate profit growth 企業増益率
corporate profits 企業収益，企業利益
excessive profit 超過利潤，不当利得，暴利

increase [improve] profit margins 利益率を高める
internal profit 内部利益
maximum profit 最大利潤，最大の利益，利益の極大化
move into profit 黒字に転換する （＝return to profit)
not-for-profit organization 非営利団体 （＝non-profit organization)
pre-depreciation profit 償却前利益
profit after taxation 税引き後利益
profit before taxation 税引き前利益
profit brought forward from the previous (business) term 前期繰越し利益金
profit center 利益中心点，プロフィット・センター
profit-earning capacity 収益力 （＝profit-making capability)
profit expectation 利益予想 （＝profit forecast, profit forecasting)
profit from capital reduction 減資差益
profit from redemption 償還利益
profit from securities revaluation 有価証券評価益
profit on foreign exchange 為替差益，外国為替差益
profit on securities sold 有価証券売却益
profit on treasury stock 自己株式処分益
profit outlook 利益予想，収益見通し，業績予想 （＝earnings forecast, profit forecast)
profit-padding 利益の水増し
profit prior to consolidation 連結前利益
profit taking 利益を確定するための売り，利益確定売り，利食い，利食い売り （＝profit taking sales)
profits for the term 当期利益金
profits from redemption 償還差益 （＝gains from redemption)
rake in massive profits 巨額の利益を上げる，大もうけする
realize a profit 利益を得る
return to profit 黒字に転換する，黒字に戻る，黒字回復する
squeeze profits 利益を圧迫する
take profits 利食い売りをする，利食いに出る，利食う
target profit 目標利益
trading profit 売買益
undivided profit 未処分利益
unfair profits 不当な利益
▶Major electric appliance manufacturers and 10

telecommunication companies turned *profits* for the year ended March 31.　3月期決算では，大手電機と情報通信10社が，黒字に転換した。

▸Mizuho Financial Group Inc. booked as *profit* a combined ¥180.5 billion from loan-loss reserves at the group's three banks.　みずほフィナンシャルグループは，傘下3銀行の貸倒れ引当金のうち合算で計1,805億円を利益として計上した。

profit and [or] loss　損益

annual profit and loss　年次損益
consolidated profit and loss account　連結損益計算書
extraordinary profit and loss　特別損益，臨時損益，非経常的損失（＝special profit and loss）
intercompany profit and loss　内部損益
operating profit and loss　営業損益
ordinary profit and loss　経常損益
profit and loss break-even point　損益分岐点（＝profit and loss point）
profit and loss for the preceding term　前期損益（＝profit and loss for the previous period）
profit and loss on securities sold　有価証券売却損益
profit or loss for the financial year　当期損益
unrealized profits and losses　含み損益

▸Under the consolidated return system, a company pays corporate tax after totaling the *profits and losses* of its affiliated companies.　連結納税制度では，企業はグループ企業［系列企業］の損益を合算して法人税を納める。

profit and loss statement　損益計算書

（＝income account, income statement, profit and loss account, statement of earnings, statement of income, statement of operations）

▸The Board of Audit asked the airport management company to submit *profit and loss statements* of its nonairport divisions.　会計検査院は，空港運営会社に非航空事業部門の損益計算書の提出を求めた。

profit decline　減益，利益の減少

▸Pulp and paper makers have seen their year-on-year *profits decline*.　製紙業界は，前年比で減益となっている。

profit driver　収益の原動力，利益を押し上げる原動力

▸Equities once again were a main *profit driver* for Nomura.　野村の収益を押し上げる原動力［主な要因］は，再び株式となった。

profit-first principle　利益至上主義

▸The *profit-first principle* may have overpowered the law-abiding spirit in the case of the company.　同社の場合は，利益至上主義のほうが順法精神より強すぎたかもしれない。

profit forecast　利益予想，収益見通し，業績予想，業績見通し（＝earnings forecast, profit outlook）

▸The financial group halved its *profit forecast* for fiscal 2008.　同フィナンシャル・グループが，2008年度の業績予想を（前回予想より）50％引き下げた。

profit growth　利益の伸び，増益

▸Although corporate sector is enjoying *profit growth*, businesses generally have yet to relax their restructuring measures to transform them into highly profitable companies.　企業部門［企業］は収益が伸びているが，一般に高収益企業［高収益体質］に転換するためのリストラの手をまだ緩めていない。

profit making　利益を上げること，利益を得ること，営利

profit-making business　収益事業，営利事業
profit-making capability　収益力（＝profit-earning capacity）
profit-making corporation　営利法人
profit-making sources　収益源

▸The group aims to strengthen its *profit-making* capability by establishing joint frameworks in product delivery and development.　同グループは，商品の配送と商品の開発を共同化して，グループ全体の収益力を強化する計画だ。

profit margin　売上利益率，売上純利益率，利率，利ざや，利幅（売上純利益率（％）＝（純利益÷純売上高）×100。「利ざや」は，金融機関の資金の調達金利と貸出金利の差）

operating profit margin　営業利益率（＝the ratio of operating profit to sales）
profit margin on sales　売上高利益率，売上高純利益率，売上総利益

▸Hitachi Ltd. aims to achieve a group operating *profit margin* of 5 percent by the end of fiscal 2009.　日立製作所は，2009年度末［2010年3月期］までに連結営業利益率5％の達成を目指している。

profit projection　利益予想，業績見通し（＝earnings forecast, profit forecast, profit outlook）

▸The company may need to further lower its *profit projections* as losses related to the battery recall may grow.　充電池回収の関連損失が拡大することもあるため，同社はさらに業績見通しの下方修正を迫られる可能性がある。

profit ratio 利益率
  profit ratio of gross capital 総資本利益率
  profit ratio of net worth 自己資本利益率, 株主資本利益率
  profit ratio of operating capital 経営資本利益率
  profit ratio of paid-up capital 払込み資本収益率

profit sharing 利益配分, 利益分配, 利益配当
  profit sharing plan 利益配分制度, 利益分配制度
  profit sharing system 利益分配制度
  ▶ESOP resembles a *profit-sharing plan*. ESOP(従業員持ち株制度)は, 利益分配制度に似ている。

profitability 名 収益性, 収益力, 営利性, 採算性, 利益率, 収益率 (＝earning power)
  achieve profitability 黒字転換を果たす, 黒字化する
  core profitability 主力事業の収益性
  corporate profitability 企業収益性, 企業の収益性
  expected profitability of new investment 新規投資の期待収益力
  increased profitability 収益性の改善, 収益性の向上, 収益力の高まり (＝improved profitability)
  investment profitability 投資収益性
  potential profitability 採算性
  regain profitability 収益力を回復する
  return to profitability 黒字に転換する
  segment profitability 事業部門別収益性
  weakened profitability 収益性の低下 (＝decreased profitability)
  ▶There are pressures on prices, margins and *profitability*. 価格や利益率, 収益性が悪化している。
  ▶We expect the deal to help slash procurement costs and raise *profitability*. 当社は, 今回の提携で, 仕入コスト[調達コスト]の削減と収益性の向上[収益力の改善]を見込んでいます。

profitable 形 儲かる, 利益を生む, 収益性[収益力]がある, 収益性が高い, 有利な, 有益な, ためになる, 役に立つ
  highly profitable company 高収益企業, 収益力[収益性]が高い企業
  most profitable season 書き入れ時
  profitable basis 収益基盤
  profitable business 収益性の高い事業, 儲かる商売[仕事], 利益が出る商売
  profitable goods 利益率の高い商品, 収益性の高い商品, 収益品
  profitable investment 有利な投資
  profitable opportunity 有利な機会
  turn profitable 黒字に転換する
  ▶Mitsubishi Motors Corp. expects to be *profitable* for the first time in four years with the introduction of new models. 三菱自動車は, 新型車の導入で, 4年ぶりの黒字転換を見込んでいる。

program 名 計画, 予定, 政策, 対策, 策, 措置, 〈政党の〉綱領, 政治要項, 制度, 番組, コンピュータ・プログラム, プログラム (⇒protection, stock option program)
  affirmative action compliance program 積極的優遇措置遵守プログラム
  asset disposal program 資産売却計画
  audit program 監査計画, 監査プログラム, 監査指示書, 監査実施手続き書
  cost containment program コスト削減計画
  expansion program 事業拡大計画
  funding program 資金調達計画
  loan program 融資枠
  product program 商品計画
  savings-stock purchase program 貯蓄株購入制度
  ▶Managers of companies with such stock option *programs* are discouraged from holding a long-term view. ストック・オプション制度を設けている企業の経営者は, 長期的な視点で企業経営に当たらなくなる。
  ▶We support *programs* that relieve job-family stress so our people can concentrate on doing their jobs and satisfying our customers. 当社は, 社員が業務の遂行と顧客の満足達成に専念できるよう, 仕事と家族のストレスを和らげるプログラムを支援しています。

progress 名 進歩, 発展, 成長, 進捗状況, 未成工事
  construction work in progress 建設仮勘定 (＝construction in progress)
  earnings progress 増益
  economic progress 経済発展, 経済進歩, 経済成長
  long-term contract work in progress 長期請負契約
  product in progress 仕掛(しかけ・しかかり)品 (＝goods in process, stock in process, work in process)
  progress payments 未成工事支出金, 未成工事の前受金
  work in progress 仕掛品 (＝product in progress, work in process)
  ▶2007 was a year of steady *progress* for the Corporation, as was 2006. 2007年度は, 当社にとっ

て2006年度と同様に着実な発展を遂げた年でした。
▶We continue to make *progress* in Asian markets. 当社は、アジア市場で拡張を続けています。

progressive cost 逓増費
progressive tax 累進課税, 累進税
project 動 計画する, 企画する, 予測する, 予想する, 見積もる
  projected deficit 赤字見通し
  projected dividend 予想配当 (⇒**per share**)
  projected P/E 予想PER (株価収益率)
  projected pension obligations 予想年金債務額 (⇒**fair value**)
▶For the full business year through next March, the company *projects* ¥27 billion in group net profit. 来年3月までの通期で、同社は270億円の税引き後利益を予想している。
▶The combined sales of the firm's large hotels and resort facilities are *projected* to top ¥150 billion. 同社の大型ホテルとリゾート施設の売却総額は、1,500億円を超える見通しだ。

project 名 計画, 企画, 対策, 案件, 事業, 開発事業, 公共事業計画, 長期目標, プロジェクト (⇒**turnover**)
  approved project 認可済み案件
  joint project 共同事業
  large project 大型プロジェクト (＝high-profile project)
  pilot project 予備計画
  project management プロジェクト管理, 計画管理, プロジェクト・マネジメント
  project plan 事業計画
  project plannning 個別計画, プロジェクト・プランニング
  R&D project 研究開発プロジェクト
  raw material development project 資源開発事業
▶A joint venture including Penta-Ocean won a contract for about ¥2.6 billion in this construction *project*. この建設工事では、五洋建設などの共同事業体（JV）が約26億円で受注した。
▶The lease-financing *project* targets individual investors such as company operators and other affluent people. このリース金融事業の対象は、会社経営者や資産家などの個人投資家だ。

project finance プロジェクト金融, 特定事業に対する金融, プロジェクト・ファイナンス
▶Financial institutions extend loans to specified projects of companies by *project finance*. 金融機関は、プロジェクト金融で、企業の特定の事業に融資している。

projected benefit obligation 予測給付債務, 見積り給付債務, 予定給付債務, 予測給付債務制度, 退職給付債務 (⇒**benefit obligation**)
  projected benefit obligation for service rendered to date 計算日までの勤務に対する予定［予測］給付債務
  projected benefit obligation in exces of plan assets 年金資産を上回る予定［予測］給付債務
▶Measurement of the *projected benefit obligation* was based on a discount rate of 8.5% and a 5% long-term rate of compensation increase in 2007. 予測給付債務は、2007年度の8.5％の割引率と5％の長期昇級率に基づいて算定されています。

projected loss 赤字予想, 予想赤字
▶Reflecting the *projected losses*, the company will pay no dividends for fiscal 2007. 赤字予想を反映して、同社は2007年度を無配とする方針だ。

projected unit credit 予測単位給付, 予測単位年金積増し
▶Annual pension cost is determined using the *Projected Unit Credit* actuarial method. 年間年金費用は、予測単位年金積増方式による年金数理計算方式で決定されています。

projected unit credit method 予測単位給付方式, 予測単位基金方式, 予測単位年金積増方式
▶We compute pension cost using the *projected unit credit method*. 年金費用は、予測単位年金積増方式で算出しています。

projection 名 見積り, 予測, 推定, 予想, 想定, 見通し, 推計 (⇒**initial projection**)
  business projection 業績見通し
  cash flow projection 資金繰りの見通し, キャッシュ・フロー予測
  earlier projection 当初予想 (＝earlier forecast, original projection)
  earnings projection 業績予想
  financial projection 財務計画, 財務見通し
  preliminary projections 暫定値
  sales projection 売上予想, 販売見通し, 予想売上
▶Banks have to set aside loan loss reserves based on *projections* of future revenues of their borrowers, not based on bankruptcies in the past. 銀行は、過去の倒産実績ではなく、融資先企業［貸出先］の将来の収益予想などを基にして、貸倒れ引当金を積み立てるべきだ。
▶The Japanese currency is about ¥5 lower than its initial *projection* of ¥120 to the dollar. 円は、当初想定した1ドル＝120円より5円程度安く推移している。

promised yield rate 予定利率 (＝promised

yield, prospective yield rate：生命保険会社が保険契約者に約束した利回り。（⇒**insurance contract**）

promising area　有望な分野

▶Sanyo plans to shift resources to more *promising areas* such as rechargeable batteries and industrial-use air conditioners, where it still earns healthy profits.　三洋電機は、充電式電池や業務用エアコンなど、同社が現在も順調に利益を上げている有望な分野に経営資源を振り向ける計画だ。

promissory note　約束手形
- **promissory notes and bills**　約束手形
- **promissory notes payable**　金融手形債務

promote 動
促進する、推進する、振興する、助長する、奨励する、販売を促進する、宣伝する、売り込む、昇進させる、昇格させる、主催する、発起する、議案の通過を促す（⇒**internal growth, representative**）

▶Board members who were *promoted* from within the company have been managing firms in Japan,　日本では、社内から昇進した取締役[従業員から持ち上がった取締役]が企業を経営している。

promotion 名
昇進、昇級、昇格、昇任、促進、推進、増進、助長、振興、奨励、販売促進、販売促進活動、創設、創立、発起（⇒**sales promotion**）
- **advertising and promotion costs**　広告宣伝費
- **employment promotion**　雇用促進
- **export promotion**　輸出振興、輸出促進
- **job promotion**　職種内昇進
- **productivity promotion**　生産性向上
- **promotion expense**　販売促進費（＝sales promotion cost）、創業費（＝organization cost）、創立費、設立費用
- **promotion system**　昇進制度
- **sales promotion cost**　販売促進費、販促費用
- **trade promotion**　貿易振興、貿易促進

▶Selling, general and administrative expenses increased largely because of advertising and *promotions*.　販売費および一般管理費は、主に広告宣伝と販売促進活動により増加しました。

property 名
財産、有体財産、資産、固定資産、有形固定資産、所有、所有権、所有地、所有物、財産権、特性、属性、物件

> 有体財産に含まれるもの ➡ 有体財産には、営業用・製造業用の固定設備としての土地(land)、建物(buildings)、機械装置(machinery)および什器備品(furniture and fixtures)と、鉱山(mine)、山林(timber tract)、油井(oil well)などの天然資源が含まれる。

- **after-acquired property**　事後取得財産
- **basic property**　基本財産
- **gain on property dividend**　現物配当処分益
- **immovable property**　不動産（＝immovables）
- **inventories and property**　棚卸し資産および有形固定資産
- **investment property**　投資不動産、投資資産
- **leased property**　リース資産
- **movable property**　動産（＝movables）
- **negative property**　消極財産（負債や支払い勘定）
- **personal property tax**　動産税
- **property additions**　固定資産の増設額、固定資産の新規取得
- **property and equipment**　有形固定資産
- **property development project**　不動産開発事業、不動産開発プロジェクト（⇒**turnover**）
- **real property tax**　固定資産税、不動産税
- **residential property price**　住宅用不動産価格
- **total property**　有形固定資産合計

▶Plant, rental machines and other *property* are depreciated over their estimated useful lives using the straight-line method.　工場設備、賃貸機械、その他の固定資産は、それぞれの見積り耐用年数にわたって定額法を用いて償却されています。

property, plant and equipment　有形固定資産、土地、建物および設備、不動産・工場設備（＝tangible fixed assets）
- **property, plant and equipment, net**　有形固定資産（純額）
- **property, plant and equipment, sold**　有形固定資産の売却、非流動資産の売却

有形固定資産に含まれるもの：

buildings	建物
construction in progress	建設仮勘定
furniture and fixtures	什器（じゅうき）備品
land	土地
leasehold improvements	賃借物の改造
machinery and equipment	機械装置、機械設備
tools	工具
vehicles	車両運搬具

▶For the three years, operating cash flows covered our additions to *property, plant and equipment* and dividend payments.　過去3年間は、営業から生じるキャッシュ・フローで有形固定資産に対する追加投資額と支払い配当金をまかないました。

proposal 名
提案、案、企画、構想、計画、申込み、オファー
- **management integration proposal**　経営統合の提案

proposal for appropriation of retained earnings 利益処分案
shareholder [stockholder] proposal 株主提案
▸Oji lowered its offer price per share from ¥860 to ¥800 under its latest *proposal*. 王子製紙は、今回の提案で1株当たり買付け価格［買取り価格］を860円から800円に引き下げた。
▸On the stockholder *proposal* requesting detailed reporting on animal experimentation, 92% of the votes cast were voted against. 動物実験に関する詳細な報告を要求する株主提案については、投票総数［投票株式総数］の92％が反対で否決された。
▸Rakuten Inc.'s management integration *proposal* will not increase TBS's corporate value. 楽天からの経営統合の提案は、TBSの企業価値の向上にはつながらないだろう。

propose 動 提案する、提唱する、企画する、申し出る、提出する、提示する、指名する、推薦する
▸*Proposed* purchase price is still far from what the investment fund is expecting. 提示された(TOBの)買付け価格は、投資ファンドの想定価格とまだ開きがある。

proprietary 形 所有者の、所有権の、私有の
　proprietary right 所有権
　proprietary trading 自己売買、自己勘定取引、ディーリング業務

proprietor 名 所有者、持ち主

prorate 動 配賦する、割り当てる、比例配分する
▸Actual indirect factory overhead was *prorated* to producing and service departments. 実際製造間接費は、製造部門とサービス部門に比例配分しました。

proration 名 配賦、比例配分（＝pro rata allocation）、割当て（＝prorating）

prospects 名 見通し、予想、先行き、将来性、見込み、可能性、期待、メド
　demand prospects 需要見通し
　earnings prospects 収益見通し、収益予想
　economic prospects 経済見通し、景気見通し
　future prospects 将来の見通し、将来性
　prospects for growth 成長見通し、成長力、業績見通し、景気見通し、景気の先行き（＝growth prospects）
　short-term prospects 短期見通し
▸Financial institutions, concerned about MMC's future *prospects*, began calling in the company's loans. 金融機関が、三菱自動車の先行きを懸念して、同社への融資回収に動いた。
▸We are confident about the long-term *prospects* for our business. 当社の長期事業見通しについては、私ども経営陣は自信を持っております。

prospectus 名 目論見書（＝listing particulars)、発行目論見書、〈会社の〉設立趣意書、事業要綱、保険案内書、案内、内容見本
　final prospectus 最終目論見書
　listing prospectus 上場目論見書
　pathfinder prospectus 募集目論見書
　preliminary prospectus 仮目論見書
　prospectus issue 目論見書の発行
　prospectus of promotion 会社設立趣意書、会社設立目論見書

　目論見書とは ➡ 有価証券の募集や売出しの際、有価証券や発行者の内容を説明した文書。株式や投資信託など有価証券を購入する投資家のための資料として、証券取引法で販売会社に交付が義務付けられている。投資信託の場合は、約款の内容や運用体制、リスク要因、申込み手数料などが記載される。

▸A *prospectus* must include certain details stipulated by the Banking Commission, such as shareholdings, a comparison of the last five annual reports, capital review and others. 目論見書には、株主情報や過去5年間の年次報告書比較、資本金の推移など、銀行委員会が定めた特定の詳細事項も記載しなければならない。

protection 名 保護、保全、保証、保障、補償、対策
　apply for protection from creditors 会社更生手続きを申請する、資産保全を申請する
　asset protection 財産保全
　blanket protection on bank deposits 銀行預金全額保証
　call protection 任意償還権不行使期間
　consumer protection 消費者保護
　customer protection 顧客保護
　debt protection 債権保護水準、債権者保護、債務返済能力
　environmental protection 環境保護
　income protection 利益保護
　debtholder [debt holder] protection 債権有者保護
　insurance protection 保険保障
　lien protection 先取特権
　price protection 価格保全
　protection of intellectual property 知的所有権の保護、知的財産の保護
　protection of personal information 個人情報保護
▸Reserves are established for price *protection* and cooperative marketing programs with distributors. 価格保全や販売業者との協調販売計画

のために，引当金が設定されています。

provide 動 提供する，供給する，与える，付与する，販売する，創出する，調達する，発生する，設定する，定める，算定する，計上する，引当計上する，発表する（⇒**contingency**）

cash provided from financing activities 財務活動に伴う資金の調達，財務活動から生じた資金

provide for ... …に備える，…に引き当てる，…を算定する，定める，規定する，計上する（⇒**Rona awards**）

provide liquidity 流動性を提供する，流動性を供給する

provide the required capital 必要資本を調達する

working capital provided from other sources その他から得た運転資本

▸Our business is asset management and we do not directly *provide* any service or manufacture any product. 当社の業務は資産の運用であり，サービスを提供するとか製品を製造するということは，直接的にはしておりません。

▸We did not *provide* for deferred taxes on the gain. 当社は，この利益に対して繰延べ税金は計上しませんでした。

provider 名 提供者，請負業者，業者，企業，インターネット接続業者，ネット接続会社，プロバイダー

cash provider 資金提供者（＝capital provider）

content provider 出店企業，コンテンツ・プロバイダー

credit enhancement provider 信用補強提供者

credit support provider 信用補填提供者，信用補完提供者

information provider 情報提供者《略 IP》

monopoly provider 独占企業

service provider サービス会社，サービス企業

solution provider ソリューション請負業者，ソリューション・サービス業者

▸To avoid sinking into a negative net worth, the firm is seeking ¥300 billion in financial aid from capital *providers*. 債務超過に陥るのを避けるため，同社は資金提供者に3,000億円の金融支援を要請している。

provision 動 引当金を計上する，引当金を繰り入れる

▸Banks have *provisioned* sufficiently against bad loans. これまでのところ，銀行は不良債権に対して引当金[不良債権引当金，貸倒れ引当金]を十分計上している。

provision 名 準備金，引当金，引当金繰入れ，引当金繰入れ額[充当額]，引当金計上，計上，拠出，提供，用意，準備，規定，条項（⇒**housing loan**）

準備金と引当金について➡「準備金」には，一般にprovisionよりreserveやallowanceが使用されることが多い。日本の場合，「準備金」は法定準備金(legal capital reserves, legal reserves, legally required reserves)である資本準備金(capital reserve)，利益準備金(profit reserve)や価格変動準備金(reserve for price fluctuation)などにだけ用いられている。これに対して「引当金」は，将来の支出にあてるためにあらかじめ準備しておく資金のことである。

additional provisions 引当金の積み増し

annual provision for pension cost 年金原価の年次計上額

bad debt provision 貸倒れ引当金

bolster provisions 引当金を積み増す（＝increase provisions）

capital provision 資金提供

contingency provisions 危険準備金（＝contingency loss provisions）

establish a provision for ... …の引当金を設定する

general provisions 一般引当金，予算総則

in provisions for ... …の引当金として

income before provisions 引当金繰入れ前利益，引当金前の利益

increase provisions 引当金を積み増す

life insurance provision 生命保険準備金

loss provision 損失引当金，損失準備金（＝loss reserve）

net interest revenue after provision for credit losses 貸倒れ引当金繰入れ後正味受取り利息

non-life net technical provisions 損害保険の正味責任準備金

operating profits before bad debt provisions 貸倒れ引当金前の業務利益，貸倒れ引当金繰入れ前の業務利益

pre-provision earnings 引当金計上前利益

provision for business restructuring 事業再編成引当金，事業再編成引当金繰入れ額（⇒**relocate**）

provision for credit losses 貸倒れ引当金，貸倒れ引当金繰入れ額

provision for depreciation 減価償却引当金

provision for disasters 災害準備金，異常危険準備金

provision for discount allowance 売上割引当金

provision for doubtful debts 貸倒れ引当金，貸倒れ引当金繰入れ額（＝bad debt provision,

provision for bad debts, provision for doubtful accounts)
provision for loss contingency 偶発損失引当金
provisions for liabilities and charges 負債・費用性引当金
retirement provisions 退職給与引当金繰入れ額
risk provision 危険引当金, リスク引当金
special provision 特別引当金
tax provision 納税引当金, 法人税等額
writeback of provisions 引当金の戻し入れ
▸Nonbank firms are forced to raise *provisions* by a recent accounting rule change. 今回の会計規則の変更で, ノンバンク(銀行以外の金融機関)各社は引当金の積み増しを迫られている。

provision for business restructuring activities 事業再編成作業の引当金
▸In the third quarter of 2007, we recorded $300 million in *provision for business restructuring activities*. 2007年第3四半期に, 当社は事業再編成作業の引当金として3億ドルを計上しました。

provision for income taxes 法人税等引当金, 法人税等充当額, 法人税等繰入れ額, 法人税等計上額, 納税引当金
▸The 2007 *provision for income taxes* was $142 million (effective tax rate of 22 percent) compared with a 2006 provision of $128 million (effective tax rate of 29 percent). 2007年の法人所得税等引当金[法人税等計上額]は, 2006年の1億2,800万ドル(実効税率29%)に対して, 1億4,200万ドル(同22%)でした。

proxy 🔢 代理人, 代行者, 代理行為, 代理権, 代理委任状, 委任状, 議決権行使委任状, 指標, 比較対象, プロキシ[プロクシー]
by proxy 代理人を立てて, 代理で, 委任状で
form of proxy 代理人様式, 委任状用紙, 委任状カード (=proxy form)
index proxy 指標
joint proxy 共同委任状
proxy card 代理人カード, 代理投票カード, 代理投票用紙 (=proxy voting card)
proxy committee 議決権代理行使委員会
proxy fight [battle, contest] 委任状争奪戦, 委任状合戦, 代理人競争
proxy for the market 市場の指標
proxy material 委任状参考資料
proxy regulation 委任状規制
proxy rule 委任状規則
proxy server 代理サーバー, プロキシ・サーバー
proxy solicitation 委任状勧誘
proxy vote 代理投票
single proxy 単独委任状
solicitation of proxies 議決権行使委任状勧誘
standing proxy 常任代理人
voting by proxy 代理人による議決権の行使
▸Over 180 million shares, or about 62 percent of total shares outstanding, were represented at the annual meeting in person or by *proxy*. 定時株主総会には, 1億8,000万株(発行済み株式総数の約62%)以上を所有する株主が出席, または委任状を提出しました。

proxy form 代理人様式, 委任状用紙, 委任状カード, 委任状 (=form of proxy; ⇒**participant**)
▸Please sign and return the enclosed *proxy form* in the envelope provided as soon as possible. 同封の委任状[委任状用紙]は, ご署名の上, 所定の封筒でできるかぎり速やかにご返送ください。

proxy statement 代理勧誘状, 代理権勧誘状, 委任状, 委任状説明書, 議決権代理行使勧誘状, プロクシー・ステートメント
▸The *Proxy Statement* includes biographies of the Board's nominees for director and their principal affiliations with other companies or organizations, as well as the items of business to be voted on at the Annual Meeting. 議決権代理行使勧誘状には, 定時株主総会で票決される議案のほかに, 取締役会で選出された取締役候補者の略歴や取締役候補者の他の会社・組織との主な協力・兼任関係などが記載されている。

proxy voting card 投票委任用紙, 代理投票用紙 (=proxy card)
▸Notices of Annual Meeting, Proxy Statement and *Proxy voting Card* are mailed to each stockholder in March. 定時株主総会開催通知, 委任状説明書と投票委任用紙は, 3月に各株主に郵送されています。

public 🔢 一般の人々, 公衆, 社会, 顧客, …界, …層
▸Japan Airlines Corp. decided to issue new shares to the *public* at ¥211 per share. 日本航空は, 公募増資の新株発行価格を1株当たり211円とすることを決めた。
▸Sale to the *public* of shares in our subsidiaries will reinforce the Corporation's value. 当社子会社の株式公開で, 当社の資産価値は今後, 拡大するものと思われます。

public 🔢 公の, 公的, 公共の, 社会的, 公開の
go public 株式公開する, 株式を上場する, 秘密情報を公開する (⇒**going public**)
public bidding 公開入札, 一般競争入札
public company 上場企業, 株式公開会社, 株

式公開企業, 上場会社 (＝publicly held company)

Public Company Accounting Oversight Board 米上場企業会計監視委員会《略 **PCAOB**》(⇒ **PCAOB**)

public corporation 株式公開企業, 公団, 公社, 特殊法人, 公共企業体, 公共団体, 公益法人

public debt 公債

public fund injection 公的資金の注入

public funds 公的資金, 公金, 公費 (＝public money, taxpayers' money)

public limited company 公開有限責任会社, 株式会社

public pension benefits 公的年金給付

public pension plan 公的年金制度, 公的年金 (＝public pension system)

public tender period 株式公開買付け期間, TOB 期間 (＝public tender offer period)

▸Google Inc. plans to go *public* by selling $2.7 billion in stock through an online auction. 米インターネット検索サービス最大手のグーグルが, ネット・オークションによる27億ドルの株式発行で新規株式公開を計画している。

public enterprise 株式公開会社, 公共企業体, 公企業

public listing 株式上場

▸The *public listing* of the firm, with the market value this creates, helps to reinforce the value of ABC Inc.'s own shares. 同社の株式上場は, ABCの市場価値を高めるとともに, ABCの自社株の株価強化にも役立っている。

public offering 株式公開, 株式公募, 公募, 公募増資, 売出し (＝going public, primary offering, public stock offering; ⇒**initial public offering**, **net proceeds**, **proceeds from the public offering**)

公募と売出しについて ➡ 一般投資家を対象に, 有価証券の取得の申込みを勧誘することを, 株式公開という。有価証券が新規発行の場合はprimary offering(募集・公募), 既発行の場合はsecondary offering(売出し)と呼ばれる。私募については, private placementの項を参照

public offering bond 公募債

public offering of bonds on fixed conditions 定率公募

▸During the first nine months of 2007, the Company completed a *publc offering* in Canada of $150 million in Debentures, due 2018. 2007年1-9月期に, 当社はカナダ国内で満期2018年の社債1億5,000万ドルの公募発行を完了しました。

public offering price 公募価格

▸We have signed an underwriting agreement with Merrill Lynch Canada Inc. for the issue of three million common shares at a *public offering price* of $18 per share. 当社は, 普通株式300万株を1株18ドルの公募価格で発行するため, メリルリンチ・カナダ社との募集引受契約に調印しました。

public ownership 株式公開, 上場企業

open up to public ownership 株式を公開する

public relations 広報, 広報活動, 広報宣伝活動, パブリック・リレーションズ, ピーアール《略 **PR**》(企業や各種団体などの業務・活動内容や商品, サービスに関する情報を社会, 消費者に伝える仕事)

public relations advertising ピーアール広告, PR広告

public relations exercise 対外宣伝

public relations officer 広報担当者, 渉外係《略 **PRO**》

public tender offer 株式公開買付け《略 **TOB**》(＝takeover bid, tender offer, TOB)

▸Investors must use a *public tender offer* if they seek to acquire more than one-third of stocks issued by any listed corporation through off-market trading. 市場外取引で上場企業が発行した株式の3分の1超を投資家が取得する場合, 投資家は株式公開買付け(TOB)を実施しなければならない。

▸The Murakami Fund responded to the *public tender offer* by selling all of its Hanshin shares to further the integration of Hanshin and Hankyu. 村上ファンドは, 阪神と阪急の経営統合を促進するため, 保有する阪神株を全株売却して株式公開買付け(TOB)に応じた。

publicly held company 公開会社, 株式公開企業, 上場会社, 上場企業 (＝publicly owned company, publicly traded company)

▸Web search leader Google Inc., in its first earnings report as a *publicly held company*, posted quarterly net income and revenue that more than doubled on strong advertising revenues. インターネット検索最大手のグーグルは, 上場会社として初の決算(7-9月期決算)で, 広告収入が伸びたため四半期純利益と売上高が前年同期の2倍超となった。

publicly owned company [**corporation**] 株式公開企業, 公開会社, 上場企業 (＝publicly quoted company, publicly traded company)

▸After an initial public offering of its common

stock in September 2006, the firm became the largest *publicly owned* equipment leasing and financing *company*. 2006年9月の普通株初公開後、同社は機器リースおよび金融部門で国内最大の公開会社になった。

pull out of ... …から撤退する、…から手を引く
▸The firm effectively *pulled out of* the energy market. 同社は事実上、エネルギー市場から撤退した。

purchase 動 買い取る、買い付ける、購入する、引き受ける、仕入れる、買収する、取得する（＝buy）
purchased cost 仕入原価
purchased fund 取得資金、市場性資金
purchased option 買いオプション
▸The company is considering directly *purchasing* a majority stake in Japan Telecom Co. 同社は、日本テレコムの過半数株式の直接取得を検討している。
▸We *purchase* essentially all cardholder receivables under an agreement with the company which issues the cards. 当社は、基本的にカード発行会社との契約に基づいてカード保有者に対する債権をすべて買い取っています。
▸We *purchased* the net assets of the company for $600,000 during 2007. 当社は、2007年度に同社の純資産を60万ドルで取得しました。

purchase 名 買取り、買付け、買入れ、購入、購買、調達、調達先、引受け、仕入れ、仕切、取得、獲得、パーチェス（⇒stock purchase plan）
bulk purchase 一括購入
corporate purchase 企業買収
equity purchase 株式取得
gross purchases 総仕入高
material purchase 材料購入、材料購入、材料仕入れ、材料受入れ
offshore purchase 域外調達
purchase and assumption method [system] 資産・負債継承方式、P&A方式
purchase and operating expenses 売上原価および営業費
purchase cost 仕入原価、購入原価（＝purchasing cost）
purchase goodwill 買入のれん
purchase of business 企業取得、企業買収、買収、営業の譲り受け
purchase of common shares for cancellation 消却のための普通株の購入
purchase of loans 債権買取り（＝purchase of debts）
purchases and sales of treasury stock 自己株式の取得および売却
redemption by purchase 買入償却
replacement purchase 買替え
returned purchase 仕入戻し品
▸*Purchases* of our strongest product line were deferred by some of our major customers. 当社の最も強力な製品ラインの購入を、一部の顧客が延期しました。

purchase method パーチェス方式、パーチェス法、買収法、買収方式（＝purchase method of combination）
▸Acquisitions of companies are accounted for using the *purchase method*. 企業の取得は、パーチェス法を採用して会計処理されています。

purchase order 発注書、注文書、購入注文書、購入指図書、仕入注文書
▸We issued a *purchase order* of merchandise to the company at a total price of US $1,000,000. 当社は、同社に総額で100万米ドルの商品注文書を発行した。

purchase price 購入価格、買入価格、買取り価格、買付け価格、取得価格、買収価格、仕入価格、仕入値段（＝purchasing price）

purchase right 購入権
▸Each outstanding share of the Company's common stock carries with it one-quarter of a preferred share *purchase right*. 当社の発行済み普通株式には、1株に付き0.25単位の優先株式購入権が付与されています。

purchaser 名 買い主、買い手、買取り人、購買者、購入者、得意先（⇒payment）
▸*Purchasers* are able to make on-the-spot payments through various financial institutions. 購入者は、各種金融機関を通じて即時決済することができる。

purchasing 名 購入、購買、仕入れ、買取り、取得
mass purchasing 大量購入、大量仕入れ
purchasing expenses 仕入費用
purchasing power gain or loss 購買力損益、購買力利得または損失、貨幣購買力損益（＝monetary gain or loss, gain or loss in purchasing power）
purchasing price 購入価格、取得価格、買取り価格（＝purchase price）
▸The RCC's main function was *purchasing* of loan credits from failed financial institutions and then collecting the money. 整理回収機構（RCC）の主な業務は、破綻金融機関からの債権買取りとその金(債権)の回収であった。

purpose 名 目的, 意図, 決意, …上, 用途 (⇒ temporary differences)
- **allowance for special purpose** 特別引当金, 特別用途引当金
- **business purpose** 事業目的
- **cash flow purpose** 資金繰りの目的
- **for financial reporting purposes** 財務報告上, 財務会計上
- **for financial statement and income tax reporting purposes** 会計上および税務上
- **for financial statement purposes** 財務諸表上の, 財務書類上の, 財務会計上
- **for general accounting purpose** 財務会計上
- **for income tax purposes** 税務会計上, 税務上
- **for plan purposes** 年金制度の目的上
- **for tax purposes** 税務上
- **general purpose financial statements** 一般目的財務書類
- **purpose loan** 目的貸付け
- **purpose of loan** 資金使途
- **specific purpose statements** 個別目的財務諸表
▸We consider temporary cash investments to be cash equivalents for cash flow reporting *purposes*. 当社は, キャッシュ・フロー報告上, 短期投資を現金等価物と見なしています.

PV 現在価値 (**present value**の略)

PV ratio 限界利益率, PV比率 (**profit volume ratio**の略)

Q q

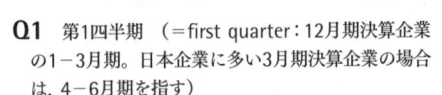

Q1 第1四半期（=first quarter：12月決算企業の1-3月期。日本企業に多い3月決算企業の場合は、4-6月期を指す）
▶In the *Q1* of 2007, we issued 19 million common shares for net cash proceeds of $244 million. 2007年第1四半期に、当社は普通株式1,900万株を発行して、2億4,400万ドルの純資金を調達しました。

Q2 第2四半期（=second quarter）
▶*Q2* operating revenues were $1,819 million. 第2四半期の営業収益は、18億1,900万ドルでした。

Q3 第3四半期（=third quarter）
▶The Corporation's *Q3* consolidated net income improved 8.7 percent to $301 million. 当社の第3四半期の連結純利益は、前年同期比8.7％増の3億100万ドルでした。

Q4 第4四半期（=fourth quarter）
▶Net income for the *Q4* of 2007 was higher than for the same period last year. 2007年第4四半期の純利益は、前年同期の水準を上回りました。

QC 品質管理（**quality control**の略）

QSPE 適格特別目的事業体（**qualifying special purpose entity**の略）

quadruple 動 4倍にする、4倍増にする、4倍になる、4倍増になる
▶Operating revenues of our telecommunications operating subsidiaries in the first quarter of 2007 *quadrupled* over the same period last year. 通信事業子会社の2007年第1四半期の営業収益は、前年同期比で4倍増加しました。

qualified 形 限定付き、条件付きの、適格の、有資格の
qualified auditor's report 限定付き監査報告書、限定意見監査報告書、限定意見報告書（=qualified audit report, qualified auditor report, qualified opinion report）
qualified pension plan 適格年金制度、適格退職年金
qualified personnel 適格従業員、有資格者（⇒ **judgment**）
qualified resident 適格居住者
qualified stock option 条件付きストック・オプション
tax qualified pension plan 適格退職年金

qualifying special purpose entity 適格特別目的事業体《略 QSPE》

quality 名 質、品質、品位、特質、特性、良質、優良、高級、内容、優良品、クオリティ
asset quality 資産内容、資産の質
credit quality 信用の質、信用度、信用力
debt quality 債券の質、債券の信用力
low quality earnings 低質の利益
management quality 経営の質
merchantable quality 商品性
order quality 受注内容
product quality 製品の品質
quality improvement 品質改善
Quality Management Institute 品質管理協会《略 QMI》
quality of earnings 利益の質、収益の質、収益内容
quality standard 品質基準、品質標準、品質規格
▶GM has been intensifying efforts to reduce costs and improve *quality*. GMは、コスト削減策と品質改善策を強化している。
▶The bank's planned acquisition of a controlling

stake in Nippon Shinpan Co. will only have a limited impact on the credit *quality* of the bank. 同行が日本信販の支配持ち分（発行済み株式の50％超）の取得を計画しているが、これによる同行の信用力への影響はごく限られるものと思われる。

quality control 品質管理《略 QC》（＝quality management)
　companywide quality control 全社的品質管理
　quality control activity QC活動 （＝quality movement)
　quality control circle QCサークル
　Statement on Quality Control Standards 品質管理基準書
　total quality control 全社的品質管理, 総合品質管理
　▶Mitsubishi Fuso will strive to regain lost consumers' confidence by drastically restructuring its *quality control* section. 三菱ふそうは、品質管理部門の抜本改編により、失った消費者の信頼回復に取り組む方針だ。

quality management standards 品質管理基準
　▶Fujiya and Yamazaki Baking Co. signed a memorandum of understanding on Yamazaki's assistance, which will be based on U.S. *quality management standards*. 不二家と山崎製パンは、米国の品質管理基準に基づく山崎製パンの支援に関する基本合意書に署名した。

quantity 名 量, 数量, 大量
　contract quantity 契約数量
　economic order quantity 経済的発注量
　increase the quality and quantity of products 製品の品質向上［高級化］と量の拡大を図る
　inventory quantities 棚卸し資産数量
　minimum order quantity 最低発注量, 最低発注数量
　order quantity 注文量, 注文数量
　output quantity 生産量, 生産数量 （＝production quantity)
　production quantity 生産量
　quantity buying 大量仕入れ, 大量購入
　quantity discount 数量割引 （＝volume discount)
　quantity shipped 出荷数量, 積載数量, 積送数量
　quantity system 定量発注システム
　sales quantity 販売数量
　unit quantity 単位量, 単位数
　▶Labor is now evaluated only in terms of *quantity*, or how many hours a worker toils, by the homogenization of labor. 労働の均質化により、労働は現在、量によって、つまり労働時間の長さによってだけ評価されるようになった。

quarter 名 四半期（1年の4分の1、つまり3か月を指す。暦年の第1四半期は、1月1日から3月31日までの3か月のこと)
　fiscal quarter 会計四半期
　for the quarter 当四半期
　for three consecutive quarters 3四半期連続して、3四半期連続
　from the previous quarter 前期比
　quarter-end close 四半期末終値
　the April-June quarter 4－6月期（日本の3月期決算企業の第1四半期にあたる)
　the first quarter 第1四半期
　the first quarter as a whole 四半期全体
　the fourth quarter 第4四半期
　the last quarter 第4四半期, 前期
　the preceding quarter 前期 （＝the previous quarter)
　the second quarter 第2四半期
　the third quarter 第3四半期
　▶For the *quarter*, shipments, revenues and earnings exceeded those of a year ago. 当四半期は、出荷高、収益と利益が前年同期を上回りました。

quarter point 0.25％
　▶The latest rate increase marked the 15th consecutive *quarter-point* adjustment since June 2004. 今回の利上げで、2004年6月から15回連続0.25％の調整となった。

quarterly 形 四半期の, 四半期ベースの, 四半期別, 四半期ごとの, 年4回の, 前期比
　on a quarterly basis 四半期ベースで （⇒ **straight bond)**
　quarterly consolidated business results 四半期連結決算 （＝quarterly consolidated settlement of accounts)
　quarterly earnings 四半期利益
　quarterly earnings report 四半期決算, 四半期決算報告, 四半期報告, 四半期報告書
　quarterly earnings statement 四半期決算, 四半期報告 （＝quarterly statement of earnings)
　quarterly financial data 四半期財務情報
　quarterly financial information 四半期財務情報
　quarterly financial reporting 四半期財務報告
　quarterly financial statements 四半期財務諸表, 四半期財務書類
　quarterly group net profit 四半期連結純利益, 四半期連結税引き後利益 （⇒**strong sales)**
　quarterly income statements 四半期損益計算書

quarterly increase 四半期の伸び率, 前期比伸び率

quarterly information (unaudited) 四半期情報 (未監査)

quarterly operating profit 四半期営業利益

quarterly release system 四半期開示制度

quarterly reporting of interim earnings 四半期報告

quarterly settlement 四半期決算

quarterly statement 四半期報告書 (=quarterly report)

quarterly statement of earnings 四半期報告, 四半期報告書

quarterly 副 年4回, 四半期ごとに, 3か月ごとに, 毎季に

▸Some listed companies have already started issuing earnings reports *quarterly*.　上場企業の一部は, 業績報告書の四半期発表をすでに開始している。

quarterly dividend 四半期配当, 四半期配当金 (⇒during the year)

▸On November 1, 2007, the board of directors approved a 45% increase in the *quarterly dividend* on common stock.　2007年11月1日, 取締役会は, 普通株式の四半期配当の45%増額を承認しました。

quarterly earnings per common share 普通株式1株当たり四半期純利益, 1株当たり四半期純利益

▸The sum of *quarterly earnings per common share* may not be the same as earnings per common share for the year.　普通株式1株当たり四半期純利益の合計は, 事業年度の普通株式1株当たり純利益と同額とならない可能性もあります。

quarterly growth 四半期の伸び, 四半期の伸び率, 四半期の成長［成長率］

▸The latest GDP figures marked the fifth consecutive *quarterly growth* in the domestic economy.　GDP速報値によると, 国内経済は5四半期連続のプラス成長となった。

quarterly net loss 四半期純損失, 四半期税引き後損失, 税引き後四半期赤字

▸UFJ Holdings, Inc. posted a *quarterly net loss* of ¥91 billion as costs to clean up its bad loans mounted.　UFJホールディングスは, 不良債権処理費用が増加したため, 税引き後で910億円の四半期赤字となった。

quarterly net profit 四半期純利益, 四半期税引き後利益, 税引き後四半期黒字

▸Citigroup's *quarterly net profit* will be significantly lower than the same period a year earlier.　米大手銀行シティグループの四半期純利益は, 前年同期を大幅に下回る見込みだ。

quarterly performance 四半期業績

▸This improved *quarterly performance* was due mainly to the company's contribution.　当四半期の業績改善は, 主に同社の貢献によるものです。

quarterly profit 四半期利益

▸*Quarterly profit* for the period ending Aug. 31 rose to $2.85 billion, or $6.13 per share, compared to $1.55 billion, or $3.26 per share, a year earlier.　6－8月期決算の四半期利益は, 前年同期の15億5,000万ドル(1株当たり3.26ドル)に対して, 28億5,000万ドル(1株当たり6.13ドル)に増加しました。

quarterly report 四半期報告書, 四季報 (= quarterly statement: 四半期ごとの企業の決算報告書; ⇒annual report, Form 10-Q)

　四半期報告書とは➡「quarterly report」と呼ばれる四半期報告書は, SECに登録している米国企業の場合は毎年, 四半期ごとにSECに提出する義務がある。

　四半期とは1年の4分の1, つまり3か月を指し, 暦年の第1四半期は1月1日から3月31日までの3か月を意味する。ただし, ここで重要なことは, 暦年(calendar year)と事業年度(business year, financial year, fiscal year)との違いである。暦年は文字どおり暦上の1月から12月までの1年を指すのに対して, 事業年度は各企業によって, また国によっても違う。日本では4月1日から翌年の3月31日までを1事業年度(企業の会計年度)としているところが多く, アメリカでは事業年度と暦年が同じで, 1月1日からスタートして12月31日に事業年度が終了するのが一般的である。そのため, 日本企業の決算期は通常3月, 米国企業の決算期は12月となる。

　なお, 事業年度が暦年と同じ場合に第1四半期(the first quarter)といえば1－3月期(January-March quarter)を指し, 第2四半期(the second quarter)といえば4－6月期(April-June quarter), 第3四半期(the third quarter)は7－9月期(July-September quarter), 第4四半期(the fourth quarter)は10－12月期(October-December quarter)を指す。また, 事業年度を半年(半期: half year)で区切って上期［上半期］と下期［下半期］に分けることもあり, この場合, 上期は英語でthe first half of the year, 下期はthe second half of the yearという。

　四半期ごとにSECへの提出が義務付けられているこれらの四半期報告書の様式はForm 10-Q (様式10-Q)で, 米国企業の場合, 提出期限は35日以内となっている(2002年7月に成立した企業改革法(サ

ーベンス・オクスレー法：Sarbanes-Oxley Act) に基づくSECの措置として, 2002年8月29日から, 従来の45日以内が35日以内に短縮された)。

ただし, 第4四半期は不要で, 記載する財務書類(財務諸表：financial statements) は要約版でよく, 一般に年次報告書で要求される財務書類注記(notes to financial statements) も省略できる。この要約財務書類(summarized financial statements) は監査(audit, auditing) を受ける必要がなく, 未監査(unaudited) の状態で提出することができ, 年次報告書と違って株主への四半期ごとの財務情報(quarterly financial information) の通知は義務付けられていない。

▶Though these changes are not yet reflected in this *quarterly report*, their impact will be felt in the performance of tomorrow. これらの変革[改革]の成果は, 当四半期の業績にはまだ反映されていませんが, そのインパクトは今後の業績に現われることと思います。

quarterly results 四半期業績, 四半期決算
(＝quarterly business results, quarterly settlement of accounts)
▶We are always reminded of our long-term corporate goals when we look to our *quarterly results*. 各四半期の業績を検討するにあたって, 私たちがつねに想起するのは, 当社の長期的な企業目標です。

quasi money 準通貨
▶*Quasi money* refers to time deposits and other types of savings at banks that can not be immediately cashed. 準通貨とは, 定期性預金のほかに, 即時に換金できない銀行預金のことをいう。

quasi subsidiary 準子会社
quick estimation 速報, 四半期速報
quote 動 見積もる, 値段[相場]をいう, 値をつける, 価格を提示する, 上場する
quoted company 上場会社, 上場企業 (＝listed company, publicly quoted company)
quoted investment 上場有価証券 (＝listed investment)
quoted market price 時価, 市場相場
▶The fair values of the Company's financial instruments have been determined based on *quoted* market prices and market interest rates, as of December 31, 2007. 当社の金融手段の公正価格は, 2007年12月31日現在の市場の相場と市中金利に基づいて決定されています。

quoted price 相場, 市場相場価格

R r

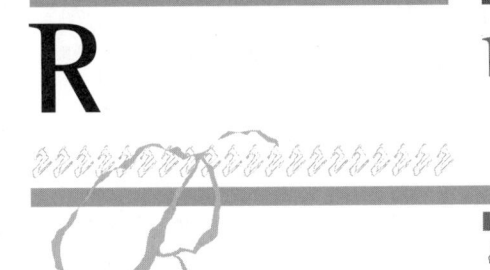

R&D 研究開発（research and developmentの略）
  R&D base 研究開発拠点
  R&D expense 研究開発費
  R&D functions 研究開発部門
  R&D intensive industry 研究開発集約型産業
  R&D project 研究開発プロジェクト
▶Investing about $30 million in *R&D*, we created new manufacturing techniques that eliminated ozone-depleting substances. 研究開発に約3,000万ドルを投じて、当社はオゾン層破壊物質を削減する新製造技術を開発しました。

R&D expenditures 研究開発費
▶We expense *R&D expenditures* as incurred until technological feasibility is established. 研究開発費は、技術面での実現可能性が確立されるまでは、発生時に費用処理しています。

R&D spending 研究開発費 （＝R&D expense, spending on research and development）
▶Most of our *R&D spending* is incurred in Canada. 当社の研究開発費の大半は、カナダで発生しています。

rack up 達成する、確保する （＝achieve）
▶In the July-September period, the company will *rack up* an extra cost of ¥51 billion for recalls of lithium-ion batteires for laptops. 7－9月期は、同社のノート型パソコン用リチウムイオン電池回収の特別費用が510億円に達する見込みだ。

raise 動〈資金などを〉調達する、〈料金・価格・資金などを〉引き上げる、上方修正する
  amount raised 調達額
  raise capital 資金を調達する、資本を調達する、資金を引き上げる、増資する、資金繰りをする
  raise cash through a private placement 第三者割当てで資金を調達する
  raise earnings substantially 収益を大幅に増やす
  raise equity 増資する
  raise external funds 外部資金を調達する （＝raise capital, raise money）
  raise funds 資金を調達する、資金を集める （＝raise capital, raise money）
  raise prices 値上げする
  raise the dividend 増配する、配当を引き上げる （＝increase the dividend）
  raise tier-one capital ティア1自己資本を調達する
▶It has been our practice since 1975 to *raise* the dividend every year. 1975年以来の慣行として、当社は毎年、配当引上げを実施してきました。
▶JAL plans to *raise* about ¥200 billion by issuing up to 750 million new shares both at home and abroad. 日航は、最終的に国内と海外で7億5,000万株の新株を発行して、約2,000億円調達する計画だ。
▶The funds were *raised* via loans from private-sector banks. 資金は、民間銀行からの借入金で調達された。
▶These ongoing efforts to *raise* productivity are part of our commitment to meet the challenge of intense competition. 現在実施しているこれらの生産性向上策は、熾烈な競争という課題に対応するための当社の取組みの一環です。
▶Time Warner had been seen as the front-runner for MGM, but Sony *raised* its offer. タイムワーナーがMGM買収の最有力候補とみられていたが、ソニーが提示額を引き上げた。

raising 名 資金の調達、募集、値上げ、延長

capital raising plan 資本調達計画, 資金調達計画
fund raising 資金調達, 資本調達, 募金 (＝fund procurement)
new equity raising 新株発行, 増資 (＝equity raising)
price raising 値上げ

rally 動 反騰する, 回復する, 盛り返す, 上昇する, 急騰する (＝rebound)
▸The recent stock market *rally* has boosted returns on the insurance premium management of four major life insurers. 最近の株式相場の上昇[株高]で, 4大生保各社の保険料運用収益が増加した.

rally 名 〈株価の〉反騰, 反発, 急騰, 上げ相場, 強気相場,〈景気などの〉持ち直し, 回復, 上昇, 上昇局面

range 名 範囲, 幅, 領域, 種類, 品揃え, 製品群, 限界, 射程, 射程距離, レンジ
 a new range of PCs パソコンの新製品群
 a wide range of product range 幅広い製品構成
 asset depreciation range 可能法定耐用年数, 法定耐用年数
 full [broad, whole, wide] range of 広範な, 広範囲の, 多種多様な, 幅広い
 in the range of ... ...の範囲内で
 long-range cash [fund] planning 長期資金計画
 middle range technology 中間技術
 price range 価格帯, 値幅, 協定価格帯
 product range 製品構成, 製品の機種, 種類, 製品群, 品揃え, 製品の幅, 車種
 range of funding options 資金調達の選択の幅
 range of industries 業種
 range of loss 損失の範囲, 損失の範囲額
 range trading もみ合い
 short-range business planning 短期経営計画
 target range 目標圏, 目標レンジ
 trading range 取引圏, 相場圏, ボックス圏, 取引レンジ
▸We offer the full *range* of telecommunications services. 当社が提供している電気通信サービス[通信サービス]は, 広範にわたっています.

rank 動 地位を占める, 並ぶ, 評価する, 位置付ける, ...の順位を決める, 等級をつける
 be ranked as ... ...と位置付けされる, ...と評価される
 be ranked top among ... ...でトップにランクされる, ...でトップを占める
 rank with ... ...と肩を並べる
▸Toyota *ranks* fifth, when compared with the U.S. magazine Forbes' ranking of global companies in terms of profits. 米フォーブス誌の世界企業利益ランキングと比較して, トヨタは5位にランクされる.

rank and file 平社員, 一般従業員, 一般職員, 一般労働者, 一般組合員, 一般大衆

rank-and-file 形 平社員の, 一般従業員の, 一般職員の
 rank-and-file employee 一般社員, 一般従業員, 平社員, 一般職員
▸Larger-than-planned *rank-and-file* employees have applied for early retirement in a program designed to cut 1,100 jobs. 1,100人の人員削減計画で, 計画を上回る数の一般従業員が希望退職に応募した.

rate 名 割合, 率, 金利, 歩合, 料金, 値段, 運賃, 相場, 等級, 速度, 進度, 程度, レート (⇒ **exchange rate, interest rate, prime rate**)
 basic rate 基本料金, 基本給(base salary), 基礎賃率(basic wage rate), 基準率, 所得税の基礎税率
 hourly rate plan 時間給制, 時間給制度
 loan rate 貸出金利
 market rate 市場金利, 市場相場, 市場レート, 銀行間相場
 rate cutting 料率引下げ, 賃率引下げ
 rate hike 利上げ, 金利引上げ, 料金引上げ, 値上げ
 rate of depreciation 減価償却率, 減価償却費率 (＝depreciation rate)
 rate of earnings 収益率
 rate of earnings on total capital 総資本純利益率
 rate of operation 操業度, 操業率 (＝rate of output)
 rate of stock turnover 棚卸し資産回転率, 商品回転率 (＝rate of stock-turn)
 rate sensitive assets and liabilities 金利感応資産・負債
 selling rate 売り相場
 yen rate 円相場, 円為替レート
▸Leading moneylending businesses make huge profits by securing loan funds from financial institutions at annual average *rates* of less than 2 percent. 大手の貸金業者は, 金融機関から平均年2％以下の金利で融資資金を調達して, 高い収益を上げている.

rate of return 利益率, 収益率,〈株式の〉配当利回り,〈債券の〉直接利回り, 利回り
 rate of return on asset 資産利益率
 rate of return on equity 株主資本利益率, 資本利益率
 rate of return on invested capital 投下資本

利益率
rate of return on investment 投資収益[利益]率, 資本利益率, 投資の運用利回り
rate of return on plan assets 年金資産の運用利益率
▶The weighted average discount rate used in determining the assumed long-term *rate of return* on plan assets was 8 percent for 2007. 年金資産の長期予想運用利益率[長期予想収益率]の算定に用いた加重平均割引率は, 2007年度は8%でした。

rating 名 格付け, 評価, 信用度, 視聴率 (⇒ credit rating, debt rating)
assign a rating of B2 B2の格付けを付与する
base rating 基礎格付け, 基本格付け
BBB long-term rating トリプルBの長期格付け
bond rating 債券格付け, 社債格付け (＝debt rating)
credit-risk rating 信用リスク格付け
experience rating 実績格付け, 実績格付け方式, 経験料率方式
financial strength rating 財務力格付け, 支払い能力格付け
implicit rating 間接格付け
independent rating agency 独立格付け機関, 独立した格付け機関 (＝independent credit rating agency)
investment-grade rating 投資適格の格付け
issuer's debt ratings 発行体の債券格付け
performance rating 人事考課 (＝service rating)
preliminary rating 予備格付け (＝provisional rating)
rating agency 格付け機関, 信用格付け機関, 格付け会社 (＝credit rating agency, rating company, rating firm, ratings service agency; ⇒ turnaround effort)
rating outlook 格付け見通し
seek a rating 格付けを申請する
▶Standard & Poor's revised upward its outlook on the long-term *ratings* on 11 regional banks. スタンダード＆プアーズは, 地銀11行の長期格付け見通しを上方修正した。

rating cuts 格下げ, 信用格付けの引下げ
▶*Ratings cuts* by rating firms can boost borrowing costs. 格付け会社が行った格下げ[信用格付けの引下げ]で, 借入コストが増大する可能性がある。

rating firm 格付け会社 (⇒rating cuts)
▶Both *rating firms* put Ford Motor Co. on review for possible downgrade. 両格付け会社は, フォードに対して[フォードの格付けを]格下げの方向で見直しに入った。

ratio 名 割合, 比率, 利益率, 収益率, 指標 (⇒ capital adequacy ratio, net worth ratio)
equity ratio 自己資本比率
liquidity ratio 流動性比率, 流動比率
ratio of debts to assets 資産に対する負債の比率, 負債・資産比率 (＝debt-asset ratio, debt to asset ratio：総資産に対する総負債の比率)
ratio of gross profit to net sales 売上高総利益率
ratio of net debt to net debt plus equity 金融債務比率
ratio of net profit to capital 資本利益率
ratio of net worth to the total assets 株主資本比率
ratio of operating profit to sales 売上高に対する営業利益の比率[割合], 営業利益率
ratio of profit to capital 資本利益率
ratio of shareholders' [stockholders'] equity 株主資本比率
▶Through continuing gains in annual earnings, it will be possible, over time, to adjust the payout *ratio* while still maintaining our dividend record. 年間利益の増大によって, 当社の配当実績を今後とも維持しながら, 時期が来たら配当性向を調整することは可能である。

rationalization 名 合理化
capacity rationalization 生産合理化, 設備合理化
industrial rationalization 産業合理化
labor rationalization 労働力の合理化
rationalization of distribution 流通合理化
rationalization of management 経営合理化
thorough rationalization 徹底した合理化
▶The firm made a $90 million provision, related to restructuring and *rationalization* of international operations. 同社は, 国際事業部門の再構築[リストラクチャリング]と効率化[合理化]に関連して, 9,000万ドルの引当金繰入れを行いました。

raw material 原料, 材料, 原材料, 素材 (⇒ material)
raw material cost 原材料費
raw materials consumption 原材料消費

RCF 手元キャッシュフロー (**retained cash flow** の略)

reacquisition 名 再取得
reacquisition price 再取得価格, 再購入価格

real 形 実際の, 実体の, 現実の, 実質の, 実質上の, 重大な, 不動産の, リアル
real deficit 実質赤字

real economy 実体経済, 実態経済
real effective exchange rate 実質実効為替レート （＝real effective FX rate）
real expenditure 実質的経費
real growth 実質経済成長, 実質伸び率 （＝real economic growth）
real profit 実質利益
real rate of return 実質収益率, 実質利回り
real value 実質価値, 実質値
▸Capital investment in the private sector is still sluggish and this will delay a full-fledged recovery in the *real* economy. 民間設備投資の動きがまだ鈍いので, 実体経済の本格的な回復は遅れる。

real estate 不動産 （⇒slump）
real estate gain 不動産売却益
real estate investment 不動産投資
real estate lending 不動産融資
real estate loss 不動産関連損失
real estate operations 不動産事業
▸The company earns revenue through *real estate* investment and through resuscitating failed financial institutions. 同社は, 不動産投資と経営破綻した金融機関を再生させることで収益を上げている。

realignment 再編成, 再編, 再調整, 再統合, 再提携, 組替え
business realignment 企業再編, 再編
industry realignment 業界再編
realignment of businesss units 事業部門の組替え
▸2006 and 2005 have been reclassified to reflect the *realignment* of various business units. 2006年度と2005年度は, 事業部門の組替えを反映させるため, 修正して再表示されています。
▸Debates have begun on the *realignment* of the NTT group's management structure. NTTグループの経営組織の再編に関する議論が始まった。
▸The new Corporate Law that went into effect in May 2006 has made company *realignment* much easier. 2006年5月から実施された新会社法で, 企業再編が以前よりはるかに容易になった。

realignment of the industry 業界再編
▸The liberalization of brokerage commissions on commodity futures trading has paved the way to potentially dramatic *realignment of the industry*. 商品先物取引の委託手数料の自由化で, 業界が劇的に再編される可能性が出てきた。

realignment strategy 再編戦略
▸The merger plan likely will affect the *realign-ment strategies* of other companies in the banking and securities industries. この統合計画は今後, 銀行・証券業界の他企業の再編戦略に影響を与えそうだ。

realizable 形 実現可能な
realizable profit 実現可能利益, 実現可能利潤
realizable value 実現可能価額（売価を基準にした資産の評価額）
▸The deferred tax assets are considered *realizable* considering past income and estimates of future income. 繰延べ税金資産は, 過去の所得と将来の推定所得を考慮すると, 実現可能であると思われます。

realization 名 実現（一般に「収益の実現」(realization of revenue）を意味することが多い。「収益」は, 財・サービスの引渡しが完了し, その対価として現金または現金等価物を受領したときに「実現」する）
income realization 利益の実現, 収益の実現
realization of gains 収益の実現
realization of profit and loss 損益の実現
revenue realization 収益の実現 （＝realization of revenue）

realize 動 実現する, 換価する, 現金に換える （⇒amount receivable or payable）
realize a profit on the property 財産を処分して利益を得る
realize capital gains キャピタル・ゲインを実現する
realize capital losses キャピタル・ロスを実現する
realize latent capital gains 含み益を実現する
▸Such income is not *realized* in cash currently but will be *realized* over the service life of the plant. これらの収益は, 当期中に現金収益としては実現せず, 当該設備の耐用年数にわたって実現します。

realized 形 実現した, 実現の要件を満たした, 実現済みの, 換価した
realized capital gains 実現資本利得, キャピタル・ゲインの実現額, キャピタル・ゲイン実現益, 実現キャピタル・ゲイン
realized gain (loss) 実現利得（損失）, 実現利益（損失）
realized gain on investment activities 投資活動による実現益
realized income 実現利益, 利益の実現 （＝realized profit）
realized loss 実現損失, 損失の実現
realized profit 実現利益 （＝realized income）

realized revenue 実現利益, 実現収益, 利益の実現
realized value 実現価値, 実現価額
realized yield 実効利回り
▶The bank's decline in net revenues reflects lower *realized* capital gains and non-accrual loans. 同行の営業利益の減少は、キャピタル・ゲインの実現額の低下と利息計上を停止した貸付け金の増大を反映しています。

real property 不動産, 不動産所有権
real property acquisition tax 不動産取得税
real property tax 固定資産税, 不動産税

reasonable 形 合理的な, 妥当な, 根拠のある, 相当な, 公正な, 適切な
reasonable assurance 合理的な確証, 合理的保証 (⇒misstatement)
reasonable basis 合理的な基礎, 合理的根拠
reasonable care 相当な注意
reasonable estimate 合理的見積り, 根拠のある見積り
reasonable price 適正価格, 合理的価格, 相当の代価
▶Our audits provide a *reasonable* basis for our opinion. 私どもの監査は、私どもの意見表明のための合理的根拠となっています。

rebate 名 割戻し, 払戻し, 返金, 還付金, 報奨金, 手数料, 戻し税, 割引, 控除, リベート
cash rebate 現金割戻し, 現金払戻し
quantity rebate 大量購入払戻し
tax rebate 税金の還付, 戻し税

rebuild 動 再構築する, 再建する, 再興する, 再生する, 回復する, 〈在庫などを〉積み増す, 建て替える, 復元する, 立て直す
▶Aeon Co. is a potential key player in efforts to *rebuild* Daiei Inc. イオンは、ダイエー再建を支援する有力な提携候補だ。

recall 動 リコール[無料回収・修理]する, 回収する, 撤回する, 取り消す, 召喚する, 呼び戻す, 解任[解職]する, 思い出す, 回想する
▶About 163,700, or 156,400 vehicles sold at home and about 7,300 vehicles exported, will be *recalled*. 国内販売分156,400台と海外輸出分約7,300台の約163,700台がリコール[改修・無償交換]される予定だ。

recall 名 欠陥車・欠陥品の回収, リコール[無料回収・修理], 無償修正, 撤回, 取消, 召喚, 呼び戻し, 復職, 〈公職者の〉解任請求, 解職[解職]権, 回想
loan recall 貸出回収
recall cost [expense] 回収費用
recall of advance 貸金回収

▶Sony booked the ¥51.2 billion battery *recall* cost for the July-September quarter. ソニーは、7-9月期に(パソコン用)充電池のリコール費用[回収費用]として512億円を計上した。

recapitalization 名 資本再編, 資本の再構成, 資本変更, 資本組入れ, 増資(「資本の再構成」は、(増資や減資のほかに、普通株の一部を優先株と組み替えたり、債券を株式と組み替えたりするなど、会社の資本構成(capital structure)を変更すること)
▶The firm plans *recapitalization* to raise funds for the construction of a new headquarters building. 同社は、新社屋の建設費用を調達するため、資本の再構成[増資]を計画している。

recapitalize 動 資本を再編する, 資本構成を修正[変更]する, 〈法定準備金などを〉資本に組み入れる
▶In an attempt to *recapitalize* itself, we raised ¥13 billion through a third-party share allotment. 資本再編のため、当社は第三者株式割当てで130億円を調達しました。

receipt 名 受領, 受取り, 領収, 収納, 受取証, 領収書, 証書, 受領額, 収入, 収入金額, 収入高, 入荷高
advance receipt 前受け金
American depositary receipt 米国預託証券
cash receipt 現金収入, 現金収入額
cash receipts and disbursements 現金収支
receipts and payments 収支状況, 現金収支
revenue receipt 売上収入
suspense receipt 仮受け金
warehouse receipt 倉荷証券
▶This accounts book indicates *receipts* and payments totaling about ¥80 million made between September and October. この会計帳簿には、9月と10月の収支状況(約8,000万円)が記載されている。

receivable 名 受取債権, 売上債権(企業の全取引から生じた売掛金や受取手形, 貸付け金, 未収金, 立替金などの受取勘定が含まれる), 売掛債権, 債権
defaulted receivables 不履行債権
finance receivables 金融債権
net receivables 純債権
nonperforming receivables 不良債権
outsranding receivables 債権残高
receivable from customers 顧客への債権
receivables financing 債権融資
receivables management 売掛債権の管理
receivables turnover 売上債権回転率, 受取勘定回転率
rentals receivables 受取リース料債権
sales of lease receivables リース債権の売却
▶Days sales outstanding in our core business de-

clined because of improved *receivables* management. 当社の主力事業の平均売上債権回転日数は、売掛債権の管理が改善したため、減少しました。
▸The improved gross margin percentage mainly reflects the maturation of the credit card *receivables* portfolio. 売上総利益率の改善は、主にクレジット・カード売掛債権ポートフォリオが成熟してきたことを反映しています。

receivable 形 受け取るべき、受領できる、支払われるべき、支払いを待っている、未収の
  commission receivable 未収手数料
  dividend receivable 未収配当金
  installment receivable 割賦売掛金、割賦未収金、割賦債権
  mortgage loan receivable 担保付き貸付け金
  refunds receivable 還付未収金
▸Accounts *receivable* balances were $1.3 million and $1.5 million at December 31, 2006 and December 31, 2007, respectively. 2006年12月31日および2007年12月31日現在の売掛金残高は、それぞれ130万ドルと150万ドルでした。

receive 動 受け取る、受領する、受け入れる、認める、受け付ける、〈資金を〉調達する、〈損害などを〉被る、歓迎する
  receive accrual accounting 発生主義会計で処理される
  receive dividends 配当金を受け取る
  receive funding from … …から資金を調達する
▸GM expects to *receive* about $14 billion from the sale of General Motors Acceptance Corp. GMは、金融子会社GMACの売却により、約140億ドルを確保する見通しだ。
▸The Corporation *received* some $200 million upon disposal of certain noncore assets. 当社は、一部の非中核的事業資産を売却して、2億ドル余りを受領しました。

recession 名 景気後退、不景気、不況、リセッション
▸The first quarter net income was slightly higher than for the same period last year, despite the effects of the lingering *recession*. 第1四半期の純利益は、長引くリセッションの影響にもかかわらず、前年同期をいくぶん上回りました。

reciprocal 形 相互の、相反する
  reciprocal arrangement 相互協定
  reciprocal share holding 株式持ち合い

reclassification 名 組換え、組換え再表示、振替、再分類

reclassify 動 組み替える、組替え再表示する、振り替える、再分類する (⇒conform to)

▸We *reclassified* certain amounts for previous years to conform with the 2007 presentation. 当社は、2007年度の表示方法[表示形式]に合わせて、過年度の金額の一部を組み替えました。

recognition 名 認識、計上、認可、許可、認知、認定、承認（会計上の「認識」は、ある会計項目を、資産・負債・収益・費用などとして会計帳簿や財務書類に正式に記帳・記載すること）
  basis of recognition 認識基準
  brand recognition ブランド認知
  expense recognition 費用の認識
  immediate recognition 即時認識、発生即費用、発生即費用原則
  immediate recognition as an expense 費用としての即時認識
  income recognition 利益の認識、利益計上
  loss recognition 損失の認識
  profit recognition 利益の認識
  recognition of gain and loss 損益の認識、利益と損失の認識
  recognition of latent reserves 含み益の実現
  recognition of pension liability 年金債務の計上
  revenue recognition 収益の認識（＝recognition of revenue）
▸Our *recognition* of these liabilities created additional deferred tax assets. 当社がこれらの債務を認識したことで、追加的な繰延べ税金資産が生じました。

recognition of revenue and expense 収益と費用の認識
▸There are timing differences in the *recognition of revenue and expense* for tax and financial statement purposes. 税務上と財務会計上とで、収益と費用の認識に期間差異がある。

recognize 動 認識する、計上する、費用処理する、認可する、許可する、認定する、承認する（＝recognise; ⇒long term contract）
  be recognized on a straight-line basis 定額法で費用処理する
  recognize income when the contract is completed 工事完成時に利益を認識する
  recognize revenues and expenses 収益と費用を認識する
  recognized in the statement of financial position 貸借対照表に計上した
▸Previously, we *recognized* costs for separations when they were identified. これまで当社は、休職については、休職が確認された時点でその費用[休職手当支払いの費用]を認識していました。

reconcile 動 調整する
▸This table shows the funded status of our postretirment benefit plans *reconciled* with the amounts recognized in the consolidated balance sheet.　この表は、退職後給付制度の基金の状態と連結貸借対照表上、認識された金額との調整を示しています。

reconciliation 名 調整, 調整表, 調整書
　bank reconciliation　銀行勘定調整
　reconciliation of results reported in accordance with generally accepted accounting principles (GAAP) in Canada with United States GAAP　カナダ会計基準と米国会計基準に従った場合に生じた差異の調整
　reconciliation of surplus　剰余金調整表, 剰余金調整書
　reconciliation of the effective tax rate and the statutory U.S. income tax rate　実効法人税率と米国法定連邦法人税率との調整
▸The *reconciliation* between those two amounts is as follows.　両者の金額の調整は、次のとおりです。

reconstruction plan　再建計画, 再建策, 経営再建策　（＝reorganization plan; ⇒**retirement**)
▸Crisis-stricken giant supermarket chain operator announced a fresh *reconstruction plan*.　経営危機に陥っている巨大スーパーが、新たな経営再建策を発表した。
▸The *reconstruction plan* was approved at a meeting of the company's board of directors.　再建策は、同社の取締役会で承認された。

record 動 記録する, 記帳する, 計上する, 評価する, 登記[登録]する, 表示する, 示す　(⇒**partnership interest**)
▸Amortization of the bond premium is *recorded* on the straight-line method.　社債プレミアムの償却は、定額法で行われています。
▸The seven major banking groups' midterm settlement of accounts is expected to *record* an estimated ¥1.95 trillion in latent gains.　大手7行・金融グループの中間決算では、推定で1兆9,500億円の含み益が出る見通しだ。

record 名形　記録, 最高記録, 過去最高, 過去最大, 成績, 登記, 登録, 動向, [形容詞的に]記録的な, 過去最高の, 空前の　(⇒**books of account**, **financial records**, **recurring profit**)
　accounting record　会計記録, 会計帳簿
　dividend record　配当実績　(⇒**ratio**)
　hit a record high　過去最高を記録する
　original record　原本記録
　post a record quarterly deficit　過去最高の四半期赤字を記録する, 四半期ベースで過去最高を記録する
　record date　配当基準日, 基準日, 名義書換え停止日, 登録日　(＝date of record)
　record earnings　過去最高益, 過去最高の利益
　record low　過去最低, 史上最低, 記録的な低水準
　record net profit　過去最高の純利益　(＝record-high net profit)
　record profit　最高益, 過去最高の利益
　stock record date　株式の名義書換え停止日
▸The FSA will issue an order to a consumer loan company to suspend business at all its branches for falsifying customers' *records*.　金融庁は、消費者金融会社に対して、顧客の取引履歴改竄で全営業店を対象とする業務停止命令を発動する見通しだ。
▸Total revenues were a *record*.　総収益は、過去最高となりました。
▸Toyota Motor Corp. announced *record* group sales and net profit for the half year to Sept. 30.　トヨタ自動車は、9月中間決算として過去最高の連結売上高と税引き後利益[純利益]を発表した。

recourse 名 償還請求, 償還請求権, 二次的の請求, 二次的支払い義務, 遡求
　endorsement without recourse　無担保裏書
　limited recourse　限定付き[制限付き]償還請求権
　recourse fund　不渡り手形の償還準備積立金
　recourse loan　遡求請求権付き貸付け金
　recourse obligation　償還義務, 二次的支払い義務
　right of recourse　償還請求権
　without recourse　遡求なし, 遡求権なし, 二次的支払い義務なし, 償還請求に応ぜず
▸This loss came from deducting *recourse* loans made to our senior management.　この損失は、当社の上級経営陣に対して行った遡求請求権付き貸付け金を控除したことで生じました。

recover 動 回復する, 〈貸出金などを〉回収する, 〈債権などを〉取り立てる
▸We expect to *recover* our negative net worth by the end of fiscal 2008.　2008年度末には、当社の債務超過は解消できる見通しです。

recovery 名 回復, 景気回復, 〈景気や市場の〉持ち直し, 相場の回復, 回収, 再建, 復興
　bad debt recovery　償却債権の取立て, 償却済み債権取立益
　capital recovery　資本の回収
　cost recovery　原価回収
　cost recovery basis [method]　原価回収法
　earnings recovery　業績回復, 収益の回復
　investment recovery　投資回収

signs of recovery 回復の兆し
zero recovery 全額回収不能
▶These listed companies literally achieved a V-shaped *recovery* after recording a combined net loss in fiscal 2001.　これらの上場企業は、2001年度に全社合計で赤字に転落した後、文字どおりV字型回復を達成した。

recurring 形 経常的な、定期的な
recurring audit 連続監査
recurring information 定期的情報
recurring margins 経常利益率
recurring operating losses 経常的な営業損失

recurring loss 経常赤字
▶The Corporation incurred ¥3 billion of *recurring losses* in its semiannual settlement of accounts.　当社は、9月の中間決算で30億円の経常赤字となりました。

recurring profit 経常利益（＝current profit, income before extraordinary items; ⇒**stream**)
　経常利益について➡売上高から販売・管理費を差し引いた営業利益に、預金の受取利息や保有株式の配当収入を加えたり、借入金の支払い利息などを差し引いたりして計算する。ただし、メーカーの工場売却や保有株式の売却による利益、リストラのための割増退職金の費用などは特別利益または特別損失と呼ばれ、経常利益には含まれない。経常利益は、日本では、企業の業績や中長期的な業況を知るのに最も適した指標とされている。
▶For JAL, a price hike of jet fuel by $1 per barrel means a drop of ¥5.5 billion in its *recurring profit* on a consolidated basis a year.　日航システムの場合、ジェット燃料の価格が1バレル当たり1ドル上昇すると、年間の連結経常利益［連結ベースで年間の経常利益］が55億円減る。

red 名 赤字（＝red ink; ⇒**after-tax balance, black, group net loss, net balance**)
be forced into the red 赤字に追い込まれる
company in the red 赤字企業、赤字法人（＝company operating in the red)
go into the red 赤字になる（＝fall into the red)
operate in the red 赤字経営する
out of the red 赤字を脱して
plunge into the red 赤字に転落する
remain in the red 赤字にとどまる
slip into the red 赤字に転落する（＝fall into the red)
▶Nomura is the first major Japanese financial institution to fall into the *red* because of problems stemming from U.S. subprime mortgage loans.　米国でのサブプライム・ローン問題で赤字に転落するのは、野村［野村ホールディングス］が日本の大手金融機関では初めてだ。
▶The company remained in the *red* for the fiscal year ended March 31, 2007 due to appraisal losses on its stockholdings.　同社の2007年3月期決算は、保有株式の含み損［評価損］で赤字にとどまった。

redeem 動 買い戻す、償還する、補填する、埋め合わせる
▶The company elected to *redeem*, prior to maturity on June 3, 2007, $120 million of first mortgage bonds on May 1, 2007.　同社は、2007年6月3日に満期が到来する前の2007年5月1日に、第一順位抵当権付き社債1億2,000万ドルを償還することを決定した。

redeemable 形 償還可能な、買戻しできる、交換できる
redeemable bond 随時償還社債、償還社債、随時償還公債
redeemable convertible preferred share 償還・転換可能優先株式
redeemable stock 償還株式（＝redeemable share)
▶Debt and preferred shares (*redeemable*) denominated in currencies other than the U.S. dollar are regarded as partial hedges of the corporation's net investments in related non-U.S. based self-sustaining operations.　米ドル以外の通貨建て債務と償還可能優先株式は、米国外に拠点を置く自立した関連事業に対する当社の純投資額の為替リスクを一部ヘッジするためのものです。

redemption 名 〈株式などの〉償還、〈投信などの〉解約（＝refundment, repayment; ⇒**secure** 動)
capital redemption 資本償還
mandatory redemption 定時償還
optional redemption 任意償還、随時償還
premium on redemption 償還プレミアム
redemption at fixed date 定時償還
redemption before maturity 期限前償還
redemption of maturity 満期償還
stock redemption 株式償還、株式の償還（＝redemption of stock)
▶In respect of our capital stock, there has not been any direct or indirect *redemption*, purchase, or other acquisition of any such stock.　当社の株式に関して、当社はこれまで当該株式の直接・間接の償還、買取りやその他の取得も行っていません。

redemption fund 償還基金

surplus for redemption fund 償還基金積立金

redeploy 動 配置転換する，再配置する，再配分する，移動する，改善する，有効利用する（＝relocate; ⇒**focus on**）
▸Operating internationally is forcing firms to reinvent their internal environments, reassess their markets, *redeploy* their resources, and change their thinking. 国際的に業務展開するにあたって，企業は社内体制の再検討や市場の再評価，経営資源の再配分，発想の転換などを迫られています。

redeployment 名 配置転換，再配備，再配置，配置替え，再配分，〈工場施設[工場・設備]の〉移動，〈工場施設の〉改善，有効利用，移動，転進（＝relocation）
▸To extend direct customer support, we launched the largest retraining and *redeployment* program in our history. 直接的な顧客支援を行うため，当社は過去[当社史上]最大規模の社員再研修・配置転換プログラムを開始しました。

redevelopment 名 再開発
▸We will establish a good, constructive relationship of trust with an eye to the *redevelopment* of the Hibiya area. 今後は日比谷地区の再開発を視野に入れて，良好で建設的な信頼関係を両社で築いて行きます。

reduce 動 減らす，削減する，低下させる，押し下げる，引き下げる，下げる，減少させる，低減する，緩和する，軽減する，解消する，控除する，短縮する
　reduce capital 減資する
　reduce funding costs 調達コストを引き下げる
　reduce gearing 負債比率を引き下げる
　reduce inventories 在庫を圧縮する
　reduce investment 投資を抑制する
　reduce overhead costs 製造間接費を削減する
　reduce production costs 生産コストを削減する
　reduce the profitability 収益性を低下させる
▸Sony wants to turn around the performance of the electronics division by *reducing* the number of products. ソニーは，製品の数を減らしてエレクトロニクス事業部の業績回復を目指している。
▸The company hopes to *reduce* production costs by boosting output volume. 同社は，生産量を大幅に増やすことで，生産コストの削減を目指している。
▸The Company's share of each associated company's income after tax is *reduced* by amortization of excess values and by the amount of dividends received. 各関連会社の税引き後利益に対する当社の持ち分は，投資超過差額の償却額及び受取配当金が控除されています。

▸U.S. and European banks gradually *reduced* their lines of credit to Japanese banks. 欧米の銀行は，邦銀に対するクレジット・ライン[貸出限度]を次第に引き下げた。

reduced 形 縮小した，減少した，割引した，…の縮小[減少，低下]（⇒**reform**⓶）
　reduced borrowing costs 調達コストの削減
　reduced losses 損失の減少，赤字縮小，赤字幅の縮小，損失幅の縮小（＝lower losses, smaller losses, reduction in losses）
　reduced profit 減益，利益の減少，利益逓減
　reduced sales 販売低下，販売の落ち込み，売上高の減少

reduction 名 削減，軽減，圧縮，短縮，引下げ，縮小，低下
　debt reduction 債務削減，債務減らし
　deficit reduction 赤字削減，財政赤字削減，赤字縮小
　expense reduction 経費削減
　income tax reductions 所得税減税
　inventory reduction 在庫削減
　personnel reduction 人員削減，従業員削減（＝staff reduction）
　price reduction 価格低下，価格の引下げ，値下げ
　reduction in [of] capital 減資，資本金の減額（＝capital decrease, capital reduction）
　reduction in operating expenses 営業経費の削減
　reduction of capital (stock) 減資（＝reduction in capital）
　reductions of long-term debt 長期債務の返済，長期債務減少
　risk reduction リスク軽減
　tax reduction 減税
　wage reduction 賃金引下げ
▸This economic recovery is mainly due to the increased exports and corporate restructuring efforts centered on debt *reduction*. 今回の景気回復の主な要因は，輸出拡大と債務減らしを中心とした企業のリストラ努力だ。

reengineer 動 業務を革新[変革]する，業務を根本的に革新する，リエンジニアリング
▸We are *reengineering* and centralizing support services for telecommunications services. 当社は現在，通信サービス部門に対する支援業務の根本的変革と集中化を進めています。

reengineering 名 業務革新，業務の根本的革新，リエンジニアリング（＝business reengineering）

reference 名 参考，参照，参照番号，照会，照会

番号, 照会人, 身元保証, 問合せ, 問合せ先, 委託, 付託, 関連, 関係, 参考人, 参考文献, 言及, 論及
accounting reference date 会計基準日
bank reference 銀行信用照会先
credit reference 信用照会先
cross reference 前後参照, 相互参照
examination by reference 照査
incorporation by reference 参照による組込み, 参照による編入
reference data 参照データ
reference level 基準レベル
reference number 参照番号, 照会番号
reference rate 指標金利
reference room 資料室
trade reference 信用照会先, 同業者信用照会先
▸All *references* to shares outstanding, dividends and per share amounts have been adjusted on a retroactive basis. 発行済み株式数と配当, 1株当たりの金額については, すべて過去に遡及して調整してあります.

refinance 動 借り換える, 切り換える, 資金を補充する, 再融資する (⇒**short-term borrowings**)
ability to refinance 借換え能力
refinance existing debt 債務[既存の債務]を借り換える (=refinance outstanding debt)
▸Interest expense declined because of benefits from *refinancing* long-term debt at favorable rates. 利息費用は, 長期負債の低金利での借換え効果で減少しました.

refinancing 名 借換え, 資金の再調達, 再融資, リファイナンス (=refinance; ⇒**call premium**)
bank refinancing 銀行融資の借換え
market access for refinancing 借換え目的の市場からの資金調達, 市場から資金調達して借り換える
mortgage refinancing モーゲージの借換え, 住宅ローンの借換え
the benefits of refinancing 借換えの効果
▸The benefits of *refinancing* were responsible for about half of the decline in interest expense in 2007. 借換えの効果は, 2007年度の支払い利息減少の約半分を占めています.

reflect 動 反映する, 示す, 記載する, 反映させる, 織り込む, 組み入れる, 適用する
▸The financial statements *reflect* the consolidated accounts of the Corporation and its subsidiaries. この連結財務書類は, 当社とその子会社の財務書類を連結したものです.
▸We did not restate our 2005 and 2006 financial statements to *reflect* the change in accounting for retiree benefits. 当社は, 2005年度と2006年度の財務書類[財務諸表]については, 退職者給付に関する会計処理の変更を反映させるための修正・再表示をしておりません.

reform 動 改革する, 改正する, 改善する, 改良する, 矯正する, 改める
▸In a move to *reform* its board of directors into a U.S.-style system of corporate governance, Sony Corp. will introduce a committee-based management system along with the revised Commercial Code. 取締役会を米国流の会社管理・運営方式に改革する動きとして, ソニーでは, 商法改正に伴って委員会ベースの経営システムを導入する.

reform 名 改革, 革新, 改正, 改善, 改良, 矯正, リフォーム
economic reform 経済改革
financial reform 金融改革
market reform 市場改革
production reform 生産革新
structural reform 構造改革
tax reform 税制改革
▸Out of the total reduced costs of about ¥110 billion, about ¥55 billion was attributed to the production *reforms*. コスト削減総額約1,100億円のうち, 約550億円は生産革新によるものだ.
▸Sony was the first company to announce a *reform* of its board under the revised Commercial Code. 改正商法に従って取締役会の改革を発表した会社は, ソニーが初めてだ.

refund 動 払い戻す, 返済する, 還付する, 弁済する, 借り換える, 償還する (=repay)
▸Deferred tax assets are essentially taxes paid in advance, which are expected to be *refunded* when the bank incurs losses. 繰延べ税金資産は本質的に前払いした税金で, 銀行が損失を被った時点で戻ってくる.

refund 名 返金, 払戻し, 〈税金の〉還付, 弁済, 弁償, 返済金, 弁済金, 借換え (=repayment)
guaranteed refund of savings deposits 普通預金[貯蓄性預金]の払戻し保証額
income tax refunds 還付税金, 法人税等の還付金
submit refund claims 税金の還付請求書を提出する, 税金の還付請求をする

refunding 名形 借換え, 払戻し, 〈税金などの〉還付, 償還, 国債入札 (⇒**deferred tax accounting, trustee**)
advance refunding 満期日前償還
bond refunding 社債借換え, 社債の借換え(発行済み社債の償還資金を得るため, 新規社債を発

debt refunding 債務借換え, 債務の借換え
issuance of refunding bonds 借換え債の発行
▸The burden of interest payments on *refunding bonds* will accumulate year after year. 借換え債の利払い負担［金利負担］は、年ごとに増える。

register 動 登録する, 登記する, 届け出る, 正式に記録する, 示す, 表す, 書留にする
▸The Securities and Exchnge Law requires investment funds to *register* and report the names of their representatives and their locations. 証券取引法は、投資ファンドに対して、投資ファンドの代表者名や所在地などの登録・届け出を義務付けている。

register 名 記録, 登録, 登記, 記入帳
note payable register 支払い手形記入帳
Register of Companies 企業登録局
register of members 株主名簿 (＝record of shareholders, stock register)

registered 形 登録された, 記名の
registered bond 記名債券, 記名社債, 登録社債
registered shareholder 登録株主
registered common shareholder 普通登録株主, 登録普通株主
▸The Company has more than 335,000 *registered common shareholders*. 当社の登録普通株主は、33万5,000人を上回っています。

registered holders of common shares 登録済み普通株主, 登録普通株主
▸*Registered holders of common shares* of the Corpration wishing to additional common shares may participate in a convenient investment plan. 当社の普通株式の追加購入を希望される登録済み普通株主は、当社の便利な投資制度に加入することができます。

registered security 登録証券 (［米］の場合, 証券取引委員会(SEC)に登録されている有価証券), 記名証券 (株式や債券などの保有者の名義が, 発行会社や登録機関の原簿に登録されている有価証券)

registrar 名 登録機関, 株主名簿登録機関, 株式登録機関, 名義書換え代理人, 登記官, 登記事務官, 記録係
registrar for stock 株式登録機関
Registrar of Companies 会社登記官

registration 名 登録, 登記, 正式記録, 登録事項, 記録事項, 登録物件, 名義書換え (⇒**shelf registration**)
▸Listing particulars are a formal statement of the company's business and financial conditions, similar to a US *registration* statement Form S-1. 上場目論見書は, 米国の登録届出書［登録目論見書］様式S-1と同じで, 申請企業の業務と財務内容に関する正式の書面だ。

registration statement 米証券取引委員会(SEC)への登録届出書, 有価証券届出書（有価証券を公募発行する際, 発行者が米取引委員会に事前に提出する書類; ⇒**shelf registration statement**)

regulate 動 規制する, 取り締まる, 統制する, 調整する, 調節する
non-regulated company 規制対象外の企業
regulated company 規制対象企業
regulated industry 規制を受ける業界
regulated market 規制市場, 市場の規制
▸A steady annual improvement in earnings of five percent or more is a reasonable goal given the weight of *regulated* companies in our asset base. 年5％以上の利益増加率の安定確保は, 規制対象企業が当社の資産構成で大きな比重を占めていることから, 妥当な目標と言えるでしょう。

regulation 名 規則, 規定, 規制, 管理, 法規, 法令, 行政規則, レギュレーション
business regulations 業務規定, 業務規則
lending regulation 貸出規制
regulation of illegal and harmful contents 違法有害コンテンツ規制
Regulation S-X 連結財務書類［財務諸表］作成規定, 財務諸表規則S-X, 規則S-X, レギュレーションS-X (様式10-Kの財務書類に関する用語, 様式, 作成方法を定めたもの)
self-regulation 自主規制

regulatory body 規制機関
▸Three *regulatory bodies* of the Stock Exchange Commission, the Listing Committee and the Banking Commission have been set up to ensure that stock market operators abide by a strict code of ethics and that transactions run smoothly. 証券取引所［株式市場］で業務を行う者が厳格な倫理規定を守り, 取引を円滑に行うため, 証券取引委員会, 上場委員会と銀行委員会の三つの規制機関が設置されている。

rehabilitate 動 再建する, 再生する, 立て直す (＝reconstruct)
▸It will not be easy to *rehabilitate* the company, which has been driven into the red by multiple factors. 同社は, 複合的な要因による赤字転落なので, 再建は容易ではない。

rehabilitation 名 再建, 経営再建, 再生, 立て直し, 修復, 回復, 復興, 更生 (⇒**capital**, **self-rehabilitation**)
corporate rehabilitation 企業再建

management rehabilitation 経営再建
- Aeon Co. or Wal-Mart Stores Inc. was considered as a partner to assist in the *rehabilitation* of Daiei Inc.　ダイエー再建に協力する事業パートナーとして, イオンや米ウォルマートが検討された。
- Corporate *rehabilitation* funds are established by creditor banks and other investors to bail out heavily indebted companies.　企業再建ファンドは, 巨額の債務を抱えた企業を救うため, 取引銀行や投資家などが設立する基金だ。
- The company is undergoing management *rehabilitation*.　同社は現在, 経営再建に取り組んでいる。

reinforce 動 強化する, 強める, 補強する, 増強する, 一段と強固にする, テコ入れする
- GM and Toyota reaffirmed that they would *reinforce* cooperative relationship.　GMとトヨタは, 両社の協力関係を強化する方針を改めて確認した。

reinvent 動 作り直す, 再発明する, 再検討する, 考え直す, 出直す　(⇒**redeploy**)

reinvest 動 再投資する
　earnings reinvested 留保利益, 利益剰余金
　reinvested income 利益剰余金
- Quarterly dividends may be *reinvested* automatically to purchase additional common shares at a discount from the average market price.　四半期配当金は, 自動的に再投資して, 平均市場価格から割り引いた価格で当社の普通株式を追加購入することができます。

reinvestment 名 再投資, 社会還元
　Community Reinvestment Act 地域社会還元法
　dividend reinvestment 配当金株式再投資
　reinvestment in business 事業への再投資
　reinvestment in fianacial assets 金融資産への再投資
　reinvestment income 再投資収益
　reinvestment of earnings 利益の再投資

REIT 不動産投資信託, リート (**real estate investment trust**の略)

relations 名 関係, 関連, リレーション　(⇒**investor relations**)
　business relations 取引関係, 業務上の関係, 事業上の関係, ビジネス関係
　community relations 地域社会との関係
　employer-employee relations 雇用者対従業員の関係
　interindustry relations table 産業連関表
　job relations 職場従業員関係
　partner relations 提携先との関係
　public relations 広報宣伝活動

- In terms of market value, the *relation* between Ito-Yokado and Seven-Eleven is a contradiction.　時価総額(株価による企業価値を示す)では, イトーヨーカ堂(親会社)とセブン-イレブン(子会社)との関係が逆転している。

relationship 名 関連, 関連, 結びつき, 取引関係
　arm's length relationship 商業ベースの取引関係
　capital relationship 資本関係
　contractual relationship 契約関係
　cooperative relationship 協力関係
　corporate relationship 企業関係
　financial relationship 財務比率
- Mitsubishi Corp. intends to reinforce its business through the *relationship* with Hokuetsu Paper in such areas as material procurement and trading of paper-pulp products.　三菱商事は, 原材料の調達や紙パルプ製品の取引などの面での北越製紙との関係により, 同社事業のテコ入れを目指している。
- While maintaining a conventional competitive *relationship*, Yomiuri, Nikkei and Asahi aim to bolster their ability to disseminate information as news media.　従来の競争関係を維持しながら, 読売, 日経, 朝日の3社は, 報道機関としての情報発信力の強化を目指している。

release 動 発売する, 販売する, 公表する, 発表する, 公開する, 〈映画を〉封切る, 解放する, 放出する, 〈借金などを〉免除する, 〈権利などを〉放棄する, 〈財産を〉譲渡する, リリースする　(⇒**results**)
- Now is the peak period for listed companies to *release* their business reports for the business year ending in March.　上場企業の3月期決算の発表が, ピークを迎えている。
- The company *released* a brief note about its group accounts.　同社は, 同社の連結決算短信[連結財務諸表短信]を発表した。

release 名 発売, 公表, 発表, 公開, 解放, 釈放, 放出, 義務の免除, 権利放棄, リリース
　news release ニュース・リリース, 記者用発表記事
　press release プレス・リリース, 新聞発表

reliability 名 信頼性, 確実性, 信憑性, 信頼度
　consistency and reliability 一貫性と信頼性
　integrity and reliability of the financial statements 財務書類の完全性と信頼性
- These capital additions provide for growth, modernization and *reliability*.　これらの追加投資は, 成長, 近代化と信頼性向上が目的です。

reliable 形 信頼できる, 信用できる, 確かな, 確実な, 期待どおりの

- The firm's financial data is not *reliable*. 同社の財務データは, 信頼性が薄い。

relocate 動 配置転換する, 再配置する, 移動する, 移転する, 移す (=redeploy)
- Our provisions for business restructuring cover the costs of closing facilities and *relocating* employees. 当社の事業再編成引当金には, 施設閉鎖や従業員再配置などの費用も含まれています。

relocation 名 配置転換, 再配置, 移動, 移転, 立地変更 (=redeployment)
  employee relocation 従業員再配置, 従業員の配置転換
  relocation allowance 引っ越し手当
  relocation of production facilities 生産拠点の移設[移転]
- Costs of $500 million associated with employee separations and *relocations* are also included in selling, general and administrative expenses. 従業員の退職と配置転換に関連する費用5億ドルも, 販売費および一般管理費に含まれている。

remaining 形 残りの, 残存する, 残余の
  remaining cash flow 残存キャッシュ・フロー
  remaining depreciable lives 残存償却年数
  remaining economic life 経済的残存耐用年数 (=remaining economic age)
  remaining life 残存期間, 残存年数, 残存耐用年数
  remaining useful life 残存耐用年数 (=residual service life)
- MUFG obtained the *remaining* 38.8 percent stock in Mitsubishi UFJ Securities through a stock swap deal. 三菱UFJフィナンシャル・グループ(MUFG)は, 株式交換取引で三菱UFJ証券の残りの株式の38.8%を取得した。

remaining interest 残存持ち分, 残りの持ち分
- We sold our *remaining interest* in the company in 2007 for a slight gain. 当社は, 2007年度に同社の残存持ち分を売却して, 少額の利益を得ました。

remaining service 残余勤続年数, 残存勤続年数 (=remaining service period)
  remaining service period 残余勤続年数, 残存勤続年数, 残存勤続期間
  remaining service to expected retirement 予想退職時までの残余勤続年数
  remaining service to full eligibility 完全受給権取得までの残余勤続年数
- We amortize prior service costs primarily on a straight-line basis over the average *remaining service* period of active employees. 当社は, 過去勤務債務[過去勤務費用]については, 主に定額法で在籍従業員の平均残存勤続年数にわたって償却しています。

remeasure 動 再測定する
- Inventories charged to cost of sales and depreciation are *remeasured* at historical rates. 売上原価に計上される棚卸し資産と減価償却費は, 取得時の為替レートで再測定されています。

remuneration 名 報酬, 給料, 代価, 報償, 謝礼, 対価 (⇒lodging expenses)
  auditor's remuneration 監査報酬
  entrepreneur's remuneration 事業主報酬
  management remuneration 経営者報酬
  monetary remuneration 金銭的報酬
  officers' remuneration 役員報酬
  remuneration cost 支払い報酬, 報償, 代価
  remuneration package 報酬, 給付, 謝礼, 代価, 報償

renewal 名 刷新, 更新, 書換え, 書換え継続, 期限延長, 自動継続, 再開, 再生, 復活, 再開発, リニューアル
  automatic renewal 自動更新
  card renewal カード更新
  renewal fee 更新手数料, 書換え手数料
  renewal option 更新選択権
  renewals and betterments 更新・改良
  urban renewal 都市再開発
- Certain land and building leases have *renewal* options for periods ranging from three to five years. 特定の[一部の]土地と建物のリースには, 3–5年の期間の更新選択権がついている。

rent 名 賃貸料, 賃借料, 地代, 超過利潤

rental 名 賃貸料, 賃借料, リース, レンタル
  annual rental 年間リース料, 年間レンタル料
  lease rentals receivable 受取リース料
  rental income 賃貸料, 賃貸収入, 受取賃貸料, リース料収入
  rental payments リース支払い額, リース料
  rental revenues 賃貸料, レンタル収益, リース料

rental commitments 賃借料
- Minimum *rental commitments*, in millions of dollars, under noncancelable leases for 2008 and thereafter are as follows. 2008年とそれ以降の解約不能リース契約に基づく賃借料の最低額(単位：百万ドル)は, 次のとおりです。

rental expense 賃借料, 賃借費用, リース料 (=rent expense)
- *Rental expense* on operating leases for the years ended December 31, 2007 amounted to $70 million. 2007年12月31日に終了した事業年度のオペレーティング・リースの賃借料は, 7,000万ドルでした。

rentals and other services レンタルその他のサービス
▸The revenues of *rentals and other services* were about level the last three years.　レンタルその他のサービス部門の収益は、過去3年間ほぼ同水準でした。

reorganization 名　再編成、再編、改編、改造、改組、改革、再生、再建、会社再建、事業再編、組織再編、組織変更、会社更生　（＝realignment;　⇒ **repositioning program**)
　capital reorganization　資本再編
　corporate reorganization　企業再編、再編、会社更生
　large-scale reorganization of the retail industry　流通業界［小売業界］の大規模再編、流通業界の大がかりな再編
　major corporate reorganization　大規模な企業再編
　quasi-reorganization　準更生
　reorganization of debt　債務再構成　（＝debt reorganization)
　reorganization scheme　再建計画　（＝reorganization plan)
▸Northwest's board is scheduled to meet Wednesday to decide on a Chapter 11 bankruptcy *reorganization*.　ノースウエスト航空の取締役会は、水曜日に会合を持って、米連邦破産法第11章による会社再建を決定する予定だ。

reorganize 動　再編成する、再編する、改造する、改組する、改革する、再生する、再建する、組織変更する
▸In the United States, a troubled company is afforded the opportunity to *reorganize* under Chapter 11 of the Federal Bankruptcy Code.　米国では、経営破綻した企業は、米連邦破産法11章に基づいて企業を再建する機会が与えられる。

repay 動　払い戻す、返済する、返還する、返金する、償還する　（＝refund)
　repay bank borrowings　銀行借入れを返済する、銀行借入金を返済する
　repay debt　債務［負債］を返済する、借入金を返済する
　repay maturing CP　満期を迎えた［満期が来た］CPを償還する
　repay principal　元本を返済する、元本を償還する
　repay the loan　ローンを返済［弁済］する、借入金を返済する
▸Proceeds from the new share issue will be used to *repay* $300 million of 10% Series 3 Notes, maturing in May 2008.　この起債［新株発行］による手取金は、2008年5月満期・利率10％のシリーズ3ノート3億ドルの償還に充てられます。
▸We *repaid* $823 million of long-term debt during the first nine months.　当社は、1－9月期に長期債務8億2,300万ドルを返済しました。

repayment 名　返済、払戻し、償還、返金　（⇒ **cash flow problems**, **debt repayment**)
　debt repayment　債務返済
　early repayment (**before due date**)　早期返済、早期完済
　loan repayment　債務返済、融資の返済、借入金の返済、ローンの返済　（＝repayment of the loan)
　lump-sum repayment　一括返済
　principal repayment　元本の償還　（＝repayment of principal)
　raising and repayment of funds　資金の調達と償還
　repayment of long term debt　長期債務の返済、長期債務支出、長期借入金返済額
　repayment of public funds　公的資金の返済　（＝public fund repayment)
　repayment of the loans　借入金の返済、ローンの返済　（＝loan repayment)
▸The company will raise more funds for loan *repayment*.　同社は、さらに債務返済の資金を調達する。
▸The financial group has already completed the *repayment* of all the public funds it received from the government.　同フィナンシャル・グループは、国から調達した公的資金をすでに完済している。

repayment of debt　債務返済、債務の支払い、借入金返済額
▸Cash used for financing activities resulted from a dividend payment and the *repayment of debt*.　財務活動に使用した現金は、支払い配当金と債務返済によるものです。

replacement cost　代替コスト、再取得原価、再調達原価、再調達コスト、取替え原価
　replacement cost method　取替え原価法
▸Current cost depreciation is based on current *replacement* costs of the assets and their estimated economic lives.　現在原価に基づく減価償却費は、資産の現在再調達コストと当該資産の見積り経済耐用年数に基づいて算定されています。

report 動　報告する、報告書を提出する、表示する、記載する、公表する、計上する、申告する、報道する、連絡する　（⇒**advisory**)
　as previously reported　前期報告額、前年度報告額

net assets at year end—as reported 期末現在の純資産：公表額, 期末純資産：公表額
report as liability 負債として計上する
report at a market value 時価で表示する, 市場価格で表示する
report huge losses 巨額の損失を計上する
report net income 純利益を計上する
report recurring losses 経常赤字になる, 経常赤字に転落する
▸Firms are allowed to annually *report* their profits from large construction projects that last several years. 複数年にまたがる大規模工事の場合, 企業は（完工前でも）単年度ごとに利益を計上することができる。
▸The firm failed to *report* a total of about ¥7 billion in taxable income. 同社は, 課税所得総額約70億円を申告しなかった。

report 名 報告, 報告書, 申告書, 報道, レポート (⇒**annual report, consolidated earnings report, earnings report**)
 accountant's report 監査報告書, 会計士報告書（目論見書添付書類）
 accounting reports 会計報告書
 advisory report 意見書
 annual meeting report 株主総会報告書
 business report 事業報告, 事業報告書, 営業報告書, 業務報告書, ビジネス・レポート
 cash report 資金報告書, 現金収支報告書
 extraordinary report 臨時報告書
 financial report 財務報告, 財務報告書, 業績報告, 有価証券報告書
 flash report 営業速報
 fund report 資金報告, 資金報告書
 periodic report 定期報告, 定期報告書
 report form 報告式, 報告式財務諸表, 監査人の報告書
 report of independent auditors 監査報告書
 report of management 経営者の報告, 経営陣の報告
 report on large shareholders 大量保有報告書
 sales report 売上報告書
 securities report 有価証券報告書 (＝**securities statement**)
 segmental report セグメント情報
 short-form audit report 短文式監査報告書
 tentative report 中間報告
 unqualified opinion report 無限定意見報告書
▸Those stockholders who attended the annual meeting received a *report* on the Corporation's current business, as well as its plans for the future. 株主総会に出席された株主の皆さまには, 当社の現在の事業と将来の計画についてご報告しました。

reportable 形 報告できる, 報告に値する, 報告義務のある
 reportable event 要報告事項
 reportable industry segment 要報告産業セグメント

reported 形 財務報告上の, 決算報告上の, 報告された, 計上された, 公表された, 計上…, 公表…
 reported earned premium 公表経過保険料
 reported equity 財務報告上の株主資本
 reported income 公表利益, 計上利益
 reported numbers 決算 (＝financial figures)
▸There is no change in the current or previously *reported* net earnings. 当年度の当期純利益と過年度に計上した当期純利益に, 変動はありません。

reported earnings 決算報告上の利益, 財務報告上の利益, 公表利益, 計上利益
▸Accounting changes sometimes have a large effect on *reported earnings* in the year of a change. 会計処理［会計処理方法］の変更は, 変更した年度の計上利益に大きな影響を及ぼすこともあります。

reported earnings per share 1株当たり計上利益
▸The decision in the fourth quarter to establish a provision of $300 million for restructuring resulted in a $0.65 reduction in 2007's *reported earnings per share*. 第4四半期に当社は, 3億ドルの事業再編引当金の設定を決定しました。その結果, 2007年度の1株当たり計上利益は0.65ドル減少しました。

reported figures 報告書上の数値, 報告書に掲げた数値
▸Previously *reported figures* have been restated. 前期までの報告書に掲げた数値は, 修正・再表示されています。

reporting 名 報告, 表示 (⇒**financial reporting, SFAS**)
 accounting for external reporting 外部報告会計
 employee reporting 従業員に対する報告
 for financial statement reporting 財務書類上, 財務諸表上
 for income tax reporting 税務上, 税務会計上
 functional reporting of expenses 職能別報告書, 職能別計算書
 income reporting 損益報告
 net of tax reporting 税引き後純額の報告, 正味

税効果の報告, 税効果考慮後の報告
periodic reporting 定期報告, 期間報告
principle of true and fair reporting 真実性の原則, 真正かつ公平な報告の原則
production reporting 生産報告
reporting currency 報告通貨(財務諸表などで金額表示の単位として用いる通貨)
reporting year 報告事業年度, 報告年度, 当年度, 当期
segmental reporting セグメント情報 (＝segmental report)
standard of reporting 報告基準

▸*Reporting* in U.S. dollars provides the most meaningful presentation of our consolidated results and financial position. 米ドルで計上[報告]したほうが, 当社の連結経営成績[連結業績]と財政状態を最も適切に表示することになります。

reporting period 報告期間, 決算報告期間, 財務報告期間, 報告事業年度(文脈に応じて「当期」や「当四半期」を指す場合もある)

▸Capital spending by companies capitalized at ¥1 billion or more climbed 10.4 percent in the *reporting period*, down from 13 percent increase the previous quarter. 資本金10億円を上回る企業の当四半期の設備投資は, 10.4%増加したものの, 前四半期の13%増と比べて減少した。

reporting qaurter 当四半期, 報告四半期

▸The pretax profits of nonmanufacturers climbed 9.1 percent in the *reporting quarter* (April–June quarter), up for the 13th consecutive quarter. 非製造業の当四半期(4–6月期)の経常利益は, 9.1%の上昇で, 13期連続増加した。

repositioning 名 事業基盤の再構築, 事業基盤の強化, 企業再編, 再位置付け, 再ポジショニング, ポジションの再設定, リポジショニング

▸For the Corporation, 2007 was a year of *repositioning*. 当社にとって, 2007年度は事業基盤再構築の1年でした。

repositioning program 事業基盤の強化プログラム, 事業基盤再構築プログラム

▸Our reorganization plan is compatible with a worldwide *repositioning program* initiated earlier in the year, aimed at strengthening our structures and procedures. この組織再編計画は, 事業機構と業務運営の強化をめざして当社が年初から世界的な規模で進めてきた事業基盤強化プログラムに沿うものです。

represent 動 表示する, 表明する, 意味する, 示す, …を象徴する, …を表す, …の代理をつとめる, …を代表する, …を代行する, …に相当する, …に当

たる (⇒**secured mortgage**)

▸Many of our employees are *represented* by unions. 当社従業員の多くは, 組合に加入しています。

▸Research and development expenses *represented* 12.0 percent of revenues in the third quarter of 2007. 2007年第3四半期の研究開発費は, 売上高の12%を占めました。

representative 名 代表者, 代理人, 代行者, 事務所, 駐在員事務所, セールスマン, 販売員, 外務員, 駐在員, 担当者 (⇒**policyholders' representative meeting**, **register** 動)

▸He was promoted to the position of *representative* director of the company. 氏は, 同社の代表取締役に昇格した。

repurchase 動 買い戻す, 再購入する (＝buy back; ⇒**cancelation**[**cancellation**], **retire**)

▸Shares were *repurchased* for cancellation in 2007. 株式は, 2007年度に買い戻して消却しました。

repurchase 名 買戻し, 再調達
equity repurchase 株式の買戻し
repurchase cost 再調達原価, 再調達価格
repurchase of bonds 社債の買戻し
share [**stock**] **repurchase** 株式の買戻し, 自社株買い (＝share buyback, stock buyback, stock repurchase)

▸Under our stock *repurchase* programs, we repurchased 11,252,000 shares during 2007 at a cost of $1,425 million. 当社の自社株買戻しプログラムに従って, 当社は2007年度に11,252,000株を14億2,500万ドルで買い戻しました。

repurchased share 買取得株式, 買戻し株式 (⇒**retire**)

reputation 名 評価, 名声, 地位, 信望, 知名度, 評判, イメージ

▸Restructuring allows us to maintain our *reputation* as the world's most innovative telecommunications corporation. 事業再編を通して, 当社は, 世界でもっとも革新的な通信機器メーカーとしての当社に対する評価を維持することもできます。

requirement 名 要件, 条件, 必要条件, 基準, 規定, 制度, 資格 (⇒**capital requirements**, **cash requirements**)
accounting requirement 会計基準, 会計処理方法, 会計義務
cash capital requirements 資金需要
employee contribution requirements 従業員拠出義務

financial requirement 資金需要
financing requirements 資金需要
funding requirements 資金需要（＝funding needs)
initial margin requirement 当初証拠金率
meet one's cash requirements 必要資金を確保する, 必要資金を賄う
reporting requirements 報告制度
sinking fund requirements 減債基金積立額
transparency requirement 透明性の規定
underwriting requirements 引受基準
working capital requirements 必要運転資金
▸We will refinance debt maturing in 2007 to meet our cash *requirements* in 2007. 当社は, 2007年に満期が到来する債務の借換えで, 2007年度の必要資金を確保する方針です。

rescue 動 救う, 救助[救出]する, 支援する, 救済する

rescue 名 救援, 支援, 救済, 救出, 救助, レスキュー
financial rescue 金融支援, 経営支援
rescue package 支援策, 救済策, 支援計画, 救助計画 （＝rescue plan)
rescue team 救助隊 （＝rescue crew [squad, unit])
rescue work 救助作業
▸The bank is orchestrating a ¥470 billion *rescue* package for ailing condominium builder Daikyo Inc. 同行は, 経営再建中のマンション分譲大手の大京に対する4,700億円の金融支援策の最終調整に入った。

research 名 研究, 調査, 研究開発, リサーチ
applied research 応用研究
basic research 基礎研究
joint research 共同研究
market research 市場調査

research and development 研究開発《略 R&D》
▸We have positioned ourselves well with our increasing investments in *research and development* and improvng product line. 当社は, 研究開発投資の拡大と製品ラインの充実に取り組んできました。

research and development cost 研究開発費
▸*Research and development costs* incurred pursuant to specific contracts with third parties are charged to earnings in the same period as the related revenue is recognized. 第三者との個別契約に従って発生した研究開発費は, 関連収益が認識された期間と同一の期間に費用として計上さ

れています。

research and development expense 研究開発費, 試験研究費 （＝R&D expense, research and development expenditure)
▸*Research and development expenses* increased 5.5 percent in 2007. 研究開発費は, 2007年度は5.5%増加しました。

research and development investment 研究開発投資, 研究開発投資額
▸*Research and development investment* was $850 million (14 percent of total revenues) in 2007. 2007年度の研究開発投資額は, 8億5,000万ドル（総売上高の14%）でした。

reserve 名 準備金, 積立金, 引当金, 充当金, 支払い準備, 予備品, 保存品, 保留, 留保, 保存, 制限, 条件 （⇒capital reserve, loan loss reserves)
accumulated reserves 累積積立金
catastrophe reserve 異常損失準備金
earned surplus reserve 利益準備金
financial reserves 財政基盤
general reserve 一般引当金, 別途積立金 （＝other reserve, special reserve, unconditional reserve)
internal reserves 内部留保, 内部留保金
inventory reserve 棚卸し資産評価引当金
legal capital reserves 法定準備金 （＝legal reserves, legally required reserves)
legal reserves 法定準備金, 準備金, 利益準備金 （＝legal earned reserves)
liability reserve 責任準備金, 負債性引当金
loan redemption reserve 借入金償還引当金
loan reserves 融資引当金, 金融機関の債権に対する引当金, 債務引当金
loss reserves 責任準備金, 損失準備金
mathematical reserve 保険料積立金
optional reserve 任意準備金, 任意積立金
other reserves その他積立金, 別途積立金 （＝general reserves, special reserves, unconditional reserves)
pension reserve 年金積立金
profit reserve 利益準備金
reserves and allowances 引当金
reserve for credit losses 貸倒れ引当金
revenue reserve 利益準備金, 利益剰余金, 任意積立金
▸Regular FSA inspections focus on whether banks' loan *reserves* are adequate. 金融庁の通常検査は, 主に銀行の債権に対する引当金が十分かどうかを検討する。
▸We provide *reserves* for these potential costs

and regularly review the adequacy of our reserves. 当社は，これらの潜在的費用に対して引当金を設定し，その妥当性を定期的に検討しています。

reserve for ... …引当金，…積立金
　reserve for amortization 償却引当金
　reserve for bad debts 貸倒れ引当金 （＝reserve for possible loan losses）
　reserve for depletion 減耗償却引当金
　reserve for depreciation 減価償却引当金，減価償却累計額 （＝accumulated depreciation, allowance for depreciation）
　reserve for ESOP debt retirement 従業員持ち株制度（ESOP）基金債務償還準備金
　reserve for losses 損失引当金
　reserve for retirement allowances 退職給与引当金
　reserve for retirement fund 退職給与積立金
▶We believe that our *reserves* for losses are adequate. 当社の損失引当金は十分な額である，と考えています。

reshape 動 刷新する，再編成する，立て直す，作り直す，作り変える，新生面を開く
▶We have slimmed down and *reshaped* our worldwide organization. 当社は，当社の世界各国の組織をスリム化して再編成しました。

residual 形 残余の，余りの
　residual equity 残余持分
　residual interest 残余権益
　residual service life 残存耐用年数
　residual value 残存価額

resignation 名 辞職，辞任，退任，辞表
　a letter of resignation 辞表，辞職願い （＝a resignation letter）
　tender [give in, hand in, send in] one's resignation 辞表を提出する
▶JAL's internal conflict has been halted at least for a while by the *resignation* of its president and chief executive officer. 日本航空の内紛は，同社の社長兼最高経営責任者の退任でひとまず決着した。

resident 名 居住者，入居者
　Canadian resident カナダ居住者
　non-resident 非居住者
　nursing home resident 老人ホーム入居者
　qualified resident 適格居住者
▶Dividends paid to owners of the Corporation's common shares who are not *residents* of Canada are subject generally to a 25 percent withholding tax. 配当金がカナダ居住者でない当社の普通株主に支払われた場合，その配当金には一般に25％の源泉所得税［源泉徴収税］が課されます。

resident 形 居住している，駐在している，専任の
　resident advisor [adviser] 専任アドバイザー
　resident branch 現地支店

resize 動 合理化する，…の大きさ［サイズ］を変える，再編する
▶We have focused on our strengths, honed our strategies, seized opportunities, trimmed costs and *resized* our operations. 私どもは，自分たちの強い分野に的を絞り，戦略を磨き，機会をとらえ，費用を削減するとともに，経営の合理化に努めてきました。

resolution 名 決議，決議案，議案，決断，決意，決定，裁決，判定，解決，解答，解明，決着，映像の鮮明度，光の解像
　extraordinary resolution 特殊決議，非常決議 （議決権を持つ株主の半数以上，議決権で3分の2以上の支持がなければ成立しない決議）
　important resolution 重要決議
　special resolution 特別決議
　stockholder resolution 株主決議 （＝shareholder resolution）
▶On the *resolution* to ratify the appointment of auditors, 99% of the votes cast were voted for. 監査人の選任を承認する議案については，投票総数（投票株式総数）の99％が賛成しました。

resource 名 資源，経営資源，財源，資金，源泉，供給源，教材，資料，手段，方策，兵力 （⇒**human resources, management resources, promising area**）
　allocation of resources 資源の配分 （＝resource allocation）
　business resources 経営資源 （⇒**outsourcing**）
　capital resources 資金の源泉
　corporate resources 経営資源，会社の資源
　financial resource(s) 資金，資本，資金力，金融力，金融資産，財務資源，財源，資金の源泉，資金源，原資 （⇒**trend**）
　human resources 人的資源，人材，人事部
　internal resources 内部資金，手元資金
　management resources 経営資源，役員人事
▶Now is time for businesses to inject their corporate *resources* into promising areas as a new source for earnings. 今は，新たな収益源として企業がその経営資源を有望な分野に投入する時期だ。
▶To meet customer needs, we coordinate *resources* across business unit lines. 顧客のニーズを満たすため，当社は事業部門の境界を越えて経営資源の調整を図っています。

responsibility 名 責任，職責，義務，責務，債務，

負担, 契約義務, 履行能力, 支払い能力 （⇒**corporate social responsibility, shift🔊**）
management responsibility 経営責任, 管理責任 （＝responsibility of management）
public responsibility 公共責任, 社会的責任, 公共性
resignation to take responsibility 引責辞任
responsibility for financial reporting 財務報告に対する責任
responsibility of the Company's management 会社の経営者の責任
shareholders' responsibility 株主責任
▶Our management executive committee has *responsibility* for policy, strategy and values. 当社の経営執行委員会は, 会社の政策[経営方針], 戦略と価値観などについての責任を負っています。

responsible 🔊 責任がある, 責任を負う, 責任の重い, 報告義務がある （⇒**integrity and objectivity of the financial statements**）
▶ChuoAoyama PricewaterhouseCoopers was *responsible* for auditing the accounts of about 5,600 companies as of the end of January 2006. 中央青山監査法人は, 2006年1月末時点で, 約5,600社の会計監査[財務書類の監査]を担当していた。
▶Management is *responsible* for maintaining a system of internal controls as a fundamental requirement for the operational and financial integrity of results. 経営者は, 営業成績および財務成績の適正性を保つ基本的条件として, 内部統制組織を維持する責任を負っています。

restate 🔊 修正する, 再表示する, 修正再表示する, 更新する （⇒**International Financial Reporting Standards**）
as restated 修正後, 訂正後残高
restate the financial statements of prior years 過年度の財務書類[財務諸表]を再表示する
Restated for two-for-one stock split effective June 5, 2007 2007年6月5日付け株式分割(1株を2株とする分割)反映後の修正再表示
▶Income taxes for 2007 have not been *restated* for this change. 2007年度の法人所得税額は, この変更による修正・再表示を行っていません。

restatement 🔊 修正, 再表示, 修正再表示, 更新, 改訂, 言い換え, 再陳述, リステートメント
　修正再表示（restatement）について➡米国では, 会計処理方法を変更した場合, 新基準を過年度(prior years)に遡って適用し, 以前に公表した過年度(prior years)の財務諸表[財務書類]の数値(figures)を修正して再表示する(to restate)会計慣行があり, 過年度の数値を修正して再表示することをrestatementと呼ぶ。その対象となるのは, 会計処理原則の変更や報告主体の変更のほかに, 不正・誤謬の修正, 新しい会計基準が発表されたときなど。
effect of restatement 修正再表示の影響, 修正再表示の影響額
restatement of balance sheet 貸借対照表の再表示
restatement of depreciation 減価償却費の修正
restatements of prior periods' financial statements 過年度財務書類[財務諸表]の再表示

restriction 🔊 制限, 規制, 制約
dividend restriction 配当制限
foreign exchange restrictions 外国為替規制
lending restrictions 貸出規制
loan restrictions 融資規制
▶*Restrictions* on share buybacks were eased in October 2001. 2001年10月に, 自社株買戻しに対する規制が緩和された。

restructure 🔊 再編成する, 再構築する, 再構成する, 再建する, 立て直す, 組織替えする, リストラする, 改編する （⇒**troubled**）
▶We need to *restructure* some of our overseas operations. 当社は, 海外事業の一部再編成を迫られています。

restructuring 🔊 事業の再構築, 事業の再編成, 再構成, 再建, 経営再建, 再編, 改革, 解雇, リストラ, リストラクチャリング （⇒**business restructuring**）
balance sheet restructuring 財務再編
capital restructuring 資本再構成, 資本の再編成
corporate debt restructuring 企業債務の再編
corporate restructuring 企業再編成, 企業再編, 会社再建, 企業リストラ, 事業機構の再編, 経営再建, リストラ
debt restructuring 債務再構成, 債務の特別条件変更 （＝refinancing debt）
financial restructuring 財務再編, 財務再構築, 金融のリストラ
large-scale restructuring 大規模再建計画
restructuring cost 事業再編成費用, リストラクチャリング費用, リストラ経費 （＝restructuring charges; ⇒**pretax provision**）
restructuring efforts 経営再建策, リストラ策 （⇒**sale**）
restructuring of debt 債務再編, 債務再構成, 債務の再構築 （＝debt restructuring）
restructuring program 再建計画, 再編計画, 再生計画, 事業再編成計画, 事業再構築計画, 再建策, 再建案 （＝restructuring package, restruc-

turing plan)
- In the fourth quarter, we decided to establish a provision of $300 million for *restructuring*. 第4四半期に, 当社は, 事業再編成のため3億ドルの引当金設定[3億ドルの事業再編引当金の設定]を決定しました。
- Restructuring should strengthen our position as the industry's low-cost manufacturer. 事業再編によって, 業界の低コスト・メーカーとしての当社の地位[経営基盤]は強化されるはずです。

restructuring charge 事業再編成費用, リストラクチャリング費用, リストラ費用 （＝restructuring cost)
- Without this fourth quarter *restructuring charge*, we earned $3.15 a share. この第4四半期の事業再編費用を除くと, 当社の利益は1株当たり3.15ドルになります。

restructuring plan 再建計画, 再編計画, 再生計画, 再建策, 再建案, リストラ計画 （＝restructuring package, restructuring program)
- Sony Corp. will ax 10,000 jobs worldwide and cut ¥200 billion in costs by the end of fiscal 2007 in a sweeping *restructuring plan*. ソニーは, 抜本的な再建策として, 2007年度末までに全世界の人員10,000人の削減と2,000億円のコスト削減を図る。

restructuring provision 事業再編引当金, 事業再編に伴う引当金繰入れ
- Before the impact of the *restructuring provision*, the earnings per common share were $1.27, an 8.6 percent decrease from the previous year. 事業再編に伴う引当金繰入れの影響額控除前の普通株式1株当たり利益は, 前年比[前期比] 8.6％減の1.27ドルでした。

results 名 成績, 業績, 決算, 決算内容, 実績, 成果, 結果, 効果, 影響, 影響額, 統計 （⇒business results, financial results)
- **annual results** 年間成績, 通期決算, 年次決算 （＝full year results)
- **company's results** 会社の業績, 会社の決算 （＝corporate business results,, corporate results)
- **consolidated results** 連結業績, 連結経営実績, 連結経営成績, 連結決算 （＝group results)
- **corporate results** 企業業績, 決算
- **earnings results** 決算
- **gross results** 経常収益
- **interim results** 中間決算 （＝interim financial results)
- **investment results** 投資成績, 投資実績, 運用成績[実績], 投資の成果 （＝investment performance)
- **payment by results** 業績給, 能率給
- **poor results** 業績の落ち込み, 業績低迷 （＝stagnant results)
- **results for the year** 当期業績, 当年度の業績
- **successful results** 好業績, 好結果, 上首尾
- Of First Section-listed companies, 819 firms excluding financial institutions and brokerages have released their annual *results*. 東証1部上場企業のうち, 金融機関と証券業を除く819社が年次決算の発表を終えた。
- Other income-net depends mostly on our cash balance and the *results* and changes in our invetments and joint ventures. 「その他の収益—純額」の大半は, 当社の現金残高と当社の投資および合弁事業の成果と変更により生じています。
- The company said it would correct its earnings *results* for the past five fiscal years. 同社は, 過去5年度分の決算訂正を発表した。
- The company's business *results* for fiscal 2007 is expected to result in a massive loss. 同社の2008年3月期決算[2007年度]の業績は, 大幅赤字[損失]が見込まれる。

resume 動 再開する, 取り戻す, 回復する, 要約する
- The bank *resumed* donations to political parties. 同行は, 政党への献金を再開する予定だ。

retail 名 小売り, 個人投資家, 小口投資家, 個人向け取引, リテール
- **retail basis** 売価基準
- **retail cost** 小売原価
- **retail method** 売価法, 売価基準法
- **retail price** 小売価格, 小売物価, 販売価格
- **retail sales** 小売販売, 小売販売高
- **retail sales volume** 小売売上高, 小売販売高, 小売販売額
- **retail trade area** 小売商圏, 小売販売圏
- The tie-up of the two companies will produce the third-largest firm in this sector of the menswear *retail* market. 両社が経営統合すると, 紳士服小売市場「業界」で第三位の会社が誕生する。

retail inventory method 売価還元法, 小売棚卸し法, 売価棚卸し法 （＝retail inventory method of accounting, retail method)
- The Company uses the *retail inventory method*. 当社は, 売価還元法を採用しています。

retailer 名 小売業, 小売企業, 小売店, スーパー
- **mass retailer** 量販小売業, 量販店
- **producer-retailer alliance** 製販同盟
- The chain of large-scale *retailers* of home ap-

pliances finally became unable to procure funds. この家電量販店は、最終的に資金調達ができなくなった[資金繰りに行き詰まってしまった]。

▸Troubled *retailer* Daiei Inc. will have to close 53 of its money-losing outlets. 経営不振の大手スーパー、ダイエーは、赤字店舗のうち53店舗の閉鎖を迫られる予定だ。

retain 動 維持する、留保する、保持する、保有する、確保する、つなぎとめる

　income retained in the business 企業内留保利益

　retain earnings 利益を留保する

　retain ownership 経営権を握る

　retained cash flow 手元キャッシュ・フロー

　retained income 任意積立金、留保利益、留保利益金、留保利益剰余金

　retained profit 留保利益、繰越し利益

　retained surplus 留保利益、留保利益剰余金

▸Independent accountants are *retained* to examine the Corporation's financial statements. 社外の独立した会計監査人[公認会計士]が、当社の財務書類を監査しています。

retained earnings 剰余金、利益剰余金、留保利益、社内留保利益金、社内留保、内部留保（＝earned surplus, retained income：過去の利益の積立てで、企業の税引き後利益から配当金や役員賞与金など社外流出分などを控除した残額をいう。英国では profit and loss account ともいう。⇒ **capital reserve**）

　consolidated retained earnings 連結留保利益（連結貸借対照表上の留保利益）、連結利益剰余金

　legal retained earnings 利益準備金

　other retained earnings その他の剰余金

　retained earnings appropriated for bond 減債積立金

　retained earnings appropriated for contingency 偶発損失準備金

　retained earnings appropriated for purchase of treasury stock 自己株式買取積立金

　retained earnings statement 利益剰余金計算書、留保利益計算書

　statement of retained earnings 利益剰余金計算書、留保利益計算書（＝retained earnings statement）

▸The company plans to dig into its *retained earnings* to prevent its net balance from sinking into the red. 純収支残高が赤字に転落するのを防ぐため、同社は内部留保を取り崩す方針だ。

retire 動 〈株式を〉消却する、〈株式を〉償還する、〈債務[借入金]などを〉返済する、〈工場などを〉除

却する、〈紙幣などを〉回収する、撤退する、引き下がる、退職する、退任する、引退する（⇒**original cost, retirement**）

　retire early 早期退職する

　retire maturing CP 満期が来たCPを償還する

　retire repurchased shares 買い戻した株式を消却する

　retire from the board 取締役を退任する

　retire [withdraw] from unproffitable operations [businesses] 不採算事業から撤退する、不採算事業を整理する

　retired life fund 退職終身基金

　sell or retire plant 工場を売却もしくは除却する

▸During 2007, two members since 1995, *retired* from the board. 2007年度で、1995年就任の当社取締役2名が、取締役を退任しました。

▸The repurchased shares were *retired* and restored to the status of authorized but unissued shares. 買戻し株式は消却して、授権未発行株式の状態に戻っています。

retired employee 退職従業員

▸In addition to pension plan benefits, the company and most of its subsidiaries provide certain health and insurance benefits for *retired employees*. 年金給付のほかに、当社と当社子会社の大半は、退職者に医療給付と生命保険給付も提供しています。

retiree 名 退職者、定年退職者、引退者、年金受給者、年金生活者（⇒**retirement incentive program**）

　cost of health care benefits for retirees 退職者に対する医療給付費用

　cost of life insurance benefits for retirees 退職者に対する生命保険給付費用

　Retiree Benefit Bankruptcy Act 退職者給付破産法

　retiree health benefits 退職者健康保険

retiree benefits 退職者給付

▸For the years ended December 31, 2007 and 2006, the costs of *retiree benefits* amounted to $7.2 million and $5.7 million, respectively. 2007年および2006年12月31日に終了した事業年度の退職者への給付費用総額は、それぞれ720万ドルと570万ドルでした。

▸In our new accounting for *retiree benefits*, we estimate and book expenses for retiree benefits during the years employees are working and accumulating these future benefits. 退職者給付についての当社の新会計処理では、従業員の勤務期間とその将来の給付額が累積される期間にわたっ

て、退職者給付費用を推定し、計上しています。
▸We added the liabilities for *retiree benefits* to our balance sheet in 2007. 当社は、2007年度に退職者給付債務を会社の貸借対照表に加えました。

retiree health care benefits 退職者健康管理給付, 退職者医療給付
▸We transferred some of these excess pension assets to fund *retiree health care benefits*. 退職者医療給付の資金を賄うため、当社はこれらの超過年金資産の一部を移転しました。

retirement 名 退職, 引退, 〈(株式の)〉消却, 償還, 返済, 除却, 処分, 廃棄 (「除却」は、耐用年数の到来や陳腐化などで使用に耐えられなくなった有形固定資産を、処分して固定資産台帳から抹消すること。⇒**shareholder**)
　allowance for retirement and severance 退職給与引当金
　bond retirement 社債償還, 社債の買入れ消却 (＝retirement of bond)
　mandatory retirement 定年退職
　probability of retirement 退職確率
　property retirement 有形固定資産の売却, 有形固定資産の廃棄
　rate of debt retirement 償還率
　reserve for retirement of preferred stock 優先株式償還準備金
　retirement annuity 退職年金
　retirement benefit plan [scheme] 退職給与制度
　retirement of debt 負債の返済, 債務返済, 債務償還 (＝debt retirement)
　retirement of fixed assets 固定資産の処分, 固定資産の除却
　retirement of shares 株式の消却, 株式の償還, 株式の買入れ消却 (＝retirement of stocks, share retirement, stock retirement：発行済み自己株式を取得して消滅させること)
　retirement plan reserves 退職給付引当金 (⇒**indemnity**)
　retirement system 除却法 (＝retirement method, retiring method)
　self-employment retirement plan 自営業者退職金制度
　Social Security retirement benefits 社会保障退職給付
　voluntary retirement 希望退職
▸The reconstruction plan includes the *retirement* of 50 percent of the firm's common shares. 経営再建策には、同社の普通株式の5割消却も含まれている。

retirement allowance 退職金, 退職給与, 退職慰労金, 退職給与引当金 (⇒**serve**)
▸*Retirement allowances* for directors are usually calculated based on employees, salaries, position and length of service. 役員退職慰労金は、一般に従業員数, 報酬, 役職や在任期間などに基づいて算出される。

retirement benefit 退職給付, 退職給与 (⇒**year of service**)
　monthly retirement benefits 年金給付月額
　retirement benefit plan 退職給与制度
　retirement benefits cost 退職給付費用
　retirement benefits paid 退職金給付支払い額
▸Monthly *retirement benefits* generally represent the greater of a fixed amount per year of service, or a percent of career compensation. 年金給付月額は、原則として在職年数に基づく一定額または職務給の一定率の額のうち、いずれか多い金額となっています。

retirement incentive program 退職勧奨制度
▸The retiree increase was a result of the *retirement incentive programs* offered in 2007. 退職者の増加は、2007年度に実施した退職勧奨制度によるものです。

retraining 名 再教育, 再研修, 再訓練 (⇒**redeployment**)
▸We are very active in the *retraining* of our employees. 当社は、従業員の再教育を積極的に行っています。

retroactive 形 遡及力のある, 遡及する, 過去にさかのぼる (＝retrospective)
　on a retroactive basis 過去に遡及して (⇒**reference**)
　retroactive adjustment 遡及修正, 遡及修正項目
　retroactive application 遡及適用, 遡及的適用 (＝retroactive imposition, retrospective application)
▸The accounting change was made *retroactive* to January 1, 2005. 会計処理の変更は、2005年1月1日に遡及して行いました。

retrospective application 遡及適用, 遡及的適用 (＝retroactive application; ⇒**International Financial Reporting Standards**)

return 動 返す, 戻す, 返還する, 還元する, 〈資本などを〉還流する, 〈利益などを〉生む, 〈収入などを〉申告する, 戻る, 復帰する, 転換する
　return to a rising trend 上昇基調に戻る
　return to break-even 収支とんとんに戻る, 赤字が解消する

return to profit 黒字に転換する
return to work 職場に復帰する
▸Roughly half of the earnings in 2007 were *returned* to the stockholders in dividends. 2007年度の利益の約半分は、配当金として株主に還元されています。

return 名 利益, 利益率, 収益, 収益率, 利回り, 運用成績, 運用収益, 還元, 申告, 申告書, 報告書, リターン

　accounting return on equity 株主資本利益率
　added return 追加収益
　after-tax return 税引き後収益率, 税引き後利益
　asset return 資産収益率, 資産利回り
　annual return 年次届出書, 年次報告書
　blue return 青色申告 (=blue form income tax return)
　cash return on investment 現金投資収益率
　earn a return 利益を上げる, 利益率を上げる
　expected return 期待収益, 予想収益, 期待収益率, 予想利益率
　external rate of return 外部収益率
　financial returns 配当金, 投資収益
　horizon return 所有期間利回り (=holding period return)
　income tax return 所得税申告書, 所得税納入申告書, 法人税申告書
　interim return 中間申告, 中間収益率
　investment return 資本利益率, 投資収益率, 運用益 (=return of investment, return on investment)
　price returns 価格収益
　rate of return on invested capital 投下資本利益率
　return of profits to shareholders 株主への利益還元 (⇒review 動)
　return on average equity 平均株主資本利益率
　return on capital 資本利益率, 自己資本利益率, 資本の見返り, 資本運用利回り (⇒average return on capital)
　return on insurance premium management 保険料運用収益 (⇒rally)
　return on net assets employed 純資産利益率 《略 RONA》
　return on net worth 株主資本利益率, 自己資本利益率
　return on sales 売上高利益率, 純利益率 (純利益=純利益÷売上)
　revised return 修正申告
　sales return 売上戻り高, 売上戻り品
　stock returns 株式総合利回り

▸We are trying as hard as we can to improve the sales, efficiency and financial *returns* of the Corporation. 私どもは、当社の売上、効率性の向上・改善と増収に全力投球しています。

return on assets 総資産利益率《略 ROA》(当期利益を総資本で割った比率) (=return on capital employed)
▸*Return on assets* is obtained by dividing net income (minus preferred stock dividends) by average total assets. 総資産利益率(ROA)は、純利益(優先株式配当金控除後)を平均総資産価額で割って[除して]求められます。

return on average shareholders' equity 平均普通株主持ち分利益率
▸The *return on average shareholders' equity* in 2007 was seven percent compared with 15 percent in 2006. 2007年度の平均普通株主持ち分利益率は、前年度の15%に対して7%でした。

return on capital employed 使用総資本利益率, 資本利益率《略 ROCE》
▸*Return on capital employed* is calculated as income divided by average total assets less average noninterest-bearing current liabilities. 使用総資本利益率は、利益を平均総資産から平均無利息流動負債を控除した金額で割って[控除した金額で除して]算出されています。

return on equity 株主資本利益率, 自己資本利益率《略 ROE》(資本金などをどれほど有効に使って利益を生んだかを示す経営指標。⇒strength)
▸*Return on equity* was 19% in 2007, compared with 21% in 2006. 2007年度の株主資本利益率[自己資本利益率]は、前年度の21%に対して19%でした。

return on investment 投下資本利益率, 使用総資本利益率, 投資収益, 投資利益率, 投資収益率, 投資利回り, 運用利回り, 投資リターン, 投下資本利益率《略 ROI》
　increase the return on investment 投資収益[利益]率を高める
　return on investment method 投資収益率法
▸The expected *return on an investment* can be estimated on the basis of its historical performance. 投資の期待収益率は、過去の運用成績に基づいて予測することができる。
▸We improved our *return on investment* in 2007. 2007年度は、投下資本利益率も向上しました。

return on plan assets 年金資産運用益, 年金資産の長期収益率
▸We assumed a long-term rate of *return on plan assets* of 8.6% in 2007. 年金資産の長期収益率

は，2007年度は8.6%でした．

return on stockholders' [shareholders'] equity　株主資本利益率，株主持ち分利益率
▸*Return on stockholders' equity* is calculated as Net income divided by average equity capital.　株主持ち分利益率は，当期純利益を平均株式資本で割って［除して］算出します．

return to stockholders [shareholders]　株主還元，株主への利益還元，株主の利益
▸We are mindful about *return to* our *stockholders*.　株主への還元［利益還元］については，絶えず念頭に置いています．

returned 形　戻された，送り返された
returned purchase　仕入戻し，仕入戻し品，戻し品，返送品
returned sales　売上戻り，戻り品

revaluation 名　再評価，評価替え，通貨切上げ
gain or loss from revaluation of inventories　棚卸し評価損益
loss from securities revaluation　有価証券評価損
profit from securities revaluation　有価証券評価益（=profit from revaluation of securities）
revaluation surplus　再評価剰余金

revamp 動　見直す，立て直す，刷新する，改良する，改造する，改訂する，修正する
▸We are forced to *revamp* our management system.　当社は，経営体制の見直しを迫られています．

reveal 動　発表する，公表する，示す，開示する，明らかにする
▸The company *revealed* a new medium-term business plan for fiscal 2007-2010.　同社は，2007-2010年度の新中期経営構想を発表した．
▸The company *revealed* the annual salaries of its four top executive officers at this year's general shareholders meeting.　同社は，今年の株主総会で代表取締役4人の年間報酬額を開示した．

revenue 名　収益，営業収益，売上，売上高，収入，歳入
収益とは ➡ 商品の販売，サービスの提供，その他企業の営業活動から生じる現金または現金等価物（cash equivalents：売掛金や受取手形などを含む）の流入額，投資から得た利子，配当ならびに固定資産の売却や交換に基づく得利，負債の減少額をいう．資本の払込みや借入金の受入れなどは，収益とはならない．なお，会計上「現金」は，銀行預金のほかに小切手，手形，郵便為替証書などを含むが，流動資産に含まれるcashは手元現金と銀行の要求払い預金を指す．

capital revenue　資本的収入
corporate revenue　企業収益
dividend revenue　受取配当金
financial revenue　財務収益，金融収益
geographic revenue　地域別売上高
incremental revenue　増分収益
nonoperating revenue　営業外収益
nonrecurring revenue　経常外利益
other revenue (expenses)　営業外収益（費用）
other revenues and gains　営業外収益および利得
revenue base　収益基盤（=revenue basis;⇒ enhancement）
revenue from investment　投資収益
revenue income　売上収入
revenue standard　収益基準
segment revenue　セグメント収益

▸The increase in *revenues* in 2007 was mainly due to increased demand for business communications products in Europe.　2007年度の売上高の増加［2007年度の増収］は，主に欧州でのビジネス通信機器の需要拡大によるものです．

revenue growth　売上高［営業収益］の伸び，収益の伸び，増収（=increase in revenues;⇒introduction）
▸*Revenue growth* from 2005 to 2007 occurred across all product lines.　2005年から2007年まで3期連続の売上高の伸びは，全製品系列にわたっています．

revenue mix　売上構成
▸The shift in *revenue mix* to other services from higher-margin rentals led to a decline in the margin percentage in 2007.　2007年度は，高利益率のレンタル事業からその他の事業［サービス］に売上構成が変化したため，利益率が低下しました．

revenues and earnings　収益と利益［純利益］，営業収益と利益［純利益］
revenues and earnings growth　収益と利益［純利益］の伸び
revenues and earnings losses　減収減益（=losses in revenues and earnings）

▸*Revenues and earnings* for financial services and leasing increased in 2007.　2007年度は，金融サービスおよびリース部門の営業収益と純利益が増加しました．

reversal 名　反発，反転，逆転，取り崩し，戻し入れ，戻り益，〈判決の〉破棄［取消し］
reversal of bad-debt reserve　貸倒れ引当金の戻り益
reversal of special allowances　特別積立金戻

reverse 動 振り戻す, 戻し入れる, 入れ替える, 取り崩す, 再修正する, 再整理する, 〈判決などを〉破棄する, 無効にする, 取り消す
▶The tax effects of timing differences originating in prior periods and *reversing* in the current period are determined at the applicable income tax rates reflected in the accounts as of the beginning of the current period. 過年度に発生し, 当期に取り崩される期間差異の税効果は, 当期首現在の勘定に反映されている当該所得税率で算定されます.

reverse split 株式併合, 株式分割 (＝reverse split of stocks, reverse stock split, share split-down)

review 動 査閲する, 評価する, 検討する, 監査する, 調査する, 審査する (「査閲」は, 監査が一般に公正妥当と認められる監査基準に従って実施されているかどうか, また所定の監査方針が遵守されているかどうかを確かめること)
▶An increase in the number of foreign shareholders prompted the company to *review* the return of profits to shareholders. 外国人株主が増えているため, 同社は株主への利益還元を見直した.
▶The audit committee *reviews* the corporation's annual consolidated financial statements and recommends their approval to the board of directors. 監査委員会は, 当社の年次連結財務書類を査閲して, 取締役会にその承認を求めます.

review 名 〈監査調書の〉査閲, 〈監査技術としての〉閲覧, 調査, 審査, 再調査, 検討, 見直し, 再考, 再審理, 報告, 報告書, 評論, レビュー (⇒**period under review**)
　business review 営業概況
　chairman's review 会長報告書
　legal review 法律見解書
　limited review 限定監査
　management review 経営監査
　peer review 相互検査, 専門家による相互審査, 相互評価, 相互批判, 同僚評価
　rating review 格付け見直し
　review of financial statements 財務諸表［財務書類］のレビュー
　review of internal control 内部統制の調査
　review of operations 営業報告書

revise 動 修正する, 改正する, 改定する, 改訂する, 見直す, 校正する, 校閲する (⇒**business projection**)
　revise downward 下方修正する (＝downgrade, revise down, slash)
　revise upward 上方修正する (＝revise up, upgrade)
▶Losses related to U.S. subprime mortgages forced Mizuho Financial Group Inc. to *revise* terms for merging Mizuho Securities and Shinko Securities. 米国のサブプライム・ローン［低所得者向け住宅融資］関連の損失で, みずほフィナンシャルグループ (FG) は, みずほ証券と新光証券の合併条件の修正を迫られた.
▶The company was forced to *revise* an original revitalization plan. 同社は, 当初の再生計画の見直しを迫られた.
▶Other banks are likely forced to *revise* their earnings projections downward because of the accelerated disposal of bad loans, business deterioration of borrowers due to the lingering recession and further decline in stock prices. 不良債権処理の加速や長引く不況による融資先の業績悪化, 株安などの影響で, 他行も業績予想の下方修正を迫られている.
▶Standard & Poor's *revised* upward the outlook on its ratings on six major Japanese insurance companies against the backdrop of their improved financial profiles. スタンダード＆プアーズは, 日本の大手保険会社6社の財務力見直し改善を背景に, 6社の格付け見通しを上方修正した.

revision 名 修正, 改正, 改訂, 変更, 見直し
　downward revision 下方修正
　massive [large, substantial] upward revision 大幅な上方修正
　slight upward revision 小幅な上方修正
　upward revision 上方修正
▶Many expect losses from bad loan disposals to increase drastically, leading to an inevitable downward *revision* of banks' business performance. 大方の予想では, 不良債権処理に伴う損失額は今後大幅に増え, 銀行の業績の下方修正は避けられない状況だ.

revitalization 名 再生, 活性化, 再活性化, 健全化, 復興, 回復
　corporate revitalization 企業再生
　management revitalization plan 経営健全化計画
　revitalization firm 企業再生会社 (＝revitalizing firm)
　revitalization plan 再生計画, 再活性化案 (⇒**revise**)
▶The government demanded banks seeking public funds to submit management *revitaliza-*

tion plans.　政府は、公的資金［資金注入］を受ける銀行に経営健全化計画の提出を求めた。

revival 名　再生、事業再生、再建、復活、回復
▸Resona Bank announced a plan to introduce *revival* accounts to manage its ¥2.3 trillion nonperforming loans separately from the healthier loans.　りそな銀行は、2兆3,000億円の不良債権を正常債権とは別個に管理する「再生勘定」を導入する方針を発表した。

revival plan　再生計画、事業再生計画、再建計画
▸Under the *revival plan*, the firm intends to issue ¥30 billion worth of preferred shares to Sumitomo Mitsui Banking.　この再生計画では、同社は、三井住友銀行を引受先として300億円の優先株式を発行する。

revive 動　再生する、再建する、立て直す、再び活性化する、〈景気などを〉刺激する、回復する、再燃する
▸The firm closed some plants as part of a strategy to *revive* its struggling operations.　同社は、不振の事業部門再建策の一環として、工場の一部を閉鎖した。

revolving credit　回転信用、回転信用状、回転クレジット、リボルビング・クレジット
　revolving credit agreement　自動更新借入契約、回転信用契約
　revolving credit system　リボルビング・システム
revolving credit facility　回転信用供与枠、回転融資枠、回転信用ファシリティ　(⇒**increase in ...**)
▸These *revolving credit facilities* are intended for general corporate purposes.　これらの回転融資枠は、一般の事業目的に使用する予定です。
▸These *revolving credit facilities* were unused at December 31, 2007.　これらの回転融資枠は、2007年12月31日現在、使用されていません。

revolving fund　回転資金
revoke 動　取り消す、無効にする、解約する　(⇒**licence**)
reward 名　報酬、報償、報奨金、褒賞金、謝礼、対価、成果、リターン
　financial rewards　金銭的な報酬
　reward to shareholders [stockholders]　株主の利益、株主への利益還元、株主還元
　rewards of investment　投資の成果
　rewards system　報奨金制度
　risk and reward　リスクとリターン
▸Gain from stock options is a *reward* for dedicated work by an employee.　ストック・オプション［自社株購入権］の利益は、従業員が熱心に勤務したことへの対価である。

right 名　権利、権限、所有権、新株引受権、正当、公正　(⇒**management right, stock appreciation right**)
　business right　営業権
　dividend right　配当請求権
　minority stockholders' right　少数株主権
　operating right　営業権　(⇒**sell** 動)
　pension right　年金権
　right of beneficiary　受益権
　right of claim　請求権
　right of minority shareholders　少数株主権
　right to benefits　受給権
　rights issue　株主割当て発行、株主割当て発行増資
　security right　担保権
　shareholders' right　株主権　(＝**stockholders' right**)
　stock acquisition right　新株予約権
　stock right　新株引受権、株式引受権、株式買受権　(＝**subscription right**)
　stockholder rights plan　株主権利制度
▸During 2007, various holders of these zero coupon notes exercised conversion *rights* for approximately 614,000 notes.　2007年度に当社は、このゼロ・クーポン債所有者から約61万4,000の債券について転換権が行使されました。
▸Stock trades involving the transfer of management *rights* has been undertaken, in principle, through a takeover bid.　経営権の移動を伴う株取引は、原則として株式公開買付け(TOB)で行われてきた。

right of indemnity　求償権
▸A nonlife insurer has used its *right of indemnity* concerning the series of faults in MMC-made vehicles.　一連の三菱製自動車の欠陥問題に関して、損保会社が求償権を行使した。

rights offering　株主割当て、株主割当て発行、株主割当て発行増資（新株発行の際、一定の割合で株主に優先的に新株を引き受ける権利を与えること）

ripple effect　波及効果
▸Housing starts have a tremendous *ripple effect* on the overall economy.　住宅着工件数は、景気全体への波及効果が大きい。

rise 動　増加する、拡大する、伸びる、上昇する、高まる
▸Against the backdrop of the rising prices of crude oil, prices of raw materials are likely to continue *rising*.　原油高を背景に［原油高で］、原材料価格の上昇は続きそうだ。
▸Net income *rose* to ¥143 billion, or ¥78 per

share, in the three months ended June. 4−6月期は, 純利益[税引き後利益]が1,430億円(1株当たり78円)に増加した.
▸The company's sales in the first quarter *rose* 12.6 percent to ¥693.7 billion. 同社の第1四半期の売上高は, (前年同期比) 12.6%増の6,937億円だった.

rise 名 増加, 拡大, 伸び, 上昇, 高騰, 向上
　rise in corporate profits 企業収益の増加
　rise in deficit 赤字の増加
　rise in oil prices 原油価格の高騰, 原油高
　rise in the yen 円高
▸We recorded a strong 12 percent *rise* in the third-quarter net income. 当社の第3四半期の純利益は, 12%増と高水準の伸びを記録しました.

rising 形 上昇する, 増加する (⇒rise 動)
　rising dollar ドル高
　rising equity value 株価上昇
　rising profits 利益の増加

rising cost コストの上昇
▸Pulp and paper makers have a hard time passing the *rising cost* of their materials onto customers. 製紙業界は, 原材料コスト上昇の価格転嫁に難航している[製紙業界は, 原材料のコスト増を顧客に転嫁するのが難しくなっている].

rising interest rate 金利の上昇
▸*Rising* long-term *interest rates* will lead directly to higher interest payments for government bonds. 長期金利の上昇は, 国債の利払い費増に直結する.

risk 名 危険, 危険性, 危険負担, 〈価格などの〉値下がり確率, リスク
　avoid prepayment risk 期限前償還リスクを避ける
　balance sheet risk 財務リスク
　bear the risk リスクを負う (＝assume the risk)
　capital risk 元本リスク, キャピタル・リスク
　collection risk 回収リスク
　credit risk 信用リスク
　diversification of risks リスク分散 (＝diversity of risks)
　diversify investment risks 投資リスクを分散する
　exchange risk 為替リスク (＝currency risk, foreign exchange risk)
　failure risk 倒産リスク
　financial risk 金融リスク, 財務リスク, 財務上[金融上]のリスク
　financing risk 資金調達リスク
　hedge risks リスクを相殺する, リスクをヘッジする

　high-risk high-return ハイリスク・ハイリターン (危険性の高い金融資産ほど高い運用益が期待できること)
　hostile acquisition risk 敵対的買収リスク
　lay off financial risk 金融リスク[財務リスク]を回避する
　manage the risk exposure リスクを管理する (＝control the risk exposure)
　management risk 経営リスク, 経営者リスク, マネジメント・リスク (＝managerial risk)
　rating risk 格付けリスク
　reduce the default risk 不履行リスクを軽減する[低減する, 低下させる, 抑える]
　risk capital 危険資本, 危険負担資本, 危険投資資本, 危険資本投資 (＝venture capital)
　risk exposure リスク, リスク・エクスポージャー
　risk hedge リスクの防止[軽減], 危険[リスク]回避手段, 損失リスクからの防衛手段[防衛策], リスク・ヘッジ
　risk reduction リスクの軽減, リスクの低下
▸We can hedge exchange *risk* through forward markets. 為替予約で, 為替リスクをヘッジすることができる.

risk management 危機管理, 危険管理, リスク管理, リスク・マネジメント
　financial risk management 金融リスク管理, 金融リスク・マネジメント

ROA 総資産利益率, 総資本利益率 (**return on assets**の略)

roadshow 動 投資家説明会を行う, 投資家向け説明会を行う
▸The firm will *roadshow* for the bond issue in Japan. 同社は, 日本での債券発行[社債発行]の投資家説明会を行う.

roadshow 名 投資家説明会, 投資家向け説明会, 募集説明会, 巡回説明会, 巡回キャンペーン, ロードショー (＝road show：証券発行会社の経営者と引受業者の担当者が, 機関投資家や有力な個人投資家を対象にして行う証券購入のメリットに関する説明会. 一般に, 発行会社の財務状況や将来の収益見通しなどを説明する. ⇒information, investor relations, IR)

robotics 名 ロボット技術, ロボット工学, ロボット
▸*Robotics* is used for delivery of mail and office supplies in this campus. この事業施設では, 郵便物や事務用品の取扱いにロボットを使っています.

robust 形 好調な, 活発な, 活況の, 目覚しい, 大幅な, 著しい, 底堅い
　robust earnings 好業績, 業績好調 (＝robust

performance, robust results)
robust economy 経済の活況, 景気好調, 底堅い景気
robust growth 大幅な伸び
robust performance 好業績, 好調な業績, 業績好調 (=robust earnings)
▶The company traced the overall sales surge to *robust performances* at new subsidiaries. 同社は, 総売上高急増の主因として新子会社の業績好調を挙げた。
robust sales 販売好調, 好調な販売
▶*Robust sales* in overseas markets, including North America, contributed to the growth in profits and sales. 北米など海外市場での販売好調が, 増収増益[利益と売上高の増加]の要因だ。
ROCE 使用総資本利益率 (**return on capital employed** の略)
ROE 株主資本利益率, 自己資本利益率, 持ち分資本利益率, 株式投資収益率 (株主資本利益率[自己資本利益率] = 純利益(net income) ÷ 純資産(owners' equity); ⇒**return on equity**)
▶Return on equity (*ROE*) is a key gauge of a company's stock investment efficiency. 株主資本利益率(ROE)は, 企業の株式投資効率を示す重要な経営指標だ。
ROI 投下資本利益率, 使用資本利益率, 投資利益率, 資本利益率 (**return on investment** の略)
rollover 图 更新, 更改, 満期書替え, 資金の回転調達, 借りつなぎ, 借換え, 支払い繰延べ, ロールオーバー
  debt rollover 債務返済の繰延べ, 債務再構成, 債務の特別条件変更 (=refinancing debt)
  lease rollover リース契約更新, 賃貸契約更新
  rollover lending ころがし貸付け
  rollover loan 借換え融資
  rollover of an existing debt 既存の債務の借換え, 借換え
  rollover of liabilities 負債の借換え
RONA 純資産利益率 (**return on net assets employed** の略)
RONA awards RONA報奨金, 純資産利益率報奨金
▶During 2007, $250 million was provided for *RONA awards*. 2007年度は, RONA報奨金に2億5,000万ドルを計上しました。
RONA incentive program 純資産利益率報奨金制度
▶The *RONA Incentive Program* is available to eligible employees who are not participating in the Company Executive Incentive Plan. 純資

利益率報奨金制度は, 会社幹部報奨金制度に参加していない有資格従業員が利用できます。
row 图 連続, 列
  for the second month in a row 2か月連続で, 2か月続けて
  for three days in a row 3日連続で, 3日連続して, 3日続けて
▶Listed companies as the whole are expected to post year-on-year increases both in sales and profits for the fourth year in a *row*. 上場企業は全体として, 前年比で4年連続の増収増益となる見込みだ。
royalty 图 〈著作権・特許権・鉱区などの〉使用料, 工業権使用料, 〈権利の〉実施料, 許諾料, 採掘料, 印税, ロイヤルティ
  maximum royalty 最高実施料
  minimum royalty 最低ロイヤルティ
  royalties revenue 使用料収益, 受取使用料
  royalty cost 支払い使用料, 使用料原価
  royalty fees on recorders 〈録音・録画機器の〉補償金[著作権使用料]
  royalty income ロイヤルティ収入
  royalty of patent rights 特許権使用料 (=patent right royalty)
  royalty payment ロイヤルティの支払い, ロイヤルティの支払い金
  running royalty 継続的使用料, 継続的実施料, ランニング・ロイヤルティ
▶For financial statement reporting, the *royalties* are recognized as income in the period earned. 財務書類上[財務諸表上], ロイヤルティは, それを稼得した期の利益として認識される。
▶Sharp Corp. revised its rewards system for inventors, allowing retired employees to receive *royalties*. シャープは, 発明者に対する報奨金制度を改定して, 退職者もロイヤルティを受け取ることができるようになった。
rule 图 規則, 規定, 規約, 通則, 法, 法規, 原則, 慣例, 通例, 支配, 裁判所の裁定[命令], 基準, 規準, ルール
  capital adequacy rule 自己資本規制, 自己資本比率規制
  compliance rules 法令・規則の遵守規則
  conduct of business rule 業務遂行基準
  cost or market rule 低価基準
  listing rules 上場基準, 上場規則, 上場要件
  net capital rule 自己資本規制比率
  one-share/one-vote rule 1株=1議決権ルール
  Rule 415 shelf registration SEC規則415に基づく一括登録

rule of fair practice 公正慣習遵守の原則
▸According to the NYSE's new *rules*, corporate boards must be composed of a majority of independent directors.　ニューヨーク証券取引所 (NYSE) の新上場基準によると, 企業 (上場企業) の取締役の過半数は社外取締役にしなければならない。

run 動　経営する, 指揮する, 管理する, 運用する, 運営する, 提供する, 操作する, 動かす, 実行する, 行う, 掲載する, 載せる; …の状態になる,〈契約などが〉有効である, 動く, 作動する, 稼働する, 進行する, 進む, 行われる, 上演される
▸With the collapse of the economic bubble in the early 1990s, many corporate managers had to devote themselves to *running* their own companies.　1990年代はじめのバブル崩壊とともに, 企業経営者の多くは自社の経営に専念せざるをえなくなった。

running 形　連続している, 連続する, 絶え間のない, 運転中の, 現在の

running average method　移動平均法 (= moving average method)

running bill　未決済手形

running cost　運転費, 運転コスト, 運営経費, 操業費, 経営費, ランニング・コスト

running expense　操業費, 経常費

running price　時価, 市価

running stock　適正在庫, 正常在庫, 運転在庫, ランニング・ストック
▸Group sales also hit a record high for the fourth year *running*.　連結売上高も, 4年連続, 過去最高となった。

S

saddled with ... …を抱えて，…を背負って，…で手いっぱい
▶The firm went bankrupt *saddled with* a ¥300 billion debt in June 2007. 同社は，3,000億円の負債を抱えて2007年6月に破産した。

salary 名 給与，給料，月給，俸給，報酬
annual salaries of a company's executives 企業役員の年間報酬額
annual salary system 年俸制
bonus and salary 賞与・給与
executive salaries 役員報酬
salaries and allowances 給料手当
salaries and salary related expenses 給料および給料関連費用
salaries and wages 給料賃金，給与・賃金 (⇒ wage)
salaries expense 給料，給与
salaries payable 未払い給与
salary payment 給与振込み，給与支払い
salary structure 給与体系 (=salary system)
salespeople salaries 販売員給与
▶*Salaries* for the managerial employees can go up or down in accordance with each employee's performance and contribution to the company. 管理職の給与は，各社員の能力［成果］と会社貢献度に応じて上下する可能性がある。

salary income 給与所得
▶Stock options must be treated as *salary income*, not occasional income. ストック・オプション［自社株購入権］は，一時所得ではなく，給与所得として扱うべきだ。

salary projection 給与計画
▶Contributions reflect actuarial assumptions regarding *salary projection* and future service benefits. 拠出金［年金掛金］は，給与計画と将来の給付額についての年金数理計算上の仮定［基礎率］を反映しています。

sale 名 販売，売買，売却，譲渡，〈証券などの〉発行，セール
approval sale 試用販売
bulk sale 一括売却［販売］，全量販売［売買］，包括譲渡，事業用資産包括譲渡 (=bulk transfer)
funds gained from the sale of shares 株式売却で調達した資金，株式発行で調達した資金
gain on sale of bonds 社債売却益
offer for sale 売出発行，間接発行
profits from the sale of businesses 営業譲渡益
sale and leaseback transaction 売却後借戻し取引，セール・リースバック取引，セール・アンド・リースバック取引 (=sale-leaseback transaction)
sale of bonds 社債発行
sale of commercial paper コマーシャル・ペーパーの発行
sale value 販売価格，売却価額，売却価値，売上高
share sale 株式発行
▶The planned *sale* of GM's stake in Suzuki Motor Corp. is believed to be part of GM's restructuring efforts. GMが保有するスズキ株の売却計画は，GMの経営再建策の一環と見られる。

sale and purchase 売買
▶The closing of the *sale and purchase* of the Shares took place at the offices of ABCD Corp. on June 10, 2007. 本株式の売買取引の実行［本株式のクロージング］は，2007年6月10日にABCDコーポレーションの事務所で行われた。

sales 名 売上, 売上高, 取引高,〈航空会社などの〉営業利益, 販売, 売買, 売却, 商法, セールス (⇒ consolidated sales, group sales)
- **bogus sales** 架空の売上, 虚偽の売上 (⇒**dress up**)
- **business sales** 企業売上高, 事業売却
- **cost of sales** 売上原価 (＝cost of goods sold)
- **credit sales** 掛売り, 信用販売, 掛売高, 掛売上高
- **foreign sales** 海外販売, 海外売上高, 国外売上高
- **gross sales** 総売上高
- **installment [instalment] sales** 割賦販売, 割賦売上高, 延べ払い
- **intercompany sales** 内部取引高
- **property sales** 資産の売却
- **sales activities** 販売活動
- **sales administrative expense** 販売管理費
- **sales and administrative expense** 販売費および一般管理費, 販売費・一般管理費
- **sales and earnings gains [growth]** 増収増益
- **sales base** 営業拠点, 販売拠点
- **sales cost** 販売費, 販売原価, 売上原価
- **sales credit** 売掛金, 未収金, 売掛債権, 売上債権
- **sales department** 営業部門, 販売部門 (⇒ strategic planning)
- **sales forecast** 売上高予想, 売上高の見通し, 販売見通し, 販売予測 (＝forecast of sales)
- **sales profit ratio** 売上利益率
- **sales revenue** 売上高, 売上収益, 総売上高, 販売収入, 販売収益
- **sales through the Internet** ネット販売, インターネット販売
- **stock sales** 株式売却, 株式の売買, 株式譲渡
- **Web sales** ネット販売

▶NEC Corp.'s *sales* of semiconductors and mobile phones have been sluggish. NECの半導体や携帯電話の販売は, 低迷している。

▶*Sales* and earnings again set record, with all three our major business segments contributing to the continuing growth. 売上高と純利益は, 当社の主力3事業部門が成長の持続に貢献し, 過去最高を更新しました。

sales effort 販売努力, 営業面の努力
▶Toyota's operating profit was pushed up mainly due to *sales efforts* and cost-reduction efforts in its production lines. トヨタの営業利益を押し上げた主な要因は, 販売努力[営業面の努力]と生産ラインのコスト削減[従業員による生産コスト削減]だ。

sales incentive 販売奨励金, 販売促進策
▶GM has replaced zero financing with other *sales incentives*, including $2002 off the price. GMは最近, ゼロ金利ローンに代わって「2002ドル割引」などの販売促進策を導入した。

sales mix 売上品目構成, 売上構成, 商品構成, セールス・ミックス
▶Pricing pressures and changes in our product *sales mix* caused the gross margin percentage to decline. 価格圧力[値下げ圧力]と当社製品の売上構成の変化で, 売上総利益率は低下しました。

sales of stock 株の売却, 株式の売買, 株式の売出し, 株式の譲渡 (⇒**stock sales**)
▶*Sales of stock* by our subsidiaries produced $45 million gain in 2007. 当社の子会社による株式の売出しで, 2007年度は4,500万ドルの利益が生じました。

sales operations 営業, 営業活動, 営業部門
▶Sanyo Electric Co. plans to spin off its domestic *sales operations*. 三洋電機は, 国内営業部門の分社化を計画している[国内営業部門を分社化する方針だ]。

sales promotion 販売促進, 販促
▶The firm attributed the improved showing to stepped-up cost-cutting efforts and *sales promotion*. 同社は, 業績改善の要因として, コスト削減努力の促進と販促を挙げた。

sales-type lease 販売型リース, 販売金融リース
▶We lease our products to customers under *sales-type leases*. 当社は, 自社製品を販売型リースで顧客にリースしています。

salvage value 残存価格, 残存価額, 転用価額 (＝residual value, scrap value; ⇒**useful life**)

same period a year earlier 前年同期 (＝same period last year)
▶Fujiya Co. posted a consolidated pretax loss of ¥7 billion in the six months through September, comapared with a loss of ¥1.3 billion in the *same period a year earlier*. 不二家の連結税引き前赤字[税引き前損失]は, 9月中間決算[4-9月期]で, 前年同期の13億円の赤字に対して70億円となった。

same period last year 前年同期 (＝same period a year earlier; ⇒**Q4**)
▶Gross capital expenditures were $1,700 million for the first nine months of 2007, compared with $1,500 million during the *same period last year*. 2007年1-9月期の資本的支出総額は, 前年同期の15億ドルに対して17億ドルでした。

same period of the previous year 前年同期 (＝same period last year)
▶The company's sales revenue for the first quar-

ter totaled ¥4.51 trillion, an increase of 10.2 percent compared with the *same period of the previous year*.　同社の第1四半期の売上高は、前年同期比10.2%増の4兆5,100億円となった。

SAR　株式評価益権、株式評価受益権（**stock appreciation right**の略）。⇒**exercisable**）

Sarbanes-Oxley Act　企業改革法（サーベンス・オクスレー法）、企業会計改革法、サーベンス・オクスレー法、SO法　（＝Sarbanes-Oxley Act of 2002)

> 企業改革法（サーベンス・オクスレー法）とは➡︎ 米エネルギー大手エンロンの経営破綻をきっかけに相次いで発覚した経営者による不正な会計操作の防止策として、2002年6月に米証券取引委員会(SEC)は、全米大企業942社の最高経営責任者(CEO)と最高財務責任者(CFO)に対して、過去の決算報告が正確であると宣誓した署名文書の提出を求めた。企業改革法は、このSECの要請を1回限りとしないで法律で恒久化することを定めたもので、2002年7月に成立した。
> 　この企業改革法（サーベンス・オクスレー法）に基づく措置として、SECはその後の8月27日、米国企業だけでなく米株式市場に上場する外国企業のCEO（最高経営責任者）とCFO（最高財務責任者）に対しても、決算報告の正確さを保証する宣誓書の提出を義務付け、8月29日から実施する新規則を決定した。
> 　このほか米国企業に対しては、年次報告書の提出期限を従来の90日以内から60日以内に、四半期報告書の提出期限を従来の45日以内から35日以内に短縮した。また、経営者による不正な会計操作や自社株売却を時間的に困難にするため、企業幹部による自社株取引の報告期限を40日以内から2日以内に大幅に短縮した。なお、企業改革法では、米国市場に上場する外国企業も含めて、決算などの虚偽報告には最長で20年の禁固刑が科されることになっている。（2002年8月28日付讀賣新聞参照）

▶The *Sarbanes-Oxlay Act* directed the SEC to implement some of the reporting changes in an attempt to force companies and their executives to be more honest with investors.　企業と企業経営者に投資家への一段と誠実な対応を義務付けるため、サーベンス・オクスレー法は、SEC［米証券取引委員会］に報告規則変更の一部実施を求めた。

savings　貯蓄、貯金、預金、年金
　retirement savings　退職年金
　savings and loan association　貯蓄金融機関、〖米〗貯蓄貸付け組合(S&L)
　savings from a debt waiver　債務免除益
　savings incentive plan　貯蓄奨励制度
　savings plan　貯蓄制度
▶We contributed $350 million to the *savings plans* for our employees in 2007.　当社は、当社従業員のための貯蓄制度に2007年度は3億5,000万ドル拠出しました。

SB　普通社債、確定利付き社債（**straight bond**の略）

Schedule 13D　届出様式13D（上場会社の発行済み株式の5%以上を取得した者が、取得後の10営業日以内に米証券取引委員会(SEC)、当該企業と、当該企業の株式を上場している証券取引所に提出することになっている報告書の書式。⇒**toehold purchase**）

scheme　事業、計画、企画、案、策、仕組み、制度、体系、方式、組織、機構、体制、概要、基準　（⇒**triangular merger scheme**）
　business scheme　業務体制
　classification scheme　分類基準
　corporate defense schemes　企業防衛策
　defined benefit scheme　確定給付年金
　occupational pension scheme　従業員年金制度
　pension scheme　年金制度
　regulation scheme　規制策
　retirement benefit scheme　退職給与制度
　share buyback scheme　自社株買い
▶The new triangular merger *scheme* was introduced in Japan in May 2007.　この新三角合併方式は、2007年5月に日本で導入された。

scope　範囲、領域、枠組み、構成、区分、余地、機会、可能性
　audit scope　監査の範囲　（＝scope of audit, scope of examination）
　economy of scope　範囲の経済
　geographic scope　営業地域
　product scope　製品構成
　scope of business　業務範囲
　scope of independent auditor's examination　独立監査人の監査範囲
　scope of opinion　意見区分
▶To improve their business performance, news organizations are working to expand the *scope* of news distribution through the Net.　メディア各社は、経営改善に向けて、ネットによるニュース配信の拡充を進めている。

scope of consolidation　連結の範囲　（＝consolidation criteria; ⇒**consolidation criteria**）

> 連結の範囲➡︎「連結の範囲」の基準としては、基本的に「他社の発行済み議決権株式(outstanding voting stock)の50%超（過半数）を直接間接に所有している場合、その会社を連結の範囲に含める」ことになっている。議決権株式の過半数を所有していても、その企業支配の関係が一時的なものや、更

生会社や破産会社など過半数所有が実質的な企業支配に当たらない場合には,連結の範囲に含めない。

scrap 動 撤回する,撤廃する,打ち切る,中止する,廃案にする,捨てる,廃品にする,スクラップにする
▶Fujita Corp. *scrapped* a plan to merge with Sumitomo Mitsui Construction Co. in March 2005. 2005年3月にフジタは,三井住友建設との経営統合計画を白紙撤回した。

scrap value 残存価格,残存価額,廃材価額 (= residual value, salvage value)
▶The asset has a useful life of 5 years and no *scrap value*. この資産の耐用年数は5年で,残存価額はゼロである。

SEC 米証券取引委員会 (Securities and Exchange Commissionの略)
　SECへの提出書類 ➡ 米証券取引委員会(SEC)に登録している企業がSECへの提出を義務付けられている主な報告書類としては,証券の発行の際に提出する届出書(registration statement)のほか,証券発行後に毎年決算期ごとに提出する年次報告書(annual report),四半期ごとに提出する四半期報告書(quarterly report),重要事項が発生した際に提出する臨時報告書(current report)などがある。
　expenses for fling with the SEC SECへの届出費用
　SEC probe SECの調査
　SEC Regulation S-X 米証券取引委員会規則S-X,SEC財務諸表規則S-X,米証券取引委員会の連結財務書類[連結財務諸表]作成規定,レギュレーションS-X
　SEC requirements SEC[米証券取引委員会]の開示要求
　SEC Rule 米証券取引委員会規則 (⇒shelf registration)

second half 下半期,下期 (= the second half of the fiscal [business] year, the second half of the year)
　the second half of the year 下半期,下期,今年度下半期[下期],今年度後半,今年後半 (= the latter half of the year, the second half)
　the second half of this fiscal year 今年度下半期,今年度下期 (= the second half, the second half of the business year)
　the second-half results 下半期決算,下期決算,下半期の業績
▶Kajima Corp., the nation's largest general contractor, returned to profit in the *second half* of the last business year. 国内ゼネコン最大手の鹿島建設が,前期[前年度]の下半期[下期]から黒字

に転換した。

second half of the current business year 今年度下半期,今年度下期
▶Sumitomo Trust & Banking Co. foresaw an additional ¥10 billion in subprime-related losses during the *second half of the current business year* through March 31, 2008. 住友信託銀行は,2008年3月31日までの下半期にサブプライム関連損失がさらに100億円増大する見通しを明らかにした。

second quarter 第2四半期
　gross profit margins for the second quarter of 2008 2008年[2008年度]第2四半期の売上利益率
　operating expenses for the second quarter 第2四半期の営業費用
　revenues for the second quarter 第2四半期の売上高
　second-quarter consolidated net income 第2四半期の連結純利益
　second quarter profit 第2四半期利益
　second quarter resuls 第2四半期の業績
▶The Corporation's wholly owned telecommunications subsidiary posted net income of $211 million for the *second quarter* of 2007. 当社が全額出資している通信事業部門子会社が,2007年度第2四半期は2億1,100万ドルの純利益を計上しました。

second-quarter operating loss 第2四半期の営業損失,第2四半期の営業赤字
▶The company posted a *second-quarter operating loss* of ¥21 billion. 同社の第2四半期の営業損失[営業赤字]は,210億円だった。

second-quarter operating revenues 第2四半期の営業収益
▶*Second-quarter operating revenues* were $1,819 million in 2007. 第2四半期の営業収益は,2007年度は18億1,900万ドルでした。

second two quarters 下半期[下期]の第3四半期と第4四半期 (⇒first two quarters)
▶In the *second two quarters* of 2007, the Corporation declared a cash dividend of $0.08 per common share. 2007年第3四半期と第4四半期に,当社はそれぞれ普通株式1株当たり0.08ドルの現金配当を宣言しました。

secondary distribution 売出し,第二次分売 (= secondary offering:不特定多数の投資家に対して,均一の条件で,すでに発行された有価証券の取得の申込みを勧誘すること)

secondary market 流通市場(trading market:投資家が発行済みの株式や債券を売買する市場),

短期金融市場(銀行引受手形や譲渡可能定期預金証書などの短期金融市場証書(money market instruments)を売買する市場), セカンダリー市場

secondary offering 売出し (＝secondary distribution：すでに発行されている有価証券(大口株主の保有株式など)を一般投資家に売り出すこと)

secondary public offering 上場後の公募

secretary 名 秘書役, 総務部長

section 名 区分, 部, 部門, セクション
 equity section 資本の部
 financial section 財務区分, 〈年次報告書の〉財務の部
 Section 1244 stock (内国歳入法)第1244条の株式
 section of stockholders' equity 資本の部

sector 名 部門, 分野, 業界, 産業, 地域, 市場, 株, セクター
 all business sectors 全業種
 banking sector 銀行業界, 銀行セクター
 business sector 事業分野, 業種, 企業セクター, 企業, 産業界, 業界
 construction sector 建設部門, 建設業界
 corporate finance sector 企業金融部門
 corporate sector 企業部門, 法人部門, 企業セクター, 企業
 corporate sector's performance 企業業績
 domestic-demand dependent sectors 内需依存株
 factory sector 製造業
 financial sector 金融部門, 金融業界, 金融・保険業, 金融セクター
 household sector 家計部門
 information and telecommunications sector 情報通信部門
 labor-intensive sectors 労働集約型産業
 leasing sector リース部門
 life insurance sector 生命保険業界, 生保業界 (＝life insurance industry; ⇒lure)
 manufacturing sector 製造業, 製造業セクター
 mining sector 鉱業株
 motor sector 自動車株
 other sectors 異業種
 primary sectors 第一次産業
 private sector 民間部門, 民間セクター, 民間企業
 public sector 政府部門, 公共部門, 公共セクター
 retail and wholesale sector 流通業
 service sector サービス部門, サービス産業
 steel sector 鉄鋼部門, 鉄鋼業界
 T-bill sector Tビル市場, 米財務省短期証券市場
 technology sector ハイテク株

▶Carbon dioxide from cars accounts for 90 percent of various greenhouse gas emissions from the transportation *sector*. 自動車から排出される二酸化炭素は, 運輸部門全体が排出する各種温室効果ガスのうち, 9割を占めている。

secure 動 獲得する, 確保する, 達成する, 実現する, 設定する, 固定する, 保証する
 be secured by ... …によって保証される, …で担保されている, …を担保にして, …を裏付けとする
 be secured on ... …を担保とする
 secure bank financing 銀行融資を受ける
 secured debt instrument 有担保債券
 secured financing 担保付き資金調達
 secured liability 担保付き負債
 secured loans 担保付き融資
 secured obligation 担保付き社債 (＝secured bond)
 secured party 担保権者

▶The bank had already *secured* it as fixed collateral. 同行は, それにはすでに根(ね)抵当権を設定していた。

▶The company was unable to *secure* sufficient funding for redemption of its corporate bonds. 同社は, 社債の償還資金の手当てがつかなかった。

secured mortgage 抵当権付き債権

▶Plan assets are represented by common and preferred shares, bonds and debentures, cash and short-term investments, real estate and *secured mortgages*. 年金資産は, 普通株式・優先株式や債券・社債, 現金・短期投資証券, 不動産, 抵当権付き債権などで構成されています。

securities 名 有価証券, 証券, 債券, 証書, 権利証書
 annual securities report 年次有価証券報告書
 cash and marketable securities at the end of the year 現金預金および有価証券期末残高
 debt and equity securities 負債証券[債務証券]と持ち分証券
 income before securities transactions 有価証券売買前利益
 income from cash and securities 金融収益と有価証券売買益
 increase (decrease) in cash and marketable securities 現金預金および有価証券の増加額(減少額)
 investment securities with remaining maturities of one year or less 1年以内に満期を迎える投資有価証券
 loss from securities revaluation 有価証券評価損

loss on securities sold　有価証券売却損
other securities　その他の有価証券
profit from securities revaluation　有価証券評価益
securities gains　証券売却益, 投資有価証券売買益
securities investment　証券投資, 有価証券投資
securities lossses　有価証券の評価損, 投資有価証券売買損
securites of affiliated company　関係会社有価証券
unrealized gains on securities　証券含み益, 有価証券含み益
▶Insider trading distorts share prices and undermines the fairness of the *securities* market.　インサイダー取引は, 株価をゆがめ, 証券市場の公正さを損なう。

Securities and Exchange Commission
米証券取引委員会《略 SEC》
　米証券取引委員会(SEC)に登録している企業がSECへの提出を義務付けられている財務書類は, consolidated balance sheet (連結貸借対照表), consolidated income statement (連結損益計算書), consolidated statement of stockholders' equity (連結キャッシュ・フロー計算書)とnotes to financial statements (財務書類注記)で構成されている。
▶The company failed to timely file its periodic reports with the *Securities and Exchange Commission* as required by Nasdaq rules.　同社は, ナスダックのルールに従って義務付けられている定期報告書を, 米証券取引委員会に期間内に提出しなかった。

Securities and Exchange Law　証券取引法
▶Financial statements are required to go through an external auditing by certified public accountants under the *Securities and Exchange Law*.　有価証券報告書は, 証券取引法で公認会計士による外部監査を受けなければならない。

securities holdings　保有証券, 保有有価証券 (保有する株式や債券)
▶Among the 10 life insurers, four reported valuation losses on their *securities holdings* of more than ¥200 billion.　生命保険10社のうち4社が, 2,000億円を超える保有株式の減損処理額を計上した。

securities market　証券市場(長期金融資産である株式や債券を取引する金融市場で, 日本では資本市場(capital market)と同義), 証券市況, 有価証券市場　(＝security market)
▶Increases in the company's stock price through stock splits made it easier for the company to raise funds through the *securities market*.　株式分割による同社の株価上昇で, 証券市場での同社の資金調達は容易になった。

securitization 名　証券化, 金融の証券化, セキュリタイゼーション
▶The two prospective partners have extensive expertise in mergers and acquisitions, as well as the *securitization* of bad loans.　提携する予定の両社は, 企業の合併・買収(M&A)や不良債権の証券化などに豊富なノウハウを持っている。

securitize 動　証券化する
securitized assets　証券化資産, 証券化した資産
securitized debt　証券化した債権
securitized home mortgages　証券化した住宅モーゲージ
securitized products　証券化商品
▶The Japan Housing Finance Agency plans to *securitize* housing loan claims bought from financial institutions.　住宅金融支援機構は, 金融機関から買い取った住宅ローンの債権を証券化する方針だ。

security 名　安全, 安全性, 保証, 保証人, 担保, 抵当, 証券, 債券, 銘柄, 保険, セキュリティ
as security for ...　…の抵当[担保, 保証]として　(＝in security for)
creation of a security interest　担保権の設定
financial security　支払い能力, 財務上の安全性
listed security　上場証券, 上場有価証券
other security investments　その他の投資有価証券
security income and expenses　有価証券損益
security money　保証金, 手付け金
unemployment security　失業保険
▶A leveraged buyout (LBO) is similar to using a mortgage to buy a house: a buyer puts some money down and borrows the rest, using the purchased asset as *security*.　レバレッジド・バイアウト(LBO)は家を買うために住宅ローンを利用するのと同じで, 買い手が購入資金の一部(頭金)を支払い, 残金は購入した資産を担保にして借り入れる仕組みになっている。

segment 動　区切る, 区分する, 細分化する　(⇒ expect, industry segment)

segment 名　事業区分, 事業分野, 事業部門, 営業区分, 区分単位, セグメント
business segment　事業分野, 事業部門, 営業区分　(＝segment of business)
customer segment　顧客層
geographic segments　地域別セグメント　(＝geographical segments)

industry segments 事業別セグメント, 産業別セグメント, 産業セグメント
information on business segment by geographic areas 地域別セグメント情報
market segment 市場区分, 市場分野
reportable industry segment 要報告産業セグメント
segment expense セグメント別費用
segment financial reporting セグメント別財務報告
segment information (unaudited) セグメント情報(未監査)
segment margin セグメント別損益, セグメント利益
segment operating profits 事業部門別営業利益
segment results セグメント業績, セグメント別業績
single industry segment 単一の事業区分
supplying segment 供給部門
▸For the first six months of fiscal 2007, the Company's power and industrial systems *segment* is likely to book an operating loss of ¥50 billion. 2007年度上期の当社の電力・産業設備事業部門は、500億円の営業損失[営業赤字]になる見通しです。
▸Revenues between industry *segments* are not material. 産業セグメント間の収益に、重要性はありません。

selected financial data 主要財務データ, 主要財務情報, 主要財務指標, 要約財務指標, 財務資料抜粋, 営業成績抜粋, ハイライト情報
selected quarterly data 主要四半期データ
self-supporting accounting system 独立採算制
self-sustaining foreign opeataions 自立した海外事業
self-sustaining operations 自立した事業
▸*Self-sustaining operations* are those whose economic activities are largely independent of those of the parent company. 自立した事業とは、その経済活動が親会社の経済活動から十分に独立している事業のことです。
sell 動 販売する, 売る, 売却する, 売り渡す, 売り込む, 納入する, 処分する, 〈債券などを〉発行する, 譲渡する (⇒**short-term borrowings**)
▸Some subsidiaries were *sold* in 2007, while new investments were made in others. 2007年には一部の子会社を売却するとともに、他の事業に新規投資を行いました。
▸The financially troubled company *sold* its operating rights to a joint company set up with GE Capital Co. 経営難に陥った同社は、GEキャピタルと設立した合弁会社に営業権を譲渡した。
▸We *sold* our 8% bonds that had a face value of $1,000,000. 当社は、額面100万ドルの8%利付き社債を発行しました。

sell off 売却する, 投げ売りする, 安く売り払う, 見切り品として処分する
▸Toshiba Corp. *sold off* its U.S. plants to Micron Technology and withdrew from DRAM production. 東芝は、米マイクロン・テクノロジーに米国工場を売却して、DRAM生産から撤退した。

sell-off 名 投げ売り, 売却, 売り, 急落
dollar sell-off ドル売り
sell-off in the market 市場の急落, 売り局面
stock market sell-off 株式相場の急落
triple sell-off トリプル安
▸Tokyo stocks fell to a three-month low as foreign investors sparked a *sell-off*. 東京株[東京株式市場の株価]は、外国人投資家が株を売り進めたため、3か月ぶりに急落した。

selling 名 販売, 売込み, 売り, 売り出し, 商法
selling and administrative expenses 販売費および一般管理費 (=general overhead)
selling and marketing expenses 販売・マーケティング費 (⇒**SG&A**)
selling commission 売上手数料
short selling 空売り
spot selling 現物売り
▸The securities company repeatedly alternated spot and short *selling* of shares of a regional bank. この証券会社は、地方銀行株の現物売りと空売りを交互に繰り返した。

selling expense [expenditure] 販売費 (=selling cost)
▸*Selling expenses* are charged against income as incurred. 販売費は、発生基準で[発生のつど]費用に計上されています。

selling, general and administrative expenses [expenditures] 販売費および一般管理費《略 **SG&A**》 (= SG&A expenditures, SG&A expenses; ⇒**total revenues**)
販売費および一般管理費に含まれるもの：

advertising expense	広告宣伝費
audit fee	監査報酬
bad debt expense	貸倒れ損失
depreciation expense	減価償却費(製造に係るものは除く)
entertainment expense	交際費
executive salaries	役員報酬

freight expense	出荷費
legal fee	弁護士報酬
promotion expense	販売促進費
rent expense	賃借料, 家賃
research and development expense	研究開発費, 試験研究費
salaries expense	給与
telephone and postage expense	通信費

▶ *Selling, general and administrative* (SG&A) expenses in the third quarter of 2007 increased by 2.5 percent from 2006. 2007年第3四半期の販売費および一般管理費(SG&A)は, 前年同期比で2.5%増加しました。

semiannual 形 半期の, 中間の, 半年ごとの, 年2回の (=biannual, semiyearly)
 semiannual dividend 中間配当, 半期配当金
 semiannual earnings 半期決算, 中間決算 (=semiannual release, semiannual results)
 semiannual income statement 中間損益計算書 (=interin income statement)
 semiannual results 中間決算 (=first-half results, interim closing, interim results)
 semiannual securities report 半期報告書
 semiannual settlement of accounts 中間決算, 半期決算 (=semiannual results, semiannual settlement)
semifinished goods 半製品, 中間製品 (=semimanufactured goods)
semimanufactured goods 半製品 (=semifinished product)
separate 動 切り離す, 分離する
▶ The company is *separating* its information-processing and distribution affiliates from its group to reduce its debts. 同社は, 負債を削減するため, 情報処理子会社と物流子会社を同社グループから切り離す方針だ。
separation 名 退職, 離職, 休職, 分離, 分割, 分解
 corporate separation 会社分割 (=corporate divestiture, demerger)
 separation of capital and administration 資本と経営の分離 (=separation between capital and management)
▶ We must book expenses for future *separations* during the years employees are working and accumulating services with the company. 社員が勤務して会社にサービスを提供し続けている期間にわたって, 当社は将来の休職に関する費用を計上しなければなりません。
separation payments 休職手当の支払い, 中途退職金の支払い
▶ Provisions for business restructuring also cover *separation payments* made as a result of special offers related to defined benefit plans. 事業再編成引当金には, 確定給付年金制度に関する特別提案を受けて行われる中途退職金の支払いも含まれています。
September midterm settlement of accounts 9月中間決算 (⇒midterm settlement of accounts)
series 名 連続, 順次, 系列, 分割発行, 指標, シリーズ (⇒repay)
 Accounting Series Release 会計連続通牒
 economic series 景気指標
 series bond 分割発行社債
 series discount 連続割引
 time series 時系列
▶ In Canada, the Corporation issued $300 million of 9% *Series* 7 Notes, due 2012. カナダで当社は, 満期2012年・利率9%のシリーズ7ノート3億ドルを発行しました。
▶ The articles of incorporation authorize the Directors to issue such shares in one or more *series* and to fix the number of shares of each *series* prior to their issue. 定款では, これらの株式をシリーズで1回以上発行する権限と, その発行前に各シリーズの発行株式数を決定する権限は, 取締役[取締役会]に与えられています。
serve 動 務める, 勤務する, 働く, 仕事をする, 〈サービスなどを〉提供する, 供給する, 〈商品などを〉売る, 運航する, 〈文書を〉渡す, 送付する, …の役に立つ, 奉仕する, 貢献する, 利用できる, …の目的にかなう, …の要求などを満たす, …の機能を果たす, …の任務[職務]を果たす, …の手段として機能する, 助長する, 促進する, 推進する, 高める
 better serve customers' needs 顧客のニーズへの対応を改善する
 serve as a hedge against inflation インフレ・ヘッジの手段[インフレに対するヘッジ手段]として機能する
 serve one's debt 債務を返済する
 serve one's interests …の利益に十分見合う
 serve one's purpose …の目的にかなう
 serve the community 地域社会に貢献する, 地域社会に奉仕する, 地域社会に尽くす
▶ The amount of retirement allowances usually is determined by the length of time directors *serve* in their post. 役員退職慰労金の金額は通常, 役員の在任期間によって決められる。
▶ We streamlined our operations and redeployed

assets to position the Corporation to *serve* its customers more effectively. 顧客サービスの効率改善[一段と効率的な顧客サービスの体制確立]をめざして，当社は業務の効率化と資産の有効利用に取組みました．

service 動 〈借金や利子などを〉支払う，〈債務を〉返済する，〈債務を〉履行する，〈債権を〉回収する，〈役務を〉提供する

▶An insurance agent is a sales person who represents a life insurance company for the purpose of soliciting applications, collecting initial premiums, and *servicing* insurance contracts. 保険募集人は，生命保険会社を代表して保険契約の勧誘，初回保険料の徴収，保険契約に関する役務を提供する販売員である．

service 名 事業，業務，サービス，役務(えきむ)，労務，勤務，服務，公務，〈借入金の〉定期返済，公債利子，〈訴状や呼出状の〉送達 (⇒**Internal Revenue Service, length of service**)

auditing services 監査業務
debt service 債務返済，元利払い
employee's service period 従業員の勤務年数
management services 経営者への提案業務，経営指導，マネジメント・サービス《略 MS》(＝management advisory services)
service contract 保守サービス契約，保守業務契約
service fee サービス手数料，受取手数料
service potentials 将来収益獲得能力，サービス・ポテンシャルズ
service yield basis 生産高比例法，生産高基準法 (＝production method, service output basis)

▶Fujita Corp. is a construction firm created after the spin-off of money-losing real estate *services* on Oct.1, 2002. フジタ社は，20002年10月1日に赤字の不動産業務を分離して設立された建設会社だ．

▶We will continue to develop innovative new *services* and offer pricing packages that add up to greater value for our customers. 当社は，今後とも革新的な新サービスを開発して，顧客に一段と高い価値をもたらす価格パッケージを提供していく方針です．

service charge 手数料，サービス料金，サービス料

▶There are no brokerage fees or other *service charges*. 仲介手数料やその他のサービス料金は，一切不要です．

service cost 勤費用，補助部門費，補助原価，用役原価，サービス部門原価 (⇒**current service cost, prior service cost**)
past service cost 過去勤務費用
service cost—benefits attributed to service during the period 勤務費用—期中の勤務により発生した給付[給付費用]
service cost—benefits earned during the period 勤務費用—当期に発生した給付[給付費用]

▶Net transition amounts and prior *service costs* are being amortized over periods ranging from 10 to 15 years. 移行時差額と過去勤務費用は，10－15年の期間にわたって償却されています．

service life 耐用年数，耐用期間，試用期間，有用期間 (＝depreciable life, durable years, useful life; ⇒**realize**)
estimated service life 見積り耐用年数
guideline service life ガイドライン耐用年数
residual service life 残存耐用年数
service pensions 年金額

▶Non-contributory defined benefit plans provide for *service pensions* based on length of service and rates of pay. 非拠出型確定給付年金制度[非拠出型給付金規定方式による年金制度]は，勤続年数と給与額に基づいて年金額を決定する．

service period 勤務期間，勤務年数 (⇒**remaining service**)

▶Prior service costs resulting from improvements in the retirement plans are amortized over the average remaining *service priod* of employees expected to receive benefits. 退職金制度の改善によって生じた過去勤務費用は，受給が予想される従業員の平均残存勤続期間にわたって償却されます．

servicer 名 債権回収会社，サービサー
servicing 名 債務返済，債務履行，利払い，債権回収，事務処理，サービシング (⇒**debt servicing**)

government bond-servicing expenditures 国債利払い費
loan servicing 利払いなどの融資処理，貸出金サービシング
loan servicing fee 融資処理手数料，貸出金サービシング手数料
mortgage servicing right モーゲージ・サービス権
servicing burden 債務返済負担

▶This joint venture will offer sales financing and *servicing* as well as raise funds for auto loans. この合弁会社は，自動車ローンの資金調達や販売金融，債権回収などを手がける．

set aside 〈準備金などを〉積み立てる，蓄えてお

く, 蓄える, 引き当てる, 設定する, 繰り入れる, 用意する,〈考えや問題を〉捨てる, 無視する, 棚上げする, 取り除く, 除外する
▶Insurers *set aside* provisions for disasters.　保険会社は, 災害準備金［異常危険準備金］を積み立てている。
▶The consumer loan company *set aside* ¥150 billion in provisions to return excessive interest charges to customers.　顧客に超過支払い利息［超過利息］を返還するため, この消費者金融会社は1,500億円の引当金を積み増した。

set up　設立する, 設定する, 準備する, 用意する, 組み立てる, 築く, 始める,〈ホームページなどを〉開設する, 開く, 創業する（⇒site）
▶Hitachi, Toshiba and Renesas Technology will *set up* a planning company to look into the feasibility of a microchip foundry.　日立製作所, 東芝, ルネサステクノロジの3社が, 企画会社を設立して, 半導体ファウンドリ計画の実行可能性を調査する。

settle 動　決済する, 清算する, 処分する, 処理する, 解決する, 決定する, 決議する, 和解する
▶Banks are about to *settle* their midyear accounts.　銀行は, これから中間決算をまとめるところだ。
▶Companies should not *settle* for good results for the first half of fiscal 2007.　企業は, 2007年度上期［2007年4-9月期］の好決算に安住してはならない。

settlement 名　決済, 清算, 決算, 処分, 解決, 決着, 決定, 妥結, 和解, 調停, 示談, 財産の譲渡, 贈与財産, 定款
　　abnormal settlement of accounts　異常決算
　　account settlement term　決算期
　　asset settlement　資産決済
　　automatic settlement　自動決済
　　biannual settlement　半期決算, 中間決算, 半期決済（=semiannual settlement）
　　business settlement　取引決済
　　cash settlement　現金決済, 現物決済, 差金決済, 即日決済
　　consolidated midterm financial settlement　中間連結決算
　　disruption of settlements　決済マヒ
　　electronic settlement　電子決済
　　electronic settlement services　電子決済業務（⇒Net trading）
　　final settlement　債務の完済
　　financial settlement　決算
　　IC card cashless account settlement system　ICカード・キャッシュ決済システム, キャッシュレス決済システム
　　installment settlement　分割払い
　　legal settlement　訴訟和解金
　　midterm settlement in May　5月中間決算
　　out-of-court settlement　示談による和解
　　settlement account　決済用預金, 決済口座（=settlement deposit, settlement-specific deposit）
　　settlement gain and loss　決算差損益
　　settlement of balance　帳尻決算
▶Disruption of *settlements*, including payments to credit card companies and encashing of promissory notes, must be prevented in case of a bank collapse.　銀行が破綻した場合, クレジット・カード会社への支払いや約束手形の現金化などの決済マヒを防がなければならない。

settlement accounts　決算
　　settlement accounts for fiscal 2008　2008年度決算
▶The firm has announced its *settlement accounts* for fiscal 2007.　同社は, 2007年度の決算［2008年3月期決算］を発表した。

settlement of accounts　決算, 収支決算, 決算報告（=account settlement）
　　the consolidated settlement of accounts　連結決算（=consolidated account settlement, consolidated results）
　　the provisional settlement of accounts　仮決算
　　the settlement of accounts for the April-June period　4-6月期決算
　　the settlement of accounts for the business year that ended in March　3月期決算
　　the settlement of accounts for the half year to September　9月中間決算
　　the settlement of accounts in the business year ending March 31　3月期決算
　　the term-end settlement of accounts　期末決算

severance 名　分離,〈雇用の〉契約解除
　　severance indemnity　退職給与
　　severance indemnity plan　退職金制度（=severance plan）
　　severance pay　退職金

SFAS　財務会計基準書（Statement of Financial Accounting Standardsの略）
▶*SFAS* No. 115 addresses the accounting and reporting for investments in equity securities that have readily determinable fair values.　SFAS［財務会計基準書］第115号は, 公正価額を容易に判定で

きる持ち分証券に対する投資に関する会計処理と報告について規定しています。

SG&A 販売費および一般管理費（＝SG&A expenses：**selling, general and administrative expenses**［**expenditures**］の略）
▸The increase in *SG&A* expenses over the last three years reflects higher selling and marketing expenses.　過去3年にわたる販売費および一般管理費の増加は、販売・マーケティング費の拡大を反映しています。

share 動 共有する, 相互利用する, 分配する, 共同負担する, 共同分担する, 分担する, 支持する, 参加する
▸The expected development cost of ¥50 billion is to be *shared* fifty-fifty between the government and the manufacturers.　500億円が見込まれている開発費は、国とメーカーが折半する予定である。
▸The three companies aim to cut the cost of manufacturing steel products and enhance their products' quality by *sharing* some of their patents.　この3社は、特許の一部を相互利用することによって鉄鋼製品の製造コストを下げるとともに、鉄鋼製品の品質向上も目指している。
▸The two chains will provide each other with merchandise and *share* distribution centers.　両チェーン店は今後、相互に商品を提供するとともに、物流センターの共通化を図る。

share 名 株, 株式, 株券, 持ち分株, 市場占有率, 市場占拠率, 負担分, シェア（＝stock; ⇒**golden share, lion's share, market share, net profit per share, new share issue**）
additional share 追加株式
all shares issued and outstanding 発行済み社外株式総数
capital share 資本金, 株式, 資本分配率, キャピタルシェア
equity share 持ち分有価証券, 持ち分株式
fund flow per share 1株当たり資金フロー
market share gain 市場シェアの拡大（＝expansion of market share）
ownership share 所有権株
share allotment 株式割当て（＝allotment of shares, share allocation）
share earnings 1株当たり利益
share exchange 株式交換
share exchange rate 株式交換比率（＝stock exchange rate）
share issue 株式発行, 新株発行
share ownership 株式所有, 持ち株数
share price 株価（＝stock price; ⇒**close**）
share register 株式名簿, 株主名簿（⇒**shareholders list**）
shares authorized 授権株式数
shares in thousands 単位：千株
shares in treasury 自己株式数, 金庫株数
shares issued 発行済み株式数
total number of shares 株式総数
▸The company increased the number of its *shares* on the market with a stock split.　同社は、株式分割で同社の流通する株式数を増やした。
▸The stock, offered at ¥235,000 a *share* in the initial public offering, opened 28 percent higher at ¥301,000.　IPO［新規株式公開］で公開価格［公募価格］が1株235,000円の同株は、公開価格を28％上回る301,000円の初値を付けた。

share buyback 株式の買戻し, 自社株発行済み株式の買戻し, 自社株買戻し, 自社株買い, 自社株取得（＝share repurchase, stock buyback）
▸*Share buybacks* are commonly aimed at raising profits per share and enhance dividend payouts to shareholders.　株式買戻しの狙いは、一般に1株当たり利益の引き上げと株主への配当支払いの増額にある。

share capital 株式資本, 株式資本金, 資本金, 株式会社の資本金（＝capital stock）
equity share capital 持ち分株式資本, 普通株式資本
issued share capital 発行済み株式資本
ordinary share capital 普通株式資本, 普通株資本
paid-up share capital 払込み資本金
preference share capital 優先株式資本

share issue limit 株式発行枠, 株式の発行可能枠［授権株式数］
▸Almost 100 companies listed on the Tokyo Stock Exchange are expected to propose a revision to their articles of incorporation to expand their respective *share issue limits* at their annual general shareholders meeting.　東証上場企業の約100社が、年次株主総会で、株式発行枠［授権株式数］拡大のための会社定款の変更を提案する見通しだ。

share split 株式分割（＝share splitting, stock split：株式分割は一般に、一時的な株価上昇を招く効果がある。⇒**stock split**）
share split-down 株式併合（＝reverse split, reverse stock split, stock split-down）
share split-up 株式分割（＝stock split-up）
▸Earnings per share in 2006 are restated for a

two-for-one *share split* on April 20, 2007. 2006年度の1株当たり純利益は, 2007年4月20日の1対2の株式分割により修正・再表示されています。

share swap 株式交換 （＝equity swap, stock swap：企業買収を行う際に買収相手と自社の株式を交換することで, 現金がなくても企業買収を進められる）
▶The company acquired six firms via a *share swap* in 2007. 同社は, 2007年に株式交換で6つの会社を買収した。

shareholder 株主 （＝stockholder）
　boost shareholder value 株主価値を高める
　equity shareholder 普通株主
　individual shareholder 個人株主
　institutional shareholder 機関投資家
　ordinary shareholder 普通株主 （＝equity shareholder）
　shareholder approval 株主の承認
　shareholder value 株主価値, 株主利益 （＝shareholders' value, value for shareholders）
　shareholders' assets 株主資本
　shareholders' interest 株主の権利, 株主利益 （⇒**trading unit**）
　shareholders' representative suit 株主代表訴訟 （＝shareholders' lawsuit：取締役が法令や定款に違反して会社に損害を与えた場合, 株主が会社に代わって取締役を相手取り会社に損害を賠償するよう求める訴訟）
▶These transactions made the Corporation the second-largest *shareholder* in the company. これらの取引[株式取得]で, 当社は同社の第2位株主になりました。

shareholder dividend reinvestment and stock purchase plan 株主配当再投当・株式購入制度
▶Shareholders wishing to acquire additional common shares of the Corporation can take advantage of the *Shareholder Dividend Reinvestment and Stock Purchase Plan*. 当社の普通株式の追加購入を希望される株主は, 株主配当再投資・株式購入制度を利用することができます。

shareholder equality 株主平等
▶Golden shares violate the principle of *shareholder equality*. 黄金株は, 「株主平等の原則」に反する。

shareholder of record 登録株主, 株主名簿上の株主, 株主 （＝stockholder of record）
▶The board of directors declared the corporation's regular quarterly dividend of $0.08 per common share, payable June 28, 2008 to *shareholders of record* at the close of business on June 11, 2008. 取締役会は, 当社の普通株式1株当たり通常四半期配当を0.08ドルとし, 2008年6月11日営業終了時の登録株主に対して2008年6月28日に支払うことを発表しました。

shareholder vote 株主投票
▶In the *shareholder vote*, there was substantial focus on whether the chair and CEO functions at the company should be split. 株主投票では, とくに同社の会長職とCEO［最高経営責任者］の職を分離すべきかどうかが大きな関心事だった。

shareholders incentives 株主優待, 株主優待制度
▶*Shareholders incentives* are designed to encourage shareholders to hold onto their stocks over the long term. 株主優待の狙いは, 株主の株式の長期保有促進にある。

shareholders list 株主名簿 （＝list of shareholders, share register）
▶The ratio of voting rights held by the company is based on the *shareholders list* as of the end of February. 同社が保有する議決権の比率は, 2月末時点の株主名簿をもとにしている。

shareholders meeting 株主総会 （＝general meeting of shareholders, general meeting of stockholders, shareholders' meeting, stockholders' meeting）
　annual shareholders meeting 年次株主総会
　emergency shareholders meeting 緊急株主総会, 臨時株主総会
▶The company has yet to receive approval for the action at its *shareholders meeting*. 同社は, 同社の株主総会でこの措置の承認はまだ得ていない。

shareholders' equity 株主資本, 株主持ち分, 自己資本, 資本, 資本の部 （⇒**stockholders' equity**）
▶Only income arising after the date of acquisition is included in *shareholders' equity*. 企業取得日後に生じた利益だけが, 資本の部に含まれています。

shareholders' value 株主価値 （＝shareholders value）
　create shareholders' [shareholders] value 株主の価値を高める （＝create value for shareholders）
　increase shareholders' value 株主の価値を高める
　maximize shareholders' value 株主価値の極大化を図る
▶The U.S. businesses give priority to maximizing

shareholders' value. 米国の企業は、株主の価値を第一に考えている。

shareholding 名 株式所有, 株式保有, 株式有率, 出資比率, 持ち株比率, 持ち株, 保有株, 保有株式 (=equity holding; ⇒stockholding)
  foreign shareholding ratio 外国人持ち株比率
  interlocked shareholdings 株式の持ち合い, 株式持ち合い (⇒cross shareholding)
  public shareholding 株式公開
  shareholding ratio 持ち株比率, 株式保有比率
  ▶Toyota will purchase some of General Motors Corp's *shareholding* in Fuji Heavy Industries Ltd. トヨタが、米ゼネラル・モーターズ(GM)が保有している富士重工の株式の一部を取得することになった。

shareowner 名 株主
  common shareowners' equity 普通株式株主持ち分
  Dear shareowner: 株主各位, 株主の皆さまへ
  ▶For the past three years we have issued new shares of common stock for our *shareowner* and employee savings plans. 過去3年間、当社の株主制度と従業員貯蓄制度のために普通株式の新株を発行してきました。

shareowner services 株主サービス
  ▶First Chicago Trust is our *shareowner services* and transfer agent. ファースト・シカゴ・トラストが、当社の株主サービスおよび名義書換え取扱機関です。

shares outstanding 社外流通株式数, 発行済み株式, 社外発行株式, 発行株式 (=outstanding shares)
  ▶The number of weighted average *shares outstanding* increases as we issue new common shares for employee savings plans, shareowner plans and other purposes. 加重平均総発行株式数が、従業員貯蓄制度や株主制度その他の目的で当社が発行する新株に応じて増加します。

sharing 名 分配, 配分, 共同分担, 共同負担, シェアリング (⇒participation, profit sharing plan)
  cost sharing 費用分担, 原価負担
  job sharing [job-sharing] 仕事分担, 分担労働, 分割勤務, 雇用共有, ジョブ・シェアリング (=work sharing)
  profit sharing 利益分配, 利益配分
  tax sharing 租税分担
  work sharing (system) ワーク・シェアリング

sharp 形 急激な, 急速な, 急な, 大幅な (⇒turn-around)
  sharp drop in earnings 業績の急激な悪化

sharp rise in stock prices 株価の急騰, 株価の急上昇

sharper competition 競争激化

sharp increase 急増
  ▶Net profit per share in the period dived to ¥6.07 from ¥41.95 in the same period a year earlier as a result of a *sharp increase* in the number of the company's outstanding shares. 当期の1株当たり純利益は、同社の発行済み株式数の急増で、前年同期の41円95銭から6円7銭に急落した。

shelf offering 一括募集

shelf registration 一括登録, 一括登録制度, 発行登録, シェルフ登録, シェルフ・レジストレーション
  「一括登録制度」では、将来発行予定の有価証券について、米証券取引委員会(SEC)に前もって登録しておくと、SEC Rule 415（米証券取引委員会規則415）に基づいて、実際の発行時に届け出をする必要はない。
  ▶No securities have been issued under this *shelf registration*. この一括登録制度に基づいて、有価証券はまだ発行されていません。
  ▶Through this *shelf registration*, the Corporation will be able to offer, from time to time, up to U.S. $300 million of its debt securities and warrants to purchase debt securities. この発行登録により、当社は3億米ドルを上限として、債務証券と債務証券の引受権付きワラントを随時、発行することができます。

shelf registration program 一括登録制度, 発行登録制度
  ▶We have U.S. $500 million of debt securities registered with the U.S. Securities Exchange Commission pursuant to a *shelf registration program*. 当社は、米証券取引委員会(SEC)の一括登録制度［発行登録制度］に基づき、5億米ドルの債務証券発行予定額をSECに登録しています。

shelf registration statement 一括登録届け出書, 発行登録届け出書 (⇒universal shelf registration statement)
  ▶During September 2007, the Corporation filed a *shelf registration statement* with the U.S. Securities and Exchange Commission. 2007年9月中、当社は有価証券の一括登録届け出書を米国証券取引委員会(SEC)に提出しました。

shift 動 移す, 変更する, 変える, 転嫁する, 入れ替える, 繰り上げる, シフトさせる, 移る, 移動する, 変わる, 変化する, シフトする
  shift downward 下降に転じる
  shift funds into other financial products 資

金を他の金融商品に変える
shift production base overseas 生産拠点を海外に移す
shift upward 上昇に転じる （⇒**manager**）
▶In 2007, we *shifted* some people and responsibilities on our Management Executive Committee, with an eye to increasing the pace of growth and globalization. 2007年に当社は, 成長速度とグローバル化の促進をめざして, 当社の経営執行委員会メンバーの一部とその担当分野の入れ替えを行いました。
▶We are not able to *shift* the raised costs of plastic parts onto product prices. プラスチック部品のコスト高[コスト上昇分]を, 製品価格に転嫁できない状況にある。

shift 名 変化, 変動, 移行, 移動, 転換, 配置転換, 交替, 交替勤務時間, 傾斜, 転嫁, 手段, 方法, 策, シフト （⇒**revenue mix**）
　do [work] a shift 交替勤務をする
　equity structure shift 資本再編成
　night shift 夜勤組
　shift in interest rate 金利の変動
　shift in market rates 相場の変動
　shift in [of] sentiment 市場の地合いの変化
　shift in the total workforce 従業員全体の配置転換
　shift of funds 資金の移動
　temporary shift in money demand 資金需要の一時的なシフト
　two shifts of eight hours 8時間の2交替勤務
▶By shrinking corporate, group, division and country headquarters, we have produced a fundamental *shift* in the total workforce. 本社, グループ, 部門と各国の本社機構を縮小することによって, 当社は従業員全体の重要な配置転換を行いました。

shifting loan 借換え

ship 動 出荷する, 発送する, 発売する, 船で送る, 輸送する, 輸出する
▶Revenue is recognized from sales or sales-type leases when the product is *shipped*. 売上または販売型リースの収益の計上時期は, 製品の出荷時となっています。

shipment 名 出荷, 出荷量, 出荷台数, 発送, 輸出, 船積み, 船積み品, 船積み量, 積み荷, 船積
　inventory to shipment ratio 在庫率, 在庫率指数
　shipment of goods 商品の出荷, 商品の発送, 商品の船積み
　shipment procedures 輸出入手続き
　unit shipments 販売台数
▶Increases in accounts receivable reflected higher levels of *shipments* in December 2007 compared to the same period in 2006. 売掛金の増加は, 2007年12月の出荷が前年同期に比べて高水準であったことを反映しています。

short-run fund planning 短期資金計画
（=short-range fund planning, short-run cash planning）

short-term 形 短期の, 短期間の, 短期満期の, 即効性の
　short-term advance from affiliated company 関係会社からの短期前受金
　short-term advance to affiliated company 関係会社への短期貸付け金, 関係会社短期前渡し金
　short-term capital gain 短期譲渡利益
　short-term capital loss 短期譲渡損失
　short-term debts 短期債務, 短期負債, 短期借入金
　short-term fund 短期資金
　short-term funding 短期資金調達
　short-term investments 短期投資（決算日後1年以内に現金化する短期的な投資）
　short-term obligations 短期債務

short-term borrowings 短期借入金, 短期債務 （=short-term loans, short term obligations）
▶The firm sold 50-year debt to refinance its *short-term borrowings*. 同社は, 短期債務[短期借入金]の借換えのため, 満期50年の債券を発行した。

short-term liability 短期負債, 短期借入金, 短期貸付け金, 短期債権
▶Net working capital—current assets less current liabilities—is a measure of our ability to cover *short-term liabilities* with assets that we expect to convert to cash soon. 正味運転資本（流動資産から流動負債を控除した額）は, 短期債務を直ちに現金化できる資産で賄う能力を表します。

showing 名 成績, 出来, 出来栄え, 表示, 展示, 上映, 上演, 外観, 体裁, 供述, 申立て （⇒**sales promotion**）
　economy's better showing 景気回復, 景気の上向き, 景気好調
　improved showing 業績改善
　strong showing 好成績, 好決算
▶The biggest factor behind the top six banks' strong *showing* is the economic recovery. 大手銀行・金融6グループの好決算の最大要因は, 景気回復だ。

shrink 動　減少する, 低下する, 縮小する
▶The firm's quarterly net loss *shrank* by more than 60 percent to ¥21.65 billion. 同社の四半期純損失は, 60%以上縮小して216億5,000万円となった。

shrinkage 名　減耗, 減損
　abnormal shrinkage 異常減損, 異常減耗
　inventory shrinkage 棚卸し減耗
　normal shrinkage 正常減耗損
　shrinkage loss 棚卸し減耗損, 棚卸し減耗費

shut down 〈工場などを〉閉鎖する, 〈操業を〉停止する　(⇒**close**)
▶The firm will *shut down* and sell 20 percent of its plants in Japan. 同社は, 日本国内工場の20%を閉鎖して売却する。

sign up 〈契約［協定］を〉結ぶ, 参加する, 応募する
▶We expect to *sign up* other distributors for the product. 当社は, 他の販売代理店とも本製品の契約を結ぶ予定です。

significant 形　重要な, 重大な, 大きな, 著しい, 際立った, 目立った, 本格的な, 相当な, かなりの, 大量の, 多額の, 大幅な, 大型の
　significant accounting policies 重要な会計方針
　significant acquisition 大型買収
　significant earnings gains 大幅な増益
　significant losses 巨額の損失, 巨額の赤字
　significant subsidiary 重要な子会社
▶During 2007, the Corporation experienced a *significant* increase in its cash requirements because of higher fixed asset expenditures. 2007年度は, 固定資産支出額が増えたため, 必要資金がかなり増加しました。

significantly 副　著しく, 大幅に
　drop significantly 大幅に減少する, 大幅に悪化する

simple 形　単純な, 簡単な, 平易な, 簡素な
　simple average method 単純平均法
　simple interest 単利
　simple labor 単純労働
　simple mean value 単純平均
　simple yield to maturity 単利最終利回り

single 形　単一の, 個々の, 唯一の
　single currency 単一通貨
　single financial market 統一金融市場
　single market 単一市場, 市場統合
　single payment 一括払
　single premium 一括払い保険料
　single proprietorship 個人企業, 個人事業主
　single unit depreciation 個別償却

sinking fund 減債基金(債券発行者が, 債券の償還に備えて償還期限前から一定額を定期的に積み立てる基金), 償却基金, 償却積立金, 別途資金
　reserve for sinking fund 減債基金積立金, 減債積立金　(＝sinking fund reserve)
　sinking fund for plant expansion 工場拡張基金
　sinking fund for redemption of bonds 社債償還基金
　sinking fund method 償却基金法, 減債基金法
　sinking fund payments 減債基金の積立て, 減債基金の繰入れ
　sinking fund requirements 減債基金積立額, 減債基金への支払い額
▶Annual maturity and *sinking fund* requirements in millions of dollars on long term debt outstanding at December 31, 2007 are as follows: 2007年12月31日現在の長期負債残高の年度別返済額と減債基金への支払い額(単位：百万ドル)は, 次のとおりです。

site 名　拠点, 施設, 事業所, 工場, 用地, 設置先, 現場, サイト, インターネット上の場所, ホームページ　(⇒**Web site**)
　auction site 競売サイト, オークション・サイト
　community site コミュニティ・サイト
　construction site 建設用地, 建設現場
　e-commerce site eコマース・サイト
　EC site ECサイト
　harmful site 有害サイト
　investment site 投資先
　joint Web site 共同サイト
　portal site ポータル・サイト
　production site 生産拠点, 生産施設, 生産先
　shopping site ショッピング・サイト
▶In August 2008, 3,500 local employees, now located in 14 separate *sites*, will finally be consolidated into the new facility. 2008年8月から, 現在14か所の事業所に配置されている3,500人の国内従業員が, 最終的にこの新事業施設に移転する予定です。
▶To support Toyota's assembly plant, Japanese auto component and material suppliers are expected to set up production *sites* in Russia. トヨタの組立工場を支援するため, 日系部品・材料メーカーがロシアに生産拠点を設けることが予想される。

six-month period ending September 9月までの6か月間, 4-9月期, 〈3月期決算企業の〉上半期

six months ended June 30 1-6月期, 〈12月期決算企業の〉上半期, 上期, 6月中間決算

six months ended Sept. 30 4-9月期, 〈3月期決算企業の〉上半期, 上期, 9月中間決算

▶The loss totaled ¥2.8 billion in the *six months ended Sept. 30*, compared with a loss of ¥18 billion a year earlier.　上半期[4−9月期]の損失総額は、前年同期の180億円に対して28億円となった。

six months through June　1−6月期、〈12月決算企業の〉上半期、上期、6月中間決算、6月中間期

▶Mergers and acquisitions involving Japanese companies reached an all-time high in the *six months through June* 2006.　2006年上期[1−6月期]の日本企業関連のM&A［企業の合併・買収］件数は、過去最高に達した。

six months through Sept. 30　4−9月期、〈3月期決算企業の〉上半期、上期、9月中間期、9月中間決算　（＝six months through September；⇒ **group net profit**）

six months to Sept. 30　4−9月期、9月中間期、〈3月期決算企業の〉上半期［上期］、9月中間決算

▶Mizuho Securities lost 27.1 billion for the *six months to Sept. 30*, compared with a profit of ¥11 billion a year earlier.　9月中間決算で、みずほ証券は、前年同期の110億円の利益に対して271億円の赤字を出した。

six months up to September　4−9月期、上半期、上期、9月中間期　（＝six months through September）

Six Sigma　シックス・シグマ

シックス・シグマ ➡ 業務改革の一環として、製品やサービスの品質向上のために米モトローラ社が開発した手法で、組織全体で製品、サービスのエラーやミスの発生確率を100万分の数回[3.4回]に抑えること。GEやIBMのほか、日本のソニー、NECや東芝も導入している。シックス・シグマは、測定・分析・改善と管理のプロセスを経て実現される。

▶Motorola's *Six Sigma* shows its corporate culture that strives to achieve perfection in quality.　モトローラ社の「シックス・シグマ」は、あくまでも品質面での完璧さを追求する同社の企業文化を示している。

skill　名　能力、手腕、技術、技能、熟練、職業能力、スキル
　bargaining skill　交渉術
　business skills　経営技術
　communication skills　コミュニケーション技能、コミュニケーション力
　conceptual skills　総合管理技術
　decision-making skill　意思決定能力
　entrepreneurial skills　経営技術
　industrial skills　産業技術
　managerial skills　経営技術、経営の手腕
　management skills　経営手腕、経営技術
　sales skills　販売能力、販売技術
　skill test　技能検定　（＝skills testing）
　skills assessment　技能評価
　skills center　技能センター
　technical skills　技能、技術力
　transfer of technical skills　技能継承

▶We are investing in enhancing the *skills* of our people and in the development of improved tools of productivity.　当社は、社員の技能向上と生産性向上に役立つツールの開発に投資しています。

skyrocket　動　急増する、急騰する、急上昇する、跳ね上がる

▶We cut a nice melon in the fourth quarter as profits *skyrocketed*.　利益が急増したので、当社は第4四半期に多額の利益配当を行った。

slash　動　削減する、減らす、低減する、引き下げる、下方修正する　（⇒**profitability**）
　slash capital expenditures　設備投資を減らす、設備投資を削減する
　slash profit forecasts　業績見通し［業績予想］を下方修正する

▶GM has posted losses and its credit rating has been *slashed* to junk status.　GMは最近赤字に陥り、信用格付けが「投機的」に落とされた。

▶The company *slashed* its profit forecasts because of costs from a massive global recall of laptop batteries.　同社は、全世界でのパソコン用充電池の回収費用が巨額なため、業績見通しを下方修正した。

▶The firm is giving up its assets in an attempt to *slash* its interest-bearing liabilities.　同社は、有利子負債を削減するため、資産を手放している。

slow down　減速する、後退する、鈍化する、停滞する、低迷する

▶The growth rates of sales and profits are expected to *slow down* in the second half of the year.　売上高と利益の伸び率は、下半期は鈍化しそうだ。

slowdown　名　〈景気などの〉減速、後退、沈滞、低迷、低下、減産、操業短縮、怠業
　demand slowdown　需要の伸びの鈍化、需要減速、需要低迷
　economic slowdown　景気減速、景気後退、景気低迷、景気鈍化
　global slowdown　世界的な景気低迷、世界的な景気減速
　inflationary slowdown　インフレ率の低下
　seasonal demand slowdown　季節要因による需要減速

▶Housing investment, a driving force for the U.S. economy until recently, has shown signs of a *slowdown*.　最近まで米景気を牽引してきた住宅投資に、減速感が見られる。

sluggish 形　不振の、低迷した、不活発な、不景気な、動きが鈍い、足どりが重い、軟調な
　sluggish demand　需要低迷（＝weak demand）
　sluggish economy　景気低迷（＝sluggish economic conditions）
　sluggish sales　販売低迷
　sluggish stock market　低迷した株式市場、株式市場の低迷、株式相場の低迷（＝slumping stock market）
▶Our business in the United States continued to be *sluggish* and showed no growth over the previous year.　米国内での当社の業績は伸びず、前年度を上回る成長を見ることができませんでした。

sluggish consumption　消費の低迷
▶This wide gap between supply and demand was caused by such factors as a plunge in demand in IT-related industries and *sluggish consumption*.　この大幅な需給ギャップは、IT関連業の需要の落ち込みや消費低迷によるものだ。

sluggish performance　業績不振
▶Banks refused to extend new loans to the company due to its *sluggish performance*.　業績不振で、銀行は同社への新規融資に応じなかった。

slump 名　暴落、急落、落ち込み、減少、低迷、不振、不況、不景気、景気沈滞、スランプ（＝sluggishness）
　slump in business　経営不振、業績不振
　slump in the dollar　ドル安
▶The prolonged *slump* in the real estate market is maintaining the decline in land prices.　不動産取引市場の長期低迷が、引き続き地下の下落を招いている。

slush fund　不正資金、賄賂資金、贈賄資金
soar 動　急騰する、急増する、大きく上回る
▶Fixed asset investment *soared* nearly 30 percent from a year ago during the July-September quarter.　7−9月期の固定資産投資は、前年同期比で3割近く増加した。

social responsibility　社会的責任
▶From the perspective of corporate *social responsibility*, the distribution industry should pay more attention to intellectual property rights in the future.　企業の社会的責任の観点から、流通業界は今後、知的財産権にも一段と配慮しなければならない。

solicit 動　勧誘する、募集する、強く求める、…するように要請する、〈資金などを〉集める、訪問販売する
　solicit clients　顧客を勧誘する
　solicit funds from …　…に資金提供を要請する、…に出資を勧誘する、…から資金を集める
　solicit orders　注文をとる
　solicit proxies　委任状を取り付ける、議決権代理行使の勧誘をする
▶As initial capital to establish an intellectual property fund, the bank plans to *solicit* between ¥5 billion and ¥6 billion from financial institutions and enterprises.　知的財産ファンドを創設するための当初資金として、同行は金融機関や事業会社から50−60億円を集める計画だ。
▶During the business suspension, the company will not be allowed to extend new loans, *solicit* new customers or call in loans.　業務停止の期間中、同社は新規融資や新規顧客の勧誘、貸出［貸金］の回収業務ができなくなる。

solicitation 名　勧誘、募集、要請、訪問販売
　insurance solicitation　保険募集（＝insurance soliciting）
　solicitation of clients　顧客の勧誘
　solicitation of proxies　議決権代理行使の勧誘、議決権行使委任状勧誘、委任状勧誘（＝proxy solicitation）
▶*Solicitation* of proxies is being made through the mail, in person, and by telecommunications.　議決権代理行使の勧誘は、郵便、経営陣により直接、または電信・電話などの通信手段で行われています。

solid 名　着実な、堅実な、底堅い、強固な、健全な、安定した
　solid demand　堅実な需要、需要の安定
　solid growth　着実な伸び、着実な［底堅い］成長
　solid management　堅実な経営、安定した経営
　solid performance　底堅い業績、堅調な値動き
▶*Solid* growth in our U.S. and Canadian markets fueled our largest dollar increases for the quarter.　当四半期は、米国とカナダ市場での着実な伸びが、売上増の最大の原動力となりました。

solution 名　解決、問題解決、問題解決策、問題解決手法、解決法、解決手段、解決策、対策、手段、〈コンピュータとアプリケーション、ネットワークの組合せによる〉システム構築、〈ユーザーの要求に応じた〉情報システムの構築、ソリューション
　comprehensive solution　包括的ソリューション
　computing solution service　業務処理・問題解決サービス
　e-business solution　Eビジネス・ソリューション
　payment solution　決済ソリューション

system solution　システム・ソリューション
Web solution　ウェブ・ソリューション
win-win-win solution　三方一両得の解決策
▸Our goal is to shape and lead the customer information *solutions* market.　当社の目標は、顧客情報ソリューション[解決策]の市場を形成し、そのマーケット・リーダーになることです。

solvency 名　支払い余力, 支払い能力, ソルベンシー（支払い期日の到来時点で支払いできる状態にあること）
　solvency position　自己資本比率
　solvency ratio　支払い能力比率, 自己資本比率, 流動性比率
　solvency rule　支払い能力規制

solvency margin　支払い余力, 支払い余力比率, ソルベンシー・マージン（＝solvency margin rate, solvency margin ratio：生命保険会社の支払い能力のことで, 保険会社の経営[財務]の健全性を判断する基準の一つ）
▸*Solvency margin* is an indicator of an insurance company's financial health.　ソルベンシー・マージン[支払い余力]比率は、保険会社の財務の健全性を示す指標の一つである。

solvency margin ratio [**rate**]　ソルベンシー・マージン[支払い余力]比率（⇒**unforeseen loss**）
▸The capital increase will bring the insurer's *solvency margin ratio* by about 25 percentage points.　基金の積み増し[基金増資]で、この保険会社のソルベンシー・マージン[支払い余力]比率は25％ほど上昇する。

source 名　源泉, 源, 〈利子・配当などの〉支払い者, 情報源, ニュース・ソース, 筋, 取材源, 関係者, 資料, 出典, 出所（⇒**vendor**）
　cash sources　資金の源泉
　deduction at source　源泉徴収
　external sources of cash　外部流動性
　financial source　財源
　funding source　資金調達源, 資金源
　funds from external sources　外部資金, 外部調達資金
　income from sources without the United States　米国外源泉所得
　income source　収入源, 所得源泉（＝income producer）
　internal sources　内部資金
　internal sources of cash　内部流動性（＝internal sources of liquidity）
　liquidity sources　資金源
　other sources of funds　その他の資金の源泉
　outside sources of funds　外部流動性
　principle of single source　単一性の原則
　production supply sources　原材料調達源
　repayment source　返済原資
　revenue sources　財源, 歳入源, 収益源, 収入源
　source and application of funds　資金の源泉と使途, 資金運用表
　source of earnings　収益源（＝earnings source, source of income, source of profits）
　source of financing　資金調達源（＝source of funding）
　source of funds　資金源, 資金の源泉
　sources and uses of funds　資金収支表
▸Financial reports and other documents published by companies are the most fundamental *sources* of information for investors and creditors.　企業が公表する有価証券報告書などは、投資家や債権者にとって最も基本的な情報源だ。

sourcing 名　調達, 業務委託, 供給, ソーシング（⇒**outsourcing**）
　double sourcing　供給源の分散
　global sourcing　グローバル・ソーシング
　raw material sourcing　原材料の供給
　world sourcing　世界市場への製品供給
▸In addition to the segment's factory expansion program, it is actively pursuing additional capacity through the *sourcing* of products from outside vendors.　当事業部門の工場拡張計画のほかに、当事業部門は外部ベンダーからの製品調達により、製造能力の強化に積極的に取り組んでいます。

SPC　特定目的会社（**special purpose company**の略）
SPE　特別目的事業体（**special purpose entity**の略）

special 形　特別の, 特定の, 特殊な, 専門の, 独特の
　special compensation payment　特別報酬の支払い《略 SCP》
　special contingency reserve　特別偶発損失準備金
　special gain or loss　特別損益
　special interim dividend　特別中間配当
　special meeting of shareholders [stockholders]　臨時株主総会
　special meeting of the board of directors　臨時取締役会会議
　special profit　特別利益
　special purpose company　特定目的会社《略 SPC》
　special reserve　特別積立金, 別途積立金, 特別引当金（＝general reserve, other reserve, un-

conditional reserve)
special year-end dividend 特別年度末配当, 特別期末配当

special benefits 特別給付
▸These *special benefits* are provided to employees accepting early retirement offers. この特別給付は、早期退職案を受諾する従業員に支払われます。

special loss 特別損失 (＝extraordinary loss)
▸The corporation reported the largest ever after-tax loss for a Japanese company due to group companies' huge *special losses*. 同社は、グループ企業全体の巨額の特別損失により、日本企業で過去最大の税引き後損失[税引き後赤字]となったことを発表した。

special resolution 特別決議
▸Approval for a triangular merger should be based on a *special resolution*. 三角合併の承認は、特別決議によらなければならない[三角合併には、特別決議による承認が必要だ]。

speculative 形 投機的な
　speculative fund 投機資金
　speculative holding 投機的保有
　speculative grade bond 投機的債券, 投機的格付け社債, 高利回り債
　speculative stock 仕手株

spend 動 支出する, 投資する, 出資する, 消費する
▸Sales also gained as the company *spent* more on machinery and equipments. 機械設備投資の拡大に伴って、同社の売上高も増加した。

spending 名 支出, 投資, 出資, 消費 (⇒**capital spending, R&D spending**)
　consumer spending 個人消費支出, 消費支出, 家計部門の支出
　corporate spending 企業の支出, 設備投資
　current spending 経常支出
　discretionary spending 裁量的経費
　household spending 個人消費
　investment spending 公共投資
　mandatory spending 義務的経費
　private spending 民間支出
　spending on goods and services 商品やサービスへの支出
　spending on R&D 研究開発費 (＝R&D spending)
▸A portion of the increase in R&D *spending* was also due to the unfavorable impact of foreign exchange on R&D expenditures most of which are incurred in Canada. 研究開発費の大半はカナダで発生しているため、米ドル為替相場の下落による影響も、研究開発費拡大の一因でした。

spin off 会社を分割する, 分社化する, 分離する, 切り離す
▸Mitsubishi Fuso was *spun off* from Mitsubishi Motors in 2003. 三菱ふそうは、2003年に三菱自動車から分社化した。

spinoff [**spin-off**] 分社化, 分社, 会社分割, 切り離し, 分離, スピンオフ (企業が事業の一部を切り離して別の会社に移すこと。⇒**service**)
▸Troubled Kanebo Ltd. returned to the black for the first time in six years on the back of a *spinoff* of its cosmetics division. 経営不振[経営再建中]のカネボウは、化粧品事業の分離などで6期ぶりの黒字転換を果たした。

split 動 分離する, 分割する, 分裂する, 離脱する, 解散する (⇒**boost**)
▸On October 1, 2007, the Corporation *split* its common stock 4 for 1. 2007年10月1日に当社は、当社発行の普通株式1株を4株に分割しました。
▸The company had its total marked-to-market value of stocks raised by *splitting* its one share into 100. 同社は、自社株1株を100株に分割して株式の時価総額をつり上げていた。

split 名 分裂, 亀裂, 不和, 分割, 株式分割 (⇒**stock split**)
▸Prior to the *split*, the company had 10,000 shares of $15 par value common stock issued and outstanding. 株式分割前、同社は額面15ドルの普通株式1万株が発行済みであった。

split off 分離する, 分離独立させる, 分割する
▸The IRCJ hopes to *split off* the real estate business to prevent the company from making up shortfalls in food supermarket earnings with income from retail space rentals. 産業再生機構が不動産事業を分離するのは、同社が食品スーパーの収益の不足分を小売店舗スペースの賃料でかさ上げするのを避けるのが狙いだ。

split-up of stock 株式分割 (＝share split-up, stock split-up)

sponsor 動 後援する, 主催する, 後押しする, 支持する, 支援する, 〈制度などを〉設ける, 〈法案などを〉主唱する, 保証する, 保証人になる, 協力する, スポンサーになる
　federally sponsored agency 連邦政府関連機関
　government sponsored agency 政府系機関
▸We *sponsor* savings plans for the majority of our employees. 当社は、大多数の当社従業員のために貯蓄制度を設けています。

sponsor 名 〈投資信託証券の〉引受人[引受業者], 〈ベンチャービジネスや慈善事業などへの〉出資者,

〈プロジェクトファイナンスの〉実質的推進者,〈債務などの〉保証人, 原資産保有者, 後援者, 後援会, 主催者, 発起人, 支持者, 広告主, 番組提供者, スポンサー

corporate sponsors スポンサー企業
official sponsor 公式スポンサー
sponsor company スポンサー企業 (=corporate sponsor)
sponsors for large advertisements 大口広告主
▶Companies inside and outside Japan expressed a desire to help Daiei's rehabilitation as a *sponsor* company. 国内外の複数企業が, ダイエー再建支援のスポンサー企業として名乗りを上げた。

spread 名 利幅, 利ざや, 上乗せ, 金利差, 開き,〈売り値と買い値の〉差, スプレッド

スプレッド ➡ 銀行の調達金利である預金金利と運用金利である貸出金利との差, 株や債券, 通貨取引などの買い呼び値(bid)と売り呼び値(offer)との差額, 有価証券の発行者への引受業者への引渡し価格と引受業者の一般投資家への売出価格との差額をいう。

interest rate spread 金利スプレッド, 利ざや
profit spread 利ざや
yield spread 利回り格差
▶Wider *spreads* were also seen in the market for commercial mortgage-backed securities. 金利差(スプレッド)の拡大は, 商業用不動産証券の市場でも見られた。

squeeze 動 締め付ける, 引き締める,〈予算や経費などを〉切り詰める, 制限する, 圧迫する, 押し下げる, 縮小する, 低下する, 減少する
▶Profits have been *squeezed* as interest rates remain near zero percent and loan demands stalls. 金利はまだゼロに近いし, 借入需要も停滞したままなので, 利益は減少している。

squeeze 名 締付け, 引締め, 切詰め, 制限, 打撃, 圧迫, 縮小, 低下, 減少
margin squeeze 利益率低下, 利益率圧迫, 利ざや縮小 (=squeeze in margins)
profit squeeze 利益減少, 利益縮小
squeeze on earnings 利益圧迫, 業績悪化

SR 社会的責任投資 (**socially responsible investing**の略)
SRI fund 社会的責任投資ファンド, SRIファンド (社会に貢献する企業は消費者や投資家から信頼を得て, 安定した利益が期待できることから, 社会への貢献度の高い企業を選んで投資する投資信託)

stabilize 動 安定させる, 固定する
stabilize food prices 食品[食糧]価格を安定させる
stabilize the economy 経済を安定させる

stable shareholder 安定株主 (=stable stockholder)
▶The company aims to protect itself from takeover attempts by securing more *stable shareholders* through a third-party share allotment. 同社は, 第三者割当て増資で安定株主を増やすことで, 買収防衛策としての効果を狙っている。

staff 名 社員, 従業員, 職員, 人員, 局員, 幹部, スタッフ
department of staff スタッフ部門
editorial staff 編集陣
engineering staff 技術スタッフ
managing staff 経営陣
staff benefits 従業員福利費
staff costs 人件費 (=staff expenses)
staff reduction 人員削減 (=reduction of staff numbers)
▶It is necessary for firms to enhance their employee retention rate and to ensure that their *staff* are the main pillar of the company. 企業は, 社員の定着率を高め, 社員を会社の主柱に育てる必要がある。

staggered board スタガー取締役会 (任期をずらした取締役で構成されている取締役会。敵対的買収への防衛手段として利用されることがある)

stake 名 出資, 出資比率, 投資金, 投資金額, 資本参加, 株式持ち分, 持ち株, 持ち株比率, 株, 株式, 利害関係 (⇒**equity stake**)
acquire [buy] an X percent stake in ... …の株式のX%を取得する
equity stake rate 持ち分比率, 出資比率
hold a 35 percent stake in ... …の株式の35%を保有する, …株の35%を保有している
increase one's stake in ... …の持ち株比率を引き上げる, …の出資比率を引き上げる (=raise one's stake in)
joint stake 共同出資, 共同出資比率
reduce one's stake in ... …の持ち株比率を引き下げる, …の出資比率を引き下げる
take a stake in ... …へ出資する
▶General Motors Corp. has reached an agreement to sell a 51 percent *stake* in its finance arm. ゼネラル・モーターズ(GM)は, 金融子会社(GMAC)の株式の51%を売却することで合意した。
▶Japan Airlines will raise its *stake* in Japan Asia Airways to 100 percent from the current 90.5 percent through an equity swap deal. 日本航空システムは, 株式交換取引により, 日本アジア航空への出資比率を現在の90.5%から100%に引き上げる[日本アジア航空を完全子会社化する]。
▶The two companies aim to maintain their joint

stake in the firm at 51 percent or more. 両社は、同社に対する両社合わせた出資比率を51%以上に維持する方針だ。

stakeholder 名 利害関係者, ステークホルダー（企業の従業員, 退職者, 労働組合や取引先, 地域社会などを指す）, 株主 （⇒trade union）
▸When a company increases profits through wage cuts, the shareholders' value will increase, but its value to *stakeholders* may decrease. 企業が賃金引下げて利益を増やした場合, 株主価値は増えるが, ステークホルダー［利害関係者］に帰属する価値は減る可能性がある。

standard 名 標準, 基準, 規格, 基準書, スタンダード （⇒accounting standards, auditing standards, ethical standard, International Financial Reporting Standards）
　capital standards 自己資本比率, 自己資本比率規制
　credit standards 融資基準, 与信基準
　de facto standard 事実上の標準, 事実上の国際基準, 事実上の世界標準, デファクト・スタンダード
　de jure standard 法による基準, 法律上の基準, 公的基準, デジュアリー・スタンダード
　disclosure standards 開示基準
　ethics standards 倫理基準
　financial standards 財務基準
　general standards 一般基準, 一般原則
　general standards of auditing 監査一般基準
　generally accepted accounting standards 一般に認められた会計基準
　internal auditing standards 内部監査基準
　origination standards 審査基準
　practice standards 業務基準
　product standards 製品基準
　quality control standard 品質管理基準
　quality standard 品質基準
　safety standard 安全基準
　standard accounts 一般投資家
　standard burden rate 標準配賦率, 製造間接費配賦率 （=standard overhead rate）
　standard cost 標準原価
　standard error ［統計］標準誤差
　standards of integrity 倫理基準
　technical standard 技術標準
　underwriting standards 与信基準
　universal standard ユニバーサル・スタンダード, 世界標準, 国際標準
　world standard 世界標準, ワールド・スタンダード （=worldwide standard）

▸All companies in the Group pride themselves on maintaining the highest *standards* of integrity in carrying out business activities. 当グループ企業は, すべて事業活動を実施するにあたって最高の倫理基準を維持することを誇りとする。

Standard & Poors 500 S&P500株価指数 （⇒Dow Jones industrial average [Industrial Average]）

standing 名 地位, 立場, 状態, 状況, 体質, 身分, 名声, 順位, 持続, 存続, ランキング表, 信用評価
　business standing 営業状態, 経営の体質
　corporate standing 企業体質
　financial standing 財政状態, 財務状況, 財務体質 （=financial position, financial status）
　legal standing 法的地位, 法的位置付け, 法的根拠

standing 形 常設の, 常置の, 常任の, 常備の, 永続的な
　standing committee 常設委員会
　standing credit 常設の信用枠
　standing expense 経常費
　standing proxy 常任代理人

start-up 名 始動, 開始, 開業, 開業準備, ベンチャー企業, 新興企業, 新会社, 新規事業, 新規企業, 新企業, スタートアップ・カンパニー （=start-up business, start-up company, start-up firm）
　start-up business 新規企業, 新興企業, ベンチャー企業, ベンチャー分野 （=start-up, start-up company, start-up firm）
　start-up costs 開業費, 開業準備費, 始動費, 運転開始費, 初期費用 （=preoperating costs）
　start-up firm 新興企業, ベンチャー企業 （=start-up company）

▸The gross margins were lower because the segment has experienced higher costs resulting from the *startup* costs associated with adding new manufacturing capacity. 売上利益が減少したのは, 製造設備の新設に伴う初期費用に起因して, 当部門のコストが増加したからです。

state 動 明示する, 公表する, 公開する, 表示する, 計上する, 評価する, 指定する, 定める, 規定する （⇒lower of cost or market）
　be stated at cost less accumulated depreciation and amortization 取得原価から減価償却累計額を控除して表示［評価, 計上］される
　be stated at the lower of standard cost or market 標準原価または時価のいずれか低いほうの金額で評価［計上, 表示］される
　stated capital 表示資本金, 表示資本額, 確定資本金
　stated in net amounts 純額表示

stated interest rate　表面利率, 約定利率
stated value　表示価額, 記載金額, 表記金額, 表記価格
stated value $1 per share　1株当たり額面額1ドル
▶Property, plant and equipment are *stated* at cost less accumulated depreciation.　有形固定資産は, 減価償却累計額控除後の取得原価で評価[計上]されています。

state-of-the-art 形　最先端の, 最新式の, 最新鋭の, 最高級の, 高度の, 最高水準の, 最新技術の, 最高技術水準の　(=cutting-edge, leading edge, sophisticated, top of the line, up-to-the-minute)
▶The Company incorporated *state-of-the-art* systems in its new facility.　当社は, 当社の新施設に最新のシステムを導入しました。

state-run 形　国営の, 国有の　(=state owned)
　state-run company　国営企業, 国有企業
　state-run enterprise　国営企業

statement 名　計算書, 財務表, 報告書, 届出書, 声明, コメント, 声明書, 規約, ステートメント　(⇒ **financial statements, profit and loss statement, proxy statement**)
　annual statement　年次報告書, 年次営業報告書
　application of funds statement　資金運用表
　balance of payments statement　国際収支表
　basic statements　基本財務諸表　(=basic financial statements)
　business statement　営業報告書
　cash flow statement　資金収支表, 収支計算書
　cash statement　現金収支計算書, 現金収支報告書, 現金有り高[在り高]表
　combined statements　結合財務諸表, 合併財務諸表
　constant dollar income statement　恒常ドル損益計算書
　date of the financial statements　財務諸表日
　distribution statement　分売届け出書
　earned surplus statement　利益剰余金計算書
　earnings statement　損益計算書　(=income statement, profit and loss statement)
　financial position statement　財政状態計算書, 財政状態表, 貸借対照表
　flow statement　フロー・ステートメント　(キャッシュ・フロー計算書や資金フロー計算書などの総称)
　flow-stock statement　フロー・ストックステートメント (資金の流れと保有高を示す計算書)
　foreign statements　外貨表示財務諸表　(= foreign currency financial statements)
　functional statement　機能別計算書
　fund [funds] flow statement　資金フロー計算書, 資金計算書, 資金運用表, 資金表　(=funds statement)
　fund statement　資金計算書　(=statement of changes in financial position)
　general purpose statement　一般目的報告書　(=general purpose report)
　graphic statements　図表式計算諸表, グラフ式計算諸表
　industry statement　産業別セグメント報告書
　interim statement　中間報告書, 中間計算書
　interim statements　中間財務書類, 中間財務諸表　(=interim financial statements)
　issue a statement　コメントを発表する
　offering statement　募集届け出書, 発行目論見書
　securities statement　有価証券報告書　(=securities report)
　social impact statement　社会影響報告書
　source and disposition statement　資金運用表
　statement of application of funds　資金運用表
　statement of assets and liabilities　資産負債計算書
　statement of capital stock　資本金変動表, 資本金計算書
　statement of capital surplus　資本剰余金計算書
　statement of financial condition　財政状態表, 貸借対照表　(=balance sheet, statement of financial position)
　statement of operations　事業報告書
　statement of retained earnings　利益剰余金計算書
　untrue statement　不実の記載
▶The Financial Accounting Standards Board adopted *Statement* No. 96, "Accounts for Income taxes" in December 1988.　財務会計基準審議会(FASB)は, 1988年12月, 基準書No.96「税効果会計」を採用した。

statement of accounts　決算報告書, 決算, 決算報告
　deficit statement of accounts　赤字決算
▶The former president is said to have instructed the firm's *statement of accounts* to include fabricated earnings.　前社長は, 同社の決算報告書に架空収益[架空の売上]を計上するよう指示したといわれる。

statement of earnings　損益計算書　(= statement of income; ⇒**foreign currency transaction**)

四半期報告書の損益計算書表示例（年度，金額は除く）：

Revenue:	総収益：
Sales	売上
Support services	支援サービス
Software	ソフトウエア
Rentals and financing	賃貸料および金融
Costs and expenses	原価および費用
Operating income	営業利益
Other income	その他の収益
Interest expense	支払い利息
Earnings before income taxes	税引き前利益
Provision for income taxes	法人所得税
Net earnings	当期純利益
Per share	1株当たり利益
Cash dividends per share	1株当たり現金配当額

Statement of Financial Accounting Standards 財務会計基準書《略 SFAS》（⇒ implement）

▶We adopted *Statement of Financial Accounting Standards* No. 106, effective January 1, 2007. 当社は，2007年1月1日から財務会計基準書第106号（「年金以外の退職後給付に関する事業主の会計処理」）を採用しました。

statement of financial position 貸借対照表, 財政状態表

四半期報告書の貸借対照表表示例（年度，金額・数値は除く）：

Assets	資産
Cash, cash equivalents and marketable securities	現金，預金および市場性ある有価証券
Receivables, inventories and prepaid expenses	売掛金，棚卸し資産および前払い費用
Total current assets	流動資産合計
Plant, rental machines and other property—net	工場設備，賃貸機械およびその他の固定資産—純額
Investments and other assets	投資およびその他の資産
Liabilities and stockholders' Equity	負債および株主持ち分
Accounts payable, taxes and other accruals	買掛金，税金およびその他の未払い費用
Short-term debt	借入金
Total current liabilities	流動負債合計
Long-term debt	長期負債
Other liabilities	その他の負債
Deferred income taxes	繰延べ税金
Stockholders' equity	株主持ち分
Stockholders' equity at Dcember 31, 2007	2007年12月31日現在株主持ち分
Net earnings	当期純利益
Cash dividends declared	現金配当金宣言額
Capital stock purchased and retired	株式の買入れ消却
Currency translation adjustments	外貨換算調整額
Other	その他
Stockholders' equity at March 31, 2007	2007年3月31日現在株主持ち分

status 名 地位，状態，状況，情勢，構造，資格，ステータス
　corporate status 法人格
　funded status 拠出状態，供出状況，積立状況
　preferred creditor status 優先債権者の地位
　tax status 税務上の取扱い
▶The life insurers' *status* as large stockholders means that when the market dives, their portfolios also take a tumble. 大株主としての生命保険会社の地位は，株価が大きく下がると資産内容も急激に悪化することを意味する。
▶This investment fund is a voluntary organization on the Civil Code and does not have corporate *status*. この投資ファンドは，民法上の任意組合で，法人格がない。

statute of limitations 出訴期限, 出訴期限法, 消滅時効, 時効

statutory 形 法定の
　statutory audit 法定監査
　statutory auditor 法定監査人，常勤監査役，監査役
　statutory surplus 法定準備金
　statutory tax rate 法定税率
　statutory workweek 法定週労働時間［日数］
▶Apart from the effects of changes in *statutory* tax rates, we do not expect the new accounting to affect future earnings materially. 法定税率変更の影響のほかは，新会計処理方法が将来の利益に大きな影響を及ぼすことはないでしょう。

step 名 措置，手段，対策，足どり，歩調，歩み，一歩，足跡，ステップ
▶While we work to sustain growth during the difficult period, we have taken strategic *steps* to position the firm for continued long-term growth. 当社は，この厳しい時期に成長の維持に取り組む一方，同社の継続的な長期発展を視座に据えて戦略的な措置を取りました。

step down 辞職する，辞任する，退任する，身を引く，引退する（＝resign）
▶The committee called for the president to *step down*. 同委員会は，社長の辞任を要求した。

stock 名 株，株式，株式資本，証券，銘柄，在庫，在庫品，ストック（＝share; ⇒ **capital stock**, com-

mon stock, preferred stock, tracking stock, treasury stock)
base stock method 基準棚卸し法 （＝base stock, base stock inventory valuation）
closing stock 棚卸し資産期末在り高
convertible stock 転換株式 （＝convertible share）
corporate stock 株式
cycle stock 循環在庫
excess stock 過剰在庫
finished product stock 製品在庫 （＝finished goods stock）
income stock 資産株, 採算株
initial stock 期首在庫, 期首在庫高
low priced stock 低位株
management stock 役員株
minimum stock level 最低在庫水準
newly issued stock 新規発行株式, 新規公開株
nonvoting stock 無議決権株, 議決権のない株式 （＝nonvoting share）
optimum stock 最適在庫量
portfolio stock 投資用株式
stock appraisal losses 株式評価損, 株式含み損
stock award plan 株式報償制度, 株式贈与制度, 株式報奨制度
stock buyout [buy-out] 株式買取り, 株の買占め
stock certificate 株券, 記名株式, 株式証券 （＝share certificate）
stock compensation plan 株式報奨制度, 株式報酬制度, 株式報酬プラン
stock-for-stock exchange rate 株式交換比率, 株式交換の交換比率 （＝stock exchange rate）
stock holding 株式保有, 株式所有, 保有株式, 持ち株, 出資比率 （＝equity holding, shareholding, stockholding; ⇒**stockholding**）
stock investment efficiency 株式投資効率 （⇒**ROE**）
stock issue 株式発行, 新株発行, 株式銘柄, 銘柄
stock market 株式市場, 証券市場, 株式相場, 株式市況, 株式売買, 株価 （＝equity market）
subsidiary stock 子会社株式
transfer of stock 株式の名義書換え, 株式の譲渡
unclaimed stock 失権株
▸The company's main bank will swap ¥40 billion in debt into *stock*. 同社の主力行が, 400億円分の債権の株式化を行う[債務の株式化に応じる]。
▸The increase in investments mainly reflects a $500 million purchase of the company *stock* in February 2007. 投資の増加は, 主に2007年2月の同社株購入の5億ドルを反映しています。

stock appreciation right 株式評価益権, 株式評価受益権, 株式騰貴権, 株式増価差額請求権 《略 SAR》
▸We grant stock options, *stock appreciation rights* (SARs), either in tandem with stock options or free-standing, in our long term incentive program. 当社は, 当社の長期勤労奨励制度で, ストック・オプション[自社株購入権]のほかに, ストック・オプションと組み合わせたまたは単独の株式評価受益権(SAR)も付与しています。

stock buyback 株式の買戻し, 自社株発行済み株式の買戻し, 自社株買戻し, 自社株買い, 自社株取得, 自社株式の取得 （＝share buyback, share repurchase, stock repurchase; ⇒**share buyback**）
▸*Stock buybacks* were limited to certain purposes, such as share retirement and stock option schemes, before the revision of the Commercial Code. 自社株買いは, 商法の改正前は, 株式の消却用やストックオプション制度向けなど特定の目的に制限されていた。

stock buyback plan 自社株取得計画, 株式買戻し計画
▸A company proposal for *stock buyback* and incentive stock option *plans* was approved at an annual meeting. 年次株主総会で, 自社株取得計画と奨励株式オプション制度の会社提案[会社側の議案]が承認された。

stock company 株式会社 （＝joint stock company, stock corporation）
▸The minimum capital requirements of ¥10 million for the establishment of a *stock company* have been eliminated under the new Corporate Law. 株式会社を設立する場合の1,000万円の最低資本金規制は, 新会社法で撤廃された。

stock dealing 株式取引, 株の売買 （＝stock deal, stock transaction）
▸In the *stock dealings*, the firm calculated a loss of ¥3.5 billion in its reports to the Tokyo Regional Taxation Bureau. この株売買で, 同社は東京国税局への申告書に35億円の損失を計上した。

stock dividend 株式配当 （＝capital bonus: 配当を現金でなく株式で交付すること）
▸The board of directors declared a 8% *stock dividend* on April 1, 2007. 取締役会は, 2007年4月1日, 8%の株式配当を宣言した[株式配当の決議を行った]。

stock exchange 証券取引所, 株式取引所, 株式交換(share exchange), 株式売買(securities exchange) （⇒**New York Stock Exchange**）

American Stock Exchange アメリカン証券取引所, アメックス《略 **AMEX**》
London Stock Exchange ロンドン証券取引所
stock exchange merger ストック・エクスチェンジ・マージャー（企業の買収・合併の手段として，存続会社が，合併で吸収される会社の株主に存続会社の株式を交付する方法。⇒**cash merger**）
Stock Exchange of Singapore シンガポール証券取引所
stock exchange offer 株式交換公開買付け，ストック・エクスチェンジ・オファー（M&Aの手段として，買収先の企業の株式を，株式などの有価証券で公開買付けする方法）
stock exchange ratio [rate] 株式交換比率（＝share exchange rate, stock-for-stock exchange rate）
Toronto Stock Exchange トロント証券取引所
▶Nasdaq launched its $5.3 billion hostile bid for the London *Stock Exchange*. 米ナスダックが，ロンドン証券取引所(LSE)に対して53億ドルの敵対的株式公開買付け(TOB)を実施した。
▶When a project plan for new product development or a new business is completed, a company would be established and placed on the *stock exchange*. 新製品の開発や新事業の事業計画に目途が立ったら，会社を設立して，株式を上場する。

stock index 株価指数
narrow based stock index 業種別株価指数
Nikkei Stock Index 300 日経株価指数300
stock index futures 株価指数先物，株価指数先物取引
stock index option 株価指数オプション

stock offering 株式発行, 株式公開, 株式公募, 株式上場 （⇒**public offering**, **public stock offering**）
initial stock offering 新規株式公開, 新規株式公募 （⇒**initial public offering**）
public stock offering 公募増資
▶We raised $2.3 billion by this *stock offering*. この株式公募［株式公開］で，当社は23億ドルを調達しました。

stock option 株式購入選択権, 株式買受権, 自社株購入権, 株式オプション, ストック・オプション （⇒**exercise price, option holder, salary income, stock appreciation right**）
ストック・オプション ➡ 報酬制度の一つで，自社株をあらかじめ決められた権利行使価格で購入する権利。自社株の株価が権利行使価格を上回れば，購入者が利益を上げることができる。ただし，ストック・オプションの問題点として，実勢株価が権利行使価格を下回る場合があることや，自社株価をつりあげる会計操作の誘因になったりすることが指摘されている。また企業会計上，人件費として計上しなければならないのに計上していない企業が多いなどの問題もある。
stock option dealing 株式オプション取引, 個別株オプション取引
stock option income ストック・オプション利益
stock option plan 株式購入選択権制度, 株式選択権制度, 自社株購入権制度, 株式オプション制度, ストック・オプション制度 （＝stock option program, stock option scheme, stock option system; ⇒**employee stock option plan**, **stock buyback plan**）
stock option program 株式購入選択権制度, 株式選択権制度, 自社株購入権制度, 株式オプション制度, ストック・オプション制度 （＝stock option plan, stock option scheme）
▶Common stock equivalents are *stock options* that we assume to be exercised for the purpose of this computation of earnings per common share. 準普通株式［普通株式等価物］は，この1株［普通株1株］当たり純利益の計算の際に行使されると仮定したストック・オプションです。
▶*Stock option* programs are seen as leading to financial window-dressing to manipulate share prices. ストック・オプション制度は，株価操作のための会計操作につながると見られている。

stock price 株価 （＝share price）
stock price disparity 株価格差
stock price per share （普通株式）1株当たり時価
▶The *stock price* disparity between Toyota and Honda is considered primarily due to the two companies' return on equity (ROE) ratios. トヨタとホンダの株価格差は，主に両社の株主資本利益率(ROE)によるものだ。

stock purchase plan 株式購入制度, 株式購入選択権制度, 株式購入権制度, 自社株購入制度 （⇒**employee stock purchase plan**）
▶ABC Inc. raised $100 million of common equity by means of its Dividend Reinvestment and *Stock Purchase Plan* and the Employees' Savings Plan. ABC Inc.は，同社の株主配当再投資・株式購入制度と従業員社内預金制度により普通株式を発行して1億ドルを調達しました。

stock-related losses 株式等関連損失
▶The major banks' *stock-related losses* ballooned 1.9 fold from a year ago because of the booking

of declines in the value of their equity holdings as appraised losses and their sale of stocks due to sluggish stock markets.　大手銀行の株式等関連損失は、株式相場の下落による保有株の減損処理や売却損などで前期の1.9倍に膨らんだ。

stock repurchase　自社株買戻し、株式買戻し、自社株買い　(=share buyback, stock buyback)
▸Under our *stock repurchase* programs, 8,611,396,000 shares were repurchased during 2007 at a cost of $992 million.　当社の自社株買戻しプログラムに従って、2007年度に861億1,139万6,000株を9億9,200万ドルで買い戻しました。

stock split　株式分割、株式の分割・併合 (1株を分割して、発行済み株式数を増やすこと。一般に、投資家を増やして必要な事業資金を集めやすくするために行われる)、無償交付　(=share split, share splitting, split-up of stock; ⇒**share**)
　reverse stock split　株式併合　(⇒**trading unit**)
　stock split-down　株式併合　(=reverse split, reverse stock split, share split-down)
　stock split-up　株式分割　(=share split-up)
　two-for-one stock split　1対2の株式分割、1対2の比率による株式分割、1株を2株に増やす株式分割　(⇒**paid-in capital**)
▸After the *stock split*, the par value of the stock was reduced by $3 per share.　株式分割後、株式の1株当たり額面は1株3ドル減少した。
▸Japan Engineering Consultants implemented a 1-for-5 *stock split* to counter Yumeshin's hostile takeover bid.　日本技術開発は、夢真の敵対的TOB［株式公開買付け］への対抗策として1株を5株に増やす株式分割を行った。

stock swap　株式交換　(=share swap, stock swapping; ⇒**share swap**)
▸Citigroup aims to be listed on the Tokyo Stock Exchange by the end of January 2008 in sync with the completion of the planned *stock swap*.　米大手金融グループのシティグループは、予定している株式交換の完了に歩調を合わせて、2008年1月末までに東京証券取引所に上場する。

stock transaction　株式取引、株取引、株の売買　(=equity trading, stock trade, stock trading)
▸Top officials of each stock exchange have a management responsibility to guarantee investors smooth *stock transactions*.　各証券取引所のトップには、投資家に円滑な株式取引を保証する経営責任がある。

stock transfer　株式名義書換え、株式譲渡　(=share transfer)
　stock transfer agent　名義書換え取扱機関、名義書換え代理人　(=transfer agent)
　stock transfer book　株主名簿、株式名簿、株式譲渡名簿、株式名義書換え簿、株主台帳、名義書換え台帳、(=transfer book)
▸The *stock transfer* will be made on Oct. 5 with Mitsui Fudosan paying ¥8,750 per share.　この株式譲渡は、三井不動産が1株当たり8,750円を支払って10月5日に行われる。

stockholder 名　株主　(=stockowner; ⇒**shareholder**)
　institutional stockholder　法人株主
　preferred stockholder　優先株株主、優先株主　(=preferred shareholder)
　stockholder plan　株主制度、株主プラン
　stockholder rights plan　株主権利制度
　stockholders' meeting　株主総会　(=general meeting, shareholders meeting, stockholders meeting; ⇒**shareholders meeting**)
　stockholders' representative suit　株主の代表訴訟
▸The approval of numerous *stockholders* must be gained for a retirement of 50 percent of common shares.　普通株式の50％消却については、多くの株主の承認を得なければならない。

stockholder of record　登録株主、株主名簿上の株主　(=shareholder of record)
▸Only *stockholders of record* at the close of business on March 15, 2008 are entitled to vote at the annual meeting.　2008年3月15日の営業終了時現在の登録株主だけが、株主総会で投票する権利があります。

stockholders' equity　株主持ち分、株主資本、資本の部、資本勘定、資本、自己資本、純資産、純資産の部　(=net worth, owners' equity, shareholders' equity：払込み資本金と利益剰余金の合計。⇒**shareholders' equity**)
　average stockholders' equity　平均株主資本
　common stockholders' equity　普通株主持ち分
　consolidated stockholders' equity　連結株主持ち分
　minority stockholders' equity　少数株主持ち分
　preferred stockholders' equity　優先株主持ち分
▸Average invested capital is defined as *stockholders' equity* plus long- and short-term debts less short-term investments (includes short-term investments categorized as cash equivalents).　平均投下資本＝資本＋長期・短期金融債務－短期投資(現預金等価物として表示する短期投資を含む)です。

stockholding 名　株式保有、保有株式、保有株、

持ち株 （=shareholding, stock holding)
▶The massive gains in *stockholdings*' latent value will raise the banks' net worth ratios markedly. 保有株式の含み益の大幅増加で，銀行の自己資本比率も大きく向上する見込みだ。

straight 形 連続した，1年前と比較した
  straight loan 通常のローン
  straight salary system 固定給制
▶It is the fifth *straight* month that the unemployment rate has surpassed that of the United States. 完全失業率が米国を上回ったのは，5か月連続である。

straight 副 連続して，1年前と比較して，ぶっ通しで

straight bond 普通社債，確定利付き社債《略 SB》(転換社債以外の普通の社債)
▶The bank will raise about ¥150 billion by issuing *straight bonds* on a quarterly basis. 同行は，四半期ベースで普通社債を発行して約1,500億円を調達する。

straight line 定額
straight-line 形 定額方式の，定額法による，直線方式の，定額の （=straight-line method)
  straight-line capitalization 直線式収益還元法
  straight-line depreciation 定額減価償却，定額償却，定額法，直線法，定額法による減価償却費（=equal-installment depreciation, straight-line method：償却資産の減価償却法の一つ)

straight-line basis 定額基準，定額法（= straight-line method)
▶Goodwill is generally amortized on a *straight-line basis* over 10 years. 営業権は通常，10年間にわたり定額法で償却しています。

straight-line method 定額法 （=straight-line basis：固定資産の取得原価から残存価額を差し引いた金額を，耐用年数で割って，1年分の減価償却費を計算する方法)
▶Depreciation is calculated generally on the *straight-line method* using rates based on the expected useful lives of the respective assets. 減価償却費は，原則として個々の資産の見積り耐用年数に基づく減価償却率を用いて，定額法で計算されています。

strategic 形 戦略的，戦略上の，戦略上重要な，戦略上役に立つ，戦略に必要な
  strategic business alliance 戦略的業務提携
  strategic implication 戦略的意義
  strategic intent 戦略的意図 （⇒**management executive committee**)
  strategic review 戦略の検討

strategic alliance 戦略提携，戦略的業務提携，戦略的同盟，製版同盟，ストラテジック・アライアンス
▶Joint venture and *strategic alliance* marked the quarter—joining the Company to partners with complementary strengths. 合弁事業と戦略的提携が当四半期のハイライトで，当社は相互補完力のあるパートナーと手を結びました。

strategic investment 戦略的投資
▶*Strategic investment* increased the potential for the Corporation's growth in worldwide markets. 戦略的投資で，グローバル市場での当社の潜在成長力は高まりました。

strategic planning 戦略計画，戦略的計画，戦略計画策定，戦略計画設定，戦略企画，戦略の策定，ストラテジック・プランニング
▶The firm's sales department now handles *strategic planning*, transactions with mass retailers and business with the public sector. 同社の営業部門は現在，営業戦略の立案や量販店，官公庁との取引を担当している。

strategy 名 戦略，策，手法，方針，ストラテジー （⇒**business strategy, global strategy, management strategy, realignment strategy**)
  acquisition strategy 買収戦略
  advertising strategy 広告戦略
  bottom-up strategy 意見上申戦略，現場意見採用戦略
  competitive strategy 競争戦略
  core strategy 基本戦略
  corporate strategy 企業戦略，経営戦略，営業戦略
  cost cutting strategy コスト削減策
  distribution strategy 流通戦略
  downstream strategy 川下戦略
  e-business strategy eビジネス戦略
  e strategy e戦略
  executive manpower strategy 幹部職員採用戦略，幹部人材養成戦略
  financial strategy 財務戦略
  funding strategy 資金調達戦略
  global marketing strategy グローバル・マーケティング戦略
  growth strategy 成長戦略
  hedge strategy ヘッジ戦略
  image strategy イメージ戦略
  investment strategy 投資戦略
  IT strategy IT戦略
  low-margin, high volume strategy 薄利多売戦略

market strategy 市場戦略, 製品市場戦略
media strategy メディア戦略, 媒体戦略
merchandise strategy 商品戦略
multibrand strategy マルチブランド戦略, 複数ブランド戦略
niche strategy すき間戦略, ニッチ戦略
portfolio strategy ポートフォリオ戦略
pricing strategy 価格戦略, 価格設定戦略
product-market [product/market] strategy 製品・市場戦略
purchasing strategy 購買戦略, 仕入戦略
retailing strategy 小売業戦略
sales strategy 販売戦略, セールス手法
solution strategy ソリューション戦略
syndication strategy シ団組成戦略
systematization strategy システム化戦略
top-down strategy 上意下達戦略, 下降型戦略
upstream strategy 川上戦略
value strategy バリュー戦略

▶In 2007 we focused on executing our *strategy*. 2007年度は, 当社の戦略実施に焦点を合わせました。

▶Japan's four megabanks are now rebuilding their global business *strategies*. 日本の4大金融グループは現在, グローバル戦略の再構築に取り組んでいる。

▶We can apply a unique management *strategy* that other companies don't have. 当社は, 他社にないユニークな経営戦略をとることができます。

stream 名 流れ, 傾向, 動向, 趨勢, 見通し, キャッシュ・フロー

come back on stream 生産を再開する
come on stream 稼働する
go on stream 生産を開始する, 稼働する
interest stream 金利の流れ, 金利のキャッシュ・フロー
on stream 生産中, 稼動中
profits stream 収益見通し (＝earnings stream)
upper end of the production stream 生産の流れ(生産から消費に至る各段階)の上流

▶Industries at the upper end of the production *stream* have higher increases in recurring profits. 生産の流れの上流にある産業のほうが, 経常利益の増加率が高い。

▶Toyota's car assembly plant in St. Petersburg is planned to go on *stream* in December 2007. ロシアのサンクトペテルブルクにあるトヨタの自動車組立工場は, 2007年12月から生産を開始する。

streamline 動 合理化する, 能率化する, 効率化する, 簡素化する, スリム化する, リストラする (⇒focus on)

▶Listed companies have improved their balance sheets by *streamlining* facilities, employees and debts. 上場企業は, 設備, 雇用と負債の過剰を解消して, 財務体質を改善した。

▶We cannot return to the black in fiscal 2008 unless we thoroughly *streamline* our business. 当社は, 徹底して経営の合理化を図らなければ, 2008年度の黒字転換は無理である。

▶We *streamlined* development work on telecommunications network systems in 2007. 当社は, 2007年度に, 通信ネットワーク・システム開発作業の効率化[合理化]を進めました。

streamlining 名 合理化, 能率化, 効率化, 簡素化, スリム化, リストラ

▶Financial institutions have no time to lose in enhancing their profitability, *streamlining* and information disclosure. 金融機関の場合, 収益力の向上や一層の合理化, 情報開示は待ったなしだ。

▶Our *streamlining* projects are being implemented through 2009. 当社の効率化プロジェクトは, 2009年度末まで実施されます。

street-name account 実質株主名を株主名簿に登録していない株主の口座

strength 名 力, 強さ, 強み, 力強さ, 体力, 勢い, 好調, 活況, 上昇, 勢力, 兵力, 人数, 長所 (⇒corporate strength)

brand strength ブランド競争力, ブランド力
business strength 経営体力, 経営力, 事業での成功
competitive strength 競争力
credit strength 信用力, 信用度, 信用の質
economic strength 経済力, 景気の力強さ, 景気の腰の強さ, 景気好調
financial strength rating 支払い能力の格付け
industrial strength 製造業の好調
marketing strength 販売力, マーケティング力
specific pockets of strength 好調な業種
strengths and weaknesses 長所と短所
technological strength 技術力
yen's strength 円高

▶One of Toyota's *strengths* is that it tailors its models to match the preferences of customers around the world. トヨタの強さの一つは, 世界各地でユーザーの好みに合った車を丁寧に作るということだ。

▶Return on equity is an indicator believed to show the real *strength* of a company. 株主資本利益率(ROE)は, 企業の本当の実力を示すとされる経営指標だ。

▶Whether equity investments, joint ventures or

other alliances, we look for partnerships that complement our own *strengths*.　出資であれ合弁その他の提携であれ，提携によって当社の強みを補完できる場合に，当社は提携先を求めます。

strengthen 動　強化する，高める，拡大する，充実させる，上昇する，向上する，改善する
▶As one step toward this corporate goal, we acquired a leading U.K. telecommunications firm to *strengthen* our position in the U.K.　この会社目標達成に向けての第一歩として，当社は英国での事業基盤を強化するため，英国の大手通信会社を取得［買収］しました。

stress 名　圧力，圧迫，困難，困難な状況，厳しい環境，厳しい経営環境，経営難，強調，力点，重点，ストレス
　financial stress　経営難，金融上の困難，財務状態の悪化，信用圧迫
　stress conditions [**situations**]　困難な状況
　under stress　困難な状況下で，厳しい状況下で，厳しい環境下で
▶The industry is under a good deal of *stress*, as evidenced by pressure on profitability and decline in stock prices over the last several months.　業界は，収益性の悪化やここ数か月の株価低迷でも明らかなように，かなり厳しい状況下にあります。

strike 名　権利行使，スト，ストライキ，〈鉱脈などの〉発見，〈石油などの〉掘り当て，突然の成功
　be (out) on strike　スト中，ストをしている
　call off a strike　ストを中止する
　come [go] out on strike　ストを開始する
　general strike　ゼネスト，総同盟罷業，ゼネラル・ストライキ
　go ahead with a strike　ストに突入する
　go on strike　ストをする，ストに突入する
　official strike　公式ストライキ，組合公認スト
　protest strike　抗議スト
　sitdown strike　座り込みスト
　stage a strike　ストを決行する
　strike action　スト
　strike ballot　スト権投票
　strike pay [**benefit**]　スト手当
　strike price　〈オプション取引の〉権利行使価格，行使価格（＝striking price）
　vote for strike action　スト権投票を行う
　wildcat strike　山猫スト（組合執行部の指令なしで組合員が勝手に行うスト）
▶U.S. factory employees went on *strike* to put pressure on the biggest U.S. automaker.　米国自動車最大手のゼネラル・モーターズ（GM）に圧力をかけるため，同社の米工場従業員がストに突入した。

strong 形　強い，強力な，力強い，強固な，堅調の，好調な，上昇基調の，優良な
　be in a strong position　優位に立っている，優位に立つ
　remain strong　堅調に推移する
　strong balance sheet　強固な財務体質，健全な財務内容，健全な財務状態
　strong demand　需要の急増，需要の大幅の伸び，需要の旺盛，需要が強いこと
　strong dollar　強いドル，ドル高
　strong earnings growth　利益の大幅な伸び，力強い利益の伸び
　strong management　強力な経営陣
　strong outperformance　大幅なアウトパフォーマンス，パフォーマンスが市場平均を大幅に上回ること
　strong price competition　激しい価格競争
　strong sales increase　売上の急増，販売の急増
　strong shareholder　安定株主
▶The balance sheet of the Corporation is *strong*.　当社の財務状態［財務内容］は，健全です。
▶U.S. President reiterated his support for a *strong* dollar.　米大統領は，「強いドル」維持を表明した。

strong performance　好業績，好調な業績，業績好調（＝strong financial performance）
▶Contributions from the telecommunications companies were higher than in the past, underlying their *strong performance*.　通信会社［通信事業会社］の貢献度は，好調な業績を反映して，過去の水準を上回りました。

strong sales　販売好調，好調な売れ行き
▶Sharp Corp's quarterly group net profit rose 27.2 percent on *strong sales* of liquid crystal display televisions and camera-equipped mobile phones.　シャープの四半期連結税引き後利益［純利益］は，液晶テレビやカメラ付き携帯電話などの販売が好調だったことから，前年同期比で27.2％増加した。

stronger performance　業績の大幅拡大，業績の大幅な伸び
▶A good order growth of 15 percent and a record order backlog of over \$3 billion for the first half of the year bolster our confidence for a *stronger performance* in the second half.　今年度上半期［上期］は受注高が15％の順調な伸び率を示し，受注残高も30億ドルを超える記録的な水準に達したため，私ども経営陣は下半期［下期］の業績の大幅拡大に自信を深めています。

structure 名 構造, 機構, 組織, 構成, 体系, 方式, 体制, 体質, 構築物, 構造物, 建造物 （⇒**capital structure, management structure**）
- **capital structure** 資本構成［構造］, 財務基盤
- **earnings structure** 収益構造
- **equity structure** 資本構成, 出資構造, 株主所有権構造
- **fiscal structure** 財政体質
- **income structure** 所得構造
- **internal control structure** 内部統制構造
- **market structure** 市場構造, 市場構成
- **ownership structure** 所有構造, 株主構造, 出資構成
- **price structure** 価格体系, 価格構造
- **rate structure** 料金体系
- **shareholding structure** 株主構成, 株主構造 （=shareholder structure）
- **term structure** 期間構造

▶Major banks are forced to review their earnings *structure*. 大手行は, 収益構造の見直しを迫られている。

struggle 動 悪戦苦闘する, 奮闘する, 苦労する, 必死になる, 取り組む （⇒**turn around**）
▶The company is *struggling* to recover earnings at its core businesses such as laser printers and digital cameras. 同社は, レーザー・プリンターやデジタル・カメラなど同社の中核事業の収益回復に取り組んでいる。

struggle 名 競争, 闘争, 紛争, 戦い, もみ合い, 取っ組み合い, 攻防戦
- **internal struggle** 内部闘争, 内紛 （=internal conflict）
- **litigating struggle** 法廷闘争
- **work-to-rule struggle** 順法闘争 （=law-abiding struggle）

struggling 形 経営不振に陥っている, 経営再建中の, 生き残りに懸命の, 生き残りに必死になっている, もたついている, 悪戦苦闘の
▶Toyota has smoothly increased its sales, compared with the *struggling* General Motors Corp. and Ford Motor Co. 販売不振のゼネラル・モーターズ（GM）やフォードに対して, トヨタは順調に売上を伸ばしている。

subject to ... …に服する, …が適用される, …に準拠する, …の対象である, …の影響を受ける, …を必要とする, …を条件とする, …を免れない, …にかぎり, …の場合にかぎって, …に従って, …を条件として, …を前提として, ただし…
▶Proceeds from exercising stock options are regarded as part of a salary and thus *subject to* a higher tax rate than for one-time income. ストック・オプションを行使して得た利益［ストック・オプション利益］は, 給与の一部と見なされるため, 一時所得より高い税率が課される。

submission 名 提出, 提示, 提示案, 提出物, 報告書, 考え, 意見, 仲裁付託合意
▶The Audit Committee reviews the corporation's financial statements and related data prior to *submission* to the full board. 監査委員会は, 当社の財務書類［財務諸表］と関連資料を, 取締役会の全体会議に提出する前に検討します。

submit 動 提出する, 提示する, 意見を述べる, 具申する
▶The firm's shareholders *submitted* proposals to disclose individual executive salaries at their general shareholders meetings. 同社の株主からは, 株主総会で役員報酬の個別開示を求める案が出された。

subordinated debenture 劣後債, 劣後社債 （=subordinated bond：債券発行会社の破産や清算に際して, 一般の債務返済後に債務弁済が開始される債券）
- **convertible subordinated debenture** 転換劣後社債
- **junior subordinated debenture** 下位劣後債
- **senior subordinated debenture** 上位劣後債

▶The two banks received the public funds by issuing *subordinated debentures* and loans. 両銀行は, 劣後債や劣後ローンを発行して公的資金（の注入）を受けた。

subordinated debt 劣位弁済債務
subordinated loan 劣後ローン
▶The bank plans to provide the money by transferring ¥100 billion in *subordinated loans* to the insurer's foundation fund. 同行は, 劣後ローン1,000億円をこの保険会社の基金に振り替えて, その資金を提供する方針だ。

subprime lender サブプライム・ローンの融資行, 信用力が比較的低い低所得者を対象にした住宅融資の融資銀行［融資行］, 住宅ローン会社 （=subprime mortgage lender; ⇒**default**）

subprime loan 低所得者を対象にした住宅融資, 低所得者層向け住宅ローン, サブプライム・ローン （=subprime mortgage, subprime mortgage loan）

> サブプライム・ローンとは ➡ サブプライム（subprime）は, 優良な借り手を対象にした「プライム」より信用力が低い, という意味である。サブプライム・ローンと呼ばれる米国の低所得者層や返済能力に問題がある個人向けの住宅ローン［住宅融資］は,

ローン返済開始から2年間くらいは金利が低いが、それ以降は一般に金利が低くなるように設定されている。そのため米国では、高金利の返済ができないサブプライム・ローンの焦げ付き問題で、株価の動揺が続いた。また、サブプライム・ローンを証券化した金融商品を販売している欧米や日本の金融機関が、多額の損失を出す事態になった。

▶Nomura booked about ¥72 billion in losses related to the U.S. *subprime loan* business in the January-June period. 野村[野村ホールディングス]は、1-6月期に米国でのサブプライム・ローン事業関連の損失として約720億円を計上した。

subprime mortgage 低所得者向け住宅ローン、低所得者層向け住宅ローン、低所得者向け住宅融資、サブプライム・ローン（=subprime mortgage loan; ⇒uncertainty）

▶UBS will post a pretax loss of up to $690 million in the third quarter mainly because of losses linked to the U.S. *subprime mortgage* crisis. スイス最大手銀行UBSの第3四半期税引前損失は、主に米国で起きた低所得者向け融資「サブプライム・ローン」問題の関連損失で、最高で6億9,000万ドルに達する見通しだ。

subprime mortgage lender 住宅ローン会社、サブプライム・ローンの融資行

subprime mortgage loan サブプライム・ローン

▶The instability of U.S. stock prices results from problems related to massive number of unrecoverable *subprime mortgage loans* extended to low-income earners in the United States. 米国の株価不安定は、米国の低所得者向け住宅ローン「サブプライム・ローン」の焦げ付き急増関連問題に起因している。

subscriber 名 〈株式の〉引受人、〈年金や電話などの〉加入者、申込者、署名者、〈新聞や雑誌の〉(予約)購読者

▶The *subscribers* changed jobs from a firm that offered the defined-contribution pension plans to one that did not offer the plans. (確定拠出年金)加入者が、確定拠出年金を導入している企業から導入していない企業に転職した。

subsequent event 後発事象 （=events occurring after the balance sheet date, post balance sheet events）

subsidiary 名 子会社、関係会社、従属会社 （= subsidiary company, subsidiary corporation; ⇒**consolidated subsidiary, wholly owned subsidiary**）

majority owned subsidiary 過半数所有子会社

marketing subsidiary 販売子会社 （=sales subsidiary)

overseas subsidiary 海外子会社 （=foreign subsidiary)

partially owned subsidiary 部分所有子会社

quasi-subsidiary 準子会社

▶Mitsubishi UFJ Financial Group Inc. turned its Mitsubishi UFJ Securities a 100% *subsidiary*. 三菱UFJフィナンシャル・グループは、三菱UFJ証券を100％子会社[完全子会社]化した。

substantial 形 かなりの規模の、大規模な、莫大な、大幅な、大型の、豊富な、実質的な、重要な、重大な

▶The market opportunity is *substantial*. 市場機会は、かなりのものです。

success 名 成功、発展、成果、勝利、サクセス (⇒**employee**)

▶Our ultimate *success* will depend on how effectively and quickly we respond to the big changes taking place in the external environment. 当社の最終的な成果は、事業環境[外部環境]に起こっている大きな変化にいかに効果的かつ迅速に対応するかにかかっています。

successful efforts method 成功成果法、成功支出額繰延べ法、成功支出、資産計上方式 （= sucessful efforts accounting)

▶We adopted the *successful efforts method* of accounting for oil and gas activities. 当社は、石油・ガス事業の会計処理については、成功成果法を採用しました。

suffer 動 〈損失などを〉受ける、損失を計上する、〈被害などを〉被る、〈打撃を〉受ける、…に見舞われる、…に巻き込まれる、耐える、低迷する、悪材料になる （⇒**appraisal loss**）

suffer a loss 損失を被る

suffer a plunge 下落する

suffer big [large] losses 大損害を受ける、巨額の損失を被る、多額の損失を計上する

suffer from a high debt load 重い債務負担に苦しむ、債務負担が重荷になる

▶The firm *suffered* a plunge in its share prices in the wake of an accounting scandal. 会計処理疑惑の結果、同社の株価が下落した。

▶The hedge fund *suffered* a loss of $6 billion this month. 同ヘッジ・ファンドは今月、60億ドルの損失を被った[計上した]。

sum 名 合計、総量、合計金額、総額、金額

single sum 一時金

sum insured 保険金額

sum total 総計、総額

sums due 満期決済額
▶This full-year dividend *sum* includes a midterm dividend of ¥70 per share. この通期配当金には、1株当たり70円の中間配当も含まれている。

sum-of-the-digits basis 級数法
▶Prior to 2005, earnings were accounted for over the collection terms of the finance receivables on the *sum-of-the-digits basis*. 2005年度以前は、収益は金融債権の回収期間にわたって級数法により会計処理していました。

sum of the years' digits method 等差等級法, 級数法, 年次級数総和法 (＝sum-of-the-years-digits method, sum of the years' digits method of depreciation)
▶We considered various methods of depreciation and selected the *sum of the years' digits method of depreciation*. 当社は、各種の減価償却方法を検討して、級数法を選択しました。

summarized financial information 要約財務情報, 財務情報要約

summarized financial results 要約財務実績, 財務実績要約

summarized financial statements 要約財務書類[財務諸表], 財務書類要約

summary 名 要約, 概要, 総括, 略式, 総合勘定, 集合勘定, 集計勘定
  five-year comparative consolidated summary of operations 最近5年間の連結営業活動の要約比較
  five year financil summary 5年間の財務状況推移
  historical summary 過去の推移, 過去の状況
  summary of earnings 損益の概要, 損益総括表
  summary of operations 損益要約表, 営業活動の要約, 要約損益計算書
  summary of significant accounting policies 重要な会計方針の要約[概要], 重要な会計処理方針の要約, 主要会計方針の要約
  summary prospectus 要約目論見書
  summary statement of business 事業説明書 (各事業部門の内容と業績の紹介)

super voting share 複数議決権株式 (＝super voting stock)
▶*Super voting shares* empower a shareholder with multiple voting rights per share. 複数議決権株式では、株主は株式1株につき複数の議決権が与えられる。

superior 形 上位の, 上級の, 優れた
  superior products and services 優れた製品とサービス
▶Our customers can count on us to consistently deliver *superior* products and services that help them achieve their personal or business goals. お客さまの信頼に応えて、当社は、つねにお客さま個人の目標または企業の目標達成に役立つ優れた製品とサービスを提供します。

supplementary [**supplemental**] 形 補足的, 補完的, 追加の, 付属の, 増補の, 補遺の, 付録の
  supplementary cost 間接費, 補足的費用
  supplementary disclosure 補足的開示情報
  supplementary financial statements 補足的財務書類[財務諸表], 補足財務情報
  supplementary rate 補充率
  supplementary retirement plan 追加退職年金制度
  supplementary schedule 付属明細表, 付属明細書
  supplementary statement 付属明細書, 補足的意見書

supplier 名 供給者, 供給会社, 供給業者, 供給下請業者, 供給源, 仕入先, 納入業者, 製造業者, メーカー, 供給国, 輸出国, 売り手, サプライヤー
  housing supplier 住宅メーカー
  leading supplier 大手サプライヤー
  local supplier 現地メーカー
  parts supplier 部品メーカー
▶Collection of receivables helps us to pay our *suppliers*. 売掛金を回収すると、当社の納入業者への支払いが楽になります。

supply 動 供給する, 提供する, 供与する
  supply funds 資金を供給[提供]する
  supply imported raw materials 輸入原材料を供給する

supply 名 供給, 供給量, 需給, 供給品, [supplies]消耗品, 貯蔵品, [supplies]政府の歳出・経費, サプライ
  construction supplies 建設資材 (＝building supplies)
  effective labor supplies 効率の高い労働力
  factory supplies 工場消耗品
  manufacturing supplies 製造用消耗品
  office supplies オフィス用品費
  operating supplies 作業用貯蔵品
  product supplies 製品需給
  productive material, work in process and supplies 原材料, 仕掛品と貯蔵品
  sources of supply 供給源
  supplies inventory 材料在庫
  supply and demand of funds 資金需給
  tight supply conditions 需給の逼迫

▸*Supply* cannot keep up with demand for some popular items.　売れ筋商品は，需要に供給が追いつけない状態だ．

▸The Corporation's subsidiaries and associated companies are leaders in the manufacure and *supply* of telecommunications equipment.　当社の子会社と関連会社は，通信機器の製造・供給の分野で主導的地位を占めています．

supply chain　供給連鎖，サプライ・チェーン（商品やサービスの顧客に届くまでの全体の流れ．原材料の調達から製品の生産・販売にいたるまでの各プロセスに係わる企業のことを指す場合もある）

▸Our *supply chain* will be strengthened further through management integration.　経営統合により，当社のサプライ・チェーンは一層強化されることになります．

support 動　支援する，援助する，支持する，サポートする　(⇒lion's share)

▸It is in our interest to *support* society's needs.　社会のニーズへの支援は，当社の利益にもつながることです．

support 名　支援，援助，支持，サポート　(＝aid, assistance; ⇒**customer support system, financial support**)

　credit support　信用補強，信用補塡，信用補完
　customer support　顧客支援
　group support　グループ支援，系列支援
　support rate　支持率　(＝approval rate [rating], popularity rating)
　technological support　技術支援

▸GM will restructure its business through Toyota's *support*.　GMは，トヨタの支援で経営を再建する方針だ．

surge 動　急増する，急騰する，高まる，殺到する，押し寄せる

▸The U.S. dollar *surged* to ¥130 level.　ドル相場が，1ドル＝130円台まで急騰した．

surge 名　急増，急騰，急上昇，殺到，大波，ブーム

▸The *surge* in prices of natural resources could ignite fears of inflation, causing countries around the world to implement tight monetary policies.　天然資源の価格急騰がインフレ懸念を呼び，世界各国が金融引締め政策を実施する可能性がある．

▸The *surge* of DSL subscribers reflects price competition by providers.　DSL［デジタル加入者回線］加入者の急増は，プロバイダーの価格競争を反映している．

surpass 動　超える，上回る，突破する，…を凌ぐ，…より優れている

▸Toyota's group net profit *surpassed* ¥1 trillion for the third consecutive year.　トヨタの連結税引き後利益［連結純利益］は，3年連続で1兆円を突破した．

surplus 名　余剰，過剰，剰余金，積立金，黒字，歳入超過額
　common and surplus　普通株式資本および剰余金
　consolidated surplus　連結剰余金
　contribution surplus　払込み剰余金　(＝contributed surplus, paid-in surplus)
　funds surplus　資金剰余金
　legal surplus　法定準備金
　moving toward surplus　黒字転換
　other surpluses　その他の剰余金
　provision for surplus　積立金繰入れ
　reserve surplus　積立金
　revaluation surplus　再評価剰余金
　statement of surplus　剰余金計算書　(＝surplus statement)
　statutory surplus　法定準備金
　structural surplus　黒字体質
　surplus appropriation statement　利益処分計算書，剰余金処分計算書　(＝appropriation statement)
　surplus for redemption fund　償還基金積立金
　surplus from consolidation and merger　合併剰余金
　surplus from reduction of capital stock　減資差益
　surplus profit　利益剰余金，超過利潤
　surplus reserve　積立金，過剰準備

▸Investment income recorded a *surplus* of ¥2.62 trillion larger than the previous year.　投資収益は，前年より黒字が2兆6,200億円拡大した．

▸The closure of the money-losing outlets will result in a *surplus* of about 2,000 employees out of about 22,000 on a consolidated basis.　不採算店舗の閉鎖に伴い，連結ベースで従業員約22,000人のうち約2,000人が余剰になる．

surplus employees　余剰人員

▸We have been able to retrain *surplus employees* and reemploy them in another area of the business.　当社は，余剰人員の再訓練と他の事業部門での再活用を実施することができました．

surplus fund　余剰資金，剰余金（自己資本のうち資本金と資本準備金以外の部分のことで，過去の利益の蓄積を示す）

▸Banks are running out of *surplus funds*.　銀行は，剰余金が底をつきかけている．

surtax 名　付加税

surviving company 存続会社, 他の企業を吸収する会社（＝surviving corporation, surviving entity, surviving firm）
▸The current system requires the shareholders of companies absorbed in mergers and acquisitions to be given stocks of *surviving companies*. 現行の制度は, 企業の吸収合併・買収で, 吸収合併される会社の株主に対して, 存続会社の株式を交付することを義務付けている。

suspend 動 停止する, 一時停止する, 中止する, 差し止める, 中断する, 離脱する, 停職する
　suspend business 業務を停止する, 営業を停止する, 取引を停止する
　suspend operations 営業を停止する, 操業を停止する
　suspend payment 支払いを停止する
　suspend the sales of nonlife insurance products 損保商品の販売を停止する
　suspend trading 取引を停止する, 売買を停止する
　suspended trading 未決取引, 売買の一時停止
▸The Financial Services Agency has ordered ChuoAoyama PricewaterhouseCoopers to *suspend* its auditing services. 金融庁が, 中央青山監査法人に対して監査業務の停止命令を出した。

suspension 名 停止, 取引停止, 取引停止処分, 差し止め, 延期, 保留, 停職, 解任
　suspension of business 業務停止, 取引停止, 営業停止（＝business suspension）
　suspension of disbursements to borrower 借入人に対する資金交付の延期
　suspension of operation 操業停止
　suspension of payment 支払い停止（＝bank suspension）
　suspension of sales 販売停止（⇒order）
　suspensions on installment plan 割賦売上高
▸The administrative order by the Financial Services Agency included the *suspension* of sales of nonlife insurance products at all of the company's outlets for two weeks. 金融庁の行政命令には, 同社全店舗での2週間の損保商品の販売停止が含まれている。

swap 動 交換する, 切り替える, 取り替える, 振り替える, 乗り換える, スワップする
　be swapped for yen funds 円資金にスワップされる
　swap convertible bonds into common shares 転換社債を普通株式に切り換える
▸The remaining debt of ¥230 billion will be converted to equity, with ¥220 billion to be *swapped* into preferred shares and ¥10 billion into common shares. 残りの債権2,300億円は株式に振り替えられ,このうち2,200億円分は優先株に, また100億円分は普通株に振り替えられる。
▸Under the triangle merger, a Japanese subsidiary of a foreign company is able to take over a Japanese firm by *swapping* some of the shares of the parent company of the subsidiary for the target's shares. 三角合併では, 海外企業の日本子会社が, 親会社の株式の一部と買収標的企業の株式を交換して日本企業を買収することができる。

swap 名 交換, スワップ（＝swapping; ⇒**equity swap contract, interest rate swap, share swap, stock swap**）
　conduct a debt-for-equity swap 債務の株化を行う, 債権の株式化を行う
　currency swap 通貨スワップ
　debt-bond swap 債務の債券化（＝debt-for-bond swap）
　equity swap 株式交換
　interest rate swap 金利スワップ
　stock swap deal 株式交換取引（＝equity swap deal, share swap deal; ⇒**remaining**）
　swap rate スワップ・レート
　swap transaction スワップ取引
▸SMBC extended loans to corporate clients on condition of buying interest rate *swaps*. 三井住友銀行は, 金利スワップを購入することを条件に, 法人顧客に融資していた。
▸The company grew through a series of mergers and acquisitions by utilizing stock splits and *swaps* and other means. 同社は, 株式分割と株式交換などの手法を駆使したM&A［企業の合併・買収］を繰り返して成長した。

swap agreement スワップ契約（相互の債務を交換する契約のこと。金利スワップと通貨スワップがある）,〈中央銀行の〉スワップ協定［相互通貨交換協定］（＝swap contract; ⇒**equity swap contract**）
　currency swap agreement 通貨スワップ契約, 通貨スワップ協定
　equity swap agreement 株式交換契約
　interest rate swap agreement 金利スワップ契約
▸The interest rate *swap agreements* mature at the time the related bank loans mature. 金利スワップ契約は, 関連銀行借入金の満期日に満了します。

swap ratio 株式の交換比率
▸The *swap ratio* has yet to be decided. 株式の交換比率は, まだ決まっていない。

SWIFT 国際銀行間通信協会, 国際銀行通信協会, スウィフト（Society for Worldwide Interbank Financial Telecommunicationの略）
▶Most cross-border money transfers between financial institutions are carried out through the international data communications network provided by the *SWIFT*.　金融機関同士の国境を越える海外送金の大半は, スウィフト［国際銀行間通信協会］が提供している国際的な金融データ通信網を介して行われている。

sync 名動　同期（する）
　in sync with ...　…と歩調を合わせて　（⇒**stock swap**)

syndicate 動　シンジケートを組織［組成］する, シンジケートで管理する
　be syndicated on a broad basis　大型のシ団組成が行われる
　syndicate a deal　シンジケート団を組成する, シ団を組成する, 案件についてシ団組成を行う

syndicate 名　〈証券発行の〉引受シンジケート団, 〈銀行の〉協調融資団, 銀行団, シンジケート
　banking syndicate　銀行の協調融資団, 銀行融資団, 銀行シンジケート団, 銀行シンジケート
　international syndicate loan　国際協調融資団, 国際シンジケート
　issue syndicate　証券発行団
　issuing syndicate of banks　銀行の発行引受団, 証券発行銀行団
　underwriting syndicate　募債引受団
▶The initial public offering (IPO) was underwritten by a *syndicate* of leading investment banks.　公開株式（IPO）は, 大手投資銀行のシンジケート団が引き受けた。

syndicated loan　銀行団による協調融資, 国際協調融資, シ・ローン, シンジケート・ローン　（＝syndicated bank loan, syndicated lending）
　commercially syndicated loan　民間協調融資
　syndicated term loan　協調ターム・ローン
　vanilla syndicated loan　単純な協調融資
▶The company took out a *syndicated loan* from 20 banks and leasing companies.　同社は, 銀行やリース会社など20社から協調融資を受けた。

synergy 名　相乗効果, シナジー効果, シナジー（＝synergy effect）
▶*Synergies* could be expected through our company's knowhow in urban redevelopment.　都市再開発の当社のノウハウによって, シナジー効果が期待できる。

system 名　組織, 機構, 体系, 方式, 体制, 制度, 設備, システム
　back-office system　事務処理システム
　business system　企業体系, 事業体系, 事務機構, 企業システム, ビジネス組織, ビジネス・システム
　crisis management system　危機管理システム, 危機管理体制
　delivery system　配送システム
　estimating systems costs　システム原価見積り
　logistics system　物流システム
　planning, program(m)ing, budgeting system　企画計画予算方式, 企画計画予算制度《略 PPBS》
　procurement system　調達システム
　profit sharing system　利益分配制度
　seniority-order wage system　年功序列型賃金体系
　system industry　システム産業
▶Toyota aims to establish a *system* to produce 10 million cars per year worldwide, including Japan.　トヨタは, 日本を含む世界各地の生産拠点で年間1,000万台の生産体制確立を視野に入れている。

T t

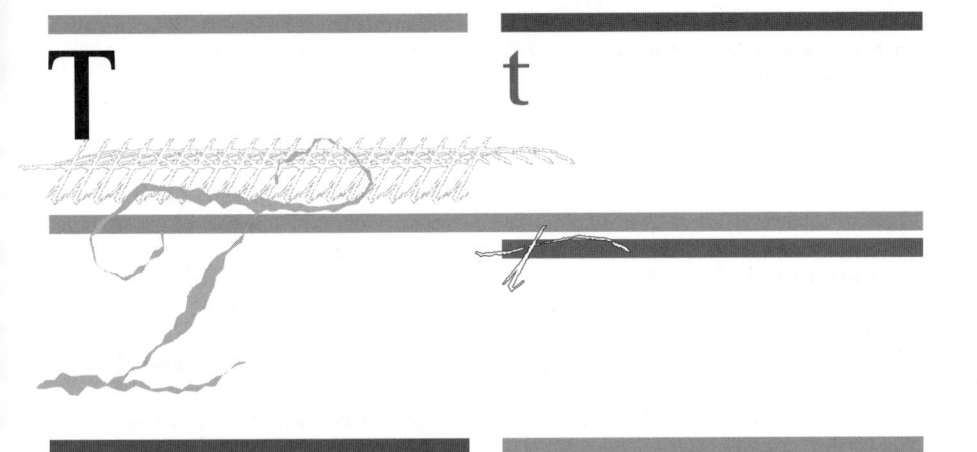

T 〈米国の〉財務省,〈英国の〉大蔵省(**Treasury Department**の略)
　T-bill 米財務省短期証券(**Treasury bill**の略)
　T-bond 米政府長期証券,財務省長期証券,財務省証券,米国債(**Treasury bond**の略)
　T-note 米財務省中期証券,中期国債(**Treasury note**の略)

table 名 表,試算表,計算表,一覧表,目録,様式,食卓
　observed life table 見積り耐用年数表
　Table A 様式A,付表A,A表(英国の通常定款(articles of association)の様式)
　table method 実査法
　table money 交際費
▶The following *table* shows the net effects of this accounting change. 以下の表は,この会計処理の変更による正味の影響額を示しています。

tactics 名 作戦,作戦行動,手段,方策,策,かけ引き,戦術
　advertizing tactics 広告戦術
　marketing tactics マーケティング戦術
　sales tactics 売上作戦
　strategies and tactics 戦略と戦術
▶The key to our success will depend on the skill with which we manage change and execute our strategies and *tactics*. 当社の成功の鍵は,変化に対応して,当社の戦略と戦術をどのように実施していくかにかかっています。

take out 〈ローンなどを〉組む,〈保険に〉入る[加入する],〈保険を〉付ける,契約する,獲得する,取得する,取り出す,持ち出す,削除する,取り除く,除去する
　take out a loan contract ローン契約を結ぶ

　take out provisions against loan losses 貸倒れ損失に備えて引当金を引き当てる
▶The number of contracts *taken out* on broadband Internet services rose by 3.74 million to 23.3 million in a year-on-year comparison. ブロードバンド[高速大容量通信]インターネット・サービスの契約件数は,前年比で374万件増の2,330万件に達した。

take over 〈企業を〉買収する,買い取る,取得する,乗っ取る,〈資産・業務などを〉引き継ぐ,継承する,〈経営権を〉獲得する,肩代わりする,占拠する
　take over a failed [troubled] business 破綻した企業の経営を引き継ぐ,経営破綻した会社を引き継ぐ
　take over the assets of ... …の資産を継承する
　take over the operations of ... …の営業譲渡を受ける
▶Misuzu Audit Corp. has asked three other major audit firms to *take over* its corporate audit operations. みすず監査法人は,他の大手3監査法人に法人監査業務の継承を要請した。
▶Off-hours trading of stocks cannot be used any more to *take over* a company. 株の時間外取引は,企業買収にはもう使えなくなった。
▶The collapsed Long-Term Credit Bank of Japan was *taken over* by Shinsei Bank. 経営破綻した日本長期信用銀行は,新生銀行が引き継いだ。

takeover [**take-over**] 名 企業買収,乗っ取り,企業取得,買収,吸収合併,〈債権などの〉譲り受け,引継ぎ,テイクオーバー (＝acquisition, tender offer; ⇒**hostile takeover**)
　agreed takeover 合意による株式公開買付け
　anti-takeover measures 買収防衛策

corporate takeover 企業買収
defend against a hostile takeover 敵対的買収に対抗する, 敵対的買収への防衛策をとる
friendly takeover 友好的買収 (=friendly acquisition)
high-leverage takeover 多額の借入れによる企業買収
prevent a takeover 乗っ取りを阻止する (=block a takeover)
takeover attempt 買収劇, 買収攻勢, 買収の企て, 買収
takeover bidder 買収提案者, 買収者
takeover defense 買収防衛手段, 防衛手段, 乗っ取り防衛手段, 買収防衛策
takeover-target company 買収標的会社
unsolicited takeover offer 一方的な企業買収提案, 敵対的買収提案
▶The two companies will hold extraordinary shareholders meetings to confirm the takeover. 両社は今後, それぞれ臨時株主総会を開いて, 買収案を正式に承認する.

takeover bid 株式公開買付け, 株式公開買付けによる企業買収, 買収提案, テイクオーバー・ビッド《略 TOB》 (=take-over bid, takeover offer, tender offer)
friendly takeover bid 友好的株式公開買付け, 友好的TOB, 株式公開買付けによる友好的買収, 友好的買収
hostile takeover bid 敵対的株式公開買付け
takeover bid period 株式公開買付けの期間, TOBの期間 (=public tender offer period)
▶Japanese companies could become targets of foreign takeover bids. 日本企業が, 外資による株式公開買付け(TOB)の標的になる可能性がある.
▶The takeover bids by Oji and Aoki are targeted at companies within their own industries. 王子製紙とアオキによる株式公開買付け(TOB)は, 同業の企業を対象にしている.

takeover offer 企業買収提案 (=takeover bid)
▶Quantas Airways has accepted an 11.1 billion Australian dollar takeover offer from a private equity consortium. カンタス航空が, 民間企業連合が提示していた111億豪ドルの買収案を受け入れた.

takeover war 買収合戦, 株式争奪戦
▶This takeover war has placed heavy financial burdens on both companies. 今回の株式争奪戦は, 両社の財務面に大きい負担をかけている.

talks 名 会談, 交渉, 協議, 話し合い

alliance talks 提携協議, 提携交渉
debt restructuring talks 債務再編交渉
exploratory talks 事前協議
labor management wage talks 労使賃金交渉
working-level talks 実務レベル協議, 実務協議, 実務者協議
▶Nissan Motor Co.'s board of directors gave its approval for exploratory talks on a proposal for struggling U.S. auto giant General Motors Corp. 日産自動車の取締役会は, 経営再建中の米自動車大手ゼネラル・モーターズ(GM)に対する提携提案の事前協議を承認した.

tangible asset 有形資産, 有形固定資産 (=physical asset)
tangible fixed asset 有形固定資産
tap 動 〈情報などを〉引き出す, 開発する, 利用する, 選ぶ, 選出する, 盗聴する
tap into the market 市場を利用する, …市場に乗り出す, 市場で起債する
tap rising demand 需要増に応える
tap the market 市場を開発[開拓]する, 市場に登場する, 市場で起債する, 市場で資金を調達する
▶Firms have begun to tap into the niche metrosexual market. 企業が, メトロセクシャル(都心に住み, オシャレに精を出す男性)のニッチ市場拡大に乗り出した.

target 動 …を目標に定める, 目標にする, 標的にする, 対象にする, 狙う, ターゲットにする
▶Seven & I Holdings Co. targets 71 percent of operating profit from convenience stores in the year ending February 2009. セブン&アイ・ホールディングスは, 2009年2月期決算のコンビニエンス・ストア部門の目標を営業利益の71%としている.

target 名 目標, 標的, 目標水準, 買収目標企業, 買収対象会社, 買収標的の会社, ターゲット
earnings target 業績目標, 利益目標, 収益目標 (=earnings goal)
growth target 成長目標 (⇒financial performance)
market target 市場標的
operating operation 運営目標, 操作目標
original target 当初の目標
profit target 収益目標, 運用益の目標
takeover target 買収の対象, 買収の標的, 買収の目標, 買収対象会社, 買収目標企業
target company 買収対象会社, 買収目標企業, 買収標的の会社, 標的企業, ターゲット企業, ターゲット・カンパニー (=target firm, targeted company)
target profit 目標利益

- Listed companies have recently become afraid of being the *target* of hostile takeover bid.　上場企業は最近, 敵対的買収の標的になるのを恐れるようになった.
- The company considers pay cuts unavoidable so as to clear its earnings *target* for the current business year to Feb. 28, 2009.　2009年2月期の収益目標［業績目標］を達成するには, 賃金カットは避けられない, と同社は考えている.

targeted company　買収の標的企業
- A *targeted company* demanded a company trying to acquire its stocks to present a business plan.　買収の標的企業は, 買収企業［標的企業の株式を取得しようとしている企業］に事業計画の提出を求めた.

tax 名　税, 税金, 租税, タックス
 additional tax　追徴税
 advertising tax　広告税（＝advertisement tax）
 applicable taxes　租税公課
 business tax　事業税, 営業税
 capital invesrment tax　資本投資税
 corporate inhabitant tax　法人住民税
 earnings befor taxes　税引き前利益
 effective tax　実効税額
 environmental tax　環境税
 estate tax　相続税, 遺産税
 fixed-rate tax reduction　定率減税
 general excise tax　一般消費税
 indirect business tax　間接事業税
 inhabitant tax　住民税
 inheritance tax　相続税
 local corporate tax　法人事業税（企業活動に対して課される地方税）
 local inhabitants tax　住民税
 local tax　地方税
 luxury tax　物品税
 negligence tax　過少申告加算税
 office tax　事業所税
 operating tax　営業税, 事業税
 ordinary tax　経常税
 overdue tax　未納の税, 延滞税
 payments of estimated tax　予定納税
 progressive tax　累進課税, 累進税
 property tax　固定資産税, 資産税, 財産税
 ratio of direct and indirect taxes　〈税の〉直間比率
 real estate tax　固定資産税
 real property acquisition tax　不動産取得税
 real property tax　固定資産税
 registration tax　登録税

regressive tax　逆進税
reserve for tax payment　納税引当金
reserve for taxes　納税引当金（＝reserve for tax payment）
sales tax　売上税, 物品販売税, 取引高税
shifting of tax　租税の転嫁, 税の転嫁（＝tax shifting）
state and local taxes　州税と地方税
state franchise tax　州法人税
stock dividend tax　株式配当課税
tax advantages　税制上の優遇措置, 節税効果（＝tax concessions, tax incentives）
tax allocation within a period　期間内税金配分
tax allowance　控除
tax amount　税額
tax asset　税金資産
tax audit　税務監査
tax avoidance　合法的な租税回避, 節税
tax base　課税基準, 課税標準, 課税ベース, 税収基盤
tax basis　申告基準, 課税標準, 税法基準（＝tax base）
tax bill　課税通知書
tax bracket　税率区分, 税率等級
tax burden　租税負担, 税負担
tax claim receivable　税金の還付請求額
tax concessions　税制上の優遇措置, 税制優遇措置（＝tax advantages, tax incentives）
tax cut　減税（＝tax reduction）
tax evasion　脱税, 課税逃れ, 税金逃れ（＝tax fraud）
tax hike　増税（＝tax increase）
tax holiday　免税期間, 免税措置, タックス・ホリデイ
tax implications　税務上の取扱い
tax investigation　税務調査
tax loss　税務上の損失, 税務上の欠損金（⇒tax benefit）
tax management　税務管理
tax on business　企業課税
tax paradise　租税天国
tax payable　未払い税金
tax payment　納税, 税金の支払い
tax point　課税時期
tax provision　納税引当金, 法人税等額
tax receivable　未収税金
tax refund　税金還付, 納税の返還（⇒tax refunds）
tax refunds　還付税額
tax relief　免税, 減税, 税額免除, 税負担の軽減,

税金の減免
tax repayment 税金還付
tax return 税務申告, 納税申告, 税務申告書, 納税申告書
tax saving 節税, 法人税などの軽減額
tax service 税務サービス, 税務
tax shelter 租税回避地, 租税回避国, 租税回避手段, 税金逃れの隠れみの, 会計操作, タックス・シェルター (=tax haven)
tax surcharge 付加税, 加算税
taxes on income 法人税等, 法人所得税
taxes, other than income taxes 租税公課
transaction tax 取引税
transfer tax 譲渡税, 財産移転税
turnover tax 売上税, 取引高税

▸Fifteen banks filed a lawsuit seeking to abolish a local corporate *tax* targeting major banks. 大手金融機関を対象にした法人事業税の取消を求めて, 15行が提訴した。

▸There are no estate *taxes* or succession duties imposed by Canada or by any province of Canada. カナダまたはカナダ国内のいかなる州でも, 遺産税または相続税を課されることはありません。

tax authorities 税務当局, 税務署

▸Proposed adjustments from *tax authorities* will not have a material adverse effect on the consolidated financial position, liquidity or results of operations of the Company. 税務当局からの修正要求で, 当社の連結財政状態, 流動性や経営成績が重大な悪影響を受けることはないようです。

tax benefit 税務上の特典,〈税額控除や所得控除などの〉税制上の優遇措置, 税効果, 節税益, 課税軽減額
　allowance for unrealizable tax benefits 繰延べ法人税資産評価勘定
　income tax benefit of operating loss carryforward 欠損金繰越しの税務上の恩典

▸After the extraordinary item, a *tax benefit* due to previous tax losses, net income applicable to common shares was $57 million. 異常損益項目 (前期の租税損金計上に伴う課税軽減額) 控除後の普通株式に帰属する純利益は, 5,700万ドルでした。

tax break 減税, 税額控除, 税率軽減措置, 租税優遇措置, 租税特別措置, 税務上の特典, 税制上の特典 (=tax cuts, tax deduction, tax reduction)
　tax break for capital gains キャピタル・ゲイン減税
　tax break on housing loans 住宅ローン減税

▸The *tax breaks* on capital gains from stock sales and on dividend income will be extended by one year. 株式譲渡益 [株式売却益] と受取配当金の税率軽減措置の期間が1年延長される。

tax convention 租税条約, 国際租税条約, 国際租税協定 (=tax treaty, taxation convention, taxation treaty)

▸This withholding tax may be reduced by an applicable international *tax convention*. この源泉所得税 [源泉徴収税] は, 国際租税条約の適用によって軽減される [引き下げられる] ことがあります。

tax credit 税額控除, 税金控除 (=tax deduction)
　deferred tax credit 繰延べ税金
　direct foreign tax credit 外国税額の直接控除
　foreign tax credit 外国税額控除
　investment tax credit 投資税額控除

▸The IRS has proposed adjustments to the Company's income and *tax credits* for these years which would result in additional tax. 内国歳入庁 (IRS) は, 当社のこれらの事業年度の収入と税額控除について, 加算税を伴う可能性のある修正を要しています。

tax-deferred share exchanges 株式交換の課税繰延べ (三角合併で, 株式交換時に課税しないで, 交換した日本子会社の親会社の株を実際に売却したときに課税すること)

tax effect 税効果 (⇒reverse 動)
　tax effect of investment credits 投資税額控除の税効果
　tax effect of operating losses 繰越欠損金の税効果
　tax effect of timing differences 期間差異による調整分, 期間差異の税効果, 税効果当期配分額 (⇒reverse)

▸The cumulative effects of accounting changes include the *tax effects* of those adjustments. 会計処理の変更による累積的影響額には, その修正による税効果が含まれています。

tax-exempt 免税の, 無税の, 非課税の, 課税されない (=tax free)
　tax-exempt bond 免税債, 非課税債券
　tax-exempt borrowings 非課税借入金
　tax-exempt expense 非課税費用, 損金 (⇒depreciation cost)

▸Firms will be allowed to treat the full amount of capital investment as *tax-exempt expenses*. 企業は今後, 設備投資については全額, 非課税費用 [損金] として処理することができるようになる。

tax expense 法人税等計上額, 法人税等費用, 税金費用, 納税額

▸The Company has $380 million of deferred investment tax credits for financial reporting purposes, which will reduce *tax expense* in future years.　当社の繰延べ投資税額控除額は、財務会計上3億8,000万ドルで、これにより将来の納税額は減少します。

tax free　非課税の［で］
▸After privatization of the state-run Japan Post, users have to pay stamp duties for services that were *tax free* in the past.　国営の日本郵政公社が民営化されてから、利用者は、これまで非課税だったサービスに対しても印紙税を支払わなければならない。

tax-free 形　非課税の, 無税の, 免税の　（＝tax-exempt, free of tax）
tax-free amortization　無税償却
tax-free disposal of bad loans　不良債権の無税償却
tax-free income　免税所得, 非課税所録

tax haven　租税回避地, 租税逃避地, 租税避難国, タックス・ヘイブン　（＝tax shelter）
▸A *tax haven* provides preferential treatment, such as an exemption from corporare tax, to its registered firm.　タックス・ヘイブン［租税回避地］は、そこに本店登記した会社については法人税の免除などの優遇措置がある。

tax incentives　税制上の優遇措置　（＝tax advantages, tax concessions）
eliminate tax incentives　税制上の優遇措置を撤廃する
foreign tax incentives　外国租税優遇措置

tax liability　税金債務, 納税額
▸Deferred *tax liabilities* are taxes we expect to pay in future periods.　繰延べ税金債務は、将来に支払う予定の税金のことです。

tax planning　納税計画, 租税計画, 節税計画, 税務計画の策定, 租税回避
tax planning strategy　税務計画戦略, 税務戦略, 戦略的税務計画, 戦略的納税計画, 税計画戦略

tax rate　税率, 課税率　（＝rate of taxation）
applicable tax rate　適用税率
average corporate tax rate　平均法人税率
basic tax rate　基本税率
corporate income tax rate　法人所得税率
current income tax rates　当期の所得税率
effective tax rate　実効税率
enacted tax rates　法定税率, 施行される税率
income tax rate　法人税率
marginal tax rate　限界税率
maximum income tax rate　所得税の最高税率
reduced tax rate　税率の軽減, 軽減税率
standard tax rate　標準税率
statutory tax rate　法定税率
withholding tax rate　源泉徴収税率
▸Our new accounting for income taxes uses the enacted *tax rates* to compute both deferred and current taxes.　法人税に関する当社の新会計処理では、繰延べおよび当期税金の計算に法定税率を使用します。

tax system　税制, 租税体系
land and financial tax systems　土地・金融税制
preferential tax system　優遇税制
securities tax system　証券税制　（＝securities taxation system）
simplified tax system　簡易課税制度

taxable 形　課税対象となる, 課税できる, 課税…　（⇒write off）
taxable goods　課税対象商品
taxable losses or expenses　有税処理
taxable profit　課税利益
taxable transaction　課税取引
taxable revenues　益金
taxable write-off　課税償却, 有税償却
▸Capital gains realized on the Corporation's common shares by individuals who are not resident in Canada for Canadian income tax purposes generally are not *taxable* in Canada.　カナダ所得税法上、カナダ居住者でない［カナダ居住者に該当しない］個人が実現した当社の普通株式のキャピタル・ゲインは、一般にカナダでは非課税扱いになります。

taxable income　課税所得, 所得金額
▸In computing the *taxable income* for federal income tax purposes, the following timing differences were taken into account.　連邦所得税算定のための課税所得を算定するにあたっては、次の期間差異を考慮しました。

taxation 名　課税, 徴税, 税収
double taxation relief　外国税額控除
dual taxation　二重課税　（＝double taxation）
self-assessed taxation system　申告納税方式
separate taxation at source　源泉分離課税
taxation formula　課税方式　（＝taxation system）
taxation treaty　租税条約　（＝tax treaty, taxation convention）
taxation office　税務署
thin capitalization taxation　過小資本税制
transfer pricing taxation system　移転価格税制（国内企業が海外に所得を移して、国内での納

税額を意図的に減らすのを防ぐ制度。日本では1986年に導入された）
two-track income taxation system 二元的所得課税方式
unitary taxation 合算課税, ユニタリー課税, ユニタリー・タックス （＝unitary tax）
▸The introduction of a tax system advantageous to banks exclusively would run counter to the principle of fairness in *taxation*. 銀行だけに有利な税制の導入は, 課税の公平原則に反することになる。

taxation bureau 国税局
▸The *taxation bureau* did not permit the company to report the money as a loss. 国税局は, この金の損金計上を認めなかった。

TCO 所有総コスト（**total cost of ownership**の略）

team 名 団, 組, 班, チーム
cross-functional team 機能横断チーム, クロス・ファンクショナル・チーム
engineering team 研究開発チーム
management team 経営陣, マネジメント・チーム
project team プロジェクト・チーム
research team 研究班, 研究チーム
self-directed team 自主管理チーム, セルフ・ディレクテッド・チーム
▸We have reinforced our management *team* with a mix of newcomers who bring proven track records and rich experiences. 当社は, 実績と豊富な経験を兼ね備えた新メンバーを迎えて, 当社の経営陣を強化しました。

telecommuting 名 在宅勤務, 通信勤務, コンピュータ勤務, テレコミューティング （＝remote work, telework, teleworking）
▸Other initiatives, like flexible work schedules, *telecommuting* and job-sharing, meet the diverse needs of individuals and the company. フレックス・タイムや在宅勤務, ジョブ・シェアリング［ワークシェア］などの他の新しい試みも, 個々の社員と会社のさまざまなニーズを満たしています。

teleconference meeting 電話会議, テレビ会議
▸In a *teleconference meeting*, the GM's board authorized the company's management to consider the proposal by Kirk Kerkorian. 電話会議［テレビ会議］で, 米ゼネラル・モーターズ(GM)の取締役会は, カーク・カーコリアン(大株主の米投資会社トラシンダを率いる投資家)の提携案を検討する権限を, 同社の経営陣に与えた。

temporal method 属性法, テンポラル法
（＝temporal approach：外貨で評価されているものは現金で, 債権・債務と時価で評価されているものは決算日レートで, 取引日の評価額で評価されているものは取引日レートで換算する外貨換算方法）
▸Financial statements of subsidiaries operating in highly inflationary economies are translated into Swedish kronor in accordance with the *temporal method*. 高度インフレ経済国で事業を展開している子会社の財務書類は, テンポラル法に従ってスウェーデン・クローナに換算されています。

temporary 形 一時的な, 臨時の, 暫定的, 仮の
temporary borrowing 一時借入金
temporary depreciation 一時償却
temporary investment 一時投資, 短期投資, 市場性ある有価証券
temporary loans 一時貸付け金, 一時借入金, 短期貸付け金, 短期借入金

temporary cash investments 短期投資, 一時投資, 短期的資金運用投資 （⇒**corporate assets**）
▸We reduced our balance of cash and *temporary cash investments* over the last two years. 当社は, 過去2年間にわたって現金と短期投資の残高を圧縮しました。

temporary differences 一時差異, 一時的差異（貸借対照表上の資産・負債の金額と課税所得計算上の資産・負債の金額との差異）
scheduling temporary differences 一時的差異の年度別内訳
taxable temporary differences 将来税務加算される一時的差異
▸Deferred income taxes reflect the impact of *temporary differences* between the amount of assets and liabilities recognized for financial reporting purposes and such amounts recognized for tax purposes. 繰延べ法人所得税は, 財務会計上で認識された資産および負債の金額と税務上で認識された当該金額との一時的差異の影響を反映しています。

tenant 名 借地人, 借家人, 賃借人, 借主, 現住者, 土地保有者, 不動産権保有者, 出店者, テナント
key tenant 核店舗, 核テナント
tenant right 借地権
tenants of online shopping mall 仮想商店街の出店者
▸The company will collect fees from the *tenants* of its online shopping mall. 同社は今後, 仮想商店街の出店者から手数料収入が得られる。

tender 動 入札する, 請け負う, 申し出る, 提出する, 提供する, 支払う

▸We *tendered* a bid on a new three-year contract with the government of Saudi Arabia. 当社は、サウジアラビア政府との新規3年契約の入札に応じました。

tender 名 入札, 応募入札, 入札書, 申込み, 提出, 提供, 提出物, 提供物, テンダー
  competitive tender 競争入札
  make a tender for ... …の入札をする
  public tender 公開入札, 一般競争入札, 競争入札, 公売, 株式公開買付け
  put out to tender 入札に付す, 入札を募る
  self tender 株式の自己買付け, 自己株の買戻し, 自社株の買戻し提案（買収を仕掛けられた場合などに、会社が株主に対して行う自社株の買戻し提案）
  tender on the Internet ネット入札, インターネットでの入札
  tender price 株式公開買付けの価格, TOB価格, テンダー価格
  the first round of tenders 一次入札
  win a tender for ... …を落札する
▸Local governments are promoting fair open bidding for public works projects by offering *tenders* on the Internet. 地方自治体は、インターネットでの入札により、公共工事[公共事業]の公正な一般競争入札を推進している。

tender offer 株式公開買付け, テンダー・オファー（=public tender offer, takeover bid, takeover offer, TOB：一般の証券取引市場の外で行われる大口証券購入の申込み）
  cash tender offer 現金公開買付け, 現金による株式公開買付け, キャッシュ・テンダー・オファー（買収先の会社の株式を現金で公開買付けする方法）
▸Following the *tender offer*, Oji Paper would acquire the remaining Hokuetsu shares through a share swap. 株式公開買付け(TOB)後に、王子製紙は、株式交換で残りの北越製紙の株を取得する。
▸The firm will extend the period during which its *tender offer* is valid to March 2 from the initial expiry date of Feb. 21. 同社は、同社の株式公開買付けの有効期限を、当初の有効期限である2月21日から3月2日まで延長する。

tender panel テンダー・パネル
  tender panel method 競争入札制度

term 名 期間, 契約期間, 専門用語, 用語, 定期不動産権, [しばしば~s]条件, 条項, 規定, 約定, 合意（⇒business term）
  accounting term 会計期間
  business year term 決算期（=business term）
  credit terms 支払い条件
  dollar terms 金額ベース, ドル・ベース, ドル表示（=dollar-denominated terms）
  in real terms 実質ベースで, 実質で, 実勢価格で
  in terms of voting rights 議決権ベースで, 議決権比率で
  in value terms 名目ベースで, 金額ベースで（=in terms of value）
  in volume terms 実質ベースで, 台数ベースで
  issue terms 発行条件（=terms of issue）
  long term contract 長期契約
  on equal terms 同じ条件で
  profit for the term 当期利益, 当期利益金
  profits and losses for the term 期中損益
  settlement term ending in March 3月期決算, 3月終了の決算期
  short-term debt 短期債務, 短期借入金
  term of payment 支払い期限, 支払い期間
  trade terms 貿易条件, 貿易支払い条件, 貿易用語, 取引用語
▸Toyota's group sales and profits hit a record high in the settlement *term* ending in March. トヨタの3月期決算で、連結売上高と利益はともに過去最高を更新した。

term-end settlement of accounts 期末決算
▸In the *term-end settlement of accounts* at the end of September, most companies use the daily average for a month of the share prices in gauging the value of latent gains or losses in their stockholdings. 9月末の期末決算で[9月中間決算で]、大半の企業は、保有株式の含み損益の評価額を算出する際に株価の月中平均を使っている。

terms and conditions 条件
▸Transfers between geographic areas are on *terms and conditions* comparable with sales to external customers. 地域間の振替えは、社外顧客への売上と同様の条件で行われています。

terminal 形 終わりの, 末端の, 定期の
  terminal value 終価, 複利終価（複利の一定利率を前提として、投資元本が投資期間の最後に到達する価値を算出したもの）

terminal funding 年金現価積立方式
  terminal funding method 年金現価充足方式

termination 名 〈契約の〉終了, 解約, 〈期間の〉満了, 解除, 〈権利の〉消滅, 解散, 退職（⇒abandonment）
  account termination 口座解約
  early termination 期限前解約
  lease termination リース解約

termination of employment 退職
termination of office 任期満了
termination benefit 退職給付
▸Provisions for business restructuring in 2007 covered $130 million for special *termination benefits*.　2007年度の事業再編成引当金には，特別退職給付の1億3,000万ドルが含まれています。

test 名　試査，〈会計記録の〉試査，調査，検定，試験，実験，基準，試練，テスト　(⇒**evidence, examination**)

> 試査とは ➡ 試験的照査の略称で，財務諸表監査の場合は，会計記録の一部を監査対象として検査し，その検査結果から全体としての会計記録[財務諸表]の適否を検討する方法をいう。試査は，test以外にtest check, test checking, testingともいう。

compliance test 準拠性テスト
debt test 負債基準
goodness of fit test 適合度検定
leverage test 負債比率
on a test basis 試査により，試査による
product test 商品テスト
role-playing test 役割演技法（セールスマンや従業員の訓練手法の一つ）
sample test 試供品テスト
test market 試験市場，テスト市場，テスト・マーケット
test marketing 試験販売，テスト・マーケティング
test run cost 試運転費
the test of accounting records 会計記録[会計報告書]の試査，財務諸表の試査
transaction test 取引調査

▸Our examinations included such *tests* and other procedures as we considered necessary in the circumstances.　私どもの監査は，私どもが状況に応じて必要と認めた会計記録の試査とその他の監査手続きを含んでいます。

thin margin 薄利，低い利益率

third-party allotment [allocation] 第三者割当て，第三者割当て増資　(＝allocation of new shares to a third party, allotment to third parties, third-party share allotment)

> 「第三者割当て」とは ➡ 役員や従業員，取引先，提携先，金融機関など発行会社と特別な関係にあるものに新株の引受権を与えて，新株を発行すること。

increase one's capital through a third-party allotment 第三者割当てで増資する
issue new shares through a third-party allotment 第三者割当てで新株を発行する
third-party share allotment 第三者株式割当

て，第三者割当て増資　(＝third party equity allotment [allocation], third-party allotment of shares)

▸The company is to float new shares under a *third-party share allotment* scheme.　同社は，第三者割当て増資計画に基づいて新株を発行する。

third quarter 第3四半期，7－9月期，〈日本の3月期決算企業の〉10－12月期

gross profit margins for the third quarter 第3四半期の売上利益率

third quarter profit 第3四半期の利益　(＝profit for the third quarter; ⇒**foresee**)

▸Consolidated net income applicable to common shares was $350 million for the *third quarter*.　第3四半期の普通株式に帰属する連結純利益は，3億5,000万ドルでした。

third quareter loss 第3四半期の損失，第3四半期の赤字　(⇒**third quarter**)

▸Ford Motor Co. reported a *third-quarter loss* of $284 million.　フォード・モーターの第3四半期決算[7－9月期決算]は，2億8,400万ドルの赤字だった。

▸Merill Lynch & Co. will post a *third quarter loss* of up to 50 cents a share after writing down $4.5 billion.　米大手証券のメリルリンチは，45億ドルの評価減を受けて，第3四半期は最高で1株当たり0.50ドルの赤字を計上する見通しだ。

third quarter net income 第3四半期の純利益

▸*Third quarter net income* was $318 million as compared with $361 million for the same period last year.　第3四半期の純利益は，前年同期の3億6,100万ドルに対して，3億1,800万ドルでした。

third quarter results 第3四半期の業績　(＝results for the third quarter)

▸The company's *third-quarter results* were based on an average rate of ¥113 per dollar.　同社の第3四半期の業績は，1ドル＝113円の平均為替レートで算定されています。

this quarter 当四半期

▸I am pleased to report a record financial performance *this quarter*.　当四半期は過去最高の業績[財務業績]を記録したことをご報告できますことを，大変うれしく思います。

this year 今年度，今期，今年

▸Ford Motor Co. lost $1.4 billion during the first half of *this year*.　フォード・モーターは，今年度上半期に14億ドルの赤字を出した。

three months ended Dec. 31 12月31日に終了した3か月間，10－12月期，〈3月期決算企業の〉第3四半期，〈12月期決算企業の〉第4四半期，12

月末終了の3か月,
- Net income rose to ¥151 billion in the *three months ended Dec. 31* from 115.2 billion a year earlier. 10−12月期の税引き後利益［純利益］は、前年同期の1,152億円から1,510億円に増加した。

three months ended March 31 3月31日終了の3か月間, 1−3月期,〈3月期決算企業の〉第4四半期,〈12月期決算企業の〉第1四半期
- Net earnings for the *three months ended March 31* were $1.0 billion in 2007. 2007年度第1四半期の純利益は10億ドルでした。

three months ended June 4−6月期,〈3月期決算企業の〉第1四半期,〈12月期決算企業の〉第2四半期
- Japan Airlines' sales rose 3.7 percent to ¥522.2 billion in the *three months ended June*. 日本航空の4−6月期は、売上高に相当する営業利益が前年同期比3.7％増の5,222億円となった。

three months ended Sept. 30 9月30日終了の3か月間, 7−9月期,〈3月期決算企業の〉第2四半期,〈12月期決算企業の〉第3四半期
- For the *three months ended September 30*, 2007, worldwide revenue was $14 billion, up 4.3 percent from the prior year. 2007年7−9月期の世界全体の売上高は、前年同期比4.3％増の140億ドルでした。

thrust 名 推進, 推進力, 推力, 前進, 攻勢, 厳しい批判, 酷評, 主眼, 主旨, 要点
  global thrust グローバル志向
  make a thrust into ... …に進出する, …に攻勢をかける
- Executive changes to increase the pace of growth and globalization accelerate a global *thrust*. 成長速度とグローバル化を促進するための役員入替えで, グローバル志向を推進しています。

tie up 提携する, 連携する, 協力する
- MFG, the nation's largest financial group, *tied up* with two major U.S. banks to strengthen its earning power. 国内金融グループ最大手のみずほフィナンシャルグループが、収益力の強化を図るため、米銀大手2行と提携した。
- The two companies are aiming to *tie up* in the hotel and resort facilities business. 両社は、ホテル・リゾート施設事業での提携を視野に入れている。

tie-up 名 提携, 合併, 統合, 経営統合, 協力, 結びつき, 業務の一時停止, タイアップ（＝alliance; ⇒business tie-up, capital tie-up）
  capital and operational tie-up 資本・業務提携
  capital and strategic tie-up 資本・戦略提携
  equity tie-up 資本提携
  strategic tie-up 戦略的提携, 戦略提携
- Both companies can enjoy synergies in terms of product development and procurement of materials by the *tie-up*. この提携によって、両社は商品開発や原材料の調達などで相乗効果を見込める。
- The *tie-up* created the world's largest banking group, with total assets of ¥190 trillion. 統合によって、総資産が190兆円の世界最大の銀行［金融］グループが誕生した。

timing 名 時期, 時間［時期, 速度］の調整・選択, 好機の選択, 潮時, 頃合い, タイミング
- The company concealed taxable income by manipulating the *timing* of the calculation in its reports to the tax authorities. 同社は、税務申告書の計上時期を操作して、課税所得を隠していた。

timing differences 〈費用収益の〉期間差異, 時間差異, 年度間差額, 期間帰属差異（⇒reverse）
  income before income taxes and taxable income—timing differences 税引き前利益と課税所得—費用収益の期間差異
  timing differences and deferred tax 〈費用収益の〉期間差異と繰延べ税金
  timing differences between pretax accounting income and taxable income 〈認識時点の違いから生じる〉会計上の利益と課税所得との期間差異
  timing differences in the recognition of revenue and expense 収益と費用の認識の期間差異（⇒recognition of revenue and expense）
- The disparity between book income and taxable income is attributable to *timing differences*. 帳簿上の利益と課税所得との差は、期間差異に起因している。

TOB 株式公開買付け（take-over bid [takeover bid]の略：応募が取得目標の株式数に達しない場合、TOBは不成立となり、応募された株式を返さなければならない。⇒takeover bid）

toehold purchase トーホールド・パーチェス（M&Aで買収対象会社［ターゲット・カンパニー］の発行済み株式を5％まで買い集めて、買収の足がかり（toehold）にすること。⇒Schedule 13D）

Tokyo Stock Exchange 東京証券取引所, 東証《略 TSE》

Tokyo Stock Price Index 東証株価指数《略 TOPIX》（＝Tokyo stock price index, Tokyo stock price index and average; ⇒TOPIX）

tool 名 道具, 用具, 工具, 工作機械, 手段, 方法, 手法, ツール

debt management tool 債務管理手段, 債務管理の手法

management tool 管理手法, 管理の手段, 経営手法

tools and equipment costs 工具・器具費, 工具器具費, 消耗工具器具備品費

tools and furnitures 工具・備品, 工具・器具

tools, furniture and fixtures 工具・器具・備品, 工具器具備品

▶Our customers look to us for the *tools* for improving productivity. 当社のお客さまは、生産性向上の切り札として当社に期待を寄せております。

tooling 名 工作, 細工, 仕上げ細工, 段取り, 工作機械一式, 装備, 生産設備, 〈製本の〉型押し

blind tooling 空押し

tooling change 段取り換え, ライン切換え

▶Engineering, *tooling*, manufacturing and applicable overhead costs are charged to costs and expenses when they are incurred. 設計, 工作, 製造および適用可能な間接費は, その発生時に原価と費用に計上されます。

top 動 上回る, 突破する, …を越える, 首位になる, 首位を占める, トップになる

▶Strong overseas performance helped Toyota's group sales *top* ¥20 trillion for the first time in the year through March. 海外の好業績で、トヨタの3月期決算は、連結売上高が（日本の製造業で）初めて20兆円を上回った。

top 形 最高の, 最高位の, 最大の, 最大限の, 最上の, 頂上の, 最上位の, 首位の, 筆頭の, 最優先の, 上部の, トップの

be at the top of the list [agenda] 最優先事項である, 最優先課題である

top brass 幹部, 高級幹部, 高級将校

top cadre 最高幹部

top companies 大手企業

top copy 原本

top-down 上意下達の, 上意下達方式の, トップダウン型の

top-down decision making トップ・ダウン型の意思決定

top executive 最高経営者, 最高執行部, 最高経営幹部, 経営首脳, 経営者, 経営トップ, [[~s]]首脳陣, 経営幹部

top grossing 興行成績がよい

top-hat scheme 高位者割増年金

top-heavy 資本過大の, 幹部［管理職・役職者］が多すぎる, 逆三角形の

top line 経常利益, 売上高, 最高レベル

top manager 経営者

top player 最大手

top secret 極秘

top shareholder 筆頭株主

▶*Top* priority is to replace the *top* management of the compnay. 最優先事項は, 同社首脳陣の一新だ。

top 名 最高位, 頂上, 首位, 最優先課題, 最優先事項, トップ

TOPIX 東証株価指数, トピックス (Tokyo Stock Price Indexの略。東証一部の時価総額を加重平均して算出する)

top management 最高経営者, 最高経営責任者, 最高経営陣, 経営者, 最高管理層, 最高経営管理者層, 経営首脳陣, 首脳陣, 首脳部, 最高幹部, トップ・マネジメント

▶Ford Motor Co. announced a shake-up of its *top management*. フォードが, トップ・マネジメントの大刷新を発表した。

total 名 合計, 総計, 総額, 総量

balance sheet total 総資産

control balance 照合合計

grand total 総計, 総合計, 累計

ground total 単純集計

net total 純計

sales totals 総売上高

total 形 合計の, 総計の, 全体の, 全体的な, 全面的な, 完全な

total amount 総額

total balance 総合収支

total borrowings 負債総額

total capital stock 資本金合計, 総資本ストック

total capitalization 総資本, 資本総額

total cost of ownership 所有総コスト《略 TCO》(情報システムの構築から維持・運用にかかる費用全体を指す)

total costing 全部原価計算, 総原価計算 (= absorption costing, full costing)

total costs and expenses 原価および費用合計

total debt 負債総額, 総負債額 (⇒total capital)

total debt as a percentage of total capitalization 資本総額に対する債務総額の比率

total debt to total capital ratio 負債構成比率, 負債総資本比率

total equity 自己資産, 総資本, 総持ち分, 総株主持ち分 (⇒total capital)

total financing activities 財務活動合計

total inventories 棚卸し資産合計

total investing activities 投資活動合計

total lendings 総貸出, 貸出総額, 貸出全体

total long-term debt 長期負債合計
total loss 全損, 損失総額, 総損失, 総欠損
total operating activities 営業活動合計
total sales 総売上高, 販総額
total shareholders' equity 資本合計
total stockholders' equity 資本合計, 株主持ち分合計, 資本の部合計 (=total shareholders' equity)
total assets 総資産, 資産合計, 総資本(貸借対照表の負債の部と純資産の部の合計)
  total assets at year-end 年度末[期末]の資産合計
  total assets employed 使用総資産
  total assets turnover 総資産回転率, 総資本回転率
total capital 総資本
▸The ratio of total debt to *total capital* (total debt plus total equity) increased to 56% at December 31, 2007. 総負債額に対する総資本(負債総額と総株主持ち分の合計)の比率は, 2007年12月31日現在で56%に増加しています。
total cost 総原価, 総費用, 原価合計, 総コスト
▸Procurement costs are an automaker's greatest expense and account for up to 60 percent of *total costs*. 調達コストは自動車メーカー最大の経費で, 最大で総コストの60%を占めている。
▸*Total costs* of telecommunication services declined this past year. 電気通信サービスの総原価は, 当年度は低下しました。
total customer satisfaction 顧客の完全な満足[満足度], 顧客の100%満足, トータル・カスタマー・サティスファクション
▸*Total customer satisfaction* remains our fundamental objective. 顧客の100%満足は, 今でも当社の基本目標です。
total liabilities 負債合計, 負債総額, 責任総額, 総責任額, トータル・ライアビリティ
  total liabilities and equity 負債資本合計
  total liabilities and net worth 総資本
  total liabilities and stockholders'[shareholders'] equity 負債および資本の部合計, 負債および株主持ち分合計
▸The company has *total liabilities* of ¥125 billion on a consolidated basis. 同社の負債総額は, 連結ベースで1,250億円に達している。
total operating expenses 総営業費用
▸*Total operating expenses* declined because of restructuring and other charges in 2007. 2007年度は, 事業再編その他の費用を計上したため, 総営業費用は減少しました。

total revenues 総収益, 総売上高, 営業収益合計 (⇒**backdrop, record**)
▸Selling, general and administrative (SG&A) expenditures in the third quarter of 2007 were 18.8 percent of *total revenues*. 2007年第3四半期の販売費および一般管理費(SG&A)は, 総売上高の18.8%でした。
tracking stock トラッキング・ストック, 部門収益連動株式
  tracking stock in a subsidiary 子会社連動株, トラッキング・ストック(子会社の業績や配当に経済価値を連動させることを意図した株式)
▸*Tracking stock* refers to shares whose dividends are paid in accordance with the performance of a company's specific subsidiary or division. 「トラッキング・ストック」とは, 企業の特定の子会社や事業部門の業績に従って配当金を支払う株式のことをいう。
trade 動 売買する, 取引する, 交換する (⇒**trading**)
▸In commodity futures trading, precious metals, petroleum products and other goods are *traded*. 商品先物取引では, 貴金属や石油製品などの商品が取引されている。
trade 名 貿易, 交易, 通商, 取引, 商売, 売買, 下取り, 交換, トレード
  accounts payable (principally trade) 支払い債務(主に営業債務)
  compared trade summary 総括精算表
  day trade デイ・トレード[デイトレード] (=day trading:買い付けたものを当日のうちに売却してしまうような回転の速い株や債券などの取引)
  gains from trade 貿易利益
  non-trade note 非営業手形
  non-trade receivables 非営業受取債権
  stock in trade 在庫品
  trade accounts payable 買掛金, 営業支払い勘定
  trade accounts receivable from subsidiaries 子会社売掛金
  trade asset 営業資産, 棚卸し資産
  trade credit 企業間信用, 企業信用, 輸出・輸入延払い
  trade discount 営業割引, 営業値引き, 業者割引, 割引
  trade expense 営業費
  trade intermediation 売買の仲介
  trade notes payable to affiliates 関係会社支払い手形
  trade notes receivable from subsidiaries 子会社受取手形

trade payable [payables] 買掛金, 支払い手形, 仕入債務, 買掛債務

trade receivable [receivables] 売掛金, 売上債権, 営業債権, 営業上の未収入金, 受取手形

▸Leading trading houses have shifted their main lines of businesses to investment from *trade intermediation*.　大手商社が, 事業の主力を売買の仲介から投資に転換した。

trade friction 貿易摩擦, 通商摩擦 (＝trade conflict, trade dispute)

▸Toyota is set to further expand its production overseas, partly to avoid *trade friction*.　トヨタは, 貿易摩擦を回避するためにも, 引き続き海外での生産能力を拡充する方針だ。

trade secret 企業秘密, 営業秘密, 業務上の秘密, トレード・シークレット

▸We are mindful of our trade secrets, our copyrighted material and those things that we can patent.　当社のトレード・シークレットや著作権の対象, 特許化の可能性があるものについては, 当社は慎重に検討しています。

trade union 労働組合, 同業組合 (＝labor union)

▸Stakeholders include employees, trading partners, and customers as well as family members of the employees, retirees, *trade unions* and even members of a community near its office or factory.　ステークホルダー［利害関係者］には, 従業員や取引先, 顧客のほかに, 従業員の家族や退職者, 労働組合, さらには営業所や工場などの近郊の地域社会の人々も含まれる。

trademarks and other intangible assets, net 商標権およびその他の無形固定資産（純額）

trading 名 取引, 売買, 商業, 貿易, 営業, トレーディング (⇒**foreign exchange trading, insider trading, margin trading, trading volume**)

algorithm trading アルゴリズム取引（コンピュータのアルゴリズム（問題解決のための処理手順）を株式売買の執行に応用したもので, あらかじめ組み込まれたプログラムに基づき, 株の値動きに応じてコンピュータが自動的に大量の売買注文を実行する）

bond trading 債券取引, 債券売買取引, 債券トレーディング

foreign exchange trading 外国為替取引

home trading ホーム・トレーディング (＝Net trading, online stock trading, online trading)

off-hours trading 時間外取引 (＝after-hours trading)

online stock trading 株のインターネット取引

public trading 公募取引

short-term trading by day traders デイ・トレーダーによる短期売買

trading assets 販売資産, 事業資産

trading balances 営業上の債権・債務残高

trading profit 売買益, 取引利益, 営業利益, 総利益, 投機利益

twenty-four-hour trading 24時間トレーディング

▸In FX margin *trading*, investors can trade around the clock via the Internet.　外国為替証拠金取引の場合, 投資家はインターネットで24時間取引できる。

▸We intend to reinforce the company's business through the relationship with the company in such areas as material procurement and *trading* of paper-pulp products.　当社は, 原材料の調達や紙パルプ製品の取引などの面での同社との関係により, 同社事業のテコ入れを目指している。

trading house 商社 (⇒**trade**)

▸Hokuetsu Paper Mills Ltd. has completed its planned new share issuance worth about ¥30 billion to major *trading house* Mitsubishi Corp.　北越製紙は, 予定していた大手商社の三菱商事を引受先とする約300億円の新株発行［第三者割当て増資］を完了した。

trading unit 取引単位

▸Even if the company conducts a reverse stock split, it will safeguard shareholders' interest by changing the minimum *trading unit* from 1,000 shares to 500.　同社が株式併合をしても, 最低取引単位を1,000株から500株に変更して株主の権利は守る方針だ。

trading volume 出来高, 売買高, 売上高, 売買額, 売買株数, 取引量 (＝volume of trading; ⇒**turnover ratio of trading**)

▸The bank's stock ended Monday's trading at ¥827 on a *trading volume* of 247.23 million shares.　同行株は, 終値827円, 出来高2億4,723万株で月曜日の取引を終えた。

transaction 名 取引, 取扱い, 業務処理, 業務, 商取引, 売買, 和解, 示談, 法律行為

accounting transaction 会計取引, 会計上の取引, 簿記上の取引

B2B transaction 企業対企業取引（B2B＝b to b, business to business）

B2C transaction 企業対消費者の取引（B2C＝b to c, business to consumer）

backlogged transaction 未決済取引

book transaction 帳簿取引
business transaction 商取引, 企業取引
capital transaction 資本取引
capital transactions 資本取引
financial transaction 金融取引, 財務取引, 資金取引
financing transaction 資金調達取引
interbranch transaction 支店間取引
internal transaction 内部取引
noncash transaction 非現金取引
nonmonetary transaction 非金銭取引, 非貨幣取引, 非金融取引
nonrecurring transactions 非経常損益
recurring transactions 経常損益
security transaction 証券取引
transaction between affiliated enterprises 系列取引
transaction cost 取引コスト, 売買コスト
transaction gain or loss 為替差損益
transaction in conflict of interest 利益相反取引
tranaction value 取引高, 売買高 (＝value of transaction)
value of transaction 売買高, 取引高
▶The company will restate its financial results as there were the problems with the way it accounted for a number of *transactions*. 同社は、一部取引の会計処理方法に問題があったため、同社の財務成績［業績］を修正再表示することになった。

transaction date 取引日
▶Other assets and other liabilities are translated at rates prevailing at the respective *transaction dates*. その他の資産とその他の負債は、各取引日の実勢為替レートで換算されいます。

transaction 動 移転する, 移す, 移し替える, 振り替える, 転送する, 譲渡する,〈名義を〉書き換える, 振り込む, 送金する, 繰り入れる, 配置転換する (⇒ paid-in capital)
▶A smaller amount of loan-loss provisions was *transferred* to profits, compared with a year before. 前年と比べて、貸倒れ引当金の戻り益が少なかった［前年と比べて、利益に振り替えた貸倒れ引当金の金額が少なかった］。
▶The firm's business was *transferred* to a new company. 同社の営業は、新会社に譲渡された。

transfer 名 〈財産などの〉譲渡, 移転,〈権限などの〉委譲, 継承,〈名義の〉書き換え, 転送, 転任, 配属, 配置転換, 出向, 振替え, 振込み, 送金, 繰入れ (⇒ stock transfer)
asset transfer 資産の譲渡, 資産のシフト

automatic transfer 自動決済, 自動振替え
bulk transfer 一括譲渡, 大量譲渡, 包括譲渡 (＝bulk sale)
business transfer 営業譲渡, 事業譲渡, 企業移転 (＝transfer of business)
capital transfer 資本移転, 資本移動
capital transfer tax 資本移転税, 資産譲渡税, 贈与税《略 CTT》
fund transfer 資金移動, 資金のシフト, 口座振替え, 送金 (＝the movement of funds)
income transfer 所得移転(国内企業が商品を通常の取引価格より安い価格で海外の関連会社(子会社や親会社)に輸出すれば、国内での所得が減る一方、商品を安く仕入れた関連会社は、所得を増やすことができる。これを、国内から海外への所得移転という)
money transfer 資金の移動 (＝transfer of money)
operational transfer 業務移管
ownership transfer 所有権の移転 (＝transfer of ownership)
share transfer 株式の名義書換え, 株式譲渡 (＝stock transfer, transfer of stocks)
transfer agent 名義書換え取扱機関, 名義換え代理人, 証券代行機関, 株式代行機関 (⇒ shareowner services)
transfer book 株式名簿, 株主名簿, 名義書換え名簿, 名義書換え台帳
transfer book closed 名義書換え停止
transfer day 名義書換え日
transfer of funds 資金移動, 資金のシフト, 口座振替え (＝fund transfer)
transfer of officials 公務員の配置転換
transfer of patent rights 特許権の移転, 特許権の譲渡
transfer of shares 株式の譲渡, 株式移転, 株式の名義書換え (＝share transfer, stock transfer, transfer of stakes)
transfer of technology 技術移転
transfer price 振替価格, 内部振替価格, 移転価格(企業の一部門が他の部門に販売するときに用いる企業内部価格)
transfer pricing 移転価格, 移転価格の決定, 移転価格税制, 振替価格操作
transfer profit 振替利益
▶The cost and service charges that relate to fixed asset *transfers* are capitalized and depreciated or amortized by the importing area. 固定資産振替えに関連する原価とサービス料は、輸入地域で資産計上され、減価償却または償却される。

▸The sharp drop in sales was largely due to the spinoff of the company's cosmetics business and the *transfer* or liquidation of 22 businesses.　売上高が大幅に落ち込んだのは、主に同社が化粧品事業を分離し、22事業を譲渡・清算したためだ。

transfer of golden shares　黄金株の譲渡
▸A company is allowed to set restrictions on the *transfer of golden shares*.　企業は、黄金株(拒否権付き種類株式)に譲渡制限を付けることができる[黄金株の譲渡に制限を設けることができる]。

transfers between geographic areas
地域区分間の移動, 地域間の振替え, 地域間の移動 (⇒term)
▸*Transfers between geographic areas* are made at prices based on total cost of the product to the supplying segment.　地域別区分間の移動は、供給部門にいたるまでに要する製品の総原価に基づく価額で行われます。

transformation 名　変化, 変形, 変換, 転換, 転化, 変革, 改革, 事業再編　(⇒reorganization)
corporate transformation　企業改革
distribution transformation　流通改革
political transformation　政権交代
▸We are engaged in a comprehensive *transformation* to ensure its competitiveness through the years ahead.　来るべき将来に備えて当社の競争力を強化するため、当社は全力を挙げて改革に取り組んでいます。

transition 名　移行, 推移, 変遷, 経過, 移行時, 移行期間, 過渡期
net trransition amounts　移行時差額　(⇒service cost)
transition obligation　移行時債務, 経過債務
transition provisions　経過規定
▸Second quarter performance was unfavorably affected by new product *transitions* and the strength of the U.S. dollars.　第2四半期の業績は、新製品への移行とドル高の悪影響を被りました。

transition asset　移行時資産, 移行時差額資産 (＝transitional asset)
▸We are amortizing a *transition asset* related to our change in pension accounting over 15 years.　当社は、年金会計変更関連の移行時差資産を15年にわたって償却中です。

transitional pension　経過年金

translate 動　換算する, 変換する, 調整する, 解釈する, 翻訳する　(⇒monetary assets, transaction date)
▸The results are *translated* into U.S. dollars.　業績は、米ドルに換算してあります。

translation 名　換算, 変換, 調整, 解釈, 翻訳
accounting translations　会計原則の調整
exchange and translation gains [losses]　為替差益[損]
foreign currency translation　外貨換算　(＝currency translation, translation of foreign currencies)
translation adjustments　換算調整額, 外貨調整額, 外貨換算修正, 為替調整額　(＝foreign currency translation adjustments)
translation of foreign balances　外貨建て残高の換算
translation of foreign exchange　外国為替換算
translation of net assets　純資産の換算
▸We show the adjustments from balance sheet *translation* as a separate component of shareowners' equity.　貸借対照表から生じる換算差損額[換算調整額]は、株主持ち分の独立した構成要素[独立した一項目]として計上しています。

translation adjustment　換算調整
accumulated foreign currency translation adjustments ― as reported　外貨換算調整[修正]―公表額
effects of foreign currency translation adjustments　外貨換算修正損益

translation differences　換算差額
▸*Translation differences* are credited to, or charged against, income in the year in which they arise.　換算差額は、その発生年度の損益として認識されています。

translation gain or [and] loss　為替換算差損益, 換算差損益, 為替差損益, 為替換算差額
▸The unrealized *translation gains and losses* on the parent company's net investment in these operations are accumulated in a separate component of shareholders' equity.　これらの事業に対する親会社の純投資額にかかわる未実現為替換算差損益[未実現為替損益]は、株主持ち分の独立項目に累計[累積計上]されています。

transnational company　超国籍企業, トランスナショナル企業
▸*Transnational companies* are at the highest level of organizational complexity.　グローバル市場で企業活動を展開しているトランスナショナル[超国籍]企業は、極めて複雑な組織で運営されています。

transparency 名　透明性　(⇒trend)
transparency and accountability of business management　経営の透明性と説明責任
transparency in decision-making　意思決定の

透明性
transparency requirement 透明性の規定
▸Major subsidiaries have each appointed outside directors as a means of actively stimulating objective discussion at board meetings and promoting greater *transparency* of business management. 主要子会社各社は, 取締役会の活性化と経営の透明性向上を図る手段として, 社外取締役を任用しています。

treasurer 名 会計役, 財務担当役員, 財務部長, 財務官, 経理部長, 会計係, 金銭出納係, トレジャラー (米大手企業では, トレジャラーは会社の資金調達や運用などの財務部門を統括する役員。⇒**controller**)
　corporate treasurer 企業の財務担当者
　treasurer's department 財務部門
treasurership 名 財務管理, 財産管理
treasury 名 国庫, 公庫, [the T-]財務省, [T-][米]財務省証券
　Treasury bill 米財務省短期証券, Tビル(通称T-billで, 単にbillとも呼ばれる)
　Treasury bond 米政府長期証券, 財務省長期証券, 財務省証券, 米国債 (＝T-bond：利息が年2回支払われる利付き証券(coupon issues))
　Treasury note 米財務省証券, Tノート, 財務省中期証券(利息が年2回支払われる利付き証券), 中期国債
treasury purchases 自己株式購入
treasury stock 金庫株, 自社株, 自己株式 (＝reacquired shares, reacquired stock, repurchased shares, repurchased stock, treasury shares：株価の低迷や乱高下を防ぐため, 企業が自社株を買い戻して, 買い取った株を保有し, 相場が持ち直したときに売ることができる株を「金庫株」という)
　accounting for treasury stock 自己株式の処理, 自己株式の会計処理
　gain on sale of treasury stock 自己株式売却益
▸In connection with the merger, the company sold 6.5 million shares of common stock held as *treasury stock*. この合併に伴って, 同社は自己株式として保有していた普通株式650万株を売却しました。
treasury stock system 金庫株制度
▸Under the *treasury stock system*, companies are allowed to buy their own stocks and keep them in reserve. 金庫株制度によると, 企業は自社株を取得して, 取得した株を保管することができる。
treatment 名 処理, 取扱い, 待遇, 措置, トリートメント
　accounting treatment 会計処理

　favorable tax treatment 税制上の優遇措置, 優遇税制, 優遇税制措置 (＝generous tax treatment)
　hedge accounting treatment ヘッジ会計処理
　off-balance-sheet treatment オフ・バランスシート取引
　tax treatment 税務上の取扱い, 税務上の扱い, 税務処理, 税制
　treatment of goodwill 営業権[のれん]の取扱い
　treatment of waste 減損処理
▸The most significant factors causing these differences between Canadian and U.S. GAAP are the *treatment* of unrealized foreign currency gains and losses. カナダ会計基準と米国会計基準の間でこれらの差異が生じている最大の要因は, 未実現為替差損益の取扱いです。
trend 名 傾向, 動向, 基調, 趨勢, 大勢, 流れ, 潮流, 流行, 波, 環境, トレンド
　be above trend トレンドを上回る
　competitive trends 競争環境
　downward trend 下落基調, 下落傾向, 低下傾向
　economic trends 経済動向, 景気動向, 景気
　inflationary trend インフレ動向
　prospective trends 今後のトレンド
　rising trend 上昇基調, 上昇傾向 (＝upward trend)
　weak trend 減少傾向
▸Another driving force behind the spinoff *trend* is mounting criticism of the lack of transparency at large corporations in the wake of Enron Corp.'s collapse. 分社化傾向の陰のもうひとつの推進力は, エンロンの経営破綻を受けて大企業の透明性[透明性欠如]に対する批判の高まりである。
▸If the current downward *trend* of stock prices continues, banks' financial resources that could be used to dispose of bad loans will decrease drastically. 株価の下落基調がこのまま続くと, 金融機関の不良債権処理の原資は激減する。
trend rate 潜在成長率, 傾向率, 傾向値
▸Increasing the assumed *trend rate* by 1% in each year would raise our accumulated post-retirement benefit obligation at December 31, 2007 by $750 million. 予想傾向値が毎年1％上昇すると, 当社の累積退職後給付債務は, 2007年12月31日現在で7億5,000万ドル増加します。
triangular merger 三角合併 (＝triangle merger)
　triangular merger scheme 三角合併方式 (2007年5月から解禁となった企業買収の仕組みで, 合併の対価として現金でなく, 買収する側の

企業の親会社の株式が使えるようになった。⇒ **swap** 動）

trim 動 削減する, 縮小する, 切り詰める,〈人員などを〉整理する, 引き下げる, 減額する （⇒**resize**）
▸The company will drastically *trim* its existing affiliates. 同社は, 既存の関連会社を抜本的に整理する方針だ。

trouble 名 経営不振, 経営破綻, 経営難, 経営危機
▸GM has been in *trouble* since last year, due to declining profits in its North America operation. GMは, 北米事業の減益で昨年来, 経営不振に陥っている。

troubled 形 経営不振の, 経営破綻した, 経営難の, 経営難に陥った, 経営危機に陥った, 問題のある, 問題の多い
　troubled business 経営の行き詰まり, 経営難, 行き詰まった経営, 経営危機の企業, 経営不振企業
　troubled company 経営不振企業, 経営破綻した企業 （⇒**reorganize**）
　troubled loan 不良債権
▸*Troubled* highly leveraged companies have found it necessary to attempt to restructure their existing debt. 負債比率が高い経営不振の企業は, 既存の債務を再構築する必要に迫られている。

true and fair view 真正かつ公正な［真正の公正な］見方, 真正かつ公正な概観
▸The annual financial statements for the financial year ending on December 31, 2007 present a *true and fair view* of the financial position as of the date thereof. 2007年12月31日に終了する事業年度［2007年12月31日終了事業年度］の年次財務書類［財務諸表］は, 同日現在の財政状態についての真実かつ公正な見方を示している。

trust 名 信託, 委託, 信頼, 信用, トラスト （⇒**investment fund**）
　balance of loan trust 貸付け信託の残高
　bond investment trust 公社債投資信託
　deed of trust 信託証書 （＝trust deed）
　employee retirement benefit trust 退職給付信託
　loan trust 貸付け信託
　pension trust 年金信託
　trust cash fund 金銭信託
　trust estate 信託財産
　trust fee 信託手数料, 信託報酬, 受託手数料
　trust principal 信託元本
　un-incorporated investment trust 非会社型投資信託
　unit investment trust 単位型投資信託, ユニット型投資信託

voting trust 議決権信託
▸A portion of this accumulated liability was provided for by group life insurance benefits and *trusts* for health care benefits funded before 2007. この累積債務の一部は, 団体生命保険給付と2007年以前に資金拠出した医療給付のための信託によって引き当てられています。

trust fund 信託基金, 信託資金, 投資信託, トラスト・ファンド
▸Pension contributions are primarily made to *trust funds* held for the sole benefit of plan participants. 年金拠出額は, 主に年金加入者の利益を唯一の目的とする信託基金に拠出される。

TSE 東京証券取引所, 東証 （Tokyo Stock Exchangeの略）
▸Companies listed on the First Section of the *TSE* have registered increases both in income and profit. 東証一部上場企業は, 増収増益となった。

TSE-listed company 東証上場企業
▸A decade ago, 96 percent of *TSE-listed companies* held shareholders meetins on the same day. 10年前は, 東証上場企業の96％が, 同じ日に株主総会を開いた。

turmoil 名 混乱, 動揺, 騒動, 騒ぎ, 不安, 危機
　credit market turmoil 金融市場の混乱 （＝turmoil in the financial markets）
　credit turmoil 信用不安
　currency turmoil 通貨危機, 為替市場の混乱
　financial turmoil 金融危機, 金融不安
▸The collapse of the subprime mortgage market and related credit market *turmoil* has resulted in $45 billion of write-downs at the world's biggest banks and securities firms. サブプライム・ローン市場の悪化や関連金融市場の混乱で, 世界の大手銀行と証券会社の評価損計上額は, これまでのところ450億ドルに達している。

turn around 好転する, 改善する, 回復する, 方向転換する,〈方針を〉変える,〈考えを〉変える,〈企業・事業を〉再生する
　turn around corporate management 企業の経営を再建する
　turn around the performance of the division 同事業部門の業績を回復する
　turn aroud the struggling manufacturer この経営不振のメーカーの事業を再生する
▸Private-sector businesses specializing in *turning around* corporate management have been established one after another. 企業経営の再建［企業再生］を専門にする民間企業が, 相次いで設立されている。

turnaround 名 転換, 方向転換, 好転, 業績改善,〈経営戦略や営業・販売, 財務などの〉改善, 企業再生, 事業再生, ターンアラウンド (⇒**sharp**)
　a sharp turnaround from a loss　赤字から大幅黒字への転換
　corporate turnaround　企業再生
　corporate turnaround fund　企業再生ファンド (=corporate reconstruction fund)
　earning turnaround　業績回復
　economic turnaround　景気回復
　major profit turnaround　利益の大幅改善, 利益の大幅回復
　turnaround situation　業績回復
▸Our business in 2007 showed a *turnaround* as earnings improved quarter by quarter.　2007年度の業績は, 四半期毎の増益にともなって, 改善しています。
▸The company posted a group pretax profit of ¥57.6 billion in the nine months to Dec. 31 in a sharp *turnaround* from a loss of ¥30 billion a year earlier.　同社の4－12月期決算は, 576億円の連結経常利益[連結税引き前利益]を計上し, 前年同期の300億円の赤字から大幅黒字に転換した。

turnaround effort　事業再生策
▸Ford is accelerating its North American *turnaround effort*.　フォードは現在, 北米事業部門の事業再生策を推進している。

turnaround plan　企業再生計画, 事業再生計画, 企業再生策
▸The U.S. rating agencies lowered Ford Motor Co.'s rating after the automaker announced a revised *turnaround plan*.　米国の格付け機関は, フォードの企業再生修正案を受けて, 同社の信用格付けを引き下げた。

turnkey 形 〈建設やプラント輸出の〉完成品引渡し[受渡し]方式の, ターンキー方式の
　full-turnkey　一括受注・発注方式, フル・ターンキー
　turnkey contract　ターンキー契約
　turnkey export　ターンキー輸出
　turnkey import　ターンキー輸入
　turnkey operation　一貫請負工事, ターンキー・オペレーション

turnover 名 売上, 売上高, 総売上高, 取引高, 出来高, 売買高, 回転, 回転率, 就労率, 転職率 (⇒**inventory turn**)
　account receivable turnover　売掛金回転率
　asset turnover　資産回転率 (=asset turnover ratio)
　average daily turnover　1日当たり平均取引高, 1日当たり平均売買高
　capital turnover　資本の回転, 資本回転率
　capital turnover point　資本回収点
　consolidated turnover　連結売上高
　equity turnover　資本回転率 (=sale to net worth)
　gross turnover　総売上高
　merchandise turnover　商品回転率 (=merchandise turnover rate)
　net-worth turnover　自己資本回転率（純売上高÷自己資本）
　sales turnover　売上高
　total assets turnover　総資産回転率, 総資本回転率
　total turnover　総売上高
　turnover of net worth　自己資本回転率, 株主資本回転率
　turnover of total capital employed　使用総資本回転率
　turnover of total operating assets　経営資本回転率
▸Revenues rose 2.6 percent on higher *turnover* from property development projects.　不動産開発事業[開発プロジェクト]の売上高の増加で, 売上高は2.6％伸びた。

turnover ratio　回転率, 売買回転率 (=turnover rate)
▸A *turnover ratio* of 50% means that it was traded once every two years.　売買回転率50％とは, 2年に1回売買されたことを意味する。

turnover ratio of trading　売買回転率
▸A *turnover ratio of trading* refers to a year's trading volume divided by an average number of listed stocks.　売買回転率は, 1年間の出来高を平均上場株式数で割った数値を指す。

two quarters　2四半期
　the first two quarters　上半期の第1四半期と第2四半期
　the second two quarters　下半期の第3四半期と第4四半期
▸In the first *two quarters* of 2007, the corporation declared a cash dividend of $0.07 per common share and in the second two quarters $0.08 for an annual total of $0.30 per common share.　当社は, 2007年第1四半期と第2四半期にそれぞれ普通株式1株当たり0.07ドル, 第3四半期と第4四半期にそれぞれ0.08ドルの現金配当を宣言し, 普通株式1株当たりの年間配当金総額は0.30ドルに達しました。

U u

umbrella 名 傘, 傘下, 保護, 包括的組織
　place ... under A's umbrella …をAの傘下に置く, …をAの傘下に収める
　under the umbrella of ... …傘下の, …に保護[援護]されている
▶Under the *umbrella* of holding company Japan Post Holdings, joined Japan Post Service Co., Japan Post Network Co., Japan Post Bank Co. and Japan Post Insurance Co.　持ち株会社の日本郵政グループ[日本郵政株式会社]の傘下に, 郵便事業会社, 郵便局会社, 郵貯銀行, かんぽ生命保険の4社が加わった。

umbrella 形 包括的な
　umbrella group 包括団体
　umbrella master agreement 包括標準契約書
unaffiliated common stock 非関連会社普通株
unamortized 形 未償却の, 償却されていない
　unamortized balance 未償却残高
　unamortized goodwill 未償却営業権
　unamortized obligation 未償却債務
　unamortized portion of service charges サービス料の未償却部分
　unamortized premium on bonds 社債発行差金
　unamortized service charges 未償却サービス料
　unamortized share-issuing expense 未償却株式発行費
▶The net change during the year in *unamortized* service charges has been eliminated in consolidation.　未償却サービス料の当期の正味増減額は, 連結決算上, 消去されています。

unaudited 形 未監査, 監査対象外
　condensed consolidated statement of operations (unaudited) 連結損益計算書要約(未監査)
　unaudited financial statements 未監査財務類, 未監査財務諸表 (＝unaudited statements)

uncertain 形 不確実な, 不確定な, 不安定な, 不確かな, 不明確な, 不透明な
▶We continue to operate in a difficult *uncertain* global economic environment.　当社は依然, 困難かつ不確実な世界の経済環境のなかで営業活動を続けています。

uncertainty 名 不確実性, 不確定, 不確定要因, 波乱要因, 不透明, 不透明性, 先行き不透明感, 不安, 不安要因
　increase the uncertainty about future profitability 将来の収益性に対する不確実性を高める
　interest rate uncertainty 金利の先行き不透明感
　remove the uncertainty 不確実性を払拭[排除]する, 不透明感を払拭する
　uncertainties in the market 市場の不確定要因, 市場の波乱要因
▶One of major *uncertainties* for the Corporation is exchange rate fluctuations.　当社にとって最大の不安要因は, 為替変動です。
▶*Uncertainty* about the global economy is increasing due to the U.S. subprime mortgage crisis.　米国のサブプライム・ローン[低所得者向け住宅融資]の焦げ付き問題で, 世界経済の不確実性が増大している。

unclaimed 形 請求されていない, 未請求の
　dividend payable unclaimed 未払い配当金, 未払い配当 (＝dividend payable)
　unclaimed check 未請求小切手
　unclaimed dividend 未請求配当金

unclaimed stock　失権株

uncollectible 名　[[〜s]]回収不能金, 徴収不能料金
▶The decrease in other costs was mainly due to lower *uncollectibles*.　その他の原価[コスト]の減少は, 主に徴収不能料金の減少によるものです。

uncollectible 形　回収不能の, 貸付け金の取立てができない, 焦げ付いた（=uncollectable）
　allowance for uncollectible accounts　貸倒れ引当金
　become uncollectible　回収不能になる, 徴収不能になる
　uncollectible loan　不良債権, 不良貸付け, 貸倒れ, 回収不能の融資（=bad loan, nonperforming loan, uncollectible receivable）
▶With the economic structure undergoing adjustment, larger numbers of loans may become *uncollectible*.　経済の構造調整に伴って, 不良債権の新規発生が高水準で続く可能性がある。

unconsolidated 形　連結から除外された, 連結の範囲に含まれない, 連結対象外の, 連結されていない, 非連結の, 単独ベースの
　unconsolidated affiliate　連結対象外の関連会社
　unconsolidated debt　単独ベースでの借入金, 非連結子会社の負債
　unconsolidated entity　非連結事業体
　unconsolidated financial statements　単独財務諸表, 単独財務書類
　unconsolidated joint venture　連結されていない合弁事業[合弁会社], 非連結合弁会社
　unconsolidated operating profit　単独ベースの営業利益, 非連結営業利益
　unconsolidated subsidiary　非連結子会社（=unconsolidated subs.）
▶Tobishima Corp. plans to cut its *unconsolidated* interest-bearing debt by 40 percent by the end of March 2007 under a new business plan.　飛島建設は, 新経営計画に基づいて2007年3月末までに非連結有利子負債を40%圧縮する計画だ。

underlying 形　基礎となる, 基礎的な, 基本的な, 根本的な, 構造的な, 裏付けとなる, 担保となる, 根底にある, 優先する
　fundamentals underlying accounting　会計の基礎概念（=fundamental accounting concepts）
　fundamentals underlying financial statements　財務諸表の基礎概念
　underlying asset　原資産, 対象資産, 担保となる資産
　underlying collateral　担保物件
　underlying demand　基本的な需要
　underlying forces　構造的要因
　underlying inflation (rate)　基礎インフレ率
　underlying motive　根底にある動機
　underlying principle　基本的な原則
　underlying receivables　裏付けとなる債権
　underlying securities　原証券
　underlying shares　現物株, 現物の株式
　underlying trends　基調, 根底にあるトレンド
▶Any transaction gains and losses on these financial instruments are generally expected to offset losses and gains on the *underlying* operational cash flows or investments.　これらの金融商品取引の損益に期待するのは, 一般にその対象となっているキャッシュ・フローや投資から生じる損失および利益との相殺です。
▶The interest rate swap agreements generally involve the exchange of fixed or floating interest payments without the exchange of *underlying* principal amounts.　この金利スワップ契約は, 一般的に元本の交換は行わず, 固定金利または変動金利による支払い利息を交換することになっています。

underreport 動　過少申告する（=understate）
▶The firm has *underreported* the ratio of stakes held by major shareholders.　同社は, これまで大株主の株式保有比率を過少申告していた。

underreporting 名　過少申告, 過少記載
▶The company announced the *underreporting* of its stake in the financial statement.　同社は, 有価証券報告書に同社株式について過少記載していたことを発表した。

undertake 動　引き受ける, 請け負う, 約束する, 着手する, 乗り出す, 進める, 取り組む, 保証する
　undertake an acquisition　買収に乗り出す
　undertake investment　投資を進める, 投資に踏み切る
▶Our alliance will *undertake* joint projects and marketing efforts.　両社の提携は, 共同のプロジェクトやマーケティング活動を約束するものです。

undertaking 名　仕事, 事業, 会社, 企業
　nonabandonment undertaking　出資維持保証
　parent undertaking　親会社
　subsidiary undertaking　子会社

underutilization of the plants　設備の遊休化

underwrite 動　〈株式や社債, 保険などを〉引受ける（⇒syndicate）

underwriter 名　証券引受人, 引受業者, 引受証券会社, 引受行, 保険業者, 保険会社, 保険代理業者,

資金提供者, スポンサー, 後援者, アンダーライター
co-underwriter 共同引受行
letters to underwriters 証券引受人への書簡, 証券引受業者へのレター
managing underwriter 幹事会社, 引受主幹事
principal underwriter 元引受人
underwriter syndication 引受業者の組成, 引受団の組成 (＝syndication of underwriters)
underwriters' allocations 引受行の割当額
underwriters' fees and commissions 証券引受会社に対する報酬と手数料
▸One of the largest *underwriters* of corporate bonds is the investment bank. 社債の最大の引受業者には，この投資銀行も入っている。

underwriting 名 〈保険や証券の〉引受け, 引受業務
firm underwriting 確定引受け
stand-by underwriting 引受募集, 残額引受発行
underwriting agreement 引受契約
underwriting amount 引受額
underwriting business 引受業務
underwriting fee 引受手数料
underwriting of corporate bonds 社債の引受け
underwriting spread 引受手数料, 引受スプレッド
underwriting standards 貸出審査基準, 与信基準, 引受基準
underwriting syndicate 募債引受団, 引受シンジケート団, 引受団, 引受シ団, シ団 (＝investment banking group, purchase group, underwriting group)
▸We must boost our capital to further expand our core business, including mergers and acquisitions and the *underwriting* of corporate bonds. 企業の合併・買収 [M&A] や社債の引受けなど当社の中核業務をさらに拡充するには，資本の増強が必要である。

undistributed earnings 留保利益, 内部留保利益, 未分配利益, 未処分利益剰余金 (⇒foreign tax credit)
▸*Undistributed earnings* of non-U.S. subsidiaries included in consolidated retained earnings amounted to $13,000 million at December 31, 2007. 連結利益剰余金に含まれている米国外子会社の未処分利益剰余金は，2007年12月31日現在で130億ドルでした。

undistributed earnings of subsidiaries 子会社の留保利益, 子会社の未分配利益

undistributed profit 未配分利益, 未処分利益, 内部留保, 留保金額

undue 形 過度の, 過大な

▸Management believes that these forward contracts should not subject the Company to *undue* risk to freign exchange movements. これらの先物取引契約で当社が過大な為替相場の変動リスクを負うことはない，と経営陣は考えております。

unearned 形 未収の, 前受けした, 未経過の
unearned income 前受け収益, 不労所得, 未経過利息
unearned interest 未経過利子, 繰延べ前利息
unearned interest income 前受け利息
unearned revenue 前受け収益, 繰延べ収益, 未稼得収益 (＝deferred income, deferred revenue)
▸*Unearned* revenue on the balance sheet fell $395 million from the previous quarter. 貸借対照表上の前受け収益は，前四半期比で3億9,500万ドル減少しました。

unfavorable 形 不利な, 好ましくない, 悪い, マイナスの
unfavorable balance 支払い超過
unfavorable effects on earnings per share 普通株式1株当たり利益に対する不利な影響額
unfavorable factor 不利な材料, マイナス要因, 悪材料
unfavorable impact 不利な影響, マイナス影響, 悪影響
unfavorable market conditions 市況の悪化, 市場環境の悪化, 不利な市場環境
▸A portion of the increase in R&D spending was due to the *unfavorable* impact of foreign exchange on R&D expenditures. 研究開発費 (R&D) 増加の一部は，研究開発費に対する為替相場の不利な影響額によるものです。
▸The company attributed the expected net profit decline to the possible *unfavorable* effects of the yen's rise against the dollar and the euro. 同社は，予想される純利益 [税引き後利益] 減少の理由として，同社に不利な円高・ドル安，ユーロ安の影響を挙げた。

unfavorably 副 不利に, 悪い方向に
unfavorably affected 不利な影響を受ける, マイナス影響が出る, 悪影響を受ける
▸Revenue and earnings were *unfavorably* affected by a stronger U.S. dollar. 収益と利益は，ドル高 [米ドル為替相場の上昇] のマイナス影響を受けました。

unforeseen loss 不測の損害
▸Solvency margin rates indicate an insurer's ability to pay out policy obligations in the event of a disaster or *unforeseen loss*. ソルベンシー・マ

ージン比率は，災害時や不測の損害が発生した場合の保険会社の保険契約債務支払い能力を示す．

unfunded 形 未拠出の （⇒**one-time pretax charge**）
　unfunded portion 未拠出部分 （＝unprovided portion）
　unfunded postretirement obligation 未拠出退職後給付債務
▸We recorded a one-time pretax charge for the *unfunded* portions of these liabilities. 当社は，この債務の未拠出部分について，税引き前臨時費用を計上しました．

union 名 労働組合，組合，ユニオン （⇒**represent**）
▸We are working with employees and the *unions* to increase their involvement and input in planning and decisions. 私たちは，従業員・組合と共に，従業員と組合が会社の企画立案や意思決定に参加して意見を述べる機会の拡大に努めています．

unissued 形 〈証券が〉未発行の
unissued shares 未発行株式（会社が発行できる株式の上限である授権株式（authorized shares）のうち，まだ発行されていない株式の総数）

unit 名 単位，構成単位，部門，事業部門，会社，支社，支店，子会社，設備一式，台，基，装置，セット，ユニット
　business unit 事業部門，事業部，事業単位
　cost unit 原価単位
　credit card unit クレジット・カード会社
　current purchasing power unit 現在購買力単位
　economic unit 経済主体
　finance unit 金融子会社
　headquarters units 本社
　operating unit 事業体
　organizational unit 組織単位
　prefabricated units プレハブ住宅
　single unit depreciation 個別償却
　unit: billion yen 単位：10億円
　unit cost 単位原価，個別原価，単価
　unit depreciation 個別償却
　unit sales 販売数量
　unprofitable unit 不採算部門
▸Each business *unit* is responsible for its own markets. 事業部は，それぞれ各事業部門の市場に関して責任を負っています．
▸NTT DoCoMo has tied up with Sumitomo Mitsui Financial Group Inc.'s credit card *unit*. NTTドコモは，三井住友フィナンシャルグループのクレジット・カード会社と提携している．

unit credit 単位給付，単位積増し，単位年金積増し （⇒**projected unit credit**）
projected unit credit cost method 予測単位年金積増し方式
projected unit credit actuarial cost method 予測単位給付評価方式
unit credit method 1人当たりの年金費用，単位給付方式，単位年金積増し方式
▸Benefits under all U.S. pension plans are valued based on the projected *unit credit* cost method. すべての米国内年金制度の給付額は，予測単位年金積増し方式に基づいて算定されています．

unit method 個別償却法，個別法 （＝unit depreciation method：棚卸し資産の評価方法の一つで，個々の資産ごとに減価償却費を計算する方法．これに対して複数の固定資産を一括して減価償却費を計算する方法を総合償却（composite-life method）という．⇒**depreciate**）
▸When we sell assets that were depreciated using the *unit method*, we include the gains or losses in operating results. 個別償却法を用いて償却した資産を売却する場合，その利益または損失は営業成績［営業損益］に含めます．

unitary tax 合算課税，ユニタリー課税，ユニタリー・タックス

universal 形 普遍的な，万国の，世界の，共通の，一般的な，総合的，ユニバーサル
　universal bank 証券業務兼営銀行，総合銀行
　universal banking ユニバーサル・バンキング（銀行の証券業兼営）
　universal partnership 共同組合
　universal pension 一律給付年金
　Universal Product Code 統一商品コード
universal service 全国均一サービス，ユニバーサル・サービス（郵便事業の場合は，全国同一料金でサービスを提供すること）
▸After privatization, the nationwide network of postal offices is maintained to offer *universal services* nationwide. 民営化後も，全国的にユニバーサルサービスを提供するため，全国の郵便局網は維持されている．

universal shelf registration statement 普遍的一括登録届け出書，普遍的一括登録書類
▸During 2007, the Company filed a *universal shelf registration statement* with the Securities and Exchange Commission covering up to $800 million of debt and equity securities. 2007年度に，当社は8億ドルを上限とする債務および持ち分証券の普遍的一括登録届出書を，米証券取引委員会（SEC）に提出しました．

unless 接 …でないかぎり

unless otherwise stated [indicated] 別段の記載がないかぎり、特段の記載がないかぎり、とくに他の記載がないかぎり
▶All dollar amounts in this document are in U.S. dollar *unless* otherwise stated. この報告書では、別段の記載がないかぎり、金額はすべて米ドルで表示されています。

unlisted 形 上場されていない、非上場の、未上場の
　unlisted company 非上場会社、非上場企業
　unlisted stock [share] 未上場株、非上場株、場外株、店頭株、未公開株
　unlisted stock company 株式を上場していない非公開会社、非上場会社 (＝unlisted joint-stock company)
▶The management of both firms purchased shares from ordinary shareholders in order to withdraw from the stock market to become *unlisted* companies. 両社の経営陣は、株式市場から撤退して非上場企業になるために、普通株主から株を買い取った。

unprofitable 形 採算の合わない、不採算な、儲からない、利益を生じない、無駄な
　unprofitable division 不採算の事業部門、不採算部門 (＝unprofitable operation)
　unprofitable operation 不採算事業 (＝unprofitable business)
　unprofitable outlet 不採算店舗 (＝unprofitable store; ⇒**restructuring plan**)
▶In September 2007, we divested our *unprofitable* outlets. 2007年9月に、当社は不採算店舗を売却しました。

unprovided portion 未拠出部分 (＝unfunded portion)
▶We recorded a one-time pretax charge of $1,800 million to record the *unprovided portions* of these liabilities. この債務の未拠出部分を計上するため、臨時の税引き前費用18億ドルを(一括)計上しました。

unrealized 形 未実現の
　unrealized equity profits 株式含み益
　unrealized income 未実現利益
　unrealized intercompany profits 未実現内部利益
　unrealized profits and losses 含み損益、未実現損益 (＝appraisal profits and losses, latent profits and losses)
　unrealized revenue 未実現収益
　unrealized exchange gains and losses 未実現の為替差損益
▶Any related *unrealized exchange gains and losses* are allocated to currency translation adjustment. これに関連する未実現為替差損益は、すべて為替換算調整勘定に配賦されています。

　unrealized foreign currency losses 未実現為替差損
▶General corporate expenses are principally cash, temporary cash investments and deferred *unrealized foreign currency losses*. 全社共通費は、主に現金預金と短期的な資金運用投資と繰延べ未実現為替差損です。

　unrealized gain 未実現利益、未実現益、未現利得、含み益、評価益 (＝appraisal gains, latent profits, unrealized profit)
　unrealized gain and loss 未実現損益、含み損益
　unrealized gains in [on] securities 有価証券含み益、証券含み益
　unrealized gains on long-term investments 長期投資評価益
▶Thanks to the increases in *unrealized gains* in their stocks, many banks expect to see their net worth increase. 株式含み益の増加で、多くの銀行は自己資本の上昇を見込んでいる。

　unrealized loss 未実現損失、含み損、評価損 (＝appraisal loss, latent loss)
　unrealized loss on investment activities 投資活動による未実現損失
　unrealized loss on marketable equity securities 市場性ある株式の未実現損失

　unrealized profit 未実現利益、含み益、評価益 (＝appraisal profit, latent gain, unrealized gain)
▶Many of the banking groups are running out of *unrealized profits* in their shareholdings. 銀行グループの多くは現在、持ち株の含み益が涸渇している。

　unrealized value 未実現評価額、未実現損益、含み損益
▶The bullish stock market in the past six months has led the *unrealized value* of bank-held stocks to swell by about ¥3 trillion. 株式市場が過去半年間、堅調に推移したことで、銀行保有株式の含み損益が約3兆円増加した。

unrecognized 形 未認識の、未実現の
　unrecognized net gain 未認識の純益、未実現純利益
　unrecognized net loss 未認識純損失
　unrecognized prior service cost 未認識過去勤務費用[債務]、過去勤務債務
　unrecognized transition asset 未認識の移行時資産、未認識の移行時差額
　unrecognized transition obligation 未認識の

移行時債務
▶The *unrecognized* transition asset related to SFAS No.87 is amortized over 15 years.　SFAS第87号(財務会計基準書第87号「年金に関する事業主の会計処理」)に係わる未認識の移行時資産は,15年にわたって償却しています。

unrecoverable 形 回復不能な
　unrecoverable loan 不良債権 (＝bad debt, bad loan, doubtful debt, nonperforming loan, uncollectible loan)

unusual 形 異常な,異例の,特別の,前例のない
　unusual dividend 特別配当,異常配当
　unusual gain and loss 特別損益,異常損益 (＝unusual profit or loss)
　unusual item 特別損益項目,異常損益項目,非正常項目
　▶The per share effects of *unusual items* in a quarter may differ from the per share effects of those same items for the year.　ある四半期の特別損益項目による1株当たりの影響額は,事業年度の同じ特別損益項目による1株当たりの影響額と異なる場合があります。

unveil 動 明らかにする,発表する,公にする,公表する,初公開する,公開する,除幕する,打ち明ける
　▶Fuji TV *unveiled* a plan to make Nippon Broadcasting System a subsidiary.　フジテレビは,ニッポン放送を子会社化する計画を発表した。

upgrade 動 昇格させる,高める,向上させる,底上げする,格上げする,格付けを引き上げる,上方修正する,グレードアップする
　▶Standard & Poor's *upgraded* the outlooks on its ratings to stable from negative on five insurance companies.　スタンダード＆プアーズは,保険会社5社の格付け見通しを「ネガティブ」から「安定的」に上方修正した。

upgrade 名 格上げ,上方修正

upgrading 名 格上げ,上方修正,引上げ (＝rating upgrade)

upstream 名 川上産業,上流部門,石油採掘部門,子会社から親会社への販売,上り,アップストリーム(「アップストリーム(上り)」は,回線の信号の流れが利用者から電話局の方向になっていること。⇒downstream)
　▶The firm is transforming itself into a seamless oil company engaged in both *upstream* and downstream operations.　同社は現在,原油の採掘[原油生産]から精製・販売まで一貫して手がける石油会社への脱皮を図っているところだ。

upward 形 上向きの,上昇する
　upward adjustment 上方修正,増額修正

upward bias 上昇傾向
upward earnings revision 業績の上方修正,業績予想の上方修正
upward mobility 昇進,昇級,出世,立身出世,栄達,上方志向[志向性]
upward of ... …以上
upward path 上昇基調,増加傾向,増加基調
upward pressure on wages 賃金上昇圧力,賃金の上昇傾向
upward trajectory 上昇軌道
▶The result of this sale was an *upward* adjustment of $30 million ($19.5 million recorded in June) in the Corporation's investment in the firm.　この売却に伴い,同社に対する当社の投資額は,6月に計上した1,950万ドルから3,000万ドルに上方修正されています。

upward 副 上方へ,さかのぼって,…以上,…以来 (⇒downward)
　slow upward trend 穏やかな上昇傾向[上昇基調],ゆるやかな増加傾向[増加トレンド]

use 動 使用する,使う,用いる,…に充てる,採用する,利用する,活用する,運用する,投入する
　be used for repaying long-term indebtedness 長期債務の返済に充てる
　financial resources used 資金の運用
　net cash used for acquisition 企業買収に使用した現金純額
　net cash used in investing activities 投資活動に投入した正味現金
　use the straight line method for financial reporting 財務会計上,定額法を用いる[採用する]
　▶This $300 million of 9% Series 7 Notes was *used* to repay the same amount of 10% Series 3 Notes, which matured in May 2006.　この利率9％のシリーズ7ノート3億ドルは,2006年5月に満期が到来した利率10％のシリーズ3ノート3億ドルの償還に充当しました。

use 名 使用,使用量,使用法,利用,活用,運用,採用,使途,用途,効用,有用,収益権
　cash use 資金の使途
　land use 土地利用
　sales and use taxes 売上税と使用税
　sources and uses of funds 資金収支
　sources of funds and uses of funds 資金の源泉と資金の運用[使途]
　unauthorized use 不正使用
　use of funds 資金の運用,資金の使用,資金の使途
　use of proceeds 資金の使途
　uses of financial resources 資金源泉の運用

▸European and U.S. companies established R&D bases in China and put their energy into developing products for *use* by Chinese consumers. 欧米の企業は, 中国に研究開発拠点を設けて, 中国仕様の製品開発に力を注いだ。

useful 形 有効な, 効果をあげる
▸Canon's cell production system was particularly *useful* in inventory control. キヤノンのセル生産方式は, 在庫管理の面でとくに効果をあげた。

useful life 耐用年数, 有効期間 （⇒**declining balance**)
　useful life of a depreciable asset 減価償却資産の耐用年数
　useful life table 耐用年数表
▸The equipment was estimated to have a *useful life* of 8 years with salvage value estimated at $5,000. この設備の耐用年数は8年で, 残存価格は5,000ドルと見積もられた。

user 名 使用者, 利用者, 顧客, 加入者, 需要家, 会員, 投資家, ユーザー
　end user 最終使用者, エンド・ユーザー
　innocent user 善意の使用者
　industrial user 産業使用者, 実需筋
　major user 大口ユーザー （＝large user, substantial user）
　users of blog service ブログ・サービスの会員
▸TEPCO's first-quarter profit almost doubled as the country's economic recovery boosted demand, especially from industrial *users*. 東京電力の第1四半期利益は, 日本の景気回復でとくに産業用需要[実需筋による需要]が伸びたため, ほぼ倍増した。

utility 名 有用性, 有益, 効用, 公益設備, 公益事業
　utility company 公益事業会社
　utility maximization principle 効用最大化の原理
　utility model 実用新案, 実用新案権
　utility plant 公益設備

V v

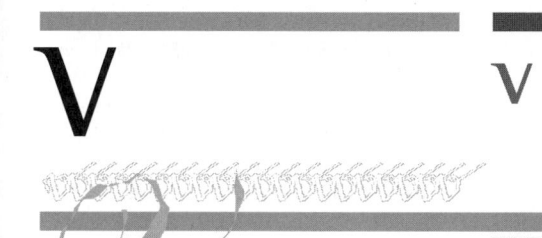

valuation 名 評価, 査定, 見積り, 評価価格, 査定価格
  accrued benefit valuation method 発生給付評価方式
  actuarial valuation 保険数理上の評価, 保険数理価値
  hidden valuation 含み資産
  inventory valuation 棚卸し資産評価
  investment valuation allowance 長期投資評価引当金
  market valuation 時価総額 (=aggregate market value, total market value：株価による企業の価値を示す「時価総額」は, 株価に発行済み株式数を掛けて算出する)
  projected benefit valuation method 予測給付評価方式
  stock valuation 株価評価
  taxable valuation 課税評価額
  valuation allowance 評価引当金, 評価性引当金
  valuation basis 評価基準
  valuation profit or loss 評価損益
  valuation reserve 評価性引当金
  valuation surplus 評価剰余金
▶At current prices, the firm's *market valuation* is more than 1.5 billion. 現在の株価でみた同社の時価総額は, 15億ドルを超えている。
valuation losses 評価損, 保有株の評価損を損失として計上する減損処理額 (=appraisal losses, evaluation losses)
▶Companies are required to post *valuation losses* on fixed assets whose market value has fallen sharply from their book value. 固定資産の時価が簿価から大幅に下落した場合の固定資産の評価損計上を, 企業は義務付けられている。
value 動 評価する, 評価替えする, 値洗いする, 重視する
  be present valued 現在価値に直す
  be valued at market 時価で評価する
  value the book at historical cost 原価で計上する
  value the book at market 時価で計上する
▶Our advanced telecommunications equipment is *valued* at approximately $130 million. 当社の先進的通信施設は, 約1億3,000万ドルと評価されています。
value 名 価値, 価格, 評価, 評価額, 金額, 相場, バリュー (⇒**book value, corporate value, create, market value, overall, par value**)
  cash value 時価
  capital value 資本価値, 資本金
  increase value for our shareholders 当社株主の価値[利益]を高める
  reported value 簿価
  share value 株価, 株式の評価
  simple mean value 単純平均
  value-added tax 付加価値税《略 VAT》
  value declared 表記価格
  value engineering 価値工学《略 VE》
  value in use 使用価値
  value-oriented management 価値重視の経営
  value strategy バリュー戦略
  value to business 企業価値
▶Financial institutions are required to report latent losses if the *value* of their stock investments falls more than 50 percent below their purchase prices. 保有株の株価が取得価格より

50%以上下落した場合, 金融機関は評価損を計上しなければならない。
▶The issuance of new shares by the company would dilute *value* of outstanding shares. 同社が新株を発行すれば, 発行済み株式の利益(1株当たり利益)は希薄化する[同社が増資すれば, 発行済み株式の価値は損なわれる]。

value-added product 付加価値製品, 高付加価値製品 (=value-added goods)
▶We need to pull in higher profits by focusing on higher *value-added products*. 当社は, 高付加価値商品に的を絞って, 高収益を上げる必要がある。

VAT 付加価値税, 付加価値割 (**value-added tax**の略)

VE 価値工学 (**value engineering**の略)

veep 副社長 (**vice president**を参照)

vendor[**vender**] 名 仕入先, 納入業者, 機材調達先, 供給元, メーカー, 販売業者, 販売会社, 売り主, 売り手, 売却元, ベンダー (⇒**sourcing**)
▶With assured long-term sources for these components from North American *vendors*, it is not economically prudent for us to produce all of these components internally. これらの部品については北米の納入業者から長期供給が保証されているため, これらの部品をすべて自社工場で生産するのは, もはや経済的に得策ではありません。

vested 形 確定した, 受給権の発生した, 既得の
　vested accumulated plan benefits 受給権確定[受給権の発生した]累積年金給付額
　vested benefit obligation 確定給付債務
　vested benefits 受給権確定給付[給付額], 受給権の発生した年金給付, 確定給付

vice president[**vice-president**] 副社長 (日本企業の部長や次長に相当する職位), 副頭取, 副会長, 副理事長, 副総裁, 副学長, 副大統領《略 VP》 (=veep)
　corporate vice-president 本社副社長
　executive vice-president 執行副社長, 業務執行副社長, 副社長, 副理事長
　financial vice-president 財務担当副社長
　senior vice president 上級副社長, 上席副社長
▶The firm named him, its senior *vice president*, as president. 同社は, 上級副社長の同氏を社長に指名した。

volatile 形 変わりやすい, 乱高下する, 変動が激しい, 変動が大きい, 変動性が高い, 不安定な, 左右されやすい (⇒**volatility**)
　less volatile 変動性が小さい
　volatile market 変わりやすい市場, 乱高下する市場, 変動が激しい市場
　volatile pricing 価格変動, 価格の変動 (=volatile prices)
▶Overseas investors are considered highly *volatile* to changes in the share price. 外国人株主は, 株価動向にかなり左右されやすいとされている。

volatility 名 変動, 変化, 乱高下, 変動性, 変動率, 将来の価格変動性, 価格変動率, 予測変動率, ボラティリティ
　excess volatility in exchange rates 為替相場の過度の変動
　exchange rate volatility 為替の乱高下, 為替相場の変動, 為替変動 (=forex volatility)
　expected income volatility 予想収益変動幅
　historical volatility 過去の変動性, ヒストリカル・ボラティリティ
　implied volatility 予想変動率, インプライド・ボラティリティ
　market volatility 市場変動性, 相場変動性, 市場の乱高下, 市場のボラティリティ
　price volatility 価格変動性, 価格変動
　stock market volatility 株式相場の変動, 株式の乱高下, 株式市場のボラティリティ
▶Our industry is a volatile one and we are subject to that *volatility*. 当業界は変動が激しく, 当社はその激しい変動の影響を受けています。

volume 名 出来高, 取引高, 売上高, 販売高, 操業度, 数量, 量(「出来高」は, 株式市場全体の売買株数を示し, 売買高ともいわれる。一般に, 株価が上昇して, 出来高も多いときは, 相場が強いとされている)
　break-even volume 損益分岐売上高
　haulage volume 輸送数量
　in volume terms 実質ベースで, 台数ベースで, 数量ベースで (=in terms of volume)
　loan volume 融資高
　low-margin, high volume strategy 薄利多売戦略
　new issue volume 起債総額
　production volume 製造高, 製造量
　profit volume ratio 限界利益率, PV比率, 売上高純利益率 (=PV ratio)
　retail volume 実質小売売上高
　sales volume 売上高, 販売高, 販売数量, 販売量, 売上数量, 取扱い高 (⇒**like-for-like basis**)
　trading volume 出来高
　volume discount 数量割引, 大口割引
　volume on the First Section of the Tokyo Stock Exchange 東証第一部の出来高
　volume of business 取引高, 売買高
▶The company was once the second-largest

provider of subprime mortgages in the United States on loan *volume*.　同社は、かつてはサブプライム・ローンの融資高で米国第2位の住宅ローン会社だった。

voluntary 形　任意の, 自主的な, 自発的な, 自由意志による, 無償の
  voluntary closure　自主廃業
  voluntary conveyance of estate in land　無償不動産譲渡
  voluntary dissolution　任意解散（＝voluntary winding up）
  voluntary partnership　任意組合
  voluntary reserves　任意積立金
  voluntary retirement　希望退職
  voluntary work　無料奉仕活動, ボランティア
▸Investors who purchased the leasing rights became members in four *voluntary* partnerships.　持ち分権(リース権)を購入した出資者は、四つの任意組合のメンバーになった。

voluntary cash payment　任意現金支払い
▸Common shares may also be purchased at the average market price by *voluntary cash payments* of as little as US $40 to a maximum of US $4,000 during a quarter.　当社の普通株式は、1四半期に最低40米ドルから最高4,000米ドルまでの範囲で、任意現金支払いにより平均市場価格で購入することもできます。

voluntary liquidation　任意清算, 任意整理
▸Shareholders did not approve of *voluntary liquidation* of the company.　株主は、同社の任意整理を承認しなかった。

voluntary separation program　任意退職計画[制度], 希望退職計画, 自発的退職プログラム
▸We offered an early retirement program and a *voluntary separation program* to our U.S.-based employees in 2007.　2007年度に当社は、当社の米国内従業員に対して、早期退職プログラムと自発的[希望]退職プログラムを提案しました。

vote 動　投票する, 票決する, 投票で決定する, 議決する,〈株式の〉議決権を行使する　(⇒**participant**)
  vote against ...　…に反対の投票をする
  vote down　否決する
  vote for ...　…に賛成の投票をする
  vote one's share　議決権を行使する
▸Shares cannot be *voted* unless the signed proxy form is returned.　署名した委任状[委任状用紙]が返送されない場合、株式の議決権を行使することはできません。

vote 名　投票, 投票用紙, 票, 得票, 票決, 決議, 投票権, 議決権, 票決権, 選挙権
  affirmative vote　賛成投票
  one vote for each share　1株につき1議決権
▸Each stockholder of record at the close of business on March 10, 2008 is entitled to one *vote* for each share held.　2008年3月10日の営業終了時に株主名簿に記載された株主は、それぞれ所有する株式1株に付き1票の議決権を行使することができます。
▸The Board of Directors recommends a *vote* AGAINST this proposal.　当取締役会は、この提案を否決されるようお願い致します。

voting 形　投票, 投票権行使, 議決権行使
  audience response voting　聴衆反応投票
  cross voting　交差投票
  cumulative voting　累積投票
  electronic voting　電子投票
  multiple choice voting　マルチ選択投票
  nonvoting redeemable preferred stock　無議決権償還優先株式
  nonvoting share　無議決権株（＝nonvoting stock）
  online voting　電子投票（＝e-vote, electronic voting：Eメールでの投票）
  parliamentary voting　議会式投票
  stockholder's voting right　株主議決権
  voting bond　議決権付き社債
  voting by proxy　代理人による議決権の行使
  voting security　議決権付き証券, 議決権のある証券
  voting upon stocks　株式に基づく投票

voting power　議決権, 投票権（＝voting right：株主が会社の総会で各種の重要な決議に参加できる権利のこと。一般に、普通株式1株につき1個の議決権が与えられている）
▸When a hostile takeover bid occurs, its target company can ask shareholders to exercise their right to acquire new shares, reducing the *voting power* of shares held by the party mounting the takeover bid.　敵対的買収者が現れたら、その買収標的会社は、株主に新株予約権(新株を購入できる権利)を行使してもらって、敵対的買収者が保有する株式の議決権の比率を引き下げることができる。

voting right　議決権, 投票権（＝voting power; ⇒**shareholders list**）
▸The firm's stake in NBS has exceeded 50 percent in terms of *voting rights*, or 46 percent in terms of shareholding ratio.　同社が保有する

VP 副社長 （⇒vice president）

voting share [stock] 議決権株式, 議決権株, 議決権付き株式 （＝voting share：議決権が付いている株式。⇒**super voting share**）

▸Citigroup Japan currently owns 67.2 percent of Nikko Cordial's outstanding shares, or 68 percent in terms of the number of *voting shares*. シティの日本法人、シティグループ・ジャパンは現在, 日興コーディアルの発行済み株式の67.2％（議決権比率で68％）を保有している。

ニッポン放送株が, 議決権比率で［議決権ベースで］50％（持ち株比率で46％）を超えた。

vulnerable to ... …の影響を受けやすい, …に弱い, …に圧迫される, 軟調の, …にさらされやすい, …に狙われやすい

be vulnerable to criticism 批判を受けやすい

be vulnerable to economic slowdown 景気低迷の影響を受けやすい

▸Floating shares are *vulnerable* to a hostile takeover bid. 浮動株は, 敵対的TOBに狙われやすい。

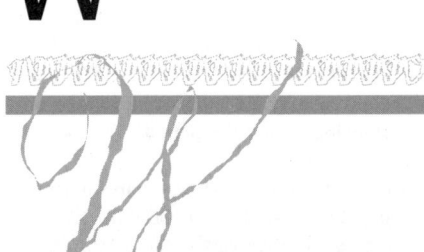

W

WACC 加重平均資本コスト（weighted average cost of capital の略．株主資本と銀行などから借りている負債を合わせた資本の平均調達コスト）
wage 名 賃金, 給料
 accrued wage　未払い賃金
 prepaid wage　前払い賃金
 salaries and wages　賃金・給与
 wage advance　賃金前払い, 賃金前貸し
 wages based on job evaluation　職能給
 wages for job classification　資格給
▶The increase in operating expenses was due primarily to increases in salaries and *wages* and to higher depreciation expenses.　この営業費用の拡大は, 主に賃金・給与の支払い額と減価償却費の増加によるものです.
waive 動 〈権利などを〉放棄する
▶The company's main banks *waived* a total of ¥110.9 billion in company debt.　同社の主力取引銀行が, 総額1,109億円の債権を放棄した.
waiver 名 〈権利の〉放棄, 〈債務の〉免除, 〈権利放棄の〉意思表示, 権利放棄証書　（⇒debt waiver, loan waiver）
▶Aoki Corp. became the first general contractor with debt *waivers* to have collapsed.　債権放棄を受けているゼネコンで経営破綻したのは, 青木建設が初めてだ.
▶In the first half, the firm booked a special profit of about ¥400 billion on debt *waivers* by its key lenders.　上半期に同社は, 主要金融機関の債務免除［債権放棄］で, 約4,000億円の特別利益を計上した.
Wall Street　米国の証券市場, 米ニューヨークの株式市場, ニューヨーク株, ウォール街の証券市場, 米ニューヨークの株式中心街, 米金融街, ウォール・ストリート
 a Wall Street economist　市場エコノミスト
 the Wall Street stock market　ウォール街の証券市場
 Wall Streeter　米証券市場関係者　（＝Wall Street watcher）
▶Goldman Sachs results topped *Wall Street* projections for a profit of $4.35 per share.　米証券大手ゴールドマン・サックスの業績は, 米金融街の1株当たり4.35ドルの利益予想を上回った.
warn 動　警告する, 予告する
warning 名　警告, 予告, 警戒, 戒め
warrant 名　新株引受権, 新株予約権, 株式買取り請求権, 倉荷証券, 権利証券, 権利証書, 権限証書, 証明書, ワラント
 bond with stock purchase warrant　新株予約権付き社債
 bond with warrant　ワラント付き社債, ワラント債
 bond with warrants attached　新株引受権付き社債　（＝warrant bond）
 detachable warrant　分離型ワラント, 分離型新株引受権付き証書
 equity warrant　新株予約権
 exercise of warrant　新株引受権の行使, ワラントの行使
 issue warrants for new shares to ...　…への新株予約権を発行する
 share warrant　株式引受権, 新株予約権, 無記名株式
 stock warrant　新株引受権, 新株予約権, 株式引受権, 新株引受権付き証券［証書］, 新株引受保証書, 株式ワラント　（＝share warrant）

warrant bond ワラント債, 新株引受権付き社債《略 WB》
▶The company plans to issue share *warrants* on May 20. 同社は, 5月20日に新株予約権の発行を予定している。
▶The market price of the stock *warrants* was $10 per warrant on April 10. 4月10日の新株引受権付き証券の市場価格は, 1単位10ドルであった。

we 代 私ども経営陣, 当社, 当行, 当店, 当監査法人
▶*We* believe the Corporation should continue to produce above-average revenue growth as well as improved profitability across most of its major product lines. 当社は引き続き業界の平均を上回る売上高の伸び率達成と, ほぼ全製品ラインにわたって収益性の改善に取り組まなければならない, と私ども経営陣は考えています。

weak 形 弱い, 弱小の, 中小の, 低迷する, 軟調の, 落ち込んだ, 低下した, 減少した, 冷え込んだ, 厳しい, 悪化した (⇒strong)
　weak economic environment 厳しい経済環境, 経済環境の悪化, 景気低迷
　weak economy 景気低迷
　weaker operating income 営業収益[営業利益]の減少[低下, 落ち込み]
　weaker sales 売上の減少, 販売の悪化, 販売の落ち込み, 販売低迷
▶Loan loss provisions for the second quarter of 2006 were $9 million, up $4.5 million over a year ago, reflecting the impact of a *weak* economy. 2006年第2四半期の貸倒れ引当金は900万ドルで, 景気低迷による影響を反映して, 前年同期を450万ドル上回りました。

wealth 形 富, 資産, 財産, 富裕, 資源, 価値のある産物
　beginning-of-period wealth 期首の財産額 (=initial wealth)
　expected wealth value 期待資産価値
　maximization of wealth 富の極大化 (=wealth maximization)
　negative wealth effect 逆資産効果
　shareholder wealth 株主の富
　terminal wealth 期末の財産額 (=end-of-period wealth)

Web site ホームページ, ウェブサイト, サイト (=homepage, Web page, website)
　create a Web site サイトを立ち上げる
　investment Web site 投資情報サイト, 投資サイト
　set up a Japanese-language Web site 日本語のホームページを設ける

subscription Web site 有料サイト, 有料ウェブサイト
▶The company expects the sales of its own products to increase as more customers visit its *Web site*. 同社は, 自社サイトを訪れる客の増加に伴う自社製品の売上増を期待している。

weighted average 加重平均, 総平均, 等価率
　weighted average number of shares outstanding during the period 期中の発行済み株式の加重平均株式数
　weighted average common shares outstanding 発行済み普通株式の加重平均株式数
　weighted average cost 加重平均原価, 総平均原価
　weighted average interest rates on short-term borrowings 短期借入金の加重平均金利
　weighted average method 加重平均法, 総平均法
　weighted average number of common shares outstanding 発行済み株式数の加重平均, 社外流通普通株式の加重平均株式数
　weighted average price 加重平均価格, 加重平均株価
　weighted average share 加重平均株式数

weighted average discount rate 加重平均割引率
▶The *weighted average discount rate* was used in determining the accumulated and accrued plan benefits. 累積年金給付債務額の算定には, 加重平均割引率が用いられた。

weighted average number of shares of common stock and common stock equivalents outstanding 発行済み普通株式と普通株式等価物[準普通株式]の加重平均株式数
▶We use the *weighted average number of shares of common stock and common stock equivalents outstanding* during each period to compute earnings per common share. 当社は, 発行済み普通株式と普通株式等価物[準普通株式]の当該期間における加重平均株式数を用いて, 1株当たり利益[純利益]を計算しています。

weighted average number of shares outstanding 発行済み株式数の加重平均, 発行済み株式の加重平均株式数
▶Earnings per common share are based on the *weighted average number of shares outstanding*. 普通株1株当たり純利益は, 発行済み株式数の加重平均に基づいて計算されています。

whole 名 全体, 全部, 通期

for the year as a whole 通年で, 通期で
the second quarter as a whole 第2四半期全体
▶For the *whole* of fiscal 2007, the firm expects its group pretax profit to expand 57.9 percent from the previous year. 2007年度通期で, 同社の連結経常利益は前年比で[前年度に比べて] 57.9%拡大する見込みだ。

wholly 副 完全に, 全部を, 全額を
wholly own 完全所有する, 全部所有する, 完全子会社化する, 全額出資する
▶Citygroup Inc. will *wholly own* Nikko Cordial Corp. by the end of January 2008. シティグループが, 2008年1月末をめどに日興コーディアルグループを完全子会社化する。

wholly-owned 形 完全所有の, 全額出資の, 100%所有の
wholly-owned foreign firm 100%外資企業

wholly-owned subsidiary 完全所有子会社, 完全子会社, 全部所有子会社, 全額出資子会社, 100%所有子会社, 100%出資子会社, 100%子会社 (＝fully owned subsidiary, fully owned unit, totally held subsidiary, wholly owned affiliate)
put ... under A's wing as a wholly owned subsidiary …を完全子会社としてAの傘下に収める
turn ... into a wholly owned subsidiary …を完全子会社化する
▶Maruha will put Nichiro under its wing as a *wholly-owned subsidiary* through a share swap. 株式交換方式で, マルハはニチロを完全子会社としてマルハの傘下に収める。

wide 形 幅の広い, …の幅の, 的を外れた
a wide range of industries 幅広い業種
wider loss 損失拡大, 赤字拡大
▶The company expects a *wider* loss for fiscal 2007. 同社は, 2007年度は赤字拡大を見込んでいる。

widen 動 拡大する, 広げる, 大きくする, 規模拡大する, 広がる, 大きくなる
▶Fujiya group loss *widened* to ¥70 billion in the six months through September. 不二家の連結赤字は, 9月中間決算で700億円に拡大した。

windfall 形 意外の, 一時的な, 一回かぎりの, 臨時の
windfall fall 思わぬ損失, 一時的損失, 意外の損失
windfall gain 思いがけない利益, 偶発利益, 過剰利得, 一回かぎりの利益 (＝windfall profit)
windfall gain or loss 偶発的損益
windfall income 一時的利益, 一時的な利益, 偶発利益
windfall loss 思わぬ損失, 意外の損失, 偶発的損失
windfall profit 臨時利益, 偶発利益, 思わぬ利益, 望外の利益, 過剰利得, タナボタ利益 (＝windfall gain)
windfall profits tax 過剰利得税, 超過所得税, タナボタ利益吸収税

windfall 名 タナボタ利益, 思わぬ利益, 思いがけない利益, 望外の利益, 臨時利益, 偶発利益, 過剰利得, タナボタ[棚ぼた], 思いがけない幸運, 追い風 (＝windfall profit)
▶The firm concealed its real intention of boosting its share price and realizing a handsome *windfall* through a sell-off of its own shares. 同社は, 自社株の株価つり上げと自社株の売り抜けで大幅な利益を得ることが, 同社の本当の目的であることを隠していた。

window-dress 動 粉飾する, 粉飾決算する (有価証券報告書の虚偽記載などで, 企業の経営を実態以上に良く見せかける行為)
▶The company may have *window-dressed* accounts over three years up to March 2006. 同社は, 2006年3月期までの3年間にわたって, 決算を粉飾していた疑いがある。

window dressing 粉飾, 粉飾決算 (＝window-dressed accounts, window-dressing accounts, window dressing settlement)
be involved in the window dressing 粉飾に関与する, 粉飾決算に関与する
financial window-dressing 会計操作
window-dressing of accounts 粉飾決算 (＝window dressing settlement)
▶Lax internal controls at the auditing firm allowed the *window dressing* of the company's accounts to go unnoticed. この監査法人の甘い内部チェック体制が, 同社の粉飾決算を見過ごした。

WIP 仕掛(しかけ[しかかり])品 (**work in process, work in progress**の略)

withdraw 動 〈預金などを〉引き出す, 〈預金などを〉引き揚げる, 〈通貨などを〉回収する, 〈市場などから〉撤退する, 取り消す, 打ち切る, 撤回する
▶The company *withdrew* from textile and food production under its revival plan. 同社は事業再生計画に基づいて, 繊維と食品の生産事業から撤退した。

withdrawal 名 撤退, 脱退, 離脱, 撤回, 回収, 〈預金の〉引出し, 引落し, 払戻し, 取消し, 解約, 〈出資者や株主に対する〉利益の分配, 資本の減少
bank withdrawal 銀行預金引出し
double withdrawal 二重引落し (＝double deduction)

partial withdrawal 一部撤退, 部分撤退
withdrawal before maturity 期日前解約
withdrawal from the core business 中核事業からの撤退, 主力事業からの撤退
withdrawal of deposits 預金の引出し, 預金の流出
▶The *withdrawal* of the company from Japan has yet to be confirmed.　同社の日本からの撤退は, まだ確認されていない。

withhold 動　源泉徴収する, 天引きする, 保留する, 抑える, 差し控える, 避ける, 公表しないでおく
　withheld amounts 源泉徴収による預り金
　withhold at source 源泉徴収する, 源泉課税する
▶Persons receiving dividends subject to Canadian withholding taxes, and who are also subject to U.S. income tax on these dividends will be entitled to either a credit or deduction with respect to the Canadian taxes *withheld* when computing their domestic tax.　カナダの源泉所得税が課される配当金の受取人が, その配当金についてさらに米国の所得税を課されるときは, 受取人の国内税額を計算する際にカナダの源泉所得税について控除(税額控除もしくは所得控除)を受けることができます。

withholding 名　源泉徴収, 給料の天引き, 売り惜しみ
　income tax withholding 源泉所得税預かり金 (＝income tax withheld of source)
　withholding at source 源泉徴収, 源泉課税
　withholding income tax 源泉徴収所得税, 源泉徴収に係る所得税, 源泉所得税

withholding tax 源泉徴収税, 源泉所得税, 源泉税, 源泉徴収税額, 源泉課税額 (＝withholding; ⇒**resident**)
　separate withholding tax system 源泉分離課税方式
　withholding tax absorbed loan 源泉課税負担型ローン
　withholding tax rate 源泉徴収税率, 源泉税率
　withholding tax refund 源泉税還付
▶Under the separate *withholding tax* system, an investor would pay only 1.05 percent of the stock's selling price as tax.　源泉分離課税方式では, 投資家は株式売却額の1.05％を納税すれば済む。

work 名　仕事, 事業, 作業, 工事, 労働, 職, [[〜s]]工場, 製作所, ワーク
　long-term construction work 長期請負工事
　partly finished work 半成工事
　place of work 職場
　spoiled work 仕損じ品

standards of field work 実施基準
temporary work 臨時雇用
work flow 仕事の流れ, 作業の流れ, ワークフロー
works charge 工場経費
works cost 製造原価
▶More than two-thirds of our employees face a growing strain in balancing *work* and family demands.　当社従業員の3分の2以上は, 仕事と家族の要求との間のバランスをとるのが重荷, と感じるようになっています。

work in process 仕掛(しかけ[しかかり])品 (＝goods in process, work in progress)《略 **WIP**》
　initial work in process 期首仕掛品 (＝beginning work in process, initial goods in process)
　work in process inventory 仕掛品棚卸し高, 仕掛品
▶Raw materials, finished goods and *work in process* are stated at the lower of average cost or market.　原材料, 製品と仕掛品は, 平均原価または時価のいずれか低いほうで計上されています。

work sharing ワーク・シェアリング, ワーク・シェア, ワーク・シェアリング・システム (＝work sharing system：1人当たりの労働時間を短縮して雇用を分かち合う制度)
　work sharing system ワーク・シェアリング, ワーク・シェアリング・システム
▶The *work sharing* system may lead to a decline in productivity.　ワーク・シェアリングは, 生産性の低下につながる可能性がある。

workforce 名　就業者, 労働力, 労働人口, 従業員, 社員, 人員, 全従業員, 全社員 (＝labor force, work force)
▶The layoffs will account for about 7 percent of its global *workforce* of 150,000.　今回の人員削減は, 全世界の従業員15万人の約7％に当たる。
▶We value and encourage diversity in our *workforce*.　当社は, 社員の多様性を尊重し, これを促進しています。

working 形　経営の, 運転する, 運用している, 営業の, 仕事上の, 作業の, 労働の, 職場での, 実用の, 実際の役に立つ, 機能している, 実動の
　working assets 運用資産
　working expense 営業費 (＝operating expense, working cost)
　working environment 労働環境, 作業環境, 職場の環境
　working fund 運転資金, 運転資本, 営業資金
　working relationship 職場の人間関係, 職場での付き合い

working capital 運転資本, 運転資金 (＝op-

erating capital)
general working capital 一般運転資金
gross working capital 総運転資本
net working capital 純運転資本, 正味運転資本
statement [schedule] of changes in working capital 運転資本変動表
working capital ratio 運転資本比率, 流動比率
working capital turnover 運転資本回転率
▶Capital stock was sold to provide additional *working capital*. 追加的運転資金の調達のため、株式を発行しました。

working capital requirements 必要運転資金, 運転資金需要
▶The greater cash flow in 2007 reflected a smaller increase in *working capital requirements* compared with 2006. 2007年度のキャッシュ・フローの増加は、前年度と比べて必要運転資金が微増にとどまったことを反映しています。

working life 勤続期間
▶Life insurance for retired employees is largely funded during their *working lives*. 退職者に対する生命保険は、勤続期間中にその大部分が積み立てられます。

workweek 名 週労働時間, 週平均労働時間
factory workweek 製造業の週平均労働時間 (=workweek in manufacturing)
five-day workweek 週5日制
statutory workweek 法定労働時間
true 5-day workweek 完全週休2日制
▶The segment was able to meet a portion of the demand for additional volume through expanded prduction lines and expanded *workweeks*. 当部門は、生産ラインの増設や週労働時間の延長などで、製品の需要増の一部に対応することができました。

world market 世界市場, グローバル市場 (=global market, international market)
▶The company announced a provision of U.S. $200 million in view of a major corporate reorganization to improve its competitiveness in *world markets*. 同社は、グローバル市場での競争力を高めるための大規模な企業再編を視野に入れて、2億米ドルの引当金設定を発表した。

worth 名形 価値, 価額, 自己資本, …に相当する量, …分, 有用性, 重要性 (⇒net worth)
bushiness worth 企業価値
fixed asets to net worth ratio 固定比率
net asset worth 純資産額
present worth 現在価値, 割引価値 (=present value)
profit ratio of net worth 自己資本利益率
total liabilities and net worth 総資本
worth of ... …相当のもの、…分の…
worth (to) current debt ratio 資本対流動負債比率, 資本流動負債比率
worth (to) fixed debt ratio 資本対固定負債比率, 資本固定負債比率
worth (to) fixed ratio 資本対固定資産比率, 資本固定[固定資本]比率, 固定比率
▶The firm chalked up ¥483 billion in sales on ¥547 billion *worth* of orders it won during the October-December quarter. 同社の10-12月期の売上高は、5,470億円の受注額で4,830億円となった。

write 動 書く, 書面にする
write down 〈帳簿価格を〉引き下げる、〈評価を〉引き下げる, 評価減を計上する, 評価損を計上する, 貸倒引当金を計上する, 償却する, 再評価する, 記録する (⇒market value, one-time charge)
inventory written down 棚卸し評価損
write down the assets to market value 資産を時価ベースで再評価する
▶Merill Lynch & Co. will *write down* $5.5 billion for bad bets on subprime mortgates and leveraged loans. 米大手証券のメリルリンチは、低所得者向け住宅融資「サブプライム・ローン」とレバレッジド・ローンの見通しが暗いため、55億ドルの評価損を計上する。

write-down [writedown] 名 評価減, 評価損, 評価引下げ, 減損
asset write-down 資産評価損, 資産の簿価格引下げ
inventory write-down 棚卸し評価減 (=inventory written down)
original write-down 当初の評価損
▶Subprime mortgage-related *write-downs* across the banking industry were more than $40 billion in the third quarter. 銀行業界全体で、米国のサブプライム・ローン(低所得者向け住宅融資)関連の評価損計上額は、第3四半期決算で400億ドルを上回った。

write off 〈債権を〉帳消しにする、〈債権を〉処理する[償却する, 放棄する], 〈評価額を〉引き下げる, 〈価格を〉引き下げる, 減価償却する, 〈費用などを〉経費として申告する
write off a production plant 生産設備を償却する
write off a 10 million yen debt 1,000万円の借金を帳消しにする
write off bad debts 貸倒れ損失を計上する

▸Losses incurred by *writing off* nonperforming loans are not generally taxable in the United States. 不良債権処理で生じた損失額は，米国では一般に課税の対象とはならない。

write-off 名 〈債権の〉帳消し，〈債権の〉処理［放棄］，消却，評価減，評価引下げ，償却，貸倒れ償却，貸倒れ損失，減価償却，〈資産の〉除却［切捨て］削除，〈帳簿の〉締切り （＝writeoff; ⇒**delinquent**）
account write-offs 貸倒れ損失
credit write-offs 不良債権の償却
debt write-off 債務の帳消し
equity write-offs 株式評価損
net write-off 正味貸倒れ償却
loan write-off 債権放棄，債務免除 （＝debt forgiveness, loan forgiveness, loan waiver）
loan write-off costs 債権処理費用，不良債権処理費用
nontaxable write-off 無税償却
write-off interval 償却期間
write-off of bad loans 不良債権処理，不良債権の償却 （＝bad loan write-off, write-off of nonperforming loans）
write-off of costs 特別損失
write-offs of appraisal losses in fixed assets 固定資産の減損処理

▸In leading economies abroad, the disposal of nonperforming loans is made in most cases through a nontaxable *write-off*. 海外の主要国では，不良債権処理は多くの場合，無税償却で行われている。

▸We keep a close watch on the status of accounts receivable, which has helped us maintain a low level of delinquent balances and *write-offs*. 当社は売掛金の状態に十分注意を払っており，これによって回収遅延残高と償却の水準が低く保たれています。

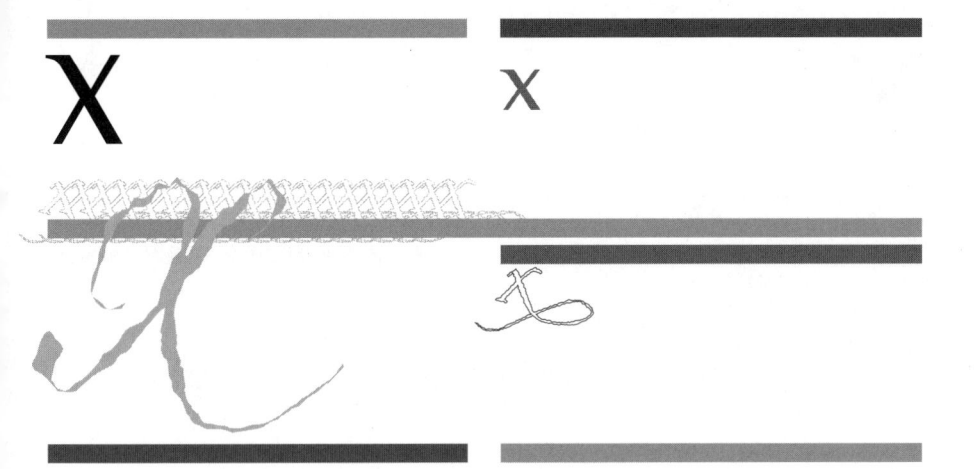

X factor 不確定要素 (＝uncertain factor, uncertainty)
X in 利息落ち (＝ex interest)
X pr 優先権利落ち (＝ex privileges)
x.a. 諸権利落ち, 全権利落ち (＝ex all)
XBRL 拡張的財務報告言語 (**extensive business reporting language**の略：財務報告用のコンピュータ記述言語)
XC 利落ち (＝ex coupon)
XD 配当落ち (＝ex div., ex dividend)
Xenocurrency 国外流通通貨, ユーロダラー
XI 利息落ち, 利落ち (＝ex interest, x-int.)
XR 権利落ち (＝ex rights, xr, x-rts.)
XW 権利証落ち, 新株引受権落ち, ワラント落ち (＝ex warrants, x-warr., xw：新株引受権利証書が付いていないこと)

Y y

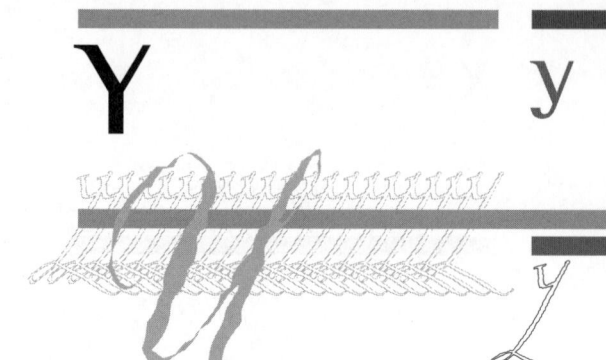

year 名 年, 年度, 事業年度, 期 (⇒**business year, current fiscal year, current year, fiscal year, full year, half year, prior year**)

　年度と年について ➡ 一般に年次報告書で「年度」とは事業年度（営業年度：business year）, 会計年度（企業の会計期間：fiscal year）のことであり,「年」は暦年のことである。事業年度と暦年は基本的に違うが, 一般に4月1日から始まって翌年の3月31日に終了する日本企業の事業年度と比べて, 米国企業の場合には事業年度の開始時期と終了時期が暦年と同じで1月1日から12月31日までの1年間となっているのが普通である（6月末, 9月末や10月末をもって終了する1年間を事業年度とする企業もある）。つまり, 事業年度＝暦年の関係にある。そこで, この関係にある12月期決算企業の場合には, とくに原文がfiscal yearやbusiness yearになっていなくても, 翻訳上「年度」を用いることも「年」を用いることもできる。

average exchange rates for the year 事業年度の平均為替レート （⇒**income statement amounts**）
base year 基準年, 基準年度, 基準年次
both on the month and on the year 前月比, 前年同月比ともに
during fiscal year or quarter 年度・期中
during the course of the current (fiscal) year 今期, 今期中, 今期は
each of the years in the three-year period ended December 31, 2007 2007年12月31日に終了した3年間の各事業年度
first half of the year 上半期, 上期
for the fourth year running 4期連続, 4年連続 （＝**for the fourth straight year**）
for the year as a whole 通年で, 通期で
from a year ago 前年比, 前年同期比, 前年同月比で
in the first half of current fisacal year 今年度上半期, 今年度上期
in the year-on-year comparison 前年同期比で, 前年同月比で
insurance year 保険年度
on a full year basis 通年で, 通期で
over a year ago 前年同期比, 前年比で
over the past year 前年同月比で
tax year 課税年度, 税務年度, 納税年度, 会計年度, 事業年度, 会計年度 （＝**fiscal year, taxable year, year of assessment**）
taxable year 課税年度
the preceding year 前年度, 前期
the third straight year 3年連続, 3期連続
the year just ended 前期
the year then ended 同日をもって終了した事業年度
the year to Dec. 31, 2008 2008年12月期
the year to March 31, 2009 2009年3月期, 2008年度
the year under review 当年度, 当期 （＝**the period under review**）
working year 営業年度, 会計年度, 決算年度
year ended February 28 2月28日終了事業年度, 2月28日終了年度, 2月期, 2月決算
year just ended 前期
year-on-year 前年同期比, 前年同月比, 前年比 （＝**over a year ago, year-over-year**; ⇒**combined pretax profit**）
year-to-year 前年同期比, 前年同月比 （＝**year-on-year**）

- Sales of the overseas subsidiaries of Japanese companies grew 17.3 percent in U.S. dollar terms in the January–March quarter from a *year* earlier. 1－3月期は，日本企業の海外子会社の売上高が，米ドル・ベースで前年同期比17.3％伸びた。
- The bank's rate of nonperforming loans against overall lendings stood at 1.41 percent, down from 2.16 percent a *year* ago. 同行の貸出全体に占める不良債権の比率は，1年前の2.16％から1.41％に低下した。

year earlier 前年，前年比，前年同期比 （＝year ago）
- The company's per-share net profit came to ¥18.24, down from ¥40.12 a *year earlier*. 同社の1株当たり純利益は，前年同期の40円12銭から減少して18円24銭となった。

year end 年末，年度末，期末，決算期末 （⇒ yearend）
　stock price at year-end 年度末［期末］の株価
　total assets at year-end 年度末［期末］の資産合計
　total employees at year-end 年度末［期末］の従業員総数
　year-end adjustment 期末修正，年度末修正，年末調整 （＝year-end adjusting）
　year-end balance 期末残高
　year-end current rates 決算日の為替レート［為替相場］
　year-end dividend 期末配当
　year-end financial position 期末財政状態
　year-end tax adjustment 年末調整
- All balance sheet items are translated at exchange rates at the respective *year-ends* of foreign subsidiaries. 貸借対照表の項目は，すべて各外国子会社の期末の為替レートで換算されています。

year ended December 31 12月31日終了事業年度，12月31日終了年度，12月31日をもって終了した事業年度，12月31日に終了した事業年度，12月期，12月期決算
- We have audited the consolidated statements of income and cash flows for the *years ended December 31*, 2007, 2006 and 2005. 私どもは，2007年，2006年および2005年12月31日をもって終了した各事業年度の連結損益計算書と連結キャッシュ・フロー計算書について監査しました。

year ending in March 3月終了事業年度，3月期
- The bank expects it would not be able to book a similar return from loan-loss reserves for the *year ending in March* 2009. 同行は，2009年3月期は，今期と同様の貸倒れ引当金の戻り益を計上できないと見ている。
- The company's confectionery division has been recording operational losses since the *year ending in March* 2005. 同社の洋菓子部門は，2005年3月期から営業赤字が続いている。

year of service 勤続年数，在職年数
- Retirement benefits are based on *years of service* and the employee's compensation. 退職給付は，勤続年数と従業員の給与額に基づいて算定されています。

year-over-year 前年同期比，前年同月比，前年比 （＝over a year ago, year-on-year）
- These revenue increases were driven primarily by the *year-over-year* growth in the number of network access services. これらの収益の伸びは，主にネットワーク接続サービスの利用件数が前年比で増加したことによるものです。

year through next March 来年3月期，来年3月までの事業年度
- The company revised upward its group net profit forecast for the *year through next March* to ¥101.8 billion. 同社は，来年3月期［今年度］の連結純利益［税引き後利益］予想を1,018億円に上方修正した。

year to March ⋯年3月期
- For the *year to March* 2009, the Company has retained its forecasts for operating profit of ¥900 billion and net profit of ¥550 billion. 当社は，営業利益9,000億円，税引き後利益5,500億円の2009年3月期［2008年度］の業績予想を変えていません。

year under review 当期，当年度
- We further improved the service for business customers in the *year under review*. 当期は，法人顧客サービスをさらに改善しました。

yearend 名 年末，年度末，期末 （⇒year end）
- Book value of the Corporation's common shares rose to $11 at *yearend* 2007. 当社普通株式1株当たり純資産［純資産額］は，2007年末現在で11ドルに上昇しています。

yearly earnings 年間利益 （＝annual earnings）

yearly sales 年間売上，年間売上高
- Rakuten boasts *yearly sales* of ¥18 billion from a virtual shopping mall and online securities brokerage. 楽天は，仮想商店街やオンライン証券などで180億円の年間売上を誇る。

yen 名 円, 円相場
  appreciating yen 円高 (=rise in the yen's value)
  depreciation of the yen 円安
  exchange value of the yen 円の為替相場
  in yen terms 円表示で, 円表示の (=in yen-denominated terms)
  long dollar positions against the yen 円売りドル買い
  yen exchange 円為替
  ▸The strong *yen* during this period has been referred to as a crisis for Japan. この時期の円高は, 日本の危機として語られている。
yen-denominated profits 円建て利益
  ▸The exchange rate of about ¥115 to the dollar has pushed up the firm's *yen-denominated profits*. 1ドル=115円前後の為替相場が, 同社の円建て利益を押し上げた。
yield 名 〈株式・債券などの〉利回り, 歩留まり, 収益, イールド
  bond yield 債券利回り, 長期国債利回り, 長期債利回り
  earnings yield 収益率, 利益率, 株式利回り, 益回り
  expected yield 期待利回り
  maturity yield 最終利回り, 償還利回り
  redemption yield 償還利回り
  stock yield 株式利回り
  stock dividend yield 株式の配当利回り, 配当回り, 株式の利回り
  yield adjustment 利回り調整 (⇒**amount receivable**)
  yield on investment 運用利回り
  yield on securities 有価証券利回り
  yield rate 歩留(ぶど)まり, 利率
  yield to call 繰上げ償還利回り
  yield to maturity 最終利回り, 満期利回り《略 **YTM**》(債券を購入して満期日まで債券を保有した場合の利回り)
  ▸The *yield* on our stock at the current price is about 4 percent—the highest in our industry. 当社の株式の時価による投資収益率は約4%で, 当業界では最高です。
yr 年, 年度 (=year)
YTM 最終利回り, 満期利回り (**yield to maturity**の略)

Z z

ZBB ゼロベース予算 (zero-base budgetの略)
ZD 無欠点 (zero defectsの略)
zero-base budget ゼロベース予算, ゼロベース予算管理《略 **ZBB**》(＝zero-base budgeting, zero-based budget：前年度の実績に関係なく, 採用された業務計画に対してだけ予算をつける方式)
zero coupon bond ゼロ・クーポン債 (＝zero coupon issue：割引債の一種)
zero defects 無欠点, 無欠陥, 無欠点運動《略 **ZD**》

zero defects movement 無欠陥運動, 無欠点運動, ZD運動, ゼロ・ディフェクト運動
zero financing ゼロ金利ローン (＝free financing, zero-interest loan, zero-interest rate loan, zero-percent financing)
zero growth ゼロ成長, 開発抑止政策
zero-interest rate policy ゼロ金利政策 (＝zero-interest policy)
▸The BOJ lifted the *zero-interest rate policy*. 日銀がゼロ金利政策を解除した。
zero recovery 全額回収不能

資料

連結財務書類の表示例
（年度，金額等の数値は除く）

1. Consolidated Statement of Earnings for the year ended December 31

連結損益計算書12月31日終了年度

(Dollars in millions per share amounts)	（単位：1株当たりの金額を除いて百万ドル）
Revenue:	総収益：
Sales	売上
Support services	支援サービス
Software	ソフトウエア
Rentals and financing	賃貸料および金融
Cost:	原価：
Sales	売上
Support services	支援サービス
Software	ソフトウエア
Rentals and financing	賃貸料および金融
Gross Profit	売上総利益
Operating Expenses:	営業費用：
Selling, general and administrative	販売費および一般管理費
Research, development and engineering	研究開発および技術費
Operating Income	営業利益
Other Income, principally interest	営業外収益，主に利息
Interest Expense	支払い利息
Earnings before Income Taxes	税引き前利益
Provision for Income Taxes	法人所得税
Net Earnings before Cumulative Effect of Accounting Change	会計処理変更に伴う累積的影響額考慮前の当期純利益
Cumulative Effect of Change in Accounting for Income Taxes	法人所得税の会計処理変更に伴う累積的影響額
Net Earnings	当期純利益
Per share amounts:	1株当たり利益：
Before cumulative effect of accounting change	会計処理変更に伴う累積的影響額考慮前
Cumulative effect of change in accounting for income taxes	法人所得税の会計処理変更に伴う累積的影響額
Net earnings	当期純利益
Average number of shares outstanding:	期中平均発行済み株式数：

2. Consolidated Statement of Financial Position at December 31:

Dollars in millions

連結貸借対照表12月31日現在

単位:百万ドル

Assets	資産
Current Assets:	流動資産:
Cash	現金
Cash equivalents	現金等価物
Marketable securities, at cost, which approximates market	市場性ある有価証券—原価評価で時価とほぼ等しい
Notes and accounts receivable-trade, net of allowances	受取手形および売掛金、貸倒引当金控除後
Other accounts receivable	その他の受取債権
Inventories	棚卸資産
Prepaid expenses and other current assets	前払い費用およびその他の流動資産
Plant, Rental Machines and Other Property	**工場設備、賃貸機械およびその他の固定資産**
Less: Accumulated depreciation	控除:減価償却累計額
Investments and Other Property:	**投資およびその他の資産:**
Software, less accumulated amortization	ソフトウエア、償却累計額控除後
Investments and sundry assets	投資および諸資産
Liabilities and Stockholders' Equity	**負債および株主持ち分**
Current Liabilities:	**流動負債:**
Taxes	税金
Loans payable	借入金
Accounts payable	買掛金
Compensation and benefits	給与および給付金
Deferred income	前受収益
Other accrued expenses and liabilities	その他の未払い費用および負債
Long-Term Debt	**長期負債**
Other Liabilities	**その他の負債**
Deferred Income Taxes	**繰延税金**
Stockholders' Equity:	**株主持ち分:**
Capital stock, par value $1.25 per share	資本金、額面1株当たり1.25ドル
Shares authorized:	授権株式数:
Issued:	発行株式数
Retained earnings	利益剰余金
Translation adjustments	外貨換算調整額
Less: Treasury stock, at cost	控除:自己株式—取得原価
Shares:	株式数:

3. Consolidated Statement of Cash Flows for the year ended December 31:

連結資金フロー 12月31日終了年度：

Dollars in millions 単位：百万ドル

Cash Flow from Operating Activities:	営業活動から生じた資金フロー：
Net earnings	当期純利益
Adjustments to reconcile net earnings to cash provided from operating activities:	純利益と営業活動から生じた資金との調整：
Depreciation	減価償却費
Amortization of software	ソフトウエア償却費
(Gain) on disposition of investment assets	投資資産の処分による(利益)
(Increase) in accounts receivable	売掛金の(増加)
(Increase) decrease in inventory	棚卸資産の(増加)減少
(Increase) in other assets	その他の資産の(増加)
Increase in accounts payable	買掛金の増加
Increase in other liabilities	その他負債の増加
Net cash provided from operating activities	営業活動から生じた資金―純額
Cash Flow from Investing Activities:	投資活動から生じた資金フロー：
Payments for plant, rental machines and other property	工場設備,賃貸機械およびその他の固定資産に対する支払い
Proceeds from disposition of plant, rental machines and other property	工場設備,賃貸機械およびその他の固定資産処分による収入
Investment in software	ソフトウエアに対する投資
Purchases of marketable securities and other investments	有価証券およびその他の投資の購入
Proceeds from marketable securities and other investments	有価証券およびその他の投資から生じた収入
Net cash used in investing activities	投資活動に使われた資金―純額
Cash Flow from Financing Activities:	金融(財務)活動から生じた資金フロー：
Proceeds from new debt	新規借入金による収入
Payment to settle debt	借入金返済のための支払い
Short-term borrowings less than 90 days—net	90日以内の短期借入金―純額
Proceeds from (payments to) employee stock plans—net	従業員ストック・プランによる収入(支払い)―純額
Payments to purchase and retire capital stock	株式の買入消却のための支払い
Cash dividends paid	現金配当支払い額
Net cash used in financing activities	金融(財務)活動に使われた資金―純額
Effect of Exchange Rate Changes on cash and cash Equivalents	現金および現金等価物に関する為替レート変動による影響額
Net Change in Cash and Cash Equivalents	現金および現金等価物の純増(減)額
Cash and Cash Equivalents at January 1	現金および現金等価物1月1日現在残高
Cash and Cash Equivalents at December 31	現金および現金等価物12月31日現在残高
Supplemental Data:	補足データ：
Cash paid during the year for:	当期現金支払い額：
Income taxes	法人所得税
Interest	利息

4. Consolidated Statement of Stockholders' Equity for the year ended December 31

連結株主持ち分計算書12月31日終了年度

Dollars in millions 単位：百万ドル

Stockholders' Equity, January 1, 2008	2008年1月1日現在株主持ち分
Net earnings	当期純利益
Cash dividends declared	現金配当金宣言額
Capital stock issued under employee plans	従業員プランによる株式の発行
Purchases and sales of treasury stock under employee and stockholder plans—net	従業員および株主プランに基づく自己株式の取得および売却—純額
Capital stock purchased and retired	株式の買入れ消却
Unrealized loss on marketable equity securities	市場性ある株式の未実現損失
Conversion of debentures	転換社債の転換
Tax reductions—employee plans	従業員プランに関連する株式に適用される税金の控除
Translation adjustments	外貨換算調整額
Stockholders' Equity, December 31, 2007	2007年12月31日現在株主持ち分

5. Consolidated Statement of Retained Earnings

連結利益剰余金計算書

Balance at beginning of year	期首残高
Net earnings	当期純利益
Dividends	配当金
—preferred shares	優先株式
—common shares	普通株式
Excess of consideration paid over stated capital	資本金相当額を超えて支払われた対価
—preferred shares redeemed	優先株式の償還
—common shares purchased for cancellation	消却のための普通株式の購入
Balance at end of year	期末残高

6. Consolidated Statement of Changes in Financial Position

連結財政状態変動表

Millions of U.S. dollars — 単位：百万米ドル

Cash and short-term investments were provided by (applied to):	現金・預金および短期投資の調達（使途）：
Operations	事業活動
Investment	投資活動
Financing	財務活動
Dividends on common shares	普通株式に対する配当金
(Decrease) increase in cash and short-term investments and borrowings	現金・預金・短期投資および短期借入金の増加（減少）
Cash and short-term investments at beginning of year	現金・預金および短期投資の期首残高
Cash and short-term investments and borrowings at end of year	現金・預金・短期投資および短期借入金の期末残高
Cash provided by operations	**事業活動による資金の調達**
Net earnings	当期純利益
Items not involving cash	資金の流出（流入）を伴わない項目
Depreciation and amortization	減価償却費
Equity in net earnings of associated company	関連会社持ち分利益
Deferred income taxes	繰延べ法人所得税
Other	その他
Dividends on preferred shares	優先株式に対する配当金
Advances from customers	顧客前受金
(Increase) decrease in working capital	運転資本の（増加）減少
Total	合計
Cash invested	**投資活動**
Expenditures for plant and equipment	有形固定資産購入
Disposals of plant and equipment	有形固定資産除却
Investment in associated company	関連会社に対する投資
Other	その他
Total	合計
Financing	**財務活動**
(Increase) decrease in long-term receivables	長期債権の（増加）減少
Increase (decrease) in notes payable	手形借入金の増加（減少）
Payment of scientific research investment royalties	科学研究投資に係わるロイヤルティの支払い額
Additions to long-term debt	長期債務の増加
Reductions of long-term debt	長期債務の返済
Redemption of preferred shares	優先株式の償還
Translation of preferred shares (redeemable)	償還可能優先株式の換算
Issue of common shares	普通株式の発行
Purchase of common shares for cancellation	消却のための普通株式の購入
Dividends from associated company	関連会社からの配当金
Other	その他
Total	合計

和英索引

A-Z

ABC　activity based costing
ABC管理　ABC
ABC管理　activity based costing
APB意見書　APB Opinions
APB意見書解釈　accounting interpretations
CP発行残高　commercial paper outstanding
DCF方式　discount [discounted] cash flow method
DIPファイナンス　DIP financing
DIPファイナンス　DIP plan
EPS増収感度　earnings per incremental share
FF金利　Federal [federal] funds rate
FF金利　key interest rate
FFレート　Federal [federal] funds rate
IR活動　investor [investors] relations
M&A案件　M&A deal
M&Aの提案　M&A bid
MPO　MPOs
PR誌　newsletter
S&P500株価指数　Standard & Poors 500
SO法　Sarbanes-Oxley Act
SRIファンド　SRI fund
TOB（株式公開買付け）価格　offer price
Tノート　Treasury note
Tビル　Treasury bill

あ

間柄　footing
相次ぐ　back-to-back
アイデア　concept
アイデア　idea
相手先商標［ブランド］製造業者　OEM
相手先商標［ブランド］製造業者　original equipment manufacturer
アイテム　item
相反する　reciprocal
アウトソーシング　outsourcing
アウトプット　output
アウトプット法　output method
アウトレット　outlet
青色申告　blue return
アカウンタビリティ　accountability
赤字　deficit
赤字　loss
赤字　red
赤字会社　below-par company
赤字額　loss
赤字決算　deficit settlement of accounts
赤字決算　net loss
赤字削減努力　gap-closing efforts
赤字続きの　loss-making [loss-making]
赤字店舗　money-losing store
赤字の　loss-making [lossmaking]
赤字の　money-losing
赤字の　negative
赤字の事業　money-losing operation
赤字予想　projected loss
赤字を抱えた　debt-saddled
赤字を出す　lose
上がり下がり　fluctuation
上がり下がりする　fluctuate
上がる　gain
明るい　favorable
明るい　positive
アキュムレーション　accumulation
明らかにする　define
明らかにする　reveal
明らかにする　unveil
悪影響　negative effect
悪影響　negative impact
悪影響を与える　negative
悪材料　negative effect
悪材料　negative impact
悪材料　negative pledge
悪材料になる　suffer
アクション　action
アクションプログラム　action program
アクセス　access
悪戦苦闘する　struggle
悪戦苦闘の　struggling
アクチュアリー　actuary
上げ相場　rally
足跡　step
足がかり　foothold
足がかり　footing
足どり　step
足取り　pace
足どりが重い　sluggish
足並み　pace
足場　foothold
足場　footing
足場　position
預かり　deposit
預り資産　customer assets
預ける　deposit
アセスメント　assessment
アセット　asset
アセットバックCP　ABCP
アセットバックCP　asset-backed commercial paper
アセットバック証券　asset-backed securities
与える　award
与える　extend
与える　grant
与える　impose
与える　provide
頭金　down payment
頭金として支払う　pay down
新しい　innovative
新しい　new
…に当たる　represent
当たる　equivalent
悪化　collapse
悪化　decline
悪化　deterioration
悪化　drop
悪化　pressure
悪化した　weak
悪化する　decline
悪化する　deteriorate
圧縮　reduction
圧迫　pressure
圧迫　squeeze
圧迫　stress
圧迫される　vulnerable
圧迫する　squeeze
アップストリーム　upstream
集める　solicit
圧力　pressure
圧力　stress
当てはめる　apply
…に充てる　use
当てる　earmark
後入れ先出し　last-in, first-out
後入れ先出し売価還元法　lifo retail method
後入れ先出し法　last-in, first-out
後入れ先出し法　LIFO
後押し　boost
後押しする　sponsor
後順位物上担保付き社債　junior mortgage bond
後払い　deferred payment
後回し　back burner
…の穴埋めをする　make up for ...
穴埋めをする　cover
アニュアル　annual
アニュアル・レポート　annual report
アファーマティブ・アクション　affirmative action
アフィリエイト　affiliate
アフター・コスト　after cost
アフターマーケット　after market [aftermarket]
アプリケーション　application
アプリケーション・ソフト　application
アポイントメント　appointment
余り　residual
網　network
アメックス　American Stock Ex-

change	
アメリカン証券取引所	American Stock Exchange
アメリカン証券取引所	AMEX
アモチゼーション	amortization
誤り	error
歩み	step
争う	compete
改める	reform
粗利	gross profit
粗利益	gross margin
粗利益	gross profit
粗利益	gross profit margin
粗利益率	gross margin
粗利益率	gross profit margin
粗利益率の低下	lower gross margins
…を表す	represent
表す	register
アルゴリズム取引	algorithm trading
…に合わせる	conform to [with] ...
…案	initiative
案	idea
案	package
案	plan
案	proposal
案	scheme
案件	deal
案件	project
安全	security
安全性	security
アンダーライター	underwriter
安定株主	stable shareholder
安定させる	stabilize
安定した	fixed
安定した	solid
案内	profile
案内	prospectus
アンバランス	imbalance

い

言い換え	restatement
イールド	yield
委員会	board
委員会	commission
委員会	committee
委員会	panel
委員団	panel
委員長	chairman
委員長	president
意外の	windfall
生かす	capitalize on
生かす	leverage
遺棄	abandonment
異議	challenge
勢い	strength
勢いをつける	pick up
域外調査	offshore purchase
域外適用管轄権	long-arm jurisdiction
生き残りに懸命の	struggling
生き残りに必死になっている	struggling
異議申立て	challenge
育成する	develop
意見	idea
意見	judgment [judgement]
意見	opinion
意見	submission
意見書	letter
意見書	opinion
意見書	opinion letter
意見の一致	accord
意見の一致	consensus
意見の発表	delivery
意見表明	opinion
意見を述べる	submit
意見をはっきり言う	assertive
移行	shift
移行	transition
移行期間	transition
移行時	transition
移行時債務	transition obligation
移行時差額	net trransition amounts
移行時資産	transition asset
意向表明	commitment
維持	maintenance
維持管理費	administrative and maintenance expenses
維持基金	foundation
意思決定	decision
意思決定	decision making
意思決定の	decision-making
意思決定能力	decision-making skill
意思決定の過程	decisionmaking process
意思決定モデル	decision model
維持修繕費	maintenance and repairs
…を維持する	continue to ...
維持する	keep
維持する	maintain
維持する	retain
意思疎通	communication
異質の	alien
維持費	maintenance charge
維持費引当金	maintenance reserve
意思表示	waiver
意思表明状	memorandum of understanding
慰謝料	compensation
…以上	upward
委譲	transfer
異常（損益）項目	extraordinary items
異常減損	abnormal shrinkage
異常項目	abnormal item
異常項目	unusual item
異常損益項目	below the line
異常損益項目	below the line
異常損益項目	unusual item
異常損失	extraordinary loss
異常損失準備金	catastrophe reserve
異常な	abnormal
異常な	extraordinary
異常な	unusual
…以上の	above
依存する	dependent
委託	commission
委託	commitment
委託	reference
委託	trust
委託証拠金	margin
委託する	assign
委託する	commit
委託する	consign
委託売買	consignment
委託販売	best-efforts selling
委託販売	consignment
委託販売品	consignment
委託品	consigned goods
委託募集	best efforts
委託募集	best efforts
委託保証金	margin
位置	location
位置	position
1行連結	one-line consolidation
一元化	integration
一元化した	consolidated
一元化する	consolidate
一元化する	integrate
一時解雇	layoff
一時解雇	temporay layoff
一次加工	primary processing
一時貸付け金	temporary loans
一時借入金	temporary borrowing
一時監査人	temporary auditor
一時帰休	layoff
一時金	one-off payment
一時金	single sum
一時雇用	temporary employment
一時差異	temporary differences
一次産品	primary goods
一時償却	temporary depreciation
一時所得	one-time income
一時停止する	suspend
一時的	one-off
一時的差異	temporary differences
一時差異の年度別内訳	scheduling temporary differences
一時的な	interim
一時的な	temporary
一時的な	windfall

一時的に介在する　mezzanine
一時的費用　one-time [onetime] charge
一時的費用　one-time charge
一時投資　temporary cash investments
一時投資　temporary investment
一時取締役　provisional director
一次入札　first round of tenders
著しい　robust
著しい　significant
著しく　significantly
一段と強固にする　reinforce
一段の　further
位置づける　rank
1日当たりの取引高　daily turnover
1日平均残高　average daily balance
1年以内回収(分)　current portion
1年以内償還(分)　current portion
1年以内返済(分)　current portion
1年以内返済予定額　current
1年基準　one-year concept
1年分　full year
1年分の　full-year
1年前と比較した　straight
1年前と比較して　straight
一番おいしいところ　lion's share
一番札　preferential bidder
一部　partially
一部　portion
一部返済金　composition
一覧後定期払い手形　bill payable at a fixed period after sight
一覧払い　payable on demand
一覧払い　sight payment
一覧払い手形　sight note
一覧表　table
一律給付年金　universal pension
一律の　flat
一流株　leader
一流企業向け最優遇貸出金利　prime rate
一流の　good
一回かぎりの　windfall
一回限りの　one-off
一回限りの損失　one-off loss
1か月　month
1か所ですべて済ませる買い物　one-stop shopping
1か所での同時まとめ買い　one-stop shopping
一括　basket
一括売出し　block offer
一括基準　aggregate basis
一括購入　B/D
一括購入　b/d
一括購入　bulk purchase
一括支払い　lump-sum payment
一括受注・発注方式　full turnkey
一括譲渡　bulk transfer

一括承認　blanket approval
一括登録　shelf registration
一括登録制度　shelf registration
一括登録制度　shelf registration program
一括登録届け出書，発行登録届け出書　shelf registration statement
一括売却[販売]　bulk sale
一括払いの　lump-sum
一括払い保険料　single premium
一括払戻金し　one-time credit
一括返済　lump-sum repayment
一括返済　maturity
一括募集　shelf offering
一貫した体制　integrated operations
一貫して　consistently
…と一貫性がある　consistent with …
一貫生産する　integrate
一貫生産体制　integrated operations
一極集中を排除する　decentralize
逸失利益　passive damages
一斉棚卸し　complete inventory
一層の　further
一体化　integration
一体化した海外事業　integrated foreign operations
一体化した事業　integrated operations
一体化する　consolidate
一体化する　integrate
一体感　integration
一致　conformity
…と一致する　consistent with …
…と一致する　match
…に一致する　conform to [with] …
一定ドル　constant dollar
一定の　fixed
一点集中購買　one-stop shopping
一般会計　general accounting
一般会計基準　GAAP
一般会計基準　generally accepted accounting principles
一般会計原則　GAAP
一般間接経費　general corporate expenses
一般管理費　administration cost [expense]
一般管理費　administration overhead
一般管理費　administrative and general expense
一般管理費　administrative and general expense
一般管理費　administrative cost
一般管理費　administrative expenses
一般管理費　central corporate expense

一般管理費および販売費　administrative and selling expenses
一般競争入札　open bidding
一般組合員　rank and file
一般経費　general expense
一般財政　current fund
一般事業目的　general corporate purposes
一般従業員　rank and file
一般従業員の　rank-and-file
一般使用者　end user
一般職員　rank and file
一般職員の　rank-and-file
一般大衆　rank and file
一般賃金　prevailing rate
一般賃率　prevailing rate
一般的な　general
一般的な　universal
一般に　generally
一般に　overall
一般に公正妥当と認められた会計原則[会計基準]　generally accepted accounting principles
一般に公正妥当と認められた会計原則[会計基準]　GAAP
一般に公正妥当と認められた監査基準　GAAS
一般に公正妥当と認められた監査基準　generally accepted auditing standards
一般に認められている　acceptable
一般に認められている保険数理法　acceptable actuarial method
一般の　general
一般の人々　public
一般費　general expense
一般物価変動　inflation
一般法人　private enterprise
一般本社経費　general corporate expenses
一般労働者　rank and file
一歩　step
一本化　integration
一本化した　consolidated
一本化する　integrate
移転　flow
移転　relocation
移転　transfer
移転価格　transfer pricing
移転価格税制　transfer pricing taxation system
遺伝子組換え食品　genetically engineered food
遺伝子工学　genetic engineering
移転する　grant
移転する　relocate
移転する　transfer
意図　idea
意図　purpose

移動	flow
移動	motion
移動	movement
移動	redeployment
移動	relocation
移動	shift
移動する	redeploy
移動する	relocate
移動する	shift
移動平均	moving average
移動平均	moving average
移動平均原価法	moving average cost method
移動平均線	moving average
移動平均法	method of moving average
移動平均法	moving-average method
移動平均法	running average method
イニシアチブ	initiative
委任	authorization
委任	commission
委任	commitment
委任事項	affairs entrusted
委任状	authorization
委任状	commission
委任状	letter of attorney
委任状	letter of proxy
委任状	power of attorney
委任状	proxy
委任状	proxy form
委任状	proxy statement
委任状カード	proxy form
委任状勧誘	proxy solicitation
委任状規制	proxy regulation
委任状規則	proxy rule
委任状参考資料	proxy material
委任状説明書	proxy statement
委任状争奪戦	proxy fight [battle, contest]
委任状用紙	proxy form
委任する	commit
委任する	delegate
イノベーション	innovation
…に違反する	infringe on [upon] …
イベント	event
意味	effect
意味する	represent
イメージ	image
イメージ	reputation
違約金	penalty
意欲	drive
…以来	upward
依頼者	client
依頼人	client
イラスト	figure
医療	health care [healthcare]
医療給付	health care benefits
医療費	health care cost

医療費用	health care cost
医療保険	health care [healthcare]
異例の	unusual
入れ替える	reverse
入れ替える	shift
インカムゲイン	current income
インサイダー	insider
因子	factor
インストールする	install [instal]
印税	royalty
引責辞任	resignation to take responsibility
インセンティブ	incentive
インターナショナル	international
インターネット	net [Net]
インターネット事業	Internet business
インターネット上の仮想商店街運営会社	Internet shopping mall operator
インターネット上の場所	site
インターネット接続業者	provider
インターネット接続サービス事業	Internet service provider
インターネットで	online [on-line]
引退	retirement
引退者	retiree
引退する	retire
引退する	step down
インダストリアル・エンジニアリング	industrial engineering
インタレスト・カバレッジ比率	interest coverage ratio
インタレスト・カバレッジ・レシオ	interest coverage ratio
院内総務	leader
インパクト	impact
インフォメーション	information
インフレ	inflation
インフレーション	inflation
インフレ率	inflation
インベスター	investor
インベスター・リレーションズ	investor [investors] relations
インベストメント	investment
インボイス	invoice
インボイスを送る	invoice
インボイスを作る	invoice

う

…より上の	above
ウェブサイト	Web site
ウォール街の証券市場	Wall Street
ウォール・ストリート	Wall Street
迂回生産	round-about production
請け合う	guarantee
受入社債利息	bond interest received
受入手数料	fee and commision received
受入手数料および支払い手数料	commission income and expense
受け入れる	accept
受け入れる	receive
請負	contract
請負業者	provider
請負工事契約	construction-type contract
請負仕事の入札	bidder for a contract
請け負う	tender
請け負う	undertake
受け付ける	receive
受取り	receipt
受取勘定	account receivable
受取金	amount receivable
受取金純額	net proceeds
受取金と支払い金	amount receivable or payable
受取債権	account receivable
受取債権	receivable
受取証	receipt
受取手形	acceptance receivable
受取手形	bills receivable
受取手形	note receivable
受取手形	notes receivable-trade
受取人	beneficiary
受取年金	pension benefits
受取配当金	dividend income
受取リース料債権	rentals receivables
受取利息	interest income
受取利息	interest revenue
受け取る	receive
受け取るべき	receivable
受ける	incur
受ける	suffer
受渡し	delivery
…を動かす	drive
動かす	run
動き	action
動き	activity
動き	development
動き	effort
動き	event
動き	fluctuation
動き	motion
動き	movement
動きが鈍い	sluggish
動く	function
動く	run
失う	lose
薄める	dilute
疑わしい	doubtful
打ち明ける	unveil
打ち上げる	launch
打合せ	arrangement
打ち切る	scrap
打ち切る	withdraw

打ち消す	offset
打ち歩	premium
打ち歩料	bond premium
内訳	breakdown
内訳	component
内訳は…	comprise
移し替える	transfer
移す	relocate
移す	shift
移す	transfer
訴え	action
訴える	accuse
移る	shift
うまく行く	pay off
うまく処理する	manage
うまく処理する	meet
生み出す	create
生み出す	generate
生む	earn
生む	generate
生む	return
埋め合わせ	offset
…を埋め合わせる	make up for ...
埋め合わせる	finance
埋め合わせる	redeem
埋め合わせをする	offset
裏書	endorsement
裏書人	endorser
裏付けとなる	underlying
売り	selling
売り	sell-off
売上	proceeds
売上	revenue
売上	sales
売上	turnover
売上原価	cost of goods sold
売上原価および営業費	purchase and operating expenses
売上構成	revenue mix
売上構成	sales mix
売上債権	account receivable
売上債権	receivable
売上債権回収期間	days sales outstanding
売上債権回収期間	DSO
売上債権回転日数	days sales outstanding
売上債権回転日数	DSO
売上債権回転率	receivables turnover
売上収入	revenue income
売上収入	revenue receipt
売上純利益率	profit margin
売上総利益	gross income
売上総利益	gross margin
売上総利益	gross profit
売上総利益	gross profit margin
売上総利益	margin
売上総利益	price margin
売上総利益率	gross profit margin
売上高	figure
売上高	operating revenue
売上高	proceeds
売上高	revenue
売上高	sales
売上高	sales turnover
売上高	sales volume
売上高	trading volume
売上高	turnover
売上高	volume
売上高1ドル当たり純利益	net earnings per revenue dollar
売上高純利益率	net income to sales ratio
売上高純利益率	net margin on sales
売上高の合計	combined sales
売上高の伸び	gain in revenues
売上高の伸び	revenue growth
売上高予測	forecast of sales
売上高利益率	net profit margin
売上高利益率	percentage profit on turnover
売上高利益率	return on sales
売上品目構成	sales mix
売上戻り	returned sales
売上戻りおよび値引き見込み額	allowance for expected returns and allowances
売上利益	gross margin
売上利益率	gross margin
売上利益率	gross profit margin
売上利益率	net margin on sales
売上利益率	profit margin
売上利益率の低下	lower gross margins
売上割引引当金	provision for discount allowance
売上割引見込み額	allowance for outstanding discounts
売り惜しみ	withholding
売掛金	account receivable
売掛金回転率	account receivable turnover
売掛金純額	net accounts receivable
売掛債権	account receivable
売掛債権	receivable
売掛債権の管理	receivables management
売掛債権売却	factoring
売り越し	selling
売込み	selling
売り込む	promote
売り込む	sell
売出し	offer
売出し	offering
売出し	placement
売出し	public offering
売出し	secondary distribution
売出し	secondary offering
売出価格	offer price
売出価格	offering price
売出発行	best-efforts issue
売出発行	offer for sale
売り出す	introduce
売り出す	issue
売り出す	launch
売り出す	market
売り出す	offer
売り建て	short position
売りつける	impose
売りつなぎ	hedge-selling
売りつなぎして損失を防ぐ	hedge
売り手	supplier
売り手	vendor [vender]
売り主	vendor [vender]
売り場	department
売りヘッジ	short hedge
売り持ち	bear position
売り持ち	oversold position
売り持ち	short position
売り渡す	sell
売る	sell
売る	serve
上乗せ	premium
上乗せ	spread
…を上回る	above
上回る	surpass
上回る	top
上向きの	upward
上向く	pick up
運営	administration
運営	charge
運営	conduct
運営	management
運営会社	operator
運営資金	current fund
運営者	operator
運営上の	administrative
運営する	manage
運営する	operate
運営する	run
運営方法	conduct
運航する	serve
運賃	rate
運転資金	operational funds
運転資金	working capital
運転資金	working fund
運転資金需要	working capital requirements
運転資金の必要額	working capital needs
運転資産	operating assets
運転資本	working capital
運転資本回転率	working capital turnover
運転資本管理	working capital management
運転資本比率	working capital ratio

運転者	operator
運転上の	operational
運転する	working
運転中の	running
運転費	running cost
運動	effort
運動	front
運動	motion
運動	movement
運用	application
運用	handling
運用	investment
運用	management
運用	operation
運用	performance
運用	use
運用管理する	manage
運用基準	guideline
運用資産	operating assets
運用資産	working assets
運用している	working
運用収益	return
運用上の	operational
運用する	invest
運用する	manage
運用する	run
運用する	use
運用成績	performance
運用成績	return
運用の	operational
運用利回り	return on investment
運用利回り	yield on investment

え

永久差異	permanent differences
永久債券	perpetual bond
永久資本	permanent financing
永久的	permanent
永久の	permanent
永久の	perpetual
永久優先株式	perpetual preferred stock
影響	effect
影響	impact
影響	results
営業	business
営業	operation
営業	practice
営業	sales operations
営業	trading
営業赤字	operating deficit
営業赤字	operating loss
営業運転	business operation
営業外項目	nonoperating elements
営業外収益	nonoperating income
営業外収益	nonoperating profit
営業外収益	nonoperating revenue

営業外収益	other income
営業外損益	nonoperating income or expenses
営業外損益区分	nonoperating section
営業外の	nonoperating
営業外費用	nonoperating expenses
影響額	effect
影響額	results
営業型リース	operating lease
営業活動	business operation
営業活動	operation
営業活動	sales operations
営業活動概況	overview of our business operations
営業活動から得られた資金	funds provided from operations
営業活動で得られる現金	cash provided by operations
営業活動によって得られる現金収入	cash provided by operations
営業活動により得た資金	funds provided by operations
営業活動によるキャッシュ・フロー	operating cash flow
営業活動による資金	fund from operations
営業活動による資金	funds from operations
営業活動による資金収入純額	net cash from operating activities
営業活動による資金の調達	cash provided by operations
営業活動を行う	do business
営業科目	line of busines
営業キャッシュ・フロー	operating cash flow
営業区分	segment
営業計画	operating plan
営業欠損金	operating loss
営業権	goodwill
営業権およびその他の無形固定資産	goodwill and other intangible assets
営業項目	line of busines
営業効率	commercial efficiency
営業資金	operational funds
営業資産	operating assets
営業している企業	going concern
営業収益	operating income
営業収益	operating profit
営業収益	operating revenue
営業収益	revenue
営業収益合計	total revenues
営業収益と純利益	revenues and earnings
営業収益と利益	revenues and earnings
営業収益の伸び	revenue growth
営業収入	operating revenue

営業純損失	net loss from operations
営業純損失	net operation loss
営業純利益	net operating profit
営業純利益	net profit from operations
営業所	office
営業上の	operating
営業上の	operational
営業上の債権・債務残高	trading balances
営業する	do business
営業する	operate
営業成績	business performance
営業成績	business results
営業成績	operating results
営業成績抜粋	selected financial data
営業責任者	account executive
営業責任者	AE
営業速報	flash report
営業損益	operating income
営業損益	operating results
営業損失	deficit
営業損失	operating loss
営業年度	business year
営業年度	fiscal year
営業年度	FY
営業の	operational
営業の	working
営業費	office expenses
営業費	operating expense
営業費	working expense
営業秘密	trade secret
営業費用	operating expense
営業品目	line of busines
営業部門	sales operations
営業報告書	account of business
営業保険料	gross premium
営業免許権	license [licence]
営業面の努力	sales effort
営業網	presence
営業用資産	operating assets
営業リース契約	operating lease
営業利益	net revenues
営業利益	operating earnings
営業利益	operating income
営業利益	operating profit
営業利益	sales
営業利益	trading profit
営業利益見通し	operating profit forecast
営業利益予想	operating profit forecast
営業利益率	operating margin
影響力	force
影響力	leverage
影響力	presence
影響を与える	affect
影響を与える	impact

影響を受けやすい	vulnerable
…の影響を受ける	subject to ...
影響を及ぼす	affect
影響を及ぼす	impact
エイジング	aging
映像	image
永続	continuity of existence
永続的な	perpetual
永続的な	standing
永続的な支払い	perpetuity
営利	profit making
営利企業	commercial enterprise
営利事業体	revenue-producing enterprise
営利性	profitability
鋭利な刃物	cutting edge
役務	service
エクイップメント	equipment
エクイティ	equity
エクイティ・ファイナンス	equity financing
エクスポージャー	exposure
エグゼクティブ	executive
1988年通商法のエクソン・フロリオ条項	Exon-Florio provision of the 1988 trade law
閲覧	access
閲覧	review
閲覧する	access
エネルギー	power
エラー	error
選ぶ	elect
選ぶ	name
選ぶ	tap
エリサ法	Employee Retirement Income Security Act
エリサ法	ERISA
得る	earn
得る	gain
得る	profit
得る	profit
エレメント	element
円	yen
演繹	deduction
延期	deferral
延期された	deferred
延期する	delay
縁故者割当て	private allocation
縁故募集	private offering
演算記号	operator
演算子	operator
エンジェル	angel
エンジニアリング	engineering
援助	cooperation
援助	support
援助する	support
エンジン	engine
円相場	yen
延滞	arrears
延滞	delinquency
延滞金	arrears
延滞金	penalty
延滞金利	penalty rate
延滞債権	arrears on loan repayments
延滞債権	overdue loan
延滞の	overdue
延滞利子	overdue interest
円建て利益	yen-denominated profits
円建て利益	yen-denominated profits
延長	extension
延長	raising
延長した	extended
延長する	extend
エンド・ユーザー	end user
円ドル相場	yen-dollar exchange rate

お

追い上げの	catch-up
追い風	windfall
追い風になる	favorable
…に追いつかない	lag
負う	carry
負う	incur
奥義	knowhow [know-how]
黄金株	golden share
黄金株の譲渡	transfer of golden shares
欧州証券規制委員会	CESR
欧州中央銀行	ECB
欧州中央銀行	European Central Bank
欧州中銀	ECB
欧州中銀	European Central Bank
旺盛な	massive
応募する	sign up
応募入札	tender
応用	application
応用システム	application
応用する	apply
応用ソフト	application
終える	close
大がかりな	massive
大型の	heavy
大型の	large
大型の	massive
大型の	significant
大型の	substantial
大株主	major shareholder
大きい	massive
大きい取り分	lion's share
大きく上回る	soar
大きくする	widen
大きくなる	widen
…の大きさを変える	resize
大きな	high
大きな	significant
大きな影響	material effect
大きな影響力のある	material
オークション	auction
オークションサイト	auction site
オークション事業	auction business
オークション出品物	auction item
オークション・ビジネス	auction business
大口株主	major shareholder
大口投資家	bloc investor
オーダー	order
…の大台	mark
大手企業	leading company
大手の	large
オーナー	owner
大波	surge
大幅な	good
大幅な	large
大幅な	massive
大幅な	robust
大幅な	sharp
大幅な	significant
大幅な	substantial
大幅に	significantly
置く	locate
置く	position
遅らせる	defer
遅らせる	delay
送り返された	returned
送り状	invoice
送り状価格の引下げ	deduction
遅れ	disadvantage
…を怠る	fail
行う	deliver
行う	effect
行う	run
行われる	run
抑える	contain
抑える	control
抑える	withhold
押し上げ	boost
押し上げる	boost
押し上げる	increase
押し上げる	inflate
押し下げる	reduce
押し下げる	squeeze
押し付ける	impose
押し寄せる	surge
オゾン層破壊	ozone depletion
落ち込み	dilution
落ち込み	drop
落ち込み	plunge
落ち込み	slump
落ち込む	drop
落ち込んだ	weak
お得意	client
おとり価格設定	leader pricing
おとり商品	leader

和英		
おとり商品	loss leader	
おとり商品政策	leader merchandising	
同じ立場・地位にある人	counterpart	
オピニオン	opinion	
オファー	offer	
オファー	proposal	
オフィサー	officer	
オフィス	office	
オプション	option	
オプション取引	option	
オプション料	premium	
オフ・バランス	off-balance-sheet	
オフ・バランス債務	off-balance sheet liability	
オフ・バランスシート	off-balance-sheet	
オフ・バランスシート取引	off-balance-sheet transaction	
オフバランスシート取引	off-balance-sheet treatment	
オフ・バランス取引	off-balance-sheet transaction	
オフバランスの偶発債務	off-balance-sheet contingencies	
オペ	operation	
オペレーション	operation	
オペレータ	operator	
オペレーティング・リース	operating lease	
覚書	minutes	
覚書	note	
重い	heavy	
思いがけない	fortuitous	
思いがけない幸運	windfall	
思いがけない利益	windfall	
思い出す	recall	
思いつき	idea	
主に	predominantly	
主に	principally	
重荷	burden	
思わぬ利益	windfall	
親会社	controlling company	
親会社	parent	
親会社	parent company	
親会社	parent company	
親会社	parent undertaking	
親会社から子会社への販売	downstream	
親会社持ち分	consolidated equity	
親子会社間の	intercompany	
及ぼす	exercise	
織り込む	reflect	
卸売り業者	distributor	
…を負わせる	entail	
負わせる	impose	
終値	close	
終値	closing	
終値	closing price	

終値	CR	
終わりの	terminal	
恩恵を受ける	benefit	
温室効果ガスの排出量	greenhouse gas emissions	
温室効果ガス排出量	greenhouse gas emissions	
オンライン	online [on-line]	
オンライン広告	online advertising	
オンライン式	online [on-line]	

か

課	department	
…界	community	
…界	public	
会	meeting	
買い上げる	buy out	
買入れ	purchase	
買入れ価格	call price	
買入価格	purchase price	
買入れ債務	account payable	
買入償却	redemption by purchase	
買入のれん	purchase goodwill	
会員	user	
外貨	foreign currency	
外貨	foreign exchange	
外貨	forex	
海外売上高	overseas sales	
海外からの	overseas	
海外子会社	foreign subsidiary	
開会式	inauguration ceremony	
海外事業	international operations	
海外事業活動	international operations	
海外収益	overseas earnings	
海外生産	offshore production	
海外調達	outsourcing	
海外の	foreign	
海外の	overseas	
海外への	overseas	
海外向けの	overseas	
買替え	replacement purchase	
外貨換算	currency translation	
外貨換算	foreign currency translation	
外貨換算差額	foreign currency translation	
外貨換算修正	accumulated foreign currency translation adjustments	
外貨換算修正損益	effects of foreign currency translation adjustments	
外貨換算調整勘定	currency translation adjustment	
外貨換算率	conversion rate [ratio]	
改革	change	
改革	improvement	

改革	innovation	
改革	reform	
改革	reorganization	
改革	restructuring	
改革	transformation	
改革する	improve	
改革する	reform	
改革する	reorganize	
買掛金	account payable	
買掛金	account-payable-trade	
買掛金	payable	
外貨建て取引	foreign currency transaction	
外観	form	
外観	showing	
概観	overview	
会議	assembly	
会議	board	
会議	meeting	
会議室	boardroom	
開業	inception	
開業	practice	
開業	start-up	
概況	overview	
開業式	inauguration ceremony	
開業準備	start-up	
開業する	locate	
概況説明	briefing	
開業費	start-up costs	
会議録	proceedings	
解禁する	liberalize	
…の会計	accounting for …	
…会計	accounting for …	
会計	account	
会計	accounting	
外形	form	
会計役	treasurer	
会計係	treasurer	
会計学	accounting	
会計慣行	accounting practice	
会計監査	accounting audit	
会計監査	auditing	
会計監査役	controller	
会計期間	accounting period	
会計期間	business year	
会計期間	fiscal year	
会計期間	period	
会計期間の概念	time period concept	
会計期間の公準	periodicity concept	
会計基準	accounting principle	
会計基準	accounting rule	
会計基準	accounting standards	
会計基準	GAAP	
会計基準の変更	accounting change	
会計規則	accounting rule	
会計規程(集)	accounting manual	
会計記録	accounts	

会計研究公報	ARB	外形標準課税	pro forma standard tax	解散する	split
会計検査	audit	会計便覧	accounting manual	改竄する	falsify
会計検査	auditing	会計簿	book	概算する	approximate
会計検査官	auditor	会計方針	accounting policy	概算する	estimate
会計検査する	audit	会計方法	accounting method	概算値を得る	approximate
会計検査役	controller	会計見積りの変更	accounting change	概算の	estimated
会計原則	accounting principle	会計連続通牒	Accounting Series Release	開始	inception
会計原則	accounting standards			開始	launch
会計原則審議会	APB	解決	arrangement	開始	start-up
会計士	accountant	解決	determination	開示	disclosure
会計システム	accounting system	解決	resolution	外資	foreign firm
会計実体	accounting entity	解決	settlement	開示基準	disclosure standards
会計実務	accounting practice	解決	solution	外資系企業	foreign firm
会計主体	accounting entity	解決策	solution	開始する	launch
会計上の	fiscal	解決手段	solution	開示する	disclose
会計上の変更	accounting change	解決する	determine	開示する	present
会計上の利益	accounting profit	解決する	settle	開示する	reveal
会計上の利益	accounting profit	解決法	solution	買占め	buyout
会計上の利益	book income	買い気配	bid	買い占める	buy out
…の会計処理	accounting for ...	解雇	layoff	買い占める	buy up
会計処理	accounting	解雇	restructuring	会社	business
会計処理	accounting practice	外国会社	alien corporation	会社	company
会計処理基準	accounting principle	外国為替	foreign exchange	会社	concern
会計処理する	account for ...	外国為替	forex	会社	corporation
会計処理する	book	外国為替	FX	会社	enterprise
会計処理の変更	accounting change	外国為替契約	foreign currency exchange contract	会社	firm
会計処理の変更	change in accounting	外国為替証拠金取引	FX margin trading	会社	incorporation
会計処理の方法	accounting principle	外国為替相場	exchange rate	会社	institution
会計処理方法	accounting	外国為替取引	foreign exchange	会社	operator
会計処理方法	accounting method	外国為替取引	foreign exchange trading	会社	organization
会計処理方法の変更	accounting change	外国為替予約	foreign currency exchange contract	会社	undertaking
会計制度	accounting system	外国企業	alien corporation	会社	unit
会計責任	accountability	外国企業	foreign firm	会社会計	corporate accounting
会計専門家	accountant	外国子会社	foreign subsidiary	会社からの独立	demerger
会計操作	accounting manipulation	外国人の	alien	会社間の	intercompany
会計組織	accounting system	外国税額控除	deduction of foreign tax	会社管理法	corporate governance
会計担当者	accountant	外国税額控除	double taxation relief	会社業績	corporate performance
会計調査公報	Accounting Research Bulletin	外国税額控除	foreign tax credit	解釈	construction
会計調査公報	ARB	外国通貨	foreign currency	解釈	translation
会計帳簿	book of accounts	外国の	alien	解釈する	construe
会計帳簿	books of account	外国の	foreign	解釈する	translate
会計手続書	accounting manual	外国の	overseas	会社経営	corporate management
会計等式	accounting equation	介護サービス	care service	会社更生	reorganization
会計に関する内部統制	internal accounting control	解散する	lay off	会社更生手続き	Chapter 11
会計年度	accounting period	解散	dissolution	会社再建	reorganization
会計年度	business year	解散	liquidation	会社資産	corporate assets
会計年度	fiscal year	解散	termination	会社設立	incorporation
会計年度	FY	概算	estimate	会社設立構想	founding concept
会計年度	period	概算書	estimate	会社設立趣意書	prospectus of promotion
会計の専門領域	accountancy	解散する	close	会社全体の一般的経費	general corporate expenses
外形標準課税	dual corporate tax system	解散する	dissolve	会社定款	corporate charter
		解散する	liquidate	会社の	corporate
				会社の沿革と組織	background and history of the company
				会社の管理・運営	corporate governance
				会社分割	demerger
				会社分割	spinoff [spin-off]

会社報告書	corporate report
会社目標	corporate goal
会社役員	corporate officer
会社役員	executive
会社役員	officer
会社を経営する	head
会社を設立する	float
会社を分割する	spin off
回収	collection
回収	payoff
回収	payout
回収	recovery
回収	withdrawal
改修	alteration
回収期間	payable period
回収基準	collection basis
改修工事	improvement
回収する	collect
回収する	recall
回収する	recover
回収する	retire
回収する	service
回収する	withdraw
回収遅延残高	delinquent balances
回収遅滞受取勘定	delinquent account receivable
回収費	collection expense [cost]
回収不能金	uncollectibles
回収不能の	uncollectible
回収不能見込み額	allowance for uncollectible receivable
解除	cancelation [cancellation]
解除	termination
解消	dissolution
解消する	absorb
解消する	dissolve
解消する	lay off
解消する	offset
解消する	reduce
解職権	recall
解職する	recall
解除条件付き利益	determinable interest
解除する	cancel
解除する	dissolve
改正	change
改正	reform
改正	revision
改正する	reform
改正する	revise
開設する	locate
開設する	open
開設する	set up
回線	line
改善	enhancement
改善	improvement
改善	pickup [pick-up]
改善	redeployment
改善	reform
改善	turnaround
改善する	develop
改善する	enhance
改善する	improve
改善する	pick up
改善する	redeploy
改善する	reform
改善する	strengthen
改善する	turn around
回線接続中	online [on-line]
回線網	network
改組	reorganization
回想	recall
改造	alteration
改造	reorganization
回想する	recall
改造する	convert
改造する	reorganize
改造する	revamp
改組する	reorganize
海損	average
解体	dissolution
解体する	dissolve
快諾	goodwill
会談	talks
改築	alteration
外注	outsourcing
外注加工費	expense arising from outside manufacture
外注する	outsource
買い注文	bid
買い注文	buy order
会長	chairman
会長	president
開通式	inauguration ceremony
買付け	acquisition
買付け	buyout
買付け	purchase
買付け価格	offer price
買付け価格	purchase price
買付け対象会社	offeree company
買い付ける	purchase
買いつなぎ	hedge-buying
買いつなぎして損失を防ぐ	hedge
買い手	purchaser
改訂	restatement
改訂	revision
改定する	revise
改訂する	revamp
改訂する	revise
回転	turnover
回転クレジット	revolving credit
回転資金	revolving fund
回転資金	revolving fund
回転信用	revolving credit
回転信用供与枠	revolving credit facility
回転信用状	revolving credit
回転融資契約	revolving loan agreement
回転融資枠	revolving credit facility
回転率	turnover
回転率	turnover ratio
会頭	president
解答	resolution
買い唱え	bid
ガイドライン	guideline
買取り	acquisition
買取り	buyback
買取り	buyout
買取り	purchase
買取り	purchasing
買取り価格	offer price
買取り価格	purchase price
買取り権付きリース	hire purchase
買取り選択権付きリース	hire purchase
買取り選択権付きリース契約	hire purchase contract
買取り選択権付きリース取引	hire purchase transaction
買取り手	acquirer
買取り人	purchaser
買い取る	buy
買い取る	buy back
買い取る	buy out
買い取る	buy up
買い取る	purchase
買い取る	take over
買い取ることができる	negotiable
介入操作	operation
解任権	recall
解任する	recall
解任請求	recall
買い主	purchaser
概念	concept
概念	idea
開発	development
開発	engineering
開発	innovation
開発会社	developer
開発業者	developer
開発契約	lease
開発事業	project
開発する	create
開発する	develop
開発する	tap
開発抑止政策	zero growth
会費	fee
回避する	lay off
外部委託	outsourcing
外部委託する	outsource
外部金融	external financing [funding]
回復	improvement
回復	pickup [pick-up]
回復	rally
回復	recovery
回復	rehabilitation
回復	revitalization

回復 revival	解約する revoke	価格先導者 price leader
回復する rally	解約できない noncancelable [noncancellable]	価格先導制 price leadership
回復する rebuild		価格帯 price range
回復する recover	解約手数料 surrender charge	価格体系 price structure
回復する resume	解約不能の noncancelable [noncancellable]	価格低下 price reduction
回復する revive		価格転嫁力 shifting power to price
回復する turn around	解約不能のオペレーティング・リース noncancelable operating lease	
回復不能減価 permanent impairment in value		価格の引下げ price reduction
		価格引下げ price cut
回復不能な unrecoverable	解約不能リース noncancelable lease	価格引下げ競争 price competition
外部資金 funds from external sources		
	概要 overview	価格変動 price movement
外部資金の調達 external financing [funding]	概要 profile	価格変動性 price volatility
	概要 scheme	価格変動率 volatility
外部資源の活用 outsourcing	概要 summary	価格保全 price protection
外部資源を活用する outsource	概要報告 briefing	価格を決める price
外部調達資金 external financing [funding]	買い呼び値 bid	価格を提示する quote
	概略的な general	かかる cost
外部取締役 outside director	概略の general	…に係わる applicable to ...
外部の人々が所有する株式 capital stock	改良 enhancement	カギ bottom line
	改良 improvement	書換え renewal
外部発行済み issued and outstanding	改良 reform	書換え transfer
	改良工事 improvement	書換え継続 renewal
外部負債比率 debt equity ratio	改良する develop	書き換える transfer
改変 alteration	改良する improve	書き記す keep
改編 reorganization	改良する reform	書き添える append
改編する restructure	改良する revamp	書留にする register
会報 proceedings	改良費 betterment expense	下級の lower
解放 release	改良費 improvement	…にかぎり subject to ...
回報 newsletter	下位劣後債 junior subordinated debenture	核 core
開放 liberalization		書く write
開放型総合保険料方式 open aggregate cost method	回線網 network	額 amount
	買う buy	格上げ upgrade
解放する release	返す return	格上げ upgrading
開放する liberalize	変える convert	格上げする upgrade
開放する open	変える shift	架空の fictious
外務員 representative	変える turn around	格差 difference
解明 resolution	…を抱えて saddled with ...	格差 disparity
買い持ち bull position	価格 figure	格下げ downgrade
買い持ち long position	価格 price	格下げ rating cuts
買い持ち overbought position	価額 value	格下げする downgrade
買戻し buyback	価額 worth	拡散指数 DI
買戻し repurchase	価格圧力 pressure on pricing	拡散指数 diffusion index
買戻し価格 call price	価格圧力 pricing pressure	学識 education
買戻し株式 repurchased share	価格維持 price fixing	確実性 certainty
買戻しできる redeemable	価格維持 price maintenance	確実性 reliability
買い戻す buy back	価格競争 price competition	確実性等価 certainty equivalent
買い戻す redeem	価格競争力 price competition	確実性等価収益率 certainty equivalent return
買い戻す repurchase	価格競争力 price competitiveness	
解約 cancelation [cancellation]	価格形成する price	確実な reliable
解約 redemption	価格決定 pricing decision	拡充する beef up
解約 termination	価格決定方針 pricing policy	拡充する boost
解約 withdrawal	価格決定モデル pricing model	各種の miscellaneous
解約可能な cancelable [cancellable]	価格支配力 pricing power	核心 core
	価格収益 price returns	革新 advance
解約可能リース cancelable lease	価格自由化 price liberalization	革新 innovation
解約可能リース契約 cancellable lease	価格条件 basis of price	革新 reform
	価格上昇 price increase	革新性 innovation
解約金 cancelation money	価格設定期間 pricing period	核心の core
解約する cancel	価格戦争 price war	革新的な groundbreaking

革新的な	innovative
…の拡大	increased
拡大	addition
拡大	expansion
拡大	extension
拡大	gain
拡大	improvement
拡大	increase
拡大	pickup [pick-up]
拡大	rise
拡大幹事手数料	expanded management fee
拡大した	extended
拡大信用供与	extended fund facility
拡大する	boost
拡大する	diversify
拡大する	extend
拡大する	grow
拡大する	improve
拡大する	increase
拡大する	rise
拡大する	strengthen
拡大する	widen
拡張	enhancement
拡張	expansion
拡張	extension
学長	president
拡張工事	extension
拡張した	extended
拡張する	extend
拡張担保	extended coverage
拡張の財務報告言語	XBRL
格付け	credit rating
格付け	rating
格付け会社	rating agency
格付け会社	rating firm
格付け機関	rating agency
格付け見解	credit opinion
格付け評価	credit rating
格付けを引き上げる	upgrade
格付けを引き下げる	downgrade
確定	determination
確定給付企業年金	defined benefit pension plan
確定給付債務	vested benefit obligation
確定給付制度	defined benefit plan
確定給付年金	defined benefit scheme
確定給付年金制度	defined benefit pension plan
確定給付年金制度	defined benefit plan
確定拠出型企業年金制度	defined-contribution corporate pension plan
確定拠出型年金	defined contribution pension
確定拠出型年金制度	401(k)-style pension scheme
確定拠出型年金制度	defined contribution pension plan
確定拠出型年金制度	defined contribution pension scheme
確定拠出制度	defined contribution plan
確定拠出制度	defined contribution plan
確定拠出年金	defined contribution pension
確定拠出年金制度	defined contribution pension scheme
確定拠出年金制度	defined-contribution annuity scheme
確定契約	firm commitment
確定債務	determinable liability
確定した	final
確定した	fixed
確定した	vested
確定する	determine
確定的な	final
確定できる	determinable
確定配当	guaranteed dividend
確定引受け	firm underwriting
確定日後一覧払い手形	bill payable at sight after a fixed period
確定利付き社債	SB
確定利付き社債	straight bond
確定利付き証券	fixed income security
確定利回り	guaranteed payback
獲得	collection
獲得	procurement
獲得	purchase
獲得主体	acquiring entity
獲得する	achieve
獲得する	chalk up
獲得する	collect
獲得する	earn
獲得する	gain
獲得する	generate
獲得する	net
獲得する	obtain
獲得する	procure
獲得する	secure
獲得する	take out
獲得する	take over
核となる	core
確認書	letter
確保する	achieve
確保する	rack up
確保する	retain
確保する	secure
額面	face
額面	face amount
額面	face amount
額面	face value
額面	par value
額面	principal amount
額面価格	face value
額面価格	par value
額面価額	face amount
額面価額	face value
額面価額	principal
額面価額	principal amount
額面額	par value
額面株	stock with par value
額面株式	par value stock
額面株式	par-value capital stock
額面株式払込み剰余金	paid-in capital in excess of par
額面金額	face amount
額面金額	nominal amount
額面超過	above par
額面超過額	premium
額面割れ投信	under-par value investment trust
確約	pledge
確約する	commit
確約する	guarantee
確約する	pledge
確立する	establish
隠れ借金	latent debts
隠れた	latent
隠れた欠陥	latent defect
家計	budget
家計部門	household sector
掛売り	charge sales
掛売り	credit sales
掛売りの顧客	charge customer
掛け金	contribution
掛金	annuity
掛金建て制度	defined contribution plan
可決する	adopt
掛けつなぎする	hedge
掛けつなぎ売買	hedge
掛けつなぐ	hedge
掛け値のない	net
かけ引き	tactics
かける	cover
かご	basket
過誤	error
加工	conversion
加工	manufacturing
加工	processing
加工する	convert
加工品	finished goods
加工品	finished product
加工品	manufactured goods
過去勤務	past service
過去勤務	prior service
過去勤務原価	prior service cost
過去勤務債務	past service liability
過去勤務債務	prior service cost
過去勤務債務	prior service liability
過去勤務費用	past service cost
過去勤務費用	prior pension cost

過去勤務費用	prior service cost
過去勤務費用	prior service pension cost
過去最高	new high
過去最高	record
過去最高の	record
過去最大	record
過去にさかのぼる	retroactive
過去の	historical
過去の事業年度	previous years
過去の事業年度	prior period
過去の事業年度	prior years
傘	umbrella
かさ上げする	inflate
加算	addition
加算：未記入の預け入れ	ADD: Deposit in transit
加算戻し	add-back
加算戻しをする	add back
加算―当期利益	ADD-Net income
瑕疵	defect
貸方	credit
貸方	creditor
貸方残高	credit balances
貸方に記入する	credit
貸金	credit
貸金回収	recall of advance
貸金業者	lender
貸し渋り	credit crunch
貸し渋り	restricted lending
貸倒れ	bad debt
貸倒れ	bad loan
貸倒れ	credit loss
貸倒れ	default
貸倒れ	loan loss
貸倒れ	nonperforming loan
貸倒れ	problem loans
貸倒れ額	credit loss
貸倒れ実績率	loan loss ratio
貸倒れ準備金	loan loss reserves
貸倒れ償却	bad debt expense
貸倒れ償却	charge-off [charge-off]
貸倒れ償却	investor charge-off
貸倒れ償却	write-off
貸倒れ損失	account write-offs
貸倒れ損失	bad debt
貸倒れ損失	bad debt expense
貸倒れ損失	loan loss
貸倒れ損失	write-off
貸倒れ損失額	loan loss charge
貸倒れ損失額	loan losses
貸倒れ損失実績	loss experience
貸倒れ引当金	allowance for credit losses
貸倒れ引当金	allowance for uncollectible accounts
貸倒れ引当金	loan loss charge
貸倒れ引当金	loan loss provisions
貸倒れ引当金	loan loss reserves
貸倒れ引当金	provision for credit losses
貸倒れ引当金	provision for doubtful debts
貸倒れ引当金繰入れ額	loan loss provisioning
貸倒れ引当金控除	less allowance for doubtful items
貸倒れ引当金控除後	net of reserve for doubtful accounts
貸倒れ引当金の戻り益	reversal of bad-debt reserve
貸倒れ引当金を計上する	wtite down
貸倒れ費用	bad debt expense
貸倒れ予想額	credit loss
貸出	lending
貸出	loan
貸出回収	loan recall
貸出期間中の上限金利	life-of-loan cap
貸出規制	lending regulation
貸出規制	lending restrictions
貸出金の劣化	impaired loan
貸出金利	lending interest rate
貸出金利	lending rate
貸出金利	loan interest rate
貸出金利	loan rate
貸出金利の上限	maximum lending rate
貸出限度	lending limit
貸出限度（額）	credit line
貸出限度額	credit limit
貸出限度額	line of credit
貸出債権	finance receivables
貸出債権	loan
貸出先	borrower
貸出残高	finance receivables
貸出残高	loan portfolio
貸出資金	loan funds
貸出資産	loan assets
貸出約定	loan commitments
貸出枠未実行残高	unused portions of commitments
貸し出す	lease
貸し出す	loan
過失	commission
過失	defect
貸付け	lending
貸付け	loan
貸付け	loan facility
貸付金	advances receivable
貸付金	indebtedness
貸付金	loan
貸付金の返還請求	call
貸付け限度（額）	credit line
貸付け先	borrower
貸付け資金	loanable fund
貸付け信託	loan trust
貸付け手数料	loan origination fees
貸付け利子	loan interest
貸し付ける	finance
貸し付ける	loan
貸し手	lender
貸し手	lessor
貸し主	lessor
貸主	creditor
貸主	lender
加重平均	arithmetic weighted average
加重平均	weighted average
加重平均価格	weighted average price
加重平均株式数	weighted average share
加重平均原価	weighted average cost
加重平均資本コスト	WACC
加重平均総発行株式数	number of weighted average shares outstanding
加重平均法	weighted average method
加重平均利回り	compound yield based on weighted average
加重平均ローン経過期間	weighted average loan age
加重平均割引率	weighted average discount rate
過剰	excess
過剰	surplus
過少記載	underreporting
過剰在庫	excess stock
過小資本税制	thin capitalization taxation
過剰就業	over-employment
過少申告	underreporting
過少申告加算税	negligence tax
過少申告する	underreport
過剰設備	excess capacity
過剰融資	excessive lending
過剰利得	windfall
過剰利得税	windfall profits tax
過剰流動性	excess liquidity
可処分個人所得	disposable personal income
可処分所得	disposable income
可処分利益	disposable profit
…を課す	entail
課す	impose
カスタマー・サービス	customer service
課する	charge
課税	assessment
課税	taxation
課税…	taxable
課税扱いとなる	chargeable
課税価額	assessed value
課税金	charge
課税軽減額	tax benefit

課税されない	tax-exempt
課税所得	taxable income
課税する	impose
課税対象となる	taxable
課税できる	taxable
課税の対象となる	chargeable
課税標準	base of taxation
課税標準	basis of assessment
課税負担手数料	tax absorption fee
課税前損失	pretax loss
課税前利益	pretax profit
課税率	tax rate
稼ぐ	earn
仮設の	fictious
画像	image
仮想現実社会	virtual community
仮想商店街	online shopping mall
仮想商店街の運営会社	Internet shopping mall operator
仮想生産	virtual manufacturing
下層の	lower
加速原価回収制度	accelerated cost recovery system
加速原価回収制度	ACRS
加速原価回収法	ACRS
加速減価償却	accelerated amortization
加速減価償却	accelerated depreciation
加速させる	accelerate
加速償却	accelerated amortization
加速償却	accelerated depreciation
加速償却制度	accelerated cost recovery system
加速償却制度	ACRS
加速償却法	accelerated cost recovery system
加速償却法	accelerated method
加速償却法	ACRS
加速する	accelerate
型	model
課題	challenge
課題	needs
課題	problem
過大計上	overstatement
過大な	undue
過大評価	overstatement
過大評価する	overvalue
過大表示	overstatement
型押し	tooling
肩代わり	assumption
肩代わりする	assume
肩代わりする	take over
型式	model
型式変更	model change
…の形で所有されている	-owned
片方	counterpart
価値	value

価値	worth
価値が下がる	depreciate
価値工学	value engineering
価値工学	value engineering
価値工学	VE
価値重視の経営	value-oriented management
価値生産性	value productivity
価値低下	depreciation
価値のある産物	wealth
価値の下落	impairment
活気	activity
活気づかせる	boost
活気づかせる	buoy
活気づけ	boost
画期的な	innovative
画期的な新製品	innovation
活況	activity
活況	strength
活況の	robust
…の合算	combined
合算	footing
合算課税	unitary tax
合算課税	unitary taxation
合算した	combined
合算した数値	combined amount
合算数値	combined amount
合算する	average
活性化	revitalization
…に合致する	conform to [with] …
活動	action
活動	activity
活動	conduct
活動	effort
活動	life
活動	movement
活動	operation
活動期間	life
活動基準管理	ABM
活動基準管理	activity based management
活動基準原価管理	activity based costing
活動基準原価計算	ABC
活動基準原価計算	activity based costing
活動度	activity
活動範囲	activity
活発化	pickup [pick-up]
活発な	brisk
活発な	heavy
活発な	high
活発な	robust
活発になる	intensify
割賦金	installment [instalment]
割賦償還	amortization
割賦償還する	amortize
割賦適用業務	application
割賦払い	installment [instalment]
割賦ローン	hire purchase lending

合併	amalgamation
合併	combination
合併	incorporation
合併	merger
合併	tie-up
合併・買収	M & A
合併財務諸表	consolidated financial statements
合併させる	affiliate
合併させる	incorporate
合併資本	joint capital
合併剰余金	surplus from consolidation and merger
合併する	affiliate
合併する	consolidate
合併する	merge
合併損益計算書	combined income statement
合併貸借対照表	combined balance sheet
活用	use
活用する	capitalize on
活用する	use
仮定	assumption
過程	process
仮定する	assume
仮定の	pro forma [proforma]
カテゴリー	category
家電製品	consumer electronics
過度	excess
過当競争	excessive [excess] competition
稼働する	run
下等の	lower
稼動率	percent of capacity use
過渡期	transition
稼得資本	earned capital
稼得する	earn
過度の	undue
かなりの	good
かなりの	healthy
かなりの	significant
かなりの規模の	substantial
加入	access
加入	participation
加入させる	affiliate
加入者	affiliate
加入者	customer
加入者	participant
加入者	subscriber
加入者	user
加入する	access
加入する	affiliate
加入する	enter
加入する	participate
加入する	take out
加入年齢方式	entry age cost method
加入年齢方式	entry cost method
金	money

金を払って退職させること	buy-out
金を払って引き取らせること	buy-out
過年度	earlier years
過年度	previous year
過年度	previous years
過年度	prior period
過年度	prior period
過年度	prior periods
過年度	prior year
過年度	prior years
過年度修正	accounting adjustment of prior periods
過年度修正	prior period adjustment
過年度修正	prior year adjustment
可能性	opportunity
可能性	potential
可能性	prospects
可能性	scope
可能性がある	potential
カバーする	offset
ガバナンス	governance
カバレッジ	coverage
過半数	majority
過半数	plurality
過半数以下の出資	minority interest
過半数株式	majority stake
過半数所有会社	majority owned company
過半数所有子会社	majority owned subsidiary
株	interest
株	issue
株	sector
株	share
株	stake
株	stock
株価	share price
株価	stock price
株価指数	stock index
株価指数オプション	stock index option
株価指数先物	stock index futures
株価収益率	PER
株価収益率	per-share earning ratio
株価収益率	price earnings ratio
株価純資産倍率	PBR
株価純資産倍率	price book-value ratio
株価純資産倍率	price book-value ratio
株価純資産倍率	price-to-book value
株価上昇	equity appreciation
株価スワップ	equity swap
株価対策	stock policy
株価評価	stock valuation
株券	share
株券	stock certificate
株式	capital stock
株式	equity
株式	share
株式	stake
株式	stock
株式委託売買手数料	brokerage commission
株式オプション	stock option
株式買入れ枠	stock-buying limit
株式買受権	stock option
株式会社	corporation
株式会社	joint stock company
株式会社	stock company
株式会社	stock corporation
株式会社の	incorporated
株式会社の資本金	share capital
株式会社の役員	corporate officer
株式買取り	stock buyout [buy-out]
株式買取り権付き社債	bond with stock purchase warrant
株式買取り請求権	warrant
株式買戻し	stock repurchase
株式金融増資	equity financing
株式公開	going public
株式公開	initial public offering
株式公開	IPO
株式公開	public offering
株式公開	public ownership
株式公開	public ownership
株式公開	public shareholding
株式公開	stock offering
株式公開会社	public enterprise
株式公開会社	public enterprise
株式公開買付け	bid
株式公開買付け	public tender offer
株式公開買付け	public tender period
株式公開買付け	takeover bid
株式公開買付け	tender offer
株式公開買付け	TOB
株式公開買付けによる企業買収	takeover bid
株式公開企業	public company
株式公開企業	public corporation
株式公開企業	publicly held company
株式公開企業	publicly owned company
株式公開企業	publicly owned company [corporation]
株式公開する	float
株式交換	equity swap
株式交換	equity swap
株式交換	share exchange
株式交換	share swap
株式交換	stock exchange
株式交換	stock swap
株式交換契約	equity swap agreement
株式交換契約	equity swap contract
株式交換公開買付け	stock exchange offer
株式交換取引	equity swap deal
株式交換取引	stock swap deal
株式交換による合併	stock-for-stock merger
株式交換による買収	share-swap acquisition
株式交換の課税繰延べ	tax-deferred share exchanges
株式交換比率	share exchange rate
株式交換比率	stock exchange ratio [rate]
株式交換比率	stock-for-stock exchange rate
株式購入権制度	stock purchase plan
株式購入制度	stock purchase plan
株式購入選択権	stock option
株式購入選択権制度	stock purchase plan
株式公募	public offering
株式公募	public stock offering
株式公募	stock offering
株式先物	stock futures
株式市況	bourse
株式市場	stock market
株式資本	capital stock
株式資本	equity capital
株式資本	share capital
株式資本	share capital
株式資本	stock
株式資本化	capitalization
株式資本金	capital stock
株式資本金	share capital
株式事務	administration of shares
株式取得	equity purchase
株式取得	equity purchase
株式取得	stock [share] acquisition
株式償還	stock redemption
株式上場	public listing
株式上場	stock offering
株式上場証券取引所	stock listings
株式譲渡	stock transfer
株式賞与制度	stock bonus plan
株式所有	equity ownership
株式所有	share ownership
株式所有	shareholding
株式所有者	stock owner
株式数	number of shares
株式数	number of shares of stock
株式数の増加	additional share
株式スワップ	equity swap
株式増価差額請求権	stock appre-

ciation right
株式総合利回り　stock returns
株式相場　bourse
株式ダウ平均　Dow Jones average [Average]
株式店頭市場　over-the-counter stock market
株式等関連損失　stock-related losses
株式騰貴権　stock appreciation right
株式投資　equity investment
株式投資　equity portfolio
株式投資　equity purchase
株式投資家　equity investor
株式投資効率　stock investment efficiency
株式投資収益率　ROE
株式登録機関　registrar
株式登録機関　registrar for stock
株式取引　stock dealing
株式取引　stock transaction
株式取引所　stock exchange
株式の買戻し　equity repurchase
株式の買戻し　share buyback
株式の買戻し　stock buyback
株式の公開公募　initial public offering
株式の交換比率　swap ratio
株式の時価総額　market capitalization
株式の自己買付け　self tender
株式の譲渡手続きと代金の払込み手続きの同時履行　closing
株式の新規公開　going public
株式の直接募集　private offering
株式の配当利回り　stock dividend yield
株式の発行　issuance of capital [stock]
株式の発行可能枠　share issue limit
株式の非公開化　going private
株式の1株当たり額面　par value of the stock
株式の評価損　stock evaluation losses
株式の分割・併合　stock split
株式の無償交付　free share distribution
株式の名義書換え　share transfer
株式の名義書換え停止日　stock record date
株式売却　stock sales
株式売却で調達した資金　funds gained from the sale of shares
株式配当　allotment
株式配当　stock dividend
株式配当課税　stock dividend tax
株式売買　stock exchange
株式売買益　capital gain

株式派生商品　equity derivatives
株式発行　equity offering
株式発行　share sale
株式発行　stock offering
株式発行可能枠　authorized capital
株式発行差金　premium on share stock
株式発行高　outstanding capital stock
株式発行費用　commission and expenses on capital shares
株式発行枠　share issue limit
株式払込み剰余金　additional paid-in capital
株式引受権　share warrant
株式引受手数料　commission
株式非公開会社　private company
株式非公開会社　privately held company
株式非公開企業　privately owned company
株式非公開の　privately held
株式評価益権　SAR
株式評価益権　stock appreciation right
株式評価受益権　SAR
株式評価受益権　stock appreciation right
株式評価損　equity write-offs
株式評価損　stock appraisal losses
株式ファンド　equity fund
株式含み益　latent stock gains
株式含み益　unrealized equity profits
株式含み損　equity holding losses
株式分割　reverse split
株式分割　share split
株式分割　share split-up
株式分割　split
株式分割　split-up of stock
株式分割　stock split
株式分割　stock split-up
株式併合　reverse split
株式併合　reverse stock split
株式併合　share split-down
株式併合　stock consolidation
株式併合　stock split-down
株式報奨制度　stock award plan
株式報奨制度　stock compensation plan
株式保有　equity holding
株式保有　shareholding
株式保有　stock holding
株式保有　stockholding
株式保有率　shareholding
株式未公開企業　privately held company
株式名義書換え　stock transfer
株式名義の書換えを停止する

close the [one's] books
株式名簿　transfer book
株式持ち合い　crossholding [cross-holding]
株式持ち合い　reciprocal share holding
株式持ち分　equity interest
株式持ち分　equity stake
株式持ち分　stake
株式持ち分　stock equity
株式持ち分　stock interest
株式利回り　stock yield
株式割当て　allocation of shares
株式割当て　share allotment
株式割当て通知書　letter of allotment
株式を公開していない　privately held
株式を非公開にすること　going private
株取引　stock deal
株取引　stock transaction
株主　owner
株主　shareholder
株主　shareholder of record
株主　shareowner
株主　stakeholder
株主　stockholder
株主各位　Dear Shareowner
株主貸付け金　loans to stockholders
株主価値　shareholders' value
株主価値の最大化　maximization of shareholder values
株主サービス　shareowner services
株主資本　equity capital
株主資本　invested capital
株主資本　ownership capital
株主資本　shareholders funds
株主資本　shareholders' equity
株主資本　stockholders' equity
株主資本回転率　sales to net worth
株主資本回転率　turnover of net worth
株主資本基盤　equity base
株主資本比率　capital-to-asset ratio
株主資本比率　net worth ratio
株主資本負債比率　gearing ratio
株主資本利益率　return on equity
株主資本利益率　return on net worth
株主資本利益率　return on stockholders' [shareholders'] equity
株主資本利益率　ROE
株主総会　general meeting
株主総会　shareholders meeting
株主総会決議　decision of a general meeting of stockholders
株主提案　shareholder proposal

株主投票	shareholder vote
株主の出資資本	equity capital
株主の皆様へ	Dear Shareowner
株主の利益	benefits of shareholders
株主配当再投資	dividend reinvestment
株主配当再配当・株式購入制度	shareholder dividend reinvestment and stock purchase plan
株主平等	shareholder equality
株主への利益還元	return of profits to shareholders
株主名簿	list of shareholders
株主名簿	shareholders list
株主名簿	stock transfer book
株主名簿上の株主	shareholder of record
株主名簿上の株主	stockholder of record
株主名簿登録機関	registrar
株主持ち分	equity capital
株主持ち分	net worth
株主持ち分	shareholders' equity
株主持ち分	stockholders' equity
株主持ち分利益	amount earned for equity
株主持ち分利益率	return on stockholders' [shareholders'] equity
株主優待	shareholders incentives
株主優待制度	shareholders incentives
株主利益	benefits of shareholders
株主割当て	issue to stockholders
株主割当て	rights offering
株主割当て発行	rights issue
株主割当て発行	rights offering
株主割当て発行	rights offering
株主割当て発行増資	rights offering
下部の	lower
株の運用	stock management
株の売買	stock dealing
株の売買	stock transaction
株の名義人	nominee
貨幣	money
貨幣項目	monetary items
貨幣性項目	monetary items
貨幣性資産	monetary assets
貨幣的ベース	monetary base
貨幣の	monetary
下方修正	downward adjustment
下方修正	downward revision
下方修正する	downgrade
下方修正する	slash
紙	paper
上期	first half
上期	first six months
上期	fiscal first half
上期の	first-half
上期の赤字	first-half loss
上期の損失	first-half loss
上期の連結税引き後利益	consolidated first-half net profit
上半期	first half
上半期	first six months
上半期	fiscal first half
上半期	H1
上半期決算	first-half account settlement
上半期損失	first-half loss
上半期の	first-half
上半期の連結純利益	consolidated first-half net profit
上半期の連結税引き後利益	consolidated first-half net profit
加盟する	affiliate
加盟する	enter
画面表示	display
貨物	goods
貨物保険	cargo insurance
空売り	short selling
空押し	blind tooling
借り上げる	lease
借入れ	advance
借入れ	borrowing
借入れ	debt
借入れ	financing
借入れ	leverage
借入れ	loan
借入金	advance
借入金	advances payable
借入金	borrowed money
借入金	borrowing
借入金	debt
借入金	funds borrowed
借入金	indebtedness
借入金	loan
借入金	note payable
借入金残高	outstanding debt
借入金償還	loan redemption
借入金償還引当金	loan redemption reserve
借入金で企業などを買い取る	leverage
借入金で投機をする	leverage
借入金による	leveraged
借入金の返済	debt repayment
借入金返済額	loan principal payments
借入金返済額	repayment of debt
借入金融	debt financing
借入金を利用した	leveraged
借入契約	loan agreement
借入限度額	line of credit
借入限度額	loan values
借入コスト	borrowing cost
借入債務	debt
借入残高	debt outstanding
借入残高	outstanding debt
借入資金による	leveraged
借入資金による企業買収	LBO
借入資金による企業買収	leveraged buyout [buy-out]
借入資本	leverage
借入資本	loan capital
借入需要	borrowing needs
借入需要	demand for loans
借入需要	financing requirements
借入需要	loan demand
借入能力	borrowing power
借入れの証券化	securitized borrowings
借入費用	borrowing cost
借入比率	financial gearing
借入比率	leverage
借入有価証券	borrowed security
借入余力	borrowing potential
借入余力	leverage
借り入れる	borrow
借入枠	line of credit
借入枠中未借入額	line of credit
仮受け金	suspense receipt
借換え	conversion
借換え	prepayment
借換え	refinancing
借換え	refund
借換え	refunding
借換え	rollover
借換え	shifting loan
借換え債の発行	issuance of refunding bonds
借換え債務の事前負担	advance refunding
借換え発行	conversion issue
借換え目的の市場からの資金調達	market access for refinancing
借換え融資	rollover loan
借り換える	refinance
借り換える	refund
借方	debit
借方	debtor
借方	Dr.
借方記入	charge
借方記入通知書	debit memorandum
借方残高	debit balance
借方残高	debtor balance
借方に記入する	charge
借方票	debit note
借り株	borrowed stock
仮決算	provisional settlement of accounts
借りつなぎ	rollover
借り手	borrower
借り手	lessee
借主	debtor
借主	lessee
借主	tenant
仮の	interim

仮の	pro forma [proforma]
仮の	temporary
仮払い金	advance
カリフォルニア州公務員退職年金基金	CalPERS
仮目論見書	preliminary prospectus
下流部門	downstream
カルチャー	culture
カルパース	CalPERS
加齢	aging
カレント・コスト	current cost
カレント・コスト減価償却費	current cost depreciation
辛うじて採算が取れる	break even
…側	interest
川上産業	upstream
川上戦略	upstream strategy
川下戦略	downstream strategy
川下部門	downstream
為替	currency
為替	exchange
為替	foreign exchange
為替換算差額	translation gain or [and] loss
為替換算差損益	translation gain or [and] loss
為替換算調整勘定	dfference of foreign currency translation
為替業務	exchange business
為替差益	exchange gain
為替差損	exchange loss
為替差損益	foreign exchange
為替差損益	transaction gain or loss
為替差損益	translation gain or [and] loss
為替市場	exchange market
為替相場	currency
為替相場	currency exchange rate
為替相場	exchange
為替相場	exchange rate
為替相場の過度の変動	excess volatility in exchange rates
為替手形	bill
為替手形	bill of exchange
為替取引	exchange deal
為替平価	par value
為替変動保険	exchange risk insurance
為替持ち高	exchange position
為替予約	exchange contract
為替リスクの軽減	hedge
為替リスクの防止	hedge
為替レート	currency exchange rate
為替レート	exchange rate
変わりやすい	volatile
変わる	shift
代わるべき手段	alternative

…観	outlook
簡易課税制度	simplified tax system
考え	idea
考え	submission
考え方	idea
考え直す	reinvent
考える	consider
換価した	realized
換価する	realize
…を喚起する	drive
喚起する	boost
環境	climate
環境	condition
環境	environment
環境	framework
環境	opportunity
環境	trend
環境の浄化整備費	cleanup costs
環境への適応	integration
環境保護	environmental protection
換金	liquidation
元金	capital
元金	principal
元金	principal amount
換金しにくい	illiquid
換金する	cash
換金性	liquidity
元金に繰り入れる	convert
換金能力	liquidity
関係	affair
関係	concern
関係	footing
関係	framework
関係	reference
関係	relations
関係	relationship
関係会社	affiliate
関係会社	affiliated company
関係会社	affiliated entities
関係会社	associate
関係会社	operation
関係会社	subsidiary
関係会社買掛金	accounts payable to affiliated companies
関係会社貸付け金	advances to affiliates
関係会社借入金	due to affiliated and associated companies
関係会社出資金	contribution to affiliated companies
関係会社投資	investment in affiliated company [concern]
関係会社有価証券	securites of affiliated company
関係会社利益持ち分	equity earnings
関係会社利益持ち分	equity earnings

関係者	affiliate
関係者	insider
関係者	interest
関係者	participant
関係者	party
関係者	player
関係者	source
…に関係する	concern
歓迎する	receive
関係を築く	establish
還元	return
還元する	return
刊行	issuance
完工	completion
慣行	practice
慣行	procedure
官公機械受注	public machinery orders
勧告の	advisory
監査	audit
監査	auditing
監査	examination
完済	payoff
監査委員会	audit committee
監査意見	opinion
管財人	administrator
管財人	manager
監査依頼会社	client
監査機関	auditor
監査基準	auditing standards
監査済み財務諸表	certified financial statements
監査済みの	audited
監査する	audit
監査する	examine
監査する	review
監査責任者	controller of audit
監査対象外	unaudited
監査手続き	due diligence
監査人	accountant
監査人	auditor
監査報告書	audit report
監査報告書	certificate of the auditor
監査報告書の日付	opinion date
監査法人	audit firm
監査法人	auditor
監査役	auditor
監査役会	board of corporate auditors
監査役会	supervisory board
監査役指名	appointment of auditors
換算	conversion
換算	equivalent
換算	translation
換算額	equivalent
換算差額	translation differences
換算差損益	translation gain or [and] loss

換算する	convert
換算する	translate
換算調整	translation adjustment
換算調整額	translation adjustments
換算レート	exchange rate
監視	monitoring
監視	oversight
幹事(引受会社)	manager
監視活動	monitoring
幹事証券会社に対する調査報告書	comfort letter for underwriter
監視する	monitor
慣習	practice
願書	application
勘定	a/c
勘定	account
勘定	accounts
勘定科目	line item
勘定科目表	chart of accounts
勘定残高	account balance
勘定残高	balance
勘定式財務諸表	account form financial statements
勘定書	account
勘定書の作成	billing
官職	appointment
官職	office
幹事を務める	manage
関心	concern
関心事	affair
関心事	concern
関心の一致	community of interest
完遂	accomplishment
関数	function
完成	completion
関税	duty
完成基準	completed contract method
完成工事高	construction of completion
完成財	finished goods
完成財	finished product
完成させる	complete
完成した	complete
完成した	finished
完成する	execute
完成品	finished goods
完成品	finished product
完成品引渡し方式の	turnkey
間接格付け	implicit rating
間接製造費	overhead cost
間接的	indirect
間接の	indirect
間接費	burden
間接費	general expense
間接費	overhead
間接費	overhead cost
間接費	supplementary cost
間接費の配賦	overhead absorption
間接費配賦率	burden rate
間接部門	overhead
完全開示	full disclosure
完全開示	full disclosure
完全開示原則	full disclosure principle
完全希薄化	full dilution
完全希薄化	fully diluted
完全希薄化	fully diluted
完全希薄化後の	fully diluted
完全希薄化1株当たり利益	fully diluted earnings per share
完全公開化	full disclosure
完全子会社	wholly-owned subsidiary
完全雇用	full employment
完全雇用	full employment
完全サービス	full service
完全受給権取得	full eligibility
完全所有子会社	fully owned subsidiary
完全所有子会社	fully owned subsidiary
完全所有子会社	wholly owned operations
完全所有子会社	wholly-owned subsidiary
完全所有の	wholly-owned
完全税効果会計	comprehensive income tax allocation
完全税効果会計	full provision basis
完全操業度	full capacity
完全操業度	full capacity
完全な	complete
完全な	full
完全な	total
完全に	fully
完全に	wholly
完全にする	complete
完全年金	full pension
完全表示	full disclosure
完全連結	full consolidation
簡素化	streamlining
簡素化する	streamline
鑑定	appraisal
鑑定	assessment
鑑定	opinion
鑑定額	assessment
鑑定価値	appraised value
監督	charge
監督	oversight
監督する	manage
観念	concept
観念	idea
完納	delivery
カンパニー制	company system
かんばん方式	JIT
かんばん方式	just-in-time
幹部	manager
幹部	staff
還付	refund
還付	refunding
幹部社員	manager
還付申請書	refund claim
還付する	refund
還付請求	claim for a refund
還付未収金	refunds receivable
元本	principal
元本	principal amount
元本	principal amount
元本残存額	remaining principal balance
元本と利息	principal and interest
元本の償還	principal repayment
元本返済	principal payment
元本保証	guaranteed principal
元本保証	principal guarantee
勧誘	solicitation
勧誘する	solicit
関与	participation
関与する	participate
元来	primarily
監理	monitoring
管理	administration
管理	charge
管理	conduct
管理	control
管理	governance
管理	hand
管理	management
管理	regulation
元利	principal and interest
管理運営する	govern
元利合計	final value
元利合計	maturity value
管理者	administrator
管理者	manager
管理上の	administrative
管理職	executive
管理職	management employee
管理処分権保持債務者	debtor in possession
管理する	control
管理する	keep
管理する	manage
管理する	monitor
管理する	run
管理的	administrative
管理の	managerial
元利払い	debt service
元利払い期間	amortization period
管理費	central and administrative expenses
管理部長	controller
管理法	governance
監理ポスト	monitoring post

還流する return
完了 accomplishment
完了基準 completed contract method
完了する achieve
慣例 rule
慣例 usual practice
関連 reference
関連 relations
関連 relationship
関連会社 affiliate
関連会社 affiliated company
関連会社 affiliated company
関連会社 associate
関連会社 associate company
関連会社 associated company
関連会社投資勘定 investment in affiliated company [concern]
関連会社普通株式 affiliated common stock
関連購買 one-stop shopping
関連性 combination
関連ハードウエア／ソフトウエア／周辺装置の市場 after market [aftermarket]
緩和する reduce

き

期 year
…期 period
ギアリング financial gearing
ギアリング gearing
議案 items of business
議案 resolution
議案提出権 initiative
議案の通過を促す promote
…に起因する attributable to …
記憶場所 location
キオプラン Keogh
機会 opportunity
機会 scope
機械 machinery
機会原価 opportunity cost
議会式投票 parliamentary voting
機械受注 machinery orders
機械受注額 machinery orders
機械設備 machinery and equipments
機械装置 machinery
機会損失 conditional loss
機会損失 opportunity loss
機会費用 opportunity cost
企画 enterprise
企画 organization
企画 planning
企画 project
企画 proposal
企画 scheme
規格 standard

企画計画予算制度 planning, program(m)ing, budgeting system
企画計画予算方式 PPBS
企画する project
企画する propose
企画立案 planning
企画力 organization
期間 life
期間 period
期間 term
機関 institution
機関 organization
期間延長 extension
期間帰属差異 timing differences
期間計画 periodic planning
期間構造 term structure
期間差異 timing differences
期間財務諸表 periodic financial accounts
基幹事業 core business
期間損失 periodic loss
機関投資家 institutional investor
期間内税金配分 tax allocation within a period
期間年金費用 periodic pension cost
期間年金費用純額 net periodic pension cost
期間年金費用純額 net periodic pension cost
期間の periodic
期間配分 allocation
期間費用 period expense
期間費用 periodic cost
期間利益 period income
期間利益 periodic income
期間利益 periodic profit
危機 crisis
危機 turmoil
機器 equipment
機器 machinery
危機管理 risk management
危機管理システム crisis management system
機器調達 procurement
機器販売 equipment sales
企業 business
企業 company
企業 concern
企業 corporation
企業 employer
企業 enterprise
企業 firm
企業 institution
企業 interest
企業 organization
企業 player
企業 producer
企業 provider
企業 undertaking

起業 entrepreneurship
企業運営 business operation
企業家 entrepreneur
起業家 entrepreneur
企業改革 corporate reform
企業改革法（サーベンス・オクスレー法） Sarbanes-Oxley Act
企業会計 corporate accounting
企業会計改革法 Sarbanes-Oxley Act
企業会計原則 Accounting Standards for Business Enterprises
企業会計原則 corporate accounting principles
企業化可能性 feasibility
企業化可能性調査 feasibility study
企業家精神 entrepreneurship
起業家精神 entrepreneurship
起業家精神が旺盛な entrepreneurial
企業価値 bushiness worth
企業価値 company's value
企業価値 corporate value
企業価値 value to business
企業化調査 feasibility study
企業家の entrepreneurial
起業家の entrepreneurial
起業家マインド enterprise
企業環境 business climate
企業間取引 B2B
企業業績 business results
企業業績 corporate earnings
企業業績 corporate performance
企業金融 corporate finance
企業グループ business group
企業グループ conglomerate
企業グループ group
企業グループ player
企業グループの経常利益 consolidated recurring profit
企業経営 business operation
企業経営 corporate management
企業経営情報 BI
企業経営内容の公開 disclosure
企業結合 combination
企業行動憲章 charter of ethics
企業固有の技術 core competence
企業固有の競争力の核 core competence
企業再建 corporate rehabilitation
企業再生 turnaround
企業再生案 turnaround plan
企業再生計画 turnaround plan
企業再編 repositioning
企業財務 corporate finance
企業財務情報 financial statements
企業資産 corporate assets
企業支配 corporate governance
企業市民 corporate citizen

| 企業収益 corporate earnings
| 企業収益 corporate performance
| 企業集団 business group
| 企業集団 group
| 企業取得 acquisition
| 企業取得 takeover [take-over]
| 企業取得と合併 M & A
| 企業情報 BI
| 企業情報の開示 disclosure
| 企業所得 corporate income
| 企業心理 business confidence
| 企業責任 accountability
| 企業戦略 business strategy
| 企業体 concern
| 企業体 entity
| 企業対企業 B2B
| 企業体質 corporate strength
| 企業担保借入買取り LBO
| 企業担保借入買取り leveraged buyout [buy-out]
| 企業統合 consolidation
| 企業統治 corporate governance
| 企業内の in-house [inhouse]
| 企業内容開示制度 disclosure system
| 企業内容の開示 disclosure
| 企業主 owner
| 企業年金 occupational annuity
| 企業年金 private enterprises annuity
| 企業年金制度 company-run pension plan
| 企業年金制度 corporate pension plan
| 企業年金法 Employee Retirement Income Security Act
| 企業年金保険 private pension
| 企業の corporate
| 企業の entrepreneurial
| 企業の会計処理 corporate accounting
| 企業の会計処理方法 corporate accounting
| 企業の合併・買収 mergers and acquisitions
| 企業の合併・買収案 M&A bid
| 企業の基本定款 articles of association
| 企業の基本定款 articles of incorporation
| 企業の基本定款 memorandum of association
| 企業の吸収合併 M & A
| 企業の経理 corporate accounting
| 企業の資金調達 corporate finance
| 企業の社会的責任 corporate social responsibility
| 企業の社会的責任 CSR
| 企業の信用等級 credit rating

企業の存続可能性 going concern
企業の体質 business climate
企業の体質 corporate culture
企業の通常定款 articles of association
企業の強み corporate strength
企業のリストラ business restructuring
企業買収 acquisition
企業買収 takeover [take-over]
企業買収専門会社 buyout firm
企業買収提案 takeover offer
企業秘密 trade secret
企業風土 business climate
企業風土 corporate culture
企業文化 corporate culture
企業分割 divestiture
企業マインド business confidence
企業目標 corporate goal
企業力 corporate strength
企業連合 combination
企業連合 consortium
基金 basic fund
基金 capital
基金 foundation
基金 foundation fund
基金 fund
基金 initial capital
基金債務 fund obligation
基金資産 plan assets
基金資産の見積り給付債務超過額 plan assets in excess of projected benefit obligation
基金設立 funding
基金増資 capital increase
基金の増額 capital increase
基金の積み増し capital increase
議決権 vote
議決権 voting power
議決権 voting right
議決権株 voting share [stock]
議決権株式 voting share [stock]
議決権行使 voting
議決権行使委任状 proxy
議決権信託 voting trust
議決権代理行使委員会 proxy committee
議決権代理行使勧誘状 proxy statement
議決権付き株式 voting share [stock]
議決権付き社債 voting bond
議決権のある証券 voting security
議決権の代理行使 substitutional exercise of voting right
議決権のない株式 nonvoting share
議決権のない優先株式 preferential nonvoting share
議決権を行使する vote
議決する vote

危険 risk
期限 maturity
期限延長 lockup [lock-up]
期限延長 renewal
危険管理 risk management
期限経過手形 overdue note
危険準備金 contingency provisions
危険性 risk
期限の経過した overdue
危険負担 risk
期限前解約 early termination
期限前償還 prepayment
期限前償還 redemption before maturity
期限前償還する prepay
期限前償還率 prepayment speed
期限前に返済する anticipate
期限前返済 early retirement
期限前返済 prepayment
期限前返済推定額 prepayment assumed
期限前弁済する prepay
機構 machinery
機構 organization
機構 scheme
機構 structure
機構 system
気候 climate
起工 groundbreaking
記号 mark
起工(式)の groundbreaking
起工式 groundbreaking
記載 entry
起債 new bond issuance
起債環境 issuing environment
記載事項 entry
記載しておく carry
記載する enter
記載する include
記載する list
記載する reflect
記載する report
起債する issue
機材調達先 vendor [vender]
起債手続き issuing process
起債発表 launch
議事 items of business
議事進行 proceedings
期日 due date
期日受渡し高 amount due
期日が到来する mature
期日前解約 withdrawal before maturity
記者会見 news conference
記者会見 press conference
希釈化 dilution
希釈化する dilute
期首 beginning
期首 BOY

機種	line
機種	model
期首株主資本	beginning equity
期首残高	balance at beginning of year
期首残高	beginning balance
期首残高	opening inventory
期首残高と期末残高	beginning and ending balances
期首仕掛(しかけ・しかかり)品	begininng work in process
期首資本	initial capital
期首棚卸し高	beginning inventory
技術	engineering
技術	skill
技術革新	innovation
技術情報	knowhow [know-how]
技術知識	knowhow [know-how]
技術費	engineering expense
技術秘訣	knowhow [know-how]
技術秘密	knowhow [know-how]
期首の	initial
期首払い年金	annuity due
期首簿価	book value at beginning of year
基準	base
基準	basis
基準	benchmark
基準	code
基準	concept
基準	criterion
基準	guideline
基準	method
基準	principle
基準	requirement
基準	rule
基準	scheme
基準	standard
基準	test
規準	norm
規準	rule
基準期間	base period
基準期間	base period
基準金利	base rate
基準金利	benchmark interest rate
基準金利	key interest rate
基準金利	key rate
基準時	base period
基準指数	benchmark
基準準備金	benchmark reserves
基準書	standard
基準測定値	measure
基準棚卸し法	base stock inventory valuation
基準棚卸し法	base stock method
基準棚卸し法	normal stock method
基準値	benchmark
…の基準となる	govern

基準にする	benchmark
基準年	base year
基準年次	base period
基準銘柄	benchmark
基準量	norm
基準利率	base rate
規準労働量	norm
議事要旨	minutes
議事録	minutes
議事録	proceedings
築く	form
築く	set up
規制	control
規制	regulation
規制	restriction
規制緩和	deregulation
規制緩和	liberalization
規制緩和する	liberalize
規制機関	regulatory body
規制市場	regulated market
規制する	regulate
規制対象外の企業	non-regulated company
規制対象企業	regulated company
規制撤廃	decontrol
規制撤廃	deregulation
規制を受ける業界	regulated industry
規制を緩和する	deregulate
規制を撤廃する	deregulate
季節調整	seasonal adjustment
季節調整	seasonal effects
季節変動	seasonal fluctuation
基礎	base
基礎	basis
基礎	foundation
基礎	fundamentals
競う	compete
寄贈	donation
寄贈基金	endowment fund
偽装する	falsify
偽造する	falsify
寄贈品	donation
基礎格付け	base rating
規則	code
規則	regulation
規則	rule
帰属	attribution
帰属主義	attributable concept
…に帰属する	applicable to …
…に帰属する	attributable to …
帰属利子	imputed interest
基礎化粧品	foundation
起訴する	accuse
基礎賃率	base rate
基礎的	underlying
基礎的仮定	basic assumption
基礎的条件	fundamentals
基礎的1株当たり利益	primary earnings per share

基礎的1株当たり利益	primary earnings per share
基礎となる	underlying
基礎年金	basic pension
基礎年金制度	basic pension plan
基礎利益	basic profit
基礎利益	core operating profit
基礎利益	fundamental profit
既存設備	existing plant and equipment
既存店ベース	like-for-like basis
既存の債務	outstanding debt
既存の債務の借換え	rollover of an existing debt
期待	expectation
期待	prospects
議題	matter
期待する	expect
期待値	expectation
期待どおりの	reliable
期待の	expected
期待外れの	disappointing
期待外れの業績	disappointing results [performance]
期待利益	anticipated profit
期待を裏切る	disappointing
期待を裏切る業績	disappointing results [performance]
基地	base
期中	during the business year
期中	during the period
期中	for the period
期中の	for the period
期中の	interim
期中平均発行済み株式数	average number of shares outstanding
期中平均発行済み株式総数	average shares outstanding
基調	trend
記帳	entry
議長	chairman
議長	president
記帳する	book
記帳する	carry
記帳する	record
規定	policy
規定	provision
規定	regulation
規定	requirement
規定	rule
規定	term
規定する	define
規定する	establish
規定する	govern
規定する	state
起動する	launch
既得権	vested interest
既得の	vested
記入	entry
記入する	book

記入する	enter
記入する	keep
機能	function
技能	accomplishment
技能	skill
機能拡張	extension
技能検定	skill test
機能している	operational
機能している	working
機能する	function
機能通貨	functional currency
機能停止	failure
機能的組織	functional organization
機能的分割	functional division
技能評価	skills assessment
機能別監査	functional auditing
機能別計算書	functional statement
…の機能を果たす	serve
機能を果たす	function
希薄後普通株式1株当たり純利益	diluted earnings per share of common stock
希薄化	dilution
希薄化後普通株式1株当たり純利益	diluted net earnings per common share
希薄化効果	dilutive effect
希薄化効果	dilutive effect
希薄化準普通株式	dilutive common stock equivalents
希薄化証券	dilutive securities
希薄化する	dilute
希薄化防止	anti-dilution
希薄化前	primary
希薄化率	dilution factor
希薄済み1株当たり利益	diluted EPS
規範	code
規範	conduct
規範	norm
基盤	base
基盤	foothold
基盤	footing
基盤	foundation
忌避	challenge
厳しい	poor
厳しい	weak
厳しいがやりがいがある	challenging
厳しい環境	stress
厳しい経営環境	stress
厳しい検査	acid test
厳しい試験	acid test
厳しい試練	acid test
厳しい批判	thrust
寄付	contribution
寄付	donation
寄付金	contribution
寄付金	donation
寄付金	donations expense
希望退職	early retirement
希望退職	voluntary retirement
希望退職計画	voluntary separation program
規模拡大する	widen
規模の縮小	downsizing
基本	base
基本	fundamentals
基本給	base rate
基本金	foundation
基本合意書	memorandum of understanding
基本財産	basic property
基本財産	principal
基本財務諸表	basic statements
基本財務書類	basic financial statements
基本思想	concept
基本税率	basic tax rate
基本設計	core
基本戦略	core strategy
基本積立金	foundation fund
基本的	primary
基本的合意	basic agreement
基本的指標	fundamentals
基本的な	core
基本的な	net
基本的な	underlying
基本的な考え方	concept
基本的な考え方	philosophy
基本的な1株利益	basic EPS
基本的に	generally
基本的に	primarily
基本的に	principally
基本的1株当たり利益	basic earnings per share
基本的1株当たり利益	primary earnings per share
基本的1株当たり利益	primary EPS
基本的普通株式1株当たり純利益	basic net earnings per common share
基本特許	pioneer patent
基本モデル	base
基本料金	base rate
基本料金	basic rate
期前償還価格	call price
期末	closing
期末	end
期末	year end
期末	yearend
期末決算	term-end settlement of accounts
期末決算	term-end settlement of accounts
期末現金残高	ending cash balance
期末在庫	ending inventory
期末残高	balance at end of year
期末残高	ending balance
期末棚卸し	ending inventory
期末棚卸し高	ending inventory
期末棚卸し高	ending inventory
期末の	final
期末の財産額	terminal wealth
期末配当	final dividend
期末払い年金	annuity in arrears
機密情報の公開	going public
機密費	classified fund
義務	accountability
義務	charge
義務	duty
義務	liability
義務	obligation
義務	responsibility
義務的経費	entitlement outlays
義務的経費	mandatory spending
義務の免除	release
義務不履行の	delinquent
記名債券	registered bond
記名社債	registered bond
記名証券	registered security
記名の	registered
決める	close
決める	determine
決める	elect
決める	name
規約	code
規約	contract
規約	rule
規約	statement
逆LBO	reverse LBO
客観性	objectivity
逆希薄化	antidilution
逆吸収合併	downstream merger
逆ざや	negative spread
逆資産効果	negative wealth effect
逆進税	regressive tax
脚注	footnote
逆転	reversal
逆の	negative
キャッシュ	cash
キャッシュ・バランス	cash balance
キャッシュ・フロー	cash flow
キャッシュ・フロー	stream
キャッシュ・フロー計算書	cash flow statement
キャッシュ・マージャー	cash merger
キャップ	cap
キャパシティ	capacity
キャピタル	capital
キャピタル・ゲイン	capital gain
キャピタル・マーケット	capital market
キャピタル・リース	capital lease
キャピタル・ロス	capital loss
キャリー取引	carry trade
キャリー・トレード	carry trade
キャルス	CALS

キャンペーン	drive	給付額計算方式	benefit formula	強化する	strengthen
キャンペーン	effort	給付関連債務	benefit-related liabilities	協議	communication
級	notch	給付金	benefit	協議	deal
救援	rescue	給付コスト	benefit cost	協議	negotiation
休暇	layoff	給付債務	benefit obligation	協議	talks
休会	closing	給付情報	benefit information	協議会	committee
急拡大する	leap	給付制度	benefit plan	協議書	deal
究極の	final	給付建て制度	defined benefit plan	供給	export
急激な	sharp	給付建て年金制度	defined benefit pension plan	供給	injection
急激に落ち込む	plummet	給付建て年金制度	defined benefit pension plan	供給	sourcing
急減	collapse	給付建て年金制度	defined benefit plan	供給	supply
急減する	collapse	給付内容	benefit coverage	供給会社	supplier
急降下	plunge	給付費	payout	供給業者	supplier
救済	bailout	給付保障	benefit security	供給契約	supply arrangement
救済	rescue	休眠会社	nonoperating company	供給源	resource
救済する	rescue	休眠の	nonoperating	供給源	supplier
救済措置	bailout	給与	compensation	供給国	supplier
吸収	absorption	給与	payroll	供給下請業者	supplier
吸収合併	absorption	給与	salary	供給者	producer
吸収合併	merger	休養期間	layoff	供給者	supplier
吸収合併	takeover [take-over]	給与外給付	fringe benefit	供給する	distribute
吸収合併する	absorb	給与計画	salary projection	供給する	provide
吸収合併する	merge	給与所得	earned income	供給する	serve
吸収する	absorb	給与所得	salary income	供給する	supply
吸収する	offset	急落	collapse	供給能力	supply capacity
救出	rescue	急落	meltdown	供給品	supply
救出する	rescue	急落	plunge	供給部門	supplying segment
救助	rescue	急落	sell-off	供給元	vendor [vender]
求償権	contribution	急落	slump	供給量	supply
求償権	right of indemnity	急落する	plunge	供給連鎖	supply chain
急上昇	boost	給料	hire	競業	competition
急上昇	surge	給料	pay	協業	cooperation
急上昇する	leap	給料	remuneration	業況感	business confidence
急上昇する	skyrocket	給料	salary	業況判断	business confidence
休職	separation	給料	wage	業況判断	DI
休職手当の支払い	separation payments	給料の天引き	withholding	業況判断	diffusion index
救助する	rescue	寄与	contribution	競業利益	competing interests
級数法	sum of the years' digits method	…業	industry	恐慌	crisis
級数法	sum-of-the-digits basis	脅威	challenge	競合	competition
急増	boost	教育	development	競合する	compete
急増	sharp increase	教育	education	競合他社	competitor
急増する	leap	強化	beef-up	強固な	solid
急増する	skyrocket	強化	consolidation	強固な	strong
急増する	soar	強化	enhancement	教材	resource
急増する	surge	業界	community	共済事業	mutual relief operations
急速な	sharp	業界	industry	共済年金	mutual aid pension plan
急騰	appreciation	業界	interest	行事	event
急騰	rally	業界	sector	業者	provider
急騰	surge	強化する	beef up	業種	line of busines
急騰する	rally	強化する	boost	凝縮した	condensed
急騰する	skyrocket	強化する	consolidate	供述	showing
急騰する	soar	強化する	enhance	業種別株価指数	narrow based stock index
急騰する	surge	強化する	improve	強制	pressure
急な	sharp	強化する	increase	矯正	reform
給付	benefit	強化する	intensify	行政	administration
給付額	benefit	強化する	reinforce	行政規則	regulation
給付額	eligible charges			行政処分	adminstrarive action
				矯正する	reform
				行政手続き	administrative pro-

ceedings	
行政の	administrative
強制和議	compulsory composition
業績	accomplishment
業績	achievement
業績	bottom line
業績	bottom lines
業績	business
業績	business performance
業績	business results
業績	earnings
業績	figure
業績	financial figures
業績	financial performance
業績	financial results
業績	operating results
業績	performance
業績	results
業績悪化企業	distressed company
業績および営業活動の検討と分析	discussion amd analysis of our results and operations
業績改善	turnaround
業績回復	turnaround situation
業績価値	achievement value
業績好調	good performance
業績好調	strong performance
業績の大幅拡大	stronger performance
業績の大幅な伸び	stronger performance
業績発表	announcement of business results
業績不振	sluggish performance
業績報告	earnings report
業績報告書	earnings report
業績見通し	earnings forecast
業績見通し	earnings projection
業績見通し	profit forecast
業績見通し	profit projection
業績予想	earnings forecast
業績予想	earnings projection
業績予想	profit forecast
業績連動型の報酬制度	merit-based pay plan [system]
競争	competition
競争	competitiveness
競争	struggle
競争相手	competition
競争相手	competitor
競争相手	contender
競争環境	competitive environment
競争条件	playing field
競争上の	competitive
競争上の優位	competitive advantage
競争上の優位	competitive edge
競争上の優位性	competitive advantage
競争上の優位性	competitive edge
競争する	compete
競争的	competitive
競争入札制度	tender panel method
競争の場	playing field
競争有利性	competitive advantage
競争力	advantage
競争力	competitive advantage
競争力	competitive edge
競争力	competitiveness
競争力での優位	competitive edge
競争力のある	competitive
競争力のある商品	competitive product
業態超え統合	cross-sectoral tie-up
業態を超えての統合	cross-sectoral tie-up
供託者	depositor
供託する	deposit
協調	cooperation
強調	stress
…を強調する	focus on …
協調融資	joint financing
協調融資	joint financing
協調融資団	consortium
協調融資団	syndicate
共通原価	common cost
共通固定費	joint capacity cost
共通固定費	joint fixed cost
共通の	common
共通の	corporate
共通の	joint
共通の	mutual
共通の	universal
共通費	common cost
協定	accord
協定	agreement
協定	arrangement
協定	contract
協定	deal
協定覚書	memorandum of understanding
協定価格	agreed price
協定書	contract
協定を結ぶ	ink an agreement
協同	cooperation
共同委任状	joint proxy
共同運営会社	joint company
共同海損分担金	contribution
共同開発	joint development
共同企業	joint venture
共同企業体	joint venture
共同企業体	JV
共同経営	partnership
共同経営者	partner
共同研究	joint research
共同事業	joint venture
共同事業体	consortium
共同事業体	joint venture
共同事業体	JV
共同社会	community
共同主幹事	co-lead manager
共同出資	joint stake
共同出資	partnership
共同出資会社	joint venture
共同出資事業	joint venture
共同出資者	joint partner
共同出資者	partner
共同出資の組織	jointly funded organization
共同所有	joint ownership
共同所有	partnership
共同所有者	partner
共同所有の	jointly owned
共同体	community
共同で	jointly
共同投資	joint investment
共同頭取	co-president
共同の	common
共同の	corporate
共同の	joint
共同の	mutual
共同引受行	co-underwriter
共同負担	sharing
共同負担する	share
共同分担	sharing
共同分担する	share
共同持ち株会社	joint holding company [firm]
共同融資	co-finance
共同連合体	consortium
京都議定書	Kyoto Protocol
競売	auction
業務	activity
業務	administration
業務	affair
業務	business
業務	business operation
業務	concern
業務	execution
業務	function
業務	job
業務	operation
業務	practice
業務	service
業務	transaction
業務粗利益	gross operating profit
業務委託	outsourcing
業務委託	sourcing
業務委託する	outsource
業務運営	business operation
業務改善	practice improvement
業務革新	reengineering
業務基準	practice standards
業務計画	operating plan
業務経費	operations expenses
業務執行	management

業務執行委員会　executive committee
業務執行役員　corporate officer
業務執行役員　officer
業務執行役員報酬　executive compensation
業務純益　net business profit
業務純益　operating earnings
業務純益　operating profit
業務上の秘密　trade secret
業務処理　transaction
業務遂行基準　conduct of business rule
業務提携　business alliance
業務提携　business tie-up
業務提携計画　business tie-up plan
業務停止　business suspension
業務展開　business development
業務展開　trading activities
業務の　operating
業務の一時停止　tie-up
業務の根本的革新　reengineering
業務を革新する　reengineer
業務を根本的に革新する　re-engineer
業務を変革する　reengineer
協約　agreement
協約　deal
共有者　joint owner
共有する　share
共有の　common
共有の　joint
強要　pressure
教養　education
業容　business
業容　business operation
供与する　extend
協力　contribution
協力　cooperation
協力　front
協力　partnership
協力　tie-up
協力する　contribute
協力する　join
協力する　sponsor
協力する　tie up
強力な　strong
許可　allowance
許可　approval
許可　license [licence]
許可　recognition
巨額の　heavy
巨額の　large
巨額の　massive
許可書　license [licence]
許可する　approve
許可する　grant
許可する　license
許可する　recognize
許可を与える　license

虚偽記載　misstatement
虚偽記載する　falsify
虚偽の　false
虚偽の　fraudulent
虚偽表示　misstatement
局　department
局員　staff
局長　director
極度　limit
局面　environment
局面　period
虚構の　fictious
寄与したもの　contributor
居住している　resident
居住者　resident
拠出　contribution
拠出　funding
拠出　provision
拠出型制度　contributory plan
拠出型制度　contributory plan
拠出型年金制度　contributory plan
拠出金　contribution
拠出金制度　defined contribution plan
拠出資本　invested capital
拠出する　contribute
拠出する　fund
拠出制年金制度　contributory plan
拠出建て年金制度　defined contribution pension
拠出建て年金制度　defined contribution plan
寄与する　contribute
巨大な　large
巨大な　massive
巨大複合企業　conglomerate
許諾　license [licence]
許諾する　grant
許諾する　license
許諾料　royalty
虚脱感　burnout
拠点　base
拠点　location
拠点　presence
拠点　site
…を拠点とする　base
拠点を置く　base
許認可　licensing
許認可　official approvals
許認可費用　permits and licenses
拒否　challenge
許容虚偽表示　torelable misstatement
許容水準　permissible level
許容できる　acceptable
許容範囲の　acceptable
切替え　conversion
切り替える　convert
切り替える　refinance
切り替える　swap

ぎりぎりの線　bottom line
切り下げる　depreciate
切捨て　write-off
紀律　conduct
切詰め　squeeze
切り詰める　squeeze
切り詰める　trim
切り抜ける　manage
切り離し　spinoff [spin-off]
切り離す　separate
切り離す　spin off
技量　hand
気力　drive
亀裂　split
記録　entry
記録　record
記録　register
記録係　registrar
記録されていない　off-the-book
記録事項　registration
…を記録する　chalk up
記録する　book
記録する　list
記録する　record
記録する　wtite down
記録的な　record
記録にのせる　enter
議論　discussion
際立った　significant
際立った業績　outstanding performance
均一の　flat
金額　amount
金額　sum
金額　value
金額後入れ先出し法　dollar value LIFO
金額後入れ先出し法　dollor value lifo
金額後出し先入れ法　dollar unit method
金額ベース　dollar terms
緊急援助　bailout
緊急貸出金利　emergency lending rate
緊急株主総会　emergency shareholders meeting
緊急資金　urgent fund
緊急事態　contingency
均衡　balance
銀行　bank
銀行　lender
銀行貸出　bank credit
銀行貸出　bank lending
銀行貸付け　bank loan
銀行貸付け金　bank loan
銀行借入れ　bank credit
銀行借入れ　bank loan
銀行借入金　bank loan
銀行借入れ枠　bank line of credit

銀行間借款　bank loan
銀行券　BN
銀行信用　bank credit
銀行信用状　bank credit
銀行信用状　banker's credit
銀行信用枠　bank line of credit
銀行代理店制度　bank agent system
銀行団　syndicate
銀行団による協調融資　syndicated loan
銀行当座貸し　bank credit
銀行の発行引受団　issuing syndicate of banks
銀行発行のクレジット・カード　bankcard
銀行保証小切手　certified check
銀行融資　bank credit
銀行融資　bank lending
銀行融資　bank loan
銀行預金全額保証　blanket protection on bank deposits
銀行与信限度額　bank line of credit
銀行与信枠　bank line of credit
銀行ローン　bank loan
金庫株　treasury stock
金庫株制度　treasury stock system
近似計算をする　approximate
金種　denomination
緊縮政策　austerity drive
金銭　money
金銭　obligation
金銭債権　monetary assets
金銭債務　debt
金銭債務訴訟　debt
金銭信託　trust cash fund
金銭出納係　treasurer
金銭的　financial
金銭の　monetary
金銭面での　financial
勤続期間　working life
勤続年数　length of service
勤続年数　year of service
吟味　acid test
勤務　duty
勤務　service
勤務期間　service period
勤務する　serve
勤務年数　service period
勤務費用　service cost
金融　credit
金融　finance
金融　financing
金融　money
金融売掛債権　finance receivables
金融緩和　easy money
金融機関　factor
金融機関　financial institution
金融機関　institution
金融機関　lender

金融機関の業務純益　consolidated operating profit
金融機関の業務純益　net operating profit
金融危機　credit crunch
金融業者　factor
金融業務　financial business
金融グループ　financial group
金融グループ　financial group
金融子会社　finance subsidiary
金融コスト　financing cost
金融サービス　financial services
金融サービス機構　FSA
金融債権　finance receivables
金融債務　debt
金融債務　net debt
金融先物　financial futures
金融先物取引　financial futures
金融支援　bailout
金融支援　financial assistance
金融支援　financial support
金融事業　financial business
金融事業を営む子会社　finance subsidiary
金融資産　financial instrument
金融資産　portfolio
金融市場　credit market
金融市場　financial market
金融市場　money market
金融収支　financial results
金融収支　net interest payment
金融手段　financial instrument
金融証書　financial instrument
金融情勢　financial condition
金融商品　financial instrument
金融情報　financial information
金融組織　financial structure
金融庁　FSA
金融手形債務　promissory notes payable
金融の　financial
金融の　monetary
金融の証券化　securitization
金融派生商品　derivative
金融派生商品　derivative financial instrument
金融派生商品　derivative instrument
金融引締め　tightening in the credit policy
金融逼迫　credit crunch
金融費用　financing cost
金融面の圧力　financial pressure
金利　interest
金利　interest rate
金利　rate
金利感応資産・負債　rate sensitive assets and liabilities
金利差　spread
金利収入　interest income

金利スワップ　interest rate swap
金利の支払い　interest payment
金利の誘導目標　key interest rate
金利負担　burden of debt service
金利変動リスク　exposure to interest rates

空気　climate
空前の　record
偶然の　fortuitous
空前の高値　new high
偶発債務　contingent liability
偶発資金　contingency fund
偶発事項　contingency
偶発事象　contingency
偶発受益者　contingent beneficiary
偶発損失　contingent loss
偶発損失　contingent loss
偶発損失　loss contingencies
偶発損失事象　loss contingencies
偶発損失事象　loss contingencies
偶発損失準備金　retained earnings appropriated for contingency
偶発損失積立金　contingent reserve
偶発損失引当金　contingent reserve
偶発損失引当金　provision for loss contingency
偶発損失引当金[準備金]　contingency reserve
偶発賃借料　contingent rent
偶発的損失　loss contingencies
偶発的な事象　fortuitous event
偶発の　contingent
偶発費用　contingent charge [cost]
偶発利益　contingent gain
偶発利益　contingent gain
偶発利益　contingent profit
偶発利益　windfall
偶発利益事象　gain contingency
偶発利得　contingent gain
クーポン　coupon
クオリティ　quality
9月期　business term ending in September
9月決算期　business term ending in September
9月中間決算　business term ending in September
区切り　segment
草分けの　groundbreaking
具申する　submit
ぐずぐずする　linger
ぐずぐずする　lingering
下り　downstream
駆動装置　drive

駆動力	drive
区分	category
区分	distribution
区分	scope
区分	section
区分上の	divisional
区分する	segment
区分単位	segment
区別	differentiation
…を区別する	earmark
組	team
組合	consortium
組合	partnership
組合	union
組合員	partner
組合せ	combination
組合せ	mix
組み入れる	capitalize
組み入れる	include
組み入れる	reflect
組換え	reclassification
組替え	realignment
組換え再表示	reclassification
組替え再表示する	reclassify
組み替える	reclassify
組立て	assembly
組立工程	line
組み立てる	set up
組別償却	group depreciation
組別償却法	group method
組む	take out
クライアント	client
クラウン・ジュエル	crown jewel
クラウン・ジュエル防衛	crown jewel defense
暮らし	life
クラス・アクション	class action
倉荷証券	warehouse receipt
倉荷証券	warrant
…と比べて	compared with ...
繰上げ償還	advance redemption
繰上げ償還価格	call price
繰上げ償還可能	callable
繰上げ償還時に支払われる割増金	call premium
繰上げ償還利回り	yield to call
繰り上げる	advance
繰り上げる	shift
繰入れ	transfer
繰り入れる	set aside
繰り入れる	transfer
クリエイティビティ	creativity
繰越し	carryforward
繰越し価額	carrying value
繰越金残存価額	balance
繰越し欠損金	loss carryforward [carry forward]
繰越し欠損金	net loss carried over
繰越し試算表	after-closing [post-closing] trial balance
クリティカル・マス	critical mass
繰延べ	carryforward
繰延べ	deferral
繰延べ	forward
繰延べ貸方項目	deferred credit
繰延べ収益	deferred credit
繰延べ収益	deferred revenue
繰延べ税額	deferred income taxes
繰延べ税金	deferred credit
繰延べ税金	deferred income taxes
繰延べ税金	deferred tax
繰延べ税金資産	deferred tax asset
繰延べ税金資産	DTAs
繰延べの	deferred
繰延べ負債	deferred liability
繰延べ法	deferral method
繰延べ法	deferred method
繰延べ方式	deferred method
繰延べ法人所得税	deferred income taxes
繰延べ法人税資産評価勘定	allowance for unrealizable tax benefits
繰延べ利益と損失	deferred gains and losses
繰り延べる	defer
繰戻し	carryback
グループ	group
グループ会社	group company
グループ企業	group company
グループ償却	group depreciation
グループ償却法	group method
グレードアップする	upgrade
クレジット	credit
クレジット・カード	credit card
クレジット・カードで買う	charge
クレジット・クランチ	credit crunch
クレジット・ライン	credit line
クレジット・ライン	line of credit
クレディター	creditor
苦労する	struggle
クロージング	closing
クロージング時現在の貸借対照表	closing balance sheet
クロージング貸借対照表	closing balance sheet
クロージング・レート	CR
グローバリゼーション	globalization
グローバル	global
グローバル化	globalization
グローバル企業	global company
グローバル市場	global market
グローバル市場	world market
グローバル戦略	global strategy
グローバルな	global
グローバル・マーケット	global market
黒字	black
黒字	profit
黒字	surplus
黒字体質	structural surplus
黒字転換	moving toward surplus
黒字の	positive
クロス・ライセンス	cross license
クロス・ライセンス契約	cross licensing agreement
くわ入れ式	groundbreaking
詳しい	full
詳しく	fully
企て	enterprise
軍	force
軍隊	force
ケアサービス	care service
経緯	experience
経営	administration
経営	business
経営	business operation
経営	business performance
経営	management
経営	operation
経営委員会	executive committee
経営側	management
経営環境	business climate
経営監視	corporate governance
経営幹部報酬委員会	executive compensation committee
経営管理	administration
経営管理	management
経営管理上の	administrative
経営危機	crisis
経営危機	financial difficulties
経営危機	trouble
経営危機に陥った	troubled
経営機構	management structure
経営基盤	position
経営基盤	presence
経営計画	business plan
経営計画	management plan
経営形態	management structure
経営権	control
経営権	control of ownership
経営権	management right
経営権	ownership
経営権に関与しない取締役	non-management Board member
経営権の変更	change of control
経営権を握る	control
経営工学	IE
経営工学	industrial engineering
経営構想	business plan
経営合理化	downsizing
経営効率	operational efficiency
経営再建	corporate rehabilitation
経営再建	rehabilitation
経営再建	restructuring
経営再建策	restructuring efforts

経営再建中の	debt-saddled
経営再建中の	struggling
経営刷新	management renewal
経営資源	management resources
経営資源	resource
経営姿勢	management style
経営執行委員会	management executive committee
経営支配株	controlling interest
経営支配権	control
経営支配権	controlling interest
経営支配権	controlling stake
経営支配権を得る	control
経営資本回転率	turnover of total operating assets
経営者	entrepreneur
経営者	executive
経営者	head
経営者	leader
経営者	manager
経営者	operator
経営者側	management
経営者による営業権取得	management buyout [buy-out]
経営者による営業権取得	MBO
経営者による自社買収	management buyout [buy-out]
経営者による自社買収	MBO
経営者の	entrepreneurial
経営者の	managerial
経営者の違反行為	management's illegal acts
経営首脳陣	top management
経営手法	business method
経営手法	management style
経営上の	administrative
経営上の	managerial
経営上の	operating
経営上の	operational
経営助言サービス	MAS
経営陣	leader
経営陣	management
経営陣	management team
経営陣と従業員による企業買収	MEBO
経営陣に対する株式の売出し	management offering
経営陣に対する株式発行	management offering
経営陣による企業買収	management buyout [buy-out]
経営陣による自社株式の公開買付け	management buyout [buy-out]
経営陣の見解	opinion of management
経営陣の刷新	management renewal
経営スタイル	management style
経営する	keep
経営する	manage
経営する	operate
経営する	run
経営成績	operating results
経営戦略	business strategy
経営戦略	management strategy
経営組織	management structure
経営多角化	business diversification
経営多角化	diversification
経営統合	integrated operations
経営統合	integration
経営統合	management integration
経営統合	merger
経営統合	tie-up
経営統合する	integrate businesses
経営統合する	integrate operations
経営統合する	merge
経営難	financial difficulties
経営難	stress
経営難	trouble
経営難に陥った	troubled
経営難の	troubled
経営の	managerial
経営の	operational
経営の	working
経営の圧迫	financial pressure
経営の健全性	financial health
経営の健全度	financial health
経営破綻	bankruptcy
経営破綻	collapse
経営破綻	failure
経営破綻	trouble
経営破綻した	bankrupt
経営破綻した	troubled
経営破綻する	collapse
経営破綻する	fail
経営判断	decision making
経営判断の	decision-making
経営風土	business climate
経営不振	financial difficulties
経営不振	trouble
経営不振企業	distressed company
経営不振に陥っている	struggling
経営不振の	troubled
経営分析	financial statements
経営法	governance
経営方式	management style
経営方針	policy
経過	transition
経過期間	age
経過期間	aging
経過規定	transition provisions
経過金利	accrual rate
計画	deal
計画	idea
計画	package
計画	plan
計画	planning
計画	program
計画	project
計画	proposal
計画	scheme
計画策定	planning
計画策定プロセス	planning process
計画する	plan
計画する	project
計画性	foresight
計画を立てる	plan
経過年金	transitional pension
経過年金	transitional pension
経過年数	age
経過報告	briefing
経過利息	accrued interest
景気	activity
景気	business climate
景気	cycle
景気	economic conditions
景気	economic environment
景気回復	economic recovery
景気回復	recovery
景気拡大	expansion
景気拡大局面	expansion period
景気後退	recession
景気循環の	cyclic
景気循環の	cyclical
景気沈滞	slump
景気づく	pick up
景気などが回復する	pick up
計器盤	panel
景気変動指数	DI
景気変動指数	diffusion index
景況	business climate
景況感	business confidence
経験	experience
軽減	reduction
軽減する	decrease
軽減する	reduce
経験の利得および損失	experience gains and losses
傾向	climate
傾向	stream
傾向	trend
傾向値	trend rate
傾向率	trend rate
警告	warning
警告する	warn
経済活動	economic activities
経済環境	economic environment
経済状況	economic conditions
経済情勢	economic conditions
経済状態	economic conditions
掲載する	include
掲載する	list
掲載する	run
経済成長	growth
経済団体	business alliance
経済的残存耐用年数	remaining economic age

経済的残存耐用年数　remaining economic life
経済的耐用年数　economic life
経済的付加価値　economic value added
経済的付加価値　EVA
経済的利益　fringe benefit
経済のグローバル化　economic globalization
経済付加価値　economic value added
経済付加価値　EVA
計算　account
計算　accounting
計算　calculation
計算　determination
計算　figure
計算　measurement
計算額　portion
計算書　account
計算書　statement
計算上の誤謬　calculation error
計算上の利息　implicit interest
計算書類　accounts
計算する　calculate
計算する　compute
計算制度　accounting system
計算体系　accounting system
計算突合せ　verification of footing and posting
計算表　table
計算方法　calculation
計算利子　imputed interest
計算利息　imputed interest
形式　form
掲示板　board
傾斜　focus
傾斜　shift
芸術・科学支援活動　mecenat
継承　assumption
継承　transfer
形状　form
計上　calculation
計上　provision
計上　recognition
計上…　reported
経常赤字　pretax loss
経常赤字　recurring loss
経常外　nonrecurring
経常外収入　nonrecurring income
経常外損益　nonrecurring gains or losses
経常外損失　extraordinary loss
経常外損失　nonrecurring charge
経常外費用　nonrecurrent expense
経常外利益　nonrecurring revenue
計上金額　recorded amount
経常黒字　current account surplus
経常経費　operating expense
計上された　reported

経常収益　current income
経常収益　gross results
経常収益　pretax profit
経常収支の黒字　current account surplus
経常収支の黒額　current account surplus
経常収入　current income
継承する　assume
継承する　take over
計上する　account for ...
計上する　accrue
計上する　book
計上する　calculate
計上する　carry
計上する　chalk up
計上する　charge
計上する　credit
計上する　declare
計上する　earmark
計上する　generate
計上する　include
計上する　list
計上する　post
計上する　provide
計上する　recognize
計上する　record
計上する　report
計上する　state
経常損益　recurring transactions
経常損益計算　above the line
経常損益計算　above the line
経常損失　pretax loss
経常的　current
経常的　ordinary
経常的な　recurring
経常的な営業損失　recurring operating losses
経常の　pretax [pre-tax]
継承破産人　debtor in possession
経常費　standing expense
経常利益　current account profit
経常利益　current profit
経常利益　line
経常利益　pretax profit
経常利益　recurring profit
計上利益　declared profit
計上利益　reported earnings
経常利益合計　combined pretax profit
係数　factor
形成する　establish
形成する　form
罫線　chart
継続期間　life
継続企業　going concern
継続雇用性　continuous employment system
継続して…する　continue to ...
継続性　consistency

継続性原則　consistency principle
継続性原則　continuity principle
継続製造指図書　process production order
継続製造指図書　standing order
継続棚卸し　continuous inventory
継続的使用料　running royalty
継続的調達と製品のライフサイクルの支援　CALS
形態　form
携帯電話会社　cell phone service provider
刑罰　penalty
経費　budget
経費　burden
経費　business cost
経費　cost
経費　expenditure
経費　expense
経費　outlay
経費　overhead burden
経費管理　overhead cost control
経費削減　cost cut
経費削減　cost reduction
経費削減　expense reduction
経費削減努力　expense reduction efforts
経費として申告する　write off
経費として認められる　deductible
景品　premium
景品引換券　coupon
契約　agreement
契約　arrangement
契約　contract
契約　deal
契約解除　severance
契約関係　contractual relationship
契約期間　term
契約義務　commitment
契約義務　contractual obligation
契約義務　responsibility
契約債務　commitment
契約者　policyholder
契約書　agreement
契約書　contract
契約上の義務　contractual obligation
契約商品　contract
契約書，協定書に署名する　ink an agreement
契約する　take out
契約手数料　commitment fee
契約の解除　dissolution
契約品　contract
契約を結ぶ　enter
契約を結ぶ　ink an agreement
経理　accounting
経理担当者　accountant
経理ハイライト　financial highlights

経理部長	accountant general
経理部長	comptroller
経理部長	controller
経理部長	treasurer
経理方針	accounting policy
計量	measurement
軽量化	downsizing
軽量化する	downsize
系列	series
系列化	integration
系列会社	affiliate
系列会社	affiliated company
系列会社	associate
系列会社	associate company
系列会社	associated company
系列化する	integrate
系列企業	affiliated company
系列企業	group company
系列取引	transaction between affiliated enterprises
系列に置く	affiliate
ゲイン	gain
ケオ・プラン	Keogh
激化する	increase
激化する	intensify
激減	plunge
激減させる	deplete
桁	digit
決意	determination
決意	drive
決意	purpose
決意	resolution
決意する	determine
結果	event
結果	product
結果	results
欠陥	defect
欠陥	disadvantage
欠陥車・欠陥品の回収	recall
決議	action
決議	decision
決議	declaration
決議	resolution
決議	vote
決議案	resolution
決議する	settle
月給	salary
結局の	net
決議録	proceedings
結語	closing
結合	combination
結合財務諸表	combined financial statements
結合財務諸表	combined statements
結合した	combined
決済	closing
決済	liquidation
決済	payment
決済	payoff
決済	settlement
決済条件	payment terms
決済する	liquidate
決済する	settle
決済手続き	clearing procedure
決算	account
決算	account settlement
決算	accounts
決算	book-closing
決算	business performance
決算	business results
決算	closing
決算	closing account
決算	corporate performance
決算	earnings
決算	earnings report
決算	figure
決算	final accounts
決算	financial figures
決算	financial results
決算	reported numbers
決算	results
決算	settlement
決算	settlement of accounts
決算	statement of accounts
決算勘定	closing account
決算期	account settlement term
決算期	book-closing period
決算期	business term
決算期末	year end
決算財務諸表	final accounts
決算財務書類	final accounts
決算書	account
決算書	financial statements
…の決算処理	accounting for …
決算処理	accounting
決算内容	results
決算配当	final dividend
決算日後	post-balance sheet date
決算日後	post-balance sheet day
決算日レート	CR
決算報告	earnings report
決算報告	settlement of accounts
決算報告	statement of accounts
決算報告期間	reporting period
決算報告書	statement of accounts
決算報告上の	reported
決算報告上の利益	reported earnings
…に結集する	focus on …
傑出した	outstanding
決心	determination
結成する	form
欠損	defect
欠損	deficit
欠損	loss
欠損金	deficit
欠損金	loss
欠損金	operating loss
欠損金の繰越し	loss carryforward
	[carry forward]
欠損金の繰越し	loss carryover
	[carry-over]
欠損金の繰戻し	loss carryback
	[carry back]
欠損金の繰戻し	tax [tax loss] carryback
決断	decision
決断	determination
決断	resolution
決断する	determine
決断力	determination
決着	resolution
決着	settlement
月中平均	daily average for a month
決定	action
決定	decision
決定	determination
決定	resolution
決定	settlement
決定する	determine
決定する	govern
決定する	settle
決定的な	final
決定できる	determinable
欠点	defect
月賦購入方式	hire purchase
月賦払い	installment [instalment]
月賦販売	monthly installment sales
月報	newsletter
結論	bottom line
懸念	concern
懸念材料	concern
下落	collapse
下落	decline
下落	decrease
下落	drop
下落	fall
下落	meltdown
下落	plunge
下落	pressure
下落基調	downward trend
下落する	decline
下落する	decrease
下落する	depreciate
下落する	drop
下落する	fall
下落する	lose
下落する	lower
下落する	plunge
権威	authority
権威者	authority
牽引車	driving force
…が原因で	due to …
牽引役	driver
牽引役	driving force
…の牽引力となる	drive
権益	interest

減益　poor earnings
減益　profit decline
原価　cost
減価　depreciation
減価　impairment
現価　present value
原価・売上高・利益関係　CVP
原価・売上高・利益関係分析　cost-volume-profit analysis
原価・営業量・利益関係　CVP
原価・営業量・利益関係分析　cost-volume-profit analysis
原価・操業度・利益分析　cost-volume-profit analysis
見解　judgment [judgement]
見解　opinion
限界　limit
限界　range
限界借入利子率　incremental borrowing rate
限界質量　critical mass
限界生産力　marginal productivity
限界税率　marginal tax rate
限界利益率　PV ratio
限界量　critical mass
原価管理　cost control
原価基礎　cost basis
原価基準　cost basis
原価基準　cost method
減額　deduction
減額　dilution
減額する　dilute
減額する　trim
原価計算　cost accounting
原価計算　cost calculation
原価計算組織　cost accounting organization
原価計算をする　cost
現価計上する　capitalize
原価合計　total cost
原価控除　cost reduction
原価構成　construction of cost
原価削減　cost reduction
原価時価比較低価法　lower of cost or market basis [method]
減価して見積もる　depreciate
原価主義　cost basis
原価主義　cost method
原価主義　method of historical cost
減価償却　amortization
減価償却　cost depreciation
減価償却　depreciation
減価償却　write-off
減価償却および償却　depreciation and amortization
減価償却期間　depreciable life
減価償却差引後　net of depreciation
減価償却資産　depreciable asset
減価償却する　depreciate

減価償却する　write off
減価償却できる　depreciable
減価償却の対象となる　depreciable
減価償却費　depreciation
減価償却費　depreciation cost
減価償却費　depreciation expense
減価償却引当金　accumulated depreciation
減価償却引当金　allowance for depreciation
減価償却引当金　depreciation provision
減価償却引当金　provision for depreciation
減価償却累計額　accrued depreciation
減価償却累計額　accrued depreciation
減価償却累計額　accumulated depreciation
減価償却累計額　accumulated depreciation and amortization
減価償却累計額控除　less accumulated depreciation
減価する　depreciate
原価総額方式　aggregate cost method
原価単位　cost unit
原価中心点　cost center
原価超過額　excess of cost
原価で　at cost
原価低減　cost reduction
原価統制　cost control
原価の流れ　cost distribution
原価の配賦　cost distribution
原価配賦　allocation
原価配分　cost allocation
原価配分　cost distribution
原価引下げ　cost reduction
原価部門　cost center
原価法　cost
原価法　cost method
原価見積り　estimated cost
原価累積額　cost accumulations
原価を見積もる　cost
研究　research
減給　pay cut
言及　reference
研究開発　R & D
研究開発　research
研究開発投資　research and development investment
研究開発投資額　research and development investment
研究開発費　R&D expenditures
研究開発費　R&D spending
研究開発費　research and development cost
研究開発費　research and devel-

opment expense
研究助成金　grant
献金　donation
献金　offering
現金　cash
現金および現金等価物の純減少　net decrease in cash and cash equivalents
現金および現金同等物　cash and cash equivalents
現金および現金同等物　cash and equivalents
現金化　liquidation
現金化する　liquidate
現金合併　cash merger
現金基準　pay-as-you-go basis
現金基準　receipts and payments basis
現金残高　cash balance
現金資金　cash flow
現金資金計算書　cash flow statement
現金支出額　cash outlay
現金収支　cash flow
現金収支計算書　cash flow statement
現金収支を伴わない　noncash
現金主義　pay-as-you-go basis
現金主義会計　pay-as-you-go accounting
現金純額　net cash
現金所要量　cash requirements
現金等価額　cash equivalents
現金等価物　cash equivalents
現金同等物　cash equivalents
現金に換える　cash
現金に換える　realize
現金の収入と支出　cash flow
現金配当　cash dividend
現金払い　cash on delivery
現金払い主義　pay-as-you-earn
現金払い主義　pay-as-you-go
現金払い主義　pay-as-you-go basis
現金払い方式　pay-as-you-earn
現金払い方式　pay-as-you-go
現金払い方式　pay-as-you-go basis
現金払い方式　pay-as-you-go formula
現金必要見込み額　cash requirements
現金必要量　cash requirements
現金預金　cash
現金預金および現金等価物　cash and cash equivalents
現金預金残高　cash balance
現金預金残高　cash balance
現金預金同等物　cash equivalents
権限　authority

権限	authorization
権限	commission
権限	power
権限	right
権限証書	warrant
権原プラント	title plant
権限を与える	authorize
権限を与える	empower
権限を委譲する	delegate
健康医療	health care [healthcare]
健康管理	health care [healthcare]
健康管理給付	health care benefits
現行の	actual
健康保険	health insurance
健康保険給付	health care benefits
検査	examination
現在価値	present value
現在価値	present worth
現在価値	PV
現在価値会計	current value accounting
現在価値会計	CVA
減債基金	amortization fund
減債基金	sinking fund
現在勤務費用	current service cost
現在原価	CC
現在原価	current cost
現在原価会計	CCA
現在原価会計	current cost accounting
現在原価に基づく減価償却	current cost depreciation
減債積立金	retained earnings appropriated for bond
…現在で	as of …
現在取替原価	current cost
…現在の	as of …
現在の	current
現在の	immediate
現在の	running
原材料	basic material
原材料	ingredient
原材料	primary materials
原材料	raw material
検査する	examine
減速	slowdown
減算	amortization
減算額	deductible amount
原産地点	point of origin
献辞	dedication
減資	capital reduction
減資	decrease of capital
原始過去勤務	past service
見識	judgment [judgement]
原始記入	original entry
原始原価	original cost
減資差益	surplus from reduction of capital stock
原資産	underlying asset
原資産保有者	sponsor
現実的	actual
堅実な	solid
現実の	actual
現実の	real
原始の	original
減収圧力	revenue pressure
減収減益	revenues and earnings losses
現住者	tenant
検証	examination
減少	decline
減少	decrease
減少	deterioration
減少	dilution
減少	drop
減少	fall
減少	loss
減少	plunge
減少	pressure
減少	slump
減少	squeeze
減少額	deduction
原証券	underlying securities
減少させる	erode
減少させる	reduce
減少した	reduced
減少した	weak
検証する	examine
減少する	decline
減少する	decrease
減少する	dilute
減少する	drop
減少する	fall
減少する	lower
減少する	plunge
減少する	shrink
減少する	squeeze
原初原価	original cost
減じる	impair
献身	dedication
減税	tax break
建設	construction
建設	foundation
建設借入金	construction loan
建設仮勘定	construction in process
建設仮勘定	construction in progress
建設仮勘定	construction work in progress
建設工事未収金	construction work account receivable
建設資材	construction supplies
建設する	engineer
建設部門	construction sector
建設用地	construction site
源泉	resource
源泉	source
健全化	revitalization
源泉課税	pay-as-you-earn
源泉課税	pay-as-you-earn
源泉課税	PAYE
源泉課税	withholding tax
源泉課税額	withholding tax
源泉課税負担型ローン	withholding tax absorbed loan
源泉課税方式	pay-as-you-go
源泉課税方式	pay-as-you-go formula
源泉所得税	withholding tax
源泉税	withholding tax
源泉税還付	withholding tax refund
源泉地	point of origin
源泉徴収	deduction at source
源泉徴収	withholding
源泉徴収	withholding at source
源泉徴収所得税	withholding income tax
源泉徴収する	withhold
源泉徴収する	withhold at source
源泉徴収税	withholding tax
源泉徴収税額	withholding tax
源泉徴収税率	withholding tax rate
源泉徴収方式	pay-as-you-go
源泉徴収方式	pay-as-you-go method
健全な	healthy
健全な	solid
源泉分離課税	separate taxation at source
源泉分離課税方式	separate withholding tax system
建造	building
現像する	develop
建造物	construction
建造物	structure
原則	principle
原則	rule
減速	slowdown
減速する	slow down
原則として	generally
原則として	principally
減損	impairment
減損	loss
減損	shrinkage
減損	write-down [writedown]
減損会計	asset impairment accounting
減損の兆候	indication of an asset's impairment
現地	field
現地監査	field audit
建築	building
現地組立方式	knockdown system
現地生産	local production
現地調達	local procurement
現地通貨	local currency
現地通貨（建て）	local currency
現地通貨建て	local currency
堅調な	good

堅調な	healthy
堅調の	strong
顕著な	outstanding
検定	authorization
検定	test
献呈	dedication
限定する	determination
限定する	narrow
限定付き	qualified
限定付き監査報告書	qualified auditor's report
限度	limit
検討	review
検討する	review
原動力	drive
原動力	driver
原動力	driving force
原動力	engine
原動力	factor
…の原動力になる	drive
限度額	limit
権能	power
現場	field
現場	site
現場監査	field audit
現場渡し	point of origin
現物受渡し	physical delivery
現物売り	spot selling
現物株	underlying shares
現物の	physical
原本記録	original record
原本書類	original papers
券面	face
券面額	face amount
券面額	face value
減耗	depletion
減耗	shrinkage
減耗控除	depletion allowance
減耗資産	depleted asset
減耗資産	depletion asset
減耗償却	depletion
減耗償却基準額	depletion base
減耗償却費	cost depletion
減耗償却費	depletion expense
減耗損失	impairment losses
現預金	cash
現預金および現金等価物	cash and cash equivalents
現預金および現金同等物	cash and cash equivalents
現預金残高	cash balance
権利	claim
権利	patent
権利	right
原理	fundamentals
原理	principle
権利証落ち	XW
権利落ち	XR
権利金	premium
権利行使	strike

権利行使価格	exercise price
権利行使価格	strike price
権利者	owner
権利証券	warrant
権利証書	securities
権利証書	warrant
権利などの剥奪	divestiture
権利の移転	negotiation
権利の行使	exercise
権利の行使可能な	exercisable
権利の主張	claim
権利の付与	grant
権利放棄	release
権利放棄証書	waiver
原料	ingredient
原料	material
原料	raw material
権力	authority
権力	power

こ

コア	core
コア・コンピテンス	core competence
コア収益	core earnings
コア・ビジネス	core business
好意	goodwill
行為	action
行為	conduct
合意	accord
合意	agreement
合意	arrangement
合意	consensus
合意	term
合意事項	agreement
高位者割増年金	top-hat scheme
合意書	accord
合意書	agreement
合意文書	accord
好影響を与える	positive
公営事業	municipal enterprise
交易	exchange
交易	trade
公益事業	utility
公益事業会社	utility company
公益事業持ち株会社	public utility holding company
公益設備	utility
公益設備	utility plant
校閲する	revise
講演	discussion
後援会	sponsor
後援者	sponsor
後援者	underwriter
後援する	sponsor
効果	benefit
効果	effect
効果	effectiveness
効果	impact

効果	results
公開	disclosure
公開	introduction
公開	marketing
公開	presentation
公開	release
更改	rollover
公開会社	listed company
公開会社	open corporation
公開会社	publicly held company
公開会社	publicly owned company [corporation]
公開株	public float
公開企業	listed company
公開企業会計監視委員会	PCAOB
公開競争	open competition
公開競売	open auction
公開公募	IPO
公開市場価値	open market value
公開市場操作	operation
公開・上場	offering
公開情報	public information
公開する	disclose
公開する	introduce
公開する	release
公開する	state
公開する	unveil
公開性	disclosure
公開入札	public bidding
公開入札	public tender
公開の	patent
公開の	public
公開有限会社	PLC
公開有限責任会社	PLC
公開有限責任会社	public limited company
…への効果がある	impact
工学	engineering
工学技術	engineering
工学技術	industrial engineering
効果的な	effective
効果をあげる	useful
交換	conversion
交換	exchange
交換	swap
交換	trade
交換可能通貨	hard currency
交換可能な	convertible
交換差金	boot
交換尻	clearing balance
交換する	exchange
交換する	swap
交換する	trade
交換できる	redeemable
交換取扱い者	operator
交換比率	exchange rate
交換不能通貨	soft currency
交換レート	exchange rate
後期	latter term
好機	opportunity

公企業	public enterprise	広告宣伝	advertising	向上	pickup [pick-up]
好機の選択	timing	広告宣伝費	advertising	向上	rise
高級	quality	広告取扱高	billing	工場	facility
恒久棚卸し法	book inventory	広告主	sponsor	工場	factory
恒久的	permanent	交互実施許諾契約	cross licensing agreement	工場	plant
恒久的投資	permanent investment			工場	site
		口座	account	工場	work
高級な	high	公債	public bond	工場間接費	factory burden
工業	industry	公債	public debt	工場間接費	factory overhead
工業界	industry	交際費	entertainment expense	向上させる	beef up
公共機関	authority	公債利子	service	向上させる	boost
公共企業体	public enterprise	好材料	positive	向上させる	enhance
鉱業権	license [licence]	好材料の	good	向上させる	improve
工業権使用料	royalty	口座解約	account termination	向上させる	upgrade
公共事業計画	project	工作	tooling	公称資本	authorized capital
興行主	entrepreneur	耕作	culture	工場主	manufacturer
工業製品	manufactured goods	工作機械	tool	工場消耗品	factory supplies
工業製品	manufactured product	工作機械一式	tooling	向上する	advance
工業製品の輸入	manufactured imports	口座残高	account balance	向上する	gain
		行使	exercise	向上する	grow
好業績	brisk business performance	工事	construction	向上する	strengthen
好業績	good performance	工事	engineering	工場設備	plant
好業績	high performance	工事	work	工場設備	plant and equipment
好業績	strong performance	行使価格	exercise price	恒常ドル	constant dollar
公共投資	capital investment	工事完成基準	competion basis	恒常ドル損益計算書	constant dollar income statement
公共の	public	工事完成基準	completed contract method		
工業品	manufactured goods			恒常ドル貸借対照表	constant dollar balance sheet
工具	tool	公式の行事	function		
…の合計	combined	公示資本	declared capital	交渉力	bargaining power
合計	aggregate	工事収益	construction revenue	控除額	deduction
合計	amount	工事進行基準	percentage of completion method	控除可能な	deductible
合計	footing			控除可能費用	deductible expenses
合計	gross	工事進行基準売上	percentage-of-completion earnings	公職	office
合計	sum			…控除後	after
合計	total	行使する	exercise	…控除後	less
…の合計額	combined	講師団	panel	…控除後	net of ...
好景気	activity	行使できる	exercisable	控除項目	deduction
合計金額	sum	工事別原価計算	job cost method	…控除後の利益	income after ...
合計検算	footing	公社債	bond	…を控除したうえで	after
合計	total	公社債投資信託	bond investment trust	控除して	less
貢献	contribution			控除する	credit
貢献	participation	公衆	public	控除する	deduct
貢献額	contribution	高収益	high performance	控除する	reduce
貢献したもの	contributor	公準	assumption	…控除前	before
…に貢献する	benefit	公準	concept	控除前の	gross
貢献する	contribute	後順位転換社債	convertible subordinated debenture	…控除前の利益	income before ...
貢献する	serve			控除をしない	gross
貢献損益	contribution profit or loss	好循環	virtuous cycle	更新	renewal
		控除	allowance	更新	restatement
貢献要因	contributing factor	控除	deduction	更新	rollover
貢献要因	contributing factor	控除	less	更新する	restate
貢献要因	contributor	控除	tax allowance	更新選択権	renewal option
公庫	treasury	交渉	bargain	更新手数料	renewal fee
広告	ad	交渉	negotiation	構図	form
広告	advertisement	交渉	talks	構図	paradigm
広告	advertising	向上	advance	高水準の	high
広告収入	advertising revenue	向上	boost	公正	right
広告収入	advertisng revenue	向上	enhancement	攻勢	thrust
広告戦術	advertizing tactics	向上	gain	更正	assessment
広告宣伝	advertisement	向上	improvement	更生	rehabilitation

構成	composition	
構成	form	
構成	mix	
構成	organization	
構成	profile	
構成	scope	
構成	structure	
構成会社	constituent company	
公正価格	fair value	
公正価額	fair value	
公正価額による年金資産	plan assets at fair value	
公正価値	fair value	
合成先物	synthetic futures	
…で構成される	comprise	
…を構成する	comprise	
校正する	revise	
公正妥当と認められている	acceptable	
構成単位	unit	
公正な	arm's length [arm's-length]	
公正な	fair	
公正な	reasonable	
公正な評価額	fair value	
厚生年金	corporate employee pension plan	
厚生年金	corporate employee pension system	
厚生年金制度	corporate employee pension plan	
厚生年金制度	corporate employee pension system	
厚生年金保険	corporate employee pension insurance	
厚生年金保険法	Japanese Welfare Pension Insurance Law	
高性能	high performance	
公正表示	fair disclosure	
構成比率	component percentage	
構成物質	material	
構成部品	component	
構成部分	integral part	
構成要素	component	
構成要素	element	
構成要素	ingredient	
構成要素	integral part	
口銭	commission	
構想	concept	
構想	idea	
構想	initiative	
構想	plan	
構想	proposal	
構造	organization	
構造	profile	
構造	status	
構造	structure	
構造改革	structural reform	
構造上の欠陥	structural defect	
構造的	underlying	
構造的な変化	structural change	
構造的不均衡	structural imbalance	
構造的マイナス要因	structural negatives	
構造物	structure	
拘束	curb	
拘束力	force	
後退	slowdown	
交替	shift	
交替勤務時間	shift	
後退する	slow down	
構築する	create	
構築する	form	
構築物	construction	
構築物	structure	
好調	strength	
好調な	brisk	
好調な	favorable	
好調な	good	
好調な	healthy	
好調な	robust	
好調な	strong	
好調な売れ行き	strong sales	
好調な業績	strong performance	
好都合な	favorable	
好都合な	friendly	
工程	process	
公定歩合	discount rate	
公的	public	
公的資金	public funds	
公的資金の注入	injection of public funds	
公的資金の注入	public fund injection	
公的年金	public pension	
公的年金	public pension plan	
公的年金給付	public pension benefits	
好転	improvement	
好転	turnaround	
好転させる	improve	
好転する	turn around	
高騰	rise	
行動	action	
行動	conduct	
行動	movement	
合同	incorporation	
行動規範	code of conduct	
行動計画	action program	
合同した	incorporate	
合同した	incorporated	
口頭で説明する	present	
高等の	advanced	
合同の	joint	
行動の規範	ethics	
行動の自由	discretion	
高度な	high	
高度な	state-of-the-art	
公にする	unveil	
購入	acquisition	
購入	procurement	
購入	purchase	
購入	purchasing	
購入価格	purchase price	
購入価格	purchasing price	
購入経験	purchase experience	
購入権	purchase right	
購入債務	account payable	
購入指図書	purchase order	
購入者	acquirer	
購入する	acquire	
購入する	buy	
購入する	procure	
購入する	purchase	
購入選択権	option	
購入注文書	purchase order	
公認	authorization	
公認会計士	certified accountant	
公認会計士	certified public accountant	
公認会計士	certified public accountant	
公認会計士	CPA	
公認会計士	public accountant	
後任監査人	successor auditor	
公認管理会計士	certified management accountant	
公認内部監査人	certified internal auditor	
公の	public	
公売	auction	
購買	purchase	
購買	purchasing	
後配株	deferred share	
購買監査	purchase [purchasing] auditing	
購買管理	purchasing management	
購買者	purchaser	
購買戦略	purchasing strategy	
購買部門	purchasing department	
購買力損益	purchasing power gain or loss	
後発事象	events occurring after the balance sheet date	
後発事象	events subsequent to balance sheet date	
後発事象	post-balance sheet event	
後発事象	post-balance sheet event	
後発事象	subsequent event	
後発事象	subsequent event	
後発事象の監査	post-balance sheet review	
後発事象の査閲	post-balance sheet review	
後半	latter half	
広範囲の	global

広範囲の	large	
広範な	comprehensive	
公表	announcement	
公表	declaration	
公表	disclosure	
公表	release	
公表…	reported	
公表経過保険料	reported earned premium	
公表された	reported	
公表しないでおく	withhold	
公表する	announce	
公表する	declare	
公表する	disclose	
公表する	issue	
公表する	name	
公表する	release	
公表する	report	
公表する	reveal	
公表する	state	
公表する	unveil	
公表データ	reported figures	
公表利益	reported earnings	
公表利益	reported income	
交付	delivery	
交付	distribution	
交付	issue	
高付加価値製品	value-added product	
交付金	grant	
交付する	deliver	
合弁	joint venture	
合弁会社	joint venture	
合弁会社	joint venture company	
合弁事業	joint venture	
合弁の	joint	
候補	contender	
公募	open offer	
公募	public offering	
公報	newsletter	
広報	PR	
広報	public relations	
広報活動	public relations	
攻防戦	struggle	
広報宣伝活動	PR	
広報宣伝活動	public relations	
広報宣伝活動	public relations	
合法の	due	
公募価格	offering price	
公募価格	public offering price	
公募債	public offering bond	
候補者	nominee	
公募増資	public offering	
公募取引	public trading	
公募入札	auction	
公募発行	public placement	
候補被指名者	nominee	
公務	public affairs	
公務	service	
被る	incur	
被る	receive	
被る	suffer	
合名会社	partnership	
項目	category	
項目	component	
項目	element	
項目	item	
公約	commitment	
公約	pledge	
公約する	commit	
公約する	pledge	
公有地譲渡証書	patent	
効用	use	
効用	utility	
小売り	retail	
合理化	downsizing	
合理化	rationalization	
合理化	streamlining	
合理化する	downsize	
合理化する	resize	
合理化する	streamline	
小売企業	retailer	
小売業	retailer	
小売棚卸し法	retail inventory method	
効率	effectiveness	
効率	efficiency	
効率化	efficiency	
効率化	streamlining	
効率化する	streamline	
効率性	efficiency	
効率的な	effective	
効率的な	efficient	
効率のよい	efficient	
合理的な	due	
合理的な	reasonable	
小売店	outlet	
小売店	retailer	
考慮	account	
考慮	assumption	
考慮	consideration	
綱領	program	
効力	effect	
効力	effectiveness	
効力をもつ	effective	
…考慮後の利益	income after …	
考慮する	assume	
考慮する	consider	
…考慮前	before	
…考慮前の利益	income before …	
高齢化	aging	
…を越える	top	
超える	surpass	
ゴーイング・コンサーン	going concern	
コード	code	
コーポレーション	corporation	
コーポレート	corporate	
コーポレート・ガバナンス	corporate governance	
コーポレート・カルチャー	corporate culture	
コーポレート・シティズン	corporate citizen [citizenship]	
コーポレート・ファイナンス	corporate finance	
コーポレート・リポート	corporate report	
ゴール	goal	
コール・オプションを買うときに支払うオプション料	call premium	
コール価格	call price	
コール借入金	call money	
コール・プレミアム	call premium	
コール・レート	call money rate	
子会社	affiliate	
子会社	arm	
子会社	dependent company	
子会社	holding	
子会社	operation	
子会社	subsidiary	
子会社	unit	
子会社から親会社への販売	upstream	
子会社支払い手形	note payable to subsidiary	
子会社純資産持ち分	equity in net assets of subsidiaries	
子会社の未分配利益	undistributed earnings of subsidiaries	
子会社の留保利益	undistributed earnings of subsidiaries	
子会社連動株	tracking stock in a subsidiary	
小型化	downsizing	
小型化する	downsize	
小型株指数	small cap index	
涸渇資産	depleted asset	
誤記	error	
小切手記入帳	check register	
小切手帳	checkbook	
小切手取引	checking transaction	
顧客	client	
顧客	customer	
顧客	public	
顧客基盤	customer base	
顧客サービス	customer service	
顧客支援サービス	customer support service	
顧客情報	client information	
顧客層	customer base	
顧客の100％満足	total customer satisfaction	
顧客の完全な満足	total customer satisfaction	
顧客の完全な満足度	total customer satisfaction	
顧客のニーズ	customer needs	
顧客の満足	CS	

顧客の満足	customer satisfaction
顧客の要求	customer needs
顧客の要求	customer requirements
顧客へのサービス	customer service
顧客への奉仕	customer service
顧客満足度	CS
顧客満足度	customer satisfaction
顧客融資契約	customor financing commiments
国営の	state-run
国外流通通貨	Xenocurrency
国際化	globalization
国際化	liberalization
国際会計基準	IAS
国際会計基準	International Accounting Standards
国際間の	international
国際競争	international competition
国際競争力	global competitiveness
国際協調融資	syndicated loan
国際業務	international operations
国際銀行間通信協会	SWIFT
国際銀行間通信協会	SWIFT
国際決済銀行	Bank for International Settlements
国際決済銀行	BIS
国際財務報告基準	IFRS
国際財務報告基準	International Financial Reporting Standards
国際事業	international activities
国際事業	international operations
国際市場	global market
国際市場	international market
国際借款団	consortium
国際上の	international
国際戦略	global strategy
国際租税協定	tax convention
国際租税条約	tax convention
国際的	international
国際的な	global
国債入札	refunding
国際標準化機構	ISO
告示	announcement
告示する	announce
国税局	taxation bureau
告訴する	accuse
告知	disclosure
小口現金	float
小口資金	petty fund
小口投資家	retail
小口の	petty
国土	land
国内営業部門	domestic sales operations
国内産の	domestic
国内需要	domestic demand
国内総生産	GDP
国内通貨(建て)	local currency
国内の	domestic
国内の	internal
告発	charge
告発する	accuse
告発する	charge
酷評	thrust
焦げ付いた	dividend payable unclaimed
焦げ付き	bad debt
個々の	individual
試み	effort
誤差	error
50%削減する	halve
故障	failure
個人企業	single proprietorship
個人消費	household spending
個人消費支出	consumer spending
個人的	individual
個人的な	private
個人投資家	retail
個人年金積立奨励制度	Keogh
個人の	individual
個人向け取引	retail
コスト	cost
コスト管理	cost control
コスト効率がよい	cost effective
コスト・コントロール	cost control
コスト削減	cost control
コスト削減	cost cut
コスト削減	cost reduction
コスト・センター	cost center
小銭	change
誇張する	inflate
コツ	knowhow [know-how]
国家財政の	fiscal
国家主席	president
国庫	treasury
固定型	fixed
固定間接費	fixed overhead
固定金利の証券	fixed income security
固定債務	funded debt
固定式の	fixed
固定資産	fixed asset
固定資産	long-lived asset
固定資産	property
固定資産支出額	fixed asset expenditures
固定資産処分損	capital loss
固定資産税	real estate tax
固定資産税	real property tax
固定資産税評価額	assessed value of fixed assets
固定資産投資	capital expenditure
固定資産投資額	capital expenditure
固定資産の減損処理	write-offs of appraisal losses in fixed assets
固定資産の除却	disposal of fixed assets
固定資産の除却費	abandonment cost
固定した	fixed
固定した	noncurrent
固定資本	fixed capital
固定する	secure
固定製造間接費	fixed overhead
固定費	overhead
固定負債	fixed liability
固定負債	long term debt
事柄	affair
事柄	event
事柄	matter
今年	this year
…ごとに	per
好ましい	favorable
好ましくない	unfavorable
小幅な伸び	marginal increase
誤謬	error
誤表示	misstatement
五分五分になる	break even
個別原価計算	specific order costing
個別償却	item depreciation
個別償却	single unit depreciation
個別償却	unit depreciation
個別償却法	unit method
個別生産システム	job order production system
個別の	independent
個別の	individual
個別法	unit method
個別目的財務諸表	specific purpose statements
コマーシャル・ペーパー	commercial paper
コマーシャル・ペーパー	CP
ごまかす	cook
コミッション	commission
コミットメント	commitment
コミットメント・ライン	commitment line
コミュニケーション	communication
コミュニティ	community
コメント	statement
顧問の	advisory
固有資産	identifiable asset
雇用	employment
雇用	job
雇用機会均等法	EEOA
雇用機会均等法	Equal Employment Opportunity Act
雇用後債務	postretirement liabilities
雇用者	employer
雇用促進税額控除	job development credit

雇用調整	layoff	コンプライアンス	compliance	債券	security
雇用調整する	lay off	梱包	package	債権	credit
雇用主	employer	コンポーネント	component	債権	debt
雇用年金	occupational pension	根本原理	basis	債権	finance receivables
雇用年金	occupational pension	根本原理	fundamentals	債権	loan
頃合い	timing	根本的な	underlying	債権	loan credits
今回の	latest	混乱	turmoil	債権	payment
根幹業務	core business			債権	receivable
今期	current business year	**さ**		再建	recovery
今期	current fiscal year			再建	rehabilitation
今期	current year	差	difference	再建	reorganization
今期	during the year	差	disparity	再建	restructuring
今期	this year	差	imbalance	再建	revival
根拠	basis	差	spread	財源	finance
根拠	foundation	サービサー	servicer	財源	resource
…を根拠に据える	base	サービシング	servicing	再建案	restructuring plan
根拠のある	reasonable	サービス	service	債券運用	bond management
根拠を置く	base	サービス部門原価	service cost	債券運用者	bond manager
コングロマリット	conglomerate	サービス料	service charge	債権回収	loan collection
根源	parent	サービス料金	service charge	債権回収	loan collection
今後	future	サーベンス・オクスレー法		債権回収	servicing
混合	mix		Sarbanes-Oxley Act	債権回収会社	servicer
今後とも…する	continue to ...	差異	difference	債権買取り業	factoring
今後の	future	差異	disparity	債権買取り業者	factor
コンシューマー	consumer	財	commodity	債権額	exposure
コンセプト	concept	財	goods	債券格付け	bond rating
コンソーシアム	consortium	再位置付け	repositioning	債券格付け	debt rating
根底にある	underlying	最大手	leader	債権株式化	debt-for-equity swap
コンテンツ	content	財貨	commodity	債権管理部門	credit department
コントローラー	comptroller	財貨	goods	債権区分	categorization of loan claims
コントローラー	controller	再開	renewal		
コントロール	control	在外子会社	CFC	再建計画	reconstruction plan
困難	stress	在外子会社	controlled foreign corporation	再建計画	reorganization scheme
困難な状況	stress			再建計画	restructuring plan
今年度	current business year	在外子会社	foreign subsidiary	再建計画	restructuring program
今年度	current fiscal year	在外従属会社	CFC	再建計画	revival plan
今年度	current year	災害準備金	provision for disasters	債権国	creditor
今年度	during the year	再開する	resume	債権国会議	consortium
今年度	this year	再開発	redevelopment	債権債務関係	obligation
今年度上期	latest fiscal first half	再開発	renewal	債券先物	bond futures
今年度上半期	fiscal first half	再活性化	revitalization	再建策	reconstruction plan
今年度上半期	latest fiscal first half	財貨の流れ	physical flow of goods	再建策	restructuring plan
		再教育	retraining	債権残高	outsranding receivables
今年度下期	second half of the current business year	細工	tooling	債券実質利回り格差	real bond yield differences
		採掘料	royalty		
今年度下半期	second half of the current business year	サイクル	cycle	債権者	creditor
		再訓練	retraining	債権者会議	creditors' meeting
今年度中間決算	latest fiscal first half	裁決	decision	再研修	retraining
		裁決	determination	債権処理費用	credit cost
今年度の	latest	裁決	judgment [judgement]	債権処理費用	loan disposal costs
コンピュータ回線で	online [on-line]	裁決	resolution	債権処理費用	loan write-off costs
コンピュータ回線を使って	online [on-line]	債券	bond	再建する	rebuild
		債券	corporate debt securities	再建する	rehabilitate
		債券	debt	再建する	reorganize
コンピュータ勤務	telecommuting	債券	debt instrument	再建する	restructure
コンピュータのネットワークで	online [on-line]	債券	debt security	再建する	revive
		債券	fixed income security	債券投資信託	bond fund
コンピュータプログラム	program	債券	note	再検討する	reinvent
コンフォート・レター	comfort letter	債券	paper	債券取引	bond trading
		債券	securities	債権の株式化	debt equity swap

債権の株式化	DES	最高財務責任者	CFO	再就職斡旋	outplacement
債権の現在価値	loan values	最高財務担当者	CFO	最終成果	bottom line
債権の査定	loan assesssment	最高財務担当役員	CFO	再修正する	reverse
債権の棚上げ	postponement of credits	最高執行責任者	COO	最終製品	finished product
		最高水準の	state-of-the-art	最終損益	bottom line
債権の届出	claim	再興する	rebuild	最終的な	net
債券発行	bond issuance [issue]	再構成	restructuring	最終的な厳しい考査	acid test
債券発行	loan	再構成する	restructure	最終的に	overall
債券発行残高	bond outstanding	最高責任者	head	最終手続き	closing
債権表示証書	note	再構築する	rebuild	最終投資家	end user
債権放棄	debt forgiveness	再構築する	restructure	最終の	final
債権放棄	debt waiver	再購入する	repurchase	最終の	latest
債権放棄	loan forgiveness	最高の	top	最終の	overall
債権放棄	loan waiver	在庫回転率	inventory turnover	最終配当	final dividend
債権放棄	loan write-off	在庫管理	inventory management	最終ユーザー	end user
債券ポートフォリオ	bond portfolio	在庫水準	inventory level	最重要事項	bottom line
		在庫として持つ	keep	最重要な	high
債権ポートフォリオ	receivables portfolio	在庫費用	inventory cost	最終利益	net profit
		在庫評価額	inventory value	最終利回り	maturity yield
債権保有者	creditor	在庫品	goods in stock	最終利回り	yield to maturity
債権保有者保護	debtholder [debt holder] protection	在庫品	goods on hand	最終利回り	YTM
		在庫品	inventory	最終利用者	end user
債権融資	receivables financing	在庫品	merchandise	歳出予算	appropriation
在庫	backlog	在庫品	stock	再取得	reacquisition
在庫	inventory	在庫品	stock in hand	再取得価格	reacquisition price
在庫	stock	在庫品	stock in trade	再取得株式	repurchased share
再考	review	在庫品評価額	inventory value	再取得原価	replacement cost
最高	cap	財産	asset	最初	beginning
最高	high	財産	goods	最小	minimum
最高	maximum	財産	property	最上位の	top
最高位	top	財産	wealth	最小株式引受限度	minimum subscription
最高位の	top	採算が合わない	loss-making [loss-making]		
最高価格先出し法	HIFO			最小限	minimum
最高価格払出し法	HIFO	採算が取れる	pay	最小値	minimum
最高価格払出し法	highest-in first-out method	財産管理	treasurership	最上の	top
		財産権	property	在職制度加入者	active plan participants
最高管理層	top management	財産権の終了	determination		
最高技術水準の	state-of-the-art	財産権の消滅	determination	在職年数	year of service
最高技術責任者	CTO	採算性	feasibility	最初の	initial
最高級の	state-of-the-art	採算性	potential profitability	最新鋭	cutting edge
最高業務運営責任者	COO	採算性	profitability	最新鋭	leading edge
最高業務運営役員	COO	採算性調査	feasibility study	最新鋭の	state-of-the-art
最高業務執行役員	CEO	採算点	break-even (point)	最新型	cutting edge
最高業務執行役員	chief executive officer	採算の合わない	unprofitable	最新型	leading edge
		財産の移転	grant	最新技術の	state-of-the-art
最高業務執行理事	CEO	財産の譲渡	settlement	最新式	cutting edge
最高業務執行理事	chief executive officer	採算の取れる規模	critical mass	最新式	leading edge
		財産目録	inventory	最新式の	state-of-the-art
最高記録	high	採算ライン	break-even (point)	最新の	emerging
最高記録	new high	採算ラインになる	break even	最新の	innovative
最高記録	record	催事	event	最新の	latest
最高経営管理者層	top management	材質	material	再審理	review
		最終赤字	net loss	…のサイズを変える	resize
最高経営者	top management	最終価値	final value	再生	rehabilitation
最高経営責任者	CEO	最終黒字	net profit	再生	renewal
最高経営責任者	chief executive officer	最終結果	bottom line	再生	reorganization
		最終決定	bottom line	再生	revitalization
最高経営責任者	top management	最終仕入原価法	method of price of last purchase	再生	revival
最高原価先出し法	HIFO			財政	budget
最高限度	cap	最終使用者	end user	財政	finance

財政赤字	fiscal deficit
財政援助	funding
再生計画	restructuring plan
再生計画	revival plan
再生紙	recycled paper
財政支出	budget outlays
財政状況	financial condition
財政状況	financial performance
財政状態	financial condition
財政状態	financial position
財政上の	monetary
再生する	rebuild
再生する	rehabilitate
再生する	reorganize
再生する	revive
再生する	turn around
財政建て直し	budget consolidation
財政的の困難	financial difficulties
財政的強み	financial strength
財政難	financial difficulties
財政難	financial pressure
財政の	fiscal
財政逼迫	financial difficulties
再整理する	reverse
最前線	cutting edge
最前線	forefront
最前線	front
最前線	front line
最前線	leading edge
最先端	cutting edge
最先端	forefront
最先端	leading edge
最先端の	latest
最先端の	state-of-the-art
最善の手法	best practice
最善の努力	best efforts
最善の努力をする条件の	best-efforts
最善の見積りと判断	best estimates and judgments
最前部	forefront
最前部	leading edge
最前列	front
再測定する	remeasure
最大	maximum
最大限の	top
最大産出高	capacity yield
最大数	maximum
最大の	top
最大の関心事	front burner
最大のシェア	lion's share
最大の比率	lion's share
最大の部分	lion's share
最大の目標	primary objective
最大量	maximum
最高値	high
採択可能	acceptable
在宅勤務	telecommuting
採択する	adopt
財団	foundation
再調査	review
再調整	realignment
再調達	repurchase
再調達原価	current cost
再調達原価	replacement cost
再調達原価	repurchase cost
再調達コスト	replacement cost
再陳述	restatement
最低	low
最低	minimum
裁定	rule
最低貸出金利	minimum lending rate
最低貸出利率	base rate
最低記録	low
再提携	realignment
最低限の経済規模	critical mass
最低購入量	minimum purchase
最低在庫水準	minimum stock level
最低在庫量	minimum stock
最低自己資本比率	minimum capital adequacy ratio
最低資本金	minimum capital
裁定する	award
最低年金計上額	minimum pension provision
最低発注量	minimum order quantity
最低発注量	minimum order size
最低必要資本金額	minimum capital requirements
最低保証金	minimum guarantee
最低落札価格	stop price
最低リース支払い額	minimum lease payments
最低リース料債権	minimum lease payments receivable
最低利益	minimum profit
最低利幅	minimum margin
最低ロイヤルティ	minimum royalty
最適在庫量	optimum stock
最適操業度	optimum output
最適ポートフォリオ	optimal portfolio
財テク	financial market
サイト	site
サイト	Web site
再統合	realignment
再投資	reinvestment
再投資収益	reinvestment income
再投資する	reinvest
歳入	revenue
歳入超過額	surplus
在任期間	length of service
再燃する	revive
サイバービジネス	cyberbusiness
栽培する	grow
再配置	redeployment
再配置	relocation
再配置する	redeploy
再配置する	relocate
再配備	redeployment
再配分	redeployment
再配分する	redeploy
再発明する	reinvent
裁判手続き	judicial procedures
最低値	low
再評価	revaluation
再評価剰余金	revaluation surplus
再評価する	wtite down
再評価積立金	appraisal surplus
再表示	restatement
再表示する	restate
細分化する	segment
再分類	reclassification
再分類する	reclassify
再編	consolidation
再編	realignment
再編	reorganization
再編	restructuring
再編計画	restructuring plan
再編策	overhaul plan
再編する	reorganize
再編する	resize
再編成	divestiture
再編成	realignment
再編成	reorganization
再編成する	reorganize
再編成する	reshape
再編成する	restructure
再ポジショニング	repositioning
債務	borrowing
債務	debt
債務	indebtedness
債務	liability
債務	loan
債務	obligation
債務	payables
債務	responsibility
財務	balance sheet
財務	finance
財務	financing
財務悪化	financial difficulties
債務一部免除契約	composition
財務運用	treasury operation
財務表	statement
財務概況	financial review
財務会計	financial reporting
財務会計基準書	SFAS
財務会計基準書	Statement of Financial Accounting Standards
財務会計基準審議会	FASB
財務会計基準審議会	Financial Accounting Standards Board
財務会計上の説明	financial review
債務過多	over-indebtedness
債務過多	over-indebtedness
債務株式化	debt-for-equity swap

財務官	treasurer
財務管理	financial market
財務管理	treasurership
債務元利返済額	debt service
財務基盤	balance sheet
財務基盤	capital structure
財務基盤	financial condition
債務救済	debt forgiveness
財務業績	financial performance
財務記録	financial records
債務金額	amounts due
財務計算書	earnings report
債務契約書	debt rating
財務構成	financial structure
財務広報	investor [investors] relations
財務広報	IR
債務国	debtor
債務再構成	reorganization of debt
債務残高	outstanding debt
財務実績	financial figures
財務実績	financial performance
財務実績	financial results
債務支払い不能者	bankrupt
債務者	borrower
債務者	debtor
財務省	treasury
財務状況	balance sheet
財務状況	financial condition
財務状況	financial health
財務状況	financial performance
財務状況	financial position
財務状況	financial review
債務証券	debt
債務証券	debt instrument
債務証券	debt security
債務証券	fixed income security
債務証券	bond
債務証券	debt instrument
債務証券	debt rating
債務証券	debt security
債務証券	obligation
財務省証券	T-bond
財務省証券	treasury
財務省証券	Treasury bond
財務状態	balance sheet
財務状態	financial condition
財務状態	financial performance
財務状態	financial position
財務状態報告書	position statement
財務省中期証券	T-note
財務省中期証券	Treasury note
財務省長期証券	T-bond
財務省長期証券	Treasury bond
財務上の	financial
財務上の健全性	financial health
財務情報	financial data
財務情報	financial information
財務情報要約	financial highlights
財務情報要約	summarized financial information
財務諸表	accounts
財務諸表	financial statements
財務諸表注記	notes to financial statements
財務諸表に対する注記	notes to financial statements
財務書類	accounts
財務書類	financial statements
財務書類[財務諸表]注記	footnote to financial statements
財務書類[財務諸表]の目的	objective of financial statements
財務書類監査	examination of financial statements
財務書類注記	notes to financial statements
財務書類に対する注記	notes to financial statements
財務書類の完全性と客観性	integrity and objectivity of the financial statements
財務書類の完全性と信頼性	integrity and reliability of the financial statements
財務書類の期間比較	comparative financial results
財務書類の連結	consolidated accounts
財務資料	financial data
財務資料抜粋	selected financial data
財務成績	financial results
財務体質	balance sheet
財務体質	financial health
財務体質	financial position
財務体質	financial strength
債務棚上げ	bailout
財務担当責任者	CFO
財務担当役員	treasurer
財務力	financial strength
債務超過	deficit
債務超過	insolvency
債務超過	liabilities exceeding assets
債務超過	negative net worth
債務超過	net capital deficiency
債務超過額	negative net worth
債務超過額	net liabilities
債務超過の	insolvent
財務データ	financial data
財務内容	balance sheet
財務内容	finance
財務内容	financial condition
財務内容	financial health
財務内容	financial strength
財務内容に関する意見書	comfort letter
財務内容に関する意見書	letter of comfort
財務の	financial
債務の肩代わり	assumed loans
債務の株式化	debt equity swap
債務の株式化	DES
財務の健全性	financial health
債務の支払い	repayment of debt
債務の範囲	liabilities base
債務の免除	debt forgiveness
財務ハイライト	financial highlights
債務比率	debt ratio
債務負担	liability exposure
債務負担	obligation
財務部長	controller
財務部長	treasurer
財務部門	treasurer's department
財務部門	treasury arm
財務部門	treasury department
債務不履行	default
債務返済	debt repayment
債務返済	debt service
債務返済	debt servicing
債務返済	loan repayment
債務返済	repayment of debt
債務返済	servicing
債務返済負担	servicing burden
債務法	liability method
財務報告	F/S
財務報告	financial reporting
財務報告	financial review
財務報告	financial statement
財務報告会計	financial reporting
財務報告期間	reporting period
財務報告書	F/S
財務報告書	financial statement
財務報告上の	reported
財務報告上の利益	reported earnings
財務報告の目的	objective of financial reporting
財務報告ハイライト	financial highlights
債務方式	liability method
債務保証	guarantee of debt
債務保証	guarantee of indebtedness
債務保証	loan guarantee
債務免除	debt waiver
債務免除	forgiveness of liabilities
債務免除	loan forgiveness
債務免除	loan waiver
債務免除	waiver of obligation
債務免除益	savings from a debt waiver
財務面での健全性	financial strength
財務面での実績	financial performance
債務履行	servicing

財務レバレッジ	financial gearing
財務レバレッジ	leverage
債務を抱えた	debt-saddled
細目	item
最安値	low
再融資	refinancing
再融資する	refinance
最優先	first priority
最優先課題	front burner
最優先課題	top
最優先事項	front burner
最優先事項	top
最優先の	top
最有力候補者	front runner [front-runner, frontrunner]
採用	use
採用する	adopt
採用する	use
材料	factor
材料	force
材料	ingredient
材料	material
材料	raw material
裁量可能キャッシュ・フロー	discretionary cash flow
裁量的経費	discretionary spending
裁量的支出	discretionary outlays
最良の見積りと判断	best estimates and judgments
最良の見積りと判断	best estimates and judgments
財力	finance
財力	financial strength
サインする	exchange
差益	capital surplus
差益	gain
差益	gross profit
査閲	review
査閲する	review
差額	balance
差額	difference
差額決済金額	net compensation amount
さかのぼって	upward
下がる	lower
先入れ先出し法	first-in, first-out basis [method]
先入れ先出し法	FIFO
先入れ先出し法	first-in, first-out basis
先入れ先出し法に基づく低価法	lower of cost (first-in, first-out) or market
先送り	back burner
先送りする	defer
先取権	priority
先物	forward
先物	futures
先物為替	forward exchange
先物為替	futures

先物契約	futures
先物契約	futures contract
先物取引	forward business
先物取引	forward dealing
先物取引	forward transaction
先物取引	futures
先物取引	futures trading
先物取引中心の	futures-driven
先行き	future
先行き	outlook
先行き	prospects
先行きの	future
先行き不透明感	uncertainty
作業	effort
作業	operation
作業	work
作業の	working
先渡し金利	forward rate
先渡し契約	forward
先渡し契約	forward contract
先渡し取引	forward
先渡し取引	forward trading
策	effort
策	exercise
策	measure
策	package
策	plan
策	program
策	scheme
策	shift
策	strategy
策	tactics
作為	action
作為	commission
削減	downsizing
削減	layoff
削減	reduction
削減する	contain
削減する	cut
削減する	downsize
削減する	eliminate
削減する	lay off
削減する	liquidate
削減する	reduce
削減する	slash
削減する	trim
削除	elimination
削除	write-off
削除する	take out
作成	execution
作成する	execute
作成する	prepare
作成する	present
作成する	produce
サクセス	success
作戦	tactics
作戦行動	tactics
作戦上の	operational
昨年	last year
昨年度	last year

避ける	withhold
下げる	cut
下げる	lower
下げる	reduce
支え	mainstay
支える	buoy
差し入れ	assignment
差し入れる	post
差し押さえ	foreclosure
差し押さえる	levy
指図する	order
差し止め	suspension
差し止める	suspend
差し伸べる	extend
…を差し引いたうえで	after
差し引いて	less
差し引いて	minus
差し控える	withhold
差引	deduction
差引	less
差引額	deduction
差引勘定	offset
…差引き後	after
…差引後	net of …
…差引後純額	net of …
…差引後の利益	income after …
差引残高	account balance
差引で	less
…差引き前	before
…差引前の利益	income before …
差し引く	credit
差し引く	deduct
詐称する	falsify
定める	appoint
定める	determine
定める	establish
定める	provide
定める	state
座談会	panel
刷新	innovation
刷新	renewal
刷新する	reshape
刷新する	revamp
殺到	surge
殺到する	surge
雑費	miscellaneous expenditure
査定	adjustment
査定	appraisal
査定	assessment
査定	valuation
査定価格	valuation
査定額	assessed value
査定額	assessment
査定価値	assessed value
査定する	assess
査定する	award
査定評価額	assessed value
作動する	function
作動する	run
サブプライム・ローン	subprime

サブプライム・ローン	loan
サブプライム・ローン	subprime mortgage
サブプライム・ローン	subprime mortgage loan
サブプライム・ローンの融資行	subprime lender
サブプライム・ローンの融資行	subprime mortgage lender
サプライ	supply
サプライ・チェーン	supply chain
サプライヤー	supplier
差別	differentiation
差別化	differentiation
差別修正措置	affirmative action
差別撤廃措置	affirmative action
サポート	support
サポートする	support
左右されやすい	volatile
左右する	determine
さらされやすい	vulnerable
騒ぎ	turmoil
傘下	umbrella
参加	access
参加	entry
参加	participation
参加意思表示	commitment
傘下入りする	affiliate
参加株式	participating capital stock
参加勧誘	challenge
傘下企業	affiliated company
参加企業	participant
参加行	participant
三角合併	triangular merger
三角合併方式	triangular merger scheme
3か月ごとに	quarterly
参加国	participant
参加者	affiliate
参加者	entry
参加者	participant
参加者	player
参加する	access
参加する	enter
参加する	join
参加する	participate
参加する	share
参加する	sign up
3月期	business term ending in March
3月期決算	business term ending in March
3月期決算	business year to March 31
3月31日までの事業年度	business year to March 31
参加登録する	enter
傘下に置く	affiliate
参加配当	participating dividend
参加優先株式	participating preferred stock
参加呼びかけ	challenge
産業	industry
産業界	industry
産業間競争	inter-industry competition
産業工学	industrial engineering
産業セグメント	industry segment
産業別セグメント	industry segment
残金	balance
参考	reference
参考人	reference
参考文献	reference
算出	calculation
産出する	deliver
算出する	calculate
算出する	compute
産出高	output
産出地帯	field
算術平均	arithmetic average [mean]
算術平均原価法	arithmetical average cost method
産出量	output
参照	reference
参照番号	reference
斬新	innovation
斬新な	innovative
賛成	approval
酸性試験	acid test
酸性試験比率	acid test ratio
賛成する	approve
山積	backlog
残存価格	salvage value
残存価格	scrap value
残存価額	residual value
残存価額	salvage value
残存価額	scrap value
残存元本額	principal outstanding
残存期間	current maturity
残存期間	remaining life
残存勤続年数	remaining service
残存償却年数	remaining depreciable lives
残存する	linger
残存する	remaining
残存耐用年数	remaining useful life
残存耐用年数	residual service life
残存持分	remaining interest
残高	amount outstanding
残高	backlog
残高	balance
残高	outstanding debt
産高比例減耗償却法	cost depletion
算定	accounting
算定	assessment
算定	calculation
算定	determination
算定	measurement
暫定推定値	preliminary estimate
算定する	assess
算定する	calculate
算定する	carry
算定する	compute
算定する	determine
算定する	provide
暫定値	preliminary projections
暫定的	temporary
暫定的な	interim
賛同	approval
賛同する	approve
参入	access
参入	entry
参入	participation
参入機会	access
参入障壁	entry barriers
参入する	access
参入する	enter
参入する	participate
算入する	include
産物	product
残務	backlog
残余期間	residual maturity
残余勤続年数	remaining service
残余勤続年数	remaining service period
残余権	remaining interest
残余権益	residual interest
残余の	remaining
残余の	residual
残余持分	residual equity

し

仕上げ細工	tooling
仕上げる	complete
仕入れ	procurement
仕入れ	purchase
仕入れ	purchasing
仕入価格	purchase price
仕入間接費	purchasing overhead
仕入原価	original cost
仕入原価	purchase cost
仕入原価	purchased cost
仕入れ債務	payable
仕入債務	account payable
仕入先	creditor
仕入先	supplier
仕入先	vendor [vender]
仕入注文書	purchase order
仕入値段	purchase price
仕入費用	purchasing expenses
仕入戻し	returned purchase
仕入れる	procure
仕入れる	purchase
試運転費	test run cost
シェア	market share
シェア	share

シェアリング	sharing
自営業者退職金制度	self-employment retirement plan
自営業者退職年金制度	Keogh
シェルフ登録	shelf registration
シェルフ・レジストレーション	shelf registration
支援	contribution
支援	rescue
支援	support
支援する	contribute
支援する	rescue
支援する	sponsor
支援する	support
塩漬け	lockup [lock-up]
塩漬け株	lockup [lock-up]
潮時	timing
市価	market price
市価	market value
時価	CC
時価	current cost
時価	fair value
時価	market price
時価	market value
時価	present market valu
時価	quoted market price
時価	running price
司会者	chairman
私会社	private company
仕掛品	WIP
仕掛品	WIP
仕掛品	work in process
仕掛品	work in process
仕掛品	work in progress
仕掛品棚卸し高	work in process inventory
資格	capacity
資格	requirement
資格	status
資格給	wages for job clasification
資格認可	licensing
仕掛(しかけ・しかかり)品	goods in process
仕掛(しかけ・しかかり)品	product in progress
時価主義会計	CCA
時価主義会計	current cost accounting
時価主義会計	current value accounting
時価主義会計	CZA
時価償却	current cost depreciation
時価償却	replacement cost depreciation
自家商標	private brand
自家製の	domestic
時価総額	aggregate market value
時価総額	market cap
時価総額	market valuation
地固め	consolidation
時価に修正した資産価額	value of assets adjusted to market
時価評価額	marked-to-market value
時価評価額	market value
直物取引	spot dealing
時間外取引	after-hours dealing
時間外取引	after-hours trading
時間外取引	off-hours trading
時間給制	hourly rate plan
時間差異	timing differences
指揮	leadership
式	form
時期	period
時期	timing
私企業	private enterprise
私企業	private enterprise
次期繰越し	C/F [c/f]
次期繰越し	B/F
次期繰越し	b/f
次期繰越し	brought forward
次期繰越し	carried forward
指揮する	run
敷地	location
時期の調整	timing
識別	differentiation
識別可能資産	identifiable asset
四季報	quarterly report
支給	issuance
至急為替	express money order
市況	market
市況	market conditions
事業	activity
事業	affair
事業	business
事業	business operation
事業	concern
事業	enterprise
事業	operation
事業	project
事業	scheme
事業	service
事業	undertaking
事業	work
事業家	entrepreneur
事業概況	outline of business activities
事業会社	operating company
事業会社	operator
事業化可能性調査	feasibility study
事業拡大計画	expansion program
事業化調査	feasibility study
事業活動で得られる現金	cash provided by operations
事業活動によって得られる現金収入	cash provided by operations
事業活動による資金の調達	cash provided by operations
事業環境	business climate
事業環境	playing field
事業環境	playing field
事業機会	market opportunity
事業機会	opportunity
事業期間	business term
事業基盤	position
事業基盤	presence
事業基盤の強化	repositioning
事業基盤の強化プログラム	repositioning program
事業基盤の再構築	repositioning
事業区分	industry segment
事業区分	segment
事業計画	business model
事業計画	business plan
事業計画	operating plan
事業コスト	business cost
事業再生	revival
事業再生	turnaround
事業再生計画	revival plan
事業再生計画	turnaround plan
事業再生策	turnaround effort
事業再生融資	debtor in possession finance
事業再生融資	DIP financing
事業再生融資制度	DIP plan
事業再編	business restructuring
事業再編	reorganization
事業再編	transformation
事業再編成	business restructuring
事業再編成作業の引当金	provision for business restructuring activities
事業再編成引当金	provision for business restructuring
事業再編成費用	restructuring charge
事業再編成費用	restructuring cost
事業再編に伴う引当金繰入れ	restructuring provision
事業再編引当金	restructuring provision
市況品	commodity
事業者	operator
事業主	employer
事業主	operator
事業主報酬	entrepreneur's remuneration
事業所	site
市況商品の派生商品	commodity derivatives
事業説明書	summary statement of business
事業戦略	business strategy
事業損失	operating loss
事業体	enterprise
事業体	entity
事業多角化	business diversification
事業団	foundation
事業単位	entity
事業提携先	partner

事業統合	integrated operations	資金過不足	net lending	資金提供	funding
事業統合	merger	資金勘定	fund account	資金提供者	underwriter
事業年度	accounting period	資金供給	liquidity allocation	資金投下	investment
事業年度	business year	資金供給	money supply	資金取引	fund deal
事業年度	fiscal year	資金供与	funding	…の資金にあてる	finance
事業年度	FY	資金供与者	creditor	資金の移動	shift of funds
事業年度	period	資金繰り	cash flow	資金の運用・調達	cash flow
事業年度	year	資金繰り	financial position	資金の回転調達	rollover
事業年度の	for the period	資金繰り	liquidity	資金の借り手	borrower
事業の再構築	restructuring	資金繰りの悪化	tightened liquidity	資金の再調達	refinancing
事業の再編成	restructuring			資金の出し手	lender
事業の種類	line of busines	資金計算書	fund statement	資金の調達	raising
事業の提携	business tie-up	資金源	funding	資金の必要額	capital requirements
事業廃止部門	discontinued operation [business]	資金源泉の運用	uses of financial resources		
				資金の流出入	cash flow
事業買収	acquisition	資金使途	purpose of loan	資金配分	fund allocation
事業費	funding	資金収支	cash flow	資金必要額	cash requirements
事業部	division	資金収支表	cash flow statement	資金負担	financial support
事業部間の	intersegment	資金収支表	sources and uses of funds	資金フロー計算書	fund [funds] flow statement
事業部制の	divisional				
事業部門	division	資金需給	supply and demand of funds	資金報告	fund report
事業部門	industry segment			資金力	financial strength
事業部門	line	資金需要	capital requirements	資金を供給する	finance
事業部門	line of busines	資金需要	demand for funds	資金を出す	finance
事業部門	segment	資金需要	financing requirements	資金を調達する	borrow
事業部門	unit	資金需要	funding requirements	資金を調達する	finance
事業分野	industry segment	資金剰余金	funds surplus	資金を伴わない	noncash
事業分野	line of busines	試金石	acid test	資金を補充する	refinance
事業分野	segment	資金洗浄	money laundering	軸	focus
事業別セグメント	industry segment	資金調達	borrowing	軸となる	core
事業モデル	business model	資金調達	capital raising	仕組み	practice
事業要綱	prospectus	資金調達	finance	仕組み	scheme
事業ライン	line of busines	資金調達	financing	仕組み証券	engineered security
事業連携	business tie-up	資金調達	fund procurement	仕組み商品	structured financial product
事業を行う	do business	資金調達	fund raising		
事業を展開する	do business	資金調達	fund raising	仕組み取引	structured deal
事業を展開する	operate	資金調達	funding	仕組む	engineer
資金	capacity	資金調達計画	funding program	時系列	time series
資金	capital	資金調達計画	fund-raising plan	刺激	impact
資金	cash	資金調達契約	financing commitment	刺激	incentive
資金	finance			刺激する	boost
資金	financing	資金調達コスト	borrowing cost	刺激する	revive
資金	fund	資金調達コスト	borrowing cost	試験	test
資金	liquidity	資金調達コスト	financing cost	資源	resource
資金	money	資金調達コスト	funding cost	資源	wealth
資金	proceeds	資金調達コスト	fund-raising cost	事件	affair
資金	resource	資金調達コストの水準	borrowing level	事件	event
資金以外の	noncash			試験研究費	experimental and research expense
資金移動	flow of funds	資金調達戦略	funding strategy		
資金移動	fund transfer	資金調達の	fund-raising	試験研究費	research and development expense
資金移動	movement of funds	資金調達能力	borrowing capacity		
資金運用	fund management	資金調達能力	funding capacity	試験市場	test market
資金運用	fund management operation	資金調達の選択肢	funding option	資源集約的技術革新	resource-intensive innovation
		資金調達必要額	financing requirements		
資金運用表	source and disposition statement			試験的	pilot
		資金調達源	funding base	資源配分	resource allocation
資金援助	financial assistance	資金調達源	funding source	試験販売	test marketing
資金化	funding	資金調達源の分布	funding distribution	指向	drive
資金化した	funded			施行	effect
		資金調達力比率	financial gearing	施行	execution

事項	affair
事項	event
事項	item
事項	matter
時効	statute of limitations
施行する	implement
…志向の	driven
自己株式	treasury stock
自己株式買取積立金	retained earnings appropriated for purchase of treasury stock
自己株式購入	treasury purchases
自己株式数	shares in treasury
自己株式の取得および売却	purchases and sales of treasury stock
自己金融	self-finance
自国通貨(建て)	local currency
自国の	domestic
事後経費	after cost
自己資金	net worth
自己資本	capital
自己資本	capital base
自己資本	equity
自己資本	equity capital
自己資本	net worth
自己資本	owned capital
自己資本	shareholders' equity
自己資本	stockholders' equity
自己資本	worth
自己資本維持契約	net worth agreement
自己資本回転率	net-worth turnover
自己資本規制	capital requirements
自己資本規制比率	net capital rule
自己資本金融	equity financing
自己資本の調達	equity financing
自己資本比率	capital adequacy ratio
自己資本比率	capital ratio [rate]
自己資本比率	capital-to-asset ratio
自己資本比率	equity capital to total assets
自己資本比率	equity ratio
自己資本比率	net worth ratio
自己資本比率	solvency position
自己資本比率規制	capital requirements
自己資本利益率	net income to stockholders' equity ratio
自己資本利益率	return on equity
自己資本利益率	ROE
自己資本利子	imputed interest
事後取得財産	after-acquired property
自己創設のれん	internally generated goodwill
仕事	affair
仕事	effort
仕事	job
仕事	undertaking
仕事	work
仕事上の	working
自己投下資本	down payment
仕事をする	serve
事後の	after
自己売買	dealing
事後費用	after cost
自己持ち分	equity
試査	test
試査	test
市債	municipal bond
施策	measure
試算	estimate
資産	asset
資産	balance sheet
資産	equipment
資産	holdings
資産	property
資産	wealth
資産運用	asset management
資産運用実績	portfolio performance
資産化	capitalization
資産化期間	capitalization period
資産化金額	amounts capitalized
資産化する	capitalize
資産型リース	capital lease
資産管理	asset management
資産管理	portfolio
資産基盤	asset base
資産計上	capitalization
資産計上金額	amount capitalized
資産計上方式	successful efforts method
資産合計	total assets
資産構成	portfolio
資産譲渡益	capital gain
資産譲渡税	CTT
資産譲渡損	capital loss
資産除却	asset abandonment
試算する	estimate
資産選択	portfolio selection
資産担保CP	ABCP
資産担保CP	asset-backed commercial paper
資産担保コマーシャル・ペーパー	ABCP
資産担保コマーシャル・ペーパー	asset-backed commercial paper
資産担保資金調達	left-hand financing
資産担保証券	ABS
資産担保証券	ABS
資産担保証券	asset-backed securities
資産内容	portfolio
資産に計上する	capitalize
資産の借り手	lessee of the property
資産の費用処理	charge-off [chargeoff]
資産の分割	divestiture
資産の分散化	diversified assets
資産売却益	capital gain
資産売却益	portfolio gains
資産売却損	capital loss
試算表	table
資産評価損引当金	asset provision
資産評価損引当金繰入れ額	asset provision
資産負債管理	ALM
資産負債管理	asset liability management
資産・負債継承方式	purchase and assumption method [system]
資産負債総合管理	ALM
資産負債総合管理	asset liability management
支持	approval
支持	support
時事解説	newsletter
支持者	sponsor
指示する	order
支持する	approve
支持する	share
支持する	sponsor
支持する	support
時事通信	newsletter
事実上の	actual
事実上の	de fact
事実上の	effective
事実の開示	disclosure
支社	unit
自社株	treasury stock
自社株買い	buyback
自社株買い	share buyback
自社株買い	share buyback scheme
自社株買い	stock buyback
自社株買い	stock repurchase
自社株買戻し	buyback
自社株買戻し	share buyback
自社株買戻し	stock buyback
自社株買戻し	stock repurchase
自社株購入権	stock option
自社株購入制度	stock purchase plan
自社株式の取得	stock buyback
自社株取得	buyback
自社株取得	share buyback
自社株取得	stock buyback
自社株取得計画	stock buyback plan
自社株発行済み株式の買戻し	share buyback
自社株発行済み株式の買戻し	stock buyback
自社ならではの強み	core compe-

tence	市場の需要　market demand	質権設定　pledge
自主開発商品　private brand product	市場の状態　market conditions	市中　market
自主規制　self-regulation	市場の不確定要因　uncertainties in the market	支柱　mainstay
自主性　independence	市場の崩壊　meltdown	市中相場　free market price
自主性　initiative	市場の暴落　meltdown	思潮　climate
支出　expenditure	市場変動性　market volatility	視聴率　rating
支出　expense	市場優先の　market-driven	質を置く　pledge
支出　outlay	市場予測　street estimates	質　quality
支出　payout	紙上利益　book profit	実価法　actual value method
支出　spending	辞職　resignation	実価法　equity method
支出金　appropriation	辞職する　step down	実業　business
支出金　payout	支持率　popularity rating	実業界　business
支出する　defray	指針　conduct	シックス・シグマ　Six Sigma
支出する　pay	指針　guideline	実験　test
支出する　spend	指数　factor	実現　realization
自主的な　free	指数　figure	実現価値　realized value
自主的な　independent	指数先物　index futures	実現可能額　realizable value
自主的な　voluntary	システム　system	実現可能性　feasibility
自主廃業　voluntary closure	システム監査人　system auditor	実現可能性調査　feasibility study
市場　field	システム構築　solution	実現可能な　realizable
市場　market	姿勢　commitment	実現可能利益　realizable profit
市場　outlet	姿勢　presence	失権株　unclaimed stock
市場　sector	自製材料　manufactured material	実現した　realized
事象　event	自製部品費　manufactured cost	実現資本利得　realized capital gains
事情　backdrop	施政方針　policy	実現済みの　realized
事情　status	施設　equipment	実現する　realize
市場アクセス　access	施設　facility	実現する　secure
市場開放　deregulation	施設　institution	実現総利益　realized gross profit
市場開放する　deregulate	施設　plant	実現損益　realized gaind and [or] loss
市場価格　market price	施設　site	実現損失　realized loss
市場価値　market value	私設の　private	実験的　pilot
市場価値　market value	事前協議　exploratory talks	実現の要件を満たした　realized
市場環境　market conditions	事前精査　due diligence	実現保有損益　realized holding gain or loss
市場環境　market environment	事前積立方式　advance funding method	実現利益　realized income
市場関連資産価格方式　market-related asset value method	事前の　pilot	実現利益　realized profit
市場機会　market opportunity	事前評価　assessment	実現利益　realized revenue
市場機会の分析・評価　opportunity assessment	思想　idea	執行　administration
市場金利　prevailing rate	持続　standing	執行　execution
市場原理　market principles	持続する　maintain	実行　action
市場原理に基づく　market-driven	持続的な経済成長　sustained economic expansion	実行　execution
市場シェア　market share	仕損じ品　defective goods	実行　exercise
市場志向の　market-driven	仕損じ品　spoiled work	実行　practice
市場性ある　marketable	事態　affair	執行委員　board member
市場占拠率　market share	事態　event	執行委員会　executive committee
市場占拠率　share	事態　matter	実行可能性　feasibility
市場占有率　market share	下請工場　subcontracting plant	実行可能性研究　feasibility study
市場占有率　share	…に従う　conform to [with] …	実行可能性調査　feasibility study
市場操作　manipulation	…に従って　subject to …	執行機関　executive
市場相場　quoted market price	…に従わせる　conform to [with] …	実行計画　action program
市場相場価格　quoted price	下取り　trade	実効証拠金率　actual margin
市場取引　marketing	下回る　lag	執行する　execute
市場に出す　launch	示談　composition	実行する　deliver
市場に出す　market	示談　settlement	実行する　execute
市場の規制　regulated market	示談　transaction	実行する　exercise
市場の急落　meltdown	示談金　composition	実行する　implement
市場の実勢金利　prevailing rate	シ団組成戦略　syndication strategy	実行する　run
市場の指標　proxy for the market	質入れする　pledge	実効税率　effective tax rate
		執行部　executive

執行役員	corporate officer
執行役員	executive
執行役員の報酬	executive remuneration packages
実効利息	effective interest
実効利回り	realized yield
実際全部原価計算	actual absorption costing
実際耐用年数	actual life
実際の	actual
実際の	effective
実際の	real
実際の役に立つ	working
実際配賦(はいふ)率	actual overhead rate
実際より多く計上すること	overstatement
実際利率	actual rate of interest
失策	oversight
実査法	table method
実施	conduct
実施	execution
実施	launch
実施義務	accountability
実施許諾	grant
実施許諾	license [licence]
実施許諾	licensing
実施許諾する	license
実施権	license [licence]
実施されている	effective
実施する	adopt
実施する	effect
実施する	execute
実施する	implement
実施中の	effective
実質赤字	real deficit
実質価値	real value
実質株主名を株主名簿に登録していない株主の口座	street-name account
実質金利	effective interest
実質経済成長	real growth
実質最終需要	real final sales
実質実効為替レート	real effective exchange rate
実質収益率	real rate of return
実質上の	real
実質上の資金調達コスト	net cost of funding
実質所得	real income
実質生産高	real output
実質的	actual
実質的経費	real expenditure
実質的推進者	sponsor
実質的な	de facto
実質的な	substantial
実質的な所有者	virtual owner
実質破産	practical insolvency
実質の	real
実質ベース	constant dollar basis
実質簿価	effective book value
実質利益	real profit
実需筋	industrial user
実施料	fee
実施料	license fee
実施料	royalty
実勢価格	market price
実勢相場	prevailing rate
実績	experience
実績	figure
実績	performance
実績	results
実績格付け	experience rating
実践	practice
実体経済	real economy
実体の	real
実体のある	physical
実体のない	intangible
実地	field
実地監査	field audit
実地棚卸し	actual inventory
実地棚卸し	physical inventory
実地の	actual
実動の	effective
実動の	working
失敗	failure
失敗企業	loser
失敗する	fail
実物監査	field audit
疾病給付	disability benefit
質への逃避	flight to quality
実務	business
実務	practice
実用新案	utility model
実用の	working
実力主義	merit-based opportunity
実例	paradigm
仕手	operator
指定	appointment
指定する	appoint
指定する	earmark
指定する	list
指定する	name
指定する	state
指摘する	accuse
私的な	private
支店	arm
支店	unit
支店勘定	branch account
支店間取引	interbranch transaction
支店貸借対照表	branch balance sheet
…の時点で	as of …
使途	application
使途	disposition
使途	use
始動	start-up
指導	guideline
指導	leadership
指導価格	leader price
指導基準	guideline
自動継続	renewal
自動更新借入契約	revolving credit agreement
指導者	head
指導者	leader
指導者の資質	leadership
指導性	leadership
指導部	leader
指導力	leadership
シナジー	synergy
シナジー効果	synergy
品揃え	range
品物	item
辞任	resignation
辞任する	step down
市の	municipal
…を凌ぐ	surpass
支配	control
支配	governance
支配	hand
支配	rule
支配(的)持ち分	controlling interest
支配会社	controlling company
支配株主	controlling shareholder
支配株主持ち分	controlling interest
支配株主持ち分	controlling stake
支配する	control
支配する	govern
支配的企業	dominant firm
支配人	manager
支配持ち分	controlling stake
支配力	power
自発的退職プログラム	voluntary separation program
自発的な	voluntary
支払い	payment
支払い	payoff
支払い	payout
支払い勘定	account payable
支払い期限	maturity
支払い期限	term of payment
支払い期限に達した	payable
支払い期限の過ぎた	overdue
支払い期日	due date
支払い期日	maturity
支払い期日到来負債	matured liability
支払い期日になる	mature
支払い期日のきた	due
支払い期日の到来した	payable
支払い義務額	expenditure
支払い義務のある	due
支払給与総額	payroll
支払い拒絶	dishonor
支払い金	amount payable

支払い金額	payment
支払い繰延べ	deferred payment
支払い繰延べ	rollover
支払い経費	expense paid
支払い債務	account payable
支払い債務	payment obligation
支払い者	source
支払い社債利息	bond interest paid
支払い準備	reserve
支払い遅延	delinquency
支払い遅延違約金	overdue penalty
支払い遅延の	overdue
支払い超過	unfavorable balance
支払い停止	default
支払い手形	note payable
支払い手形	notes payable-trade
支払手形	acceptance payable
支払手形	bills payable
支払い手数料	payment commission
支払い能力	financial strength
支払い能力	responsibility
支払い能力	solvency
支払い能力規制	solvency rule
支払い能力比率	solvency ratio
支払いの優先順位	payment priorities
支払い配当金	dividend payment
支払い日	maturity
支払い不能	insolvency
支払い不能者	insolvent
支払い不能による清算	insolvent liquidation
支払い不能の	bankrupt
支払い不能の	insolvent
支払い報酬	remuneration cost
支払い保険金	payout
支払い保証契約	bond
支払い保証小切手	certified check
支払い満期の	payable
支払い猶予期間	credit
支払い余力	solvency
支払い余力	solvency margin
支払い余力比率	solvency margin
支払い利息	interest cost
支払い利息	interest expense
支払い利息	interest payment
支払い利息・税金・営業権償却費控除前利益	EBITA
支払い利息・税金・減価償却・償却控除前利益	EBITDA
支払い利息・税金・減価償却控除前利益	EBITD
支払い利息および税金控除前利益	EBIT
支払い利息純額	net interest
支払いを待っている	receivable
支払う	defray
支払う	match
支払う	meet
支払う	pay
支払う	pay out
支払う	service
支払う	tender
支払うべき	payable
支払わせる	charge
支払われる	payable
支払われるべき	receivable
市販	marketing
地盤	footing
四半期	business quarter
四半期	quarter
四半期業績	quarterly performance
四半期業績	quarterly results
四半期決算	quarterly results
四半期ごとに	quarterly
四半期ごとの	quarterly
四半期純損失	quarterly net loss
四半期純利益	quarterly net profit
四半期末終値	quarter-end close
四半期税引き後損失	quarterly net loss
四半期税引き後利益	quarterly net profit
四半期速報	quick estimation
四半期の	quarterly
四半期の成長	quarterly growth
四半期の成長率	quarterly growth
四半期の伸び	quarterly growth
四半期の伸び率	quarterly growth
四半期配当	quarterly dividend
四半期配当金	quarterly dividend
四半期ベースの	quarterly
四半期別	quarterly
四半期報告書	quarterly report
四半期利益	quarterly profit
指標	benchmark
指標	data
指標	figure
指標	guideline
指標	index proxy
指標	measure
指標	measurement
指標	proxy
指標	ratio
指標	series
辞表	resignation
指標金利	key interest rate
指標金利	key rate
指標となる	pilot
指標銘柄	benchmark
シフト	shift
シフトさせる	shift
シフトする	shift
紙幣	bill
紙幣	note
次頁繰越し	B/F
次頁繰越し	brought forward
次頁繰越し	carried forward
私募	private offering
私募	private placement
私募債	bonds offered through private placement
私募債	private placement
私募債	private placement bond
私募債市場	private placement bond market
私募発行	private placement
私募発行	private placing
私募発行する	privately place
資本	capacity
資本	capital
資本	net worth
資本	shareholders' equity
資本	stockholders' equity
資本移転税	CTT
資本移動の自由化	open capital flows
資本化	capitalization
資本回転率	equity turnover
資本化する	capitalize
資本過大の	top-heavy
資本価値	capital value
資本株式	capital stock
資本化リース	capital lease
資本勘定	stockholders' equity
資本基盤	capital base
資本基盤	capitalization
資本・業務提携	capital and business partnership
資本金	capital
資本金	capital base
資本金	capital stock
資本金	common share
資本金	common stock
資本金	share capital
資本金組入れ発行	capitalization issue
資本金の欠損	impaired capital
資本金の欠損	impairment
資本組入れ	capitalization
資本組入れ	recapitalization
資本構成	capital structure
資本構成	capitalization
資本構成	equity structure
資本構成	financial structure
資本構成を修正する	recapitalize
資本構成を変更する	recapitalize
資本構造	capital structure
資本拘束	change of control
資本拘束条項	change of control clause
資本再編	recapitalization
資本再編成	equity structure shift
資本参加	equity participation
資本参加	stake
資本・産出量比率	capital-output ratio
資本支出	capital expenditure
資本支出額	capital expenditure

資本市場	capital market
資本主	investor
資本集約型	capital-intensive
資本集約的	capital-intensive
資本準備金	capital reserve
資本準備金	capital surplus
資本剰余金	additional paid-in capital
資本剰余金	capital reserve
資本剰余金	capital surplus
資本ストック	capital stock
資本総額	capitalization
資本増強	capital increase
資本損失	capital loss
資本対固定資産比率	worth (to) fixed ratio
資本対固定負債比率	worth (to) fixed debt ratio
資本対流動負債比率	worth (to) current debt ratio
資本調達	capitalization
資本調達	financing
資本調達	fund raising
資本調達の	fund-raising
資本積立金	capital surplus
資本提携	capital alliance
資本提携	capital tie-up
資本提携	equity tie-up
資本提携	equity tie-up
資本提携関係	equity alliance
資本的資産	permanent asset
資本的支出	capital expenditure
資本的支出	capital spending
資本的支出（純額）	net capital expenditures
資本的支出純額	net capital expenditures
資本的支出総額	gross capital expenditures
資本投下	capital investment
資本投資	capital expenditure
資本投資	capital investment
資本投資額	capital expenditure
資本逃避	flight
資本として使用する	capitalize
資本に組み入れる	recapitalize
資本の価値構成	value composition of capital
資本の欠損	impaired capital
資本の減少	withdrawal
資本の固定	lockup [lock-up]
資本の再構成	recapitalization
資本の部	component of stockholders' equity
資本の部	equity section
資本の部	section of stockholders' equity
資本の部	shareholders' equity
資本の部	stockholders' equity
資本変更	recapitalization
資本リース	capital lease
資本利益率	return on capital
資本利益率	return on capital employed
資本利益率	ROI
資本利得	capital gain
資本を再編する	recapitalize
市民としての企業	corporate citizen [citizenship]
事務	administration
事務	affair
事務管理	administration
事務所	office
事務所	representative
事務上の誤り	clerical error
事務処理	processing
事務処理	servicing
事務と管理のための諸費用	clerical and administrative expenses
指名	appointment
指名競争入札	bidding among designated companies
指名権	power
指名する	adopt
指名する	appoint
指名する	name
指名する	propose
締切り	closing
締切り	footing
締切り	write-off
締め切る	close
…を示す	post
示す	define
示す	present
示す	record
示す	reflect
示す	register
示す	represent
示す	reveal
締付け	squeeze
締め付ける	squeeze
…を占める	account for ...
…を占める	comprise
…を占める	generate
…に占める比率	as a percentage of ...
下期	last half
下期	latter half
下期	second half
下期の第3四半期と第4四半期	second two quarters
下半期	H2
下半期	last half
下半期	latter half
下半期	latter term
下半期	second half
下半期の第3四半期と第4四半期	second two quarters
諮問委員会	advisory board
諮問機関	advisory board
諮問の	advisory
社員	employee
社員	hire
社員	partner
社員	people
社員	staff
社員	workforce
社会	community
社会	public
社会還元	reinvestment
社外調達	outsourcing
社外調達する	outsource
社会的	public
社会的責任	social responsibility
社会的責任投資	SRI
社会的責任投資ファンド	SRI fund
社外取締役	independent director
社外取締役	outside director
社外取締役選任	appointment of outside directors
社外発行株式	shares outstanding
社外流通株式数	shares outstanding
借記	charge
借記する	charge
弱小の	weak
借地権	tenant right
借地・借家契約	lease
借地人	tenant
弱点	defect
弱点	disadvantage
尺度	benchmark
尺度	criterion
尺度	measure
尺度	measurement
尺度とする	benchmark
釈放	release
借用証書	bond
社債	bond
社債	debenture
社債	debenture stock
社債	debenture stock
社債借換え	bond refunding
社債権者	bond holder
社債券発行高	debentures issued
社債償還	bond redemption
社債償還	bond retirement
社債償還基金	fund for retirement of bond
社債転換	bond conversion
社債の買戻し	repurchase of bonds
社債の格付け	debt rating
社債の残存期間	remaining life of the issue
社債の償還資金	funding for redemption of corporate bonds
社債の償還日	due date
社債の担保	collateral for bonds
社債配当	bond dividend
社債発行	bond issuance [issue]

社債発行	issue of bonds
社債発行差金	bond discounts
社債発行差金	bond premium
社債発行差金	bond premium
社債発行差金	discounts on bonds payable
社債発行差金	unamortized premium on bonds
社債発行費	bond expenses
社債発行費	bond issue expenses
社債発行費	expense on bonds
社債発行割増金	bond premium
社債プレミアム	bond premium
社債利息	bond interest
社債利息	debenture interest
社債割増金	bond premium
社債割増発行差金	premium on bonds payable
車種	model
ジャスダック	Jasdaq
ジャスト・イン・タイム	just-in-time
社説	leader
社団	company
社長	chairman
社長	head
社長	president
借家人	tenant
借款	loan
借款	loan grants
借金	borrowing
借金	charge
借金	debt
借金	liability
借金する	borrow
借金などを完済する	pay off
借金を返す	pay off
借金を背負っている	debt-saddled
射程	range
射程距離	range
社内管理	internal control
社内企業制	company system
社内調査	in-house investigation
社内手続き	administration process
社内取締役	employee director
社内取締役	inside director
社内の	in-house [inhouse]
社内の	internal
社内留保	retained earnings
社内留保利益金	retained earnings
社風	corporate culture
社報	newsletter
謝礼	fee
謝礼	remuneration
謝礼	reward
ジャンク債	junk
首位	top
首位になる	top
首位の	top
首位を占める	top
主因	driver
主因	driving force
事由	event
自由意志による	voluntary
収益	earning
収益	earnings
収益	income
収益	proceeds
収益	return
収益	revenue
収益	yield
収益稼得活動	revenue-earning activity
収益基準	revenue standard
収益基盤	revenue base
収益権	use
収益資産	earning assets
収益性	earning power
収益性	performance
収益性	profitability
収益性がある	profitable
収益性が高い	profitable
収益性資産	earning assets
収益生成過程	return generating process
収益性の悪化	pressure on profitability
収益と純利益	revenues and earnings
収益と純利益の伸び	growth in revenues and earnings
収益と費用の認識	recognition of revenue and expense
収益と利益	revenues and earnings
収益と利益の伸び	growth in revenues and earnings
収益の期間帰属	attribution of revenue to periods
収益の原動力	profit driver
収益の実現	realization of gains
収益の資本還元	capitalization
収益の増加	earnings growth
収益の認識	revenue recognition
収益の伸び	earnings growth
収益の伸び	gain in revenues
収益の伸び	revenue growth
収益伸び率	earnings growth
収益費用の対応	revenue-cost matching
収益分布	revenue distribution
収益報告	earnings report
収益見通し	earnings projection
収益見通し	profit forecast
収益予想	earnings forecast
収益予想	earnings projection
収益率	profitability
収益率	rate of return
収益率	ratio
収益率	return
収益率の伸び	earnings growth
収益力	earning power
収益力	profitability
収益力がある	profitable
収益を上げる	chalk up
収益を押し上げる原動力	profit driver
終価	final value
終価	future value
終価	FV
終価	terminal value
自由化	decontrol
自由化	deregulation
自由化	liberalization
集会	assembly
重加算税	heavy additional tax
自由化する	deregulate
自由化する	liberalize
終価率法	future value table
周期	cycle
什器	facility
周期的な	cyclic
周期的な	cyclical
周期的な	periodic
従業員	employee
従業員	manpower
従業員	people
従業員	personnel
従業員	staff
従業員	workforce
従業員貸付け金	advances to employees
従業員株式買取り権制度	employee stock option plan
従業員株式購入制度	employee stock purchase plan
従業員株式購入制度	ESPP
従業員株式購入選択権制度	employee stock option plan
従業員株式購入選択権制度	ESOP
従業員株式報酬制度	employee stock compensation
従業員株式保有制度	employee stock ownership plan
従業員給付	employee benefit
従業員数	manpower
従業員ストック・オプション制度	employee stock option plan
従業員待遇委員会	committee on employee benefits
従業員退職所得保障法	Employee Retirement Income Security Act
従業員手形貸付け金	note receivable due from employee
従業員などの名簿	book
従業員年金	employee pension
従業員年金制度	occupational pension scheme
従業員の経営権買取り	worker buyout
従業員1人当たり生産高	per-

従業員名簿	payroll
従業員持ち株制度	employee stock ownership plan
従業員持ち株制度	employee stock purchase plan
従業員持ち株制度	ESOP
従業員持ち株制度	ESPP
就業者	workforce
集金	collection
集計勘定	summary
終決	determination
終結すべき	determinable
集合	basket
集合勘定	summary
自由裁量	discretion
自由裁量権	disposition
自由裁量の	discretionary
自由参入	free entry
収支	account
収支	balance
収支がとんとんになる	break even
収支計算書	cash flow statement
収支決算	settlement of accounts
…を重視する	focus on ...
重視する	value
充実させる	strengthen
充実した	full
充実した	massive
重質の	heavy
収支とんとん	break-even (point)
自由剰余金	free surplus
就職口	job
終身雇用	lifetime employment
終身年金	perpetual annuity
終身年金	perpetuity
終身の	perpetual
修正	adjustment
修正	alteration
修正	restatement
修正	revision
修正後発事象	adjusting events after the balance sheet date
修正項目	adjustment item
修正再表示	restatement
修正再表示する	restate
修正財務諸表	modified accounts
修正申告	revised return
修正する	adjust
修正する	restate
修正する	revamp
修正する	revise
修正申込み	counter offer
習俗	practice
従属会社	dependent company
従属会社	subsidiary
従属する	dependent
重大局面	crisis
重大な	heavy
重大な	real
重大な	significant
重大な	substantial
重大な影響	material effect
重大な関心事	front burner
住宅エクイティ	home equity
住宅金融	housing loan
住宅金融支援機構	Japan Housing Finance Agency
住宅建設投資	invetment in home building
住宅取得控除	credits for mortgage payments
住宅着工	housing start
住宅着工件数	housing start
住宅着工戸数	housing start
住宅融資証券	MBS
住宅融資証券	mortgage-backed security
住宅融資証券事業	mortgage-backed securities business
住宅用不動産価格	residential property price
住宅ローン	housing loan
住宅ローン	mortgage
住宅ローン会社	subprime lender
住宅ローン会社	subprime mortgage lender
住宅ローン市場	residential mortgage market
集団	group
集団訴訟	class action
集団代表訴訟	class action
…に執着する	focus on ...
集中	focus
集中化	focus
集中させる	concentrate
…に集中する	focus
集中する	concentrate
重点	stress
充当	appropriation
充当可能な	available
充当金	appropriation
充当金	reserve
周到な準備	foresight
習得	experience
自由土地保有	freehold
自由な	free
州内会社	domestic corporation
州内法人	domestic corporation
12月期	business term ending in December
12月期決算	business term ending in December
12月期決算	calendar year
12月決算期	business term ending in December
12月終了事業年度	business term ending in December
収入	earnings
収入	proceeds
収入	receipt
収入	revenue
収入金額	receipt
収入高	receipt
就任	assumption
就任式	inauguration ceremony
就任する	assume
私有の	private
私有の	proprietary
収納	receipt
集配業務	collection and distribution services
修復	rehabilitation
十分な	due
十分な	full
十分な	good
十分な開示	full disclosure
十分に	fully
週平均労働時間	workweek
周辺資産	noncore assets
自由保有権	freehold
住民税	local inhabitants tax
重役	board member
重役	executive
集約化	integration
重役会	board
重役会	board of directors
集約する	consolidate
収用	appropriation
充用	appropriation
重要	matter
重要事項	material respect
重要資産売却作戦	crown jewel defense
重要性	account
重要性	concern
重要性	worth
重要である	concern
重要な	large
重要な	material
重要な	significant
重要な	substantial
重要な差異	material difference
重要な点	material respect
収能力	capacity
重要部分	forefront
収容力	capacity
終了	close
終了	end
終了	termination
終了する	end
就労	employment
週労働時間	workweek
就労率	turnover
収録する	include
受益	benefit
受益金	benefit
受益者	beneficial owner
受益者	beneficiary
主眼	thrust

主幹事	lead manager
主義	basis
主義	concept
主義	method
主義	philosophy
主義	principle
需給	supply
受給権確定［受給権の発生した］累積年金給付額	vested accumulated plan benefits
受給権確定給付［給付額］	vested benefits
受給権の発生した	vested
受給資格がある	eligible
受給資格取得済み在職制度加入者	fully eligible active plan participant
受給者	beneficiary
需給の逼迫	tight supply conditions
縮小	decline
縮小	decrease
縮小	pressure
縮小	reduction
縮小	squeeze
縮小した	reduced
縮小する	cut
縮小する	decline
縮小する	decrease
縮小する	downsize
縮小する	narrow
縮小する	shrink
縮小する	squeeze
縮小する	trim
熟成	aging
熟練	skill
熟練技術	accomplishment
授権	authorization
授権	commission
授権株式	authorized capital
授権株式	authorized shares [stock]
授権株式数	authorized capital
授権株式数	authorized shares [stock]
授権株式数	number of shares authorized
授権株式数	share issue limit
授権株式数	shares authorized
授権株式総数	authorized capitalization
授権資本	authorized capital
授権社債	bond authorized
授権普通株式数	authorized common stock
授権優先株式数	authorized preferred stock
受講者	participant
取材源	source
主催者	sponsor
主催する	promote

主催する	sponsor
取材する	cover
主債務者	principal
主旨	thrust
趣旨	effect
主軸	core
種々雑多な	miscellaneous
主唱する	sponsor
主成分	basis
受贈	donation
受贈金	donation
主題	matter
受諾	acceptance
受諾	compliance
受諾する	accept
受託責任	stewardship accountability
手段	implement
手段	leverage
手段	measure
手段	resource
手段	shift
手段	solution
手段	step
手段	tactics
手段	tool
…の手段として機能する	serve
受注	order entry
受注	order entry
受注会社	bid winner
受注業者	bid winner
受注残	order backlog
受注残高	backlog
受注残高	factory backlog
受注残高	order backlog
受注残高	order backlog
受注残高	orders on hand
受注品	order
受注仕様生産	CTO
受注生産	BTO
受注生産	build to order
受注生産方式	BTO
受注生産方式	build to order
受注高	order
受注内容	order quality
主張する	assertive
出荷	delivery
出荷	handling
出荷	shipment
出荷基準	delivery basis
出荷数量	quantity shipped
出荷する	ship
出荷台数	shipment
出荷量	shipment
出願	application
出願手数料	application fee
出向	transfer
出資	capital investment
出資	contribution
出資	equity contribution

出資	equity investment
出資	funding
出資	investment
出資	participation
出資	spending
出資	stake
出資維持保証	nonabandonment undertaking
出資企業	investor
出資金	annuity
出資金	capital
出資金	capital investment
出資金	contribution to capital
出資者	equity partner
出資者	investor
出資者	owner
出資者	sponsor
出資する	capitalize
出資する	contribute
出資する	finance
出資する	fund
出資する	invest
出資する	spend
出資比率	equity stake
出資比率	ownership
出資比率	shareholding
出資比率	stake
出所	source
出席者	participant
出訴期限	statute of limitations
出訴期限法	statute of limitations
出典	source
出店	outlet
出店者	tenant
出店する	open
出費	outlay
出品物	entry
出力	output
主導	drive
主導	initiative
…主導型	driven
主導権	initiative
主導的地位	cutting edge
主導的地位	leading edge
…主導の	driven
取得	acquisition
取得	procurement
取得	purchase
取得	purchasing
取得営業権	purchased goodwill
取得価格	acquisition price
取得価格	book value
取得価格	purchase price
取得価額	original cost
取得原価	acquisition cost
取得原価	historical cost
取得原価	original cost
取得原価基準	cost basis
取得原価超過額	excess of cost
取得原価で	at cost

(資産の)取得原価と正味実現可能額のうち低いほうの価額	lower of cost and net realizable value
取得原価に基づく減耗償却	cost depletion
取得資金	purchased fund
取得時の	historical
取得時の為替レート	historical cost
取得者	acquirer
取得する	acquire
取得する	buy
取得する	obtain
取得する	procure
取得する	purchase
取得する	take out
取得する	take over
主として	primarily
首脳	leader
首脳陣	leader
首脳部	top management
首尾一貫して	consistently
手法	engineering
手法	knowhow [know-how]
手法	method
手法	practice
手法	strategy
手法	tool
寿命	life
寿命	life cycle
種目	item
授与	commission
授与	presentation
需要	demand
需要	needs
需要間競争	demands competition
需要家	customer
需要家	user
主要株主	major shareholder
需要管理	demand side management
主要企業	leading company
主要財務指標	selected financial data
主要財務情報	selected financial data
主要財務データ	selected financial data
主要事実	matter
主要四半期データ	selected quarterly data
主要政策金利	key interest rate
主要取引銀行	main bank
主要な	large
需要見通し	demand prospects
需要予測	demand forecast
授与者	investor
授与する	award
樹立する	establish
受領	receipt
受領額	receipt
受領する	receive
受領できる	receivable
主力	core
主力	mainstay
主力株	leader
主力行	main bank
主力事業	core business
主力事業	main business
主力事業の収益	core earnings
主力商品	mainstay
主力戦略	core strategy
主力取引銀行	main bank
種類	category
種類	denomination
種類	form
種類	range
手腕	skill
順位	notch
順位	standing
…の順位を決める	rank
純受取利息	net interest income
純売上高	net sales
純運転資本	net working capital
純運転資本	net working capital
純運用資産	net assets employed
純営業収益	net operating revenues
純営業利益	net operating profit
純益	net
純益を上げる	net
巡回キャンペーン	roadshow
巡回説明会	roadshow
純額	net
純額	net amount
純額表示	net presentation
純額表示	stated in net amounts
純貸出高	net advance
純借入債務	net funded debt
循環	cycle
循環	flow
循環の	cyclic
循環の	cyclical
純キャッシュ	net cash
純キャッシュフロー	net cash flow
純キャッシュフロー	net cash flow
…に準拠する	conform to [with] …
…に準拠する	subject to …
準拠性	compliance
準拠性	conformity
純金融負債	net financial liabilities
純計	net total
純現金支出	net cash outflows
純現金収入	net cash inflows
純現在価値	net present value
準更生	quasi-reorganization
準子会社	quasi subsidiary
準子会社	quasi-subsidiary
純誤差脱漏項目	net errors and omissions line
純債権	net receivables
純財産	net asset value
純債務	net debt
順次	series
純資金	net proceeds
純資金収入額	net cash flow
純資産	book value
純資産	capital
純資産	equity
純資産	net asset
純資産	net asset value
純資産	net worth
純資産	stockholders' equity
純資産額	book value
純資産額	net asset value
純資産額	net asset worth
純資産価値	equity
純資産価値	NAV
純資産価値	net asset value
純資産の部	stockholders' equity
純資産利益率	return on net assets employed
純資産利益率	RONA
純実現・未実現キャピタル・ゲイン	net realized and unrealized capital gains
瞬時電子取引	CALS
純支払い利息	net interest deficit
純資本所得	net capital gain
遵守	compliance
純収益	net revenues
純収支	net cash
純収支	net cash flow
純収支残高	net balance
純収入	cash flow
純収入	net cash flow
純収入	net income
遵守性	compliance
順序	method
順序	order
純償却額	net charge-offs
純所得	net income
純粋の	net
純粋持ち株会社	pure holding company
純生産性	net productivity
純増	net increase
純損益	bottom line
純損失	net loss
純損失収益性	bottom line
純損失の合計	combined net loss
純調達額	net borrowing needs
順調な	healthy
準通貨	quasi money
純投資額	net investment
純投資ヘッジ	net investment hedges
順応	conformity
純売却益	net proceeds
純販売利益	net margin

準備	arrangement
準備	provision
準備金	provision
準備金	reserve
準備する	prepare
準備する	set up
準備調査	feasibility study
純費用	net charge
純負債	net debt
純負債額	net debt position
純負債額	net indebtedness
純負債比率	gearing
純負債比率	negative net gearing
純負債比率	net gearing
準普通株式	common stock equivalents
順法闘争	work-to-rule struggle
純簿価	net book value
純有形資産	net tangible assets
純利益	absolute profit
純利益	bottom line
純利益	bottom line results
純利益	earnings
純利益	net earnings
純利益	net income
純利益	net income
純利益	net profit
純利益	proceeds
純利益に占める持ち分	equity in net earnings
純利益により得た資金	funds provided from net earnings
純利益率	net income ratio
純利息	net interest
純流動資産	net liquid assets
純量	net
準劣後請求権	mezzanine subordination
ジョイント	joint
ジョイント・ベンチャー	joint venture
ジョイント・ベンチャー	JV
省	department
使用	employment
使用	use
…上	purpose
掌握する	control
小委員会	panel
上位請求権	senior claim
上位の	superior
上位劣後債	senior subordinated debenture
上映	showing
上演	presentation
上演	showing
上演される	run
商会	firm
照会	reference
紹介	introduction
障害	failure
紹介する	introduce
生涯賃金	life-long earning
照会人	reference
生涯年金	life annuity
照会番号	reference
昇格	promotion
奨学金	foundation
奨学金	grant
昇格させる	promote
昇格させる	upgrade
使用価値	value in use
使用可能な	available
浄化費用	cleanup costs
償還	amortization
償還	call
償還	redemption
償還	refunding
償還	repayment
償還	retirement
召喚	recall
償還・転換可能優先株式	redeemable convertible preferred share
償還価格	call price
償還可能な	callable
償還可能な	redeemable
償還株式	redeemable stock
償還基金	redemption fund
償還基金	redemption fund
償還基金積立金	surplus for redemption fund
償還期限	maturity
償還義務	recourse obligation
償還条項	call provision
償還する	call
償還する	pay off
償還する	redeem
償還する	refund
償還する	repay
償還する	retire
召喚する	recall
償還請求	recourse
償還請求権	recourse
償還できる	callable
償還プレミアム	call premium
償還プレミアム	premium on redemption
償還優先株	redeemable preferred shares
償還優先株式	callable preferred stock
償還利回り	redemption yield
商機	opportunity
試用期間	service life
償却	amortization
償却	depreciation
償却	write-off
消却	cancelation [cancellation]
消却	retirement
消却	write-off
償却額	amortization
償却額控除後	less amortization
償却可能な	depreciable
償却期間	write-off interval
償却基金	sinking fund
償却されていない	unamortized
償却実績	write off experience
償却する	amortize
償却する	cancel
償却する	charge off
償却する	depreciate
償却する	write off
償却する	wtite down
消却する	cancel
消却する	retire
償却性の	depreciable
償却積立金	sinking fund
償却費	depreciation
償却前利益	pre-depreciation profit
償却率	percent depreciated
昇級	promotion
上級の	superior
上級副社長	senior vice president
上級役員	senior executive
消去	elimination
商況	business climate
商業	business
商業	trading
状況	affair
状況	climate
状況	condition
状況	experience
状況	standing
状況	status
商業為替手形	commercial draft
商業資産	commercial assets
商業者商標	private brand
商業証券	commercial paper
商業証券	CP
状況説明	briefing
商業手形	commercial note
商業手形	commercial paper
商業手形	CP
商業ベースの	arm's length [arm's-length]
商業用不動産証券	asset-backed securities
消極的な	negative
消極的のれん	negative goodwill
消極のれん	negative goodwill
消去仕訳	work sheet elimination
消去する	eliminate
使用許諾	license [licence]
使用許諾	licensing
使用許諾契約	licensing agreement
使用許諾する	license
消去と修正	elimination and adjustments
賞金	premium

衝撃	impact
衝撃を与える	impact
証券	bill
証券	equity
証券	investment
証券	issue
証券	note
証券	paper
証券	securities
証券	security
証券	stock
使用権	license [licence]
条件	climate
条件	condition
条件	offer
条件	requirement
条件	reserve
条件	term
条件	terms and conditions
上限	cap
上限	guideline
上限	maximum
証券化	securitization
証券会社	brokerage
証券会社	brokerage firm
証券化資産	securitized assets
証券化した債権	securitized debt
証券化商品	securitized products
証券化する	securitize
証券業	brokerage
証券業務兼営銀行	universal bank
上限金利	cap
証券広報	investor [investors] relations
証券市況	securities market
証券市場	securities market
証券市場	security market
条件付き支払項目	conditional payment
条件付き証券	contingent issues
条件付きストック・オプション	qualified stock option
条件付き認可	conditional approval
条件付きの	qualified
証券投資	securities investment
証券投資	security investment
…を条件として	subject to ...
…を条件とする	contingent
…を条件とする	subject to ...
証券取引	security transaction
証券取引所	bourse
証券取引所	stock exchange
証券取引所上場手続き	exchange listing procedures
証券取引所の立会場	boardroom
証券取引法	Securities and Exchange Law
証券仲買会社	brokerage
証券の発行市場	primary market for securities
証券売却益	securities gains
証券発行団	issue syndicate
証券引受業者に対する調査報告書	comfort letter for underwriter
証券引受人	underwriter
証券引受人への書簡	comfort letter for underwriter
証券保有高	position
証拠	evidence
照合	adjustment
照合	comparison
照合	matching
条項	provision
条項	term
照合合計	control balance
証拠金	margin
証拠金	margin requirement
証拠書類	document
証拠資料	evidence
証拠物件	evidence
照査	checking audit
照査	examination by reference
詳細に	fully
上市	launch
少子高齢化	declining birthrate and graying society
使用資本利益率	ROI
商社	firm
商社	trading house
使用者	employer
使用者	user
成就	accomplishment
…に照準を合わせる	concentrate
証書	letter
証書	receipt
証書	securities
…の上昇	increased
上昇	advance
上昇	appreciation
上昇	boost
上昇	enhancement
上昇	expansion
上昇	gain
上昇	improvement
上昇	increase
上昇	pickup [pick-up]
上昇	rally
上昇	rise
上昇	strength
上場	initial public offering
上場	IPO
上場	listing
上場	public listing
上昇圧力	upward pressure
上場会社	listed company
上場会社	publicly held company
上場会社	quoted company
上場株式	listed share
上場企業	listed company
上場企業	public ownership
上場企業	publicly held company
上場企業	publicly owned company [corporation]
上場企業	quoted [listed] company
上場企業	quoted company
上場基準	eligibility criteria for listing
上場基準	listing requirement
上場基準	listing rules
上昇基調	upward path
上昇基調の	strong
上昇軌道	upward trajectory
上昇局面	rally
上昇傾向	upward bias
上昇傾向にある	positive
上場後の公募	secondary public offering
上昇させる	increase
上昇させる	inflate
上場されていない	unlisted
上場される	list
上昇した	increased
上場証券	listed security
上場証券取引所	stock exchange listing
上場申請	listing application
上昇する	advance
上昇する	appreciate
上昇する	gain
上昇する	rally
上昇する	rise
上昇する	rising
上昇する	strengthen
上昇する	upward
上場する	introduce
上場する	launch
上場する	list
上場する	quote
上場直前の公募	initial public offering
上場停止	delisting
上場手数料	listing fee
上場廃止	delisting
上場派生商品	exchange-traded derivatives
上場目論見書	listing particulars
上場目論見書	listing prospectus
上場有価証券	quoted investment
上場を停止する	delist
上場を廃止する	delist
生じる	accrue
昇進	promotion
昇進	upward mobility
昇進させる	promote
昇進する	leap
昇進制度	promotion system
昇進の機会	opportunity of advancement
少数	minority

少数株主　minority shareholder
少数株主権　minority interest
少数株主損益　minority interest
少数株主持ち分　minority equity
少数株主持ち分　minority interest
少数株主持ち分　minority interest
少数株主持ち分利益　minority interest
少数支配　minority control
少数者に支配されている　closely held
少数派　minority
少数民族　minority
少数民族の優遇措置　affirmative action
少数持ち分の買取り　minority buy-out
少数利益　minority interest
使用する　use
情勢　affair
情勢　climate
情勢　condition
情勢　development
情勢　environment
情勢　status
常設委員会　permanent committee
常設の　permanent
常設の　standing
常設の信用枠　standing credit
使用総資本回転率　turnover of total capital employed
使用総資本利益率　return on capital employed
使用総資本利益率　return on investment
使用総資本利益率　ROCE
消息　information
状態　condition
状態　position
状態　standing
状態　status
…の状態になる　run
承諾　approval
承諾　authorization
承諾　compliance
承諾する　accept
承諾する　approve
承諾する　grant
商談　bargain
商談　negotiation
常置の　standing
省・庁・課　office
省・庁・局・部　board
使用できる　operational
商店　outlet
焦点　focus
…に焦点を当てる　focus on …
…に焦点を合わせる　focus on …
焦点を合わせる　focus

…に焦点を置く　focus on …
…に焦点を絞る　focus
譲渡　assignment
譲渡　disposition
譲渡　grant
譲渡　negotiation
譲渡　transfer
譲渡可能資産　negotiable aset
譲渡可能定期預金証券　CD
譲渡可能定期預金証書　certificate of deposit
譲渡可能な　negotiable
譲渡可能船荷証券　negotiable bill of lading
譲渡所得　capital gain
譲渡済み金額　amount pledged
譲渡する　amortize
譲渡する　grant
譲渡する　release
譲渡する　sell
譲渡する　transfer
譲渡税　transfer tax
譲渡性預金　NCD
譲渡性預金　negotiable certificate of deposit
譲渡損失　capital loss
譲渡抵当　mortgage
商取引　transaction
承認　allowance
承認　approval
承認　authorization
承認　recognition
昇任　promotion
使用人　employee
承認された　approved
承認済みの請求書　approved invoice
承認済み予算額　appropriation
承認する　approve
承認する　authorize
承認する　recognize
常任代理人　standing proxy
常任の　standing
正念場　acid test
商売　business
商売　trade
消費　spending
消費財　consumer product
消費支出　consumer outlays
消費者　consumer
消費者金融　consumer lending
消費者信用残高　consumer installment credit
消費者製品　consumer product
消費者製品　consumer product
消費者物価　consumer prices
消費者保護　consumer protection
消費する　spend
常備する　keep
常備の　standing

消費の低迷　sluggish consumption
商標　brand
商標権およびその他の無形固定資産（純額）　trademarks and other intangible assets, net
消費量　expenditure
商品　commodity
商品　goods
商品　item
商品　merchandise
商品　product
商品開発　product development
商品群　line of products
商品群　product line
商品券　coupon
商品構成　sales mix
商品先物　commodity futures
商品先物　commodity futures
商品先物市場　commodity futures
商品先物取引　commodity futures trading
商品市場　commodity market
商品性　merchantable quality
商品相場　commodity market
商品取引所　commodity exchange
商品の共同開発　joint product development
商品の種類　line
商品やサービスへの支出　spending on goods and services
商品ライン　line of products
商品ライン　product line
上部の　top
商法　sales
商法　selling
使用法　use
情報　code
情報　content
情報　data
情報　information
情報開示　disclosure
情報隔壁　firewall [fire wall]
情報技術　IT
情報源　source
情報システムの構築　solution
上方修正　upgrade
上方修正　upgrading
上方修正　upward adjustment
上方修正　upward revision
上方修正する　raise
上方修正する　upgrade
情報の公開　disclosure
情報の内容　content
情報の中身　content
上方へ　upward
情報漏洩防止システム　firewall [fire wall]
正味　net
正味受取利息　net interest revenue
正味運転資本　net working capital

正味価額 equity	将来 future	職業紹介 placement
正味貸倒れ償却 net write-off	将来起こりそうな potential	職業能力 skill
正味借入金 net borrowing	将来価値 future value	職業倫理規程 code of professional ethics
正味キャッシュ net cash	将来キャッシュ・フロー future cash flow	職種内昇進 job promotion
正味キャッシュ・フロー net cash flow	将来財務情報 prospective financial information	職責 duty
正味繰越し額 net carrying amount	将来収益獲得能力 service potentials	職責 responsibility
正味経過保険料 net premiums earned	将来性 future	食卓 table
正味現金 net cash	将来性 potential	食肉処理 beef-up
正味財産 capital	将来性 prospects	食肉処理する beef up
正味財産 net asset	将来の future	職人 hand
正味財産 net worth	将来の価格変動性 volatility	職能 function
正味最低リース料 net minimum lease payments	将来の資金繰り future cash flow	職能給 wage on job evaluation
正味残高 free balance	将来の見積り雇用後給付 estimated future postemployment benefits	職能給 wages based on job evaluation
正味資産 net asset	将来の見積り退職後給付 estimated future retiree benefits	職能別報告書 functional reporting of expenses
正味資産 net worth	勝利 success	職場 job
正味資産額 net asset value	上流部門 upstream	職場 place of work
正味収入保険料 net premium revenues	使用料 fee	職場外訓練 off-the-job training
正味帳簿価額 net book value	使用料 hire	職場での working
正味入金額 net proceeds	使用料 royalty	職場内訓練 OJT
正味の net	使用量 use	職場内訓練 on-the-job training
正味の影響 net effects	使用料収益 royalties revenue	植物 plant
正味負債 net liabilities	奨励 incentive	職務 business
正味負債 net liabilities	奨励 promotion	職務 duty
正味負債額 net amount owed	奨励金 premium	職務 function
正味簿価 NBV	奨励する promote	職務 job
正味簿価 net book value	奨励報酬 incentive award	職務 office
正味簿価 net book value	奨励報償制度 incentive compensation plan	職務給 career compensation
正味簿価 net carrying value	除外する set aside	職務給 job rate
正味保険料収入 net premium revenues	所轄官庁 oversight agency	職務給 pay according to function
正味利益 net advantage	書簡 letter	職務給 wages [pay] according to function
正味流動資産 net current assets	初期 beginning	職務評価 job evaluation
常務執行役員 senior executive officer	初期の initial	…の職務を果たす serve
証明書 letter	除却 abandonment	職務を果たす function
証明書 warrant	除却 disposal	職歴平均給与方式 career-average pay
消滅 termination	除却 retirement	助言の advisory
消滅時効 statute of limitations	除却 write-off	諸権利落ち x.a.
消滅すべき determinable	除却する retire	所在地 location
消耗させる deplete	除却法 abandonment method	書式 form
消耗品 supply	除却法 retirement system	書状 letter
賞与 bonus	除去 elimination	助成 furtherance
譲与 grant	除去する eliminate	助成金 bonus
剰余金 net income	除去する take out	助成金 grant
剰余金 retained earnings	職 employment	助長 furtherance
剰余金 surplus	職 job	助長 promotion
剰余金 surplus fund	職 position	助長する promote
剰余金処分 appropriation	職 post	助長する serve
剰余金処分計算書 surplus appropriation statement	職 work	職階給 wage on job classification
剰余金調整表 reconciliation of surplus	職員 employee	職権 commission
賞与支給額 bonus payments	職員 personnel	職工 hand
賞与引当金 accrued bonuses	職員 staff	所得 earnings
賞与引当金 bonus payment reserve	職業 business	所得 income
	職業斡旋 placement	所得 melon
	職業訓練 job training	所得 proceeds
		所得から控除できない non-deductible

| 所得金額 taxable income
| 所得算入 nondeductible
| 所得税 income tax
| 所得税費用 income tax expense
| 所得税率 income tax rate
| 所得比例年金 earnings-related pension
| 処罰 penalty
| ジョブ job
| 処分 action
| 処分 appropriation
| 処分 disposal
| 処分 disposition
| 処分 liquidation
| 処分 penalty
| 処分 retirement
| 処分 settlement
| 処分価額 disposal value
| 処分可能な available
| 処分する liquidate
| 処分する sell
| 処分する settle
| 処分できる disposable
| 除幕式 dedication
| 除幕式 inauguration ceremony
| 除幕する unveil
| 署名 execution
| 署名者 subscriber
| 署名する execute
| 書面にする wtite
| 所有 holding
| 所有 ownership
| 所有 property
| 所有期間利回り horizon return
| 所有権 fee
| 所有権 ownership
| 所有権 property
| 所有権 proprietary right
| 所有権 right
| 所有権株 ownership share
| 所有権者 owner
| 所有権の proprietary
| 所有構造 ownership structure
| 所有財産 holding
| …によって所有されている -owned
| 所有者 owner
| 所有者 ownership
| 所有者 proprietor
| 所有者支配 owner control
| 所有者の proprietary
| 所有者持ち分 net worth shareholder's equity
| 所有する own
| 所有総コスト TCO
| 所有地 property
| 所有比率 ownership
| 所有物 property
| 所有持ち分 holding
| 所有有価証券 portfolio
| 処理 charge

処理 conduct
処理 disposal
処理 liquidation
処理 processing
処理 treatment
処理 write-off
処理する account for …
処理する include
処理する liquidate
処理する settle
処理する write off
処理手順 procedure
処理の managerial
書類 document
書類 paper
白地裏書 endorsement in blank
シリーズ series
自立 independence
自立した independent
自立した海外事業 self-sustaining foreign opeataions
自立した事業 self-sustaining operations
資料 data
資料 material
資料 paper
資料 resource
資料 source
熾烈な fierce
試練 test
試練の challenging
シ・ローン syndicated loan
芯 core
新… new
新案 model
人員 manpower
人員 personnel
人員 staff
人員 workforce
人員削減 downsizing
人員削減 job cut
人員削減 layoff
人員削減する downsize
人員配置 placement
新会社 start-up
…を侵害する infringe on [upon] …
新株 new shares
新株先買権 preemptive right
新株の無償交付 free distribution
新株発行 issuance of new shares
新株発行 new share issue
新株発行 new share offering
新株発行による資金調達 equity financing
新株発行費 stock issue cost
新株引受権 preemptive right
新株引受権 right
新株引受権 stock right
新株引受権 stock warrant
新株引受権 warrant

新株引受権落ち XW
新株引受権付き社債 bond with warrants attached
新株優先引受権 preemptive right
新株予約権 equity warrant
新株予約権 preemptive right
新株予約権 stock acquisition right
新株予約権 warrant
新株予約権付き社債 bond with stock purchase warrant
新株予約権付き社債 bond with stock purchase warrant
新株割当て allotment of new shares
審議会 board
審議会 panel
新規株式公開 initial public offering
新規株式公開 IPO
新規株式公募 initial public offering
新規株式公募 IPO
新規株式発行 new share issue
新規借入れ new borrowing
新規企業 start-up
新企業 start-up
新規公開売出し unseasoned offer
新規公募 initial public offering
新規公募 IPO
新規事業 start-up
新規資金調達 new borrowing
新機軸 innovation
新機軸 innovative
新規資本 fresh capital
新規上場する float
新規に発行する float
新規の new
新記録 high
新工夫 innovation
震源地 focus
人件費 personnel costs
人件費 wage burden
振興 incentive
振興 promotion
進行 movement
振興企業 start-up
振興企業 start-up business
進行基準 percentage of completion method
振興する promote
進行する run
新興の emerging
申告 declaration
申告 return
申告書 report
申告書 return
申告所得 declared income
申告する declare
申告する report
申告する return

申告納税	self-assessment
申告納税方式	self-assessed taxation system
審査	assessment
審査	review
人材	manpower
審査会	panel
審査基準	origination standards
審査する	assess
審査する	review
審査団	panel
人事	personnel
人事管理	personnel administration
シンジケート	syndicate
シンジケートで管理する	syndicate
シンジケート・ローン	syndicated loan
シンジケートを組織する	syndicate
シンジケートを組成する	syndicate
人種差別撤廃	integration
進出	advance
進出	participation
進出	presence
進出する	advance
進出する	participate
人種統合	integration
進取の気性	enterprise
新手法	innovation
心身の衰弱	burnout
進水させる	launch
申請	application
真正かつ公正な概観	true and fair view
真正かつ公正な見方	true and fair view
申請者	application
申請する	enter
申請する	file
新制度	innovation
新制度などの導入	innovation
新生の	emerging
新製品	new product
新生面開拓の	groundbreaking
新生面を開く	reshape
新世代ネット企業	new generation Internet firm
新設合併	consolidation
新設住宅着工戸数	housing start
新設する	create
親切な	good
親善	goodwill
心像	image
新高値	new high
信託	trust
信託元本	trust principal
信託基金	trust fund
信託銀行	trust bank
信託契約	trust deed
信託財産	trust estate
信託資金	trust fund
信託受益権	beneficiary right to the trust
信託証書	deed of trust
信託手数料	trust fee
診断	evaluation
慎重性の原則	conservatism
進捗状況	progress
進呈	presentation
人的資源	manpower
進展	advance
進展	development
進展	movement
進度	rate
新入社員	hire
信任	confidence
新年度	coming year
心配	concern
新発債	newly issued bond
新発債	primary paper
新発明	innovation
審判	judgment [judgement]
信憑性	reliability
人物	figure
新聞	paper
進歩	advance
進歩	development
進歩	improvement
進歩	progress
信望	reputation
進歩した	advanced
進歩する	advance
信用	claim
信用	confidence
信用	credit
信用	goodwill
信用	trust
信用拡大	credit expansion
信用格付け	credit rating
信用格付け機関	credit rating agency
信用格付け機関	rating agency
信用格付けサービス	credit rating service
信用格付けの引下げ	rating cuts
信用貸出限度	credit limit
信用危機	credit crunch
信用業務	credit business
信用供与	facility
信用供与契約	commitments to extend credit
信用供与限度	credit line
信用供与限度	line of credit
信用供与限度額	credit limit
信用供与承認	credit approval
信用供与枠	credit facilities
信用供与枠	credit line
信用供与枠	line of credit
信用限度	credit limit
信用限度	credit limit
信用限度	credit line
信用限度	line of credit
信用需要	credit demand
信用状	credit
信用状	L/C
信用状	letter of credit
信用照会先	credit reference
信用状開設依頼書	application
信用状態	credit standing
信用状の受益者	letter of credit beneficiary
信用状未使用残高	outstanding letters of credit
信用損失	credit loss
信用損失	credit loss
信用貸借対照表	credit balance sheet
信用できる	reliable
信用度	credit standing
信用度	rating
信用取引	margin trading
信用派生商品	credit derivatives
信用逼迫	credit crunch
信用評価	credit assessment
信用評価	standing
信用不安	credit crunch
信用補完	credit enhancement
信用補強	credit enhancement
信用補強	credit support
信用保証枠	credit line
信用補填	credit enhancement
信用補填	credit enhancement
信用補填提供者	credit support provider
信用リスク	credit risk
信用リスク	impaired risk
信用力	credit profile
信用力	credit standing
信用力	credit strength
信用枠	borrowing facilities
信用枠	credit facilities
信用枠	credit facilities
信用枠	facility
信頼	confidence
信頼	goodwill
信頼	trust
信頼性	reliability
信頼できる	reliable
信頼度	reliability
尽力	effort

す

図	figure
図案	figure
吸い上げる	offset
推移	development
推移	transition
推計	estimate
推計	projection

推計する estimate	据える position	スワップする swap
遂行 accomplishment	すき間 niche	スワップ取引 swap deal
遂行 conduct	スキル skill	スワップ取引 swap transaction
遂行する execute	救う rescue	
遂行する implement	少なくとも fully	**せ**
随時償還社債 redeemable bond	スクラップにする scrap	
水準 level	優れた superior	税 duty
水準 mark	…より優れている surpass	税 tax
水準 norm	図形 figure	成果 accomplishment
推奨者 endorser	スケールの大きい massive	成果 achievement
推進 furtherance	筋 source	成果 effectiveness
推進 improvement	筋道 method	成果 payoff
推進 promotion	進める run	成果 performance
推進 thrust	進める advance	成果 product
推進する accelerate	進める undertake	成果 results
推進する boost	スタートアップ・カンパニー start-up	成果 reward
推進する improve		成果 success
推進する promote	スタイル figure	正価 net
推進する serve	スタガー取締役会 staggered board	成果が上がらない negative
推進力 drive	スタッフ staff	税額控除 credit
推進力 driver	廃れた obsolete	税額控除 tax break
推進力 driving force	スタンダード standard	税額控除 tax credit
推進力 guiding force	スタンバイ協定 standby arrangement	正確に fully
推進力 thrust		成果主義型給与制度 performance-based pay system
推薦する propose	ステークホルダー stakeholder	
垂直的合併 vertical merger	ステータス status	成果主義型賃金体系 performance-based pay system
垂直的多角化 vertical diversification	ステートメント statement	
	ステップ step	成果主義型の賃金制度 merit-based pay plan [system]
垂直的分業 vertical division of labor	すでに発生している outstanding	
	捨てる scrap	成果主義型の報酬制度 merit-based pay plan [system]
推定 estimate	捨てる set aside	
推定 expectation	スト strike	生活 life
推定 projection	ストック stock	生活循環 life cycle
推定する assume	ストック・オプション stock option	正規の full
推定する estimate	ストップ・リミット stop limit	請求 claim
推定する expect	スト破り監視員 picket	請求金額 charge
推定値 estimate	ストライキ strike	請求権 claim
推定の estimated	ストラテジー strategy	請求されていない unclaimed
推定費用 estimated cost	ストラテジック・アライアンス strategic alliance	請求事項 claim
推定量 estimate		請求書の送付 billing
水平的 horizontal	ストラテジック・プランニング strategic planning	請求する charge
推力 thrust		請求する demand
スウィフト SWIFT	ストレス pressure	請求することができる chargeable
数字 figure	ストレス stress	請求優先権 priority of claims
趨勢 stream	スピード pace	制御 control
趨勢 trend	図表 chart	制御盤 panel
数値 amount	スピンオフ spinoff [spin-off]	税金 charge
数値 figure	スプレッド spread	税金 tax
スーパー retailer	すべて連結の範囲に含めてある fully consolidated	税金控除 tax credit
数量 figure		税金債務 tax liability
数量 quantity	スポンサー sponsor	税金資産 tax asset
数量 volume	スポンサー underwriter	税金費用 income tax expense
数量割引 quantity discount	スポンサーになる sponsor	税金費用 income taxes
数量割引 volume discount	スランプ slump	税金費用 tax expense
据置き型の deferred	スリム化 streamlining	政権 administration
据え期間 life to call	スリム化する streamline	政権 leadership
据えきの deferred	スワップ swap	制限 limit
据え置く defer	スワップ協定 swap agreement	制限 reserve
据え置く keep	スワップ契約 swap agreement	制限 restriction
据え置く maintain	スワップ主導型の swap-driven	制限 squeeze

制限解除	decontrol	生産系列	production line	正式契約書の作成・署名	closing
税減額効果	benefit	生産合理化	capacity rationalization	正式に記録する	register
制限する	squeeze	生産効率	productivity	正式に登録する	enter
制限を受けない	free	生産子会社	manufacturing operations	正式の	due
…に制限を設ける	determine	生産国	producer	正式の	full
成功	success	生産コスト	manufacturing cost	政治資金規正法	Political Funds Control Law
税効果	interperiod tax allocation	生産コスト	production cost	政治資金収入	political fund revenues
税効果	tax benefit	生産サイクル	production cycle	脆弱な	vulnerable
税効果	tax effect	生産支援会社	production support company	税収	taxation
税効果後	net of income tax effect	生産システム	manufacturing system	政治要項	program
成功支出	successful efforts method	生産システム	production system	正常債権	sound loan
…と整合する	consistent with ...	生産者	producer	正常費用	normal expense
成功成果法	successful efforts method	清算事由	liquidation event	税制	tax system
成功報酬	contingent fee	清算する	close	税制上の特典	tax break
成功報酬	contingent fee	清算する	liquidate	税制上の優遇措置	tax advantages
税込みの	pretax [pre-tax]	清算する	settle	税制上の優遇措置	tax benefit
税込み利益	pretax profit	生産する	manufacture	税制上の優遇措置	tax incentives
制裁	penalty	生産する	produce	生成する	generate
制裁金	penalty	生産性	efficiency	税制優遇	preferential tax treatment
制作	creativity	生産性	productivity	成績	achievement
制作	production	生産性向上	productivity improvement	成績	mark
政策	deal	生産性向上	productivity promotion	成績	record
政策	drive	生産性の向上	productivity gain	成績	results
政策	effort	生産設備	factory	成績	showing
政策	initiative	生産設備	plant	製造	manufacture
政策	measure	生産設備	plant and equipment	製造	manufacturing
政策	package	生産設備	producer's plant and equipment	製造	production
政策	plan	生産設備	production capacity	製造間接費	burden
政策	policy	生産設備	tooling	製造間接費	factory burden
政策	program	生産線	production line	製造間接費	factory burden
製作	manufacture	生産高	output	製造間接費	factory expense
製作	manufacturing	生産高比例法	activity method	製造間接費	factory overhead cost
製作	output	生産高比例法	output method	製造間接費	manufacturing indirect cost
製作	production	生産高比例法	service yield basis	製造間接費	manufacturing overhead
政策金利	key interest rate	生産・調達・運用支援統合情報システム	CALS	製造間接費	overhead
政策金利	key rate	生産年数	productive life	製造間接費	overhead expense
政策決定	decision making	生産能力	capacity	製造間接費配賦額	absorbed burden
政策決定の	decision-making	生産能力	production capacity	製造間接費配賦額	absorbed overhead
製作者	manufacturer	清算配当	final dividend	製造間接費配賦額	applied factory burden
製作所	work	生産品	manufactured goods	製造間接費配賦額	applied overhead
製作する	manufacture	生産品	product	製造技術	knowhow [know-how]
製作する	produce	生産物	commodity	製造業	factory
製作費	output cost	生産方式	production system	製造業	factory sector
清算	liquidation	生産要素	productive factor	製造業	manufacturing sector
清算	settlement	生産余力	production capacity	製造業者	manufacturer
生産	manufacture	生産ライン	production line	製造業者	producer
生産	manufacturing	生産量	output	製造業者	supplier
生産	output	生産量	output volume	製造拠点	production base
生産	production	生産力	productive force	製造原価	factory cost
精算	adjustment	生産力	productivity	製造原価	manufacturing cost
生産委託契約	OEM	静止画像	still image	製造原価	output cost
生産委託契約	original equipment manufacturing	正式記録	registration		
生産関連会社	manufacturing operations				
生産拠点	production base				

製造原価	production cost
製造工程	manufacturing process
製造コスト	manufacturing cost
製造コスト	production cost
製造指図書	manufacture order
製造事業	manufacturing operations
製造者	manufacturer
製造所要時間	manufacturing cycle time
製造する	manufacture
製造する	produce
製造費	production cost
製造物責任	product liability
製造部門	manufacturing operations
製造部門	manufacturing process
製造部門費	producing department cost
製造用消耗品	manufacturing supplies
製造ライン	production line
成長	expansion
成長	growth
成長	progress
成長する	grow
成長潜在力	growth potential
成長の機会	growth opportunity
成長の機会	growth opportunity
成長見通し	growth forecast
成長率	growth
制定する	establish
制度	facility
制度	framework
制度	package
制度	plan
制度	program
制度	requirement
制度	scheme
制度	system
正当	right
正当な	due
正当な注意	due diligence
正当な努力	due diligence
正当な評価	appreciation
制度加入者	plan participant
制度資産	plan assets
正の	positive
製版同盟	strategic alliance
製販同盟	producer-retailer alliance
整備	development
整備	enhancement
整備	improvement
税引き価格	price minus tax
税引き後	net of tax
税引き後赤字	after-tax loss
税引き後赤字	net deficit
税引き後赤字	net loss
税引き後営業利益	NOPAT
税引き後金額	net
税引き後黒字	after-tax profit
税引き後支払い利息控除前利益	earnings before interest and after tax
税引き後支払い利息控除前利益	EBIAT
税引き後四半期赤字	quarterly net loss
税引き後四半期黒字	quarterly net profit
税引き後収益率	after-tax return
税引き後純額の報告	net of tax reporting
税引き後純利益	net profit after tax
税引き後所得	after-tax income
税引き後損失	after-tax loss
税引き後損失	after-tax loss
税引き後損失の合計額	combined net loss
税引き後で	after-tax
税引き後の	after-tax
税引き後の	net
税引き後の影響	after-tax effect
税引き後法	net of tax method
税引き後利益	after-tax balance
税引き後利益	after-tax balance
税引き後利益	after-tax earnings
税引き後利益	after-tax gain
税引き後利益	after-tax profit
税引き後利益	earnings after taxes
税引き後利益	EAT
税引き後利益	net income
税引き後利益	net profit
税引き後利益	post-tax profit
税引き後利益の赤字	negative net worth
税引き後利益の合計額	combined net profit
税引き後利益率	after-tax margin
税引き後利子控除前利益	earnings before interest and after tax
税引き後利子控除前利益	EBIAT
税引き前純利益	net profit before tax
税引き前所得	pretax income
税引き前損失	pretax loss
税引き前当期利益	income before income taxes
税引き前の	pretax [pre-tax]
税引き前引当金	pretax provision
税引き前利益	earnings before income taxes
税引き前利益	income before income taxes
税引き前利益	pretax accounting income
税引き前利益	pretax earnings
税引き前利益	pretax profit
税引き前臨時費用	one-time pre-tax charge
整備する	develop
整備する	maintain
製品	development
製品	equipment
製品	finished goods
製品	finished product
製品	finished product
製品	goods
製品	goods produced
製品	manufacture
製品	manufactured goods
製品	product
製品開発	product development
製品価格	product price
製品関連費用	product related expenses
製品金融の取決め	product financing arrangement
製品群	range
製品系列	line of products
製品系列	product line
製品原価	production cost
製品構成	line of products
製品構成	product line
製品在庫	finished goods inventory
製品在庫	finished product stock
製品寿命	life cycle
製品寿命	product life
製品種目	line of products
製品種目	product line
製品性能	product performance
製品による資金調達方法	product financing arrangement
製品の共同開発	joint product development
製品販売	product sales
製品品目	line of products
製品品目	product line
製品ポートフォリオ	portfolio of products
製品ポートフォリオ管理	product portfolio management
製品輸入	manufactured imports
製品ライフサイクル	life cycle
製品ライン	line of products
製品ライン	product line
政府	administration
正副2通のうちの1通	counterpart
政府支出金	appropriation
税負担率	effective tax rate
政府の歳出・経費	supply
政府部門	public sector
成分	component
成分	element
成分	ingredient
成分表示	ingredient
生保・再保険事業	life and rein-

surance business
製法 process
税務計画の策定 tax planning
税務署 tax authorities
税務上の欠損金 tax loss
税務上の損失 tax loss
税務上の特典 tax benefit
税務上の特典 tax break
税務調整 adjustment for taxable income
税務当局 tax authorities
生命 life
声明 statement
声明書 statement
生命保険 life insurance
生命保険会社 life insurer
生命保険給付 life insurance coverage
制約 restriction
誓約 commitment
誓約 pledge
制約する impair
誓約する pledge
制約を受けない free
整理 adjustment
整理 consolidation
整理 divestiture
整理 liquidation
整理する close
整理する consolidate
整理する divest
整理する liquidate
整理する trim
成立 completion
成立 execution
税率 tax rate
税率軽減措置 tax break
整理統合した consolidated
整理統合する consolidate
整理ポスト liquidation post
勢力 force
勢力 player
勢力 strength
税を課される chargeable
セール sale
セールス sales
セールスマン account executive
セールスマン AE
セールスマン representative
セールス・ミックス sales mix
…を背負って saddled with ...
世界化 globalization
世界企業 global company
世界経済 global economy
世界市場 global market
世界市場 world market
世界戦略 global strategy
世界的規模の global
世界の global
世界の universal

世界の景気 global economy
セカンダリー市場 secondary market
積送する invoice
責任 accountability
責任 charge
責任 duty
責任 liability
責任 responsibility
(…する)責任がある accountable
責任がある responsible
責任者 head
責任者 manager
責任準備金 liability reserve
責任生産量 norm
責任総額 total liabilities
責任の重い responsible
責任を負う assume
責任を負う responsible
責任をとる assume
責務 commission
責務 concern
責務 responsibility
石油採掘部門 upstream
石油精製・販売部門 downstream
セキュリタイゼーション securitization
セクション section
セクター sector
セグメント segment
セグメント間の intersegment
セグメント帰属資産 identifiable asset
セグメント固有資産 identifiable asset
施主 owner
是正する correct
接客 customer service
積極的是正措置 affirmative action
積極的な positive
積極的のれん positive goodwill
積極的優遇措置 affirmative action
積極的優遇措置 affirmative action
積極的優遇措置遵守プログラム affirmative action compliance program
接近する access
設計 engineering
設計する engineer
設計する plan
設計・調達と建設 engineering, procurement and construction
設計・調達と建設 EPC
説示 charge
節税益 tax benefit
節税計画 tax planning
接続 access
接続する access
接続料金 access charge
設置先 site

設置する establish
設置する install [instal]
設定する carry
設定する create
設定する establish
設定する form
設定する post
設定する provide
設定する secure
設定する set aside
設定する set up
セット unit
折半出資 equal partnership
設備 capacity
設備 equipment
設備 facility
設備 plant and equipment
設備 system
設備一式 unit
設備拡張 expansion
設備拡張計画 planned expansion
設備稼動率 capacity ratio
設備機器リース equipment lease
設備更新 equipment replacement
設備購入債務 equipment purchase obligation
設備装置 plant and equipment
設備貸与 leaseback
設備適正価額 equipment fair value
設備投資 capex [CAPEX]
設備投資 capital expenditure
設備投資 capital investment
設備投資 capital spending
設備投資 equipment investment
設備投資 investment in plant and equipment
設備投資 outlays for capital equipment
設備投資額 capital expenditure
設備投資の抑制 less investment in plant and equipment
設備の処分 disposal of facilities
設備の廃棄 disposal of facilities
設備の遊休化 underutilization of the plants
設備配置計画 arrangement plan
設備利用 capacity utilization
説明 account
説明会 briefing
説明会 presentation
説明する account for ...
説明責任 accountability
設立 float
設立 foundation
設立時の initial
設立趣意書 prospectus
設立する create
設立する establish
設立する form

設立する set up	前期繰越し carried down	全社一般資産 corporate assets
設立定款 articles of incorporation	前期繰越べ欠損金 deficit at the beginning of a period	全社員 workforce
設立当初の original		全社共通費 general corporate expenses
背中合わせの back-to-back	前期修正項目 prior period item	
是認 approval	前期損益修正益 prior period adjustment profit	全社的品質管理 companywide quality control
狭まる narrow		
狭める narrow	前期損益修正損 loss from prior period adjustment	船主 owner
セミナー briefing		全従業員 workforce
責める accuse	前期損益修正損 prior period adjustment loss	占取する enter
競り bid		選出 election
競り bidding	前期の対応額 comparative figures	戦術 tactics
競り bidding war	前期の比較対応数値 comparative figures	選出する adopt
競り売り auction		選出する elect
競り手 bidder	前期比 from a year earlier	選出する tap
ゼロ金利政策 zero-interest rate policy	前期比 from the year before	先取特権 lien protection
	前期比 over the previous year	先取特権 preemptive right
ゼロ金利ローン zero financing	前期比 quarterly	専心 dedication
ゼロ・クーポン債 zero coupon bond	前期比で compared to a year earlier	前身 forerunner
		前進 advance
ゼロ成長 zero growth	前期比で from a year ago	前進 thrust
ゼロ・ベース予算 ZBB	前期までに掲げた数値 previously reported figures	前進する advance
ゼロ・ベース予算 zero-base budget		全世界一体化 globalization
	前期までの各事業年度 prior years	全世界的 global
ゼロ・ベース予算管理 zero-base budget	前期までの事業年度 previous years	全世界の global
		前線 front
善意 goodwill	前期までの報告書に掲げた数値 previously reported figures	漸増する incremental
善意の使用者 innocent user		漸増的な cumulative
全額 full amount	選挙 election	全体 whole
全額回収不能 zero recovery	選挙権 vote	全体的な global
全額出資子会社 wholly-owned subsidiary	占拠する take over	全体的な total
	先駆 forerunner	全体として overall
全額出資の fully funded	先駆者 forerunner	全体の entire
全額出資の wholly-owned	前月比 month-on-month	全体の gross
全額消去 full elimination	前月比で month-on-month	全体の overall
全額所有子会社 fully owned subsidiary	宣言 declaration	全体の total
	宣言する declare	選択 election
全額払込み済み株式 fully-paid capital stock	先見性 foresight	選択 option
	全権能と権限 full powers and authority	選択科目 option
全額払込み済み株式 full-paid capital stock		選択権 election
	先見の明 foresight	選択権 option
全額引受方式 underwriting method	宣言配当金 declared dividend	選択肢 alternative
	全権利落ち x.a.	選択肢 option
全額を wholly	先行的 pilot	選択手段 option
全科目連結 line-by-line consolidation	宣告 declaration	選択する elect
	全国均一サービス universal service	選択の余地 option
前期 last quarter		前兆 forerunner
前期 last year	前後参照 cross reference	前提 assumption
前期 preceding fiscal year	潜在株式調整後利益 fully diluted earnings per share	…を前提として subject to ...
前期 preceding quarter		宣伝する promote
前期 preceding year	潜在成長率 potential	宣伝文句 advertising jingle
前期 previous year	潜在成長率 trend rate	先頭 cutting edge
前期 prior period	潜在的な latent	先頭 forefront
前期 prior year	潜在的な potential	先頭 front
前期 year just ended	潜在能力 potential	先頭 leading edge
前期以前 prior periods	潜在力 potential	先導企業 leading company
前期以前 prior years	全社合わせての赤字 combined net loss	選任 election
前期繰越し B/D		専任アドバイザー resident adviser [adviser]
前期繰越し b/d	全社一般経費 general corporate expenses	
前期繰越し brought down		前任監査人 predecessor auditor
前期繰越し C/D [c/d]		選任する appoint

選任する	elect	全部	whole	戦略の策定	strategic planning
専任の	resident	全部監査	complete auditing	全力を挙げる	commit
専念	dedication	全部原価	absorbed cost	全力を傾ける	concentrate
前年	last year	全部原価	absorption cost	前例のない	unusual
前年	preceding year	全部原価	full cost		
前年	year earlier	全部原価計算	full cost accounting		
専念する	commit	全部原価プラス価格決定法	full-cost plus method	**そ**	
前年度	last fiscal year			層	level
前年度	last year	全部原価法	full cost basis	…層	public
前年度	preceding fiscal year	全部原価法	full cost method	添う	meet
前年度	preceding year	全部所有子会社	wholly-owned subsidiary	相違	disparity
前年度	preceding year			総売上高	gross sales
前年度	previous year	全部で	overall	総売上高	sales totals
前年度	prior period	全部の	full	総売上高	total revenues
前年度	prior year	全部配賦原価	fully allocated cost	総売上高	turnover
前年度以前	previous years	全部配賦原価	fully allocated cost	総運転資本	gross working capital
前年度以前	prior periods	全部連結	full consolidation	総営業費用	total operating expenses
前年度以前	prior years	全部連結	full consolidation		
前年同期	prior year	全部連結されている	fully consolidated	増益	earnings growth
前年同期	same period a year earlier			増益	profit growth
前年同期	same period last year	全部を	wholly	総益金	gross income
前年同期	same period of the previous year	専務取締役	senior managing director	…の増加	increase in …
				…の増加	increased
前年同期比	from a year earlier	鮮明度	resolution	増価	appreciation
前年同期比	from the year before	全面時価評価法	full fair value method	増加	accumulation
前年同期比	over a year ago			増加	addition
前年同期比	over the previous year	全面的	full	増加	advance
前年同期比	year earlier	全面的な	global	増加	enhancement
前年同期比	year-on-year	全面的な	total	増加	gain
前年同期比	year-over-year	専門家	authority	増加	growth
前年同期比で	compared to a year earlier	専門家	player	増加	improvement
		専門家集団	panel	増加	increase
前年同月比	over a year ago	専門家の報告書	expertise	増加	pickup [pick-up]
前年同月比	year-over-year	専門技術	expertise	増加	rise
前年と比べて	over the previous year	専門技術	knowhow [know-how]	総会	general meeting
		専門知識	expertise	総会	meeting
前年度までの各事業年度	prior years	専門知識	knowhow [know-how]	増改築積立金	additions and betterments [improvements] reserves
前年度までの事業年度	previous years	専門の	special		
		専門用語	term	増加額	accrual
前年度までの事業年度	prior periods	占有	assumption	増加額	appreciation
		占有	holding	総額	aggregate
前年比	from a year ago	占有する	assume	総額	aggregate amount
前年比	from a year ago	戦略	strategy	総額	amount
前年比	from a year earlier	戦略企画	strategic planning	総額	figure
前年比	from the year before	戦略計画	strategic planning	総額	gross
前年比	over the previous year	戦略計画策定	strategic planning	総額	sum
前年比	year earlier	戦略計画設定	strategic planning	総額	total
前年比	year-over-year	戦略上重要な	strategic	総額原価法	aggregate cost method
前年比で	compared to a year earlier	戦略上の	operational		
		戦略上の	strategic	総額で	overall
前年より	over the previous year	戦略上役に立つ	strategic	総額の	full
前納する	prepay	戦略提携	strategic alliance	総額連結	full consolidation
前半	first half	戦略的	strategic	増加させる	boost
全般的な	general	戦略的業務提携	strategic alliance	増加した	increased
全般的な	large	戦略的計画	strategic planning	増加資本	additional capital
全般的に	generally	戦略的財務広報	investor [investors] relations	増加する	accrue
前半の	first-half			増加する	advance
全部	fully	戦略的投資	strategic investment	増加する	gain
		戦略的同盟	strategic alliance	増加する	grow
		戦略に必要な	strategic	増加する	increase

増加する	rise
増加する	rising
総括	summary
総括原価	full cost
総括原価主義	full cost principle
総括精算表	compared trade summary
総株式数	capital stock
増加部分	accrual
早期完済	full repayment before maturity
早期退職	early retirement
早期退職奨励金	buyout
早期退職制度	early retirement program
早期退職制度	early retirement program
早期退職優遇制度	early retirement and buyout packages
早期定年	early retirement
早期投資	early investment
早期返済	early repayment (before due date)
創業	foundation
操業	activity
操業	operation
増強	beef-up
増強	boost
創業する	set up
操業する	operate
増強する	beef up
増強する	boost
増強する	intensify
増強する	reinforce
操業短縮	slowdown
操業度	capacity
操業度	volume
操業度	volume level
操業費	running expense
送金	transfer
送金する	transfer
総計	aggregate
総計	amount
総計	sum total
総計	total
総計で	overall
総計の	gross
総計の	total
総経費	general expense
総経費	overhead
総決算	bottom line
増減	change
総原価	full cost
総原価	total cost
総合勘定	summary
総合耐用年数	composite life
総合的	general
総合的	universal
総合的な	comprehensive
総合的な	global
総合的な	overall
総合保険料方式	aggregate cost method
総コスト	total cost
相互調達	mutual procurement
相互通貨交換協定	swap agreement
相互の	mutual
相互の	reciprocal
相互保険	mutual insurance
相互利益協定	combination
相互理解	communication
相互利用する	share
操作	manipulation
操作	operation
相殺	compensation
相殺	elimination
相殺	offset
総裁	president
相殺額	offset
相殺項目	offset item
相殺誤差	compensating error
相殺消去	elimination
相殺消去する	eliminate
相殺する	average
相殺する	net
相殺する	offset
造作	fixture
創作する	create
創作性	creativity
操作上の	operational
操作する	control
操作する	manipulate
操作する	operate
操作する	run
操作する人	operator
操作の	managerial
増資	additional share
増資	capital increase
増資	capital increment
増資	fresh capital
増資	injection of equity
増資	new share issue
増資	new shares
増資	recapitalization
増資株	additional share
増資計画	capital boost plan
増資交渉	negotiations on the capital increase
総資産	identifiable asset
総資産	total assets
総資産利益率	return on assets
総資産利益率	ROA
総資本	total assets
総資本	total capital
総資本利益率	net income to total assets ratio
総資本利益率	ROA
増収	gain in revenues
増収	revenue growth
総収益	gross income
総収益	gross sales
総収益	total revenues
操縦する	manipulate
増収増益	growth in revenues and earnings
増収増益	increse in revenues and profits
総収入	gross income
創出する	create
創出する	provide
相乗効果	synergy
総所得	gross income
増進	enhancement
増進	gain
増進	promotion
増進する	gain
総数	aggregate
総数	amount
総生産高	aggregate output
造成する	develop
総責任額	total liabilities
創設	promotion
増設	addition
創設する	establish
創造する	create
創造する	generate
創造性	creativity
創造力	creativity
相続財産権	fee
相続税	estate tax
増大	boost
増大	enhancement
増大	gain
増大	growth
増大	increase
総代会	meeting of representatives of policyholders
総代会	policyholders' representative meeting
増大した	increased
増大する	gain
増大する	grow
増大する	increase
送達	delivery
送達	service
送達する	deliver
装置	drive
装置	equipment
装置	package
装置	unit
増築	addition
総長	president
想定	assumption
想定	projection
贈呈	presentation
想定する	assume
贈呈する	present
争点	issue
騒動	turmoil

相当額	equivalent
…に相当する	approximate
…に相当する	represent
相当する	equivalent
…に相当する量	worth
相当な	healthy
相当な	reasonable
相当な	significant
相当の	due
相当の注意	due diligence
相当分	equivalent
挿入語句	parenthesis
相場	market
相場	market price
相場	quoted price
相場	rate
相場	value
相場師	operator
相場操縦	manipulation
相場の回復	recovery
相場をいう	quote
装備	tooling
総費用	total cost
送付する	serve
増分収益	incremental revenue
増分主義予算	incremental budget
増分の	incremental
増分利益	incremental profit
総平均	weighted average
総平均法	weighted average method
総保険料	gross premium
増補の	supplementary [supplemental]
総務部長	secretary
総輸入元	distributor
贈与	donation
贈与財産	settlement
贈与税	CTT
総利益	trading profit
創立	foundation
創立	promotion
創立する	establish
総量	amount
総量	sum
総量	total
贈賄資金	slush fund
総和法	aggregate method
ソーシング	sourcing
遡求	recourse
遡求権付きの売却	factoring with recourse
遡求権なし	nonrecourse
遡求権なしの売却	factoring without recourse
遡及修正	backlog adjustment
遡及修正	backlog adjustment
遡及修正	retroactive adjustment
遡及償却	catch-up depreciation
遡及償却額	backlog depreciation
遡及する	retroactive
遡及請求権付き貸付け金	recourse loan
遡及力のある	retroactive
遡及的適用	retrospective application
遡及適用	retroactive application
遡及適用	retrospective application
即座の	immediate
即時決済	immediate settlement
即時決済	on-the-spot payment
即時認識	immediate recognition
即時年金	immediate anuity
即時の	immediate
促進	furtherance
促進	improvement
促進	promotion
促進策	incentive
促進する	accelerate
促進する	advance
促進する	improve
促進する	promote
促進する	serve
属性	attribution
属性	property
属性法	temporal method
測定	determination
測定	measurement
測定基準	benchmark
測定する	determine
測定値	measurement
測度	measure
速度	pace
速度	rate
速報	quick estimation
速報値	advanced figures
速報値	earlier reported estimate
底	low
底上げする	upgrade
底堅い	robust
底堅い	solid
損なう	dilute
損なう	impair
底値	low
素材	basic material
素材	material
素材	raw material
組織	institution
組織	machinery
組織	organization
組織	scheme
組織	structure
組織	system
組織化	organization
組織替えする	restructure
組織構成	organizational structure
組織再編	reorganization
組織する	form
組織体	entity
組織体	organization
組織的運動	drive
組織内の	in-house [inhouse]
組織変更	reorganization
組織変更する	reorganize
阻止する	contain
素質	potential
訴訟	action
訴訟	proceedings
訴状	bill
訴訟記録	minutes
訴訟実務	practice
訴訟手続き	practice
訴訟手続き	proceedings
訴訟手続き	process
訴訟和解金	legal settlement
租税	tax
租税回避	tax planning
租税回避地	tax haven
租税計画	tax planning
租税公課	applicable taxes
租税条約	tax convention
組成する	form
租税体系	tax system
租税逃避	tax haven
租税特別措置	tax break
租税避難国	tax haven
租税優遇措置	tax break
措置	action
措置	measure
措置	proceedings
措置	program
措置	step
措置	treatment
即金主義	pay-as-you-earn
即金主義	PAYE
即金で支払う	pay down
即効性の	short-term
即刻の	immediate
率先	initiative
備え	hedge
その他	other
その他から得た運転資本	working capital provided from other sources
その他の	other
その他の収益	other income
その他の負債	other liabilities
その他の包括利益累計額	accumulated other comprehensive income
その他負債	other liabilities
ソリューション	solution
ソルベンシー	solvency
ソルベンシー・マージン	solvency margin
損益	gain and loss [gain or loss]
損益	income
損益	profit and [or] loss

損益および留保利益結合計算書 combined income and retained earnings statement
損益計算書 earnings report
損益計算書 income statement
損益計算書 profit and loss statement
損益計算書 statement of earnings
損益計算書の金額 income statement amounts
損益の確定 lockup [lock-up]
損益の実現 realization of profit and loss
損益分岐点 break-even (point)
損益法 deferred method
損害 damage
損害 disadvantage
損害 loss
損害額 damage
損害額 loss
損害査定 damage assessment
損害査定 damage assessment
損害査定費 loss adjustment expense
損害塡補 indemnity
損害賠償 compensation for damages
損害賠償 compensation for losses
損害賠償 damage
損害賠償 damage compensation
損害賠償額 damage
損害賠償金 damage
損害賠償金 damage payments
損害賠償請求 claims for damages
損害賠償責任 liability for damages
損害賠償訴訟 damage suit
損害賠償未収金 damage claims receivable
損害費用 damage costs
損害保険 casualty insurance
損害保険 nonlife insurance
損害保険会社 nonlife insurer
損害保険の正味責任準備金 non-life net technical provisions
損金 charge against revenues
損金 deduction
損金算入 deduction
損金算入できる deductible
損金不算入の租税課税 non-deductible tax
存在 presence
存在感 presence
損失 deficit
損失 disadvantage
損失 loss
損失拡大 wider loss
損失金 deficit
損失の繰延べ loss carryforward [carry forward]
損失の認識 loss recognition
損失引当金 loss provision
損失引当金 reserves for losses
損失負担 exposure to losses
損失分担方式 loss-sharing system
損失補償 indemnity
損失補償契約 indemnity
損失予想額 loss projections
損失予防策をとる hedge
損失予防手段 hedge
損失を計上する suffer
損失を被る lose
存続 life
存続 standing
存続会社 surviving company
存続期間 life
存続期間 life span
尊重する consider
損得なしになる break even
損費として処理する charge off
損保 nonlife insurer
損保会社 nonlife insurer
損耗 impairment

た

ターゲット target
ターゲットにする target
ターンアラウンド turnaround
ターンキー方式の turnkey
…台 mark
台 unit
第1回株式公募 initial public offering
第1四半期 first quarter
第1四半期 Q1
第2四半期 Q2
第2四半期 second quarter
第2四半期の営業赤字 second-quarter operating loss
第2四半期の営業収益 second-quarter operating revenues
第2四半期の営業損失 second-quarter operating loss
第3四半期 Q3
第3四半期 third quarter
第3四半期 fourth quarter
第4四半期 Q4
第4四半期の業績 fourth quarter results
第4四半期の純利益 fourth quarter earnings
第4四半期の利益 fourth quarter earnings
タイアップ tie-up
代案 alternative
第一次産業 primary sectors
第一順位の primary
第一人者 front runner [front-runner, frontrunner]
第一の original
第一面 front
第一線 forefront
第一線 front line
対売上高純利益率 net margin on sales
対応 action
対応 matching
対応 measure
対応する meet
対価 compensation
対価 consideration
対価 fee
対価 remuneration
対価 reward
退化 deterioration
代価 charge
大会 meeting
対外 foreign
対外 overseas
退化する deteriorate
大規模な heavy
大規模な large
大規模な massive
大規模な substantial
耐久財 durable goods
耐久財 durable product
耐久財 durables
耐久消費財 durable product
怠業 slowdown
代金 charge
代金 consideration
代金 proceeds
代金取立て collection
代金取立手形 bill for collection
代金引換え渡し cash on delivery
代金引換渡し COD
代金引換渡し collect on delivery
待遇 treatment
体系 framework
体系 scheme
体系 structure
体系 system
体験 experience
代行者 proxy
代行者 representative
…を代行する represent
対抗馬 contender
大黒柱 mainstay
対策 effort
対策 measure
対策 package
対策 policy
対策 program
対策 project
対策 protection
対策 solution
対策 step
第三者委員会 third party committee

第三者株式割当て　third-party share allotment
第三者間取引にかかわる　arm's length [arm's-length]
第三者預託　escrow
第三者割当て　allocation of new shares to a third party
第三者割当て　private placement
第三者割当て　third-party allotment [allocation]
第三者割当て増資　third-party allotment [allocation]
第三者割当て増資する　privately place
第三者割当て発行する　privately place
大事業　enterprise
体質　culture
体質　standing
体質　structure
…に対して　compared with …
貸借　lending
貸借勘定　balance
貸借契約　charter
貸借対照表　balance sheet
貸借対照表　position statement
貸借対照表情報　balance sheet information
貸借対照表に計上されない　off-balance-sheet
貸借対照表に表示されない　off-balance-sheet
貸借対照表の作成　preparation of balance sheet
貸借対照表日後　post-balance sheet day
貸借対照表日後に発生した事象　post-balance sheet event
貸借対照表日後の査閲　post-balance sheet review
対照　comparison
対象　matter
対象　objective
代償　compensation
代償　remuneration
…の対象である　subject to …
…を対象とする　cover
対象にする　target
代償の　compensatory
退職　retirement
退職　separation
退職　termination of employment
退職慰労金　retirement allowance
退職勧奨制度　retirement incentive program
退職給付　retirement benefit
退職給付　termination benefit
退職給付債務　projected benefit obligation
退職給付引当金　retirement plan reserves
退職給与　retirement allowance
退職給与　retirement benefit
退職給与　severance indemnity
退職給与引当金　allowance for retirement and severance
退職給与引当金　retirement allowance
退職給与引当金繰入れ額　retirement provisions
退職金　retirement allowance
退職金　severance pay
退職金制度　severance indemnity plan
退職後　postretirement
退職後給付　postemployment [post-employment] benefits
退職後給付　postretirement benefit
退職後給付会計　accounting for postemployment benefits
退職後給付債務　postretirement benefit obligation
退職後給付純期間費用　net periodic postretirement benefit cost
退職後給付制度　postretirement benefit plan
退職後給付に関する会計処理　accounting for postemployment benefits
退職後給付についての会計処理　accounting for postemployment benefits
退職後給付費用　postretirement benefit cost
退職後の健康管理給付　postretirement health care benefit
退職後の健康保険給付金　postretirement health care benefit
退職者　retiree
退職者医療給付　retiree health care benefits
退職者給付　retiree benefits
退職者給付会計　accounting for retiree benefits
退職者給付についての会計処理　accounting for retiree benefits
退職者健康管理給付　retiree health care benefits
退職者健康保険　retiree health benefits
退職従業員　retired employee
退職従業員　retired employee
退職終身基金　retired life fund
退職する　retire
退職年金給付　pension benefits
退職年金債務　obligations under pension and deferred compensation plans
退職年金増加額　postretirement award
対処する　manage
…に対する比率　as a percentage of …
…に対する割合　as a percentage of …
体制　leadership
体制　scheme
体制　structure
体制　system
大勢　trend
代替コスト　replacement cost
代替策　alternative
代替的会計基準　alternative accounting principle
大多数　majority
態度　presence
対投資家関係　investor [investors] relations
大統領　president
タイトル　heading
第二次分売　secondary distribution
退任　resignation
退任する　retire
退任する　step down
滞納　arrears
滞納　default
滞納金　arrears
滞納の　delinquent
大半　majority
代表者　representative
…を代表する　represent
代表として派遣する　delegate
代表取締役　representative director
代物弁済　accord
大部分　lion's share
大部分　majority
大変金になる　lucrative
タイミング　timing
耐用期間　life
耐用期間　service life
耐用年数　age
耐用年数　durable years
耐用年数　life
耐用年数　life period
耐用年数　period of depreciation
耐用年数　service life
耐用年数　service life
耐用年数　useful life
耐用年数表　useful life table
代理委任状　proxy
代理勧誘状　proxy statement
代理業務　commission
代理権　proxy
代理権勧誘状　proxy statement
代理行為　proxy
代理店　distributor
代理投票　proxy vote
代理投票用紙　proxy voting card

代理人	escrow
代理人	proxy
代理人	representative
代理人カード	proxy card
代理人様式	form of proxy
代理人様式	proxy form
滞留債権	delinquent account
大量	quantity
大量購入払戻し	quantity rebate
大量仕入れ	quantity buying
大量の	heavy
大量の	large
大量の	massive
大量の	significant
大量保有報告書	report on large stockholders [shareholders]
体力	financial strength
体力	strength
…の代理をつとめる	represent
ダウ（工業株30種）平均	Dow Jones industrial average [Industrial Average]
ダウ工業株30種平均	Dow Jones industrial average [Industrial Average]
ダウ工業株平均	Dow Jones industrial average [Industrial Average]
ダウ・ジョーンズ平均	Dow Jones average [Average]
ダウ・ジョーンズ平均株価	Dow Jones average [Average]
ダウ平均	Dow Jones average [Average]
ダウ平均	Dow Jones industrial average [Industrial Average]
ダウンサイジング	downsizing
ダウンストリーム	downstream
絶え間のない	running
耐える	suffer
高	amount
高い	good
高い	high
高入先出し法	HIFO
多角化	diversification
多角化	diversity
多角化	expansion
多角化企業	conglomerate
多角化する	diversify
多角経営	diversified management
多角的合併	multi-merger
多額の	heavy
多額の	massive
多額の	significant
多額の利益配当	melon
高く評価する	appreciate
高値	high
高まり	increase
高まる	grow
高まる	intensify
高まる	rise
高まる	surge
高める	boost
高める	create
高める	enhance
高める	improve
高める	increase
高める	intensify
高める	serve
高める	strengthen
高める	upgrade
兌換券	convertible note
多岐にわたる	general
多業種企業	multi-industry firm
多極分散する	decentralize
宅地開発業者	developer
宅地造成業者	developer
巧みに操る	manipulate
巧みに運営する	engineer
巧みに管理する	engineer
巧みに計画する	engineer
巧みに処理する	engineer
蓄えておく	set aside
蓄える	set aside
打撃	squeeze
妥結	settlement
多国籍企業	multinational enterprise
確かな	reliable
出し手レート	offered rate
他社に負けない	competitive
多数	majority
多数	plurality
多数意見	consensus
多大の	massive
戦い	struggle
ただし…	subject to …
立会所	boardroom
立ち上げる	enter
立ち上げる	launch
立入り	entry
立入り権	license [licence]
立ち入る	access
立ち入る	enter
立場	capacity
立場	footing
立場	presence
立場	standing
立場の明確な表明	commitment
脱大型コンピュータ現象	downsizing
タックス・ヘイブン	tax haven
…に達する	amount to …
達成	accomplishment
達成	achievement
達成	completion
達成	execution
達成基準	norm
達成する	achieve
達成する	chalk up
達成する	deliver
達成する	execute
達成する	gain
達成する	meet
達成する	rack up
達成する	secure
脱退	withdrawal
…建て	denominated
建て替える	rebuild
立て直し	rehabilitation
立て直す	rebuild
立て直す	rehabilitate
立て直す	reshape
立て直す	restructure
立て直す	revamp
立て直す	revive
建物	building
建物維持費	building maintenance expense
妥当な	reasonable
棚上げ状態	back burner
棚上げする	set aside
棚卸し	inventory
棚卸し表	inventory
棚卸し減耗	inventory shortage
棚卸し減耗費	inventory shortage
棚卸し差損費	inventory shortage
棚卸し資産	inventory
棚卸し資産回転率	inventory turn
棚卸し資産回転率	inventory turnover
棚卸し資産期末在り高	closing stock
棚卸し資産期末有り高	ending inventory
棚卸し資産期末保有高	ending inventory
棚卸し資産原価	inventory cost
棚卸資産原価	inventoriable cost
棚卸し資産の取得原価	inventory cost
棚卸し資産引当金	inventory reserve
棚卸し資産評価	inventory valuation
棚卸し資産評価額	inventory value
棚卸し資産評価引当金	inventory reserve
棚卸し高	inventory
棚卸し評価	inventory valuation
棚卸し品	inventory
棚ぼた	windfall
タナボタ利益	windfall
他人資本	borrowed capital
他人資本調達	debt financing
頼みの綱	mainstay
…のために	due to …
ためになる	profitable
多様化	diversification
多様化する	diversify
多様性	diversity

多様性	productivity
多量の	massive
団	team
単位	entity
単位	unit
単位：100万ドル	in millions
単位：10億ドル	in billions
単位：ドル	in dollars
単位：パーセント	in percentages
単位：百万ドル	millions of dollars
単位型投資信託	unit investment trust
単位給付	unit credit
単位給付方式	unit credit method
単位原価	unit cost
単一の	flat
単一の事業区分	single industry segment
単位積増し	unit credit
単位年金積増し	unit credit
段階	notch
段階	process
段階的に解消する	phase out
段階的に削減する	phase out
段階的に撤廃する	phase out
段階的に廃止する	phase out
段階的に閉鎖する	phase out
短期貸付け金	short-term liability
短期借入金	note payable
短期借入金	short-term borrowings
短期借入金	short-term debts
短期借入金	short-term liability
短期借入金純額	net short-term borrowings
短期借入金純額	net short-term borrowings
短期借入金の加重平均金利	weighted average interest rates on short-term borrowings
短期間の	short-term
短期金融市場	money market
短期金融市場	secondary market
短期金利	Federal [federal] funds rate
短期繰延べ法	deferral of prepayments for future services
短期債	short end
短期債権	short-term liability
短期債務	short-term borrowings
短期債務	short-term debts
短期資金	hot money
短期資金計画	short-run fund planning
短期証券	short paper
短期的資金運用投資	temporary cash investments
短期的な	immediate
短期投資	temporary cash investments
短期投資資金	hedge fund
短期の	current
短期の	short-term
短期負債	current liabilities
短期負債	short-term debts
短期負債	short-term liability
短期物	front end
短期満期の	short-term
探索的調査	exploratory research
探索の	exploratory
短縮	reduction
短縮する	reduce
単純希薄化1株当たり利益	primary earnings per share
単純希薄化による1株当たり利益	primary earnings per share
単純協業	simple cooperation
単純集計	ground total
単純平均	simple mean value
単純平均法	arithmetical average cost method
短所	defect
団体	community
団体	corporation
団体	group
団体	organization
団体規約	articles of association
団体保険	group insurance
担当記者	hand
担当者	representative
単独委任状	single proxy
単独経常利益	parent recurring profit
単独財務諸表	unconsolidated financial statements
単独ベース	parent
単独ベースの	unconsolidated
単独ベースの売上高	parent sales
単独ベースの営業利益	parent operating profit
単独ベースの営業利益	unconsolidated operating profit
単独ベースの経常利益	parent-only pretax profit
単独ベースの収益	parent basis earnings
単独ベースの収益見通し	parent-basis earnings outlook
単独ベースの税引き前利益	parent-only pretax profit
段取り	organization
段取り	plan
段取り	tooling
段取り換え	tooling change
担保	charge
担保	collateral
担保	coverage
担保	guarantee
担保	mortgage
担保	pledge
担保	security
担保・抵当品	pledge
担保価値	collateral value
担保からの元本支払い[元本返済]	collateral principal payment
担保金	margin
担保権	charge
担保権	security right
担保権の実行	foreclosed collateral
担保権の順位	priority between mortgages
担保財産	collateral
担保資産	pledged asset
担保品	collateral
担保付き債券	mortgage bond
担保付き資金調達	secured financing
担保付き社債	debenture stock
担保付き社債	collateral bond
担保付き社債	mortgage bond
担保付き社債	secured obligation
担保付き負債	secured liability
担保付き融資	mortgage
担保付き融資	secured loans
担保提供者	mortgagor
担保となる	underlying
…を担保に入れる	cover
担保に入れる	pledge
担保に供する	pledge
担保範囲	coverage
担保評価	collateral assessment
担保評価額	collateral value estimates
担保品	collateral goods
担保物	guarantee
担保物件	collateral
担保物件	underlying collateral
担保不動産	mortgage
担保余力	net worth of collateral
端末利用者	end user
単名手形	single name paper
単利	simple interest
単利	simple interest
単利現価	simple present value

ち

地位	appointment
地位	capacity
地位	position
地位	post
地位	presence
地位	profile
地位	reputation
地位	standing
地位	status
地域	geographic area
地域	sector
地域間の移動	transfers between

地域間の売掛金		中途解約
geographic areas	地代 rent	tlement
地域間の売掛金 interarea accounts receivable	縮める narrow	中間決算 midterm report
	秩序 order	中間決算 midterm settlement of accounts
地域間の振替え transfers between geographic areas	知的財産 intellectual property	
	知的財産権 intellectual property	中間決算 midyear accounts
地域間振替え interarea transfers	知的財産権 intellectual property right	中間決算 semiannual results
地域区分間の移動 transfers between geographic areas		中間決算 semiannual settlement of accounts
	知的財産権紛争 intellectual property dispute	
地域社会 community		中間決算報告 interim financial results report
地域社会ベースの community-based	知的資産 intellectual asset	
	知的所有権 intellectual property	中間決算報告 interim report
地域セグメント geographic area	知的所有権 intellectual property right	中間決算報告 midterm earnings report
地域別売上高 geographic revenue		
地域別区分 geographic area	地歩 footing	中間決算報告 midterm report
地域別セグメント情報 geographical [geographic] segment information	地歩 position	中間財 intermediate goods
	地方 climate	中間製品 semifinished goods
	地方自治の municipal	中間損益計算書 semiannual income statement
地域密着型の community-based	地方税 local tax	
チーム team	知名度 name	中間的に介在する mezzanine
地位を占める rank	知名度 reputation	中間に位置する mezzanine
チェックする monitor	チャージ charge	中間の half-yearly
遅延 arrears	着実な solid	中間の interim
遅延 delay	着手 launch	中間の semiannual
遅延金利 delayed interest	着手する embark	中間配当 semiannual dividend
チェンジ・オブ・コントロール条項 change of control clause	着手する launch	中間報告 interim report
	着手する undertake	中間報告 midterm report
遅延損害金 penalty charge	着想 idea	中間報告 tentative report
遅延利息 delayed interest	チャプター・イレブン Chapter 11	中期 midterm
遅延利息 penalty interest	チャレンジ challenge	注記 footnote
近い close	チャンス opportunity	注記 note
違い difference	注意 note	中期経営計画 intermediate planning
地価公示価格 posted prices of land	仲介 brokerage	
	仲介業 brokerage	中期経営戦略 midterm management strategy
力 ability	仲介手数料 brokerage	
力 force	中核 core	中期国債 T-note
力 leverage	中核企業 core business	中期国債 Treasury note
力 power	中核業務 core business	駐在員 representative
力 strength	中核事業 core business	駐在員事務所 representative
力強い strong	中核事業 main business	駐在している resident
力強さ strength	中核事業 principal areas of activity	仲裁付託合意 submission
…に力を注ぐ focus on …		中止 abandonment
力を注ぐ concentrate	中核事業収益 core earnings	中止 cancelation [cancellation]
地球温暖化ガスの排出量 greenhouse gas emissions	…を中核事業にする focus on …	中止事業 discontinued operation [business]
	中核戦略 core strategy	
地球規模の global	中核的の業務 core competence	中止する cancel
地球全体の global	中核的自己資本比率 core capital rate [ratio]	中止する scrap
地球的規模化 globalization		中止する suspend
蓄財 accumulation	中核的な core	注釈 note
蓄積 accumulation	…を中核に据える focus on …	中小の weak
蓄積 backlog	中核能力 core competence	中心 core
蓄積した accumulated	中間 half	中心 focus
蓄積する accumulate	中間 half year	中心 forefront
遅行指標 lagging indicator	中間 midterm	中心相場 prevailing rate
遅行する lag	中間会計期間の interim	中心的な core
知識 idea	中間期の利益 interim profit	…中心の driven
知識 information	中間決算 first-half account settlement	中心レート prevailing rate
恥辱 dishonor		中枢 core
地帯 climate	中間決算 half-fiscal year account	中断 abandonment
遅滞 arrears	中間決算 midterm earnings report	中断する suspend
遅滞 delay	中間決算 midterm financial set-	中途解約 cancelation before ma-

turity	
中途解約不能の	noncancelable [noncancellable]
中途解約不能リース	non-cancelable lease
中途退職金の支払い	separation payments
注入	injection
…に注目する	focus on ...
注目の的	focus
注文	order
注文残高	backlog
注文執行	order execution
注文者	owner
注文主導型の	order-driven
注文書	order
注文書	purchase order
注文処理	order entry
注文する	order
注文生産方式	build to order
注文品	order
注文履行費	order-filling cost
注文履行費予算	budget for order-filling cost
中立的買収	neutral acquisition
…帳	book
超一流企業	AAA company
調印	execution
調印式	closing
調印する	execute
超過	excess
超過負債	excess
超過の	excess
超過引受オプション	over-allotment option
超過利潤	excessive profit
超過利潤	rent
長期	long range
長期	long run
長期	long term
長期請負契約	long term contract
長期受取勘定	long-term receivable
長期受取債権	long-term receivable
長期格付け	long-term debt rating
長期貸付け金	long term loans
長期貨幣性資産	long-term monetary assets
長期借入金	long term debt
長期借入金	long term loans
長期借入債務	long term debt
長期金融売掛債権	long-term finance receivables
長期金融債権	long-term finance receivables
長期金融市場	capital market
長期金利	long-term interest rate
長期勤労奨励制度	long-term incentive program
長期経営計画	long-term planning
長期計画	long-term planning
長期傾向	long run trend
長期契約	long term contract
長期工事契約	long term contract
長期国債の借換え	funding
長期債化	funding
長期債権	long-term receivable
長期債務	long term debt
長期債務の増加	additions to long-term debt
長期資金調達	long-term financing
長期資産	long-lived asset
長期資本	capitalization
長期資本収支	net long-term capital flow
長期奨励報酬制度	long-term incentive program
長期性資産	long-lived asset
長期的動向	long run forces
長期的な	permanent
長期的費用	long range cost
長期的費用	long-run cost
長期投資評価引当金	investment valuation allowance
長期の	noncurrent
長期の無形資産	noncurrent intangible assets
長期の無形資産	noncurrent tangible asset
長期負債	deferred liability
長期負債	fixed liability
長期負債	long term debt
長期負債対総資本比率	long-term debt-to-total capital
長期保有資産	long-lived asset
長期未払い金	long-term accounts payable
長期目標	project
長期融資	long term loans
長期予算	long range budget
長距離	long range
帳消し	write-off
帳消しにする	make up for ...
帳消しにする	offset
帳消しにする	write off
超国籍企業	transnational company
調査	examination
調査	research
調査	review
調査	test
調査する	examine
調査する	monitor
調査する	review
調査団	panel
調査報告書	comfort letter
徴収	collection
徴収する	collect
徴収する	levy
聴衆反応投票	audience response voting
徴収不能料金	uncollectibles
長所	strength
頂上	top
頂上の	top
帳尻	balance
調整	adjustment
調整	arrangement
調整	reconciliation
調整	translation
徴税	taxation
調整項目	balancing item
調整後当期利益	ACE
調整後当期利益	ACE
調整書	reconciliation
調整する	adjust
調整する	correct
調整する	reconcile
調整する	regulate
調整する	translate
調整表	reconciliation
調節する	adjust
調節する	regulate
挑戦	challenge
挑戦の	challenging
調達	funding
調達	procurement
調達	purchase
調達	sourcing
調達額	amount raised
調達可能な	available
調達先	purchase
調達資金	proceeds
調達手段	funding
調達する	fund
調達する	obtain
調達する	procure
調達する	provide
調達する	raise
調達する	receive
調停	settlement
超低金利	ultralow interest rates
帳票	document
重複	overlap
重複関係	overlap
重複上場する	dual-list
重複部分	overlap
帳簿	book
帳簿外の	off-the-book
帳簿価格	book value
帳簿価額	book value
帳簿価額	carrying amount
帳簿価額	carrying amount
帳簿価額	carrying value
帳簿価格株式購入制度	book value stock purchase plan
帳簿価格株式プラン	book value stock plan

帳簿価額法	book value method
帳簿価額方式	book value approach
帳簿監査	book audit
帳簿控除方式	account method
帳簿上の価格	book value
帳簿上の剰余金	book surplus
帳簿上の損失	book loss
帳簿上の損失	book loss
帳簿上の利益	book income
帳簿上の利益	book profit
帳簿上の利益	book profit
帳簿棚卸	book inventory
帳簿棚卸し高	book calculation of inventory
帳簿棚卸法	book inventory method
帳簿棚卸法	book inventory system
帳簿取引	book transaction
帳簿に載せる	book
帳簿利益	book profit
帳簿を締める	close the [one's] books
帳面	book
潮流	trend
…と調和する	match
調和する	dovetail
調和すること	dovetailing
貯金	savings
直接投資	equity investment
直接投資	equity method investment
直接入札	unsolicited bidding
直接融資	straight financing
直接利回り	flat yield
直接利回り	rate of return
直線式収益還元法	straight-line capitalization
著作物	content
貯蔵品	supply
貯蓄	savings
貯蓄株購入制度	savings-stock purchase program
貯蓄制度	savings plan
貯蓄率	savings level
直結	online [on-line]
賃上げ	pay rise
賃貸しする	lease
賃借りする	lease
賃金	hire
賃金	pay
賃金	payroll
賃金	wage
賃金外給付	fringe benefit
賃金上昇圧力	upward pressure on wages
賃金所得	wage income
賃金制度	pay plan
賃金制度	pay system
賃金台帳	payroll
賃金前払い	wage advance
賃借する	hire
賃借人	lessee
賃借人	tenant
賃借費用	rental expense
賃借料	hire
賃借料	hire charge
賃借料	occupancy expense
賃借料	rent
賃借料	rental
賃借料	rental commitments
賃借料	rental expense
陳述	delivery
沈滞	doldrums
沈滞	slowdown
賃貸借	lease
賃貸借	leasing
賃貸借契約(書)	lease
賃貸性リース	operating lease
賃人	lessor
賃貸人の既存資産	existing assets of the lessor
賃貸料	rent
賃貸料	rental
賃貸料	rental revenues
陳腐化	obsolescence
陳腐化資産	obsolete asset
陳腐化した	obsolete
陳腐化棚卸資産	obsolete inventory
陳列	display
陳列する	order

つ

追加	addition
追加株式	additional share
追加給付	fringe benefit
追加資本	fresh capital
追加的運転資金	additonal working capital
追加的な	additional
追加投資	addition
追加投資	additional investment
追加の	further
追加の	supplementary [supplemental]
追加払込み資本	additional paid-in capital
追加方式の	cumulative
追徴課税	penalty tax
追徴金	assessment
…についていけない	lag
通貨	cash
通貨	currency
通貨	money
通貨換算	currency translation
通貨供給量	money supply
通貨切り上げ	revaluation
通貨交換レート	currency exchange rate
通貨の	monetary
通貨膨張	inflation
通関申告	entry
通関手続き	entry
通期	entire business year
通期	entire fiscal year
通期	full business year
通期	full fiscal year
通期	full year
通期	whole
通期	whole [entire] business year
通期業績見通し	full-year forecast
通期純利益	full-year net income
通期税引き後利益	full-year net income
通期の	annual
通期の	full-year
通期の業績	full-year earnings
通期の業績予想	full-year forecast
通期の収益	full-year earnings
通期の純利益	full-year consolidated net profit
通期の純利益予想	full-year net income forecast
通期の税引き後利益	full-year consolidated net profit
通期の税引き後利益予想	full-year net income forecast
通期の連結営業利益	full-year group operating profit
通期配当	full-year dividend
通期予想	expectations for the year as a whole
通期予想	full-year forecast
通商	trade
通常の	common
通常の	general
通常の	ordinary
通常の営業過程	normal course of business
通常の業務過程	normal course of business
通常の事業活動	normal course of business
通常の事業過程	normal course of business
通商摩擦	trade friction
通信	communication
通信勤務	telecommuting
通信情報・伝達事項	message
通信文	message
通信網	network
通則	rule
通知書	note
通知手数料	advising charge
通年	full year
通年の	full-year
ツール	tool

| 通例 rule
| 使いこなす manage
| 使い捨ての disposable
| …が使いやすい －friendly
| 使いやすい friendly
| 使う use
| …につき per
| 月 month
| 突合せ comparison
| 突合せ footing
| 突合せ matching
| 就く assume
| 償いの compensatory
| 作り変える reshape
| 作り出す create
| 作り出す form
| 作り直す reinvent
| 作り直す reshape
| ツケ negative legacy
| つけ込む capitalize on
| 付け値 bid
| つける position
| 付ける carry
| 付ける cover
| 付ける effect
| 付ける take out
| 続けざまの back-to-back
| 続ける keep
| 勤め employment
| 勤め口 position
| 務める serve
| つなぎとめる retain
| 積置き配当 cumulative dividend
| 積立て funding
| 積立額 amounts funded
| 積立金 appropriation
| 積立金 fund
| 積立金 reserve
| 積立金 reserve surplus
| 積立金 surplus
| 積立金 surplus reserve
| 積立金繰入れ addition to reserves
| 積立金繰入れ provision for surplus
| 積立金を払い戻す pay out
| 積み立てた funded
| 積立年金制度 funded pension plan
| 積立利益 accumulated earnings
| 積み立てる fund
| 積み立てる set aside
| 積み荷 shipment
| 積み増し accumulation
| 積み増しの incremental
| 積み増す book
| 積み増す boost
| 積み増す rebuild
| 積む gain
| 強い high
| 強い strong

強い影響を与える determine
強気材料 positive
強気市場 bull market
強気相場 rally
強気の good
強気の positive
強くなる intensify
強く求める solicit
強さ strength
強含みの positive
強み advantage
強み strength
強める intensify
強める reinforce
釣合い balance
つり上げる inflate
釣銭 change

て

…で due to ...
手当 allowance
手当 benefit
手当 bonus
手当 compensation
手当 pay
提案 bid
提案 initiative
提案 motion
提案 offer
提案 plan
提案 presentation
提案 proposal
提案する float
提案する propose
提案をする offer
ディーリング dealing
低下 decline
低下 decrease
低下 depletion
低下 deterioration
低下 drop
低下 pressure
低下 reduction
低下 slowdown
低下 squeeze
低価格製品 low-end product
低価基準 lower of cost or market
低価基準 lower of cost or market basis [method]
定額基準 straight-line basis
定額拠出制度 defined contribution plan
定額減価償却 straight-line depreciation
定額償却 amortization
定額法 equal installment depreciation
定額法 straight-line
定額法 straight-line basis

定額法 straight-line method
定額前渡資金 imprest fund
定額料金 flat rate
低下させる erode
低下させる reduce
低下した weak
低価主義 lower of cost or market basis [method]
低下 fall
低下する decline
低下する decrease
低下する depreciate
低下する deteriorate
低下する drop
低下する fall
低下する lower
低下する plunge
低下する shrink
低下する squeeze
低価法 lower of cost or market
低価法 lower of cost or market basis [method]
定款 articles of incorporation
定款 charter
定款 settlement
提議 motion
定期実地棚卸し periodic physical inventory
提起する enter
定義する define
定期的な periodic
定期的な recurring
定期的に返済する amortize
定期の terminal
定期不動産権 term
定期返済 service
定期報告 periodic report
定期報告 periodic reporting
提供 cooperation
提供 donation
提供 offering
提供 provision
提供 tender
提供者 provider
提供する advance
提供する deliver
提供する extend
提供する fund
提供する offer
提供する present
提供する provide
提供する run
提供する serve
提供する service
提供する tender
提供物 tender
低金利ローン low cost loan
テイクオーバー takeover [takeover]
テイクオーバー・ビッド takeover

bid	提示する submit	低費用 low cost
低位株 low priced stock	定時総会 annual meeting	定評のある approved
提携 alliance	提出 presentation	ディファクト de fact
提携 cooperation	提出 submission	低迷 decline
提携 front	提出 tender	低迷 doldrums
提携 partnership	提出する enter	低迷 drop
提携 tie-up	提出する file	低迷 plunge
提携カード affiliated card	提出する present	低迷 slowdown
提携関係 alliance	提出する produce	低迷 slump
提携企業 partner	提出する propose	低迷した poor
提携協議 alliance talks	提出する submit	低迷した sluggish
提携契約 alliance pact	提出する tender	低迷する decline
提携交渉 tie-up negotiation	提出物 submission	低迷する plunge
提携先 partner	提出物 tender	低迷する slow down
提携させる affiliate	提唱する propose	低迷する suffer
提携者 affiliate	停職する suspend	低迷する weak
提携者 partner	低所得者層向け住宅ローン sub-prime loan	定率公募 public offering of bonds on fixed conditions
提携する affiliate	低所得者層向け住宅ローン sub-prime mortgage	定率法 declining balance
提携する join	低所得者向け住宅融資 subprime mortgage	定率法 declining balance
提携する tie up	低所得者向け住宅ローン sub-prime mortgage	定率法 diminishing balance method
締結 execution	低所得者を対象にした住宅融資 subprime loan	定率法 method of fixed percentage on cost
低減 layoff	ディスカウント discount	定率補助金 percentage grant
低原価 low cost	ディスカウント・キャッシュ・フロー方式 discount [discounted] cash flow method	低利融資 low-interest loans
逓減減価償却法 declining depreciation method	ディスクロージャー disclosure	定量的非財務情報 quantified non-financial information
逓減減価法 diminishing balance method	ディストリビューション distribution	定量発注システム quantity system
逓減残高法 diminishing balance method	ディストリビュータ distributor	定例株主総会 AGM
逓減償却法 diminishing balance method	ディスプレー display	データ data
低減する lay off	訂正する correct	データ figure
低減する lower	提訴 charge	出遅れる lag
低減する reduce	逓増費 progressive cost	手落ち oversight
低減する slash	停滞 deterioration	手加減する cook
低コスト low cost	停滞する deteriorate	手形 bill
低コストの competitive	停滞する slow down	手形 note
低コスト労働力 low cost labor	…で手いっぱい saddled with …	手形 paper
体裁 showing	程度 extension	手形買取り手数料 negotiation charge
停止 suspension	程度 notch	手形貸付け loan on note
提示 offer	程度 rate	手形借入金 note payable
提示 presentation	抵当 guarantee	手形交換尻 clearing house balance
提示 submission	抵当 mortgage	手形債権 acceptance payable
提示案 submission	抵当 pledge	手形債権 acceptance receivable
提示価格 offer price	抵当 security	手形債権 note payable
提示価格 offered price	抵当権 mortgage	手形などを譲渡できる negotiable
提示額 offer	抵当権設定 mortgage	手形の期限が来る fall
定時株主総会 AGM	抵当権設定者 mortgagor	手形の提示 presentation
定時株主総会 annual meeting	抵当権付き債権 secured mortgage	手形引受手数料 acceptance commission
定時株主総会開催の通知 Notice of Annual Meeting	抵当権付き社債 mortgage bond	手形振出人 drawer
定時償還 mandatory redemption	抵当証書 mortgage	手形保有高 draft holdings
定時償還 redemption at fixed date	…を抵当とする cover	手形割引 note receivable discount
停止する shut down	抵当流れ foreclosure	手紙 communication
停止する suspend	抵当に入れる pledge	手紙 letter
提示する float	定年退職 mandatory retirement	出来 showing
提示する offer	定年退職者 retiree	適格債権 eligible receivables
提示する post		
提示する present		
提示する propose		

適格特別目的事業体	QSPE
適格特別目的事業体	qualifying special purpose entity
…に適格な	applicable to ...
適格年金制度	approved pension scheme
適格年金制度	approved pension scheme
適格年金制度	qualified pension plan
適格の	eligible
適格の	qualified
適合	compliance
適合	conformity
…に適合させる	conform to [with] ...
…に適合する	conform to [with] ...
適合する	dovetail
適合すること	dovetailing
適合性	conformity
適合度検定	goodness of fit test
出来事	affair
出来事	event
適した地位	niche
適した場所	niche
適所	niche
適正価値	fair value
適正在庫	right inventory
適正在庫	running stock
適正な	due
適正な	fair
適正表示	fair presentation
適切な	due
適切な	reasonable
敵対する	hostile
敵対的	hostile
敵対的M&A	hostile takeover
敵対的TOB	hostile bid
敵対的株式公開買付け	hostile bid
敵対的買収	hostile bid
敵対的買収	hostile takeover
敵対的買収者	hostile acquirer
敵対的買収提案	hostile bid
敵対の買収に対する防衛手段	poison pill
出来高	trading volume
出来高	trading volume
出来高	turnover
出来高	volume
出来高払い	incentive
出来栄え	showing
適法の	due
適用	application
…に適用可能な	applicable to ...
適用業務	application
…が適用される	govern
…が適用される	subject to ...
適用する	apply
適用する	implement
適用する	reflect
適用税率	applicable tax rate
適用範囲	coverage
適用利息	imputed interest
…できるようにする	empower
テコ	leverage
テコ入れする	reinforce
テコの作用	leverage
出先	field
手順	method
手順	procedure
手数料	charge
手数料	commission
手数料	fee
手数料	premium
手数料	service charge
手数料収入	commission payments
手数料収入	commission revenue
手数料費用	commission expense
テスト	test
撤回	recall
撤回	withdrawal
撤回する	recall
撤回する	scrap
撤回する	withdraw
哲学	philosophy
手付け金	consideration
手付け金	down payment
手付け金	margin
手付金	deposit
手付金として支払う	deposit
…に徹する	driven
撤退	withdrawal
…から撤退する	pull out of ...
撤退する	retire
撤退する	withdraw
手続き	procedure
手続き	proceedings
手続き	process
手続き	processing
徹底的な	close
デット	debt
デット・エクイティ・スワップ	debt equity swap
デット・エクイティ・スワップ	debt-for-equity swap
デット・エクイティ・スワップ	DES
デット・エクイティ・レシオ	debt equity ratio
デット・ファイナンス	debt finance
撤廃	elimination
撤廃する	eliminate
撤廃する	scrap
手取金	proceeds
出直す	reinvent
テナント	tenant
手抜かり	oversight
手配	arrangement
手配する	effect
手放す	divest
デビット	debit
デフォルト	default
デフレーション	deflation
デフレーションの	deflationary
デベロッパー	developer
デマンド	demand
手持ち	hand
手持ち在庫	stock on hand
手持ち資金	fund in hand
手持ち数量	quantity on hand
手持ち注文	backlog
手持ちの受注分	orders on hand
手元	hand
手元キャッシュフロー	RCF
手元キャッシュフロー	retained cash flow
手元資金	internal resources
手元流動性	liquidity at hand
デュー・ディリジェンス	due diligence
デリバティブ	derivative
デリバティブ	derivative financial instrument
テレコミューティング	telecommuting
テレビ会議	teleconference meeting
…から手を引く	pull out of ...
…店	outlet
転化	transformation
転嫁	shift
展開	development
展開	environment
展開する	develop
転嫁する	shift
転換	conversion
転換	shift
転換	transformation
転換	turnaround
転換価格	conversion price
転換型優先株	convertible preferred shares
転換価値	conversion value
転換可能な	convertible
転換株式	convertible stock [share]
転換期間	conversion period
転換権付きクラスA優先株式	convertible class A preferred stock
転換権付き優先株式	convertible preferred stock
転換社債	CB
転換社債	convertible bond
転換社債	convertible bond payable
転換社債	convertible debenture
転換社債	convertible note
転換社債型新株予約権付き社債	moving strike convertible bond
転換社債型新株予約権付き社債	

MSCB
転換条項 conversion clause
転換条項 conversion privilege
転換する convert
転換する return
転換性のある convertible
転換できる convertible
転換優先株式 convertible preferred stock
転換優先株式 convertible preferred stock
転換劣後社債 convertible subordinated debenture
転換劣後社債 convertible subordinated debenture
転記する carry
転記する post
電気通信事業者 operator
電機メーカー electric appliance maker
典型 norm
典型 paradigm
伝言 message
展示 display
展示 showing
電子決済 electronic settlement
電子書籍 e-book
電子投票 electronic voting
電子投票 online voting
電子マネー electronic money
転職斡旋 outplacement
転職率 turnover
転進 redeployment
転送 transfer
転送する transfer
伝送路 line
テンダー tender
テンダー・オファー tender offer
テンダー・パネル tender panel
伝達 communication
店頭市場 over-the-counter market
店頭市場の over-the-counter
店頭取引の over-the-counter
店頭の over-the-counter
店頭売買の over-the-counter
店頭販売 over-the-counter sale
転任 transfer
転売禁止 lockup [lock-up]
天引きする withhold
伝票 note
添付した accompanying
添付の脚注 appended footnote
テンポ pace
填補 absorption
店舗 office
店舗 outlet
展望 outlook
填補する absorb
テンポラル法 temporal method

店舗立地 store location
転用価額 salvage value
転用認可 conversion approval
転落する plunge
電力 power
電話会議 teleconference meeting
電話交換手 operator
電話線 line

と

問合せ reference
問合せ先 reference
同意 accord
同意 agreement
同意 approval
同意語 equivalent
同意書 agreement
同意する accept
同意する approve
統一 integration
統一する integrate
統一体 entity
統一ドル constant dollar
統一ドル会計 constant dollar accounting
動因 drive
当会計年度 current fiscal year
当該年度 applicable to the year
等価交換の原則 equal value principle
投下資本 invested capital
投下資本 invested fund
投下資本利益率 return on investment
投下資本利益率 return on investment
投下資本利益率 ROI
投じする invest
同価値である equivalent
…を統括する head
統括する manage
統括本部 headquarters
等価物 equivalent
等価率 weighted average
当監査法人 we
当監査法人の意見では in our opinion
登記 entry
登記 record
登記 register
登記 registration
当期 current year
当期 during the year
当期 for the year
当期 period under review
当期 year under review
騰貴 advance
騰貴 appreciation
騰貴 enhancement

討議 discussion
動機 incentive
動議 motion
道義 morality
道義 principle
同期(する) sync
登記官 registrar
当期業績 current results
当期業績 results for the year
当期原価 current cost
当期歳入 current revenue
当期仕入高 purchases for the period
当期支払い額 current maturity
当期収益 current revenue
当期収入 current revenue
当期純損失 net loss
当期純利益 current net earnings
当期純利益 current net income
当期純利益 line
当期純利益 net earnings
当期純利益 net income
当期純利益 net income for the year
当期純利益 net profit
当期剰余金 net profit
登記する record
登記する register
騰貴する appreciate
道義性 morality
投機的な speculative
投機的保有 speculative holding
当期に during the period
同期に during the period
当期の current
当期の勤務費用 current service cost
当期費用 current cost
当期分 current
等級 rate
等級をつける rank
同業異種間の horizontal
同業組合 trade union
同業者 competitor
同業者 counterpart
同業者 interest
東京証券取引所 Tokyo Stock Exchange
東京証券取引所 TSE
投機利益 trading profit
当期利益 bottom line
当期利益 current income
当期利益 net figure
当期利益ベース net level
当期連結純損失 group net loss
当期連結純利益 group net profit
道具 implement
道具 tool
統計 data
統計 figure

統計	results
同系会社	associate
当行	we
統合	alliance
統合	consolidation
統合	integration
統合	merger
統合	tie-up
動向	condition
動向	cycle
動向	environment
動向	event
動向	experience
動向	movement
動向	overview
動向	performance
動向	record
動向	stream
動向	trend
統合化	dovetailing
統合事業	integrated operations
統合した	combined
統合した	consolidated
統合する	consolidate
統合する	integrate
統合する	merge
当座資金	current fund
当座資産	quick assets
当座資産比率	liquid asset ratio
洞察力	foresight
等差等級法	sum of the years' digits method
当座の	current
当座比率	acid test ratio
当座預金	demand deposit
当座預金	open account
当座預金残高	outstanding current accounts
倒産	bankruptcy
倒産	collapse
倒産	failure
倒産	insolvency
動産	goods
動産	movable property
動産・不動産純額	premises and equipment net
倒産した	bankrupt
倒産した	insolvent
倒産する	collapse
倒産する	fail
投資	capitalization
投資	exposure
投資	investment
投資	spending
投資およびその他の資産	investments and other property
投資家	account
投資家	investor
投資家	player
投資家	user
投資会社	investor
投資額	investment
投資家説明会	briefing
投資家説明会	roadshow
投資家説明会を行う	roadshow
投資活動	investing activities
投資家向け広報	investor [investors] relations
投資家向け広報	IR
投資家向け広報活動	investor [investors] relations
投資家向け広報活動	IR
投資家向け情報公開	investor [investors] relations
投資家向け説明会	briefing
投資家向け説明会	roadshow
投資家向け説明会を行う	roadshow
投資側	investor
投資勘定	investment
当事業年度	current business year
当事業年度	current fiscal year
投資金	stake
投資金額	stake
投資銀行	investment bank
投資減税	investment tax credit
投資国	investor
投資コスト	investment costs
投資顧問	asset management
投資顧問	manager
投資顧問の	advisory
投資事業	investment
投資資金	invested fund
投資資金	investment fund
投資資産	investment
投資資産	investment portfolio
投資資産	portfolio
投資資本	investment capital
投資資本構成	investment portfolio
投資者	investor
当事者	party
投資収益	net interest earnings
投資収益	return on investment
投資収益	revenue from investment
投資収益性	investment profitability
投資収益率	investment profitability
投資収益率	return on investment
投資信託	investment trust
投資信託	investment trust fund
投資信託	mutual fund
投資信託	trust fund
投資信託基金	investment trust fund
投資信託財産	investment fund
投資する	capitalize
投資する	invest
投資する	spend
投資税額控除	investment tax credit
投資損益	equity earnings
投資損失引当金	allowance for investment losses
投資適格の格付け	investment-grade rating
投資の内容	investment portfolio
当四半期	reporting qaurter
当四半期	this quarter
投資ファンド	investment fund
投資物	investment
投資不適格	junk
投資不適格レベル	junk territory
投資ポートフォリオ	investment portfolio
当社	we
同社の普通株式に帰属する当期純損失	net loss applicable to common shares for the company
党首	head
党首	leader
投資有価証券	investments in securities
東証	Tokyo Stock Exchange
東証	TSE
東証株価指数	Tokyo Stock Price Index
東証株価指数	TOPIX
投資用株式	portfolio stock
東証上場企業	TSE-listed company
当初資本	initial capital
当初の	initial
当初の	original
当初の評価損	original write-down
当初の見通し	initial projection
当初の目標	original target
当初満期	original maturity
当初見積り	initial estimate
当初見積り額	initial estimate
当初予想	earlier forecast
当初予想	earlier projection
当初予想	initial estimate
当初予想	initial projection
当初予想	original [initial] estimate
投資利益	earnings
投資利益率	investment profitability
投資利益率	return on investment
投資利益率	ROI
投資リスク	investment risk
投資リターン	return on investment
投資利回り	return on investment
投信	investment trust
統制	control
統制解除	decontrol
統制環境	control environment
統制する	regulate

統制撤廃　decontrol
当然支払われるべき　due
闘争　struggle
統率する　manage
統率力　leadership
統治　governance
統治能力　governance
頭注　heading notes
盗聴する　tap
当店　we
同等である　equivalent
同等物　counterpart
同等物　equivalent
道徳　ethics
道徳　morality
道徳性　morality
道徳の　ethical
頭取　president
投入　injection
導入　import
導入　introduction
導入　launch
投入原材料　input materials
投入する　capitalize
投入する　invest
投入する　launch
投入する　use
導入する　establish
導入する　introduce
導入する　launch
当年度　current business year
当年度　current fiscal year
当年度　current year
当年度　for the year
当年度　year under review
統廃合する　consolidate
投票　election
投票　vote
投票　voting
投票委任用紙　proxy voting card
投票権　vote
投票権　voting power
投票権行使　voting
投票する　vote
投票で決定する　vote
投票用紙　vote
同盟　alliance
同盟関係　alliance
同盟国　alliance
透明性　transparency
当面の　immediate
当面の業績見通し　immediate earnings outlook
動揺　turmoil
騰落　fluctuation
同量である　equivalent
登録　entry
登録　record
登録　register
登録　registration

登録株主　registered shareholder
登録株主　shareholder of record
登録株主　stockholder of record
登録機関　registrar
登録された　registered
登録事項　registration
登録事務官　registrar
登録社債　registered bond
登録証券　registered security
登録申請　application for registration
登録済み普通株主　registered holders of common shares
登録する　record
登録する　register
登録届出書　registration statement
登録普通株主　registered holders of common shares
登録物件　registration
登録免許税　registration and license tax
討論会　panel
通しの　consecutive
通し番号　consecutive numbers
トータル・カスタマー・サティスファクション　total customer satisfaction
トータル・ライアビリティ　total liabilities
トーホールド・パーチェス　toe-hold purchase
ドキュメント　document
得　percentage
得意客　client
得意客　customer
得意先　client
得意先　customer
得意先　goodwill
得意先　purchaser
独自性　initiative
特質　quality
特殊な　special
特性　profile
特性　property
特性　quality
独創性　creativity
独創力　creativity
独創力　initiative
特定口座　specified account
特定事業に対する金融　project finance
特定の　special
特定の銘柄品　brand
特定分野　niche
特定目的会社　SPC
特定目的会社　special purpose company
独特の　special
特に優れた　outstanding
特売品　leader

得票　vote
特別給付　special benefits
特別決議　special resolution
特別損益　unusual gain and loss
特別（損益）項目　extraordinary items
特別損益項目　unusual item
特別損益項目　unusual item
特別損失　extraordinary loss
特別損失　one-off charge
特別損失　one-off loss
特別損失　special loss
特別損失　write-off of costs
特別退職勧奨制度の費用　charges for special pension options
特別の　additional
特別の　extraordinary
特別の　special
特別の　unusual
特別配当　bonus
特別配当　bonus dividend
特別配当　melon
特別配当　unusual dividend
特別配当株　bonus share [stock]
特別発行　bonus issue
特別引当金　allowance for special purpose
特別目的事業体　SPE
特別利益　extraordinary income
特別利益　one-off gains
匿名組合員　dormant partner
毒薬条項　poison pill
特約店　outlet
独立　independence
独立会計士の監査意見　opinion of independent accountant
独立企業間の　arm's length [arm's-length]
独立系　independent
独立採算制　pay-as-you-go
独立採算制　pay-as-you-go basis
独立採算制　self-supporting accounting system
独立した　arm's length [arm's-length]
独立した　independent
独立した構成要素　separate component
独立性　independence
独立第三者間の　arm's length [arm's-length]
独立当事者間の　arm's length [arm's-length]
独立取締役　independent director
独立の　free
閉ざされた　closed
年　year
年換算　annualized terms
閉じた　close
土台　basis

土台	foundation	トラスト	trust	取り出す	take out
土地	land	トラスト・ファンド	trust fund	取立てができない	dividend payable unclaimed
土地，建物および設備	property, plant and equipment	トラッキング・ストック	tracking stock	取立て代理業	factoring
土地・金融税制	land and financial tax systems	トランスナショナル企業	transnational company	取り立てる	recover
土地保有者	tenant	取扱い	handling	取り付ける	install [instal]
土地保有税	land-holding tax	取扱い	management	取り除く	divest
特許	license [licence]	取扱い	transaction	取り除く	set aside
特許	patent	取扱い	treatment	取り除く	take out
特許協力	patent cooperation	取扱い手数料	handling charge	取引	activity
特許権	patent	取扱い手数料	lifting charge	取引	bargain
特許権	patent property	取り扱う	cover	取引	business
特許権交換による特許	cross license	取り扱う	manage	取引	deal
特許権使用料	license fee	トリートメント	treatment	取引	dealing
特許権侵害	patent infringement	取替え価格	replacement price	取引	exchange
特許実施権	patent licensing	取替え原価	replacement cost	取引	negotiation
特許証	patent	取替原価法	replacement cost method	取引	trade
特許状	charter	取り替える	exchange	取引	trading
特許侵害	patent infringement	取り替える	swap	取引	transaction
特許請求の範囲	claim	取り交わす	exchange	取引関係	account
特許相互利用契約	cross licensing agreement	取決め	agreement	取引完了	closing
特許抵触	patent infringement	取決め	appointment	取引関連偶発債務	transaction-related contingencies
特許認可手続き	licensing practice	取決め	arrangement	取引銀行	creditor
特許物件	patent	取決め	deal	取引契約	bargain
特許を与える	license	取り決める	close	取引契約	commitment
取っ組み合い	struggle	取り崩す	reverse	取引圏	trading range
特恵の	preferential	取組み	commitment	取引コスト	transaction cost
特権	patent	取組み	drive	取引先	account
特権株	golden share	取組み	effort	取引先	client
突然の成功	strike	取り組む	commit	取引先	customer
突入	plunge	取り組む	struggle	取引先	relationship
突破する	surpass	取り組む	undertake	取引参加者	transaction participant
突破する	top	取消し	dissolution	取引執行力	skill in trade execution
突発事項	infrequent item	取消し	recall	取引所	bourse
突発事象	infrequent event	取消し	withdrawal	取引所	exchange
トップ	leading edge	取消し不能の	noncancelable [noncancellable]	取引条件	business terms [terms and conditions]
トップ	top	取消し不能保証	noncancelable guarantee	取引所分売	distribution overhead
トップ企業	front runner [front-runner, frontrunner]	取り消す	cancel	取引所分売	exchange distribution
トップになる	top	取り消す	dissolve	取引する	deal
トップの	top	取り消す	recall	取引する	do business
トップ・マネジメント	top management	取り消す	reverse	取引する	trade
トップ見出し	leader	取り消す	revoke	取引税	transaction tax
トップランナー	front runner [front-runner, frontrunner]	取り消す	withdraw	取引制限	trading limit
届出書	statement	取締役	board member	取引高	sales
届出様式13D	Schedule 13D	取締役	director	取引高	tranaction value
届け出る	register	取締役会	board	取引高	turnover
届ける	deliver	取締役会	board of directors	取引高	volume
とび抜けた	outstanding	取締役会会議	meeting of board of directors	取引高	volume of business
土俵	playing field	取締役会会長	chairman of the board	取引単位	trading unit
乏しい	lean	取締役会長	chairman of board of directors	取引調査	transaction test
乏しい	poor	取締役会の全体会議	full board	取引停止	suspension
富	wealth	取締役会の提案	board proposal	取引停止処分	suspension
…を伴う	entail	取り締まる	regulate	取引の収支	bottom line
ドライブ	drive			取引発生日の	historical
				取引日	transaction date
				取引ポスト	trading post
				取引明細付き勘定照合表	de-

scriptive statement	
取引利益	trading profit
取引量	deal flow
取引量	trading volume
トリプルAの会社	AAA company
トリプルAの格付けの会社	AAA company
取りまとめ	arrangement
取り戻す	resume
努力	effort
努力	exercise
努力の成果	effort
ドル	dollar
ドル価値後入れ先出し法	dollar value LIFO
ドル価値後入れ先出し法	dollar-value LIFO method
ドル価値法	dollar value LIFO
ドル価値法	dollar value method
ドル相場	dollar
ドル建て	dollar-denominated terms [basis]
ドルベースでの直接投資	dollar amount of direct investment
トレーダー	player
トレーディング	trading
トレード	trade
トレード・シークレット	trade secret
トレジャラー	treasurer
トレンド	trend
鈍化する	slow down
問屋	distributor

な

…でないかぎり	except
…でないかぎり	unless
内国会社	domestic corporation
内国歳入庁	Internal Revenue Service
内国歳入庁	IRS
内国歳入法	Internal Revenue Code
内国歳入法	IRC
内国歳入法典	Internal Revenue Code
内国法人	domestic corporation
内需	domestic demand
内需依存株	domestic-demand dependent sectors
内製	inhouse processing
内線	extension
内挿	interpolation
内部会計統制	internal accounting control
内部監査	internal audit
内部監査委員会	committee on internal auditing
内部監査人	internal auditor
内部管理体制	internal management system
内部資金	internal resources
内部者	insider
内部情報	privileged information
内部成長	internal growth
内部成長	organic growth
内部チェック	internal control
内部チェック体制	internal control
内部調査	in-house investigation
内部調達資金	internally generated funds
内部統制	internal control
内部統制機構	internal control system
内部統制組織	internal control system
内部統制手続き	control procedure
内部統制目的	control objective
内部の	in-house [inhouse]
内部の	intercompany
内部の	internal
内部留保	retained earnings
内部留保	undistributed profit
内部留保利益	undistributed earnings
内密	confidence
内容	matter
内容	mix
内容	quality
内容の特定	disclosure
内容見本	prospectus
内容目次	contents
仲買	brokerage
仲買業	brokerage
中だるみ	doldrums
なかなか消えない	linger
長引く	lingering
中身	mix
流れ	flow
流れ	movement
流れ	process
流れ	stream
流れ	trend
流れ作業	production line
投げ売り	sell-off
投げ売りする	sell off
なし崩し償却	amortization
成し遂げる	effect
…になじみやすい	–friendly
ナスダック	Nasdaq Stock Market
ナスダック証券市場	Nasdaq Stock Market
名前	name
…の名前を挙げる	name
波	trend
並ぶ	rank
並べる	order
成り行き	event
成り行き注文	order without limit
…から成る	comprise
…になる	amount to …
名を挙げる	list
難題	challenge
軟調な	sluggish
軟調な	vulnerable
軟調の	weak
難問	challenge
難問	problem

に

ニーズ	needs
荷為替信用状	documentary credit
二元的所得課税方式	two-track income taxation system
二次市場	after market [aftermarket]
二次的支払い義務	recourse
二次的請求	recourse
二次的な	indirect
2四半期	two quarters
二重課税	dual taxation
二重責任	dual responsibility
二重帳簿	two sets of account books
日時	date
日用品	commodity
日経平均株価（225種）	key Nikkei Index
ニッチ	niche
二等分する	halve
荷主	cargo owner
荷主	owner
二の次	back burner
2倍になる	double
日本の合同会社	LLC
日本版401k	401(k)-style pension scheme
日本版401k	defined contribution pension
ニュー	new
入会	entry
入会金	fee
入会金	footing
入会する	enter
入荷高	receipt
入国	entry
入札	auction
入札	bid
入札	bidding
入札	issuance
入札	offering
入札	tender
入札価格	bid price
入札価格	bidding price
入札行	bidder
入札業者	bidder
入札参加企業	bidder
入札者	bidder

入札書	tender
入札する	tender
入札手続き	bidding procedures
入札費	bidding expense
入札方式	bidding system
入札保証	tender guarantee
入質	pledge
入質する	pledge
入手	procurement
入手可能な	available
入手する	access
入手する	gain
入手する	obtain
入手する	procure
入場	entry
入場料	fee
ニュース	information
ニュース・ソース	source
ニューズ・レター	newsletter
ニューヨーク株	Wall Street
ニューヨーク証券取引所	New York Stock Exchange
ニューヨーク証券取引所	NYSE
入力	entry
入力する	enter
任意	discretion
任意解散	voluntary dissolution
任意組合	voluntary organization
任意組合	voluntary partnership
任意現金支払い	voluntary cash payment
任意償還価格	call price
任意償還不行使期間	call protection
任意償還条項	call provision
任意償還プレミアム	call premium
任意清算	voluntary liquidation
任意整理	voluntary liquidation
任意退職計画	voluntary separation program
任意積立金	free reserve
任意積立金	retained income
任意積立金	voluntary reserves
任意の	discretionary
任意の	free
任意の	voluntary
任意の委員会	voluntary committee
認可	approval
認可	authorization
認可	license [licence]
認可	licensing
認可	recognition
認可された	approved
認可済み案件	approved project
認可する	approve
認可する	recognize
認可を与える	license
任期満了	termination of office
認識	idea
認識	recognition
認識基準	basis of recognition
認識する	recognize
認証定款	charter
人数	strength
認知	recognition
認定	recognition
認定する	establish
認定する	recognize
任務	challenge
任務	charge
任務	commission
任務	concern
任務	duty
任務	function
任務	post
…の任務を果たす	serve
任命	appointment
任命	commission
任命書	commission
任命する	appoint
任命する	name

ね

値上がり	advance
値上がり	price increase
値上がり益	capital gain
値上がりする	advance
値上げ	price increase
値上げ	price raising
値上げ	raising
値上げ取消高	mark up cancelation
値洗い	mark-to-market
値洗いする	mark to market
値洗いする	value
値入れ	markon
値入れ率	markon
値動き	performance
値動き	price performance
ネーム	name
ネガティブ	negative
ネゴシエーション	negotiation
値下り確率	risk
値下り銘柄	loser
値下げ	price cut
値下げ	price reduction
値下げ圧力	price pressure
値下げ取消高	mark down cancelation
値段	figure
値段	price
値段	rate
値段をいう	quote
値段をつける	price
捏造する	falsify
ネット	net
ネット・オークション	online auction
ネット・キャッシュ	net cash
ネット銀行	Internet bank
ネット銀行	Net bank
ネット広告	online advertising
ネット事業	Internet business
ネット上で	online [on-line]
ネット上のセキュリティ・システム	firewall [fire wall]
ネット接続会社	provider
ネット専業銀行	Net bank
ネット専業銀行業務	Internet-based banking venture
ネット専業証券会社	online securities brokerage
ネットで	online [on-line]
ネット取引	Net trading
ネット取引	online trading
ネット配信	Net distribution
ネットバンク	Net bank
ネット販売	Net trading
ネットワーク	network
値幅制限	daily price limit
値幅制限	price limit
値幅制限	price movement restriction
値引き	allowance
値引きして売る	discount
根(ね)保証	basic guarantee
ねらい	idea
狙う	target
値をつける	quote
年	year
年	yr
年1回の	annual
年2回の	semiannual
年4回	quarterly
年4回の	quarterly
年間売上	yearly sales
年間売上高	yearly sales
年間の	annual
年間の	during the year
年間の	for the period
年間配当	full-year dividend
年間利益	yearly earnings
年金	annuity
年金	benefit
年金	pension
年金	savings
年金額	service pensions
年金加入者	pension subscriber
年金基金	pension fund
年金給付	pension benefits
年金給付	plan benefits
年金給付債務額	accrued plan benefits
年金給付累積額	accumulated plan benefits
年金供給協定	pension scheme
年金拠出額	pension contributions
年金原価	pension cost

年金原価計上額 provision for pension costs
年金現価充足方式 terminal funding method
年金現価積立方式 terminal funding
年金現価積立方式 terminal funding
年金コスト pension cost
年金債務 pension liability
年金債務 pension obligation
年金債務控除後 net of pension liabilities
年金資金 pension fund
年金資産 pension asset
年金資産 pension plan assets
年金資産 plan assets
年金資産運用益 return on plan assets
年金資産の長期収益率 return on plan assets
年金システム pension system
年金終価 amount of annuity
年金終価 amount of annuity
年金受給権確定従業員 fully vested employees to pension plan
年金受給権者 annuitant
年金受給資格 qualifying conditions
年金受給者 annuitant
年金受給者 pensioner
年金受給者 retiree
年金受領権 annuity
年金商品 accumulation product
年金数理計算上の actuarial
年金数理計算方式 actuarial cost method
年金数理上の actuarial
年金数理上の現在価値 actuarial present value
年金数理上の負債総額 full actuarial liability
年金数理人 actuary
年金生活者 pensioner
年金生活者 retiree
年金制度 pension plan
年金制度 pension scheme
年金制度 pension system
年金制度資産 pension plan assets
年金制度資産 plan assets
年金制度費用 benefit plans expense
年金積立額 funding contributions
年金積立金 pension fund
年金の支払い pension payout
年金費用 annuity cost
年金費用 pension cost
年金費用 pension expense
年金負債 pension liability
年金プラン純資産 net plan assets

年金保険 annuity insurance
年金保険制度 annuity
年金保険の販売 pension insurance sales
年金保険料 pension premium
年金未支給額 accumulated plan benefits
年功序列型賃金体系 seniority-order wage system
年功序列賃金構造 pay-for-age structure
年次営業報告書 annual report
年次株主総会 AGM
年次株主総会 annual meeting
年次株主総会 annual shareowners [shareholders, stockholders] meeting
年次株主総会招集通知 Notice of Annual Meeting
年次級数総和法 sum of the years' digits method
年次計算書類 annual accounts
年次決算報告書 annual report
年次財務諸表 annual accounts
年次財務諸表 final accounts
年次財務書類 annual accounts
年次財務書類 final accounts
年次社員総会 AGM
年次総会 annual meeting
年次の annual
年次報告書 annual report
年次有価証券報告書 annual securities report
年初 BOY
年数 age
年数 life
年数 period
年数調べ aging
年度 business year
年度 calendar year
年度 fiscal year
年度 FY
年度 period
年度 year
年度 yr
年度・期中 during fiscal year or quarter
年度間税配分 interperiod tax allocation
年度間差額 timing differences
年度初め BOY
年度末 end
年度末 year end
年度末 yearend
年賦金 annuity
年賦償還 amortization
年賦償還 redemption by yearly installment
年報 annual report
年報 newsletter

年俸制 annual salary system
年末 year end
年末 yearend
年利 per annum rate
年率 annualized terms
年率換算 annualized terms
年齢 age
年齢調べ aging

の

納期 due date
納税額 tax expense
納税額 tax liability
納税計画 tax planning
納税引当金 provision for income taxes
納入 delivery
納入 payment
納入期間 delivery interval
納入業者 supplier
納入業者 vendor [vender]
納入する deliver
納入する sell
ノウハウ expertise
ノウハウ knowhow [know-how]
納品 delivery
納品書 delivery note
納付金 contribution
納付金 fee
納付する contribute
能率 efficiency
能率化 streamlining
能率化する streamline
能率的な efficient
能力 ability
能力 capacity
能力 power
能力 skill
能力給 pay according to ability
能力給制度 performance-based pay system
ノート note
残り balance
残りの remaining
残りの持ち分 remaining interest
載せる run
…を除いて except
…を除いて net of ...
…を除く less
望ましい成果を十分得るための確固たる基盤 critical mass
ノックダウン方式 knockdown system
ノッチ notch
乗っ取り buyout
乗っ取り takeover [take-over]
乗っ取る buy out
乗っ取る take over
延ばす extend

伸ばす create	廃棄 retirement	sures
伸ばす grow	廃棄する dissolve	買収防衛策 poison pill
伸ばす increase	売却 disposal	買収方式 purchase method
…の伸び increase in …	売却 disposition	買収目標企業 target
伸び gain	売却 divestiture	排出権 allowance
伸び growth	売却 liquidation	排出割当て allowance
伸び improvement	売却 sale	排除 elimination
伸び increase	売却 sales	賠償 compensation
伸び pace	売却 sell-off	賠償 indemnity
伸び pickup [pick-up]	売却益 proceeds	賠償金 compensation
伸び rise	売却可能証券 available-for-sale securities	賠償金 indemnity
伸び悩み pressure		賠償責任 liability
伸び悩みの flat	売却後借戻し取引 sale and lease-back transaction	排除する eliminate
伸び悩みの poor		配信 distribution
伸び率 growth	売却収入 proceeds	配信する distribute
伸び率 percentage gain	売却する divest	配送 delivery
伸びる grow	売却する liquidate	配送する distribute
伸びる increase	売却する sell	倍増する double
伸びる rise	売却する sell off	配送センター distribution center
延払い deferred payment	売却元 vendor [vender]	配属 transfer
上り upstream	配給 distribution	配達 delivery
乗り換える swap	配給 issuance	配達人 distributor
乗り切る manage	配給 marketing	配達する deliver
乗り出す undertake	配給する distribute	配置 location
ノルマ norm	背景 backdrop	配置替え redeployment
のれん goodwill	背景説明 briefing	配置する position
のれん intangible asset	廃材価額 scrap value	配置転換 redeployment
場 meeting	廃止事業 discontinued operation [business]	配置転換 relocation
場 opportunity		配置転換 shift
…の場合にかぎって subject to …	敗者 loser	配置転換 transfer
…の場合を除いて except	買収 acquisition	配置転換する redeploy
	買収 bid	配置転換する relocate
は	買収 buyout	配置転換する transfer
	買収 purchase	配当 allocation
把握する monitor	買収 takeover [take-over]	配当 distribution
パーセンテージ・ポイント percentage point	買収案件 bid	配当 dividend
	買収会社 acquirer	配当 payout
パーセント percent	買収価格 purchase price	配当落ち XD
パーセント percentage	買収企業 acquirer	配当基準日 record date
パーセント・ポイント percentage point	買収者 acquirer	配当金 cash dividend
	買収条件 climate for acquisition	配当金 dividend
パーチェス purchase	買収する acquire	配当金 payout
パーチェス法 purchase method	買収する buy	配当金株式再投資 dividend reinvestment
パーチェス方式 purchase method	買収する buy out	
パートナー partner	買収する purchase	配当金再投資 dividend reinvestment
パートナーシップ partnership	買収する take over	
パートナーシップの利権 partnership interest	買収戦略 buyout strategy	配当金収入 dividend income
	買収対象会社 target	配当金の支払い dividend payment
パートナーシップ持ち分 partnership interest	買収対象会社 target company	配当金の支払い dividend payout
	買収提案 bid	配当再投資 dividend reinvestment
パーレン parenthesis	買収提案 bidding	
ハイア・パーチェス hire purchase	買収提案 buyout offer	配当支払い dividend payment
廃棄にする scrap	買収提案 takeover bid	配当支払い dividend payout
売価 market price	買収の標的 bid target	配当支払い額 dividend payment
売価還元法 retail inventory method	買収の標的企業 targeted company	配当支払い率 dividend payout
		配当所得 dividend income
倍加する double	買収標的会社 target	配当性向 dividend payout
売価棚卸し法 retail inventory method	買収ファンド buyout fund	配当性向 payout percentage
	買収法 purchase method	配当性向 payout ratio [rate]
廃棄 dissolution	買収防衛策 anti-takeover mea-	配当宣言 declaration of dividend

配当宣言日　declaration date	配分　sharing	破綻　collapse
配当必要額　required distribution	配分額　appropriation	破綻　failure
配当率　dividend ratio [rate]	配分　portion	破綻　insolvency
配当率調整型優先株式　adjustable rate preferred stock	…に配分される　applicable to …	破綻した　bankrupt
	配分する　allocate	破綻した　insolvent
配当率逓増優先株式　increasing rate preferred stock	売申込み　offer	破綻者　bankrupt
	培養　culture	破綻する　collapse
配当率入札方式優先株式　uction rate preferred stock	売呼び値　offer	破綻する　fail
	ハイライト情報　selected financial data	8月期決算　business year ending in August
配当利回り　dividend yield		
配当利回り　rate of return	配慮　concern	8月終了の事業年度　business year ending in August
配当を行う　issue	入る　enter	
売買　deal	入る　take out	発案　idea
売買　dealing	パイロット　pilot	発案　initiative
売買　market	破棄　cancelation [cancellation]	発会式　inauguration ceremony
売買　marketing	破棄する　reverse	発議　initiative
売買　sale	波及効果　repercussion effect	発議　motion
売買　sale and purchase	波及効果　ripple effect	発揮する　exercise
売買　sales	拍車をかける　accelerate	罰金　penalty
売買　trade	莫大な　substantial	バックログ　backlog
売買　trading	薄利　thin margin	パッケージ　package
売買　transaction	薄利多売戦略　low-margin, high volume strategy	発見　strike
売買一任勘定資金　discretionary fund		発効　effect
	励み　incentive	発行　float
売買益　trading profit	派遣する　dispatch	発行　issuance
売買益　trading profit	破産　bankruptcy	発行　issue
売買回転率　turnover ratio	破産　failure	発行　offering
売買回転率　turnover ratio of trading	破産　liquidation	発行　sale
	破産した　bankrupt	初公開する　unveil
売買額　trading volume	破産者　bankrupt	発行価格　issuance price
売買可能な　marketable	破産者　insolvent	発行価格　issue price
売買株数　trading volume	破産する　fail	発行価額　offer price
売買契約　commitment	破産する　liquidate	発行額　issuance volume
売買する　merchandise	破産宣告　declaration of bankruptcy	発行株式　shares outstanding
売買する　trade		発行株式数　issued shares
売買選択権　option	破産宣告を受けた者　bankrupt	発行体に関する公表データ　public data on issuer
売買高　trading volume	破産手続き　bankruptcy	
売買高　turnover	破産手続き　bankruptcy procedure	発行企業　issuing enterprise
売買高　value of transaction	破産手続き　bankruptcy procedure	発行規模　size of the issuance
売買取引　dealing	破産手続き　receivership proceedings	発行債　issue
売買約定　commitment		発行差金　original issue discount
廃品にする　scrap	初め　beginning	発行市場　issue market
配布　distribution	初め　inception	発行市場　primary market
配賦　absorption	初めの　initial	発行条件　issue terms
配賦　allocation	始める　set up	発行条件　terms of the offering
配賦　application	場所　location	発行済み　outstanding
配賦　distribution	バスケット方式集合　basket	発行済み株式　issued shares
配賦　proration	はずみをつける　pick up	発行済み株式　outstanding equities
…に配賦可能な　applicable to …	派生した　derivative	
配賦原価　applied cost	派生商品　derivative	発行済み株式　outstanding shares
配賦原価　distributed cost	派生商品　derivative financial instrument	発行済み株式　shares outstanding
配布する　distribute		発行済み株式資本　issued share capital
配賦する　absorb	派生商品　derivative product	
配賦する　allocate	派生商品取引　derivative transaction	発行済み株式資本　issued share capital
配賦する　apply		
配賦する　prorate	働き　activity	発行済み株式資本金　issue capital
配分　allocation	働き　function	発行済み株式資本金　issued share capital
配分　allotment	働き口　job	
配分　appropriation	働く　function	発行済み株式数　issued shares
配分　distribution	働く　serve	発行済み株式数　number of shares

発行済み株式数　issued
発行済み株式数　number of shares of stock outstanding
発行済み株式数　number of shares outstanding
発行済み株式数　shares issued
発行済み株式数の加重平均　weighted average number of shares outstanding
発行済み株式の加重平均株式数　weighted average number of shares outstanding
発行済み株式の時価総額　capitalization
発行済み議決権株式　outstanding voting stock
発行済み資本　issued capital
発行済み資本金　paid-in capital
発行済み社外流通株式　common shares outstanding
発行済み普通株式　common shares outstanding
発行済み普通株式　outstanding common stock
発行済み普通株式　outstanding ordinary shares
発行済み普通株式の加重平均株式数　weighted average common shares outstanding
発行済み普通株式の平均株式数　average common shares outstanding
発行済み普通株式の平均数　average common shares outstanding
発行済みワラント　warrant outstanding
発行する　float
発行する　issue
発行する　offer
発行する　sell
発行体　borrower
発行体　issuing enterprise
発行体　issuing enterprise
発行体の債券格付け　issuer's debt ratings
発行手数料　opening commission
発行登録　shelf registration
発行部数　issue
発行目論見書　offering statement
発行目論見書　prospectus
発行枠　maximum limits
発射する　launch
発生　accrual
発生基準で　as incurred
発生給付評価方式　accrued benefit valuation method
発生経費　accrued expenses
発生原価　incurred cost
発生減価　accrued depreciation
発生債務　obligations incurred

発生させる　create
発生させる　incur
発生事項　event
発生した　accrued
発生時点で　as incurred
発生時に　as incurred
発生主義　accrual basis
発生主義　accrued basis
発生主義　accrued method
発生主義の原則　accrual principle
発生済み利息　accrued interest
発生する　accrue
発生する　generate
発生する　provide
発生費用　incurred expense
発生利息　accrued interest
発送　shipment
発送する　dispatch
発送する　ship
罰則　penalty
バッチ処理　batch processing
発注者　owner
発注書　purchase order
発注する　order
発展　advance
発展　boost
発展　development
発展　progress
発展　success
発展させる　develop
発展させる　improve
発展する　advance
発展する　grow
発電容量　capacity
初値　share price on the first day
初値を付ける　open
発売　introduction
発売　launch
発売　release
発売する　introduce
発売する　launch
発売する　release
発売する　ship
発表　announcement
発表　launch
発表　presentation
発表　release
発表する　announce
発表する　declare
発表する　disclose
発表する　issue
発表する　provide
発表する　release
発表する　reveal
発表する　unveil
発表の場　outlet
発明の開示　disclosure
パテント　patent
歯止めをかける　contain
話し合い　talks

跳ね上がる　leap
跳ね上がる　skyrocket
パネル　panel
幅　range
…の幅の　wide
幅広い　wide
幅広い　comprehensive
パフォーマンス　performance
パフォーマンス制度　performance plan
パフォーマンス・プラン　performance plan
パブリック・プライベート・パートナーシップ　PPP
パブリック・リレーションズ　public relations
バブル　bubble
バブル期　bubble economy period
速さ　pace
払込み　payment
払込み資本　contributed capital
払込み資本　equity capital
払込み資本　paid-in capital
払込み資本金　paid-in capital
払込み資本金　paid-up share capital
払込み資本剰余金　additional paid-in capital
払込み剰余金　additional paid-in capital
払込み剰余金　contributed surplus
払込み剰余金　contribution surplus
払込み剰余金　paid-in surplus
払い込む　contribute
払戻し　payoff
払戻し　refund
払戻し　refunding
払戻し　repayment
払戻し　withdrawal
払い戻す　refund
払い戻す　repay
パラダイム　paradigm
バランス　balance
バランス・シート　balance sheet
バランス・シート　BS
バランス・シート管理　asset liability management
バランス・シート管理　ALM
バランスト・スコアカード　balanced scorecard
波乱要因　uncertainty
張り合う　compete
バリュー　value
バリュー戦略　value strategy
班　team
範囲　coverage
範囲　extension
範囲　range
範囲　scope

範囲外　below the line	反騰　rally	被裏書人　endorsee
反映させる　reflect	反騰する　rally	非営利団体　not-for-profit organization
反映する　reflect	半年ごとの　semiannual	
半額にする　halve	販売　marketing	冷え込んだ　weak
半期　half	販売　sale	被害　damage
半期　half year	販売　sales	被害額　damage
半期決算　biannual settlement	販売　selling	非会社型投資信託　un-incorporated investment trust
半期決算　semiannual earnings	販売員　representative	
半期決算利益　interim profit	販売会社　vendor [vender]	比較　comparison
半期の　half-yearly	販売型リース　sales-type lease	比較可能性　comparability
半期の　interim	販売業者　vendor [vender]	比較財務書類　comparative financial statements
半期の　semiannual	販売金融リース　sales-type lease	
反希薄化　antidilution	販売好調　strong sales	比較生産性　comparative productivity
半期報告　interim report	販売後市場　after market [aftermarket]	
半期報告　midterm report		比較貸借対照表　comparative balance sheet
半期報告書　interim report	販売先　placement	
半期報告書　semiannual financial statement	販売資産　trading assets	比較対象　proxy
	販売奨励金　incentive	被獲得主体　acquired entity
半期報告書　semiannual securities report	販売奨励金　sales incentive	比較優位　comparative advantage
	販売する　distribute	比較優位　comparative advantage
半期利益　interim profit	販売する　market	比較優位　competitive advantage
バンク　bank	販売する　offer	比較優位性　comparative advantage
番組　content	販売する　provide	
番組　program	販売する　release	比較優位性　competitive advantage
番組提供者　sponsor	販売する　sell	
番組の内容　content	販売促進　promotion	非課税　tax free
バンク・ローン　bank loan	販売促進　sales promotion	非課税で　tax free
判決　action	販売促進活動　promotion	非課税の　nontaxable
判決　decision	販売促進策　sales incentive	非課税の　tax-exempt
判決　determination	販売代理店　distributor	非課税の　tax-free
判決　judgment [judgement]	販売高　volume	光の解像　resolution
判決債務者　judgment debtor	販売手数料　placement commission	被監査会社　client
判決による債権者　judgment [judgement] creditor		悲観的な　negative
	販売店　distributor	非管理職従業員　occupational employee
半減させる　halve	販売努力　sales effort	
万国の　universal	販売の垂直統合　vertically integrated marketing	非管理職従業員　occupational employee
半数所有会社　associate		
半製品　half-finished goods	販売費　distribution expense	非関連会社普通株　unaffiliated common stock
半製品　semifinished goods	販売費　selling expense [expenditure]	
半製品　semifinished goods		引き合う　pay off
半製品　semimanufactured goods	販売費および一般管理費　selling, general and administrative expenses [expenditures]	引上げ　increase
販促　sales promotion		引上げ　upgrading
反則金　penalty		引き上げる　boost
反対の　negative	販売費および一般管理費　SG&A	引き上げる　increase
判断　assessment	販売網　distribution network	引き上げる　raise
判断　decision	販売を促進する　merchandise	引き揚げる　withdraw
判断　determination	販売を促進する　promote	引当金　accrual
判断　estimate	反発　pressure	引当金　allowance
判断　judgment [judgement]	反発　rally	引当金　provision
判断　opinion	半分　half	引当金　reserve
判断する　assess	半分に引き下げる　halve	引当金　reserves and allowances
判断する　determine	半分に減らす　halve	引当金繰入れ　provision
反ダンピング措置　antidumping actions	範例　paradigm	引当金繰入れ額　provision
	販路　market	引当金計上　provision
判断力　judgment [judgement]	販路　outlet	引当金計上前利益　pre-provision earnings
範疇　category		
判定　decision	**ひ**	引当金控除後　less allowances
判定　evaluation		引当金控除後価額　gross-less-allowance valuation
判定　resolution	ピーアール　public relations	
判定を下す　deliver	引いて　minus	引当金充当額　provision

引当金法	allowance method
引当金を繰り入れる	provision
引当金を計上する	provision
引当計上する	provide
引き当てる	set aside
…を率いる	head
引き入れる	embark
引き受け	acceptance
引受け	assumption
引受け	purchase
引受け	underwriting
引受額	underwriting amount
引受額	underwriting commitment
引受基準	underwriting requirements
引受業者	sponsor
引受業者	underwriter
引受業務	underwriting
引受業務	underwriting business
引受銀行	merchant bank
引受契約	underwriting agreement
引受行	underwriter
引受債務	acceptance commitment
引受証券会社	underwriter
引受シンジケート団	syndicate
引き受けた	assumed
引受団	underwriting group
引受手数料	underwriting commission
引受手数料	underwriting fee
引受手数料	underwriting spread
引受人	guarantee
引受人	sponsor
引受人	subscriber
引受募集	stand-by underwriting
引き受ける	accept
引き受ける	acquire
引き受ける	assume
引き受ける	buy
引き受ける	commit
引き受ける	incur
引き受ける	purchase
引き受ける	undertake
引き受ける	underwrite
引き起こす	create
引き起こす	generate
引き起こす	incur
引き起こす	procure
引落し	debit
引落し	withdrawal
引き落とす	deduct
引き下がる	retire
引下げ	reduction
引き下げる	cut
引き下げる	decrease
引き下げる	lower
引き下げる	reduce
引き下げる	slash
引き下げる	trim
引き下げる	write off
引き下げる	wtite down
引締め	squeeze
引き締める	squeeze
引出し	withdrawal
引き出す	tap
引き出す	withdraw
引き継いだ	assumed
引継ぎ	assumption
引継ぎ	takeover [take-over]
引継ぎ負債	assumed liability
引継負債	liabilities assumed
引き継ぐ	assume
引き継ぐ	take over
引き続き…する	continue to ...
非居住者	nonresident
非拠出	noncontributory
非拠出型確定給付年金制度	noncontributory defined benefit plan
非拠出型給付金規定方式による年金制度	noncontributory defined benefit plan
非拠出型退職給付制度	noncontributory plan
非拠出型追加的退職給付制度	noncontributory supplemental retirement benefit plan
非拠出型の	noncontributory
非拠出年金制度	noncontributory plan
引渡し	abandonment
引渡し	delivery
引き渡す	consign
引き渡す	deliver
非金銭活動	noncash activities
非金銭項目増加(減少)	add (deduct) noncash items
非金銭取引	nonmonetary transaction
非金銭の	noncash
非金融無形資産	nonfinancial intangibles
非金利収入	nonfinancial earnings
低いほう	lower
低い利益率	thin margin
引け	close
非経常損益	nonrecurring transactions
非経常(的)項目	extraordinary items
非経常的損益項目	nonrecurring items
非経常的な	nonrecurring
非継続企業	quitting concern
非継続事業	discontinued operation [business]
ピケ隊員	picket
引け値	close
引け値	closing price
引け値	CR
引ける	close
非原価項目	non-cost item
非現金項目	noncash items
非現金項目純額	net non-cash items
非現金項目増加(減少)	add (deduct) noncash items
非現金資産	noncash asset
非現金の	noncash
非現金費用	noncash expense
非公開会社	closed company
非公開会社	private company
非公開会社	privately held company
非公開会社化	going private
非公開企業	nonpublic company
非公開の	closed
非公開の	private
非控除	nondeductible
非控除費用	nondeductible expense
非財務情報	nonfinancial financial information
非財務諸表情報	nonfinancial statement section
非財務書類情報	nonfinancial statement section
非参加株	nonparticipating stock
非参加	nonparticipating
非参加優先株式	nonparticipating preferred stock
非市場性商品	nonmarketed commodity
ビジネス	business
ビジネス開発	business development
ビジネス活動をする	do business
ビジネス機会	market opportunity
ビジネス手法	business model
ビジネス戦略	business strategy
ビジネスチャンス	opportunity
ビジネスの展開	business development
ビジネスモデル	business model
被支配会社	controlled company
被指名者	nominee
非主力事業	noncore business
費消	expenditure
非償還優先株式	nonredeemable preferred stock
非上場会社	private company
非上場会社	privately held company
非上場会社	unlisted company
非上場会社	unlisted stock company
非上場企業	unquoted [unlisted] company
非上場債	unlisted note
非上場の	privately held

非上場の	unlisted
秘書役	secretary
非所得控除	nondeductible reserves
被推薦人	nominee
非正常項目	unusual item
非戦略的業務部門	nonstrategic business
非戦略的事業	nonstrategic business
非戦略的事業部門	nonstrategic business
非戦略的事業部門	nonstrategic division
非戦略部門	nonstrategic division
微増	marginal increase
非遡及	nonrecourse
非遡及債務	nonrecourse obligation
非中核事業	noncore business
非中核の事業資産	noncore assets
非中核の資産	noncore assets
日付	date
…の日付で	as of ...
…の日付に	as of ...
必死になる	struggle
必需品	needs
必達目標	commitment
ビッド	bid
筆頭株主	largest shareholder
筆頭の	top
ヒット商品	hit product
逼迫	pressure
必要	needs
必要運転資金	working capital requirements
必要運転資金	working capital requirements
必要額	needs
必要経費	necessary expenses
必要最低資本額	authorized minimum
必要資金	cash requirements
必要資本金額	capitalization requirements
必要条件	requirement
…を必要とする	subject to ...
必要とする	cost
必要とする	demand
必要とする	entail
必要な条件	ingredient
必要量	needs
…比で	compared with ...
否定的な	negative
非適格年金	nonqualified plan
秘伝	knowhow [know-how]
非転換社債	nonconvertible bond
非転換優先株式	nonconvertible preferred stock
人	head
被投資会社	investee
被投資会社	investee company
1株当たり	per share
1株当たり買付け価格	offer price per share
1株当たり価値	per-share value
1株当たり完全希薄化後純利益	fully diluted earnings per share
1株当たり希薄化前純利益	primary earnings per share
1株当たり計上利益	reported earnings per share
1株当たり計上利益	reported earnings per share
1株当たり資金フロー	fund flow per share
1株当たり四半期純利益	quarterly earnings per common share
1株当たり資本額	equity per share
1株当たり純資産	book value per share
1株当たり純資産	book value per share
1株当たり純資産	BPS
1株当たり純資産	net assets worth per share
1株当たり純資産額	book value per share
1株当たり純資産額	BPS
1株当たり純資産価値	net asset value per share
1株当たり純損失	loss per share
1株当たり純損失	per-share net loss
1株当たり純有形資産価値	net tangible assets per share
1株当たり純利益	earnings per share
1株当たり純利益	EPS
1株当たり純利益	net earnings per share
1株当たり純利益	net income per share
1株当たり純利益	net profit per share
1株当たり正味配当金	net dividend per share
1株当たり当期純利益	earnings per share
1株当たり配当	dividend per share
1株当たり配当	DPS
1株当たり配当額	dividend per share
1株当たり配当額	DPS
1株当たり配当金	dividend per share
1株当たり配当金	DPS
1株当たり簿価	book value per share
1株当たり利益	earnings per common share
1株当たり利益	earnings per share
1株当たり利益	EPS
1株当たり利益	share earnings
1株当たり利益の二重表示	dual presentation of earnings per share
1株当たり連結純利益	per-share group net profit
…に等しい	contain
人手	hand
人手	manpower
人々	people
…に一役買う	contribute
1人当たり	per head
非難する	accuse
被任命者	nominee
被買収会社	acquired company
被買収企業	acquired company
非反復的	nonrecurring
備品	fixture
非分離型の新株引受権付き社債	bond with nondetachable stock warrant
秘密	confidence
秘密保持	confidence
非銘柄商品	generic brand
費目	expense item
100%子会社	fully owned subsidiary
100%子会社	wholly-owned subsidiary
100%出資子会社	wholly-owned subsidiary
100%所有子会社	wholly-owned subsidiary
100%所有の	wholly-owned
百分率	percent
百分率	percentage
百分率財務諸表	common-size financial statements
百分率損益計算書	common-size income statement
百分率貸借対照表	common-size balance sheet
票	vote
費用	charge
費用	cost
費用	expense
表3	back cover inside
表4	back cover
評価	appraisal
評価	assessment
評価	calculation
評価	estimate
評価	evaluation
評価	mark
評価	opinion
評価	rating
評価	reputation

評価	valuation
評価	value
評価益	appraisal gain
評価益	appreciation
評価益	book profit
評価益	latent gain
評価益	latent profit
評価益	unrealized gain
評価益	unrealized profit
評価替え	mark-to-market
評価替え	revaluation
評価替えする	mark to market
評価替えする	value
評価価格	valuation
評価額	appraisal value
評価額	appraised value
評価額	assessment
評価額	value
評価価値	appraised value
評価基準	valuation basis
評価切り上げ	appreciation
評価減	impairment
評価減	write-down [writedown]
評価減	write-off
評価減を計上する	wtite down
評価剰余金	appraisal surplus
評価剰余金	appreciation surplus
評価剰余金	valuation surplus
評価する	assess
評価する	calculate
評価する	estimate
評価する	monitor
評価する	rank
評価する	record
評価する	review
評価する	state
評価する	value
評価性引当金	valuation reserve
評価増	appreciation
評価損	appraisal loss
評価損	book loss
評価損	latent loss
評価損	unrealized loss
評価損	valuation losses
評価損	write-down [writedown]
評価損益	valuation profit or loss
評価損失の記帳	allowance for inventory price decline
評価損を計上する	wtite down
評価替剰余金	appraisal surplus
評価引当金	valuation allowance
評価引下げ	write-down [writedown]
評価引下げ	write-off
評価モデル	valuation model
表記価格	value declared
表記する	list
票決	vote
票決権	vote
票決する	vote
表現形式	form
費用効果が高い	cost effective
費用効率がよい	cost effective
費用削減	cost cut
費用削減	cost reduction
表示	disclosure
表示	display
表示	presentation
表示	reporting
表示	showing
表示価額	stated value
標識	mark
表示形式	presentation
表示資本金	stated capital
表示する	cover
表示する	include
表示する	list
表示する	present
表示する	record
表示する	report
表示する	represent
表示する	state
表示端末装置	display
…表示の	denominated
表示方法	manner of presentation
表示方法	presentation
費用・収益の対応	matching
標準	criterion
標準	level
標準	mark
標準	norm
標準	standard
標準価格	standard price
標準原価	standard cost
標準誤差	standard error
標準誤差	standard error
標準税率	standard tax rate
標準的方式	norm
標準配賦率	standard burden rate
…を表象する	represent
費用処理する	expense
費用処理する	recognize
費用対効果分析	cost-benefit analysis
標的	mark
標的	target
標的にする	target
平等雇用機会法	EEOA
平等雇用機会法	Equal Employment Opportunity Act
費用として計上する	expense
費用として控除される	deductible
費用に計上する	expense
費用の流れ	cost distribution
費用の認識	expense recognition
費用の配賦	cost distribution
費用配分	cost distribution
評判	reputation
費用負担	burden
費用便益評価	cost benefit evaluation
費用便益分析	benefit-cost [benefit/cost] analysis
費用便益分析	cost-benefit analysis
費用または損失として処理する	charge off
費用見積り	estimated cost
表	chart
表	listing
表	table
表の作成	listing
表明する	represent
表面	front
表面に出ない	latent
表面利率	nominal interest
表面利率	stated interest rate
評論	review
開き	disparity
開き	spread
開く	open
開く	set up
平社員	rank and file
平社員の	rank-and-file
ピリオド	period
比率	measure
比率	mix
比率	percentage
比率	ratio
非流動資産	noncurrent assets
非流動的	noncurrent
非流動負債	noncurrent liabilities
比例配分	proration
比例配分する	prorate
比例連結	proportional [proportionate] consolidation
非連結	nonconsolidated
非連結子会社	unconsolidated subsidiary
非連結事業体	unconsolidated entity
非連結の	unconsolidated
非連結ベースの	nonconsolidated
広がる	widen
広げる	widen
品位	quality
品質	quality
品質改善	quality improvement
品質管理	QC
品質管理	quality control
品質管理基準	quality control standard
品質管理基準	quality management standards
品質管理手続き	quality processes
品質基準	quality standard
品質競争	quality competition
品質向上	quality enhancement
品質低下	deterioration
品質保証引当金	liability for ser-

日本語	英語	日本語	英語	日本語	英語
	vice guarentees	フォームS-1	Form S-1	副会長	vice president [vice-president]
貧弱な	lean	フォームS-8	Form S-8		
品目	item	フォワード	forward	副学長	vice president [vice-president]
		付加	addition		
ふ		賦課	absorption	復元する	rebuild
		賦課	assessment	複合企業	conglomerate
部	department	部・課	division	複合企業財務諸表	conglomerate financial statements
部	section	部会	committee		
ファーム	firm	賦課課税方式	official assessment method	複合企業体	conglomerate
歩合	percentage			複合体	conglomerate
歩合	rate	付加価値	added value	複合的合併	conglomerate merger
ファイアウォール	firewall [fire wall]	付加価値額	added value	複合的資本構成	complex capital structure
歩合制	percentage	付加価値計算書	added value statement	服地	material
ファイナンス	finance			複式記入	double entry
ファクター	factor	付加価値税	added value tax	副社長	veep
ファクタリング	factoring	付加価値税	added value tax	副社長	vice president [vice-president]
ファクタリング業者	factor	付加価値税	value-added tax		
ファシリティ	facility	付加価値税	VAT	服従	compliance
不安	concern	付加価値製品	value-added product	復職	recall
不安	crisis			複数議決権株式	super voting share
不安	turmoil	付加給付	fringe benefit	…に服する	subject to ...
不安	uncertainty	付加給付	fringe benefit		
不安材料	concern	付加給付制度	fringe benefit plan	副総裁	vice president [vice-president]
ファンダメンタルズ	fundamentals	賦課金	assessment		
不安定な	uncertain	不確実性	uncertainty	副大統領	vice president [vice-president]
不安定な	volatile	不確実な	uncertain		
ファンデーション	foundation	不確定	uncertainty	復調する	pick up
ファンド	fund	不確定な	uncertain	副頭取	vice president [vice-president]
不安要因	uncertainty	不確定年金	contingent annuity		
フィー	fee	不確定の	contingent	副本	counterpart
フィージビリティ	feasibility	不確定要因	uncertainty	含み益	appraisal gain
フィージビリティ・スタディ	feasibility study	不確定要素	X factor	含み益	appraisal profit
		不可欠な一部	integral part	含み益	book profit
フィールド	field	賦課原価	incurred cost	含み益	latent gain
不一致	disparity	付加する	accrue	含み益	latent profit
不一致	division	付加する	append	含み益	latent value
封切る	release	賦課する	levy	含み益	paper profit
封鎖	closure	付加税	surtax	含み益	unrealized gain
風潮	climate	不活発な	sluggish	含み益	unrealized profit
風土	climate	賦課的	chargeable	含み資産	hidden assets
風土	culture	付加的機能	option	含み資産	hidden valuation
ブーム	surge	付加的な	additional	含み資産	latent asset
増えた	increased	付加的払込み資本	additional paid-in capital	含み資産	off-the-book property
フェデラル・ファンド金利	Federal [federal] funds rate			含み損	appraisal loss
		賦課的労務費	chargeable labor cost	含み損	book loss
フェデラル・ファンド適用金利 Federal [federal] funds rate				含み損	embedded losses
		不稼動債権の比率	nonperforming loan percentage	含み損	latent loss
フェデラル・ファンド・レート Federal [federal] funds rate				含み損	paper loss
		不可分の一体	integral part	含み損	unrealized loss
増える	increase	賦課方式	assessment plan	含み損益	appraisal profits and losses
増える	pick up	賦課方式	pay-as-you-go financing plan		
フォーカス	focus			含み損益	latent gains or losses
フォーム	form	賦課方式	pay-as-you-go formula	含み損益	latent profits and losses
フォーム10-K	Form 10-K	付加利子	imputed interest	含み損益	paper profit or loss
フォーム10-Q	Form 10-Q	不況	doldrums	含み損益	unrealized profits and losses
フォーム20-F	Form 20-F	不況	recession		
フォーム8-K	Form 8-K	不況	slump	含み損益	unrealized value
フォームF-1	Form F-1	部局	arm	含みを持つ	latent
フォームF-4	Form F-4	不均衡	disparity	…を含む	comprise
		不均衡	imbalance	含む	contain

含む	cover
含む	include
服務	service
膨らませる	inflate
複利	compound interest
複利	compound interest rate
複利	compounded interest
複利現価	compound present value
福利厚生費	fringe benefit
福利厚生費制度	welfare compensation plan
副理事長	vice president [vice-president]
複利終価	future amount
複利年金終価	amount of annuity
不景気	doldrums
不景気	recession
不景気	slump
不景気な	sluggish
符号	mark
総…	general
総…	gross
負債	borrowing
負債	charge
負債	debit
負債	debt
負債	gearing
負債	indebtedness
負債	leverage
負債	liability
負債	obligation
負債・費用性引当金	provisions for liabilities and charges
負債および株主持ち分	liabilities and stockholders' equity
負債および資本	liabilities and capital
負債額	indebtedness
負債金融	debt finance
負債金融	debt financing
負債合計	total liabilities
不採算事業	money-losing operation
不採算事業	unprofitable operation
負債残高	debt outstanding
不採算店舗	money-losing store
不採算店舗	unprofitable outlet
不採算な	unprofitable
不採算の	money-losing
不採算部門	unprofitable division
不採算部門	unprofitable unit
負債・資本比率	debt equity ratio
負債・資本比率	DER
負債総額	total liabilities
負債調整率	gearing proportion
負債対資本比率	debt equity ratio
負債に陥る	incur
負債による資金調達	debt finance
負債による資金調達	debt financing
負債の借換え	rollover of liabilities
負債倍率	debt equity ratio
負債比率	debt equity ratio
負債比率	debt ratio
負債比率	equity capital to total debt ratio
負債比率	financial gearing
負債比率	gearing
負債比率	leverage
負債比率	liability ratio
負債比率が低い企業	conservative-leveraged company
負債法	liability method
負債法	liability method
負債方式	liability method
負債持ち分比率	debit equity ratio
負債を抱えた	debt-saddled
不実の記載	untrue statement
不実表示	misstatement
節目	benchmark
部署	post
不振	doldrums
不振	slump
不振の	poor
不振の	sluggish
…に付随する	contingent
不正確な	false
不正資金	slush fund
不正資金の洗浄	money laundering
不正侵入防止機能	firewall [fire wall]
不正侵入防止装置	firewall [fire wall]
不正操作	manipulation
不正な	fraudulent
不正な財務報告	fraudulent financial reporting
不足	crisis
不足	deficit
不足額	balance
不足額	deficit
付属する	accompanying
付属設備	improvement
付属定款	bylaw
付属電話機	extension
付属の	supplementary [supplemental]
不測の事態	contingency
不測の損害	unforeseen loss
不足分	difference
付帯給付	fringe benefit
付帯費用	chargeable expense
付帯物	fixture
付託	reference
不確かな	contingent
不確かな	doubtful
不確かな	uncertain
再び活性化する	revive
負担	assumption
負担	burden
負担	liability
負担	responsibility
負担額	liability
負担金	burden charge
負担金	contribution
負担させる	charge
負担すべき	chargeable
負担する	absorb
負担する	assume
負担する	defray
負担する	incur
負担する	pay
負担能力	coverage
負担部分	contribution
負担分	share
部長	manager
普通	capital stock
普通株	common share
普通株	common stock
普通株	straight equity
普通株式	common share
普通株式	common stock
普通株式1株当たり純資産価値	net asset value per share
普通株式資本および剰余金	common and surplus
普通株式増加数	incremental common stock
普通株式相当証券	common stock equivalents
普通株式等価物	common stock equivalents
普通株式に帰属する当期純利益	net earnings applicable to common shares
普通株式発行総数	common shares outstanding
普通株式1株当たり四半期純利益	quarterly earnings per common share
普通株式1株当たり純資産	book value per common share [stock]
普通株式1株当たり純利益	earnings per common share
普通株式1株当たり純利益	earnings per share
普通株式1株当たり利益	earnings per common share
普通株資本金	common share
普通株資本金	common stock
普通株主	common stockholder
普通株主	equity shareholder
普通株主持ち分利益	amount earned for equity
普通株主持ち分利益	amount earned for equity
普通議決権株式	common voting stock

普通社債	SB
普通社債	straight bond
普通登録株主	registered common shareholder
普通の	common
普通の	ordinary
物価	price
物価高騰	inflation
物価上昇	inflation
物価上昇率	inflation
物価水準	price level
復活	renewal
復活	revival
復帰する	return
物件	property
復興	recovery
復興	rehabilitation
復興	revitalization
不都合	disadvantage
物質	material
物質的な	material
物的生産能力	physical productive capacity
物的な	material
物的流通	physical distribution
ぶっ通しで	straight
プットオプション付き転換社債	convertible bonds with put option
プットオプション付き普通株式	puttable common stock
物品	commodity
物品	goods
不釣り合い	disparity
物理的耐用年数	physical life
物流	physical distribution
物流コスト	physical distribution cost
物流システム	logistics system
物流センター	distribution center
物流・販売支援会社	distribution and marketing support company
物流・販売支援会社	distribution and marketing support company
物流網	distribution network
不定の	infinite
浮動株	floating shares
浮動株	free float
浮動株数	float
不動産	immovable property
不動産	real assets
不動産	real estate
不動産	real property
不動産開発業者	developer
不動産権保有者	tenant
不動産・工場設備	property, plant and equipment
不動産取得税	real property acquisition tax
不動産証券	mortgage-backed security
不動産証券化事業	mortgage-backed securities business
不動産証券事業	mortgage-backed securities business
不動産所有権	freehold
不動産所有権	real property
不動産担保[抵当]貸付け金	loans secured by real real estate
不動産担保債	mortgage bond
不動産担保付き債券	debenture
不動産仲介	listing
不動産仲介契約	listing
不動産投資信託	REIT
不動産取引の報告書	escrow statement
不動産の	real
浮動担保	floating charge
浮動担保	floating charge
浮動的な	floating
不働の	idle
不透明	uncertainty
不透明性	uncertainty
不透明な	uncertain
歩留まり	yield
歩留まり	yield rate
船積み	shipment
船積み	shipment
船積み量	shipment
船荷	shipment
船で送る	ship
負の	negative
負の遺産	negative legacy
負の効果	negative effect
負の効果	negative impact
負の側面	negative effect
負の側面	negative impact
負ののれん	negative goodwill
不払い	nonpayment
賦払い	hire plan
不備	defect
不備	disadvantage
不平等	disparity
部品	component
部品製造指図書	parts production order
部分	component
部分	percentage
部分	portion
部分的に	partially
普遍的一括登録書類	universal shelf registration statement
普遍的一括登録届け出書	universal shelf registration statement
普遍的な	universal
不便な点	disadvantage
付保範囲	coverage
不明確な	uncertain
不名誉	dishonor
部門	arm
部門	category
部門	department
部門	division
部門	function
部門	operation
部門	process
部門	section
部門	sector
部門	unit
部門間の	intersegment
部門計算	sectional calculation
部門収益連動株式	tracking stock
部門責任者	section head
部門の	departmental
部門の	divisional
増やす	enhance
増やす	increase
富裕	wealth
浮揚させる	buoy
扶養親族	dependent
付与する	accrue
付与する	grant
付与する	provide
プライベート	private
プライベート・ブランド	private brand
プライマリー	primary
プライマリー市場	primary market
プライム・レート	prime rate
…のプラスになる	benefit
プラス	positive
プラス要因	positive
プラン	package
プラン	plan
ブランド	brand
プラント	plant
ブランド商品	brand
ブランド店	brand
ブランド品	brand
プランニング	planning
不利	disadvantage
振替え	reclassification
振替え	transfer
振替価格	transfer price
振替操作	transfer operation
振替手数料	transferring charge
振替利益	transfer profit
振り替える	convert
振り替える	reclassify
振り替える	swap
振り替える	transfer
不履行	failure
不履行債権	defaulted receivables
不履行の債務	delinquency
振込み	payment
振込み	transfer
振り込む	transfer
振出し	issue
振出人	drawer
振り出す	issue

不利な	poor
不利な	unfavorable
不利立場	disadvantage
不利に	unfavorably
振戻し	add-back
振り戻す	add back
振り戻す	reverse
不良	defect
不良貸出	bad loan
不良貸付け	bad debt
不良貸付け	bad loan
不良貸付け	loan loss
不良貸付け	nonperforming loan
不良債権	bad debt
不良債権	bad loan
不良債権	impaired asset
不良債権	impaired loan
不良債権	loan loss
不良債権	nonperforming loan
不良債権	nonperforming receivables
不良債権	problem exposures
不良債権	problem loans
不良債権	uncollectible loan
不良債権	unrecoverable loan
不良債権額	loan loss charge
不良債権額	problem loans
不良債権残高	delinquent balances
不良債権残高	outstanding non-performing loans
不良債権処理	bad loan disposal
不良債権処理	write-off of bad loans
不良債権処理額	credit cost
不良債権処理額	loan loss charge
不良債権処理損	loan loss charge
不良債権処理の負担	burden of disposing of bad loans
不良債権の処理	disposal of non-performing loans
不良融資	bad loan
フリンジ・ベネフィット	fringe benefit
部類	category
フル稼働	full capacity
フル・コスト	full cost
プレーヤー	player
プレゼンス	presence
プレゼンテーション	presentation
プレッジ	pledge
プレミアム	premium
フロー	flow
ブローカー	brokerage
フロースルー方式	flow-through method
フロート	float
プロキシ	proxy
プロキュアメント	procurement
プロクシー	proxy
プロクシー・ステートメント	proxy statement
付録の	supplementary [supplemental]
プログラム	program
プロジェクト	project
プロジェクト金融	project finance
プロジェクト・ファイナンス	project finance
プロセス	process
プロダクション	production
プロダクティビティ	productivity
プロダクト	product
プロダクト・ライン	line of products
プロダクト・ライン	product line
プロバイダー	provider
プロファイル	profile
プロフィール	profile
プロポーション	figure
フロント	front
不和	split
不渡り	dishonor
不渡り小切手	dishonored check
不渡り手形	dishonored bill
不渡り手形	unpaid note
不渡りにする	float
…分	portion
…分	worth
雰囲気	climate
分化	differentiation
文化	culture
分解	separation
文化活動への貢献・寄与	mecenat
文化支援	mecenat
文化支援事業	mecenat
分割	division
分割	separation
分割	split
分割上の	divisional
分割する	split
分割する	split off
分割発行	series
分割発行社債	series bond
分割払い	deferred payment
分割払い	installment [instalment]
分割払い購入方式	hire purchase
分権する	decentralize
分散	diversity
分散化	diversification
分散化された資産	diversified assets
分散化した資産	diversified assets
分散化する	decentralize
分散する	decentralize
分散する	diversify
分散投資	diversification
分散投資	portfolio diversification
分散投資して損失リスクを少なくする	hedge
分散投資する	diversify
分子	numerator
分社	spinoff [spin-off]
分社化	spinoff [spin-off]
分社化する	spin off
文書	data
文書	document
文書	letter
文書	paper
粉飾	manipulation of accounts
粉飾	window dressing
粉飾決算	window dressing
粉飾決算	window-dressing of accounts
粉飾決算する	window-dress
粉飾する	dress up
粉飾する	window-dress
分析	evaluation
分析する	monitor
紛争	struggle
分担	portion
分担金	contribution
分担する	share
奮闘する	struggle
分売	distribution
分配	distribution
分配	division
分配	marketing
分配	sharing
分売案内書	offering circular
分配金	dividend
分売する	distribute
分配する	deal
分配する	distribute
分配する	share
分売届出書	distribution statement
分配利益	distributed earnings
分布	distribution
分別	judgment [judgement]
分母	denominator
文面	message
分野	category
分野	division
分野	field
分野	front
分野	niche
分野	sector
分離	separation
分離	severance
分離	spinoff [spin-off]
分離型の新株引受権付き社債	bond with detachable stock warrant
分離型モーゲージ証券	stripped mortgage securities
分離型ワラント	detachable warrant
分離する	separate
分離する	spin off
分離する	split
分離する	split off
分離独立させる	split off

分類	breakdown
分類	category
分類	distribution
分類基準	classification scheme
分類貸借対照表	classified balance sheet
分裂	division
分裂	split
分裂する	split

ベア・ハッグ	bear hug
閉会	closure
平価切上げ	appreciation
平価切下げ	depreciation
平均	average
平均	norm
平均売掛債権滞留日数	days sales outstanding
平均売掛債権滞留日数	DSO
平均株主資本利益率	return on average equity
平均原価時価低価法	lower of average cost or market
平均原価または時価のいずれか低いほう（の金額）	lower of average cost or market
平均残高	average daily balance
平均資本利益率	average return on capital
平均の	average
平均発行済み株式数	average number of shares outstanding
平均発行済み株式総数	average number of shares outstanding
平均普通株主持ち分利益率	return on average shareholders' equity
米金融街	Wall Street
平均余命	mean expectation life
併合	merger
米国外子会社	operations located outside the U.S.
米国公認会計士協会	AICPA
米国公認会計士協会	American Institute of Certified Public Accountants
米国債	T-bond
米国債	Treasury bond
米国の証券市場	Wall Street
閉鎖	closing
閉鎖	closure
米財務省証券	T-note
米財務省証券	Treasury note
米財務省短期証券	T-bill
米財務省短期証券	Treasury bill
閉鎖会社	closed corporation
閉鎖会社	private company
閉鎖型総合保険料方式	closed aggregate cost method

閉鎖式投資信託会社	closed-end company
閉鎖する	close
閉鎖する	shut down
米証券取引委員会	SEC
米証券取引委員会	Securities and Exchange Commission
米上場企業会計監視委員会	PCAOB
米政府長期証券	T-bond
米政府長期証券	Treasury bond
平坦化	flat
米内国歳入庁コード401(k)	401(k)
米ニューヨークの株式市場	Wall Street
米ニューヨークの株式中心街	Wall Street
閉幕	closure
平面図	plan
兵力	force
兵力	resource
兵力	strength
米連邦公開市場委員会	Federal Open Market Committee
米連邦準備制度理事会	Fed
米連邦準備制度理事会	Federal Reserve Board
米連邦準備理事会	Federal Reserve Board
米連邦破法11章	Chapter 11
ベーシス・ポイント	basis point
ベース	base
ベース	basis
ペース	pace
…をベースにする	base
ペーパー	paper
ヘッジ	hedge
ヘッジ資金	hedge fund
ヘッジ損益	hedging gains and losses
ヘッジ取引	hedge transaction
ヘッジ・ファンド	hedge fund
ヘッジ・ファンドの売り買い操作	buying and selling operations by hedge funds
別途資金	sinking fund
ペナルティ	penalty
ベネフィット	benefit
減らす	cut
減らす	decrease
減らす	reduce
減らす	slash
減る	decrease
ヘルスケア	health care [healthcare]
便益	benefit
変化	change
変化	fluctuation
変化	movement
変化	shift

変化	transformation
変化	volatility
変化がない	flat
変革	innovation
変革	transformation
変額商品	variable product
変額年金	variable annuity
変化する	shift
変換	transformation
変換	translation
変換可能な	convertible
変換する	translate
返還する	repay
返還する	return
便宜	accommodation
便宜	facility
返金	repayment
返金する	repay
変形	transformation
変更	alteration
変更	change
変更	revision
変更する	shift
変更定款	revised articles of incorporation
弁護士	attorney
返済	payment
返済	refund
返済	repayment
返済	retirement
弁済	payment
弁済	refund
弁済期限	maturity
返済期日	due date
返済金	refund
弁済金	refund
返済原資	repayment source
返済する	pay
返済する	pay off
返済する	refund
返済する	repay
返済する	retire
返済する	service
弁済する	liquidate
弁済する	pay
弁済する	refund
返済遅延	delinquency
返済不能の	insolvent
返済利息	paid interest
弁償	refund
変遷	transition
変造	alteration
変造する	falsify
ベンダー	vendor [vender]
ベンチマーク	benchmark
ベンチャー企業	start-up
ベンチャー企業への個人投資家	angel
変動	change
変動	float

変動	fluctuation
変動	movement
変動	shift
変動	volatility
変動が大きい	volatile
変動が激しい	volatile
変動為替相場	flexible exchange rate
変動為替相場	floating exchange rate
変動金利	flexible rate
変動金利	floating interest rate
変動金利	floating interest rate
変動金利	floating rate
変動金利のキャッシュ・フロー	floating cash flow
変動しない	fixed
変動する	flexible
変動する	floating
変動する	fluctuate
変動性	volatility
変動性が高い	volatile
変動相場	floating exchange rate
変動相場	floating rate
変動相場制	float
変動相場制である	float
変動相場制に移行する	float
変動相場制にする	float
変動費	floating cost
変動率	volatility
変動利付き債	floating rate bond
変動利率	floating rate
変動レート	floating rate
編入	incorporation
編入する	incorporate
弁論	proceedings

ほ

ポイズン・ピル	poison pill
補遺の	supplementary [supplemental]
ポイント	percentage point
法	code
法	rule
法案	bill
貿易	trade
貿易	trading
貿易摩擦	trade friction
法貨	functional currency
崩壊	collapse
崩壊	fall
崩壊する	collapse
崩壊する	fall
望外の利益	windfall
包括主義利益	all-inclusive profit
包括損失	comprehensive loss
包括担保	floating charge
包括提携	comprehensive tie-up [alliance]
包括的組織	umbrella
包括的提携	comprehensive alliance
包括的な	comprehensive
包括的な	global
包括的な	umbrella
包括的年次財務報告	comprehensive annual financial report
包括標準契約書	umbrella master agreement
包括法案	package
包括補助金	block grant
包括利益	comprehensive income
包括利率	implicit interest rate
放棄	abandonment
放棄	forgiveness
放棄	waiver
放棄	write-off
法規	regulation
法規	rule
放棄する	divest
放棄する	release
放棄する	waive
放棄する	write off
俸給	salary
防禦壁	firewall [fire wall]
方向転換	turnaround
方向転換する	turn around
報告	account
報告	report
報告	reporting
報告	review
報告会計士	reporting accountant
報告期間	reporting period
報告基準	standard of reporting
報告義務がある	responsible
報告義務のある	reportable
報告された	reported
報告事業年度	reporting period
報告事業年度	reporting year
報告四半期	reporting qaurter
報告書	letter
報告書	newsletter
報告書	report
報告書	return
報告書	review
報告書	statement
報告書	submission
報告書上の数値	reported figures
報告書に掲げた数値	reported figures
報告書を提出する	report
報告する	report
報告制度	reporting requirements
報告責任	accountability
報告通貨	reporting currency
報告できる	reportable
報告に値する	reportable
防護策	hedge
方策	measure
方策	resource
方策	tactics
方式	basis
方式	method
方式	plan
方式	procedure
方式	scheme
方式	structure
方式	system
奉仕する	serve
報酬	commission
報酬	compensation
報酬	fee
報酬	pay
報酬	payoff
報酬	remuneration
報酬	remuneration package
報酬	reward
報酬	salary
報酬制度	pay plan
報酬比例部分	earnings-related component
法主体	entity
放出	release
放出する	release
報償	compensation
報償	remuneration
報償	reward
報奨	incentive
報償金	compensation
報奨金	incentive
報奨金	incentive award
報奨金	premium
報奨金	reward
褒賞金	reward
報奨金制度	incentive plan
報奨金制度	rewards system
報奨制度	bonus system
報奨制度	incentive plan
報償費用	compensation expense
方針	basis
方針	initiative
方針	line
方針	philosophy
方針	policy
方針	principle
方針	profile
方針	strategy
法人	corporation
法人	firm
法人	institution
法人化する	incorporate
法人金融	corporate finance
法人事業税	corporate tax
法人所得	corporate income
法人所得	corporation income
法人所得税	income tax
法人所得税	income taxes
法人所得税会計	accounting for income taxes

法人所得税費用	income tax expense
法人税	corporate tax
法人税	corporation income tax
法人税	income tax
法人税額	income tax expense
法人税繰入れ額	provision for income taxes
法人税控除前利益	income before income taxes
法人税考慮前利益	income before income taxes
法人税, 住民税および事業税	income taxes
法人税等	income taxes
法人税等計上額	provision for income taxes
法人税等計上額	tax expense
法人税等充当額	provision for income taxes
法人税等に関する会計処理	accounting for income taxes
法人税等の期間相互配分	interperiod tax allocation
法人税等の期間配分	interperiod tax allocation
法人税等の支払い額	income tax payments
法人税等引当金	provision for income taxes
法人税等費用	tax expense
法人税等引当金	provision for income taxes
法人税の期間内配分	intraperiod income tax allocation
法人税率	income tax rate
法人設立	incorporation
法人設立費	incorporation fee
法人組織の	incorporate
法人組織の	incorporated
法人団体	incorporation
包装	package
包装費	package cost
法定監査	statutory audit
法定監査人	statutory auditor
法定金利の上限	legal ceiling on interest rates
法定実効税率	effective tax rate
法定資本	capital stock
法定準備金	legal capital reserves
法定準備金	legal reserves
法定準備金	legal surplus
法定準備金	statutory surplus
法定税率	enacted tax rates
法定税率	statutory tax rate
法定の	statutory
法定有効期間	legal life
法定労働時間	statutory workweek
法的権限	power
法的効力	force
法的存在者	entity
法的手続き	proceedings
法的枠組み	legal framework
報道	report
報道する	cover
報道する	report
冒頭部分	front
法の不備	defects in the law
豊富な	substantial
方法	method
方法	plan
方法	shift
方法	tool
泡沫	bubble
法務部	legal department
方面	front
訪問販売	solicitation
訪問販売する	solicit
暴落	collapse
暴落	crisis
暴落	meltdown
暴落	slump
暴落する	collapse
法律見解書	legal review
法律行為	transaction
法律事務	practice
法令	regulation
法令遵守	legal compliance
ボード	board
ポートフォリオ	portfolio
ボーナス	bonus
ホームページ	site
ホームページ	Web site
簿価	book value
簿価	carrying amount
簿価	carrying value
簿価	original cost
簿価	reported value
簿外口座	off-the-book account
簿外債務	hidden liability
簿外債務	off-balance sheet liability
簿外債務	off-the-book debts
簿外債務	off-the-book liabilities
簿外資金調達	off-balance-sheet financing
簿外資産	off-balance-sheet asset
簿外資産	out-of-book assets
簿外取引	off-balance-sheet transaction
簿外取引	off-the-book deal
簿外取引	off-the-book transaction
簿外の	off-balance-sheet
簿外の	off-the-book
簿外負債	liability off the book
簿外負債	off-balance sheet liability
他の	other
他の企業を吸収する会社	surviving company
簿価法	book value method
保管	charge
補間	interpolation
保管銀行	custodian bank
保管する	keep
補完的	supplementary [supplemental]
補強	beef-up
補強	enhancement
補強する	beef up
補強する	reinforce
募金	fund raising
募金運動	drive
保険	insurance
保険	security
保険案内書	prospectus
保険委付	abandonment
保険会社	insurer
保険会社	underwriter
保険会社の経常収支残高	pretax balance
保険型年金	insured pension plan
保険加入者	policyholder
保険業者	insurer
保険業者	underwriter
保険金	claim
保険金	claims paid
保険金	insurance
保険金	premium
保険金額	insurance
保険金額	life insurance coverage
保険金額	sum insured
保険金支払い費	claim adjustment expense
保険金の支払い	payout
保険金費用の認識	claim cost recognition
保険契約	insurance
保険契約	insurance contract
保険契約	policy
保険契約金額	life insurance coverage
保険契約者	insurance policyholder
保険契約者	policyholder
保険計理士	actuary
保険者	insurer
保険証券	policy
保険条件	insurance
保険証書	policy
保険数理原価法	actuarial cost method
保険数理士	actuary
保険数理上の	actuarial
保険数理上の計算価値	actuarially computed value
保険数理上の現在価値	actuarial present value
保険数理専門家	actuary

保険数理による原価計算法 actuarial cost method	補償 protection	補塡する finance
保険代理業者 underwriter	保証額 guarantee	補塡する fund
保険つなぎ hedge	保証金 bond	補塡する redeem
保険の総額 outstanding balance of contracts	保証金 deposit	骨組み framework
	保証金 guarantee money	…にほぼ等しい approximate
保険料 contribution	保証金 security money	保有 holding
保険料 insurance	保証金 security payment	保有数 inventory
保険料 insurance premium	補償金 compensation	保有株 holding
保険料 premium	補償金 indemnity	保有株 holdings
保険料運用収益 return on insurance premium management	保証契約 guarantee	保有株 shareholding
	保証債務 liabilities for [on] guarantee	保有株 stockholding
保険料収入 premium income	保証債務 liability for guarantee	保有株式 portfolio
保険料収入 premium revenue	保証債務 sFguarntee liabilities	保有株式 shareholding
保険料建て方式 defined contribution plan	保証債務 warranty claim	保有株式 stockholding
	保証社債 assumed bond	保有株の評価損を損失として計上する減損処理額 valuation losses
保険料積立金 mathematical reserve	保証書 guarantee	
	保証状 guarantee	保有株の評価損を損失に計上する減損処理額 appraisal loss
保護 protection	保証証書 bond	
保護 umbrella	保証する guarantee	保有契約 outstanding balance of contracts
募債引受団 underwriting syndicate	保証する secure	
	保証する sponsor	保有契約高 outstanding balance of contracts
保持 holding	保証する undertake	
ポジション position	保証付き社債 guaranteed bond	保有財産 holding
ポジション presence	保証手数料 guarantee fee	保有証券 securities holdings
ポジションの再設定 repositioning	補償取引 compensation deal	保有する own
保持する keep	保証人 guarantee	保有する retain
保持する retain	保証人 insurer	保有高 holdings
ポジティブ positive	保証人 security	保有有価証券 securities holdings
保釈 bond	保証人 sponsor	ボラティリティ volatility
保守 maintenance	保証人になる sponsor	掘り当て strike
保守・点検 maintenance and inspection	補償の compensatory	ポリシー policy
	保証配当 guaranteed dividend	保留 back burner
募集 effort	補助金 grant	保留 reserve
募集 offer	補助原価 service cost	保留する withhold
募集 offering	補助の pilot	ボロワー borrower
募集 primary offering	補助部門費 service cost	本格的な significant
募集 raising	ポスト post	本業 core business
募集 solicitation	補正する adjust	本業 main business
募集価格 offer price	補正する correct	本業の core
募集価格 offering price	保全 protection	本支店勘定 inter-office account
募集する solicit	保全する maintain	本社 headquarters
募集説明会 roadshow	補足財務情報 supplemental [supplementary] financial information	本社 headquarters units
募集届出書 offering statement		本社 home office
募集・販売 placement		本社資産 corporate assets
補修部品市場 after market [aftermarket]	補足的 supplementary [supplemental]	本社費用 central corporate expense
		本社費用 central corporate expense
募集目論見書 pathfinder prospectus	保存 reserve	
	保存する keep	本店 headquarters
保守主義 conservatism	保存品 reserve	本店 home office
保守主義の原則 conservatism	母体 parent	本店勘定 head office account
保守する maintain	歩調 step	本人 principal
保証 bond	発起 promotion	本音 bottom line
保証 endorsement	発起する promote	本部 headquarters
保証 guarantee	発起人 sponsor	本部資産 corporate assets
保証 protection	発足式 inauguration ceremony	本部費 central corporate expense
保証 security	発端 inception	翻訳 translation
保障 protection	ポテンシャル potential	翻訳する translate
補償 compensation	…を補塡する make up for …	
補償 indemnity	補塡する cover	

ま

- マーク　mark
- マーケット　market
- マーケットシェア　market share
- マーケティング　marketing
- マーケティングおよび販売費　marketing and sales expenses
- マーケティング・販売費　marketing and sales expenses
- マーチャント・システム　merchant system
- 毎季に　quarterly
- 埋蔵地帯　field
- 毎年の　annual
- マイナス　disadvantage
- マイナス　minus
- マイナス影響　negative effect
- マイナス影響　negative impact
- マイナス効果　negative effect
- マイナス効果　negative impact
- マイナスの　negative
- マイナスの　unfavorable
- マイナスの営業権　negative goodwill
- マイナス要因　negative pledge
- …前　before
- 前受け金　advance receipt
- 前受金　advance
- 前受けした　unearned
- 前受収益　prepaid income
- 前受け収益　prepayment received
- 前受収益　unearned income
- 前受収益　unearned revenue
- 前受収益　deferred credit
- 前受収益　deferred revenue
- 前受け利息　unearned interest income
- 前貸し　advance
- 前貸し金　advance
- 前金　advance
- 前金　front money
- 前倒し　front-loading
- 前倒し計上　advance accounting
- 前倒し執行　front-loading
- 前倒しする　front-load
- …前の利益　income before …
- 前払い　advance
- 前払い　prepayment
- 前払い金　advance
- 前払い金　advance payments
- 前払い金　imprest
- 前払いする　advance
- 前払いする　prepay
- 前払い退職後健康保険費用　prepaid postretirement healthcare costs
- 前払い注文　order and advance
- 前払い賃金　prepaid wage
- 前払い賃借料　prepaid rental
- 前払い手数料　prepaid commission
- 前払い特許権使用料　prepaid royalty
- 前払い年金原価　prepaid pension cost
- 前払い年金コスト　prepaid pension cost
- 前払い年金費用　prepaid pension cost
- 前払い費用　prepaid expenses
- 前払い費用　prepayment
- 前払い費用　prepayment paid
- 前払い法人税　advance corporation tax
- 前払い法人税　advance corporation tax
- 前払い保険料　advance premium
- 前払い保険料　prepaid insurance
- 前払い保険料　up-front premium
- 前渡し金　advance
- 前渡し金　down payment
- 前渡し金　imprest
- 前渡し　advance
- 前渡しする　advance
- 任せる　consign
- 賄う　cover
- 賄う　fund
- …に巻き込まれる　suffer
- 負け組　loser
- 負け組企業　loser
- 負ける　lose
- 増す　enhance
- 増す　gain
- まずまずの　fair
- 抹消　cancelation [cancellation]
- 末端の　terminal
- …に的を絞る　focus on …
- 的を外れた　wide
- マニュファクチュアリング　manufacturing
- …を免れない　subject to …
- マネー　money
- マネー・サプライ　money supply
- マネージャー　manager
- マネー・マーケット　money market
- マネー・ロンダリング　money laundering
- 招く　incur
- マネジメント　management
- マネジメント・チーム　management team
- マネジメント・バイアウト　management buyout [buy-out]
- マネジメント・バイアウト　MBO
- マネジメント・バイイン　MBI
- マネタリー　monetary
- マネタリー・ベース　monetary base
- 守る　keep
- 丸括弧　parenthesis
- 満期　due date
- 満期　maturity
- 満期一括償債　bullet deal
- 満期書替え　rollover
- 満期決済額　amount due
- 満期決済額　sums due
- 満期後社債　matured bond
- 満期支払い　amount due
- 満期支払い金　payment(s) due
- 満期支払い高　amount due
- 満期償還　redemption of maturity
- 満期手形　matured note
- 満期になる　mature
- 満期の経過した　overdue
- 満期の過ぎた　due
- 満期日　due date
- 満期日　maturity date
- 満期日前償還　advance refunding
- 満期日前償還　advance refunding
- 満期保証　maturity guarantee
- 満期保有証券　held-to maturity securities
- 満期保有目的債券　held-to maturity securities
- 満期利回り　YTM
- マンパワー　manpower
- 満了　termination

み

- …に見合う　match
- ミーティング　meeting
- 見落とし　oversight
- 未解決の　outstanding
- 見返り信用状の　back-to-back
- 未監査　unaudited
- 未監査財務書類　unaudited financial statements
- 未拠出退職後給付債務　unfunded postretirement obligation
- 未拠出の　unfunded
- 未拠出部分　unfunded portion
- 未拠出部分　unprovided portion
- 見切り品として処分する　sell off
- 未経過の　unearned
- 未経過費用　expenses paid in advance
- 未経過利子　unearned interest
- 未決済小切手　outstanding checks
- 未決済小切手取立て中の手形・小切手類　float
- 未決済債務　obligation outstanding
- 未決済手形　running bill
- 未決済取引　backlogged transaction
- 未決済の　outstanding
- 未決定の　outstanding
- 未決取引　suspended trading

見越し額 accrual
見越し計上する accrue
見越し項目 accrual
見越して使う anticipate
見越し負債 accrued liabilities
見越す capitalize on
見込まれる純利益 expected net profit
見込み prospects
見込み額 allowance
見込み損失 anticipated loss
見込み利益 anticipated profit
見込む assume
見込む expect
見込む foresee
未成工事支出金 progress payments
未実現益 unrealized gain
未実現為替差損 unrealized foreign currency losses
未実現収益 unrealized revenue
未実現純利益 unrecognized net gain
未実現損益 unrealized gain and loss
未実現損益 unrealized value
未実現損失 unrealized loss
未実現内部利益 unrealized intercompany profits
未実現の unrealized
未実現の unrecognized
未実現の為替差損益 unrealized exchange gains and losses
未実現評価額 unrealized value
未実現利益 unrealized gain
未実現利益 unrealized income
未実現利益 unrealized profit
未実現利得 unrealized gain
未収金 account due
未収金 account receivable
未収収益 accrued income
未収収益 accrued receivables
未収収益 accrued revenues
未収手数料 accrued commission receivable
未収手数料 commission receivable
未収手数料 commission receivable
未収入金 account receivable
未収の accrued
未収の receivable
未収の unearned
未収の債権 claim
未収配当金 dividend receivable
未収払戻し金 claim for reimbursement
未収保険金 due and deferred premiums
未収保険料 deferred premium
未収利息 accrued interest
未収利息 accrued interest receiv-

able
未償還債務 debt outstanding
未償還社債 bond payable
未償還の outstanding
未償還負債 debt outstanding
未償還負債 outstanding debt
未償却営業権 unamortized goodwill
未償却株式発行費 unamortized share-issuing expense
未償却サービス料 unamortized service charges
未償却債務 unamortized obligation
未償却残高 carrying value
未償却残高 unamortized balance
未償却の unamortized
未上場株 unlisted stock [share]
未上場の unlisted
未使用信用枠 uncommitted line of credit
未処分利益 undistributed profit
未処分利益 undivided profit
未処分利益剰余金 undistributed earnings
未処理欠損金 unappropriated deficit
未処理の outstanding
未処理部分 backlog
ミス error
ミスマッチ mismatch
未請求配当金 unclaimed dividend
未成工事 progress
未整備 defect
満たす meet
ミックス mix
密接な close
未積立年金費用債務 liability for pension expense not funded
見積り appraisal
見積り estimate
見積り expectation
見積り projection
見積り valuation
見積り額 accrual
見積り給付債務 projected benefit obligation
見積り金額 estimate
見積り原価 estimated cost
見積り財務情報 pro forma [proforma] financial information
見積り財務諸表 forward financial statements
見積り書 estimate
見積り耐用年数 estimated life
見積り耐用年数 expected useful life
見積り耐用年数表 observed life table
見積り超過額 excess over esti-

mate
見積りの estimated
見積りの expected
見積りの pro forma [proforma]
見積り費用 estimated cost
見積り有効期間 estimated life
見積もる approximate
見積もる estimate
見積もる expect
見積もる project
見積もる quote
見通し expectation
見通し forecast
見通し forecasting
見通し foresight
見通し outlook
見通し profile
見通し projection
見通し prospects
見通し stream
見通しの expected
認められている acceptable
認める accept
認める grant
認める receive
見直し review
見直し revision
見直す revamp
見直す revise
見なし配当 imputed dividend
見なす consider
源 source
身につける gain
ミニマム minimum
未認識過去勤務費用 unrecognized prior service cost
未認識純損失 unrecognized net loss
未認識の unrecognized
未認識の移行時債務 unrecognized transition obligation
未認識の移行時資産 unrecognized transition asset
未納金 arrears
未配分利益 undistributed profit
未発行株式 unissued shares
未発行の unissued
未払い額見越し accrual
未払い勘定 payable
未払い金 account payable
未払い金 accrual
未払い金 arrears
未払い金 debt service
未払い固定資産税 accrued property taxes
未払い債務 accrued liabilities
未払い残高 outstanding balance
未払い残高 outstanding debt
未払い賞与 bonuses payable
未払い賃金 accrued wage

未払い賃借料勘定　rent payable account
未払い手数料　accrued commission
未払い手数料　commission payable
未払い年金費用　accrued pension cost
未払い年金費用　accrued pension cost
未払い年金費用　unfunded accrued pension cost
未払いの　accrued
未払いの　deferred
未払いの　outstanding
未払い配当金　accrued dividend
未払い費用　accrual
未払い費用　accrued charges
未払い費用　accrued liabilities
未払い負債　accrued liabilities
未払い負債　accrued liabilities
未払い負債額　debt outstanding
未払い負債額　outstanding debt
未払い報酬　accrued compensation
未払い法人税　accrued income taxes
未払い法人税等　accrued taxes on incme
未払い保険料　premium due
未払い利息　accrued interest
未払い利息　accrued interest payable
未払い利息　back interest
身分　standing
未分配利益　undistributed earnings
…に見舞われる　suffer
身元保証　reference
未来　future
未来価値　future value
未来の　future
未履行債務　commitment
未履行の　outstanding
身を引く　step down
実を結ぶ　pay off
民営化　privatization
民営会社　private company
民営の　private
民間機械受注　private machinery orders
民間企業　private company
民間企業　private enterprise
民間支出　private spending
民間の　private
民間部門　private sector
民間持ち株会社　private industrial holding company
民需　private demand

む

無益資産の評価と償却　valuation and amortization of intangibles
無額面　nonpar
無額面株　stock without par value
無額面株式　nonpar stock [share]
無額面株式　nonpar value capital stock
無額面株式　nonpar value stock
無議決権株　nonvoting share
無議決権株　nonvoting share
無議決権株　nonvoting stock
無議決権クラスB優先株式　nonvoting class B preferred stock
無議決権償還優先株式　nonvoting redeemable preferred stock
無議決権償還優先株式　nonvoting redemable preferred stock
無記名債券　blank bond
無形固定資産　intangible asset
無形固定資産　intangibles
無形財産　intangibles
無形財産取引税　intangibles tax
無形資産　intangible asset
無形資産　intangible asset
無形資産　intangibles
無形の　intangible
無欠陥　zero defects
無欠陥運動　zero defects movement
無欠点　ZD
無欠点　zero defects
無欠点運動　zero defects
無限定意見報告書　unqualified opinion report
無限の　infinite
無効にする　reverse
無効にする　revoke
無視する　set aside
無借金経営　pay-as-you-go policy
無借金の　pay-as-you-go
…と矛盾しない　consistent with …
無償株　free share
無償給付　grant
無償交付　free issue
無償交付　stock split
無償資金　grant
無償修正　recall
無償増資　free distribution of common shares
無償の　free
無償の　voluntary
無償不動産譲渡　voluntary conveyance of estate in land
難しい　challenging
結びつき　relationship
結びつき　tie-up
結ぶ　sign up

無税償却　nontaxable write-off
無税の　nontaxable
無税　tax-exempt
無税　tax-free
無体権　intangible right
無体項目　intangibles
無体資産　intangible asset
無体の　intangible
無駄な　unprofitable
無駄のない　lean
無担保裏書　endorsement without recourse
無担保借入れ　unsecured borrowing
無担保債　debenture bond
無担保債券　debenture
無担保社債　debenture bond
無担保社債　debenture bond
無担保社債　unsecured corporate debenture
無配　no dividend
無配の　nonparticipating
無料回収・修理　recall
無料回収・修理する　recall
無料の　free
無料奉仕活動　voluntary work

め

明確にする　define
銘柄　brand
銘柄　issue
銘柄　security
銘柄　stock
名義　name
名義書換え　registration
名義書換え代理人　registrar
名義書換え停止　transfer book closed
名義書換え取扱機関　stock transfer agent
名義書換え取扱機関　transfer agent
名義書換え日　transfer day
名義上の株式保有　nominee
名義上の株主　owner of record
明示する　disclose
明示する　state
名称　denomination
名称　name
命じる　order
名声　reputation
名声　standing
明白な　patent
名簿　listing
命名する　name
名目貨幣基準　nominal dollar basis
命令　bidding
命令　order
命令　rule

命令を出す	order
メイン・バンク	main bank
メーカー	factory
メーカー	industry
メーカー	manufacturer
メーカー	producer
メーカー	supplier
メーカー	vendor [vender]
メーカー希望小売価格	sticker price
目先の	immediate
目先の業績改善	immediate improvement
メザニン型の	mezzanine
目覚しい	robust
メセナ	mecenat
目立った	outstanding
目立った	significant
目玉商品	leader
メッセージ	message
目途	prospects
メリット	advantage
面	front
免許	license [licence]
免許	licensing
免許状	letter
免許状	license [licence]
免許手数料	license fee
免許料	license fee
免許を与える	license
免除	cancelation [cancellation]
免除	forgiveness
免除	waiver
免除された	free
免除する	release
免税の	tax-exempt
免税の	tax-free
免責の補償	indemnity against liability
メンテナンス	maintenance

も

儲からない	unprofitable
儲かる	lucrative
儲かる	pay
儲かる	profitable
設ける	create
設ける	establish
設ける	impose
設ける	locate
設ける	sponsor
申込み	application
申込み	bid
申込み	bidding
申込み	offer
申込み	proposal
申込み	tender
申込み国	bidder
申込み者	application
申込み者	subscriber
申込みを締め切る	close the [one's] books
申し込む	enter
申し込む	offer
申立て	motion
申立て	showing
申立てる	file
申立てる	present
申し出	offer
申し出る	enter
申し出る	propose
申し出る	tender
網状組織	network
燃え尽き	burnout
燃え尽き症候群	burnout
モーゲージ	mortgage
モーゲージ証券	mortgage-backed security
モーゲージ担保証券	MBS
モーゲージ担保証券	mortgage-backed security
目次	contents
目前の	immediate
目的	end
目的	goal
目的	objective
目的	purpose
目的貸付け	purpose loan
…の目的にかなう	serve
目標	goal
目標	mark
目標	objective
目標	target
目標水準	target
…を目標に定める	target
目標にする	target
目録	inventory
目録	table
目論見書	prospectus
目論見書の発行	prospectus issue
模型	model
もたついている	struggling
…をもたらした要因	contributing factor
…をもたらす	drive
…をもたらす	entail
もたらす	achieve
もたらす	earn
もたらす	net
持ち合い株	crossheld shares
持ち合い株式	crossheld shares
持ち合う	crosshold [cross-hold]
用いる	use
持ち株	holdings
持ち株	shareholding
持ち株	stake
持ち株	stockholding
持ち株会社	holding company
持ち株会社	holdings
持ち株会社の監査人	primary auditor
持ち株比率	equity position
持ち株比率	holding
持ち株比率	holdings
持ち株比率	ownership
持ち株比率	shareholding
持ち株比率	shareholding ratio
持ち株比率	stake
持ち株比率状況	equity ownership conditions
持ち込み	introduction
持ち高	position
持ち出す	take out
持ち直し	rally
持ち直し	recovery
持ち主	proprietor
持ち場	post
持ち分	equity
持ち分	equity stake
持ち分	interest
持ち分株	share
持ち分株式資本	equity share capital
持ち分権	equity
持ち分権	equity interest
持ち分権	leasing right
持ち分資本	equity capital
持ち分資本利益率	ROE
持ち分証券	equity securities
持ち分比率	equity stake rate
持ち分プーリング	pooling of interest [interests]
持ち分プーリング法	pooling of interest [interests]
持ち分プーリング法	pooling of interest [interests] method
持ち分プーリング方式	pooling of interest [interests] method
持ち分法	equity basis
持ち分法	equity method
持ち分法収益	equity method profits
持ち分法適用会社	associate
持ち分法利益	equity holding income
持ち分法利益	equity method income
持ち分有価証券	equity securities
持ち分有価証券	equity share
持ち分利益	equity in net earnings
持つ	own
目下の	immediate
モデル	model
基	unit
戻された	returned
戻し入れる	reverse
戻す	return
元引受人	principal underwriter
求める	call

求める demand	…の役に立つ serve	有価証券報告書 securities report
戻る return	役に立つ profit	有価証券報告書 securities statement
モニターする monitor	役に立つ profitable	有価証券明細表 portfolio
モニタリング monitoring	役目 function	有価証券利息 security interest
物 deal	役目を果たす function	有価証券利回り yield on securities
模範 model	役割 function	有機的成長 organic growth
模範 paradigm	…にやさしい –friendly	有機的成長 organic growth
もみ合い struggle	安い competitive	有機的成長率 organic growth
模様替え alteration	安く売り払う sell off	遊休資金 idle cash
モラル morality	安値 low	遊休資金 idle money
盛り上がる pick up	安値を付ける plunge	遊休資産 idle property
盛り返す rally	薬効 effectiveness	遊休施設 idle facility
もれなく記入する complete	雇い人 employee	遊休生産能力 idle capacity
問題 affair	雇い主 employer	遊休設備 idle equipment
問題 concern	雇う hire	遊休設備 idle plant
問題 issue	やりがいのある仕事 challenge	遊休設備 surplus equipment
問題 matter	やり取り communication	遊休の idle
問題 problem	やり取りする exchange	遊休不動産 idle real estate
問題解決 solution		優遇税制 preferential tax system
問題解決策 solution	**ゆ**	優遇税制措置 preferential tax treatment
問題解決手法 solution	優位 advantage	優遇措置 advantage
問題債権 problem loans	優位性 advantage	有形固定資産 property, plant and equipment
問題点 issue	優位性 leadership	有形固定資産 physical asset
問題のある troubled	優位な立場 leadership	有形固定資産 plant and equipment
問題の多い troubled	優位に predominantly	有形固定資産 property
問題の核心 bottom line	誘因 incentive	有形固定資産 tangible asset
問題融資先 problem borrower	有益 utility	有形固定資産 tangible fixed asset
	有益な healthy	有形資産 physical asset
や	有益な profitable	有形資産 tangible asset
野外撮影場 location	有害な negative	有形資産 tangible asset
役員 board member	有価証券 negotiable instrument	有形の material
役員 director	有価証券 securities	有形の physical
役員 officer	有価証券 valuable paper	有限責任会社 LLC
約因 consideration	有価証券市場 securities market	有限責任組合 LLP
役員会 board of directors	有価証券損益 security income and expenses	有限責任事業組合 LLP
役員借入金 loan from officer	有価証券担保貸付付き金 loans secured by stock and bonds	有限責任パートナーシップ LLP
役員室 boardroom	有価証券投資 portfolio investment	融合 merger
役員人事 management resources	有価証券届出書 registration statement	友好関係を結ぶ affiliate
役員退職慰労引当金 allowance for retirement benefits for directors and corporate auditors	有価証券の発行者の引受業者への引渡し価格と引受業者の一般投資家への売出価格との差額 spread	有効期間 useful life
		有効性 effectiveness
		有効性 efficiency
役員報酬 executive compensation	有価証券の評価損 securities losses	有効性 force
役員報酬委員会 executive compensation committee	有価証券の保有状態 position	有効である run
役職 appointment	有価証券評価損 loss from securities revaluation	友好的TOB friendly tender offer
役職 position	有価証券評価損 loss from valuation of securities	友好的株式公開買付け friendly takeover bid
役職員 executive	有価証券報告書 annual report	友好的株式公開買付け friendly tender offer
躍進する leap	有価証券報告書 F/S	友好的な friendly
約束 appointment	有価証券報告書 financial statement	友好的買収 friendly acquisition
約束 commitment	有価証券報告書 financial statements	友好的買収 friendly offer
約束 obligation	有価証券報告書 portfolio	友好的買収 friendly takeover
約束する commit		有効な effective
約束する undertake		有効な efficient
約束手形 note		有効な useful
約束手形 promissory note		
約定 commitment		
約定 term		
約定品 contract		
…に役に立つ –friendly		

有効利用	redeployment
有効利用する	redeploy
ユーザー	customer
ユーザー	user
融資	accommodation
融資	advance
融資	credit
融資	exposure
融資	facility
融資	finance
融資	financing
融資	funding
融資	lending
融資	loan
融資	loan finance
有資格の	eligible
有資格の	qualified
融資慣行	lending practice
融資期間	lending period
融資規制	loan restrictions
融資業務	lending service
融資金額	amount financed
融資限度	line of credit
融資限度額	credit line
融資行	lender
融資先	borrower
融資先	commitment
融資先	debtor
融資先	loan recipient
融資先企業	borrower
融資先企業	debtor company
融資先企業	loan recipient
融資残高	outstanding credits
融資残高	outstanding loan
融資者	lender
融資承認	commitment
融資する	finance
融資する	loan
融資総額	exposure
融資高	loan volume
融資団	financial group
融資手続き	loan making process
融資引当金	loan reserves
融資保証	advancing guarantee
優秀な	good
優勝候補	front runner [front-runner, frontrunner]
融資枠	credit facilities
融資枠	credit line
融資枠	facility
融資枠	loan program
融資枠の設定	commitment line
融資を受ける	borrow
融通	accommodation
融通手形	accommodation bill
融通手形	accommodation paper
融通目的	accommodation purpose
優勢	advantage
優勢に	predominantly
優先	priority
優先…	preferred
優先株	preferred share
優先株	preferred stock
優先株株主	preferred stockholder
優先株式	preferred share
優先株式	preferred stock
優先株式資本	preference share capital
優先株式に対する配当金	dividend on preferred shares
優先株式に対する配当金	dividends on preferred shares
優先株式の償還	preferred shares redeemed
優先株式の配当宣言額	preferred dividends declared
優先株式の発行	issuance of preferred shares
優先株式配当金	preferred share dividends
優先株主持ち分	preferred stockholders' equity
優先権	priority
優先権利落ち	X pr
優先権を与えられた	preferred
優先権を持つ	preferred
優先債権者	creditors by priority
優先債権者の地位	preferred creditor status
優先事項	front burner
優先事項	priority
優先出資証券	preferred securities
優先順位	priority
優先する	govern
優先する	underlying
優先的	preferred
優先的考慮事項	front burner
優先的選択権	option
優先入札者	preferred bidder
…優先の	driven
優先の	preferential
優先配当金	preferred dividends
有体財産	property
有体動産	goods
有担保債券	secured debt instrument
誘導する	engineer
有能な	efficient
誘発する	generate
有望資産売却戦略	crown jewel defense
有望な分野	promising area
有用	use
有用期間	service life
有用性	utility
有用性	worth
有利	advantage
有利子の	interest-bearing
…に有利な	-friendly
有利な	favorable
有利な	lucrative
有利な	profitable
有利な立場	leverage
優良	quality
有料サイト	subscription Web site
優良手形	fine paper
優良な	blue-chip
優良な	strong
優良の	good
優良発行体	premium borrower
優良品	quality
有料付属品	option
有力企業	leading company
ユーロ・ダラー	Xenocurrency
輸出	export
輸出	shipment
輸出国	supplier
輸出する	ship
輸出製品	export
輸出地の取引銀行による荷為替手形の買取り	negotiation
輸出品	export
譲り受け	takeover [take-over]
譲受人	endorsee
輸送機器	transport machinery
輸送機器	transportation machinery
輸送数量	haulage volume
輸送する	ship
委ねる	consign
ユニオン	union
ユニタリー課税	unitary tax
ユニタリー・タックス	unitary tax
ユニット	unit
ユニバーサル	universal
ユニバーサル・サービス	universal service
輸入	import
輸入製品	import
輸入代理店	distributor
輸入品	import
よい結果を生む	pay off
用意	provision
用意する	prepare
用意する	set aside
用意する	set up
容易に現金に転換できない	illiquid
容易にする	enhance
要員	personnel
要因	element
要因	factor
要因	force
要因	ingredient
要因	player
…の要因になる	contribute
用役原価	service cost

要求 challenge	要約する resume	与信承認 credit approval
要求 demand	要約目論見書 summary prospectus	与信手続き credit procedures
要求 needs	予期する anticipate	与信費用 credit cost
要求水準 norm	預金 account	与信枠 credit facilities
要求する charge	預金 cash	与信枠 exposure limit
要求する demand	預金 credit	予想 assumption
…の要求などを満たす serve	預金 deposit	予想 estimate
要求払い預金 demand deposit	預金 savings	予想 expectation
要求払い預金と手元現金 cash at bank and in hand	預金小切手 certified check	予想 forecast
	預金残高証明書 certificate of bank balance	予想 forecasting
用具 tool		予想 outlook
要件 requirement	預金者 depositor	予想 projection
用語 term	預金者側残高 book balance	予想 prospects
様式 form	預金証書 CD	予想赤字 projected loss
様式 table	預金証書 certificate of deposit	予想貸倒れ損失 potential loan losses
様式10-K Form 10-K	抑制 control	
様式10-Q Form 10-Q	抑制 curb	予想貸倒れ損失額 potential loan losses
様式20-F Form 20-F	抑制する contain	
様式8-K Form 8-K	抑制する control	予想される純利益 expected net profit
様式F-1 Form F-1	抑制する curb	
様式F-4 Form F-4	予見 forecast	予想純利益 expected net profit
様式S-1 Form S-1	予見する foresee	予想する anticipate
様式S-8 Form S-8	予告する warn	予想する assume
養殖 culture	横の horizontal	予想する estimate
要する cost	横ばい状態の flat	予想する expect
要する demand	横ばいの flat	予想する forecast
要請 solicitation	横割りの horizontal	予想する foresee
…するように要請する solicit	予算 budget	予想する project
要素 element	予算管理 budgeting	予想損失 anticipated loss
要素 factor	予算上の budgetary	予想耐用年数 probable life
要素 ingredient	予算手続き budgetary procedure	予想超過収益率 forecast excess returns
様態 form	予算の計上 budgetary appropriation	
用地 land		予想長期収益率 expected long-term rate of return
用地 location	予算編成 budgeting	
用地 site	予算編成方針 budget guideline	予想の anticipatory
要点 bottom line	予算目標 budget goal	予想の assumed
要点 thrust	予算を組む earmark	予想の expected
用途 purpose	余剰 excess	予想配当 projected dividend
用途 use	余剰 surplus	予想変動率 implied volatility
容認 acceptance	余剰資金 excess liquidity	予想利益 anticipated profit
容認する accept	余剰資金 surplus fund	予想を裏切る disappointing
容認できる acceptable	余剰人員 surplus employees	予想を裏切る業績 disappointing results [performance]
用品 equipment	余剰生産 surplus production	
用品 item	余剰の excess	予測 estimate
要報告産業セグメント reportable industry segment	余剰利益 melon	予測 forecast
	与信 credit	予測 forecasting
要報告事項 reportable event	与信期間 credit period	予測 outlook
要約 summary	与信基準 credit criteria	予測 profile
要約財務指標 selected financial data	与信基準 credit underwriting policy	予測 projection
		予測給付債務 PBO
要約財務情報 summarized financial information	与信基準 lending standards	予測給付債務 projected benefit obligation
	与信基準 underwriting standards	
要約財務情報 summarized financial information	与信業務 credit activities	予測給付債務制度 projected benefit obligation
	与信限度 borrower limit	
要約財務諸表 abstract of financial statements	与信限度 credit limit	予測される将来の雇用後給付 estimated future postemployment benefits
	与信限度(額) credit line	
要約財務書類 summarized financial statements	与信限度額 line of credit	
	与信残高 exposure	予測される将来の退職後給付 estimated future retiree benefits
要約された condensed	与信者 credit grantor	
要約書 briefing	与信承認 credit approval	予測する estimate

予測する　forecast
予測する　project
予測単位基金方式　projected unit credit method
予測単位給付　projected unit credit
予測単位給付方式　projected unit credit method
予測単位年金積増し　projected unit credit
予測単位年金積増方式　projected unit credit method
予測変動率　volatility
予知　forecast
余地　potential
余地　scope
予兆　forerunner
予定　plan
予定　program
予定給付債務　PBO
予定給付債務　projected benefit obligation
予定原価　estimated cost
予定されている　due
予定する　assume
予定通り進行しない　lag
予定納税　payments of estimated tax
予定配賦　application
予定利率　guaranteed yield
予定利率　promised yield rate
予納法人税　advance corporation tax
予備格付け　preliminary rating
予備品　reserve
予備調査　feasibility study
予備貯蔵　backlog
予備的合意書　memorandum of understanding
呼び値　bid offer price
予備の　pilot
呼び戻し　recall
呼び戻す　recall
予報　forecast
予報　outlook
予報する　forecast
予約　appointment
（予約）購読者　subscriber
予約する　book
予約取引　forward
…により　due to …
拠り所　mainstay
余力　potential
…による　attributable to …
…によれば　per
弱い　vulnerable
弱い　weak
弱気材料　negative
弱気市場　bear market
弱気の　negative
弱含みの　negative

弱める　dilute
弱める　impair
4倍増にする　quadruple
4倍増になる　quadruple
4倍にする　quadruple
4倍になる　quadruple

ら

来期　coming year
ライセンシング　licensing
ライセンス　license [licence]
ライセンス供与　licensing
ライセンス供与する　license
ライセンス契約　licensing
ライセンス料　license fee
来年度　coming year
ライバル　competition
ライバル　competitor
ライバル　contender
ライバル企業　competitor
ライフ　life
ライフサイクル　life cycle
ライン　line
落札価格　accepted bid
落札価格　bid
落札業者　bid winner
落札業者　winner of the bidding
落札予定会社　bid winner
落成式　inauguration ceremony
ランキング表　standing
乱高下　fluctuation
乱高下　volatility
乱高下する　fluctuate
乱高下する　volatile

り

リアル　real
リース　lease
リース　leasing
リース　rental
リース契約　lease
リース契約　lease obligation
リース権　leasing right
リース債権　lease receivable
リース債務　lease obligation
リース資産　leased property
リース支払い額　lease payments
リース収益　leasing income
リースする　lease
リース賃借人　lessee
リース賃貸人　lessor
リース取引　lease
リースに係わる正味現金投資額　net cash investment in a lease
リースによる借戻し　leaseback
リースバック　leaseback
リース物件　leased property
リース料　lease payments

リース料　rental expense
リース料収入　leasing income
リース料の支払い　lease payments
リーダー　leader
リーダーシップ　leadership
リーダー性　leadership
リート　REIT
…による利益　income from …
…利益　income from …
利益　advantage
利益　benefit
利益　bottom line
利益　credit
利益　earning
利益　earnings
利益　gain
利益　income
利益　interest
利益　melon
利益　payoff
利益　percentage
利益　profit
利益　return
利益圧迫　squeeze on earnings
利益が得られる　lucrative
利益が発生する　benefit
利益共同体　community of interest
利益供与　payoff
利益参加社債　participating bond
利益至上主義　profit-first principle
利益準備金　earned surplus reserve
利益準備金　legal retained earnings
利益準備金　revenue reserve
利益剰余金　accumulated earnings
利益剰余金　accumulated income
利益剰余金　accumulated income
利益剰余金　accumulated profit
利益剰余金　earned surplus
利益剰余金　reinvested income
利益剰余金　retained earnings
利益剰余金　surplus profit
利益剰余金計算書　earned surplus statement
利益剰余金計算書　retained earnings statement
利益処分　appropriation
利益処分　below the line
利益処分案　proposal for appropriation of retained earnings
利益処分計算書　appropriation statement
利益処分計算書　surplus appropriation statement
利益処分計算書　surplus appropriation statement
利益相反　conflict of interest
利益相反行為　conflict of interest
利益相反取引　transaction in conflict of interest
…の利益になる　benefit

利益になる	pay
利益になる	profit
利益の大きい	lucrative
利益の減少	profit decline
利益の質	quality of earnings
利益の増加	growth in profits
利益の伸び	earnings growth
利益の伸び	profit growth
利益の分配	withdrawal
利益配当	dividend
利益配当	profit sharing
利益配分	profit sharing
利益発生期間	period benefited
利益不参加の	nonparticipating
利益分配	profit sharing
利益横ばい	flat profits
利益予想	earnings forecast
利益予想	profit forecast
利益予想	profit projection
利益率	margin
利益率	margin percentage
利益率	profit margin
利益率	profit ratio
利益率	profitability
利益率	rate of return
利益率	ratio
利益率	return
利益率改善	margin improvement
利益率改善	margin improvement
利益率低下	margin squeeze
利益率低下	pressure on margins
利益を上げる	earn
利益を上げること	profit making
利益を与える	benefit
利益を生む	profitable
利益を得る	benefit
利益を得ること	profit making
利益を生じない	unprofitable
リエンジニアリング	reengineering
リエンジニアリング	reengineering
利落ち	ex interest
利落ち	XC
利落ち	XI
利害関係	concern
利害関係	conflict of risk
利害関係	interest
利害関係	stake
利害関係がある	concern
利害関係者	interested parties
利害関係者	stakeholder
利害の一致	community of interest
利害の衝突	conflict of interest
利害の対立	conflict of interest
利害の調整	community of interest
力作	effort
力点	stress
利権	interest
履行	execution
履行	performance
履行期限	term of execution
履行期日	due date
履行義務のある	due
履行する	execute
履行する	meet
履行する	service
履行能力	responsibility
リコール	recall
リコールする	recall
リサーチ	research
利ざや	margin
利ざや	profit margin
利ざや	spread
利ざや改善	margin improvement
利ざやの拡大	margin improvement
…の利子	interest on …
利子	interest
理事	board member
理事	director
理事	manager
理事会	board
理事会	board of directors
理事会	meeting
利子支払い	interest payment
利子支払い保証倍率	interest coverage ratio
利子収入	interest revenue
利子税金控除前利益	EBIT
利子費用	interest cost
利子費用	interest expense
利潤	earnings
利潤	gain
利潤	profit
利潤をもたらす	pay
利殖	accumulation
離職	separation
利子率	interest rate
リスク	crisis
リスク	risk
リスク管理	risk management
リスク危険度	exposure
リスク限度額	exposure threshold
リスク資産総額	exposure
リスクマネジメント	risk management
リスクを回避する	hedge
リステートメント	restatement
リストラ	downsizing
リストラ	restructuring
リストラ	streamlining
リストラクチャリング	restructuring
リストラクチャリング費用	restructuring charge
リストラ計画	restructuring plan
リストラ策	overhaul plan
リストラする	downsize
リストラする	restructure
リストラする	streamline
リストラ費用	restructuring charge
リセッション	recession
…の利息	interest on …
利息	interest
利息	interest rate
利息落ち	X in
利息落ち	XI
利息収益	interest income
利息収益	interest revenue
利息収入	interest income
利息収入	interest revenue
利息条件付きの	interest-bearing
利息制限法	Interest Limitation Law
利息の返済	interest payment
利息払い	debt servicing
利息費用	interest cost
利息費用	interest expense
リターン	return
リターン	reward
離脱	withdrawal
離脱する	split
離脱する	suspend
…率	factor
率	percent
率	rate
立案	planning
立案する	plan
利付き債券	active bond
利付きの	interest-bearing
立証する	establish
律する	govern
立地	location
立地決定	location decision
立地条件	location
立地変更	relocation
立地要因	location factor
立派な演説	effort
リテール	retail
利点	advantage
利点	benefit
利点	incentive
利点	percentage
利得	benefit
利得	gain
利得	payoff
利得	profit
リニューアル	renewal
理念	concept
理念	philosophy
利幅	profit margin
利幅	spread
利払い	interest payment
利払い	servicing
利払い税引き前利益	EBIT
利払い余力率	interest coverage ratio
利払い利息・税金・減価償却控除前利益	EBITD
リファイナンス	refinancing

リフォーム	reform	流動性選好	liquidity preference	利用する	capitalize on
リポジショニング	repositioning	流動性と資本の源泉	liquidity and capital resources	利用する	tap
リボルビング・クレジット	revolving credit	流動性に乏しい	illiquid	利用する	use
利回り	rate of return	流動性の供給	liquidity injection	量的拡大	quantitative expansion
利回り	return	流動性の高い	liquid	利用できる	serve
利回り	yield	流動性の高い投資	liquid investment	料率引下げ	rate cutting
利回り改善	yield improvement	流動性の高さ	liquidity	リリースする	release
利回り格差	yield spread	流動性のない	illiquid	利率	interest rate
利回り調整	yield adjustment	流動性預金	floating deposits	リレーション	relations
リミット	limit	流動的	current	理論的枠組み	paradigm
略号	code	流動的	floating	厘	percentage point
略式	summary	流動負債	current liabilities	臨界	critical mass
略式財務諸表	abridged accounts	流動負債	floating debt	臨界質量	critical mass
理由	account	流動負債	floating liability	臨界量	critical mass
流行	currency	流入法	flow-through method	輪郭	profile
流行	trend	留保	reserve	臨時株主総会	extraordinary shareholders meeting
流出	flow	留保金額	undistributed profit	臨時雇用	temporary work
流通	currency	留保する	retain	臨時税引き前費用	one-time pre-tax charge
流通	distribution	留保利益	accumulated earnings	臨時損益	nonrecurring profit and loss
流通	marketing	留保利益	accumulated income		
流通	negotiation	留保利益	accumulated profit	臨時(損益)項目	extraordinary items
流通可能の	negotiable	留保利益	retained earnings		
流通業	distributor	留保利益	retained profit	臨時の	contingent
流通業者	distributor	留保利益	retained surplus	臨時の	current
流通経路	distribution channel	留保利益	undistributed earnings	臨時の	extraordinary
流通させる	distribute	流用する	convert	臨時の	temporary
流通市場	after market [aftermarket]	量	amount	臨時の	windfall
流通市場	secondary market	量	quantity	臨時発行証券	contingent issues
流通市場	secondary market	量	volume	臨時費用	contingency
流通市場	trading market	利用	access	臨時費用	nonrecurring cost
流通市場価格	secondary-market value	利用	employment	臨時費用	one-time [onetime] charge
流通市場の取引	secondary flows	利用	use	臨時利益	extraordinary income
流通証券	negotiable paper	領域	field	臨時利益	windfall
流通する	floating	領域	niche	臨時利益	windfall profit
流通性	liquidity	領域	range	隣接した	immediate
流通性のある	negotiable	領域	scope	倫理	ethics
流通センター	distribution center	了解覚書	memorandum of understanding	倫理	morality
流通ネットワーク	distribution network	両替	conversion	倫理基準	ethical standard
		両替	exchange	倫理規定	code of ethics
流通網	distribution network	両替資金	change fund	倫理性	morality
流通網	float	両替する	convert	倫理体系	ethics
流通網	distribution network	両替する	exchange	倫理的業務活動	ethical business conduct
流動	current	利用可能な	available		
流動化	liquidation	料金	charge	倫理の	ethical
流動資金	current fund	料金	fee		
流動資金	liquid fund	料金	rate		
流動資産	current assets	利用限度額	bank line of credit		
流動資産	floating asset	利用限度額	credit line	累加した	cumulative
流動資産	liquid asset	良好な	favorable	累加配当	cumulative dividend
流動資本	floating capital	良好な	good	累計支出額	accumulated expenditure
流動資本	liquid capital	良質	quality		
流動する	floating	利用者	user	累計的	cumulative
流動性	current	領収	receipt	累計的損益計算書	cumulative income statement
流動性	liquidation	領収書	receipt		
流動性	liquidity	…を利用する	leverage	類似会社	comparable company
流動性がある	liquid	利用する	access	累進課税	progressive tax
流動性需要	liquidity demand	利用する	apply	累積	accumulation

累積赤字　accumulated deficit
累積額　accumulated amount
累積株　cumulative stock
累積換算調整額　cumulative translation adjustment
累積給付　accumulated benefit
累積給付額　accumulated plan benefits
累積給付債務額　accumulated plan benefits
累積効果　cumulative effect
累積効果　cumulative effect
累積債務　accumulated liability
累積した　accumulated
累積した　cumulative
累積する　accumulate
累積退職後給付債務　accumulated postretirement benefit obligation
累積積立金　accumulated reserves
累積の影響　cumulative effect
累積的影響額　cumulative effect
累積的会計修正　cumulative accounting adjustment
累積的な　cumulative
累積的優先株式　accumulated preferred stok
累積年金給付債務額　accumulated and accrued plan benefits
累積配当　accumulated dividend
累積配当　cumulative dividend
累積未払い配当　accumulated dividend
累積優先株式　cumulative preferred stock [share]
累積利益　accumulated earnings
累積利益　accumulated income
累積利益配当　accumulated dividend
ルール　rule

れ

例　paradigm
レイオフ　layoff
レイオフを進める　lay off
例示　comparison
0.1ポイント　notch
0.50％　half a percentage point
0.25％　quarter point
レート　rate
歴史的　historical
歴史的原価　historical cost
歴史的原価　original cost
暦年　calendar year
レギュレーション　regulation
レスキュー　rescue
レター　letter
列　row
劣位　disadvantage
劣位弁済債務　subordinated debt
劣化　deterioration
劣化　impairment
劣化　physical deterioration
劣化した貸出金　impaired loan
劣化する　impair
劣後株　deferred share
劣後債　subordinated debenture
劣後社債　subordinated debenture
劣後請求権　junior claim
劣後転換社債　convertible subordinated debenture
劣後普通株式　junior common stock
劣後ローン　subordinated loan
レッサー　lessor
レッシー　lessee
レバレッジ　leverage
レバレッジド・バイアウト　LBO
レバレッジド・バイアウト　leveraged buyout [buy-out]
レバレッジド・リース　leveraged lease
レビュー　review
レベル　level
レポート　report
廉価買取選択権　bargain purchase option
連携　alliance
連携　partnership
連携する　tie up
連結　combination
連結　consolidation
連結　group
連結売上高　consolidated revenues
連結売上高　consolidated sales
連結売上高　group operating revenue
連結売上高　group sales
連結営業赤字　group operating loss
連結営業黒字　group operating profit
連結営業収益　group operating revenue
連結営業収入　group operating revenue
連結営業損失　group operating loss
連結営業利益　consolidated operating profit
連結営業利益　group operating profit
連結営業利益率　consolidated operating profit margin
連結会計　accounting consolidation
連結会社　consolidated company
連結株主持ち分　consolidated stockholders' equity
連結から除外された　unconsolidated
連結業績報告書　consolidated earnings report
連結業務利益　consolidated operating profit
連結計算書　consolidated statement
連結計上する　consolidate
連結経常損失　group pretax loss
連結経常利益　consolidated business profits
連結経常利益　consolidated pretax profit
連結経常利益　consolidated recurring profit
連結経常利益　group pretax profit
連結計上利益　consolidated current account profit
連結決算　consolidated accounting period figures
連結決算　consolidated accounts
連結決算　consolidated earnings report
連結決算　consolidation
連結決算報告　consolidated earnings report
連結決算報告書　consolidated earnings report
連結子会社　consolidated subsidiary
連結財務諸表　consolidated accounts
連結財務諸表　consolidated financial statements
連結財務諸表注記　notes to consolidated financial statements
連結財務書類　consolidated accounts
連結財務書類　consolidated financial statements
連結財務書類注記　notes to consolidated financial statements
連結されていない　unconsolidated
連結事業体　consolidated entity
連結資金計算書　consolidated funds statement
連結した　combined
連結した　consolidated
連結資本的支出純額　consolidated net capital expenditures
連結収益　combined revenue
連結収益　consolidated revenues
連結主体　consolidated entity
連結純売上高　group net sales
連結純損失　consolidated net loss
連結純損失　group net loss
連結純利益　consolidated earnings
連結純利益　consolidated net income
連結純利益　consolidated net

profit
連結純利益　group net income
連結純利益　group net profit
連結純利益の合計額　combined group net profit
連結する　consolidate
連結税引き後赤字　consolidated after-tax deficit
連結税引き後赤字　consolidated after-tax loss
連結税引き後赤字　consolidated net loss
連結税引き後赤字　group net loss
連結税引き後売上高　group net sales
連結税引き後黒字　consolidated after-tax profit
連結税引き後損失　consolidated after-tax loss
連結税引き後損失　consolidated net loss
連結税引き後利益　consolidated after-tax profit
連結税引き後利益　consolidated net profit
連結税引き後利益　group after-tax profit
連結税引き後利益　group net income
連結税引き後利益　group net profit
連結税引き後利益の合計額　combined group net profit
連結税引き前損失　group pretax loss
連結税引き前利益　consolidated pretax profit
連結税引き前利益　group pretax profit
連結損益計算書　consolidated income statement
連結貸借対照表　consolidated balance sheet
連結貸借対照表　consolidated balance sheet
連結対象外関連会社　unconsolidated affiliate
連結対象会社　consolidated company
連結対象外の　unconsolidated
連結対象関連会社　consolidated affiliate
連結対象子会社　companies consolidated
連結対象子会社　consolidated subsidiary
連結対象にする　consolidate
連結対象の　consolidated
連結対象の関連会社　consolidated affiliate

連結対象の持ち分法適用会社　consolidated affiliate
連結中間決算報告　group interim report
連結中間決算報告書　group interim report
連結超過額　consolidated excess
連結当期純利益　consolidated net income
連結当期利益　consolidated earnings
連結納税　consolidated taxation
連結納税申告　consolidated return
連結納税申告　consolidated tax return
連結納税申告書　consolidated return
連結納税申告書　consolidated tax return
連結納税引当金　consolidated tax provision
連結の範囲　consolidation criteria
連結の範囲　scope of consolidation
連結の範囲に含まれない　unconsolidated
連結の方針　consolidation policy
連結のれん　consolidated excess
連結配当性向　consolidated payout ratio
連結範囲の基準　consolidation criteria
連結ベース　consolidated basis
連結ベースの売上高　consolidated sales
連結ベースの税引き後利益　consolidated net profit
連結方針　basis of consolidation
連結方針　consolidation policy
連結持ち分　consolidated equity
連結持ち分　consolidated stockholders' equity
連結有利子負債　consolidated interest-bearing debt
連結利益　consolidated earnings
連結利益　consolidated income
連結利益　consolidated profit
連合　alliance
連合の　joint
レンジ　range
連続　row
連続　series
連続監査　running audit
連続した　consecutive
連続した　straight
連続して　straight
連続している　running
連続する　running
連続性　continuity
連続の　back-to-back
連続割引　series discount

連帯の　joint
レンタル　rental
連邦改正破産法第11章　Chapter 11
連邦公開市場委員会　FOMC
連邦雇用者責任法　Federal Employers' Liability Act
連邦準備制度理事会　FRB
連邦所得税　federal income tax
連邦取引委員会　Federal Trade Commission
連邦取引委員会　FTC
連邦破産法第10章　Chapter 10 of the National Bankruptcy Act
連邦法人税　federal income tax
連邦法人税率　federal statutory tax rate
連邦法定税率　federal statutory tax rate
連絡　communication
連絡する　report
連絡網　network

ろ

ロイヤルティ　royalty
老化　aging
老朽　aging
老朽　obsolescence
老朽化　aging
老朽化　deterioration
老朽化する　deteriorate
老朽設備　obsolete equipment
労災保険　worker's compensation insurance
労作　effort
労使　labor management
労使関係　labor management relations
労使協約　deal
労使協約　labor agreement
労働　work
労働協約　labor agreement
労働組合　trade union
労働組合　union
労働市場の開放　liberalization of the labor market
労働人員　manpower
労働人口　workforce
労働の　working
労働力　manpower
労働力　workforce
労働力管理　manpower management
労務　service
労務管理　labor management
労力　manpower
ロードショー　roadshow
ロールオーバー　rollover
ローン　financing
ローン　loan

ローンチ	launch
…にログインする	enter
ロケーション	location
ロジスティクス	logistics
炉心	core
ロス	loss
ロス・シェアリング方式	loss-sharing system
路線	line
ロックアップ	lockup [lock-up]
ロボット	robotics
ロボット技術	robotics
ロボット工学	robotics
論及	reference
論拠	basis
論点	issue
論文	paper
論理の一貫した	consecutive

わ

ワーク	work
ワーク・シェア	work sharing
ワーク・シェアリング	work sharing
ワーク・シェアリング・システム	work sharing
賄賂	payoff
賄賂資金	slush fund
和解	accord
和解	composition
和解	settlement
和解	transaction
和解する	settle
和議	composition
枠組み	framework
枠組み	paradigm
枠組み	scope
分け前	percentage
分け前	portion
私ども経営陣	we
私どもの意見では	in our opinion
渡す	deliver
渡す	serve
渡り合う	compete
ワラント	warrant
ワラント落ち	XW
ワラント債	bond with stock purchase warrant
ワラント債	warrant bond
ワラント付き社債	bond with warrant
割合	percent
割合	percentage
割合	rate
割合	ratio
割当て	allocation
割当て	allotment
割当て	assignment
割当て	portion
割当て	proration
割当金	allotment
割当予算額	appropriation
割り当てる	allocate
割り当てる	consign
割り当てる	prorate
割引	discount
割引額	discount
割引キャッシュ・フロー法	DCF
割引キャッシュ・フロー法	discount [discounted] cash flow method
割引現価	discounted present value
割引現在価値法	DCF
割引現在価値法	discount [discounted] cash flow method
割引した	reduced
割引する	discount
割引制度	discount plan
割引手形	acceptance receivable discounted
割引手形	note receivable discounted
割引手数料	discount commission
割引発行債	discount bond
割引発行社債	bond issued at a discount
割引率	discount
割引率	discount rate
割引料	discount
割引料	discount charge
割振り	allocation
割り振る	allocate
割増価格	premium
割増金	premium
割増手当	premium bonus
割増発行社債	bond issued at a premium
悪い	poor
悪い	unfavorable
悪い方向に	unfavorably
ワンストップ・サービス	one-stop service
ワンストップ・ショッピング	one-stop shopping
ワン・トゥ・ワン・マーケティング	one-to-one marketing

2008年9月10日　初版発行

財務情報英和辞典

2008年9月10日　第1刷発行

著者　　　　　　　菊地義明（きくち・よしあき）

発行者　　　　　　株式会社三省堂　代表者八幡統厚

印刷者　　　　　　三省堂印刷株式会社

発行所　　　　　　株式会社三省堂

〒101-8371
東京都千代田区三崎町二丁目22番14号

電話　編集　（03）3230-9411
　　　営業　（03）3230-9412

振替口座　00160-5-54300
http://www.sanseido.co.jp

〈財務英和・544pp.〉

落丁本・乱丁本はお取替えいたします

ISBN 978-4-385-11031-8

[R]本書の全部または一部を無断で複写複製（コピー）することは，著作権法上での例外を除き，禁じられています。
本書からの複写を希望される場合は，日本複写権センター（03-3401-2382）にご連絡ください。

テクニカルライター英和辞典　[増補新装版]

光明誠一［編］　B6変型判　752頁

ネジやクギから大型機械・装置・プラントまで、具体的な「物」の構造や機能を、正確で簡潔な英文で記述するための英和辞典。約1万1千語収録。和英索引6千項目付き。

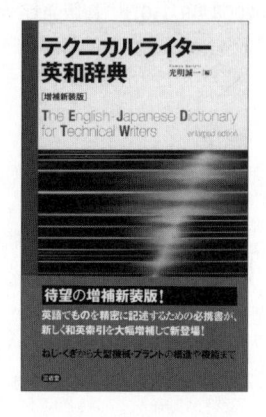

グランドコンサイス英和辞典

三省堂編修所［編］　A5変型判　3,024頁

理工・医学・社会科学・ITから生活・スポーツまで、あらゆる分野を網羅した英語データベース！一冊もの英和最大の36万項目収録。

グランドコンサイス和英辞典

三省堂編修所［編］　A5変型判　2,528頁

見出し語・複合語・派生語21万項目、用例11万項目を収録。あらゆる分野を網羅した最大級の和英データベース！